MENANDER
A COMMENTARY

MENANDER
A COMMENTARY

BY

A. W. GOMME, F.B.A.

LATE PROFESSOR OF GREEK
IN THE UNIVERSITY OF GLASGOW

AND

F. H. SANDBACH, F.B.A.

EMERITUS PROFESSOR OF CLASSICS
IN THE UNIVERSITY OF CAMBRIDGE

OXFORD
AT THE UNIVERSITY PRESS
1973

Oxford University Press, Ely House, London W. 1

GLASGOW NEW YORK TORONTO MELBOURNE WELLINGTON
CAPE TOWN IBADAN NAIROBI DAR ES SALAAM LUSAKA ADDIS ABABA
DELHI BOMBAY CALCUTTA MADRAS KARACHI LAHORE DACCA
KUALA LUMPUR SINGAPORE HONG KONG TOKYO

ISBN 0 19 814197 1 X

© *Oxford University Press 1973*

*Printed in Great Britain
at the University Press, Oxford
by Vivian Ridler
Printer to the University*

PREFACE

PROFESSOR A. W. GOMME's admiration for Menander was known from several articles and from the final chapter of his *Essays in Greek History and Literature*. It was less well known that for many years before his death he had been planning to make this author more accessible to the undergraduate student of the classics by providing an annotated text. This was intended to include not only the plays and scenes recovered in whole or in part through the discoveries that for practical purposes began with Nicole's publication of the *Georgos* papyrus in 1898, but also fragments preserved in the literary tradition, if long enough to illustrate Menander's manner of writing. At various times he had been assisted in the task by his Glasgow colleagues W. E. Muir and J. Carnegie, but latterly he was working alone. At the time of his death he had in typescript a draft commentary on *Heros*, *Epitrepontes*, *Perikeiromene*, and *Samia*; on the rest of his project he had made some unorganized notes. He lived to see *Dyskolos*, but was unable to take account of it; he was necessarily ignorant of the subsequent discoveries that have brought new knowledge and new problems.

When I was asked by the Clarendon Press to complete Gomme's work, which they had undertaken to publish, I soon found it impossible to preserve much of his draft commentary completely unaltered. In the first place, Gomme himself had indicated that many notes should be reconsidered or omitted. Secondly, it was clear from his papers, as from internal evidence, that many others had by successive additions grown to a state such that rewriting was necessary to secure logical order and clarity. Similarly, when I thought it desirable to extend a note by the inclusion of new matter, this often brought with it a need for recasting. As a result only a minority of notes on the four plays mentioned above are exactly in the form that he left them; they may perhaps be recognized by those who are familiar with his style. It would not in general be practicable to distinguish his contributions from mine (although the first-person pronoun always denotes me)

and even if it were practicable it would not benefit the user of the
book. It is right that Gomme should have the main credit for
what is good; for all that is wrong I accept responsibility. There
were, however, some opinions maintained by him which I could
not adopt, but which deserved a hearing. I have then recorded
the view as being his, and added the reasons which cause me to
disagree. I have also reproduced without comment some of his
attempts to reconstruct by imagination parts of plays that are lost.
This was an exercise that he enjoyed and thought valuable, but
one for which I profess neither inclination or ability.

It was originally intended that this commentary should be
accompanied by a text. Gomme had prepared one for his four
plays; it reproduced in part that of Jensen (*Sam., Perik.*), in part
that of Körte's third edition (*Epitr., Heros*), making some modifica-
tions, mainly by the omission of the more hazardous supplements.
The Delegates of the Press decided, however, that in view of the
growth of the material since Gomme's death it would be desirable
to publish the text separately as an Oxford Classical Text. The
lemmata of the commentary are taken therefore from that
edition (1972).

It may be useful to recall the principles on which the text was
constituted. It is based on the belief that the ordinary reader of
a play wishes to know where he is passing from the certain to the
conjectural, not to be informed of holes in the papyrus; it is of
no profit to him to read κ[α]ί and [τ]οῦτο and νὴ τοὺς θ[εούς
rather than καί, τοῦτο, and νὴ τοὺς θεούς; on the contrary there
is a danger that, having become accustomed not to notice the
brackets in such cases, he will tend to disregard also those that
enclose speculative supplements. Even professional scholars may
be found to quote as Menander's the words of Wilamowitz.
Accordingly square brackets are used only where a doubt, however slight, can remain about the correctness of the supplement.
Similarly, dotted letters are used only where neither the remains of
a mutilated letter nor the context allow a certain identification.
Körte once called for a text constructed on these lines (*SB Leipzig*
1908, 149) and Gomme had at one time been minded to supply
one, but abandoned the idea on the ground that it would lead
to an overloaded apparatus criticus, 'a nuisance to everyone and
fatal to the beginner'. I hope that this will prove to have been
an illusory fear.

The recent discovery of new papyrus texts of passages previously known in a mutilated form has brought a salutary reminder of how difficult it often is to restore correctly even a few
missing letters. The supplements placed in my text are less
numerous than they would have been a few years ago; and even
so the reader is urged to treat everything in square brackets with
some measure of reserve.

Gomme had put in hand, aided by Mr. D. A. Campbell,
a renumbering of the lines of the three plays of which the Cairo
papyrus preserves large parts. He argued that the traditional
method of numbering consecutively the surviving lines, without
attention to the gaps, meant that if a new fragment were discovered, the numeration would need to be altered. In Körte's
edition of *Epitrepontes* there is already a double numeration: a
new discovery would lead to a triple one. The length of the gaps
in the Cairo codex can usually be calculated to an approximate
number of lines; so, if in our numeration we make allowance
for what is lost, a newly found fragment can be fitted in without
disturbance, provided there is an overlap. I have, with some
hestitation, followed Gomme in this so far as *Epitrepontes* and
Perikeiromene are concerned, printing also in the right-hand
margin Körte's numeration, now currently used. The new
numeration has the advantage of making it immediately clear
to what part of the play any passage belongs. Gomme's re-
numeration of *Samia*, about which he had himself earlier been
doubtful (*JHS* lix [1939], 310), was made obsolete by the
evidence of the Bodmer papyrus and Mitilini mosaic. It would
now be possible to renumber the play nearly correctly by his
method; but I have refrained from doing this. The gaps that
still remain are so short that if missing lines are recovered, they
can be numbered 000*a*, 000*b*, and so on, as has been done for
142*a*–142*m*, without any alteration to the present numeration.
The play has in fact been renumbered by J.-M. Jaques in his
edition. In *Sikyonios* the stichometric indications in S at 151 and
254 (Kassel) would be a guide to renumbering 110–279, but
this being considerably less than half the entire number of lines
preserved in whole or part the operation is hardly justifiable.

Every commentator on Menander must be vastly indebted
to his predecessors. For the older discoveries, besides the editions

of Jensen (1926) and Körte (1938), I have, like Gomme, found particular profit in the material collected by Capps, *Four Plays of Menander* (1910), although his text is at many points to be disregarded. Van Leeuwen's *Menandri Fabularum Reliquiae*[3] (1919) is not to be neglected. Wilamowitz's *Menander: Das Schiedsgericht* (*Epitrepontes*) (1925), although not free from mistakes, is stimulating and individual: Gomme owed much to it, although he was often moved to dissent.

If it is invidious thus to single out the books of a few dead scholars and to neglect the great amount of valuable work by many authors that is to be found in articles, it is still more invidious to treat the living in the same manner. I will nevertheless mention a few of those to whom I am indebted, again confining myself to books. T. B. L. Webster's *Studies in Menander* (1950, 2nd edn. 1960) contains as much that is important as is speculative or obsolete; his *Studies in Later Greek Comedy* (1953, 2nd edn. 1969) also has much that demands attention. C. Dedoussi's commentary on the Cairo *Samia* (1965) is helpful. My debts to the numerous editors of *Dyskolos* are recognized in the introduction to that play. My notes on it were in the main written before the appearance of E. W. Handley's outstandingly good edition (1965). I have tried to acknowledge what I have subsequently taken from him. Perhaps more should have been taken, but my commentary does not aim at the completeness of his. Many of the mentions made of him concern passages on which we do not agree; this was inevitable since his is the standard edition of the play, and it should be understood as testimony to its importance. The editions in the series Kleine Texte of *Sikyonios* by R. Kassel (1965) and of *Aspis* and *Samia* by C. Austin (vol. ii, 1970) assemble an invaluable collection of parallel and illustrative passages, from which I have freely borrowed.

It is an even more pleasant duty to thank those numerous scholars who have sent me offprints and information or given me their opinions on disputed points. I owe a particular debt to M. J.-M. Jacques, who kindly provided me with a copy of the *Samia* apographon and discussed many passages from it and from the Cairo MS. of that play. Professor E. G. Turner has helped me in many ways; I am especially indebted to him for allowing me to use the proofs of volumes of *Oxyrhynchus Papyri* and otherwise introducing me to new texts before their publication. He also lent me photographs of a large part of the Cairo codex, made from negatives obtained in 1971 by Dr. R. A. Coles and Professor L. Koenen; these caused me to modify several notes. I am moreover grateful to him and to Professor E. W. Handley for permission to treat some lines of *Dis Exapaton* which will have their definitive publication in Supplement 22 of the *Bulletin of the Institute of Classical Studies* (University of London). Dr. Colin Austin called my attention to a number of articles and finally read a draft of the whole commentary apart from the introduction; I have greatly profited from his valuable suggestions and his detection of numerous errors.

Lastly I must express my thanks to the staff of the Clarendon Press for their unstinted helpfulness at all stages in the production of this book.

F. H. SANDBACH

Trinity College, Cambridge
July 1972

CONTENTS

ABBREVIATIONS

Denniston, *GP*	J. D. Denniston, *The Greek Particles*² (Oxford, 1954).
Gomme, *Essays*	A. W. Gomme, *Essays in Greek History and Literature* (Oxford, 1937).
Goodwin, *MT*	W. W. Goodwin, *Syntax of the Moods and Tenses of the Greek Verb*² (London, 1889).
K–G	R. Kühner–B. Gerth, *Ausführliche Grammatik der griechischen Sprache, Satzlehre*³ (Hanover and Leipzig, 1897).
LSJ	H. G. Liddell–R. Scott–H. S. Jones, *A Greek–English Lexicon*⁹ (Oxford, 1925–40).
Meisterhans³	K. Meisterhans–E. Schwyzer, *Grammatik der attischen Inschriften*³ (Berlin, 1900).
Page, *GLP*	D. L. Page, *Greek Literary Papyri* (London, 1950).
RE	Pauly–Wissowa, *Real-Encyclopädie der klassischen Altertumswissenschaft*.
Schwyzer	E. Schwyzer, *Griechische Grammatik* (Munich, 1939–53).
Webster, *StM*	T. B. L. Webster, *Studies in Menander*² (Manchester, 1960).

The abbreviations of ancient authors' names and of titles of journals will, I hope, be intelligible. The more drastically abbreviated appear in the form used in *L'Année Philologique*; for the sake of convenience I set out a few that may cause hesitation:

PCPS	*Proceedings of the Cambridge Philological Society.*
REA	*Revue des Études Anciennes.*
SIFC	*Studi italiani di filologia classica.*
ZPE	*Zeitschrift für Papyrologie und Epigraphik.*

References of the form '[Author] frag. 27 K' are to Kock's *Comicorum Atticorum Fragmenta*. The fragments of Menander from the indirect tradition are always quoted from Körte's *Menandri quae supersunt, pars altera*, posthumously edited by A. Thierfelder (2nd edn., Leipzig, 1959). When it is necessary for the sake of clarity the reference takes the form 'frag. 27 K–T'.

INTRODUCTION

I. MENANDER'S LIFE AND WORKS

MANY of the poets of the Middle and New Comedy were foreigners who settled in Athens, but Menander was an Athenian of good family, the son of Diopeithes and Hegestrate,[1] born in 342/1 B.C.[2] He is said to have learned his craft from an association with Alexis, whom an improbable story made his paternal uncle,[3] and to have been a pupil of the Peripatetic philosopher Theophrastus.[4] In a short life—his death, allegedly by drowning when swimming at the Piraeus,[5] is to be placed not later than 290/89, perhaps as early as 293/2[6]—he wrote 105 plays.[7] Not all of these can have been performed at the major Athenian festivals; some may have been destined for country festivals, since there were theatres in several of the demes; others for performance in other Greek cities. Just as

[1] Suda s.v. Μένανδροc; Com. Gr. Frag. ed. Kaibel, p. 9.

[2] IG xiv. 1184, a stone that has disappeared, puts his birth in the archonship of Sosigenes (342/1), and his death when 52 (or in his 52nd year) in that of Philippos (293/2) and in the 32nd year of Ptolemy I Soter (also 293/2). These dates are clearly irreconcilable, yet all are supported. Strabo xiv. 638 says that he was an ephebus along with Epicurus (who was born 342/1) and the anonymous author of περὶ κωμῳδίαc probably reported that his first play was produced when he was still an ephebus (i.e. not more than twenty) in the archonship of Philokles (322/1); the MS. has Diokles, which cannot be right. The same author may have agreed that he died when 52 (or in his 52nd year); the MS. has 56. Jerome places his death in 292/1, but the Armenian version of Eusebios in 293/2. Aulus Gellius xvii. 21. 42 also puts it at about 292. The best-attested date is that of his birth, established by two, perhaps three, apparently independent lines of evidence; the evidence about the date of his death and his age may all come from a single original source. Jacoby, followed by Körte, supposed that the Alexandrians, not finding his name in the official lists of competitors after 293/2, erroneously assumed that he died in that year. This may be the true explanation. Yet no one knows whether the reason ancient scholars had for saying he was 52 (or in his 52nd year) was a good one.

[3] Suda s.v. Ἄλεξιc.   [4] Diog. L. v. 36.

[5] Schol. on Ovid, Ibis 591–2.   [6] See note 2.

[7] Aulus Gellius xvii. 4. 5 quotes the iambic line πρὸc τοῖcιν ἑκατὸν πέντε γράψαι δράματα from Apollodoros' Chronica (frag. 77 Jacoby); according to Gellius others made the number 108 or 109. Anon. περὶ κωμῳδίαc and Suda also give 108, and there was a story that Terence was drowned when bringing back from Greece 108 comedies of Menander that he had translated (!) (Suetonius, Vita Terenti, p. 294 R). The numbers may have been exaggerated by mistakenly counting as separate plays what were alternative titles for the same play.

Athens in this age imported dramatists, she also exported plays. It is possible, too, that some of his plays never found a producer. In his lifetime he was not the most popular of playwrights, gaining only eight recorded victories.[1] Whatever the reason for his lack of contemporary success, Menander became immensely popular with later generations, and was regarded as the pre-eminent author of New Comedy. More than that, the scholar Aristophanes of Byzantium (*c.* 257–180 B.C.) placed him second only to Homer among all the poets of Greece.[2] In Quintilian's résumé of Greek and Roman literature he is given four paragraphs, when no other writer but Homer gets more than one, except Euripides, who has two.[3] Homer and Menander are the first authors that Ausonius recommends to his grandson.[4] No doubt as learning decayed fewer and fewer of the plays were readily available, and in the Dark Ages of the eighth and ninth centuries even these were lost.[5] Their subject-matter, in which love played a large part, will not have been thought edifying, and they were not part of the traditional school curriculum. It seems certain that the later Byzantine scholars knew nothing of Menander but certain short extracts in anthologies, citations in grammarians and lexica, and quotations in surviving authors.

These fragments came to the western world, the scholars of which were able to add to them several plays by Plautus and Terence that were based on Menandrean originals. But these, even if they had been faithful translations, would have been an inadequate substitute for the original Greek; and they were not faithful translations, but adaptations to suit the Roman theatre. They can give some help, but it is imperfect help, towards understanding Menander, who remained a great name, but little known, until the end of the nineteenth century. The first

---

[1] Apollodoros apud Aul. Gell. xvii. 4. 6; 'Rara coronato plausere theatra Menandro', Martial v. 10. 9; 'doctior urbe sua', Manilius v. 475.

[2] *IG* xiv. 1183.   [3] *Inst. Or.* x. 1. 69–72.   [4] *Epist.* xxii. 44.

[5] D. Del Corno, 'Selezioni menandree', *Dioniso* xxxviii (1964), 130; R. Cantarella, *Dioniso* N.S. xvii (1954), 22; A. Dain, *Maia* xv (1963), 278. The St. Petersburg parchment was made into a palimpsest in the eighth century.

Why Menander disappeared remains something of a puzzle. One may suppose that in the eighth century Byzantium was the only place where conditions in any way favoured the preservation of classical texts; and that the Menandrean texts were so few that chance could lead to their complete destruction. This is Cantarella's view. I would hazard the further suggestion that Menandrean codices, having been much read, were worn and looked fit candidates for the scrap-heap.

discovery of a passage long and complete enough to allow appreciation of the poet's dramatic quality came with publication in 1898 of some eighty almost whole lines of *Georgos*, giving nearly all of one scene. But the truly important step was the appearance in 1907 of a find made two years earlier, portions of five plays; from two, *Heros* and an unidentified play, less than a single scene apiece, but considerable parts of *Epitrepontes*, *Perikeiromene*, and *Samia*.

At Aphroditopolis, near the Egyptian Thebes, there lived in the sixth century A.D. a lawyer named Flavius Dioskoros, who was also a writer of verses.[1] When his house was excavated by Gustave Lefebvre, a store of documents was found in the last room he explored. Some of these were kept in a jar and had been protected by the insertion of sheets from a codex that had contained plays by Menander. Other leaves and fragments from the codex were lying in the floor. The earliest editions were far from satisfactory; fragments were not all assigned to the right plays, the more damaged parts of the papyrus were incorrectly or insufficiently read, and many supplements were printed that today no one would suppose to be correct. It is not surprising that some scholars found that their expectations were cheated and that the new discoveries showed Menander's reputation to be overinflated. Others recognized high literary merit, and successive editions and works of interpretation have made us better equipped to pass a judgement on the poet's work.[2]

For fifty years after the publication of the Aphroditopolis papyrus only small scraps of new material came to light, but then M. Bodmer secured from Egypt parts of a codex which contain *Dyskolos* almost complete. This play was published in 1959, the first, and as yet the only, whole play to be recovered. It was followed in 1965 by large parts of *Sikyonios*, extracted by a skilful technical feat from the wrappings of a mummy at the Sorbonne, and some badly damaged remains of *Misumenos* from the Oxyrhynchus collection. Thereafter other small fragments came to

---

[1] J. Maspero, *REG* xxiv (1911), 426–81.

[2] Texts: Körte[2] 1912, Körte[3] 1938 (reprinted with addenda, 1957), Sudhaus[2] 1914, van Leeuwen[3] 1919, Allinson 1921, Jensen 1929, Del Corno 1967. Commentary and interpretation: Wilamowitz, *Menander, das Schiedsgericht* (1925), Capps, *Four Plays of Menander* (1910), Gilbert Murray, *Aristophanes* (1933), pp. 221–63, A. Körte, article 'Menandros' in *RE* xv (1931), 707–61, T. B. L. Webster, *Studies in Menander*[2] (1960). This is a brief selection only.

light, and in 1969 M. Bodmer published large parts of *Samia*, some of which overlapped what was previously known, and of *Aspis*. New finds are still possible, but in the hands of fortune.

II. THE LATIN ADAPTATIONS

The material thus recovered from Egypt gives enough knowledge of Menander to make it profitable to inquire how much of the original is to be seen through the Latin dress of several plays by Plautus and Terence, and allows cautious use of them in forming a picture of the Greek dramatist. But the first task is to set out the plays concerned. The majority of scholars agree that there are eight, Plautus' *Aulularia*, *Bacchides*, *Cistellaria*, and *Stichus*, Terence's *Adelphoe*, *Andria*, *Eunuchus*, and *Heautontimorumenos*.

Aulularia is not proved to have a Menandrean original, but if Menander did not write the play on which it is based, the author must have closely imitated him. The case for Menander has been strengthened by the recovery of *Dyskolos*, to which *Aulularia* has striking resemblances.[1] It has been argued that the two Greek

---

[1] *Aul.* 23 ff. ~ *Dysk.* 36 ff.; *Aul.* 89 ff. ~ *Dysk.* 426; *Aul.* 283 ff. ~ *Dysk.* 891 f.; in both plays a rich man offers to marry an undowered girl. W. G. Arnott, *Phoenix* xviii (1964), 232, points out that the motivation of Euclio's return at Act II is like that of Sostratos' return in *Dysk.* Act II, and that there is a likeness between the scenes *Aul.* 182 ff. and *Dysk.* 269 ff. See also the article by W. Kraus cited on p. 5 n. 2 below. Chorikios xxxii. 73 includes among a list of Menander's characters Ϲμικρίνηϲ, ὁ δεδιὼϲ μή τι τῶν ἔνδον ὁ καπνὸϲ οἴχοιτο φέρων. This is not exactly the same as *Aul.* 300, 'diuom atque hominum clamat continuo fidem, de suo tigillo fumus si qua exit foras', but it is credible that Plautus substituted a simpler joke for Menander's. For a recent discussion of *Aulularia* see W. Ludwig, *Philologus* cv (1961), 44, who emphasizes the likeness to *Dyskolos*, ibid. 247 ff., W. Schäfer, *Menanders Dyskolos* (1965), pp. 96–110; also F. Klingner, *Studien z. griech. u. römischen Literatur*, pp. 114–25, E. Burck, *Wien. Stud.* lxix (1956), 265.

I myself feel that *Aulularia* is in construction inferior to *Dyskolos*. (*a*) Although the Lar assures us that he is behind the events, we have to take his word for it, and he is mentioned once only in the play proper, at 386. Contrast Pan's part in *Dyskolos*. (*b*) Sostratos and Euclio both leave at the end of Act I and return unsuccessful in Act II. But whereas Sostratos' failure to find Getas is explained, and the explanation prepares for the slave's later entrance, Euclio's disappointment is never accounted for. (*c*) Euclio twice gives away, to the same eavesdropper, the intended hiding-place for his crock. The similarity of the two scenes argues a lack of inventiveness. (*d*) Lykonides' conduct is inadequately motivated. Although he had shown no interest for nine months in the girl he had ravished, the prospect of her marrying his uncle makes him suddenly want her for his wife. It is true that other men in New Comedy (*Samia*, *Georgos*, Ter. *Adelphoe*) procrastinate over

plays were not far apart in date. *Moribus praefectum mulierum* (*Aul.* 504) refers, it is said, to the office of γυναικονόμος, which was abolished at Athens in 307; the allusion is more likely to have been made soon after its institution there, which was the work either of Demetrios of Phaleron, soon after 317, or of the government of 322–318.[1] Fraenkel, however (*Plautinisches im Plautus*, p. 139) makes a strong case for regarding the phrase as a Plautine addition.

It must be admitted, however, that it is not easy to identify a Menandrean original. Webster's Ἄπιστος is improbable, the often favoured Ὑδρία less so.[2] If Θησαυρός was the original of Luscius' *Thesaurus*, referred to by Terence, *Eun.* 10, Donatus' account of Luscius' plot shows it to have had no likeness to *Aulularia*; if it was not, the surviving fragments, although not irreconcilable with *Aul.*, do not positively suggest the derivation.

Bacchides is generally agreed to be an adaptation of Δὶς Ἐξαπατῶν.[3] For the Greek original, of which 494–551 are an adaptation, see p. 118. Plautus' changes have increased the importance of the slave Chrysalus, and have vulgarized both the first surviving scene and the end of the play.[4] But Menander's

a marriage which they desire, but they all have fathers whose consent is unobtainable or doubtful. Lykonides' father is dead, so that nothing stands in his way.

In view of these imperfections and the difficulty of identifying the Greek original some caution seems called for. Nevertheless, a Menandrean model appears probable, and some of the weaknesses detailed above may be due to omissions by Plautus of material that he found otiose.

[1] D. Del Corno, *Dioniso* xxxvi (1962), 136.

[2] The only fragment from Ἄπιστος (58) is hard to reconcile with *Aul.*, although an attempt is made by K. Gaiser, *Wien. Stud.* lxxix (1966), 191. If *Pap. Ant.* 15 (see p. 722) gives the opening of Ἄπιστος, the identification is impossible. For Ὑδρία see most recently W. Kraus, *Serta Philologica Aenopontana* 1962, pp. 185 ff. (Innsbrücker Beiträge 7–8). The title is discussed by W. Ludwig, *Philologus* cv (1961), 252 ff.

[3] W. Görler's doubts, *Μενάνδρου Γνῶμαι* (1963), p. 11, do not carry him so far as to deny that some play by Menander was Plautus' original.

[4] E. Fraenkel, *Plautinisches im Plautus*, p. 10, demonstrated that Chrysalus' great monologue (925–78) is entirely Plautine. If the Roman crudities, which are easily separable, are stripped from 35–108, a delightful scene comes to light, in which the innocent Pistoclerus falls to Bacchis' wily appeal to his loyalty to his friend. The relation of the final scene (1120–1206) to the original is uncertain. A conclusion in which the fathers accepted the *fait accompli* and joined their sons at a party with the Bacchis sisters is not unlikely; but it is not credible that Mnesilochus should be expected to accept his friend's father as his girl's lover when the whole plot has depended on his and her exclusive attachment. 'Neque adeo haec faceremus, ni ante hac uidissemus fieri | ut apud lenones riuales filiis fierent patres', writes

hand is still clearly visible in the brilliant narrative of 251–325, and in the contrasts of character: father with father, son with son, slave with slave, and again each father with each son and each son with each slave. Character was no doubt a more prominent element of the original play than of the Latin adaptation, but the intrigues of the clever slave must have provided a large part of its interest: this is unique among the surviving plays by or after Menander.

Cistellaria is a version, unfortunately much mutilated, of Menander's Ϲυναριϲτῶϲαι.[1] The plot is most skilfully contrived, so that the characters' motives and movements combine to carry the story forward: there is a great variety of scene, charming, touching, or amusing, and the grace of Menander's dialogue is in great part not obliterated by the Latin version. Notable is the predominance of the female characters.

For attempts to reconstruct the Greek original, see W. Süss, *Rh. Mus.* lxxxiv (1935), 161, lxxxvii (1938), 97, Webster, *StM* 91, Kuiper, *Grieksche originealen en Latijnische navolgingen*, p. 167, W. Ludwig, *Entretiens Hardt* xvi. 47. The Mitilini mosaic (see below, p. 12 n. 2) gives the names Philainis, Plangon, and Pythias: these are the *lena*, Selenium, and Gymnasium of Plautus, cf. H. J. Mette, *Lustrum* xi (1967), 139.

Stichus is, by the evidence of the didascalia, based on Ἀδελφοί; this must be the so-called Ἀδελφοί α' (*P. Oxy.* 2462), the second play of that name being the original of Terence's *Adelphoe*. It contains some vigorous writing by Plautus and the figure of Gelasimus, the parasite, is amusingly presented, although without depth or sympathy. But the play is so devoid of plot, point, or character-drawing that one is tempted to doubt whether it is more than distantly connected with Menander.[2] It ends with a hilarious drinking-party among slaves, reminiscent of the

Plautus (1209–10), unable to distinguish between a brothel slave and a free *hetaira*. The elimination of the *soror* from the last scene would avoid the presence of four speaking actors on the stage.

[1] *Cist.* 408 was quoted by Festus as from 'Plautus in Sinaristosis', E. Fraenkel, *Philologus* lxxxvii (1932), 117, who thus confirmed the guess of B. Prehn, *Quaest. Plaut.* 10. That the original was by Menander was already known, since frag. 382 (558 Kock) corresponds to *Cist.* 89–93.

[2] Webster, *StM* 139–45, attempts to recognize and reconstruct incidents of Ἀδελφοί, but comes nowhere near divining a reasonable plot. Fraenkel, op. cit., pp. 278–92, assigns most of the play to Plautus' own invention. See also Mette, *Lustrum* x (1966), 36.

revelling that frequently concludes Old Comedies. The recovery of *Dyskolos* makes it more credible that Ἀδελφοί here offered Plautus something that he could develop in his own manner.

It has been claimed that *Poenulus* is based on a Menandrean original. The Greek title was Καρχηδόνιος and plays of this name by Menander and by Alexis are known to have existed. The dispute[1] seems to me to have been determined in favour of Alexis by the discovery of *P. Oxy.* 2654 (p. 153 of OCT), which gives a passage from Menander's play that implies a different plot from that of *Poenulus*, and probably a scene in Athens, not Calydon. Alexis had previously been supported by G. Zuntz, *Mnem.* 3rd ser. v (1937), 61 (frag. 100, *Poen.* 1318), and W. G. Arnott, *Rh. Mus.* cii (1959), 252 (frag. 263, *Poen.* 522–5). There are similarities between passages in Menander and in *Poenulus* (*Mis.* 218 f. ∼ *Poen.* 1296 ff., *Sik.* 312 ff. ∼ *Poen.* 1099 ff., and others noted by Webster, *StM* 132 f.), but poets of the New Comedy borrowed and adapted one another's motifs, and borrowing by Menander from Alexis (or vice versa) is not to be rejected.

K. Gaiser, *Poetica* i (1967), 436, argues that *Miles Gloriosus* is based on Menander's *Ephesios*, for which he guesses *Alazon*, Plautus' name for the Greek original (*MG* 86), to have been a variant. He supposes that Milphidippa and Acroteleutium replace an original 'Pleusicles'[2] (disguised as a female slave) and 'Philocomasium' (disguised as Dicaea) who continued to use the secret passage between the houses of 'Pyrgopolinices' and 'Periplectomenus'. This would do something to give unity to the plot, but implies considerable alteration in the latter part of the play. The earlier part seems to me long-winded and lacking in subtlety, and if a Menandrean play was the original, Plautus can in many parts have kept little but the general outline of incident. Little interest is aroused in Periplectomenus, whose long *apologia*, occupying the centre of the play, seems to be there for its own sake rather than for any dramatic relevance. It is impossible to deny that the mature Menander (the date of the original is after 300 B.C.) may on occasion have written a rather ramshackle play, but the reasons for identifying the original of

---

[1] For bibliography see G. Maurach, *Philologus* cviii (1964), 247.

[2] A name in inverted commas is not the true name, which is unknown, of the character in the Greek original, but that of his representative in the Latin adaptation.

Miles with his *Ephesios* are far from being cogent. Of the five
fragments from *Ephesios* two only consist of more than a couple of
words: 'Sceledrus' may have envisaged that he would be sold
as a punishment for letting 'Philocomasium' escape (frag. 171);
'Periplectomenus' and 'Pleusicles' may have discussed the price
of fish (frags. 172, 173). Webster, *StM* 151, makes a case for
a Menandrean origin of *Truculentus*, but without full conviction,
and in *Studies in Later Greek Comedy*², p. 150, prefers Philemon. In
the latter work, pp. 210 ff., he puts some inconclusive arguments
for Menandrean originals of *Curculio* and *Pseudolus*.

To turn to Terence, the prologues to *Andria* and *Eunuchus*, and
the didascalia to *Heautontimorumenos* and *Adelphoe*, together with
the evidence of Donatus, show that these plays are based on
originals by Menander. But changes of uncertain extent have
been made in them all; Terence himself admits it. *Andria* has
received elements from Περινθία as well as Ἀνδρία, *Eunuchus* has
characters from Κόλαξ grafted into the plot of Εὐνοῦχος, and
Adelphoe has a scene from Diphilos' Ϲυναποθνήϲκοντεϲ, which
necessitated the omission of parts of the first two acts of Ἀδελφοί β'.
The intrigue of *Heautontimorumenos* seems to have been made more
complicated.

The modern literature is extensive, and, besides referring to
Jachmann's article in *RE* s.v. Terentius, I mention only a few
of the more important subsequent discussions:

(1) *Andria*: H. Drexler, *Hermes* lxxiii (1938), 39–65; edition by
    A. Thierfelder (1951); A. Mazzarino, *Da Menandro a Terenzio*
    (1947).
(2) *Eunuchus*: U. Knoche, *NGG* n.f. i (1936), 145 ff., n.f. iii (1938),
    31 ff., *Hermes* lxxvi (1941), 251 ff.; H. Drexler, *Hermes* lxxiii
    (1938), 73 ff., lxxvi (1941), 75 ff., *Gnomon* xviii (1942), 19 ff.;
    A. Klotz, *Würzb. Jahrb.* i (1946), 1 ff.; W. Ludwig, *Philologus* ciii
    (1959), 1 ff.; H. Marti, *Lustrum* viii (1963), 63–72.
(3) *Adelphoe*: H. Drexler, *Die Komposition von Terenz' Adelphen u.
    Plautus' Rudens* (1934); O. Rieth, *Die Kunst Menanders in den
    'Adelphen' des Terenz* (1964).
(4) *Heautontimorumenos*: H. J. Mette, *Gymnasium* lxix (1962), 401–3.

Terence made deliberate changes for artistic reasons. He dis-
liked some forms of dramatic convention that Menander had
accepted. Therefore he did away with the expository prologue,
and he reduced the number of soliloquies addressed to the

audience. He avoids recognition scenes and the bestowing of dowries. He omits much of the detail which gives life, individuality, and personality to Menander's characters: one may compare his

> post deinde,
> quod iussi dari bibere et quantum imperaui,
> date   (*Andria* 483–5)

with the original

> καὶ τεττάρων
> ὠῶν μετὰ τοῦτο, φιλτάτη, τὸ νεοττίον,   (frag. 37)

or

> agrum in his regionibus
> meliorem neque preti maioris nemo habet   (*Heaut.* 63–4)

with

> καὶ τῶν Ἅλῃϲι χωρίον
> κεκτημένοϲ κάλλιϲτον εἶ, νὴ τὸν Δία,
> ἐν τοῖϲ τριϲίν γε, καὶ τὸ μακαριώτατον,
> ἄϲτικτον.   (frag. 127)

The detail of the Greek is there to indicate the inquisitiveness of the speaker, who prides himself on his interest in his fellow human beings: 'humani nil a me alienum puto.' To be sure, the Roman spectators could not be expected to have heard of Halai, and few of a city audience would have any personal acquaintance with mortgaging land. Nevertheless Terence was probably not merely suiting his public, but also deliberately suppressing detail that appeared to him irrelevant and unnecessary. He may well have thought that the paradox of the self-tormentor was sharper if his farm had no superior than if it were only 'in the first three'. Again, it was the practice of Greek dramatists to avoid the presence on the stage of more than three speaking characters at once; Terence thought this restraint unnecessary, and even more often than Plautus gives a part to a fourth or even a fifth person.

All these changes are deliberate, whether for the better or for the worse. Some other changes are undoubtedly for the worse. Terence had only a limited understanding of or respect for Menander's characters. A partial excuse is to be found in the fact that he was dealing with a foreign society and men who had lived over a hundred years before his time. This must have made it difficult to appreciate the way in which Menander gave his characters individual and appropriate styles of speech. But it does not pardon such a volte-face as the last scene of *Eunuchus*, which is quite out of keeping with the earlier treatment of Phaedria and Thais, and may have been suggested by very different characters in Κόλαξ.

It is unfortunate that none of the recovered fragments of Menander comes from any of the four plays adapted by Terence: the detailed comparison would be instructive. But even the general comparison that is feasible supports Caesar's verdict when he addressed the latter as 'dimidiate Menander'.[1]

III. MENANDER'S THEATRE

(i) *Buildings*

Menander's plays were mostly written for production in Athens. When reading them, we should try to think of them, not as books, but as dramatic performances, to imagine them enacted on the stage, before a holiday audience, seated in the open-air theatre. Yet many of the details must elude us, and others are a matter of probability rather than certainly established.[2] The nature of the stage itself in the 'Theatre of Lykurgos' at the end of the fourth century has been hotly disputed. Later in the Hellenistic age it was, as in many other theatres, a high narrow platform some thirteen feet above the level of the orchestra, access being by ramps at the side, and through the *skene* or stage-building behind. Such stages could be found in some cities, e.g. Epidauros, even in Menander's time. But at Athens the evidence points to the preservation of the low stage, communicating easily with the orchestra.[3] Some uncertain support is to be found in the plays

---

[1] Suetonius, p. 34, ed. Reifferscheid: 'Tu quoque tu in summis, o dimidiate Menander, | poneris, et merito, puri sermonis amator. | lenibus atque utinam scriptis adiuncta foret uis | comica, ut aequato uirtus polleret honore | cum Graecis.' A sober comparison of the two dramatists is made by W. Ludwig, 'The Originality of Terence and his Greek Models', *GRBS* ix (1968), 169.

[2] For a full discussion see A. W. Pickard-Cambridge, *Theatre of Dionysus at Athens*, particularly ch. iv; also P. D. Arnott, *Greek Scenic Conventions*, and T. B. L. Webster, *Greek Theatre Production*.

[3] T. B. L. Webster, *Griechische Bühnenaltertümer*, p. 20, argues that the high stage was introduced during Menander's career. But (1) professional actors would not have found an insuperable difficulty in acting on different kinds of stage in different cities, and (2) Plut. *Demetrius* 34, which recounts how Demetrios addressed the people, καταβὰc ὥcπερ οἱ τραγῳδοὶ διὰ τῶν ἄνω παρόδων, is hard to interpret with confidence; Pickard-Cambridge, p. 159, calls the passage 'hazy' and 'valueless'.

themselves. *Dysk.* 143–52, in which the characters discuss the rapidly approaching Knemon, implies that they can see him coming up one of the long *parodoi* which led into the orchestra, and that a ramp or a few steps will bring him on the stage. The formula for introducing the chorus at its first appearance, οἷς μὴ 'νοχλεῖν εὔκαιρον εἶναί μοι δοκεῖ, *Epitr.* 171, is made for a situation where there is no great difference of level between actors and chorus.[1] *Theophorumene* 26 ff. have been used as decisive evidence for easy transition from stage to orchestra, but are less than cogent (see note there and T. B. L. Webster, *Greek Theatre Production*, p. 22).

It is probable then that the stage of the theatre at Athens in Menander's time was a low platform in front of the *skene*; if there was a *proskenion*, it was only a shallow projection to which scene-painting or hangings could be attached; it is not known how much use was made of such things. In the *skene* there were three openings, which could represent the doorways of houses, etc. Most plays require only two houses, but *Perikeiromene* probably needs three.[2] *Dyskolos* needs the third entrance to represent the cave, the original of *Aulularia* needed it for a temple.[3] Pollux iv. 124 implies that when only two houses were represented the central door was used for that of the protagonist, and the right-hand one for the secondary character. This evidence, probably true of some performances at some period, does not necessarily apply to Menander's Athens.

The width of the stage, with its three doorways, was in the theatre of Lykurgos 66 feet. Beyond this there was at each side a projecting structure, $16\frac{1}{2}$ feet deep and 21 to 23 feet across, which must have marked its limits. These structures, called by modern scholars *paraskenia*, are something of a puzzle. It seems likely that they were open colonnades through which actors approaching from the *parodoi* could pass. They must have restricted the view of the stage from the seats at the sides of the auditorium. Is it possible that audiences for plays were no longer large enough for those seats to be needed?[4]

---

[1] This seems to be a late play. But supporters of the high stage can suggest that the chorus, not more than fifteen in number (see below), appeared on it for their performances in the intervals.

[2] *Pace* Körte, *Hiereia* does not, so far as we know.

[3] So also Plautus, *Curculio.*

[4] The theatre would hold a maximum of about 17,000 spectators.

In front of the stage was the circular orchestra, with a diameter of 66 feet, into which the *parodoi* led, as well as to the stage. There was, it seems, a convention by which the *parodos* on the audience's left was, unless some other indication was given, thought to come from the harbour or the country, that on the right from the market or the town. In the orchestra the chorus performed between the acts, and here a series of doubts arises. What was the nature of its performance? Did it sing as well as dance? If it sang, what did it sing? Had its reduced importance led to a reduction in its number? Did it remain in the orchestra during the acts, or come and go at each interval? I know no evidence or argument that makes possible a confident answer to any of these questions.[1]

The stage represented the space outside the houses of the characters; if the scene is in a town or village it will be thought of as a street. Indoor scenes were therefore rarely portrayed;[2]

---

[1] The appearance of the chorus is marked in our texts, from the earliest, by the word *XOPOY*. This may stand for *XOPOY MEΛOC*—a papyrus fragment of tragedy (*P. Hibeh* i. 4) has *XOPOY M[* —or for *KOMMATION XOPOY*, as in the Ravenna and Venice MSS. of Aristophanes at *Plutus* 771. But the word *MEΛOC* might have been dropped when and if singing was dropped. Plaut. *Rudens* 290–305 may represent a song, written by Diphilos, and exceptionally preserved in the text. My own guess is that the chorus sang, but that the words, having no connection with the plot of the play, were not preserved in the written text.

Aristotle, *Pol.* 1276ᵇ1–6, seems to imply that in his day the comic chorus, once of twenty-four members, numbered no more than fifteen at the most, being equal in size to the tragic. At Delphi in the late third century there were seven or four *choreutai* (Dittenberger, *Sylloge* ii. 424. 42 and 690), but Delphi was not Athens, and a century had elapsed since Menander's time. He can call his chorus μειράκια πάμπολλα (*Perik.* 261).

[2] Some scholars, e.g. T. B. L. Webster, *Greek Theatre Production*, pp. 24 ff., believe that certain scenes, although represented on the stage, are to be thought of as taking place indoors. The most probable instance is Philematium's toilet and the following drinking-scene in *Mostellaria* 156–430; but part of the stage remains the street (313 ff., 326), and the characters go *in* to the house (397, 405).

A difficult problem is raised by Menander's *Synaristosai*. The Mitilini mosaic shows, under the heading cυναριcτωcων με(ρος) α (Act I), the women sitting at table (S. Charitonidis–L. Kahil–R. Ginouvès, *Antike Kunst*, Beiheft 6 (1970), 41, Plate 5). The same scene in reverse appears in the untitled mosaic by or after Dioskurides of Samos, found at Pompeii and now in the Naples Museum (L. Curtius, *Die Wandmalerei Pompejis*, Plate X; A. W. Pickard-Cambridge, *Theatre of Dionysus*, fig. 86). This meal must have taken place indoors. Yet the first scene of Plautus' *Cistellaria* represents the departure of Gymnasium after the meal, which is described, not acted; all this can very well be thought of as taking place in the street; there is no reason for supposing that Menander's play opened in any other way, and frag. 385 seems to correspond to *Cist.* 19. It is perhaps possible that the mosaics illustrate not what was seen on the stage in Act I, but what was there described. There is there are none in our surviving remains of Menander, unless *Dyskolos* 691–758 is one, staged by means of the *ekkyklema* or platform rolled out through the doorway. This limitation was less hampering to the dramatist than it would be to a modern English writer. Life took place out of doors in Greece far more than it does in our climes. But some plots required indoor scenes, and then they are either reported (e.g. *Dysk.* 666–88, *Perik.* 318–24, *Epitr.* 878–900, *Mis.* 186 ff.), or begin indoors and continue out of doors as one of the characters departs, when the earlier part of the conversation is supplied by conjecture from that which is heard (e.g. *Dysk.* 784–96, *Sam.* 369–98, probably *Perik.* 708 ff.).

(ii) *Actors*

The actors were dressed realistically in accord with the age and status of the persons they represented; the grotesque exaggerations of Old Comedy had disappeared.[1] But they still wore masks,[2] some of which caricatured the features of the old and of slaves. Facial expression being thus out of the question—and it would hardly have been visible in the great theatre—actors were dependent upon gesture and expressive voice for their effects: it was the latter that attracted most attention in antiquity.[3] Neither can now be reconstructed in detail, but one thing is likely, namely that in dialogue the actors faced the audience more than they do in modern realistic drama.[4] Both the need to

a similar possibility over *Phasma*, of which the mosaic is most readily interpreted as showing the internal door between the two houses; it is hard to believe that the door in the *skene*, which served as the house's front door, was made to represent this inside door also. Another conceivable explanation is that *Synaristosai* began with a tableau: the women were revealed at table behind the open doors of the house, if they were wide enough, and then came out to speak the first lines. For a fuller discussion by several scholars see *Entretiens Hardt* xvi. 35–9.

[1] It can, however, not be asserted that no dramatist in Menander's time used any element of caricature in costume, nor even that Menander refrained absolutely. But there is nothing in the surviving texts to suggest that he looked to this for any of his effects.

[2] This is a matter on which much has been written; I am not competent to deal with it, and refer to C. Robert, *Die Masken der neueren attischen Komödie*, M. Bieber, *History of the Greek and Roman Theater*[2], A. W. Pickard-Cambridge, *The Dramatic Festivals of Athens*[2], pp. 223–30, and T. B. L. Webster, *Greek Theatre Production*, pp. 73 ff.

[3] Pickard-Cambridge, op. cit., pp. 167–76.

[4] 'It is by no means certain that the modern method of speaking dialogue was even known to Shakespeare's stage. When the naturalist movement reached its

be audible in the large theatre and the accepted presence of the spectators will have contributed to this.

In the theatre of the early twentieth century the stage was a box from which one side had been removed, to allow the audience to watch and overhear actors, who pretended not to know that they were observed. At least, that was the theory, although the phrase 'playing to the gallery' is a reminder that some actors were less than conscientious in keeping the convention. The separation between players and spectators was the more marked because of the contrast between the bright lighting of the stage and the darkness of the auditorium. In the Greek theatre there was no such contrast; actors and audience were under the same sky and the architectural design included them in a single space; the audience had indeed reached their seats by the *parodoi* that were to be used by the actors. That being so, the spectators were more immediately present at the events going forward in front of them, and the actor in New Comedy draws them in to participate. He informs them of what has happened off-stage, he confides in them, may even put questions to them,[1] although he gives no opportunity for an answer. This link between actor and audience is an inheritance from Old Comedy, and from Old Comedy is inherited, too, the traditional vocative used in addressing the spectators: ἄνδρες. Even where this vocative is not used it is often necessary to imagine that a monologue was no less addressed to the audience; one would not always be right to see the modern stage-convention, by which the character talks to himself, in order that the audience may as it were overhear his thoughts. A speech which a *reader* is inclined to take as a soliloquy in this sense may after a time reveal itself by the vocative as an address to the audience,[2] and the character of a speech that is introduced by ἄνδρες may in no way differ from one that is not.[3] The conventional soliloquy is, however,

climax in the last quarter of the nineteenth century, reformers of the drama all over Europe found that it was necessary to train actors not to speak dialogue "out front" ', B. L. Joseph, *Elizabethan Acting* (1951), p. 130.

[1] *Dysk.* 657, perhaps 194. If *Aul.* 715–17 is Menandrean and not Plautine, the audience's assistance may be invoked: 'obsecro uos ego mi auxilio | oro obtestor sitis et hominem demonstretis quis eam apstulerit. | quid ais tu? tibi credere certum est, nam esse bonum ex uoltu cognosco.' Similarly at *Cist.* 678, 'mei homines, mei spectatores, facite indicium si quis uidit, | quis eam apstulerit', etc. See E. Fraenkel, *Beobachtungen zu Aristophanes*, p. 21. [2] e.g. *Dysk.* 643 ff., *Epitr.* 878 ff.
[3] *Dysk.* 666 ff. and 522 ff.; *Epitr.* 878 ff. and 419 ff.; *Sam.* 682 ff. and 664 ff.

not unknown.[1] An intermediate type may be seen in Knemon's entrance-speech, *Dysk.* 153 ff.: here he is literally talking to himself (149), a habit into which solitary persons easily fall.[2] Whether the playwright intended this speech to pass into an address to the audience, there is nothing to show, any more than at 442–57. But true soliloquy, of the kind that would be as natural or more natural, if thought rather than spoken, is given to Daos at 218 ff., and to Sostratos at 381 ff., and there are many other passages of this nature. Often enough one may hesitate, and may then suppose that the ancient actor would, unless under the poet's instructions, have had to decide whether to speak the lines to himself or to the audience. There is no reason to assume that he would have any prejudice in favour of speaking to himself.

Terence, probably in the quest for realism that led him to abandon the expository prologue, reduced the number of monologues, at times introducing persons whose sole purpose was to save a character from the necessity of addressing the audience directly.[3] There are only two places where the spectators are appealed to: the introductory prologue, which is not part of the play, and the final words *uos ualete et plaudite* (or even a mere *plaudite*). By contrast, in the appeal for applause in *Dyskolos* the audience is supposed to have *shared* the pleasure of the characters at their success in overcoming Knemon. This involvement of the spectators was impossible in the Roman theatre, where a set of entertainers of low social class performed a play about the doings of a lot of foreigners. But in Athens it encouraged the use of the monologue, in the composition of which Menander shows the greatest skill.

Monologues must also have offered the actor an occasion for the display of his powers, and it is relevant that there was a prize for the best *protagonistes* or leading actor, recorded in inscriptions alongside that for the best play. The prize for the comic actor was established at the Lenaia in the middle of the fifth century; it was introduced at the Dionysia between 329 and 312 B.C., that is about the time when Menander began his career.[4]

---

[1] *Perik.* 184–90 seems a clear instance.

[2] Cf. *Stoicorum Veterum Fragmenta* (ed. von Arnim), i. 616, πρὸς δὲ τὸν μονήρη καὶ ἑαυτῷ λαλοῦντα "οὐ φαύλῳ" ἔφη (sc. Κλεάνθης) "ἀνθρώπῳ λαλεῖς."

[3] Antipho in Ter. *Eunuchus*, Sosia in *Andria*.

[4] A. W. Pickard-Cambridge, *Dramatic Festivals*[2], p. 94.

The *protagonistai* were probably assigned to the five competing dramatists by lot. There is acute disagreement among scholars on the question whether the playwrights were also bound by a rule that they were not to employ more than three speaking actors, who by doubling parts might represent all the characters in a play, except in so far as a super might represent a character in a scene during which he did not speak. The use of masks would make such a system feasible, and it might have been introduced to make the conditions as equal as possible for all contestants. Our evidence is inadequate to make any conclusion certain, but if there was such a restriction it must have affected the construction of plays, and an attempt must be made to treat the problem briefly.[1]

That tragedians had to make do with three actors seems clear (Aristotle, *Poetics* 1449[a]15, Pickard-Cambridge, *Dramatic Festivals*, 2nd edn., pp. 138–48). Many of Aristophanes' plays need a fourth actor, but there never was a word *tetartagonistes*; *tritagonistes*, 'third player', remains the word to indicate the actor with the least important role. Records of the festival Soteria at Delphi from about 275 B.C. onwards show that the visiting groups or guilds of actors each have three τραγῳδοί or three κωμῳδοί. This is the sum of the external evidence, and clearly it proves nothing about the conditions in Menander's Athens.[2] Although the travelling companies performed old plays, they may have chosen those for which three actors would suffice; and the fact that three actors can perform a play does not show that it was written to be performed by that number.

The only hope of discovering whether Menander wrote for three actors is by examining his plays. This, however, is not likely to lead to any firm general conclusions. Even if it should

[1] For fuller treatments see K. Rees, *The so-called Rule of Three Actors* etc. (1908); idem, *Cl. Phil.* v (1910), 291; E. Legrand, *Daos*, pp. 365 ff. (E. T. 289 ff.); A. W. Pickard-Cambridge, *The Dramatic Festivals of Athens*[2], pp. 135 ff.; R. C. Flickinger, *The Greek Theater and the Drama*[4], pp. 173–88; K. Schneider, *RE* Suppl. viii. 190–3.

[2] Dr. Austin has called my attention to an unpublished scrap of a play, *P. Berol.* 21119 of the second century A.D. This indicates two speakers by marginal letters *B̄* and *Δ̄*. In other papyri (*P. Oxy.* 2458, *PSI* 1176, *P. Rylands* 484, *P. Hibeh* 180) one or more of the marginal letters *Ā*, *B̄*, *Γ̄* indicate speakers, and are plausibly supposed to refer to three actors. Hence it is reasonable to guess that *Δ̄* assigns a speech to a fourth actor. Even if this is right, too hasty conclusions should not be drawn. The play may not be New Comedy and, even if it is, one cannot infer with certainty more than that four actors were not unknown in plays of that period.

appear that some plays require a minimum of four actors, it would still be possible that others were written so that they could be performed by three; and if some plays seem to be written for three actors, others might have been intended for a larger company. Moreover, only a small fraction of his writing survives, even if the Latin adaptations are taken into account; and they have made changes which make their evidence difficult to handle.

Perhaps the most powerful argument is the fact that nowhere in our remains is there a scene where four speaking persons are on the stage at once. There is not even an instance where (say) A, B, C, and D appear together, A, B, and C converse, and then after the departure of A and B conversation is continued by C and D. It is true that to write four-part dialogue is not easy, but it is surprising that if Menander had four actors available he did not accept the challenge. The rule that Horace expressed in the phrase 'nec quarta loqui persona laboret' must have had some reason; and none can be as satisfactory as the absence of a fourth actor. The Roman adaptations of Greek comedies contain many scenes with four or even five speaking parts. It is usually easy to see that this is or may be due to the Latin author, but there are one or two places where there must have been great changes if there were three speakers only in the original. The most difficult is Plaut. *Rudens* 1045–1181, from which Ampelisca may easily be eliminated, but the four other speakers seem all to be needed.[1] Yet even if occasional exceptions exist, it is an almost universal rule that Greek plays never have more than three speakers on the stage at once; and the most obvious explanation is that the dramatist normally disposed of only three actors.

There are a number of scenes which it is tempting to explain by supposing that no fourth actor was available. At *Dyskolos* 378–92 the three men do not set off for the fields together. Daos goes first, at 378, and Gorgias may follow at 383, leaving Sostratos to deliver a few lines alone. This will allow the first two to return by the other *parodos* as Sikon and Getas at 393 and 401.

[1] Plautus' ability to make changes in the points at which characters appear has been proved by the fragment of *Dis Exapaton* that corresponds to *Bacchides* 526 ff. I suspect that in Diphilos' play 'Trachalio' left after 'Gripus' handed 'Daemones' the box, and sent out the women: the same actor will here have played 'Trachalio' and 'Palaestra'.

At *Sikyonios* 385 Dromon and Kichesias leave by a *parodos*. Before following them at 396 Stratophanes gives some detailed instructions about his luggage. It is hard to believe that they were all of dramatic importance. His speech may have as one object to give an actor who had gone off at 385 time to reappear at 397 from the house as Moschion. Other places where there is a very convenient, although quite justified, exit are the departure of Kallippides at *Dysk*. 860 (Simiche enters 874), of the cook at *Sam*. 390 (Nikeratos enters 399), of Parmenon at *Sam*. 694 (Nikeratos enters 713), of Theron at *Sik*. 367 (Stratophanes enters 377).

The time taken by an experienced actor to change his mask and costume, often only his cloak, can be very short. A longer period would be needed to walk, or even run, from one *parodos* to the other, when that was required, a distance of sixty yards in the theatre of Dionysos. Nevertheless I believe that all surviving plays could be performed by three actors, provided that the stage could remain empty for a short time, as it can in the modern theatre.[1]

If comedies were performed by three actors, it must have often been necessary that a character was shared between two actors. Thus in *Aspis* one actor must have played both Daos and Smikrines in Act II, but different actors are required for Acts I and III; in *Epitrepontes* Acts III and V Onesimos and Smikrines will be played by two actors, in Act IV by one; in *Perikeiromene* Act II different actors must play Moschion and Sosias, in Act III the parts are played by the same man. Similar splitting of parts will be necessary in *Samia* and *Dyskolos*. Such a procedure has appeared incredible to some modern scholars. Although masks would hide the face, the difference of voice and perhaps of stature could not be disguised. But this must have been tolerated by the audiences of the touring companies of the third century, and it is an unjustified assumption that it would have been intolerable to Athenians fifty years earlier.

The evidence appears to me to favour the three-actor rule, but to be inconclusive. Some scholars, while accepting it in principle, would allow minor exceptions, suggesting that some small parts

[1] This assumes that Getas in *Mis*. 259–69, Glykera in *Perik*. 1006–26, and Sophrone in *Epitr*. 1062–1131 are all *personae mutae*: see notes ad loc. In *Epitr*. time is scanty at 376–82 if Daos returns as Onesimos, but perhaps it was Smikrines who took on the slave's part.

may have been given to a fourth actor, perhaps a novice. There is no evidence for this: the fourth actor is introduced to minimize what moderns feel to be the difficulties inherent in splitting parts between actors, and assigning very different roles to the same actor. If a fourth actor was allowable, it is no more than a guess that he was restricted to speaking a few lines only.[1]

Schemes to divide *Dyskolos* between three actors are given by G. P. Goold, *Phoenix* xiii (1959), 144 ff., J. G. Griffith, *CQ* n.s. x (1960), 113 ff., and Handley in his edition, pp. 25 ff.; a scheme for four actors by Griffith loc. cit.; one for six by H. J. Mette in his edition, p. 32. Of other plays only *Samia* is so nearly complete that the operation is feasible. Here, if there are three actors, one could play Demeas and Parmenon in Act I, another Moschion, Chrysis in Acts III and IV, and Parmenon in Acts II and III, and a third Nikeratos, the cook, Chrysis in Act I, and Parmenon in Act V.

(iii) *Conventions*

It is known that the choral interludes divided *Dyskolos* and *Samia* into five acts (μέρη); it is extremely likely that the same was true of *Aspis, Epitrepontes, Perikeiromene, Sikyonios*. There is no play which can be seen to have had any other number of acts, and it is therefore likely that the convention was already established which caused Horace to write

neue minor neu sit quinto productior actu (*AP* 189).

Why this practice was adopted is not known. The interludes were used to represent the passage of time, which could be as short or as long as the playwright wished. A character may come and go between two places in the town within a single act, but a longer journey must take place in an interval between acts.[2]

Menander frequently constructed acts so that they ended not

---

[1] Cf. K. J. Dover, *Aristophanes, Clouds*, lxxviii.

[2] It is not clear whether Menander ever caused more to happen in these intervals than could be accommodated in the time supposed to pass between the beginning and end of the play. The cook in *Dyskolos* is, I think, hired in Phyle (αὐτόθεν 263) not in Athens: the action of *Epitrepontes* extends over two days and the scene is not known. But it would be surprising if Menander bothered about accurate realism in this matter, seeing that he is prepared to allow a brief absence from the stage to cover actions that must have taken much longer to perform (e.g. *Perik.* 311–15, *Sam.* 361–8).

with a climax, but with the introduction of a character who was
to play an important part in the next act (e.g. *Sam.* Act III, *Mis.*
Act III, *Perik.* Act I) ; thus he secures continuity.[1] But although
similarities can be found in the layout of certain plays, there is no
universal pattern.[2] The knot may be untied as early as the
fourth act (*Epitr.*), or apparently so (*Dysk., Sam.*), the play being
prolonged by an unexpected difficulty; on the other hand the
solution may not come until the fifth (*Mis., Sik.*).

In many, perhaps in most, of Menander's plays there was a
prologue spoken by some supernatural figure: Pan in *Dyskolos*,
the Hero in *Heros*, Misapprehension in *Perikeiromene*, Luck in
Aspis, Proof ("Ελεγχος) in some unknown play (frag. 717), unknown figures in *Phasma, Sikyonios, Synaristosai*, and the original
of Plaut. *Aulularia*.[3] They were used by him, as by his contemporaries, to put the audience in possession of the background of
basic facts, and when, as often happened, none of the characters
knew the whole of the circumstances, a non-human prologue-
speaker was needed.[4] A modern author might allow the facts to
transpire from various sources as the play proceeded; the ancient
audience was given the advantage of knowing the truth that
was concealed from the persons of the play and of being able to
appreciate the importance or the irrelevance of their actions.
Whether Menander ever adopted the modern method and kept
the spectators in the dark, as Terence did in *Adelphoe*, cannot be
known; I think it unlikely.

Both divine and human prologue-speakers are to be found in
Euripidean tragedy and doubtless served as a precedent for the
writers of comedy. But tragedy gave no model for Menander's
not infrequent device of beginning his play with a human scene
and following it with an explanatory divine prologue (*Aspis,
Heros, Perikeiromene, Synaristosai*, and probably elsewhere too).
There is, however, something similar in some of Aristophanes'
earlier plays, where the exposition follows an opening scene
of baffling nature (*Knights, Wasps, Peace*), and in Euripides'

---

[1] E. W. Handley, *Entretiens Hardt* xvi. 11, with more examples.
[2] A. Blanchard, *REG* xxxiii (1970), 38 has some interesting observations on
desis and *lysis*, but tries to apply too rigid a scheme.
[3] Divine prologues seem to me to be required in *Epitrepontes, Eunuchos, Andria,
Perinthia*, and possible in *Georgos, Adelphoi β′, Misumenos*.
[4] The only human speaker of a prologue yet known in Menander is Moschion
of *Samia*.

Iphigeneia in Aulis; in all these plays, however, the exposition is given by a character present in the first scene.

To plunge *in medias res* and to postpone the exposition until interest has been aroused has obvious theatrical advantages. But a postponed divine prologue, which interrupts the sequence of events, is clearly a device that would not recommend itself to a whole-hearted supporter of realism. Menander's realism, however, is strongly limited. Personifications like Misapprehension and Proof are obviously products of his poetic imagination, not divinities in whom true belief is expected.

The prologues are written with great skill. The situation is set out in an easy, conversational style, which is neither arid nor overloaded with facts. The essentials are given in such a way that they hold the interest and will not be forgotten. It is noteworthy that with few exceptions the prologue does not name the characters;[1] for the purposes of the plot it does not matter what they are called.[2]

IV. MENANDER'S PLAYS AND THE LIFE OF HIS TIME

Aristophanes of Byzantium wrote

> ὦ Μένανδρε καὶ βίε,
> πότεροc ἄρ' ὑμῶν πότερον ἀπεμιμήcατο.[3]

Some modern critics complain that Menander did not represent life, but only a small section of domestic life. Some historians regret the absence of evidence in him about the political events in which they are interested. There are other scholars who imagine that political activity at Athens had dwindled away, and that Menander represents the predominant interests of an unpolitical, philistine bourgeoisie. 'In this provincial town that Athens now was, the old patriotic pride and absorption in the questions of the day . . . could no longer exist . . . Public life no longer provided an outlet for energy and ambition.'[4]

[1] In two complete and three incomplete Menandrean prologues only two characters are named (*Dysk.* 6, *Aspis* 110); Euclio is named in the prologue to *Aulularia*. Some other authors followed the same principle: the prologue to Plaut. *Mercator* has no names, that to *Rudens* only that of Daemones.

[2] Minor, but yet important, characters may not get a name until the play is well advanced. Thus in *Dyskolos* Sikon's name is not used until 889.

[3] Syrian. *in Hermog.* ii. 23 Rabe.

[4] A. P. Shipp, ed. Terence, *Andria*, p. 2.

Such criticisms are misguided. The decisive date in the history of Athens as a city-state is neither the battle of Chaironeia nor the death of Alexander the Great, but 262 B.C., with the fatal defeat in the war launched by the decree of Chremonides (Gomme, *Essays*, p. 223). During Menander's lifetime Athens, reduced to the position of a minor power, was struggling with the problem of survival in the enlarged world dominated by the warring dynasts who were Alexander's successors. The fundamental division among the Athenians was between those who looked for security by accepting the protection of Macedon and those who wished to pursue an active independent policy. To some extent this was also a division between oligarchs and democrats, and between rich and poor, although it must not be supposed that all rich men were pro-Macedonian oligarchs.

In 322 B.C. the Athenians, having lost command of the sea, had to surrender unconditionally to Antipater. A drastic change of constitution followed, secured by the presence of a Macedonian garrison at the Peiraeus. All political activity, including the important jury-service, was reserved for those with a property qualification of twenty minae, enough to exclude more than half the citizen population. These continued to enjoy their purely civil rights, but could no longer look for any payments from public funds.[1] There was a brief restoration of democracy after Antipater's death, but in 317 B.C. Cassander once again enforced a limited franchise, although with the more liberal qualification of ten minae, and appointed Demetrios of Phaleron as 'Supervisor (ἐπιμελητής) of the City'. Each of these changes was accompanied by the execution or suicide of prominent politicians.

Demetrios, who had been a pupil of Theophrastos, founder of the Peripatetic school, was entrusted with the revision of the

---

[1] Diodorus Siculus xviii. 18. 5 reckons the disfranchised at 22,000. Plutarch, *Phocion* 28, makes them 'over 12,000'. W. W. Tarn, *CAH* vi. 460, N. G. L. Hammond, *History of Greece to 322 B.C.*, p. 649, A. W. Gomme, *Population of Athens*, p. 78, accept the higher figure; W. S. Ferguson, *Hellenistic Athens*, p. 22, A. H. M. Jones, *Athenian Democracy*, p. 79, the lower. There is a judicious discussion by C. Pelekidis, *Histoire de l'éphébie attique*, Appendix I, who shows that the weight of evidence favours an adult male citizen-population of about 20,000 in the later fourth century. Plutarch is then probably right and Diodorus' figure an exaggeration, as will also be his statement that 12,000 emigrated to Thrace. Gomme suggested that real property alone counted for the qualification. It may be guessed that the poorer part of the population, no longer receiving a theoric payment, did not attend the theatre in great number and that this had some effect on the nature of the plays written.

laws. Some of his measures, directed towards securing good order (γυναικονόμοι and νομοφύλακες), were to be cancelled by the democrats as soon as they returned to power; but his abolition of the choregia and the trierarchy was allowed to stand. During the greater part of Menander's career, therefore, his plays were produced not by enforced private generosity but under the aegis of a public *agonothetes*. Although Demetrios liked to present himself as a restorer of democracy, to the majority of Athenians he appeared a tyrant.[1] When in 307 B.C. Antigonos, who held Asia Minor, moved against Macedon, they welcomed his son Demetrios Poliorketes as a liberator. Democracy was restored, and Menander, who had been among the expelled ruler's friends, was saved only by the intercession of Poliorketes' cousin Telesphoros. The new regime was not extremist; it allowed a number of important offices to be filled by election, not lot, and preserved the powers of the Areopagos. But it prepared for war; had some military success, followed by disasters; was rescued once again by Demetrios Poliorketes, whose help was paid for by the death or exile of those who had opposed his supporters. His defeat at Ipsos in 301 B.C. left Athens once again exposed to Macedonian power and the democrats lost control to a pacifist leadership. The death of Cassander in 298/7 gave Demetrios another opportunity. The ruling faction at Athens began to kill his supporters; the democrats established themselves in the Peiraeus, and the 'moderates', under the dictatorial leadership of Lachares, held the city, where they resolutely sustained a long siege, until starvation forced them to surrender in 294. Menander died not much later, and it is unnecessary to continue the story further: it is one of a see-saw between pro-Macedonian and nationalist forces.[2]

Public life, therefore, was not at a standstill. It was bitterly and sometimes bloodily contested and success went to those who could obtain effective outside help. Comedy had in any case abandoned the political field for a generation or more before Menander began to write. He can hardly have had any regrets: the politics

---

[1] For the latest estimate see A. Columbini, *Misc. greca e romana* (1965), p. 177, who points out that ancient opinions become more favourable the further their authors are removed in time from the fourth century.

[2] See W. S. Ferguson, *Hellenistic Athens* (1911), W. W. Tarn in *CAH* vi and vii, *RE* suppl. x, col. 82 (brief but up to date); and for the period 312 to 262 B.C. the judicious account of A. D. Momigliano, *Riv. stor. it.* lxxi (1959) = *Terzo Contributo* etc., pp. 28–32.

of his time were far too grim and frustrated to make a suitable
subject for an audience that wished to be entertained on a public
holiday.[1] That he was not unaware of the political stresses of his
time appears from a short passage of *Sikyonios* (155 ff.). Similarly
the account in *Aspis* of the freebooting expedition in Lykia shows
a knowledge of other sides of life than the domestic.

Nevertheless it is within domestic or private life that he found
the subjects for his comedy. Plutarch observed that Eros ran
through them all (frag. 134 Sandbach, vii. 130 Bernardakis),
and it certainly is a factor in all the plays where the plot is known
in any degree. But Eros, which is sexual attraction and a desire
for possession, is not in itself the predominant subject: how could
it be when its object was often a citizen girl with whom the lover
could have little or no association until he obtained her as a wife?
Each new discovery brings more evidence of the danger of
generalizing about Menander's plays. Some have a strongly
marked general theme: *Adelphoe* B, Terence's *Adelphoe*, is about
the right way to bring up a son, *Dyskolos* is about co-operation
and isolation, *Samia* a study in relations between father and son.
In *Epitrepontes*, although it has a serious theme of loyalty between
husband and wife, the plot is forwarded to a great extent by
scenes between 'minor' characters, who are depicted for their
own sakes. *Sikyonios* appears to be a play of incident, with clearly
marked characters, a story excellently told, but with no moral.
Misumenos again seems to have been a play full of incident, built
round the central situation of the soldier who is hated by the
captive girl whom he loves. Gomme wrote (*Essays*, p. 284) that
'what is at bottom wrong with [Terence's] *Andria*, *H.T.* and
Eunuchus . . . is that unlike the three later plays and still more
unlike those of Menander, they are not *about* anything'. Only
some of Menander's plays are about a subject of wider interest
than the characters who embody it, but they are all about
characters who have an individuality: 'we are', to quote Gomme
again, 'in a world of reasonable men and women, with human
feelings and emotions; and these men and women are most subtly
observed'. Not only do they give the illusion of being real people,

---

[1] But allusions to politics were occasionally made by Menander's contemporaries,
Alexis frags. 94, 111, Archedikos frag. 4 K, above all Philippides frag. 25 K.
Menander may have been too much of an artist to seek for applause by appealing
to political feeling: but a new find could upset such a guess.

but they are presented in a way that encourages the spectator's interest: in their conversation, even in their monologues, they do not so much explain themselves as drop the clues from which he can make his inferences about them. The range of characters treated in this realistic manner is wide, and there are memorable figures among the slaves, many of whom have parts much more fully realized than those usually given to servants in the plays of say Ibsen, Wilde, or Shaw. Middle Comedy had satirized certain types, the cook, the soldier, the pimp, the *hetaira*, the parasite, and attached to them stock characteristics. Menander accepted these figures, but was not bound by their conventional attributes; the *hetaira* need not be a 'meretrix mala', and the soldier need not be a braggart. Polemon of *Perikeiromene* is without a trace of boastfulness, but drawn as an original and emotional human being; Thrasonides of *Misumenos* may have recounted his military exploits: the play emphasizes not that but his self-restraint and consideration for Krateia. Even the noted loquacity, boastfulness, and inquisitiveness of cooks are hinted at rather than emphasized, and, when present, are integrated into the dynamic movement of the scene (e.g. *Sam.* 283–95, *Dysk.* 409 ff., 489–500, 643–7). In *Dyskolos* they are far from the only elements in the make-up of Sikon, who is cautious, imaginative, and good-natured until he is crossed. In some cases the stock characteristic is inverted: the cook of *Misumenos* says not a word, at least at his entrance, and the cook of *Aspis* tells a tale of unemployment and frustration. Menander's art is not that of caricature. He presents figures that have the appearance of real life.

Real life, however, although far more varied and complicated than life in Menander's plays, is to a great extent uninteresting. He concentrated on certain fields that experience had shown to make good material for comedy. In these fields he was dealing with emotions that the average man had experienced in himself or in others or could at least imagine. The situations may often be unusual, but they are not such that they cannot be understood by the ordinary man, not such that he would be at an emotional loss in them. They concern the relations between individual men and women that affect their own personal happiness. The characters feel deeply over these things, but because the spectator has a superior viewpoint the sympathy that he must entertain for them is tinged with amusement. He knows that the situation

is not as black as it looks to them, that they are distressing themselves through some misapprehension, or that some unknown fact
will come to light that will solve their problems. He knows that
all will come right in the end: it is a comedy that he is watching,
and sometimes the prologue has assured him of a happy result
(*Perik.* 165 f., *Aspis* 97, 143 ff.).

Personal relations occupied much of an Athenian's attention
and success in them was both something that his own efforts
could forward and something that could bring happiness to
himself and to his friends. To know how other people think, feel,
and behave is a necessary foundation for success. Menander was
an acute observer of the human being, and set before the
spectator a series of object-lessons. But one must add that his
analysis does not go deep; his characters are credible, lifelike,
and individual, but he does not penetrate far below the surface.
It is unusual that Knemon's misanthropy is traced back to his
experience of human behaviour, and in *Samia* Moschion's gratitude to his adoptive father has little effect on his actions.

But besides these figures on which the spectator can exercise
his powers of observation Menander provides some advice on
how to behave. It is done tactfully, and he does not provide
neatly turned moral sentiments; or, if he does, they are given
a touch of irony by their context or the character who utters
them. But there is a persistent current of suggestion that men
would get on better if they would be tolerant, kind, and co-
operative, if they would see things as they are, recognizing that
most human beings are a mixture of virtues and faults. Plutarch
speaks (*QC* 712 b) of 'the undercurrent of excellent plain sentiments that soften the hardest character and bend it to complete
reasonableness. The blending of jest and earnest would seem to
have no other aim than simultaneous pleasure and profit. . . . It
would not be surprising if Menander's polished charm exercised
a reforming influence by making men's characters reflect his
fairness and kindness.' Menander's popularity was perhaps not
due only to his literary skill, but also to his having an acceptable
moral attitude, so that, in a sense that Aristophanes probably
did not intend, life imitated Menander.

Yet, when all that has been said, Menander's plays are primarily entertainments, and it is for their dramatic and literary
merits that they are read. The reader must be encouraged to

find those for himself, but some hints may be given of what he should look for.

First, the plays are well constructed, in the sense that the plot develops naturally from the situation and the characters. That is not to say that it *need* develop as it does; although each action is intelligible, it is the dramatist who causes it to take place at the moment when it will carry the plot forward as he wishes. One aspect of this virtue is that exits and entrances are usually plausible: the difficulty of avoiding any suspicion that they are contrived can easily be underestimated, and if the dramatist had to write for three actors only his task was all the harder. Then the incidents of the plot are often unexpected, not infrequently contrary to the expectations that have been aroused. A well-known story represents Menander as replying to a friend who was surprised that, with the festival near, he had not composed his comedy, 'Indeed I have composed it: the plot is worked out; all I have to do is to write the verses to go with it.'

But although this story rightly insists on the importance of structure, it must not be allowed to depreciate the merits of Menander's language. The versification is in itself highly skilful; the illusion of natural speech is maintained, but the emphasized words tend to fall in emphatic positions—the beginning of the line, or the end when there is a runover; there is constant variety in the placing of stops, in the use of resolution, in the substitution of anapaests for iambi; the trimeter approaches the strictness of tragic style and departs from it in accord with the underlying sense. Then the language is appropriate to the characters; there are no violent contrasts, but vocabulary and structure are subtly individualized. At the same time he writes with great economy when he wishes, the more so with advancing maturity; he can carry the action forward with astonishing speed, while at the same time illuminating the characters or feelings of his personages. By contrast—and there is a great deal of variety in his plays—monologues may sometimes protract and embroider what could have been stated concisely, although there are others which display a turmoil of varied reflection.

These are all merits that could be appreciated by a spectator who knew nothing of Greek comedy. But there are others that require such a knowledge. Menander was working in a tradition that gave him incidents and characters. For an educated spectator it must have been a pleasure to see how he modified these and was always making something new out of the traditional material.

V. MEN AND WOMEN IN ATHENIAN SOCIETY

Many of Menander's plays feature a marriage; and, if the scene is laid at Athens, they must accord with the laws and customs familiar to contemporary Athenians. Since these had certain peculiarities, it is desirable to give a brief account of them,[1] in so far as they are relevant.

Marriage, in the strict sense of the word γάμος, which made the woman a γαμετὴ γυνή, could take place only between partners who were each of citizen birth on both sides. Only the offspring of such a marriage were called 'legitimate', γνήcιοι, and they alone were eligible for enrolment in phratry and deme; the former qualified for admission to various religious occasions with an important social side, the latter for citizenship itself. It was a crime for a citizen and an alien to purport to be in this relationship: on conviction, the alien was sold into slavery.[2] This institution had as its avowed aim the maintenance of purity in the citizen stock. In the plays there recurs, with slight verbal variations, the formula παίδων ἐπ᾽ ἀρότῳ γνηcίων, 'for the begetting of legitimate children'. The formula did not of course completely cover what a husband might expect of a wife. It expresses that aspect of the marriage that is of interest to the world at large.

Marriage of this sort could take place only at the instance of the male member of the bride's family who was her κύριος, and an essential step in the process was called ἐγγύη; there is a corresponding verb ἐγγυᾶν.[3] The usual translation is 'betrothal', and in Latin adaptations of Greek plays the term *spondere* is used. The exact significance is not clear, and has been much discussed.[4] But ἐγγυᾶν means 'place in the hand', 'entrust'; the act is

---

[1] I take much of this from H. J. Wolff, 'Marriage Law and Family Organization in Ancient Athens', *Traditio* ii (1944), 43 ff. See also A. R. W. Harrison, *The Law of Athens*, i, pp. 1–60.

[2] This makes it impossible that Athens should be the scene of *Perikeiromene*. Polemon, a Corinthian, could not marry Pataikos' daughter, if *he* were an Athenian.

[3] *Dyskolos* 762, 841.

[4] There is a good discussion by Harrison, op. cit., pp. 6–9. On the one hand no further act was required from the girl's κύριος; on the other ἐγγύη cannot constitute marriage, for Demosthenes' father 'betrothed' his own wife during

an essential step in constituting the marriage state, although that does not become effective until the bride is physically transferred to her new κύριος;[1] this transference usually took place shortly, but might be postponed if circumstances demanded. In all this the bride was entirely passive; no action was required of her, nor was she expected to have any wishes. This was natural in view of the seclusion in which young girls were brought up.[2]

Fundamental to Athenian ideas of marriage was that the wife did not sever her connection with her own family. The word for giving in marriage was ἐκδιδόναι, which in other contexts denotes not an absolute transference, but a handing over for a limited purpose, e.g. a letting on lease, or the hiring out of a slave. In the case of the wife, that purpose is the begetting of legitimate children. Control of her passes for the time being to her husband, who becomes her κύριος. But if the purpose of the marriage is frustrated by repudiation or death, the wife reverts without ado to her own family, and comes under the control of a male relative. Within this framework it is intelligible that a father might in some circumstances put an end to his daughter's marriage and take her back under his own control, even against her wishes;[3] he would be resuming a right that he had never absolutely transferred.

If, however, the purpose of the marriage has been fulfilled, and the wife has provided a son to ensure the continuance of the house into which she has married, the situation is changed. It

his lifetime to Aphobos. I think the difficulties arise through attempts to find in Athenian marriage law the definiteness to be expected in modern laws.

[1] Wolff, op. cit., p. 42. The statement that ἐγγύη was essential is not quite true. One situation, which lies in the background of *Dyskolos* and is openly envisaged in *Aspis*, precluded it. If a man died leaving a daughter but no son, true or adopted, she could be claimed in marriage by her next-of-kin within specified degrees. The estate went with her in trust, as it were, for the expected children and she was called ἐπίκληρος; the procedure by which the next-of-kin established his right was known as ἐπιδικασία. *Aspis* shows that the same situation might arise on the death of a man who had no grown-up brothers and was κύριος of his sister; she too might be ἐπίκληρος. For some of the possible complications which might prevent her having this position see A. R. W. Harrison, *Law of Athens*, i. 132–8.

[2] But in *Perikeiromene*, where Glykera has been living with Polemon before her citizen birth is established, it is effectively her consent, although legally no doubt that of her father, that makes the marriage possible. Such circumstances must have been quite unusual.

[3] This is implied by *Epitrepontes, Stichus* (Ἀδελφοί α΄), and the Didot *rhesis*; in real life, Dem. xli. 4.

was left to her to decide, if her husband died, whether she remained with the son[1] or reverted to her own family.

An Athenian might live with a woman, not as his wife, but as his παλλακή, 'concubine'. The English word has unfortunately a more pejorative tone than the Greek. Such a union might be with another Athenian, although this may have been unusual, with a foreign woman, or with a slave. In the first case the children were free, but suffered certain disabilities; they did not become full members of the family and so could not inherit their father's property nor could the sons join his phratry, although they may have been allowed to enter the deme and so become citizens; daughters, however, could be given in full marriage.[2] The offspring of an alien woman were free but alien, those of a slave were slaves.[3]

A third form of relation is that with a *hetaira*. The essential difference is that whereas a παλλακή is expected to be faithful to her man during their union, which will last unless something unforeseen breaks it up, a *hetaira* accepts successive lovers or even two or more at once. She may give herself solely to one man for a period, but this is seen as a temporary arrangement.[4] The name *hetaira* covers a very wide range of women; some are slaves, belonging to a πορνοβοcκόc, who will hire or sell them at a wide range of prices according to their gifts[5] (Habrotonon in *Epitrepontes*, the girl in *Kolax*), others are free but poor and bound to take any clients they can (*Samia* 177), others are rich and successful, able to choose between lovers, and obtaining high rewards (Thais in Terence's *Eunuchus*, named Χρυcίc in Menander's Εὐνοῦχοc, Bacchis in Ter. *Heautontimorumenos*).

It is important to grasp that, as is illustrated by *Samia* and *Perikeiromene*, there was no social barrier between the wife and the

---

[1] Thus Myrrhine in *Dyskolos*, on separation from Knemon, went back not to her own family, but to her son by her previous marriage.

[2] Wolff, op. cit., p. 82. The main evidence is in Isaios iii.

[3] But could, of course, be manumitted.

[4] e.g. Bacchis' sister in *Bacchides* (Δὶc 'Εξαπατῶν) had hired herself to a soldier for a year (frag. x. cf. 43). There can be no firm line between the παλλακή and the *hetaira*. None is provided by an orator's remark that we take *hetairai* for pleasure, *pallakai* for household physical comfort (τῆc καθ' ἡμέραν θεραπείαc τοῦ cώματοc), and wives for childbirth, [Dem.] lix. 122.

[5] It could be profitable to train a small attractive child, [Dem.] lix. 18, δεινὴ δὲ φύcιν μικρῶν παιδίων cυνιδεῖν εὐπρεπῆ, καὶ ταῦτα ἐπιcταμένη θρέψαι καὶ παιδεῦcαι ἐμπείρωc.

free 'concubine', and that no discredit attached to the man who lived with a *pallake*. Nor did it offend the sense of propriety that a respectable woman should occupy that position, which is quite different from that of the more or less promiscuous *hetaira*. A man may be as faithful to his 'concubine' as to his wife, and treat her with as much respect. Nevertheless the status is an inferior one, because it is not included in the structure of the family, on which the city depends. An Athenian woman would not willingly accept, if she had an alternative, a position which excluded her children from rights in the family and the state. Nor had she the advantages, to be discussed, of bringing a dowry.

The giving of a dowry, προῖξ, was a usual but not essential part of a regular marriage. No doubt there were many poor men who were unable to provide any dowry, but its absence might give rise to the suspicion that the union was concubinage, not marriage.[1] The practice springs from a hard-headed facing of realities. The wife brings new expenses to the family she enters, and it is reasonable and felt by her own relations as right[2] that she should also bring some contribution to meet them. On the other hand the dowry operates to her advantage. It places her husband under a moral obligation to provide for her the standard of life she may expect.[3] Moreover, since the dowry must be returned in case of a divorce, the husband has a financial interest in keeping the marriage in being.[4] The wife is also provided for in the event of her husband's death without issue by her; again she takes her dowry back to her own family.

Since there was no registration of marriages, the introduction of a son to phratry and deme depended on the evidence of those members of those bodies who knew that the marriage had taken place according to the proper forms and that the mother's parents were both citizens. No man was, as the orators say, likely to hand over a dowry without witnesses, and their possible usefulness extended to confirming, if necessary, the facts about the marriage. A further set of witnesses was secured by the marriage-feast,[5] to which it was usual to invite many relations. Some bridegrooms, at least, also entertained the members of their phratry; in some phratries this may have been expected of them.[6]

Social conditions in Athens made it virtually impossible for

---

[1] Plautus, *Trinummus*, 690–1.   [2] Ibid. 681 ff.   [3] Theophrastos, *Char.* xxviii. 4.
[4] Isaios iii. 28.   [5] Dem. xxx. 21.   [6] Isaios viii. 18.

a young man to meet a marriageable girl in private. The daughter of well-to-do parents in particular would be confined to the women's quarters if there were visitors, and have little occasion to go outside the house except to attend religious ceremonies. Even the wife of a well-to-do household had little reason to leave the home, which provided the centre of her activities;[1] and the larger it was, the more self-sufficient it would be. Accordingly, in some plays the young man falls in love with a girl whom he sees at a festival: but he has no chance of making her acquaintance unless she is fatherless, permanently or temporarily, and living with a woman who will allow him some access to her.[2]

Several Greek comedies, *Samia, Georgos, Fab. incert.*, cf. *Andria, Adelphoe, Truculentus*, contain a situation in which a young man is in love with a young woman who before the play opens, or even in the course of it, is delivered of a child of which he is the father. Yet this stage has been reached without their being married. To the modern reader this is strange, because traditionally importance is attached to a child's being born in wedlock, and he is inclined to think the young man heartless. Greek assumptions were different, and need explanation.

The young man involved in these plots is the son of a man of some means, and dependent on his father. The father's consent to the son's marriage may have been, as some believe, legally necessary; certainly it was in practice required.[3] Athenian society offered no obvious ways by which a young man without capital could support a family. He could, of course, enlist as a mercenary soldier, but that was no suitable occupation for a family breadwinner. Nor, if the law gave the father a veto, was it an unreasonable law. He was responsible for the economic well-being of himself, his children, and his further descendants, and the introduction

---

[1] L. A. Post, 'Woman's Place in Menander's Athens', *TAPA* lxxi (1940), 420 ff., assembles and judiciously discusses much material. 'The women's quarters were more a sanctuary than a prison'; cf. Plato, *Laws* 781 c. Besides religious occasions, there was visiting of neighbours' wives. Isaios vi. 10 says that Euktemon's wife and daughters were known to most of his fellow demesmen; this will mean that they were known by sight.

[2] So in *Synaristosai*, Plaut. *Cist.* 89 ff.

[3] By contrast, it is unlikely that a father could legally require his son to marry, but some fathers in comedy take it for granted that their sons will do as they are told and accept a bride chosen for them, e.g. *Perik.* 1025, *Georgos* 7, Ter. *Heautontim.* 1055 ff.

of a new member into the family with the probability of grand-children, who would in course of time have their claims on the estate, was a matter of direct concern to him. He would normally wish to see that the wife brought with her a dowry that would make a reasonable contribution towards these new obligations.

In the plays the father's consent is always in doubt because the girl is poor. In *Samia* it cannot even be asked, because he is abroad. There was nothing that Moschion could do, and but for the stroke of fortune by which the child could be passed off as that of his father's mistress, there would have been no alternative but to expose it. But usually the son hesitates because he fears a refusal. He may indeed hope that he is more likely to persuade his father if he can actually show him a grandson; that human feelings will then prevail over economic calculation.[1] To wait for the birth of the child may offer the best chance of gaining consent for the marriage.

The situation must also be considered from the point of view of the girl and her mother—her father is in these plots always dead or absent. Athenian law exposed to a civil suit or a criminal prosecution the perpetrator of a rape on a citizen girl. Rape, not seduction, is sometimes explicitly said to be the beginning of the story and must be supposed in other cases.[2] If the girl had been a consenting partner, that would have lowered her in the eyes of the fourth-century Athenian. On the other hand, although rape was regarded as a disgraceful act, it was by no means an unpardonable or unthinkable one. Eros was recognized as a blinding and overmastering force that could sweep young men forward,[3] as it had so often caused the gods of mythology to ravish beautiful human maidens. Now was the victim's mother to set the law in motion? Either civil suit or prosecution would be dropped if the young man married the girl, and this might be the objective of an action. But it must never be forgotten that in

---

[1] *Adelphoe* 333: 'qui se in sui gremio positurum puerum dicebat patris, | ita obsecraturum ut liceret hanc sibi uxorem ducere.'

[2] Modern moral attitudes, which condemn rape and often tolerate seduction, lead to misunderstanding and sometimes to misrepresentation. Thus even A. R. W. Harrison, who is well aware of ancient views, slips into writing 'Menander's *Arbitr.*, which concerns a girl who has been seduced' (*Law of Athens*, i. p. 192).

[3] e.g. *Aulularia* 737: 'deu' mihi impulsor fuit . . . fateor peccauisse . . . te oratum aduenio ut animo aequo ignoscas mihi.'

Athens, perhaps even more than in a modern state, the law applicable to the facts of a situation was not necessarily applied. In the circumstances we are considering the mother would first be obliged, since she had no right to conduct a case herself, to induce her κύριος (or some other man) to undertake the suit or prosecution. Then if that difficulty were surmounted, the other side might decide to fight, and a rich litigant had many resources, legal and illegal, to use against a poor one. Even if a civil suit were successful, the girl's prospects of another marriage might not be rosy. It is therefore not to be wondered at that if the young man excuses his act by his passion, protests his desire to marry the girl, and declares that given time and opportunity he will bring his father round to approve the match, the mother should accept this chance of getting a willing husband for her child rather than seek the incalculable outcome of an appeal to the law.

In a number of plays of the New Comedy, although in fewer than might be guessed from some modern critics, the plot depends on the exposure of an unwanted child, who has the good fortune to be rescued by some humble personage. This motive was adopted from tragedy, e.g. Sophocles' *Tyro*, or Euripides' *Ion* or *Melanippe Desmotis*; the tragedians, however, will not have invented it, but found the stories existing in mythology. Whether such exposure of children was practised in Athens of Menander's time has been much discussed.[1] The evidence for it comes mainly from the plays, which may be thought merely to use a traditional motive, not to give a picture of current life. Certainly the happy ending, by which the child is restored to its true parents, must have been an almost unknown occurrence. Why then suppose that the rest of the story is any more true to life?

There is no doubt that exposure was not infrequent in the Greco-Roman era, and that legitimate children, born in wedlock, were its victims, as well as the illegitimate.[2] That it was by no means unknown that an exposed infant should be picked up and

---

[1] A few discussions: Daremberg et Saglio, s.v. Expositio; La Rue van Hook, *TAPA* li (1920), 134; A. W. Gomme, *Population of Athens*, Note C; G. van N. Niljoen, *Acta Classica* ii (1959), 58; J. Rudhardt, *Mus. Helv.* xx (1963), 17; A. C. van Geytenbeek, *Musonius Rufus and Greek Diatribe*, pp. 80–7.

[2] Musonius frag. xv, εἰ πάντα τὰ γινόμενα τέκνα θρεπτέον, Hierokles apud Stob. iv. 24. 4, Plutarch, *Mor.* 497 e, Philo, *De spec. leg.* iii. 110–19, Dio Prusensis iv. 25, Aelian, *VH* ii. 7.

reared appears from a talk by Favorinus reported by Aulus Gellius xii. 1. 23, 'ipsius quoque infantis adfectio animi, amoris, consuetudinis in ea sola unde alitur occupatur et proinde, ut in expositis usu uenit, matris quae genuit neque sensum ullum neque desiderium capit.' For an earlier period, about 230–100 B.C., W. W. Tarn, *Hellenistic Civilisation*, 3rd edn., pp. 100–2, collects the evidence of inscriptions from several places and concludes that 'infanticide on a considerable scale, particularly of girls, is not in doubt'. It may still be denied that the practices of later times and other places were already usual in the fourth and third centuries B.C. at Athens. That illegitimate infants were often abandoned would seem *a priori* to be likely;[1] but whether married parents refrained from bringing up children is a question on which there is little evidence. The smallness of many families may have been due to caution in intercourse or to abortion. P. Jardé, *Les Céréales* etc., p. 137, claimed that in 61 families completely known from the orators there were 87 sons and 44 daughters, from which he concluded that exposure of female children must have been common. But his figures cannot be relied upon.[2] We have therefore nothing but the evidence from drama. When Poseidippos made a character say θυγατέρα δ' ἐκτίθησι (sc. πᾶς) κἂν ᾖ πλούσιος, frag. 11 K, he was no doubt exaggerating, but there must surely have been something to exaggerate. Sostrata at Terence *H.T.* 626 says to her husband, 'meministine me esse grauidam et mihi te maximo opere edicere, | si puellam parerem, nolle tolli?'; this must have been a credible action on the part of one who is represented as a sympathetic character.[3] Juppiter, disguised as Amphitryo, tells Alcumena to acknowledge their future child, 'uerum quod natum erit tollito' (Plaut. *Amph.* 499–501); this must imply that the decision whether a child born in wedlock was to be raised rested with the father. It may therefore be concluded that the exposure or infanticide of legitimate offspring, and in particular of daughters, was by no means unknown at the end of the fourth century.

[1] Exposure is taken for granted at Ter. *Hec.* 400. Exposed infants were common in eighteenth-century London; the Foundling Hospital was established in 1745, and saved the lives of some.
[2] Complete enumeration of a family is rarely certain.
[3] Cf. probably Ter. *Phormio* 647.

VI. METRE

[The following notes are intended to do no more than give basic information. An excellent full treatment may be found in Handley's edition of *Dyskolos*, pp. 56–73.]

The variety of metre found in Aristophanes, in Plautus, and to a lesser extent in Terence is absent from Menander. The only metres he used commonly were the iambic trimeter and the trochaic tetrameter. It has been maintained that the tetrameter was given up in his later plays. Certainly there are none in the surviving parts of *Epitrepontes*, but the difficulty of dating most of his plays and the part of chance in determining whether tetrameters, if they existed, were quoted by later authors ought to lead to caution.[1] In *Dyskolos* the last scene is in iambic tetrameters; *Kolax* (frag. 7) and *Leukadia* (frag. 258 K–T) contained anapaests; *Phasma* (frag. 3) had ithyphallics and *Theophorumene* (q.v.) probably some other metre, perhaps dactylic hexameters.

Trochaic metre is regarded by Aristotle as κορδακικώτερος, 'tending to a lively vulgarity', *Rhet.* iii. 1408ᵇ36. In tragedy trochaic tetrameters are often used in lively and excited scenes; a single line is frequently divided between two speakers. But in Euripides' *Iphigeneia in Aulis* a long speech in which Iphigeneia solemnly and calmly declares her reasons for accepting death is cast in this metre (1368–1401). So in Menander there are lively trochaic scenes with frequent change of speaker (*Perik.* 267–353, *Sam.* 421–615, 670 ff.), but also Knemon's serious *apologia pro vita sua* (*Dysk.* 708–47), which passes into a scene with rapid exchanges. In *Sikyonios* 110–49 the exchanges are quick, but there is nothing farcical about the matter. There are other passages in the fragments of New Comedy which would seem to belong to serious contexts, e.g. Philemon frag. 213 K, Diphilos frag. 24 K, Menander frags. 208–9, perhaps frag. 309. Perhaps it can be said that passages in this metre are distinguished in tone from the adjacent iambics, but not always in the same way; they may be marked by excitement, or urgency, or a seriousness that

---

[1] Cf. C. Dedoussi, Πλάτων xi (1959), 404. Trochaic tetrameters are recorded from Ἁλιεύς (? after 305), Ἀσπίς, Γεωργός, Δύσκολος (317), Ἐπαγγελλόμενος, Ἡνίοχος (? 312), Θησαυρός, Θρασυλέων, Θυρωρός, Καρχηδόνιος, Ναύκληρος, Ὀλυνθία (314/13), Ὀργή (321), Παλλακή (probably), Περικειρομένη, Σαμία, Σικυώνιος, Ὑδρία, Ὑποβολιμαῖος, Φάσμα, Φιλάδελφοι, and perhaps Πλόκιον, Ῥαπιζομένη, and Συναριστῶσαι. Webster, *StM* 107, guesses all these to be early plays.

is to be taken seriously. All these characters go well with the comparatively strict metrical form.[1]

It is not known how the delivery of trochaic tetrameters differed from that of the usual iambic trimeter. The greater regularity of the metre must have had some effect upon the actor's manner. But there is no evidence to prove that trochaics were accompanied by the *aulos*, as were the iambic tetrameters of the last scene of *Dyskolos*. Xenophon, *Symp*. 6. 3, writes ὥσπερ Νικόστρατος ὁ ὑποκριτὴς τετράμετρα πρὸς τὸν αὐλὸν κατέλεγεν, but these were not necessarily trochaics, nor in comedy, and even if they were, his action may have been unusual.[2]

Iambic trimeters allow of great metrical variation. The skill of Menander's composition will appear if they are read aloud. There is constant change in the length of phrases, the placing of stops, and the amount of departure from the forms of tragedy.[3] The verse gives emphasis to the right words, yet their order is normally that of speech.

Iambic trimeter

The iambic trimeter of comedy differs from that of tragedy in the following main points:

(1) A caesura is not obligatory: there may instead be diaeresis after the third foot:

τὰς πλησίον Νύμφας στεφανοῦσαν Cώστρατε,

or not even that:

οὕτως ἔχω· παραλαμβάνει τις τῶν φίλων.

(2) There is no observance of 'Porson's law', by which the fifth foot must be an iambus if it contains more than one word (prepositives and postpositives being reckoned as part of the following or previous word respectively):

τῆς Ἀττικῆς νομίζετ' εἶναι τὸν τόπον.

---

[1] On the various uses of this metre see M. Imhof, *Mus. Helv.* xiii (1956), 125 ff., C. Dedoussi, Πλάτων xiii (1961), 59.

[2] Pickard-Cambridge, *Dramatic Festivals*², pp. 158–60, 165. He does not mention the practice of the Roman stage, where it is certain that many trochaics, if not all had an accompaniment on the *tibia*.

[3] Even in his tetrameters Menander is more varied than Aristophanes; see J. W. White, *Verse of Greek Comedy*, § 106.

(3) Dactyls are freely allowed in the first foot, even if broken after the second syllable:

οὐδὲ μετρίως, εἴ coι τοιοῦτος φαίνομαι.

Dactyls in the third foot are occasionally broken after the second syllable:

τούτων κακῶν μηδὲν ὑπὸ τηθίδος τινός.

Dactyls are freely allowed in the fifth foot, but are normally broken after the first syllable.[1]

(4) Anapaests are allowed in any foot except the last. In Menander an anapaest is not formed by two words of which the first is partially in the preceding foot. The apparent exceptions can, and sometimes must for other reasons, be emended, but for frag. 397. 3:

οἷον τὰ {μὲν} νηςιωτικὰ ταυτὶ ξενύδρια.[2]

Except in the first foot anapaests are not frequently divided even when they begin with a word, and the division is usually obscured by elision or by the word's being a prepositive,[3] e.g. *Epitr.* 286 ἐμὲ δ' οὐδὲ ἕν, *Dysk.* 68 περὶ ταῦτα, 151 τὸν Ἀπόλλω; more remarkable are *Heros* 22 νέος ὤν, *Epitr.* 299 πρὸς ὃν οὑτοcί, *Sam.* 100 πίκρα πάντ'.

(5) A syllable containing a short vowel and preceding a mute and liquid is short, i.e. both consonants are pronounced with the succeeding vowel; the few exceptions can be explained as due to a momentary elevation of style.[4]

(6) Except in quotation from tragedy, θεός is never monosyllabic.[5] Less use is made of crasis.

Trochaic tetrameter

The catalectic trochaic tetrameter is built from the metron $- \cup - \underline{\cup}$, and in its basic form runs $- \cup - \underline{\cup} - \cup - \underline{\cup} - \cup - \underline{\cup} - \cup \underline{\cup}$. In all the examples yet known from Menander (except *Sam.* 484) there is diaeresis after the second metron, e.g. πρὸς τὸ κερδαίνειν ἔχουcιν | οὐδὲν εὔνουν ᾠόμην. Authors of the Old Comedy do not

---

[1] But μὰ τοὺς δώδεκα θεούς, *Kol.* 116, *Sam.* 306; and cf. *Asp.* 138, *Epitr.* 381.

[2] H. J. Mette, *Lustrum* x. 113, supposes that two lacunae have reduced two original lines to one; a possible but unlikely way of restoring normality.

[3] J. W. White, *Verse of Greek Comedy*, §§ 116–22, 160–2, W. G. Arnott, *CQ* N.s. vii (1957), 188 ff., E. W. Handley, *Dyskolos* 63–6.

[4] ὅπλα *Epitr.* 324, τέκνον *Misum.* 214, μελάθροις *Sam.* 517, perhaps μίτρα *Perik.* 823.

[5] Unless at *Perik.* 827, where it will, if so scanned, be paratragic.

observe this rule,[1] and it may be noted that in *Sik.* 136[2] the diaeresis is apparent to the eye only, being followed by a postpositive:

$$\hat{\eta}\lambda\theta\epsilon \; \pi\epsilon\rho\grave{\iota} \; \tauο\acute{\upsilon}\tau\omega\nu \; \grave{\alpha}\pi\acute{\alpha}\nu\tau\omega\nu \; \mu\upsilonι \; \tauό\tau' \; \epsilon\mathring{\upsilon}\theta\grave{\upsilon}\epsilon \; \gamma\rho\acute{\alpha}\mu\mu\alpha\tau\alpha.$$

The first or third syllable of the metron (except the last syllable of the line) may be resolved into two shorts, giving a tribrach or an anapaest. Resolution of the *anceps* fourth syllable and dactyl for trochee are very rare, but attempts to remove all instances by emendation do not succeed.[3] There are three[4] plausible examples of these anomalies in Menander so far:

Sam. 731   δεῦρο δ᾽ ἡμῖν ἐκδότω τιc δᾷδα καὶ cτεφάνουc, ἵνα
Perik. 340   οὐ γὰρ ὡc αὐλητρὶ]c οὐδ᾽ ὡc πορνίδιον τρικάθλιον
Sik. 135   ἐπυθόμην :: πολλῶν ταλάντων Cτρατοφάνη κατὰ cύμβολα.

Unlike tragedy, comedy does not observe the law that there is no word-break at the end of the first or third metron if that metron ends with a long syllable.

Iambic tetrameter

The catalectic iambic tetrameter is built from the metron $\underset{\smile}{-} - \smile -$, and in its basic form runs $\underset{\smile}{-} - \smile - \mid \underset{\smile}{-} - \smile - \mid \underset{\smile}{-} - \smile - \mid$ $\smile - \underset{\smile}{-}$. There is either diaeresis after the second metron or caesura after the first syllable of the third.[5] Resolution of the *anceps* first syllable of the metron is found in Aristophanes but not in the only scene in this metre from Menander (*Dysk.* 880–958). Nor does Menander follow Aristophanes in allowing anapaests in the second half of the metron.[6]

VII. THE MANUSCRIPTS

The ancient book originally took the form of a roll of papyrus, made by joining a series of sheets side to side. On these sheets the writing was in columns and the lines were parallel to the long edges of the roll. In this form each play would normally occupy one roll. Many of the smaller fragments of Menander

[1] In tragedy, there is an exception (with change of speaker) in Soph. *Phil.* 1402.
[2] So also in frag. 150.
[3] M. Dale, *Lustrum* ii (1957), 40; for removal, M. Platnauer, *CR* n.s. i (1951), 132, G. P. Goold, *Phoenix* xiii (1959), 154. Dactyls are found even in tragedy, Eur. *Or.* 1535, *IA* 882.
[4] *Dysk.* 774 may be another, but see note there. *PSI* 1176. 15 (Page, *GLP* 278) has the metron τοῖc Cαμόθρᾳξι, but the authorship is uncertain.
[5] But *Dysk.* 895 may be an exception.   [6] e.g. *Frogs* 937.

come from such rolls, and the Sorbonne *Sikyonios* preserves a large part of one. In later antiquity the roll was superseded by the codex, which has leaves like a modern book and could be large enough to take several plays. Menander appears in the new form first in the third century A.D., and from the fourth century in no other. The codex could be made up in various ways; in leaves secured by stitching, like the Bodmer papyrus (see below, p. 47), in sheets folded in two and placed inside one another, as in the papyrus of *Misumenos* published by E. G. Turner (*BICS* suppl. no. 17), or most neatly in quaternios, as in the Cairo papyrus described below. Skin was occasionally used instead of papyrus, even in Egypt.

Only slowly did written texts come to consult the convenience of the reader. The most striking example is that it never became the regular practice to indicate the names of the speakers. The earliest manuscript of comedy in which this is done is dated to the first or second century A.D. (*P. Oxy.* 211); thereafter the giving of names may be complete, sporadic, or totally lacking. In the manuscripts of the Christian era change of speaker is most frequently shown by a dicolon, two points one above the other, to separate the speeches, and a paragraphus, or short stroke extending into the left-hand margin, below the line in which or at the end of which the change is made. The paragraphus would appear to be superfluous and is in fact omitted in some manuscripts. It seems, however, that it was the original method of indicating change of speaker, to which the dicola were later added. Paragraphi were adequate for tragedy, where change of speaker is predominantly at the line-end, but not for comedy, where intralinear change is common. This change was sometimes indicated by leaving a small space between words, as here and there in the early Sorbonne *Sikyonios*. Not only might such spaces easily be overlooked in copying, but this method also left it unclear whether there was a change at the end of the line as well as within it.

Manuscripts which use the system of dicola seem to make remarkably few mistakes with it, and those more often by omission than by adding them wrongly. We may guess that they descend from carefully written copies that preserved, better than does the Sorbonne *Sikyonios*, the division of speeches in some way shown in the original text, which may have been the poet's autograph.

The names of speakers, however, were not part of the transmitted text, but were added later by individual enterprise. Future discoveries may provide examples earlier than are known at present, but there is evidence that names were absent from the early texts. W. G. Rutherford, *A Chapter in the History of Annotation*, pp. 115–17, made a collection of Aristophanic scholia which imply that the texts possessed by their authors did not indicate the names of speakers, and the scholiast on Soph. *Ajax* 354 explicitly says that when there is doubt the persons may be distinguished by attention to their characters (ibid. 108). No more authority attaches to the lists of dramatis personae prefixed to plays in some manuscripts; they, too, seem to have been made up from a study of the words of the text.[1]

The moral of this for the editor is that he should not render a superstitious respect to the names of speakers. Nor should he be quick to disagree with his ancient predecessor, whoever first provided them. That person probably was guided by a knowledge of far more of Menander's plays than the modern scholar; he may even have seen a performance in which the assignment of speeches depended on an old theatrical tradition among the 'artists of Dionysos'. The editor should be equally cautious about disregarding a dicolon: some few are certainly erroneous, but it is probable that the vast majority descend correctly from the dramatist's own text. It is much more likely that the manuscript makes a mistake by omitting a dicolon where there should be one, and there are in fact many passages where a change of speaker must be recognized although there is no sign of it in the papyrus.

The dicolon was used in some papyri to mark change of person addressed as well as change of speaker. It should then not be

[1] J. Andrieu, *Le Dialogue antique*, p. 94. The attempt of F. Stoessl, *Philologus* c (1956), to show that the dramatis personae of Euripides' *Heraclidae* go back to the author is unsuccessful. Eurystheus' herald, anonymous in the text, is named Kopreus not because in a list of characters Euripides gave him the name he denied him in the play, but (as Andrieu says) from scholarly knowledge of *Iliad* xv. 639, just as the anonymous herald of Aeschylus' *Agamemnon* is called Talthybios in the list of characters. Stoessl is no more successful in arguing that the list of characters and indications of speakers in the Bodmer papyrus of *Dyskolos* go back to Menander himself (*SB Öst. Akad. d. Wiss.* vol. 234. 5); see e.g. *CR* N.S. xii (1962), 27, *JHS* lxxxiii (1963), 168.

For unwarranted names in the lists attached to plays by Aristophanes, see Coulon's edition, intro., p. xxxi. Besides Andrieu, op. cit., pp. 259–70, J. C. B. Lowe, *BICS* ix (1962), 27 ff., examines with care the evidence for indications of speaker in all types of ancient Greek drama.

accompanied by a paragraphus (so the Cairo MS. at *Perik.* 188, 190, the Bodmer MS. at *Dysk.* 177, etc.), unless the line also contains a change of speaker.

Two MSS. of which the remains are extensive deserve fuller description.

The Cairo codex

C (Cairensis 43227), found at Aphroditopolis, is of the fifth century A.D., well written in a regular rounded book-hand. Accents and breathings are rarely indicated, except in *Perik.* 508–30, where they have been added by a second hand. Elisions, however, are carefully marked by an apostrophe, except that elision of a preposition is never marked. Observation of this rule is important when making restorations. There may be no instance of the scribe's carelessly omitting an apostrophe: at *Epitr.* 543 he falsely took εμαυτης as a genitive (see note ad loc.). Jensen and Körte list four verses in which he writes an apostrophe where there should be none; a mistaken intention rather than carelessness is to be seen at *Sam.* 321 αλλ'ως; *Perik.* 151 αποτ'αυτοματου may indicate crasis rather than elision of τε; the apostrophe read by Körte after καθεν in *Epitr.* 381 may be a colon (Lefebvre); in *Perik.* 272, although Körte asserts that the MS. has οδ'εδιωκ, Jensen reports the apostrophe as doubtful, and the facsimile almost excludes it. In a dozen places a mute is written for an aspirate before a following aspirate, e.g. *Heros* 43 ειρηκ'υπεςχηται. *Scriptio plena*, i.e. the writing in full of a word that must be elided, is rare. Iota, where we write it subscript, is either adscript or more frequently omitted. At the end of a line, but there only, ν is sometimes written by a horizontal stroke over the preceding vowel.

Textual errors of a kind that can be easily detected are fairly common: wrong vowels, duplication or transposition of words, addition of extraneous words, omission of letters or syllables. All these can be cured; omission of whole words has occasionally occurred and is more difficult to remedy. Comparison with B, where that can be made, shows that there has also been some deliberate alteration of words. Where C is the sole surviving MS. detection of this is impossible.

Change of speaker is indicated in the usual manner by a dicolon in the text and a paragraphus, occasionally omitted by error, beneath the beginning of the line. Here and there, and apparently without consistent principle, the name of the speaker is added in abbreviated form. Such names are frequent in the fragment of *Heros*, but only one occurs in *Samia*. This suggests that at some time in the history of the text a reader began to add names but became less and less thorough as he went on.

The codex was made up in quaternios, or groups of four sheets; these make eight leaves, which carry writing on both sides and so give sixteen pages. The material was manufactured by hammering together two layers of prepared reed laid at right angles to one another: one surface therefore shows fibres parallel with the writing, the other fibres perpendicular to it. It has been the custom to call the former side the *recto*, the latter the *verso*, misapplying terms long used with another meaning: the recto is properly that side of a leaf which lies to the right when a book is opened. The modern terms, 'with horizontal fibres', 'with vertical fibres', are unambiguous but clumsy; I have compromised by writing 'recto' and 'verso'. It is a feature of the Cairo codex, shared with many papyrus codices, that the sheets are so arranged that facing pages both have either horizontal or vertical fibres; there was thus no contrast in their appearance.

This way of making up a book has enabled scholars to go some way in reconstructing the codex. The leaf preserved from the beginning of *Heros* is numbered $\kappa\theta$ ($= 29$) to the right of the 'recto', λ ($= 30$) in the centre of the 'verso'. *Heros* was, then, preceded by some other play. It was followed by *Epitrepontes*. The proof is this: the fragment Z ('recto'), which is certainly to be assigned to the early part of Act IV, is numbered ς ($= 6$) in the top *left-hand* corner. This number must indicate the sixth quaternio and be on its first page, i.e. p. 81 of the whole codex. The page numbers on the leaf from *Heros* are not only differently placed, but are additions by a second hand, made in an ink which has faded badly. Since the average contents of a page are 35 lines, pages 31–80 would contain about 1,750 lines. It follows that *Epitrepontes* succeeded *Heros*.

Bearing in mind the alternation of horizontal and vertical fibres, it becomes possible to assign the fragments of *Epitrepontes* to their pages in the codex, as follows. The letters and numerals (D 1, 2, etc.) are those given by Lefebvre to the fragments as marks of identity: D 1 indicates one side of fragment D, D 2 the other; D 3, 4 are the two sides of the other leaf forming part of the same sheet as D 1, 2. β is a fragment from a whole sheet, containing parts of both pages:

	Pages of codex	Lines of OCT edition
missing (h.v.)	65, 66	—
D 1.2 (v.h.)	67, 68	218–90
C 1.2 (h.v.)	69, 70	291–364
B 1.2 (v.h.)	71, 72	365–432
B 3.4 (h.v.)	73, 74	433–502
C 3.4 (v.h.)	75, 76	503–74
D 3.4 (h.v.)	77, 78	575–644
Y 1.2+R 1.2 (v.h.)	79, 80	645–65 [666–79] 680–99 [700–13]
Z 1.2 (h.v.)	81, 82	714–25 [726–48] 749–59 [760–84]
missing (v.h.)	83, 84	[785–852]
H 1.2 (h.v.)	85, 86	853–933
β 1.2+Q 1.2 (v.h.)	87, 88	934–89 [990–1002]
β 3.4+U 1.2 (h.v.)	89, 90	1003–59
H 3.4 (v.h.)	91, 92	1060–1131
missing (h.v.)	93, 94	—
,, (v.h.)	95, 96	—

Perikeiromene probably followed. The first surviving leaf, E 1–2 (v.h.), contains an earlier part of the play than J, which is a double sheet (v.h.h.v.) from the centre of a quaternio and contains the end of Act I. E 1–2 therefore was the second leaf of this quaternio. It is highly probable, although it cannot be proved, that this quaternio immediately succeeded the sixth, since the space is about what is required for the missing end of *Epitrepontes* and the missing beginning of *Perikeiromene*. We may tentatively reconstruct as follows:

H 3.4 (v.h.)	91, 92	*Epitr.* 1060–1131
missing (h.v.)	93, 94	[*Epitr.* end]
,, (v.h.)	95, 96	[*Perik.* hypothesis etc. vv. 1–50]
Quat. 7		
missing (h.v.)	97, 98	[*Perik.* 51–120]
E 1.2 (v.h.)	99, 100	*Perik.* 121–90
missing (h.v.)	101, 102	[*Perik.* 191–260]
J 1.2 (v.h.)	103, 104	*Perik.* 261–330

J 3.4 (h.v.)	105, 106	*Perik.* 331–406
missing (v.h.)	107, 108	[*Perik.* 407–79]
E 3.4 (h.v.)	109, 110	*Perik.* 480–550
missing (v.h.)	111, 112	[*Perik.* 551–620]

Quat. 8

missing (h.v.)	113, 114	[*Perik.* 621–90]
K 1.2 (v.h.)	115, 116	[*Perik.* 691–707] 708–25 [726–41] 742–60
missing (h.v.)	117, 118	[*Perik.* 761–830]
„ (v.h.)	119, 120	[*Perik.* 831–900]
„ (h.v.)	121, 122	[*Perik.* 901–70]
„ (v.h.)	123, 124	[*Perik.* 971–1040]
„ (h.v.)	125, 126	—
„ (v.h.)	127, 128	—

The fragments of *Samia* are contained on five sheets of a quaternio, as follows:

G 1.2 (h.v.)	193–256
I 3.4 (v.h.)	257–323
F 1.2 (h.v.)	324–93
missing (v.h.)	—
„ (h.v.)	—
F 3.4 (v.h.)	418–86
I 1.2 (h.v.)	487–557
missing (v.h.)	—

Since the beginning of *Samia* is missing in this codex, this quaternio cannot have been the first; nor can it have been the second, for the seventh leaf of that was occupied by the opening of *Heros*. Quaternios 3–8 are accounted for by the rest of *Heros*, *Epitrepontes*, and *Perikeiromene*, with some space at the end of quaternio 8 for the beginning of a new play.

That play was not *Samia*, the third act of which began in the middle of the last page of a quaternio; the words of Demeas at the top of G 1 are at least a dozen lines after the act's beginning. If *Samia* followed *Perikeiromene*, that quaternio would be the ninth; accordingly the first two acts would run, if the pages were all occupied, to over 600 lines, say 550 in quaternio 9 and 70 at the end of quaternio 8. Such lengthy acts are excluded by the evidence of B, M. Bodmer's codex.

Editio princeps: G. Lefebvre, *Fragments d'un manuscrit de Ménandre*

(1907). Text and photographs: G. Lefebvre, *Papyrus de Ménandre* (1911).

The Cairo papyrus was carefully examined by A. Körte, who published his findings in *Berichte d. sächs. Gesellschaft d. Wiss.* lx (1908), 87 ff., and in his editions of 1910 and 1912, and twice by C. Jensen (*Rh. Mus.* lxv [1910], 539 ff. and 635 ff., *Hermes* xlix [1914], 382 ff.). Lefebvre made use of Jensen's first article and of Körte's for his re-examination of the papyrus, and included in his text of 1911 all their results of which he felt convinced. S. Sudhaus then conducted his own careful examination, and published his results in *Menanderstudien* (1914) and in his text *Menandri reliquiae nuper repertae* (1914). The outbreak of war prevented him from correcting the proofs of the latter. The last complete examination of the papyrus was conducted by O. Guéraud, who had been commissioned to edit Menander (a project that never came to fruition) and who published his results in *Bulletin de l'Institut français d'archéologie orientale* xxvii (1928), 127 ff. This unfortunately escaped the notice of Jensen, and of German scholars in general, until Körte's third edition was on the point of going to press in 1938: Körte was able to make some reference to it in his apparatus, but his text could not be changed. Guéraud found that he could almost always verify the readings of Körte, Jensen, and Lefebvre; even where he disagreed, he could see that they had a case. But he found the reports of Sudhaus less reliable, and charitably put down his faults to over-conscientiousness. 'Il n'a pas voulu s'exposer à omettre de lire un seul point d'encre, et c'est ce qui l'a conduit à lire même ce qui était illisible, même ce qui n'existait pas.' Guéraud also utters a warning against over-confidence in the interpretation placed even by the more reliable editors on what they saw: e.g. a vertical stroke, eaten into by a hole at the side, will give the illusion of being part of a round letter; letters are not always well made and, if then mutilated, will inevitably be misinterpreted; diacritical marks, elision, or punctuation can be mistaken for remains of letters. There are parts of the Cairo MS. where the papyrus is tattered, the ink is faded, and the surface rubbed and dirty. It is astonishing that anything has been deciphered, and although a probable text may be established on the consensus of palaeographers' opinion, it ought to be remembered that they are not infallible.

The Bodmer codex

B (*P. Bodmer* 25–4–26) is mostly in the library of M. Bodmer at Cologny, Geneva. A small scrap is in Cologne (*P. Colon.* 904) and another in Barcelona (*P. Barc.* 45). It is assigned by most scholars to the latter half of the third century A.D., although some would place it in the early fourth century. It was originally a single-quire codex of sixteen sheets, sixty-four pages. The sheets were cut from a roll and the text inscribed before they were bound.[1] Occasionally the writer, when inscribing the left-hand page, allowed some lines to extend more than half-way across the whole sheet. The sheets were then folded down the vertical central line and secured by thread through holes on this line. Page 14 of the quire thus formed contains several over-long lines; their final letters appeared on page 51, an inconvenience to the reader. After a time the sheets began to split down the fold and an attempt was made to hold them by more stitching. Later, when the splitting had gone further and leaves had become loose, a new binding was put in hand. The pages were numbered, but the two leaves (which were still connected) of the central sheet were placed back to front, so that what should have been pp. 31–2 became pp. 33–4. The pile of leaves was then stitched through at a distance of about 1 cm. from the left-hand edge. Although the book was thus preserved, it was also made unusable, since it cannot have been fully opened.[2]

The codex contained on pp. 1–18 *Samia*, on pp. 19–39 *Dyskolos*, on pp. 40–end *Aspis*. Leaves 22, 23, 27, i.e. pp. 43–6, 53–4, were for some reason left blank. The first four leaves (pp. 1–8) of *Samia* have been much damaged, and similarly the last five (pp. 55 ff.) of *Aspis* are lost or fragmentary. The rest is almost all well preserved. It seems probable that, except for p. 37, the text is the work of a single copyist, but his writing varies in its forms: sometimes he drops briefly into a semi-cursive style, and

---

[1] *Ed. pr.* of *P. Bodmer* 25, p. 12, points out that it is possible that the text was inscribed before the sheets were cut from the roll; but this would have been a procedure of some inconvenience and no apparent advantage.

[2] This assumes that the stitching was tight. If it was loose, it would have been possible to slide the leaves on the thread, to see their inner edges. But there is no sign of wear at the holes, so that the book, even if usable, was not used. The account of B given above is derived from the *ed. pr.* of *P. Bodmer* 25 and 26.

he will abandon one predominant form of a letter in favour of some other.[1]

Most accents are marked on pp. 1–4 and 21–2; elsewhere they are sporadically used, but disappear almost entirely after p. 26. Breathings are marked with rather more, but still imperfect, consistency. They too are absent after p. 26. Elisions, except of prepositions, are usually marked throughout; an apostrophe also appears at times in the middle of words, e.g. μετ'ιεναι, πετ'τειν.

Change of speaker is denoted in the usual way by dicolon and paragraphus. Speakers' names are usually given when they first appear in any scene, and here and there afterwards, on no ascertainable principle (*pace* F. Stoessl, 'Personenwechsel in Menanders Dyskolos', *SB Öst. Akad. d. Wiss.* vol. 234. 5 (1960); see *CR* n.s. xii [1962], 27). Occasionally the dicolon is used to mark a change of person addressed. There are many marks of punctuation: high, median, or low dots. *Scriptio plena* occurs occasionally.

Detectable textual errors are more frequent than in C: bad spelling (confusion of ε and αι, of o, ω, and ου, and of η, ι, υ, ει, and οι), omission of letters or words, and misreading of consonants are all common. Many mistakes have been corrected, often and perhaps usually by the original writer. Useful analyses of types of error are to be found in the editions of *Dyskolos* by Handley (pp. 49–52) and Jacques (p. 52), and in Austin's *Aspis et Samia* (pp. 60–5).

Editiones principes:

P. Bodmer 4. V. Martin, *Papyrus Bodmer IV, Ménandre: Le Dyscolos* (1958 on title-page, published 1959), with complete photographs reduced in size by roughly one-fifth. A further scrap was published with *P. Bodmer* 26 (1969), see below.

P. Barc. 45. R. Roca-Puig, *Bol. R. Ac. Buen. Letr. Barc.* xxxii (1967–8), 5 (in Catalan), with photographs. Re-edited, *Estudios Clásicos* xii (1968), 375, with photographs.

P. Colon. 904. R. Merkelbach, *Zeitschr. f. Papyrologie u. Epigraphik* i (1967), 103, with photographs, then unidentified.

---

[1] C. A. Nelson and J. L. Raymond, *Bull. Am. Soc. Pap.* iv (1967), 43, try to distinguish two, or even four, principal copyists, chiefly by differences in the forms of κ and υ. But I think these were due to the whims of a single writer, who occasionally forgot which form he was using and reverted momentarily to the other.

P. Bodmer 25. R. Kasser (with the collaboration of C. Austin), *Papyrus Bodmer XXV, Ménandre: La Samienne* (1969), with complete photographs reduced in size by 27 per cent and including *P. Barc.* 45.

P. Bodmer 26. R. Kasser (with the collaboration of C. Austin), *Papyrus Bodmer XXVI, Ménandre: Le Bouclier* (1969), with complete photographs reduced in size by 27 per cent and including *P. Colon.* 904.

The last two volumes do not give an edited text but a transcript in which words have been divided and a few supplements added. The first critical edition is by C. Austin, *Menandri Aspis et Samia* i (1969), in the series Kleine Texte für Vorlesungen und Übungen.

TABLE OF PAPYRI

		Date	*Editio princeps*	Pack[1]	
B	*P. Bodmer* 4	A.D. iii/iv	V. Martin (1959)	1298	*Dyskolos*
	P. Bodmer 25		R. Casser and C. Austin (1969)	—	*Samia*
	P. Bodmer 26		do.	—	*Aspis*
	P. Barc. 45		R. Roca-Puig (1967)	—	*Samia*
	P. Colon. 904		R. Merkelbach (1967)	—	*Aspis*
B 1	*P. Berol.* 9767	i B.C.	W. Schubart and U. von Wilamowitz (1907)	1310	*Kitharistes*
B 2	*P. Berol.* 13281	A.D. iii	U. von Wilamowitz (1918)	1315	*Misumenos*
B 3	*P. Berol.* 13932 (F 1 belongs to same codex)	A.D. v	W. Schubart (1950)	1318	*Misumenos*
B 4	*P. Berol.* 21106	i B.C.	H. Maehler (1967)	—	*Georgos*
B 5	*P. Berol.* 21199	A.D. vi/vii	H. Maehler (1969)	—	*Dyskolos*
C	*P. Cair.* 43227	A.D. v	G. Lefebvre (1907)	1301	*Heros Epitrepontes Perikeiromene Fabula incerta Samia*
F	*P. Flor.* 100	A.D. iv	G. Vitelli (1910)	1307	*Georgos*
F 1	*P. Flor.* 126 (B 3 belongs to same codex)	A.D. v	G. Vitelli (1913)	1318	*Aspis*
F 2	*P. Soc. Ital.* 1280	A.D. ii	M. Norsa and G. Vitelli (1935)	1309	*Theophorumene*
G	*P. Gen.* 155	A.D. v/vi	J. Nicole (1898)	1306	*Georgos*
H	*P. Heidelberg* 219	A.D. ii	A. Gerhard (1911)	1305	*Perikeiromene*
H 1	*Membr. Hermupolitana*	A.D. iii/iv	B. Grenfell and A. Hunt (1905)	1299	*Dyskolos*
I	*P. IFAO* 89	A.D. iii	B. Boyaval (1970)	—	*Misumenos*
L	*P. Lipsiensis* 613	A.D. iii	A. Körte (1908)	1303	*Perikeiromene*
M	*P. Musei Britannici* 2823a	A.D. iv	H. J. M. Milne (1930)	1308	*Georgos*
O	*P. Oxy.* 211	A.D. i/ii	B. Grenfell and A. Hunt (1899)	1304	*Perikeiromene*
O 1	*P. Oxy.* 409	A.D. ii	B. Grenfell and A. Hunt (1903)	1311	*Kolax*
	P. Oxy. 2655		E. G. Turner (1968)	—	
O 2	*P. Oxy.* 855	A.D. iii	B. Grenfell and A. Hunt (1908)	1317	*Perinthia*
O 3	*P. Oxy.* 1013	A.D. v/vi	A. Hunt (1910)	1314	*Misumenos*

[1] R. Pack, *The Greek and Latin Literary Texts from Graeco-Roman Egypt*, 2nd edn., 1962.

		Date	Editio princeps	Pack	
) 4	P. Oxy. 1236	A.D. iv	A. Hunt (1914)	1302	Epitrepontes
) 5	P. Oxy. 1237	A.D. iii	B. Grenfell and A. Hunt (1914)	1312	Kolax
) 6	P. Oxy. 1238	A.D. i	A. Hunt (1914)	1647	Sikyonios
) 7	P. Oxy. 1605	A.D. iii	B. Grenfell and A. Hunt (1919)	1316	Misumenos
) 8	P. Oxy. 2467	A.D. iii	E. G. Turner (1962)	1300	Dyskolos
) 9	P. Oxy. 2654 P. Colon. 5031	A.D. i	E. G. Turner (1968) L. Koenen (1969)	—	Karchedonios
) 10	P. Oxy. 2656	A.D. iv	E. G. Turner (1968)	1320a	Misumenos
) 11	P. Oxy. 2657	A.D. iii	E. G. Turner (1968)	—	Misumenos
) 12	P. Oxy. 2825	A.D. i	E.G. Turner (1971)	—	Phasma
) 13	P. Oxy. sine numero	A.D. iii/iv	E. W. Handley (1968) in part	—	Dis Exapaton
) 14	P. Oxy 2829	A.D. iii/iv	M. Weinstein (1971)	—	Epitrepontes
) 15	P. Oxy. 2830	A.D. iii	E. G. Turner (1971)	—	Perikeiromene
) 16	P. Oxy. 2831	A.D. ii	E. G. Turner (1970)	—	Samia
) 17	P. Oxy. 2943	A.D. ii	—	—	Samia
	Membr. Petropolitana 388	A.D. iv	C. G. Cobet (1876) in part, V. Jernstedt (1891)	—	Epitrepontes Phasma
	P. Sorbonne 72	iii B.C.	P. Jouguet (1906)	1656	Sikyonios
	P. Sorbonne 2272		A. Blanchard and A. Bataille (1965)	—	
	P. Sorbonne 2273		do.	—	
	P. Soc. Ital. 99	A.D. ii	G. Vitelli (1910)	1654	Encheiridion
	P. Ross. Georg. 10	A.D. ii	G. Zereteli (1909)	1313	Koneiazomenai

APPENDIX

	P. Oxy. 1235	A.D. ii	A. Hunt (1914)	1321	Summary of Hiereia, Imbrioi
1	P. Brit. Mus. 2562	A.D. iii/iv	H. J. M. Milne (1934)	—	List of 17 plays
2	P. Oxy. 2462	A.D. ii	E. G. Turner (1962)	1297	List of 19 plays
3	P. IFAO 337	A.D. ii	B. Boyaval (1970)	—	Fragment of a summary, incl. Dis Exapaton

The following list gives brief descriptions of the manuscripts which contained texts of identified plays in this edition. The means used to indicate change of speaker are recorded wherever there is evidence. The first edition is given, and also references to revised texts, excluding those to be found in the standard editions.

So far as concerns those fragments that are of unidentified plays and therefore of authorship in some degree uncertain, a short account of the manuscript is to be found at the beginning of the notes on each piece.

B   *P. Bodmer* 4+25+26, *P. Colon.* 904. See above, p. 47.

B 1   *P. Berol.* 9767. Parts of 3 columns. 33–4 lines to the column. Dicola.
       Ed. pr.: W. Schubart and U. von Wilamowitz, Berliner Klassikertexte v. 2. 115, Plate VI. See also Schubart, *Pap. Graec. Berol.* 11a.

B 2   *P. Berol.* 13281. Lower part of one leaf. Paragraphi, dicola, one name.
       Ed. pr.: U. von Wilamowitz, *SB Berlin* 1918, 747. Revised texts: Körte–Thierfelder, *Menandri Reliquiae* ii. 286 (1954), H. Maehler, *Lustrum* x (1966), 154, C. Austin, *Oxyrhynchus Papyri* xxxiii (1968), 17.

B 3   *P. Berol.* 13932. A parchment fragment, from the same codex as F 1.
       Ed. pr.: W. Schubart, 'Griechische literärische Papyri' (*Berichte d. Sächs. Akad. d. Wiss.* xcvii [1950], 47). Revised texts as for B 2.

B 4   *P. Berol.* 21106. Part of 7 lines.
       Ed. pr.: H. Maehler, *Museum Helveticum* xxiv (1967), 77.

B 5   *P. Berol.* 21199. Beginnings of 6 lines, ends of 6.
       Ed. pr.: H. Maehler, *Zeitschrift f. Paläographie und Epigraphik*, iv (1969), 113.

C   *P. Cairensis* 43227. See above, p. 42.

F   *PSI* 100. A narrow strip. Over 30 lines to the page (? *c.* 50). Paragraphi, dicola, 2 *notae personarum*.
       Ed. pr.: G. Vitelli, *Pap. Soc. It.* i (1910), 168. See also E. L. de Stefani, *SIFC* xx (1913), 1.

F 1   *PSI* 126. Second sheet of a quaternio. 28 lines to the page. Paragraphi, dicola.
       Ed. pr.: G. Vitelli, *Pap. Soc. It.* ii (1913), 27. Re-edited, M. Norsa and G. Coppola, *Riv. indo-greco-itala* vi (1922), 35.

F 2   *PSI* 1280. Two columns, each of 15 lines. Of the first only a few letters preserved. Dicola.
       Ed. pr.: M. Norsa and G. Vitelli, *Annali della R. Scuola norm. sup. di Pisa* iv (1935), 1. Photograph and transcript, M. Norsa, *La scrittura letteraria greca*, Plate 9*d*. Re-edited, V. Bartoletti, *PSI* xii, 135–8, A. Garzya, *Dioniso* N.s. xvi (1953), 64.

G   *P. Gen.* 155. One leaf, 43–4 lines. Some dicola, 3 paragraphi, 1 colon. Frequent errors of spelling, or worse.

Ed. pr.: J. Nicole (1897 [1898 on title-page]). Transcript and text by Grenfell and Hunt (1898) ; transcript and photograph, New Palaeographical Society, Plates 74 and 75 (1906).

H   *P.. Heidelberg* 219. Ends of 18 lines. No evidence on distinction of speakers.

     Ed. pr.: G. A. Gerhard, *SB Heidelberg* 1911, 4, 1–11.

H 1   *Membr. Hermupolitana.* A scrap in the Bodleian Library, Oxford (MSS. graec. class. g 50 (P)). Possibly dicola.

     Ed. pr.: B. Grenfell and A. Hunt, *Mélanges Nicole* (1905), p. 220.

I   *P. IFAO* 89. Centre of upper part of a column. No evidence on distinction of speakers. From the writing Turner guesses this to be a schoolboy's exercise.

     Ed. pr.: B. Boyaval, *Zeitschrift f. Papyrologie u. Epigraphik* vi (1970), 1, with photograph. Re-edited, L. Koenen, ibid. 99.

L   *P. Lips.* 613. Double sheet (4 pages originally numbered *NA, NB, ΞA, ΞB*, i.e. 51, 52, 61, 62). 30 to 31 lines to the page. Paragraphi, dicola. Elision normally marked.

     Ed. pr.: A. Körte, *SB Leipzig* lx (1908), 145, with photographs.

M   *P. Mus. Brit.* 2823a. 3 scraps, one identified by containing a few words from Stobaios iv. 32b. 24, who quotes the lines as from Menander's *Georgos*.

     Ed. pr.: H. J. M. Milne, *Journal of Egyptian Archaeology* xvi (1930), 192.

O   *P. Oxy.* 211. Column of 51 lines, with a few letters from preceding column. Paragraphi and spaces. A second, perhaps contemporary, hand added dicola, some names of speakers, and some stage directions. He also corrected the text and added or deleted some paragraphi.

     Ed. pr.: B. Grenfell and A. Hunt, *Oxyrhynchus Papyri* ii (1899), 11, with photograph of 976–1008.

O 1   *P. Oxy.* 409, 2655. 3 columns of 34 lines. Paragraphi, dicola.

     Ed. pr.: *P. Oxy.* 409, B. Grenfell and A. Hunt, *Oxyrhynchus Papyri* iii (1903) with photograph (see also ibid. v [1908]), *P. Oxy.* 2655, E. G. Turner, *Oxyrhynchus Papyri* xxxiii (1968), with photograph.

O 2   *P. Oxy.* 855. Part of a column, with traces of the preceding column. Paragraphi, dicola, some names.

     Ed. pr.: B. Grenfell and A. Hunt, *Oxyrhynchus Papyri* vi (1908).

O 3   *P. Oxy.* 1013. Lower part of a page and some fragments. Paragraphi, dicola, one name by first hand, three by second.

     Ed. pr.: A. Hunt, *Oxyrhynchus Papyri* vii (1910). New readings, E. G. Turner, *Oxyrhynchus Papyri* xxxiii (1968).

O 4   *P. Oxy.* 1236. Damaged page of a parchment codex; parts of 21 or 22 lines on each side; originally there were 44. Dicola, one name.
Ed. pr.: A. Hunt, *Oxyrhynchus Papyri* x (1914).

O 5   *P. Oxy.* 1237. Badly damaged upper parts of two columns. Paragraphi, dicola, 2 names.
Ed. pr.: B. Grenfell and A. Hunt, *Oxyrhynchus Papyri* x (1914).

O 6   *P. Oxy.* 1238. 9 curtailed lines from one column. Paragraphi, dicola, 4 names.
Ed. pr.: A. Hunt, *Oxyrhynchus Papyri* x (1914), with photograph.

O 7   *P. Oxy.* 1605. Narrow strip with beginnings of 27 lines and a few letters from preceding column. Paragraphi, one name added by second hand, no dicola preserved.
Ed. pr.: B. Grenfell and A. Hunt, *Oxyrhynchus Papyri* xiii (1919).

O 8   *P. Oxy.* 2467. Ends of 10 lines and 8 lines.
Ed. pr.: E. G. Turner, *Oxyrhynchus Papyri* xxvii (1962).

O 9   *P. Oxy.* 2654. Parts of 3 columns. Paragraphi, some spaces, 2 dicola.
Ed. pr.: E. G. Turner, *Oxyrhynchus Papyri* xxxiii (1968), with photograph.
P. Colon. 5031. Parts of 9 lines from each of 2 columns. Paragraphi.
Ed. pr.: L. Koenen, *Zeitschrift für Papyrologie und Epigraphik* iv (1969), 170, with photograph. Identified as part of the same roll as *P. Oxy.* 2654, ibid. vi (1970).

O 10   *P. Oxy.* 2656. 5 pages, all damaged, some badly, from a codex, 36–40 lines to the page. Paragraphi, dicola, and some names.
Ed. pr.: E. G. Turner, *BICS* Supplement xvii (1965), with infra-red photographs. Re-edited, *Oxyrhynchus Papyri* xxxiii (1968).

O 11   *P. Oxy.* 2657. Remains of two columns, of about 50 lines. Paragraphi, dicola in mid line only.
Ed. pr.: E. G. Turner, *Oxyrhynchus Papyri* xxxiii (1968), with photographs.

O 12   *P. Oxy.* 2825. Parts of 4 columns. Paragraphi, sometimes a space.
Ed. pr.: E. G. Turner, *Oxyrhynchus Papyri* xxxviii (1971), with photographs.

O 13   *P. Oxy.* sine numero. 3 columns each of 51 lines, the upper parts much damaged. Paragraphi, dicola, a few names. *Ed. pr.*: E. W. Handley, *Menander and Plautus* (1968). To be fully published in *BICS* xxii, with photograph.

O 14   *P. Oxy.* 2829. Eleven fragments. Paragraphi and dicola. *Ed. pr.*: E. G. Turner, *Oxyrhynchus Papyri* xxxviii (1971).

O 15   *P. Oxy.* 2830. Beginnings of 20 lines from one column. Paragraphi and dicola, one name. *Ed. pr.*: E. G. Turner, *Oxyrhynchus Papyri* xxxviii (1971).

O 16   *P. Oxy.* 2831. A few letters from 6 lines. *Ed. pr.*: E. G. Turner, *Aegyptus* xlvii (published 1970), 187, with photograph.

O 17   *P. Oxy.* 2943. Beginnings of 22 lines from one column, a few letters from the preceding column. Paragraphi and dicola.

P   *Membr. Petrop.* 388. Parts of three leaves, one from *Phasma*, two from *Epitrepontes*. 'Verso' overwritten in eighth cent. with a text in Syriac; later used to bind a book, found in 1844 by Tischendorf in the monastery of Sinai. Paragraphi, sometimes a gap and colon, two dicola added (mistakenly) by second hand. *Ed. pr.*: of 'recto', C. G. Cobet, *Mnem.* n.s. iv (1876), 285; of both sides, V. Jernstedt, *Acta Univ. Petropol.* xxvi (1891), which I have not seen. See further H. Hutloff, *De Menandri Epitrepontibus* (Berlin, 1913), and S. Sudhaus, *Hermes* xlviii (1913), 24. Photograph of one page (*Epitr.* 127–46) in Capps's edition, of another (*Phasma* 26–52) in Körte's 2nd edn. (1912).

S   *P. Sorbonne* 72+2272+2273. Parts of 21 columns, of 21 to 25 lines apiece. Used to make papier mâché for mummy cases. Paragraphi, sometimes spaces, two dicola (? afterthoughts). Offsets of ink, arising from the folding of the papyrus in making the papier mâché, may mislead where letters are incompletely preserved. *Ed. pr.*: A. Blanchard and A. Bataille, *Recherches de Papyrologie* iii (1964), 103 (for *P. Sorb.* 72, P. Jouguet, *BCH* xxx [1906], 103), with complete photographs. Re-edited: R. Kassel, *Kleine Texte*, no. 185 (1965). Cf. also R. A. Coles, *Emerita* xxxiv (1966), 131.

Z   *P. Ross. Georg.* i. 10. Ends of 20 lines from one column, a few letters from the next. Paragraphi, dicola. Remains of marginal notes.

Ed. pr.: G. Zereteli, *Journal des Ministeriums für Volksaufklärung* (Abt. Klass. Phil.) 1909, 89. Re-edited: G. Zereteli and O. Krüger, *P. Ross. Georg.* i (1925).

Doubtful fragments

There are many comic fragments in papyri that may be from plays by Menander; the later the papyrus, the higher the initial chance that it contains his work. Many of these are scraps of no great interest, and a selection only of the more important has been printed in the OCT and commented on here. They are:

*P. Antinoop.*15. A.D. iv. Pack² 1659. Possibly Ἄπιϲτοϲ.

P. Didot (Paris, Louvre, no. 7172). ii B.C. (I). Pack² 1319. Modern opinion tends against this, but it is in the editions of Jensen and Körte.

    (II). Pack² 1320. Not unworthy of Menander.

P. Ghôran II (*P. Sorbonne* 72). iii B.C. Pack² 1657. *Fab. incert.* VII Mette.

P. Hamburg 656. iii B.C. Pack² 1643. Included, as uncertain, by Körte–Thierfelder, *Menander*, vol. ii, p. 272.

P. Oxy. 10. A.D. ii/iii. Pack² 1677.

I have also included a few lines from a play found in two rolls of the third century B.C.:

P. Petrie 4.
P. Hibeh 5+*P. Rylands* 16a+*P. Heidelberg* 180, 184.

Between them these rolls give parts of nearly 400 lines, but very little is intelligible. Among the characters is a cook named Libys, and a person of that name may have had a part in *Hydria* (frag. 404 K–T), with which Austin would identify this play. Others are named Daos, Strobilos, Demeas, and Nikophanes.

I have omitted the following fragments, of which the first is almost certainly by Menander, and several others very probably by him. None of them has much to offer:

PSI 99. A.D. ii. Pack² 1654. Ends of 34 lines; speakers: Straton, Kerdon, and Doris. The first two names were borne by characters in *Encheiridion*, with which D. Del Corno therefore identified this play, *Parola del Passato* cxxi (1968), 20.

P. Berol. 13892 (= *P. Schubart* 23). A.D. iii. *Fab. incert.* II Mette. Contains the name Kantharos, like *P. Antinoop.* 15. Edited by J. W. B. Barns and P. H. J. Lloyd-Jones, *JHS* lxxxiv (1964), 31–3.

P. Hibeh 180. iii B.C. Pack² 1324. *Fab. incert.* III Mette.

P. Antinoop. 55. A.D. iv. Pack² 1642. *Fab. incert.* IV Mette. Although the remains, to be found in *Lustrum* x. 186–91, are extensive, only three short separated passages offer a continuous text.

P. Oxy. 1239. A.D. iii. Pack² 1648. *Fab. incert.* V Mette. Ends of 21 lines, of which the last two probably contained the formula with which *Dyskolos* and *Sikyonios* end.

P. Oxy. 2658 A.D. ii. *Fab. incert.* VI Mette. Beginnings of 28 lines.

P. Hibeh 6. iii B.C. Pack² 1666. 'Interpretation . . . is obscure and uncertain', Page, *GLP* 287.

Other small fragments, which offer no clue to authorship, include:

P. Hibeh 12, 181, *P. Oxy.* 429, 430, 431, 677, 678, 862, 2329, *PRIMI* 8.

Menandrean authorship of the following seems to me on the whole unlikely:

P. Argent. 53, *P. Berol.* 9941, *P. Oxy.* 11, *PSI* 1176 (Page, *GLP* 277).

For a complete text of the doubtful fragments see C. Austin, *Comicorum Graecorum fragmenta in papyris reperta (1838–1971)*, Berlin and New York, 1972.

COMMENTARY

ASPIS

B   *P. Bodmer* 26 and *P. Colon.* 904, parts of the same codex, preserve nearly half the play (1–146, 149–400, 405–544).

F 1   *PSI* 126 has 120–35, 145–60, 378–408, 410–29. Before discovery of B made identification of the play possible these lines were named *Comoedia Florentina*.

See the edition of C. Austin, *Menandri Aspis et Samia* (Kleine Texte für Vorlesungen und Übungen), vols. i (1969) and ii (commentary, 1970). Some further points are to be found in K. Gaiser, *Menander, Der Schild oder die Erbtochter* (1971), a translation with introduction.

Dramatis Personae

Kleostratos, a young man
Daos, an elderly slave, personal attendant on Kleostratos
Smikrines, an old miser, uncle of Kleostratos
Chairestratos, younger brother of Smikrines
Chaireas, stepson of Chairestratos
A friend of Chaireas
A cook
A waiter
Luck, a goddess

Besides these speaking characters there is Spinther, the cook's slave, and others may have appeared. Kleostratos' sister, whom Chaireas loves, and Chairestratos' daughter, who becomes Kleostratos' bride, are essential to the plot, but it is unlikely that they came on the stage before the final scene, and they need not have done so then.

Scene: Athens.

Plot

The plot is fairly simple. There were three brothers, Smikrines, Chairestratos, and a third unnamed, who has died, leaving a son Kleostratos and a daughter. Kleostratos has gone to the wars, to improve his finances, and put his sister in charge of Chairestratos, who has a daughter and a stepson, Chaireas, the child of his second, and present, wife. Chairestratos is, when the play opens, about to marry his niece to his stepson, himself providing the dowry. Kleostratos' slave Daos appears and recounts to Smikrines, the first member of the family he meets, the death of his young master. He has with him most of the booty that the latter had taken in Asia. Kleostratos' sister is his 'heiress', and Smikrines proposes to exercise his right as nearest male relative to take her in marriage, to secure this property. Chairestratos and Chaireas are greatly distressed: the latter, it turns out, is in love with the girl. Daos suggests a plan to divert Smikrines. If Chairestratos should appear to die, his daughter will be his 'heiress', and carry with her a fortune worth fifteen times that of Kleostratos. Smikrines will drop his intended bride, and marry her off to the first comer, who will be Chaireas, in order to be free to claim Chairestratos' daughter. Chaireas leaves, to return with a friend who is disguised as a doctor; but first Daos brings Smikrines news of Chairestratos' sudden illness. The 'doctor' foresees that it will be fatal. Some 200 lines are then missing, and what remains after the gap, from the later part of Act IV and from Act V, is very mutilated. Smikrines appears to learn of his brother's 'death', and then Kleostratos returns, as had been promised in a prologue delivered by Luck. The last act must have contained, besides the wedding of Chaireas and the girl, that of Kleostratos and his cousin, and also the discomfiture of Smikrines.

Although there are some good scenes, *Aspis* is not one of Menander's best plays. The characters, so far as they can be judged from the two acts and a half that remain, lack depth and originality. Smikrines is unusual in being wholly bad; his greed and hypocrisy are unrelieved by any feature that can win him sympathy. The slave Daos, on the other hand, appears to be without faults, always acting with devotion, human feeling, and ingenuity. The action of the play is not at all points perfectly fitted to the personages. Smikrines would not be interested in the details of the long story that Daos tells him in the opening scene; and the quotations from tragedy with which Daos ornaments his report of Chairestratos' illness, though amusing, do not serve his purpose, since they might well arouse suspicions that he was only play-acting.

But, when this has been said, it must be recognized that much of the writing is first-rate and that the play would go well on the stage. Daos' story in the opening scene is vividly told, and Smikrines' few interjected remarks most effectively hint at his character. After the divine prologue, Smikrines' intention to get hold of his nephew's estate is revealed under a dress of self-justification and met by an ironical refusal to comment by Daos, whose opinion is nevertheless implicitly made clear. In the second act Daos' plan for defeating Smikrines is cleverly revealed; he does not say 'If you were thought to be dead, Smikrines would drop your niece to get your daughter: so this is what you must do'; he begins with what Chairestratos must do, which appears puzzling because its object is to seek, and is therefore of greater interest to a spectator. In Act III Daos' citations of tragedy and the foreign 'doctor's' professional manner form two amusing scenes, in which Smikrines can no longer dictate the course of events.

ACT I

(i) 1–96: *Daos and Smikrines*

1: Daos enters, followed by a crowd of captives, men and girls, and baggage animals (140–1); for 17½ lines, of which the first 9 are in perfect tragic metre, he emotionally addresses the young master he has left for dead. A reader would suppose him to be alone, but 18–20 suggest that he entered on the stage accompanied by Smikrines, who shares his belief that the young man is dead. It is true that Smikrines could have inferred that from 13–18, if he had emerged from his house unnoticed not later than 13. But the exchanges 18–21 seem unsuitable to the theory that Smikrines and Daos here first meet after a long absence (130), unless their curtness is a sign of Smikrines' lack of humanity, revealed by his very first words.

οὐδέ of line 2 demands a preceding negative, Denniston, *GP* 190, e.g. ἐγὼ μὲν οὐκ ἄλυπον ἡμέραν κτλ.

2 ὦ τρόφιμε: 'Young master', *Epitr.* frag. 1 n.

3 παραπλήϲι' ὡϲ: 'I do not draw up my accounts in the same way as I once hoped when I was setting out.' παραπλήϲια is adverbial rather than the direct object of διαλογίζομαι. Although παραπλήϲιοϲ and ὅμοιοϲ are usually constructed with a dative, an adverbial relative is sometimes used; thus π. ὡϲ εἰ, Hdt. iv. 99, ὁ. ὡϲ εἰ, Hdt. i. 155, Plato, *Laws* 628 d, π. καθάπερ, *Epist.* 321 a, ὁ. ὥϲπερ, Aesch. *Ag.* 1311, Xen. *Cyr.* i. 4. 6, etc. At the end ἐξορμωμένων, 'as we set out' (K–G ii. 110) is a possible alternative.

4 εὐδοξοῦντα: 'In high repute', [Eur.] *Rhes.* 496, Xen. *Mem.* iii. 6. 16, Dem. xx. 142, Aischines ii. 66, 118, seems more likely than εὐδοκοῦντα, 'being happy', a word first found in Polybios, with whom it is a favourite.

5–6: 'Pass your life in some grace and dignity.' τε joins this clause to the succeeding καὶ τὴν ἀδελφὴν κτλ. ἀπὸ ϲτρατείαϲ is in Aesch. *Ag.* 603, *Eum.* 631, also of return from a campaign.

7: Cf. frag. 213, ἄρχων, ϲτρατηγόϲ, ἡγεμών, δήμου πάλιν ϲύμβουλοϲ. But here ϲύμβουλοϲ will indicate a member of an advisory council attached to a commander, as in Thuc. v. 63, or to a provincial governor, as in Xen. *Hell.* iii. 1. 13. Daos seems to suppose that in civilian life Chairestratos would keep the title of the military office he had once held.

9 καταξίῳ: A word from tragedy, found also in inscriptions from the second century B.C. The poor farmer at Eur. *El.* 46 regards himself as οὐ κατάξιος of Elektra.

10 ποθεινὸν ἥκοντ': Ar. *Ach.* 886, ἦλθες ποθεινή, Eur. *IT* 515, ποθεινός γ' ἦλθες.

12 εὐνοιας χάριν: Lit. 'in return for my goodwill towards you', but the meaning is 'for my services, inspired by my goodwill'. The use of χάριν for ἕνεκα, although found in Plato, is mainly tragic. In Menander it occurs elsewhere only in the dubious fragment 683, χρημάτων χάριν, in the paratragic stichomythia of *Perik.* 801, τίνος χάριν, and by a certain supplement in the paratragic line *Sik.* 170. **παραλόγως τ' ἀνήρπασαι**: 'Are snatched away against all expectation'. ἀναρπάζω is often used of kidnapping; its use here of the action of Death is imaginative, but cf. Soph. *El.* 848, ὃς γὰρ ἔτ' ἦν, φροῦδος ἀναρπασθείς.

14 ὦ Κλεόστρατε: See *Dysk.* 823 n.

15: Cf. Eur. *HF* 1098, ἔγχη τόξα τ' ... ἃ πρὶν παρασπίζοντ' ἐμοῖς βραχίοσιν ἔσῳζε πλευρὰς ἐξ ἐμοῦ τ' ἐσῴζετο.

16 σεσωμένος was the Attic form, preserved by S at *Sik.* 121, where see n., but usually corrupted in MSS., as here, to σεσωσμένος. But Aelius Dionysius c 12 Erbse says οἱ δὲ νεώτεροι (which includes writers of New Comedy) σέσωσμαι.

17 τὴν: B has της, perhaps by memory of ης in ησθα. Similarly in 4 σωθουντα is due to unconscious memory of ευδοξουντα.

19 ὦ Δᾶε: ὦ strikes a note of simulated emotion. But the adjective ἀνελπίστου indicates no sorrow; it is left for Daos to supply feeling with δεινῆς. **ἢ τίνι τρόπῳ;** appears to be an absolute equivalent of πῶς; such tautology is not infrequent in tragedy.

20–1: Stobaios has στρατιώτην, B στρατιώτης, which Austin emends to στρατιώτηι. Either construction (acc. or dat.) is possible: 'it can hardly happen that a soldier finds ...', cf. e.g. Arist. *Pol.* 1286ᵃ35, or 'it is hard for a soldier to find ...'

21 πρόφασις: 'Cause', with the connotations of being 'external' and 'sufficient'. εὑρεῖν suggests 'discover by search' when taken with σωτηρίας πρόφασιν, 'light upon' when taken with ὀλέθρου πρόφασιν.

23: Lykia was a province of SW. Asia Minor, to the E. of Karia. It is mountainous country, but a long flat narrow plain cuts back deep inland near the western boundary. This is watered by the river that the Greeks called Xanthos, the Yellow River (the modern R. Koca), already known to Homer, *Il.* vi. 171, xii. 313. According to Strabo xiv. 3. 6, it was formerly called Sirbis. Near the sea was a town also called Xanthos by the Greeks, and Arñna in Lykian. The Lykians had, however, become partially Hellenized by the later fourth century, and Greek was used in many inscriptions (*RE* 2 Reihe ix. 1375–1408). There is no historical evidence to indicate what might have been the object of a campaign there in Menander's lifetime, except that Ptolemy is said to have captured Lykia from Antigonos in 309 B.C. (Diod. Sic. xx. 27). From the story that Daos tells, the Greeks might have been engaged in nothing more than a piece of private freebooting, and in the disorganized period following the death of Alexander that was perhaps possible in this country, isolated as it was by mountain-ranges from the neighbouring territory.

Daos begins like a messenger in tragedy, cf. Aesch. *Persae* 447, νῆςός τις ἐςτὶ πρόςθε Cαλαμῖνος τόπων, Soph. *Trach.* 237, ἀκτή τις ἔςτ' Εὐβοίς.

24 ἐπιεικῶς . . . πολλαῖς: 'A fair number', cf. 35, *Epitr.* 423 n.

27 ἦν: This is the idiomatic use of the imperfect ἦν to express a fact now recognized, but which was true, although overlooked, all along; Goodwin, *MT* § 39. ὡς ἔοικε here replaces ἄρα, more usual in this construction. Daos produces a platitude, but this suits his somewhat pompous style, illustrated again at 21–2, 164–6, 191 (γνῶθι cαυτόν).

30 τὸ καταφρονεῖν: Sc. τῶν βαρβάρων, cf. Thuc. ii. 11. 4, τὸ ἔλαςςον πλῆθος δεδιὸς ἄμεινον ἠμύνατο τοὺς πλέονας διὰ τὸ καταφρονοῦντας ἀπαραςκεύους γενέςθαι, and Xen. *Hell.* iv. 1. 17, καταφρονητικῶς δέ ποτε καὶ ἀφυλάκτως διὰ τὸ μηδὲν πρότερον ἐςφάλθαι. **τὸ μέλλον:** 'Towards what was to come', cf. Thuc. iv. 71. 1, ἐδόκει ἡςυχάςαςι τὸ μέλλον περιδεῖν.

31 τὸν χάρακα: χάραξ, a stake, was used to mean a palisaded camp, in which sense it was masculine, whereas it was feminine when meaning a vine-stake, *Dysk.* 113.

32 ἐπώλουν: To whom did they sell their booty and of what did it consist? The neuter αἰχμάλωτα will cover both household goods, as in Xen. *Hell.* iv. 1. 26, and prisoners, as in *Anabasis* iv. 1. 13, *Hell.* iv. 6. 6. Presumably slave-dealers had followed the army in hopes of business.

χρήματα . . . ἀπελθών: 'Every man had a lot of money or valuables when he came back from the country.' This text, printed by Austin, is satisfactory for sense. B has απελθειν (cf. ελθειν for ελθων at 295) and Lloyd-Jones suggested ἐπελθεῖν, 'every man was able to fall on many valuables', but had no parallel for such a use of the word. For his conjecture ⟨Cμ.⟩ Ἄπολλον, ὡς καλόν Austin cites Lykophron frag. 1 Nauck *TGF²*.

35 ἑξακοcίουc: See 83. χρυcοῦc: Originally a χρυcοῦc was a gold stater (δαρεικόc) of about 130 g. weight, and very common in Asia. But a slightly heavier coin minted first by Philip of Macedon (whence it is called *philippus* in Latin) drove this out. In third-century papyri the word is used to mean not a coin, but 20 drachmae, and this meaning may already be found here. ποτήρια: Probably of silver. For drinking-vessels as booty, cf. Xen. *Anab.* iv. 3. 25, 4. 21, *Hell.* iv. 1. 24.

37 Ῥόδον: Rhodes is about 50 miles by sea from the mouth of the R. Xanthos.

41–3: Austin calls my attention to an ambiguity. Did the barbarians remain out of sight of the sentries by keeping a hill in front of them, that is between themselves and the Greek camp? Or did they occupy a hill in front of the camp, and escape the notice of scouts who reconnoitred the lower ground only? The former seems to me more likely, and to have some support from a passage adduced by Austin: Xen. *Cyr.* iii. 3. 28, where Cyrus, approaching an Assyrian camp, disguised his strength, κώμαc τε καὶ γηλόφουc ἐπίπροcθεν ποιηcάμενοc.

43 αὐτομόλων: Probably slaves who ran away, cf. Thuc. vii. 27. 5, ἀνδραπόδων πλέον ἢ δύο μυριάδεc ηὐτομολήκεcαν.

46–7: By ἅπαν τὸ cτρατόπεδον Daos cannot mean every Greek soldier in the army, for at 64–5 we learn of some who were not in the camp on the fatal night, but scattered on their looting forays, cf. Xen. *Hell.* iii. 2. 3 for such nocturnal absence. The words mean 'everyone in the camp'. All these (*a*) were in their tents (none standing guard) and (*b*) had come from a well-stocked countryside. γίνεται is impersonal: 'there happened what you would expect.' οἷον εἰκόc: *Sam.* 42.

48 ἐβρύαζον: Priscian, *Inst.* v. 193 Hertz. has βρύειν Μένανδροc τὸ μεθύειν ἐν τῇ Ἀcπίδι. Since there is a verb βρύειν, Menander may have used it elsewhere in the play, but the correction βρυ⟨άζ⟩ειν is likely. Although the army was no doubt drinking heavily, the verb βρυάζειν, which literally means 'swell up', has a wider metaphorical meaning, 'revelling'. It was used by Epicurus, paradoxically, of his own simple enjoyments, frag. 181, βρυάζω τῷ κατὰ τὸ cωμάτιον ἡδεῖ, ὕδατι καὶ ἄρτῳ χρώμενοc, cf. Plutarch, *non posse suauiter*, 1090 a, ἀξιοῦμεν αὐτοὺc . . . μὴ φάναι χαίρειν καὶ βρυάζειν τοὺc ἐν πόνοιc ὑπερβάλλουcι καὶ νόcοιc γιγνομένουc, Duris frag. 24 Jacoby, αἱ γυναῖκεc ἐβρύ⟨αζ⟩ον ἐν τῇ Δωρίδι cτολῇ, Aemilianus, *AP* ix. 756. In Ar. *Knights* 602 ἀνεβρύαξαν is suspect (ἀνεφρυάξανθ' Walsh).

49 γάρ conveys assent: 'Yes, very bad, for . . .'

52 ff.: The first survivors of the massacre, which had taken place some time after nightfall, arrive at Daos' camping place about the middle of the night. This is rather surprising, since Daos had made an early start (ἔωθεν 40) and presumably marched all day. But the first comers were probably on horseback; the infantrymen kept on coming in during the rest of the night (cf. the order in 61). Daos' convoy, on the other hand, including young girls and beasts of burden (? donkeys), would not have moved very fast.

55 ἀνδραποδίων: This diminutive of ἀνδράποδον was used by Hypereides frag. 227 (Pollux iii. 77) and Diphilos frag. 80 K. For the position of τῆc cf. *Dysk.* 408 n., H. van Herwerden, *Mnem.* xxxvii (1909), 164 n. 3.

58: The correction εὐτυχῶc is supported by *Dysk.* 400, ἀλλ' ἐcτὶν εὐτυχῶc τὸ νυμφαῖον τοδ[ί. Turner's ἐκ τύχηc is good Greek, but not yet paralleled in Menander.

60 ἠθροιζόμεcθα: This form of 1st pers. plural passive is common in tragedy, for metrical convenience, but unusual in Menander; frag. 767, οὐχ ὅθεν ἀπωλόμεcθα cωθείημεν ἄν, is perhaps the only other example.

ἐπέρρεον: 'Came streaming up', cf. e.g. Hdt. ix. 38, ἐπιρρεόντων τῶν Ἑλλήνων.

61 ὑπαcπιcταί: In the army of Alexander the Great the ὑπαcπιcταί were a corps of light-armed infantry, who are often found leading the assault when a fortification is taken by storm. Their operations called for greater courage and initiative than did those of the ordinary infantryman, fighting in the massed phalanx. In this flight they are able to run faster than the heavy-armed cτρατιῶται, although they are, of course, behind the cavalry. See Addenda.

62 ὡc ὤνηco: 'How lucky for you that . . .', cf. Theokritos xv. 55, ὠνάθην μεγάλωc ὅτι . . ., Lucian, *Prometheus* 20, ὤνηco διότι . . . Smikrines spares no word of sympathy for the wounded.

63 χάρακα βαλόμενοι: 'Having thrown up a palisade'; cf. for the phrase Dem. xviii. 87, Plut. *Aem.* 17, Polybios iii. 105. 10.

65 προνομαῖc αἷc εἶπον: 'Forays I spoke of', i.e. at 31–3. For the attraction of the relative, which should logically be ἅc, cf. 134, τῆc γυναικὸc ἧc ἔχει. The noun (several times in Xenophon) and the (later) verb προνομεύω were both used indiscriminately of foraging and general plundering. **ἐπεγίνοντο**: 'Kept on joining us', cf. Thuc. iii. 77, παραινούντων τῶν Ἀθηναίων cφᾶc τε ἐᾶcαι πρῶτον ἐκπλεῦcαι καὶ ὕcτερον ἐκείνουc ἐπιγενέcθαι. The survivors of the massacre were strengthened by the addition, in packet after packet of men, of those who had escaped because they were not in the camp but out raiding in the countryside. ἐπιγίγνεϲθαι with a dative usually means 'come up *to attack*' (LSJ s.v. II. 2), but this is not a necessary implication, cf. [Xen.] *Cyneg.* vi. 19, ἐὰν . . . μὴ οἷόϲ τ᾽ ᾖ κυνοδρομῶν ἐπιγίνεϲθαι αὐταῖϲ, sc. ταῖϲ κυϲί, and Arist. *EN* 1174ᵇ34: pleasure is an ἐπιγιγνόμενόν τι τέλοϲ, 'a supervening perfection', οἷον τοῖϲ ἀκμαίοιϲ ἡ ὥρα.

66 προήγομεν πάλιν: 'We started to go out again', i.e. from our strong-point. B has προϲηγομεν, 'we began to approach'. This must mean 'to approach the old camp', but the lack of any mention of that camp is awkward. προϲ- and προ- are commonly confused by B.

68 οὐϲ ἔλαβον: It is important that the Lykians had taken some prisoners: Kleostratos will prove to have been among them.

69 αὐτὸν μὲν: Daos has in mind a continuation with τὴν δ᾽ ἀϲπίδα, but Smikrines' interruption causes him to change the form of his statement.

70: Reeve, quoted by Austin, adduces Amm. Marc. xix. 9. 9, 'nostrorum cadauera mox caesorum fatiscunt ac diffluunt adeo ut nullius mortui facies post quatriduum agnoscatur.' The alert spectator will realize that a man is less certainly recognized by his shield than by his face.

73: Although the scholiast on Aristophanes or his source seems to have taken ϲυντετριμμένην with the preceding words, I think Handley's correction gives more effective sentences than does Kassel's. The facts relevant to the question πῶϲ οἶϲθα; are that he was (1) lying there dead (2) recognizable by his shield. The damage to the shield is not to the point here. But one must note *Dysk.* 126, διόπερ . . . μοι δοκεῖ.

75 ὁ χρηϲτόϲ: As so often, ironical, e.g. *Sam.* 408, *Epitr.* 1066. The commander abbreviated the funeral rites unnecessarily: there was no real danger from the Lykians, who had retired to the mountains. All the same he had the remains buried hastily (ϲπουδῇ πάνυ, 78) and then at once withdrew (ἀνέζευξε εὐθύϲ, 79). Unfortunately this interpretation is not the only one possible. ϲπουδῇ can mean 'with all zeal' as well as 'in haste' and ἀναζευγνύναι can be used of breaking camp for a forward move (e.g. Thuc. viii. 108, Plut. *Agesilaus* 22) as well as for a retreat (e.g. Hdt. viii. 60, Plut. *Coriolanus* 31).

76: I accept Kassel's change of κλαιειν to καίειν (or the fourth-century Attic κάειν). The commander foresaw that there would be an unnecessary expenditure of time if the bones of the cremated were individually collected for burial, a procedure that would necessitate individual cremations. He avoided this by a mass cremation and mass burial, preventing individual funeral pyres. κλαίειν καθ᾽ ἕνα would be relevant only if it could mean not merely 'weep for', but the whole funeral process of weeping and cremating; and that I doubt. The haste of the funeral and its mass nature are not merely picturesque detail. They ensure that Daos had little opportunity for checking the identity of the corpse, e.g. by the clothes it was wearing.

77: The verb ὀcτολογεῖν occurs once only elsewhere, in a passage that leaves it dubious whether it can take as object the man whose bones are gathered, Isaios iv. 19, οὔτ᾽ ἀποθανόντ᾽ ἀνείλετ᾽ οὔτ᾽ ἔκαυcεν οὔτ᾽ ὠcτολόγηcεν. If it can, Kassel's change of ἑκάcτοιc to ἑκάcτουc is plausible: the delay will arise through collecting the bones of each man individually. If the dative is maintained, then it is said that time will be spent by each burial-party severally. That is doubtless true, but the commander's concern is for the delay to the force as a whole, not to individual units.

80 διεπίπτομεν: 'We slipped through', cf. Xen. *Hell.* iii. 2. 4, ἀπεχώρηcαν ἐν τῇ μάχῃ διαπεcόντεc, Polybios i. 34. 11, διέπεcον εἰc τὴν Ἀcπίδα. The imperfects διεπίπτομεν, ἐπλέομεν concentrate attention on the *processes* of 'slipping through' and of 'travelling by sea'. Daos did not carry out the instructions that had been given him, because the supposed death of his master had made them pointless. He had been told to deposit the valuables with the friend in Rhodes for safe keeping: now that his master could not reclaim them, there was no reason for depositing them; his duty was clearly to take the property home to form part, no doubt almost the whole, of the dead man's estate.

82 ἀκήκοαc μου πάντα: Austin notes how similar phrases often end a long speech, Soph. *Ajax* 480, πάντ᾽ ἀκήκοαc λόγον, *Phil.* 389, Aesch. *Ag.* 582, *Eum.* 710. Smikrines without pretence turns to what interests him, the gold; the rest of the story excites no comment.

84: 40 minae = 24 kg.

85 κληρονόμε: Daos shows by this form of address that he understands Smikrines' interest in the details of the treasure to be that of a prospective heir. On the legal position see below, 149 n. Smikrines' denial does not ring true, and the doubts it raises will attach also to his exclamation at 90 that his nephew 'should have lived'. Kassel and Austin prefer to give οὐ πλείονοc to Smikrines, as a question; but the isolated vocative κληρονόμε is not convincing.

88-9 ἔνεcτ᾽ ἐνταῦθ᾽: 'Are in here', i.e. in boxes, to which Daos points, carried by the slaves.   ὄχλον . . . οἰκεῖον: 'This crowd of persons', i.e. the prisoners of 36-7, 55, 'that you see belongs to you.'

90 ὤφελε ζῆν: Klearchos in Xen. *Anab.* ii. 1. 4 opens a speech with ἀλλ' ὤφελε μὲν Κῦρος ζῆν. Smikrines' remark may be conventional as well as insincere. Daos replies with a heartfelt ὤφελε.

92 οἷς ἥκιστα χρῆν: 'Those who ought least to hear it' are the young man's relatives, who will be most affected. For οἷς ἥκιστ' ἐχρῆν, applied to those closely connected, see *Mis.* 249 n. The change of B's χρη to χρῆν (or even ἐχρῆν) seems necessary. As V. Schmidt argues, οὐ χρή is used of what ought not to be done and what the speaker hopes will not be done, οὐκ ἐχρῆν of what is done, although it ought not to have been done.

93–6: Against 93 B has a marginal note ηϲυχη (= ἡϲυχῆ, 'quietly'), to indicate, as at 467, that the speech is an 'aside', not to be heard by the other character(s) on the stage. Cf. Schol. Ven. Ar. *Frogs* 606, ἡϲυχῆ δὲ ταῦτα λέγει. Del Corno, *ZPE* vi (1970) 214, plausibly suggests that the word is misplaced, Smikrines' aside beginning with νυνὶ δέ.

93 βουλήϲομαι: Jebb on Soph. *OT* 1077 explains that the present wish is represented as continuing in the future; this is rightly regarded by Page on Eur. *Med.* 259 as artificial: 'The tense is modified by the futurity of the content of the wish.' Page compares the vulgar English 'I shall be pleased to accept.'

95 εἴϲω παριέναι: One would expect this to mean 'go in to visit them', as in Eur. *Hel.* 451, where Menelaos wishing to enter Theoklymenos' palace says ἔϲω πάρειμι, but the sequel shows that Smikrines enters his own house. Moreover, if B's future participle ϲκεψόμενος is right, εἴϲω παριέναι must mean 'go into my house', although there is no one there whom he would wish to meet, for he would not enter that of Chairestratos in order to deliberate. Possibly a change should be made to ϲκεψάμενος: 'My present intention is that I too should go in to visit them when I have considered how I can behave most gently towards them.'

96 προϲενεχθείη τις ἡμερώτατα: By τις Smikrines means himself, and it is surprising that he should consider how to behave in a 'gentle' way towards his relations. Perhaps he has already conceived the plan, which he will soon put forward, of marrying Kleostratos' sister, realizes that it will be unwelcome, and wonders how he can propose it with the minimum of brutality. The word ἡμερώτατα, emphatic by its position, must remain in the audience's mind; they will wonder what he meant by it; for, although his character has as yet only been hinted at, those hints have not suggested any fine feelings. For the phrase cf. Dio Cassius lvii. 18, ἡμερώτατα τῷ οἰκείῳ προϲεφέρετο.

(ii) 97–148: *Prologue by the goddess Luck*

97: A goddess enters, to deliver a 'postponed' prologue, a feature of several of Menander's plays; see introduction, p. 20. This prologue is a dramatic convenience, for she is able to explain the relationships between the characters and also the existing situation. To do this in dialogue would no doubt have been possible; to do it naturally and dramatically would have been difficult, perhaps impossible. But the goddess not only informs the audience of facts known to all the characters, she also tells them of something known only to Kleostratos, who is not yet present, namely that he was not killed in Lykia, but is on the point of reappearing in Athens. Menander thus gives up the possibility of a dramatic surprise. It was traditionally more important that the audience should not be in the dark about any essential fact in the story. They are even told in advance (143 ff.) that the machinations of Smikrines will be defeated, much as in *Perik.* Misapprehension broadly hints that all will come well and the foundlings be restored to their relations. τι . . . δυσχερές: 'Something unpleasant' means the death of Kleostratos. Divinities keep away from the pollution of death (Barrett on Eur. *Hipp.* 1437–9).

102: This 'other mercenary' was perhaps said to be in Kleostratos' tent.

104 ἐπέχων: The meaning of this verb, and it has many, would be determined by the missing words at the end of the previous line. Possibly οὐδὲ ἕν ἐπέχων, 'without a moment's delay', but more likely 'continuously', as in Ar. *Peace* 1121, παῖ' αὐτὸν ἐπέχων, Thuc. ii. 101. 5. ἐσήμαινε: Sc. ὁ σαλπικτής: the verb is sometimes so used without a subject, Hdt. viii. 11, Eur. *Heracl.* 830, Xen. *Anab.* iii. 4. 4, etc. There is a somewhat similar scene in Xen. *Anab.* vii. 4. 16, a night attack by natives; at the signal given by a young trumpeter the Greeks rush out of the houses where they are quartered.

105 τὸ πάρον . . . πλησίον: 'The armour that was to hand by him'.

106 τούτου: Daos, who has only just left the stage. He is οὗτος again in 110. Similarly τήνδε τὴν ἀσπίδα is 'this shield you have just seen'.

112 σωθήσεται: 'Will arrive safely', LSJ s.v. II. 2. ὅσον οὐ means 'just not', 'almost'; so ὅσον οὐδέπω is 'just not yet', i.e. 'very soon now'.

116 ὑπερπέπαικεν: 'Beats all men in badness'. The perfect tense expresses the present result of Smikrines' past bad actions. Cf. Dem. l. 34, τοσοῦτον ὑπερπέπαικας πλούτῳ τοὺς ἄλλους.

118 τῶν ἐν τῷ βίῳ αἰσχρῶν πεφρόντικ' οὐδέν: 'He hasn't given a moment's thought to the shameful actions in his life.'

121 μονότροπος: 'Solitary'. The word was used as the title of plays by the comedians Phrynichos, Anaxilas, and Ophelion. The solitary man is one of the figures of comedy. Knemon of *Dyskolos* belongs to this class. Like Knemon and Euclio of *Aulularia*, Smikrines parsimoniously keeps a single old woman as maid of all work.

122 ἐν γειτόνων: 'In the neighbouring house', cf. *Dysk.* 25 n., *Perik.* 147. Austin has a valuable note on the phrase and its later confusion with ἐκ γειτόνων.

123 ἀδελφός: There is no certain way of determining whether to write ἀδελφός, 'his (only) brother . . . younger than he', or ἀδελφός, 'a brother . . . a younger brother'. But as the plot assumes that there is no other surviving brother, it is I think likely that the point was made here in the prologue; accordingly I print ἀδελφός.   τοῦδε calls for a deictic gesture.

125 τῷ μειρακίῳ: i.e. Kleostratos.   χρηστὸς . . . καὶ πλούσιος like the commander in *Sik.* 14.

129: Vitelli reports a grave accent in F 1 on the ι of αυται, but either the report or the accent must be mistaken, in view of the following enclitic τε. The common conjunction of αὐτός and the reflexive makes it tempting to read αὐταί θ' ἑαυταῖς, but the position of τε is slightly easier with αὗται. The girls have been brought up together in the respectable seclusion of a rich family.

130–6: Chairestratos' intention was to marry his ward to his stepson. The repeated imperfect ἔμελλε, 'was intending', suggests that the intention was being frustrated. 'Ward' seems a proper word to use, since he must either have been entrusted by her brother with power to dispose of her in marriage, or have felt that the power had passed to him through the young man's prolonged absence. Plaut. *Trinummus* 573 may be compared: there, when a father is away, the right of betrothal may be exercised by a brother.

τὰ οἰκεῖα must be Kleostratos' private property, and the fact that it is 'quite moderate' leads his uncle to provide a dowry himself. μέτριος, to be sure, is usually a term of praise; the sense 'poor' is not attested by LSJ before the fourth century A.D. In frag. 8 ὁ μετρίως πράττων is opposed to ὁ πένης. In [Dem.] xxxiii. 4 the speaker is a merchant who has given up travelling, μέτρια δ' ἔχων engages in the shipping business. But one who had been obliged to go soldiering to find a dowry for his sister cannot have had much property.

133 cυνοικίζειν: A common word for legal marriage, cf. 10, *Heros* 43 n., *Pap. Didot* 40.

135 ἐπεδίδου: This verb is used of giving a dowry ('in addition to the bride'), e.g. 268, LSJ s.v. 2.

137–8: The text of F 1 is inscribed on ruled guide-lines; hence it is probable that there was a regular number of lines to the page, and the second page had 28 on each side. It follows that there were in all probability 12 lines in F 1 between 135 and 145. Arnott suggests that something has dropped out in B hereabouts, *Zeitschr. f. Pap. u. Epigraphik* iv (1969), 162; there is, however, no other sign that anything is missing.   **νυνί,** as the sequel shows, means 'this very day'.

139: Menander, like other comic poets, sometimes introduces γάρ late in the sentence; Denniston, *GP* 96–7, gives examples from Aristophanes and later comedy.

141 σκευοφόρα: Sc. κτήνη, 'baggage-animals', like the donkeys that accompany Stratophanes in *Sikyonios*.   **παιδίσκαι:** A reminder that the ὄχλος of captives included both sexes.   **ἐπικλήρου:** 'Heiress', see intro. p. 29 n. 1. All the property just enumerated will go with her.

142 χρόνῳ προέχων: 'Being ahead in years'. For this sense of χρόνος cf. Soph. *OC* 374, χρόνῳ μείων γεγώς.

146 ἐπὶ τἀρχαῖα: Cf. Ar. *Knights* 1387, εἰς τἀρχαῖα δὴ καθίσταμαι, 'I return to my previous state', cf. *Clouds* 593, Isokr. iv. 156, πάλιν εἰς τἀρχαῖα καταστῆσαι.

147–8: One may doubt whether to make τίς an interrogative dependent on τοὔνομα φράσαι, or independent as I have printed it. But editors are wrong in attaching πάντων κυρία κτλ. to Τύχη and making that phrase part of the answer; if it were, we should have ἡ πάντων κυρία. Aischines ii. 131 has τὴν τύχην, ἣ πάντων ἐστὶ κυρία. Cf. also Philyllios frag. 8 K.   **βραβεῦσαι:** βραβεύειν, properly 'to give a decision as umpire', came to mean 'control', 'direct', e.g. Plut. *Pelop.* 13, πρᾶξιν . . . βραβευθεῖσαν . . . ὑπὸ τῆς Τύχης, Alkiphron, *ep.* ii. 4. 2, τὸ ζῆν . . . ὑπὸ τῆς Τύχης βραβεύεται, Heliod. vii. 6. 4, τύχη τις τὰ ἀνθρώπεια βραβεύουσα. πάντων τούτων depends on κυρία, and the two infinitives are epexegetic.

Τύχη: C. H. Moore, *Cl. Phil.* xi (1916), 1, adversely criticizes Menander for not revealing the identity of the speaker at the beginning of the prologue; the same 'fault' occurs in *Perikeiromene*, whereas in *Aulularia, Casina, Cistellaria, Rudens,* and *Trinummus* (and now one can add *Dyskolos*) the divinity reveals its name at once. This overlooks the fact that the dramatist may *wish* to keep his audience wondering, perhaps looking at the mask and costume for some clue. Here the words in which Luck reveals herself give a virtual promise that she is going to play a determining part in the events that are to follow.

The importance of Chance or Luck in human affairs was of old a common topic among the Greeks (cf. frag. 417 n.) and Aristotle devotes chapters 4–6 of *Physics B* to showing that it is not a true cause of events. Numerous fragments of comedy show how ready men were in the fourth and third centuries to 'explain' events as due to chance, an explanation favoured by the etymological connection of τύχη with τυγχάνειν, 'happen'. The vast changes that followed the conquests of Alexander must have contributed to the feeling that there was a power at work greater than human volition; in his essay on τύχη Demetrios of Phaleron asked who fifty years before could have foreseen these changes (*F. Gr. Hist.* 228. 39). The workings of chance should be blind (e.g. frag. 463) and are usually so regarded, but human inconsistency cannot avoid the idea that the force that brings luck, good or bad, can be influenced or propitiated. From this it is an easy, perhaps a simultaneous, step to ascribe to it a personality, thoughts, plans, and emotions. Thus from Menander we can quote, besides the 'Mind of Luck' in frag. 517, the apostrophe ὦ μεταβολαῖς χαίρουσα παντοίαις Τύχη, cόν ἐcτ' ὄνειδος τοῦτο (frag. 630) and *Koneiaz.* 13 ff. Cults of Τύχη, or of some particular Τύχη, e.g. that of a city, sprang up in Hellenistic times and sculptors gave her human form. A shrine of Ἀγαθὴ Τύχη existed in Athens as early as 335/4 B.C. (*IG* ii². 333c). This passage is, however, the only one in comedy where Τύχη is *clearly* personified, and there is no reason for supposing that Menander conceived of her as any more real than Ἄγνοια of *Perikeiromene*. On Τύχη see M. P. Nilsson, *Gesch. d. gr. Religion*, ii. 190 ff., *Greek Piety* (Eng. trans.), p. 86, U. von Wilamowitz, *Glaube d. Hellenen*, ii. 298 ff.

(iii) **149–163**: *Smikrines alone*

149: The goddess having left, Smikrines comes out of his house. He explains that he has not required any account of the property brought back from Asia, since it would not be practicable to cheat him of any of it. It is not obvious what right he has to his nephew's property, since for inheritance sisters took precedence over uncles (Harrison, *Law of Athens*, i p. 144), but when he continues by saying that he will tell his brother to drop the marriage he was intending for his niece, this should be a hint to an Athenian spectator that he had in mind the exercise of his own right to claim her in marriage and so gain control of his nephew's estate.

150 φέρει: Daos.

151 ὁποία: The change to indirect interrogative after a previous direct one is common, the reverse change, exemplified at 199, less so, K–G ii. 516.

152 ἐνθάδε: 'Here', Chairestratos' house.

153 βασκαίνειν: Properly 'to cast the evil eye on one' comes to mean 'malign', as here, or with the dat. 'grudge', 'envy'; see LSJ s.v.

154: 'The full facts will out so long as the bearers are servants.' Servants would have no interest in concealing any attempt by their masters to cheat by misrepresenting the total to be shared.

156 οἶμαι μὲν οὖν αὐτούς: αὐτούς, like αὐτοῖς (159), must mean Chairestratos and his household. μὲν οὖν may be corrective, Smikrines pushing aside the idea of possible cheating and substituting the view that 'they' will *willingly* act rightly and loyally. But it is tempting to recognize an instance of οὖν emphasizing a prospective μέν; see Denniston, *GP* 473, who quotes, however, no instance from comedy and only one from the orators. Transitional μὲν οὖν, introducing a consequence of what has just been said, is unlikely because of ἑκόντας: a man cannot be said to act aright willingly if he does so because he knows his servants would give the game away if he did otherwise.

ἐμμενεῖν: 'Abide by', a common sense, LSJ s.v. 2.

158 οὐθεὶς ἐπιτρέψει: 'No one will let them have it their own way'; cf. Ar. *Plut.* 915, μὴ 'πιτρέπειν ἐάν τις ἐξαμαρτάνῃ.

159 προειπεῖν: 'Give them notice', 'warn them'.

160–3: 'Perhaps it is odd even to talk about this marriage; for they are not thinking about a wedding now that this bad news has come. But I will call Daos out: he (not being a relative of the dead Kleostratos) will be the only member of the household who will listen to me.'

If ἐστὶν is right, the unexpressed subject can hardly be Chairestratos, who has not been mentioned, but rather some undetermined conception, e.g. τὰ πράγματα. But εἶναι ἐν, 'be busy with' (see LSJ s.v. ἐν A. II. 1), normally has a personal subject, so that the correction εἰσὶν has much probability.

162 τὴν θύραν γε κόψας: Smikrines may not be able to command attention, but he can at any rate knock at the door.

(iv) 164–215: *Smikrines and Daos*

164: Daos appears. No reason is even suggested for his coming out, unless we are to suppose him to wish to get away from the mourning women. Usually in Menander there is an easily discoverable cause for every entry, although there is no necessity that it should bring the entry about exactly at the point where it occurs. But occasionally, as here, the character's appearance is seemingly not accounted for, or, if there is any hint, it is so discreet that we may suspect we have imagined it. Thus Onesimos at *Epitr.* 382 *may* come out of the house because he wants to get away from the irritating slowness of the cook, and Nikeratos at *Sam.* 713 to escape the nagging of his wife.

Daos' words, spoken into the house as he comes out, are addressed to the women, who include the supposedly dead youth's sister. They may well be forgiven, he says, for acting as they are doing, that is presumably for wailing and lamenting the death, but they should, so far as they can, bear what has happened like human beings. That is to say, a human being has reason and knows that death is sooner or later the lot of all men.   ἐκ τῶν ἐνόντων: Cf. Dem. xviii. 256, λόγους . . . οἷς ἐκ τῶν ἐνόντων ὡς ἂν δύνωμαι μετριώτατα χρήσομαι.

ἀνθρωπίνως: Cf. [Plut.] *Consolatio ad Apollonium* 118 b, πείθοντες τὰ κοινὰ τοῦ βίου συμπτώματα κοινῶς φέρειν καὶ τὰ ἀνθρώπινα ἀνθρωπίνως, and Men. frag. 650 K–T, ἀνθρωπίνως δεῖ τὰς τύχας φέρειν, ξένε. The 'human' way to bear the loss of those dear to one is to remember that to die is man's lot. Daos' humane concern for the women's grief serves to show up Smikrines' attachment to material possessions. Although it comes out only slowly that he is planning to secure the dead man's property, he almost immediately begins to talk about his own. This should, he says, have gone after his death to Kleostratos in its entirety. Here we have a difficulty, which has been noted also by E. Karabelias, *Rev. hist. de droit français et étranger*, lviii (1970), 369, in a valuable article which discusses at length the legal aspects of the play. It is clear that the brothers Chairestratos, Smikrines, and Kleostratos' dead father were all sons of the same father. This is explicitly stated of the latter two (115) and must be understood to be true also of Chairestratos, whose family relation to Kleostratos is the same as that of Smikrines (124). If Chairestratos were a brother on his mother's side only, he would belong to a different γένος. This is supported by the fact that Smikrines is related in the same way to Chairestratos' daughter and to Kleostratos' sister (352, cf. 179): this would not be true if he had been maternal uncle of the former and paternal uncle of the latter. The laws of inheritance preferred several classes of paternal relatives to maternal uncles, and although a maternal uncle *might* have a claim to the hand of an ἐπίκληρος, it could not have been assumed without explanation (355).

But if all three brothers had the same father, how can Smikrines say that his own property ought, according to the law, to have passed entirely to Kleostratos? The law provides for succession when a will has not been made, and Athenian law provided that an estate should in the first instance go in equal shares to brothers by the same father or, if they were dead, to their sons *per stirpes*. Hence Smikrines' property would have been equally shared between Kleostratos and

Chairestratos, if he were still alive, which as younger brother he probably would be. Indeed Smikrines assumes at 182 that Chairestratos will survive him, and will, unless steps are taken to prevent it, obtain his property. Perhaps Smikrines misrepresents the legal position in order to support his own intention to prevent his brother from inheriting. If he had said 'By law Chairestratos ought to have had half my property and Kleostratos the other half', that would have been a poor basis for continuing 'I don't intend to let Chairestratos have any'. By making a will, which would have been legal since he had no children, he could have made Kleostratos his sole heir; and it may be that if challenged on the legal position he would have replied that that had been his intention.

169 διοικεῖν ταῦτα: ταῦτα means the plunder from Lykia, which is in the forefront of Smikrines' mind, although he does not admit that it is the object of the manœuvre he is about to propose.

171 τί γάρ; 'You ask what'; cf. *Sam.* 129 n.

173 τί μου: γ' ἐμοῦ, printed by Austin, is nearer B's τ' εμου, but there is no function for γε. On second thoughts he preferred Handley's τί μου, *ZPE* iv (1969), 162.

175 οὐδὲ μετριάζει: Lit. 'he isn't even moderate', i.e. 'he doesn't even come half-way'; the miserly Smikrines feels that his brother, as the younger, should come more than half-way, and complains that in fact he tries to get more than an equal share (πλεονεκτοῦντα). No indication is given of the nature of the business over which Chairestratos is accused of unfairness. But it could be supposed for example that the paternal estate had not been completely divided. M. L. West suggests οὐδέν for οὐδέ, 'he is nowhere moderate', a possible sense, but, as Austin points out, οὐδὲ μετρίως recurs, *Dysk.* 314, 962.

176 οἰκοτρίβα: See *Sik.* 78 n.   **νόθον:** A bastard child had either no rights or effectively no rights in his father's property; Harrison, *Law of Athens*, i p. 148.

177 οὐκ οἶδ' ὅτῳ: *Pace* Austin, this may be true. Smikrines is not on good terms with his brother, and may know no more of the marriage than he has learned by seeing preparations for it. I suspect that he does not know Chaireas, who is introduced to him at 262 (Χαιρέας ὁδί); he is described at 117 as knowing none of his relations.

178 ἐπανενεγκών: 'Referring to me', cf. *Dysk.* 760.

181 ἀλλοτρίως ἔχων: 'Behaving as if not a member of my family'; cf. *Dysk.* 241.

183: Cf. Eur. *Alc.* 656, ἄλλοις δόμον λείψειν ἔμελλες ὀρφανὸν διαρπάσαι.

184: These 'men he knows' are perhaps imaginary; he has had no opportunity of talking with anyone since learning that the girl had become ἐπίκληρος and that her hand could be claimed. But it is possible that earlier he had been advised to ask for or even to take her in marriage. He might have demanded, in the absence of her brother, to exercise the rights of κύριος, and have assigned her to himself.

He would not, merely by marrying the girl, prevent his property from passing to his brother, who would remain his heir. But the birth of a son, who would be the new heir, would alter the situation completely.

187 λέγειν πως: Arist. *Ath. Pol.* 9 (quoted by Austin) writes διὰ τὸ μὴ γεγράφθαι τοὺς νόμους ἁπλῶς μηδὲ σαφῶς, ἀλλ᾽ ὥσπερ ὁ περὶ τῶν κλήρων καὶ ἐπικλήρων. If the girl was ἐπίκληρος and Smikrines was her nearest male relative, he was entitled to marry her. But the facts had first to be established by the legal process of ἐπιδικασία. Hence Smikrines is justified in not making an absolute statement that the law said that he should marry her. An *obligation* to marry an orphan girl existed only if she had a property of less than 500 dr., and could be escaped by providing her with a dowry. E. Karabelias, op. cit., p. 381, correctly says that the process of ἐπιδικασία is irrelevant to Menander's plot, and therefore not mentioned, so far as we know.

188: Daos cannot be expected to offer any advice on the correct legal procedure; he could help only with the personal relations with Chairestratos and his wife, in whose house the girl lives. But even there it is hard to see what he could do. Perhaps Smikrines wishes Daos to discourage any attempt to continue with the intended marriage between the girl and Chaireas: his own marriage with her will be more 'correctly' achieved (ὀρθῶς) if the other is not pursued. **ἔδει:** The imperfect, like the English 'you ought', carries the suggestion that Daos is not doing what is his duty, Goodwin, *MT* § 417. This is unfair and unpleasant.

189: The addition of ὦ before Cμικρίνη is palaeographically plausible, and although ὦ is not usually attached to vocatives, it is occasionally used to add an emotional touch, appeal or remonstrance, *Dysk.* 823 n. It must be noticed, however, that B has αλλοτριος (yet the confusion of o and ω is common as in ορθος for ορθως in 188) and οὐκ ἀλλότριος ⟨εἶ⟩ would make good sense. Daos will become Smikrines' property along with the rest of Kleostratos' estate (214), and ought to consider his new master's interests.

190 ῥῆμα: Frag. 215, ῥῆμά τι ἐφθέγξατ᾽ οὐδὲν ἐμφερὲς ... τῷ "γνῶθι cαυτόν", Philemon frag. 152 K, τὸ "γνῶθι cαυτόν" ... τὸ ῥῆμα τοῦτο.

τι μεμεριμνημένον: 'The result of careful meditation'. The verb
μεριμνᾶν is sometimes used of philosophical activity, e.g. Ar. frag. 672,
ὃς τὰ μὲν ἀφανῆ μεριμνᾷ, Xen. *Mem.* i. 1. 14, τῶν τε περὶ τῆς τῶν πάντων
φύσεως μεριμνώντων τοῖς μὲν δοκεῖν ἓν μόνον τὸ ὂν εἶναι, ibid. iv. 7. 6,
κινδυνεῦσαι δ' ἂν ἔφη καὶ παραφρονῆσαι τὸν ταῦτα μεριμνῶντα οὐδὲν
ἧττον ἢ Ἀναξαγόρας. There is at first sight something absurd in so
describing a platitudinous precept, but a platitude may be based on
much evidence, and it is useful to be reminded of that, so that its
value is not overlooked through its familiarity.

192 μὴ πονηρῷ: Daos modestly describes himself as 'not dishonest',
but he insists that he should be asked for his opinion only on matters
that concern him as a servant.   **τούτων . . . λόγον:** 'An expression
of opinion about these things'; for the genitive, cf. Plat. *Apol.* 26 b,
θεῶν, ὧν νῦν ὁ λόγος ἐστίν, Dem. iv. 33, τῶν πράξεων παρὰ τοῦ στρατηγοῦ
τὸν λόγον ζητοῦντες. The more usual construction is περί and gen.

194–6: These lines seem too much damaged to allow of likely restoration. In 195 θεράποντός ἐστι, 'is the duty of a servant', is tempting,
but Kasser says it is excluded.

197: cημεῖ' ἐπέcτηcεν is possible, and might mean 'placed seals upon
them', cf. 358. But the verb used there (ἐπιβάλλειν) is the normal one
for sealing (Ar. *Birds* 559, *Thesm.* 415, LSJ s.v. I. 3), and ἐφίcταναι
suggests setting up a stone to mark ownership of, or a mortgage on,
property, as in Dem. xli. 6, ὅρουc ἐπιcτῆcαι . . . ἐπὶ τὴν οἰκίαν, *IG*
ii². 1183. 39, ὅρον ἐφιcτάναι. For stones as cημεῖα see LSJ s.v. 5. But
landed property is hardly in question here, and I prefer the supplement ἔπεcτι(ν) (Austin), perhaps followed by a new sentence beginning
ὅcα (Barigazzi). Rost and Turner suggest writing τίcιν, possible but
uncertain since the context is not established. Similarly the clause
ἂν κελεύῃ τίc με may go either with the preceding or with the following
sentence.

200–2 τοῦ παρόντος: Persons present would be possible witnesses,
should occasion arise.   **κλήρου:** 'A matter of inheritance', not τοῦ
κλήρου, 'Kleostratos' estate'.   **ἐπικλήρου:** 'An heiress', one to whom
the κλῆρος attaches and so passes to her future husband.   **διαφορᾶc
οἰκειότητος:** 'Difference in relationship'; Smikrines has not made
much of this, and indeed at 189 stated that his brother and he were
on the same footing; but his claim to the girl's hand rests on the
assumption that, as the elder brother and senior member of the
family (172), he is her next-of-kin.

206: The discovery that the customs of one nation shock the nationals
of another was an old one: Διccοὶ λόγοι 2. 9–18. The Greeks' contempt
for Phrygians is marked by the proverb Φρὺξ ἀνὴρ πληγεὶς ἀμείνων

καὶ διακονέςτεροc (*Suda* s.v.). They were regarded as cowardly and effeminate (242 below, Eur. *Or.* 1369–1536, Tertullian, *de anima* 20, 'comici Phrygas timidos illudunt.') That one of this race should criticize Greek customs, and seem to have right on his side, is a pleasant paradox.

210 λέγειν ὁμοῦ τι: 'To be saying more or less' or 'almost to be saying'. For this use of ὁμοῦ τι cf. Dem. xxvii. 11, ὁμοῦ τι τάλαντον, Antiphanes frag. 217 K, ὁμοῦ τι πρὸc τέλοc δρόμου περῶν, Plut. *Mor.* 86 c, ὁμοῦ τι τοῖc αὐτοῖc ὀνόμαcι, and other passages quoted by V. Schmidt in Austin's ed. vol. ii. This has developed from the use of ὁμοῦ to mean 'near', *Georg.* 88 n. The change of τι to τό, once suggested by me (Austin's edn., p. 103), is wrong. Handley's proposal to write πράγματ' ἢ makes Smikrines' speech less fragmented, but that is not necessarily a merit. If τοιουτότροπόν τι stands alone, λέγειc may be understood with it.

211 τούτων τινὰ: One of the (male) members of the family that lives here. Why does Smikrines guess, quite rightly, that none of them is at home? Perhaps because it had been necessary for Daos to check the women's lamentations (92).   **ὀπτέον:** 'See', i.e. 'talk to', cf. *Dysk.* 236 n.

214 παρεγγυᾶν, 'put in the care of', is used with some irony by Daos.
    οἵῳ μ' ἀφ' οἵου: There are dependent clauses in prose where the relative οἷοc is thus doubled, Xen. *Cyr.* iv. 5. 29, Plat. *Symp.* 195 a, *Phaedr.* 271 b, διδάcκων οἷα οὖcα ὑφ' οἵων λόγων . . . πείθεται. But to parallel the exclamatory repetition one must apparently go to tragedy: Eur. *Alc.* 144, ὦ τλῆμον, οἵαc οἷοc ὢν ἁμαρτάνειc.

215 τί c' ἠδίκηκα τηλικοῦτο; 'What wrong have I done you as great as the harm you are doing me?' For 'wronging' the gods cf. Baton frag. 2 K, τί τηλικοῦτον ἀδικεῖc τοὺc θεούc; Alexis frag. 70 K, ἀδικεῖ τε τὸν Ἔρωτ' ἐμφανῶc θνητὸc θεόν.

(v) 216–249: *Daos, Cook* (exit 233), *Waiter* (enters 233)

216–49: This is a lively scene, but at first sight it seems in no way to give new information, to forward the plot, or to be integrated into the structure. Its purpose seems merely that of introducing the cook, who has a traditional part in comedy. This cook has the loquacity of his tribe, but differs from its conventional representative in that, whereas other cooks boast of their skill and success, he complains of his constant bad luck; and whereas they are normally introduced as they arrive at their employer's house, he appears as he leaves in frustration. His abuse, however, of his assistant for neglecting opportunities of pilfering takes up a traditional theme: some other cooks in comedy show this readiness to steal; Page, *GLP*, p. 272, Euphron frags. 1 K and 10 K, Dionysios frag. 3 K, Plaut. *Aul.* 322, *Pseud.* 790.

But since Menander frequently so constructs his plays that the final scene of an act introduces some element required for the progress of the plot in the next act, one looks for some kind of connection between this scene with the cook and the coming act. This may be found in the fact that it brings a vivid reminder that the wedding of Kleostratos' sister was on the very point of taking place that day. This makes Smikrines' conduct in stopping it more inhumane, and Chaireas' disappointment, to be displayed in the next act, even more likely to arouse the audience's sympathy.

Handley, *Entretiens Hardt* xvi. 15, remarks that the scene illustrates Menander's readiness to present the same event through more than one pair of eyes. The cook's view of the bad news and the consequent lamentations is very different from that of Daos.

216: 'If I do ever get a job'; the implication is that he is generally unemployed. Photios s.v. ἔργον has λαβεῖν ἔργον τὸ μιcθῶcαι ἑαυτόν, Ameipsias frag. 1 K ἐγὼ δ' ἰὼν πειράcομαι | εἰc τὴν ἀγορὰν ἔργον λαβεῖν.

218 κυοῦcά τιc λάθρᾳ: Strictly this should be κνήcaca, for the pregnancy preceded and did not accompany the state of having given birth. Perhaps the indignant cook's language is meant to sound strained here, as it certainly is at 224–6 below.

219: B's text may be defended by Eur. *Cycl.* 334, ἀγὼ οὔτινι θύω πλὴν ἐμοί, θεοῖcι δ' οὔ, which has the same irregular division of the tribrach and the same unusual short vowel υ in θύω. Long ῡ gives a broken anapaest, which Lloyd-Jones would retain. The short υ is also found in Ar. *Ach.* 792 (spoken, to be sure, by a Megarian) and Strato frag. 1 K (twice). In Eur. *El.* 1141 Denniston accepts Nauck's θύῃ for θύειν.

220 δυcποτμίαc: The word was previously known only from later prose (first in Dionysios of Halikarnassos), but since δύcποτμοc, 'illstarred', although found in *Misumenos* A 5 (= frag. 6 Körte), ἆρ' ἐρῶντα δυcποτμώτερον, in the main belongs to tragedy, its use by the cook of his bad luck probably has a touch of absurdity.

222 μαχαίραc: The cook's knife is his typical tool, *Sam.* 284.

223 δι' ἡμερῶν δέκα: After an interval of ten days (without work), LSJ s.v. διά A. II. 2.   δραχμῶν τριῶν depends on ἔργον, a genitive of value, as in Isaios ii. 35, δέκα μνῶν χωρίον.

224–6: The cook exaggerates: no corpse had come from Lykia and no force had been used. The ending of two successive clauses with

82 COMMENTARY

ταύτας, having the same reference, has aroused suspicion. Austin first changed the second ταύτας to αὐτάς, but later suggested converting the first to γ' αὐτάς. I should prefer to write the first as τ' αὐτάς, with τε postponed: but why should not ωιμηντ'εχειν have been written? Handley thought of including both words ταύτας in the same clause, making them first and last, cf. *Sam.* 551 ἐμὲ ... ἐμέ (*BICS* xvi [1969], 103), but B separates ταυτας and νεκρος by a colon.

227 ἱερόcυλε: For this term of abuse cf. *Dysk.* 640, *Sam.* 678, *Perik.* 176.

229: For the theft of oil cf. *Pap. Heidelberg* 184, frag. 11, κἀν ταῖς cπογγιαῖς ἐλᾳδία ... ἐκφέρουcι, and Page, *GLP* p. 172. A cook in Dionysios frag. 3 K says to his assistant μέμνηcο τῶνδε, as a command. Cf. also Polybios xv. 34. 6, παραλαβὼν εὐφυέcτατον καιρόν (quoted by Del Corno).

230 Cπινθήρ, 'Spark', is the name of the παιδάριον (222); it belongs to a cook in Theopompos frag. 32 K and in Ariston, *AP* vi. 306; Aristeides is the statesman who earned the sobriquet of ὁ δίκαιοc, Plut. *Aristides* 6; Aischines iii. 181. ὄψομαί c' ἐγὼ ἄδειπνον: Cf. the threat of Bdelykleon to his slaves, Ar. *Wasps* 435, εἰ δὲ μὴ ... οὐδὲν ἀριcτήcετε.

232 τραπεζοποιόc: *Dysk.* 647 n. Since there is no reason why a τραπεζοποιόc should be more needed at a funeral feast (περίδειπνον) than a cook (cf. Hegesippos frag. 1 K, where a cook speaks of occasions when he serves at a περίδειπνον), this must be a sarcastic remark by the cook, made when the τραπεζοποιόc does not immediately follow him: 'the τραπεζοποιόc is probably staying for the funeral feast!' With these words he probably leaves the stage.

233–5: B gives this to the τραπεζοποιόc, who will not be a subordinate of the cook, but hired independently, cf. *Sam.* 289. Austin explains that he speaks to the women of the house as he emerges (since he first comes on the stage here, the part can be taken by the actor who plays Smikrines) and that he plays upon the senses of κόπτεcθαι, which may mean 'to beat the breast' or 'to be wearied or bored' (*Sam.* 285 n.). If he is not paid for the trouble he has had, he will be on a par with them, for they are κοπτόμεναι (in the first sense) without pay and he will be κοπτόμενοc (in the second) without pay.

Alternatively he may address the cook, if that character has not already gone. Then he will come out beating his breast, and hoping to be paid for thus mourning. If he is not paid for that, then he will be as unrewarded as the cook and Spinther. This is less likely, since it does away with the play on two senses of κόπτομαι, a traditional joke for which the ingenuity of dramatists found new forms. Here, on the former interpretation, the person of the τραπεζοποιόc replaces that of the cook, and the sense 'beat the breast' that of 'cut with a knife'.

238 ff.: There is no indication in B of the speaker, but a Thracian cook is less likely than a Thracian τραπεζοποιός. He is probably a slave, rather than a freedman, but perhaps one carrying on his trade for himself and paying his master an ἀποφορά, see *Epitr.* 377 n.

239 τοιόνδε is a word not found elsewhere in New Comedy, but δ is as good as certain, and no other supplement suggests itself. Why, however, should the servitor use this word and not τοιοῦτο? ἀπόπληκτε: Cf. *Perik.* 496 n. The vocative is used again as a term of abuse, *Sam.* 105, Strato frag. 1, 35 K.

241 ποταπός: This spelling, for ποδαπός, may be due to a copyist; but Alexis frag. 230 K is transmitted by Athenaios as ποταπὸς ὁ Βρόμιος; cf. id. frag. 173 K, where the spelling ποταποc is early enough to have given rise to the corruption δέсποτα πῶc in Athenaios 386 a. There is no real evidence when this form, not infrequent in the MSS. of authors of our era, came into use. Phrynichos (39) Rutherford) condemns it, and one would restore ποδαπός here, did not a suspicion remain that ποταπός is an intentional vulgarism.

242 οὐδὲν ἱερόν: Theokr. v. 22 has ἔcτι μὲν οὐδὲν ἱερόν, where the scholiast calls this a proverbial expression ἐπὶ τῶν μηδενὸς ἀξίων, explaining by a story that Herakles, seeing a statue of Adonis, remarked "οὐδὲν ἱερόν". A similar phrase, also applied adjectivally to human beings, is οὐδὲν ὑγιές, e.g. Ar. *Thesm.* 394, τὰς οὐδὲν ὑγιές. ἀνδρόγυνοс: 'A womanish creature', *Sam.* 69 n. There may be an allusion to the self-castration of the Phrygian Galli. For the sexual 'manliness' of the Thracians and particularly the Getai see frag. 794. Here their manliness is supposed to take the form of bold theft. Then παρὰ προcδοκίαν it is added that the mills, places of punishment (*Heros* 3 n.), are full of them. Reeve ingeniously suggests that the last sentence should be given to Daos with ὑμῶν for ἡμῶν. His riposte would then resemble that in Ephippos frag. 2 K, μεθύοντες ἀεὶ τὰς μάχας πάсας μάχονται. :: τοιγαροῦν φεύγουс' ἀεί.

244 ἀνδρεῖον τὸ χρῆμα: 'They're brave creatures', cf. 314, μιαρὸν τὸ χρῆμα, 'a foul creature!', Ar. *Wasps* 933, κλεπτὸν τὸ χρῆμα τἀνδρός.

245-9: Daos announces the approach of the chorus, whom he calls ὄχλον ἄλλον; perhaps they are a crowd 'other' than the captives, who were taken indoors at 92. But the cook and his assistant could perhaps be called an ὄχλος in the sense of 'a nuisance', cf. *Sik.* 150, ὄχλος εἶ. The last lines are addressed to the intoxicated men. For their sentiment Austin quotes Eur. *Alc.* 785, τὸ τῆς τύχης γὰρ ἀφανές . . . εὔφραινε cαυτόν, πῖνε. Having uttered his approval, Daos withdraws into Chairestratos' house. For the chorus, whose performances separate the acts, but who have no other function in the play, see introduction, p. 12.

ACT II

(i) 250–284: *Smikrines, Chairestratos, Chaireas*

250: Smikrines, who had gone at 213 to the market-place to look for his brother or nephew, returns with them both. Although the young man Chaireas does not, I believe, speak before 275, perhaps not until left alone at 284, he must be present from the beginning. This is shown by the deictic pronoun όδί at 262, and by the fact that he knows of Kleostratos' supposed death, of which he can have learned only from Smikrines or Chairestratos.

252: Smikrines snubs his younger brother's interest in the funeral arrangements. They will be for *him* to arrange. There is finality in the future perfect: 'They will have been arranged.'

253 ὁμολόγει τὴν παρθένον μηδενί: 'Promise the girl to no one'; this use of ὁμολογῶ is unparalleled in classical Greek in the active voice; but the passive is used in Thuc. viii. 29, πλέον ἀνδρὶ ἑκάστῳ ἢ τρεῖς ὀβολοὶ ὡμολογήθησαν. I take ὁμολογεῖν to be wider than ἐγγυᾶν, 'formal betrothal', and to include any informal agreement to give the girl in marriage, like that at *Sam.* 114 ff.

254: Cf. *Sam.* 454 for this phrase.

257 μετριότητος: The μέτριος does not go too far; for an old man to marry a girl is to go too far; 'moderation' would not allow him to go beyond a middle-aged woman.　**διὰ τί, παῖ;** Can Smikrines address Chairestratos, even though he is the younger, as παῖ? Or was the previous remark made, as Webster and Mette suggested, by the young Chaireas? The following ἐμοὶ μὲν παντελῶς δοκεῖς γέρων would well suit a young man; yet it is not inappropriate for Chairestratos; a younger brother can say to an elder: 'You seem to me to be an old man.' The obstacle to accepting Webster's view is that Chaireas' speech, 284–93, will be more effective if he first breaks silence with it. The difficulty about παῖ, if a real one, could be surmounted if the word was used, not as a true vocative, but as an exclamation of surprise, as seems to be the case in the phrase τί τοῦτο παῖ; (*Dysk.* 500 n.).

260 πρεσβύτερος: 'Elderly' does not suggest as advanced an age as γέρων.　**ἀνθρωπίνως . . . ἔνεγκε**: 'Treat this situation humanely' or 'like a human being'. φέρω with an adverb does not always have the sense 'endure', but is more like 'take' in such phrases as 'take it slowly', 'take it calmly'; thus often χαλεπῶς φέρειν, πικρῶς φέρειν.

262 ὁδί: Cf. 177 n.   **cύντροφοc:** 'Brought up under the same roof '.

264 μηδὲν ζημιοῦ: 'Suffer no loss'. Smikrines is offered 'all these ὄντα', all this property that Daos has brought. The offer would give him the same property as he would acquire by claiming the girl as an ἐπίκληρος. But it would be a profitable bargain, since he would be freed from the expense of keeping a wife. The dowry that Chairestratos proposes to give the girl is less than the sum̤she would bring a husband as an ἐπίκληρος, but it is generous and would satisfy a husband who had no claim through kinship to marry her. But property that went with a woman was always regarded as being for the benefit of her children, and her sons got control of it when two years past puberty (Harrison, *Law of Athens* i, p. 113 n. 2). Hence if Chairestratos' plan were carried through, a child born to the girl might argue that the arrangement had cheated him out of the property that was his right. I do not know that there is any evidence to show what rights, if any, the law gave him, but even if there were none, he or someone suing on his behalf might hope to win a jury's sympathy and the verdict.

267 αὐτήν: 'By herself', i.e. without the property; this sense of αὐτός is illustrated by LSJ s.v. I. 3. Chairestratos goes on to explain that it will not be difficult to find her a husband without the property, because he will provide a dowry from his own resources.

269 Μελιτίδη: Cf. [Lucian] *Amores* 53, Μελιτίδην ἢ Κόροιβον οἴει με πρὸς θεῶν; Melitides was an archetypal figure for a man of feeble understanding (Diogen. vii. 12, ἀνοητότερος Ἰαβύκου καὶ Κοροίβου καὶ Μελιτίδου, Apostolios v. 27, where Leutsch–Schneidewin collect instances). Eustathios *in Odysseam* x. 552 (1669. 50) says he could not count beyond five and did not know which of his parents had given him birth (but see *Suda* s.v. γέλοιος). Some scholars spell his name Μελητίδης, as a patronymic from Μέλητος (see LSJ s.v.); Μελίτης ought to give Μελιτάδης. They may be right. Their grammar is good, but perhaps better than that of those who used the name, which is nowhere spelled with η in surviving MSS.

273 τούτου: Sc. τοῦ παιδίου, unlike τούτῳ in 271, which means Chaireas.   **κατάβαλε:** 'Drop it', i.e. 'forget it'. This is not a common sense of the word. Aelian frag. 111 recounts how, when a guest broke a valuable glass, his host Apicius said to him οὐ καταβαλεῖς τὸ πραχθὲν καὶ σεαυτὸν ἡμῖν παρέξεις φαιδρότερον συμποτήν; Dem. xviii. 103 uses the word of 'dropping' a proposed law.

274 "οἴει;" λέγεις; ' "Do you think?" you say?' The implication is that 'think' is not strong enough; Smikrines is sure of it. Similarly *Dysk.* 7–10, οὐ χαίρων τ' ὄχλῳ· "ὄχλῳ" λέγω; ... λελάληκεν ἡδέως ἐν τῷ βιῴ οὐδεν⟨ί⟩, but there the stronger statement is explicitly made. Here Smikrines indicates his certainty by passing on without further words to what follows from it: he will take the girl, and therefore wants a schedule of the property at once. He does not conceal his suspicions that Chairestratos might, if there were no such schedule, make away with some of it. The schedule is to be brought by Daos, whom he trusts as disinterested (155). In the event Daos does not bring it: he will be too occupied to do so, and indeed there is no evidence that he was ever given instructions to make it. His failure will be interpreted by Smikrines as a sign that he is working with Chairestratos (393).

275: It is possible to maintain B's δή μοι by supposing that Chaire-stratos interrupts before Smikrines reaches his verb, e.g. ἀποδῷ. If the next line were preserved it might support, but could not invalidate, this solution. Austin writes δῶι μοι; any mistake is possible, but δη for δωι is not a very likely one.

276: Only nine or ten letters are lost at the beginning of the line, so that an omission either there or in the latter part seems probable. *Exempli gratia* I have added ποτε, as omitted by haplography. B has μ' εδει: and 'what ought I to have done?', sc. to avoid this catastrophe, is excellent sense. One cannot be confident, however, that the apostrophe has any authority, and με δεῖ, 'what ought I to do?', is something Chairestratos could well say. After this, Smikrines speaks a line almost entirely lost, and goes into his house.

279–81: A likely sense is 'I expected to leave you as my heirs, you as husband of Kleostratos' sister, Kleostratos as husband of my daughter', e.g. cὲ μὲν λαβόντα ταύτην [προcεδόκων,] αὐτὸν δ' ἐκεῖνον τὴν ἐμήν, [τῆc οὐcίαc Handley] ὑμᾶc καταλείψειν τῆc ἐμαυτοῦ κυρίουc.

283 ἃ μήποτ' ἤλπιcα: 'Such as I would never have expected'. Chairestratos enters his house, but his stepson does not follow. He reflects that, being deprived of his expected bride, he has worse troubles than his stepfather has. But any feeling that this is too self-centred is allayed by the fact that he puts pity for his dead friend in the forefront of his thoughts. The repeated address to the supposedly dead man recalls to the audience that they have been promised his return, which will put an end to Chaireas' troubles.

(ii) 284–298: *Chaireas*

284–6 τὸ μὲν cὸν ... πάθοc: Cf. *Dysk.* 236 n. But here ἐcτί, which is part of the phrase κατὰ λόγον ἐcτί, 'it is reasonable', is placed at the end of the sentence.

286 οὐδὲ εἷc . . . οὕτωc ἠτύχηκεν: For similar protestations of unique misfortune see *Perik.* 535, *Sam.* 12, *Mis.* A 4 (= frag. 6 Körte), *P. Antinoop.* 15. 1, Ter. *Hec.* 293.

287 τούτων: Chairestratos and his family, who have lost only a relative, not a bride as well.

288 περιπεcών: The English 'having fallen in love' does not imply misfortune, although we 'fall into' traps, error, despair, etc. But περιπίπτω is almost always used of encountering with evils. So here for Chaireas love is not in itself a thing he would have chosen (it was not αὐθαίρετον, cf. Eur. frag. 339 N, οὐκ αὐθαίρετοι βροτοῖc ἔρωτεc), but he had hoped that it would lead to happiness if he were united in marriage to the girl.

289 φίλτατ' ἀνθρώπων ἐμοί: The same phrase at Ar. *Clouds* 110, where see Dover's note; he quotes Soph. *El.* 1126, ὦ φιλτάτου μνημεῖον ἀνθρώπων ἐμοί. Four successive lines here in tragic metre indicate the seriousness of the speaker's feeling.

290 οὐθὲν προπετὲc οὐδ' ἀνάξιον οὐδ' ἄδικον: The three adjectives all refer to the same act that he did not do, the rape or seduction of the girl, which would have been precipitate in itself, unworthy of him and his moral standards, and a wrong to her and her family.

292: The omission of αὐτην, object both of cυνοικίcαι and of κατέλιπεc, is remarkable and still more so the construction of ἐδεήθην with the acc. τὸν θεῖον for the normal genitive. Another instance, usually quoted as unique, is Thuc. v. 36, ἐδέοντο Βοιωτοὺc ὅπωc, but the scholiast has ἐδέοντο Βοιωτοὺc οὕτω ποιῆcαι, whence Stahl suggested the omission of some infinitive, e.g. παραcκευάζειν, of which Βοιωτούc would be the object. Herondas v. 19, however, has τῶν cε γουνάτων δεῦμαι, which it is artificial to interpret as τῶν cε γουνάτων (ἱκετεύω), δεῦμαι. Austin quotes Longus ii. 23. 4, τοῦτον ἐδεήθημεν ἐπίκουρον γενέcθαι. The influence of other verbs of asking that are followed by acc. may have affected δέομαι; similarly κελεύω is occasionally followed by dat., like, e.g., ἐπιτάττω, *Perik.* 474 n.

293: Although she had no legal standing in the matter, Chairestratos' wife had apparently had her say in it.

294 μακάριοc: A word often used of the bridegroom, cf. *Sik.* 379 n.

295 οἰηθεὶc cφόδρα: The aorist of οἴομαι is rare in all drama. In comedy only in Ar. *Knights* 860, Antiphanes frag. 194 K (an unintelligible and perhaps corrupt riddle), and 400 below.

296 οὐδ' ἰδεῖν: 'I shall not even be able to see (her)', for she will be shut away in Smikrines' house; αὐτήν is to be supplied from αὐτῆς of the next clause.

298: 'That judges my claim worthless from now on'; cf. Eur. frag. 618 N, τὸν ὄλβον οὐδὲν οὐδαμοῦ κρίνω βροτοῖς, Aesch. *Pers.* 497, θεοὺς ... νομίζων οὐδαμοῦ. Pearson, on Soph. frag. 106, collects other examples.

(iii) 299–390: *Chaireas, Daos, Chairestratos*

299: The voice of Daos is heard from the house, as he attempts to revive the spirits of Chairestratos, who has collapsed in his distress. His call to Chaireas for help may be made without appearing at the door, which had possibly been left open or half-open by Chairestratos, who would expect the young man to follow him. With some hesitation I think that he then tells Chairestratos to open the door wider, and to show himself, and finally appears with him, bringing him out on the stage at 305.

Del Corno, *ZPE* vi (1970), 216, argues that Chairestratos had collapsed *outside* his house and that Daos here appears and tries to take him in to console his household (τοὺς φίλους) over the death of Kleostratos. Such an interpretation could be put on his words, but it is an unlikely one, since there has been nothing to put the audience in mind of the mourners within.

That an actor behind the door of the *skene* could speak so that his words could be heard by the audience is shown by many passages, e.g. 500 below (see note), *Perinthia* 2, Aesch. *Ag.* 1343–5, Ar. *Ach.* 407–9, Terence, *Andria* 473. Austin supposes Daos to come out and call Chaireas, to urge him to open the door (from outside) and make himself visible to Chairestratos. But if Chaireas is standing in the doorway at 303, how are we to understand the action of 304–5?

300: 'You can't despair or be doing nothing.'

302 ἐν τούτῳ: Does this mean 'everything depends on Chairestratos', or 'on not allowing Chairestratos to despair', i.e. ἐν τῷ μὴ ἐπιτρέπειν? Either masc. or neuter is possible, cf. LSJ s.v. ἐν A. I. 6.

306 μελαγχολῶ: *Dyskolos* 88 n. Chairestratos' madness is of the depressive variety.

307 ἐν ἐμαυτοῦ: *Sam.* 340 n.   ἀκαρὴς πάνυ: *Perik.* 356 n.

308 καλός: Ironical, LSJ s.v. IV.   ἔκστασιν: 'Distraction', lit. 'stepping out of the normal self', cf. *Epitr.* 893, frag. 136, πάντα δὲ τὰ μηδὲ προσδοκώμεν' ἔκστασιν φέρει. For the verbal phrase ἐξέστηκα (ἐμαυτοῦ) see *Sam.* 279, 620.

311 δυνήσεται δέ: The prospect of Smikrines' marriage is not a new one to Daos, since it had been broached to him by Smikrines himself. Daos must ask whether he will be able to carry the project through, hoping that Chairestratos may have some means of stopping it. But Chairestratos' reply shows that, if Smikrines insists he will marry the girl, that settles the matter. **ὁ καλὸc κἀγαθόc:** Ironical, as in *Dis Exapaton* 91, Alexis frag. 107 K, where a crowd of dangerous revellers are referred to by the phrase τῶν καλῶν τε κἀγαθῶν ἐνθάδε cυνόντων.

312 καὶ ταῦτα: 'And that when I am offering him all that Kleostratos has sent'; LSJ s.v. οὗτοc C. III. 2.

313 ὢ μιαρώτατοc: K–G i. 46, a construction common in tragedy, e.g. Eur. *Or.* 90, ὢ μέλεοc, and in comedy; cf. Ar. *Wasps* 900 and *Thesm.* 649, ὢ μιαρὸc οὗτοc, *Frogs* 921. Confusion of ω and ο is common in B. Since the previous sentence has its subject, ὁ καλὸc κἀγαθόc, Daos could not supply ὁ μιαρώτατοc to complete it. **μιαρὸν τὸ χρῆμα:** Like 244, ἀνδρεῖον τὸ χρῆμα, 'the creature's a blackguard'. **οὐ μὴ βιῶ:** *Sam.* 428 n. What Chairestratos had expressed as a hope or a wish at 282–3 is now more emphatically a determination to die. It prepares the way for the scheme that Daos will propose at 330 ff.; see F. Stoessl, *Rh. Mus.* cxii (1969), 220.

316–19: Assignment of speeches is disputed. Somewhere a dicolon must have been omitted in B. Arnott's proposal to insert ⟨Δα.⟩ after ἔνεcτι, which becomes the only word spoken by Chairestratos, if the dicolon after ἐργῶδεc is disregarded, has the disadvantage that it may be unparalleled for a slave to swear by Athene; he argues that she is appealed to as goddess of invention, not as the goddess of the city. Arnott also accepted Austin's insertion of ⟨Χα.⟩ before πάνυ, a change sufficient in itself to give sense to the passage. See Addenda.

324: The supplements ἐπτ[οημένον (Austin) and ἐπτ[ερωμένον (Lloyd-Jones) both mean 'carried away by excitement'. Neither word occurs elsewhere in New Comedy.

327 ἀλόγιcτοc: 'Unthinking', 'unreasoning', as in Plato, *Apol.* 37 c, *Gorgias* 522 e, ὅcτιc μὴ παντάπαcιν ἀλόγιcτοc . . . ἐcτιν.

329–30 τραγῳδῆcαι κτλ.: 'Stage a tragic unpleasant misfortune'. For ἀλλοῖον, 'not of the sort one would like', cf. Arkesilaos in Diog. Laert. iv. 44, where εἴ τι γένοιτο ἀλλοῖον means 'if I should die'. πάθοc also is used of death somewhat euphemistically, e.g. Hdt. ii. 133, μετὰ τῆc θυγατρὸc τὸ πάθοc. It has this sense in 332, where the νεανίcκοc is Kleostratos. **ὑπεῖπαc:** At 314–15.

331 δόξαι: The dependent infinitive does not come until the end of the sentence (336); for this position of associated words, first and last in the clause, see *Dysk.* 236 n.

336–7: For the sentiment cf. Eur. frag. 1071, λῦπαι γὰρ ἀνθρώποιςι τίκτουςιν νόςους, Soph. frag. 663 Pearson, τίκτουςι γάρ τοι καὶ νόςους δυςθυμίαι, Philemon frag. 106 K, διὰ λύπην . . . γίγνεται πολλοῖςι καὶ νοςήματ᾽ οὐκ ἰάςιμα.

336 γενέςθαι περιπετῆ: This phrase, as an equivalent of περιπίπτειν, 'fall in with', constructed with a dative of the evil met with, was previously known only from later authors, e.g. Plutarch, *C. Gracchus* 10, *Pompey* 62, etc.

338 πικρὸν εὖ οἶδα: A man who resents things and is vindictive is πικρός; he may be thought of as experiencing λύπη. Thus it is plausible that Chairestratos, being πικρός, should suffer λύπη and the consequent illness. But it is odd that he should combine this character with being χρηςτὸς πάνυ (125), as also that it should be Daos who knows Chairestratos to have a character to suit the deception, since it is Smikrines who must be convinced by it. Hence there is attraction in Kassel's change to εὖ οἶδε, sc. Cμικρίνης. Yet Smikrines, who 'does not know his relations' (117), is not altogether a suitable subject for the verb. Daos, on the other hand, might mention Chairestratos' tendency to πικρότης and μελαγχολία as likely to lend verisimilitude to the story he will tell of his illness.

341: φρενῖτις, the illness that will in fact be chosen (446), is inflammation of the diaphragm (Diokles frag. 38), not of the brain (LSJ s.v.); the φρένες are the diaphragm, Plato, *Tim.* 70 a, Arist. *PA* 672^{b}11. But mental derangement was regarded as a possible symptom of this disease, Lucian *Symp.* 20, Plut. *QC* 693 a, ἄνθρωπος . . . φρενιτίζων (-ετ- MSS.) καὶ μαινόμενος.

345 ἐγκέκλειςαι is perfect, a tense which would associate with the preceding presents, βοῶμεν, κοπτόμεθα. But if the word is to be joined with the following προκείςεται, it should be the future perfect, ἐγκεκλείςει.

348–9 ἐπίκληρος . . . ἐπιδίκῳ: See introduction, p. 29 n. 1.

350 coì μέν: Austin retracted his change to cῆι μέν, which to be logical would require ἔcται for ἐcτί; the sixty talents belong to Chairestratos now, but if he 'dies' *will* 'belong' to his daughter. ἀμφοῖν (352), 'the two of them', is perfectly intelligible even with coί in 350.

351 τέτταρα: The money brought home amounted to two talents; the rest will be made up by the silver articles, the slaves, etc.

353 πέτρινος: 'To be made of rock' is elsewhere a metaphor for hard-heartedness (Aesch. *PV* 242) or immobility (Eur. *Med.* 28), but here for stupidity or being impervious to new ideas; a meaning known with the more prosaic λίθος, Ar. *Clouds* 1201, ἀβέλτεροι . . . ὄντες λίθοι, Apollod. Caryst. frag. 9 K, σύ με παντάπασιν ἥγηςαι λίθον (the sense of which appears from Terence's version, *Hec.* 214, 'me omnino lapidem non hominem putas'). The sense of Anaxippos frag. 3 K, ἢ τοῦτον λέγεις, τὸν πέτρινον, is quite uncertain.

354 παρόντων μαρτύρων τριςχιλίων: The point is that even if there were 3,000 men present to witness his cupidity he would, having the choice between the two girls, take the richer and discard the poorer on anyone who would take her.

356 οἰμώξετἄρα: 'He'll be sorry for it'; the fut. of οἰμώζω occurs half a dozen times in Aristophanes, with or without ἄρα, as a kind of threat or perhaps curse. In *Thesm.* 248 we have οἰμώξετἄρ' εἴ τις κτλ. ; here the cause is given not by an if-clause but by the dative τῷ δοκεῖν, 'he'll be sorry for imagining that'. Kassel and Austin prefer to think that B has wrongly divided the speeches. They make Chairestratos say merely οἰμώξετἄρα, whereon Daos continues τῷ δοκεῖν, i.e. (λήψεται) τῷ δοκεῖν, 'he'll marry her, in imagination'. This may be right.

357 διοικήςει: B gives διοικῆςαι: the infinitive (of purpose) would depend on περίειςι: in classical Greek this construction, with verbs of going, belongs to poetry, Goodwin, *MT* § 772, and is not common even there. Hesitantly I think a change must be made and prefer διοικήςει (several scholars) to διοικήςας, suggested by Page.

358: Putting seals on the doors, to prevent valuables being removed. Even foodstuffs might be secured in this way, see Aristophanes, *Thesm.* 418–28. A collection of passages that refer to this practice is made by J. Diggle, *Euripides Phaethon*, note on line 223. A seal, as a substitute for a lock, has both advantages and disadvantages. It is no physical obstacle to entry, but unlike a lock, the manipulation of which need leave no trace, by being broken it gives immediate warning of an unauthorized entry, and cannot be replaced so long as the man who made it retains the signet with which he marked it.

361: The sense is probably 'keeping him off from coming near'; Smikrines must not be allowed to examine the 'corpse'. But although μή is very possible, and now approved by Kasser, it is not certain. Kasser and Austin originally read ἵνα, following which Kassel suggested καλοῦν]τες, supposing that the mourners would be confident that Smikrines would not accept their invitation. The invitation would seem to me an unnecessary risk, and I prefer the other reading and interpretation. Moreover ἵνα προσέλθῃ would, I think, express a real intention on the part of the mourners that Smikrines should approach; 'inviting him to approach' would be καλοῦντες προσελθεῖν.

367 εἰςπράττει may be 3rd person singular active, or 2nd person singular middle. The two voices are used without distinction of meaning. Lloyd-Jones suggests that Daos proposes that they will bring an action against Smikrines for theft of Chairestratos' property: the loser in such an action was liable to pay twice the amount he was held to have stolen, Dem. xxiv. 114, Harrison, *Law of Athens* i, p. 207 n. 2.

367–76: Punctuation and assignment to speakers are not certain. πάνυ may go with the preceding words, or with what follows. Austin's text neglects the dicolon after κενῆς in 373. There is no cogent reason why the following sentences should not be given to Chairestratos. They may perhaps be more plausibly assigned to Daos, the inventor of the plan of deceit. Chaireas, however, adds some details of his own invention (376–9), and it is possible that Chairestratos thinks of employing a quack doctor.

To suppose the loss of a dicolon after τρόπου (368) would result in what seems to me a more credible piece of dialogue. (Δα.) τιμωρί]αν— λαβεῖν cφοδροτέραν; (Χα.) λήψομαι νὴ τὸν Δία [ὃν] μ' ὠδύνηκέ πωποτ' ἀξίαν δίκην—διὰ κενῆς. (Δα.) πράττειν ⟨δὲ⟩ δεῖ ἤδη. It is Chairestratos rather than Daos who has been exposed to Smikrines' rancour, and if Lloyd-Jones's explanation of 367 is right, it is Chairestratos who will exact retribution. I think that μ is as consonant as ς with the traces shown in the photograph before ω in 371.

In 376 καὶ μὴν ἔδει may belong either to Daos or to Chairestratos. The fact that B marks Daos as the speaker of ταχὺ μὲν οὖν in 379 may suggest that he is not the speaker in 376.

372 ταῖς ἀληθείαις: The plural seems not to differ from the singular τῇ ἀληθείᾳ in meaning; cf. *Epitr.* 578 n.   λύκος χανών: Paroemiographers give λύκος ἔχανεν as a phrase used of those who are cheated of their hopes (Leutsch–Schneidewin, *Corpus Paroem. Gr.* i. 273, ii. 510); those who will may believe the explanation that a wolf goes for its victim with open mouth, and if it fails to make a catch, has gaped to no purpose. The phrase was used by Aristophanes frag. 337, Eubulos frag. 15 K, Euphron frag. 1 K, τοῦ γὰρ μὴ χανεῖν λύκον διὰ κενῆς cὺ μόνος ηὕρηκας τέχνην.

374 ξενικὸν . . . ἰατρόν: The technical skill of doctors made them, like sophists, who claimed to teach political and oratorical skill, welcome visitors in towns not their own. There were schools of medicine in Sicily and in Kos and in Knidos, in all of which places a man might acquire his professional knowledge. All these places were Doric-speaking, and Doric-speaking doctors appear in Krates frag. 41 K, Alexis frag. 142 K (this doctor seemingly an Athenian who puts on a Doric accent), Epikrates frag. 11 K (a Sicilian). Agesilaos was treated by a Syracusan doctor at Megara, Xen. *Hell.* v. 4. 58.

375 ἀcτεῖον: The word means 'witty', 'charming', even just 'good of its sort' (see LSJ) : here perhaps it indicates one who will 'see the joke' and help to play it.   **ὑπαλάζονα:** Like many compounds of ὑπο-, a *hapax*, 'a bit of an impostor'.   **οὐ πάνυ:** Lit. 'not quite', means (by understatement) 'absolutely not'.

376 τί δὲ τοῦτο; 'What d'you say to this?'

377 προκόμιον αἰτήcομαι: προκόμιον, 'false hair', occurs among a long list of feminine wear in Ar. frag. 320. A χλανίc was a fine cloak, *Dysk.* 257 n., and to wear one might be suitably ostentatious for this 'doctor'. It is intelligible that Chaireas might have to borrow both hair and cloak ; the stick is more surprising, but it was an older man's possession, not a youth's.

379 ξενιεῖ: 'Will speak like a foreigner', Dem. lvii. 18.   **ταχὺ μὲν οὖν:** μὲν οὖν often means 'no, but rather . . .'; here, however, that sense is unsuitable. Perhaps the sense is 'yes, but quickly'; or else μὲν οὖν emphasizes ταχύ as it does πάνυ or κομιδῇ, 'really quickly', like 'really completely'.

381 ἀπόθνηcκ' ἀγαθῇ τύχῃ: 'Die and good luck to you'; ἀγαθῇ τύχῃ is often joined to imperatives, e.g. Dem. iii. 18, ταῦτα ποιεῖτ' ἀγαθῇ τύχῃ. Van Leeuwen supposed that the phrase ἀγαθῇ τύχῃ was used to neutralize the unpropitious command ἀπόθνηcκε. I think that primarily the speaker is joking, by associating the courteous words with an apparently hostile imperative. Kassel wished, against B, to assign μηδένα . . . πρᾶγμα to Daos, but the plural ἀφίετε is not suitable to this : the 'dead' Chairestratos will be in no position to prevent servants leaving the house ; it is Daos and Chaireas who will have to keep up the game.   **382: See Addenda.**

383 τίς δ' ἡμῖν ξυνείcεται: B assigns this to Chaireas, but I think Gaiser is right in arguing that to be mistaken. Chaireas must leave at 379, sped on his way by the words ταχὺ μὲν οὖν. From 380 Chairestratos and Daos are alone. Chairestratos' warning (381–3) not to let anyone out of the house (he might give the game away) prompts the inquiry who is to be in the secret.

384 ταῖc παιδίcκαιc: Chairestratos' daughter and Kleostratos' sister.

If these relations do not weep, will the 'death' be convincing? But the wish to spare them pain is consistent with Chairestratos' 'goodness' (125).

386 παροινεῖν: The word is mostly used of violent behaviour, *Dysk.* 92–5 n., but here it probably indicates no more than verbal violence, insult. Stobaios iv. 27 is entitled οὐ χρὴ παροινεῖν εἰς τοὺς τετελευτηκότας, and in Philostratos, *Heroicus* 295. 8 insulting the dead Ajax is called παροινία.

387–90: These lines are given to Chaireas by Austin, who accepts B's attribution of 383. But even if Chaireas has not already left, they suit Daos better, for it is he who will enjoy the διατριβή that is here forecast. Chaireas, if present at all in the coming scenes, will be there as a *muta persona.* As so often, the concluding lines of one act look forward to, and prepare for, the initial passages of the next.   **εἴcω τις ἀγέτω τουτονί:** Why should Chairestratos need taking into his own home? I can only suggest that he is already beginning to act the part of a sick man. 388–90 offer some difficulty. At one time I accepted Austin's view that the subject of ἕξει is Chairestratos (τουτονί). But he is to be shut away out of sight of all that will be going on, and will have no διατριβή; if he has any ἀγωνία, that will not be dependent on the plausibility of the 'doctor'. The subject must be τὸ πάθος, and that will, I think, mean 'the (fictitious) calamity of Chairestratos' death', rather than 'the emotion I shall display'. This calamity is to be attended, 'you may be sure [ἀμέλει, cf. *Sam.* 223 n.], by διατριβὴ οὐκ ἄρρυθμος ἀγωνία τε'. The adjective may go with διατριβή, or with ἀγωνία (τε being postponed), or more probably with both nouns. Literally οὐκ ἄρρυθμος means 'not ill-shaped', and here seems to be a substitute for καλή: it will be 'a pretty entertainment' (Plutarch, *Antony* 29 records how the Alexandrians cυνέπαιζον οὐκ ἀρρύθμως οὐδ' ἀμούcως with Antony when he engaged in βωμολοχία). But the entertainment will have its serious side; the conspirators have to get the better of Smikrines, and this will involve ἀγωνία, 'a contest or struggle to win'. As an alternative, ἀγωνία might mean the (pretended) anguish that Daos will display; this is less likely, as being in no way consequent on the plausibility of the doctor. The clause ἂν ἐνcτῇ μόνον does not express any doubt about the occurrence of the 'calamity'; the meaning is that its occurrence is all that is needed to bring about the entertaining struggle.

390: Daos enters the house with Chairestratos, who is led by the slave summoned to take him (387). Chaireas leaves, to find the friend who will play the part of the doctor. The pause before the next act is filled by a performance executed by the chorus.

ACT III

(i) 391–398: *Smikrines*

391: Smikrines comes out of his house. ταχύ γ': Sarcastic: Daos has not brought the inventory (ἀπογραφήν) of the valuables, nor given any thought to Smikrines. For the sarcastic use of ταχύ γε cf. Ar. *Clouds* 646–7, ἄγροικος εἶ καὶ δυςμαθής. ταχύ γ' ἂν δύναιο μανθάνειν περὶ ῥυθμῶν, Aischines i. 181, ταχύ γ' ἂν Τίμαρχον . . . εἴαςε πολιτεύεςθαι, and Denniston, *GP* 128–9.

393: Daos, Smikrines concludes, is acting with 'these men', i.e. with Chairestratos and his associate(s). But he welcomes this, since Daos' omission has given him the excuse not to show a generous, friendly spirit when inquiring into the assets, but to promote his own interests. For the phrase πρόφαςιν εἴληφ(α) ἄςμενος, cf. *Dysk.* 135, πρόφαςιν οὗτος ἄςμενος εἴληφεν. F 1 has αςμενως; the adverb was sometimes substituted by copyists for the adjective, see LSJ s.v. But ἀςμένως is required by the metre at Alexis frag. 142 K, ἀςμένως ἠκούςαμεν.

395 φιλανθρώπως: Not 'like a public benefactor' (Page). φιλάνθρωπος (cf. *Sam.* 35, *Pap. Didot* i. 41, *Dysk.* 105 n.) is frequently used of the relation of one individual to another, covering a wide range of English words: 'kind, friendly, generous, courteous'; here perhaps 'altruistic' will do.

397 τὰ γὰρ οὐ φανερά: 'What they are not declaring'. Smikrines assumes dishonesty, and welcomes the opportunity of complaining at the slowness in providing the list; this will enable him to demand to see and count the property himself. For the pragmatic distinction between φανερά and ἀφανὴς οὐςία see *Dysk.* 811 n.

398 δραπέτου: There is no reason to suppose Daos to have been a runaway; as in *Karch.* 35, the word is mere abuse like τοιχωρύχος or ἱερόςυλος.

(ii) 399–432: *Smikrines and Daos*

399 ff.: Smikrines had come out with the intention of going to make trouble for Daos and Chairestratos. The former now appears unsought, but with a tale of woe that distracts Smikrines from his purpose. At first he pretends not to see the old man, but addresses his story to high heaven. Whether he openly recognized him in the lost and mutilated lines after 403 is doubtful; he may pretend first to pay him attention at 419, with the vocative Cμικρίνη. **ὦ δαίμονες**: A substitute for the hackneyed ὦ θεοί of tragedy.

402 cκηπτὸc . . . ῥαγδαῖοc: cκηπτός (also *Sam.* 556) can mean not only 'thunderbolt' but also a sudden storm of wind, as in Soph. *Ant.* 418, and probably Dem. xviii. 194. Since ῥαγδαῖοc (from ῥάττειν) is properly applied to violent beating rain, the latter sense is appropriate here. Elsewhere in comedy ῥαγδαῖοc occurs only as applied by metaphor to violent persons.

404: Kassel suggests ὦ δαῖμον᾽, ὄν. Trag. adesp. 17 Nauck begins ὦ δαῖμον, ὅc (as does Alkiphron, *ep.* iii. 13. 1), Aesch. *Persae* 845 and Eur. frag. 444 N, ὦ δαῖμον, ὥc. There must have been at least one quotation from tragedy among the lost and damaged lines, in view of πάλιν in 408.   **405:** See Addenda.

407: The opening line of Euripides' *Stheneboia* (frag. 661 N), used by Aristophanes in the 'lekythos'-scene, *Frogs* 1217, and frequently quoted; in the fourth century by Aristotle, *Rhetoric* 1394ᵇ2, the comedians Nikostratos (frag. 28 K) and Philippides (frag. 18 K), and an anonymous, *P. Oxy.* 2086.

408: For the restoration Blume quotes *Fab. incert.* 56, ὦ πολυτίμητοι θεοί, ἐρρωμένου πράγματοc.

409–10: Restoration is uncertain. The last surviving letters are plausibly read by Austin as καια[; he suggests καὶ ἀ[. Δᾶε κακόδαιμον is just possibly self-address. W. S. Anderson, *Phoenix* xxiv (1970), 229, thinks that the question ποῖ τρέχειc; shows Daos to have been running up and down the stage during the preceding lines. Possibly, but I prefer to see him taking, at the end of 409, some 'blind', hurried steps that bring him on top of Smikrines. Whereas the two were apart before, they are now close together, certainly at 419, probably from 410. When trying to imagine the stage action, one should remember that it is difficult to speak intelligibly while running. At *Dysk.* 81 the fleeing Pyrrhias comes to a halt at the end of his first line, at the latest; the question ποῖ κακόδαιμον; at 84 is prompted by a new movement on his part. In Plautine scenes like *Curculio* 280 ff. one must suppose a pretence of running, with frequent halts interposed.

411: Chairemon frag. 2 N, from his Ἀχιλλεὺc Θερcιτοκτόνοc, a line made famous by Theophrastos in his *Callisthenes*.

412–13: Aesch. *Niobe* (frag. 156 N, 273, 15–16 Mette), attacked by Plato, *Rep.* 380 a, and twice cited by Plutarch (*Mor.* 17 b, 1065 b) to exemplify the regrettable theology to be found in poetry. The exclamation ὑπέρευγε (cf. εὖγε) is found also at *Epitr.* 525 and by a certain emendation at *Theophorumene* 30; ὑπέρευ modifies a verb, ὑπέρευ λέγειc, *Perik.* 982. θεός is scanned as a monosyllable, as often in tragedy: probably it was so scanned in *Niobe*.

414 ὁ cεμνά—: Sc. εἰπών. This is the most likely emendation of B's οcεμνεα, which will have preserved a mistake cεμνε, corrected by a superscript α. Daos is interrupted by Smikrines before he can finish his sentence. (F 1's reading is quite uncertain; Vitelli thought he saw a word ending]ρεα before γνωμολογειc.) **γνωμολογεῖc;** 'Are you reciting maxims?'

415 οὐδὲ παύcεται; Perhaps 'won't he even stop?' sc. let alone answer my question, or possibly οὐδέ introduces an indignant question, as δέ often does. Denniston, *GP* 198, suggests this explanation of Ar. *Knights* 1302, οὐδὲ πυνθάνεcθε ταῦτα; See Addenda.

415–18: There were two tragedians named Karkinos, father and son, Sicilians. The younger, who was favoured by Dionysios II, was by far the more famous, gained eleven victories at Athens, and is doubtless the author of the central quotation here, and perhaps of the two others also. None of them is in Nauck *TGF*.

In 417 F 1 has πουφηcιν, and this may be right, if μιᾷ is dropped (Wilamowitz). A similar explanatory μιᾷ is found in the Trincavelli text of Stobaios, iii. 15. 3, ἐν ἡμέρᾳ δὲ μιᾷ διαφορῆcαι ῥᾴδιον (Diphilos frag. 100 K); που is common with quotations, e.g. Philemon quoted by Satyros, *P. Oxy.* 1176 p. 150, Εὐριπίδηc πού φηcιν οὕτωc. ἐν ἡμέρᾳ μιᾷ is, of course, a phrase often paralleled: in Menander, *Dysk.* 186, 864, *Karch.* 8 (= frag. 228 K–T). K.Tsantsanoglou, Ἐπιcτ. Ἐπετηρὶc Φιλοcοφ. Cχολῆc Πανεπιcτ. Θεccαλονίκηc, ix (1965), 255, calls attention to a short gnomologium on f. 200 of codex 95 from the Monastery of Zaborda, the codex which contains the 'Thessaloniki' Photios. This gnomologium has an entry Μενάνδρου κωμῳδία, and, below it, the verses cκιὰ τὰ θνητῶν· ἐν μιᾷ γὰρ ἡμέρᾳ | τὸν εὐτυχῆ τίθηcι δυcτυχῆ θεόc. Tsantsanoglou argues that they must originally have been taken from a tragedy without any lemma, and that Μενάνδρου κωμῳδία was added by someone who recognized that they were partially contained in *Aspis*. Clearly this is possible, and if true will support (but not require) the retention of μιᾷ and the dropping of που. But other explanations are possible: Menander may have used the complete two lines in another play, or the original anthologist may have taken the quotation from *Aspis* and filled it out with cκιὰ τὰ θνητῶν, taken from somewhere else, to make two complete lines, cf. *Epitr.* 563 n. Tsantsanoglou does not notice that Isidoros of Pelusium, *epist.* 5. 244, has cκιὰ γὰρ τὰ θνητῶν λέγει ἡ κωμῳδία (Nauck, *TGF* p. 783).

The sentiment of the passage is repeated in Philemon frag. 213 K, τύχηc δὲ μεταβολὰc οὐκ ἀγνοεῖc | ὅτι τὸν εὔπορον τίθηcι πτωχὸν εἰc τὸν αὔριον.

420 cχεδόν τι is often 'used to soften a positive assertion' (LSJ);

'perhaps I might say he's dead' would represent the absurdity of the original. ἀδελφὸc . . . cou is the familiar equivalent of ὁ cὸc ἀδελφόc. For the separation cf. *Epitr.* 934, ἐπακροώμενοc ἔcτηκαc ἱερócυλέ μου, *Sam.* 568, τὸ παιδίον λήψεταί μου, and see K. J. Dover, *Greek Word Order*, pp. 18 f., on the way in which post-positives may fail to occupy what seems to us their 'natural place'. The emphatic cοῦ printed by Körte is out of place.

422 χολή: An excess of bile was supposed to induce madness, *Dysk.* 89 n., and so was grief, e.g. Philemon frag. 106 K, διὰ λύπην καὶ μανία γὰρ γίγνεται πολλοῖcι καὶ νοcήματ᾽ οὐκ ἰάcιμα, αὐτοὺc δ᾽ ἀνῃρήκαcι διὰ λύπην τινεc. **ἔκcταcιc φρενῶν:** The patient was 'out of his mind', cf. Eur. *Or.* 1021, ἐξέcτην φρενῶν. **πνιγμόc:** 'Choking', the only purely physical symptom mentioned.

424–7 οὐκ ἔcτιν οὐδὲν κτλ.: The opening of Euripides' *Orestes*. Daos is interrupted before he can complete the sentence, which continues οὐδὲ cυμφορὰ θεήλατοc, ἧc οὐκ ἂν ἄραιτ᾽ ἄχθοc ἀνθρώπου φύcιc. **τὰc γὰρ cυμφορὰc κτλ.** appears as Euripides frag. 944a Snell, but 427 strongly suggests that the words come from Chairemon. Daos, however, if we write τὸ δέ in 427, may be understood to ascribe the passage from Euripides to Chairemon and the other passage to Euripides. Since *Orestes* was a well-known play, this would amuse the better educated. Wilamowitz, and also F. G. Allinson, *TAPA* lii (1921), 69, suspected that τὰc γὰρ cυμφορὰc κτλ. was a quotation invented by Daos, and impudently ascribed to Euripides. The idea that the audience would know Euripides' ninety-two plays so completely that they would detect the imposture is an illusion such as neither scholar usually entertained. Handley wrote τόδε Χαιρήμονοc, but when οὗτοc and ὅδε are so opposed, the first usually refers to what precedes them, the second to what follows, K–G i. 646.

428 οὐ τῶν τυχόντων: 'Not everyday writers', cf. *Dysk.* 678, 684, frag. 680, οὐ τοῦ τυχόντοc ἀνδρόc.

429: Probably both B and F presented a line with a foot too many. Most editors write οὔχετ᾽ οὖν for οιχεταιμενουν, but the interpolation of μέν is unparalleled in Menander papyri and μὲν οὖν is excellent: 'Has any doctor come?' 'On the contrary, Chaireas has gone to fetch one.' It is better to drop οὐθείc, following Vitelli, as an addition intended to make the meaning plain.

430–1: The disguised friend appears, and Daos urges him to hurry. He may be supposed to move with professional dignity; so the doctor in Plaut. *Men.* 888 seems to the old man, waiting impatiently, to be crawling. A paragraphus below 431 shows that the 'doctor' returned a brief answer. βέλτιστε is a common form of polite address to a stranger, *Epitr.* 224, 308, 370, *Sam.* 384, *Dysk.* 144, 319, 338, 342, 476, 503.

432: Another line from Eur. *Orestes* (232): 'Sick men's helplessness makes them hard to please.' The line does not appear particularly relevant. Can it be taken as a hint to Smikrines that no intervention by him will be welcome?

(iii) **433–464:** *Smikrines and 'Doctor'*

433–5: Smikrines' reasons for not entering the house are sound and suit his unfriendly character: that he should keep out is all to the good from the conspirators' angle. Somewhere in the gap of *c.* sixteen lines that follows the 'doctor' came out again, pretending to have examined the patient.

439–64: The doctor speaks in a literary Doric, probably to suggest that he is from Sicily, which produced many medical men. But Doric-speaking Kos was another medical centre. At the end, if B may be believed, he lapses into Attic forms, σύ for τύ and perhaps θανάτους for θανάτως. Whether this is deliberately done by Menander or due to scribal error, as I suppose, must be uncertain. In 448 θάλπεν gives a form of the infinitive found in many Doric dialects (Schwyzer, i. 807), but ὀνυμάζειν (445) is inconsistent; again the question arises, poet or copyist? But the hyperdoric νόσαμα (464) will be Menander's and perhaps deliberate.

The introduction of foreign dialects seems to have been an occasional feature of Greek comedy at all periods, but was perhaps more common in Old Comedy. From Aristophanes may be cited the Megarian and the Boeotian in *Ach.*, the Spartans in *Lys.*, the Scythian in *Thesm.*, from Krates some Dorian (frag. 41 K). In Middle Comedy Eubulos had a Boeotian (frag. 12 K). Whether Alexis or Plautus is responsible for the Punic in *Poenulus* may be disputed.

The doctor uses several words intended to indicate his foreign origin or technical knowledge. φρενῖτις is a medical term, Hippokrates, *Aph.* iii. 30; Diokles frag. 38 quoted on 341. πάμπαν is a favourite word of Aristotle, but not found in Attic writers (outside tragedy). βιώσιμος is a rarity in the sense 'likely to live'; Theophrastos *HP* ix. 12. 1, and then again in Arrian, e.g. *Anab.* ii. 4. 8, τοὺς μὲν ἄλλους ἰατροὺς οὐκ οἴεσθαι εἶναι βιώσιμον. ἀνερεύγεται gives the first instance of this compound; the simple verb ἐρεύγομαι, 'belch', (in Attic ἐρυγγάνω) is mainly found in poetry, but also in Hippocratic writings, *Morb.* ii. 69, *Mul.* i. 41. ἀναφρίζειν was known only from Phrynichos, *PS* p. 46 B. θάλπειν is also not an Attic word, Rutherford, *New Phrynichus*, p. 169.

445 μὲν ὦν: μέν is probably prospective and emphasized by ὦν (Denniston, *GP* 473, notes that this is commoner in Hippokrates and Aristotle than elsewhere). 'We *call* it phrenitis, but we cannot *cure* it' is what the 'doctor' suggests he intends to say. The Greeks called *phrenitis* a number of disorders that modern medicine would distinguish; probably meningitis was among them. The common symptoms were high fever, delirium, and vomiting (Littré (ed.), *Hippocrates*, ii. 571); Hippokrates, *Epidem.* i. 2. 6, says φρενιτικοῖcι μὲν cπαcμοί, καὶ ἰωδέα ἐπανεμεῦcιν· ἔνιοι ταχυθάνατοι τουτέων.

446: There is a single point in B after τουτο, probably a mistake for a dicolon. μανθάνω without object is not uncommon, e.g. 211 above, *Sam.* 375. Fraenkel wished to read τοῦτο μανθάνω, comparing 442, 443; it is impossible to say whether he was right.

447–9: Austin suggests that 447 might be given to Smikrines as a question. This involves supposing B's dicolon at the end of 446 to be mistakenly placed there instead of after cωτηρίαc. I think this must be accepted, since a categorical statement here by the 'doctor' leaves no room for the announcement of 450, which is identical in content. Ar. *Thesm.* 946, has κοὐκ ἔcτ᾽ ἐτ᾽ ἐλπὶc οὐδεμία cωτηρίαc, but Menander may easily have invented the line afresh: the final three words, which recur in Thuc. i. 65, ἐλπίδα οὐδεμίαν ἔχων cωτηρίαc, are probably a stock locution.

448: θάλπειν literally means 'to warm or heat'; it is used of the effects of passion, particularly that of love, Bacchylides frag. 16. 2, Aesch. *PV* 590, 650, Soph. frag. 474 Pearson, Herondas ii. 81, perhaps Theokritos xiv. 38, *P. Oxy.* 212. 16. But warmth may be comforting, and so Sophocles' Elektra can say to Chrysothemis, ἐc τί μοι βλέψαca θάλπει τῷδ᾽ ἀνηκέcτῳ πυρί; (*El.* 888); the fire is the fire of hope, which gives her false comfort, cf. *Ajax* 478, ὅcτιc κεναῖcιν ἐλπίcιν θερμαίνεται. There seems to be a still further extension, to a meaning that approaches that of 'deceive', in Ar. *Knights* 210, αἴ κα μὴ θαλφθῇ λόγοιc. The Sophoclean passages indicate the force of the word here, 'to give false comfort', and the usage is plainly metaphorical; a good parallel is Aesch. *PV* 684, cήμαινε μηδέ μ᾽ οἰκτίcαc cύνθαλπε μύθοιc ψευδέcιν. It is tempting to call these usages metaphorical, but they have a basis in literal physical fact, real or supposed, and it is hard to say how far that is remembered.

450 τοι: Perhaps Doric for coι, an ethic dative. The particle τοι is not found in Menander except in compounds (μέντοι etc.); but if it was not heard in Attic speech of his time, it may have been used in Doric. Yet it may be doubted whether a Doric speaker would in such a sentence know whether he was using a particle or an ethic dative, Denniston, *GP* 537.

451: On the vomiting of bile cf. Nikophon frag. 12 K, πυρετός . . . ἐμεῖν ποιεῖ χολήν, Nikandros, *Theriaka* 435, ἀπερευγόμενος ἔμετον χολοειδέα. ἐπισκοτεῖν means 'to throw a shadow or darkness on something.' The failing of vision is one of death's harbingers.

453 ἀναφρίζει: 'Foams up through the mouth'. Austin suggests that the preceding word was πυκνόν. Proceleusmatics being suspect (*Georgos* 84 n.), this would imply a third-foot dactyl divided before the last syllable, as at *Dysk*. 386, 476.

454 ἐκφορὰν βλέπει: 'He looks like being carried out to the grave.'

455 προάγωμες, παῖ: The 'doctor' addresses his attendant slave.

σέ, σέ: I know no instance of the repetition of a pronoun without any intervening word, although *Sam.* 675 is plausibly emended to read σὲ γάρ, ⟨σὲ⟩ περιμένουσι.   μετακαλῆις: Cf. δοκῆις (462). These may be hyperdoricisms, the only attested forms for the singular of verbs in -έω being -εῖς, -εῖ. See Austin's note.

458 τὼς τέως: 'As hitherto'. For the possibly Doric τως for ὡς cf. the Megarian in Ar. *Ach*. 762, τὼς ἀρωραῖοι μύες. But the form, due to a false analogy with τώς = ὥς, is already found in Attic dramatists, Aesch. *Septem* 637, perhaps *Ag.* 242, Soph. *Ichn.* 39, 296.

The 'doctor' can hardly open the conversation with an unprovoked assertion about Smikrines' prospects of life. That comes only at 462 when he has been provoked, probably by a failure to accept without reservation his prognosis of death for Chairestratos. As a long shot, possibly κληρονόμος ὢν οὐκ ἂν βιώῃς τως τέως: 'With his money you will be able to live more extravagantly.'

459–60: The 'doctor' seems to take offence at this speech, replying, e.g.: 'Laugh at me, if you like; I know my trade.' Hence Smikrines may have said, e.g., 'Pray for his recovery; doctors are not always right.' Thus the lines may be speculatively supplemented as follows: ἐρρωμένως τιν'] αὐτὸν εὔχου τρόπον ἔχειν · | [καὶ γὰρ παρὰ λόγο]ν πολλὰ γίνεται. :: γέλα | [αἴ λῆις, κρατεῖν δέ] φαμι τᾶς ἐμᾶς τέχνας.

464 φθιτικόν: Doric for φθισικόν, 'consumptive'. Cf. frag. 538. 7.

θανάτους βλέπεις: 'You look like death.' The use of the plural of one man's death is found in lyrics in tragedy, e.g. Soph. *El.* 205, τοὺς ἐμὸς ἴδε πατὴρ θανάτους αἰκεῖς διδύμαιν χειροῖν, and perhaps also Plato, *Rep.* 399 a, ἢ εἰς τραύματα ἢ εἰς θανάτους ἰόντος ἢ εἴς τινα ἄλλην συμφορὰν πεσόντος, but there various possible forms of death may be meant. M. L. West suggested θανάτως, but the form -ως was not universal in Doric as acc. plur. ending in o-stems; -oc was used in Kos and -ovc at Syracuse, Bechtel, *Griech. Dialekt.* ii, pp. 230, 572.

465: Smikrines disregards the prognostications of the doctor, who probably departs here. The old man's next remarks await elucidation. Perhaps the first sentence means: 'I well imagine (ἦ που, Denniston, *GP* 286) the women are plundering his possessions as if they were taking goods from a foreign enemy', i.e. behaving as soldiers do in a foreign country. For the use of φέρω without an object cf. Lysias xx. 17, ὥϲπερ ἔνιοι ἥρπαζον καὶ ἔφερον. 'Orders are given to the neighbours through the water-channels': ὑδρορρόαι are said by LSJ to be watercourses whether on the ground or on the roof. For the latter sense they cite only Ar. *Wasps* 126, where ground-level drains may be meant. Elsewhere drains on the ground *are* meant, Ar. *Ach.* 922, 1186, Alkiphron iii. 47, probably Polybios iv. 57. 8. There may be some topical allusion that is now irrecoverable.

467: Daos may have come out with the doctor, but it is perhaps more likely that he appears here. The note ηϲυχη (cf. 93) above θορυβηϲω shows that his remark is not for Smikrines' ears.

ACT IV

(i) **469–490:** *Smikrines and another*

469: Either 'they are crying "he's gone..."', as at 343, or 'they are crying aloud. He's gone.'

471: The *nota persona* may, but need not, show that Smikrines enters here. The corrupt letters δεδρακιχ' have not received any plausible correction. δέδρακε, 'has run away', is possible.

474–90: The fragmentary remains of these lines give no hold for reconstruction. ἐγγυᾶν at 484 possibly refers to the betrothal of Kleostratos' sister to Chaireas, which Smikrines may now contemplate, seeing the prospect of a richer prize in Chairestratos' daughter.

(ii) **491–515:** *Kleostratos and Daos*

491–508: Kleostratos returns from Lykia, and after a moment's delay is recognized by Daos. The speakers of 474–90 have all left the stage, and Kleostratos probably opens with a greeting to his motherland, e.g. ὦ φιλτάτη Γῆ μῆτερ, as in frag. 287. See also *Sam.* 101 n. At 499 Daos probably answers a knock. He does not at first know Kleostratos; it is possible that he does not open or fully open the door and so does not see him. If so, at 504 Kleostratos may, after the exclamation ὦ θεῖε, 'uncle!', continue ἄνοιγε τὴν θύραν, ἄνθρωπέ μοι κακόδαιμον.

He will not yet know that this man is Daos. When Daos in 506 uses the address μειράκιον he still cannot know his master, but the cry of ὦ Ζεῦ marks his recognition, cf. *Mis.* 210, ὦ Ζεῦ, τίν' ὄψιν οὐδὲ προσδοκωμένην ὁρῶ; He continued with something that caused Chaireas surprise, e.g. 'you were a corpse'.

496: E.g. εἰ δ' αὖ διαπ[εσὼν (Handley) τοὺς πολεμίους ζῆ μόνον] ὁ Δᾶος, εὐτυχ[έστατον πάντων τότ' ἂν]νομίσαιμ' ἐμαυτόν.

499 παιητέα: Cf. *Epitr.* 1075, ἡ θύρα παιητέα. There 'banging' on the door (the usual verb for knocking at a door is κόπτειν) was a sign of Smikrines' bad temper; here it indicates the exuberance of Kleostratos' feelings on his return. The action will not recommend him to those who are acting the part of a family bereaved. For the end of the line Austin suggests τίς τὴν θύραν, as in Herondas i. 3, and quotes Plaut. *Rud.* 414, 'quis est qui nostris tam proterue foribus facit iniuriam? :: ego sum.'

508 ἔχω ϲε: Cf. *Mis.* 214, ἔχω ϲε, τέκνον, and similarly at an unexpected reunion, Eur. *Alc.* 1134, *Electra* 579, *Ion* 1440, *IT* 829.

512 ἀνοίγετε: Perhaps open the room where Chairestratos is in hiding.

514 ἐγρηγορώϲ: Austin suggests that this is Chairestratos, recalled to life. One could also imagine some such sentiment as 'wide awake I now see what we, your friends, did not even dream of'.

(iii) 516–44

The position of the line-ends, to the right of the page, confirms that these are trochaic tetrameters. The first speaker is probably Daos, who foretells a double marriage: Chairestratos will give his own daughter to Kleostratos and his niece to Chaireas. The second speaker perhaps comes on at 526; is he Chaireas, who is here informed of his friend's safe return ('Where is he?' he asks)? It may be guessed that the rest of the act, which was short, displayed the discomfiture of Smikrines, who may be seen approaching at 534 and who enters at 540, to be the speaker of the following lines, expressing his intention to give Chaireas Kleostratos' sister. At 539 Turner suggests οἰκεῖος ἀνήρ ἐϲτί μοι τρόπον τινά. Chaireas could say this, since he is intending to marry Smikrines' niece, except that ἐϲτί for ἔϲται or γίνεται is dubious. *Dysk.* 903–4 might equally suggest ϲωφρονιϲτέος γὰρ ἀνὴρ κτλ.

520: Austin suggests τὸν χρόνο]ν, comparing [Lucian], *Am.* 54, παρέλκειν πλείω χρόνον.

522: Lloyd-Jones's ἀδελφιδῆν for ἀδελφην is very probable (*ZPE* ii [1968], 154). Chairestratos will give his niece to Chaireas, as he had originally intended (hence πάλιν). Perhaps her returned brother would in the letter of the law now be her κύριος, but it is easy to imagine that he would allow her uncle to continue to perform the marriage for which he had made all arrangements.

526 τὸν γείτονα: Probably Smikrines.

530 cῶc Κλεόcτρατος (Handley) is likely. The adjective is used again in *Epitr.* 409, frag. 711.

537 ἄν τε, and not, e.g., θύρ]αν τε, is necessary if the median diaeresis is to be maintained. The only exception in Menander is *Sam.* 484.

Fragment 1. It is profitless to guess what occasion there can have been for these reflections. Although the lines are quoted by Stobaios in his chapter entitled ψόγος τυραννίδος, the speaker has in mind subordinate commanders in charge of garrisons or of cities as much as independent autocrats. Meineke's change of οἱ to ἤ is unnecessary: the asyndeton makes the sentence more forcible. Without the context one does not know whether Porson's suspicion of οὕτω was justified. He suggested οὗτοι, cf. Ar. *Wasps* 634, ὑπονοοῦϲιν οὗτοι ῥαιδίωϲ τρυγήϲειν; whichever is right, ῥᾳδίωϲ probably goes with προϲιέναι.

Fragment 2. Iberia was the country between the Black Sea and the Caspian, roughly the modern Georgia, described by Strabo, xi. 3. 1–6. A woman of this nationality may have been mentioned, but the feminine adjective can also be applied to things.

Fragment 3. This seems to be the only instance of the aorist of the simple verb μύζω, 'mutter, say μῦ μῦ', but ἐπέμυξαν is found at *Il.* iv. 20, viii. 457; at Diog. L. x. 118 MSS. are divided between μύζει and μύξει in a context where future tenses predominate.

Fragment 4. κανδύτανες: 'Portmanteaux', see *Sik.* 388 n.; perhaps they contained the clothes that were part of Kleostratos' booty.

Gaiser, *Menander Der Schild*, pp. 9–10, revives the guess of R. Herzog, *Hermes* li (1916), 315, that an alternative title of this play was Ἐπί-κληρος. Two plays by Menander seem to have been so called. One was probably also entitled Χρηϲτή and cannot be identified with *Aspis* (frag. 152 K–T). Gaiser suggests that frags. 155 and 156, from the 'first' *Epikleros*, belong to *Aspis*, and that Smikrines was reported as wanting a cock out of his house for fear it should scratch up his buried treasure (cf. Plaut. *Aul.* 465–72).

GEORGOS

G   *P. Genavensis* 155. This was the first complete leaf of a Menandrean codex to be discovered. The writing is inelegant, with frequent ligatures, and the size of the letters varies so greatly, but with a tendency to increase towards the end of the line, that it is not always possible to be certain how many letters have been lost in gaps. The scribe copied from a defective manuscript, as he deliberately left blanks at the end of 3 and the beginning of 34. Indeterminate marks at the foot of the page after 87 seem not to be traces of a lost verse.

B 4 *P. Berolinensis* 21106 is a scrap with parts of 25–31.

F   *PSI* 100 is a narrow strip that overlaps the text of G.

M   *P. Mus. Brit.* 2823 a consists of three scraps, one of which contains a few words from frag. 93 Kock, quoted by Stobaios iv. 32 b 24 from Menander's *Georgos*. The others are presumably from the same play, but they throw no light on it and have not been printed in OCT.

The claim of A. Barigazzi, *Athenaeum* xxxiv (1956), 340 ff., that *P. Oxy.* 2329 contains a passage from *Georgos* is effectively criticized by D. Del Corno, *Menandro*, p. 397[3].

H. Weil, *REG* xi (1898), 121; Wilamowitz, *NJA* iii (1899), 513 = *Kl. Schr.* i. 224; K. Dziatzko, *Rh. Mus.* liv (1899), 497, lv (1900), 104; A. Kretschmar, *De Menandri reliquiis nuper repertis* (1906), pp. 5–56; F. Préchac, *Mélanges archéol. et hist.* xxvii (1907), 277; Webster, *StM* 47.

That the contents of G come from the latter part of the first act is certain, since it has on its 'recto', i.e. side with horizontal fibres, the page-number η (6) and on its 'verso' ζ (7). Apparently five pages preceded; since the surviving leaf has 44 lines on one side and 43 on the other, they will have contained not more than about 230 lines, not enough for an act and a half. If one page were filled by hypothesis, list of characters, etc., the remaining four would have about 175 lines, which with the surviving 95 lines would constitute an act of about 270 lines. This is exceptionally long, and Wilamowitz guessed that a life of Menander was prefixed to the play (*Kl. Schr.* i. 242, 247). A further complication is that the first side of the leaf has the even number 6, whereas an odd number would be expected. Körte

thought that the first side of the first leaf was not numbered, having
been left blank. A mistake in numbering, the omission of a number
having resulted in the writing of η where ε was required, is not very
likely. If, whatever the explanation, three pages of text have been
lost, the first act will have had about 225 verses, a probable figure:
Dyskolos Act I has 232, *Aspis* 249, *Samia* about 215.

Plot

This was a play, which like *Samia*, *Plokion*, and the original of *Aulularia*,
presented rich and poor neighbours. A poor woman Myrrhine, presumably a widow, had a daughter (? Hedeia) and a son (Gorgias).
The daughter was violated by the rich neighbour's son, who probably
hoped that something would turn up that would enable him to get
his father's consent to a marriage. But on returning from a business-
trip he found his father in the midst of preparations to marry him
to his half-sister. In the first surviving scene he declares himself at
a loss how to avoid this marriage. Next Myrrhine appears with
another woman, Philinna, perhaps her old nurse (cf. ὦ τέκνον 25, 84),
who indignantly denounces the young man's treachery in abandoning
the girl and marrying someone else. The rich man's slave Daos now
enters, bringing produce from the country: he tells the women that
Gorgias, who has been working there on or near the farm of a well-
to-do old man named Kleainetos, has won the farmer's gratitude by
nursing him back to health after an accident; Kleainetos has promised
to marry Gorgias' sister, and they are on their way to fetch the bride.
Daos expects Myrrhine to welcome this match, so unexpectedly
favourable from the financial aspect, but as soon as he has gone she
reveals to Philinna that the proposal is a disaster, for the girl is far
gone in pregnancy. The remaining fragments do not allow any reconstruction of the plot. At the beginning of the second act Gorgias
has arrived and learned of his sister's condition: she may even have
given birth to a child in the interval (but the words τὴν Ἄρτεμιν [112]
and τὸ παιδίον [116] might be prospective). Perhaps Gorgias does not
at this point know who is guilty (cf. frag. 1). At a later stage someone,
perhaps Kleainetos, advises him to put up with the wrong done to
his sister (frag. 2), and warns him that a poor man's grievance does
not get favourable hearing (129–33). No doubt in the end the rich
young man married the poor girl, and in this Kleainetos, who must
be the γεωργός of the title, played a large part. Beyond that lies the
region of guess-work; nevertheless the many scholars may be right who,
taking a hint from 58 (οἱονεὶ νομίςας ἑαυτοῦ πατέρα), think that
Kleainetos proved to be the father of Gorgias and his sister. This
would certainly remove the obstacle to her marrying the rich young

man, and might allow the play to end with a triple wedding, as in
Hiereia, the other pairs being Kleainetos and Myrrhine and Gorgias
and the neighbour's daughter. There is, however, a consequence to
be faced about such a plot. It is impossible that the respectable
Myrrhine should have brought up two openly illegitimate children.
She must either have fathered them (? twins) on her late husband or
have been married to Kleainetos and in some way separated from him.
For the second alternative compare Körte's reconstruction of *Hiereia*.
It may be asked what preceded the first surviving verses. If about 130
lines are to be accounted for, there must have been a good deal. A prologue by a divine figure is likely, if this is a play in which the human
actors are largely ignorant of their true relations. It would be unusual
if this was followed by another long monologue, delivered by the
young man; but in *Aspis* a monologue of fifteen lines does follow the
divine prologue.

Quintilian, *Inst. Orat.* xi. 3. 91, writes: 'Cum mihi comoedi quoque
pessime facere uideantur quod etiam si iuuenem agant, cum tamen in
expositione ['in a narration'] aut senis sermo, ut in Hydriae prologo,
aut mulieris, ut in Georgo, incidit, tremula uel effeminata uoce pro-
nuntiant'. Somewhere in the play, therefore, some young man reported what a woman had said. Many scholars do not hesitate to
assert that this occurred in the earlier part of the monologue with
which the surviving fragments begin.

(i) 1–21: *The rich young man*

1–3: ἐδοκουν is followed in G by a blank, πραττων and ὑποφοβουμενος,
however, occupy about the normal position for a verse-end. It is more
likely that something is missing after πράττων than that that word is
itself corrupt, but it is quite uncertain whether ὑποφοβούμενος is or is
not the last word of the line.

3 ἦν . . . ἐδόκουν: Choiroboskos quoted just enough of the line for his
purpose, viz. to establish that ἦν is here 1st person sing., the older Attic
form being ἦ. For this he needed the verb ἐδόκουν, but one cannot
tell whether the clause ended with that word or not. Plutarch,
Demetr. 4, οὔτ' ὢν οὔτε δοκῶν πονηρός, shows that the missing part of
the line need not have been grammatically connected with what
survives. ἦν was in fact already used by Euripides, E. Harrison, *CR* lvi
(1942) 6 ff., Rutherford, *New Phrynichus*, pp. 242–3. One may guess that
the speaker explained his inaction by the absence in the country of
the girl's brother, from whom he would have to ask her hand.

4–12: The irregularity of the writing makes it impossible to determine
certainly how many letters were lost at the beginning of the lines.

Grenfell and Hunt guess 6, and 6±1 seems about right, since 8–10 can confidently be restored καταλαμ]βάνω, τὸν πατέ]ρα, and αὐτὸς ὅ], while in 6 ἀπόδη]μον is probable. Moiris, it is true, says that the Attic word was ἔκδημος, but although ἀπόδημος does not occur elsewhere in surviving Attic texts, ἀποδημεῖν and ἀποδημία are common. Since in 5]c is slightly to the left of]μ in 6, Wilamowitz's νῦν δ' ἔτυχε], printed by Körte, is too long, as is his καὶ γὰρ τότ]ε in 4. Moreover the broken anapaest (τόθ' ὁ μειρ) is unacceptable. In Menander elision justifies a break after the second short syllable only (Epitr. 286, Perik. 178, frag. 620. 10, perhaps Sik. 420). For 5 ἔτυχέ τι] or possibly ἔςτι δέ τι] seems long enough; the former would go well with Grenfell–Hunt's ἐν ᾧ δέ in 4

6 ἐπὶ πρᾶξιν: 'On a piece of private business', cf. Hymn. Apoll. 397, ἐπὶ πρῆξιν . . . ἔπλεον.

7 γινομένους . . . γάμους: It is a recurring dramatic motif (convenient for the stage, whether true to life or not) that a father arranges an immediate marriage for his son, without warning. He may have a motive for haste, as Apoecides has in Plautus, Epidicus 190, or Simo in Terence, Andria. It is possible that in this play the father had some suspicion of his son's interest in the girl next door and wished to scotch it at once. News of a traveller's return often precedes his appearance, e.g. Sam. 59, Plautus, Bacch. 170, Stichus 272, and presumably did so in this play: otherwise the father could not have started the wedding-preparations. Note that this line, if it is correctly restored, has four anapaests.

8 ςτεφανουμένους: This is palaeographically an easier correction of εςτεφανους than van Leeuwen's ἐςτεμμένους. Even if one might expect the garlanding of the gods to have been completed at the very beginning of the preparations, one can hardly assert that it *cannot* have proceeded along with them. The present participle is therefore possible.

10: The marriage of half-brother and half-sister, if the common parent was the father, was allowed by Athenian law, and convenient in avoiding the division of family property. No such marriages actually take place in any surviving comedy, although some modern scholars have favoured them in their reconstructions of lost plays.

10–12: Restoration is difficult, because G omitted one or more words in 11. The text usually printed is ὁμοπατρία γάρ ἐςτί μοι | [ἐκ τῆς] ⟨ἐκείνῳ⟩ νυν[ὶ] γυναικὸς τρεφομένης | γεγονυῖ' ἀ]δελφή. (1) γεγονυῖα is almost certainly too long; Préchac's γεγῶςα, better in this respect, is a form unknown in Menander. One must, however, in this badly written papyrus, reckon with the possibility of an error of spelling, e.g. γόννια. (2) The phrase τρέφειν γυναῖκα is unusual; one might perhaps find it in a context where charges on a man's income were under discussion. But τρέφειν is commonly used of bringing up children. Hence it is probable that, as Nicole believed, τρεφομενης is a mistake for τρεφομένη, having been attracted by the adjacent genitive γυναικος. One might then write μεθ' ῆς] ⟨ἔχει⟩ νυνὶ γυναικὸς τρεφομένη | [ἠβῶς' ἀ]δελφή, cf. Dem. lvii. 37, ἐκ μὲν ῆς πρῶτον ἔσχε γυναικός, or ἐκ τῆς] ⟨γαμετῆς⟩ νυνὶ γυναικός τρεφομένη.

Perhaps the phrase γυναικὸς τρεφομένης made Wilamowitz (Kl. Schr. i. 234) and Körte think she was a 'concubina' (i.e. παλλακή). It would be surprising if the young man's father intended to 'marry' him to an illegitimate child, as the girl would then be if the scene of the play is Athens; and the young man would surely have been entitled to resist. There cannot be any duty to marry, unless the bride is of citizen status, when it may be regarded as a duty to provide a legitimate heir to carry on the family. See introduction, pp. 28, 30.

13–16: The sense of the first part of line 13 is certain, though the words are not. The young man must say that he cannot see the solution to his problem. πλὴν οὕτως ἔχω then looks forward; he recognizes one fixed point: he will not wrong his sweetheart by some course of action (cf. Dysk. 379, οὕτως ἔχω: 'I shall die if I don't get the girl', and ibid. 58). What is this course? It involves explaining nothing (14) and some action over τὸν γάμον (15), which one would take to be that with the half-sister (7), mentioned again in the same words at 21, rather than any marriage he may have promised the girl he has violated.

In 15 Nicole read λ[.]πων, and Grenfell and Hunt transcribed λιπων without any sign of uncertainty, but the anonymous transcript of the New Palaeographical Society, published in 1906 and said to be 'based on a collation of Grenfell and Hunt's text with the original' is]λ[.]πων. On the facsimile there is no trace of any letters before ων and the papyrus is torn so that nothing can be left but their lower extremities. But λιπών, or a compound, must be accepted as probable; the evidence may have been clearer in 1898. λιπὼν τὸν γάμον will mean 'not proceeding with the marriage' (cf. [Dem.] lix. 60, ἔλιπεν . . . τὸν ὅρκον καὶ οὐκ ὤμοσεν).

Accepting this, Körte prints οὐκ ἂν φυγὼν ἐξ οἰ]κίας οὐδὲν φράσας | [οὕτω] λιπὼν δὲ τὸν γάμον τὴν φιλτάτην | ['Ηδεῖ]αν ἀδικήσαιμ' ἄν: 'I would not wrong my dearest by running away from home without saying anything and so not proceeding with the marriage.' There are objections to this: (1) The absence of the article with οἰκίας, paralleled only in trochaic tetrameters, Perik. 292, 342. Sudhaus tried to overcome this by writing ἀπιὼν μὲν ἐκ τῆς οἰκίας, but οὐ γὰρ εὐσεβές requires a preceding negative. (2) οὐδὲν φράσας must be understood

as 'saying nothing to my household', whereas the continuation
κόπτειν δὲ μέλλων τὴν θύραν shows that what the speaker rejects is the
possibility of saying nothing to his love; Robert's οὐδὲν φράcαc αὐτῇ
surmounts this, but involves a feeble contrast between that phrase and
λιπὼν τὸν γάμον. (3) One would expect the young man to say 'I don't
know how to deal with this crisis. But my position is this—I would
not break my promise to my love and marry my sister', not '. . . my
position is this—I would not run away without saying a word'. With
hesitation, I suggest a reconstruction like this: οὐ δῆτα τῶν τῆc οἰκίαc
οὐδὲν φράcαc, οὕτω λιπὼν δὲ τὸν γάμον, τὴν φιλτάτην Ἡδεῖαν ἀδικήcαιμ'
ἄν: 'I would not injure my dearest by explaining nothing of the events
in my house but letting the marriage with her drop just like that.'
This has the disadvantage of requiring τὸν γάμον here not to refer to
the same marriage as τὸν γάμον of 21. An undeservedly neglected
solution, which avoids this difficulty, is that of H. Richards, CR xii
(1898), 433, who proposed, e.g., ἐξῆλθον (? better ἐλήλυθ') ἐκ τῆc
οἰ]κίαc οὐδὲν φράcαc | [cιγῇ] λιπὼν δὲ τὸν γάμον. τὴν φιλτάτην | [οὐκ]
ἄν ⟨ποτ'⟩ ἀδικήcαιμ' ἄν. But there is no certain parallel in Menander
for repeated ἄν, see Dysk. 187 n.

16 Ἡδεῖαν: A proper name might fit at the beginning of the line,
but since there is room for three letters only before αν, it is hard to find
one. Wilamowitz's Ἡδεῖαν (cf. Kirchner, Prosop. Att. 6370–4, Diog.
Laert. x. 7) assumes the spelling ηδιαν, or ηδεαν.

19: Although 4 suggests that the absence of the brother had been in
some way awkward, it would now in these circumstances be embarrassing to meet him.

(ii) 22–96: *Myrrhine, Philinna, Daos* (enters 35 with *Syros*)

22–41: The words suggest the following action: the two women enter
from the spectators' right, as coming from the town. Myrrhine's house
is on the other side, but they do not go to it immediately, because
Philinna moves indignantly towards the house of the young man
(right or centre). This delay causes them to be cut off from Myrrhine's
house by the approach of Daos from the left, as coming from the
country. Instead of pushing past him, Myrrhine suggests standing
back. Accordingly he does not immediately see her. Only when he
turns to the young man's house, into which he orders Syros to take
the provender they are bringing, does he catch sight of her.

22: Philinna, probably Myrrhine's old nurse (25, 54, 84), presumably
does not live with her, since she is unacquainted with the family
situation. Perhaps, like the nurse in *Samia*, she is a freedwoman. What

causes the two women to come upon the stage here? K. Dziatzko, *Rh. Mus.* liv (1899), 509, suggested that Myrrhine might have gone to fetch Philinna to help in the crisis, and that the women enter from the town. This must be right. Philinna does not know of the girl's advanced pregnancy (see 87). The two women cannot therefore come out of Myrrhine's house in order that Philinna may go for a midwife. Nor, if she were leaving for any other reason, could Myrrhine say to her πάντα τἀμαυτῆc λέγω, *at the moment they are about to part*, if she had kept back her daughter's condition. But if they here arrive, with a prospective conversation ahead, the words are quite natural. When Myrrhine says ἐν τοῖcδ᾽ ἐγὼ νῦν εἰμι, she may be supposed already to have explained that her daughter has the young man as a lover, perhaps that she is pregnant, but that the young man is on the point of marrying another.

26 ἀλάζον᾽: 'Cheat, liar'; *Σ Frogs* 280, *Clouds* 102, ἀλάζονac ἰδίωc τοὺc ψεύcτac καλεῖ. The word implies false pretences, not necessarily boasting.

28 τί "χαιρέτω"; 'What do you mean by "let him be"?', cf. *Sam.* 351.

31: The text is uncertain. B4 confirms G's τοcουτουc against the conjecture τοιούτουc found in the German editions. Van Leeuwen read τί δαὶ τοcούτουc κατατεμὼν προcέρχεται | ὄζουc κτλ. But δαί is doubtfully Menandrean and κατατέμνειν usually means 'chop up', not 'cut down' or 'cut off'. I suggest, without conviction, (Μυ.) γαμεῖ· τοcούτουc κατατεμὼν προcέρχεται ὄζουc ὁ θεράπων κτλ. The numerous branches of greenery are a proof that a marriage-festival is toward. Or is there an interrupted sentence: γαμεῖ τοcούτουc—(sc. ὅρκουc ὁμόcαc); (Μυ.) κατὰ τύχην προcέρχεται ἡμῖν κτλ.?

32 βραχύ: Probably 'a short distance', although the word can mean 'for a short time', *Epitr.* 188.

33: The photograph seems to show β[..]ι, as is transcribed by Pal. Soc., but βούλει is too long, unless spelled βολι or βωλι. The construction of βούλει with the subjunctive is common in Attic, e.g. Ar. *Knights* 36, βούλει φράcω; Plato, *Phaedr.* 228 e.

34 καλόν γ᾽ ἂν εἴη: If Myrrhine speaks these words, her motive is more likely to be propriety than a desire to eavesdrop (Waddell) or any fear of meeting Daos. But O. Guéraud, *Bull. Inst. français d'archéol. orientale* xxvii (1927), 117, noted that in the only other place (Xenarchos frag. 8 K) where καλόν γ᾽ ἂν εἴη occurs in comedy, it is ironical: 'That would be a fine thing!' He argued, with some likelihood, that the phrase here belongs to Philinna: 'What do we care for him! It would be a fine thing for us to get out of his way!' H. Richards, *CR* xii (1898), 433, also saw irony.

35 ἀγρὸν . . . μέτρον: Stobaios, *Ecl.* iv. 15 b 23, quotes as from Menander's *Georgos* the lines ἀγρὸν εὐcεβέcτερον γεωργεῖν οὐδένα οἶμαι· φέρει γὰρ ὄcα θεοῖc ἄνθη καλά, κίττον, δάφνην· κρίθαc δ᾽ ἐὰν cπείρω, πάνυ δικαίωc ἀπέδωχ᾽ ὅc᾽ ἂν καταβαλῶ. Waddell suggests that Daos, having heard these lines spoken earlier in the play by Kleainetos, now 'humorously varies the expression'; but it is hardly credible that Kleainetos had appeared previously. It is in fact difficult to suppose that both passages occurred in the same play. Wilamowitz first adopted, but later rejected, Nicole's suggestion that they belong to different versions of the play. Perhaps the easiest solution is that in the text of Stobaios two passages from different plays have been telescoped, e.g., Μενάνδρου Γεωργοῦ· ἀγρὸν . . . φέρει γὰρ [μυρρίνην . . . οὐ πλέον. τοῦ αὐτοῦ (name of play) . . . φέρει γὰρ] ὄcα θεοῖc ἄνθη κτλ.

It is possible that after 36 a line has fallen out, which explained, as in the parallel passage, that the plants mentioned were used in the cult of the gods. Many attempts have been made to invent such a line, which might also give a more satisfactory meaning to ἄνθη τοcαῦτα. The most successful is that of H. Weil, *Journal des Savants* (1897), 657, φέρει γὰρ μυρρίνην, κίττον, ⟨δάφνην, αὐτόματος οὕτως, ὅcα θεοῖc θύειν (better δοῦναι)⟩ καλόν, ἄνθη, τοcαῦτα. For a defence of the text as it stands, see R. Kauer, *Wiener Stud.* xxvi (1904), 209, who argues that myrtle is so closely associated with Aphrodite, ivy with Bacchus, Apollo, and the Muses, that the joke about the land's 'piety' would be easily intelligible, cf. Alkiphron iii. 17, ἔφερεc ἂν τοῖc θεοῖc κίττον καὶ δάφναc καὶ μυρρίναc καὶ ἄνθη ὅcα cύγκαιρα. With the traditional text τοcαῦτα is exclamatory, 'what a quantity of flowers!', see L. Radermacher, *Rh. Mus.* N.S. lv (1900), 482. Theophylaktos Simokates *ep.* 27 has ἀντὶ πυρῶν μυρρίναc, ἀντὶ κριθῶν κίττον: he knew this play.

37: Cf. Xen. *Cyr.* viii. 3. 38, γῄδιον . . . πάντων δικαιότατον . . . ὅ τι γὰρ λάβοι cπέρμα καλῶc καὶ δικαίωc ἀπεδίδου αὐτό τε καὶ τόκον οὐδέν τι πολύν.

38 ἀπέδωκεν: Gnomic aorist.   **ὀρθῶc καὶ δικαίωc,** a stock formula, e.g. Antiphon i. 10, Dem. xviii. 255, *IG* ii². 228. 14.

39 ὁ Cύροc: for nom. with article and imperative, cf. frag. 257, ἐπίθεc τὸ πῦρ, ἡ ζάκοροc.   **ὅμωc:** I.e. 'little though it is that we bring'.

40: Sudhaus's ⟨ἅ⟩πανθ᾽ ὅcα has little advantage palaeographically over Nicole's πάνθ ὅ⟨πο⟩cα, and introduces a proceleusmatic. Even if this foot is metrically admissible (see 84 n.) it is too rare to be welcome in an emendation. But ὅποcοc occurs once only in Menander (*Aspis* 151) and there is an indirect interrogative; the word disappears about

300 B.C. from Attic inscriptions, Meisterhans[3], p. 237. Perhaps πάνθ', ὅca ⟨γε⟩.

41 χαῖρε πολλά: Daos is similarly effusive at 84, ἔρρωcο πολλά. G's original reading νὴ καὶ cύ γε has parallels at Sam. 129, Pap. Ghôran ii. 165, and Lucian, Timon 46, Dial. Mort. 20. 3, Dial. Deor. 20. 7. The reason why νη was altered to νυ is obscure. Grenfell–Hunt guessed that νυ was a remnant of πανυ, which they printed, the divided anapaest being defensible, although unusual (intro. p. 38).

42 γεννικὴ καὶ κοcμία γύναι: Most scholars follow Wilamowitz, Kleine Schriften i. 236, in believing that Daos speaks insolently to Myrrhine (non sine tecto despectu Körte, laetum nuntium se afferre simulans Jensen). This is surely a mistake. Daos brings a poor woman news of an advantageous match for her daughter: he cannot believe this to be anything but good news. There is no indication that he is aware of his young master's interest in her, and no reason why the spectators should assume he had knowledge of it. Nor need his congratulations on escaping from poverty be anything but sincere. It is comic that his good news begins with an alarming accident; but that he is not thereby making fun of Myrrhine is shown by his attempt to reassure her, θάρρει (49). No more does he make fun of her here. Slaves can appreciate good breeding and behaviour, cf. the Daos of Heros 40, who speaks of Plangon as ἐλευθέριοc καὶ κοcμία. If the laugh is on anyone, it is on the slave for using a high-flown phrase; but it is one that fits him, for he fancies himself as a master of the Greek language. That the adj. γεννικόc carries no sneer is shown by Dysk. 321, γεννικὸν ὁρῶ cε τὸν τρόπον; cf. also frag. 951. 10, γενναία γύναι, spoken by the grateful slave Parmenon.

43 τί πράττειc; 'How are things with you?'

45 γεῦcαι: 'Give a taste of', cf. Herondas vi. 11, c' ἔγευc' ἂν τῶν ἐμῶν χειρῶν, Alexis frag. 179 K, καὶ γὰρ βούλομαι | ὕδατός cε γεῦcαι, Anaxippos frag. 1. 27 K, γεύcω δ' ἐὰν βούλῃ cε τῶν εὑρημένων.

46 οὗ: 'Where', as in Aspis 122, Perik. 404, frag. 59 K–T. This loose construction, 'Kleainetos, where your son works', is much easier in English than in Greek. Van Leeuwen's defence of it by reference to K–G ii. 401[3] has generally been approved. But K–G do not include οὗ in their list of adverbs used as substitutes for a relative with preposition (e.g. παρ' ᾧ); ὅπου is included but said to be unusual and poetical; moreover they say that a personal antecedent is unusual. Reinach suggested ᾧ for οὗ (cf. καθεωρουν in 42) with a construction exemplified by Hdt. ii. 124, ἐργάζεcθαι ἑωυτῷ κελεύειν πάντας Αἰγυπτίουc.

48 χρηςτῶς πάνυ: 'Well and truly', cf. Ar. *Eccl.* 638, ἄγξους' εὖ καὶ χρηςτῶς . . . τὸν γέροντα. Menander is imitated by Aelian *ep.* 2, ἐπέκοψε τὸ ςκέλος πάνυ χρηςτῶς καὶ θέρμη ἐπέλαβεν αὐτοῦ καὶ βούβων ἐπήρθη. **ςκάπτων:** Digging with a mattock (δίκελλα, 65) to break up the earth between the vines.

49 τάλαιν' ἐγώ: See *Sam.* 245 n. The expression need not imply any great emotion, but if Myrrhine and Kleainetos had once been married or connected in some other way of which she was aware, there could be more concern in the exclamation than Daos would guess.

51 θέρμα: I follow Rutherford, *New Phrynichus*, p. 414, in thinking this a neuter, formed from θέρομαι, and found in the MSS. of Plato, *Theaet.* 178 c (accented θερμά, by confusion with the adjective) and Ar. frag. 690, ὁ δ' ἔχων θέρμα καὶ | πῦρ ἧκεν (Kock prints θέρμαν, converting the fragment to anapaests). It is usually and unnecessarily taken to be a feminine by-form of the noun θέρμη, used by several authors in the same sense, 'fever'.

53: Although the scholiast on Ar. *Peace* 59, followed by *Suda* s.v., has ὁ Μένανδρός φηςι πολλάκις (Παλλακῇ Kock) ἐκκορηθείης cύ γε, this is the only surviving instance of the imprecation ('may you be swept away like the dirt you are') in his works. But Alkiphron iii. 26, ἀλλ' ἐκκορηθείης ὅτι | ἄκαιρος εἶ καὶ λάλος, may be a quotation from him. οἷα κτλ. gives the reason for the preceding words (see LSJ s.v. οἷος II. 2).

54 γρᾴδιον: On diminutives see *Perik.* 389 n.; this recurs at *Mis.* 228.

56 οἱ μὲν οἰκέται καὶ βάρβαροι: Although βάρβαρος can mean 'cruel', e.g. *Epitrep.* 898, the sense here may well be that Kleainetos' slaves were not Greeks and were un-Greekly callous. For καί linking appositionally related words see Denniston, *GP* 291, *Dysk.* 3.

57 ἐφ' οἷς ἐκεῖνός ἐςτιν: 'In whose hands he is', present tenses because his household still consists of slaves only. **οἰμώζειν μακράν:** The usual phrase is οἰμώζειν μακρά, *Epitr.* 150, 1068, *Perik.* 370, but μακράν is found in good MSS. at Ar. *Birds* 120 (RVA) and *Plut.* 111 (RV).

58: Körte and others boldly deduce from this line that Gorgias really was the son of Kleainetos, who had once ravished Myrrhine.

60 ἐκτρίβω usually means 'rub out, destroy', but cf. ἔκτριμμα, 'towel'.

62 ἀνέςτης': 'Got him on his feet', after the imperfects of repeated action.

63 φίλον τέκνον: Editors give this to Myrrhine, but it comes just as well, if not better, from Philinna, who is as uninhibited in sentimentality as in indignation; cf. *Sam.* 242, where the old nurse exclaims φίλτατον τέκνον about the child of her former charge. εὖ δῆθ' οὑτοcί (Grenfell–Hunt) sc. ἐποίει is the obvious correction of G's ευδηταγ'ουτωcει. The objection that the deictic οὑτοcί could not be used of the absent Gorgias is now refuted by *Dysk.* 559. For δῆτα used with an oath see Denniston, *GP* 276, and in sentences that endorse a previous speaker's words, ibid. 277.

64: G's text is unmetrical and the remedy uncertain. Sudhaus's ⟨ἐπ⟩αναλαβών gives the word an unknown sense, Körte's ⟨ὁ δ'⟩ ἀναλαβών, although it provides for the change of subject, gives the unusual sequence δὲ ... γάρ, for which no good parallel is to be found in Denniston, *GP* 72. Perhaps αναλαβων was written in mistake for αναλαμβανων (the reverse mistake, *Dysk.* 15); while recuperating (pres. part.) Kleainetos had time to ask the boy questions. Cf. Plut. *Mor.* 576 B, ἔκ τινοc πληγῆc περὶ τὸ cκέλοc ἀναλαμβάνοντοc αὐτόν.

69: It is notable that Gorgias is called μειράκιον and νεανίcκοc without distinction, cf. *Dysk.* 27 n.   κοινουμένου: Editors generally have διερχομένου, but it is rash to ascribe this form to Menander; Attic used ἰών, not ἐρχόμενοc, except for ὑπερχόμενοc in the sense 'beguiling', Kühnert–Blass, *Gr. Gr.* i. 2. 430, Rutherford, *New Phrynichus*, p. 103.

74 νοῦν ἔcχε: 'He showed sense'; cf. νοῦν ἔχειc, *Aspis* 174, *Sam.* 605, *Dysk.* 736, 958, νοῦν ἔχετε, *Dysk.* 129, *Sik.* 167. Daos has reserved his 'good news' to the end, and delivers it in five surprising words, which must cause Myrrhine concealed consternation.

75: 'The sum total of my story is this', cf. frag. 740, 10. τοῦτο looks forward to 76 ff.

77: The traces of a letter before λαβων are hard to interpret and have been read as ο, c, or ν. I hesitantly accept the last reading (Jensen) as being the most recent; it implies αὐτή]ν; the possibility of the word-order is guaranteed by [Dem.] *in Neaeram* 38, ἀφικνεῖται αὐτὴν ἔχων. εὐθὺ]c, if possible, would make good sense.

Daos concludes his speech with pompous self-satisfaction: note four consecutive lines in tragic metre, the grand word δυcνουθέτητοc, and the personification of Poverty as an animal. W. Görler, Μενάνδρου Γνῶμαι, p. 80, observes that in tragedy messengers' speeches often end, as here, with a gnome. Daos' gnome is not particularly well suited to Myrrhine's situation: it is late in the day to recommend her a pauper's life in the country. This unsuitability chimes with Daos' general lack of tact.

80: The idea that poverty is better hidden in the country recurs in frag. 336.

83: Probably a stately phrase, cf. the sausage-seller's speech, Ar.

Knights 642, ὦ βουλή, λόγους ἀγαθοὺς φέρων εὐαγγελίcαcθαι πρῶτον ὑμῖν βούλομαι.

84 ἐρρῶcο: A formula for parting, often found at the end of letters, *Perik.* 170 n. Körte retains the reading of G, which involves a proceleusmatic (◡ ◡ ◡ ◡) in the fourth place. The admissibility of this foot in Greek comic trimeters is hotly disputed, but much of the evidence quoted for it is unreliable (see H. J. Newiger, *Hermes* lxxxix [1961], 175, who lists earlier discussions). Here it is possible that a copyist wrote the familiar reply καὶ cύ γε, cf. 41, whereas in fact Myrrhine, in her distraction, answered curtly καὶ cύ, as does Sostratos at *Δὶc 'Εξαπατῶν* 104, although for a different reason.

85 τρίβουcα: G appears to have o corrected to ι. Wilamowitz read cτροβοῦcα, but τρίβουcα is supported by Aristainetos' imitation, *ep.* ii. 5, ὦ τῆc ἀπορίαc δι' ἣν περιπατῶ τρίβουcα τὰc χεῖραc.   **τί γάρ;** 'You ask me why?': see *Epitr.* 262 n.

88 ὁμοῦ: Cf. frag. 760, Harpokration 137. 36, ὁμοῦ . . . ἀντὶ τοῦ ἐγγύc. ἔcτι δὲ πολὺ παρ' Ἀττικοῖc. καὶ Μένανδρόc που· ἤδη γάρ ἐcτι τοῦ τίκτειν ὁμοῦ. Schol. Ap. Rhod. ii. 121 quotes as Menander's the line ὁμοῦ δὲ τοῦ τίκτειν παρεγένεθ' ἡ κόρη (frag. 760 K–T).

PSI 100 gives a few letters from the ends of lines 79–87, and continues in the same way to 98. The end of the act falls between 96 and 97. 92 ends .....]εται and 96 ....]c'εγω, which is consistent with an ending not unlike that of *Perik.* 261, e.g. 'A band of youths προcέρχεται . . . Let us go in. I will tell you more.'

The new act probably began with the entry of Gorgias from the country; he will have come to prepare his sister to receive her unexpected bridegroom. From the remains of his soliloquy it appears that something disturbs him (τί ποιή[cω;, 102). Then Philinna appears and there are traces of a conversation that begins (104) Φιλιν | πρὸ τῶν θυρῶ[ν . . . (105) Γοργ | οὐδεὶc γάρ εἰμ' ἕ[τεροc, but only quite uncertain guesses can be made of its import.

Frag. 1. Perhaps advice from Kleainetos to Gorgias, who may have threatened an action against the young man for the rape of his sister.

1 εὐκαταφρόνητον: For the neuter cf. *Dysk.* 129, ὑπέρπικρον δέ τι ἐστὶν πένηc γεωργόc, 296, πτωχὸc ἀδικηθείc ἐcτι δυcκολώτατον.

4 cυκοφάντηc: One who brings a false accusation in the hope that his victim will think it safer to buy him off than to contest the case; see *Epitr.* 218 n.   **τριβώνιον:** A rough, poor cloak, as in Ar. *Plut.* 842.

Frag. 2. This and the two following fragments may also be parts of the same speech of advice; yet these lines are unusually high-flown in style. τὴν ὑμετέραν πενίαν is the equivalent of ὑμᾶς πένητας ὄντας. Then in τοῦτο ἠδίκηκεν οὗ τυχὸν μεταλήψεται, τοῦτο means πενίαν, but whereas the man injures the *poor*, he is in danger of participating in *poverty*; the *sententia* is verbally neat, but involves a change in the denotation of πενία. Finally the metaphor of the last line is a striking one, perhaps from seasonal rivers that dry up, lit. 'change for the worse' ('ebb and flow' of LSJ introduces the idea of tides, more familiar to us than to Greeks). ῥεῦμα occurs nowhere else in New Comedy. I suspect that this rhetoric was meant by Menander to be a little absurd; was it put in the mouth of Daos (cf. 42 n.)?

Frag. 3. This is quoted by the anthologist Orion, as from Menander. The preceding quotation has the lemma ἐκ τοῦ γεωργίου (sic), but with a marginal note ἀπὸ τῶν ἀποτρεπόντων (sic); it is frag. 9 of *Epitr.* The lemma probably belongs to this fragment, and has been misplaced. Stobaios has lines 1–2, and assigns them to *Georgos*. The speaker may be Kleainetos.

2 ἀδικεῖcθαι κτλ.: 'Best knows how to suffer injuries without losing his self-control'. The advice is of course not to refrain from all retaliation, but to keep one's temper.

4 μικροψυχίας: Arist. *EN* 1125ᵃ3 says that the μεγαλόψυχος bears no grudges, but will overlook offences. On the other hand, to overlook insults to one's family is ἀνδραποδῶδες, ibid. 1126ᵃ7.

Frag. 4. The speaker is probably Kleainetos, whose candid confession that he does not know all the ways of the town will lend more weight to what he will say from the experience that his years have brought him.

Frag. 5. There is no clue to the speaker, but the lines must be addressed to the young man who speaks 1–21. His lack of determination must then have continued beyond the first act, since the passage can hardly have preceded 7 ff.

1 ἐμβεβρόντηcαι: 'Are you out of your mind?' lit. 'thunderstruck', Lat. *attonitus*; cf. ἐμβρόντητος *Perik.* 273, ἐμβροντηcία *Sam.* 411, ἐμβρόντητε *Dysk.* 441, Dem. xviii. 243.   **γελοῖον, ὅc:** Cf. *Heros* 76, ὡς οἰκτρόν, ἢ τοιαῦτα δυcτυχῶ.

Frag. 7. Quoted as an instance of the pejorative use of πράγματα. As they stand, the words may form the end of one trochaic tetrameter and the beginning of the next; there is no need to take them as a lyric Telesillum, as Webster does, *StM* 107. But the quotation may mutilate an iambic line.

DIS EXAPATON

O 13 *P. Oxy.* sine numero. Reconstructed from thirteen fragments by E. W. Handley with the aid of W. E. H. Cockle. Parts of three columns, each apparently of fifty-one lines, from the back of a roll. The text of Menander was written in the later third or early fourth century; much is difficult to read owing to holes and the disappearance of ink.

Partial publication: E. W. Handley, *Menander and Plautus* (1968), pp. 22–4. *Editio princeps* of the whole: *BICS* supplement 22, 'New Fragments of the *Dis Exapaton* of Menander'. I am indebted to Professor Handley for a provisional transcript and text.

This fragment is the original of lines 494–562 of Plautus' *Bacchides*, a play generally agreed to be based on Menander's *Dis Exapaton* (see p. 5). It is of great interest, being the first extended passage which corresponds to a part of a Roman adaptation of Menander or indeed of any Greek play. Previously the longest such fragment was of sixteen lines (*Plokion*, frag. 333 K–T), of which Aulus Gellius preserves Caecilius' version. Plautus' treatment is surprisingly free. In all probability he did not always show so much independence (for example, even in this play Chrysalus' story, *Bacch.* 249–336, must hold fairly close to the Menandrean original), but there is here a warning of the dangers involved in trying to form an idea of a Greek play from the Latin adaptation.

Plot

It will be convenient to give a brief summary, resting on the assumption that basically Plautus' play is evidence for Menander's. (Plautus has changed some of the names, and I give his version in inverted commas.) A young Athenian, Sostratos ('Mnesilochus'), has been to Ephesos, along with a slave, Syros ('Chrysalus'), to collect a large sum of money owed to his father. While there, he met a *hetaira*, 'Bacchis', with whom he fell in love. She had hired herself for a year to a soldier, who took her to Athens. Sostratos wrote to his friend Moschos ('Pistoclerus'), asking him to find where 'Bacchis' was living. Moschos discovered that she had just arrived with the soldier, but had gone to visit her sister, another *hetaira*, also called 'Bacchis'. This sister sees in Moschos a desirable young man, and lures him to a dinner in her house, on the pretext that he will be able to protect his friend's girl against the soldier, who may try forcibly to extend her period of service. Moschos' *paidagogos*, Lydos, is indignant and grows more so as the dinner proceeds and Moschos begins openly to succumb to the sister's charms. He rushes off to inform Moschos' father, 'Philoxenus', of his son's misbehaviour. Meanwhile Sostratos has returned to Athens with his father's money. Syros is the first to appear, and learns from Moschos that the girl is found, but that a considerable sum of money is needed quickly to cancel her bargain with the soldier. Sostratos' father, 'Nicobulus', appears and Syros is quick-witted enough immediately to spin him a story of how, being threatened by the danger of a piratical attack, they had thought it wiser to leave the money on deposit in Ephesos. 'Nicobulus' goes off to meet Sostratos, but misses him. Sostratos returns to fall in with Lydos and 'Philoxenus'; from Lydos he learns that Moschos is making love to 'Bacchis', and is horrified by his friend's supposed disloyalty. The others think that he is upset by Moschos' conduct in becoming a *hetaira*'s lover, and (this is where the Oxyrhynchus fragment begins) entrust him with the task of reproving and rescuing the young man. Left alone, Sostratos determines to hand over all the money to his father, who soon comes back from his vain search for his son. Sostratos tells him that he has the money; 'Nicobulus' expresses surprise at the story he has been told by Syros, but the matter is not pursued, and the two go off. The act ends. The next act opens with the reappearance of 'Nicobulus' and Sostratos; after a time the former departs, leaving Sostratos to express his irritation with 'Bacchis' and ambiguous feelings about Moschos. The latter now comes out of the sister's house; he had heard from Syros that Sostratos had arrived; he cannot conceive why he has not yet come to' Bacchis'. He sees Sostratos, who greets him coldly, and almost immediately begins to utter reproaches. From this point only Plautus' version is available. It will suffice to say that the supposed disloyalty is cleared up, and that 'Chrysalus' (Syros) embarks upon another plan, which cheats the old man out of the money that his son needs.

Plautus has cut out the scene in which 'Nicobulus' returns and Sostratos tells him that he has brought the money home from Asia. In his play 'Mnesilochus' goes indoors, saying that he will give his father the money. As a result 'Nicobulus' is never seen to return home, unless he does so silently and without seeing his son at 393. There 'Mnesilochus', after speaking of his father, says 'sed eccum uideo incedere'. But Leo thought the words spurious, the result of a wish to omit 393–403; *eccum* would then refer not to 'Nicobulus' but to 'Philoxenus', who in the guise of *patrem sodalis* opens line 404.

In Menander's play the handing over of the money is supposed to have taken place during the choral interlude between the acts. In the Roman theatre there was no chorus, and Plautus was obliged to provide some alternative method of allowing for the necessary passage of time. He did so, rather inadequately, by bringing 'Pistoclerus' on (526) before 'Mnesilochus' reappeared (530). This results in the almost complete suppression of the dialogue between Sostratos and his father at the beginning of the new act and of the monologue in which Sostratos had expressed his feelings towards 'Bacchis' and Moschos. *Bacchides* 530ᵇ–531 recall Δὶc 'Εξαπατῶν 91–2, but for the most part the monologue is replaced by a long conversation between the two young men (534–59). For the relation between *Bacchides* and Δὶc 'Εξαπατῶν see E. W. Handley, *Menander and Plautus, passim*, C. Questa, *Entretiens Hardt* xvi, 191 ff. Questa summarizes earlier work in the introduction to his edition (1965).

1–10: Very little remains of these lines, which have not been printed in OCT.

11 ἐκκάλει: 'Call him [Moschos] out' of the *hetaira*'s house.

12 ἐναντίον: I.e. face to face, brought to face you. Cf. Eur. *Hipp.* 946–7, δεῖξον . . . τὸ còν πρόcωπον δεῦρ' ἐναντίον πατρί.

13: Handley printed and still prefers αὐτόν τε cῶcον οἰκίαν φίλην φιλῶν. But the emphatic position of αὐτόν seems inexplicable, and I think Rea must be right in seeing, not φίλην, but θ' ολην; αὐτόν τε . . . οἰκίαν τε gives a phrase of familiar form, 'save him and with him the whole family of your friends'.

14: Lydos would like to be left behind to second Sostratos in the upbraiding of his young master.

15–16 αὐτῷ must be emphatic in this position. Sostratos had already shown his disapproval of Moschos in his absence: now he is to speak sharply to him when he gets him face to face.   **ἔλαυνε:** There seems to be no exact parallel; the meaning is probably 'keep on at him, harass him', cf. Eur. *Andr.* 31, κακοῖc πρὸc αὐτῆc cχετλίοιc ἐλαύνομαι, Dem. xxi. 135, cὺ δ' ἀπειλεῖc πᾶcιν, ἐλαύνειc πάντας, Timotheos, *Persae* 223, ἐλᾷ τε αἴθοπι μώμῳ, and Libanios, *orat.* lxii. 72.

ἀκρατῆ: Moschos, Lydos believes, has no control over his passions. He may, like the Aristotelian ἀκρατήc, know what is right, but he does not do it.

18: 'Now he's gone', i.e. now at last, an unusual sense of ἤδη. Ter. *HT* 978, 'abiit?', *Hec.* 444, 'ille abiit', 510, 'abiit', similar phrases that note an exit, support this interpretation. But τούτου in the next line means Moschos, and οὗτοc could have the same reference: 'he's already gone for good', i.e. it is too late to save him. In favour of this note that φροῦδος is a word not found in Attic prose or New Comedy; it is a favourite of tragedy, and ἐcτὶ φροῦδος is therefore to be seen as an emotional phrase, better suited to Moschos' conduct than to Lydos' departure.

ἐμπλήκτου is a possible supplement, 'he's crazed and she'll hold on to him', but ἔμπληκτοc in Attic usually means 'unstable, impulsive', Plato, *Lysis* 214 c, Soph. *Ajax* 1358, Eur. *Tro.* 1205.

18–30: Agitation makes Sostratos' monologue disjointed. Unless the papyrus should be emended to read καθεξει⟨c⟩cωcτρατον, he speaks of the girl in the third and in the second person in immediately adjacent verbs: 'She'll get him under her thumb! You snapped up Sostratos first!' Here he uses the third person of himself; shortly he will address himself in the second (23); and then turn to the first (25, 29).

19 καθέξει: κατέχειν plus genitive, 'have the mastery of', is not common in the fourth century, and elsewhere the object is a thing or a locality, not a person.

προήρπαcαc: οὐκέτι γὰρ ἁρπαcθήcομαι ὑπὸ cοῦ, says Polemon to Pannychis ṃn Lucian, *Dial. Mer.* ix. 4.

21 ἰταμή: The ἰταμός does not sit still but boldly takes the initiative or the offensive; Sostratos foresees that 'Bacchis', when accused, will fight back and swear her innocence by all the gods.

23 κακὴ κακῶc: Sc. ἀπόλοιτο. Sostratos makes a movement to enter the *hetaira*'s house to tell the girl he has finished with her, but retreats at the thought that she may be too persuasive. Then he thinks he will divest himself of his father's money. She will soon stop using her charms on a man with empty pockets.

24 δουλο[: Perhaps 'I am completely her slave'.

25 ὡc κενόν: 'As a man with empty pockets', cf. 92. Xen. *Cyr.* iii. 2. 25, ἔλαβεν ἀμφοτέρουc ὡc φίλουc.

27 πιθανευομένη: The restoration is confirmed by the recurrence of the word at 93. Previously known only from Artemidoros' dreambook ii. 32, it seems to mean 'making herself persuasive or winning'. For this use of πιθανός cf. Dioskorides *AP* v. 53, ἡ πιθανή μ᾿ ἔτρωcεν Ἀριcτονόη, Asklepiades *AP* v. 158, Ἑρμιόνη πιθανῇ ποτ᾿ ἐγὼ cυνέπαιζον, and *Perik.* 999 n.

29 νεκρῷ λέγουcα μῦθον: A certain restoration from Plautus, *Bacchides* 518, 'quam si ad sepulcrum mortuo narret logos'. The phrase is known from the paroemiographers: Diogenianus vi. 82, νεκρῷ λέγουcα μύθουc εἰc οὖc, cf. id. iii. 34, Makarios vi. 10, cf. also Ter. *Phormio* 1015, 'uerba fiunt mortuo'.

30 ff.: The first of the exchanges between father and son are almost entirely lost. But 'Nicobulus' must have expressed his concern at the failure to bring back his money, and Sostratos at 50 seems to tell him that he has no reason to criticize his guest-friend; all the money has been brought back; there had been no plot. 'Nicobulus' should pay no attention to Syros' story.

48 τὸν τόκον: One may guess that the guest-friend had added interest to the capital deposited with him, cf. 57 n.

49 μηδὲ ἕν . . . ἐγκάλει χρηστῷ ξένῳ: According to the story told by 'Chrysalus', the guest-friend in Ephesos ('Archidemides') to whom 'Nicobulus' had entrusted his money had denied receiving it and, after being forced by a lawsuit to disgorge, had instigated a piratical plot to regain it, *Bacchides* 258–86.

53 ἐκείνῳ λόγῳ: 'The tale told you by Syros.' The absence of the article is strange.

54 παρώρμησε: 'Instigated', sc. the pirates, as 'Archidemides' was alleged to have done after the loss of the lawsuit.

55–6: In Plautus 'Theotimus' is a person invented by 'Chrysalus', who said that 'Mnesilochus' (= Sostratos) had deposited his father's money with him for safety. This is probably the first mention in this scene of the name, since Sostratos' father cannot have repeated the whole story told him by the slave. Hence τί "πρὸς Θεότιμον" ; 'What do you mean by "with Theotimos"?' (cf. *Sam.* 374, τί "καί" ; *Georgos* 28, τί "χαιρέτω" ;) is a more likely supplement than οὐ πρὸς Θεότιμον, 'Not with Theotimos', which would imply agreement that Theotimos existed. αὐτὸς ἐφύλαττεν: 'Your friend looked after the money himself.'

57 διφορεῖ: Literally the word is used of trees that bear two crops in a year, Theophrastos, *CP* i. 14. 1. Here the phrase 'so far as income (means of livelihood) goes he bears twice a year' must mean 'he is a profitable man to invest your money with'. χρηστὸς κτλ.: 'He's a very good chap: he used his brains.' If χρηστόν is right, 'he thought of some very good plan'.

59 ἀκολούθει: Where is the gold? Perhaps deposited somewhere in the town; since Syros had informed Sostratos of the trick he had played, it would have been imprudent to return home with it. The coming interval between the acts will cover a journey to fetch it.

60–3: The anxiety of Sostratos' father to get his money was shown at 52. He still cannot quite believe that he will, and suspiciously asks: 'Are you playing some game with me?' Then, assured that all is well, he says that if he gets the money he'll have no complaints; and he

will not waste time by quarrelling with his son first. It is important
that the old man, who is to be cheated in the sequel, should be unsympathetically portrayed. The act ends with this emphasis on his
love of money, greater it may be suspected than his love of his son.

61 οὐκοῦν ἀκολουθῶ: 'I'm coming with you, then.' He comes because
of the promise in λαβέ, cf. Ar. *Eccl.* 851–3, πρὸς ταῦτα χωρεῖθ' . . . : :
οὐκοῦν [R, οὔκουν Γ] βαδιοῦμαι δῆτα. Handley prefers interrogative
οὔκουν ἀκολουθῶ; 'Aren't I coming, then?'. Denniston, *GP* 436, shows
that in many passages of drama the choice between οὐκοῦν, introducing a statement, and interrogatory οὔκουν is difficult.

At the foot of the column, against the last line of the act, is a numeral
read by Handley as *TΞΔ*, i.e. 364. The problems raised by this figure
are discussed in *Entretiens Hardt* xvi. 223–6. *A priori* the most probable
solutions are that the number is that of the verses either in the two
acts already written or in the immediately preceding second act. But
the former solution implies that *Bacchides* 109–493 correspond to about
130 lines of Menander, probably 150 at the most, which cannot be
enough; even if some elaboration by Plautus is very probable, it
can hardly have been on this scale. If 364 is the number of lines in
Menander's second act, the first 311 will correspond to 384 in
Plautus' version. An act of 364 lines would be about eighty lines longer
than the longest yet known (*Epitr.* Act III), but such an unusual length
seems easier to swallow than the other solution.

ACT III(?)

64–90: Sostratos and his father come on, but the conversation between
them is too mutilated to allow of any but the most speculative reconstruction. At the end the father says that he will go to the market-
place on some business; Sostratos has been given something else to do
(i.e. to reprove his friend Moschos).

91 καὶ μήν introduces a new point, but it is impossible to say whether
it is one that arises in continuation of the father's remarks or in that
of Sostratos' private thoughts. The text that follows is difficult; but
if πᾶν ὅ is right in 94, the next two lines must be a thought that
Sostratos imagines the girl to entertain. The actor would be helped
in his task of conveying this by the fact that the word αὐτίκα is
explicitly said to be her thought; a change of voice there, and again
for 95–6, would make things clear. But the written text (without any
inverted commas) is not so easily intelligible, and it is not surprising
that Plautus made no attempt to translate this speech.

The divided anapaest ὃ κόμιζ- is not unparalleled, cf. *Sam.* 154, 377, ὃ λέγεις, 658, ἃ φλυαρεῖς; to read πάνυ for πᾶν ὅ brings difficulties of interpretation that I cannot solve. **καλήν τε κἀγαθήν:** For a similar use see *Aspis* 311 n.

93 πιθανευομένην: See 27 n.   **προσδοκῶσαν κτλ.:** 'Expecting— "immediately" she says to herself—all the gold I'm bringing'.

95 πάνυ κομίζει: 'He brings this all right', cf. Antiphanes frag. 179 K, σῦκα μὲν νὴ τὸν Δία πάνυ φέρει.   **ἀξιῶς τ' ἐμοῦ:** Handley guessed that the girl was called *Chrysis* and that the phrase alludes to this, *Menander and Plautus*, p. 21. This seems too subtle a point for the theatre. All she means is that she gets the high price that she is worth.

97: Handley prints αὐτή (i.e. ἡ αὐτή), but αὕτη seems at least as good.   **καλῶς ποοῦσά γε:** 'Good work by her!' cf. *Aspis* 394, *Dysk.* 629, *Perik.* 989, ? *Epitr.* 427, Ar. *Plut.* 863.   **ἱκανῶς** is probably to be taken with εὑρέθη: 'She has been found clearly enough to be what I once thought her.'

99: ἐλεῶ is possible; Sostratos may simultaneously be sorry for his friend and angry at his disloyalty.

100: Sostratos' readiness to blame the girl rather than his friend is reminiscent of Demeas' readiness in *Samia* to blame Chrysis rather than Moschion (328 ff.).

102: Moschos' words may, as Handley suggests, be spoken over his shoulder to the girl in the house, as he comes out. But the similar passage, *Samia* 690, εἶτα ποῦ 'στιν, εἰπέ μοι, suggests rather that he is expressing his surprise to the world at large. εἶτα introducing a question may mark surprise, indignation, sarcasm, etc.; see LSJ s.v. II, *Dysk.* 153, *Sam.* 502, *Epitr.* 468, 1100, *Perik.* 712.

104 καὶ σύ: This is curt, cf. *Georgos* 84, like ναί in 106.

105 ὑπόδακρυ: The word was previously known only as a gloss in Hesychios on γλαμυρός, 'bleary'; but ὑποδακρύειν, 'weep a little', is in Lucian, *Dial. Deor.* vi. 2.

107: Restoration is uncertain. Handley suggested εἶτ' οὐ παράγεις; (too long, but he supposed the omission of a letter), 'Aren't you coming in then?' That fits well with what follows: 'No, the trouble is under that roof, to be sure.' But it is less appropriate as a sequel to Sostratos' admission that he has had some bad news. Accordingly I prefer εἶτ' οὐ λέγεις; 'Then aren't you going to tell me what it is?' (cf. *Sik.* 146), to which Sostratos replies, attaching his words to his previous ναί, 'Yes, and it's under that roof, of course.'   **ἀμέλει:** Cf. *Sam.* 223, 371.

112 οὐκ ἠξίουν γοῦν: 'I didn't *expect* it myself either', cf. *Sam.* 708.

Fragment 1. The young man is presumably Moschos.

Fragment 2. Both βουληφόρως and ὅραϲιν are recherché words. The adverb is quoted from no other place, and the adjective βουληφόροϲ is mainly epic, applied to princes and leaders. ὅραϲιϲ, properly the 'act of seeing', is Aristotelian, but the word seems to have been taken up in later times as a substitute for the more banal ὄψιϲ (see LSJ). The speaker here doubtless has his tongue in his cheek, and will be a slave. The supplement ὤ is uncertain; many other monosyllables are possible, including δή. If ὤ is right, it is a not very usual addition to the vocative, and in keeping with the rest of the language.

Webster, *StM* 86, somewhat hazardously suggests that the fragment is the original of Ter. *Ad.* 385 ff., and that Fulgentius falsely assigned it to *Dis Exapaton.*

Fragment 3. παράϲτα for παράϲτηθι recurs at *Theophorumene* 28.

Fragment 4. Plautus, *Bacchides* 816, shows that this line was used by the slave Syros to provoke his elderly master. It is a more epigrammatic statement of the sentiment expressed by Silenos in Aristotle's popular *Eudemus* (frag. 6 Ross, 44 Rose³,) ἄριϲτον γὰρ πᾶϲι καὶ πάϲαιϲ τὸ μὴ γενέϲθαι, τὸ μέντοι μετὰ τοῦτο καὶ τὸ πρῶτον τῶν ἀνθρώποιϲ ἀνυϲτῶν τὸ γενομένουϲ ἀποθανεῖν ὡϲ τάχιϲτα.

DYSKOLOS

B   *P. Bodmer* 4, see introduction, p. 47.
Editio princeps: V. Martin, *Ménandre: Le Dyscolos* (1959) (1958 on title-page), with complete photographs.

H 1 *Memb. Hermupolitana*, Bodleian Library, Oxford, (MSS. graec. class. g 50 (P)), cent. A.D. iii. Parts of 140–50, 169–74.
Editio princeps: B. Grenfell–A. Hunt, *Mélanges Nicole* (1905), p. 220.

O 8 *P. Oxy.* 2467, cent. A.D. iii. Fragments of 263–72, 283–90.
Editio princeps: E. G. Turner, *Oxyrhynchus Papyri* xxvii (1962).

B 5 *P. Berol.* 21199, cent. A.D. vi–vii. Beginnings of 452–7, ends of 484–9.
Editio princeps: H. Maehler, *ZPE* iv (1969), 113.

The most important edition is that by E. W. Handley, *The Dyskolos of Menander* (1965), with extensive introduction and commentary. Other editions are numerous, the most profitable being:

H. Lloyd-Jones, (Oxford Classical Text, 1960), text only, with index verborum.

W. Kraus, *Menanders Dyskolos* (1960), with useful notes on the text.

J. Martin, *Ménandre: L'Atrabiliaire* (1961), with appreciative commentary.

J.-M. Jacques, in the Budé series (1963), with good introduction.

I have also profited in varying degrees from those of M. Treu (1960), H. J. Mette (1960, 2nd edn. 1961), J. Bingen (1960, 2nd edn. 1964), C. Diano (1960), C. Gallavotti (1959, 2nd edn. 1959), O. Foss (1960), B. A. van Groningen, (Verhand. d. Kon. Nederlandse Akad. v. Wetenschappen, Afd. Letterkunde, lxvii. 3, 1960), F. Stoessl (*Kommentar zu Menanders Dyskolos*, 1965), W. E. Blake (1966).

There are a great number of articles and dissertations. A clear bibliography is given by C. Corbato in two numbers of *Dioniso*, xxxvii and xxxviii (1963, 1964). Of later works mention is due in particular to A. Schäfer, *Menanders Dyskolos* (Beiträge z. Klass. Philologie 14, 1965).

A Rhodian amphora of the second century B.C., described by L. Kahil, *Antike Kunst*, Beiheft 6 (1970), 101, is inscribed ΔΥCΚΟΛΟΥ and on the other side ΜΕ ᚺ. Mme Kahil suggests, with some hesitation, that the pot was used in the third act of some stage production.

She admits that the inscription may be only some joke. There is no other evidence for revivals of *Dyskolos*, unless the *Dyscolus* ascribed to Plautus was a translation. Nevertheless the play clearly remained in circulation among readers until a late date. It was known to Alkiphron (? late second cent.), Aelian (early third cent.), Libanios (fourth cent.), and Aristainetos (fifth cent.), and its title at least to someone who in the third or fourth century A.D. made a list of fifteen plays by Menander (*P. Brit. Mus.* 2562) and to Agathias (*AP* v. 218) in the later sixth century. Finally the Berlin fragment (B 5) seems to be at present the latest Menandrean MS. that is known.

Hypothesis

The hypothesis to *Heros* is, like this, twelve lines in length, but claims no author. The metrical hypotheses to Aristophanes' plays, each ten lines in length, are in some MSS. ascribed to 'Aristophanes the grammarian', i.e. the famous Alexandrian scholar from Byzantium (*c.* 257–180 B.C.). This is patently false, and there is no good reason to suppose them to be versified summaries of hypotheses written by him in prose. But, as an editor of Aristophanes and a warm admirer of Menander, he was a suitable person on whom to father these concoctions. See Wilamowitz, *Einleitung in d. gr. Tragödie*, p. 145 and T. O. H. Achelis, *Philologus*, lxxii (1913), 439, lxxiii (1914–16), 122, and a bibliography in Handley's edition, p. 122, to which now add R. Pfeiffer, *History of Classical Scholarship*, pp. 190–4.

1 μέν, ἦν: This correction of μόνην is so easy (cf. 409, 679) that we need not saddle the author with the view that Knemon had contracted an earlier marriage, or with a recondite phrase for 'motherless'.

2 ἔγημεν should not be maintained here. The author is unlikely wilfully to have indulged in a broken anapaest, which could have been avoided by elision, and this papyrus often adds a nu ephelkustikon against the metre, e.g. 377. But ἔγημ' ἔν' ἔχουcαν υἱόν is possibly what was intended. There are, however, no marks of elision, which this papyrus usually indicates.   τάχος is a line-filler: the prologue does not say whether his wife left Knemon soon or late.

3: To scan ἀγρῶν with first syllable long is contrary to comic practice, but the hypothesis to Ar. *Knights* has the even more remarkable τινὰ Κλέωνα.

4: Comedy, and Attic writers in general, preferred cφόδρα to cφοδρῶc, but the preference need not be foisted on the author of the hypothesis by writing cφόδρ' ὡc. cφοδρῶc ἐρῶν is good later Greek, e.g. Athenaios 594 c.

5 ἀντέπιφθ': 'Resisted'; ἀντιπίπτω in the sense 'oppose' more frequently has a non-personal subject, but personal subjects occur,
e.g. Polybios in *Suda* s.v. ἀλογιςτία, *Acta Apost.* 7. 51 τῷ πνεύματι τῷ
ἁγίῳ ἀντιπίπτετε. The writer of the hypothesis is inaccurate here,
since Sostratos never succeeded in asking Knemon for his daughter's
hand.

6 ἔπιθεν: This is the simplest change for the unmetrical ἔπειθεν, but
one cannot parallel such a poetic form in the extant comic hypotheses.
τὸν ἀδελφὸν οὖν ἔπειθεν would be more in accord with their style. Ar.
Plut. 949, however, has πιθών in a comic trimeter.

7 οὐκ εἶχ' ὅ τι λέγοι ἐκεῖνος: Sc. the brother. The original reading
ποεῖ is not grammatical. The v.l. λέγοι may have some authority;
otherwise one can write ποῇ (D. Mayer ap. Treu), deliberative subjunctive vividly retained for the optative although in past sequence,
or perhaps ποοῖ (cf. Ar. *Knights* 1131).

8–12: The true action of the play is here replaced by a banal conventional ending: Sostratos wins his bride by rescuing her surly father,
who is thus reformed in character, makes it up with his wife, and
arranges marriages for his daughter and his son. All this is avoided
by Menander.

10: The imperfect ἐδίδου, for the expected aorist or present, will be
metri gratia. The corrupt ἐρῶν cannot be corrected with certainty.
ἑκών is not improbable, although it would misrepresent the play; cf.
θέλων, *Heros*, prol. 12.

Didascalia

This may be derived from Aristophanes of Byzantium, who composed
similar historical notices on tragedies. It is the only example as yet
known attached to the *text* of a play by Menander, but such a notice
of the *Imbrians* is prefixed to the summary of that drama, *P. Oxy.* 1235
(OCT p. 306). We may suppose all except the last sentence to be
based on the official inscriptions at Athens, the remains of which are
printed by Pickard-Cambridge, *Dramatic Festivals of Athens*², pp. 101 ff.
R. Pfeiffer, *History of Classical Scholarship*, pp. 191–2, inclines to the view
that Aristophanes published a text of Menander and that 'even the
description of the plot may be in substance his work'. His view
deserves respect, but it will be prudent to withhold assent, so long as
the evidence remains as slender as it is today.

Δημογένους: The emendation (for διδυμογενης) is all but certain
(R. K. Sherk, *Arethusa* i [1968] 103). Demogenes' archonship is dated
317/16. But the Marmor Parium (*F. Gr. Hist.* II B 239 B 14, cf.

II D p. 735) states that Menander won his first victory in the archonship of Demokleides (316/15). The difference is plausibly resolved by
supposing this to mean his first victory at the Great Dionysia, to which
Jacoby believes the Marmor Parium always refers when recording
first victories. For other less likely explanations see M. Gigante,
Parola del Passato lxvi (1959), 211, and for some uninhibited specula-
tions F. della Corte, *Maia* N.s. ii (1960), 83, D. Marzullo, *Atti dei
Lincei, Rendiconti* xv (1960), 62, C. Gallavotti, *Riv. Fil.* xxxviii (1960), 1.
R. Cantarella, *Menandrea*, 55, suggests that καὶ ἐνίκα should be placed
after Cκαφεύc, to make the actor Aristodemos the subject; prizes
for comic actors were introduced somewhere between 329 and 312
(B. Snell, *Nach. d. Akad. Wiss. Göttingen* [1966], 29).

Ἀριστόδημος Cκαφεύc: Aristodemos is otherwise unknown; he will
have taken the part of Knemon, and perhaps others (see intro. p. 16).
Aristodemos of Metaponton, a tragic actor, was a generation earlier.
Ed. pr. emended cκαφευc to Cκαρφεύc: Skarphe or Skarpheia was an
important town in Lokris, about 7 m. E. of Thermopylae. S. N.
Koumanoudis, however, *Rev. Phil.* xxxv (1961), 99, defends Cκαφεύc
as the ethnic of Cκάφαι, a small place in Boeotia, whose inhabitants
moved into Thebes at the beginning of the Archidamian war. *Hell. Oxy.*
xvi, xvii (*F. Gr. Hist.* II A pp. 26–7) describe them as cυντελούντων
εἰc τὰc Θήβαc, 'counting as part of Thebes'. Although the name may
have continued to be used at Thebes, it would at first sight be surprising if it were also employed abroad, as if, for example, an Athenian
at Thebes were described as an Acharnian. Koumanoudis, however,
points to some funerary inscriptions of the mid fourth century from
Eleusis, where seven women, who are associated with Thebans, are
described as Cκαφλικαί (*Polemon* v [1955], 150). Strabo ix. 2. 24 mentions a place Cκάφλαι (emended in our editions to Cκάρφη, to agree
with Steph. Byz. s.v. Ἐτεωνόc and Eustathios on *Il.* ii. 497) near
Thebes. Koumanoudis argues that Cκάφλαι and Cκάφαι are identical,
and that it must be supposed that Eleusis harboured a colony of
refugees from Cκάφλαι–Cκάφαι, who had not accepted the merger with
Thebes and who retained their ethnic name, Cκαφλικοί or Cκαφεῖc.
All this makes it impossible to say confidently that the papyrus is
wrong here. Nevertheless Skarphe, with its much larger population,
is *a priori* more likely to have supplied a leading comic actor than the
hypothetical refugee colony, and the papyrus is unreliable for spelling.
Another famous comic actor came from Skarphe—Lykon, who was
playing in the 320s (Plut. *Alex.* 29, Athen. 538 f.); Aristodemos may
have been a compatriot.

Μιcάνθρωπος: Other plays by Menander with alternative titles were

Ἀνδρογύνος (Κρής), Ἀρρηφόρος (Αὐλητρίς or Αὐλητρίδες), Ἀχαιοί (Πελοποννήcιοι), Μιcούμενος (Θραcωνίδης), Ὑποβολιμαῖος (Ἄγροικος), Cαμία (Κηδία), and perhaps Ἀνατιθεμένη (Μεccηνία). In one instance of alternative titles, Antiphanes' Ἄγροικοι or Βουταλίων, Athenaios reports (358 d) that the second was given to a revised version, and he says that Diphilos' Εὐνοῦχος or Cτρατιώτης was a revision of his Αἱρηcιτείχης (496 f.) : but it would be unsafe to generalize that all alternative titles imply a revision. One could imagine a reader finding a name for a copy of a play that had no title: the play that follows *Dyskolos* in the Bodmer papyrus had none at its head; or a bookseller might hope to mislead purchasers with a novel title.

List of characters
The list gives the characters in the order in which they appear in the play. Originally descriptions were attached to four only, viz. Πάν θεός, παρθένος θυγατὴρ Κνήμων(ος), Cίκων μάγειρος, Cιμίκη γραῦς. The same writer then added ὁ παράcιτος and all the other descriptions, crossing out θεός and replacing it by ὁ θεός. He also placed a β before the name of Sostratos, an α before that of Pyrrhias, a false correction of order. J. Martin suggests that he had come across a new MS., with a list of characters in which Sostratos and Pyrrhias had been accidentally interchanged, and that he rashly 'corrected' his previous list; from the same MS. he may have taken the descriptions ὁ παράcιτος etc. and possibly some of the corrections made in the text of the play. All this may be true; one cannot tell.

The list does not include named *mutae personae*—Myrrhine (Gorgias' mother), Plangon (Sostratos' sister), Donax, Parthenis (slaves). Nor does it include one who has an unrecognized speaking part—Sostratos' mother (see 430 n.). The papyrus assigns her lines to Getas. Her absence from the list of characters is no support for that. There is no reason to suppose the list to have any authority, any more than those prefixed in MSS. to tragedies and the plays of Aristophanes. J. Andrieu, *Le Dialogue antique*, p. 94, has shown that these were drawn up from a study of the text, and not always intelligently; for example, Hermes is made a character in the *Clouds*, as if he in person, not his statue, were addressed at 1478. All the evidence points to the plays' having been handed down for generations without any identification of the speakers (see p. 40). The first step will have been to identify them in the margins of the text; the lists of characters will then have been drawn up on the basis of those identifications. The attempt of F. Stoessl to argue that certain lists, including that of *Dyskolos*, go back to the dramatist himself (*Philologus*, c [1956], 207 ff., *Personenwechsel in Menanders Dyskolos*, SB. Öst. Ak. Wiss. 234, 5) does not convince me.

As is usual in Menander some of the names recur in other plays and indicate something about the person. This applies to the three names that show their possessors to be slaves: *Daos*, *Getas* (both ethnic names, see *Heros*, p. 387), and *Pyrrhias* (also in *Perinthia* and *Sikyonios* and in the Latinized form *Byrrhia* in Ter. *Andria*), perhaps a name given to red-heads from the north.

Sikon is the name of a cook also in Sosipatros frag. 1 K, and Aristophanes' posthumous play Αἰολοςίκων represented Aiolos as a cook. It is derived from Ϲικελόϲ, the name of the barbarian natives of Sicily, and is found as a slave name, e.g. Ar. *Eccl.* 867, Alexis (?), *Asotodidaskalos* 4, but also as that of a free man, perhaps a freedman, in an inscription, Kirchner, *Prosop. Att.* 12650. Nothing in this play determines Sikon's status, whether free or slave: that he is paid proves nothing, for he might be a slave working on his own account but paying a fixed sum to his owner, like Syriskos in *Epitr.* (380). Those who will may believe Athenaios' statement (658 e) that no cooks in New Comedy, except in Poseidippos, were slaves. The cook Cylindrus in Plaut. *Menaechm.* is certainly a slave, but he may have been made one by Plautus. On this subject see A. Giannini, *Acme* xiii (1960), 159 (n. 220) and 186.

Chaireas is described as a παράϲιτοϲ. It is not true that all other bearers of the name have this character. The Chaireas of *Fab. incert.* plays a principal part in an intrigue which appears to approach blackmail, and might, although I do not believe it, conceivably be a 'parasite' of the type of Phormio in Terence's play. But the Chaireas of *Aspis*, although he too lends himself to a deception, is a sympathetic young man of good character. Chaireas of *P. Oxy.* 2533 seems to be a young lover who marries his love, as is true of Terence's Chaerea in *Eunuchus*. The Chaireas of *Koneiaz.* is nothing but a name, and the status of Chaireas in Alexis frag. 21 is not determinable. The Chaireas of this play does not have the traits usually associated with the parasite, toadyism, sponging, and greed. But he shows himself not to be a true friend to Sostratos, and was therefore classed as a 'parasite', that being the only category available in the conventional repertoire of comic types.

In fact, although he shows no signs of self-seeking and is far from being a flatterer, there are aspects of his behaviour that recall the more conventional parasite. First, there is the way in which he boasts, without its being quite necessary, of his abilities and technique (58–68). Then this technique is one of helping his 'friends' to obtain women, whether wives or lights-of-love. When Mercury in Plaut. *Amphitruo* helps Juppiter in his *amours*, he describes his actions by the word *subparasitor* (515, 993; D. Guilbert, *Ét. class.* xxxi [1963], 55).

Menander thus gave Chaireas traits that his audience could recognize as belonging to the traditional parasite, although they are not the most characteristic. These traits suggest that he is not a true friend, but one who cultivates Sostratos with some idea of advantage to be gained. It is possible that he was also given a mask that would indicate his connection with the parasite-type.

Sostratos is a name plausibly restored in a fragment of an anonymous comedy, *Pap. Hibeh* 6, frag. f, but nothing shows the character's status. The lover Mnesilochus of Plaut. *Bacchides* was called Sostratos in the original, Δὶς Ἐξαπατῶν.

Gorgias is a poor boy who works on the land in *Heros* and *Georgos* also. In view of Greek methods of etymology, which looked to find in the name of a thing suggestions of its nature—thus ἐρᾶν and ὁρᾶν were connected, for love feeds upon or arises from the sight of the beloved—one may guess that Gorgias was associated with γεωργός. More scientifically the name should be connected with the adj. γοργός, 'active, strenuous'. T. Williams, *Mnem.* 4th ser. xviii (1965), 269, advances a bold theory that Gorgias was a by-form of Gorgason, the name of a healing divinity, and finds a surviving influence of this in the parts played by each of the three owners of the name.

Kallippides is a name with an aristocratic ring—it was one of those suggested by Strepsiades' well-born wife for their son (*Clouds* 64)—but not a rarity; at least five historical Athenians bore it, *Pros. Att.* 8049–53.

Simiche is a diminutive of cιμός, 'snub-nosed'. The name belongs to a free woman from Mykonos in a Delian inscription of 280 B.C. (*IG* xii. 2. 161 B 23). A slave so called occurs in Aelian, *VH* xii. 43, and in fiction in Lucian, *Dial. Mer.* 4, *Cataplus* 22, Alkiphron, *ep.* iv. 13. 11. (In the last three places the MSS. spell Cιμμίχη, but in Attic we have Cιμίας not Cιμμίας, and so should have Cιμίχη, as in the best MS. (A) of Photios s.v., see *Epitr.* 630 n.) Both in the text (636, 926, 931) and in the margin the papyrus consistently spells Cιμικη. Maas's ingenious suggestion that, being a barbarian, Simiche was unable, like the Scythian policeman in Ar. *Thesmophoriazusae*, to pronounce an aspirate, and that Knemon had imitated her own mispronunciation of her name, need not be taken seriously; after all, her first words are ὦ δυcτυχήc, ὦ δυcτυχήc, ὦ δυcτυχήc, not ὦ δυcτυκήc κτλ. The repeated error of the papyrus, for error it must be, is, however, remarkable. Although confusion of χ and κ is met with in papyri (Mayser, *Gramm. gr. Pap.* I. i. 171) it is not frequent, for the sounds of the two letters diverged in later Greek. The two other instances in this play can be explained, δεδιωκ' (118) as due to the influence of ἐδίωκε, and τοιχωρυκοι (447) as due to dissimilation of the aspirates, although this usually operates in the other direction, as in ἐτύθην for ἐθύθην. The corruption of Cιμιχη to Cιμικη may have been facilitated by the fact that diminutives in -ίχος, although common in Attic and Doric, are rare in other dialects and in the κοινή (K. Latte, *De saltationibus*, p. 105). A copyist might be tempted to see the more familiar termination -ικός; χ and κ can look somewhat similar. See Addenda.

Turning to the *personae mutae*, *Myrrhine* is the name of married women in *Perik.*, *Heros*, *Georg.*, cf. Plaut. *Casina*, Ter. *Hecyra*; *Plangon* of a citizen girl in *Dysk.* (see n. on. p. 203), *Heros*, *Sam.*; *Donax* of a slave in *Sikyonios* and Ter. *Eunuchus*. *Parthenis* is not paralleled in drama.

Finally *Knemon* himself has a name that is unique, hitherto unparalleled from real life, but used by Lucian for a character in *Dial. Mort.* 8 and by Heliodoros for a young Athenian in his romance. It has no obvious connection with the character of the misanthrope, and is of the nickname type, applicable to one who has remarkable lower legs. The name *may* have carried some suggestion to the audience; for example, [Arist.] *Physiognomica* 810ᵃ28 makes a well-developed κνήμη a sign of strength of character (εὔρωστοι τὴν ψυχήν). Stoessl would derive the name from the Homeric κνημός, 'shoulder of a mountain', in view of Knemon's hill-farm.

(i) 1–49: *Prologue by Pan*

These lines are well treated by A. Schäfer, *Menanders Dyskolos*, pp. 31–4; see also W. Ludwig, *Entretiens Hardt* xvi. 84–91.

In some plays a prologue spoken by a divinity was a necessity. The Greek playwright liked his audience to be in possession of the essential facts of the situation from the outset. They were then in a better position to understand and to savour the events on the stage. If some of these facts were not known to any of the characters, a divine prologue was the only way of conveying them to the spectators. In *Dyskolos* there is only one such unknown fact, and the divine prologue is mainly a convenient way of informing the public where the play is supposed to take place, who the principal characters are, and how they are already connected. It serves as a substitute for a programme or playbill, and avoids the difficulty of smuggling into the dialogue facts needed more for the audience's sake than for that of the characters. There is the further dramatic advantage that Knemon's behaviour as recounted and then displayed in the first scene is intelligible, as of a piece with the longstanding quarrelsome misanthropy of which the prologue tells; the audience will be in no danger of putting it down to insanity, as does Pyrrhias, or to a temporary provocation, such as Chaireas suggests.

The fact, known by no one, which only a prologue can reveal, is that Sostratos fell in love at sight because he was inspired to it by Pan. This gives a particular flavour, which might be called comic irony, to the passages where the unwitting Sostratos invokes that god (311, 572) and to that where he takes to himself all the credit for his success (862–5). Moreover the dream sent by Pan to Sostratos' mother (407 ff.), vital in its effects to the course of the action, is explained by the god's interest in bringing about the girl's marriage; it is not the gratuitous coincidence it would otherwise appear to be.

When, after speaking the prologue, Pan retires into his cave, he is not seen again, but he is not forgotten. Besides the passages just mentioned, there is the presence of his worshippers, the Πανισταί who form the chorus; he is saluted by Sikon at 401, and during the whole latter part of the play there is coming and going from his shrine, which is the scene of the concluding revels (as is emphasized at 876)— appropriately so, since he was a god of rustic jollity. The Homeric hymn calls him πολύκροτον ἡδυγέλωτα, and he is addressed by the chorus of Sophocles' *Ajax* as θεῶν χοροποί᾽ ἄναξ (698, cf. Photiadis, *Greece & Rome*, 2nd ser. v [1958], 112). This continuing presence of Pan may even have had its visual expression in the shape of his statue on the stage. It is implied by 51 that statues of the Nymphs stood outside the cave, and Sostratos' words at 572, ἀλλὰ μὴν προσεύχομαι ἀεὶ παριών cοι, will be more effective if addressed to a visible statue than to the unseen power within the cave. One may compare Eur. *Hipp.* 116, προσευξόμεσθα τοῖσι σοῖς ἀγάλμασιν, δέσποινα Κύπρι, where the actual presence of a statue is confirmed by 101, τήνδ᾽, ἣ πύλαισι σαῖς ἐφέστηκεν Κύπρις. On the frequent use of statues as stage furniture see P. D. Arnott, *Greek Scenic Conventions*, pp. 65 ff.

There are reminders of the Nymphs, too, with whom he lives. Knemon's daughter garlands them (51) and fetches water from them (197), Knemon himself repines at their neighbourhood, which brings unwelcome visitors (444), Getas sees their intervention when Knemon falls into the well (643), and Sikon tells how, at the party, their water was mixed with the wine (947). All these touches are designed to give the impression that Pan and the Nymphs did not merely initiate the action, but continued to participate in the events. The human drama is graced by the presence of divine personages. It is thus removed a little from the realm of mundane every-day probabilities, and realism is coloured by romance.

Pan, a god of wild uncultivated places, worshipped by shepherds and huntsmen, was often associated with the Nymphs who, as spirits of water and trees, provided shade and refreshment for the flocks. Both frequently had shrines in caves, e.g. the Nymphs, *Od.* xiii. 103;

DYSKOLOS

Pan on the Akropolis at Athens, Eur. *Ion* 492; both together on Parnassos and Kithairon, at Lebadeia (Farnell, *Cults*, v. 431 ff., 464 ff.), and in Attica at Oinoe (*JHS*, Arch. Reports for 1957, p. 6, for 1958, p. 4). Two dedicatory reliefs from a cave on Pentelikon show Hermes, Pan, Nymphs, and worshippers; on one of these the cave itself is represented (U. Hausmann, *Griechische Weihreliefs*, pp. 60–1). Since in this play Pan causes Sostratos to fall in love, it is interesting that a fourth-century bell-krater shows Pan seated in a cave along with the Nymphs and Eros (Beazley, *Attic Red-Figure Vase-Painters*[2], p. 1452).

The shrine at Phyle, a deme on the Boeotian frontier, high on Mt. Parnes, is mentioned by Harpokration, s.v. *Φυλή*, and Aelian, *Ep. rust.* 15 (who may know it only from reading this play). There is no reason for refusing to identify Menander's shrine with a small and inaccessible cave at some distance from the village, where dedications to Pan and the Nymphs have been found (W. Wrede, *Ath. Mitteilungen* xlix [1924], 155, F. Brommer, *RE* suppl. viii. 993–4; it is illustrated in Bingen's second edition). For the purposes of his play Menander represents it as capacious and close to Knemon's house. Such few of the audience as might have visited it would not be offended by the departure from geographical realism.

1 τῆc Ἀττικῆc: The prominent position of these words is noteworthy. J. Martin suggests as a reason that the play is about typically Attic countryfolk, cf. 604. Even were this to be admitted, their Atticness is little emphasized. Perhaps plays laid in foreign parts (like *Perik.*) were common enough for it to be reasonable to announce in the first words that Attica is the scene of this play.

Possibly there is a topical point. Cassander had placed a Macedonian garrison in the fort of Phyle, which did not revert to the Athenians until 307 B.C. (Plutarch, *Demetrius*, c. 27). It seems unlikely to me, however, that Menander wished to remind his audience that Phyle was, in spite of harbouring a foreign prince, really Athenian soil.

νομίζετε: The speaker of a Euripidean prologue often immediately informs the audience who he is and where he is, e.g. *Bacch.* 1, *ἥκω Διὸc παῖc τήνδε Θηβαίων χθόνα | Διόνυcοc*. Although Euripides shows much ingenuity in disguising the conflict with naturalism that is involved, the practice cannot avoid some air of artificiality. Menander here openly accepts the reality that what the audience sees at the beginning of the play is the permanent background and an actor X, to be changed by imagination into the required scene and dramatic personage. Pan here in his opening words is still half the actor, and becomes fully Pan only after he has converted the background to Phyle and the cave of the Nymphs.

3 καὶ τῶν δυναμένων: 'Those who can farm the rocks' are not additional to, but identical with, the men of Phyle; cf. *Georg.* 56 n., Eur. *Bacch.* 919, δίccαc δὲ Θήβαc καὶ πόλιcμ' ἑπτάcτομον. πέτραc γεωργεῖν: Lucian, *Phalaris* 2, and, if Kock's frag. adesp. 380 is a fantasy, Theophylaktos Simokates, *Epist.* 5, may have taken the phrase from here, but it may also have been one in common use, cf. πέτραc cκάπτοντα in the anecdote from Aristotle quoted on 605. Of the territory of Phyle today C. T. Murphy writes: 'The country is mountainous but well-watered, and there are green fields interspersed among the bare and rocky slopes' (*CJ* lix [1964], 316).

5 τὸν ἀγρὸν τὸν ἐπὶ δεξιά: 'The farm on my right'. By the normal convention of the Attic stage that side which was on the audience's right was the 'town' side, the other the 'country' side. Since Gorgias lives nearer to Cholargos and therefore to Athens than Knemon does (32–3), his house will be on the right and Knemon's to the left. Hence the latter lies on the right of Pan when he emerges from the central cave to deliver the prologue, and this suits the rule that actors, when speaking of left and right, mean their own left and right (Haigh, *Attic Theatre*, p. 194).

Two unorthodox views, which require ἐπὶ δεξιά here to mean 'on the audience's right', deserve consideration. After all, a rule may have exceptions, and in performance a gesture would make all plain. J. H. Quincey, *Notes on the Dyskolos*, p. 3, observes that at 909 Getas, helping to carry Knemon out of his house, gives the order ἐπὶ δεξιάν, 'right turn'. If Knemon's house were on the audience's left, an actor's right turn would carry him towards the side of the stage, and Quincey maintains that the final scene must have been acted in the centre, not at the side, of the stage. Even if we allow that in 909 δεξιός can indicate actor's right, but audience's right in 5, the assumption about the final scene is an uncertain one. It is quite intelligible that Getas and Sikon should set Knemon down on that side of his door which was furthest from the shrine, since they do not wish their goings-on to attract the notice of those in it. Moreover it may be noticed that when at the end of the play Knemon is carried in triumph into the shrine, it will be scenically more effective if there is some distance to be covered. (Alternatively, as Handley observes, if Knemon must be brought to the centre of the stage, εἰc δεξιάν might be spoken by or to an actor facing the stage-building.) The other unorthodox view is that of G. Rambelli, *Menandrea*, 35, who proposes an asymmetrical arrangement with Knemon's house in the middle and the cave on the audience's left. His reason is that Knemon's fields must lie on the 'country' side, and we hear that 'necessity' causes him to pass by Pan's shrine (11–12) and salute the god. But to this it may be replied that when Knemon returns from his fields (153 ff.) he does *not* greet Pan. Presumably, however solitary he may have been, there were occasions when he had to go to the village and would thus pass the cave if it occupied the central position. It must, however, be admitted that to place Knemon's house centrally brings advantages for the action in the first act. When Pyrrhias enters in wild flight (81) he finds Sostratos and Chaireas near Knemon's door (87, 99), from which he fails to drag them. The flight could be more effective if it covered half the stage before being arrested. Then when Knemon is seen approaching, Sostratos retires a short way from his door (148) and is not noticed by Knemon, although still 'by' his door (167), for a long time after his entry from the left. This would be easier if Knemon's house were not itself on the left. At the beginning of Act III, if Knemon's house is central, the procession of worshippers must pass him as he stands in his doorway. Some may think this objectionable; I do not. But I do not believe that any arguments based on the way that we might like to stage the play are strong enough to make us disregard the normal usage of ἐπὶ δεξιά, which requires that the cave should be in the centre.

6 ἀπάνθρωπος: In Aesch. *PV* 20, τῷδ᾽ ἀπανθρώπῳ πάγῳ, the word means 'remote from men'. Knemon lives as far from the village as he can; but more importantly he is spiritually remote from his fellow men, unsocial. The word carries, however, a further connotation of 'inhumanity'. This sense is common in later Greek, e.g. in Plutarch, and was already established, as can be seen from *Mis.* 187, ὠμότητος ... ἀπανθρώπου. Hesychios s.v. has cκληρός, ἀνόητος, ἄφρων, ἀνελεήμων. Cοφοκλῆς. Pearson (frag. 1020) claims that this vindicates the sense 'inhuman' for the fifth century, but we cannot be certain, lacking Sophocles' text, that Hesychios interpreted it rightly.

7 οὐ χαίρων τε: Cf. *Sam.* 560, οὐ προήcεcθαί τε, and *Perik.* 128 n.

8 ἐπιεικῶς χρόνον πολύν: 'A pretty long time', like ἐπιεικῶς μάχαιc | πολλαῖc, *Aspis* 24, 'a pretty good number of battles', cf. *Epitr.* 423 n.; hyperbaton, however mild, is noteworthy in Menander's style; here it emphasizes the separated words ἐπιεικῶc ... πολύν. Later Knemon is called a γέρων, which suggests a man of over sixty.

10 οὐδενί: The change from οὐδέν is logical; this sentence corrects the phrase οὐ χαίρων ὄχλῳ, which is retracted as an understatement: 'Why, he has never chatted willingly to *anybody*, and never opened a conversation with anyone.' It is true that a god need not employ perfect logic; to say 'he has never chatted willingly *at all*' implies 'to anybody', and this would be made explicit by οὐδένα in οὐ προσηγόρευκε πρότερος δ᾽ οὐδένα. But to speak so would obscure the point, and clarity is to be expected from a prologue-speaker.   ἡδέως means 'with pleasure to himself' rather than 'to others', cf. 270, 658, and, e.g., Dem. xviii. 64, ἡδέως ἂν ἐροίμην, 'I'd be glad to ask'. In Theophrastos, *Char.* 24. 6, it is a mark of the arrogant man (ὑπερήφανος) προσελθεῖν πρότερος οὐδενί.

11 ἐμὲ τὸν Πᾶνα: Object of προσηγόρευκε rather than of παριών; of necessity Knemon speaks to Pan, because as a neighbour he has to pass his shrine. Although the emphasis lies on the grudgingness of the salutation, the phrase shows that Knemon is not entirely dead to religious feeling. See further on 433.

12 τοῦτ᾽ αὐτῷ μεταμέλει: μεταμέλει is usually impersonal, with no subject, but cf. Ar. *Clouds* 1114, οἶμαι δέ σοι ταῦτα μεταμελήσειν.

13 τῷ τρόπῳ τοιοῦτος: Knemon's marriage, essential to the plot, may seem out of character. Menander boldly anticipates that criticism by making the point himself. οὖν is resumptive, 8–12 being an elaboration not strictly necessary to the story.

13–20: It is interesting to see how Menander used some of these motifs to an entirely different purpose in another play, Ter. *Adelphoe* 866, 'ego ille agrestis saeuos tristis parcus truculentus tenax duxi uxorem: quam ibi miseriam uidi! nati filii, alia cura.'

16: Since παῖδας καταλείπομαι (middle) is a Greek usage (e.g. Plato, *Symp.* 209 d), the alteration to υὸν . . . καταλελειμμένου μικρόν proposed by Foss may be right; it has the advantage of giving the same subject to the two perfect participles. Yet the reading of the papyrus, although in such a matter it has little authority, is not impossible. τότε for ποτε is, however, a necessary change; since all sons were 'once small', the fact would not be worth remark.

18: Cf. frag. 60, νύκτα γὰρ προσλαμβάνει (of a talkative woman). This supports the excision of τῆς rather than of τό, a course also recommended by the sharper point of 'the greater part of the night' as compared with 'much of the night', and by the avoidance of a broken anapaest. The omission of the article with νύξ is common (K–G i. 606), but where one particular night is involved the article is often used: contrast, e.g., Plut. *Mor.* 704 a, πολὺ μέρος περὶ ταῦτ᾽ ἀναλίσκων τῆς νυκτός, 'much of that night', with Eur. (*Antiope*) frag. 183, νέμων τὸ πλεῖστον ἡμέρας τούτῳ μέρος, 'most of every day'. The deletion of τό is supported by W. G. Arnott, *Mnem.* 4th ser. xix (1966), 396 and many others. Handley and Schäfer follow *ed. pr.* in excising καί: they may be right; but καί seems desirable after οὐ μόνον, as in frag. 622, οὐ γὰρ τὸ μὴ πράττειν κατὰ νοῦν ἔχει μόνον λύπην, παρέχει δὲ φροντίδας καὶ τἀγαθά. In the phrase οὐ μόνον . . . ἀλλὰ (καί) the καί is normally omitted only if the second member includes the first or is seen as a contrast rather than an addition, K–G ii. 257. One would expect the same to hold good for the less usual οὐ μόνον . . . δέ.

17 ζυγομαχῶν: Lit. 'fighting with a yoke-companion', a metaphor from horses or oxen harnessed together. The word properly implies fruitless struggle against that which cannot be escaped, as at 250.

20 ἔτι μᾶλλον: Sc. ἔζη κακῶc. The child did not reconcile the parents; indeed it may be guessed that it was one of the wife's faults that she had borne a daughter, not the son that every Greek desired.

22 ἀπῆλθε: An ill-treated wife might leave her husband (ἀπολείπειν) with the consent of the archon, but separation by agreement, which is intended here, was also possible: Lipsius, *Attisches Recht*, ii. 487, Harrison, *Law of Athens* i, pp. 39–44.

23 χωρίδιον: For the quantity (ῐδ) cf. frag. 436 and οἰκίδιον, *Perik.* 389, ἀργυρίδιον, Ar. *Plutus* 147, 240, δικαστηρῐδιον, *Wasps* 803. χωρῐδιον is the diminutive of χωρίον, 'piece of land'; the termination -ιδιον, if an extension of a stem in ι-, ιο-, or ια-, is usually -ῐδιον, otherwise usually -ῐδιον, but there are numerous exceptions to both rules; see W. Petersen, *The Greek Diminutives in -ιον*, pp. 215–18.

24 ὕπαρχον ἦν: Like the English 'there was a little holding belonging to him', this 'periphrastic' idiom indicates that the holding belonged to him not merely at the time when his mother joined him, but had done so previously. The construction is studied by G. Björck, *HN ΔΙΔΑCΚΩΝ* (Uppsala, 1940). **ἐνθαδὶ ἐν γειτόνων:** Pan points (deictic ἐνθαδί) to the house represented by the door on his left. The phrase ἐν γειτόνων (*Perik.* 147, *Phasma* 13, *Aspis* 122) arose by an ellipse of οἰκίᾳ, but here it is used without thought of that, much as one might say in English that so-and-so owns a field 'next door' to mine. **κακῶc:** I.e. at a poor standard of living; cf. frag. 57, τὰ κακῶc τρέφοντα χωρί' ἀνδρείους ποεῖ.

26 τὴν μητέρ', αὐτόν: For the order cf. [Dem.] *in Neaer.* 42, τοῦτόν τε καὶ αὐτὴν τρέφει καὶ παιδάρια τρία (cf. *in Boeot.* 51, τρέφουcα μεθ' αὐτῆc τούτουc καὶ θεραπαίναc cυχνάc); as a parallel for three nouns joined by a single τε V. Martin quotes Eur. *El.* 334, αἱ χεῖρες, ἡ γλῶcc', ἡ ταλαίπωρόc τε φρήν (other examples, Denniston, *GP* 501). Those who think that the emphasis should lie on Gorgias' supporting others rather than himself will accept Lloyd-Jones's emendation αὐτοῦ or Photiadis' αὑτοῦ. Exceptions occur to the normal rule that the reflexive αὐτοῦ is placed between the noun and its article, e.g. *Epitr.* 890, τὴν κεφαλήν . . . αὐτοῦ, Ar. *Clouds* 905, τὸν πατέρ' αὐτοῦ δήϲαϲ, Xen. *Hell.* vii. 3. 12, [Dem.] xl. 32, ἐπιτεμὼν τὴν κεφαλὴν αὐτοῦ; in all those instances the word is pleonastic, as it would be here.   ἕνα: εναμα of B may be a conflation of variants ἕνα and ἅμα; the former is better, as insisting on Gorgias' poverty.

27 μειρακύλλιον: Although a deteriorative force usually attaches to the suffix -ύλλιον, the word is here not derogatory, as in Ar. *Frogs* 89, *Epitr.* 169, etc., but hypocoristic, 'a fine lad', as in Anaxandrides frag. 33 K. μειράκιον was sometimes used to cover the whole range from παῖϲ to ἀνήρ or νεανίϲκοϲ (Epiktet. *Diss.* iii. 9. 8), i.e. the years from fourteen to twenty-one, as by Hippokrates, quoted in Philo, *De Opificio Mundi*, c. 36, παῖϲ δ' ἄχρι γονῆϲ ἐκφύϲιοϲ, ἐϲ τὰ δὶϲ ἑπτά· μειράκιον δ' ἄχρι γενείου λαχνώϲιοϲ, ἐϲ τὰ τρὶϲ ἑπτά, cf. Xen. *Symp.* 4. 17, παῖϲ, μειράκιον, ἀνήρ, πρεϲβύτηϲ, and also 967 of this play. But to Menander the word might indicate an age between that of ἔφηβοϲ and full manhood, frag. 724, παῖϲ γέγον', ἔφηβοϲ, μειράκιον, ἀνήρ, γέρων. One became an ἔφηβοϲ at eighteen, so that a μειράκιον in this restricted sense will be about twenty or a little more. W. H. Porter, *Plutarch's Life of Aratus*, p. 51, shows that this is Plutarch's use of the word, e.g. Octavian at nineteen is οὔπω πάνυ μειράκιον (*Brut.* 27); but Demetrios is 'still a μειράκιον' at twenty-two (*Demetr.* 5). That these names can shade into one another is shown by *Georg.* 67–9, where Gorgias is called both μειράκιον and νεανίϲκοϲ, cf. Lysias iii. 10.

29 προάγει: 'Experience of difficulties is bringing him on', but a general gnome is implied: 'Experience brings early maturity.' It marks off the end of this section of the narrative: we now return to Knemon.

30 αὐτός . . . μόνος: 'All alone', as 331.

31 καὶ γραῦν θεράπαιναν: The way this is thrown in as an afterthought minimizes the old woman's importance; she is no real detraction from Knemon's solitariness.   ξυλοφορῶν: For wood as saleable produce of an estate, cf. [Dem.] (xlii) 7.   ϲκάπτων: To break up the earth with a mattock more deeply than the shallow plough could do, or where the plough could not go, was a tiring form of labour typical of Athenian cultivation.

32 ἀπὸ τούτων ἀρξάμενοϲ: The actor would indicate Gorgias' house. The aorist is idiomatic in such phrases, cf. Plato, *Symp.* 173 d, δοκεῖϲ μοι ἀτεχνῶϲ πάνταϲ ἀθλίουϲ ἡγεῖϲθαι . . . ἀπὸ ϲαυτοῦ ἀρξάμενοϲ.

33 Χολαργέων: Cholargos was a city deme, of the Akamantid tribe, on the north side of the town, beyond the Kerameikos, *RE* (2. Reihe)

vii. 369. The exact site is not agreed; see Handley's note. This passage suggests that it lay where the road from Phyle entered the city.
34 ἐφεξῆc πάνταc: 'Each and all', cf. Dem. xxii. 61, ἐξῆc ἅπανταc. R. Renehan, *Greek Textual Criticism*, p. 104, collects instances of this idiom.

35 ὁμοία τῇ τροφῇ: Since the immediate context insists so strongly on Knemon's unpleasantness, some scholars have felt that this phrase would mean that the girl, too, was unpleasant, and Lloyd-Jones accepts Lewis's change to γέγον᾽ ἀνομοία. The change is not needed: to a Greek the isolation of the household would bring about a desirable innocence in the girl. Xenophon makes Ischomachos say with satisfaction that his wife had before marriage been brought up ὅπωc ὡc ἐλάχιcτα μὲν ὄψοιτο, ἐλάχιcτα δ᾽ ἀκούcοιτο, ἐλάχιcτα δ᾽ ἔροιτο (*Oec.* vii. 6). Later in this play Sostratos finds it a merit that the girl's τροφή has been away from feminine influence, so that she knows nothing of τῶν ἐν τῷ βίῳ τούτων κακῶν (384–6).

36 φλαῦρον: Not elsewhere in comedy after Aristophanes, although in Plato and Demosthenes. It is impossible to say what colour the word had for Menander's audience. Photios says φλαῦρον γάρ ἐcτι τὸ μικρὸν κακόν, φαῦλον δὲ τὸ μέγα, but it may be doubted whether this is more than a grammarian's fancy.

36–9: Cf. Plaut. *Aul.* 23 ff. *Lar familiaris* speaks: 'Ea mihi cotidie | aut ture aut uino aut aliqui semper supplicat, | dat mihi coronas. eius honoris gratia | feci etc.' **cυντρόφουc:** 'That live with me'; for this sense cf. Soph. *El.* 1190. **κολακεύουc᾽:** There is no disapproval in the word, which is here used as if it were θεραπεύουcα; this is not usual, but cf. *Perik.* 314, frag. 382, a lover φοιτῶν καὶ κολακεύων ⟨ἐμέ τε καὶ⟩ τὴν μητέρα, Ephippos frag. 6, Aelian, *ep. rust.* xix, θεοὺc ἐκολάκευον. **ἐπιμελῶc . . . ἐπιμέλειαν:** The repetition seems to be accidental. **τε** to add a new *sentence* is not unparalleled in Menander, 541 and 731 of this play, *Epitr.* 917, although unusual in fourth-century prose (Denniston, *GP* 499); the meaning seems to be 'and so', as in Thucydides (K–G ii. 242). **καὶ μάλα:** καὶ reinforces μάλα. **εὐπόρου:** In the fourth century εὔπορος and ἄπορος became common synonyms for πλούcιος and πένηc; perhaps originally they were felt to be less emotionally charged.

40–1 ταλάντων . . . πολλῶν: Genitive of price; the separation of the words lends them emphasis. **ἀcτικόν:** Dem. lv. 11 speaks of a farm neglected by its owner, δυcχεραίνοντοc ὅλωc τοῖc τόποιc καὶ μᾶλλον ἀcτικοῦ. Here it is the owner's son who spends his time at the family's house in Athens. This is essential to the plot, which demands that he should not be known to Knemon or Gorgias.

42 θήραν: The usual quarry in Attica was the hare, although some deer were to be found. Provided damage to growing crops was avoided, hunting was freely allowed, outside a close season (ἀναγρία), over private land. If this is surprising, it may be remembered that the farmer would benefit from the killing of animals that ate his crops.

κυνηγέτου τινός: Is this (a) Pyrrhias, called τὸν cυνκυνηγόν at 71, (b) Chaireas, perhaps called τὸν cυνκυνηγέτην at 48, (c) someone else unnamed? (c) may be ruled out, as serving no purpose. As for (a), a mention that Pyrrhias accompanied Sostratos on this expedition is unnecessary; the fact certainly explains how he can be sure of finding the right house when sent with a message to the girl's father, but it is imparted just where it is needed, at 71; there is no occasion for anticipating it here. What of (b)? The words in 48, τὸν ἐρῶντα τόν τε cυν [. . ., 'I see approaching the lover and the . . .', strongly suggest that both Sostratos and Chaireas have already been mentioned. Moreover, no convincing alternative has been found for the supplement cυγκ[υνηγέτη]ν.

On the other hand, there is nothing in the scene 50 ff. to suggest that Chaireas had accompanied Sostratos hunting; nor would one expect the impulsive Sostratos to sleep on his adventure before imparting it to his friend, if that friend had been in his company the previous day. This, however, may be an improbability ἔξω τοῦ δράματος, to be accepted as necessary if the play is to start early in the morning. One may also feel surprise that Chaireas should be described as 'a huntsman' or 'a hunting friend'. But could a slave be described simply as κυνηγέτης τις, 'a slave who manages the dogs'? In [Xen.] *Cyneg.* the master manages the dogs, and the slave who accompanies him carries the nets and is called ἀρκυωρός. I suspect that in the absence of anything to point the other way a κυνηγέτης is a free man who goes hunting, not his slave-assistant.

A decision is uncertain, but the strongest evidence is that of 48, which points to Chaireas. If he is the κυνηγέτης of 42, the next line may be completed by φίλο]υ, or ἄλλο]υ, or ἑτέρο]υ; or, supplying a welcome connective particle, by καί πο]υ or εἶτ' ο]ὖ. The last is the most attractive: the god implies that he had guided Sostratos to the scene; I do not see why he should insist, yet mark it by the word που as a guess, that the youth had arrived accidentally. If Pyrrhias is the κυνηγέτης, δοῦλο]υ is impossible (*Heros* 20 n.), ἄλλο]υ and ἑτέρο]υ unlikely, εἶτ' ο]ὖ the most probable reading.

The conversation of 50–5 shows, it is true, that Chaireas was not present when Sostratos saw the girl; but the two companions might have been separated while hunting. An indication, but no proof, that Chaireas accompanied Sostratos on his hunting expedition is to be found in Libanios, *Decl.* xxvii, a work which derives many motifs from this play; in c. 25 the δύϲκολοϲ asks his city-loving son ϲυμπότηϲ εἰμί ϲοι, ϲυϲτρατιώτηϲ, ϲυγκυνηγέτηϲ; Plutarch, *quomodo adulator* 52 b, says that a κόλαξ, if he gets hold of a man fond of hunting, enthusiastically goes out with him; but his true concern is not with the game, but to enmesh the hunter.

43 παραβαλόντα: Intrans., 'entering, coming to'.

44 ἔχειν πωϲ ἐνθεαϲτικῶϲ = ἐνθεάζειν (Hdt. i. 63) = ἔνθεοϲ εἶναι. The more usual ἐνθουϲιάζειν or ἐνθουϲιᾶν seems to have the same meaning; at least Plutarch uses ἐνθουϲιαϲμόϲ and ἐνθεάζεϲθαι indifferently at *QC* 623 c. Possession by Pan (or by Hekate or by the Mother of the Gods) is suggested by the chorus in Euripides' *Hippolytus* as a possible reason for the behaviour of the love-sick Phaedra (141). The idea that love is a form of divine possession is so familiar that it hardly needs illustration, but one may quote Xen. *Symp.* i. 10, ὑπὸ τοῦ ϲώφρονοϲ ἔρωτοϲ ἔνθεοι, Plato, *Symp.* 180 b, θειότερον γὰρ ἐραϲτὴϲ παιδικῶν· ἔνθεοϲ γάρ ἐϲτι.

The missing beginning of the line might be expected to connect Sostratos with the girl. *Ed. pr.* suggested αὐτῆϲ, but the top of a final c should be visible and is not. (The construction, a genitive dependent on ἐνθεαϲτικῶϲ ἔχειν, may be defensible; ἐρωτικῶϲ ἔχειν τινοϲ (Plato, *Symp.* 222 c) is no true parallel, since ἐρᾶν takes a genitive. Better is Machon 351 Gow, διὰ τό πωϲ | τὸν Ἀνδρόνικον ἡδέωϲ αὐτῆϲ ἔχειν, where ἡδέωϲ ἔχειν is the equivalent of ἐρᾶν. Another instance of a loosely constructed genitive occurs in Xen. *Hell.* v. 4. 25, ἀπολυτικῶϲ αὐτοῦ εἶχον, 'were disposed to acquit him'.) Exiguous traces of ink before εχειν are hard to reconcile with any letter except μ or α or with a mark of punctuation. Bingen's ἔρωτ]α ἔχειν seems to me the best suggestion yet made. The addition of πωϲ to an adverb in -ωϲ is common in this play (95, 201, 249, 387, 777, 835). Since it occurs elsewhere in Menander only in frag. 153, he may have deliberately abandoned it as a tiresome trick of speech. There are at most three other instances in comedy: Ar. *Knights* 196, Metagenes frag. 2 K, and perhaps Philemon frag. 4 K.

46 βουλήθητε δέ: The point, such as it is, seems to be that Pan unexpectedly takes literally the formula ἐὰν βούληϲθε, 'if you like', and adds 'but *do* like'. The whole sentence seems to be repeated in the prologue of *Sikyonios* (24–5). It has some resemblance to the injunction to the audience to attend that is found in some prologues to Latin plays: Plaut. *Amphitryo* 151, 'adeste'; *Asin.* 14, 'date . . . operam'; *Poen.* 126, 'adeste'; *Trin.* 22, 'adeste'; Ter. *Andr.* 24, 'adeste aequo animo et rem cognoscite'; *Eun.* 44, 'date operam . . . animum attendite'; *Phorm.* 31, 'date operam, adeste, aequo animo'.

48–9: A regular triangular tear has led to the loss of a maximum of nine letters in 48 and of eight in 49, including those of which traces remain. cυνκ[υνηγέτη]ν will fill the former gap, and nothing else has been suggested that is plausible, although some scholars have searched for a word to indicate that Chaireas is a hanger-on (*parasitos*) of Sostratos, as the list of dramatis personae states. For the latter gap, no word gives better sense than c[υγκοινουμ]ένους, 'consulting', but it is too long. To support a restoration by supposing a mis-spelling is a last resort, but mistakes are frequent in this papyrus, for example at 61 the scribe originally wrote δι for δει, and it is not wildly impossible to guess that he originally omitted a letter in cυγκοινουμένους. cυννοουμένους (Fraenkel) is unlikely because the pair immediately enter in animated conversation; αὐτοὺς . . . cυμβαλουμένους (J. Martin), 'themselves about to contribute something to your information', is ingenious but does not convince me.

(ii) 50–80: *Sostratos and Chaireas*

Sostratos and Chaireas enter by the *parodos* on the audience's right, as coming from the town. Sostratos is ἀcτικὸc τῇ διατριβῇ. He is to be understood, from the opening question, just to have pointed out to Chaireas the place where he had seen the girl the previous day, and fallen in love with her.

50 ἐνθένδε: This is the reading of one branch of the tradition of Ammonios and of Symeon's unpublished Cυναγωγή, as quoted by Nickau. (The other branch has ἔνθέν γε, which was corrected by Valckenaer.) Ammonios and Symeon both derive from a work on Greek usage by a scholar of the second century A.D. There is no case for rejecting his reading ἐνθένδε in favour of B's ἐνταῦθα because accident has corrupted the rest of the quotation in the later works. It is in fact preferable as being *lectio difficilior* and unlikely to have replaced ἐνταῦθα by accident or by design. On the other hand, since its interpretation offers difficulties, there was a motive for substituting the other word. There seem to be two ways in which it can be interpreted: either (*a*) ἐνθένδε goes with ἰδών, and Chaireas means 'seeing from this spot where we are standing', or (*b*) ἐνθένδε goes with the following words 'seeing a girl from that house', with a gesture towards Knemon's house. (*a*) is straightforward Greek, but makes no obvious point, unless it be that on the previous occasion Sostratos had kept his distance and not been seen by the girl. The word ἐνθένδε would then give the actors a cue to halt as soon as they were in view of the audience. (The whole of the succeeding conversation, however, cannot be static; the pair crosses the stage before 81, when they are near Knemon's door: perhaps this movement could be effectively combined with Chaireas' professions, 61–8.) (*b*) ἐνθάδε is frequently used with reference to a house represented on the stage, and although I do not know another example of ἐνθένδε so used, the equivalent ἐντεῦθεν is found 913, *Perik.* 374. If this interpretation is adopted ἐνθένδε is somewhat freely constructed; strictly one should say ἐνθένδε (ἰοῦcαν καὶ) cτεφανοῦcαν or τινα ἐνθένδε παῖδα. But the freedom may be pardonable. Dramatically the word would be very justifiable, since the door of Knemon's house is to be prominent throughout the act, the climax of which is the appearance from it once again of his daughter.   ἐλευθέραν: There can be no question of marriage, which Sostratos intends, unless the girl is of free birth; but how had he learned her status? One can only say that the wish had been father to the thought.

Ammonios quotes the passage to illustrate the confusion between εὐθύ, εὐθύc, and εὐθέωc. εὐθύc goes with the phrase ἐρῶν ἀπῆλθεc, 'you at once emerged in love'. Sostratos did literally 'come away' but the primary sense of ἀπῆλθεc is probably not that. ἀπελθεῖν sometimes means 'get off', 'come off', as in the English 'come off best', and this sense is likely here, as in frag. 568. 6, οὐδὲν πέπονθεν, ἀλλ' ἀπῆλθε καταγελῶν. R. Kassel, *Rh. Mus.* cvi (1963), 300, quotes Isokr. *Trap.* 57, ἐν τοῖc ἰδίοιc cυμβολαίοιc . . . πλέον ἔχοντεc ἀπέρχεcθε.

54: Whether Menander intended it or not, an actor could make the assonance of cκω-, -γω, -κω, -χω suggest a lover's sighs. Did Aristophanes intend a similar effect with *Frogs* 58, μὴ cκῶπτέ μ' ὦδελφ', οὐ γὰρ ἀλλ' ἔχω κακῶc? Cf. L. A. Post, *AJP* lxxx (1959), 412, lxxxii (1961), 96.

55 διόπερ refers to κακῶc ἔχω, not to Chaireas' interjection ἀλλ' οὐκ ἀπιcτῶ.

56 πρακτικόν: The πρακτικόc is the man who knows how to deal with any particular situation, Arist. *EN* 1141ᵇ7.

58 οὕτωc ἔχω looks forward, as at 379: 'My position is this.'

59–60 ἁρπάcαc suggests carrying off a slave-*hetaira* from her owner, cf. *Kolax* 131, Ter. *Adelphoe* 90, 'eripuit mulierem quam amabat'; κατακάω refers to forcing a door by burning it, a procedure that might be adopted by the ardent lover of a free *hetaira* (Theokritos ii. 128), as well as to obtain the property of a πορνοβοcκόc, Plaut. *Persa* 569, Herondas ii. 35 (where see Headlam's note). Chaireas paints his headlong energy not only by asyndeton but also by the absence of any logical order in his verbs.

62–3: Typically of Menander's style the *sententia* is introduced not for its own sake, but to illustrate the pompous and untimely self-importance of Chaireas. ἐν τῷ ταχέως: Cf. *Mis.* 275, τοῦ ταχέως; there is an ellipse of some undetermined verb, e.g. πράττειν.

66 βίον: If this meant 'her way of life', as in 21, it would overlap with τρόπους. 'Financial position', as in 306, seems more likely, especially in view of the importance of the dowry in most marriages.

67 ἤδη: 'Now (but not in the former case'). καταλείπομαι middle, since Chaireas has an interest in the sort of memory of his behaviour his friend will always retain.

68 ὡς ἂν διοικήςω: Lit. 'in whatever way I manage' (aor. subj.), but in English we should say, e.g., 'a memory that depends on the way I manage'; cf. Plato, *Symp.* 181 a, ὡς ἂν πραχθῇ, τοιοῦτον ἀπέβη, 'its nature depends on the way it is done'. διοικεῖν is usually followed by an acc.; for the construction here cf. Isokr. *Paneg.* 38, μέλλοντας καὶ περὶ τῶν ἄλλων καλῶς διοικήςειν, and Aristotle's will in Diog. Laert. v. 12 and 13, περὶ τῶν ἄλλων διοικεῖν, περὶ τοῦ παιδίου διοικεῖν. B's text is therefore quite defensible; but Handley prefers to give διοικήςω an object by reading ὅς' ἄν (the confusion of o and ω is very frequent in this papyrus). W. Kraus, *Gnomon* xl (1968), 343, is perhaps right in replying that the friend will not remember *everything* that Chaireas does, but more generally *how* he manages things.

69 οὐ πάνυ κτλ.: The only instance in this play where an 'aside' forms the second part of a speech. καὶ νῦν γε: 'And *this* is an occasion on which we ought to get all this information.' Sostratos disregards the unwelcome advice, confessing that he has already taken positive action by sending Pyrrhias to broach the matter; there is a *fait accompli*, marked by the perfect tense of πέπομφα.

71 τὸν cυνκυνηγόν: 'Who came hunting with us', if 42 was rightly explained.

73 τῷ κυρίῳ τῆς οἰκίας: The head of the household might have been some other male relative, if the girl's father had been dead.

75 ἥμαρτον: The frank acknowledgement of error is to Sostratos' credit, cf. Ctesipho's *peccavi*, Ter. *Adelphoe* 276. But the error he acknowledges is not that which caused Chaireas' consternation: Chaireas was shocked at the precipitance of his advance, not at the possible discourtesy of entrusting it to a slave.

76 ἥρμοττ': Kamerbeek's correction of ηρμοcτ' is necessary because the intrans. ἁρμόττειν means 'be appropriate', the passive ἡρμόςθαι 'to be adjusted'.

78 ff.: For this somewhat artless way of preparing for a character's entry cf. Soph. *OT* 289, πάλαι δὲ μὴ παρὼν θαυμάζεται, but there Teiresias' appearance is delayed for another ten lines. In both places the effect is to suggest that something has gone wrong with the speaker's plans, a suggestion soon confirmed. Here the excitement of Pyrrhias' arrival will prevent the audience from reflecting that Sostratos had no good reason for thinking him slow to return. He had been chased off by Knemon and so had no opportunity of spending on his errand the time he might have been expected to spend. But Sostratos is a lover and therefore impatient. οἴκαδε παρεῖναι . . . μοι: This must be 'report to me at our house in town', not at the family's country-house. Since Sostratos has been described as ἀςτικὸς τῇ διατριβῇ, we think of him as coming from the town. The fact that Pyrrhias was dispatched at dawn also suggests a long journey, not one from a neighbouring farm. It appears later that Sostratos cannot have spent the night in the country; otherwise he would have known of his mother's dream and the upset it had caused (260 ff.). We must imagine then that he had changed his mind, in a lover's restlessness, and gone out himself to Phyle without waiting for the return of Pyrrhias, whom he would expect to meet on the road. εἰρήκειν: Pluperfect because the verb refers to a time earlier than the perfect τεθαύμακα, 'I am surprised', πάλαι, 'and have been for some time'.

80 μοι is probably to be taken with παρεῖναι, πυθομένῳ τἀνταῦθα being interposed by lively anticipation, just as in 78 ἥτις ἐcτί comes between διατριβήν and αὐτοῦ.

(iii) 81–144: *Pyrrhias, Sostratos, Chaireas* (exit 134)

81: Pyrrhias enters from the left, running in terror. The running slave is a stock figure of comedy (Ter. *Heauton.* 37), here used naturally and effectively. πάρες: 'Let me pass', cf. Page, *GLP* 48. 7, πρὸς θεῶν πάρες, διώκομαι γάρ.

82 τί τοῦτο παῖ: Diano would give this to Chaireas, and to make him speak first suits his predominance in the foregoing scene. But Menander, like Aristophanes, is sparing with genuinely three-sided dialogue. Normally, if three characters are on the stage, A converses first with B, then with C. There are of course exceptions (e.g. 364–80, *Perik.* 467–81), and interjections by a third party into a duologue are common. Nevertheless ordinary technique suggests the assignment of all the responses in 82–6 to the same character, and that will be

Sostratos, who must be addressed at 86, ἀπαλλαγῶμεν, ἱκετεύω cε. Treu gives τί ἐcτι; and μὰ Δία to Chaireas, arguing that the πρακτικόc could not stand idly by. But one of the points in this scene is that for all his boasts he proves to be quite useless.

84 βάλλει: 2nd person passive.   ποῖ; 'Where are you off to?', cf. Arist. *Plut.* 417, ποῖ; ποῖ; τί φεύγετον; Page, *GLP* 48. 13, ποῖ cυ, ποῖ; *Samia* 324, ποῖ cυ, ποῖ, μαcτιγία; C. Gallavotti, *Riv. fil.* xci (1963), 72, would see a use of ποῖ like that in Ar. *Lysistr.* 383, μῶν θερμὸν ἦν; ποῖ θερμόν; (cf. ibid. 193), which rejects a suggestion as nonsensical. But to make a true parallel we should here have to have ποῖ βάλλει;

85 τί δαὶ λέγειc; The particle δαί, well known from Aristophanes and Euripides, expresses surprise or wonder. Since it has not yet been found elsewhere in Menander or in the fragments of New Comedy except once in Diphilos frag. 17 K, many editors read τί δέ. B has δ' αἰ, which is interpreted as δ'αι changed to δε, but may be δαι changed to δ' αει. Choice is difficult: on the one hand αι for ε is not uncommon in this papyrus, even in a familiar word (αιτεραν for ετεραν, 516) and the false substitution of δαί for δέ can be illustrated from Ar. *Ach.* 912, where it is unmetrical; on the other hand the comparatively unfamiliar δαί might be read as δ' αἰ or 'corrected' to δέ.

88 Ὀδύνηc γὰρ υόc: M. Gigante, *Riv. fil.* N.S. xl (1962), 185, quotes Palladas, *AP* ix. 394, Χρυcέ, πάτερ κολάκων, ὀδύνηc καὶ φροντίδοc υἱόc; this is a verbal, but not a real, parallel, since Palladas' meaning is not that gold is afflicted with, but that it is earned by, pain and care. What is required is a parallel for the idea that the son is characterized by the quality personified in the parent: this is found in the Greek Bible, e.g. Luke 10 : 6, υἱὸc εἰρήνηc, but there one must reckon with the influence of a Semitic idiom (see Moulton–Milligan, *Vocabulary of the Greek Testament*, p. 649). In true Greek authors the nearest parallels are Soph. *OT* 1080, Τύχηc παῖδα, Aristophanes frag. 573, Χαιρεφῶντα Νυκτὸc παῖδα, Anaxandrides frag. 38 K, Ἄρεοc παιδίον; the sons here are lucky, nocturnal, warlike. Eur. *Troades* 766–9, quoted by J. Martin, *Actes du Congrès Budé* (1963), p. 356, seems to me less relevant. Something a little closer is to be found in Latin plays: Plaut. *MG* 1292 'mulier profecto natast ex ipsa Mora', i.e. women are dilatory,, and *Stichus* 155, 'Famem ego fuisse suspicor matrem mihi', i.e. I am always hungry. Fraenkel, however, argues (*Plautinisches im Plautus*, p. 290) that both these lines are Plautine additions to the Greek original; in *Elementi Plautini*, p. 434, he takes the same view of *Epidicus* 673–4, 'ille quidem Volcani iratist filius: | quaqua tangit omne amburit'.

Pyrrhias may mean either that Knemon is ὀδυνηρόc, i.e. causes distress to others, or that he suffers distress. The former seems more likely in this context. True, Chaireas later suggests that Knemon was temporarily distressed (ὀδυνώμενος), but that is in order to make excuses for the old man. Here Pyrrhias is concerned to show that Knemon is dangerous.

The fanciful ᾿Οδύνης υἱός is somewhat strangely associated with the alternatives ἢ κακοδαιμονῶν ἢ μελαγχολῶν, and there is much attraction in the view of L. A. Post, *AJP* lxxxii (1961), 100, and C. Gallavotti, *Riv. fil.* xci (1963), 72, that Pyrrhias means by ᾿Οδύνης υἱός not Knemon, but himself, for whom he is very sorry. This would have a parallel in *Stichus* 155, quoted above. Gallavotti proposes to read ᾿Οδύνης γὰρ υἱὸς ἢ Κακοδαιμονίας τις ἦ (after Post's ἢ κακοδαιμονῶν τις ἦ) but this leaves an unsatisfactory sequel: one cannot say μελαγχολῶν ἄνθρωπος for μελαγχολῶν τις ἄνθρωπος. Better to write ᾿Οδύνης ἄρ' υἱὸς ἦν· κακοδαιμονῶν τις ἢ μελαγχολῶν κτλ. The imperfect with ἄρα is used of a fact that, true all along, has just been discovered, Denniston, *GP* 36. Although ἦ was more favoured by Aristophanes for the 1st person, ἦν is the only form attested for Menander, cf. *Georgos* 3 n., or as yet found in the papyri, unless this is the first contrary instance.

κακοδαιμονῶν: 'Possessed by an evil spirit', cf. Ar. *Plutus* 372, where the word is, as here, associated with μελαγχολᾶν.   **μελαγχολῶν:** The investigations of H. Flashar, *Melancholie und Melancholiker* (Berlin, 1966), show that in the earlier works of the Hippocratic Corpus blackness of bile, caused by a thickening of its substance, is a symptom of bodily and mental disturbance; the idea that black bile is a normal secretion, distinct from yellow bile, first occurs about 400 B.C., in περὶ φύσιος ἀνθρώπου; an excess of black bile was supposed to bring mental derangement, of a manic as well as of a depressive type. In Plato, *Rep.* 573 c, the 'tyrannical man' is μελαγχολικός because he thinks he can 'rule gods and men'; the μελαγχολικός knows no restraint, Arist. *EN* 1150ᵇ25. Aristophanes' use of the verb, *Birds* 14, *Plutus* 12, 366, 903, shows it to have become popularized, without any technical meaning, to cover any form of being out of contact with reality, cf. [Dem.] xlviii. 56, Plato, *Phaedr.* 268 e. For more professional views of μελαγχολία see Flashar's book, and in particular Alexander of Tralles, i. 591 Puschmann, Galen xix. 699 Kühn, Aretaios s.v.; all these regard the insanity as being mainly depressive, but allow angriness to be a symptom.

89: B gives a rough breathing to ἄνθρωπος and a smooth to οἰκῶν. It is hard to believe that this is right, but Handley refers to Herondas vi. 52, ὁ δ' ἕτερος ἐγγὺς τῆς συνοικίης οἰκέων τῆς 'Ερμοδώρου τὴν πλατεῖαν ἔκβαντι ἦν μέν κοτ', ἦν τις, and to four other passages (all poetical) there quoted by Headlam–Knox for the absence of the expected article with οἰκῶν and similar participles. I therefore follow B, hesitantly. Handley himself regularizes the construction by writing μελαγχολῶν ἄνθρωπος, οἰκῶν [ἐνθάδ]ε τὴν οἰκίαν, πρὸς ὅν μ᾽ ἔπεμψας—; the sentence breaks off before reaching its verb. This seems to me a form of expression perhaps too deliberate for the excited and breathless Pyrrhias. Lloyd-Jones makes a new sentence begin with οἰκῶν, envisaging something like οἰκῶ[ν τυγχάν]ει τὴν οἰκίαν πρὸς ἥν (Maas) μ᾽ ἔπεμψας.

90: The traces in the papyrus suit either ἔπεμπες or ἔπεμψας. The imperfect of πέμπω, like that of κελεύω, is frequently used where the aspect of the verb would appear to demand the aorist. The reason seems to be that the verb is felt to indicate the *beginning* of an action which will be completed only with the completion of the mission or execution of the order (Schwyzer ii. 277).

91 μεγάλου κακοῦ: Probably an exclamatory genitive, cf. *Epitr.* 396, Ἄπολλον καὶ θεοί, δεινοῦ κακοῦ. To precede it ὦ θεοί (Page) is possible, but elsewhere known from Menander only in the mouth of Habrotonon (three times) in *Epitr.*, and in the possibly paratragic lines *Perik.* 807, 827. Kamerbeek's ἵνα τύχω is attractive but speculative.

δακτύλους: 'Toes'.

92–5: Restoration of these lines is so difficult that the suspicion arises that there may have been some error in the papyrus. παροινεῖν means to behave with the sort of brutality that might be displayed by a man in drink, to maltreat, to insult, and is often used of actual physical assault. There is no necessary implication that drink is in fact to blame, although it may be. The word is therefore very appropriate to Knemon's actions, as Pyrrhias will shortly describe them, and it would be natural to suppose that this is its reference. The difficulties are that (1) ἐλθών is not easily applied to Knemon, (2) a paragraphus below 92 shows that Pyrrhias is not the speaker, unless *two* changes of speaker can be accommodated in the brief lost portion of the line; but Pyrrhias alone yet knows that Knemon πεπαρῴνηκε. Hence most scholars suppose that Pyrrhias is the *subject* of πεπαρῴνηκε, and that one or other of the young men guesses that he had brought the attack on himself by insulting behaviour. There is thus reached a type of restoration well exemplified by Kraus's text: (Cω.) ἀλλ᾽ ἴσως | ἐλθών τι πεπαρῴνηκε δεῦρο. (Χαι.) παραφρονῶν | εὔδηλός ἐςτι. (Cω.) νὴ Δία. To such a solution there are serious objections. (1) The young men do not know that Pyrrhias has been assaulted, only that he has arrived running from an invisible and perhaps imaginary pursuer and that he claims that he has been sent to visit a madman. To guess that he had committed some wantonly insulting act is hardly a natural reaction to this. (2) That a slave should insult the man to whom he has been sent on an errand is a strange guess, and there is nothing in Pyrrhias' character to make it a plausible one. (3) If the accusation is made, it is very odd that no one pays any attention to it, not even Pyrrhias. (4) The accusation blunts the effect of 138 ff. There Sostratos, disappointed at being let down by Chaireas, whom he cannot upbraid, relieves his feelings by an outburst of suspicion about Pyrrhias' conduct. The dramatic force of this unexpected outburst would be spoiled if he had previously expressed a belief that Pyrrhias had misbehaved.

These considerations lead to the conclusion, maintained by van Groningen, Quincey, Sbordone, and Treu, that πεπαρῴνηκε has Knemon for its subject. Moreover, Pyrrhias alone has the knowledge to use the word. But ἐλθών must surely refer to Pyrrhias and, since there is a paragraphus below 92, be spoken by someone else. A dicolon, then, must have been lost after ἐλθών or after τι. ἐλθών can be used of a man who goes on an errand to get information, e.g. *Perik.* 355, ἵν' ἴδω τί ποιεῖ καὶ λέγω ἐλθών, and it may be that Sostratos made some inquiry after the success of Pyrrhias' errand; that was, after all, what he was interested in. Yet there is no room for an inquiry, unless interrupted. However, Pyrrhias is excited enough to interrupt. *Exempli gratia* one might write

> . . . ἅπαντας. (Cω.) εἰπὲ τί
> ἐλθών — ⟨Πυ.⟩ τί; πεπαρῴνηκε. δεῦρο.

'But tell me, your errand, what—?' 'What? He beat me up! Come this way.' It would then be tempting to allow Pyrrhias to continue παραφρονῶν εὔδηλός ἐστι, but there is a dicolon after ἐστι and a paragraphus below the line, and the following words almost certainly belong to him. Possibly (Cω.) δέδιέ γε, εὔδηλός ἐστι, to which Pyrrhias, who makes no bones about his fright, could enthusiastically and comically assent:

> νὴ Δί' ἐξώλης ἄρα
> Cώστρατ' ἀπολοίμην.

For this way of assenting, which involves the ellipse of εἰ μὴ οὕτως ἐστί or the like, cf. Eubulos frag. 117 K, νὴ Δί', ἀπολοίμην ἄρα. But all this is speculative. For the form πεπαρῴνηκεν, with reduplication of the prefix as well as internal augment, cf. δεδιωκηκώς, *Perik.* 272.

95 [ἔχε] δέ πως φυλακτικῶς: This supplement is likely; the construction is familiar (44, 777, probably 249) and the sense is good: Pyrrhias, who is about to launch on his story, warns his master to keep an eye open for the possible arrival of the maniac. Some scholars have felt that ἀλλ' οὐ δύναμαι λέγειν should be a reply to an invitation to speak, and that Sostratos should ask for Pyrrhias' story. Hence Blake suggested [λέγε] δέ πως φυλακτικῶc, attributing the words to Sostratos. But it is not very plausible that Sostratos should advise Pyrrhias to be on his guard. (Stoessl, accepting λέγε, improbably makes Pyrrhias address himself.) If the reconstruction suggested above (92–95 n.) is right, Pyrrhias *has* been asked for his story; and it is effective that at the moment when he might be expected to begin it, he should plead shortage of breath and allege an inability to speak.

96 προсέстηκεν . . . τὸ πνεῦμα: Cf. [Arist.] *Probl.* 864ᵃ12, τὸ φάρμακον . . . τὸ πνεῦμα . . . προсίсταν, 870ᵃ30, αἱ πρὸс τὸ cιμὸν ('uphill') πορεῖαι . . . τὸ πνεῦμα προсιстᾶсιν. The fact that B has]cέстηκε throws no doubt on the restoration; two lines below it has προсῆλθε. There one must in fact emend to προῆλθε: προέρχομαι is the standard word for coming out of a house (cf. 2, 499, 899, *Epitr.* 857, *Sam.* 262, frag. 100); προсέρχομαι in *Perik.* 317 provides no exception, for there the point is not that Daos comes *out* of the house, but that he comes *up* to his master. Confusion of προс and προ occurs in this play at 391, 898, and in my view at 753; it is a common error in MSS. of all dates.

98: Dr. Austin informs me, from autopsy of B, that ζητεῖν (not ζητεῖτ') is necessary.

100 λοφιδίου: The diminutive is 'deteriorative', expressing Pyrrhias' ruffled temper rather than any smallness of the hill.

101 περιφθειρόμενον: φθείρομαι can be substituted for ἔρχομαι by way of imprecation or contempt, e.g. Eur. *Andr.* 708, εἰ μὴ φθερῇ τῆсδ' ὡс τάχιст' ἀπὸ стέγηс, *Perik.* 526, οὐκ εἰсφθερεῖсθε θᾶττον ὑμεῖс ἐκποδών, *Sam.* 158, ἀποφθείρου ταχύ, cf. ibid. 282, Lykurgos c. 40, ἐπὶ γήρωс ὁδῷ περιφθειρομένουс. Perhaps περιφθείρομαι might, like περιέρχομαι, be followed by the accusative ἀχράδαс (cf. *Heros* frag. 8, περιηγήсομαι τὰс ἀχράδαс); this view is adopted by Lloyd-Jones, who then writes ἦ πολύν κτλ. With some hesitation, I follow him for the reasons given below. Affirmative ἦ without a following main verb is rare (it occurs in *Rhesus* 899); ἦ πολύс, on the other hand, is a common conjunction of words and is occasionally found, as it would be here, late in the sentence and used to introduce a participle: Aesch. *Eum.* 144, ἐπάθομεν, φίλαι—ἦ πολλὰ δὴ παθοῦсα, Pindar, *Pyth.* ix. 22, ἦ πολλὰν . . . εἰρήναν παρέχοιсα, Denniston, *GP* 281.

Hesychios has περιφθείρεсθαι· τὰс φθεῖραс сυλλέγειν. C. Corbato, *Studi Menandrei*, pp. 77 ff., follows ed. pr. in supposing this to be taken from our passage and to be a correct interpretation of it. The φθεῖρεс are in his opinion some parasitic insect living upon wild pears, and Knemon was, in Pyrrhias' retrospective view, engaged either in cleaning the trees or in collecting wood. A long argument does not seem to me to make the interpretation plausible.

102 κύφων': κύφων (the scholiast on Ar. *Plut.* 606 recognizes an alternative accentuation κυφών, and B writes κυφῶν') was an instrument of punishment described by the scholiast on *Plut.* 476 as a piece of wood placed on the neck and shoulders in such a way as to make the victim stoop (κύπτειν). The word can also be applied to the victim himself, and as a mere term of abuse (Lucian, *Pseudologistes* 17, ὄλεθρον, κύφωνα, βάραθρον). It is possible that Knemon was gathering a load of wood (cf. 31, ξυλοφορῶν) among his wild pears and that Pyrrhias describes him as a κύφων, since it made him stoop in the same way. πολύν, however, seems a strange epithet; one would expect μέγαν or βαρύν. Perhaps it can be explained by supposing Pyrrhias to have had in mind a literal phrase like πολὺ πλῆθος ξύλων, and then to have substituted κύφωνα. Jacques writes πολύν—κύφων', as a definite anacoluthon. Editors who write ἀχράδας ἢ πολὺν κύφωνα . . . συλλέγοντα leave Pyrrhias in a strange uncertainty whether Knemon was gathering pears or humping wood. This is avoided by Lloyd-Jones's version ἢ πολύν, which makes ἀχράδας the object of περιφθειρόμενον, not of συλλέγοντα. But perhaps too much sense should not be expected of the angry and agitated Pyrrhias.

Handley supposes that κύφων was used colloquially to mean 'something horrible', 'as bad as the pillory', just as ἀγχόνη, 'noose', may mean 'something as bad as throttling', e.g. Ar. *Ach.* 125. There is no known parallel for this, but Hesychios has τάσσεται δὲ καὶ ἐπὶ πάντων τῶν δυσχερῶν καὶ ὀλεθρίων, cf. Photios s.v., χρῶνται δ' ἤδη τῇ λέξει ἐπὶ πάντων τῶν δυσχερῶν. The intensifying epithet πολύν might be justified by πολὺς γέλως, πολὺς ὄλβος, etc. Although this interpretation gives πολὺν κύφωνα a sense that is in itself credible, the whole phrase is strange: 'collecting wild pears—or something thoroughly horrible'. Handley quotes such phrases as ζητρεῖον ἢ κακόν μέγα (Theopompos frag. 63 K), μύραιναν ἢ κακόν τι . . . μέγα θαλάττιον (Antiphanes frag. 211 K). But whereas a prison or a sea-serpent is unpleasant, there is nothing wrong with wild pears. They were eaten (Pherekrates frag. 186 K, Telekleides frag. 32 K), and according to Dioskorides i. 168 rendered fungi harmless if stewed with them. I see no probability in J. Taillardat's suggestion, *Les Images d'Aristophane*, p. 153 n. 3, that Knemon will be doubled up with pain through constipation induced by the wild pears (cf. Hippokrates vi. p. 563 Littré), nor in that of W. Morris, *Bull. of American Soc. of Papyrologists*, iv (1967), 55, who wishes to read τυφῶν'. One may agree with J. Martin: 'La verdeur populaire du langage de Pyrrhias pose aux philologues des problèmes délicats.'

ὡc ὀργίλωc: 'How angrily he speaks', cf. the comment *nimis iracunde*, Plaut. *Asin.* 470.

103 τί, ὦ μακάριε: These words are assigned to Pyrrhias by B, which has a dicolon after οργιλωc. Nevertheless it must be mistaken. ὦ μακάριε is ironical, and irony suits neither his status nor his state of mind. On the other hand ὦ μακάριε can be addressed to an angry man, see *Perik.* 469, *Pap. Ghôran* ii. 151 (Schroeder, *Novae Comoediae Fragmenta*, p. 35, Page, *GLP* p. 304), Plut. *Phocion* 9, cf. *Marius* 2, in ironical remonstrance. Here Pyrrhias is asked why on earth he is so angry. It is possible that the dicolon after ὀργίλωc was intended to mean that the speaker turned from his companion to Pyrrhias. Who that speaker was is a matter of taste: the remains of a *nota personae* are ambiguous. The faint air of superiority seems to me to suit Chaireas; Handley compares his exclamation ὡc ταχύ at 52. Schäfer follows Lloyd-Jones in supposing that both the young men comment, making Sostratos say ὡc ὀργίλωc, Chaireas τί ⟨δ'⟩, ὦ μακάριε;

106 φιλάνθρωποc: 'Courteous, friendly', cf. Dem. xviii. 298, φιλανθρωπία λόγων. Tromp de Ruiter, *Mnem.* lix (1932), 271, collects a great number of passages containing this word. The meaning centres on 'kindness'. Here Pyrrhias regarded himself as doing Knemon a good turn, and wished to make this clear at once. ἐπιδέξιοc: Perhaps 'dexterous'; the word's connotations are not altogether clear, but it may suggest cleverness, pleasantness, and urbane gentlemanly behaviour. Arist. *EN* 1128ª17 has τοῦ δὲ ἐπιδεξίου ἐcτὶ τοιαῦτα λέγειν καὶ ἀκούειν οἷα τῷ ἐπιεικεῖ καὶ ἐλευθερίῳ ἁρμόττει. Machon 344 Gow provides a verbal parallel, ἐπιδέξιον βουλόμενον εἶναι τὸν cατράπην.

107–8: Some have seen a corruption here. Lloyd-Jones localizes it at ἰδεῖν τί cε, but this phrase, 'see you about something', is supported by *Perik.* 159, where see n. ἥκω δέ for ἥκω τι is a simple correction (perhaps too simple), giving the sense 'I come to see you about something, forwarding an affair in your interest'; for inceptive δέ see Denniston, *GP* 172, and for the construction Soph. *OC* 12, μανθάνειν γὰρ ἥκομεν. An early attempt to defend B's text was that of Thierfelder, who would translate: 'I come for a reason, eager that you should see an affair in your interest'; but ἰδεῖν is strange for μαθεῖν. Handley improves on this with: 'I've come to you about something, sir—I'm anxious for your sake to see you about a thing.' The involved and clumsy word-order could be explained as due to Pyrrhias' wish to be tactful and make a good impression. I should, however, prefer not to associate τι and πρᾶγμα but to translate: 'I've come to you about something, sir,—to see you about something, promoting an affair in your interest.' J. A. Willis (*apud* Handley) calls attention to

Plato, *Prot.* 314 e, Πρωταγόραν γάρ τι δεόμενοι ἰδεῖν ἤλθομεν, and 316 b, πρός cε τι ἤλθομεν (in both passages Burnet adopts τοι from some *recentiores*). τι is occasionally repeated pleonastically: Xen. *Cyr.* i. 6. 11, οἴει τι, ἔφη, ἧττόν τι τοῦτο εἶναι αἰcχρόν; cf. Fraenkel, *Beobacht. zu Aristophanes*, p. 89; but this is hardly the explanation of the double τι here. Another way of avoiding τι . . . πρᾶγμα is that of A. Garzya, *Dioniso* xl (1966), 30, who puts a full stop after cπεύδων and makes ὑπὲρ coῦ πρᾶγμα the beginning of an interrupted sentence. This does not convince me. cπεύδων ὑπὲρ coῦ πρᾶγμα: Cf. Eur. *Hec.* 120, ἦν δὲ τὸ μὲν còν cπεύδων ἀγαθόν. Not a tactful opening; a stranger who approaches saying that he has a proposition to your advantage arouses more suspicion than confidence.

108 ἀνόcιε as a word of abuse recurs at 122, 469, 595; and nowhere else in comedy.

109: For δέ in questions see Denniston, *GP* 173: 'Usually there is a note of surprise, impatience, or indignation.'

110 τί μαθών; 'What's the idea?'

111 ἀφίῃc': If B is followed, we must read ἀφίῃcιν, with short ι, found elsewhere in Menander only by a dubious conjecture, at *Epitr.* 1112. In view of the frequency with which B adds a ν ephelkustikon instead of eliding, it is better to keep the normal scansion here. The only other examples in comedy of ῐ are ξυνίημι, Ar. *Birds* 946, and Philemon frag. 123 K (= Strato frag. 1 K).

112 ἐc κόρακαc: One might suppose an ellipse of a curse on Knemon, but it is not necessary to see anything but a vague imprecation, 'oh, damn it!', cf. *Heros* 70, Ar. *Wasps* 852, 982. **ἀλλὰ c' ὁ Ποcειδῶν:** The same curse is uttered by the victim of an assault at 504.

113 χάρακα: A stake, such as was used to support vines; in this sense the word is fem., according to Ammonios, *diff.* 509 Nickau, masc. when a stake in a palisade, cf. *Aspis* 31. To speculate why a stake was at hand seems unnecessary; but anyone wishing to do so may welcome Handley's suggestion that Pyrrhias uses the word as an exaggerated description of Knemon's walking-stick, the old man's βακτηρία.

 πάλιν: This could mean that Knemon picked up again a stake (or his stick) that he had dropped in order to take hold of the clod. But it is perhaps more likely that Pyrrhias somewhat confusedly means 'he took a stake (and attacked me) again'.

114 ταύτῃ μ' ἐκάθαιρε: B has ἐκάθαιρε ταύτην, which could mean 'he was trimming it': in Plato, *Rep.* 361 d, ἐκκαθαίρειν is used of a sculptor who trims away stone in making a statue. But it is unlikely that Pyrrhias would include such an irrelevant detail in his indignant narrative. We must see in καθαίρω the slang sense 'beat' (cf. English 'a dusting'), exemplified at 901, cf. Theokr. v. 119 and Hesychios καθαρθῆναι· μαστιγωθῆναι. In fact B has a marginal note μαστιγγ[, a mis-spelling for μαστιγ[. *Ed. pr.* retained ταύτην, supposing the word to mean τὴν κεφαλήν, indicated by a gesture; and J. Taillardat, *Les Images d'Aristophane*, p. 518, suggests that it means τὴν πυγήν. Since it is unlikely that Knemon confined his blows to any particular target on Pyrrhias' body, I somewhat doubtfully adopt Handley's emendation. Jacques throws doubt on the imperfect and prints ταύτῃ 'με καθαίρει with a split anapaest (and similarly Taillardat suggests ἐκάθαρε ταύτην). But apart from the fact that the imperfect is a common narrative tense, it is here very much in place, because the action ('he started to beat me') is not completed, unlike that of the preceding present tenses. Lysias iii. 17 offers a good parallel: ἐντυγχάνω . . . ἐπιλαμβάνομαι . . . ἔτυπτον.

114: Cf. *Sik.* 100, ἐμοὶ δὲ καὶ τούτῳ τί πρᾶγμ' ἐστιν;

116 ὀξύτατον . . . τι: W. G. Arnott, *Mnem.* 4th ser. xix (1967), 397, cites Heliod. iv. 7. 11, ὀξύ τι καὶ μέγα ἀνέκραγε.

117 τὸ δὲ πέρας: Like τὸ τέλος, τὸ πέρας is sometimes used adverbially, 'finally', as in *Epitr.* 287, 533, 891. But here the following γάρ rules out that use and suggests the ellipse of some verb such as ἄκουε, μάνθανε: 'listen to the end of the story.'

120: τὸ δασύ is not necessarily as impenetrable as a 'thicket'; land planted with olives is so called, Lysias vii. 7. **σφενδονῶν:** The construction of this verb is with acc. of target, dat. of missile, contrary to the English 'sling a stone at someone'. The passage is imitated by Aelian, *ep. rust.* 13, βάλλεις οὖν ἡμᾶς ταῖς βώλοις καὶ ταῖς ἀχράσι, and 14, ἔνθεν τοι βάλλω τοὺς εἰσφοιτῶντας εἰς τὸ χωρίον καὶ βώλοις καὶ λίθοις.

123 ἀνήμερον: A word previously unknown in comedy, but found in Aesch. *PV* 716, ἀνήμεροι γάρ, οὐδὲ πρόσπλατοι ξένοις. Is it too elevated a word for Pyrrhias, whose language is lively and picturesque, not literary? One cannot be confident that it is, and it will be prudent not to follow those editors who overrule B's evidence and assign the phrase to Sostratos or Chaireas. If, however, it is to be overruled, there are many possible ways of distributing the words from ἀνήμερον to γέρων; one that might deserve consideration is (Χαι.) ἀνήμερόν τι πρᾶγμα τελέως. (Πυ.) ἀνόσιος γέρων. At 117 Chaireas said μαινόμενον . . . τελέως, and this might be intended as a characteristic turn of speech (so Bingen). To assign the whole from ἀνήμερον to γέρων to Chaireas results in the division of 123 between three speakers. In this play the only trimeter so divided is 212 (L. Strzelecki, *Eos* li [1961], 261).

R. Kassel, *Gnomon* xxxiii (1961), 134, argues that ἀνήμερον . . . γέρων is a single phrase, 'an ungodly old man is a savage thing', or rather, since ἀνόcιοc is merely abusive, 'a thoroughly damnable old man is a savage thing'—not a likely *sententia*; 129–30 give no real parallel.

ἱκετεύω c', ἄπιτε: See *Epitr.* 430 n.

125: The easiest way to restore the metre is to add ὅδ' before ὀδυνωμενοc (mis-spelled ουδυνωμενοc in B), provided that a reason can be found for using ὅδε of someone not present on the stage. Most alleged examples from Menander of this use are textually uncertain (185 below, *Kolax* 120, 122, *Epitr.* 986), leaving only *Aspis* 123, where a deictic gesture towards Smikrines' house would be possible, and *Sam.* 37, where a gesture, although not impossible, seems unlikely. 'The pronoun is deictic, evolved by a people used to talking with their hands, and there must be *some* reason for a gesture of immediacy', A. M. Dale, *JHS* lxxxiv (1964), 166, discussing tragic instances. Here a gesture towards Knemon's farm (cf. τὸν ἀγρόν . . . τουτονί, 5) is perhaps conceivable; but I accept the supplement ὅδ' in default of anything else truly plausible.   **νῦν τετύχηκε** well illustrates the fact that the Greek perfect is not a past tense; the verb expresses the present consequence of a past 'chance'.

128 πρακτικώτερον: Chaireas lives up to his reputation for giving practical advice (56). It is comic that he advises inaction. B's original reading πρακτικώτατον makes good sense; the change to the comparative must have been a deliberate correction to agree with the exemplar or some other text. This gives the comparative better authority: it should be kept.

129 εὐκαιρία may have been a vogue word of Menander's day; cf. Ter. *HT* 364, 'in tempore ad eam ueni, quod rerum omniumst primum', and Theophrastos' amusing portrait of the ἄκαιροc, *Char.* 12.   **νοῦν ἔχετε:** Imperative, addressed primarily to Sostratos, like 123, ἱκετεύω c', ἄπιτε, but including Chaireas. The plural form makes it impossible to take ἔχετε as indicative; as yet Chaireas alone has, in Pyrrhias' view, shown any sense.

130 πένηc: See 327 n.

132 μόνοc: Chaireas proposes to take the affair into his own hands, as he had suggested at 65 would be the correct procedure. His failure to do anything today is not to be allowed to diminish his importance.

134 διάτριβε: 'Let the time pass'; the word can be used either of

wasting, or of occupying, one's time. Here it seems to be neutral.
καὶ cú is to be taken with ἀπελθών, 'going home like me'.

135: Cf. *Aspis* 394, πρόφαϲιν εἴληφ' ἄϲμενοϲ. The absence of stage
directions from the papyrus here is regrettable, since it is left uncertain whether Chaireas departs at 134. That he does so seems likely,
since the previous lines clearly prepare for his going, and 135–8
cannot be intended for his ears. Jacques, however, argues that these
lines are an aside and that Chaireas does not finally depart until at
147 Knemon is imagined as in sight. This enables him to assign 145–6
to Chaireas and so justify the paragraphus there (see n. ad loc.).
But the solution brings its own difficulties: (1) it is necessary to disregard the fact that H 1 assigns 145 to Sostratos; (2) if we assume the
three-actor rule, the same actor plays Chaireas and Knemon. Is there
time between 147 and 153 (at the latest) for him to depart by the
right *parodos*, change his mask and costume, and enter by the left
parodos? A departure at 134 would make this much easier.

138 ἐπιβολήν, meaning 'design', known from Polybios and later
authors, is a likely supplement. Page's βουλὴν ἐμήν is improbable; τὴν
ἐμὴν βουλήν would be expected, cf. W. G. Arnott, *Class. Journ.* lviii
(1962), 127.

140–1: Supplements are uncertain, but the general sense seems clear,
and those printed in OCT will not be seriously misleading.

142–6: There should be no doubt that cὺ δὲ τούτῳ λάλει is spoken by
Pyrrhias to Sostratos, who replies: 'I couldn't'; I'm never a persuasive
talker.' It follows that ὑπάγω, βέλτιϲτε is also spoken by Pyrrhias.
βέλτιϲτε is normally a polite address to a man whose name is not known
(*Sam.* 81 is an exception), and is therefore probably directed towards
the approaching Knemon: 'I am retiring, sir.' There is no parallel in
New Comedy for its use by a slave to his master. It remains uncertain,
however, whether αὐτόϲ is to be taken (*a*) with ὑπάγω, or (*b*) with
πάρεϲτί γ' οὑτοϲί (Lloyd-Jones), or (*c*) is a question interjected by
Sostratos (Handley, Bingen²).

The problem has been confused by reports of readings of H 1 made
by scholars who had seen only photographs. Inspection of the fragment (from which the ends of the lines are lost) leaves me unconvinced
that there was any *nota personae* before 143 or any paragraphus
anywhere. 144 has no dicola, and I think no punctuation, although
a high point after αγω may be guessed rather than seen. Before 145
something was written, probably an abbreviated form of Sostratos'
name; τ is likely, and I should like to see]ωϲτρ'. H 1 is then consonant
with (*a*), but speaks against (*c*) and to some extent against (*b*), since
this MS. has punctuation after δυναιμην (145) and θυραϲ (149). B has

dicola at the end of 143 and 144, and perhaps after βέλτιστε. To suppose all to indicate a change of speaker leads to an unacceptable distribution of parts. But if the dicolon at the end of 143 marks a change of person addressed, there is no difficulty. Pyrrhias turns from Sostratos to Knemon: 'I'm retiring of my own accord, sir'; there should then be, and perhaps is, another dicolon to mark that he turns back to his master: 'But *you* chat with him.' The evidence of B then speaks against (*b*). Since it has lost the beginning of the line, we do not know whether it had a dicolon after αυτος and so supported (*c*). The available evidence, that of H 1, favours (*a*), which may be right. Yet (*b*) is so much more effective that it has been adopted in OCT.

(iv) 145–152: *Sostratos alone*

146: B has a paragraphus below the line and a dicolon after]νι. There must be some error here if 144 has been rightly interpreted. All difficulty is solved by disregarding both signs, but this is high-handed. Another possibility is that a dicolon has been omitted after λαλεῖν, and that the end of the line is a question by Pyrrhias. Yet he seems to make his exit at 144.

Very hesitantly, I prefer to disregard dicolon and paragraphus and would choose to fill the gap with Kraus's ποῖον λέγει[ν δὲ τῷδ' ἔ]νι; If Pyrrhias is the speaker, ποῖον λέγει[ς cὺ τουτο]νί or something similar would be more suitable.

148 ὡς δ' ἐcπούδακε: Ar. *Thesm.* 571, γυνή τις ἡμῖν | ἐcπουδακυῖα προcτρέχει, Philemon frag. 79 K, a hen that has picked up something too big to swallow περιτρέχει κύκλῳ | τηροῦcα τοῦτο, καταπιεῖν δ' ἐcπούδακεν, ἕτεραι διώκουcιν δὲ ταύτην. These passages do not justify the meaning 'hurry'; rather 'he is bent on business'.

149: The word before βοᾷ is uncertain. Against Lloyd-Jones's ingenious ἀλλ' Ἄρη βοᾷ (cf. Ar. *Plut.* 328) is the absence in B of an apostrophe. The traces do not exclude ἀλλὰ γάρ (*pace* Jacques; see the same combination of αγ in 180), which is usually read. The fact that Knemon is talking loudly to himself as he walks is evidence that he is not in his right mind (for this common meaning of ὑγιαίνειν cf. *Perik.* 470, Ἀr. *Plut.* 364, and Damoxenos frag. 2 K, καὶ νῦν δ' οὐχ ὑγιαίνειν μοι δοκῶ). γάρ will then introduce an anticipatory reason. But in this usage we normally meet ἀλλά . . . γάρ, not ἀλλὰ γάρ; Denniston, *GP* 99, can find only three, or perhaps four, examples of the latter. This passage may provide another, but ἀλλὰ καί seems possible (cf. ακ in 138), and is as good in sense, 'but he's actually talking out loud'.

151 μέντοι: Confirmatory, as is usual in Menander, not adversative.

μὰ τὸν Ἀπόλλω: Unless joined with ναί (thus commonly ναὶ μὰ Δία, also ναὶ μὰ τοὺς θεούς, Xen. *Cyr.* ii. 2. 2, ναὶ μὰ τὰς Νύμφας, Eupolis frag. 74 K, and comic variants like ναὶ μὰ τὰς κράμβας, ibid.), μά is in Attic confined to negative sentences, although there may be an ellipse of the negative phrase, e.g. μὰ Δία stands alone as a denial. If this were the only contrary instance, one could confidently accept the correction νὴ τὸν Ἀπόλλω; but μά recurs in a positive assertion at 639 (see note) and perhaps at 718 (see note). The positive usage is also found in Aristainetos i. 10, Achilles Tatius viii. 5, Lucian, *Cal.* 14, Libanios xxvi. 23, 31 (Δύσκολος γήμας λάλον γυναῖκα, a work which has echoes of this play), Alkiphron *ep.* iv. 18. 1 and 19. 1 (letters from and to Menander); these late authors may have copied something they found in their texts of Attic Comedy. In Plaut. *Captivi* 880, μὰ τὸν Ἀπόλλω is affirmative and confirmed by metre, but associated with the Doric oath ναὶ τὰν Πραινέστην; affirmative μά is frequent in the Life (G) of Aesop (e.g. cc. 8, 15, 25, 26, 48, 52), which B. E. Perry, *Aesopica* i, shows to have been composed in Egypt in the first century A.D.

152 μὴ οὐχί: The double negative is illogical, and in Ar. *Plut.* 252 we read τί γὰρ ἄν τις οὐχὶ πρός σε τἀληθὲς λέγοι; and in Eur. *IA* 1423 τί γὰρ τἀληθὲς οὐκ εἴποι τις ἄν; Hence many editors follow Fraenkel in expunging μή. But there is no obvious reason for its interpolation, unless Lloyd-Jones is right in supposing it to have been suggested by νη in the line above, and its presence may be due to the influence of phrases like τί κωλύει μὴ οὐ λέγειν, or αἰσχρόν ἐστι μὴ οὐ φάναι (Plato, *Prot.* 352 d), which are near in meaning. Cf. Plato, *Theaet.* 153 a, τίς οὖν ἂν . . . δύναιτο ἀμφισβητήσας μὴ οὐ καταγέλαστος γενέσθαι; (so W (?), Eusebios, Stobaios; μὴ καταγέλαστος BT).

Another apparently false double negative in the papyrus of Hypereides, *pro Euxenippo* xx. 26, λέγειν μὴ οὐ τὰ ἄριστα, may be seen as a parallel either for the interpolation of a second negative or for an illogical popular use of two negatives. Handley calls attention to Plato, *Phil.* 12 e, πῶς γὰρ ἡδονή γε ἡδονῇ μὴ οὐχ ὁμοιότατον ἂν εἴη; (so TWD). But Hackforth, *Plato's Examination of Pleasure*, p. 15, following H. Jackson, repunctuates πῶς γὰρ ἡδονῇ γε ἡδονή; μὴ (= *num*) οὐχ ὁμοιότατον ἂν εἴη τοῦτο αὐτὸ ἑαυτῷ;

(v) 153–178: *Sostratos, Knemon*

153: Nine lines have intervened since Knemon was first sighted, during which the audience waits with growing suspense for his arrival. What will he look like? What will he do? What will he say? One may suppose that the maker of his mask had devised something striking, and the poet has found quite unexpected words for him. He starts talking about Perseus, the last subject anyone would have forecast.

When Jacques writes that 'the reference to Perseus, like all similar mythological allusions, may come from tragedy', he cannot be refuted, but it must not be supposed that the Athenians knew no mythology unless they had seen it on the stage; one can hardly *assert* that the references to Perseus here and to Atlas at 683 are derived from Euripides' *Andromeda* (cf. L. A. Post, *AJP* lxxxii [1961], 96).

εἶτ' οὐ: J. Martin well compares three other passages where εἶτ' οὐ introduces a similar appeal: frag. 718, εἶτ' οὐ δικαίως προσπεπατταλευμένον γράφουσι τὸν Προμηθέα πρὸς ταῖς πέτραις; Antiphanes frag. 159 K, εἶτ' οὐ σοφοὶ δῆτ' εἰσὶν οἱ Σκύθαι σφόδρα, οἳ γενομένοισιν εὐθέως τοῖς παιδίοις διδόασιν ἵππων καὶ βοῶν πίνειν γάλα; Aristophon frag. 11 K, εἶτ' οὐ δικαίως ἐστ' ἀπεψηφισμένος ὑπὸ τῶν θεῶν τῶν δώδεκ' εἰκότως τ' Ἔρως;

156 τοιοῦτο κτῆμα: 'Such a fine possession', i.e. the decapitated Medusa's head. The correction ᾧ λίθους, rather than ὃ λιθινούς, is supported by Aelian's imitation, *ep. rust.* 14, μακάριον δὲ ἥγημαι τὸν Περσέα κατὰ δύο τρόπους ἐκεῖνον, ὅτι τε πτηνὸς ἦν καὶ οὐδενὶ συνήντα ὑπεράνω τε ἦν τοῦ προσαγορεύειν τινὰ καὶ ἀσπάζεσθαι. ζηλῶ δὲ αὐτὸν καὶ τοῦ κτήματος ἐκείνου εὖ μάλα ᾧ τοὺς συναντῶντας ἐποίει λίθους. οὗπερ οὖν εἴ μοι τις εὐμάρεια κατατυχεῖν ἐγένετο, οὐδὲν ἂν ἦν ἀφθονώτερον λιθίνων ἀνδριάντων.

161 ἐπεμβαίνοντες: The connotations of this double compound are either hostility or taking a stand, occupying something. Both are suitable here.

162: Most editors join ἤδη with the previous line, and I side with them. But there is no other complete sentence in Menander that ends in ἤδη, and such a position is unusual elsewhere. The likeness obtained with 165–6 may appeal to some, and be thought repetitious by others.

παρ' αὐτήν κτλ.: This is in effect ironical; the relative clause ὃς οὐδ' ἐργάζομαι adduces a fact to show how far from the truth the first clause is, cf. 868, *Sam.* 413. There is an echo of this passage, combined with 115, in Libanios, *Decl.* xxvii (Δύσκολοι ὤλισθεν). 5, ὅς, ἵνα μηδὲ ἄκων τινὶ περιτύχω, οὐδὲ τὴν δημοσίαν εἴωθα βαδίζειν ὁδόν, and in Aelian, *ep. rust.* 14, ἔνθεν τοι καὶ τοῦ χωρίου τὸ παρὰ τὴν ὁδὸν μέρος ἀργὸν εἴασα. For νὴ Δία in an ironical statement Handley quotes Dem. xix. 222, ἀλλὰ διὰ τί σοῦ κατηγορῶ; συκοφαντῶ νὴ Δία, ἵν' ἀργύριον λάβω παρὰ σοῦ.

163 διατρίβειν: Clearly 'hang about', 'waste my time', for Knemon proceeds to say that he does not 'even' work there, cf. 134 n.

164: Handley (following Kraus and Kamerbeek) defends B's text, τοιοῦτο τὸ μέρος χωρίου, taking τοιοῦτο to be predicative, 'although it is as it is, i.e. better land than that up the hill'. I do not find this convincing, since in the context there is no mention, to which τοιοῦτο could refer, of the quality of the roadside land. Handley himself admits to being disturbed by the omission of the article with χωρίου: his suggested explanations are unsatisfactory.

166 ὦ πολυπληθείας: Pollux iv. 163 quotes this word from Demosthenes and Hypereides.

168–71: B's readings, ἆρα τυπ⟨τ⟩ήςεις γε με and ἐμοὶ χαλεπαίνει, appear to me defensible, although not certainly right. ἆρα τυπτήςεις γε με (a phrase that recurs with a slight modification at *Sam.* 574, ἀλλὰ τυπτήςεις με;) is a response to a threatening gesture, intended to remind the aggressor to keep the law. Sostratos has withdrawn only 'a little' (148), so that Knemon, as he approaches, can effectively make a threatening movement. To Sostratos' warning question Knemon makes no direct reply but, as Handley well puts it, talks *at* him. Sostratos' next remark, 'he is angry with *me*' (note the emphatically placed ἐμοὶ) shows him to realize that he is faced not merely with an angry man but with a man who is angry with him in particular. He then turns to Knemon and tries to appease him by claiming that he has business there and is not one of those who inflict themselves on Knemon's privacy without cause. Compare the gaoler of Plato, *Phaedo* 116 c, who says to Socrates οὐκ ἐμοὶ χαλεπαίνεις, γιγνώςκεις γὰρ τοὺς αἰτίους, ἀλλ' ἐκείνοις. Nevertheless this interpretation seems a little forced and Handley may be right to accept both the emendations that have been proposed, *ed. pr.*'s ἆρα τυπτήςει γε με and van Groningen's ἐμοὶ χαλεπαίνεις; In any case Sostratos' hastily concocted fiction does nothing but increase Knemon's irritation.

168 γέ με: Rather than γ' ἐμέ, cf. *Samia* 574, ἀλλὰ τυπτήςεις μ'; Ar. *Plut.* 21, οὐ γάρ με τυπτήςεις.

169: Libanios, *Decl.* xxvi (Δύςκολος γήμας λάλον γυναῖκα). 4, λαβὼν ἀπὸ τῆς κλίνης σχοινίον ἐλθὼν ἂν εἰς ἐρημίαν ἐπί τι δένδρον ἀπηγχόμην.

173 ςτοάν: A covered colonnade, where people might meet for a variety of purposes. The Cτοὰ Ποικίλη, or Painted Stoa, gave its name to the Stoics, since Zeno taught there. νενομίκατε plural, 'you and your friends', and perfect with present meaning, 'it is your view', cf. 833 n. ἢ τὸ τοῦ Λεώ: B's corrected reading can be interpreted as ἢ τὸ τοῦ λεώ or ἢ τὸ τοῦ Λεώ. λεώς is generally used of the assembled people and is, outside poetry, more or less restricted to the vocative plural, in phrases like ἀκούετε λεώ, ἴτε λεώ. It is perhaps not impossible that τὸ τοῦ λεώ means, as G. Monaco suggests (*SIFC* xxi [1959], 236), 'the place where the people assembles'. But no parallel is known, and unless one turns up, probability must be considered to lie with the linguistically satisfactory alternative τὸ τοῦ Λεώ, proposed by S. Koumanoudis, *Platon* xxi (1959), 91. Leos was a hero; the position of his shrine is unknown, but R. E. Wycherley, *Mnem.* 4th ser. xviii (1965), 282, points out that a dedication to him has been found in the NE. corner of the *agora* (*Hesperia* ix [1940], 59 n. 8), so that it may have been here; if so, it may have been a habitual rendezvous. Koumanoudis thought, however, that the reference was to the Λεωκόρειον, which commemorated his daughters and was a famous landmark in or near the northern part of the *agora*. It may be noted that Ποικίλη Cτοά and Λεωκόρειον are associated, as places where men might be met, by Theophylaktos Simokates, *qu. nat.* 1. But τὸ τοῦ Λεώ must mean the shrine of Leos, cf. τὸ τοῦ Πανός, Ar. *Lys.* 911. Hence Wycherley would read τὸ τῶν Λεώ, 'the shrine of the daughters of Leos'. To show that this shrine was associated with dubious company he quotes Dem. liv. 7–8 (a brawl there), Apostolios x. 53 (*Paroem. gr.* ii. 500), λεωκόριον οἰκεῖς· ἐπὶ τῶν λιμωττόντων, Alkiphron iii. 15. 1 (a haunt of *hetairai*). There is not enough evidence to support a confident decision.

175 ἀπαντᾶν: Lloyd-Jones's brilliant emendation explains the construction of πρός with accusative in the previous line: 'If you want to see someone, arrange to come to *my* door to meet him; yes, by all means, and build a seat there, etc.' ἀπαντᾶν is more usually constructed with εἰς, but cf. frag. 700, ἀναμενῶ ϲε πρὸς τοὔλαιον ('where oil is sold'). For the phrasing compare Heliod. ii. 7, ἀναμεῖναί τινας ἐν ταύτῃ ϲυντεταγμένῳ. This text implies that Knemon's house will become a regular rendezvous, so that the amenity of a seat will be welcome. Its construction will be once for all (aorist imperative), but the arrangements to meet will be repeated (present imperative).

176 θῶκον: A reason for the use of the Ionic form θῶκος is hard to find, and perhaps it is a mere error for the Attic θᾶκος. Knemon will mean a bench on which people can sit while waiting.

177 ϲυνέδριον: Perhaps 'a meeting-house'. The word more frequently means 'council', 'board', but also a 'council-chamber', and it may denote a private place of meeting, Polybios ii. 39. 1, ἐνεπρήϲθη τὰ ϲυνέδρια τῶν Πυθαγορείων. But in Plato, *Prot.* 317 d, the company 'construct' a ϲυνέδριον extempore by collecting benches and couches; and it may be that Knemon thinks not of a building, but of extensive seating, as opposed to the single θῶκος. Something of this kind seems also to be intended in Pherekrates frag. 64 K, where the seller of perfumes sits under a parasol, κατεϲκευαϲμένον (middle) ϲυνέδριον τοῖϲ μειρακίοιϲ. The dicolon after the word indicates that Knemon ceases to address Sostratos, and talks to himself.

178 ἐπηρεαϲμόϲ: 'Malicious interference'; Arist. *Rhet.* 1378ᵇ18 defines ἐπηρεαϲμόϲ as ἐμποδιϲμὸϲ ταῖϲ βουλήϲεϲιν, οὐχ ἵνα τι αὐτῷ, ἀλλ' ἵνα μὴ ἐκείνῳ.

(vi) **179–188:** *Sostratos alone*

179: Lit. 'this affair is no matter of a trifling effort, but of one more intense'. The genitive is hard to classify. Dr. Austin calls my attention to Dem. viii. 48, δοκεῖ ταῦτα . . . καὶ πόνων πολλῶν καὶ πραγματείαϲ εἶναι, and Plato, *Gorgias* 461 a, οὐκ ὀλίγηϲ ϲυνουϲίαϲ ἐϲτί, *Laws* 708 d, χρόνου πολλοῦ, passages which grammarians include under the heading of 'possessive genitives'. A more usual form of expression is seen in frag. 680, ἀναδραμεῖν δὲ τὴν ἁμαρτίαν | οὐ τοῦ τυχόντοϲ ἀνδρόϲ, ἀλλ' ἀξιολόγου, where the genitive indicates the agent in whose power it is to act (Schwyzer, ii. 123–4). Perhaps the general concept is one of 'belonging to'.

180 γ': If this is the correct addition, γε is to be taken with the whole phrase τουτὶ τὸ πρᾶγμα, cf. 414 n.

182 τὸν τοῦ πατρόϲ: 'My father's slave'. Sostratos expects to find him at his father's house in the neighbourhood (40).

183 ἔχει ⟨τι⟩ διάπυρον: 'Fieriness' does not seem a quality likely to conciliate Knemon, nor does Getas display it in the sequel: the tormenting of the disabled Knemon in Act V hardly deserves this description. I am loath to join W. Kraus, *Anzeiger f. Altertumswissenschaft* xv (1962), 7, in condemning Menander for carelessness. Perhaps the word διάπυροϲ is here used in the sense of 'energetic' or 'spirited': Plutarch, *Mor.* 805 a, says that embassies to the Emperor need a man διαπύρου καὶ θάρϲοϲ ἅμα καὶ νοῦν ἔχοντοϲ. ἔχει ⟨τι⟩ διαπονεῖν, he knows how to stick to a job and finish it', would suit this context, where Sostratos has just declared that no ordinary pains are needed; it would also suit the character of Getas, one of long-suffering patience (402–9, 476–9, 546–51, 563–9, ? 886).

185 τὸ τοῦδ': Although ὅδε is not normally used by Menander except of someone on the stage, Knemon has so recently left that it may be permissible here, as in *Aspis* 123 n. The alternative correction τούτου δ' introduces an unnecessary δέ. The correct remedy for the missing long syllable (or two short ones) is uncertain. If the optative ἀπωϲαιτ' of B is right, there is no alternative to τάχ' ἄν; but the phrase οἶδ' ἐγώ suggests a more positive statement than τάχ' ἂν ἀπώσαιτο. Hence many editors, seeing the common confusion of αι and ε, read ἀπωσετ(αι). If this is right, several supplements are possible: I adopt Diano's πᾶν exempli gratia. Ed. pr.'s ὡc gives a construction for οἶδα not yet known in Menander.

186 μέν: The opening of the door in 188 prevents this sentence from receiving the expected δέ clause. If we may guess at Sostratos' intended speech, his meaning may have been: 'For, although I do not approve of delay, I do not *myself* see what's to be done.'   χρόνον ἐμποιεῖν: Cf. Dem. xxiii. 93.

187: The minimum correction is Handley's πόλλ' ἄν for πολλα δ' αν; the repetition of ἄν, although paralleled in other authors, has no warrant as yet in Menander and πόλλ' ἐν of ed. pr. is more probable. The phrase ἐν ἡμέρᾳ μιᾷ recurs at 864, *Aspis* 417, *Karch.* 8.

188 τὴν θύραν πέπληχε: The phrase may indicate that the girl comes out in haste, see *Sam.* 300–1 n. Sostratos will by now be on the point of going off to the right; he will thus not stand between the girl and the cave, towards which she moves at 197.

(vii) **189–218:** *Sostratos, Knemon's daughter* (exit 214), *Daos* (enters 206)

189: Cf. *Sam.* 398 n., Eur. *Phoen.* 373, οἴμοι τῶν ἐμῶν ἐγὼ κακῶν. In such phrases the genitive depends, it would seem, by origin on a 'suppressed' verb, of which ἐγώ is the subject. This verb would express a feeling caused by the thing of which the name is in the genitive. But it is not to be supposed that speakers had the historic sense to recognize this, or that they had any verb in mind (Schwyzer, ii. 133–4).

Knemon's unexpectedly early return has caught his household unprepared. The spectator will not notice what an analytical reader may observe, that no good reason is provided for this early return. He had not pursued Pyrrhias hot-foot, but arrived after an interval, talking generalities and not directly mentioning the trespasser. At the time one accepts his coming, because Pyrrhias' belief that he is being chased prepares one for it. Knemon's actual entry, in which he shows no concern for the pursuit of Pyrrhias, makes an effective dramatic surprise. But if he is not chasing Pyrrhias, why does he return home, unless the time has come for knocking off work?

190 κάδον: Defined by Ammonios *diff.* 73 Nickau as ᾧ ἐκ τοῦ φρέατος ἀνιμῶcι τὸ ὕδωρ. Where the material is mentioned at all it is usually bronze, but that may be because an earthenware κάδος was more usual. For references see *Studi della scuola papirologica* (R. Acc. Milan), iii. 137. The Greek well was not usually equipped with a windlass; the bucket, let down on a rope by hand, could therefore be dropped.

192 ὦ Διοσκόρω φίλω: The children of Zeus, Castor and Pollux, are gods called upon for help, Ar. *Eccl.* 1069, or thanked for help, *Peace* 285. B has διοσκουρω, but the Attic form is Διοσκόρω, Phrynichos 212, confirmed by the metre in all other passages in dramatic verse where the name occurs, except the lyric Eur. *IA* 769.

193 θερμὸν ⟨δ'⟩ ὕδωρ: For washing, cf. Amphis frag. 7 K. θερμόν alone can mean hot water (e.g. Ar. *Clouds* 1044), and it is *conceivable* that ὕδωρ is an intruded explanation, but to restore the line on that assumption is unnecessary ingenuity when simpler remedies are to hand. I adopt the simplest.

194 ἐξιών is perhaps just intelligible. When Knemon went out, he said to his daughter 'Get some water warmed up for me', meaning not that she should do it immediately but that she should have the water ready for his return. He had come back unexpectedly soon, through chasing the intruder Pyrrhias off his land, and so she had been caught unprepared. But although it is not difficult to imagine this story, it has no advantage over the more obvious way of motivating the girl's appearance, namely that Knemon, on arriving home, had called for hot water. Hence there is much probability in the suggestion of Zuntz, *CR* N.s. xx (1970), 7, that ἐξιών is a mistake for εἰσιών.

194: As in 193, restoration is uncertain. ἄνδρες, τί δρῶ; (Barrett) is attractive. It is reasonable that Sostratos should be in doubt what to do, since Athenian manners would not normally allow a stranger to address a respectable girl. Aristophanes has τί δρῶ; (*Plut.* 222, *Thesm.* 70, 925), but δρᾶν is not used elsewhere by Menander except at *Sam.* 568. Barigazzi's ἄνδρες, τέρας is supported by Damoxenos frag. 3 in Athen. 15 b, ἐφαίνετο τέρας τι κάλλους, ἄνδρες. For the appeal to the audience, see introduction, p. 14.

195: Handley tries to rehabilitate *ed. pr.*'s generally despised supplement κακὴν κακῶς by quoting Eur. *Cycl.* 268, ἦ κακῶς οὗτοι κακοὶ οἱ παῖδες ἀπόλοινθ' οὓς μάλιστ' ἐγὼ φιλῶ. Here there can be no deliberate suggestion by Silenos that the satyrs *are* κακοί. Nevertheless, his use of the phrase is intended to be comically inappropriate, and I do not find it an adequate parallel. A collection of the instances of the formula κακὸν κακῶς is given by B. Gygh-Wyss, *Das nominale Poly-ptoton usw.*, pp. 80–2.

196: A dicolon after ἐκείνην is probable, but not certain (J. Martin thinks one has been deleted); there is no paragraphus under the line. It is a hard choice whether to disregard the dicolon, if such it be, and to give the second half of the line to the girl, or to supply a paragraphus and give it to Sostratos. To me the words seem slightly more natural in the girl's mouth. If they do belong to her the line may have ended with the feminine oath μὰ τὼ θεώ (Demeter and Persephone), but Gallavotti's μάτην λαλεῖν, preferred by Handley, makes good sense: 'There's no time for useless chatter.' If Sostratos is the speaker, he must have ended either μὰ τοὺς θεούς or μὰ τὸν Δία.

198 ἄρα: 'As they well may be doing', cf. 665 n. and *Epitr.* 295.

199: The line has been variously completed. δ[οῦναι θέλῃς is widely accepted and may be right, but θέλειν is at the best a rare word in Menander, cf. 269 n. The general sense is not in doubt, and so I print a possible but uncertain supplement in OCT.

200: The obvious way to fill the gap is with τ[ὴν ὑδρίαν], but τὴν χύτραν (cooking-pot) is possible, if Knemon's frugal economy denied his household the proper vessel for fetching water, just as it failed to provide a spare bucket.

201: B gives ναὶ πρὸς θεῶν to the girl, and although the words would be suitable enough in Sostratos' mouth, if she showed maidenly hesitation (503, Ar. *Clouds* 784, etc.), they are no less suitable to her. What follows defies certain restoration. Several editors read ἄνθρωπε, but this mode of address always carries a note of superiority or contempt. Quincey's ἄρυσόν γ' is only made long enough for the gap by introducing an unwanted γε, which would sharpen the tone of command, Denniston, *GP* 125. Although the verb ἀνύειν is not found elsewhere in Menander and only once in New Comedy, Anaxilas frag. 37 K, Barigazzi's ἄνυσον δ' is as likely as anything, cf. Ar. frag. 102, ἀλλ' ἄνυσον, οὐ μέλλειν ἐχρῆν, and Plautus, *Rudens* 438: 'SCEP. cedo mi urnam. AMP. cape, propera, amabo, ecferre.'

202: 'Country girl though she is, she has the manners of a lady.' B rightly gives the next sentence also to Sostratos: ὦ πολυτίμητοι θεοί is known only as a masculine exclamation. The lover prays to be preserved, because he is in danger of 'dying of love' if he is unsuccessful, cf. 379–80. Elsewhere in Menander this exclamation always precedes the phrase to be emphasized (*Dysk.* 381, 479, *Aspis* 408, *Fab. inc.* 56, frag. 97, where Körte–Thierfelder's punctuation needs amending), and the heavy stop is therefore best placed before it here. This position of the words is, however, not obligatory: Antiphanes frag. 145 K has them parenthetically and late.

203 τίς ἂν ἐμὲ cώcαι δαιμόνων; Lloyd-Jones silently (and perhaps rightly) alters ἐμέ to με. But the emphatic ἐμέ can be defended, if Sostratos is supposed to think that he is saving the girl and the old woman from their difficulties, but that a god's intervention is needed to save *him*. For cώζειν in the sense of bringing a lover safely to his goal, cf. 378 n. δ[αιμόνων] is an uncertain supplement, but cf. *Epitr.* 855, τίς ἂν θεῶν τάλαιναν ἐλεήcειέ με;: τ[ῶν πόνων], 'pangs of love', of *ed. pr.* implies a τ of unusual shape.

204 τίς ἐψόφηκεν: The noise was made by the opening, not of Knemon's door, but of Gorgias', from which Daos emerges (206). It is generally supposed that the girl, in mistaken alarm, runs back to her own house. This is not quite right. An actor could not utter the words ἔπειτα . . . ἔξω while running, and they cannot be separated from ἆρ' ὁ πάππας ἔρχεται. The girl returns towards her door after 205, when she has seen that her father is *not* emerging, and that she will not run straight into him. That she does return then is suggested by 211–12, on which see n., and perhaps by the fact that Daos does not see her when he first turns to face the audience (208). His first sentences, down to ἐcτιν, are spoken into the house, to Gorgias' mother. ὁ δέ means Gorgias. Daos' opening sentence clearly characterizes him at once as having the old retainer's privilege to grumble, and as a hard-working servant; a shirker would protract the comparatively easy household jobs to avoid the hard labour of digging. The rest of his speech prolongs the time that Sostratos remains in the cave to fill the pitcher, while the girl waits apprehensively. Its matter reminds the audience of Gorgias' poverty, touched on in the prologue (25); this is important in view of later developments, Sostratos' generous offer of friendship and his own attempted refusal of an advantageous marriage.

209–11: Cf. Ar. *Plut.* 437, πενία . . . ἢ cφῷν ξυνοικῶ. Ibid. 456, ὦ κάκιcτ' ἀπολουμένη is addressed to Πενία; cf. also Amphis frag. 23 K, Πλοῦτος . . . ἔνδον κάθηται. The concept of poverty as a resident in one's house is as early as Theognis 351,

ἆ δειλὴ πενίη, τί μένεις;
. . . ἀλλ' ἴθι καὶ δόμον ἄλλον ἐποίχεο,

cf. Plato, *Symp.* 203 d, ἐνδείᾳ cύνοικος, Kritias frag. 29 Diels–Kranz.

τηλικοῦτο: This form of the neuter, for the usual τηλικοῦτον, occurs in *Aspis* 215 and Alexis frag. 244. Not exactly 'Why do we find you so great a burden?', but 'Why have we lighted on you in such measure?', i.e. 'Why are we so poor?'

211 ff.: One cannot be certain what action is intended here. Perhaps Sostratos emerges from the shrine with the words λάμβανε τηνδί, to find that the girl has retreated to her own doorway, fearful of being found out of doors by her father; she then calls to him φέρε δεῦρο. One may compare the scene in Plautus' *Rudens* where Sceparnio returns with the pitcher to find that Ampelisca, who has been frightened, has disappeared: 'Cape aquam hanc sis. ubi es?' (465).

212: It is remarkable what life Menander has given to the girl in the few lines she speaks. In the domestic crisis that has arisen her first concern is not for herself but for her old nurse. Then the address to the Nymphs, ὦ φίλταται Νύμφαι, shows real warmth of feeling by the superlative. It can be understood that this child, brought up alone with two old people, has made imaginary friends, as such children will. Her reply to Sostratos' offer of help is naïvely direct: thinking of nothing but her predicament, she does not utter a word to call attention to herself or to indicate any interest in him. Her one idea is to get the water (φέρε δεῦρο) and, that achieved, she disappears without a word of acknowledgement. J. Martin and Kraus assign φέρε δεῦρο . . . πατρός to Daos, whom they suppose to intervene to prevent contact between the girl and the stranger. But since the words λάμβανε τηνδί are the first to draw his attention to what is going on, this would require lightning action on his part. Nor is there any reason why he should tell the girl to take care of her father, whom he has no cause to love, cf. 247. In Sostratos' mouth the words are appropriate; he wants the old man to be in a good temper, and moreover gladly imagines the girl to be kind and helpful, qualities he will value in a wife.   βούλεθ': *Fab. incert.* 62, quoted by Handley in support of B's ἐβούλετο, only emphasizes its improbability. τί ποτε ἐβούλετο; is there asked because the man's past actions are inexplicable in view of his present ones. In the present situation 'What was he after in coming here at all?' is not a plausible immediate reaction to the unexpected sight of the young man in conversation with the girl, even if the question might be asked after reflection. 'What is he up to?' is the only credible question here. There is no reason for believing that the *scriptio plena* of B goes back to Menander himself; the spelling ποτ'εβουλετοουτοςι may merely represent a reader's interpretation of ποτεβουλεθουτοςι. τί ποτε βούλεται; recurs at *Aspis* 403.

213: B has a dicolon after πατρος, marking that the following words are addressed by Sostratos not to the girl, but to himself, cf. 177 n.
      ἐπιμελοῦ: Is this what Sostratos said, or should it be ἐπιμέλου? ἐπιμέλομαι is the predominant form in papyri of the third century, hence Witkowski, *Epist. privat. gr.* 9, prints ἐπιμέλου δὲ καὶ ϲαυτοῦ ὅπωϲ ὑγιαίνηϲ (260 B.C.). But ἐπιμελοῦμαι prevails in Attic inscriptions (Meisterhans³, p. 175) and is guaranteed by metre at *Heros* 26, *Georg.* 62.

215: B assigns παῦε θρηνῶν κτλ. to Pyrrhias, and all editors except Blake have given κατὰ τρόπον τί; to Sostratos. This will not do. Sostratos might ask *how* things will turn out all right; he cannot ask *what* will turn out all right, since he must know perfectly well what Pyrrhias means. The question belongs to Daos, as was seen by E. Grassi, *Atene e Roma* N.s. vi (1961), 144. He overhears ἔσται κατὰ τρόπον, and his suspicions are aroused; what is this promised success?

Grassi further saw that the papyrus has fallen into a natural and tempting error by making Pyrrhias the speaker of παῦε θρηνῶν κτλ. This and μὴ φοβοῦ κτλ. are addressed to himself by *Sostratos*, cf. *Sam.* 326, 349. Pyrrhias went off at 144, to all appearance; Knemon sees no one about but Sostratos, and there is nothing to hint that the slave remains lurking somewhere in the background. (Some make him hide in the cave, but action of this sort without any clue in the text is unparalleled.) This might be accepted if what Pyrrhias is supposed to say were in character or dramatically useful. But Pyrrhias has in the earlier scene not shown any interest in Sostratos' success, and he has no reason for here enjoining optimism. Nor would he be likely to counsel Sostratos to return: his one idea has been to put a good distance between himself and Knemon, and he could not be sure that Sostratos would not bring him back as well as Getas. Characters can, no doubt, show a change of front, but they do not change front without reason at the very moment when they disappear from the play for good.

The very phrase παῦε θρηνῶν is evidence that Sostratos is the speaker. θρῆνος, θρηνῶ, etc., are mainly poetic words; θρῆνος is unknown in comedy, θρηνεῖν occurs in a magniloquent passage of Phrynichos (frag. 69 K), in lyrics in Aristophanes, *Birds* 211, in a paratragic context, *Clouds* 1260, and in anapaests in Alexis frag. 162 (φθόγγους ἀλύρους θρηνεῖν, clearly paratragic). To call a single οἴμοι κακοδαίμων a θρῆνος, 'a dirge', is exaggerated language, which Sostratos can properly use in irony at his own expense—to jest at his own expense is characteristic of him, cf. his narratives 522 ff. and 666 ff.— but which is quite out of place in Pyrrhias' mouth.

Sostratos in the early part of this act showed no self-confidence. But seeing the girl again, this time he spoke to her, perhaps after an initial hesitation. Inspired by this, he becomes more decisive, and assures himself that all will turn out well. He still does not rely upon himself, but will consult with Getas. But his confidence grows, and at 267 he is ready to try what he can do without help.

The supposed presence of Pyrrhias creates severe difficulties for those who believe that Menander had only three speaking actors at his disposal. According to G. P. Goold, *Phoenix* xiii (1959), 147, the same man played the girl and Pyrrhias, withdrawing into Knemon's house at 206, speaking φέρε δεῦρο off-stage, and reappearing from the shrine at 214. Webster, *StM* 225, had a more elaborate scheme, but later, *CR* n.s. xv (1965), 17, saw the truth, independently of Grassi.

κατὰ τρόπον τί; A. C. Moorhouse, *Studies in the Greek Negative*, p. 147, observes that when a question repeats a previous speaker's word or phrase, the interrogative is often postponed, e.g. Eur. *Bacch.* 661 f., ἥκω Κιθαιρῶν' . . . ἥκεις δὲ ποίαν;

217: Sostratos, leaving for his father's house in the village, must pass in front of Daos, but he has no reason to concern himself with him. Daos, however, misses an opportunity of intervening, for which he is later taken to task (235).

218: ὡc may be exclamatory (Handley) or, as I prefer, mean 'because', introducing the reason for asking the preceding question, as in Soph. *Phil.* 914, τί ποτε λέγεις, ὦ τέκνον; ὡc οὐ μανθάνω.

(viii) 219–232: *Daos alone*

220 ὦ Κνήμων: See 823 n.   **πονηρόν:** 'A bad business', as *Her.* 17, *Perik.* 390.

222 f.: If the phrase can be dissected, μόνην is governed by ἐᾷc and ἀφεὶc ἐν ἐρημίᾳ go together: 'leave her by herself, letting her go free in a lonely place'; for ἀφεὶc ἐᾶν, cf. Soph. *Ajax* 754. The emendation ὡc προcῆκον ἦν introduces a common phrase of Hellenistic and later Greek, e.g. C. B. Welles, *Royal Correspondence in the Hellenistic Period*, 14. 3, ἐπιμελούμενοc ὡc προcῆκον ἦν, Philemon frag. 4 K, ὃ μὴ προcῆκον ἦν. An earlier example is Isaios vii. 14, υόc, ὅν . . . δι' ἐπιμελείαc εἶχεν, ὥcπερ καὶ προcῆκον ἦν. Some editors adopt ὡc προκειμένην ('the idea is that Knemon's treatment of the girl is tantamount to exposing her as a baby', Handley). Parallels of sorts are available to meet the linguistic difficulties of this, but I should hesitate to ascribe to Daos such a flight of fancy.

224 καταμανθάνων: A present participle indicates a time simultaneous with that of the main verb to which it is attached. Hence Peek doubted the simple correction, accepted by most editors, and wished to read τουτὶ ⟨δὲ⟩ καταμαθών. This is undoubtedly normal Greek and may be right. But the present tense of verbs of perceiving, learning, etc. is often used to indicate not the act of perception, but the resulting possession of knowledge, K–G i. 135. So καταμανθάνων may mean not 'while learning', but 'knowing, as having learnt', and thus be properly attached to προcερρύη. Moreover the rule that a present participle shows simultaneity is occasionally broken: Xen. *Anab.* iv. 7. 13, αἱ γυναῖκες ῥιπτοῦσαι τὰ παιδία, εἶτα ἑαυτὰς ἐπικατερρίπτουν.

225 προcερρύη: 'Sneaked up', cf. Plut. *Amat.* 760 a, τῶν οἰκετῶν τινὸς προcρυέντος ἔξωθεν τῇ τραπέζῃ καὶ τὸν οἶνον ὑφαιρουμένου.

226 ἕρμαιον: 'A godsend', cf. Dem. xxxviii. 6, τὴν ἡμετέραν ἀπειρίαν . . . ἕρμαιον νομίcαντες.   **οὐ μὴν ἀλλά** 'normally denotes that what is being said cannot be gainsaid, however strong the arguments to the contrary', Denniston, *GP* 28, who says that the combination is unknown in verse apart from οὐ μὴν . . . ἀλλά at Eur. *IT* 630, and in prose almost confined to Plato, Isokrates, Demosthenes, and Aristotle, οὐ μὴν ἀλλά . . . γε (as here) being chiefly found in the first two. Daos is no run-of-the-mill slave, whether in loyalty or in language, cf. 207–11 and 228, where ἐν ἐπιμελείᾳ . . . γενώμεθα replaces the usual ἐπιμέλειαν ἔχωμεν. The force of οὐ μὴν ἀλλά here seems to be 'although this is really her father's business, there is nothing for it but to tell her brother'.

227 τὴν ταχίcτην: Sc. ὁδόν, cf. *Perik.* 265.

229: To the reader this line seems flat after τὴν ταχίcτην (227). Its function seems to be to provide a link with the announcement in 230 of the approach of the chorus.

230 Πανιcτάc: B's reading παιανιcτας involves two irregularities, the shortening of αι and a broken anapaest. The former is credible (see Handley's note) and the latter might be tolerated if necessary, although there is no parallel in Menander. But, although παιανιcταί are known from imperial times in Egypt, Rome, and the Piraeus (see LSJ), it seems far more likely that the revellers approaching the shrine of Pan are Πανιcταί, or Pan-worshippers. Πανιαcταί are first recorded from Rhodes in the second century B.C. (*IG* xii. (1). 155.75) and Πανιcταί not at all; but similar alternative forms are met with: ἡρωιcταί *IG* ii². 1339, ἡρωιαcταί *IG* vii. 2725, Βακχιcταί *IG* xii. (3). 1296, Βακχιαcταί Philod. Scarph. in *Coll. Alexandr.* p. 169. Πριαπιcταί are recorded in Crete in the first century B.C. J.-M. Jacques, *Bull. Budé*, (1960), p. 420, calls attention to the reverse error, Πανιcμόc for Παιανιcμόc in [Plut.] *de fluviis* 5. 2.

The arguments on both sides are fully set out by Handley, who retains παιανιcταί on the grounds that no argument against it is fatal and that the word may have some appropriateness unknown to us.

232: The chorus, representing members of a society for the worship of Pan, enter and perform a dance; this is nothing but an interlude, for they have no connection with the plot. We now have four plays (*Aspis, Dysk., Epitr., Perik.*) in which the chorus's first appearance is similarly introduced; 232 here is identical with *Epitr.* 171. See further introduction, p. 12.

ACT II

(i) 233–258: *Gorgias and Daos*

233: The second act begins, like the first, with a device much favoured by Menander, the entry of two characters in mid-conversation (784 below, *Aspis* 250, *Heros* 1, *Epitr.* 218(?), 979, 1062, *Perik*, 267, *Sam.* 61, 283, 369, *Georgos* 22, *Phasma* 26, *Sik.* 150, 312). Here he is less successful in making it natural; it is hard to believe that the talk between Gorgias and Daos had only just reached the point where the former utters his remonstrance. δέ shows that the two men are continuing a conversation already begun, cf. *Georgos* 22 (ἀλλά). W. Görler, *Philologus* cv (1961), 299, shows a curious similarity of structure between *Dysk.* 233–381 and Ter. *Eun.* 817–922.

234 φαύλως: 'Casually', LSJ s.v. II. 3.

235 Δᾶ', which might fall out by haplography, is the likeliest supplement. It has the possible advantage of introducing the character's name as soon as possible: Gorgias, too, is named at the first opportunity in 247, as Sostratos and Chaireas at 51, 54—but Sikon remains anonymous until 889, the last scene of the play. The repetition of Δᾶ' at 240 is no obstacle, cf. *Epitr.* 1063, 1071, *Perik.* 267, 276 (both first entrances of master and slave).

235 ἰδεῖν, like English 'see', can mean 'talk to', cf. 174, 305, frag. 95. 19, *Perik.* 159; Σ Thuc. iv. 125 explains ἰδεῖν by διαλεχθῆναι. It is not possible to take ὅςτις ποτ' ἦν ἰδεῖν together, to mean 'see who on earth he was', since ἰδεῖν cannot be substituted for πυθέςθαι and one cannot *see* who a stranger is unless he wears a label. For ὅςτις ποτ' ἦν, 'whoever he may have been', cf. 486.   **τοῦτο** is the object of ποιοῦντα; therefore τοῦτο ... εἰπεῖν is not a unit and the postponement of τε is surprising, the more so as nowhere else in Menander except *Sam.* 445 is it certainly preceded by a unit of more than two words (possibly three in *Kith.* frag. 5, where ἀκούςματ' εἰς τρυφήν τε is the traditional reading). Associated words, like τοῦτο and ποιοῦντα here, are sometimes widely separated when placed first and last in the clause, as at *Epitr.* 130–1, βιάζεται ... αὐτόν, Soph. *Phil.* 618, καὶ τούτων κάρα τέμνειν ἐφεῖτο τῷ θέλοντι μὴ τυχών, *OT* 1056, τὰ δὲ ῥηθέντα βούλου μηδὲ μεμνῆςθαι μάτην (Jebb misunderstands), Eur. *Hipp.* 24, ἐλθόντα γάρ νιν Πιτθέως ποτ' ἐκ δόμων ςεμνῶν ἐς ὄψιν καὶ τέλη μυστηρίων Πανδίονος γῆν, *IT* 1360, τίνος τίς ὢν ςὺ τήνδ' ἀπεμπολᾷς χθονός, Dem.

xviii. 158, ὑφ᾽ ἑνὸς τοιαῦτα πέπονθεν ἡ Ἑλλὰς ἀνθρώπου, Pap. Hibeh 6. 28 (Page, *GLP* p. 290), Ἕλλην βεβαίως φαίνεταί τις τοὺς τρόπους Δημέας ἄνθρωπος, Machon 64 Gow, ὑπερβολῇ λέγουσιν τὸν Φιλόξενον τῶν διθυράμβων τὸν ποιητὴν γεγονέναι ὀψοφάγον. ὅπως μηδεὶς ὄψεταί σε τοῦτο ποιοῦντα would be a well-known form of warning; it is here put into *oratio obliqua* after εἰπεῖν.

239 ἴσως, as often in Aristotle, implies no real doubt, but avoids the appearance of dogmatism.

240 οἰκειότητα: Photios, s.v. οἰκείαν, reports that Aristophanes of Byzantium noted that Menander loosely used the word οἰκεῖος of blood-relations, whereas its correct meaning was 'connection by marriage' (as at 904). ἐμῆς: The only argument against this reading (for εμμη[.]) is that μέλει is normally accompanied by a dative, and it may be a cogent one. The rule, however, is not absolute: Eur. *HF* 595, μέλει μὲν οὐδέν εἴ με πᾶς᾽ εἶδεν πόλις. Another objection that has been raised to ἐμῆς is that in New Comedy 'my father' is normally either ὁ πατήρ or ὁ πατήρ μου (e.g. *Perik.* 306) or ὁ ἐμὸς πατήρ (e.g. *Perik.* 274), and that other relationships (e.g. 'your son', 'his daughter') are similarly expressed. But there are very relevant exceptions. When the emphasis is, as here, on the relationship itself, and the phrase does not simply denote a person, the noun may be used without the article: *Epitr.* 341–2, γαμῶν ἀδελφήν τις διὰ γνωρίσματα | ἐπέσχε, μητέρ᾽ ἐντυχὼν ἐρρύσατο, *Sam.* 698, *Georg.* 59, *Hypobolimaios* frag. 428, and with an instructive variety, frag. 453, μητὴρ τέθνηκε ταῖν ἀδελφαῖν ταῖν δυοῖν | ταύταιν· τρέφει δὲ παλλακή τις τοῦ πατρὸς | αὐτάς, ἅβρα τῆς μητρὸς αὐτῶν γενομένη. There is no reason why a possessive pronoun should not be attached to the noun that has no article, and indeed there is an instance: *Perik.* 777, ἀδελφὴ δ᾽ ἔστ᾽ ἐμὴ | αὕτη. Similarly at *Mis.* 212 Krateia exclaims πατὴρ ἐμός; 'My father?' The absence of articles in frag. 334, οὐκ ἐμοὶ μόνον, υἱῷ πολὺ μᾶλλον, θυγατρί, may be explicable if the meaning is 'not to me alone, her husband, but also to her *son* and her *daughter*'. The suitability of ἐμῆς without article to this passage may outweigh the unusualness of μέλει without a dative. If it does not, ἔμοιγ᾽ is more likely than ἡμῖν. The latter would necessarily stand for ἐμοί, since Gorgias cannot say 'you and I still care for my sister': Daos is in fact being criticized for his lack of interest. But the following ἡμᾶς and ἡμεῖς are true plurals, 'me and my household'. The change from ἡμεῖς, 'I', to ἡμεῖς, 'we', would be awkward. Confusion of οι and η occurs at 473, λεβοιτιον, ει for ε at 338, 599, 904, 955. ἐπιμέλει (B) is impossible. Neither 'do you look after my *sister*?' nor 'you do look after my *sister*' is sense in the context. W. J. Verdenius, *Mnem.* 4th ser. xxi (1968), 433, suggests ἐπιμελεῖ (dative), 'you can't escape relationship if you take care of my sister', but this is no better.

242 μή: B's μηδέ is senseless and creates a broken anapaest. Gorgias, as in the preceding lines, speaks in asyndeton.

245 ὁ ἔξωθεν: 'The outsider'.

247 ὦ τᾶν: The etymology of this peculiarly Attic form of address (tragedy, comedy, Plato, Demosthenes) is unknown (G. Björck, *Das Alpha Impurum*, pp. 275 ff.). It frequently carries a shade of meaning that may be irony (cf. Hesychios s.v.), impatience, or remonstrance, and is therefore an unusual way for a slave to address his master. In *Knights* 1036 the Paphlagonian so speaks to Demos, whom he is accustomed to control, and a serf so addresses Iolaos in remonstrance, Eur. *Heracl.* 688. Daos, an old slave who has known Gorgias from childhood, may be allowed some freedom of expression. For the combination of ὦ τᾶν with a vocative, cf. *Pap. Ghôran* ii. 154 (Schroeder, *Nov. Com. Frag.* p. 36, Page, *GLP* p. 304), ὦ τᾶν, Φαίδιμε. The usage of the phrase is fully investigated by G. J. de Vries, *Mnem.* 4th ser. xix (1966), 235 ff.

The tone of protest in ὦ τᾶν has generally been disregarded in attempts to fill the beginning of the line. Gorgias must have said something to which Daos takes exception because it will require him to approach Knemon's door, and Knemon will 'string him up' (κρεμᾷ, 'future'). It may be thought that to keep an eye on possibly mischievous strangers will not cause him to approach the door. Therefore Kamerbeek, *Mnem.* 4th ser. xvii (1964), 161, suggests εἰcιτέον; but Daos would surely not be in danger if accompanied by Gorgias. Moreover, in New Comedy only close relations walk uninvited into other people's houses; others knock on the door, as doubtless in real life. The former objection applies also to Kassel's κόψωμεν (Schäfer, *Menanders Dyskolos*, p. 121). Proposals to withdraw, like Handley's ὑπάγωμεν or Austin's ἔλθωμεν, *CR* N.S. xviii (1968), 276, also involve no danger to Daos. The best I can suggest of this kind is ἴθι κόψον, cf. Plaut. *Bacch.* 578, but I cannot see why Gorgias should not knock himself. Is it possible that Daos understands Gorgias' speech as a command not to treat Knemon's household as ἀλλότριος, but to make contacts there as occasion offers, and protests that this would be dangerous?

249 κρεμᾷ: Although a slave might be punished by literal suspension (and perhaps be beaten at the same time, Dover on Ar. *Clouds* 870), the verb can be used of hanging against something, e.g. Hypereides, quoted by Pollux iii. 79, κρεμάcαc ἐκ τοῦ κίονοc ἐξέδειρεν; it is applied to Euripides' kinsman when fastened to the plank, Ar. *Thesm.* 1027.

1053.   δυϲχρήϲτωϲ γε: γε shows that Gorgias agrees with an implication of Daos' speech, and in what follows he indicates that there is no use in trying to talk to Knemon. This is further evidence that Daos protested against some suggestion which involved an attempt to do so.

249–52: Although the gaps to be filled are small, no agreement has been reached, or is likely to be reached without further evidence, about the reconstitution of the text.

(*a*) It is uncertain whether the missing verb in 250 (presumably some part of ἔχω) had as its subject (1) Gorgias or Daos or (2) Knemon. (1) Plut. *Aem.* 19 uses ἔχοντα δυϲχρήϲτωϲ of a man lamed by a kick from a horse, and if the parallel is apt the meaning here must be that Gorgias or Daos was, is, or will be helpless in dealing with Knemon. The suitable choices are εἶχον, ἕξω, and ἕξειϲ; the last is the least suitable, since Gorgias is more likely to consider his own experience or prospects with Knemon than those of Daos. Certainly if ζυγομαχῶν is taken as part of this clause, Daos will not be the subject; it is not his place to wrangle with Knemon. (2) There is no reason why δυϲχρήϲτωϲ ἔχειν should not mean 'be unmanageable', since δύϲχρηϲτοϲ is used, e.g., of unmanageable dogs by [Xen.] *Cyneg.* iii. 11. In that case either ἔχει or ἕξει is possible.

(*b*) Does ζυγομαχῶν (see 17 n.) go with what precedes or what follows? The former seems more likely with εἶχον, ἕξω, and perhaps with ἕξειϲ, the latter with ἔχει or ἕξει. 'If one struggles with him, one will be able neither to constrain him nor to persuade him' is a very possible sentiment. I doubt whether it is possible to regard ζυγομαχῶν as anticipated from the first οὔτε clause only; this would imply that Gorgias did not envisage the antithetical οὔτε . . . οὔτε construction until after beginning his sentence.

(*c*) In 250–2 some of the lines of approach that have been suggested involve insuperable difficulties. (1) One possible line is best represented by the text of Lloyd-Jones and Jacques: τοῦτον οὔθ' ὅτῳ τρόπῳ | ἀναγκάϲαι τιϲ εἰϲ τὸ βέλτι[ον ῥέπει]ν | οὔτ' ἂν μεταπείϲαι νουθετῶν ο[ἶδ' οὐδὲ εἷ]ϲ. ἀναγκάϲαι is an emendation of B's αναγκαϲειε, the more familiar form of the optative, but unmetrical here as causing a broken anapaest; with it ἄν must be supplied from the next clause, a rare form of expression, for which see K–G i. 249. (The supplement from a *preceding* ἄν, as at 744, is much easier.) Conversely in 252 ὅτῳ τρόπῳ must be supplied from 250, so that the whole sentence is decidedly awkward. Then the supplement in 251 seems too short, and that in 252 is certainly too long, for the gap. Perhaps one must have recourse to the supposition of a mis-spelling in 252, e.g. ουδειϲ for οὐδὲ εἷϲ.

In 251 τρέπειν would be weak, and βέλτιον φρονεῖν unsuitable, with ἀναγκάcαι. (2) Handley supposes that ὅτῳ τρόπῳ is not interrogative, but means 'in any way whatever' (LSJ s.v. ὅcτιc IV. 2. d), and diffidently completes 252 with ο[ἴ᾽ ἂν φίλο]c. This simplifies the structure, but still leaves the unusual absence of ἂν from the first clause. To avoid this, it would be better to write ἀναγκάcει (future). (3) Corruption cannot be excluded, and, if it is assumed, another possible solution would be to write οὔθ᾽ ὅτῳ τρόπῳ | ἀναγκάcει τιc εἰc τὸ βέλτιον cτρέφων | οὔτ᾽ αὖ μεταπεῖcαι νουθετῶν οἶδ᾽ οὐδὲ εἶc, constructing οἶδε first with an indirect question in future tense, then with an infinitive.

255 ἔπιcχε: This intransitive use is found at Eur. *Electra* 758, where Denniston points out that intrans. ἐπίcχω occurs in Plato, *Parm.* 152 b, *Phaedr.* 257 c. There is therefore no need to think the use here paratragic. Schwyzer, i. 798, 800, argues that ἐπίcχε is the regularly formed aor. imperat. of ἐπέχω, and that the normally used (ἐπί)cχεc may be formed on the analogy of θέc. But μικρόν is consistent with the continuative present imperative, as well as with the instantaneous aorist; not 'stop!' but 'hold on a little!' (Note, however, 906, μικρὸν πρόcμεινον, *Pap. Ant.* 55 frag. a 'verso' 7, ἐπίμεινον βραχύ.) Cf. also ἡ[cύχω]c ἐπίcχετε, *Pap. Hibeh* 6, 10 = Page, *GLP* p. 288, which may be interpreted as pres. imperat. of ἐπίcχω rather than aor. of ἐπέχω.

256 ὥcπερ εἶπον: B has ωcπερανειπον, giving a broken anapaest. If read as ὥcπερ ἀνεῖπον, 'as I proclaimed', this also provides no sense, and if as ὥcπερ ἂν εἶπον, 'as I should have said', an unlikely one. The intrusion of αν may be explained as an anticipation of ανακαμψαc. Daos does not refer by 'just as I said' to anything he has said on the stage, but to what he had told Gorgias when he went to fetch him; having heard Sostratos express the intention of returning, he had reported that to his master, and urged that they too should come back to secure the girl's safety. Having been criticized for his immediate inaction, he here emphasizes that on *this* point he had been right. In comparison ὡc ἂν εἶπον, 'as I should have said', (?) if asked, preferred by J. Martin and Jacques, lacks force.

257 χλανίδα: A fine cloak, regarded as luxurious: Dem. xxxiv, *In Phormionem* 45, cὺ μὲν χλανίδα φορεῖc . . . καὶ τρεῖc παῖδαc ἀκολούθουc περιάγειc. A man who has lost his money says τὴν χλανίδα πάντεc, ὡc ἔοικεν, οὐκ ἐμὲ προcηγόρευον· οὐδὲ εἶc νῦν μοι λαλεῖ, Poseidippos frag. 31 K.

258: The dicolon after οὗτοc is not absolutely certain. It would, however, be foolish of Daos to insist on the obvious villainy of Sostratos, since he would thus accuse his own previous inaction. The latter half of the line better suits Gorgias, who later shows himself convinced that

Sostratos' intentions were of the worst.   ἀπὸ τοῦ βλέμματος:
'from the look in his eye'. A βλέμμα may be friendly, Eur. *HF* 306,
or soft and melting, Philetairos frag. 5 K, or betray that a man is in
love or intoxicated, Antiphanes frag. 235 K. Here Gorgias thinks
that he can see at once (εὐθύς) that the other man's look marks him
as a rascal.

(ii) **259–392**: *Sostratos, Gorgias* (? exit 381), *Daos* (exit 378)

260: Sostratos' familiarity with his mother's superstitious habits has
prevented him from asking any details, so that he knows neither of
the dream that so closely concerns him, nor that his mother will
come to sacrifice at Pan's cave. Hence he is surprised to see Getas
there at 551, but with characteristic impulsiveness turns the sacrifice
to his own purposes (558).

262 τὸν δῆμον: Phyle.

263 αὐτόθεν: This word, generally disregarded by translators, may
mean 'immediately' or 'from the very place' (cf. *Sik.* 12); the latter
seems probable here: the cook is to be hired locally (although later
he boasts of his clientele in the city, 490). On the hiring of cooks see
below, p. 290.

264 ἐρρῶσθαι φράσας: Like χαίρειν λέγειν, 'put out of one's mind', cf.
520, Antiphanes frag. 88 K, Demosthenes xviii. 152, ἐρρῶσθαι φράσας
πολλὰ Κιρραίοις καὶ Λοκροῖς, xix. 248, ἐρρῶσθαι πολλὰ φράσας τῷ σοφῷ
Σοφοκλεῖ.

267 διαλέξεσθαι: The aor. infin. of B would mean 'I think I have
conversed'. For the construction with fut. infin. 'it is my intention
to . . .', cf. 229. MSS. occasionally give an aorist where a future would
be expected, but corruption is always likely, as here, K–G i. 195.
In Attic inscriptions the aorist is διελέχθην, the future διαλέξομαι
(Meisterhans³, p. 193), and διαλέξασθαι is quoted by Pollux ii. 125
from Aristophanes (frag. 343) as being a remarkable form. This
confirms the necessity for making the easy change.

268: 'That I shall not be able even to debate any longer what to do'.
To plan is better than to be at a loss what to do, but even to plan
seems inadequate to Sostratos: the time has come for action.

269 ἐθελήσαις: Before the discovery of *Dyskolos* the only forms of this
verb known in Menander were from the present θέλω (not the traditional Attic ἐθέλω), and they were comparatively rare—eight instances
of which one was in a quotation from tragedy (*Aspis* 413), two in the
formula ἂν θεὸς θέλῃ or ἂν θεοὶ θέλωσιν (*Georg.* 45, frag. 39), two in
suspect citations (frag. 45, frag. 499), one in the doubtful Didot

rhesis (29), one in an uncertain supplement (*Heros* 53), and one in a passage quoted by Clement of Alexandria: his MSS. give οὐκ ἐθέλων, which is emended to ἄρ' οὐ θέλων (frag. 97, q.v.). In this play we have the aorist ἠθέλησα here and at 767, and fut. ἐθελήσω at 854. In each case the speaker is Gorgias; can it be that the forms are old-fashioned, and appropriate to this serious-minded country youth? In each case the usage is perfectly correct by Attic norms, 'consent' as opposed to 'wish'. In the fragments of Middle and New Comedy ἐθελήσω does not occur at all, and ἠθέλησα once only, and there in paratragic surroundings, Kriton frag. 3 K.

270 cπουδαιότερον: The comparative is intensifying, 'quite serious', cf. ἀπειρότερον, 345, and the common θᾶττον.

272: Gorgias, whose language always tends to stiffness, here speaks in a comically formal, almost pompous, style, beginning with an elaborate period of thirteen lines; yet he does not get through without an anacoluthon (τοῖς πράττουσι . . . ἐλθόντας . . . προςδοκᾶν). His rhythm is strict, too; only four of the first seventeen lines could not stand in a Euripidean tragedy—contrast the freedom of rhythm and variety of construction when Sostratos moralizes, 797–812. He begins, also, with a solemn gnome, like a character in a tragedy, although (as is remarked by W. Görler, Μενάνδρου Γνῶμαι, p. 74) it is subordinated to νομίζω. Contrast the way in which Sostratos covers up his maxims with a dress to make them suit the occasion, but even so provokes the protest τί μοι λέγεις γνώμας; Gorgias' oration may be summarized as follows: 'Neither good fortune nor bad lasts for ever. Only so long as the fortunate man is not carried away by his good luck and tempted to wrong-doing does his fortune last. If a poor man remains honest, he is finally trusted and may expect a better share in life. Do not therefore put your trust in your wealth, nor despise poor men like me; but act so that you may deserve always to prosper.' This is not a triumph of logic, for Gorgias starts by saying that *all* men experience a change of fortune, and ends by holding out the ideal of having good fortune for ever: moreover, it is in his view only the *honest* poor who may expect to improve their lot. But it is important as showing that he has not given in and accepted poverty as his permanent and necessary condition: he is in a way prepared for the improvement that this day will quite unexpectedly bring.

273 τούτου: Sc. τοῦ εὐτυχεῖν or τοῦ πράττειν κακῶς. Handley appositely quotes Thuc. i. 6. 5, πυγμῆς καὶ πάλης ἆθλα τίθεται, καὶ διεζωςμένοι τοῦτο δρῶςιν.

274 μέχρι τούτου is an irregular antecedent of ὅςον ἂν χρόνον.

275 εὐθενοῦντα: 'Flourishing'; the word is not found elsewhere in comedy except in Kratinos frag. 327 K, but is used by Demosthenes, e.g. *De Corona* 286, εὐθενούντων τῶν πραγμάτων. Gorgias wishes to be impressive, but with τὰ τοῦ βίου falls into unnecessary verbiage.

277 τοῦθ': Sc. τὸ ἄδικόν τι ποιεῖν.

279 λαμβάνει: It is unnecessary to change this to λαμβάνειν (*ed. pr.*), since Gorgias may temporarily fail to maintain his long piece of *oratio obliqua*.

The view that human fortune is mutable was one on which the Greeks were notoriously fond of insisting. It is here developed by the addition that wrong-doing brings success to an end, and honesty brings an escape from poverty. It is not likely that Menander held this naïve view, but he may have wished it were more often true than in fact it was. The idea that honesty is in the end rewarded is found elsewhere, e.g. Plato, *Republic* 613 c, Eur. *Ion* 1621, εἰς τέλος γὰρ οἱ μὲν ἐσθλοὶ τυγχάνουσιν ἀξίων.

281 φέρωσι . . . τὸν δαίμονα: It was a popular idea that each man had attached to him a spirit (δαίμων) which determined or implemented his fate. But it is hard to be sure that Gorgias has that in view: he may use δαίμων as a substitute for τύχη, which is often given divine status.   **εὐγενῶς:** Since bravery is part of the ideal of the Greek gentleman, εὐγενῶς sometimes has the connotation 'bravely', *Sam.* 356, Eur. *Cycl.* 201, κατθανούμεθ' εὐγενῶς.

282 ποτ' . . . χρόνῳ: 'In process of time', cf. Xen. *Hell.* iv. 1. 34, χρόνῳ ποτέ, Hdt. ix. 62, χρόνῳ κοτέ, Herondas iv. 33, χρόνῳ κοτ' ὤνθρωποι κῆς τοὺς λίθους ἔξουσι τὴν ζόην θεῖναι, Ar. *Clouds* 865, ἦ μὴν σὺ τούτοις τῷ χρόνῳ ποτ' ἀχθέσει (paratragic), Soph. *Ajax* 1082, πόλιν χρόνῳ ποτὲ | ἐξ οὐρίων δραμοῦσαν εἰς βυθὸν πεσεῖν. Again Gorgias' rhetoric carries him beyond the bounds of ordinary speech.

πίστιν: Whose confidence will the poor man win, that of other men or that of the supernatural powers? Since there is no mention of other men, it is perhaps easier to suppose the meaning to be that he will by continued good conduct win the confidence of his δαίμων, or of the δαίμων that is τύχη, who may then reward him. It may not be possible exactly to parallel this, but see *Epitr.* 1096 ff.; writers often give an original turn to the δαίμων theory; thus Plato in the myth of the *Republic* (617 d) makes the soul choose its own δαίμων, to whom it is ever after bound, and a character in Menander turned the δαίμων into a guide to the mystery of life (frag. 714).

Handley considers that it is a question of business credit; the poor man, if he shows himself respectable, may be able to borrow money to start some enterprise. He cites with approval Thierfelder's comparison of Dem. xxxvi. 44, πίϲτιϲ ἀφορμὴ τῶν παϲῶν ἐϲτὶ μεγίϲτη πρὸϲ χρηματιϲμόν, 'a good credit is the greatest asset in business'.

E. R. Dodds, followed by Lloyd-Jones, writes Χρόνῳ and supposes the man to win the confidence of a personified Time. Time, it is true, is sometimes made responsible by Greek authors for events, but the personal relation involved in πίϲτιϲ does not seem likely with the abstraction Time. S. Eitrem, *Symb. Osl.* xxxvii (1961), 153, thinks men put their trust in time to bring about an improvement.

283 μερίδα: μερίϲ is used of a share in a meal or in property; here it will be a share in the good things of life.

284–7: These lines are quoted by Stobaios, *Ecl.* iii. 22. 19, as part of an extract from Menander (frag. 250). They do not follow logically on the seven verses that there precede them, the last three of which are elsewhere (*Ecl.* iv. 51. 8) ascribed to the Κυβερνήτηϲ (Κυβερνῆται was probably the true title). It is more likely that the MSS. of Stobaios have amalgamated two originally separate citations than that Menander used the same lines in *Dysk.* and in Κυβερνῆται.

285 πίϲτευε τούτῳ: 'Have confidence in your wealth', sc. that it will always remain with you. **πτωχῶν:** Although πτωχόϲ properly means 'beggar', it is loosely used of the very poor. In a famous passage of Aristophanes, *Plutus* 552, Poverty (Πενία) is made indignantly to draw a distinction between the πτωχόϲ and the πένηϲ: πτωχοῦ μὲν γὰρ βίοϲ . . . ζῆν ἐϲτιν μηδὲν ἔχοντα, τοῦ δὲ πένητοϲ ζῆν φειδόμενον καὶ τοῖϲ ἔργοιϲ προϲέχοντα, περιγίγνεϲθαι δ' αὐτῷ μηδέν, μὴ μέντοι μηδ' ἐπιλείπειν. Gorgias is not in fact πτωχόϲ, being the owner of a small estate and a slave; he exaggerates rhetorically in order to make more invidious the contrast between his poverty and Sostratos' wealth. There is another exaggeration, for a different purpose, at 795, where the rich Kallippides recoils from the idea of a double matrimonial alliance with 'beggars'.

286 διευτυχῶν ἀεί: 'Continue always in prosperity', cf. frag. 740. 3, διευτυχῶν ἀεί.

287 τοῖϲ ὁρῶϲιν: 'To those who watch you': Gorgias means the public; the rich are in the public eye.

288 ἄτοπόν τι: ἄτοποϲ, 'odd', is euphemistically used for 'bad', 'wicked', e.g. Baton frag. 3 K quoted in 743 n., Sextus Empiricus, *PH* iii. 201, τοὺϲ Ϲτωικοὺϲ ὁρῶμεν οὐκ ἄτοπον εἶναι λέγονταϲ τὸ ἑταίρᾳ ϲυνοικεῖν. W. G. Arnott, *Phoenix* xviii (1964), 119, has an interesting examination of this usage. W. Görler, *Philologus*, cv (1961), 302, well remarks that Gorgias reacts to the inadequate word by coming into the open with ἔργον . . . φαῦλον, emphatic by separation.

290: Gorgias' fears are illustrated by a (? true) story in Pausanias iv. 20. 6: γυναῖκα εἶδεν ἐφ᾽ ὕδωρ ἐλθοῦσαν, ἐρασθεὶς δὲ διαλεχθῆναί τε ἐτόλμησε καὶ δοὺς δῶρα cυγγίνεται. The modern Sarakatsan shepherds, who often preserve ancient Greek modes of thought and behaviour, associate water-fetching with sexual adventures or misadventures; J. K. Campbell, *Honour, Family, and Patronage*, p. 86. ἐζηλωκέναι: 'To have set your heart on', cf. the contrary ἀρετὴν ζηλοῦν, Dem. xx. 141, Lys. xi. 26, and Dem. ii. 15, ὁ μὲν δόξης ἐπιθυμεῖ καὶ τοῦτ᾽ ἐζήλωκε. The tone may be above that of everyday talk, as elsewhere in Menander the word has its ordinary sense of 'envy'.

292 κατεργάcαcθαι: This correction, which makes the verb depend on καιρόν, a word often followed by an infinitive, is at least highly probable. Handley maintains κατεργάcεcθαι, dependent like πείcειν on νομίζων, but as Kraus says, one would then expect ἐπιτηρήcαc (*Gnomon* xl [1968], 344).

293 Ἄπολλον: An exclamation of dismay, which causes Gorgias to retract the violence of θανάτων ἄξιον πολλῶν with οὐ δίκαιόν ἐcτι γοῦν κτλ., 'Well, it isn't *right* . . .'

294: Bekker, *anecd.* 457. 18, *Suda* s.v. ἄcχολοc. ἀcχολοῦμαι καὶ ἀcχολεῖται καὶ ἀcχολεῖcθαι· πάντα ταῦτα Μένανδροc λέγει (frag. 828). The active is found in the same sense in Aristotle and Philemon; Alexis and Epicurus used the middle.

297 δυcκολώτατον: Similarly Aristophanes' wasps say (1105) that no animal when teased is δυcκολώτερον than they; the poor man, if wronged, is 'a very difficult customer' because he is assured of public sympathy (cf. Ter. *Phor.* 275, 'iudicum qui saepe . . . propter misericordiam addunt pauperi') and, being ready to suppose himself insulted as well as injured, is likely to be more resentful and vindictive, cf. τοῖc ἐχθροῖc ἀνιαροί, Ar. *Plutus* 561, and contrast the opposite sentiment in *Georg.* 129 ff. The use here of the word δύcκολοc, otherwise applied only to Knemon, is accidental, cf. 597 n. ἐλεινόc: The Attic form, cf. Porson, *Euripidis Tragoediae* ed. J. Scholefield, pp. 4–5, is probable. Neither here nor at *Sam.* 371, the only other certain instance in New Comedy, does the metre require the Ionic form, usual in the κοινή. It may, however, be that the papyri are right, and that Menander already used the longer, uncontracted, and finally victorious form. Yet the MSS. of Aristophanes give ἐλεεινοί at *Frogs* 1063 where ἐλεινοί is necessary for metre's sake.

298 εἰc ἀδικίαν: The only example quoted by LSJ of this construction of λαμβάνω, 'take for, take as', is Philostratos, *Imag.* ii. 32, εἰ ἐc κόρην λαμβάνοιτο; but Salmasius conjectured it in frag. 539. 3, εἰc (ἀεὶ

MSS.) μέμψιν ἰδίαν αὐτὸν ἐπαναγκὲς λαβεῖν.　ὕβριν: The supplement is favoured by Arist. *Rhet.* 1378ᵇ14, Lucian, *Timon* c. 28, Ter. *Ad.* 605, 'omnes quibus res sunt minus secundae mage sunt nescioquomodo | suspiciosi; ad contumeliam omnia accipiunt magis', a version of frag. 8 K–T, πρὸς ἄπαντα δειλὸν ὁ πένης ἐστὶ γὰρ | καὶ πάντας αὐτοῦ καταφρονεῖν ὑπολαμβάνει, and above all by Philippides frag. 26 K, ὁ γὰρ εἰς τὸν ἀcθενῆ βίᾳ τι, Πάμφιλε, | ποιῶν ὑβρίζειν οὐχ ἁμαρτάνειν δοκεῖ.

300 εὖ γε, δέςποθ', κτλ. is assigned by *ed. pr.* and Lloyd-Jones to Pyrrhias, but there is no reason to suppose him to be present in this scene. If the three-actor rule holds he would in any case have to be a *persona muta*; even if it does not, there is no parallel for a single speech contributed by someone whose presence is otherwise never hinted at. Accordingly the majority of editors rightly assign the words to Daos. But there is less agreement about their bearing, and this must depend upon the supplement at the end of the line. οὕτω πολλά cοι ἀγαθὰ γένοιτο and similar phrases are used in making requests; if μοι is substituted for cοι, the phrase is confirmatory of an assertion, e.g. *Epitr.* 362, 1070, *Perik*, 404. *Ed. pr.* here supplied cοι; Jacques, who accepts this, supposes Daos to applaud his master's speech (εὖ γε) and then to be interrupted as he was about to implore him not to listen to Sostratos. This supposes an extraordinary ability in the audience to divine what he was about to say, and it is by no means the only, or even the most natural, thing he could say. Rather he should be eager that Sostratos *should* be heard; for if Sostratos can establish his respectability, his own omission to warn him off will no longer appear to have been a serious failure in duty. If one interprets in this way, εὖ γε expresses approval of Sostratos' request for a hearing, which Daos thus seconds. This avoids the slight awkwardness by which, on the other theory, Daos' 'Bravo!' does not follow immediately on his master's speech. This awkwardness led van Groningen to give εὖ γε to Gorgias, as an assent to Sostratos' request, a use for which there seems to be no parallel.

If we read πολλά μοι ἀγαθὰ γένοιτο, then εὖ γε may express approval either of Gorgias' speech or of Sostratos' proposal. The latter view avoids the unexplained delay in comment; the former can be paralleled by Ter. *Phorm.* 398, where Getas approves his master Demipho with 'eu, noster, recte'. The balance of probability is obscure, but I incline to prefer μοι to cοι, so that Daos will not repeat in other words the wish οὕτως εὐτυχοίης uttered by Sostratos; there might even be some point in the contrast between his wishing himself well and Sostratos' altruistic phrase. I prefer, too, to believe that Daos applauds Sostratos' request for a hearing.

301 καὶ cύ γ' ὁ λαλῶν: Editors generally complete the line with πρόcεχε δή (cf. Amphis frag. 6 K) : Sostratos must then reprove Daos for his intervention; for λαλεῖν of unnecessary talk cf. 504, 512. Whatever view is taken of Daos' remark, ὁ λαλῶν is strange, because the person who has really done the talking is not he, but Gorgias. Moreover it is Gorgias, not Daos, whose attention Sostratos must demand. I conclude that καὶ cύ γε attaches to ἄκουcον, and that Sostratos ignores the slave's interruption; ὁ λαλῶν will then carry a criticism of Gorgias' tirade uttered in ignorance of the facts: this will be made more explicit if the line is completed by πρὶν μαθεῖν. In another scene of unjustified suspicion, *Pap. Ghôran* ii. 152, Page, *GLP* p. 304, we read A. οἶδα πάντα. B. πρὶν μαθεῖν; Compare also Ar. *Plutus* 376, κατηγορεῖc γὰρ πρὶν μαθεῖν τὸ πρᾶγμά μου (and in different contexts, but also of hasty action, Soph. *Phil.* 370, πρὶν μαθεῖν ἐμοῦ, [Eur.] *Rhes.* 76, ταχύνειc πρὶν μαθεῖν τὸ δρώμενον). There is a considerable space after the letter ρ, with no trace of ink; this suits ρ[ι better than ρ[ο, cf., e.g., τριc in 603 and τροφ- in 607. For καὶ cύ γε in the mouth of one who insists on a hearing cf. Ar. *Plutus* 103, καὶ cύ γε, ἀντιβολῶ, πιθοῦ, 473, καὶ cύ γε διδάcκου.

302–14: Sostratos' reply is quite unlike Gorgias' set speeches, being in short phrases; the sentences seem to shape themselves as they are uttered, and give a convincing picture of sincerity.

303: The first surviving instance of this lover's epigram, cf. Kallimachos, *epigr.* 42. 6, εἰ τοῦτ' ἐcτ' ἀδίκημ', ἀδικέω, Ter. *Andr.* 896, 'ego me amare hanc fateor; si id peccare est, fateor id quoque'.

304 τί γὰρ ἄν τιc εἴποι; I.e. 'What else can I say?' For πλήν to introduce a modification of an absolute negative (or equivalent rhetorical question) cf. *Epitr.* 483, οὐδὲν οἶδα, πλὴν ἰδοῦcά γε γνοίην ἂν αὐτήν, *Perik.* 504, οὐκ οἶδ' ὅ τι λέγω . . . πλὴν ἀπάγξομαι, *Georg.* 13, frag. 622. 5.

306 ὧν ἐλεύθεροc: One would think this hardly needed saying by one who was wearing a fine cloak; it may indicate Sostratos' modesty, which also comes out in the understatement βίον ἱκανὸν ἔχων.

308 ἄπροικον: Since a dowry had usually to be returned if a marriage broke up—indeed the husband was often required to give a guarantee for its return by pledging real property (M. I. Finley, *Land and Credit in Ancient Athens*, pp. 79, 266)—it formed a safeguard for the wife against hasty divorce (Isaios iii. 36) ; Sostratos offers as a substitute a solemn promise to cherish his wife always.

The original of Plaut. *Aulularia* is generally believed to have been a play by Menander not far removed in time from *Dyskolos*. There at 478 the rich Megadorus, who intends to marry a girl without dowry, says: 'Nam meo quidem animo si idem faciant ceteri opulentiores, pauperiorum filias ut indotatas ducant uxores domum, et multo fiat ciuitas concordior et inuidia nos minore utamur quam utimur.' The idea of fostering social concord in this way may have been in the air at this time, and have appealed to or even been fostered by Demetrios of Phaleron. Sostratos is no doctrinaire social reformer, but he acts from his generous heart in a way that the reformer would approve. Other plays by Menander where a rich man's son marries a poor girl are *Samia* and Ἀδελφοί β′ (Ter. *Adelphoe*).

310 κακοτεχνεῖν: Usually 'to use *fraudulent* artifices', here apparently no more than 'to plan mischief'.

311 οὗτός μ' ὁ Πάν: It is possible that there was a statue of Pan outside his cave, as there is one of Apollo somewhere on the stage (659). This would add vividness to Sostratos' address to Pan, 571–3. P. D. Arnott, *Greek Scenic Conventions*, pp. 65–9, shows how frequently statues were used on the Greek stage.

312 ἀπόπληκτον: *Perik.* 496 n. Does Sostratos wish himself bodily paralysis or mental disablement or both? Since the Nymphs and Pan are both frequently associated with frenzy (cf. *panic*), presumably he asks that his wits be taken from him. But Pan could be taken as responsible for an apoplectic fit (Eur. *Med.* 1172).   **αὐτοῦ:** 'Here, on this very spot' often has a further indication of place added; 'by the house', i.e. Knemon's.

314 οὐδὲ μετρίως: 'I am upset, in no small measure either.' It is characteristic of Sostratos' uncertainty and lack of self-confidence that his reaction to Gorgias' suspicions is not indignation, but agitation.

315 κἀγώ: Not 'if I, too, spoke more violently than was called for', but 'if *I* spoke more violently etc.', Denniston, *GP* 320.

317 μεταπείθεις ταῦτα: πείθεις ταῦτα would mean 'you persuade me of this that you say'; the preposition μετα- adds that a change of mind is involved.   **φίλον μ' ἔχεις:** To a Greek friendship was more clearly defined than to a modern Englishman: another man either was or was not φίλος, and if he was, an expectation of mutual aid existed, see T. W. Earp, *Way of the Greeks* (1929), pp. 31–2. Here behind Gorgias' somewhat ingenuous declaration there is to be recognized a sudden attraction to Sostratos, an attraction that 615 shows to be reciprocated; but note that Sostratos replies to the declaration of friendship with an immediate claim for help.

319 βέλτιστε is a polite and respectful, often conciliatory, form of address, applicable to a stranger, twice repeated (338, 342) in this scene by Gorgias, who wishes to repair his unfortunate earlier attitude. Sostratos continues to use μειράκιον (299, 311, 342), and later, when the young men are on even terms, working side by side in the fields, Gorgias also employs the latter form of address (539). Although clearly in no way offensive, it is frequently associated with a situation where the person addressed has something to learn (frags. 250, 538, and everywhere in this play except 539 and 729; even in these two places Gorgias may use it because he feels he could give Sostratos a lesson in digging, and Knemon in order to suggest that Gorgias had better keep quiet).

320–2 τί χρήϲιμοϲ; 'What do you mean by useful?', cf. *Sam.* 374, τί "καί"; Eur. *Alc.* 807, τί "ζῶϲιν"; The dialogue here is so abrupt as to have aroused suspicion. One must suppose that by τί χρήϲιμοϲ; Gorgias indicates not failure to see for what Sostratos wants his assistance (which would be obtuse), but doubt that he can help. To this Sostratos replies that he is γεννικὸϲ τῷ τρόπῳ. Unfortunately the word is too uncommon in a straightforward sense (*Georg.* 42 n. and Plato, *Phaedr.* 279 a, of Isokrates) for its precise force to be appreciated, but its congeners γενναῖοϲ and εὐγενήϲ suggest the man who not only has high motives but also acts firmly upon them. By saying that Gorgias is γεννικόϲ, Sostratos implies that he will play the part that a friend should, by intervening vigorously with his stepfather. Gorgias recognizes the implication and may interrupt, before it can be made more explicit, with his frank explanation of why he sees the situation as hopeless. This explanation seems to me to be adequate, so that there is no need to have recourse to emendation, either by supposing the loss of a line after 319 (Kraus) or 321 (van Groningen) or by disregarding the paragraphus and dicolon of 321, reading ὁρῶν for ὁρῶ, and so making Gorgias speak continuously from τί χρήϲιμοϲ; onwards (Fraenkel).

322 πρόφαϲιν . . . ἐμφανίϲαι: These words are similarly contrasted, *Sam.* 354–5. For the separation of πρόφαϲιν . . . κενήν cf. 236 n. For κενὴ πρόφαϲιϲ cf. Dem. xviii. 150.

326 ϲχεδὸν οἶδα: ϲχεδόν softens the assertion 'I know (but not perhaps as well as you)'. Eur. *Troades* 898, ϲχεδὸν μὲν οἶδα ϲοὶ ϲτυγουμένη, Ar. *Plut.* 860, ἐγὼ ϲχεδὸν τὸ πρᾶγμα γιγνώϲκειν δοκῶ. **ὑπερβολή τιϲ:** Lit. 'there is a sort of overshooting belonging to this trouble', i.e. 'this trouble beats all', cf. *Sam.* 461. Similar uses of ὑπερβολή are common in the orators, e.g. Dem. xix. 66, εἴ τιϲ ὑπερβολὴ τούτου, xxvii. 38, ταῦτ' οὐχ ὑπερβολή;

327 δυεῖν: This form begins to replace δυοῖν in Attic inscriptions during the last quarter of the fourth century, Meisterhans³, p. 157.

It appears that although Knemon makes the impression of being a poor man, and lives like one, that is unnecessary: his farm is of moderate value. An estate of forty-five minae ($\frac{3}{4}$ talent) is difficult to live on, [Dem.] xlii. 22; one of seventy minae is that of a poor man (πένης), Dem. xxviii. 8; yet one of only twenty minae provides the minimum qualification for citizenship at the time of *Dyskolos*.

One owner of an estate of one talent possessed one male slave and two female, Isaios viii. 35; an estate of five talents is worked by seven slaves. However hard Knemon may have worked, he cannot have farmed his land adequately single-handed; in fact we are told that he leaves some of it uncultivated (163). A. H. M. Jones, *Athenian Democracy*, p. 79, reckons that an average estate of two talents would be of about thirty-five acres, but that is an average; Knemon's hill-farm would necessarily be larger than the average of estates of the same value.

332 ἄνθρωπον ... οὐδένα: For this expression cf. Dem. liv. 16, [Dem.] lix. 10, xliii. 17.

333 μεθ' αὑτοῦ τὴν κόρην ... ἔχων: This fact, introduced to paint Knemon's character—he has some human affection for his daughter— later serves to determine Sostratos to go and dig with Gorgias (360).

τὰ πολλά: 'For the most part'; this adverbial use (Thuc. ii. 87. 6) does not occur elsewhere in Menander, and is infrequent in Middle and New Comedy. (I can find only Anaxandrides frag. 34 K (iambic tetrameters), *monost.* 417, 699 Jaekel, and ? Dionys. frag. 2, 26 K.) It is conceivable that the phrase is old-fashioned.

339 ἀναγκαίους: 'Kinsfolk': the etymological origin may be to the fore; kinsfolk are called ἀναγκαῖοι, as *necessarily* connected; here Gorgias cannot escape his relationship with Knemon, but Sostratos need not try to contract one.

340 οἶς: The antecedent is ἡμᾶς, not ταῦτα.

343: The idea that love is for the idle is found also in Theophrastos frag. 114, ἐρωτηθεὶς τί ἐστιν ἔρως, "πάθος" ἔφη "ψυχῆς σχολαζούσης". Terence, *HT* 109: 'Nulla adeo ex re istuc fit nisi ex nimio otio.' Gorgias gives his sentiment a characteristically fine phrase: ἀνάπαυσις occurs in comedy only in frag. adesp. 115 K, where also the language calls for a smile, ἐκ κόπου γλυκεῖ' ἀνάπαυσις, ἐξ ἀλουσίας δ' ὕδωρ, and in Daos' elevated speech, *Aspis* 12.

345: Browning's emendation is confirmed by Aristainetos ii. 17, οὐπώποτε (Cobet: οὔπω τε) ἠράσθης; ... σφόδρα γοῦν ἀπειρότερον διαλέγῃ. Aristainetos frequently works in quotations from Menander and other authors and will have been quoting deliberately. The same cannot be said of Heliodoros, who at vi. 5. 5. has οὐπώποτε ἠράςθης; His language often reminds one of phrases met in comedy, but I do not think there is evidence of conscious quotation. οὔ μοι δοκεῖς (cf. 787) must refer back over the intervening question to οὐπώποτ' ἠράςθης; if this is too difficult, we could change to οὔ μοι δοκεῖ γε, sc. ἀνάπαυςιν διδόναι.

347 τῷ θεῷ: Sostratos does not put a name to the god who controls him; the audience knows it to be Pan.

348 οὐδέν is too short, but seems almost inevitable. Perhaps it was written ουδεεν, i.e. οὐδὲ ἕν, as οὐδείς is written ουδεεις at 324. We cannot *restore* οὐδὲ ἕν because a dactyl is not normally, perhaps never, followed by an anapaest, J. W. White, *Verse of Greek Comedy*, p. 49.

349 οὔκ, εἰ λάβοιμι: 'My distress will *not* be in vain if I should get the girl to wife':: 'You'd not get her.' οὔκ, εἰ, although less common than οὔκ, ἀλλά, is by no means infrequent, e.g. Eur. *HF* 719, Soph. *Phil.* 109, *OT* 583, Ar. *Peace* 828; similarly οὔκ, ἤν, Eur. *Hec.* 399, Ar. *Plut.* 321. The space before βοιμι is insufficient for seven average letters, but the usual ligatured ει need take no more room than ε. This tells against most other suggested supplements. πῶς ἂν λάβοιμι (*ed. pr.*) and εἰ γὰρ λάβοιμι (Page) make Sostratos disregard μάτην κακοπαθεῖς. οὐκ ἂν λάβοιμι (Diano, etc.) is a question that Sostratos would hardly put at this stage in the conversation: it would argue either dim wits or a faint heart.

350 ff.: The general sense seems to be: 'You will not win her, and you will realize this if you come with me; we shall meet him in the fields; I shall interpose a word about getting the girl married, for that's a thing I'd gladly see done.' But restoration is impossible because 350 is corrupt; no word ending in -ννα can have stood here. Van Groningen and Mette suggest that B had cυναcυνκολουθηcαc, i.e. cυνακολουθήcαc with a repeated cυν; if that is so, it must also have omitted a word, since there is space for only six or seven letters. In 351 παράγῃς or παράcτῃς is more likely in the context than παρ' αὐτῆς, although palaeographically there is nothing to choose; either would require ἐάν (or ἄν) in one of these lines. In these circumstances there is a wide field for conjecture, and dozens of proposals have been made, none convincing enough to be worth record here. My own suggestion would be γνώcει⟨δὲ καὶ⟩ c]ὺ [[να]] cυν⟨α⟩κολουθήcαc ἐμοὶ | [τοῦτ', ἂν] παράcτῃς. I am glad to find that Jacques suggests something very similar. For the separation of γνώcει . . . τοῦτο, cf. 236 n.

351 πληcίον . . . ἡμῶν: For the separated position cf. 236 n. Gorgias and Knemon work different parts of the same νάπη or mountain-valley.

352: Cf. *Sam.* 64, ἐμβαλεῖc περὶ τοῦ γάμου λόγον, Longus i. 19, ἐνέβαλε λόγον περὶ τοῦ Χλόηc γάμου, iii. 29, ἐμβάλλει λόγον περὶ γάμου.

355 μαχεῖται: 'Quarrel with', cf. Theophr. *Char.* 14. 9, 23. 8, τῷ παιδὶ μάχεcθαι ὅτι τὸ χρυcίον οὐκ ἔχων αὐτῷ ἀκολουθεῖ.

358: How does Gorgias know that Knemon is not there? Had he seen him depart in pursuit of Pyrrhias? But this would upset the normal routine of the day, which Knemon is here expected to follow. The difficulty would be overlooked on the stage, and it is necessary for the sequel that Sostratos should *wait* for Knemon and be disappointed.

359 ἣν εἴωθεν: Sc. ὁδόν. **ὦ τᾶν**: For the colour of this address (often irony or remonstrance) see 247 n. Here I think the point is that Gorgias is unreasonably trying to scare Sostratos when, after all, the girl will be with her father; how then *could* he not be keen to go? Gorgias' reply is somewhat unsympathetically matter-of-fact.

361 ἕτοιμοc is normally not accompanied by the present tense of εἶναι, cf. 370; but see 307, *Aspis* 329, and *Epitr.* 515 where ἕτοιμόc εἰμι is a probable conjecture. No supplement here is more probable than ⟨εἰμ'⟩. **οἳ λέγειc**: 'To the place you speak of', i.e. the νάπη of 351. These words are marked off in B by a dicolon, but it is a puzzle how anyone could wish to assign them to Gorgias. They are repeated two lines below, and the repetition seems to have no dramatic value. Can it be that we should emend here to read ⟨Γο.⟩ εὖ λέγειc? Blake proposed βάδιζ'· ἕτοιμός εἰμ'. ⟨Γο.⟩ οἷον λέγειc, conceivably right if Gorgias is shocked, not at Sostratos' readiness to fall in with his plan, but at his motive for doing so, the hope of seeing the girl.

362 cυναγωνίcαι μοι: 'Take my side.' The word is common in Demosthenes, perhaps a little colourful here. Parenthetic ἀντιβολῶ (cε), familiar in Aristophanes, is not yet known from New Comedy elsewhere. Perhaps it had become less common in ordinary talk, and therefore stronger in effect.

363: Although B does not cause Daos to intervene until 365, there are two reasons for assigning this speech to him also: (*a*) it is a rudely phrased objection to a course of action which Gorgias seems to have envisaged himself just before—350 ff.; (*b*) it implies the reason given at 365–6, and it would be both improper and contrary to ancient dramatic technique for Daos to give that reason if it was his master who had been asked for it.

365 τί δὴ γὰρ οὐχί; The transposition of B's unmetrical γὰρ δή gives a phrase known from *Sam.* 79, Eur. *Or.* 1602, Plato, *Parm.* 138 b,

140 e, Denniston, *GP* 211. τί γὰρ . . . δῆτα occurs at Ar. *Clouds* 403.
ταῖς βώλοις: Note the article, 'with those clods of his'.
366 ὄλεθρον ἀργόν: 'A loafing pest'. Demosthenes calls Philip
ὄλεθρος Μακεδών, ix. 31, and Aischines ὄλεθρος γραμματεύς, xviii. 127.
ἀποκαλεῖν usually means to give someone a disparaging name, e.g.
Xen. *Mem.* i. 2. 57, τοὺς κυβεύοντας . . . ἀργοὺς ἀπεκάλει.

366 ff.: Since Daos' attitude to Sostratos is hostile in 364 and 371–3,
there is some force in Kraus's view, according to which the helpful
suggestion that by joining in the digging Sostratos might get Knemon's
ear must be attributed, against B, to Gorgias. Nevertheless the papyrus
can be defended. (1) If the speaker is Daos, the suggestion, although
represented by him as helpful, need not be so intended in reality : what
he wishes is to exhaust and discourage Sostratos, as he explains at
371 ff. (2) Gorgias, in suggesting that Sostratos should accompany
him to the fields, desired to prove that any hope of a marriage was
out of the question, not to forward the plan. If these lines are spoken
by him, we must accept that he changes his ground. Although that
is not out of the question, there is no other sign of it : at 363 τίνα
τρόπον; shows that he has at least no positive idea of helping, and at
371 τί κακοπαθεῖν cαυτὸν βιάζῃ; looks as if he still thought the position
as hopeless as at 349, μάτην κακοπαθεῖc. Not until 380, moved by
Sostratos' last protestation, does he almost grudgingly wish him
success, εἴπερ λέγειc ἃ φρονεῖc, ἐπιτύχοιc.

On the other hand one cannot accept van Groningen's idea that
the phrases of 367 ff. are 'durs ou offensants' and therefore suitable
only to Daos. καὶ παρὰ cοῦ does not mean 'even from you', but 'from
you', Denniston, *GP* 320; καὶ cύ is frequently thus emphatic, e.g. Dio
Prus. iii. 1 (to Trajan), Cωκράτηc . . . ὃν καὶ cὺ γιγνώcκειc ἀκοῇ πρὸ
πολλῶν ἐτῶν γενόμενον.

Here Menander employs the common dramatic device of laying
a false trail; the suggested event does not occur, Knemon and
Sostratos never meet in the fields, and Knemon never listens to
Sostratos. But at a later stage (754 ff.) they meet and Gorgias tries to
introduce Sostratos as a hard-working farmer; Knemon shows no
interest, and it is no longer necessary that he should.

367 εἰ τύχοι γάρ: A. Oguse, *Bull. Fac. Lettres Strasbourg*, (1964), 201,
showed that this is the right punctuation, comparing many passages,
including Eur. *Or.* 780, εἰ τύχοι, γένοιτ᾽ ἄν, Dem. xv. 16, τάχ᾽ ἄν, εἰ
τύχοιεν, cωφρονέcτεροι . . . γένοιντο, xxiii. 58, τάχ᾽ ἄν, εἰ τύχοι, καὶ
τούτων cυμβάντων, 143, τάχ᾽ ἄν, εἰ τύχοι, καὶ τοιοῦτό τι cυμβαίη. In the
last three passages εἰ τύχοι is associated with τάχ᾽ ἄν, as also in xxiv. 36,
xxxvi. 55; here it reinforces ἴcωc, a word of the same meaning.

369 αὐτουργόν: A man who works his land himself, not relying on slave-labour (but not necessarily entirely without it), Eur. *Or.* 920, αὐτουργός, οἵπερ καὶ μόνοι cῴζουcι γῆν. Thuc. i. 141 contrasts the Athenians with the Peloponnesians, who being αὐτουργοί cannot engage in long campaigns. Such a one might help a neighbour either on an exchange basis or for pay. As at *Epitr.* 910, *Georg.* 66, τῷ βίῳ, 'in way of life', adds little to the adjective to which it is attached.

370 πειθαρχεῖν: 'Obey authority', only here in Menander. Sostratos puts himself under the orders of the helpful slave.

371 τί κακοπαθεῖν κτλ.: Why is there no answer to this question? Either because Sostratos' reply is one of action, probably to divest himself of his cloak, or because the question is an 'aside'. I prefer the latter, for Gorgias would appear singularly naïve if he hoped to affect Sostratos by this remark, which echoes what he had ineffectually said at 348. Lloyd-Jones removes the problem by reading αὐτόν for ϲαυτόν, supposing that Gorgias puts the question to Daos. But I doubt whether βιάζῃ is then the right verb and whether κακοπαθεῖν can have a reference other than that of 348. Handley also makes Gorgias address Daos, but retains ϲαυτόν: 'Gorgias cannot see why the slave wants to inflict a day's work on himself.' But Gorgias and Daos would surely have returned to the fields in any case. In any event Sostratos cannot stand idle during Daos' speech (371–4), which I take to be addressed to Gorgias, not an aside to the audience. He must move apart, do something to prepare himself for digging, and then, being ready, ask for a mattock. It is possible that he here deposits his cloak in the shrine, from which he may recover it in the interval between Acts IV and V: as Handley remarks, it would be appropriate to the renewed emphasis there on his wealth *vis-à-vis* the poverty of Gorgias. He will hardly take it to the fields over his arm (? with the intention of dropping it before coming within sight of Knemon).

375 ἔκφερε δίκελλαν: This implies that Sostratos knows Gorgias and Daos to belong to the second house represented on the stage. It is not a point likely to trouble the audience, but when going off at the end of Act I Sostratos had passed in front of the door where Daos was standing and (however preoccupied) could have observed him. The δίκελλα, a two-bladed or two-pronged mattock, is the characteristic tool of the farm-worker, used like a pickaxe (527). Not only could it be employed in stony ground and among trees, but it provided deeper cultivation than the shallow wooden plough of the Greeks. A similar tool was called *bidens* by the Romans. Both were made in differing weights and in differing shapes, either with two wide blades or with two tines. An excellent illustration of the heavy two-tined variety is given by a mosaic in Constantinople, showing two men using the δίκελλα; one is at the end of his stroke, the other has the tool swung right back over his head (K. D. White, *Agricultural Instruments of the Romans*, pp. 47–52, Plate 3, D. Talbot Rice, *The Great Palace of the Empress*, Plate 47; see also Handley on *Dysk.* 527).

378 ἀπέcωcαc: If we follow B in giving this to Daos, the meaning seems to be 'you have saved me', sc. from the back-breaking labour with the mattock. But building a dry-stone wall is not light work either, and Daos is no shirker (207, 372, 541). An alternative is to read ἀπέcωcά c', 'I have preserved you', sc. from being assaulted by Knemon. But Daos does not wish Sostratos well, regarding him as a source of trouble; after 371–4 such a remark strikes oddly. The best solution is to interpret the colon after δοc as meaning that Sostratos turns from Daos to Gorgias, and to suppose the loss of a dicolon after ἀπέcωcαc. 'You have saved my life', says Sostratos, and then continues at 379: 'If I don't get the girl, I shall die.' Gorgias, therefore, by offering him a chance of approaching her father, has saved his life. For ἀπέcωcαc addressed to one who saves a lover from despair, cf. Lucian, *Dial. Meretr.* ii. 4; the word is rendered by *seruare* in Latin, Plaut. *Curc.* 628, *Men.* 1065, *Merc.* 112, *Poen.* 917.   **τρόφιμε:** See *Epitr.* frag. 1 n. Although Gorgias clearly owns his farm and his slave, who correctly calls him δεcπότηc at 300, Daos here addresses him as he would have done when he was still a child, the master's son.   **διώκετε:** 'Follow', cf. *Sam.* 198, *Sik.* 384, Xen. *Hell.* i. 1. 13, Ἀλκιβιάδηc δὲ εἰπὼν καὶ τούτοιc διώκειν αὐτόν, Plato, *Phaedo* 61 b 8, Εὐήνῳ φράζε . . . ἐμὲ διώκειν ὡc τάχιcτα.

379 οὕτωc ἔχω looks forward to the following sentence, as at 58. B's παραποθανεῖν although a *hapax* is not utterly impossible, in view of the not uncommon παραπόλλυcθαι. (Reiske's conjecture τῶν τότε παραποθανόντων for τῶν τε γὰρ ἀποθ. in Dio Cassius frag. 102, Boissevain i. p. 346, is not certainly right.) If the emendation οὕτωc ἔχω γάρ is accepted, the meaning is 'you have saved my life, since I shall die if I don't get the girl.'

381 ff.: Does Gorgias here leave the stage (*ed. pr.*, Vicenti, Treu, J. Martin, Jacques, van Groningen, Mette) or remain to listen to Sostratos' speech (Lloyd-Jones, Gallavotti, Diano)? ὡc οἴει in 382 may be addressed to one who has just left, and the speech reads more and more like a soliloquy as it proceeds. On the assignment of parts approved by Goold and Handley the actor who played Gorgias must leave at 381 in order to assume the mask of Sikon, who enters at 393 by the other *parodos*. But he need not go so soon if he is to take the part of Getas, who does not arrive until 420.

382 γάρ: This seems to refer back to 379–80, Sostratos continuing his train of thought and ignoring the intervening remark of Gorgias, Denniston, *GP* 63. Otherwise one must suppose an ellipse of 'I hope indeed for success', ibid. 61. It is impossible to say whether cύ 'goes with' ἀποτρέπεις or with οἴει; and only a grammarian would ask. It is not emphatic.

383 παρώξυμμαι: 'I am spurred on'; the same contrast with ἀποτρέπειν occurs in Dem. xxi. 37.

385 ff.: There are a number of difficulties here. (1) B has τῶν ἐν τῷ βίῳ τούτων κακῶν, which is perfectly good Greek, paralleled by frag. 401, which praises life in country solitude: ἥ τε κατὰ πόλιν αὕτη τρυφὴ λάμπει μέν, εἰc δ᾽ ὀλίγον χρόνον, and *Aspis* 335, τῶν ἄφνω τούτων τινὶ κακῶν. τούτων can mean 'these we know of' (LSJ C. 3. b) and need not be emended to τούτῳ. (2) If B's δεδεικαμενη conceals some form of the verb δεδίττομαι (or δεδίcκομαι), then δειδικαμένη, found in Appian, *BC* v. 79, εἴτε τι cημεῖον δειδικάμενοc, is the nearest. The only known Attic aorist is δεδιξαμένη (Dem. xix. 291, cf. the Atticist Lucian, *Zeuxis* 4), and this may have been corrupted in B to the later form. There are, however, considerations which raise doubt about this solution: (*a*) in Attic Greek elsewhere the verb is a transitive middle, meaning 'alarm'; in later authors, to be sure, the meaning 'be frightened' occurs, but only with forms that they may have taken to be passive; (*b*) it is strange that this one item, timidity, should be picked out from all the evils that feminine upbringing was supposed to implant, luxury, deceitfulness, vanity, etc.; (*c*) strange, too, that ὑπο τηθίδοc should be attached to a verb in the middle voice. Hence there is much to be said, so far as sense goes, for *ed. pr.*'s δεδιδαγμένη; although palaeographically this is not an easy corruption, it is a conceivable one. (3) μαίαc may, in view of τηθίδοc, 'aunt', mean 'grandmother', cf. Hesychios, τήθην οἱ Ἕλληνεc τὴν πατρὸc ἢ μητρὸc μητέρα, οἱ δὲ παλαιοὶ ἀκύρωc μάμμην καὶ μαῖαν. But the word can be applied to any old woman (Aristoph. Byz. frag. 140 Nauck): Phaidra so addresses her old nurse, Eur. *Hippolytus* 243. When the young woman in Ar. *Eccl.* 915 tauntingly calls her elderly rival μαῖα, 'granny' would do. The meaning in Antiphanes frag. 159 K, where most of a line is lost, is quite uncertain; perhaps 'midwife', as in Plato, *Theaet.* 149 a, and medical authors. Handley suggests that τηθίc may have been used not only of true aunts, but of any elderly female relative, and thinks that μαῖα too is here vague, and would include any old woman called upon to look after a girl.

388: B's μετavτουπατροc may be explained as due to the insertion of the article τοῦ (cf. 151, 769) and the misreading of α as αυ. **ἀγρίου:**

Sostratos, wishing to think the best of his future father-in-law, explains his ferocity as a hatred of ill-doers; he puts the best possible construction on 355, λοιδορούμενος τοὺς βίους οὓς ἄγουςι. Surprisingly, he turns out to be not so far from the mark, as will be learned from Knemon's *apologia*, 718 ff. There is an imitation of the passage in Aelian, *ep. rust.* 15, if Jacques rightly emends there to ἄγριος ὢν καὶ ⟨μιсο⟩πόνηρος τὸν τρόπον (μονήρης Hercher).

390 τάλαντα τέτταρα: Roughly two cwt. or 100 kg. Cf. Sosikrates frag. 1 K, ὅταν γὰρ οἶμαι λευκὸς ἄνθρωπος, παχύς, | ἀργός, λάβῃ δίκελλαν εἰωθὼς τρυφᾶν | πεντεςτάτηρον, γίνεται τὸ πνεῦμ' ἄνω, an exaggeration in the opposite sense, for a *stater = mina* (Pollux ix. 57) = nearly three-fifths of a kilogramme.

391 προαπολεῖ: B has προςαπολει, which Barrett on *Hipp.* 1374–7 defends, thinking the meaning to be 'will finish off', without any implication of earlier harm. The confusion of προ- and προς- is common in this MS., see 98 n.; I take the meaning to be that the heavy mattock will finish him before he has the chance of a word with Knemon.

392 καταπονεῖν: Cf. frag. 526, πάντα γὰρ ταῖς ἐνδελεχείαις καταπονεῖται πράγματα.

(iii) 393–401: *Sikon, with a sheep*

393 καλόν: 'No ordinary beauty'; the irony of the phrase appears when it is unexpectedly followed by a curse (Kraus). No exact parallel has been quoted, but a change to κακόν is in itself unlikely (καλόν being *lectio difficilior*), and spoils a good point.

Note the complete lack of liaison between this scene and the preceding one: the other examples of this in Menander are after 486, 521, 665, 873, *Epitr.* 1061, *Georg.* 21, *Mis.* 269, *Aspis* 490, *Sam.* 95.

394 ἄπαγ' εἰς τὸ βάραθρον: Cf. 575, where it is clear that ἄπαγε is addressed to no one in particular; therefore it is not addressed to the sheep in this passage. The curse is a previously unknown variant on ἄπαγ' ἐς κόρακας, *Perik.* 396, *Dysk.* 432. The βάραθρον was a cleft into which criminals were thrown as a means of execution.

395–6: Since θρῖον is particularly used of the leaf, and κράδη of the branch, of the fig-tree, θαλλόν of the shoots of the olive, punctuation after θαλλοῦ is probable.

396: δ' εсβιαν of B is doubly, perhaps trebly, suspect: (1) the prepositional phrase is otherwise unknown; (2) two verbs in asyndeton, followed by a third with δέ, make an unusual construction (Denniston, *GP* 164, knows only two examples, of which Ar. *Knights* 79 is uncertain;

the MSS. disagree where to place δέ, which may therefore be interpolated); (3) εc should be εἰc, although this is a typical spelling mistake. Hence Lloyd-Jones emended to πρὸc βίαν, Fraenkel to ἐκ βίαc (cf. *Heros* 79). But the corruption is a strange one, and εἰc with a noun or adjective is frequently used to express manner in place of an adverb (LSJ IV. 3), e.g. εἰc τάχοc. It is best to keep εἰc βίαν, with some reserve.   ἀποcπᾷ: Apparently intrans. (cf. Xen. *Anab.* i. 5. 3), 'it twists away off my shoulders'; for the middle cf. Eur. *Hecuba* 225, μήτ' ἀποcπαcθῇc βίᾳ.

398 τοὐναντίον δὴ γέγονε: B's δ'ηγαγον shows a confusion of α and ε as at 207, omission of a letter, and resultant faulty word-division.

For τοὐναντίον, 'the opposite of what one would expect', Barber quoted Antiphanes frag. 233 K, τοὐναντίον γὰρ νῦν ποιοῦcιν οἱ θεοί· | ἐὰν ἐπιορκήcῃ τιc, αὐτὸc εὐθέωc | ὁ δίδουc τὸν ὅρκον ἐγένετ' ἐμβρόντητοc. Cf. also Heliodoros i. 25. 3, γίνεται τοὐναντίον. Gallavotti, *Riv. fil.* xliii (1965), 139, adduces instances from Aeneas of Gaza, who seems to have known this play. So here instead of the cook cutting up the sheep, he is 'cut to pieces' by the sheep. Menander has given new life to an old joke on the literal and metaphorical meanings of (κατα)κόπτω: usually it is the cook who 'makes mincemeat' of his associates, *Sam.* 283–93, Alexis frag. 173, μὴ κόπτε με | ἀλλὰ τὰ κρέα, Sosipatros frag. 1. 20 K, Anaxippos frag. 1. 23 K; here he himself is the victim.

399 νεωλκῶν: Ancient ships were regularly pulled up the beach, but they might be drawn considerable distances overland. The adverbial addition of τὴν ὁδόν, 'along the road', suggests that Sikon has in mind such a more exceptional effort. Examples are the track with rollers across the Isthmus of Corinth, and the effort of the Tarentines against the Romans, Polybios viii. 29.

401 τὸν Πᾶνα χαίρειν: Probably addressed to Pan's statue, see 311 n. and 433 n. The phrase presumably depends on κελεύω or some such word understood. Plato's *Ion* opens τὸν "Ιωνα χαίρειν.   **παῖ Γέτα:** This form of address, although it no doubt betrays some feeling of superiority, does not show that Sikon is himself not a slave, since Getas uses it in addressing Donax, 959. Cf. Ar. *Plut.* 624, παῖ Καρίων.

(iv) 402–426: *Sikon and Getas*

405 cτρώματα: Rugs to sit or recline on. The motif of the slave overburdened with luggage was an old one at the time of the *Frogs* (1 ff.). Menander characteristically retains it, but in an attenuated form and integrated into the play. Here it (*a*) explains Getas' late arrival, (*b*) marks his propensity to grumble at women, cf. 460, 568, (*c*) prepares for the entry of a large company at the beginning of Act III.

406: When a line is both mutilated and corrupt, it is rarely possible to restore it in a way that will command universal assent.

1. Metre may be restored by writing αὐτά for ταῦτα. Then the gap can be filled by, e.g., τί δ᾽ ἐγ[ωγε; (Cικ.) ἐπ]έρεισον. This solution is adopted by Bingen.

2. ταῦτα may be transposed. Handley writes τί δ᾽ ἐγ[ωγε; (Cικ.)] ταῦτ᾽ ἐπέρεισον δεῦρο, supposing B to have had εγωγε: επερεισον. He explains the emphatic ταῦτα as referring to the cooking utensils, which interest Sikon, rather than the whole load. τί δ᾽ ἐγωγε; he would translate 'What about me?' In the passages he quotes as parallels similar phrases (Ar. *Peace* 1116, τί ἐγὼ δέ; *Thesm.* 70, τί οὖν ἐγὼ δρῶ; *Thesm.* 925, *Plut.* 1197) are put in the mouths of persons who are left inactive, or out of it, when others have expressed an intention of doing something. That is not the situation here; and we have no evidence that Getas was carrying cooking utensils as well as rugs. Page proposed τί δ᾽ ἐγ[ωγ᾽ οὐ; (Cικ.)] δεῦρ᾽ ἔρεισον ταῦτα; 'What am I not carrying?' With the change of αὐτά for ταῦτα this is possible. Against Jacques's τί δ᾽ ἐγ[ὼ δρῶ;] one may note that as yet δρᾶν appears once only in Menander: *Sam.* 568, τί δράcω; (where see note).

3. In 407 γάρ suggests that an explanation is being offered of what Getas said in 406. Can that have been τί δ᾽ ἐγ[ὼ νῦν] δεῦρο; sc. φέρω? 'For another dream would send us off to the other side of Attica'.

4. Blake points out that the only remaining dicolon is after ἰδού. To maintain it, he suggests that Getas tells Sikon to come and hold up the luggage (δεῦρ᾽, ἔρεισον ταῦτα) while he gets out from under it, and that Sikon answers ἰδού. But he has no better proposal to fill the gap than τί δ᾽ ἐγὼ δρῶ;

407 ἐνύπνιον may be the noun used adverbially as in *Ar. Wasps* 1218, ἐνύπνιον ἐcτιώμεθα; or the noun in apposition to Πᾶνα; or the adjective, cf. Aesch. *Septem* 710, ἐνυπνίων φαντασμάτων ὄψεις and *AP* xii. 124 (Gow and Page, *Hell. Epigr.* p. 802), ἐνύπνιος ἦλθε. There is the same doubt at *Perik.* 358 and elsewhere.

408 Παιανιοῖ: This locative case is parallel to, e.g., Μεγαροῖ. The deme of Paiania (neut. plural) was on the E. side of Hymettos, about twenty miles from Phyle; this is the first evidence that Pan had a shrine there. E. Vanderpool, *Am. Journ. Arch.* lxxi (1967), 309, guesses it to have been at a cave some two miles N. of the village. For the position of τόν, cf. 264, *Georgos* 26, *Aspis* 55. τούτῳ goes with θύcοντεc; it receives emphasis by being brought forward.

409: Sikon correctly sees the implication that the journey to Phyle has been occasioned by a dream.

410 μή με κόπτε: κόπτω means 'weary', particularly by loquacity; cf. Hegesippos frag. 1. 3 K, μὴ κόπτε με, Alexis frag. 173. 12, both addressed to cooks. The loquacity of cooks was a stock stage characteristic: here Menander modifies it, turning it to an inability to listen to a story without interruption; at the same time he combines it with *inquisitiveness*, as in *Epitrepontes*. μή μοι is a far commoner collocation than μή με (907), which may have caused B's mistake. To keep μοι as an ethic dative, taking κόπτε to have an unexpressed object (e.g. τὰ ὦτα), 'don't, pray, be a bore', is improbable in face of the parallels.

εἶπον, imperative of weak aor. εἶπα, of which εἶπας is the only common form in Attic, occurs occasionally: frag. 675, Plato, *Meno* 71 d.

412 ἀπολεῖς: 'You'll be the death of me.' This is surely possible, as at Ar. *Wasps* 849, *Clouds* 1499, *Plut.* 390, *Eccl.* 775, although the usual phrase is ἀπολεῖς με (which Mette would restore). At Ar. *Frogs* 1245 the MSS. are divided between ἀπολεῖς and ἀπολεῖ c', and the latter may be right.

B in fact here has απολεισ', and Blake defends ἀπολεῖ c', but does not explain why Getas should expect his story to deal Sikon such a blow.

The symbolic dream in Greek drama, tragedy and comedy alike, is normally used as a means of heightening expectation. It either looks forward to something that has not yet happened, Plaut. *Merc.* 125, *Rud.* 583, or refers to something that has occurred but has still to be revealed to the dreamer, Aesch. *Pers.* 176, *Choeph.* 527, Soph. *El.* 417, or combines both functions, Eur. *Hec.* 68, *IT* 44. The dream here belongs to the second category, but is very differently used. Whereas in tragedy such dreams build up an atmosphere of impending catastrophe, Sostratos' mother's dream is if anything reassuring to the spectators, who are made to feel that Pan, who had in the prologue declared his benevolence, is still pulling the strings. But its function is not primarily that, but one of dramatic architecture, since it shows that the arrival of the sacrificial party, essential for the plot and for a happy outcome of Sostratos' affairs, is not a contrived coincidence but the result of one and the same divine instigation. In these circumstances a bare recital of the dream would be undramatic. Menander has cleverly retained interest by superimposing another stock motive, that of the inquisitive cook, who excitedly drags the story out of Getas. It is one to cause alarm to Sostratos' friends, especially if the view of Artemidoros (ii. 37), that to dream of Pan portended danger, was already current: in any event, the shackles he fastened on

Sostratos must be of sinister import. It was commonly believed that the catastrophe presaged by a dream could be averted by sacrifice and rites of purification; the motive occurs frequently in tragedy, e.g. Aesch. *Persae* 215 ff., *Choephoroi* 21 ff.

413 τρόφιμε: See *Epitr.* frag. 1 n.

414 κομψῷ νεανίcκῳ γε: γε emphasizes the element κομψῷ in the unified group κομψῷ νεανίcκῳ (Denniston, *GP* 150), cf. Ar. *Plut.* 21, cτέφανον ἔχοντά γε, Eur. *Helen* 837, ταὐτῷ ξίφει γε, *Cyclops* 283, αἰcχρὸν cτράτευμά γε. **κομψῷ:** See *Perik.* 298 n. **περικρούειν:** The leg-irons are closed round the ankle by hammering. Previously this usage of the verb was not known before Plutarch, *an vitiositas* 499 a.

415 διφθέραν: See *Epitr.* 229 n. Nothing in the text shows that Sostratos did wear such a skin cloak—he would have had to borrow one from Gorgias. It is only a dream symbol, like the fetters; they symbolize his enslavement to love, it stands for the hard labour he undertakes.

416 ἐν τοῦ πληcίον τῷ χωρίῳ: 'On the farm of his [i.e. Pan's] neighbour'. Both Knemon and Gorgias were Pan's neighbours; literally Sostratos worked on Gorgias' land, but simultaneously his toil in the dream has a symbolical reference to the pains of love that centre on Knemon's farm. For the position of the genitive A. P. Treweek (*apud* Handley) refers to Thuc. iii. 81. 5, ἐν τοῦ Διονύcου τῷ ἱερῷ (for more examples see K–G i. 618); it throws emphasis on τοῦ πληcίον, rightly, since the remarkable thing is that Sostratos should dig in this remote spot, not that he should dig *on a farm*. **ἄτοπον** probably combines the meanings 'odd' and 'bad', cf. 288 n.

419 πάλιν αἶρου: The dramatic reason why Getas had to put his burden down was that the actor would have been intolerably handicapped if he had had to stoop under it during the whole of the previous lively exchanges. **μεμάθηκα:** 'Now I understand.'

420 cτιβάδαc: Couches of leaves or similar material, to be covered by the cτρώματα, or rugs, brought by Getas. Longus iv. 38, describing a feast outside a cave sacred to Pan and the Nymphs, writes πρὸ τοῦ ἄντρου cτιβάδαc ὑπεcτόρεcαν ἐκ χλωρᾶc φυλλάδοc. **ποῶμεν:** This is a more likely correction of ποήcωμεν than ποήcω, since B elsewhere introduces false futures (see next n.: -ωμεν may be a mis-spelling for -ομεν); on the other hand the insertion of μεν is neither paralleled nor easily explicable.

422 θύειν γε: Since B elsewhere substitutes future for present (541, 780) I prefer to emend θύcειν to θύειν rather than θῦcαι; but either change gives possible Greek. γε is here limiting: nothing shall stand in the way of the *sacrifice*, whatever its success may prove to be. This thought leads on to ἀλλ' ἀγαθῇ τύχῃ, a prayer that all may turn out well. No particular verb need be supplied with the phrase, although one cannot say that it is *wrong* to supply θύωμεν. J. Martin gives ἀλλ' ἀγαθῇ τύχῃ to Getas, as a formula of agreement (*Sam.* 297 n.); there is no advantage in this.

423 ὀφρῦς ἄνες ποτ': ποτε implies impatience. The phrase ὀφρῦς ἀνιέναι, 'relax the brow', is not found elsewhere, but cf. Lucian, *Icaromenippus* 23, μειδιάσας οὖν ὁ Ζεὺς καὶ μικρὸν ἐπανεὶς τῶν ὀφρύων. Arching of the eyebrows is known today as a sign of scepticism, or it may here indicate that Getas feels badly treated; cf. *Epitr.* 632 ff. n.

424 χορτάςω: χορτάζειν is properly used of feeding cattle; when applied to persons it means 'fill'. A character in Athenaios, iii. 99 f, criticized for using the passive χορτασθῆναι instead of κορεσθῆναι, quotes in his own support a number of passages from comedy, remarking *inter alia* that Menander used the word in his Τροφώνιος.

425: B's οὖν may be defensible, see Handley's note and particularly Plato, *Apol.* 22 b: 'I am in fact one who praises you.' Assentient γοῦν (Denniston, *GP* 454) would certainly be in place: 'Yes to be sure I always praise you', cf. *Perik.* 1001, πιθανώτερος πολλῷ φανεῖ γοῦν. But I incline to adopt Jacques's coῦ τ' εἰμὶ καὶ τῆς ⟨cῆc⟩ τέχνης, although it assumes two errors. He compares *Georgos* 70, coῦ τε καὶ τῆς cῆc πενίας. For the phrase cf. Heliodoros ii. 8. 4, ἑαυτήν τε καὶ ⟨τὴν⟩ τέχνην ἐξεμίσθου.

426 ἀεί ποτ': This combination marks what has been true at any time, e.g. Thuc. vi. 82. 2, οἱ Ἴωνες αἰεί ποτε πολέμιοι τοῖς Δωριεῦσι.   **οὐχὶ πιστεύω** is spoken to the audience rather than to Sikon.

XOPOY: In contrast with the lines that precede the entry of the chorus before the first interlude, there are no words in the text to introduce the second and subsequent interludes. This seems to have been the standard practice and suggests that, as one would expect, the chorus remained in the orchestra during the acts. But how did it leave at the end of the play? In some of Aristophanes' plays the chorus leaves with the actors; in *Clouds* and *Thesm.* it baldly announces that the play is over and that it is going. In New Comedy perhaps it left wordlessly at the end; or it may have danced out at the finish of the interlude before the last act.

ACT III

(i) **427–441**: *Knemon, Sostratos' mother* (enters 430 with *Plangon* and *Parthenis*), *Getas* (enters 434)

427 τὴν θύραν κλείсаса: Similarly Euclio, going to market, says to his old maidservant Staphyla 'aedis occlude', Plaut. *Aul.* 274; there is a long development of the theme, ibid. 89–104. To bolt the door in the daytime was unusual, as is shown by Theopropides' surprise at Plaut. *Mostellaria* 444. Euclio wishes it bolted because he is afraid for his treasure; Knemon's command is a sign of misanthropy. Knemon's appearance is expected, having been foretold by Gorgias (359); the audience will note that this is an occasion on which he does *not* take his daughter to the fields with him (360); Sostratos will be disappointed of seeing her again.

The fact that the chorus has become a purely conventional survival is shown by Knemon's conduct here. He pays no attention whatever to the presence of the tipsy Panistai, but is shortly to be greatly upset by the arrival of a respectable household party.

428 скότουс: Genitive of time, like ἑσπέρας, μεсημβρίας, etc.

The audience know that Knemon cannot be allowed to remove himself from the scene for good. The phrase stimulates their curiosity to see how his intention will be reversed. At the same time it is a stroke of character-drawing, illustrating his devotion to toil (31).

430–41: This scene has been much debated, since Ritchie maintained (J. H. Quincey etc., *Notes on the Dyskolos of Menander* [1959], p. 6) that B is here at fault in failing to recognize Sostratos' mother as a speaking character and falsely dividing her part between Getas and someone unnamed, but presumably Sikon. Those who defend the credit of B are driven, in my opinion, to contrived expedients, and I adopt Ritchie's view, with certain modification of detail which may meet some of the objections to it that have been raised. On the antecedent probability of a mistake in B it must be remembered that texts of plays were, so far as we know, transmitted for at least two centuries before names of speakers were introduced. Nor is the absence of Sostratos' mother from the initial list of characters any support for B's assignment of parts: assignment of parts must have preceded the drawing up of lists of characters.

Ritchie's arguments are: (1) that when a group of persons appear on the stage, convention requires that at least one should speak; (2) that the order to Plangon to hurry should come from one of this group, not from Getas, to whom B assigns it: he is in the shrine and (it may be added) appears only when the flute music announces the

party's arrival; (3) that the fussy concern over religious ceremony
(432, 440) suits the picture already drawn (260 ff., 407 ff.) of the
mother, but is out of character for Getas; (4) that the exclamatory
τάλαν of 438 (a certain emendation for τάλαιν') is used exclusively
by female characters. The last argument is uncertain, because τάλαν
might be taken as agreeing with πρόβατον, but (1), (2), and (3) are
I believe conclusive, as has been recognized by Lloyd-Jones, Mette,
Bingen, J. Martin, Blake, and Jacques among editors. It may be
added that the introduction of a speaking mother has two further
advantages. Knemon reacts at once to the appearance of the party:
he does not delay until it has brought Getas out, a slowness that would
be a little surprising. Secondly, the mother, who from what we have
already heard, is a formidable character, does not preserve an unexplained silence while Getas takes charge of the proceedings.

   Ritchie's conclusion has been resisted, and the arguments of
van Groningen, Post, and Handley deserve attention. The first supposed that Getas accompanies the arriving party, which does not
necessarily include the mother. The mother is, however, present later
(867), without her arrival's having been even hinted at elsewhere. And
since Getas was last seen entering the cave with the luggage, it would
be contrary to all custom (and logic) if his next appearance were from
anywhere but the cave. The intervals between the acts do not cancel,
as they may in modern plays, the whereabouts of the characters. Post,
AJP lxxxiv (1963), 43, 203, makes the mother arrive first, and enter
the shrine; Getas then comes out to hurry Plangon in—she is required
to 'inaugurate the basket' before the sacrifice. In giving orders to all
and sundry Getas is to be regarded as the mother's mouthpiece. But
the silent action thus imagined at the beginning of the scene is unlike
Greek technique, and there is no reason for supposing that the
ceremony of the basket required the presence of the daughter of the
household. Handley resorts to no artificialities to explain the appearance of Getas from the shrine; he just happened to come out,
being tired of waiting. Certainly Menander has no hesitation about
allowing coincidence to bring people on the stage at the moment the
plot demands, e.g. Daos at 206. But here it would put a strain on
credulity if (*a*) the party happened to arrive just as Knemon left
his house and (*b*) Getas happened to come out of the cave just as the
party arrived. There is no parallel in New Comedy for such a double
coincidence, all the more striking because at the beginning of an
act there is no dramatic momentum to disguise it. There follows
in Handley's scheme, as in those of all defenders of the MS., the appearance of Sikon. This would be motivated by his hearing the strains
of the pipe. But it is dramatically without point. What he says

(434*b*–437*a* in Handley's version) could perfectly well be said by
Getas. It is not like Menander's economical construction to bring on
a character to make a single short speech of no particular importance.
Handley is apparently uneasy at the thought that Getas, seeing
the approach of his mistress with a train of servants, should neglect
her, but brusquely command her young daughter to 'get a move on'.
He argues therefore that Plangon is probably another servant, whom
Getas can properly order about. The improbability of this is maintained in 430 n.

While accepting Ritchie's brilliant recognition that Sostratos'
mother speaks here, I find his division of speakers not entirely acceptable. (1) ὦ Ἡράκλεις, ἀηδίας must be Knemon's interjection, not
a grumble by Getas at being kept waiting. ὦ Ἡράκλεις is an expression of consternation, and ἀηδία is a strong word: 'Heavens, this is
disgusting!' See LSJ s.v. and *Sam.* 434. (2) 438. Ritchie gives ναί . . .
τέθνηκε γάρ to Getas. Since γοῦν and γάρ can hardly stand in the same
clause, we should have to adopt (with Thierfelder) the punctuation
ναὶ μὰ τὸν Δία· τὸ γοῦν πρόβατον· μικροῦ τέθνηκε γάρ. Here the restrictive γοῦν follows awkwardly on the strong affirmation that *everything*
is ready. This objection applies also to Lloyd-Jones, who gives all
from ναί . . . εἴcιτε to Getas. The exchanges are more natural if we
give all from τὸ γοῦν to the mother, punctuating τὸ γοῦν πρόβατον
—μικροῦ τέθνηκε γάρ, τάλαν—οὐ περιμένει τὴν cὴν cχολήν. This of course
is addressed to Getas, not Plangon, as Ritchie believes. See further
note on 438. (3) Still less can ποῖ κέχηνας, ἐμβρόντητε cύ be addressed
to Plangon; the bride-to-be cannot be a target for abusive terms.
If it befits a lady to use such language, it may be addressed to one of
the servants, cf. *Sam.* 105. Similarly Kynno's servant stands gaping
(ὧδε χὦδε χαcκούcη) when given an order outside Asklepios' temple,
Herondas iv. 42, cf. Ar. *Lys.* 426. But there are other possibilities: the
more probable are (1) Getas speaks to a servant, (2) Getas, as he
goes, speaks (? *sotto voce*) to Knemon, who may well stand gaping
and thunderstruck. This latter is Lloyd-Jones's solution and I adopt it.
Note must be taken, however, of the observations of J. G. Griffith, *CR*
N.S. xviii (1968), 8; he enumerates twenty-four other instances in
comedy of a vocative adjective followed by cύ, and concludes that such
phrases are used only between 'social equals'. If we grant that gods
and free men are social equals, and that cooks occupy an ambiguous
position, free by status but consorting with slaves, Griffith's observation
is true for the eighteen instances where the status of the speakers is
known. He concludes that Getas must address a servant, and thinks
(without justification) this fatal to Ritchie's view that the mother has
a speaking part. I think that Griffith's material shows that, if Getas

addresses Knemon as ἐμβρόντητε cύ, the phrase is even more imper-
tinent than appears at first sight. (It would be possible to give to
Sikon the whole of the part here assigned to Getas; he addresses
Knemon as ἱερόcυλε cύ at 640. But I do not think it suits him as well
as it suits Getas.)

430 Πλάγγων: 'Doll', a name borne in real life by women of all
stations. But as the name is given in *Heros* and *Samia* to free-born
girls, this Plangon too will be free-born, and identifiable with Sostratos' sister, mentioned later in the play (794). Handley argues that
because the Plangon of *Heros* is working as a servant and Plangon of
Sam. is poor, this Plangon is likely to be a fellow domestic of Getas';
he also says that there is no reason why Sostratos' sister should be
named. The latter argument tells against the former: if there is no
reason for naming the sister, there is even less for naming a domestic,
who has no function to perform in the play. The sister becomes
important in Act V; that is why attention is momentarily directed to
her here. The deftly economical touch establishes her presence with
the party.   θᾶττον is not comparative in sense, when combined with
an imperative, but means something like 'and quickly, too', cf. 454,
ἄνοιγε θᾶττον, 596, 866. So Plangon is here told not to 'walk faster',
but to 'get going'. She may have stopped to look around.

432 ἐc κόρακαc: B has εicκορακαc, but the Attic dialect anomalously used
ἐc, not εἰc, in this imprecation and in the euphemism ἐc μακαρίαν (Hellad.
ap. Phot. *Bibl.* 535 *b*). εἰc was originally ενc and the group ενcκορακαc
developed to ἐc κόρακαc, just as ἐν Cκαμβωνιδῶν is found written
εcκαμβωνιδων, Meisterhans³, p. 111.   **Πάρθενι:** The flute-girl is not
necessarily a member of the household; like her namesake in Lucian,
Dial. Mer. 15, she may have been hired for the occasion, as Habrotonon of *Epitrepontes* was hired to play for a party of ladies at the
Tauropolia. It is her music that brings Getas out of the shrine.
Handley suggests the possibility that she only pretended to play, the
music being really supplied by the piper who accompanied the
chorus: this is conceivable, but a mere guess.

433 Πανός: Cf. Ar. *Knights* 106, cπεῖcον ἀγαθοῦ δαίμονοc; the
genitives are possessive, possibly with the ellipse of a noun (μέλοc,
cπονδήν), 'play the tune that is Pan's', 'make the libation that belongs
to the Agathos Daimon'; see Schwyzer, ii. 124. It is not clear that
any particular tune was appropriate to visiting the shrine of Pan, but
it is possible; see Handley's note.

434 ἀπεcώθητέ γε: 'You have arrived safely'; no specific danger is
understood, but the remark is natural when made to anyone who

arrives later than expected. γε may emphasize the idea of safe, as opposed to punctual, arrival.

437 ναὶ μὰ (τὸν) Δία is much less common in New Comedy than in Old, being known only here and *Perik.* 317, 380, *Aspis* 167.

438 οὐ περιμένει τὴν cὴν cχολήν: Cf. Plato, *Rep.* 370 b, ἐάν τις τινὸς παρῇ ἔργου καιρόν, διόλλυται . . . οὐ γὰρ οἶμαι ἐθέλει τὸ πραττόμενον τὴν τοῦ πράττοντος cχολὴν περιμένειν. Whether to write περιμένει (pres.) or περιμενεῖ (fut.) is a problem with no certain answer. In Plato, *Symp.* 172 a, the recorded MSS. seem to have οὐ περιμένεις, if they give any accent, but editors show a preference for περιμενεῖς. The mother supports her inquiry whether everything is ready by saying that certainly there is no time to be lost over the sacrifice of the sheep, which she presumably sees tethered outside the shrine. Her phrase contains not a reproach for, but a warning against, dawdling: a pleasant and characteristic touch in the mouth of a woman who has kept others waiting. Jests about the poor condition of sacrificial animals were common in comedy, *Sam.* 399 n. Here the sting is that the cook has provided the sheep, and spent as little as possible on it. The joke that the sacrificial victim is likely to die, presumably of starvation or old age, recurs in Plaut. *Aul.* 567, 'caedundum conduxi ego illum:: tum tu idem optumumst loces ecferendum; nam iam credo mortuost.' This may, therefore, well have had its counterpart in a Menandrean original.

B's τάλαιν' is impossible; elision at the line-end is unknown in New Comedy, and confined in earlier verse to words such as δέ, τε, με. The reading was perhaps introduced by someone who supposed the next line to be directed to Plangon; he will be responsible for the dicolon which precedes the word.

440 κανᾶ: Baskets containing sacrificial necessities, see *Perik.* 997 n. The plural, like that of χέρνιβας, is probably a sign of the unusual devotion of this woman (J. Martin); normally no one needs more than one (e.g. *Sam.* 222, Ar. *Peace* 948, Eur. *HF* 926), but see Eur. *El.* 800.   θυλήματα are grains mixed with wine and oil, sprinkled on the sacrificial meats, cf. Ar. *Peace* 1040, ἐγὼ δ' ἐπὶ cπλάγχν' εἶμι καὶ θυλήματα; according to a god in Pherekrates' Αὐτόμολοι, this was to disguise the stinginess of the offering (frag. 23 K).

441 ἐμβρόντητε: 'Thunderstruck'; this vocative of abuse recurs in Ar. *Eccl.* 793, Philemon frag. 44 K, and Dem. xviii. 243. So far as its form goes, the word may as well be feminine as masculine (cf. *Pap. Hibeh* 6. 42, Page, *GLP* p. 290).

(ii) **442–455**: *Knemon alone*

442–55: Knemon's speech allows for a passage of time during which the sacrifice takes place; when they come to cook the sheep, the discovery follows that the stew-pot has been forgotten. From a realistic point of view far more time would be required for the off-stage events than for Knemon's words: but such a lack of correspondence is usual in Greek drama (introd. p. 19 n. 2). What Knemon says serves to underline his devotion to hard work, his suspiciousness, and his unfriendliness to the neighbouring gods. But it also introduces a new point: his dislike of his fellow men is rooted in a belief in their selfishness, here illustrated by the way in which they treat themselves as the chief beneficiaries when sacrificing to the gods. This prepares for his *apologia*, 718 ff.

443 ἀργόν: Cf. 31, ἀεὶ πονῶν; Knemon hates idleness.

445: With hesitation I adopt the emendation κακὸν | ἀεὶ παροικοῦc', 'are always a trouble as neighbours'. This supposes that αει was written αι, and that there was a dittography of παρ. κακόν is occasionally used, without the article or any adjective such as μέγα or τι, as a noun, e.g. Ar. *Frogs* 552, κακὸν ἥκει τινί, and may be so used here. Handley gives parallels for the form of expression and suggests that they all imply a comparison. If this were true, they would be imperfect parallels. But when Philokleon says καπνὸc ἔγωγε ἐξέρχομαι (Ar. *Wasps* 144) he does not mean 'I am coming out like smoke', but quite literally 'I am smoke coming out'.

446 καταβαλὼν τὴν οἰκίαν: Some of the materials, particularly the timber, would be re-used for the new house.

448 κοίταc: Boxes or baskets for food, 'hampers', cf. Hesychios s.v.
φέρονται: Middle (Kraus), 'bring with them for their own use', cf. Xen. *Mem.* iii. 14. 1, τῶν μικρὸν (sc. ὄψον) φερομένων, Eur. *Cycl.* 88, τεύχη φέρονται κενά, βορᾶc κεχρημένοι. Athenaios' φέροντεc is due to failure to recognize this usage. B's [κοιτ]αιφερονται (passive) is impossible because it disregards the reflexive ἑαυτῶν.

450 πόπανον: A kind of cake, burnt in sacrifice. Knemon here associates two different lines of thought: (*a*) that the gods are best pleased by simple sacrifices, (*b*) that the average sacrificer looks to his own interests rather than those of the gods. The same combination is to be seen in frag. adesp. 372, ψαιcτά, λιβανωτόν, πόπανα· ταῦτ' ὠνήcομαι· | οὐ τοῖc φίλοιc θύω γάρ, ἀλλὰ τοῖc θεοῖc. For (*a*) compare Theopompos' story, quoted by Porphyry, *de abstinentia* ii, pp. 145–6 Nauck, of Klearchos, who was declared by the Pythia to serve the

gods best of all men and was found to sacrifice regularly with λιβανω-
τοῖc καὶ ψαιcτοῖc (= θυλήμαcιν) καὶ ποπάνοιc; (b) is a traditional
theme in comedy, cf. Pherekrates, quoted in 440 n. Note that this
trimeter has four resolved feet, an unusual plenty; J. W. White, *Iambic
Trimeter in Menander*, p. 159.

451 ὀcφὺν ἄκραν: ὀcφύc is the hinder part of the back and ὀcφὺc ἄκρα
doubtless includes the tail; this may once have been regarded as
peculiarly endowed with life and therefore valuable (H. Wagenvoort,
'Zur magischen Bedeutung des Schwanzes', *Serta Phil. Aenopontana*,
pp. 273 ff., Schol. Aesch. *PV* 496, εὐκίνητος γὰρ οὖcα καὶ cπέρματα
ἔχουcα θύεται τοῖc θεοῖc), but to fourth-century eyes it looked a scurvy
offering; cf. Eubulos frag. 130 K, αὐτοῖc δὲ τοῖc θεοῖcι τὴν κέρκον
μόνην | καὶ μηρὸν ὥcπερ παιδεραcταῖc θύετε, Menander frag. 264,
ἐγὼ μὲν οὖν ὤν γε θεὸc οὐκ εἴαcα τὴν | ὀcφὺν ἂν ἐπὶ τὸν βωμὸν ἐπιθεῖναί
ποτε | εἰ μὴ καθήγιζέν τιc ἅμα τὴν ἔγχελυν.

452–3: Clement quotes the lines with ὀcτέα τὰ (read ὀcτᾶ τε) ἄβρωτα
and ἀναλίcκουcι, a verb which can be used of consuming meat. B is
supported by Athenaios and is more vigorous with καταπίνουcι. In
favour of ὀcτᾶ one might quote com. adesp. 1205 K: τίc ὧδε μῶροc . . .
ὅcτιc ἐλπίζει θεοὺc | ὀcτῶν ἀcάρκων καὶ χόληc πυρουμένηc | ἃ καὶ κυcὶν
πεινῶcιν οὐχὶ βρώcιμα | χαίρειν ἀπαρχαῖc; nevertheless bones are already
implied in ὀcφὺν ἄκραν, and the definite accusation that the gods get
tail and gall-bladder *because* they are inedible suits Knemon well.

Theophrastos in his περὶ εὐcεβείαc recommended bloodless sacrifices
and a virtuous heart, and since Menander was his pupil, his influence
has been seen here. It may be so, but the themes adopted all have
closer parallels elsewhere, and to put them in Knemon's mouth is
not to recommend them.

454 ποητέον: The more obvious τηρητέον is too long for the gap. In
fact, as the sequel shows, Knemon sets to work on an indoor job
(584). He has here to call on his servant to open the door because
she has bolted it, in accordance with his orders (427). He had left it
unbolted when he had gone out early in the morning, since he enters
without difficulty at 178. There is no significance in this: the poet
would not wish to repeat the motif of unbolting the door, which
would in fact have spoiled the effect at 178.

(iii) 456–465: *Getas alone*

456: Emerging from the shrine Getas speaks back to one of the servants.   λεβήτιον, diminutive of λέβηc, is a large vessel such as
a cook would use for boiling or stewing.   ἐπιλέληcθε supposes a

common spelling mistake in B, -αι having been written for -ε: 'The lot of you, you're telling me, have forgotten the stew-pot.' Other suggestions are ἐπιλέληcται and ἐπιλελῆcθαι. The first is dubious because whereas the use of ἐπιλέληcμαι as a middle is known from Ar. *Clouds* 631 onwards, the use as a passive is first found in the Septuagint; the second is possible, but less lively than the correction adopted in OCT, which gives parenthetic φήc.

457 ἀποκραιπαλᾶτε: In Plut. *Antony* 30 ἀποκραιπαλᾶν means 'sleep off a debauch', cf. Bekker, *Anecd.* 429. 5, ἀποκραιπαλιcμόc· τῆc κραιπάληc ἀπαλλαγὴ καὶ μέθηc, but the compound might be parallel to, e.g., ἀποναρκᾶν, 'grow numb', and mean 'get intoxicated': either meaning suits the context here, but the former is preferable.

460: The combination of γάρ with the adjuration μὰ τοὺc θεούc is difficult and perhaps unparalleled. At Ar. *Knights* 366, νὴ τὸν Ποcειδῶ κἀμὲ γάρ, Bothe's τἄρ' is generally accepted, and τἄρ' should perhaps be read here, although τοι is at the best unusual in Menander, see *Sam.* 150 n. Cf. Ar. *Wasps* 299, μὰ Δί' οὐ τἄρα προπέμψω.

461 θεραπαινίδια: At *Sam.* 251 θεραπαινίδιον is probably 'a young slave-girl'; that sense is possible here, but the diminutive certainly also carries a derogatory force. The word does not occur elsewhere in comedy.

462 κινητιᾶν: This word is a substitute for βινητιᾶν, as κινεῖν for βινεῖν (e.g. Ar. *Knights* 877, 879, *Clouds* 1102). Although the analogy of χεζητιᾶν, οὐρητιᾶν, μαθητιᾶν, etc. would lead one to suppose that βινητιᾶν meant βινεῖν ἐπιθυμεῖν, in fact it always means βινεῖcθαι ἐπιθυμεῖν (even in Lucian, *Pseudol.* 27). One may compare the passive sense of μαcτιγιᾶν, 'want a whipping'. κινητιᾶν is found also in the *Life of Aesop* c. 32 (B. E. Perry, *Aesopica*, i. 47). In frag. 174 (Kock) of Plato Comicus, Meineke, *Fragmenta Comicorum Graecorum*, ii. p. 675, gives κινητιᾶν as if it were the MS. reading; but the source, Athenaios 442 a, has βινητιᾶν (like Kock), as W. G. Arnott has kindly confirmed from a microfilm of the codex Marcianus in his possession.

The obvious meaning of διαβαλεῖν ἐὰν ἴδῃ τιc is that, if anyone notices (and tries to act on what he sees), the girls tell tales (to their master or mistress). G. Pascucci, *Atene e Roma* iv (1959), 102, argues that διαβαλεῖν means 'cheats his expectations'. *Suda* s.v. has τὸ ἐξαπατᾶν καὶ παραλογίζεcθαι, quoting Thuc. i. 133 and the comic poet Krates (frag. 47 K). In the passages Pascucci cites, however, (Hdt. v. 50, 97, viii. 10, Ar. *Birds* 1648, *Thesm.* 1214: add Isaios xi. 4) the word always means 'mislead by misrepresentation', as it may well do in Archippos frag. 36 K, τὸν γὰρ γέροντα διαβαλοῦμαι τήμερον. Such a connotation would be out of place here, and the obvious interpretation is therefore more likely. (διαβάλλειν does not necessarily imply false-hood.)　παῖδες καλοί: A formula not previously known, but re-peated at 912, so that καλῶ (*ed. pr.*) is not a compelling conjecture. After the appealing diminutive παιδίον, Getas reverts in irritation to the plain παῖδες (464). παῖδες καλοί recurs in a different context at *Sam.* 733.

464: The missing τί could, so far as palaeographic reasons go, be plausibly replaced after τουτί (Page), and one may compare Ar. *Peace* 181, τουτὶ τί ἐϲτι τὸ κακόν; *Birds* 1036, τουτὶ τί ἐϲτιν αὖ κακόν; But in phrases of this sort τί ἐϲτι may form an inseparable unit, as at 218 (cf. 431).

465: ἡήν occurs elsewhere only at *Perinthia* 15, where it is probably an embarrassed exclamation. Here, if rightly restored, it must indicate puzzlement and perhaps like ἦν at *Samia* 313 some apprehension. Servants do not normally *run* to answer the door; hence Getas may wonder what is up. G. Luck, *Rh. Mus.* cviii (1965), 269, maintains that the exclamation should be given a rough breathing. It is a long-drawn-out form of ην (Schwyzer, ii. 566), of which Photios says s.v. δαϲέωϲ ὅταν ἠθικῶϲ λέγεται . . . τὸ δὲ ψιλὸν ἀντὶ τοῦ ἰδού, i.e. ην has a rough breathing when expressive of emotion, a smooth when it is the equivalent of ἰδού. The same distinction can be seen in Latin between *hem!* and *en* or *em*.

In the first Delphic Paean (*Coll. Alex.* 142 ff.) we find such spellings as ταασδε and μααντειειον to indicate that the syllable is sung to two notes and occupies twice the normal time. Probably we should see in ηην the representation of one long-drawn vowel, rising in pitch and occupying the time of two normal long syllables. Kraus would read ἦ ἦ, which at Eur. *HF* 906 and Ar. *Clouds* 105 seems to show alarm or disapproval. Note that Theophrastos makes it characteristic of the ἀγροῖκοϲ that he answers the door himself (*Char.* 4. 9).

(iv) 466–486: *Getas* (exit 480) *and Knemon*

466: The papyrus is at fault over the change of speakers. The earlier editors made Knemon end with εἰπέ μοι, supposing the omission of both dicolon and paragraphus. Post's division, adopted in the text, is based on the argument that the slave Getas, with a request to make, would not use the rude address ἄνθρωπε but βέλτιϲτε, as he does at 476, even after further insults, and that Knemon at 108 uses a like phrase in ἀνόϲιε ἄνθρωπε. It may be observed that parenthetic εἰπέ μοι at the end of a line is frequent in Menander (510 below, *Aspis* 85, *Epitr.* 237, 864, *Perik.* 383, 387, *Sam.* 170, 677, *Georg.* 33, but at *Sam.* 453, 690, the phrase ends both line and clause). For its insertion

between closely cohering words cf. Baton frag. 5. 11 K, ἐόρακας οὖν
φιλόσοφον εἰπέ μοι τινά.   μὴ δακῇς: Also at *Sam.* 384. For Knemon's
reply cf. Archippos frag. 35 K: *B.* μῶν ἔδακέ cε τιc; *A.* ἔδακε; κατὰ
μὲν οὖν ἔφαγε. Xen. *Anab.* iv. 8. 14 has τούτουc ... καὶ ὠμοὺς δεῖ
καταφαγεῖν, *Hell.* iii. 3. 6 καὶ ὠμῶν ἐcθίειν αὐτῶν.

468: The missing syllable can be variously supplied: ⟨τῶν⟩ θεῶν, as
again at 503, μὴ ⟨δή⟩, cf. *Perik.* 976, μὴ ⟨μή⟩, cf. Ar. *Wasps* 1418,
μή ⟨με⟩, cf. Ar. *Lysistrata* 948. There is little to choose.

469 cυμβόλαιον ... τι: The word, applicable to any contract,
is used particularly in connection with loans, e.g. *Dem.* xxxii. 7,
Lysias xii. 98. But it may be used loosely, as in Eur. *Ion* 411, to mean
'business-dealing', and that is how Knemon intends it. Getas takes
it in the narrow sense: he is no importunate creditor. For a cυμβόλαιον as an occasion for visiting a man cf. [Dem.] xlvii. 19, ἐμοὶ γὰρ
πρὸς Θεόφημον cυμβόλαιον μὲν οὐδὲν πώποτε ... ἐγένετο ... ὥcτε ...
ἐλθεῖν ἐπὶ τὴν οἰκίαν τὴν τούτου. *Ed. pr.* prints interrogative τί; which
seems less likely for sense; and the postponement of τί is only partially
paralleled in the formula cοὶ δὲ κἀμοὶ πρᾶγμα τί ἐcτι; (114 above).

472 λεβήτιον: It is stated in Cramer's *Anecd. Oxon.* iii. 273 that one
reason for using a diminutive is to make what one asks for sound
less important, ἐὰν ὃ αἰτῇ τιc cμικρύνῃ, ἵνα μὴ μεγάλην ποιήςῃ τὴν
χάριν ... ὡc ἔχει τὸ παρὰ Μενάνδρῳ λεβήτιον. One might think that
this ingenious observation, if made with regard to this passage, is
proved groundless by Getas' use of the word at 456, but he may
there be quoting the maids, who wish to minimize their carelessness.
L. Amundsen, *Symb. Osl.* xl (1965), 15, gives instances of the use of
diminutives in private letters when a request is made. A good example
is *P. Cairo Zenon* 59030, which reports that on the failure of a request
for the loan of a ἱππάριον, it had been necessary to buy a ἵππον.

B, having correctly had λεβητιον in 472, twice gives λεβοιτιον in 473,
a strange error. But it is highly improbable that, as some believe,
Menander intended a mispronunciation by his characters: the
sounds η and οι were quite different in his time. Observe that 472
has neither caesura nor diaeresis after the third foot. The effect is one
of comical anticlimax. The next line, with its three equal divisions,
is also of strikingly unusual shape.

473 κλητῆρας: Witnesses to the delivery of a summons; compare
the scene in Ar. *Clouds* 1214 ff. when the money-lender, wishing
to summons Strepsiades, brings a friend κλητεύcοντα. Knemon is
the last person to appreciate Getas' attempt to ease the situation by
facetiousness.

474 θύειν με βοῦς: It was unusual for a private individual to sacrifice an ox. Cf. Straton frag. 1. 20 K, οὐ θύω βοῦν, ἄθλιε. But not impossible: Poseidippos frag. 26 K, διακονοῦμεν νῦν γάμους· τὸ θῦμα βοῦς· ὁ διδοὺς ἐπιφανής, ἐπιφανὴς ὁ λαμβάνων; and the μικροφιλότιμος of Theophrastos (*Char.* 21), having sacrificed an ox, takes care that all visitors to his house shall know it. It may not be amiss to remind the English reader that snails are, like oxen, eaten in Mediterranean countries, cf. Galen vi. 668, κοχλίας δὲ ὁσημέραι πάντες ῞Ελληνες ἐσθίουσιν.

475: A dactyl in the third foot divided – ∪ | ∪ is rare, but cf. 386 and frag. 162, μηδὲ προσάγου, *Perik.* 272.

476 εὐτύχει: This is a phrase for saying good-bye, cf. *Epitr.* 370. It is not certain that any part of Getas' speech before 479b–480, which is clearly not for Knemon's ears, is addressed to the infuriated old man. But the impudent retort οὐδὲ κοχλίαν ἔγωγέ σε is more effective if not made *sotto voce*; and it is perhaps more likely that the laying of the blame on the women is addressed to Knemon than that Getas assures himself in a soliloquy of what he knows to be untrue (cf. 457–9). Also, if 476–80 are entirely soliloquy, it is hard to see what Knemon does with himself the while.

480 ἔχις πολιός: 'Grey-haired viper'; the viper bites unexpectedly. Cf. Dem. xxv. 52, πορεύεται διὰ τῆς ἀγορᾶς ὥσπερ ἔχις ἢ σκορπίος, and ibid. 96. Jacques's proposal to read ἔχις ⟨ὁ⟩ πολιὸς ἄνθρωπος has met with little favour.

481 ἀνδροφόνα θηρία: For ἀνδροφόνος as a term of abuse, cf. Amphis frag. 30 K, Philippides frag. 5 K; for θηρία, cf. *Perik.* 366, ἱερόσυλα θηρία, Ar. *Knights* 273 etc., [Dem.] xxxiv. 52.

482 ἡμῶν: Ed. pr. changed to ὑμῶν, but unnecessarily. One may compare Knemon's language at 167, πρὸς ταῖς θύραις ἔστηκεν ἡμῶν. Since the words are unemphatic they are enclitic (and should probably be accented ἥμων, W. S. Barrett, *Hippolytus*, p. 425); this explains the position of ἡμῶν here, for enclitics have a certain tendency to come early in a clause, K. J. Dover, *Greek Word Order*, p. 14. A further reason against ὑμῶν is that the phrase ὑμῶν (ἡμῶν) τις is rarely divided, E. Fraenkel, *Beobachtungen zu Aristophanes*, p. 97. νομίζετε is addressed to the spectators; the word ὁρᾶν is therefore appropriate.

483 λάβω: This change from B's λαβὼν gives a much easier sentence, with two if-clauses, the second subordinate to the first (Goodwin, *MT* § 510). If λαβών is kept, the sentence is anacoluthic, the ἄν being repeated; the repetition is much more intelligible in *P. Didot* i. 27, 30.

484 ἕνα τῶν πολλῶν: For this derogatory phrase, 'a person of no importance', cf. Dem. *in Meid.* 96, παρὰ τὴν πενίαν καὶ ἐρημίαν καὶ τὸ τῶν πολλῶν εἶc εἶναι, Isokr. ii. 50; similarly in Latin, e.g. Cic. *Fin.* ii. 62, 'tenuis . . . unusque ex multis'.

(v) 487–499: *Sikon alone*

487 ff.: Once, with van Groningen, I believed that Getas accompanied Sikon on to the stage here. The reasons for this are: (1) that 515, οἷόν ἐcτ' ἐπιδεξίωc αἰτεῖν· διαφέρει νὴ Δία, is more readily understood as a sarcasm by Getas than as an ironical remark at his own expense by Sikon; (2) that 500, πάλιν αὖ cύ; on the face of it means that Knemon here meets Getas for a second time; (3) that it is possible, on this assumption, to divide the dialogue 501–5 strictly as shown by B between a cursing Getas, who gets a beating, and an obstinately polite Sikon; (4) that 488–99 arouse the expectation that Sikon will bring a wasps' nest about his ears, and that it would be dramatically effective to cheat that expectation by directing Knemon's wrath on Getas, who would have approached too near in his hope of enjoying Sikon's expected discomfiture; (5) that this would give point to Sikon's retort at 892, ἐγὼ δ' ἔπαcχον ἀρτίωc; without requiring recourse to a dubious obscenity. But against (1) it may be noted that Sikon makes fun of himself over his trouble with the sheep, κατακέκομμ' ἐγὼ ὁ μάγειρος (398); that the metaphor βεβωλοκόπηκεν (515) suits his style of speech better than that of Getas; and that a change of speaker, of which the papyrus gives no indication, would be necessary somewhere between νὴ Δία (516) and ἀρά γε (518). Against the other points must be set two difficulties. (*a*) An exit of Getas is nowhere suggested. (*b*) At 575 he speaks as if he had not seen Simiche before. But perhaps she did not respond to the order in 502 to bring the strap. Since the dialogue is explicable as a duologue between Knemon and Sikon (see notes on 500, 510), and there is no balance of advantage in introducing Getas, it is best to conclude that Sikon's opening words are spoken to an unseen Getas still in the cave and that his succeeding lines are addressed to the audience. A difficulty certainly remains in ὑμεῖc (497), which can hardly mean the spectators, unless we could supply something like ὑμεῖc δέ ⟨με⟩ κρεμᾶν ποτ' ἐλέγετε; But if ὑμεῖc does not mean the spectators, it implies an unexpected turn by Sikon towards the cave.

488: *Ed. pr.* wrote τυχὸν ἤτειc cκατοφάγωc, translating 'tu as dû faire ta demande sans délicatesse'. If cκατοφάγοc were always a mere term of abuse, it would hardly form an adverb, any more than τοιχωρύχοc or ἱερόcυλοc. But it also has a positive meaning, perhaps 'sticking at nothing' (see *Sam.* 550 n.), and in this sense an adverb might be formed. Nevertheless it is tempting to see the well-attested vocative cκατοφάγε, followed by exclamatory ὡс. τυχὸν ᾔτειс then gives no sense, unless it can be understood to mean 'perhaps you *demanded* the loan'. For the corruption ητειcκαταφαγ' cf. Athen. 107 f, where καὶ πρίcκουc καταφάγου is written for καπρίcκουc cκατοφάγουc.

The apostrophe in B cannot be used to support the vocative, since the writer sometimes made mistakes over word-division (e.g. 877 αντ'ειπαc, 953 αλλ'η, 663 αλλ'υποτατοc) and may here have seen κατάφαγ(ε) ὡс, senseless though that is.

494 ὑπακούω is commonly used in the sense of 'answer a knock at the door', usually absolutely, but in Plato, *Crito* 43 a, with a dative of the person whose knock is answered. The dative τῇ θύρᾳ here may be unparalleled (Stoessl). Theophrastos, *Char.* 28. 4, has acc., αὐταὶ τὴν αὔλειον ὑπακούουcι, and perhaps also at 4. 9.

494 f.: B writes μητερ without a mark of elision and should therefore intend the vocative; πάτερ will then also be intended, and one might write with Marzullo, Shipp, etc. "πάτερ" ⟨ἐγὼ⟩ καὶ "παππ[ια". Unfortunately the letter before the gap is almost certainly α not π. The vocative πᾶπα cannot conveniently be found a place in the line, and it is best to suppose that we have to deal with accusatives, and restore as in OCT.

495 τῶν διὰ μέcου: The political centre (Thuc. viii. 75) is not relevant here; possibly 'of the middle class' (Arist. *Pol.* 1296ᵃ8, ὅπου γὰρ πολὺ τὸ διὰ μέcου). Priestesses were often chosen from good families, so that the address might flatter a bourgeoise. But a middle-class woman would hardly answer her door, having slaves to perform the office. The most probable meaning is 'middle-aged', for which sense of μέcοc cf. the proverb ἔργα νέων, βουλαὶ δὲ μέcων, εὐχαὶ δὲ γερόντων, quoted by Hypereides frag. 60, and parodied by Strabo xiv. 5. 14.

496 ἐκάλεc' ἱερέαν: There is no line in Menander where an anapaest follows a dactyl or a tribrach, and most instances have disappeared from modern texts of Aristophanes (*Birds* 108, ποδαπὼ τὸ γένοc; (Πε.) ὅθεν αἱ τριήρειc may be excused by the change of speaker). The third syllable of the word for priestess here will therefore be short, as it always is in tragedy and probably in comedy, although metre leaves the quantity undetermined in Ar. *Thesm.* 759, anon. in Page, *GLP* 48. 5, Men. *Sik.* 242, 258, 279. Spelling and accentuation are, however, uncertain. ἱερειᾶ (cf. βαcιλειᾶ) and ἱερεᾶ (cf. Ionic ἱερέη, whence by contraction ἱερῆ) are clearly legitimate forms. But when Attic inscriptions give, as they occasionally do, ιερεα for the normal ιερεια (Meisterhans³, p. 40), they may indicate ἱερεᾶ, and this may have been the usual pronunciation of what was written ιερεια. The spelling ιερεα is found in the MS. of *Sikyonios* 279, in the papyrus, also third century B.C., of Euripides' *Erechtheus* (frag. 65. 97 Austin), and is transmitted in Soph. frag. 456.

496–8: No supplements here are overwhelmingly probable, and the difficulty is increased by the corruption in 497. It is clear that the θεράπων is politely addressed as βέλτιστε. The obvious supplement in 496 is νεώτερος, to continue the progression from elderly to middle-aged; but Menander may have avoided the obvious.

After κρεμαν B has a letter almost undamaged except for a blob of ink, which makes its interpretation uncertain. ν or η looks possible, γ (Jacques) less probable, υ even less so. Most suggested supplements fall into two classes: (*a*) those that suppose the meaning to be 'you and your like (are good for nothing and) deserve a beating', e.g.: ὑμεῖς δ' ⟨οὐ⟩ κρεμάννυσθ' ἄξιοι; (*b*) those that suppose it to be 'you and your like use menaces (when you try to borrow)', e.g.: ὑμεῖς δέ ⟨γε⟩ κρεμᾶν ἤδη φατέ. (*a*) appears to me the more probable. An original line is followed by Blake's ὑμεῖς δ' ἐκκρεμάννυσθ' ἐκ τύχης, 'you depend on chance'.

At 498 Winnington-Ingram ingeniously suggested ὦ τῆς ἀμαθίας, "παιδίον παῖδες" καλεῖν. ἐγώ "πρόελθε κτλ.". But the words παιδίον, παῖδες must, as usual, accompany the knocking on the door, necessary at this point in order that Knemon may be disturbed at his work and come out. It seems, in fact, that he appears in time to be addressed as πατρίδιον in 499. It is uncertain whether ἐγώ goes with what precedes, being the beginning of a sentence broken off at the sight of Knemon, or whether it is the subject of βούλομαι, πρόελθε πατρίδιον being parenthetical, or whether it is the beginning of a sentence explaining Sikon's need for a cooking-pot, so that if the sentence had been completed πρόελθε . . . βούλομαι would have been a parenthesis.

(vi) **500–421:** *Sikon and Knemon* (exit 514)

500 πάλιν αὖ σύ: It is often supposed that Knemon in his anger mistakes Sikon for Getas. Yet it may be that the phrase does not mean '*You* again!' but indicates that Sikon is doing what another has done before, cf. 167, πάλιν τις οὑτοσί κτλ. This is not excluded by 501, οὐκ εἴρηκά σοι πρὸς τὴν θύραν μὴ προσιέναι, since Knemon imagines (507) that he has given public notice of this ban.

500 π[αῖ, τί τ]οῦτο; The supplement is uncertain, because initially there may be not π, but τα, and because even with π there are other ways of filling the gap. It is, however, likely, because παῖ, τί τοῦτο; is a known exclamation to express surprise and one that is fitting here. It is found at *Mis.* 216 (probably), *Sam.* 691, 715, *Pap. Ant.* 55, frag. *a*

verso i. 5; the form τί τοῦτο, παῖ; occurs at *Sam.* 360, *Perik.* 316,
frag. 100 K–T, Machon 215 Gow. In the first three of the latter
passages a slave is or may be addressed. (At *Sam.* 360 the speaker
knows he is alone on the stage, but vocative παῖ cannot be excluded,
see n. there.) But at *Mis.* 216 there is neither slave nor young man; at
Sam. 691 and 715 there is a young man, but it is far from clear that
he is addressed. At Machon 215 the phrase is used by one free
courtesan to another, a circumstance in which vocative παῖ is probably
not in place. One may also notice *Sam.* 678, παῖ, τί ποιεῖς Μοςχίων;
where it is unlikely that Parmenon, struck or threatened by his young
master, calls him 'boy'. *Mis.* 216 proves, and these other passages
suggest, that the phrase became purely exclamatory and was not felt
as an address to any παῖς. This has a parallel in the American exclamation 'Oh boy!', which does not require the presence of any boy,
any more than does the modern Greek exclamation παιδί μου, to
which Mr. G. Speake drew my attention; and a similar development
is to be seen in the Latin exclamation *eugepae!*, presumably borrowed
from a colloquial Greek εὖ γε, παῖ. It is even possible that the word παι
was not in origin a vocative, but an exclamation (? to be accented
παί) of which παπαί and παππαπαί are longer forms. Here, then,
Sikon may be supposed to utter this cry of surprise, as Knemon
seizes him, although Knemon is no παῖς; similarly at *Mis.* 216 Getas
cries παῖ, τί τοῦθ'; at the sight of the sixty-year-old Demeas with
Krateia in his arms.

If the initial letters are τα, the only possibility seems to be ταὐτὸ
τοῦτο. The meaning of this, in Sikon's mouth, is obscure. Kraus
suggested that he intended to continue with the verb ἥκω, 'this errand
on which I have come is the same as that of the other man'; he quotes
Plato, *Prot.* 310 e, αὐτὰ ταῦτα ἥκω. Interrupted sentences are usually
plainer to complete and understand, and this would not be a disarm-
ing way to begin.

If the alternative πῶς; τί τοῦτο; is right, a pause must be imagined
between the two questions. By πῶς; Sikon intends, 'What do you
mean by πάλιν αὖ σύ;?' Knemon does not answer, but seizes him,
whereupon he cries τί τοῦτο; W. G. Arnott's suggestion πᾶπα— (Κν.)
τοῦτ' ἐρεθίζεις μ', *Greece and Rome*, 2nd ser. xv (1968), 6, has some
attraction, but necessitates supposing that the dicolon after τουτ is
misplaced.

503 ἄφες: ἀφῶ would be more usual, but the repetition of the actual
imperative used is found in *Pap. Ghôran* ii. 147, Page, *GLP* p. 302,
περίμενε. (Φαιδ.) ''περίμενε'';

504 ἧκε πάλιν: An ironical imperative, 'come back (for some more

blows)'. I doubt whether the old woman ever came with the strap
or, if she did, whether it was used. 515–17 suggest that Sikon was
punched.   καί in indignant questions seems to be adverbial,
'actually', Denniston, *GP* 311.

505 χυτρόγαυλον: The word was known from Pollux and inscriptions, and must denote an earthenware vessel, perhaps bucket-shaped.
The exact point of Sikon's asking for this and not a λεβήτιον escapes
us. It may be that it was a not very usual piece, one that a man might
be flattered to be asked for; if so, the request would only irritate
further the irascible Knemon, who is attached to his simplicity of life.
Handley suggests that Sikon regards it as more tactful to ask for
a utensil that had not been previously refused, but would serve his
purpose as well.

  For the motif of refusing to lend to a neighbour cf. Plaut. *Aul.* 95,
'cultrum, securim, pistillum, mortarium, quae utenda uasa semper
uicini rogant, fures uenisse atque apstulisse dicito', Theophrastos, *Char.*
10 (the μικρολόγος), καὶ ἀπαγορεῦσαι τῇ γυναικὶ μήτε ἅλας χρηννύειν
μήτε ἐλλύχνιον μήτε κύμινον μήτε ὀρίγανον μήτε ὀλὰς μήτε στέμματα
μήτε θυηλήματα.

  It is easier to suppose the common mistake of transposition than
the corruption of αἰτηϲόμενος to αἰτούμενος. The use of the future
participle to express the intention attached to a verb of motion is
much more common than that of the present. For the present participle
cf. *Mis.* 32, λυτρούμενος ἥκεις, Eur. *Suppl.* 120, τούτους θανόντας ἦλθον
ἐξαιτῶν.

507: Cf. Alexis, frag. 174, οὐκ ἔχων δὲ τυγχάνω | οὐκ ὄξος, οὐκ ἄνηθον,
οὐκ ὀρίγανον, | οὐ θρῖον, οὐκ ἔλαιον, οὐκ ἀμυγδάλας, and still more.
Choiroboskos in Theodos. i. 259 Hilgard quotes as from Menander
οὐκ ἔχω οὔθ' ἅλας οὔτ' ὄξος οὔτ' ὀρίγανον (frag. 671). There is no
reason why this should not be a mutilated quotation from some other
play. To substitute ὀρίγανον here for ἀλλ' οὐδέν is gratuitous, and does
not improve the sense, while introducing a broken anapaest for which
frag. 397. 3 is the only parallel (intro. p. 38). The scansion ὀρῑγανον,
alleged in a frag. of Timotheos the dithyrambist (frag. 23, Page,
Poetae Melici Graeci, 799), is not probable in comedy.

510 νὴ ϲὺν κακῷ γε: To change νή to ναί is rash in view of the fact
that papyri of Menander offer such an affirmative νή (without the
name of a god) at *Epitr.* 1120, *Karch.* 33, *Sam.* 385, 389, see also *Georg.*
41 n. and Satyros, *Vita Euripidis*, frag. 39 col. xiii, νὴ γελοίως γε, to
which Dr. Austin called my attention. It is more likely that ϲὺν κακῷ
means 'to your hurt' (a threat) than 'to my hurt', but if so the words
must be *sotto voce*.

512 χαῖρε πολλά: A warm salutation (cf. *Mis.* 213, *Georg.* 41), here ironical.

513 οὐ βούλομαι χαίρειν: A like surly phrase is attributed to Timon by Kallimachos, *epigr.* 3, μὴ χαίρειν εἴπῃς με, κακὸν κέαρ, ἀλλὰ πάρελθε· | ἴcον ἐμοὶ χαίρειν ἐcτὶ τὸ μή cε πελᾶν. For Sikon's retort, cf. Plaut. *Persa* 851: 'Nolo mihi bene esse. (Le.) ne sit.'

515 βεβωλοκόπηκεν: 'He has given me a fine pounding.' βωλοκοπεῖν literally 'to break up clods'. In the following phrases Sikon is ironical at his own expense.

517 ἐφ' ἑτέραν θύραν: It is a question here, as at 925, whether this means 'to another house' or 'to a back door of this house'. The latter interpretation, on the face of it less appropriate to the situation in which Sikon finds himself, is supported by Plut. *Pomp.* 643 e, ἀποκλείcαc τὴν αὔλειον (the front door) ἑτέραιc θύραιc ᾤχετ' ἀπιών, cf. *QC* 645 e, and Apollodoros frag. 13 K (of political speakers, *sens. obsc.*), τὴν γὰρ αἰcχύνην πάλαι πᾶcαν ἀπολωλέκεcαν καθ' ἑτέραc θύραc. But I think Sikon means 'shall I go to another house?'; one other is visible to the audience, that of Gorgias. **ἔλθῃ τιc:** Deliberative subjunctive, see *Epitr.* 511 n.

517 cφαιρομαχοῦc': 'Engage in sparring practice', 'practise for the prize-ring'. cφαιρομαχία was boxing with the hands protected by cφαῖραι, instead of the ἱμάντεc or thongs of leather which were wound round the hand and forearm in actual contests: Plato, *Laws* 830 a, πύκται γε ὄντεc . . . ὡc ἐγγύτατα τοῦ ὁμοίου ἰόντεc, ἀντὶ ἱμάντων cφαίραc ἂν περιεδούμεθα, ὅπωc αἱ πληγαί τε καὶ αἱ τῶν πληγῶν εὐλάβειαι διεμελετῶντο. The word is associated with practice-bouts, probably from its earliest occurrence (possibly 394 B.C., *IG* xiv. 1097) in Aristomenes' play *Dionysus in Training*, Διόνυcοc Ἀcκιτήc (*CAF* i. 692); see also Aelius Aristides xlvii, p. 322 Jebb, Statius, *Silvae* iv. *praef.*, where it is coupled with *lusio palaris*, 'sword-play against a dummy', and Seneca, *ep. mor.* lxxx. 1. (The Roman authors show that in their time *sphaeromachia* could draw spectators, and *P. Oxy.* 1050, of the second or third century A.D., mentions cφαιρομάχοι along with pancratiasts and a boxer as participants at an athletic contest.) In spite of Seneca's reference to blood (which after all can flow from the nose), it is clear that the cφαῖραι must have been of the nature of boxing-gloves, not iron balls or lead weights, as is often absurdly stated; for an illustration see E. N. Gardiner, *Greek Athletic Festivals*[2], fig. 182. It is impossible, however, to assert that they were *identical* with the ἐπίcφαιρα of Plut. *Mor.* 825 e, τῶν μὲν γὰρ ἐν ταῖc παλαίcτραιc διαμαχομένων ἐπιcφαίροιc περιδέουcι τὰc χεῖραc, ὅπωc εἰc ἀνήκεcτον ἡ ἄμιλλα μηθὲν ἐκπίπτῃ, μαλακὴν ἔχουcα τὴν πληγὴν καὶ ἄλυπον.

The verb occurs in Polybios xvi. 21. 6, who tells how Tlepolemos, regent of Egypt about 200 B.C., τὸ μὲν πλεῖστον μέρος τῆς ἡμέρας κατέτριβε cφαιρομαχῶν καὶ πρὸς τὰ μειράκια διαμιλλώμενος ἐν τοῖc ὅπλοιc, also in Plato, *Laws* 830 e, where it is said that the young must be trained for war by field-day exercises that approach the reality, and πᾶcαν μιμουμένουc τὴν πολεμικὴν ὄντωc cφαιρομαχεῖν τε καὶ βολαῖc, ὡc ἐγγύτατα τῶν ἀληθῶν χρωμένουc ὑποκινδύνοιc βέλεciν. I cannot believe that the latter passage is textually sound, and therefore refrain from any attempt at explanation, calling attention only to a different and perhaps relevant form of cφαιρομαχία, Pollux ix. 107, schol. Plato, *Theaet.* 146 a, Eustathios 1601, 25.

The best treatment of cφαιρομαχία is by S. Meudner, *Gymnasium* lx (1953), 20. The evidence was assembled, with much irrelevant matter, by H. Frère, *Mélanges Ernout*, pp. 141 ff.; but his treatment is obscure.

519 ὀπτᾶν: Cooking by dry heat (roasting, grilling) was regarded as an inferior method to braising, stewing, or boiling, Athenaios 656 a. For κράτιcτον, 'the best plan', cf. 593, Ar. *Plut.* 412.

520: λοπάc is a shallow dish, often with a lid, in which the meat could be boiled or stewed. The word ζεῖν is associated with it in Euphron frag. 8 K and Damoxenos frag. 2. 50 K, παφλάζειν, 'seethe, bubble', in Eubulos frag. 109 K, and ἑψητοί in Ar. frags. 52, 282 K, Eupolis frag. 5 K. B. A. Sparkes, 'The Greek Kitchen', *JHS* (1962), 130, translates 'casserole' and illustrates surviving examples on Plate VI, 3 and 5. C. Dedoussi on *Sam.* 365 points out that λοπάδεc, λοπάδια are elsewhere frequently associated with fish, and never with meat. Sikon, therefore, means that he will make do with the wrong utensil; the guests will not have to put up with nothing but roast meat. It is uncertain whether καί or μοι should be deleted; καί is intruded at 920, but μοι might be an explanatory addition.

521 τοῖc οὖcι τούτοιc: 'These utensils that there *are*'.

(vii) 522–545: *Sostratos alone*

522: The stage is momentarily empty before Sostratos returns the way he had left near the end of Act II. He opens his monologue with a wry parody of the generalization which sometimes introduces a narrative monologue (W. Görler, Μενάνδρου Γνῶμαι, pp. 44 ff.). The words ἐπὶ Φυλὴν ἐλθέτω are thought by Treu to be a deliberate echo of Sikon's ἐρρῶcθαι λέγω Φυλαcίοιc; and this has appealed to some scholars.

523: The latter part of the line can be corrected with confidence.

Turner saw that the construction follows that of Antiphanes frag. 282 K, οἴμοι κακοδαίμων, τὸν τράχηλον ὡς ἔχω. Usage then requires τρισκακοδαίμων, nominative, not vocative, since it is exclamatory, and that it should be preceded by an exclamation. Hence ὤ must be retained, and κυνηγετήςων is too long by a syllable. The choice lies between κυνηγετῶν and κυνηγέτης. In support of the former compare the substitution in B of future for present at 420, 541, 780; in favour of the latter *Heros* frag. 8, τοῖς ἐξ ἄςτεως κυνηγέταις ἥκουςι.

525 ἐμπεςὼν πολύς: 'Falling with all my might upon the task'.

526 νεανίας ἐγώ τις: 'With a young man's vigour'. Vigour and ardour are often connotations of the word, e.g. at Ar. *Wasps* 1333 the revellers from whom old Philokleon has stolen their flute-girl threaten him with legal proceedings, κεἰ ςφόδρ᾽ εἶ νεανίας. But Sostratos is still a μειράκιον and has not yet reached his full strength, τῇ δὲ τετάρτῃ πᾶς τις ἐν ἑβδομάδι μέγ᾽ ἄριστος | ἰςχύων (Solon frag. 19. 7 Diehl).

528: The right correction of εγαιπλειον is hard to find. For sense the most probable suggestion yet made seems to me to be Blake's ἐνέπαιον, but confusion of γ and ν does not occur elsewhere in B. I find less objection in the lack of any evidence that ἐμπαίειν was used of striking a mattock into the ground. Without confidence, I print ἔπαιον, supposing progressive corruption: επαιον⟩ επλειον⟩ εγαιπλειον. The nearest parallel is Lucian, *Timon* 40, μᾶλλον δὲ παῖε ... ςκάπτε, ὦ Τίμων, βαθείας καταφέρων (sc. πληγάς). If the correction is right, one may notice that the sound of ἐξαίρων ἄνω ςφόδρα τὴν δίκελλαν suggests the long upward heave of the mattock, followed by the vigorous down-stroke of βαθὺ | ἔπαιον, 'I struck in deep.'

Handley reads ὡς ἂν ἐργάτης βαθὺ⟨ς⟩ (*ed. pr.*) ἐπὶ πλέον (Lloyd-Jones) ἐπεκείμην φιλοπόνως and understands 'as though an experienced hand, I worked away most industriously'. He points out that ἐπὶ πλέον can in Hellenistic Greek be used without any overt comparative force to mean 'exceedingly', e.g. Aratos, *Phaen.* 1048, χειμῶνός κε λέγοιεν ἐπὶ πλέον ἰςχύςοντος, Theokr. iii. 47, οὐχ οὕτως "Ωδωνις ἐπὶ πλέον ἤγαγε λύςςας, 'brought to an excess of madness', Diog. L. iv. 41, ἐπὶ πλέον ἐραςθῆναι, 'to be strongly in love'. I do not feel convinced, however, that ἐπὶ πλέον ... φιλοπόνως is Menandrean Greek; moreover, although βαθύς can certainly be applied as an epithet to one who has a profound or a crafty mind, it does not seem appropriate to the man whose skill is in digging.

529 καὶ μετεςτρεφόμην τι: 'I began to turn round a little as well (as digging).'

531: B's ποτέ must mean 'at times'. Handley writes τότε, i.e. when

Sostratos turned round he took the opportunity to rub the small of his back. The change is slight and may be right.

533: The postponement of δέ to fifth place in the clause is paralleled in frag. 380, ἐν τῷ πρὸc αὐτὸν δ' ἀναλογιcμῷ, *Aspis* 204.

534 οὐδεὶc ἤρχετο: Even in compounds the imperf. of ἔρχομαι is rare in Attic, and in some cases textually doubtful; περιήρχετ' in Ar. *Thesm.* 504 is perhaps the most plausible example, see Rutherford, *New Phrynichus*, p. 103. The uncompounded form is unknown before Phylarchos (late third century B.C.), who used ἤρχοντο (*F. Gr. Hist.* 81 frag. 44), but he was probably not an Athenian by origin. It is not easy to see the need for an imperf. here, unless the meaning is that no one was in the offing, on the way, let alone had actually come (K–G ii. 1. 144). One would have more confidence in the form if ἠρχόμην did not stand just above; the copyist's eye may have wandered. W. G. Arnott, *Mnem.* 4th ser. xix (1967), 397, sees 'intentional assonance'.   **κατέκαε**: Understand με, 'was burning me up'.

ἀπεξυλούμην ἀτρέμα δ': 'But I was quietly going as hard as wood.' ἀτρέμα, often ἀτρέμαc before vowels, in Homer means 'without moving', but it developed the sense 'quietly, gently' when used with verbs, e.g. Plato, *Gorg.* 503 d, ἀτρέμα cκοπούμενοι, [Xen.] *Cyneg.* 5. 31, ἀτρέμα διαπορεύηται, Dem. xxxvii. 55, ὁ ταχὺ βαδίζων . . . ὁ ἀτρέμαc, cf. Ar. *Clouds* 390, ἀτρέμαc πρῶτον, παππὰξ παππάξ, κἄπειτ' ἐπάγει, παπαπαππάξ. I somewhat hesitantly prefer this sense to 'I was going immovably as hard as wood', which is perhaps not impossible. With adjectives the word means 'moderately', 'slightly' (Arnott, *BICS* xv [1968], 121, collects a number of passages), but that is less suitable here.

B has ατρεμαδ'ε. To write ἀτρέμα δ' is easy and may be right, δέ being postponed, as in the previous line. In spite of stretching and hollowing his back (λορδοῦν), Sostratos began to get as stiff as a poker. Bingen withdrew his conjecture ἀτρέμαc, which would suppose progressive corruption, ατρεμαc⟩ ατρεμαε⟩ ατρεμαε̃⟩ ατρεμαδ̇'ε.

536 ὥcπερ τὰ κηλώνεια: An image used by Aristophanes in the probably corrupt frag. 679, ὥcτ' ἀνακύπτων καὶ κατακύπτων τοῦ cχήματος εἴνεκα τοῦδε | κηλωνείου τοῖc κηπουροῖc (εἰκόνα . . . κηλώνειον Edmonds) and by Libanios, *Decl.* xxvii. 25, ἵν' ὥcπερ τὰ κηλώνεια τὴν δίκελλαν ἀναφέρῃc. A κηλώνειον was a pivoted beam used for raising water (illustrated in Daremberg and Saglio s.v.). The rope carrying the bucket was attached to the longer arm, and a counterweight to the shorter; hauling on the rope allowed the bucket to descend into the well; the rope was then released and the counterweight caused it to bring the full bucket to the surface.

539 ἐγώ: Sc. ἔφην, cf. *Epitr.* 262.

540 αὔριον κτλ.: This may, as editors other than Diano suppose, be Gorgias' reply. For an unindicated change of speaker in reported dialogue cf. *Sam.* 256. But it is perhaps better that Sostratos should state his intention of persisting with the plan next day than that Gorgias should assume it. Moreover, if Sostratos says no more than τί οὖν ποῶμεν; εὐθύς is singularly pointless; the question is exactly what might be expected. But it is right that he should jump at the justification for ending his labour, and characteristic of his sense of humour and self-criticism that he should make the point that he did so.

541 ἐῶμεν: B's reading, εασομεν οτε, gives a proceleusmatic (∪ ∪ ∪ ∪) in the fourth place. The admissibility of this foot is dubious, see *Georg.* 84 n., and it can here be very easily avoided by assuming a mistake made elsewhere in this papyrus, ποιήcω for ποιω 780, ποιηcωμεν for ποιωμεν 420. The influence of τηρήcομεν will account for the error.

ὅ τε Δᾶος παρῆν: Clearly τε is easier if it attaches this sentence to ἐγὼ εὐθύς, sc. ἔφην (as with the punctuation adopted) than if it connects it with an entirely suppressed verb of saying implied by αὔριον . . . ἐῶμεν. **cκαπάνην:** 'Digging', as in Theophr. *HP* ii. 7. 1.

543 ἔφοδος: A probable supplement; the word is often military, 'approach' or 'assault', but not always (see LSJ); no metaphor need be intended here.

545 ἕλκει κτλ.: The interest of Sostratos' story may not entirely have stilled the question, why has he returned? We now learn that there is no good reason, but the lover irrationally haunts the place where his love lives. For the dramatic technique (story first, explanation of presence last) cf. *Perik.* 172–80.

(viii) 546–573 *Sostratos and Getas*

546: Getas comes out of the cave. His opening words are directed at Sikon inside, but no doubt he will very soon speak towards the audience.

547 ζωπυρῶ: *Et. Gud.* 234. 25, ζωπυρεῖν κυρίωc τὸ τοὺς ἄνθρακας φυcᾶν, ὡc τὸ "τρισκατάρατε, ζωπύρει τοὺς ἄνθρακας." Μένανδρος ἐν Ἀρρηφόροιc (frag. 65).

548–9: No restoration here is obviously right. The first letter in 548 of which there is a trace may be μ or π or less probably ν. Kraus's suggestion δέχομαι, φέρω, πλύνω, κατατέμνω cπλαγχνά is as good as any: 'I receive (from Sikon, who cuts up the sheep), carry off, clean, mince up the innards.' Cleaning the entrails occurs elsewhere among the preliminaries of a feast, e.g. Ar. *Plut.* 1168, πλῦνέ γε   . τὰc κοιλίαc, frags. 200, 686, Alexis frag. 186, πλυτέον εὖ μάλα.

549 μάττω: The verb is particularly used of kneading a mixture of water and barley-flour, which was then eaten without being baked, Plato, *Rep.* 372 b. It is tempting to take ἅμα with μάττω rather than κατατέμνω, but H. Juhnke, *Hermes*, lxxxix (1961), 122, points out that in Menander ἅμα nearly always follows its verb. περιφέρω τὰ κ[ρέα (Lloyd-Jones, cf. Xen. *Cyr.* ii. 2. 2) and τἀρ[τιδία (Kraus) are both open to the objection that the meal appears not yet to have begun (554), but is still being cooked. This is avoided by Arnott's τὰ κ[εράμια, 'the cooking pots'. The deictic τ]ουτονί (? τοι]ουτονί) is hard to explain. Kraus suggests νὴ τουτονί (ναὶ μὰ τουτονί Jacques) as an oath by Pan, whose statue may have been on the stage. Is it conceivable that Getas, blinded by the smoke, cannot see what god is presented and therefore omits his name? See further on 659.

550–1: Many scholars have suggested reading ὄνοc for ὅλοc, in view of Ar. *Frogs* 159, where the laden Xanthias says ἐγὼ γοῦν ὄνοc ἄγω (ἄγων ΦS Photios) μυcτήρια. According to the scholiast there a donkey 'celebrating the mysteries' is a donkey burdened by the luggage of those going to Eleusis. Xanthias may complain of being a beast of burden: Getas' complaint is not that, but that he is a factotum. There is, it is true, room for doubt whether the expression in Aristophanes is properly understood, see M. Tierney, *Mélanges O. Navarre*, pp. 395 ff. But if it is not and we do not know its origin, that is reason for being slow to believe that ὄνοc ἄγει τὴν ἑορτήν is a possible variant on Aristophanes' phrase. Another reason for rejecting the emendation is that if Menander had wished to compare Getas to a donkey here, he would not have done so at 403. He does not repeat his jokes in the same play. The gap in 550 makes certainty impossible: I incline to think that ὅλοc should be ὅλωc, taken either with τυφλόc or with the following sentence, which is sarcastic: 'It seems I'm keeping the holiday!' The association of the word ἑορτή with the concept of 'no work' is illustrated by LSJ s.v. 2 and 3.

552 cὺ δ' εἶ τίc; The phrase is found at *Epitr.* 391, Ar. *Plut.* 242, anon. *P. Hibeh* 5 (Page, *GLP* p. 294). The failure of Getas to recognize Sostratos is explained by his being blinded by the smoke, which also serves to explain his leaving the shrine (cf. Ar. *Plut.* 821, ἐμὲ δ' ἐξέπεμψεν ὁ καπνόc· οὐχ οἷόc τε γὰρ | ἔνδον μένειν ἦν). In Terence failure to recognize another character becomes a cliché, requiring no motivation (*Andria* 965, cf. 236–67, 301–10, 337–44, *Ad.* 299–320, *Eun.* 81–6, *Phorm.* 179–96, 230–53, 738–40, 845 ff.).

τρόφιμος: 'Young master', see *Epitr.* 134 n., and for the absence of the article 883 n.

553 τί γάρ; As at 636, this seems to mean: 'You ask me "what?"' Cf. *Epitr.* 261 n.

557 διαδραμών: 'When I've been on an errand', cf. *Epitr.* 462. Thierfelder rightly takes ἐνθαδί with the following words. Its position makes it emphatic. Sostratos originally had no use for the sacrifice (264), but finding that it is to take place *here*, sees how to turn it to his own purposes: he will use it to form a closer alliance with Gorgias, with a view to the intended repetition of the day's attempt to win over Knemon.

559 γάρ, ἐλθών: B's παρελθών is impossible; neither 'passing in' nor 'passing by' makes sense. ὡς ἔχω, lit. 'just as I am', is here passing into the meaning 'without delay', Thuc. iii. 30. 1, ἐμοὶ δοκεῖ πλεῖν ἡμᾶς ἐπὶ Μυτιλήνην πρὶν ἐκπύστους γενέσθαι, ὥσπερ ἔχομεν, Ar. *Eccl.* 533, Antiphanes frag. 199 K. Hesychios has ὡς ἔχω· εὐθέως. I do not think that there is any suggestion that Sostratos rejects the idea of recovering his cloak before going. The deictic τουτί is remarkable, Gorgias not being on the stage or even in his house.

561 ἱερῶν κεκοινωνηκότες: Plato, *Laws* 738 d, recommends common sacrifices as a means to solidarity, ὅπως ἂν ... φιλοφρονῶνταί τε ἀλλήλους μετὰ θυσιῶν καὶ οἰκειῶνται.

563 τί φής; Getas has previously heard nothing of any marriage. He must be supposed either not to hear 561–2, or to disregard the news in his preoccupation with his own meal.

564 πορευθείς: Perhaps no more than metrically convenient as an alternative to ἐλθών of 559.

565: Ar. *Ach.* 389–90 has λαβέ δ' ἐμοῦ γ' ἕνεκα ... τιν' Ἄιδος κυνῆν: 'Get, for all I care, a helmet of invisibility.' Here we appear to have something a little different; Getas says bitterly and sarcastically: 'I hope for my sake there may be 3,000 of you!' But Webster's change to the imperative γένεσθε would bring the two passages into line.

567 καλὸν γὰρ κτλ.: Sarcastic, of course. Nothing has been said to suggest that the sheep was particularly small, but the motif of the skinny sacrificial sheep was common enough (*Sam.* 399 n.) to make Getas' remark intelligible. πάνυ should perhaps be taken to modify καλόν, not, as I have punctuated in OCT, ἄξιον (Schäfer).

568: The addition of τά before γύναια is essential; and that involves the suppression of τιν (? a dittography of ειν). ἄξιον ἰδεῖν· ἀλλά recurs at the beginning of a trimeter, *Perik.* 522. Handley defends B's reading in the following way. (a) ἄξιον ἰδεῖν τινα, 'worth someone's seeing', quoting Tucker on *Frogs* 552 for 'allusive τιc'. But to whom is the allusion supposed to be? (b) γύναια ταῦτα, like οὗτος ἀνήρ, used when talking 'at' someone. But the women are not present to be talked at. (c) γύναῖα, a not impossible but exceptional scansion (see my n. on *Epitr.* 348).

569 ἔχει: Sc. τὰ γύναια. Getas ironically says that the women, being a decent lot, will go shares at any rate (γε) with him in some dish. For the ironic use of ἀcτεῖοc cf. *Sam.* 657 n.

570 ἁλὸς πικροῦ: Cf. Homer, *Od.* xvii. 455, οὐ cύ γ' ἐξ οἴκου cῷ ἐπιcτάτῃ οὐδ' ἅλα δοίης, [Theokritos] xxvii. 61, οὐδ' ἅλα δοίης. The origin of this proverbial phrase is obscure (see Gow on Theokritos loc. cit.), but Menander seems to have understood it in the sense that salt was so cheap that no ordinary person would grudge it; 'bitter' salt is inferior and unrefined, containing a large quantity of magnesium salts; R. J. Forbes, *Studies in Ancient Technology*, iii. 164 f. Leonidas of Tarentum, *AP* vii. 736, writes of an ascetic ἢ καί τοι γλήχων ἢ καὶ θύμον ἢ καὶ ὁ πικρὸς | ἀδυμιγὴc εἴη χόνδρος ἐποψίδιοc. **καλῶc ἔcται:** 'All will go well today'; Sostratos is probably as deaf to Getas' forebodings as Getas is unconcerned about Sostratos' love-affair; his presentiment concerns himself, not Getas' meal.

571 μαντεύcομαι: Pan was in some places an oracular deity, Farnell, *Cults*, v. 464–5, and even instructed Apollo in the art, Apollodoros i. 4. 3. Sostratos assures him that on this occasion he will not be called on for a prophecy; Sostratos will do the prophesying. The future μαντεύcομαι, which has aroused suspicion, may be so explained. Then with a feeling that he has been a little off-hand, he calls attention to the fact that, as always, he is now paying his respects as he passes by. ἀλλὰ μήν adds a new point, emphatically or insistently, sometimes with an adversative, sometimes with a confirmatory force (Denniston, *GP* 341); here there would seem to be adversative colour. Denniston calls it 'rare in verse', but this is an exaggeration if comedy is included (*Perik.* 512, *Sam.* 117, 546, 575, *Fab. inc.* 45, Alexis frag. 167 K, Nikostratos frag. 8 K, Dioxippos frag. 2 K, Ar. *Birds* 385, *Frogs* 258).

573 φιλανθρωπεύcομαι: Editors suppose that Sostratos promises to treat Pan kindly, and some find in his use of the word φιλανθρωπεύεcθαι to a god either humour or a sign of the decay of religion or both. I believe that he declares his intention to act the kind host to Gorgias and Daos. One may compare the way in which Philip of Macedon tried to ingratiate himself with the Theban envoys, according to

Demosthenes xix. 139, ἐν θυσίᾳ τινι καὶ δείπνῳ πίνων καὶ φιλανθρωπευό-
μενος πρὸς αὐτούς. The noun φιλανθρώπευμα is used of an invitation
to dinner, Plut. *Mor.* 816 b–c, cf. 970 a.

Expressing his optimism and hospitable intentions Sostratos goes
off to summon Gorgias. His prophecy that all will be well contrasts
sharply with the immediate entry of Simiche in great distress.

(ix) 574–587: *Simiche and Getas*

574: The structure of this line (cf. 472) is the comic condiment to the
emotion of its words. Aristophanes had, not surprisingly, found funny
the line of the tragedian Achaios, χαῖρ' ὦ Χάρων, χαῖρ' ὦ Χάρων,
χαῖρ' ὦ Χάρων (*Frogs* 184); Plaut. *Trinummus* 1094, 'o Callicles, o
Callicles, o Callicles', may have been taken from Philemon.

575 ἄπαγ' εἰς τὸ βάραθρον: That this imprecation is not specifically
addressed to Simiche is shown by the following words, which refer
to her in the third person; cf. 112 n., 394 n. τοῦ γέροντός τις γυνή:
Getas does not say 'a servant', θεράπαινα, but uses a word that would
cover a wife or a παλλακή. He thereby expresses his low opinion of
Knemon, whom he knows as a badly dressed old man who opens his
own door: he is prepared to believe him to be living with old Simiche
as his woman.

576 ff.: The position of τοῦ δεσπότου, which depends on λάθρᾳ, is
remarkable. Foss suggests that the disorder of Simiche's words is due
to her agitation; compare [Longinus], περὶ ὕψους 22, who calls hyperbaton χαρακτὴρ ἐναγωνίου πάθους ἀληθέστατος (J. H. Kells, *CR* N.S.
xi [1961], 189 n. 1).

579: B appears (Turner: others doubt this) to have written α above
the ε of ενηψα: either ἀνῆψα or ἐνῆψα would be possible; the former is
the more usual verb (see LSJ), and has been adopted in OCT.

　τὴν δίκελλαν: The article implies that Knemon possessed only one.
His house is, moreover, so ill equipped that it does not contain the
hook normally used for recovering buckets (see 599–600 n.).

581: In OCT I hastily followed most editors in giving ὀρθῶς to Getas,
although B has no dicolon after it, probably none before it, and certainly no paragraphus below the line. B's text may be right, if Simiche
means that she dropped the mattock 'straight' down the well, so that
it fell vertically. Spoken by Getas ὀρθῶς is strange, for it usually
expresses assent to a statement or a proposal; but he has no reason
for assenting to the statement that the rope had broken, having no
knowledge of his own. F. Stoessl, *Philologus*, cvi (1962), 126, suggests
οὕτως, which might be better taken with ἐνςέςεικα than with εὐθύς,

as he takes it.   ἐνcέcεικα: Cf. 632. The two passages show that
ἐνcείω, properly 'shake into', had popularly developed the sense 'let
drop into'. After the preceding aorists, which indicated past events,
the perfect expresses the present state of affairs, 'I've let it drop'.
θ' ἀθλία: Jacques's change, for τ' ἀθλία, is I think required; see *Epitr.*
431 n., 563.

582 μετὰ τοῦ κάδου is defensible, although changed by Lloyd-Jones
to μετὰ τὸν κάδον. Probably the rope broke under the combined weight
of the mattock and the bucket, full of water.

583: 'What is still left for you to do is to throw yourself in'; ῥῖψαι is
made vivid by being brought forward (hyperbaton) before τὸ λοιπόν cοι.

584 κόπρον: One is to understand that Knemon and his animals
lived under the same roof. A mattock, with blades or tines more or
less at right angles to the shaft, does not seem the ideal tool for
shifting dung. Perhaps this is another indication that Knemon's
household had only the minimum equipment.

586: It would be effective if Getas were to interrupt Simiche's tale
with the warning that Knemon is coming, and she must run; but
not so much more effective than the division of words given by the
papyrus that there is justification for overriding its indication.

(x) 588–602: *Simiche, Knemon, Getas*

587: It is possible that γραῦ should be assigned to Knemon as he
bursts out; cf. 925, γραῦ· ποῦ 'cτὶν ἡ γραῦc; In any case his appearance
motivates Getas' μᾶλλον δ' ἀμύνου, 'defend yourself, it is too late for
flight'.   ὦ πονηρά: 'Poor wretch', cf. *Heros* 6 n., Ar. *Frogs* 852,
ὦ πόνηρ' Εὐριπίδη, in an injunction to flee the Aeschylean hailstorm.
Handley would take ὦ πονηρά . . . γραῦ together, with parenthetic
ἀποκτενεῖ cε—possible.

588: Menander never explains how Knemon discovered that the
mattock was down the well; in the excitement no explanation is
needed.   τοιχωρύχοc: The word is, as in Aristophanes (e.g. *Clouds*
1327), a mere term of abuse; the literal meaning 'housebreaker,
burglar' is quite inappropriate. Female burglars will have been even
more uncommon in ancient Athens than in modern London.

591: Ar. *Wasps* 396, Bdelykleon, trying to escape from the upper
storey, καθιμᾷ | αὑτὸν δῆcαc. Knemon proposes to fasten Simiche to
the rope and let her down the well to recover his mattock. Why does
he not pursue this plan? Instead he climbs down himself. The audience

has to guess why he changes his mind. Simiche's protest brings the angry reply that he will use the very rope that is in his hands; Getas' malicious comment reminds him that it is rotten. This is the first check to his plan. He might think of getting another rope, but Simiche suggests getting help from Daos. Superficially his retort means '*You get me in this mess and propose to call Daos to get me out of it*', but behind this lies an angry refusal to compromise his position of self-sufficiency. Reminded of this, he determines that he will recover the mattock unaided. His abusive rejection of Getas' offer of help is a sign that confirms his motive.

595 ἀνηρηκυῖά με: This correction is supported by *Sik.* 82, ἀνῄρηκάς με. The exaggeration, 'when you have destroyed me', is in character, cf. 160, νῦν δ' οὐ βιωτόν. ἀνόcι(ε), an adjective of two terminations. Some editors have preferred ἀνόcι(α) ἀνειρηκυῖα, γραῦ, supposing that Knemon regards calling on Daos for help as an unholy act; but the verb, 'proclaim', is unsuitable. See also 108 n.

596 οὐ coὶ λέγω; Lit. 'is it not you I am talking to?', a sarcastic manner of expressing impatience, cf. *Epitr.* 1077, οὐχ ὑμῖν λέγω;

596 ff.: Greek idiom requires τάλας ἐγώ, not ἐγὼ τάλας, and so either the words at the beginning of 597 must be interchanged, or τάλας must be restored at the end of 596. Since θᾶττον βάδιζ' εἴcω is likely to be a complete phrase, the second alternative is probable. It is then tempting to adopt Winnington-Ingram's further supplement and read [τάλας] ἐγώ, τάλας τῆc νῦν ἐρημίαc, [τάλας] ὡc οὐδὲ εἷc, comparing for the end a comic poet, perhaps Philemon, in Page, *GLP* p. 280, ἐγὼ μὲν ὕβρισμαι, Λάχηc, ὡc οὐδὲ εἷc ἄνθρωποc ἕτεροc πώποτε. But the interpretation of the text so constituted offers more difficulty, I believe, than is realized by some who adopt it. ἐρημία, 'isolation', is a key word of the play: Knemon longs for it (169) and Gorgias points out that it was nearly his undoing (694, and cf. 222); it is strange if Knemon here laments his beloved isolation, especially as immediately before and after he explicitly rejects help, whether suggested (595) or offered (600). To speak of 'a sigh at his self-chosen loneliness' (Treu) or 'an inner feeling of self-pity' (Handley) does little to explain the anomaly. There is a further difficulty. The only probable remedy for the un-metrical form in which B presents 597 is to read either τῆc νῦν ἐρημίαc or ἐρημίαc τῆc νῦν (Handley prefers the latter, perhaps poetic or elevated language). Knemon then refers to a *present* ἐρημία, something that is not permanent, cf. Isaios ii. 12 where ἡ παροῦcα ἐρημία is used of a man who had sent his wife away. But Knemon's way of life had continued for some time, his ἐρημία was nothing new. If Winnington-Ingram's restoration is right, can it be that the present ἐρημία is the

DYSKOLOS

absence of his mattock? The phrase would be an exaggerated one, inadequately paralleled by Ar. *Birds* 1483, ἐν τῇ λύχνων ἐρημίᾳ; but Knemon's language is generally violent and exaggerated. For the use of a key word without its usual reference compare δυςκολώτατον in 296. For the genitive of cause attached to τάλας, cf. Ar. *Plut.* 1044, τάλαιν' ἐγὼ τῆς ὕβρεος.

A different approach is that of Jacques, who reads [τάλας] ἐγώ, τάλας. τῆς νῦν ἐρημίας [ἐρῶ] ὡς οὐδὲ εἷς. This makes τῆς νῦν intelligible: Knemon loves the isolation he *now* enjoys, opposing it in thought to the human contact that would arise if he were to ask Daos for help.

599–600: No conjecture made on the assumption that καὶ cχοινίον means 'even a rope' is plausible. καί will mean 'and'. What then was the other object offered? Shipp and others suggest a ἁρπάγη, defined by Ammonios p. 22 (73 Nickau) as ἐν ᾗ ἐκ τῶν φρεάτων τοὺς κάδους ἐξαίρουςιν (cf. Buchmann, *Anecd. Gr. Paris.*, ii. 376. 25, τὸ ἄγκιστρον δι' οὗ τῶν φρεάτων τὰ ἀγγεῖα ἐξαίρομεν). Although a rope might be available, having been used to secure Getas' bundle of rugs, etc., one would not at first sight expect a hook to be part of the luggage of a picnic-party. Pollux vi. 88, however, mentions as an item in a cook's equipment a κρεάγραν, ἣν καὶ ἁρπάγην ἐκάλουν. Ar. *Eccl.* 1002, τί δῆτα καὶ κρεάγρας τοῖς κάδοις ὠνοίμεθ' ἄν; shows that it could be used for lifting buckets. According to the scholiast on Ar. *Knights* 772, it was shaped like a hand with bent fingers, and could be used for extracting pieces of meat from the boiling pot (Daremberg and Saglio iii. 11 give an illustration).

Other specific nouns seem to be less likely as supplements: κλίμακα, κάδον, βρόχον have been suggested. πάνθ' ἃ δεῖ (Kraus) makes unnecessary the particular offer of a cχοινίον as well; ἄλλα τε is too vague to be convincing.

601 εἴ τι μοι λαλεῖς: Fraenkel's supplement follows *Sam.* 388, (Δημ.) κατάξω τὴν κεφαλὴν ἄνθρωπέ cου, ἂν μοι διαλέγῃ. (Μαγ.) νὴ δικαίως γε. Many editors adopt μοι δίδως ('offer') of *ed. pr.*, as more specifically appropriate to the situation. The choice is uncertain.

602 καὶ μάλα δικαίως: Hesychios explains this phrase by καὶ πάνυ εἰκότως. Compare *Sam.* 388–9, quoted on 601, and *Epitr.* 249.

(xi) 603–610: *Getas alone*

603 ὦ τρισκακοδαιμων is in itself unexceptionable, but in view of the common confusion in B of ω and ο the true reading may be εἰσπεπήδηκεν πάλιν | ὁ τρισκακοδαίμων. οὗτος οἷον ζῇ βίον κτλ. Cf. *Perik.* 977, πῶς βιώσομαι | ὁ τρισκακοδαίμων; perhaps *Karch.* 9, περὶ τίνος λαλεῖ | [ὁ τρισκακοδαίμ]ων;

604 εἰλικρινής: 'Unadulterated'; neither the adjective nor the adverb occurs elsewhere in comedy, or indeed outside prose, if LSJ is correct. The choice here between εἰλικρινής and εἰλικρινῶς is not easy, and to choose the adjective may be no more than a personal preference. Plato, *Menex.* 245 d has διὰ τὸ εἰλικρινῶς εἶναι Ἕλληνας καὶ ἀμιγεῖς βαρβάρων, while Arrian, *Tact.* 4, speaking of light-armed cavalry called Ταραντῖνοι, says that some never engage at close quarters, οἳ δὴ καὶ εἰλικρινεῖς Ταραντῖνοί εἰσιν (Hercher proposed εἰλικρινῶς).

605: B's σκαφον is a form also found in Hesychios s.v., whether by pure scribal error or because this was a popular mispronunciation. Thyme is not a native of Attica; θύμον, according to J. André, *Rev. phil.* xxxiv (1960), 52, is *Satureia thymbra* L. (savory); σφάκος, 'sage' is *Salvia calycina*.

Libanios, *Decl.* xxvii. 18 appears to have a reminiscence of this passage, γεωργῶ . . . ὄχθον τραχύν, θύμον φέροντα (Kraus: γεωργοῦντα) καὶ σφάκον.

606: B's ἐπίσταται is possible Greek, 'he understands torment', but ἐπισπᾶται, 'wins himself torment', goes better with οὐδὲν ἀγαθὸν λαμβάνων, of which it is the contrary, and is also more vigorous. The error is a minimal one; it probably occurs again at Soph. *Ajax* 869. One may compare Libanios iv. 166, κακὸν ἑκὼν ἐπεσπασάμην, which may be taken from some comedy (*CAF* iii. 671), and Aesch. *Persae* 477, τοσόνδε πλῆθος πημάτων ἐπέσπασεν. Post suggests, *AJP* lxxxiv (1963), 47, that there is a reminiscence of the anecdote told of Peisistratos and the farmer on Hymettos, παντελῶς πέτρας σκάπτοντα. Asked τί γίγνεται ἐκ τοῦ χωρίου, he replied ὅσα κακὰ καὶ ὀδύναι (Arist. *Ath. Pol.* 16. 6). In this play the contempt for the labours of an agricultural life suits the rich man's domestic slave; at the same time the Athenians had a traditional admiration for the hard-working countryman, and the description of Knemon as a 'genuine Attic farmer' is a subtle suggestion that there is some good in him, a suggestion that prepares the way for the shift of sympathy required in the next act.

608 ἐπικλήτους: Cf. Plut. *Mor.* 707 a, τὸ δὲ τῶν ἐπικλήτων ἔθος, οὓς νῦν σκιὰς καλοῦσιν, οὐ κεκλημένους αὐτούς, ἀλλ' ὑπὸ τῶν κεκλημένων ἐπὶ τὸ δεῖπνον ἀγομένους. Socrates at Agathon's party in Plato's *Symposium* is an example. Getas talks as if Sostratos were a guest at his mother's party, and were now himself introducing further uninvited guests.   **ἐργάται:** Gorgias and Daos, whom Getas does not distinguish as master and slave, but lumps together as 'labourers'. We may suppose them to be dressed much alike, cf. [Xen.] *Resp. Athen.* 10, ἐcθῆτα γὰρ οὐδὲν βελτίω ἔχει ὁ δῆμοc αὐτόθι ἢ οἱ δοῦλοι— although more than a century had elapsed since that was written.

(xii) **611–619**: *Sostratos, Gorgias* (with *Daos*), *Getas*

610 οὖτοc τί κτλ.; Sostratos ignores this question; presumably he neither hears it nor is intended to hear it. It is probably couched in the third person, since ἄγομαι middle, 'I take with me', is not exemplified in fourth-century comedy. The emphatically placed οὖτοc expresses impatience. Presumably Getas here returns to his work in the shrine; the text nowhere marks his exit.

611–13 οὐκ . . . ἄλλωc ποῆcαι are words commonly used when issuing an invitation; in Ar. *Birds* 133 the ideal host adds to his invitation to a wedding-feast καὶ μηδαμῶc ἄλλωc ποήcῃc. E. Fraenkel, *Beobachtungen zu Aristophanes*, p. 69, gives further illustrations of the formula. If we accept B's distribution of speakers, πάντ' ἔχομεν must mean 'we have all that is needed', i.e. food enough for all. But it is then obscure why Sostratos should burst out with the indignant protest ὦ Ἡράκλειc κτλ. In a modern play such an outburst might be caused by a silent gesture of refusal, but that is not the way of Greek drama, which is verbally explicit. Ritchie suggested giving ὦ Ἡράκλειc to Getas, who sees his chances of a share in the feast receding with the arrival of more guests. But this would add nothing to his characterization; he has already made his protest. Moreover the usual expression of dismay, when it stands isolated, is Ἡράκλειc not ὦ Ἡράκλειc, which is introductory of something. It is here in fact difficult to separate ὦ Ἡράκλειc from what follows, because δέ in the question has an indignant or impatient tone (Denniston, *GP* 173); and this usage is often found in questions that succeed an exclamation (ibid. 174). A more likely solution is to give πάντ' ἔχομεν to Gorgias, and with Webster, Post, and Quincey, *JHS* lxxxvi (1966), 637, suppose this to be an idiomatic but somewhat boorish expression of refusal, which could provoke Sostratos' indignant reply. (The evidence for the existence of such an expression is, however, thin. In *Pap. Hibeh* 6. 32 (Page, *GLP* p. 288) an offer of provisions (τἀναγκαῖα) for a journey is received with the words ἔχομεν ἅπαντα, whereupon the speaker is rebuked by Ἄπολλον, ὡc ἄγροικοc εἶ. But here there is no need to see any idiom: ἅπαντα may mean ἅπαντα τἀναγκαῖα.) Gorgias' unwillingness to accept a favour and proud assertion of ability to stand on his own legs prepares the way for his attempt to refuse an advantageous marriage at the beginning of Act V. But in both places his resistance quickly collapses. Here it does so when he is shown to be offending against the pattern of behaviour that society reasonably expects; I suggest in my note on 835 ff. that there, also, he is accused of socially inadequate conduct.

To avoid supposing that B has failed to mark a change of speaker, Handley makes πάντ' ἔχομεν a quotation, by which Sostratos reproduces the words that Gorgias is supposed just to have uttered before coming on the scene. This is neat, but would it ask too much of the actor?

613 ὅλωc: Cf. 861 n.

615 cοι πάλαι φίλοc: Cf. Eur. frag. 902, τὸν ἐcθλὸν ἄνδρα, κἂν ἑκὰς ναίῃ χθονός, | κἂν μήποτ' ὄccοιc εἰcίδω, κρίνω φίλον, and Iamblichos, VP 237, τὸν λόγον . . . ὡc ἄρ' οἱ cπουδαῖοι ἄνδρες καὶ προcωτάτω γῆc οἰκοῦντεc φίλοι εἰcὶν ἀλλήλοιc πρὶν ἢ γνώριμοί τε καὶ προcήγοροι γενέcθαι.

616: Gallavotti suggests that B's ταυταδ' is a conflation of alternatives ταῦτα and τάδε: he adopts τάδε, Handley ταῦτ'. I prefer to suppose that δ' is due to the common aversion of scribes to asyndeton; they often introduce δέ to avoid it, cf. 678 n., 737 n. In any case the pronoun refers to the two mattocks and any other gear that the pair are carrying. Notice the lack of inhibitions on Sostratos' part: he gives orders to another man's slave, and invites him to lunch. Gorgias without apology countermands the invitation: he has his own ideas about how his slave should be employed. The impulsiveness and the ungraciousness of the two young men are once again illustrated.

617: It is not likely that the spectator would, if Daos came to the party, trouble himself over Myrrhine's being left alone. What, then, is the point of this injunction? There is no *particular* reason for here emphasizing Gorgias' filial solicitude, although it helps to build up the picture of this worthy young man. The spectator might notice, too, that unlike Getas, Daos does not grumble at being deprived of a meal. His silence is of course inevitable, since the part must be played by a κωφὸν πρόcωπον: but Menander may have made a virtue of necessity. Perhaps the principal object of the line is just to get rid of a character who is not wanted again. If Daos accompanied Sostratos and Gorgias into the shrine, he might be expected to come out with his master at the cry for help, and would then have to follow him into Knemon's house. But the presence of a third pair of hands would spoil the story of the rescue. Moreover he would have to get back home again, a trivial but tiresome complication, especially if the number of persons available as κωφὰ πρόcωπα was limited: the scene where the rescued Knemon is brought out already requires two, to take the parts of the daughter and Myrrhine.

ACT IV

(i) **620–638**: *Simiche, Sikon, Gorgias* (635–8, with *Sostratos*)

623 cπονδάc: Libations were poured at the end of a meal, in preparation for the wine that followed, as well as before it. Cf. frag. 239, τὰc τραπέζαc αἴρετε, μύρα cτεφάνουc ἑτοίμαcον, cπονδὰc πόει. The lunch has taken place during the *entracte*, so far as eating goes; its later stages are now interrupted by the catastrophe to Knemon, but resumed in Act V.

624 οἰμώζετε: Although Simiche's lamentation might interfere, as being ill omened, with the pouring of the libations, Knemon's abuse and violence had not been allowed to impede those made before the meal. I think that οἰμώζετε may be imperative, and that between them the three verbs constitute Sikon's reply to the appeal for help. 'Heavens, let us make our libations in peace. You abuse us, you beat us—you can go to hell!'

Although there is a paragraphus below this line, it contains no dicolon; it is not therefore at once clear whether οἰμώζετε or ἐκτόπου ends Sikon's speech. On the first alternative, Simiche despairs of getting help, since they live in such an out-of-the-way place, the ἐρημία of 597. But although this, the literal, meaning of ἔκτοποc occurs in tragedy (Soph. *Trach.* 32), the usual colloquial sense is 'extraordinary', and it is therefore more plausible to give ὦ τῆc . . . ἐκτόπου to Sikon: 'What an extraordinary house!'

627: Notice the tenses; he was climbing down (κατέβαινε, imperfect), then he slipped (ὤλιcθε, aorist), and now has fallen (πέπτωκε, perfect). Fourth-century Attic wells with recessed toe- and finger-holds are illustrated in *Bull. Corr. Hell.* lxxxiv (1960), 646, lxxxvii (1963), 693.

628–9 οὐ γὰρ . . . Οὐρανόν: It is not possible to take this as a single sentence, since it is almost unknown for an oath to be attached to a question, even where the question is the virtual equivalent of a statement; a question is emphasized by πρὸc τῶν θεῶν or a similar phrase. The only exception I can quote is Eubulos frag. 117 K, ἀλλὰ νὴ Δία | χρηcτή τιc ἦν μέντοι τίc; Here ἀλλὰ νὴ Δία has its common function of indicating a supposed objection, and is not a normal confirmatory oath. Kassel, Thierfelder, and others suggest breaking the sentence by giving οὗτοc to Simiche, cf. *Heros* 27. There is no warrant for this in B, unless its cφοδραι is a remnant of cφοδρα:, and the question 'Not the very bad-tempered old man?', while admitting of an answer, does not require one. This solution cannot be ruled out, but cannot be preferred to one that gives the whole passage to Sikon, as B does, and divides it into a question and an asseveration. But where is the question to end? at γάρ, at γέρων, at cφόδρα, or at οὗτος? Since cφόδρα in Menander more frequently follows than precedes the word it modifies, the first two places are the less likely and, if the division is made after cφόδρα, οὗτος is over-emphasized. For these reasons, but with hesitation, I place the stop after οὗτος. It must be observed, however, that if οὗτος were οὕτως—and confusion of ο and ω is very common in B—it could very well stand emphatically first: by falling down the well, Knemon has exhibited unusual good conduct.

The usual phrase for expressing approval is καλῶς ποιεῖν, and Quincey (*JHS* lxxxvi [1966], 143) may be right in emending καλά γ' to καλῶς. νὴ τὸν Οὐρανόν, found six times in Aristophanes, appears here alone as yet in Menander, although μὰ τὴν Δήμητρα καὶ τὸν Οὐρανόν occurs in *Pap. Ant.* 15. By contrast Menander has νὴ τὸν ῞Ηλιον six times, Aristophanes not at all. Fashions in swearing may change, but it may be possible to detect a growing lack of confidence in the divinity of the sky.

630 còν ἔργον ἐcτί: The addition of ἐcτί (as in Ar. *Lys.* 315, *Frogs* 589) saves the phrase from undue solemnity. Without the verb we have Aesch. *PV* 635, *Eum.* 734, Kratinos frag. 108 K, (paratragic), *Λήδα*, còν ἔργον, Ar. *Birds* 862, ἱερεῦ, còν ἔργον, θῦε τοῖς καινοῖς θεοῖς, *Peace* 426, ὑμέτερον ἐντεῦθεν ἔργον, ἄνδρες, etc. I doubt whether P. T. Stevens, *CQ* xxxi (1937), 189, is right to count the phrase còν ἔργον as colloquial.

631 ὅλμον: Eustathios on *Iliad* xi. 147 explains ὅλμος as a hollow wooden or stone vessel used for pounding beans etc. At Ar. *Wasps* 201 a ὅλμος is heavy enough to be used to secure the door against Philokleon's attempts to escape. Parthenios 14 tells the story of a Milesian woman Kleoboia who, in the situation of Potiphar's wife, caused the young man to go down a well to rescue her tame partridge, whereupon ἐπιcείει cτιβαρόν αὐτῷ πέτρον. Another story of a woman who stoned a man in an empty well is told by Plutarch, *Mul. Virt.* 260 b.

633: This proverbial expression, Apost. vii. 40 (Leutsch–Schneidewin *Paroem. gr.* ii. 405 : ἐν φρέατι κυνομαχεῖν. ἐπὶ τῶν ἀποφυγεῖν οὐκ ἐχόντων καὶ μοχθηρῷ τινὶ προσπαλαιόντων, cf. *Suda* s.v. ἐν φρέατι κυcὶ μάχεcθαι, Hesychios s.v. ἐν φρέατι κυνομαχεῖν, Zenob. iii. 45), may be connected with a fable about a gardener who was bitten by his dog when he tried to rescue it from a well, *Corpus Fabul. Aesopicarum*, i. 148, ii. 169 Hausrath, B. E. Perry, *Aesopica*, p. 368.

635: B gives ωγοργιαπουτιcποτει: πουποτειμιγηcεγω. Correction is uncertain, and without much confidence I follow the *ed. pr.* which

gives ποῦ γῆς ποτ' εἶ; (Γο.) ποῦ γῆς ἐγώ; This supposes that ποτ' εἰμι
was added by way of explanation, to make a complete sentence. For
such an addition there is no parallel in the present text, and the
ellipse of εἰμί is too usual to require clarification. J. Martin thought
that ποῦ ποτ' εἰμὶ γῆς ἐγώ; should be kept, in view of the fact that the
phrase is found at *Perik.* 793 as an expression of bewilderment (ποῦ
γῆς εἰμί; is the question of a man who has just fainted at *Sik.* 369);
he proposed to read ὦ Γοργία, ποῦ ποῦ ποτ' εἰμὶ γῆς ἐγώ; τιсποτει
must then be regarded as a miswriting of πουποτει, observed and
corrected, but not cancelled. The dicolon is an obstacle to this view;
it can only be explained as misplaced from a correct position before
the first που, where it would mark the fact that ποῦ πότ' εἰμι γῆς ἐγώ;
is a question addressed to the air, not to Gorgias. Although ποτε
more frequently follows the first of two repeated interrogatives (e.g.
Soph. *Phil.* 175 πῶс ποτε πῶс . . .), it is found also after the second,
Eur. *Or.* 278, ποῖ ποῖ ποθ' . . .

It is to be noted that Simiche does not know Gorgias to be in the
cave. Her summons ὦ Γοργία will be directed towards his house and
he will respond from an unexpected direction. It is just possible that,
if *ed. pr.*'s correction is right, Simiche cries ποῦ γῆς ποτ' εἶ; because
he does not immediately appear at his own door; she might suppose
him to be at home, for this is the time of the midday meal.

638 ἡγοῦ κτλ.: Who speaks? If B's dicolon after δευρ indicates change
of speaker, the alternatives are (1) Simiche to Gorgias (Mette),
(2) Sostratos to Gorgias (Martin etc.). (2) is impossible, for Sostratos
knows nothing of the nature of the crisis: summoned by Gorgias, he
may follow him; he cannot give him instructions. (1) is possible, and
the abruptness of the phrase might be excused by the urgency of the
moment. Another possibility is (3) that the dicolon indicates change
of addressee; then the words are spoken by Gorgias to Simiche. There
is an indication that this is what B intends: δευρ' is written, whereas
scriptio plena is the rule at change of speaker. Against this Kraus has
objected that Gorgias would know his way to the well, and need no
leading. I doubt whether this reflection would occur to a spectator or
that, if it did, it would be justified. Gorgias may not have been in
Knemon's house for many years: he was not living there when his
mother left it (22).

(ii) **639-665:** *Sikon alone*

639 μὰ τὸν Διόνυсον: Cf. 151 n. Sense requires that the oath should
be taken with the preceding clauses, not the following negative one.
it should not be necessary to warn the reader that it is Sikon, not

the poet in his own person, who sees the hand of divine vengeance at work.

641: ἐμπίπτειν is commoner than εἰcπίπτειν (and cf. hypothesis 7 εἰc φρέαρ . . . ἐμπεcών), but the latter occurs, e.g. Thuc. iii. 98, ἐcπίπτοντεc ἐc χαράδραc, in the literal sense here required: the chances here favour εἰcπεcών rather than ἐμπεcών, which supposes a greater error of transcription.

642: To give water to the thirsty and show the way to the traveller were regarded as fundamental human duties: the Jews were supposed to have abjured them, Juvenal xiv. 103–4.

643 νυνὶ μέν: It is unusually difficult to see what contrasted thought is implied by this 'μέν solitarium'; perhaps something like 'and on other occasions I hope he may get his deserts' or 'I may be revenged on those who treat me badly'.

645 διέφυγεν: Gnomic aorist.

646 ἱεροπρεπήc: The very word, 'suitable to a religious function', is as high-sounding as the claim that Sikon makes for his art. Since it is part of a cook's duties to *sacrifice* the animal he may be regarded as a minor religious functionary. Athenion frag. 1. 40 K has a cook who makes this claim: καταρχόμεθ' ἡμεῖc οἱ μάγειροι, θύομεν, | cπονδὰc ποιοῦμεν, τῷ μάλιcτα τοὺc θεοὺc | ἡμῖν ὑπακούειν. At the beginning of the line the supplement ἀλλ' εἰc is as likely as any; there is room for it if written with ligatures; the construction has a parallel in Philippides frag. 26 K, quoted in 298 n. κακῶc . . . πόει might be suggested, with separation of the words as exemplified in 236 n.

647 τραπεζοποιόν: See Hesychios s.v., οὐχ ὁ μάγειροc, ἀλλ' ὁ τῆc πάcηc περὶ τὰ cυμπόcια παρακευῆc ἐπιμελούμενοc. His duties are given by Antiphanes frag. 152 K, προcέλαβον ἐλθὼν τουτονὶ | τραπεζοποιόν, ὃc πλυνεῖ cκεύη, λύχνουc | ἑτοιμάcει, cπονδὰc ποιήcει, τἄλλ' ὅcα | τούτῳ προcήκει. cπονδὰc ποιήcει is puzzling, since one would expect the cook himself to perform this ceremony, as in *Kolax* frag. 1. Gulick (ed. Athenaios 170 d), following Kock, translates 'will prepare the libations', but this is unconvincing. There may have been some point in Antiphanes that is lost to us. W. G. Arnott points out that the compound is like μηχανοποιόc, indicating an operator, not a manufacturer.

648 ἆρα μή: 'It can't be that . . .?' Denniston, *GP* 47. Although occurring in Antiphon 5. 4, ἀποιμώζειν is chiefly found in tragedy, cf. particularly Eur. *Med.* 31, αὐτὴ πρὸc αὑτὴν πατέρ' ἀποιμώζῃ φίλον.

650: It is useless to guess what was said in this gap, which is due to the fact that the top of a sheet has been lost. Four seems the most likely number of missing lines, but it must not be regarded as beyond doubt, any more than that five have been lost after 702 from the other side of the sheet.

654 ff.: It is probable that these lines suggested some way in which Knemon might be rescued. If so, it will not have anticipated what transpires to have happened in fact. One can imagine something like δηλονότι καθύπερθ᾽ ἐμβαλόντες cχοινίον | οὕτως ἀνιμήcουcιν αὐτόν. This would make clearer Gorgias' courage in taking the risk of descending into the well himself.

656 ff.: If τίν[α is right (it is not quite certain), ἀcτείαν, 'charming, delightful', is probably Sikon's answer to his own question. The punctuation adopted by Lloyd-Jones and by Handley (ἀcτείαν ἐγὼ μέν. ἡδέωc ἴδοιμ᾽ ἂν κτλ.) disregards the probable opposition between ἐγὼ μέν and ὑμεῖc δέ, and gives a slightly disjointed sequence. Certainty is unattainable here.

657 βεβαμμένου: The space barely allows βεβ[ρεγ]μένου, and there is no reason why βεβαμμένοc should be confined, as Kraus maintains, to the sense 'dyed'; see Epikt. ii. 9. 20. For βάπτω, 'dip', cf. 200.

659 Ἀπόλλω τουτονί: Cf. frag. 801, Ar. *Thesm.* 748 for the same oath, and (with μά) *Sam.* 309, *Mis.* 314. Something that represented Apollo Aguieus stood outside the Athenian's house-door, see Ar. *Wasps* 875, ὦ δέcποτ᾽ ἄναξ, γεῖτον ἀγυιεῦ, τοὐμοῦ προθύρου προπύλαιε, where the scholiast says that it took the form of a pillar with a conical top: πρὸ τῶν θυρῶν ἔθοc εἶχον κίοναc εἰc ὀξὺ λήγονταc ὡc ὀβελίcκουc ἱδρύειν εἰc τιμὴν Ἀπόλλωνοc Ἀγυιέωc. Similarly the Berlin Photios has Ἀγυιεύc· ὁ πρὸ τῶν αὐλείων θυρῶν κωνοειδὴc κίων, ἱερὸc Ἀπόλλωνοc. καὶ αὐτὸc ὁ θεόc. Farnell, *Cults*, iv. 149, is inclined to believe Harpokration, who says s.v. Ἀγυιᾶc that this pillar was a Doric practice and that in Attica it was replaced by an altar, quoting as authority Kratinos and Menander. Helladios (fourth century A.D.), summarized by Photios, *bibl.* 535 *b*, says that it was called Ἀγυιᾶc Λοξίαc, Sophocles frag. 370 Pearson speaks of ἀγυιεὺc βωμός, and Pollux iv. 123 writes ἐπὶ δὲ τῆc cκηνῆc καὶ ἀγυιεὺc ἔκειτο βωμὸc ὁ πρὸ τῶν θυρῶν. But Helladios apparently believed pillar and altar to be adjacent: τὸν Λοξίαν γὰρ προcεκύνουν, ὃν πρὸ τῶν θυρῶν ἕκαcτοc ἱδρύοντο καὶ πάλιν βωμὸν παρ᾽ αὐτῷ cτρογγύλον ποιοῦντεc. That there was a pillar as well as an altar seems to be implied by the plays, in which the god is spoken of as present, Eur. *Phoen.* 631, καὶ cύ, Φοῖβ᾽ ἄναξ Ἀγυιεῦ, καὶ μέλαθρα, χαίρετε, Ar. *Wasps* 875, Men. *Sam.* 444, Plaut. *Bacch.* 172-3, 'saluto te, uicine Apollo, qui aedibus propinquos nostris accolis'. Yet he may have been thought of as present in the altar, cf. F. Schwenn, *Gebet und Opfer*, p. 130. The statement of Hesychios s.v. Ἀγυιεύς that the altar had the shape of a column deserves no credit. See Fraenkel on Aesch. *Ag.* 1081, MacDowell on *Wasps* 875.

659–65: Although Sikon appears to tell the women in the shrine to continue with the interrupted libation, in order that he may stay to see the unfortunate Knemon, he must in fact himself go in at 665, for his mute presence during the following scenes would be intolerable. His departure into the shrine is indeed quite natural, for he cannot expect Knemon to come out of his house and so provide the spectacle he would wish for. A prayer accompanies a libation, cf. *Kolax* frag. 1, Ar. *Peace* 433–5, etc.; but for Knemon's accident, it might have been in terms as general as those are, but now Sikon is able to suggest a particular and topical subject for intercession. ὑπὲρ τούτων may be anticipatory of 661–2, or may mean 'on behalf of these men, i.e. the rescuers'.

665 ἄν τις ἆρα: ἆρα is the equivalent of ἄρα, *metri gratia*. Denniston, *GP* 45, cites ἦν ἆρα from [Eur.] *Rhesus* 119; Demosthenes xxii. 57 has εἴ τισιν ἆρα δοκοῦσιν ἐπιτήδειαι 'κεῖναι παθεῖν; as here, the meaning seems to be 'as they may do', cf. Theokritos vii. 105, εἴτ' ἐστ' ἆρα Φιλῖνος, 'as it may well be'.

(iii) **666–690**: *Sostratos alone*

666 ff.: For this way of beginning a monologue compare Ar. *Clouds* 627 ff., μὰ τὴν Ἀναπνοὴν μὰ τὸ Χάος μὰ τὸν Ἀέρα, οὐκ εἶδον οὕτως ἄνδρ' ἄγροικον οὐδένα (or οὐδαμοῦ).

666: Consecutive soliloquies by two characters neither of whom is dramatically related to the other have been thought contrary to Greek dramatic technique, G. Jachmann, *Plautinisches und Attisches*, p. 76 n. 1. It is natural that such a succession should normally be avoided, but here they are unified by both referring to the same off-stage incident.

669 μικροῦ must be taken with ἀποπεπνιγμένον, 'drowned', but the words are strangely separated. μικροῦ can be regarded neither as an afterthought nor as an unimportant supplement. Perhaps Sostratos, who knows how to make the best of a story, deliberately reserves the word in order to mislead the audience momentarily into thinking Knemon dead.   τῆς γλυκείας διατριβῆς: 'What a delightful time I've spent!' or 'What a delightful amusement!'

671 κατεπήδησεν: No doubt Gorgias literally 'jumped down'. Cf. Plato, *Prot.* 349 e, οἶσθ' οὖν τίνες εἰς τὰ φρέατα κολυμβῶσιν θαρραλέως;

Laches 193 c, ὅσοι ἂν ἐθέλωσιν εἰς φρέαρ καταβαίνοντες καὶ κολυμβῶντες καρτερεῖν ἐν τούτῳ τῷ ἔργῳ, μὴ ὄντες δεινοί . . . ἀνδρειοτέρους φήσεις τῶν ταῦτα δεινῶν;

672 τί γὰρ ἐμέλλομεν; Parenthetic, 'what else was to be expected of us?', a fairly rare usage, but cf. Plato, *Rep.* 349 d, τί μέλλει; 'What else do you expect of him?' Adam there adduces *Hipp. Min.* 377 d, *Rep.* 566 d, 605 c. πλήν is attached to οὐδὲν ἐποοῦμεν. J. Martin suggests that τί ἐμέλλομεν; has the more ordinary sense, 'Why were we dilatory?', but if that question were asked it would need an answer.

675 χρυςοῦς: A nearly contemporary instance of this ironical usage is provided by a phrase of Epicurus quoted by Diog. Laert. x. 8., Πλάτωνα χρυσοῦν (ἐκάλει). The adjective can be seriously used as an epithet of gods. Plato makes an ironically ambiguous use of it at *Phaedr.* 235 e, φίλτατος εἶ καὶ ὡς ἀληθῶς χρυσοῦς εἴ με οἴει λέγειν ὡς Λυσίας τοῦ παντὸς ἡμάρτηκε. ἐγὼ δὲ ὁ χρυσοῦς in Alkiphron ii. 14 [iii. 17] will be taken from some comedy, if not from this. For other examples see E. Degani, *RCCM* v (1963), 291.

676 τροφός: The nurse of drama regularly tries to act as comforter of the woman she has reared, when the latter is in distress. Sostratos adopts this role, instead of helping Gorgias.

677 ἄγαλμα, most frequently 'a statue', may also mean 'a picture'. Bekker, *Anecdota*, 82. 11, has ἀνδριάς· καὶ ἐπὶ γραφῆς. [i.e. ἀνδριάς can be used of a painting] Πλάτων Πολιτείᾳ (iv. 420 c), Μένανδρος Δυσκόλῳ. We may see here a garbled reference to this passage, since it is unlikely that the word ἀνδριάς occurred in this sense in any of the missing lines of the play; e.g. ἀνδριὰς καὶ ⟨ἄγαλμα· καὶ⟩ ἐπὶ γραφῆς. To compare human beauty to a work of art is a conventional phrase, cf. Plato, *Charmides* 154 c, πάντες ὥσπερ ἄγαλμα ἐθεῶντο αὐτόν (a beautiful youth), [Theokr.] xxxiii. 28, ἀλλ' ὡς ἄγαλμ' ἐσεῖδον, Plaut. *Epidicus* 624, 'estne consimilis quasi quom signum pictum pulchre aspexeris?'

678 τοῦ δὲ πεπληγμένου: 'Hard-hit', 'taken a knock', cf. Dem. xxv. 41: Aristogeiton persecutes private individuals, ἴασι δ' οἱ πεπληγμένοι. The broken anapaest in the fourth foot as given by B is suspect; asyndeton would not be impossible, and intrusive δέ is a common feature of MSS., cf. 187, 736, 740. Alternatively δέ may be removed, as Austin suggests (*CR* n.s. xviii [1968], 275), to a position after ἔμελε.

679 ἢ τινος: 'Than of anything', cf. Dem. xix. 35, πραοτέρους γενέσθαι τινός, xxi. 66, κἂν ἄμεινον ἀγωνίσωμαί τινος.

680 ἐκεῖνον: Van Groningen, *Mnem.* 4th ser. xii (1959), 289, thinks this pronoun refers to Gorgias; M. L. West, *Gnomon* 1962, 253 takes the same view, finding it 'unnatural' that it should refer to the person denoted by the participle in 678. But ἐκεῖνος regularly refers to one who is less in the forefront of attention (J. H. Kells, *CR* N.S. xiv [1964], 233); in the forefront of Sostratos' attention lies, not Knemon, but his daughter. ἐνώχλει: The imperfect of ἐνοχλῶ is normally ἠνώχλουν; Menander here used a more logical but less established form, found in the MS. of Arist. *Ath. Pol.* 11 (ἐνώχλουν), and in the good codex S of Demosthenes, iii. 3. 5.

681 εἰς ἀπολώλεκα: The perfect tense indicates present responsibility for a past action, 'I am *almost* responsible for having finished him off all on my own': so Kraus. Most editors articulate B's letters as εἰσαπολώλεκα; although not otherwise known, this compound seems in itself possible, meaning 'I lost him into the well', cf. εἰσαφίημι. But it is not very likely in the context, because Knemon was at all relevant times already *in* the well.

682: Apparently a second, sound rope has been found, to assist Gorgias' rescue operations, unless Knemon himself had used a rope secured to something at the well-head. The well has of course no winding-gear.

683: To compare Gorgias bearing up Knemon to Atlas supporting the earth is an exaggeration that suits Sostratos' lively imagination; οὐχ ὁ τυχών, 'no ordinary', is also a favourite phrase with him (179, 678). Mythological comparisons, often elaborate, were much used by Plautus (Fraenkel, *Plautinisches im Plautus*, pp. 8 ff., 59 ff.), but this is as yet the only instance in Menander where a character is metaphorically identified with a mythological figure (as opposed to a simile such as *Kol.* 124, ὅσους Ὀδυσσεὺς ἦλθεν εἰς Τροίαν ἔχων). *Samia* 337 is somewhat different.

685 ἀνενήνοχε: Perfect, 'finally got him right to the top'; in ἐξελήλυθα the force of the tense is 'I came out and here I am'.

685 ἐκεῖνος: Again, as at 680, there is the question whether Gorgias or Knemon is meant, but here it is more difficult to answer. Either was of less importance to Sostratos than the girl. But the story may point to Knemon. Once he had got out, Sostratos had no cause to haul on the rope and could turn his undivided attention to the girl; Gorgias could be relied on to climb out without help.

687: Cf. Achilles Tatius i. 5. 2, μικροῦ προσελθὼν τὸν πατέρα κατεφίλησα (quoted by Arnott, *Mnem.* 4th ser. xix [1966], 398).

688: Many scholars have completed the line with ἐνθεαστικῶς from

44. This is the least likely of all supplements, since Sostratos does not know that his love is divinely inspired. There is little to choose between the other alternatives (none of which may hit the truth) given in the app. crit. of OCT. As a long shot, I note that Aristainetos, who elsewhere echoes this play, has ἐκθύμωc ἐρῶ (ii. 15).

689 παρασκευάζομαι δή—: apparently Sostratos was getting himself ready, inopportune though the occasion was, to ask for the girl in marriage.

(iv) 690–758: Knemon, Sostratos, Gorgias (with Knemon's
daughter, and Myrrhine from about 706)

690: There is no reason for bringing Knemon out of his house, except that the next scene must be played in view of the audience. Menander makes no attempt to secure verisimilitude. No excuse is better than an inadequate one. Moreover if, as is argued below, Knemon was brought out by the *ekkyklema*, the use of that conventional device for showing an interior obviated the need for any excuse.

It is not easy to determine the way in which Knemon's appearance was staged. The highly probable supplement εἰcκυ]κλεῖτ' εἴcω με at 758—inescapable unless there is corruption in the text there—implies that he is on something which can be wheeled. That this is a chair (Lloyd-Jones) is excluded by the fact that he can be 'laid down' (740, κατάκλινόν με). Some kind of bed or couch might be suggested, but a wheeled bed was not a usual article of furniture in ancient Athens, and it would be exceedingly odd if Knemon, whose general standard of living did not rise above a bare minimum, possessed such a thing; in the final scene moreover he appears to be carried, not wheeled, out of his house (909, θὲc αὐτοῦ, 920 κατατέθηκεν).

A number of scholars (including V. and J. Martin, Foss, Treu, van Groningen) think that Knemon walked out of his house supported by Gorgias (and perhaps his daughter). Apart from neglecting 758, this is hard to reconcile with 701, βούλει μ' ἀναcτῆcαι; although some do it by making Knemon sit down at some point in the preceding ten lines. None of these scholars explains how to get him off the stage after he has lain down at 740. An alternative, adopted by Jacques (and reached independently by me), is that he was brought out on the *ekkyklema* or rolling platform. To be sure, the very existence of this device in the Attic Theatre has been called into question (see A. W. Pickard-Cambridge, *Theatre of Dionysus in Athens*, 100–22). To my mind, however, P. D. Arnott, *Greek Scenic Conventions*, 78–88, makes a strong case for the traditional view that it was used at Athens in the fifth century,

both seriously in tragedies and by way of parody in Old Comedy
(*Acharnians* 406 ff., *Thesm.* 95, 269, but probably not *Clouds* 181–95,
see Dover's ed., p. lxxv); see also an excellent discussion by N. C.
Hourmouziades, *Production and Imagination in Euripides*, 93 ff. There
can, of course, be no question of parody here; the scene which begins
here has a colour less comic than that of any other part of the play,
and there would therefore be no disharmony if it were introduced by
a conventional device that properly belonged to tragedy. This interpretation has the advantage that it accounts in a simple way for
certain features of the text which, although perhaps not inexplicable
otherwise, are not easily explained. (1) There is no conceivable reason
for bringing the injured Knemon out of his house, and none is offered.
One could say that since the dramatic necessity of playing the scene
in view of the audience involves this breach of verisimilitude, the poet
was wise not to call attention to the improbability by any excuse,
which must have been inadequate. If, however, the *ekkyklema* was an
accepted convention for displaying an interior, and was used here, no
difficulty arises. (2) The *ekkyklema* would allow, perhaps demand, the
grouping of figures in a tableau. To the unexpected appearance of
such a tableau there could be no more appropriate response than
Sostratos' exclamation ἐκτόπου θ[έας; this would be a 'spectacle' in
the proper sense of the word. (3) If Gorgias transports Knemon outside
his house, it is odd that he should do so merely to ask him if he wants
anything. The question invites the reply that he wants to be taken
indoors. But if we have a tableau representing an indoor scene, it is
the most natural question to ask a man who has been put to bed after
an accident.

It may be objected that if Knemon on the *ekkyklema* is to be thought
of as indoors, he cannot converse (702, 753) with Sostratos, who is
outside the house. This is logic, but not the logic of the theatre. To
quote Arnott (p. 87, apropos of Eur. *HF* 1029, 1069, 1099): 'Obviously
the *ekkyklema* shows what has been done inside the house; but, once
rolled out, it loses all sense of place and serves merely as a focal point
for the ensuing action.' Pickard-Cambridge's case against the *ekkyklema* leans heavily on the supposed impossibility that what was
'indoors' could later be 'outdoors'.

The fact that Knemon's appearance is heralded by one of the
phrases which announce the normal entrance of an actor, τὴν θύραν
ψοφοῦσιν, is no objection to the view that the *ekkyklema* was used. At
Ar. *Thesm.* 95, cίγα : : τί δ' ἐcτίν; : : Ἀγάθων ἐξέρχεται similarly suggests a normal entrance; and at Eur. *HF* 1029, ἴδεcθε διάνδιχα κλῆθρα
κλίνεται ὑψιπύλων δόμων does not prepare the hearer for anything
unusual. Indeed the effect of the tableau will be the greater if it

involves a surprise, if the door opens to allow the passage of the *ekkyklema* instead of the expected actor.

Little reliance can be placed on Pollux, but when he says (iv. 128) that the *ekkyklema* 'must be assumed to stand by each door, as it were by each house' (χρὴ τοῦτο νοεῖcθαι καθ' ἑκάcτην θύραν οἱονεὶ καθ' ἑκάcτην οἰκίαν [= Scholiast on Clem. Alex. *Strom.* vii. 76]), he *may* preserve a tradition that it was used in New Comedy, of which it is characteristic that more than one house was represented in the setting. But ancient scholars may have supposed, perhaps rightly, that Old Comedy was sometimes staged in the same way and employed more than a single door.

692 τεθάρρηκ': Barrett quoted the dialogue between Theseus and the dying Hippolytos, Eur. *Hipp.* 1456, (Θη.) μὴ νῦν προδῷc με, τέκνον, ἀλλὰ καρτέρει. ('Ιππ.) κεκαρτέρηται τἀμά. ὄλωλα γάρ, πάτερ. But whereas κεκαρτέρηται τἀμά is a striking phrase, meaning 'I have endured all that I shall endure', τεθάρρηκα is common in the sense 'I am of good heart' and no member of the audience (not being an editor of the *Hippolytus*) could understand it to mean 'my days of confidence are over'. J. C. Kamerbeek, *Mnem.* 4th ser. xix (1966) 421, suggests τεθάρρητ', which avoids this criticism and is closer to the Euripidean parallel. But it may be doubted whether this unique passive suits Knemon's plain style of speech. Although the passage of Euripides may have been at the back of Menander's mind, he has made something quite different of it here. Knemon is of good cheer, not because he is confident of recovery, but because he is not in future going to be a nuisance. This has an unexpected air of altruism, but as the scene proceeds it emerges that what he intends (if he does not remove himself by dying) is to retire from active life that might bring him into contact with his neighbour, and to get his daughter off his hands. The isolation that he has always sought will in fact be even more complete.

695 παραπόλωλαc: The compound sometimes carries a connotation of unnecessary or regrettable death. **ἀκαρής,** see *Perik.* 356 n. As a historical curiosity and a warning against the dangers of inadequate and unreliable information it may be noted that Meineke made a 'Eupolidean' out of the quotation of this line in *Et. Magn.* thus: ⟨- ᴜ -⟩ ὁρᾷc, ἀκαρής παραπόλωλαc ἀρτίωc. **καταζῆν,** 'live out your life': the verb often connotes absence of trouble or danger.

697 χαλεπῶc μὲν ἔχω: Cf. Plato *Symp.* 176 a, πάνυ χαλεπῶc ἔχω ὑπὸ τοῦ χθὲc πότου, *Theaet.* 142 b, χαλεπῶc μὲν γὰρ ἔχει καὶ ὑπὸ τραυμάτων. '*Although* I am in a poor way, fetch your mother', may seem strange. But it is characteristic that Knemon does not think of getting Myrrhine

(709) as a nurse; she is wanted as a witness to the family business, which he intends to transact at once, poorly though he feels.

698 ff.: Allocation of speeches is difficult. B has no dicola from χαλεπῶc to λαβοῦca, but a paragraphus below 698. The alternatives are these. (*a*) The paragraphus is mistaken. In this case there is no need to substitute ὡc ἔνι τάχιcτα (Maas, Zuntz) for ὡc ἔνι μάλιcτα, a phrase common in Hellenistic and later Greek in a great variety of contexts; here it would mean something like 'urgently'. One may suspect that ὡc ἔνι μάλιcτα was in the original of Ter. *Ad.* 699 ff., 'uxorem accersas: abi . . . iam quantum potest.' (*b*) The paragraphus is right, and two dicola have been omitted, the first after μητέρα—Lloyd-Jones claims that it can be seen there, but I am unconvinced—and the second either after μάλιcτα or after ἔοικε. If the second lost dicolon came after ἔοικε, Gorgias must speak τὰ κακά . . . ὡc ἔοικε after crossing the stage to his own house; the words cannot be meant for Knemon's ears. The sentence is, however, more appropriate to Knemon, since he alone yet knows what lessons he has learned, and will repeat them in 713–16. From Gorgias the words could only be a surprisingly sweeping generalization from a single incident, unless he believes that, taught by his accident, Knemon is sending for his wife to look after him in future. I prefer, therefore, the alternative that, if a dicolon is lost, it is lost after μάλιcτα. But I consider it more likely that Gorgias does not speak at all. He often fails to respond in words (363, 612 ff., 873) and it is not necessary that a person dispatched on an errand should say that he is going (e.g. *Perik.* 755, *Sik.* 395); on the other hand ὡc ἔνι μάλιcτα was frequently tagged on to the end of sentences.

700 θυγάτριον: The diminutive is a sign of affection, perhaps unusual; she is θύγατερ at 740.

701 μακάριε ἄνθρωπε: Sostratos comically felicitates Knemon on receiving this attention at the hands of the girl with whom he has fallen in love. Cf. Ter. *HT* 380, 'eo. quid istic? :: manebit :: hominem felicem!' Whether Sostratos intended his exclamation to be heard or not, it calls Knemon's attention to his presence, and it is highly probable that the old man responds with his wonted rudeness. Sostratos' prospects of becoming his son-in-law look no brighter than before. For μακάριε | ἄνθρωπε cf. *Sam.* 285–6, ἄθλιε | ἄνθρωπε.

703–10: In the gap (see 650 n.), Gorgias returns with his mother, who must be the Μυρ]ρίνη of 709; this name always belongs in comedy to an older married woman (*Heros, Perik., Georgos,* cf. Plaut. *Casina,* Ter. *Hecyra*). There is no space for Sostratos to have given any satisfactory reply to Knemon's question. The entry of Myrrhine will probably

have coincided with the change from iambics to trochaic tetrameters;
Gorgias may have spoken, Myrrhine certainly did not: she is a
κωφὸν πρόςωπον. Absurd though this may seem to anyone accustomed
to the naturalism of the modern stage, it is dramatically defensible.
We have no interest in Myrrhine, of whose character we know nothing;
it cannot matter what she says. What does matter is what Knemon
will find to say to her after their long separation, and of that a gap
in the text cheats us.

By a hasty generalization from *Perik.* and *Samia* it used to be said
that trochaic tetrameters were appropriate to lively and farcical
scenes; it now appears that they were not confined to such. Knemon's
apologia pro uita sua and the girl's betrothal are the most serious scenes
of the play. The metre is also found in frags. 208, 209 (from Θυρωρός),
which give 8½ lines of a misanthropic speech against relatives; they
may have formed part of a manifesto like Knemon's.

S. Luria, *Romanitas* iv (1962), 171, proposes to insert here frag. 647,
ἡδύ γ' ἀποθνήςκειν ὅτῳ ζῆν μὴ πάρεςθ' ὡς βούλεται. Handley makes the
same suggestion, quoting Libanios xxvi. 30, εἰ οὖν δεῖ με λυπούμενον
ζῆν, μὴ ζῆν μοι βέλτιον. Kraus suggested that Julian, *Misopogon* 342 a,
κατὰ τὸν τοῦ Μενάνδρου Δύςκολον αὐτὸς ἐμαυτῷ πόνους προςετίθην,
might refer to one of these lost lines.

711: Kraus's εὐκτόν, although attractive in meaning, will not fit the
traces. δίκαιον is very likely; and a possible sense would be 'I have not
given up the way of life I have chosen—it might not have been right
for me to do so—and none of you could make me change my mind.'

712 cυγχωρήςετε: 'you are going to let me have my way.'

713: ὅτι γε, adopted by some editors, is less likely than ὅςτις, as being
metrically unusual; there is no other example of a tribrach in this
place in *Dyskolos*; elsewhere in Menander only *Sam.* 550, 713, *Perik.*
292.   τῶν ἁπάντων: Partitive genitive; the effect is '*alone* of all
men'.

714: αὐτάρκεια was a recognized Greek ideal: ἡ δὲ αὐτάρκεια καὶ τέλος
καὶ βέλτιςτον, Arist. *Pol.* 1253ᵃ1, for whom it is one recommendation
of the 'intellectual life' that it is the one in which a man is most self-
sufficient. But Aristotle maintains that man is essentially a social
animal, and that a being so self-sufficient as to have no need of
society would be either a god or a beast (ibid. ᵃ28). It is only a whole
society that can be self-sufficient (*EN* 1097ᵇ8). This lesson Knemon
appears to have learnt from his accident: there must be mutual help.
He goes on to argue that what had prevented him from realizing this
before was his belief that men's selfishness made mutual benevolence

impossible: in this, too, he had been wrong, as is shown by Gorgias' disinterested help.

715 ἄϲκοπον: B has αϲκαπτον, by error for ἄϲκεπτον, cf. the contrary error ϲκέπτει for ϲκάπτει (207). ἄϲκεπτον easily arises from ἄϲκοπον, since it is the more familiar form and ο/ε, π/πτ (142, 466, 699) are sometimes confused; one need not suppose it to have been an intrusive gloss. ἄϲκοποϲ in the passive sense, 'invisible, unintelligible, incomprehensible', is almost entirely confined to tragedy, but Theophrastos frag. 73, ἄϲκοποϲ ἡ τύχη, is a good contemporary prose parallel to its use here to mean 'unforeseeable'. Treu *apud* Handley cites Ps.-Phokylides 117, ἄϲκοπόϲ ἐϲτι βροτῶν θάνατοϲ, τὸ δὲ μέλλον ἄδηλον. ὀξεῖαν, 'swift', see LSJ s.v. IV.

717: The restoration printed seems certain, although some critics have tried to introduce γυναῖκα, perhaps moved by the apparent tautology of εἶναι and παρεῖναι. But Philemon frag. 118 K, ὡϲ ὄντα τοῦτον καὶ παρόντ᾽ ἀεὶ ϲέβου, provides a parallel.

718 μὰ τὸν Ἥφαιϲτον: It is possible to treat οὕτω . . . ἔχουϲιν or οὕτω . . . ἐγώ as a parenthesis, and so preserve the normal rule that oaths with μά are confined to negative sentences. I have adopted the former punctuation, but with the reservation that it seems a somewhat artificial proceeding. See 151 n.

718–20: Cf. Plut. *de cohibenda ira*, 456 f, μιϲοπονηρίαν τὸ δύϲκολον οὐκ ὀρθῶϲ τίθενται.

718 διεφθάρμην: a likely correction: the sense 'to be perverted in mind' is that familiar in the accusation of Socrates, διαφθείρει τοὺϲ νέουϲ. More usually a word is added to indicate the field of perversion, e.g. Aesch. *Ag.* 932, γνώμην μὲν ἴϲθι μὴ διαφθεροῦντ᾽ ἐμέ, Eur. *Hel.* 1192, λύπῃ ϲὰϲ διέφθαρϲαι φρέναϲ, etc. Without such a word Plut. *Agis* 18, διεφθαρμένοϲ ἦν ὑπὸ κενῆϲ δόξηϲ ὁ Κλεόμβροτοϲ. The pluperfect indicates a state in past time.

719: This line can be variously interpreted according to its punctuation. If B's text is kept, it may be translated 'seeing all their ways of life, how they have their calculations set on gain' *or* 'seeing all their ways of life, their calculations, how they are disposed to gain'. If the asyndeton is removed by the easy addition of θ᾽ (of which the diastole may survive in B) between two similar letters, c and o, then there are the alternatives 'seeing how they have set all their ways of life and calculations on gain', *or* 'seeing their ways of life and calculations, how they are disposed to gain'. Fortunately the choice does not seriously affect the sense.

721–2 τοῦτο δὴ ἐμποδών: I.e. prevented him from looking earlier for someone to be his aid.

723 εὐγενεστάτου: Cf. 281 n., but Gorgias has shown more than bravery in his willingness to disregard the past; he has shown true nobility of character.

724: A syllable is lacking in the second half of the line. If in the first half οὐκ ἐῶντ⟨ά τ'⟩ is right, that syllable might be καί (Goold), since οὐκ ἐῶντα would be treated, as is shown by the position of τε, as a single word, the equivalent of κωλύοντα.

725 εἰς οὐδὲν μέρος means no more than εἰς οὐδέν, cf. *Perik.* 297 n.

726 ἡδέως: Cf. 10 n.

727: This is a puzzling passage, about which the only thing that is clear is that ἄλλως should be ἄλλος. No further change is necessary on any of three assumptions; (a) a line has been lost, so that the original sense was '⟨He did not say⟩ what anyone else would have said'; (b) there is an aposiopesis in 729 after νῦν, so that the meaning is 'What anyone else would have said, and with justification, namely "You won't let me approach you . . . nor will I help now"—(this he did not say).' In favour of (b) is the question τί δ' ἐστί; which could easily interrupt a sentence. The ellipse of εἶπεν with ὅπερ ἂν ἄλλος is not impossible, K–G i. 244. (c) A. M. Dale (quoted by Handley), accepting the same ellipse of εἶπεν, supposes that ὅπερ means 'whereas', a sense found in Apollonios Dyskolos; Schneider, *Gramm. Gr.* 1. ii. 126–7 collects instances. The acc. of respect, 'with regard to which', thus develops an adversative meaning. Better known is the causal meaning of ὅ, e.g. Eur. *Phoen.* 155, 263, LSJ s.v. ὅς A. b. IV. 2, Ar. *Eccl.* 338 (perhaps paratragic). This is a possible explanation, but since this use of ὅ is not found in New Comedy, hardly to be accepted without reservations. No correction that involves a further change seems to me both to make a better text and to have palaeographic likelihood, unless it be Eitrem's ἕτερ' ἂν ἄλλος, 'anyone else would have acted differently'.

728: ἡμῖν: 'My mother and me'.

729 τί δ' ἐστί; 'What's the matter?'; it must be supposed that Gorgias makes to protest against this view that he is the only man able to put proper humanity above past slights, and so causes Knemon to break off from his commentary on the past, and having done so, go on to his plans for the future. On the address μειράκιον see 319 n.

ἐάν τ': τε is required to correspond to τε in 731; in B it has been misplaced after μειράκιον and altered to δ'.

730 ἴcωc: 'Probably', cf. 239 n. B so corrects an original οιον. Kassel's ἴcθ' ὡc is no more likely. Jacques prefers to follow Diano in regarding the correction as conjectural, and substituting his own conjecture οἴωc. The meaning will then be 'and I imagine I shall die miserably, seeing what a state I am in now'.

731 ff.: U. E. Paoli, *Mus. Helvet.* xviii (1961), 53, writes well on the legal background to this scene. It was not unusual for a man without a male heir of his body to provide for the inheritance of his property by adopting a son from among his relations or connections. This adoption and the testamentary disposition were executed simultaneously. For another case where the adopted son took over the property while the adopting father was still alive, as Gorgias does here, see Isaios vii. 15; the speaker says that his adoptive father πάντα τὰ αὑτοῦ διοικεῖν παρέδωκεν, ὡc αὐτὸc μὲν οὐδὲν ἂν ἔτι πρᾶξαι τούτων δυνηθείc. **ἅ τ' ἔχων:** The connection by τε of the imperative νόμιcον to the indicative ποοῦμαι is noteworthy. Perhaps 'think them all yours' can be regarded as an anacoluthic substitute for 'I give you them all.' Handley writes ἅ τ' ἔχων . . . ἄνδρα ⟨τ'⟩, with a harsh or even improbable result. Lloyd-Jones accepts Page's ἅ γ' ἔχων, in which the force of γε is hard to see.

732 παρεγγυῶ: 'I entrust her to your care', cf. Hdt. iii. 8, τοῖcι φίλοιcι παρεγγυᾶ τὸν ξεῖνον, *Aspis* 214. There is no reason to suppose with Paoli that the word specifically confers on Gorgias the right of ἐγγύηcιc, promising in marriage; that right is rather given in the succeeding lines.

733: Either δ' αὐτῇ or τ' αὐτῇ is a possible correction. For οὗτοc with the same reference as an immediately preceding ὅδε cf. Eur. *Medea* 1046 and Page's note there. **εἰ γὰρ κτλ.:** 'even if I should get quite well, I shall never be able to find her a husband myself.' More elaborate emendations result in a less satisfactory sense. Knemon represents his recovery as a remote possibility, and flatly denies his ability to secure a son-in-law.

736 cὺν τοῖc θεοῖc, 'by the grace of God', goes with νοῦν ἔχειc, cf. *Perinthia* frag. 9 (7 Koe.), οὐδ' αὐτόc εἰμι cὺν θεοῖc ὑπόξυλοc; to take it with πρᾶττε, νοῦν ἔχειc being parenthetical, is no improvement. τἆλλα is the most likely correction of B's τὰ δ' ἄλλα; intrusive δέ is a common error, made the more likely here by the preceding μέν 'solitarium'. If this is adopted, Knemon tells Gorgias to manage everything in his own way, except that he is to let his new father live a solitary life. Van Groningen's τὰ δ' ἐμά is a possible alternative, meaning that Gorgias is to take on what have been Knemon's responsibilities.

737 κηδεμών . . . εἰκότως: I prefer to punctuate after rather than before εἰκότως, a word often found at the end of sentences. Whoever might be adopted by Knemon would become the girl's guardian— Gorgias is *suitably* her guardian, since she is his sister. τοῦ κτήματος depends on θῆμιςν, cf. 236 n. *Ed. pr.* adds τε after κηδεμών, but asyndeton is quite intelligible here. In this section of his speech Knemon utters short and jerky phrases, perhaps acting up to his imagined critical condition. In the first and third sections he manages quite involved sentences. Menander was a man of the theatre and knew how to provide variety in the long monologue.

738 ἐπιδίδωμι is the *vox propria* for the giving of a dowry, see LSJ. Half the estate as dowry seems a large proportion, but it is possible that when the heir was an adoptive son it was thought right that a natural daughter should have a greater share than otherwise. Paoli appeals to Isaios, iii. 49–51: Eudios, an adoptive son, endowed the natural daughter with one-sixth of the estate, μηδὲ τὸ δίκαιον (Paoli: δέκατον MSS.) μέρος ἐπιδούς. Eudios is accused of injustice, not of illegality; there will not have been any law, as Paoli suggests, providing for a dowry of half the estate. Handley rightly points out that διαμετρήςας implies surveying the land and marking off half of it with boundary stones.   ⟨cύ⟩: Palaeographically this is the easiest supplement. Menander frequently adds cύ to 2nd person imperatives.

⟨θ⟩ἥμιcυ: The article is frequently, but not invariably (e.g. Plato, *Laws* 806 c, Xen. *Anab.* i. 9. 26), added to ἥμιcυ used as a noun; similarly in English we say both 'the half' and 'a half'. Maas's correction of B is easy and is adopted in OCT, cf. Ar. *Lys.* 116, ἐμαυτῆς παρατεμοῦςα θἥμιcυ.

739 διοίκει: 'look after'; a personal object is unusual with this verb, but cf. Demosthenes, xxiv. 202, ἀλλὰ νὴ Δία τὴν ἀδελφὴν καλῶς διῴκηκεν, Epicurus frag. 71 Arrighetti 177 Usener, cὺ οὖν, ἄν τι γένηται, τὰ Μητροδώρου παιδία διοίκηςον, Isaios vii. 6.

740: Having completed his dispositions, Knemon naturally wishes to rest; but his change of position marks the beginning of the third part of his long speech.   τῶν ἀναγκαίων: Cf. [Isokr.] i. 41, δύο ποιοῦ καιροὺς τοῦ λέγειν, ἢ περὶ ὧν οἶςθα ςαφῶς ἢ περὶ ὧν ἀναγκαῖον εἰπεῖν· ἐν τούτοις γὰρ μόνοις ὁ λόγος τῆς ςιωπῆς κρεῖττον. B's δ' after τῶν is unwanted, cf. 678 n.

743: The sense must be 'if all men were like me', yet there is hardly space for εἰ τοιοῦτ]οι; perhaps B had ειτουτοι, cf. 758 n. Diano's εἴ γ' ὅμοι]οι would mean 'if all men were alike'. For the sentiment cf. Baton frag. 3K, εἰ τοῦτον ἔζων πάντες ὃν ἐγὼ ζῶ βίον, οὔτ' ἄτοπος ἦν ἂν οὔτε μοιχὸc οὐδὲ εἷc, Plaut. *Aul.* 478, 'si idem faciant ceteri . . . et multo fiat ciuitas concordior'; for the theme of social justice following on a *impossibile* cf. Alexis frag. 212 K, εἴ τιc ἀφέλοι τοῦτ' ἀφ' ἡμῶν τὸ μέροc ἀπὸ τοῦ cώματοc (sc. τὴν γαcτέρα), οὔτ' ἂν ἀδικοῖ γ' (Ahrens for ἀδικοῖτ') οὐδὲν οὐδεὶc οὔθ' ὑβρίζοι τᾶν (Ahrens for ὑβρίζοιτ' ἄν) ἑκών.

746 ἀλλ': Lloyd-Jones, following Roberts, thought the traces incompatible with this and read οὐκ, to the great weakening of the sense. But there is a trace of a letter that cannot be ο or υ; and λλ, if written in ligature (as often, e.g. 663, 764, 772), is as likely as κ, which normally descends below the line, as the broken letter does not. Kassel punctuates after οὕτω, perhaps rightly; *ed. pr.* after ἀρεcτά, which is less vigorous.

Gorgias and his mother and sister are not litigious, warmongers, or criminals, nor is there any ground for supposing them sympathetic to these blots on society. This line must be addressed to the audience, oddly though this may strike the modern reader; see intro. p. 14 on this feature of Greek comedy. It accords with this that βούλομ' εἰπεῖν, with which Knemon's manifesto begins, recalls the phrases with which the chorus of Old Comedy sometimes introduce their recommendations to the people or the judges (*Knights* 565, 595, *Clouds* 115, *Birds* 1076, 1101).

749 cοὶ cυνδοκοῦν: 'With your agreement', cf. Xen. *Hell.* ii. 3. 51 cυνδοκοῦν ἅπαcιν ἡμῖν. A similar accusative absolute is found in δόξαν, ἐξόν, etc.

750 οὗτοc implies impatience: 'Look here! I've said no less and no more than I meant.' Contrast between λέγω and φρονῶ is familiar: Dem. xviii. 282, ὁ μὴ λέγων ὃ φρονεῖ, Deinarchos i. 47, ἕτερα μὲν λέγων, ἕτερα δὲ φρονῶν.

751 γάρ: i.e. 'I must bother you, because . . .', cf. Denniston, *GP* 74. Eur. *Hel.* 446, μηδ' ὤθει βίᾳ:: πείθῃ γὰρ οὐδὲν ὧν λέγω, provides a good parallel for this rather uncommon usage.

752: It is quite uncertain how this line is to be filled. Some suggestions, αἰτῶν ⟨γαμεῖν⟩ τιc (Kraus) or αἰτῶν τιc ⟨οὗτοc⟩ (Handley), cause the line to be divided between the speakers at the half-way point. As this was done in 751, it is perhaps unlikely that the same division was repeated in 752; Menander has a strong liking for variation in such breaks. Nowhere in these trochaic tetrameters is there a change of speaker at the same point in two successive lines. But there are two instances, 917/18 and 930/1, in the iambic tetrameters of the last scene, and eleven in the trochaics of *Samia*, including three where there is a double repetition, 530/1/2, 561/2/3, and 580/1/2.

753 ὁ ποῖος; 'Whom are you talking about?', cf. *Epitr.* 392, *Sik.* 378. I take it as likely that the dicolon after ουτοcι marks a turn by Gorgias from Knemon to Sostratos. It is just possible that it marks a change of speaker, Knemon calling Sostratos forward, and that the dicolon at the end of the line shows that he then turns again to Gorgias. **πρόcελθε:** B has προελθε, which *ed. pr.* erroneously transcribed as προcελθε, and so inadvertently printed the correct reading. προc-έρχομαι, 'come up', is common in Menander and New Comedy, προέρχομαι is used only of coming out of a building. προέρχομαι is of course familiar elsewhere in the sense 'come forward to speak', but I think the prefix is due to the fact that the speaker comes *out* of the crowd or group where he was. The contrary error προcῆλθε for προῆλθε occurs at 96, where see n.

754: μέν 'solitarium': the possible antithesis would perhaps be 'but did he get his sunburn by working in the fields?' For this is substituted 'Is he a farmer?' It is not clear whether B has a dicolon at the end of the line: none is transcribed by *ed. pr.*, but there appear to be two dots, exceptionally high for a dicolon. Further, Handley has pointed out that καὶ μάλ' ὦ πάτερ may not, as has been generally assumed, belong to Gorgias, but to Sostratos, cf. 171. Stratophanes at *Sikyonios* 379 addresses as πάτερ the man he hopes to make his father-in-law. This being so, there are many possibilities for dividing the speeches; the reader may work out the permutations, remembering that 755 may be either a statement by one or other of the young men or a question from Knemon.

755 τὴν ἡμέραν: 'The whole day long'; for the more usual τὴν ἡμέραν ὅλην, cf. Theophrastos, *Char.* xvi. 2, οὕτω τὴν ἡμέραν περιπατῶν. Austin points out that Aristophanes has τὴν νύκτα at *Thesm.* 494, elsewhere always ὅλην τὴν νύκτα.

756 is the top surviving line of a page. Lloyd-Jones follows Barrett in thinking that the tail of a letter in a higher line, now otherwise lost, cuts into the τ. This is very doubtful.

758 εἰcκυκλεῖτ': Cf. Ar. *Thesm.* 265, εἴcω τιc ὡc τάχιcτά μ' εἰcκυκλεῖ τιc. ἐγκυ-κλεῖτ', where Agathon is, I believe, on the *ekkyklema*. The space in B is barely adequate for εικcκυ]κλειτ, but a letter may have been omitted. ἐγκυ-κλεῖτ' (Mette) and ἀλλὰ κλεῖτ' (Diano) are highly improbable.

(v) 759–775: *Sostratos and Gorgias*

758–64: the discovery of a missing scrap of B (*Pap. Bodmer* xxvi. 48) has narrowed the field for conjecture here, but there is still some un-certainty. First let us consider the allocation of speeches. οὐδὲν ὁ πατὴρ ἀντερεῖ must belong to Sostratos, since Knemon's consent has already been made very clear; moreover the paragraphus below 761 proves that there was a change of speaker in the line, the last part of which belongs to Gorgias. *Ed. pr.* (Austin–Kasser) give the preceding clause (760) also to Sostratos, writing ἐπανε[νεγκ]ε ταυτᾳ [γ] ὡϲ τ[α]χ[ιϲτ εμοι]. They offer no translation of this, which would appear to mean 'Refer *these* matters to me as soon as possible', a phrase I find difficult to understand in the context. If it is right, Gorgias must have said previously: 'It remains to promise my sister in marriage.' Beyond that it is quite uncertain who says ἐπιμελοῦ τούτου, Gorgias to Myrrhine or Sostratos to the girl, 'Take care of him', or even Knemon to Gorgias, 'See to it.' The dicolon after τούτου probably indicates a change of speaker, but since the beginning of the line is lost one cannot be sure that there was a paragraphus; if there was none, the dicolon will indicate a change of person addressed.

As an alternative Sostratos may say to Gorgias 'It remains for you to promise your sister in marriage' and Gorgias reply 'Refer these affairs, Sostratos, to those to whom you should', e.g. ἐπανέ[νεγκ]ε ταῦτα, [C]ώϲτ[ραθ', οἷϲ ϲε δεῖ. This involves disregarding a low spot of ink, which *ed. pr.* interpret as the foot of χ. For the sense, *Aspis* 178 may be compared. There Smikrines complains that his brother has not consulted him (οὐκ ἐπανεγκών), the eldest of the family, about the marriage of their niece.

In 762 the gods are called on as witnesses in the absence of any friends or relations of either party. In 763 difficulty arises from the missing initial syllable and the dubious word which Kasser and Austin would read as πλ[η]θη; of the λ there is left only part of an unusually vertical left-hand stroke.

It is commonly supposed that 763 contained a promise to pay a 'just' dowry, since elsewhere after the formal words of betrothal the amount of the dowry is stated, 843 below, *Perik.* 1015, *Mis.* 446, *P. Oxy.* 2533. C. Préaux, *Chron. d'Égypte* 1960, 228, suggests that Gorgias substitutes a scrupulous ὅϲα δίκαιόν ἐϲτι because he does not know the exact value of the estate, of which he has been told that half must be given as the dowry. This is unconvincing, since at 845 he specifies the sum as 1 talent, without having had in the meantime any opportunity to make a valuation. Lines 764 ff. do not suggest that 763 dealt with a 'just' dowry. It would be clumsy of Gorgias to tell Sostratos that he had secured the proper dowry because he had shown himself an honest and determined man. It was the girl, not the dowry, that Sostratos had taken up the mattock to win. A more likely sentiment is that in winning the girl Sostratos is getting something he has deserved (ἐνεγκεῖν, cf. LSJ s.v. φέρω VI. 3). Can it be that B wrote ἐcτιπιcθη, but that the true text is ⟨τήνδ'⟩ ἐνεγκεῖν ⟨c'⟩ ὡc δίκαιόν ἐcτ' ἐπείcθην? ἐγγυῶ: Betrothal (ἐγγύηcιc) could be carried out by a father, an uncle, or a brother by the same father (ὁμοπάτωρ); Gorgias, although only a uterine brother in fact, is fictionally made ὁμοπάτωρ by his adoption. So long as the father was available, an uncle or brother would not normally perform the act of betrothal. Plaut. *Trinummus* 573 affords an example of a brother's doing it in the father's absence. Hence Knemon must here delegate his rights to Gorgias (732–3) as much as he transfers his property to him (731–2).

764 οὐ πεπλαcμένῳ γὰρ ἤθει: Cf. *Pap. Ant.* 15. 16–17 αὐτῆc ἐλευθέρῳ γὰρ ἤθει καὶ βίῳ δεθεὶc ἀπλάcτῳ. Arnott, *Hermes* xcvi (1968), 384, calls attention to Aristainetos, *ep.* 1. 2, where ἦθοc πεπλαcμένον is used, doubtless culled from this play.

767 τούτῳ τῷ μέρει is no more than τούτῳ, cf. 725 n., *Epitr.* 234 n. ἀνήρ, 'a true man', LSJ s.v. IV. Gorgias' sententious remark comes out in a typically involved and pompous formulation. ἐν δὲ τούτῳ τῷ μέρει is anticipatory of the ὅcτιc clause. Handley well compares Thuc. vi. 14, τὸ καλῶc ἄρξαι τοῦτ' εἶναι, ὃc ἂν τὴν πατρίδα ὠφελήcῃ etc. The postponement of ὅcτιc is unusual, but cf. frag. 725, κακῶc ἀκούων ὅcτιc οὐκ ὀργίζεται. The strange order at the end of the sentence brings together εὐπορῶν and πένητι, with the former in an emphatic position at the beginning of the line.

769: Page's μεταβολήν is more logical than μεταβολάc of *ed. pr.*, since one particular change, from riches to poverty, is in view. But logic is not always supreme; see Philemon frag. 213 K, τύχηc δὲ μεταβολὰc οὐκ ἀγνοεῖc | ὅτι τὸν εὔπορον τίθηcι πτωχόν εἰc τὴν αὔριον. Perhaps the idea is that a variety of misfortunes can bring this reversal of condition. The plural τύχηc μεταβολαί occurs elsewhere—Hipparchos frag. 2 K, Menander frag. 348, 630—and is therefore slightly more probable than the sing. in this passage. It must be confessed that τυχ[is an uncertain reading. Blake's π[αθών is possible, but does not account, as τύχηc does, for the intrusive article τηc. ἐγκρατῶc, 'with self-control', i.e. not giving way to despair, cf. frag. 634, οὐκ ἐὰν | ἀναcπάcαc τιc τὰc ὀφρῦc "οἴμοι" λαλῇ | ἀλλ' ὃc τά ⟨γ'⟩ αὑτοῦ πράγματ' ἐγκρατῶc φέρει.

771: Restoration at the end is uncertain. I adopt a supplement that is merely otiose, rather than one that adds a point we do not know Menander to have made.

773 δ': B has τ'; failure to aspirate when the vowel is elided is paralleled at 254, 360, 375. *Ed. pr.* changes to the more obvious δ' (the opposite error occurs at 729). τε is, however, defensible if Sostratos offers two reasons for not enlarging on his good intentions, modesty and the opportune arrival of his father.

If anyone is inclined to ask why Gorgias knows Kallippides by sight but not Sostratos, the latter is ἀστικὸς τῇ διατριβῇ (41), while the old man, if such a good farmer, must often visit his farm.   εἰς καλόν: Cf. *Sam.* 280, Plat. *Symp.* 174 e, εἰς καλὸν ἥκεις.

774: We appear to have in νὴ Δία a dactyl, which the trochaic tetrameter does not normally admit. But in Ar. *Knights* 319, νὴ Δία κἀμέ constitutes a trochaic metron, and in Menander frag. 303, νὴ Δία καὶ γενήςομαι gives a broken anapaest in iambics. The common phrase νὴ τὸν Δία τὸν μέγιστον (or cωτῆρα) may also be relevant, but not necessarily so, since it may have constituted a single mouthful. If we are to believe ancient grammarians, these metrical irregularities could be removed by substituting an alternative dissyllabic form of the oath, νὴ Δί; see Photios s.v., νὴ Δὶ καὶ νὴ Δία, ἑκατέρως, cf. Herodian ii. 217. 16, 903. 30 Leutsch. There are, however, a few other dactyls in trochaic tetrameters, of which some but not all involve the syllable -δι-, e.g. *Perik.* 340, πορνίδιον, *Sam.* 731, καὶ ϲτεφάνους, Ar. *Ach.* 318, τὴν κεφαλήν, *Eccl.* 1156, ἡδέως διὰ τόν, which cannot be plausibly removed (see A. M. Dale, *Lustrum* ii. 40; and on the other side G. P. Goold, *Phoenix* xiii (1959), 154). Trisyllabic νὴ Δία cannot therefore be excluded. The case for a dissyllabic νὴ Δία (whether νὴ Δί or νὴ Δία) is strongly argued by J. Werres. *Die Beteuerungsformeln in der attischen Komödie*, 7–8: he points out that in Aristophanes' iambic trimeters trisyllabic νὴ Δία would give a broken anapaest in 8 places out of 13, whereas elided νὴ Δί', occurring 87 times, does so only once (*Thesm.* 609).

The division of the anapaest (πά)νυ | μὲν οὖν after the first syllable is paralleled by *Perik.* 337 (τυ)χὸν | ἴcως, and *Sam.* 605 (δι)ὰ | κενῆς, all phrases where the words closely cohere.

(vi) 775–763: *Sostratos, Gorgias, Kallippides* (exit 780)

775: It is an insoluble question whether Gorgias knows Kallippides as a fair-dealing man, or says that he deserves to be rich since he is a good farmer. But in any case the economy may be noted by which a touch is added to Gorgias' character—his admiration for good farming—and Kallippides is made a person in his own right, not just Sostratos' father.   ἀπολέλειμμ': Lit. 'I am left out', i.e., 'I have missed the lunch'; cf. [Dem.] xxxiv. 38, τριῶν καιρῶν . . . οὐδενός . . . ἀπολελείμμεθα, 'we have missed none of the three opportunities',

DYSKOLOS 253

Lucian, *Dial. Mar.* 15. 1, ἡδίστου θεάματος ἀπελείφθης. ἴcωc: The English equivalent is 'I'm sure', cf. 239.

776: *Ed. pr.* restored this line by writing καταβεβρωκότες γὰρ ἤδη, which may be right. But the omission of the first syllable of 775 suggests the possibility that the beginning of both lines was illegible at some stage in the transmission. Gallavotti's lively version, which suits this theory, has been adopted in OCT: 'having eaten up the sheep for certain'. δή, attached to verbs, usually lends an emotional tone, Denniston, *GP* 214, K–G ii. 126.

777 εἰς ἀγρόν: This must mean 'to my farm'. The absence of the article is noteworthy. The phrases εἰς ἀγρόν, ἐξ ἀγροῦ, ἐν ἀγρῷ are usually translated 'to, from, in the country', but they normally imply 'to, from, at the farm'. Kallippides' words show that he has not come *direct* from his farm; whether he has come from it at all is in no way indicated.

Although the name γοργι´ in the margin might apply either to 777 or to 778, the former line is nearer and so more likely to be meant. Foss, however, suggests that Πόσειδον κτλ. better suits Sostratos. Opinions on this may differ, although it may be noticed that Gorgias elsewhere uses no oaths but an occasional νὴ Δία or μὰ Δία.

Kallippides' hunger, quite understandable when he is so late for lunch, makes a mildly comic scene, so that the act ends on a note of relaxation from the seriousness which pervades the greater part of it. It also serves the dramatic purpose of bringing about a pause in the action, to be filled by the last choral interlude.

ὀξυπείνως: The adjective, 'ravenous', first occurs in Antiphanes and Eubulos, writers of Middle Comedy.

778: This suggested to Aelian, *ep. rust.* xv, the phrase ἐμπιών . . . ἔςῃ τι καὶ πραότερος.

779 τί τοῦτο; Kallippides is surprised to find Sostratos outside the cave, and infers that the lunch is finished.

781: The missing syllable can be supplied in various ways. αὐτῷ has been suspected since, if it means 'him', τῷ πατρί in the same clause is superfluous; on the other hand 'your father himself' hardly fits the context. Either Fraenkel's οὕτω or Page's αὐτός is attractive. But it is possible to take τῷ πατρὶ κατὰ μόνας as part of the if-clause, understanding the ellipse of an infinitive of a verb of saying.

782 κατὰ μόνας: 'By yourself'. Thuc. i. 32, κατὰ μόνας ἀπεωσάμεθα Κορινθίους. At the end B has εξερχει (or just possibly εξερχετ[αι]) a strange corruption of ἐξέρχομαι, perhaps due to assimilation to the 2nd person of περιμενεῖς. Van Groningen ingeniously suggested that the division of speeches is wrong, and that we should read (*Γο.*) . . . ἔνδον περιμένει c', οὐ γάρ; (*Cω.*) οὐκ ἐξέρχεται | ἔνδοθεν. I do not find this supposedly sarcastic reference to Kallippides' appetite convincing, and it does not fit the succeeding sentence. But if Gorgias promises to stay at home, Sostratos can logically answer: '*Then* I shall call you over in a short while.'

783 τοίνυν is not often placed later than second word, unless the preceding words are closely associated (Denniston, *GP* 579); *Perik.* 270 provides another exception to the rule. Lloyd-Jones and Handley rightly make Gorgias enter Knemon's house, where the rest of the family is; ἔνδον (782), 'at home', will, in the absence of any specific indication to the contrary, refer to a man's own house, but now that Gorgias is an adopted son, Knemon's house is his house—πάντα ϲαυτοῦ νόμιϲον εἶναι.

ACT V

(i) **784–821**: *Sostratos and Kallippides*

784: This is a fine dramatic opening. The audience is momentarily misled into thinking that Kallippides has raised objections to the marriage. His reply undeceives them, but leaves them wondering what has gone wrong, and necessarily bewildered by Sostratos' answer 'I don't consider that you have met my wishes.' Not until 794 do they discover what lies behind the conversation, namely that Kallippides has rejected a suggestion that Gorgias should marry his daughter.

785: Handley punctuates τί δὲ οὐ ϲυγκεχώρηκα; This has attractions as a complete rejection of the charge that Kallippides has not done all that Sostratos would wish. But could Kallippides utter the words? He *knows* perfectly well that he has *not* agreed to the suggestion made about Gorgias' marriage. τί δέ; οὐ ϲυγκεχώρηκα; on the other hand is a possible evasive reply: 'What? Haven't I agreed?' sc. to your marriage. To place the question-mark not after ϲυγκεχώρηκα, but after λαμβάνειν (*ed. pr.*), gives a less lively speech.

788: Perhaps paraphrased by Aristainetos ii. 9, γινώϲκων ὡϲ ἀϲφαλέϲτερον καθίϲταται γάμοϲ ἐκ πόθου τινὸϲ τὴν πρόφαϲιν εὐτυχήϲαϲ (frag. com. adesp. 180 K). The sentiment would be more striking to a fourth-century audience than it is today.

It is a puzzle why in B τουτο is added above the line. I adopt the view that it is an interpolation (cf. εὐθύϲ in *Sam.* 225), whether first made here or in some other MS. If, however, τοῦτο is correct, there are various ways of restoring metre, e.g. (1) νὴ τοὺς ἔγωγε τοῦτο γινώςκων ἔφην (Gallavotti, cf. frag. 311, οὐ μὰ τήν and Ar. *Frogs* 1374, μὰ τόν, with ellipse of the name of the divinity), (2) νὴ τοὺς θεοὺς ἔγωγε τοῦτο γνοὺς ὅτι (Handley), (3) νὴ τοὺς θεοὺς ἔγωγε τοῦτ᾽ ἔγνων ἀεί (Page). None of these is any more likely than the text printed in OCT, which supposes that there is here another instance of the common trimeter-ending γινώςκων (-ειν, -εις) ὅτι.

789 οὕτως: In support of his conjecture (for ουτος) Kassel quotes Plato, *Phaed.* 67 a, οὕτως, ὡς ἔοικεν, ἐγγυτάτω ἐςόμεθα τοῦ εἰδέναι, ἐὰν ὅτι μάλιςτα μηδὲν ὁμιλῶμεν τῷ ςώματι.

790: τοῦτο . . . πονεῖν of B is impossible; one would require e.g. πάντα . . . πονεῖν. τοῦτο ποιεῖν = γαμεῖν.

793 τοῦτο: The pronoun is explained by οὐκ ἀντιδώςειν τὴν ἐμήν, but it has the common 'reference backwards', standing for what Kallippides is supposed to have been saying before his entrance on the stage. *Ed. pr.*'s τούτῳ is possibly right, but not a necessary change, for it is easy to understand the indirect object.

794 αἰςχρὸν λέγεις is given by B to Kallippides. He can hardly mean 'your suggestion is a shameful one'. Perhaps the words are a question: 'Do you call my refusal something to be ashamed of?' Alternatively, if the dicolon is mistaken, Sostratos could mean 'That's a shameful thing to say!'

795 πτωχούς is an emotional exaggeration, see 285 n.

797 ἀβεβαίου πράγματος: Cf. Alexis frag. 281 K, τῶν γὰρ ἀγαθῶν τὸν πλοῦτον ὕςτατον τίθει· | ἀβεβαιότατον γάρ ἐςτιν ὧν κεκτήμεθα. | τὰ δ᾽ ἀλλ᾽ ἐπιεικῶς ('usually') τοῖς ἔχουςι παραμένει. The rhetorical devices used by Sostratos in the speech he starts here are easy to see; they are well set out by J. Blänsdorf, *Archäische Gedankengänge in den Komödien des Plautus*, 288.

798–802: B's text is unsatisfactory at three places. (1) περιμενοῦντα, 'wait for', is unexpected for παραμενοῦντα, 'stay with'; cf. the similar passage of Alexis frag. 281, quoted in the previous note; (2) the singular τούτου strikes oddly into the series ταῦτα . . . πάντα . . . τούτων, and the majority of editors find it impossible, although Handley defends it as a natural inconsequence in an excited speech; (3) μήτε φθονοίης is senseless. Lines 798–812 are quoted by Stobaios as coming from Menander's *Dyskolos*. In general, when he cites a play by name, he appears to follow a book-text, good or bad, without adapting it (W. Görler, Μενάνδρου Γνῶμαι, 107). Here in his MSS. the opening lines run as follows: εἰ μὲν γὰρ οἶσθα ταῦτα παραμενοῦντά cοι | εἰς πάντα τὸν χρόνον φύλαττε μηδενὶ | ἄλλῳ μεταδιδούς, αὐτὸς ὧν δὲ κύριος. | εἰ δὲ μὴ cεαυτοῦ, τῆc τύχηc δὲ πάντ' ἔχειc, | τί ἂν φθονοίηc, κτλ. At first sight this makes sense, and in view of the frequent errors in the papyrus, it is tempting to accept the whole of it, except for the unmetrical εἰ δὲ μή for which Meineke's εἰ μὴ δέ can be substituted. There are, however, objections to this. (1) The corruption of ἄλλῳ to τούτου is inexplicable, whereas ἄλλῳ might be substituted for the dubious τούτου. (2) 'To be in control' (κύριος) of money cannot be contrasted with giving part of it away: control includes the ability to give away, e.g. a bride is given away by her κύριος. (3) εἰ μὴ δέ for εἰ δὲ μή is unexampled; the nearest parallel is Timokles frag. 8 K, where ἵνα μὴ δέ is read by emendation from ἵνα δὲ μή. Besides these objections to Stobaios' text, it is easily explicable as the product of deliberate change. If ει at the beginning of 801 were, very excusably, taken as 'if', parallel to εἰ μέν in 798, ωνδεμηcυκυριοc would yield no sense. To alter the meaningless phrase to αὐτὸc ὧν δὲ κύριος would be of a piece with altering τούτου to ἄλλῳ, and the change of ειμηδε to εἰ δὲ μή might be part of the same man's handiwork.

If we start from B's text and look for something that could be corrupted to τούτου, there is a good candidate in τοῦ coῦ (Kapsomenos, Quincey). μήτε φθονοίηc is more intractable; I have hesitantly adopted the change to μή τι: the construction with the optative (wish) instead of subjunctive (prohibition) is unwelcome. Handley gives two prose examples where the optative 'assumes a jussive force', but in both the element of wishing has a predominant place. Perhaps Sostratos may tactfully substitute a hope for a prohibition, but it is remarkable how few parallels are to be found and how weak they are; see Goodwin, *MT* § 725, K–G i. 229. One may contrast the frequency with which (e.g.) λέγοιc ἄν replaces λέγε. Stobaios' τί ἂν provides unexceptionable Greek, and might be accepted were it not that it leaves μητε unexplained. I suspect that μή τι φθονήcηc is what Menander wrote. The anacoluthon εἰ μέν . . . ὧν δέ is quite in Sostratos' supple style of speech, cf. ἐγὼ μέν . . . λήψομαι . . . πῶc δέ . . . cὺ φῄc; (791–3). The formal responson εἰ μέν . . . εἰ δέ would be more in Gorgias' line.

801: τύχη is here on the way towards personification; Körte spells the word with a capital letter in frag. 116 and Τύχη delivers the prologue in *Aspis*. It is well known that the power of Luck or Chance so fascinated the Hellenistic world that Τύχη became a goddess to be worshipped and propitiated. Theophrastos quoted with approval Chairemon's line, τύχη τὰ θνητῶν πράγματ' οὐκ εὐβουλία, and many passages of New Comedy show how in Menander's time everyone was talking of τύχη, some insisting on its importance, others denying it. On the whole subject see M. P. Nilsson, *Geschichte d. gr. Religion²*,

ii. 207 ff., Wilamowitz, *Glaube d. Hellenen*, ii. 298 ff., Legrand, *Daos*, p. 397.

804: There is little to choose between παρελομένη (Stobaios) and ἀφελομένη (B). But B is often careless, and Stobaios' reading will not here be due to deliberate change: it also deserves preference as the rarer compound. With this reading notice the alliteration—a rhetorical touch that may raise a smile (Fraenkel on Aesch. *Ag.* 268)—unless Handley is right in printing not πάντα but ταῦτα, which he and Gallavotti see in B: very blotted tops of letters are all that remain.

805–6: E. Fraenkel, *Beobachtungen z. Aristophanes*, p. 91, defends the repeated cε, appealing to Ar. *Birds* 544, cὺ δέ μοι . . . ἥκεις ἐμοὶ cωτήρ, frag. 132, ἔδει δέ γε cε . . . μὴ παρέχειν cε πράγματα, Ap. Rhod. iv. 385, Ar. *Ach.* 383, Soph. *OC* 1278.

806 εἰ κύριος: There is perhaps a formal inconsistency with 800, ὧν δὲ μὴ cὺ κύριος εἰ. In both places κύριος means 'having control over', but whereas here it is limited by the words ὅcον χρόνον to temporary control, in 800 Sostratos was speaking of ultimate control.

807 αὐτόν: 'Yourself', i.e. without waiting for Fortune to dispose of your money.

809 τοῦτο γὰρ ἀθάνατον: It is intentionally striking to say that 'help to others never dies', but the phrase is suggested by the application of ἀθάνατος to words meaning 'memory', 'gratitude', μνήμη Lysias ii. 81, χάρις Hdt. vii. 178, Men. frag. 479. The end of the line was uncertain in B according to the original photograph, but that in *ed. pr.* of *P. Bodmer* 26 clearly shows πταιcαcτυχη[, agreeing with Stobaios.

811: The words πλοῦτος ἀφανής may have suggested the technical terms ἀφανὴς οὐcία and ἐμφανὴς (or φανερὰ) οὐcία. These do not, as is sometimes said, correspond to our distinction between personal and real property; although land, buildings, and slaves belong by their nature to the second category, that of visible property, cash, deposits, and loans may be one or the other, according to whether the owner acknowledges his ownership (see Daremberg and Saglio, s.v. Aphanes Ousia, and A. R. W. Harrison, *The Law of Athens*, i, pp. 230–1).

812 κατορύξας ἔχεις: Not a mere periphrasis for a perfect, but 'keep buried'. Sostratos unequivocally states that his father has a buried treasure. In a society at a primitive stage of economic development, this would be no unusual way of keeping one's reserve wealth, as is shown not only by stories of discoveries of buried hoards (Menander, Θησαυρός, Plaut. *Aulularia*) but also in real life by Demosthenes xxix. 49, τὰ μὲν χρήμαθ', ὅσα κατέλιπεν ὁ πατήρ, ἐκείνῃ τῇ ἡμέρᾳ κατωρύττετο, although here there was a primary desire to conceal possession of the wealth. That hoards were not uncommon is implied by Plato, *Euthyd.* 288 e, ἆρ' οὖν ἄν τι ἡμᾶς ὀνήςειεν, εἰ ἐπισταίμεθα γιγνώςκειν περιόντες ὅπου τῆς γῆς χρυςίον πλεῖςτον κατορώρυκται, and in Ar. *Plut.* 237 Wealth says ἢν μὲν γὰρ ὡς φειδωλὸν ('a thrifty man') εἰςελθὼν τύχω, | εὐθὺς κατώρυξέν με κατὰ τῆς γῆς κάτω, | κἄν τις προςέλθῃ χρηςτὸς ἄνθρωπος φίλος | αἰτῶν λαβεῖν τι ςμικρὸν ἀργυρίδιον, | ἔξαρνός ἐςτι μηδ' ἰδεῖν με πώποτε.

813 οἶcθ' οἶός εἰμι: The text is disputed. B gives οἶcθ' οἶός ἐcτι, which was defended by van Groningen. He supposed the subject to be ὁ πλοῦτός μου, i.e. the buried treasure mentioned in the previous line. But it is not the nature of this treasure that is relevant here, but that of Kallippides, who is not the man to carry with him to the grave the wealth that should be his son's. Hence the reading of *ed. pr.*, οἶός εἰμι, is reasonable and supported by R. Kassel, *Gnomon* xxxiii (1961), 138, and by Blake. Others, including Handley, prefer the slighter change to οἶόν ἐcτι, 'you know how things are'. The evidence as yet cited for this phrase is slender, being *Perik.* 342, where Wilamowitz's supplement οἶcθ'] οἶ[όν ἐ]cτιν, οἶμαι is not improbable, but yet not certain.

814 οὐ cυγκατορύξω: In a play by Luscius Lanuuinus, perhaps founded on Menander's Θηςαυρός, a father did cause a fortune to be buried with him, trying to ensure that his son would discover it only ten years later (Donatus on Ter. *Eun.* 9), and cf. Plaut. *Aul.* 6–12.

816 ἀγαθῇ τύχῃ: Cf. 422 and *Sam.* 297 n. Should δοκιμάcας be taken with the preceding words, 'do you wish to secure as a friend a man whose worth you have examined?', or with the succeeding, 'do so, since you have examined his worth'? Editors are divided and the choice uncertain. To examine a man's credentials and then to set about securing his friendship sounds cold-blooded and calculating to a modern ear. But 'friendship' to a Greek involved so many obligations that it might reasonably be approached in a spirit we should consider suitable to entering a business partnership. There is an interesting discussion of the subject in Xen. *Mem.* ii. 6, introduced by the phrase δοκιμάζειν φίλους ὁποίους ἄξιον κτᾶcθαι. Plut. *Mor.* 482 b quotes a phrase of Theophrastos, οὐ φιλοῦντα δεῖ κρίνειν, ἀλλὰ κρίναντα φιλεῖν (cf. Cic. *de amicitia* 85).

817: πόριζε and βάδιζε are probably variant readings, and the end of the line has been excluded. πόριζε gives an obvious sense, but may be too nearly synonymous with δίδου of the next line to be right. βάδιζε, 'off with you', i.e. to Gorgias, appears more likely (cf. *Sam.* 159, 661,

Epitr. 376). **γνώμας:** The word has the sense of 'practical or moral maxims', often with a connotation of 'sententiousness', whence scholars' English 'gnome, gnomic'. The usefulness of γνῶμαι was recognized in the theory of teachers of rhetoric, who invented the technical term γνωμολογία (Plato, *Phaedr.* 267 c, where it is joined with διπλασιολογία and εἰκονολογία; the subject is treated at length in Arist. *Rhet. B* 1394ᵃ19 ff.). Here Sostratos has advanced several not unfamiliar sentiments: (1) A man is not the true owner of his wealth; Eur. *Phoen.* 555 ff., οὔτοι τὰ χρήματ' ἴδια κέκτηνται βροτοί, | τὰ τῶν θεῶν δ' ἔχοντες ἐπιμελούμεθα, | ὅταν δὲ χρῄζωσ' αὔτ' ἀφαιροῦνται πάλιν. More generally, the mutability of human affairs is a commonplace. (2) A man should use his wealth for good purposes and to help his friends, not hoard it: Pindar, *Nem.* i. 31 ff., οὐκ ἔραμαι πολὺν ἐν μεγάρῳ πλοῦτον κατακρύψας ἔχειν, | ἀλλ' ἐόντων εὖ τε παθεῖν καὶ ἀκοῦσαι φίλοις ἐξαρκέων. (3) Friends are better than wealth; Eur. *Or.* 1155, οὐκ ἔστιν οὐδὲν κρεῖττον ἢ φίλος σαφής, | οὐ πλοῦτος, οὐ τυραννίς (*Orestes* was a popular play, to which there are several allusions in *Sikyonios*). A copious collection of ancient gnomes on unused wealth was made by H. Herter, *Rh. Mus.* xciv (1951), 14.

818–19: A dicolon is missing somewhere. If at the end of 818, a para-graphus has been omitted also; I have preferred to suppose the lesser error, loss after the second ἑκών. For the interrogative repetition of a word cf. 918 οὐκ ἔστιν; *Epitr.* 1114, θυγατριδοῦν; *Sam.* 558, περιπατήσω;

818 δίδου, μεταδίδου: W. G. Arnott, *CQ* N.s. v (1955), 214, remarks that it is surprisingly unusual for a simple verb to be followed by the same verb compounded with a prefix (to his examples add Asklepi-ades, *AP* v. 162, οἴχομαι . . . διοίχομαι). Here the point is that Sostratos will not merely 'give away'; he will associate Gorgias with himself, 'give him a share'.

819 ἑκών: There may be more in this than a desire on Sostratos' part for the comfort of being in harmony with his father; he may have in view the desirability of making sure that there will be no change of mind, cf. [Dem.] lvi. 2, τοῖς νόμοις . . . οἳ κελεύουσιν, ὅσα ἄν τις ἑκὼν ἕτερος ἑτέρῳ ὁμολογήσῃ, κύρια εἶναι.

(ii) **821–855:** *Sostratos, Kallippides, Gorgias*

821: It is interesting that the Greek, unlike the modern Englishman, has no hesitation about eavesdropping on a private conversation. Dramatically, this avoids the necessity of any repetition to Gorgias of what the spectators already know. It is improbable that Gorgias was seen by the audience before this point: that would have distracted their attention. His appearance now is the more effective for being unexpected. He had been about to come out (why?—an audience has no time to ask) but, hearing voices, stopped at the door (πρὸc τῇ θύρᾳ), which may not have been completely closed. For a similar case see Plaut. *Merc.* 477, 'omnia ego istaec auscultaui ab ostio.'

823 τί οὖν; Thierfelder would give this to Sostratos, comparing *Sam.* 379, *Fab. incert.* 17. But τί οὖν; can occur in a continuous speech, Sosipatros frag. 1. 43 (by emendation). And it is possible that it is intended, with its slightly pompous effect, to be characteristic of Gorgias, cf. 284, 363. Page's c' ⟨ὦ C⟩ώcτρατε is palaeographically neat, but perhaps wrong. In this play in ordinary conversational address ὦ is not attached to a name in the vocative. But it is found in appeals (ὦ Γοργία 635, ὦ Πάν 573) and in a rhetorical address to the absent Knemon (220), cf. *Aspis* 14. Elsewhere in Menander it occurs where there is a note of appeal (*Her.* 19, *Perinth.* 3, *Georg.* 22) or remonstrance (*Her.* 72, ?*Kith.* 81, *Aspis* 189, *Mis.* frag. 7 [4 Körte]) or with a gnomic speech (*Georg.* frag. 3, *Kith.* frag. 1). This is also the practice of the κοινή (Schwyzer, ii. 61⁴). Plato's practice is the opposite; he usually adds ὦ to the vocative. If ὦ is right here, it must indicate solemnity in Gorgias' manner.

829 καλῶc ἔχει μοι: A formula of polite refusal, cf. *Perik.* 516 n.

830 τρυφαίνειν, although a previously unknown word, is defensible (Kraus, Handley) on the analogy of such pairs as κραδαίνειν/κραδᾶν, μαργαίνειν/μαργᾶν, ὀργαίνειν/ὀργᾶν (Ernst Fraenkel, *Griech. Denomina-tiva*, 20). λυccαίνειν for λυccᾶν occurs only in Soph. *Ant.* 633, χλιδαίνεcθαι for χλιδᾶν only in Xen. *Symp.* 8. 8. Nevertheless the emendation τρυφᾶν ἐν, which assumes errors paralleled elsewhere in B, may be correct. In view of the tendency of poets of the New Comedy to use the same or similar phrases, it is supported by Euphron frag. 12 K, ἐν ταῖc γὰρ ἑτέρων βούλετ' ἀτυχίαιc τρυφᾶν. I accept the normalizing correction δοκεῖ for δοκῶ, but note that Menander's contemporary Hippolochos is represented by the MS. of Athenaios 129 a to have written 'Ροδίαι, ἐμοὶ μὲν γυμναὶ δοκῶ, πλὴν ἔλεγόν τινεc αὐτὰc ἔχειν χιτῶναc, which Kaibel maintains. Men. frag. 61 K–T, ὅλην ἐπίνομεν τὴν νύκτα διὰ cὲ καὶ cφόδρ' ἄκρατόν μοι δοκῶ, is less striking.

831: τρυφαίνειν or τρυφᾶν in 830 must have a pejorative tinge, but that does not mean that a quite different verb is to be supplied here (διάγειν or φείδεcθαι, Handley). Gorgias is ready to admit the pleasant-ness of an easy life, if it has been earned by one's own efforts.

832–3: Notice the play of tenses in κρίνειc, κέκρικα. 'Are you judging . . . ?' 'My judgement is . . .' By his use of the perfect, with its sense of a continuing state, Gorgias indicates the firmness of his judgement.

833 ff.: Textual uncertainty makes this one of the most difficult passages of the play. As it stands 834 makes no sense, but the inversion, usually adopted, of πολλά and μικρά gives a possible meaning. It is true that nothing has been said about the size of the dowry to go with Kallippides' daughter, but in the conversation which Gorgias overheard Sostratos had proposed by implication that he should be made εὔπορος (807), and in 825 he assumes that the dowry would be such as to bring him a standard of life to which he was not accustomed. The principle now enunciated, that a poor man should not accept a fortune, goes no further in fact than the determination to earn his own living of 830. But it sounds less convincing, couched in this antithetical and rhetorical form, characteristic of Gorgias (cf. 245, 250 ff., 348). It calls forth a reply which may have combined admiration with some criticism that led Gorgias to abandon his principles and accept his fortune.

[I do not feel entirely satisfied with the above explanation, and tentatively suggest reading λαβεῖν δέ, μικρὰ τἄμ' ἔχοντ', οὐκ ἄξιον, λαβεῖν then has the sense 'take as wife', as previously in 786, 791, 795, 828 (cf. 307, 349), and justice is done to the emphatic position of ἐμαυτόν: 'My *person* is worthy of her, but my fortunes make me an unsuitable husband.']

The rest of the passage remains baffling in spite of all attempts to divine the sense. The suspicion must arise that this is due to some corruption, perhaps even the loss of a line. The difficulties are increased by two uncertainties: (1) below 835 there is a horizontal stroke which may be a misplaced paragraphus or, more likely, the top of an initial π; (2) 839 is corrupt, a short syllable being missing before ἀπόπληκτος. All that can be confidently said is that the words ἐπειδὴ συμπεπεισμένον μ' ὁρᾷς belong to Kallippides, and τούτῳ μ' ἀναπέπεικας to Gorgias, who thus confesses his change of mind and accepts the proffered bride. But it remains a mystery what this argument was that was adequate to shift him. If obliged to supplement the lines, for the sake of a performance, I should write them as follows:

> νὴ τὸν Δία τὸν μέγιστον εὐγενῶς γέ πως
> παράλο]γος εἶ :: πῶς; :: οὐκ ἔχων βούλει δοκεῖν
> ἀγαπᾶν]· ἐπειδὴ συμπεπεισμένον μ' ὁρᾷς,
> πάρεικ]ε. ⟨::⟩ τούτῳ μ' ἀναπέπεικας· διπλασίως
> ἦν ἂν νοc]ῶν—πένης ⟨γὰρ⟩ ἀπόπληκτός θ' ἅμα—
> φεύγων ὅ]ς ὑποδείκνυσιν εἰς σωτηρίαν.

'You are nobly paradoxical in wishing to appear satisfied with your lack of means.' . . . 'I should be sick in mind as well as in purse, if I were to avoid the one man who offers me a way out of my difficulties.'

It is noble of Gorgias not to be ashamed of his poverty, but ineffective of him to neglect the opportunity of removing it. Cf. Thuc. ii. 40, τὸ πένεσθαι οὐχ ὁμολογεῖν τινὶ αἰσχρόν, ἀλλὰ μὴ διαφεύγειν ἔργῳ αἴσχιον. διπλασίως is probably to be constructed with what follows, since Gorgias can hardly have been given two reasons to cause his change of mind.

But some completely different approach may be right, e.g. Handley writes:

> νὴ τὸν Δία τὸν μέγιστον εὐγενῶς γέ πως
> π[ερίερ]γος εἶ :: πῶς; :: οὐκ ἔχων βούλει δοκεῖν
> ἔχειν.] ἐπειδὴ συμπεπεισμένον μ' ὁρᾶς—
> αὐτῷ δ]ὲ τούτῳ μ' ἀναπέπεικας διπλασίως—
> μὴ φεῦγ' ⟨ἔτ'⟩] ὢν πένης ⟨τις⟩ ἀπόπληκτός θ' ἅμα
> ὅς' ὁ γάμο]ς ὑποδείκνυσιν εἰς σωτηρίαν.

περίεργος must then mean 'unnecessarily fussy' ('excess of conscience', as he translates, is hardly justified by the word's usage). But I do not understand οὐκ ἔχων βούλει δοκεῖν ἔχειν, although it has been widely accepted, since Gorgias has flatly stated that he *is* poor. Moreover ἔχειν would require unusually wide writing to fill the space.

839 ἀπόπληκτος: 'Out of my mind', cf. [Dem.] xxxiv. 16, ἀπόπληκτον . . . καὶ παντελῶς μαινόμενον.

840 ὑποδείκνυσιν . . . σωτηρίαν: The phrase recurs at Plut. *Marius* 428 b. This suggests that the word before σωτηρίαν is not εἰς but εἶς; the sense would be good, 'someone or something alone offers a prospect of saving Gorgias from poverty'. On the other hand, Jacques quotes Libanios, *Progymn.* 10. 4. 4, λεπτὴν ἔχοντες εἰς σωτηρίαν ἐλπίδα to support the supplement ἐλπί]δ' ὑποδείκνυσιν εἰς σωτηρίαν.

841: This line probably belongs to Sostratos, who by the word ἡμῖν associates himself with his father. Although Kallippides must in fact pronounce the formula of marriage, it was Sostratos who had arranged it.

842 παίδων ἐπ' ἀρότῳ γνησίων: Cf. *Perik.* 1013 n., *Sam.* 727, *P. Oxy.* 429, 1829, and Prokopios, *ep.* 135, παίδων ἐπ' ἀρότῳ γνησίων, ἡ κωμῳδία φησί. On the size of the dowry see *Epitr.* 134 n.

846: Whereas μὴ σὺ λίαν would be an acceptable elliptical phrase, 'don't do too much'. B's μηδαυ (so written without apostrophe) can hardly be resolved into μηδ' αὖ since μηδέ is out of place. μηδαυ is probably a misreading of a cursive μηδως or μηδεν. The quantity of ι in λίαν is indeterminate in 6 places elsewhere in Menander, but in frag. 786 it is long, as here, if Körte's text is correct; but that is doubtful. It is mostly indeterminate in the comic fragments also, but twice long (Theopompos frag. 29 K, Mnesimachos frag. 3 K), twice short (Aristophon frag. 11 K, adesp. incert. 1205 Kock, 91 Nauck).

B fails to indicate where Gorgias' speech ends. If, as at 591, 624, a dicolon has been omitted at the end of the line, we cannot read ἀλλ' ἔχω τόδε χωρίον, because the article τό would be lacking. Hence some have suggested τό γε χωρίον. The change is not persuasive, since corruption of γε to δέ is not yet paralleled in Menandrean papyri. Others suppose a dicolon to be omitted after ἔχω, and Kallippides to reply τὸ δὲ χωρίον κέκτης' ὅλον cύ. It is not clear what the function of δέ would be here, and since intrusive δέ is found elsewhere (187, 736, 678 n., Sam. 77, τὸ δὲ παιδίον at the line-end), another instance of intrusion may be seen here, perhaps the work of someone who, believing, rightly or wrongly, that Kallippides' reply began with τὸ χωρίον, inserted the particle to show this.

847: Once again Gorgias' silence gives his consent to a generous proposal. Sostratos' offer to take the girl without a dowry (308) will be carried out, and Gorgias' property will not fall far short of the dowry he will receive with Plangon.

849 ἀλλὰ χρή: The tradition of the ancient grammarians, collected in Menander frag. 820, states that this is a formula of assent; they give as equivalents καὶ μάλα and ἔcτω. A fuller form is found in Plato, ἀλλὰ χρὴ ταῦτα (or οὕτω) ποιεῖν, e.g. Theaet. 145 c, 184 b, Rep. 328 b, Laws 641 e.

850 ff.: Since we do not know what was said in these lines it would be rash to follow Quincey and Shipp, who assign τὴν νύκτα . . . ποήcομεν to Kallippides, in defiance of B, which has no sign of a change of speaker in 852. Nevertheless they may well be right, for the phrase ποεῖν γάμους is normally used of the head of the household. Yet Sostratos, as a spoilt son, might speak for his father (cf. 841).

The gap could be filled e.g. τὴν νύκτα [παρὰ τῷ Πανὶ ταύτην, Γοργία,] | πάντες μεν[οῦμεν, αὔριον δὲ το]ὺς γάμους | ποήcομεν.

853 κομίcατε: By the plural Myrrhine and the girl, although not on the stage, are associated with Gorgias.

(iii) **855–873**: *Sostratos, Kallippides* (exit 860), *Gorgias* (enters 866 with *Myrrhine and Knemon's daughter*)

858: The hoary jest at the bibulous propensities of women is hardly redeemed by the neatness with which Kallippides reverses his son's phrase. The connotation of παννυχιοῦμεν for the old sensualist is to be seen from the other occurrences of the word in comedy: Ar. *Clouds* 1069, and frag. 695, παννυχίζων τὴν δέσποιναν ἐρείδεις; cf. Lucian, *Dial. Meretr.* xiv. 1. Aelian, *ep.* xv, makes his Kallippides suggest to his Knemon that he may have a tumble with a girl at Pan's shrine, οὐδὲν ⟨ἂν⟩ ἀπεοικὸς εἴη καὶ τοιοῦτό τι πραχθῆναι ἐν τῇ τοῦ Πανὸς θυσίᾳ. καὶ γάρ τοι κἀκεῖνος ἐρωτικὸς εὖ μάλα.

860: Kallippides goes into the shrine. If he remained on the stage, he would divert attention from Sostratos; but apart from that, if there are three actors only, he has to change costume to reappear as Simiche at 874.

861 οὐδενὸς . . . ὅλως: For ὅλως reinforcing a negative pronoun, cf. frag. 59. 8, οὐδὲ εἷς . . . ὅλως, 597, ὅλως μηθέν, 397 (= *Perinthia* frag. 4), οὐδεμίαν . . . ὅλως, *Samia* 558, μηδὲν . . . ὅλως, *Kith.* 68, ὅλως οὐδ' ὀντινοῦν. Similarly with an interrogative, rhetorically replacing a negative, 613 τίς ἀνθρώπων ὅλως . . .;

We have to choose between εὖ φρονοῦντα of B and εὖ πονοῦντα, Grotius's emendation of the reading of Stobaios' MSS., εὖ ποιοῦντα. The former makes good sense, 'the man who thinks aright should never despair'; but 'the man who works hard and thoroughly should never despair' is not inferior. But since the section of Stobaios where the lines are quoted is περὶ φιλοπονίας, there was some danger that φρονοῦντα might be altered to πονοῦντα; there is no reason why the reverse change should have been made here in B.

862 ἁλωτά: 'Attainable'. The sense is unusual, and Sostratos is to be thought of as turning a fine phrase; the metaphor of the huntsman's quarry lies in the background. For a parallel, see Soph. *OT* 111, τὸ δὲ ζητούμενον | ἁλωτόν, ἐκφεύγει δὲ τἀμελούμενον.

864 ἐν ἡμέρᾳ μιᾷ: So Sostratos' optimism at 187 has been justified. But his self-satisfaction has its comic side. The audience must realize that luck has notably seconded his efforts.

866 θᾶττόν ποθ' must indicate some impatience, cf. 423 n., 430 n. Perhaps we should imagine that the ladies have taken their time over their preparations for attending the party. The fact that Gorgias has been off the stage for ten lines only does not rule this out, for off-stage and on-stage time do not necessarily proceed at equal speeds; see intro. p. 19 n. 2.   δεῦτε δή: δεῦτε functions as a plural imperative

'come here', being formed on the adverb δεῦρο, 'hither', by means of
the 2nd person plural ending -τε: the word is not known from comedy,
and hence δεῦρο has been proposed (Sydney; I do not believe with
van Groningen that it was written as a correction in the papyrus).
But it is not likely that the comparatively unfamiliar form was introduced by mistake or conjecture; moreover since it is found in the
New Testament, Epictetus, and Plutarch (see LSJ), it may have
already been used colloquially in Menander's time.

867 μῆτερ, δέχου ταύτας: Lloyd-Jones makes Sostratos' mother come
out of the shrine here. There is no reason why she should. More
probably Sostratos leads Myrrhine and her daughter to the mouth
of the cave, and speaks these words into the interior.   **οὐδέπω:** for
the ellipse (of e.g. ἥκει), cf. *Sam.* 196 and Ar. *Thesm.* 846, ἰλλὸς
γεγένημαι προσδοκῶν· ὁ δ' οὐδέπω.

868 ὃς ἱκέτευεν: Relative clauses are occasionally so used to confirm
(as here and *Sam.* 413) or reject (162 above, *Perik.* 471) the implication of a preceding question or statement. The corresponding English
phrases are 'Why, I . . .' or 'Why, he . . .', etc. Cf. K–G ii. 435.

870: B has omitted a dicolon somewhere. I prefer to ascribe ἀλλὰ
πολλὰ χαιρέτω to Sostratos, as ἡμεῖς δ' ἴωμεν follows it so naturally,
and also because the cheerfulness of it suits him well, whereas the
laconic τοιοῦτος is in character for Gorgias, who is resigned to the
old man's ways. Thierfelder compares Ter. *Andria* 919, 'sic, Crito,
est hic: mitte.'

871: Gorgias would have completed his sentence with some verb like
συνδιατρίβειν. His feelings of delicacy here have been thought to pre-
clude his having entered the cave with Sostratos at the end of Act III;
for the women were in the cave then also. But to associate with strange
women at a meal and at a wine-party may be very different things.
In spite of frag. 761, εὐκαταφρόνητος τῇ στολῇ | εἴσειμι, καὶ τοῦτ' εἰς
γυναῖκας, I doubt whether Webster is right (*StM*² 232) in supposing
Gorgias to be ill at ease because of his working clothes. Sostratos
reassures him by reminding him that he is now 'one of the family',
this suggests that his scruples were about entering the company, not
of women, but of the women of another household.

872 τίς ὁ λῆρος; The words cohere, so that the broken anapaest is
only apparent, cf. *Perik.* 388.   **οἰκεῖα:** See 240 n.

(iv) 874–884: *Simiche and Getas* (enters 879)

874 νὴ τὴν Ἄρτεμιν: The oath by Artemis, although found seven
times in Aristophanes, does not occur elsewhere in the remains of

Middle and New Comedy; it is used once in Machon, 297 Gow. Conceivably there is some point, of which we cannot now be sure, in its use here by the old woman.

876 πρὸς τὸν θεόν must be emphatic by its position (cf. what is said on p. 134 about Pan's importance). Handley suggests that Knemon's refusal is insulting to the god as well as ungracious to the family.

878: The completion of the line is difficult. *Ed. pr.* supposed a sentence to end at νῦν, and wrote εὖ πάθοις. But εὖ πάσχειν means 'to be treated well', and such a wish follows awkwardly on the prophecy of misfortune. Kraus's εὖ πέσοι is more likely, 'may it turn out well', but I know no example of this impersonal use of εὖ πίπτειν. Webster ingeniously proposed μεῖζον ἢ νῦν εὐπαθεῖν; Knemon will have to put up with something worse than merry-making and indulgence, things he counts as evil. But at this stage all think him too ill for making merry: I should prefer to write εὖ παθεῖν, understanding Simiche to mean that Knemon would regard it as an evil if he were the object of kindly attention. This may, however, make a sentiment somewhat too subtle for Simiche, and Blake may be right with εὖ πάνυ, i.e. εὖ πάνυ μεῖζον. Cf. Xenarchos frag. 7 K, ἐξεπίτηδες εὖ πάνυ.

879 ἐγὼ προσελθὼν ὄψομαι: *Perik.* 181 has ἐγὼ προελθοῦσ' ὄψομαι, so that one wonders whether either passage should be altered to bring the two into line. But in *Perik.* Doris may mean 'I will go *first* and see', and Getas here intend 'I will go *to him* and see', so that the papyrus reading is defensible in both places. Yet if we keep προσελθών here, it is doubtful whether δεῦρο can be taken with it; the first three words are probably spoken to the company in the cave, and δεῦρο could hardly be substituted for ἐκεῖσε: a deictic gesture is not in place. προελθών . . . δεῦρο, however, ('I will come out here and see') would be easy. It is quite uncertain how to restore the missing words at the end of the line; probably – ◡ – is lacking, since Barrett's view that the line was a tetrameter is unlikely. The metre will not have changed until the playing of the piper, indicated *after* this line, caused it to do so.   αὐλεῖ: For the use of the verb without a subject perhaps cf. *Theoph.* 28. The fuller αὐλεῖ τις ἔνδοθεν is found in RV as a stage-direction after Ar. *Frogs* 311, αὐλεῖ after *Birds* 222. Verbs similarly used without a subject are θύειν Hdt. ii. 87, σαλπίζειν, σημαίνειν Xen. *Cyr.* i. 2. 17, iii. 4. 4, ἀναγιγνώσκειν Dem. xx. 27; Schwyzer, ii. 621, K–G. i. 32. Here the piper may be on the stage, see n. on 959; he accompanies the following scene, and he must be supposed to disregard the command to stop given in 881. Contrast Plaut. *Stichus* 762-8, where the metre reverts to iambic senarii while the *tibicen* takes a drink. It is quite natural that there should be pipe-music at the party in Pan's shrine; Getas, having a task to perform, declares he cannot yet give himself to singing or dancing to its strains; this is the realistic background that serves as an excuse for the fact that the whole of the scene is unrealistically played to an accompaniment from the pipe. The accompanist is thus introduced more subtly than by Aristophanes, *Eccl.* 890, cὺ δέ, φιλοττάριον αὐλητά, τοὺς αὐλοὺς λαβών, ἄξιον ἐμοῦ καὶ coῦ προcαύληcον μέλοc. Nevertheless the piper addressed is not one of the party, but what one may call the theatre piper, who has accompanied the songs of the chorus, and who now strikes up unexpectedly and at first sight inopportunely. Beazley, *Hesperia* xxiv (1955), 305, describes all the vases that show a piper in the company of a chorus or of actors. It happens that they all seem to represent tragedy or satyr-play.

880–958: This scene is written in catalectic iambic tetrameters. The use of this metre in comedy is discussed by Körte, *RE* s.v. Komödie. Aristophanes has it frequently both in choral recitative and in lively scenes of debate (e.g. *Knights* 335–66, *Thesm.* 531–73, *Frogs* 905–70). 'It had great vogue with the poets of the Old Comedy' (J. W. White, *The Verse of Greek Comedy*, § 188); it was used to describe drinking-parties by Plato (frag. 69) and Philyllios (frags. 3–4). A handful of examples are known from Middle Comedy; from New Comedy the only other is Diphilos frag. 1 K. Menander was therefore perhaps a little old-fashioned in using this metre, and ending his play with a lively scene in which realism was abandoned at least in so far as it was acted to the time of a musical accompaniment from the player of the *aulos*. But the whole conception of the scene has an element of fantasy: Getas and Sikon carry Knemon out of his house and, as he lies helpless after his accident, rag him with preposterous requests to borrow equipment; then, after painting a picture of the delights of the party in the cave, try to pick him up and make him dance, finally forcing him to consent to be carried in to join the others.

By this Menander found a solution for a dramatic problem; whether it was an adequate solution may be a matter for dispute. At the end of the fourth act Sostratos' marriage was assured. But it is not for nothing that the play is called *Dyskolos*: Knemon and his way of life, cut off from social contact, make a subject at least as important as Sostratos and his love. Now in the fourth act Knemon has by his apologia done a great deal to rehabilitate himself in the spectators' eyes: he has made a specious claim that his solitariness was due to his recognition of the world's villainy, and his attempt at self-sufficiency to a belief that one could not rely on help from others. He has admitted his error in this and proposed to make himself dependent on Gorgias, to whom he hands over his property, allowing him to dispose of the daughter in marriage to Sostratos, the person whom the audience wishes to see successful. All these things must effect a swing of sympathy towards him. But he cannot be allowed to win a victory and be left in possession of the field. He is not an admirable character, and he has no intention of behaving amiably or co-operatively in his retirement; for this he must be made to suffer, if the justice of comedy is to prevail. His antisocial behaviour must bring him misfortune and make him the subject of ridicule. His discomfiture at the hands of Getas and Sikon becomes possible because he will not join the party in the cave and even sends Simiche away, 'so that he may be quite alone'. They, in turn, are moved to take a revenge for their treatment when, in the third act, they had tried to borrow a cooking-pot from him, and their failure then now suggests the method of revenge. Those scenes, in the middle of the play, which appeared at the time not to advance the plot, but to be mere amusing illustrations of Knemon's character, thus turn out to be necessary preliminaries to the play's required conclusion.

The way in which the last scene is written, with the music and strict rhythm, which remove it from the confines of realism, enables the spectator to enjoy it as good fun without paying attention to what might otherwise be disturbing. The tormenting of a man who is physically incapacitated, even if he is less badly injured than he believes, would, if played quite seriously, be unpleasant. Moreover, although a comedy should be regarded as something complete in itself, so that one ought not to ask what its persons will do when it ends, unless the dramatist tells us, yet he ought not to make any prophesies that are improbable or impossible, given the characters that he has depicted. Now in this play Knemon and his unsocial way of life must be shown as defeated by the normal view that takes man to be a social animal, and this defeat is symbolized when he is borne off to join the party in the cave. Getas declares that 'he must be tamed' (903) and at the end of the scene says that the spectators share his pleasure in 'having won his struggle with the old man'. The spectators are thus induced to have the comforting feeling that Knemon is both defeated and reformed. But Menander does not say that he was reformed, nor even suggest that he could be reformed. The old man's last words regard the good fellowship of the party as something to be 'put up with'. He goes there under duress, and there is nothing to indicate that he will not fall back into his self-chosen spiritual isolation as soon as he can, just as he did after he had in the previous act accepted the necessity of material help from Gorgias. That help was not to involve co-operation. He handed over everything to his adopted son, farm and daughter, and asked only to be left in peace. There is, therefore, some contrast

between the suggestion of a 'happy ending' and what might be foreseen from a realistic appreciation of Knemon's character. That inconsistency is obscured because the last scene is not written in a fully
realistic manner, but requires the audience to accept the fancy that
speech may be in a strict rhythm, to a musical accompaniment, and
that the accompanist is in league with the characters. The departure
from logic discourages any desire to look for strict consistency with
the rest of the play. But a hostile critic might say that there is some
dishonesty in thus giving a feeling that all is well in the end, when an
attentive spectator must realize that Knemon has no intention of
making any fundamental change in himself.

880: For ἄθλι' οὗτος cf. Theokr. v. 76, βέντιcθ' οὗτος. But punctuation between the two words is also possible.

881: Handley suggests that we need not believe Getas' statement
that he has been sent to look to Knemon, but that he makes an
excuse to escape from the party in order to torment the old man.
There is not the slightest warrant for this in the text. It is a necessity
of drama that one believes what the characters say unless there is
some indication to the contrary. The long-suffering Getas has been
given yet another job, and it is only when he discovers that Simiche
is leaving her master and that he has got him alone that he conceives
the idea of taking a revenge.

It is uncertain whether the final word should be ἐπίcχεc 'stop!',
addressed to the flute-player, who has continued to play in spite of
the remonstrance, or ἔπιcχε 'hold on!', i.e. 'don't play until I return'
cf. 255 n. Simiche's καὶ . . . γ', 'Yes, and', attaches her remark to the
first part of the line.

882 τιc ἄλλοc, i.e. 'one of you, not me'.

883 τροφίμη: 'The young mistress', this feminine of τρόφιμος 'master's
son' (see 553 n.), found also in *Sikyonios* 8, 361, Charito 1. 12, is
quoted by LSJ only from Pollux 3. 73, who understands it to mean
δέσποινα; the absence of the definite article, as at 553, is noteworthy;
but δεσπότην is found without the article at *Perik.* 359, and κεκτημένην
ibid. 262.

884 προσειπεῖν: So of words of parting, Eur. *Heracl.* 573, προσειποῦς'
ὕστατον πρόσφθεγμα δή, perhaps also *Sam.* 694. ταύτῃ is emphatic:
Simiche wishes to talk with the girl, not sit with Knemon.

(v) **885–908:** *Getas and Sikon* (enters 890)

886 τούτου: Editors (except Kraus) write τοῦτον, but Getas cannot
say that he has *long* decided (or wanted) to take *this* opportunity,

for the opportunity has arisen only a moment before, with the departure
of Simiche. What he has long looked forward to is 'the opportunity
of *this*', i.e. of 'looking after' Knemon. υ and ν are equally possible.
διαπορ[ῶ τί χρὴ δρᾶν (Maas) may be good sense; the wreck of the
next lines makes it impossible to say. But the trace of the last surviving
letter does not strongly suggest ρ. Possibly διαπον[εῖν ἔδει με, 'I had to
go on waiting at the party.' I prefer ἔδει to Barigazzi's ἐχρῆν, since
Menander elsewhere uses the latter of what *ought* to be done (or to
have been done) but is not or has not been done. The next two lines
are beyond restoration. It is possible, as J. Martin suggests, that
Getas here peeps into Knemon's house to assure himself that the old
man is in bed. Somewhere he must do so, or he could not answer
Sikon's question at 893.

890: 'What a pastime I think I've got!' rather than 'what fun I
propose to have' (Handley), which would require a future infinitive.
(The passages quoted in LSJ s.v. οἴομαι VI. 3 do not support the use
of a present infinitive; in Lysias xii. 26 Madvig rightly expelled οἴει
as an interpolation.)

892 οὐ λαικάσει: The same imprecation is found in Straton, frag. 1.
36 Kock (Page, *GLP* 266), cf. Kephisodoros frag. 3 K, λαικάσομ' ἄρα,
'I'll be — ' d.' 'Graeci aliquem contemptus significandi causa λαικάζειν
iubebant, id est fellare', Housman, *Hermes* lxvi (1931), 408.   **ἐγὼ
δ' ἔπασχον:** With some hesitation I accept the generally held view
that πάσχω is here used *sensu obsceno*, cf. Lat. *pathicus*. This equivocation
is found neither in Aristophanes nor in any other comic author, and
the usage itself (unknown to LSJ) is rare in classical Greek; the
nearest parallels I know are Theopompos ap. Athen. 517 e, οὐδὲν δ'
αἰσχρόν ἐςτι Τυρρηνοῖς οὐ μόνον αὐτοὺς ἐν μέςῳ τι ποιοῦντας, ἀλλ' οὐδὲ
πάςχοντας and Aischines i. 41, τὸ πρᾶγμα ὃ προηρεῖτο ἐκεῖνος μὲν
ποιεῖν, οὗτος δὲ πάςχειν. In later Greek we have e.g. [Arist.] *Probl.*
879b31, πάςχειν ἐπιθυμοῦςιν, Plut. *Amat.* 768 e, τοὺς ἡδομένους τῷ
πάςχειν, Luc. *Dial. Mer.* v. 2, αὐτὸ πάςχειν, Diog. L. v. 76, ὑπὸ
Κλέωνος πεπονθέναι. But unless this is the point, Sikon's question is
very flat. The emphatic ἐγώ may suggest the implication 'it was *you*,
if anyone, who — '. On this interpretation, Sikon does not immediately
see that the words ὧν ἀρτίως ἔπαςχες refer to his rough treatment by
Knemon earlier in the day. The indecency is not brought in for its
own sake; it indicates that wine has removed Sikon's inhibitions but
not the fertility of his imagination, and so prepares the ground for
the coming scene The dramatic use of *Perik.* 482 may be compared
(see n.). But the similar jest, also concerning a cook, Plaut. *Aul.* 283
'mequidem hercle non diuides' etc., serves no dramatic purpose; it

has certainly been elaborated and may have been totally invented by Plautus.

893 ἔχει δὲ πῶς; The papyrus is torn away immediately after the ϲ, so that it is impossible to say whether another word followed, or whether we should read ἔχει δὲ ⟨δὴ⟩ πῶς; comparing e.g. Eur. *HF* 1246, δράϲειϲ δὲ δὴ τί; In either case the order of words emphasizes ἔχει, 'and his *condition*? how is he?'

894: The loss of the end of 893 leaves it uncertain whether there was change of speaker there. If a change is assumed, Getas' reply implies that Knemon could be made to suffer more. Sikon then asks for a reassurance that, even if not *in extremis*, he is at least unable to get out of bed.

895 ἀναϲτῆναι ⟨γάρ⟩: This correction gives a line unique in this scene in that it has no diaeresis after the second metron nor caesura after the first syllable of the third. Hence some prefer to read ἀναϲτῆν' ⟨αὐτόϲ⟩, 'get up by his own efforts'. But Aristophanes has lines without diaeresis or this caesura, e.g. *Clouds* 1353, 1354, 1380, 1381; and the elision of -ναι in aor. 2 infin. may not be permissible in Menander (cf. *Perik.* 343 n.).

896 εἰϲιών, i.e. going into the house where Knemon is lying. If this plan were executed, the audience would lose the benefit of it. The true object of Getas' modification, to bring Knemon outside first, is to allow them to share in the fun. From Getas' point of view it has no rational object. But the actions of men under the influence of drink are often due to apparently irrational whims.

896-7: B marks a change of speaker after αἰτήϲομ' εἰϲιών τι. But this requires the same speaker to state his intention of going in and then immediately modify it by the suggestion of bringing Knemon out. It seems more likely that one speaker modifies the proposal of the other.

897 τὸ δεῖνα: This phrase (on which see A. C. Moorhouse, *CQ* N.S. xiii (1963), 24 ff.) is often used to introduce a sudden thought, 'do you know what?' e.g. Ar. *Birds* 648, ἀτάρ, τὸ δεῖνα, δεῦρ' ἐπανάκρουϲαι πάλιν, *Lysistr.* 921, 926, καίτοι, τὸ δεῖνα, προϲκεφάλαιον οὐκ ἔχειϲ, etc. *Ed. pr.* filled out the line with πρῶτον ⟨ὦ τᾶν⟩, but there seems to be no place for protest or irony (see 247 n.), and I prefer Handley's ⟨τί δ' ἄν,⟩ τὸ δεῖνα, which follows the model of Ar. *Wasps* 524, τί δ' ἤν, τὸ δεῖνα, τῇ διαίτῃ μὴ 'μμένῃϲ;

898 αὐτοῦ: 'Here', as in 312.

899 οὕτω: 'With things so arranged', i.e. having got him outside.

ἐπιφλέγωμεν: There are no clear parallels for the use of this word. It may mean 'let us inflame him (with rage)', cf. Ar. *Clouds* 992, κἂν σκώπτῃ τίς σε, φλέγεσθαι, and Ter. *Phormio* 186, 'incendam' ('I should inflame him'); or it may be used, somewhat like the obsolete slang 'roast' (= 'ridicule'), in the sense of 'put in a hot spot', cf. Timotheos, *Persae* 222, ὁ γάρ μ' εὐγενέτας μακραίων Cπάρτας . . . δονεῖ λαὸς ἐπιφλέγων ἐλᾷ τ' αἴθοπι μώμῳ, ὅτι παλαιοτέραν νέοις' ὕμνοις μοῦσαν ἀτιμῶ.

900 ff.: From here to the end of the play there is much uncertainty about the assignment of speeches. This uncertainty may well have been felt in antiquity: the speaker is indicated twice only in B, Getas at 901, Knemon at 919, and at neither place could there have been any doubt. The difficulties are greater because a number of dicola have certainly been omitted (912, 913, 924, 945, 957) or misplaced (906, 927); it is not unlikely that there are other mistakes. If the transmission of the text ever went through a stage like that of the *Sikyonios* papyrus, where changes of speaker were marked only by paragraphi and occasional small spaces between words, the correct insertion of dicola would have presented a baffling problem to an ancient reader or scholar. The solutions adopted here must be regarded as tentative.

To deal first with the passage 910–30, it is clear that first one of Knemon's tormentors attacks him (910 ἐγὼ προάξω πρότερος . . . 918 ἀποτρέχω δή) and then the other (920 . . . 925 ἐφ' ἑτέραν βαδίζω θύραν); then the first returns, addressed at 927 by τί βούλει; and is followed by the second, who repeats the request for draperies (930, cf. 923). But which takes the initiative? According to the indications of B it is Sikon. Getas must speak 903, κηδεύομεν γὰρ αὐτῷ. Between this and 910 five dicola intervene; hence it is Sikon who says ἐγὼ προάξω πρότερος. It would be absurd to maintain as certain that B's dicola are correct and that none have been omitted. Yet that B's text is correct in giving 910 to Sikon is confirmed in two ways. First, it was he who suggested (896) that he should annoy Knemon with requests. It is natural that he should take the lead in putting the plan into action. Secondly, it is appropriate that the cook should ask for cooking-vessels (914) and Getas, who had brought the rugs for the party (405), for carpets and hangings (922–3).

910–30 offer a simple choice between alternatives: either Sikon or Getas takes the initiative. Reasons have been given for choosing Sikon. Most editors (including Lloyd-Jones, J. Martin, Jacques, Handley) choose Getas, but do not explain why. When we turn to 904–9 the possibilities are much more complex. One may start by setting out the text implied by B.

(Γετ.) κηδεύομεν γὰρ αὐτῷ.
οἰκεῖος ἡμῖν γίνετ'. εἰ δ' ἔςται τοιοῦτος ἀεί,
ἔργον ὑπενεγκεῖν. (Cικ.) πῶς γὰρ οὔ; (Γετ.) λαθεῖν μόνον ἐπιθύμει
αὐτὸν φέρων δεῦρ' εἰς τὸ πρόςθεν. πρόαγε δὴ cὺ μικρόν.
(Cικ.) πρόςμεινον ἱκετεύω cε. μή με καταλιπὼν ἀπέλθῃς.
καὶ μὴ ψόφει πρὸς τῶν θεῶν. (Γετ.) ἀλλ' οὐ ψοφῶ μὰ τὴν Γῆν.
εἰς δεξιάν. (Cικ.) ἰδού. θὲς αὐτοῦ. νῦν ὁ καιρός. εἶεν.
ἐγὼ προάξω πρότερος.

One change seems certain: μικρόν must belong to πρόςμεινον, cf. *Epitr.* 364, βραχὺ | πρόςμεινον, ἱκετεύω c', and 858, μικρόν, γύναι, πρόςμεινον. The words are spoken by one who is about to enter the house, in response to the invitation πρόαγε δὴ cύ, and who fears that the other either will not follow or will not wait outside, but will make off, leaving him with the sole responsibility. This nervous character is, according to B, Sikon, and that suits the caution he has already displayed at 894 and 900. There are however other speeches that seem less appropriately assigned. (1) λαθεῖν μόνον ἐπιθύμει αὐτὸν φέρων δεῦρο looks as if it should be addressed to Getas, whose proposal it was to bring Knemon out. (2) μὰ τὴν Γῆν is an oath perhaps less suitable to Getas than to Sikon. It is comparatively rare (twice in Aristophanes, seven times in the fragments of Middle and New Comedy, nowhere else as yet in Menander). Sikon has an extensive vocabulary, and in our Menander he alone swears by Οὐρανός (629). (3) One may doubt whether B is right in not making any change of speaker after ἰδού in 910.

There are many possible ways of meeting one, two, or all of these points. What seems to me the most likely is

(Γετ.) ἔργον ὑπενεγκεῖν, πῶς γὰρ οὔ; (Cικ.) λαθεῖν μόνον ἐπιθύμει
αὐτὸν φέρων δεῦρ' εἰς τὸ πρόςθεν. ⟨Γετ.⟩ πρόαγε δὴ cύ. ⟨Cικ.⟩
μικρὸν
πρόςμεινον ἱκετεύω cε. μή με καταλιπὼν ἀπέλθῃς.
⟨Γετ.⟩ καὶ μὴ ψόφει πρὸς τῶν θεῶν. (Cικ.) ἀλλ' οὐ ψοφῶ μὰ τὴν Γῆν.
⟨Γετ.⟩ εἰς δεξιάν. (Cικ.) ἰδού. ⟨Γετ.⟩ θὲς αὐτοῦ. νῦν ὁ καιρός. ⟨Cικ.⟩
εἶεν.
ἐγὼ προάξω κτλ.

In favour of this it may be noted that the series of imperatives πρόαγε δὴ cύ ('You go first then'), μὴ ψόφει, εἰς δεξιάν, θὲς αὐτοῦ are all assigned to Getas; that is all the imperatives directly connected with bringing Knemon out are spoken by the originator of the scheme.

901 καθαίρῃ: 113 n.

902 τὸ δ' ὅλον: Apparently used, as frequently in *Magna Moralia* (see Susemihl's index), as equivalent to ὅλως, 'he absolutely must be tamed'. This may be the meaning in frag. adesp. 339 Kock, τὸ δ' ὅλον οὐκ ἐπίσταμαι κιθαρίζειν. The usual sense, 'in general' (LSJ) is not appropriate here. Handley's suggestion (not placed in his text) of putting a stop after ἡμῖν, 'the whole situation is in our power', would probably (as he notes) require ἔστ' ἐφ' ἡμῖν.

903 κηδεύομεν . . . οἰκεῖος ἡμῖν: Getas identifies himself with the family he serves.		**τοιοῦτος:** 'As he is'.

905 ὑπενεγκεῖν: The absence of ὑποφέρω elsewhere in Comedy will be an accident, but the use of the aorist rather than the continuous present is remarkable. Cf., however, Arist. *Pol.* 1267ᵃ21: a city's wealth should not be οὕτως ὀλίγην ὥστε μὴ δύνασθαι πόλεμον ὑπενεγκεῖν μηδὲ τῶν ἴσων καὶ τῶν ὁμοίων.		**λαθεῖν μόνον ἐπιθύμει:** I maintain what I think is B's reading, but without confidence. There are two exceptional features: (1) the use of the imperative ἐπιθύμει, 'long to avoid notice' is strange; one would expect 'try to' or 'take care to'. (2) The tribrach is divided, irregularly for iambics, after the second syllable. τίνα τρόπον in 919 is not a parallel, for those two words adhere closely. According to J. W. White, *Verse of Greek Comedy*, § 175, there are only three such tribrachs in Aristophanes' iambic tetrameters: *Clouds* 1056 and *Knights* 893 are palliated by elision, and *Clouds* 1440 by tmesis (ἀπὸ γὰρ ὀλοῦμαι).

Jacques believes B to have ἐπιθυμου (the writing is cramped and the last letter mutilated) and prints προθύμου (Fraenkel), which does away with both difficulties. Nevertheless I think that the unusual ἐπιθύμει may pass in Sikon's mouth, and am not sure that the metrical oddity is decisive against it.

906 πρόαγε δὴ σύ: Handley points out that this is a courtesy used when two people are going somewhere together: one invites the other to lead the way: Plato, *Phaedr.* 227 c, 229 a. At 866 προάγετε δή is hardly intended as a courtesy, but polite phrases can be uttered in a way that lends them barbs. The action here is uncertain. Handley supposes that Getas, having uttered the polite phrase, does not act in accordance with it, 'but makes a dash for the door, leaving Sikon protesting in the rear'. My own view is given in the note on 900 ff.

908 καὶ μὴ ψόφει: The normal use of ψοφεῖν in comedy is of the noise made in opening a door to come out. That is because a person on the stage will usually perceive by sight that another goes in, but his ears give him warning that someone is coming out. But the door will make the same noise for an entry as for an exit. Here the conspirators must be quiet as they enter, not to avoid attracting the attention of Gorgias in the shrine, but so that Knemon may first awake bewildered outside his house. Other noise besides that of the door may be intended: in Eur. *Or*. 137, μὴ ψοφεῖτε means 'tread softly'. If Sikon misunderstood the word ἔπασχες in 891, did he misunderstand μὴ ψόφει here? See Machon 158 Gow, ἀπεψόφησε (= ἀπέπαρδε).

I believe that after this line the stage is momentarily empty, both conspirators having entered the house, but the gap will be bridged by the continuing strains of the pipe. But it is only an assumption that both enter. If Knemon is brought out on a bed, they will both be needed to carry it. But there is no mention in the text of a bed; its existence can only be deduced from the improbability that he could be picked up bodily and carried out without waking. If that improbability was in fact allowed, in a scene which is somewhat fanciful, perhaps Menander was prepared to make the improbability a large one and cause him to be carried out by one of the conspirators alone, over his shoulder. Other methods of transport have been suggested: in a rug or on a mattress (Diano) or in a chair (Lloyd-Jones). Both would require two bearers. I think it more likely that Knemon had no bedstead than that he possessed a chair suitable for sleeping in. His house was ill equipped (190, 597 ff.).

(vi) 909–964: *Getas, Sikon, Knemon*

909 εἰς δεξιάν: See note on 5.

910 καὶ τὸν ῥυθμὸν cù τήρει: Gallavotti, rightly in my opinion, makes this an order to the piper whose music accompanies this scene: 'Watch your time.' Van Groningen thought that one of Knemon's tormentors told the other to watch the rhythm of his knocking, so that he might imitate it when his turn came, Kraus (whom Handley seems to follow) that he tells him to watch the manner or 'shape' of his actions (cf. LSJ s.v. ῥυθμός VI). Handley also notes a suggestion that the piper had in fact ceased to play or played softly after ἐπίσχες (880), and is here given the cue to resume. We know too little of ancient theatrical practice to be able to say whether unaccompanied iambic tetrameters were ever used.

911: Page, generally followed by editors until Handley dissented, maintained that this line should be expunged as an incorrect version of 912. Against this it may be said that the appealing παῖδες καλοί, with which 912 opens, comes better after a number of unanswered calls. 911–12 will then be a rather longer version of the series we have

in 459–64: παιδίον . . . παῖδες . . . παῖδες καλοί . . . παιδίον . . . παῖδες.
Knemon's repetition of οἴχομ' οἴμοι has a parallel of sorts in that of
τίς ἄν με στήςειεν ὀρθόν; (914, 928).

913: Sikon pretends that Knemon's repeated groans, doubtless louder
on the second occasion, make him aware of the latter's presence. He
asks whether he belongs to the house where he has been knocking,
cf. *Perik.* 374. Knemon shows no sign of remembering his previous
encounters with Sikon and Getas: it is easy to imagine that the shock
of his accident has made him forget.

914–16: The articles for which Sikon asks are all things that might be
used at a large party where a dinner was followed by wine-drinking.
For λέβητες see 456 n. τρίποδες are small round-topped tables, usually
with three legs; τράπεζαι are also usually three-legged, but had larger
rectangular or trapezoid tops. The latter were used for the meal, the
former for dessert and wine (*RE* xv. 937 ff.). Compared with the
couches (κλῖναι) they were small and of light construction, being thus
unlike modern dining-room tables, which are larger and heavier than
the chairs. A symposion scene on a well-known Campanian crater of
c. 340 B.C. (G. M. A. Richter, *Handbook of Greek Art*, fig. 469) shows
both types of table and also the vessel for mixing wine with water,
κρατήρ (928), a little taller than broad and widening to the top.
Sikon's demands are preposterously exaggerated. Whereas he had
previously asked for a single diminutive λεβήτιον, he now requires
plural λέβητες. Page proposed λέβητά c' αἰτοῦμαι παρ' ὑμῶν, lit. 'I ask
you (sing.) for a cauldron from your lot'; Sikon would address
Knemon as if he were a slave in someone's household. The difficulty
is that 916 παῖδες τοῖς ἔνδον ⟨εἰς⟩αγγείλατε suggests that the preceding
requests have been directed, not to Knemon, but to the imaginary slaves
who answer the door. Blake suggested that cε might be addressed to
one such imaginary slave, but it is awkward to leave Knemon's
question 'And what do *you* want?' unanswered. I think the most
satisfactory solution is that Sikon answers the question by 'I am
asking for cauldrons from your lot', and then continues to direct his
demands into the house 'You've got them . . . and seven small tables
etc.'

914 cκάφην: Aristophanes' fantasy might have associated sage
(cφάκον B) with cooking-pots and tables; in New Comedy more logic
is to be expected. Some word (but which?) beginning cκαφ-, and
meaning a bowl or tray is required: cκάφη and cκαφίς are well
attested in this sense, cκάφος (neut.) hardly at all. Cf. the reverse
metathesis at 605, cκαφον for cφακον.   **παρ' ὑμῶν:** 'From your
household'.

918: Either ἀ⟨λλ' ἀ⟩κήκοας μυριάκις or ⟨οὐκ⟩ ἀκήκοας μυριάκις; will supply the missing syllable. The latter is more forcible, but Knemon, just recalled to consciousness, is not at his strongest in his first replies. Palaeographically the former error is perhaps marginally more probable, and I therefore suppose it, without confidence.

920 εἰς τὸ πρόσθε: B has προσθε here, but εἰστοπροσθεν at 906, cf. *Sam.* 168, 214. In this phrase metre makes πρόσθεν necessary at *Theoph.* 26, but there is no reason for changing πρόσθε here or at *Mis.* 68. The interpretation of the end of the line is uncertain. B is corrupt, but ἄπαγε δὴ cὺ καὶ δή is highly probable as a correction. With considerable hesitation I adopt the view that a dicolon is lost before καὶ δή, which forms the reply to the imperative ἄπαγε, cf. Denniston, *GP* 251 (but the verb is usually repeated, e.g. Ar. *Clouds* 778, εἰπὲ δή :: καὶ δὴ λέγω). Sikon presumably suited his action to the word at ἀποτρέχω δή (918). Knemon's lament covers the time occupied by his withdrawal. Then, as he goes away, Getas comes up, and Knemon, on noticing him, tells him to be off. Getas replies καὶ δή, 'there you are, I am going', but instead of retiring quietly falls upon the near-by door with his fists, calling for the imaginary servants. The dicolon after κατατέθηκεν marks, not a change of speaker, but that Knemon turns from addressing the air to dismissing the new intruder. A similar view is taken by J. H. Newiger, *Gymnasium* lxxiv (1967), 543.

Other interpretations: Jacques gives the whole phrase ἄπαγε δὴ cὺ καὶ δή to Knemon, supposing it to be addressed to Sikon, who (in his view) here comes up to take over from Getas the business of tormenting the old man. He takes καὶ δή to mean 'immediately', cf. Ar. *Wasps* 492, ὥστε καὶ δὴ τοὔνομ' αὐτῆς ἐν ἀγορᾷ κυλίνδεται, and Hesychios, καὶ δή· ἐπὶ τοῦ ἤδη. Mette, *GGA* ccxiv (1962), 131, thinks that Sikon says to Getas (who has for Mette taken the initiative up to now) 'You stand aside, and right now.' Handley follows this, but in his note favours either giving καὶ δή to Getas, as a response, or if Sikon is to retain the words, making them 'a preface . . . to the knocking'. Blake makes Knemon direct ἄπαγε δὴ cὺ at the retreating Getas; but the phrase comes a line and a half too late for that.

922 δάπιδας: Woven rugs such as might be put on couches, for comfort and display.

923 πόθεν; 'Impossible!' **παραπέτασμα:** Oriental tapestries, used as curtains or hangings, were among Greek luxuries, boasted of by Theophrastos' Vain Man (*Char.* 21. 15), cf. Ar. *Frogs* 938, οὐχ ἱππαλεκτρυόνας μὰ Δί' οὐδὲ τραγελάφους ἅπερ cύ, | ἃν τοῖσι παραπετάςμασιν τοῖς Μηδικοῖς γράφουσι. The line is remarkable for having three resolved feet.

924: Barrett's supplement, ἑκατόν] ποδῶν τὸ μῆκος. (Κν.) ἑκατόν; εἴθε μοι γένοιτο | [ἑνὸς πο]θεν, is clever, but (apart from the fact that it involves (1) changing B's division of speakers, (2) an anapaestic foot unparalleled in this scene) makes Knemon wish for a hanging as uselessly short as one of 100 ft. length would be exaggeratedly long. The wish is also out of character; Knemon's lack of gear is due to parsimony, not poverty; it is not part of his make-up to want imported tapestries. Gallavotti suggests that Knemon wishes for a strap, ἱμάς (cf. 502); Kraus's objection that, unable to rise, he could not use one, may make too much of his incapacity. If the objection is valid at all it would apply equally to Kassel's λίθος (supported by Schäfer by reference to Hor. Sat. ii. 7. 116, 'unde mihi lapidem?' and Knemon's earlier conduct); one must at least sit up to defend oneself effectively, whether with a stone or a strap. I incline to think ἱμάς πο]θεν the most probable restoration in 925, although the papyrus shows no traces that would support this reading; there is apparently not room for λίθος πο]θέν.

925 βαδίζω: Perhaps deliberative subjunctive, cf. 516, perhaps indicative and a statement.

926 ἀπαλλάγητε: Although at the moment annoyed by Getas only, Knemon rightly regards him as one of a pair; cf. the way in which, with less justification, he treats Sostratos as one of a gang, 173. His respite is only momentary. Both tormentors return, led by Sikon. B marks off the curse by dicola after σιμικη and θεοι, and has paragraphi below 926 and 927. If the intention is that one of the tormentors curses Knemon, that must be a mistake. Rather the dicola mark change of person addressed. When Simiche does not reply, Knemon levels a curse at the retreating or temporarily silent Getas, and then turns with τί βούλει; to Sikon. δέ joins the curse to ἀπαλλάγητε δή.

928 κρατῆρα χαλκοῦν μέγαν: For examples see W. Lamb, *Greek and Roman Bronzes*, plate 82; the size and magnificence that might be attained is illustrated by the great vessel (c. 500 B.C.) found at Vix in France, over 5 ft. tall (Richter, *Handbook of Greek Art*, fig. 300).

931 ff.: Assignment of parts is again uncertain. I have adopted the view that Sikon has the leading part from here to 954, where Getas, the prime mover in this last scene, takes over for its conclusion. There is an occasional interjection by Knemon or Getas, and such an interjection at the lost end of 935 may account for the paragraphus below the line. But it is clear that there are several possible ways of dividing 931–9; with 940 Sikon certainly speaks.

930: Palaeographically the easiest change is to write πα⟨τρ⟩ίδιον, οὐδ' ὁ κρατήρ; (Barigazzi and others). But 'Not even the mixing-bowl, father?' is an awkward sequel to 'You really have the curtain!', unless we assume that Knemon made a gesture of dissent after the first sentence.

If we suppose that the dicolon after παπια should be after πατριδιον we get ἔcτιν . . . τὸ παραπέταcμα, παπία, πατρίδιον. (Κν.) οὐδ' ὁ κρατήρ, 'We haven't the mixing-bowl either.' This is perhaps possible Greek, but is not alluring. A bolder remedy is (Κν.) μὰ τὸν Δί', οὐδ' ὁ κρατήρ, 'No, nor the bowl either'. The corruption of ματονδι to παιδιον is surprising, but conceivable, especially if in some copy δι had been omitted and then added above the line: μα̂τον. The result of this change is so good that I am tempted to adopt it. Each rascal makes one demand, for bowl and curtain respectively, and Knemon denies possession of both objects, in the reverse order. This is an excellent symmetrical arrangement, which I would not surrender in favour of Kraus's modification, accepted by Handley, (Κν.) μὰ τὸν Δί'. (Γετ.) οὐδ' ὁ κρατήρ; He adopted it because B has a dicolon after κρατήρ, although not before οὐδέ. But if Knemon says οὐδ' ὁ κρατήρ, the following dicolon may indicate that τὴν Cιμίχην ἀποκτενῶ is soliloquy, not addressed to Getas and Sikon. In favour of Kraus's division Handley quotes Ar. frag. 318, ἢ νῆcτιc ὀπτᾶτ' ἢ γαλεὸc ἢ τευθίδεc :: μὰ τὸν Δί' οὐ δῆτ' :: οὐδὲ βατίc;

931: Van Groningen remarked on the strangeness of κάθευδε (ed. pr. for B's καθευθε). The command to go to sleep is immediately followed by a command to listen, and ten lines later by μὴ κάθευδε. I do not think that κάθευδε can be weakened to mean 'keep quiet'; καθεύδειν is of course used metaphorically of someone who is 'asleep', when he ought to be mentally active (LSJ II), but that is not what is required of Knemon here. I once suggested that καθευθε should be καθιζε (CR N.S. xii (1962), 26), but Professor Arnott pointed out to me the existence of the imperative κάθου, from κάθημαι, attested by Hesychios as Menandrean and found in Ar. frag. 620, οἰμώζων κάθου, Anaxandrides frag. 13 K, Alexis frag. 224 K. I would now read κάθου cύ. Menander often attaches cύ to an imperative; in this play at 556, 616, 738 (where it has fallen out after ου), 753, 840, 920, 957. With this reading Knemon half struggles to his feet as he threatens to kill Simiche, but is forced to sit. This gives variety to the scene; he does not lie down throughout. His change of posture here marks the beginning of a new section: the clowning is over, he must now listen to a continuous and comparatively serious speech. One may compare the way in which the sections of his own great speech are marked by changes of position at 700 and 740. Moreover the sitting posture prepares for 954, where he is suddenly and unexpectedly jerked to his feet to join the dance: this would be difficult, perhaps impossible, if he were still recumbent (see note there).

932: Metre may be restored by reading either (a) γυναῖκα μιϲεῖϲ or (b) μιϲεῖϲ γυναῖκαϲ. Logic favours (a). There is no sign that Knemon had a greater hatred of women in general than of men; indeed a woman, his daughter, was the only person he tolerated (334), but he *had* quarrelled with his wife. One might also see in this line a kind of résumé of the prologue: dislike of crowds (7), of his wife (17), of the shrine next door (12). Against this may be set, first the fact that elsewhere in Menander 'your wife', 'his wife', and so on, is ἡ γυνή, with the article. Even in *Epitr.* 914 γυναῖκα may be understood as 'a woman', rather than 'my wife'. Possibly the absence of the article here could be excused by the metre, iambic tetrameters not trimeters. Secondly, it may be argued that the relation to πάντα ταῦτ' ἀνέξει ('you will put up with all these annoyances to which we are subjecting you') of the preceding three clauses in asyndeton is that they explain why Knemon has no choice in the matter, not that they justify his treatment. He has shunned the crowd (432 ὄχλος τις), sent away all the women of his household (867–9), and refused to join the party; hence he is alone and defenceless. (T. Williams, *Mnem.* 4th ser. xvi (1963), 120, defends μιϲεῖϲ γυναῖκαϲ as a typical exaggeration, aided by a tradition that the solitary misanthrope was specifically a misogynist also; but his evidence seems to me to be inadequate.)

I cannot match the confidence with which some scholars declare for one or other of the above alternatives, but prefer (b), mainly because of the difficulty in the lack of an article involved in (a), but also because the energy of three parallel clauses, each beginning with its verb, seems superior to the artificiality of a chiasmus.

934 πρῖε: Probably 'bite your lips in rage'. The phrase is to be associated with Soph. frag. 897 Pearson, ὀδόντι πρῖε τὸ στόμα, Ar. *Frogs* 927, μὴ πρῖε τοὺς ὀδόντας, *Wasps* 287, μηδ' οὕτω σεαυτὸν ἔσθιε μηδ' ἀγανάκτει. The passive (or middle) clearly means 'be enraged' in *AP* ix. 77, πριομένα κάλλει Γανυμήδεος εἶπέ ποθ' Ἥρα, possibly in Men. frag. 695, ἔνδοθεν δὲ πρίεται.

938–9: Aristainetos i. 27, οὐ περιβολῆς, οὐ φιλημάτων slightly supports Quincey's supplements; cf. also *Mis.* 221, τίνα περιβάλλειν καὶ φιλεῖν οὗτος [δοκεῖς;], and Heliodoros v. 44, περιπλοκῶν τε καὶ φιλημάτων.

940 ἄνωθεν is improbable with ηὐτρέπιζον, but possibly goes with what precedes, a verb of saying being understood; one could supplement μακρὸν (rather than μικρόν, with Handley, Jacques) δ' ἄνωθεν, 'they started far back in telling their stories', cf. *Epitr.* 240, μικρόν γ' ἄνωθεν (but there λέγε precedes), Aischines i. 170, μικρὸν δ' ἄνωθεν ἄρξομαι, Plut. *Marius* 45, ἄνωθεν ἀρξάμενοι. If emendation may be considered, μικρὸν δ' ἄπωθεν ηὐτρέπιζον cυμπόcιον κτλ. would make sense: 'At a little distance I was getting ready for the *men's* drinking-party.'

941 τοῖc ἀνδράcιν is opposed, it would seem, to αἱ γυναῖκεc of 937, and τούτοιc cannot belong to these words. It is the opening of an un-completed sentence, interrupted as Sikon suspects that Knemon is not paying attention. **μὴ γάρ:** (1) Shipp, Kraus, J. Martin, Handley, etc. take this as a question by Knemon 'am I not then to sleep?'; if such a feeble reaction on Knemon's part is credible, it must be a sign that his spirit is breaking. (2) Marzullo supposes a prohibition; Knemon tells his tormentors not to shake him. But γάρ is then strange. (3) The best solution is that the words are spoken by Getas, and are confirmatory of μὴ κάθευδε, 'no, don't', as in Plato, *Rep.* 509 c, ἑκὼν οὐκ ἀπολείψω :: μὴ γάρ, cf. *Theaet.* 205 e.

942: the missing word (? words) is quite uncertain, as is whether it belonged to Knemon or to Sikon. If βούλει was not preceded by a negative, the cook must wilfully misinterpret Knemon's groan as a sign that he is sorry to miss the feast. This is neither impossible nor compelling.

943 cπονδὴ παρῆν: B's cπονδὴ γὰρ ἦν 'there was a bustle', makes fair sense (γάρ 'after an expression conveying a summons to attention', Denniston, *GP* 59) and has a good parallel in Plaut. *Stich.* 677, 'ibi festinamus omnes, lectis sternendis studuimus munditiisque appa-randis', which may be translated from Menander's Ἀδελφοί α'; cf. also *festinant*, Plaut. *Casina* 763, 792. But, unlike the emendation, it has no particular point. The pouring of a libation was an essential preliminary to a cυμπόcιον. Plato Comicus frag. 69 K, in the account of a drinking-party referred to on 870, has cπονδὴ μὲν ἤδη γέγονε. For παρῆν, 'was ready', compare Eubulos frag. 112 K, ὡc γὰρ εἰcῆλθε τὰ γερόντια τότ' εἰc δόμουc, εὐθὺc ἀνεκλίνετο, παρῆν cτέφανοc ἐν τάχει, Straton frag. 1. 40 K, παρῆν (sc. χέρνιψ.) Here the libations were ready in the vessel from which they would be poured.

The following words are slightly damaged but the traces are not consistent with any Greek words but ἐcτρώννυντο χαμαὶ cτιβάc. This indicates the correctness of Jacques's emendation ἐcτρώννυτο cτιβὰc χαμαί rather than Barigazzi's ἐcτρώννυον cτιβάδαc χαμαί, or Quincey's ἐcτρώννυον χαμαιcτιβεῖc which introduces a not-impossible hapax. (ἐcτρωννύετο will not pass in Attic, so that ἐcτρωννύετο χαμαὶ cτιβάc will not do.) Blake objects to the singular cτιβάc, which is a couch made of leaves, brushwood, or similar material. But the men for which this was being prepared were only three in number, Sostratos, Kallippides, and Gorgias, and might have shared a single large cτιβάc. The plural cτιβάδεc (-άδαc), however introduced, creates an anapaest, unparalleled in this scene, although found in Aristophanes' iambic tetrameters.

The difficulty that remains is that τραπέζαc ἔγωγε involves a surprising ellipse of a verb (? ποιῶ; cτρώννυμι is not appropriate), and that in any case, when Sikon has earlier declared his superiority to the τραπεζοποιόc (646–7), it is odd that he should here claim that laying the tables is his function. E. W. Whittle, *CP* lvii (1962), 265, may be right in supposing the loss of a line between 943 and 944; this would have contained a verb to govern τραπέζαc and an activity for Sikon. It must, however, be remembered that what is described is a *symposium*, not a dinner. For the latter the cook would have to be busy with his dishes in the kitchen, but at the *symposium* the table would have sweetmeats, nuts, fruit, etc., and the cook *might* regard it as his business to set out these delicacies. The omission of a verb to govern τραπέζαc might be explained by the assumption that τοῦτο γάρ κτλ. is parenthetical, but that Sikon never returns to the expected verb because he breaks off to ask ἀκούειc; 'Are you listening?'

945 μαλακόc: Although μαλακῶc ἔχειν means 'to be ill', the adjective μαλακόc appears not to be used in that sense. Aristotle, *EN* 1150ᵃ31 opposes μαλακία to καρτερία, cf. Plato, *Rep.* 556 b, μαλακοὺc καρτερεῖν πρὸc ἡδονάc. I believe that Getas here detects, or affects to detect, signs of weakening on Knemon's part, a hankering to indulge himself at the symposium. In Plaut. *Bacch.* 73, Bacchis says to Pistoclerus, who fears for his morals if he joins her party, 'malacissandus es': although this is probably a Plautine addition to the scene, it illustrates the connotations of μαλακόc. Handley suggests that there is a joking reference to 943, ἐcτρώννυτο cτιβάc; 'an excessive liking for soft furnishings' was a sign of 'effeminate luxury'. If he is right, the joke is obscure, for cτιβάδεc (see 420 n.) are only luxurious as opposed to the bare ground and Knemon has shown no liking for them, excessive or otherwise.

946–53: In the description of the feast Sikon, who has already shown himself to be a man of metaphors and colourful language, rises to the use of plainly poetic vocabulary, in lines that are metrically strict, in that they contain only one resolution. An elevated style had been used by earlier poets in describing feasts and drinking scenes, e.g. Plato frag. 189 K, Antiphanes frag. 52, 174, 237 K; lack of context for such fragments makes it impossible to say whether they intended more than a purely comic effect. Here Menander clearly uses the poetic style to heighten the excitement and draw an alluring picture of the merriment in the cave.

946 εὔιον γέροντα: 'A Bacchic old one, already of venerable age'; B has an explanation, misplaced against 945, τον διονυcον. More prosaically the phrase means 'wine of an old vintage'; it is easier because γέρων is sometimes applied adjectivally to οἶνοc: Alexis frag. 167, ἤδη cαπρόc, γέρων γε δαιμονίωc, cf. Eubulos frag. 124 K, Θάcιον ἢ Χῖον λαβὼν | ἢ Λέcβιον γέροντα νεκταροcταγῆ. **πολιόc**, lit. 'grey-haired', sometimes has the connotation 'venerable', e.g. Plato, *Tim.* 22 b, μάθημα χρόνῳ πολιόν· **ἔκλινε** (replacing the usual ἐνέχει) continues the metaphor; the old man is 'put to rest', not 'poured in'. Wine was poured into the cup first (ὑποχεῖν) and water added (ἐπιχεῖν), see Athenaios 782 a.

947 κύτος, 'vessel' or 'jar' is, like νᾶμα and πρόcπολοc (950), a word from tragedy. Plato Comicus, parodying tragic language, wrote ἴηcιν εὐθὺς κύλικος εἰς κοῖλον κύτοc (frag. 189 K). Earlier comedians used high-flown descriptions of everyday things to raise a laugh; Menander, deftly avoiding exaggerated absurdity, uses the old device to give a touch of idyllic romance to his picture; one is reminded of some of Aristophanes' lyrics.

948 ἐδεξιοῦτ': δεξιοῦμαι+dat. means 'raise the right hand in greeting to someone'; here it must mean 'toasting', cf. [Eur.] *Rhesus* 419, πυκνὴν ἄμυcτιν . . . δεξιούμενοι.

949 ὥcπερεὶ 'c ἄμμον: This is perhaps the least objectionable solution of a difficult problem. I reject the emendation ψάμμον for the letters cαμμον, since there is no close similarity between carrying sand and keeping cups filled with wine. But sand is a notorious absorbent of liquid, and the sense may be 'it was as if you were carrying wine to sand'. This could properly be expressed either by ὥcπερεὶ εἰς ἄμμον φοροίηc or by ὥcπερ ἂν εἰς ἄ. φ. 'it was just as you might carry' or by ὥcπερ ἂν εἰ εἰc ἄ. φ. The last form may have arisen by confusion of the other two or by an ellipse, ὥcπερ ἂν (εἴη εἰ) εἰς ἄ. φ. (LSJ s.v. ὥcπερ εἰ II). The letters of our text can be explained in two ways: we must suppose either an illogical suppression of εἰ and write ὥcπερ εἰc ἄμμον, or a synaloepha of εἰ and εἰc, to be represented by εἰ 'c. In Ar. *Lys.* 605 χωρεῖ 'c τὴν ναῦν stands in modern texts (after Bentley), although the MSS. have χωρεῖ εἰc, and at *Thesm.* 1224 Cobet's τηδὶ διώξει; 'c τοὔμπαλιν τρέχειc is required. But B's spelling is unreliable, so that ωcπερειc may be a mere error for ωcπερειειc. Neither here nor in Aristophanes can εἰ 'c be interpreted as indicating prodelision of ἐc, for that form of the preposition is confined in comedy to the phrases ἐc κόρακαc, ἐc μακαρίαν. Gallavotti ingeniously suggested ὥcπερ εἰ Cάμιον φοροίηc. But an anapaest is nowhere else substituted in this scene for a spondee (cf. 924 n.), and the sense intended is not very clear: presumably 'they enjoyed the local wine as much as if it had been Samian wine'.

As object of φοροίηc the word ταῦτα is suspiciously vague; it is more likely to be that of μανθάνειc. The question ταῦτα μανθάνειc cύ; might be assigned with plausibility to Getas, but it is not a necessary change.

950 βραχεῖcα: Lit. 'soaked', i.e. tipsy, cf. Eur. *El.* 326, μέθη δὲ βρεχθεὶc τῆc ἐμῆc μητρὸc πόcιc . . . ἐνθρῴcκει τάφῳ. B gives βρεχειcα, a spelling of the aorist passive known from Egyptian papyri of the second century A.D., but unlikely to have been used by Menander, since it appears to be a hybrid between two legitimate forms: ἐβρέχθην, found in Attic writers, and ἐβράχην, previously known only from prose authors of the second century A.D. or of uncertain date (see LSJ). Compare such pairs as ἐcτρέφθην/ἐcτράφην.

950–2: The phrases προcώπου ἄνθοc κατεcκιαcμένη and χορεῖον εἰcέβαινε ῥυθμόν straddle over the line-endings and make one long swinging sentence of these three lines, which thus contrast with the short *cola* of 946–8. **εὐήλικοc:** The analogy of ἔφηλιξ, παρῆλιξ, cυνῆλιξ shows that the rare word εὐῆλιξ here means 'of an excellent age', i.e. a young adult. (In [Polemon], *Physiognomica* 5 εὐήλικεc, if not an error for εὐμήκειc, must mean 'tall'.) The girl's face had the 'bloom' of youth (ἄνθοc), and she was 'shaded with respect to it': the shade will have been cast by a veil or a garland or her hair (cf. Archilochos frag. 25, ἡ δέ οἱ κόμη ὤμουc κατεcκίαζε, Anakreon frag. 347 Page) or any combination of these things. Then she 'stepped into a dance rhythm', at the same time 'hesitating and trembling', for she was 'ashamed' of so departing from the modest behaviour expected of a girl; cf. Teles p. 38 Hense, μέλλων καὶ τρέμων.

953: Another girl joined hands with her (cυγκαθάπτειν is a new word) and they made a dance. **κἀχόρευεν:** van Groningen supported the change to κἀχόρευον, made also by Maas, arguing that a single dancer does not constitute a χόροc, and that it takes at least two to χορεύειν. Although this is true, the verb is commonly used in the singular, meaning 'dance with another or others', and may be so used here. The proposed change, although possibly right, is not necessary.

954: This line takes a surprising turn: no one would expect that the address ὦ πρᾶγμα πάνδεινον παθών would be followed by the command to dance with them, χόρευε. One can imagine that Getas lays a com-miserating hand on Knemon, and then suddenly with Sikon's aid jerks him to his feet. This is only possible if the old man is already sitting up. There can be no pause in the middle of the line, for all this is recited to the strict time of the music. ὦ πρᾶγμα πάνδεινον παθών: There is nothing poetic about this phrase unless it be the construction of ὦ with a participle; the words themselves are ordinary, cf. *Sam.* 557, πάνδεινα ποιεῖ πράγματα, Demosthenes liv. 33, πάνδεινον ἔςται πρᾶγμα. cυνεπίβαινε: The relevant meaning of ἐπιβαίνω, used absolutely, is 'get a footing', 'stand on one's feet', e.g. of a wounded man, *Iliad* v. 666. So here the compound will mean 'get on your feet along with us' or 'with our help'.

955–6: 'What on earth are you after, you wretches?' cries Knemon, and Getas replies only 'Do more to get on your feet with us; you're a clumsy fellow'; they resume the dance to his protest: 'For heaven's sake, don't.'

So I understand the line, but other interpretations may be right. (1) At the beginning B has τυπτε, which it is tempting to expand to τύπτετε; (Fraenkel, etc.). But I think this is a will-o'-the-wisp. The plain brutality of intimidating the old man by blows would be out of place in a scene where sociability is to prevail over solitariness, and I suspect that the audience would have found repulsive the spectacle of a free man being beaten by a slave. It is better to assume τιποτε >τιπτε >τυπτε (for υ replacing ι cf. 873, ουκ'εια for οικεια; but the sounds represented by the letters were not yet identical, W. S. Allen, *Vox Graeca*, 65). The double interrogative in τί ποτε τί is to be paralleled by such passages as *Sam.* 324, ποῖ cὺ ποῖ μαcτιγία; But it may be better to articulate τί ποτ' ἔτι (Householder), 'What more do you want?'

(2) Handley does not commit himself to any specific action here; he leaves open the possibility that Knemon is not hoisted up, but continues to lie on his bed. He takes μᾶλλον not as intensive with cυνεπίβαινε, but as 'a weak adversative': 'join in rather than protest'.

(3) Handley also supposes ἄγροικος εἶ to mean 'your manners!', being a reference to the old man's refusal to dance. He quotes *P. Hib.* 6, Page *GLP* p. 288, where the phrase Ἄπολλον, ὡς ἄγροικυς εἶ is addressed to a young man who has refused an offer of money and provisions. This may be right, but I prefer to suppose that Knemon's 'clumsy stupidity' refers to the failure of his feet to follow the rhythm of the dance into which he is being dragged. Since the townsman ascribes awkwardness and stupidity to the rustic, the adjective ἄγροικος is found associated with cκαιός, Ephippos frag. 23 K, with δυcμαθής, Ar. *Clouds* 646, and when Strepsiades will not learn about rhythms he is ἀγρεῖος καὶ cκαιός (655). Theophrastos, *Char.* iv, defines ἀγροικία

as ἀσχήμων ἀμαθία. Here Getas finds that Knemon has a countryman's 'stupidity' over dancing.

958: B originally had κεικακα, converted to τακεικακα, i.e. τἀκεῖ κακά, by writing τα above κει. The explanation of this is not obvious. Perhaps τἀκεῖ and τὰ κακά are variant readings, that have been conflated, less probably κακά is an explanation of τἀκεῖ. I see no grounds for a rational choice. In any case the sense is the same. Knemon continues to regard human society as burdensome, but as a choice of evils the company in the cave is better than that of Sikon and Getas.

959 ὦ καλλίνικοι: The victory of Getas and Sikon is an augury for the success of the play. We have here a muted echo of the more boisterous conclusions of some of Aristophanes' plays. Compare in *Ach.* 1227 ff. the repeated τήνελλα καλλίνικος, a phrase which recurs at the end of *Birds* (1764); and so in *Eccl.* and *Lysistr.* the chorus engage in a song and dance ὡς ἐπὶ νίκῃ, to celebrate their success and to wish victory for the dramatist. Cf. L. B. Lawler, *Orchesis Kallinikos*, *TAPA* lxxix (1948), 254.   **παῖ Δόναξ**: A slave of this name occurs also in *Sikyonios* (385) and another is a member of Thraso's storming-party in Ter. *Eun.* 772. 'Reed' would be a suitable name for a piper, and since the piper ceases to play with the change from tetrameters to trimeters, it has been thought that Donax is the piper, now free to make one of the bearers. This is, I think, an improbable fancy. Donax is rather one of the slaves belonging to the party brought by Sostratos' mother. The name may have been given to men of fine physique, as a large man today may be nicknamed 'Tiny'.   **cύ γε**, 'yes, you', has met with much doubt, but Soph. *Phil.* 977, 'Οδυccέωc, cάφ' ἴcθ', ἐμοῦ γ', ὃν εἰcορᾷc, provides a parallel of a sort. Maas ingeniously proposed Cύρε; but the appearance of another slave would be unnecessary since a man, whether on a bed or not, is carried as conveniently by two as by three bearers. Lloyd-Jones's cύ τ' ὦ Cίκων (cf. cὺ δ' ὦ Cίκων at a line-end, Ar. *Eccl.* 867) cannot be safely rejected, but ὦ with the vocative raises doubt, see 823 n.

961 παρακινοῦντά τι: There are three possible ways of understanding this: (1) 'causing any trouble', cf. Dem. xv. 12, πρὸς τὸ μηδ' ὁτιοῦν παρακινεῖν, (2) 'shifting your ground', cf. Plato, *Rep.* 540 a, εἰ ἐμμενοῦcιν . . . ἤ τι καὶ παρακινήcουcι; (3) 'behaving insanely', cf. Plato, *Phaedr.* 249 d, νουθετεῖται ὡς παρακινῶν.

962 αὖτις: The 'Attic' form αὖθιc, normal in the κοινή, is thought to have arisen through the influence on an original αὖτιc, retained in Ionic, of αὖθι, with which it is confused by Alexandrian poets (so Boisacq, *Dictionnaire étymologique*, and Frisk, *Etym. Wörterbuch*). The

explanation is not very convincing, since it supposes that a word in
everyday use was influenced by one that belongs to the poetic epic.
It is remarkable that the papyri of Menander give αυτις 3 or 4 times
(*Dysk.* 962, *Epitr.* 579, *Sam.* 626, (?) 637) against two occurrences of
αυθις (*Epitr.* 972, *Sik.* 64). But the MSS. of Stobaios give αὖθις in
Theoph. frag. 1. 2 and αὖθις is also in the Didot papyrus (i. 30).
Pearson, *Sophocles* (OCT), Praef. xvi, notes that not only do the MSS.
of the tragedians often have αὖτις, but that it also occurs twice in the
papyrus of the *Ichneutae* (227, 229); he suspects that Sophocles used
either form at will.

963: The simplest solution is that of Gallavotti, to change τηνικαδω to
τηνικάδ'. ἰώ. The hiatus after ἰώ is perhaps not intolerable, cf. Ar.
Birds 406, ἰώ, ἔποψ. The division of the tribrach after the second
syllable is a more serious objection; although it may be palliated by
elision, it is made more remarkable by the punctuation. But it is
possible that the abrupt shout ἰώ excuses the licence. If this solution
is rejected, a variety of more or less arbitrary remedies are to hand,
some keeping τηνικάδε, others changing it to τηνικαῦτα (τηνίκα is not
Attic). A further complication is that both words can mean 'on this
occasion' as well as 'on that occasion', and can therefore be taken
either with what follows or with what precedes. Taking them with
what follows, we could have e.g. τὸ τηνικάδε ⟨δ' οὖν⟩ ἐκδότω or τὸ
τηνικα⟨ῦτα⟩ δ' ἐκδότω (*ed. pr.*); with what precedes, τὸ τηνικάδε.
⟨νῦν δ'⟩ ἐκδότω (Kraus) or τὸ τηνικα⟨ῦτ'. ἀ⟩λλ' ἐκδότω (London,
Thierfelder; Handley also hesitantly suggests ὦ ἐκδότω). Blake gives
τὸ τηνικάδ⟨ε γ'.⟩ ὦ⟨δ'⟩ ἐκδότω. *Non liquet.*

964: B marks change of speaker after δᾷδα and not at the end of the
line. But the final address to the audience must be made by Getas,
since Sikon is occupied in carrying Knemon. This would not, however, make it impossible for him to hand the old man a garland,
perhaps picked up from an altar or a statue (cf. 311 n.) in passing or
brought by a super. The two words τουτονὶ λαβέ may therefore belong
to him. But if the paragraphus is a mistake, the dicolon might indicate
that Getas, having called for garlands, now turns to address Knemon.
For the ellipse of στέφανον, cf. Ar. *Thesm.* 380, περίθου νυν τόνδε, *Eccl.*
171, τονδὶ λαβοῦσα.

The garlands are wear for revellers (cf. Plato Comicus frag. 69 K,
στέφανον ἔπειθ' ἑκάστῳ | δώσω φέρων τῶν ξυμποτῶν), and the torch,
too, is associated with going to a party, cf. Ar. *Eccl.* 1149, *Plut.* 1041,
στεφάνους γέ τοι καὶ δᾷδ' ἔχων πορεύεται. Here sober sense may see
little point in having a torch for the short journey to the cave, but
besides marking that the day is over and night has fallen, it lends the

play's conclusion the traditional atmosphere of the κῶμος. A torch or torches appear in the exodos of Ar. *Eccl.* (1149), *Plut.* (1194, ἀλλ' ἐκδότω τις δεῦρο δᾷδας), *Frogs* (1525), *Clouds* (1490), Men. *Sikyonios* (418), *Samia* (731), *Misumenos* (458), and in a play by Antiphanes (frag. 199 K); garlands in *Sam.*, *Sik.*, *Mis.*, *P. Oxy.* 1239 (*Menandri Fab. Incert.* v Mette).

(vii) 965–969: *address to audience by Getas*

967: It would seem that the *plaudite* of Latin comedies is derived from their Greek originals; but it could not in the altered conditions of the Roman theatre be followed by an appeal for victory. There is a similar request for applause at the end of *Samia* (735), *Sikyonios* (421), and in frag. 771, ἐξείραντες (not ἐξάραντες, Fraenkel, *Beobachtungen zu Aristophanes*, p. 155) ἐπικροτήσατε. Kraus finds in this line evidence that there were no women in the audience, contrary to the conclusions of Pickard-Cambridge, *Dramatic Festivals*², pp. 263–5, 269. Yet if women were present, decorum might forbid them to applaud.

968–9: This couplet is quoted by the scholia on Aristides (Dindorf p. 301), and alluded to by Himerios, *or.* xix. 3; the last line was adapted by Dioskoros of Aphroditopolis (cf. intro. p. 3). The couplet also concluded *Misumenos* and *Sikyonios*; it has been recognized by Handley and Corbato in *P. Oxy.* 1239 (*BICS* xii [1965], 62, *Studi Men.* 94) and may have stood at the end of other plays, just as the formula for introducing the chorus could be repeated, cf. 231 n. Moreover, dramatists must have closely approached one another in the wording of their appeals for victory and requests for applause: the last words of Poseidippos' *Apokleiomene* were [ἡ] δὲ φιλόγελως θεὰ | [Νίκη με]θ' ἡμῶν εὐμενὴς ἔπ[οι]τ' ἀεί (*Pap. Heidelberg* 183, cf. E. Vogt, *RhM* cii [1959], 192).

968 εὐπάτειρα: Nike is by origin Athena Nike, so that her father is Zeus, cf. Himerios, *or.* xix. 3, Νίκη, Διὸς τοῦ μεγάλου παῖ, εὐπάτειρα καὶ φιλόγελως. Although Wilamowitz said that only a pedant would inquire into her paternity, we may suppose that Menander agreed with Himerios, not with Hesiod, who made her the daughter of a giant, Pallas, and of Styx (*Theogony* 384). One is reminded of the anapaests ὦ μέγα σεμνὴ Νίκη τὸν ἐμὸν βίοτον κατέχοις καὶ μὴ λήγοις στεφανοῦσα that conclude Eur. *IT*, *Or.*, and the spurious end of *Phoen.*, and are interpolated in some MSS. of *Hipp.* (Barrett on *Hipp.* 1462–6 argues that these are everywhere actors' supplements, and would account in the same way for the repetition in five plays of πολλαὶ μορφαὶ τῶν δαιμονίων. I do not think that Wm. Calder III, *Cl. Phil.* lx [1965], 281, shakes his case against these tags in tragedy.)

EPITREPONTES

C   *P. Cairensis* 43227 contains 218–699, 714–25, 749–59, 853–958, 969–89, 1003–23, 1037–57, 1060–1131. All between 582 and 759, 853 and 981, 989 and 1060 is badly mutilated; only here and there does the sense appear.

P   *Membranae Petropolitanae* (Petr. graec. 388) contain 127–48, 159–77. They were at Petrograd, now Leningrad.

O 4   *P. Oxyrhynchica* 1236 is a mutilated parchment page containing parts of 880–901, 923–43.

O 14   *P. Oxyrhynchica* 2829 has the middle of 218–31, the beginnings of 232–56, and some remains of 310–22, 347–61. There are six other very small scraps which cannot be placed.

Pap. Berol. 21142 (ined.) of the second century A.D., knowledge of which I owe to Dr. C. Austin, has the beginnings of eleven lines (and an illegible letter that begins the twelfth) running as follows: εἰς ἕτερα ν[, ἤδη 'cτι πει[, Χαριcίωι πρ[, ἀλλὰ λέλυτα[ι, πίνειν μ[, βινεῖν ε.[, οὐθεὶc κελ[ευ, προcτάξατ.[, ἀγάπα κολα[, ἐπιcτọλη[, εἰρην[. This is dialogue, since there is a paragraphus below every line but the tenth. As the name Charisios occurs in no other known play, the fragment may be from *Epitrepontes*. A place might be found for it in the first scene between Onesimos and Karion, or conceivably between 146 and 150; the scene between Pamphile and Smikrines, after 759, seems unlikely. Unfortunately, even if it does belong to *Epitrepontes*, it is uninformative.

Annotated editions: U. von Wilamowitz-Moellendorf, *Menander, Das Schiedsgericht* (1925), V. de Falco, *Menandri Epitrepontes* (1st edn. 1945; 3rd edn. 1961).

Scene: a street in an Attic deme. Two houses seen, those of Charisios and Chairestratos.

Dramatis Personae, in suggested order of appearance:
    Karion, caterer and chef
    Onesimos, personal servant to Charisios
    Chairestratos, a friend of Charisios
    Habrotonon, a girl harpist, enslaved to a brothel-keeper
    Smikrines, father of Pamphile
    Syros (or Syriskos), a charcoal-burner
    Daos, a shepherd

Simias, perhaps not a speaking part (see n. on 603–36)
Pamphile, daughter of Smikrines and wife of Charisios
Charisios, a young man, husband of Pamphile
Sophrone, one-time nurse to Pamphile; perhaps not a speaking
part (see n. on 1119–20)

The deme is nowhere identified in what remains of the play.
Gomme thought it might lie at the foothills of Hymettos (e.g. near
the modern monastery of Kaiseriane), though he observed that
Hymettos was not, for the greater part, wooded (242) in Menander's
day any more than it is now (Plat. *Critias* 111 c). In Alkiphron *Epist.*
iii. 27 a married woman who, like Pamphile, has to get rid of a child
born five months after marriage, causes it to be exposed on Mount
Parnes; Syriskos' occupation of charcoal-burning is a reminder that
Acharnai, famous for its charcoal-burners, lay at the foot of that
mountain. Wilamowitz (*Schiedsgericht*, 50–1) objects that Acharnai is
rather far from the city, from which he believed Smikrines to make
three journeys in one day. If such considerations of realism are applicable, they apply even more forcibly to the suggestion of H. J. Mette,
Hermes xc (1962), 383, that the scene will be near the still more
distant Ἁλαὶ Ἀραφηνίδες (see 451 n.), since Charisios and Pamphile
both attended the Tauropolia there before their marriage. I doubt,
however, whether realistic calculation of time and distance should be
applied to events off stage (intro. p. 19 n. 2) and, even if they should be,
believe that only two of Smikrines' journeys fall in one day (introductory note to Act III).

The persons of the play all with the exception of Smikrines bear
names in common use at Athens, but by dramatic convention these
names indicate their status or character. *Karion*, a derivative of Κάρ,
'Karian', said by Aischines ii. 157 to be a name often borne by
characters in comedy, is given elsewhere to cooks (Euphron, *Syn-
ephebi*—an apprentice—Plaut. *Miles* 1397); it was often a slave name
(e.g. Ar. *Plutus*), and cooks are constantly found in comedy associating
on familiar terms with the slaves who assist them; the last scene of
Dyskolos offers a striking example. In spite of what is said by Athenaios,
quoted in the note on Sikon, p. 131, some of these cooks may be slaves
themselves, living independently but paying part of their earnings to
their masters, or they may be freedmen. Elaborate cooking was not
an everyday feature of life even in a wealthy Greek household; when
the occasion demanded it, a cook was hired and prepared the meal
with the aid of the regular servants. *Onesimos, Syros (Syriskos)*, and *Daos*
are all common slave names. The first, 'Helpful', may be compared
with such names as Cωcίας, Χρηcτή, Πιcτός; the two latter are ethnic
names, the Daoi seeming to be a Phrygian people (*Aspis* 206). The

giving of ethnic names to slaves was common, e.g. Getas, Thratta (both in *Heros*), Lydos (*Dis Exapaton*), but some could be borne by citizens, e.g. Skythes (Kirchner, *Prosop. Att.* 12736–7). Similarly Parmenon, normally a slave name, occasionally belonged to a citizen (ibid. 11640, 11642–3). The same is true of *Habrotonon*, which as in *Perik.* is here given to a slave *hetaira*: the name is derived from an aromatic plant (*artemisia*), supposed to have aphrodisiac qualities (Pliny, *NH* xxi. 162). *Sophrone* denotes an old nurse (*Heros*, Terence *Eunuchus*, *Phormio*). *Smikrines* is usually a tight-fisted old man (*Aspis*, ?*Sik.*, Plaut. *Aulularia*). The name *Charisios* for a young man is not known from any other play, but is found in *P. Berol.* 21142, which may be a fragment of *Epitrepontes*. *Chairestratos* was the name of a leading young man in Εὐνοῦχος, Terence's Phaedria, of a man of uncertain age in *Pap. Ghôran* II (Page, *GLP* p. 304), and of an older one in *Aspis*. *Pamphile* was a name historically borne by *hetairai* as well as respectable women, but it is that of the heroine in Ter. *Adelphoe*, of the young girl in *Eunuchus*, and of a young wife in Plaut. *Stichus*.

Ten quotations in ancient writers, which are either given as from *Epitrepontes* or plausibly assigned to it, cannot be accurately placed. Fragments 1–6 are generally believed to have come before the first surviving scene. Fragments 1 and 2 are probably from the opening of the play: fragments 3 and 5 seem also to be from the first act. Fragments 4 and 6 are placed here with some plausibility. For fragments 7 and 8 see after 759; fragments 9 and 10 are printed at the end of the play.

Fragment 1. It is possible that these lines opened the play as Onesimos, who had been sent to hire a cook in the town, entered with him. Dr. Austin has pointed out to me that πρὸς θεῶν may have a parallel in *Dis Exapaton*, which opened with the words πρὸς τῶν θεῶν, μειράκιον (*ZPE* vi [1970], 6). But clearly some other verses may have preceded.

The name of the cook, Karion, was restored by Wilamowitz from a passage of Themistios (*or.* xxi. 262 C) that clearly refers to fragment 2. After quoting οὐδὲν γλυκερώτερον (*sic*) ἢ πάντ' εἰδέναι, he continues ὁ μάγειρος ὁ κωμῳδικός . . . ἐπέτριβε τοὺς δαιτυμόνας ἐξαλλάττων τὰ ἡδύσματα. ἀλλ' οὐκ ἐνταῦθα Καρίωνος τὸ κακὸν τὸ μέγα, ὅτι μοχθηρὰ ἡ τέχνη αὐτοῦ καὶ ἀλλόκοτος, ἀλλ' ὅτι πονηρὸν ἀνθρώπιον ἦν καὶ οὐκ ἐπὶ τῷ ἔργῳ εἰς τὰς οἰκίας παρερχόμενον, ἀλλ' ἵνα λαλήσῃ καὶ ψιθυρίσῃ . . . καὶ ἐξενέγκῃ . . . καὶ τὰ ἀπόρρητα τῆς οἰκίας. This shows not only that Karion was represented as a gossip but also that, like many cooks of comedy, he boasted of the refinements of his art; this aspect may appear in fragment 5. It is conceivable that Onesimos was led by Karion to tell how he had found out that Pamphile had borne a child during her husband's absence, five months after her marriage, and exposed it with the help of her old nurse Sophrone; how he had reported this to Charisios on his return and how his master had left his home for that of his friend Chairestratos, summoning Habrotonon to console him. Capps, *AJP* xxix (1908), 422, argues that Charisios' intention will have been to force Pamphile to leave him; he refrains from divorcing her by sending her away, since that might call her character into question. A high-minded man, such as Charisios is represented to be, might have intended this result, and this could have been explained in a divine prologue (see below). The actual remains of the play contain nothing to support Capps's theory, for which, however, Ter. *Hec.* 148–56 offers a good parallel.

ὁ τρόφιμος: In New Comedy regularly used by slaves of the master's son, normally of the young master still living at home, but here of one who has now married and set up on his own (cf. *Dysk.* 378). In a rich household a son would often have his personal slave, and it may be implied that Onesimos had filled that position with Charisios before, as well as after, his marriage. τρόφιμος can have a passive sense, 'child being reared', cf. Eur. *Ion* 684, and one may suppose this to be the origin of so calling the son of the house; but some Greeks at least thought the meaning to be active, 'providing rations', see Schol. Aristid. p. 53 Dind., σημαίνει καὶ τὸν θρέψαντα καὶ τὸν τραφέντα. θρέψαντα τὸν δεσπότην, ὡς παρὰ Μενάνδρῳ.

ὁ νῦν ἔχων τὴν Ἁβρότονον: Karion already knows the story from local gossip; and, as Wilamowitz notes, he is intrigued that he is to arrange a dinner for Charisios, but not at Charisios' own house. Note the article (almost 'our friend Habrotonon'), and that it is feminine though the name is neuter in form, cf. ἡ Γναθαίνιον, ἡ Γλυκέριον, Machon 335, 511 Gow.

ψάλτριαν: Although ψάλτριαι and αὐλητρίδες are sometimes associated (frag. 264) and the legal maximum charge for a slave of either profession was the same, viz. 2 drachmas (Arist. *Ath. Pol.* 50. 2), there may have been some difference of esteem, since the κιθάρα was, and the αὐλός was not, regarded as a suitable instrument for the free man to play (cf. the story of Athena's rejecting the αὐλός); and it is noteworthy that girls who are being trained to be *hetairai* but later turn out to be of citizen birth learn the stringed instrument, (Plaut. *Rud.* 43, Ter. *Eun.* 133) and that Phaedria in Ter. *Phormio* buys and frees a *citharistria* to make her his mistress.

Fragment 2. This fragment is quoted with καὶ πάλιν between the two parts, which implies that they were not consecutive, or not spoken by the same person. De Falco gives καὶ σύ ... εἶ to Onesimos, which is not out of the question.   περίεργος: 'Officious, meddlesome', as at 262, and in particular 'inquisitive', as here and *Sam.* 300. Whether Onesimos was, in this first scene, delighted with the success of his curiosity, or already feeling that all was not well between him and his master, we do not know. It would be like Menander to make Karion congratulate Onesimos, unaware of the latter's embarrassment.

Fragment 3. Meaning and occasion are quite uncertain; although editors assign the words to Onesimos, they might be spoken by Chairestratos or even Habrotonon. Since Photios quotes the passage to illustrate the use of ἀλύειν to mean μηδὲν πράττειν that meaning is more likely than the older sense 'be distraught, perplexed'. κατακείμενος may mean 'reclining at table, or 'lying on his bed' (cf. *Perik.* 551).   ὁ δέ probably refers to Charisios, but possibly to Chairestratos or even Karion. It may be noted that the speaker is not necessarily addressing the person (? Karion) who is the subject of ποιεῖς; for he may be recounting what he, or someone else, had previously said.

Fragment 4. ἐχῖνος: 'A kind of large jar, with a wide mouth: mentioned by Menander in the *Epitrepontes*' (Erotianos p. 41. 18 Nachm.).

Fragment 5. ἐπέπασα: An aorist of repeated action (Goodwin, *MT* § 56; akin to the gnomic use), as it is followed by ἐὰν οὕτω τύχῃ, 'if it should so befall'. The phrase must contain a jest, for τάριχος is (1) a cheap food, not a suitable material for culinary art, (2) already salted. This second fact puts out of court Wilamowitz's view (*Schiedsgericht*, 51) that the fragment comes from a speech in which Smikrines contrasted his own economical life with Charisios' extravagance. Themistios, quoted on frag. 1, says that Karion 'varied his seasonings'; to put salt on salt fish would be a seasoning 'unpleasantly out of the ordinary (ἀλλόκοτος)'. That Karion made jokes at somebody's expense in this play is shown by Athenaios 659 b, οἱ μάγειροι σκωπτικοί τινες, ὡς παρὰ Μενάνδρῳ ἐν Ἐπιτρέπουσιν.

Fragment 6. It is usually supposed that these lines were spoken by Smikrines, and formed part of the scene of which 127 is the first line preserved. Neither supposition is by any means certain. Capps thought that they belong to Karion. A man who is without occupation eats twice as much if healthy as he does if in a fever, but to no purpose, because he is equally unproductive.

After the opening scene, which cannot have been a short one, between Onesimos and Karion, what happened? It is generally supposed that

there was a 'delayed prologue', as in *Aspis*, *Heros*, *Perikeiromene*, and
other plays, spoken by some divinity. However much of the background may have been given by Onesimos, he cannot have explained
the key points that Charisios was in fact the father of Pamphile's
supposedly illegitimate child, and that this child, although exposed,
had been rescued by a slave who had given it to another slave, whose
master was Chairestratos. It would be contrary to what is known of
Greek dramatic practice to keep the audience in the dark about these
facts, allowing them to share their discovery with Pamphile and
Charisios. In theory, Menander might in this play (as Gomme maintained) have innovated by letting the spectators learn the truth
simultaneously with the characters. That he did not, is made as good
as certain by the arbitration scene from which the play is named.
That long dispute over the ownership of some trinkets found with an
exposed baby would lose its dramatic effect if the audience were unaware that the baby had any connection with the characters who had
already been introduced. Moreover, it is a typical piece of Greek
irony that Smikrines, who adjudicates, is unaware that on his decision
depends the fate of his own grandson. It is essential, if the scene is to
have its full force, that the audience should see the danger in which he
stands of unknowingly condemning the infant to a life of slavery.

(i) **127–141**: *Smikrines, Chairestratos (apart)*

The Petrograd parchment contains the end of the last scene of Act I
(see 169 n.). Where it begins, Smikrines is speaking in a soliloquy;
he can hardly have been long on the stage in view of Chairestratos'
remark at 131, which seems to be a reaction to his appearance on the
scene, not to his words. He has come to visit his daughter, whom his
son-in-law, he hears, has abandoned in order to carouse in low company; but in accordance with his parsimonious nature his indignation
is directed against the extravagance rather than the disloyalty of this.
What preceded his entrance, there is no means of knowing. Something
had brought Chairestratos on the stage; if he had a companion, that
person perhaps re-entered the house at Smikrines' approach, while
Chairestratos drew aside to remain unseen.

127 ff.: πίνει δὲ πολυτελέστατον, Sudhaus's supplement for the end of
the preceding verse, gives the certain sense, Smikrines being more
concerned with the cost than the quantity of the wine consumed.

αὐτὸ τοῦτ' . . . τοῦτό γε: 'This is what astounds me . . . it is this
which is well-nigh incredible.' Note ὑπέρ in the sense more usually
borne by περί, not uncommon from the fourth century but found as
early as Hdt. iv. 8. 1.

ἀπιστίᾳ: Gomme agreed with most editors in accepting the interpretation supported by H. Fränkel, *AJP* lviii (1937), 456, according to which ἀπιστία is passive, 'incredibility', and the whole phrase means '*this* is as good as incredible, that a man has to force himself to drink when he is paying a top price for his wine, i.e. getting a first-rate wine.' Fränkel supposed that Charisios was not only, as will appear, uninterested in Habrotonon but had also shown a disinclination to drink, news of which had somehow reached Smikrines.

I find this latter supposition difficult to accept, because there is no sign elsewhere that Smikrines thinks of Charisios as a reluctant reprobate: on the contrary, he pictures him on the alcoholic path to ruin (755, cf. 588, 681). It seems to me more likely that the parsimonious old man is surprised that anyone can even force himself to drink, let alone do it willingly, when his wine costs so much. (Does not this also better account for καί?). Charisios' drunkenness may be passed over, but not his extravagance.

Neither of the passages quoted by Fränkel to support the passive sense of ἀπιστία is relevant, for in both the word has the active meaning 'distrust, disbelief': Herakleitos frag. 86 D–K, ἀπιστίῃ διαφυγγάνει γινώσκεσθαι, Aesch. *Ag.* 268, πέφευγε τοὔπος ἐξ ἀπιστίας. But the adj. ἄπιστος often means· 'incredible' (LSJ s.v. I. 2) and a corresponding use of ἀπιστία is not only likely, but found in Isokr. xvii. 48, τὴν ἀτοπίαν καὶ τὴν ἀπιστίαν ὧν . . . ἐπεχείρει λέγειν. Phrases like ταῦτ' ἀπιστίαν, ταῦτ' ὀργὴν ἔχει, Dem. x. 45, do not, of course, show the passive sense. Wilamowitz conjectured ἀπληστία, 'greediness', a word that does not fit the context.

εἰ καὶ βιάζεται . . . ἑαυτόν: 'That a man should really bring himself to drink when he buys wine at an obol the half-pint'. For the separation of βιάζεται and ἑαυτόν cf. *Dysk.* 236 n. Pherekrates frag. 1 K omits the reflexive pronoun, ἐγὼ κατεσθίω μόλις τῆς ἡμέρας πένθ' ἡμιμέδιμνα, ἐὰν βιάζωμαι. In normal years wine could be had at one-sixth of an obol for a κοτύλη (about half a pint); in times of scarcity the price could be three times as great (Dem. xlii. 20, Körte, *Gnomon* i [1925], 22). No doubt one could pay even higher prices than one obol for superior wines, cf. Plut. *Mor.* 470 f (4 obols for imported Chian shocks a friend of Socrates). In Alexis frag. 15 K someone, in giving the accounts of a party, mentions wine at 10 obols the χοῦς (of 12 κοτύλαι). It seems, therefore, that Smikrines' surprise and indignation are comic, the price of one obol a κοτύλη being by no means unheard of.

132 διασκεδᾷ τὸν ἔρωτα: The obvious meaning is that Smikrines will break up Charisios' affair with Habrotonon, and this implies that Chairestratos is unaware that in fact there is nothing between them.

It is possible, of course, that other *hetairai* were present besides Habrotonon, and that Chairestratos foresees an end to his party and all the love-making that is to be expected. Webster, *StM* 36, suggests that Chairestratos means by ἔρωτα his own love, and that he had in a previous scene explained that, as Charisios was uninterested in Habrotonon, he had himself conceived a passion for her. But if the party for which Charisios had hired her broke up, why should he not then hire her for his own use? It must be emphasized that nothing in the actual remains of the play (as opposed to conjectural supplements) indicates that Menander met the sentimental demand that Habrotonon should get a lover, still less (as some have wished) a husband. Yet when Chorikios, *apol. mim.* 71, speaks of a Chairestratos who loved a harp-player, he may have *Epitr.* in mind, though it is rash to assert it. He was probably referring to a well-known play (Körte, *Hermes* lxxix [1944], 207), but Chairestratos was a name used in Menander's Ἀcπίc and Εὐνοῦχος and in *Pap. Ghôran* ii, perhaps elsewhere also.

133 τί δὲ . . . οἰμωζέτω; Körte, following Hutloff, assigns these words to Smikrines, on the ground that there is a space and a colon after ερωτα (just as there is at the change of speaker after διδωcι, 137, and γλυκυτατε, 143). Smikrines will then not yet be concerned about the safety of his daughter's dowry, but declare that Charisios' extravagance is no concern of his; it is his son-in-law's behaviour to Pamphile that troubles him, although in complaining of it he again reverts to the topic of extravagance. The sense of this is good. On the other hand the space and colon after ἔρωτα are exactly paralleled in 140 after λελόγιcται (Harsh, *AJP* lxii [1941], 103), where there can be no change of speaker; and Hutloff believed that he could distinguish *CMI* (invisible in the facsimile) in the margin opposite line 134, indicating that Smikrines' speech begins with προῖκα. The sense thus given is perhaps less probable, although approved by Wilamowitz: 'I don't care if he does break up the party' must be taken as a phrase of puerile defiance on Chairestratos' part. The paragraphus below 133 does not favour either alternative, since it may indicate a change of speaker within that line, at the end of it, or in both places.   πάλιν shows that Smikrines has already cursed Charisios (or Chairestratos Smikrines), and makes Körte's οἰμωζέτω preferable to Wilamowitz's οἰμώξεται.

134 ff. τάλαντα τέτταρα: (1) Three talents recurs as a handsome dowry in other plays (*Perik.*, *Dysk.*, possibly *Koneiaz.*), two talents in *Aspis*, *Mis.*, and *P. Oxy.* 2533. Smikrines, an austere and parsimonious rather than a miserly character, has gone a little beyond this in endowing his daughter. (2) It is a stock idea that a rich wife makes her

husband her servant (cf. Anaxandrides frag. 52 K, Antiphanes frag.
320 K, Menander frags. 333, 334 K–T). Hence it has been supposed
by some (Capps, Wilamowitz, etc.) that Smikrines tartly observes that
this is certainly not the case with Charisios. He might be thought of
as considering the size of his daughter's dowry as more exceptional
than it was. But G. Méautis, *Le Crépuscule d'Athènes et Ménandre*, p. 183, is
possibly right in denying that a father-in-law would suggest that his
son-in-law should have taken this humble position. T. Williams,
Wiener Studien lxxix (1961), 42, argues that οἰκέτης must mean 'sharer
of a household' (Zuntz); the plural can mean 'members of a household' (Hdt. viii. 106, Xen. *Anab.* iv. 6. 1), not slaves only; this will
then be an exceptional use of the singular in the same sense (cf.
W. J. Verdenius, *Mnem.* 1956, 231, who adduces οἰκέτις in Theok.
xviii. 38, exceptionally meaning 'housewife'). (3) In Greek marriage
contracts from Egypt the husband undertakes not to live apart from
his wife, μηδ' ἄλλην οἰκίαν οἰκεῖν ἧς οὐ κυριεύcει (ἡ δεῖνα) (*Pap. Teb.*
974 of the second century B.C., 104 of 92 B.C.). ἀπόκοιτος occurs in
a formula used of the wife, (καὶ τῇ δεῖνα) μὴ ἐξέcτω ἀπόκοιτον μηδὲ
ἀφήμερον γίνεcθαι (ibid. and *P. Gen.* 21 of the second century B.C. =
Wilcken, *Chrestomathie*, ii. 284). Williams suggests that Athenian
marriage was regarded as implying these obligations of cohabitation
that were to be made contractual in Egypt. For ἀπόκοιτος of the
husband cf. a fragment, probably by Menander, in *Pap. Ant.* 15,
μί[αν οὐ γεγ]ένημαι νύκτ' ἀπόκοιτος πώποτε | ἀπὸ τ[ῆc γυναι]κόc;
Lucian, *Bis Accusatus* 27, cυνῆν ἀεὶ μηδὲ μίαν νύκτα ἀπόκοιτος γιγνόμενος.
(4) M. I. Finley, *Studies in Land and Credit* etc., pp. 79, 266, considers
that the dowries of New Comedy are comically exaggerated and bear
no relation to those of real life. This may well be true of some met in
Plautus' and Terence's adaptations—20 talents in *Cistellaria* (561),
10 in *Andria* (951) and *Mercator* (704); but these do not necessarily
preserve the figures of their originals, since Romans were accustomed
to greater riches than Greeks. In fragment 333 a dowry of 10 talents
is clearly regarded as exceptional. Evidence for actual dowries mostly
comes from the orators, a generation or more before our comedies:
few exceed one talent, but Demosthenes' sister received 2 talents out
of a total estate of 14 talents (xxvii. 4–5). It is not impossible that the
size of dowries increased in the latter part of the fourth century.
Fortunes were larger (W. S. Ferguson, *Hellenistic Athens*, pp. 68 f.) and
no longer subject to the burden of liturgies: released from these, rich
men may have been more generous to their daughters, particularly to
only daughters, which the heroines of New Comedy often seem to be.
A series of inscriptions from Mykonos (*Recueil des inscr. jurid. grecques*,
i. 48), dated to the period of Macedonian ascendancy, gives a range

of dowries of which the highest are $2\frac{1}{3}$ and 2 talents; the richest men of Mykonos were probably small fry by Athenian standards. 3 talents will in Menander's time have been perhaps an unusually generous, but not an incredibly large, dowry for a rich man to give.

136 δώδεκα τῆς ἡμέρας δραχμάς: It is unfortunately not clear how extravagant this payment was, assuming that it was for the services of Habrotonon alone. According to Arist. *Ath. Pol.* 50. 2, a sumptuary law forbade the payment of a higher fee than 2 dr. for engaging a ψάλτρια, cf. Hypereides, iv. 3 Kenyon (before 324 B.C.), but it may no longer have been in force, or enforced. *Samia* 392 speaks of *hetairai* going to dinner-parties for 'only 10 dr.', but these are free women, who may have been more expensive than slaves. Yet charges of this nature may not have been unheard of even for slaves. Plaut. *Asinaria* 230, 752 has a slave *hetaira* hired for a year for 2,000 dr., i.e. about 6 dr. a day, and a long contract would no doubt be at a cheaper rate than a short one; the prices paid for accomplished *hetairai* were high, ranging from 20 to 60 minae; (20 minae: *Pseudolus* 51; 30 minae: *Rudens* 45, *Mostellaria* 300, [Dem.] lix. 29; 40 minae: *Epidicus* 52, *Curculio* 343; 60 minae, *Persa* 662), whereas skilled male artisans might fetch much less, e.g. Demosthenes reckons his knife-makers as worth 'at least 3 minae on the average'. Even though prices of male slaves were somewhat higher fifty years later, to argue that it must have been extravagant to pay 12 dr. for a *hetaira* when a skilled man's wage was only 2 dr. is to think in terms of morals rather than economics. On the whole it seems likely that, as over the wine, Smikrines' indignation is a measure of his parsimony, rather than evidence that Charisios was really paying an excessive price.

139 πρός: Adverbial, as in 349, a use frequent in Plato and Demosthenes at the end of a clause.

140: Two obols had been the allowance paid to needy citizens at the time of the Peloponnesian war, and had been supposed to support man and wife: this was known as the διωβέλιον. The rise in prices will have made this sum insufficient by Menander's time, hence ποτέ. Demosthenes iv. 28 (351 B.C.) still optimistically reckons 2 obols a day a minimum ration allowance for troops, but about 330 B.C. slaves' keep is reckoned at 3 obols a day (*IG* ii–iii². 1672), and the ephebes received 4 obols (Arist. *Ath. Pol.* 42. 3).   πτισάνη was made by damping and pounding barley, then drying it in the sun. It was flavoured with salt, and eaten with the liquid extracted in the pounding (*Geoponica* iii. 9). The supplement ⟨πρὸς⟩ πτισάνην (Sudhaus) is preferred by H. Teykowski, 'Der Präpositionsgebrauch bei Menander' (Diss. Bonn, 1940), 24; whereas Wilamowitz thought πρός inadmissible,

and wrote ⟨γ' εἰc⟩. Either preposition seems to be good Greek, e.g.
Plato, *Prot.* 322 b, πρὸc μὲν τροφὴν ἱκανή, Xen. *Hiero* iv. 9, ἱκανά
ἐcτιν εἰc τὰ ἀναγκαῖα δαπανήματα.

(ii) **142–172**: *Chairestratos, Habrotonon* (?), *Smikrines* (exit 163)

142 ff.: Someone comes out of Chairestratos' house to say that
Charisios is waiting for him. This person is not, immediately at least,
explained to the audience in any way, or addressed by name; it is
likely therefore that he or she has been on the stage before, possibly
as Chairestratos' companion earlier in the scene (see 127 n.). Opinions
differ as to who this character is. The address γλυκύταθ' rules out
Karion, Onesimos, or any of Chairestratos' servants. Webster suggests Habrotonon, who probably uses γλυκύτατε at 953, and I follow
him, noting only that although the word is commonly used by women,
it is not peculiar to them ([Plato], *Hipparchus* 227 d, Ar. *Acharnians*
462). Most editors suppose the new arrival to be Simias, mentioned
at 630, whom they take to be another of Charisios' friends; whether
rightly so is discussed in the note on 603–36. Since γλυκύτατε in this
passage appears to be an uncalled-for endearment, it seems more
likely that it is uttered out of habit by the *hetaira* Habrotonon than by
the friend Simias, if such he be; compare the indiscriminate use of
'darling' by some women today.

144: Wilamowitz cleverly conjectured ὡc ἄθλιόc τιc [φιλόcοφοc βλέπει
cκύθρωφ'] and claimed that the first φ was recognizable on the photograph. This is not certain enough to be printed. In the next line there
are at least three possibilities: (1) ὁ τριcκακοδαίμων is the subject of
a preceding verb, and means Smikrines; ψάλτριαν will then begin
a sentence by Chairestratos or his companion (Sudhaus, *Menanderstudien*, p. 6); (2) ὁ τριcκακοδαίμων begins a speech by Chairestratos
and means Smikrines; Sudhaus in his edition printed ὁ τριcκακοδαίμων
ψάλτριαν τὴν ἔνδον οἰκοῦcαν γυναῖκα and added a note 'ueretur ne
domo extrudat'; but one would I think expect τὴν ψάλτριαν; (3) ὁ
τριcκακοδαίμων begins a speech by Smikrines and means Charisios
(Webster): 'the unfortunate chap has taken a harpist' would be
possible, but no way of fitting in γυναῖκα has been suggested.

149–60: Körte says that about 10 lines are missing after 148, and
Gomme accepted this. But it is no more than a guess, based on the
supposition that the Petrograd codex had about 30 lines to the page.
Turner has recently shown from analogous codices that there is no
reason why it should not have had as many as 50, *Greek-Roman-and-
Byzantine Studies* x (1969), 311. The length of the gap may then be

anything from 10 to 30 lines, and this uncertainty makes it all the more doubtful how 159–60 are to be interpreted.

I suspect that, having used in the scene down to 142 the motif of the character who overhears another and comments on his remarks, Menander did not make much further play with it after Habrotonon joined Chairestratos. Rather Smikrines will have seen this girl who has supplanted his daughter, and immediately addressed her in harsh terms. 159–60 will then be the end of this passage, e.g. (Ἀβρ.) οὕτως ἀγαθόν τι ϲοι γένοιτο, μὴ λέγε τοιοῦτον. (Ϲμ.) οὐκ ἐς κόρακας; οἰμώξει μακρά. Having disposed of her, Smikrines then explains either to the audience or to Chairestratos his intention of going in to talk to his daughter. Smikrines uses the phrase οἰμώξει μακρά to Sophrone at 1068, and these are its only instances as yet in Menander, who may have felt it to be a phrase characteristic of this old man, cf. *Entretiens Hardt* xvi. 122, 131.

The disappearance, with the left-hand edge of the column, of possible paragraphi and the absence of dicola makes the distribution of speeches very uncertain. Capps states that there is a colon after γένοιτο. If this is so, it may mark a change of speaker, e.g. (Ϲμ.) μὴ λέγε | μηδὲ ἐν ἔτ'.

There have been various other suggestions to explain 159–60. A possible interpretation is that Chairestratos asks his companion (or is asked by the companion) not to tell Smikrines that Charisios is staying in Chairestratos' house; the old man may know no more than that his son-in-law has left home and is indulging in 'extravagant' living. Kuiper suggested a preceding line such as οὔκουν λέγειν χρή, ποῦ 'ϲτι νῦν Χαρίϲιος. He also thought that in 160 the companion persisted, saying e.g. λέγοιμ' ἄν, and was cursed by Chairestratos. Wilamowitz argued that the curse must be directed at Smikrines, who must therefore have spoken the missing beginning of the line; he suggested πορεύϲομ' 'I will go on in' (*Perik.* 184 n.), although this awkwardly anticipates εἴϲειμι νῦν εἴϲω (161).

163 προϲβαλῶ: A military term, 'launch an attack', used similarly in *Sam.* 421. **τοῦτον,** sc. Charisios; in 164 αὐτῷ is Charisios and τοῦτον Smikrines; on the stage there would be no difficulty in making clear the reference of the pronouns.

165 ff. κίναδος: Said to be a word, of Sicilian origin, for 'fox': it is used by Sophokles, Aristophanes, Andokides, and Demosthenes to mean 'a cunning rogue'. The missing word in 166 may be ἀνάϲτατον 'topsy-turvy', recorded as Menandrean by the Berlin Photios 122. 19 (Kock), or διάϲτατον 'divided against itself' (Sudhaus). But the import is not clear, still less that of the succeeding exchanges. It looks, however, as if Chairestratos said that Smikrines' arrival would cause an

upset in Charisios' house, and Habrotonon (if it is she) replied that
she could wish it would cause one in many others as well. Challenged
on this, she answers, 'Well, one house, next to it', by which Chairestratos rightly understands her to mean his own. Her reason for this
must be that she has not received the attention she expected from
Charisios, and something must have been said earlier to make the
present remarks intelligible. When later in the play, at 434, she complains that Charisios *no longer* lets her *even* take a place at his side, that
may imply that earlier she had reported a coldness that was less
strongly marked.

169 ὡς καὶ μειρακυλλίων ὄχλος κτλ.: Cf. *Dysk.* 230–2, which employs
an almost identical formula; where the entry of the chorus is announced by one of the characters this always, so far as we know, marks
the end of the first act; cf. *Perik.* 261 n. Later interludes by the chorus
have no introduction.

These lines are the clearest evidence that in Menander, and probably in other writers of New Comedy, the chorus need no longer have
anything to do with the play. If there were even the slightest necessary
link, the roistering youngsters of whom it here consists would be most
fit company at the party which is being prepared in Chairestratos'
house. As it is, they are to be avoided (Gomme, *CQ* xxx [1936], 64).
It may be added that a chorus of guests would have been awkward
to handle, since as a chorus they are required outside the house and
as guests indoors; and that the chorus of strangers that the play provides are very naturally not welcomed by Chairestratos, who would
not wish to extend his hospitality to several, perhaps fifteen, unknown
tipsy young men.

A small fragment (VI) of O 14 probably comes from this part of
the play. It is plausibly restored to give ἀπ]ọ[κ]οιτος ἐξ ὅτου[περ?,
and two lines later]ων ἐμοί: τί φηcι; με[. Weinstein says that the
meaning must be that Charisios has not lived with Pamphile since
their marriage. Menander may have contrived such a separation, but
all we have evidence for is that he had not lived with her since his
discovery that she had borne a child, probably in his absence, that he
believed not to be his. The fragment may come from the gap after
145, while Chairestratos and Habrotonon are still listening unseen to
Smikrines. Another possible place is between 177 and 218, where the
speakers would be Smikrines and Onesimos.

ACT II

(i) **172–177:** *Onesimos* (?) *alone*

The beginnings of six lines from the opening of Act II are preserved by the Petrograd parchment. The absence of paragraphi suggests that the scene was a monologue, and the words ὁ δεcπότηc that
it was spoken by a servant, probably Onesimos (Muir, *CR* liii [1939],
63, Sudhaus, *Menanderstudien* [1913], p. 10). Less likely is Wilamowitz's
idea that the speaker is Smikrines who, irritated by his inability to
influence Pamphile against her husband, delivers himself of a jeremiad,
'Nothing can be relied on; the master is flouted by his slave, the old
man by the young, fathers by daughters, etc.'

The third leaf of the parchment bears a few letters which may or
may not belong to this scene or to this play: they yield no sense.
How many lines are missing between 177 and the beginning of the
Cairo papyrus is quite uncertain—but enough, if Onesimos is the
speaker of the monologue, for him to conclude, for Smikrines to come
out of the house, perhaps lamenting Pamphile's obduracy, for an
exchange between him and Onesimos, certainly for the latter's withdrawal. Webster, *StM* 37, points out that when Smikrines returns at
579, Onesimos fears that 'he has learned the truth from someone in
the city' and prepares to get out of his way. This strongly suggests
that Onesimos has told him some lie, and more or less proves an
earlier meeting between them, probably at the beginning of this act.
But when Webster follows Jensen in supposing that Onesimos had
persuaded Smikrines that Charisios and Pamphile were reconciled,
that introduces an improbable piece of deception. It is easier to guess
that he misled the old man about his son-in-law's whereabouts.
Jensen's view is associated with his hazardous restoration of 583 ff.

(ii) **218–375:** *Smikrines* (exit 370), *Daos, Syriskos* (with wife)

The next scene is that from which the play takes its name. Two slaves,
a shepherd and a charcoal-burner, dispute the ownership of some
trinkets which had been found with an exposed child; should they
belong to the finder or to the other, who had accepted the child from
him? They approach the first passer-by to arbitrate; by a coincidence
he is, without knowing it, the child's grandfather. If he should adjudge
the trinkets to the finder, he will unwittingly doom his grandchild not
to be restored to his parents, but to be brought up in slavery. The
scene is brilliantly written, and the two slaves sharply distinguished:
Daos slow in decision, but tenacious, shrewdly self-centred, and with

an effective simplicity of speech, Syriskos (? Syros) more subtle and ingratiating, capable of more complicated periods, and proudly employing many of the devices of the practised orator. A long but sensitive account of the scene is given by J. W. Cohoon, 'Rhetorical Studies in the Arbitration Scene of Menander's *Epitrepontes*', *TAPA* xlv (1914), 141–230. He points out that probably no law covered the ownership of the trinkets; it was a question of equity, such as was often submitted to private arbitration.

Hyginus, *fab.* 187, tells the story of Alope, daughter of the king Kerkyon, who bore a child (Hippothoon) to Poseidon. It was exposed and found by a shepherd, who gave it to another; the latter laid claim to the articles found with the child, and the matter came before the king for judgement. Recognizing a piece of Alope's apparel, he had her executed and the child exposed again. (Its further adventures and Alope's metamorphosis into a spring are irrelevant here.) The majority of scholars suppose that Hyginus followed Euripides' *Alope* in the part of the story here recounted, and that Menander took the idea for his scene from that play. Although only a hypothesis, this is a good deal more likely than Wilamowitz's suggestion (*Schiedsgericht*, pp. 129 ff.) that an unknown mythographer was inspired by Menander; see the criticisms of F. Wehrli, *Motivstudien zur griechischen Komödie*, p. 119. There is no evidence that Menander introduced any verbal echoes of Euripides to call attention to the parallel, and the whole ethos of the scene, which is far more important than the basic situation, must be quite different from that of a tragedy.

This scene is represented on a fine mosaic (? iv cent. A.D.) in Mitilini, *BCH* lxxxvi (1962), 875, which has the heading *ΕΠΙΤΡΕ-ΠΟΝΤΩΝ ΜΒ* (μέρος β', or Act II). The picture is reproduced in colour in Plate 4 of *Antike Kunst*, Beiheft 6, by L. Kahil and others, and discussed ibid. 44. The characters are named *CΥΡΟC* (*not CΥΡΙCΚΟC*), *CΜΕΙΚΡΙΝΗC* and *ΑΝΘΡΑΚΕΥC*. There is also a woman with a child in her arms. Some mistake has been made, for it is not Daos who is the charcoal-burner. Nevertheless, it is very possible that the mosaic correctly gives the name of the slave as *Cύρος*, although applying it to the wrong person. *Cυρίσκος* may be a diminutive, used derogatorily (270 n.) I shall, however, follow custom and call the character Syriskos, not Syros. The actor labelled Syros has a very short tunic, characteristic of slaves in comedy; the so-called 'charcoal-burner', however, has a long garment. This suggests that the latter represents the more important of the two slaves, i.e. Syriskos.

218: Daos, a shepherd, and a charcoal-burner, Syriskos, enter, disputing; the latter is accompanied by his wife, who is carrying a baby. 218 may be the first line of their dialogue, or a few lines (in which their names could have been used) may be missing. O. Schroeder, *Hermes* lxxxviii (1960), 123, suggests without much plausibility that frag. 617 gives the opening lines of the scene: κρεῖττον ὀλίγ' ἐcτὶ χρήματ' ἀνυπόπτωc ἔχειν, ἢ πολλὰ φανερῶc Δᾶε (ἃ δὲ MSS.) μετ' ὀνείδουc ἔχειν. The gnome is undramatic and inapposite. The division between speakers must be ascertained from the sense. Since Syriskos is 'the plaintiff', he must say φεύγειc τὸ δίκαιον, to which Daos answers cυκοφαντεῖc. Again, τί γάρ cοι μετεδίδουν can only be from Daos. Between these two sentences there should therefore be an even number of dicola to mark change of speaker, but C gives five, presumably one too many or one too few. The text printed in OCT is that of Körte, which disregards the dicolon after δυcτυχηc. Alternatively, it is just as possible to disregard that after τὰ μή c', and to assign the whole of 219 to Syriskos, as Körte did in his edn. of 1912. Wilamowitz thought this necessary, on the ground that ἔχειν must mean 'keep', but this is disproved by 292, where Daos indubitably says οὐ δεῖ c' ἔχειν.

Weinstein (cf. *HSCP* lxxv [1971] 135) follows Capps in supposing a dicolon to be lost after βούλομαι. Thus she divides (Δα.) ἐπιτρεπτέον τινί ἐcτι περὶ τούτων. (Cυ.) βούλομαι. ⟨Δα.⟩ κρινώμεθα. But the proposal for arbitration is more likely to come from the imaginative Syriskos than from the simple Daos. The latter also, being the man in possession, has no motive for a conciliatory move. Plautus, *Rudens* 1002 offers a parallel: the 'claimant' Trachalio suggests arbitration to Gripus, the man who is in possession of the disputed birth-tokens. These considerations lead me to go against the general principle that it is easier to suppose the loss of a dicolon than its erroneous insertion.

cυκοφαντεῖc: 'You are blackmailing me.' A frequent practice of a cυκοφάντηc was to *threaten* prosecution, and squeeze money out of the timid. It was possible to call his bluff, for, if he once started a case, he had to go on with it or suffer a heavy penalty. Cf. *Sam.* 578; *Perik.* 378 n.   **δυcτυχήc**: ἄθλιοc, a word of somewhat similar meaning, is commonly used in the vocative in a purely derogatory sense, and in the nominative in genuine commiseration. No vocative form of δυcτυχήc is found, cf. Choiroboskos in Theod. i. 176. 41 Hilg., and perhaps we should always write ὦ δυcτυχήc, as an exclamatory nominative, at frag. 137, *Heros* frag. 7, as well as *Dysk.* 574, 919. In none of these places is δυcτυχήc used as a word of abuse, nor is there any place in New Comedy where it means anything but 'unfortunate'. It may here be employed as a quasi-insult, Daos commiserating with Syriskos on his 'misfortune' in being a blackmailer. See Addenda.

219 c' . . . c': Wilamowitz urges that the vowels of c(ε) and c(ά) must have been sounded, particularly in the second case, where the elision is before a word spoken by another. When he claims that the phrase would otherwise be unintelligible, he underestimates the interpretative skill of the human mind. But metrical elision at change of speaker presents a problem. There are three possibilities: (1) the first speaker completed his word before the second began, (2) the first speaker completed his word, but the second began simultaneously with the first's final syllable, (3) the first speaker did not complete his word. (1) seems unlikely, as involving the disregard of a syllable in scanning the verse; slight support for (2) as against (3) may be had from the practice of some MSS. in writing both vowels (*scriptio plena*) at such places.

220 βούλομαι: 'I would like to', 'I am delighted', rather than just 'I am willing' (ἐθέλω; but the only character in Menander who certainly uses that word is Gorgias in *Dysk.*, see 269 n.).   **κρινώμεθα:** 'Let us arbitrate', i.e. go to an arbiter; but the Greek verb is passive, lit. 'Let us be judged.'

221–2: ἱκανός: 'Competent', in a legal as well as moral or intellectual sense.   **δίκαια πάσχω,** 'I deserve what I am getting.' The δέ after δίκαια does not answer ἐμοὶ μέν, which is a case of μέν *solitarium*, 'I for my part'.   **μετεδίδουν** not μετέδωκα, 'What made me offer you a share?'; or the imperfect may be one of an action of which consequences are still to come, K–G i. 143–4.

223 ἀγαθῇ τύχῃ: The original meaning, 'may good fortune follow', was sometimes more or less forgotten, and the phrase does hardly more than indicate consent, cf. *Sam.* 297. There is no corresponding formula in English. Gomme compared the French 'à la bonne heure', now perhaps an old-fashioned way of expressing consent.

228 διάλυσον ἡμᾶς: 'Put an end to' or 'settle our quarrel'. The middle or passive (διαλύεσθαι) means 'to be reconciled'.

229 περιπατεῖτε: I.e. 'When you should be at work'.   **διφθέρας ἔχοντες:** Cf. 328. The διφθέρα was the poor man's cloak, and especially the peasant's, made of goatskin: *Dysk.* 415, Ar. *Clouds* 72; cf. Plato, *Crito* 53 d. It was, of course, not especially a *slave's* cloak—slaves were not thus distinguished in Athens: [Xen.] *Resp. Ath.* 1. 10, Plato, *Rep.* viii. 563 b; and the point here lies simply in the natural reaction of a well-to-do man when the poor want something which he thinks quite unsuitable to them.

230 ἀλλ' ὅμως: 'But all the same—', the aposiopesis is as natural in English as in Greek. Cf. *Sik.* 147, Ar. *Ach.* 402, and in continuous speech, ending a sentence, ibid. 956 ('The turn is said to occur sixteen times in Euripides', Rennie ad loc.) Note the asyndeta, Syriskos pausing after each sentence, waiting for a favourable answer.

231 πάτερ: Common as an ingratiating form of address by slaves to an elderly man, e.g. 301 below, *Dysk*. 107, but not confined to slaves, *Dysk*. 171, *Sik*. 379.

232 ff. ἐν παντὶ καιρῷ does not mean simply 'always', but on every occasion on which there may be conflict. In classical Greek καιρός regularly means *significant* occasion.

234 ff. τούτου τοῦ μέρους means no more than τούτου, just as at *Dysk*. 767 ἐν τούτῳ τῷ μέρει is the equivalent of ἐν τούτῳ. This pleonastic use of μέρος is common in later writers, especially the wordy Polybios (Wilamowitz); cf. C. B. Welles, *Royal Correspondence in the Hellenistic Period*, p. 348. It is found already in Epicurus frag. 29 Usener, 16 Arrighetti, καὶ χωρὶς τούτου τοῦ μέρους οὐκ οἶδ' ὅπως . . . Cf. *ep. ad Pyth.* 100, καὶ τοῦτο τὸ μέρος (i.e. βροντή) πλεοναχῶς γίνεσθαι. Syriskos will feel that it lends distinction to his style. The phrase κοινόν ἐστι τῷ βίῳ πάντων sounds well, but its exact meaning, if it has one, is not easy to express. Perhaps it is that readiness to support justice is something universally experienced in life. Or is the meaning that such behaviour is to the common benefit of all men's lives, i.e. that it improves their life? 'It's a common interest that touches all men's lives', Post. Capps compares Eur. *Suppl.* 539, πάσης Ἑλλάδος κοινὸν τόδε, εἰ τοὺς θανόντας . . . ἀτάφους τις ἕξει.

With τὸν παρατυγχάνοντα, 'anyone who happens to be on the spot', one may compare Solon's dictum that there will be least injustice in a state if it is resented by all citizens, not only by its victims (Diog. L. i. 59). τῶν πολιτῶν ὁ βουλόμενος therefore could bring an action against an alleged offender in a criminal case; and the great and wise Solon's law led to the activities of the *sykophantes*.

236 μετρίῳ: 'Fairish', meant as an understatement, cf. *Perik*. 512. Syriskos has just delivered himself of a gnome such as is familiar from the speeches of the law-courts. Daos proves to be not without a certain natural eloquence, but Syriskos employs many of the artifices practised by the orators. A conspectus of the rhetorical figures used is to be found in B. Keulen, *Studia ad arbitrium in Menandri Epitrepontibus exhibitum*, pp. 79 ff. **cυμπέπλεγμαι**: Probably a metaphor from wrestling cf. Aischines ii. 153, and Eur. *Bacchae* 800, ἀπόρῳ γε τῷδε cυμπεπλέγμεθα ξένῳ.

237 τί γάρ; 'Why', emphatic (perhaps a survival of γ' ἄρα, but see the discussion in Denniston, *GP*, 82–5). Other uses of τί γάρ; in Menander are 'you ask why?' (261) and 'what else?' (*Epitr*. 882, *Sam*.

581, *Phasma* 8). ἐμμενεῖτε: 'Abide by' a decision, as in Plato, *Crito* 50 c, Dem. xli. 14, ἐμμένειν οἷς ἐκεῖνοι γνοῖεν, [Dem.] lix. 45, xxxiii. 15.

238 πάντως: C assigns the word to Syriskos, but it is possible that Daos and Syriskos give their assent together.

239 cù πρότερος ὁ cιωπῶν λέγε: Smikrines snubs the forward Syriskos. The result is that, without knowing it, he causes the 'defendant' to speak before the 'plaintiff', contrary to orderly procedure, cf. Ter. *Eun.* 10–14. There is a dramatic reason for this: since the plaintiff is to deliver the more brilliant speech and to succeed in winning his case, it is more effective that he should speak second and rebut his opponent. **τὸ κωλύον:** C has τοκωλυονμε, whether O 14 also had με after κωλυον is not known. To suppress με is the easiest course, but to write τό με κωλύον, cf. *Dysk.* 753, *Kith.* 51, may be correct.

240 μικρόν γ' ἄνωθεν: In full ἄνωθεν ἀρξάμενος, but the adverb is sometimes attached to the verb of saying, e.g. [Dem.] lix. 74, ἄνωθεν διηγήσασθαι; so here it attaches to ἐρῶ, understood from λέγε. ἐρῶ is also the verb understood to govern τὰ πρὸς τοῦτον, 'my dealings with this fellow'. Daos begins abruptly, in marked contrast to Syriskos. Anon. τέχνη ῥητορική, Spengel–Hammer, *Rhetores Graeci*, i. 359, καὶ Μένανδρος ἐν τοῖς Ἐπιτρέπουσι τὴν δίκην ἄνευ προοιμίων πεποίηκεν, uses these speeches as evidence for his opinion that fourth-century speeches had no prooemia as delivered, although provided with them in their published form; hardly a justified inference.

241 καὶ σαφῆ: 'Absolutely clear'. Denniston, *GP* 319.

242 τῷ δασεῖ: The nom. would be τὸ δασύ (*Dysk.* 120), cf. Xen. *Anab.* iv. 7. 7. It is unnecessary to see here with LSJ the earliest instance of the noun τὸ δάσος, which in the koine replaced the Attic τὸ δασύ (Thomas Magister). The use of the adjective δασύς of ground covered thickly with trees or shrubs was common, especially in Herodotos. It does not here necessarily mean a forest of tall trees; perhaps only scrub-oak; but, in any case, common land, where herdsmen and charcoal-burners (257) would be equally at home. τὰ χωρία ταῦτα are the farms, private property, near the village or township which is the scene of the action.

243–4 ἐποίμαινον . . . ἡμέραν: 'I was looking after my flock, some thirty days ago now, maybe.' The sense of the English word 'ago' can be expressed in Greek by an accusative noun with an ordinal numeral, apparently an extension of the acc. of duration, e.g. Xen. *An.* iv. 5. 24, καταλαμβάνει τὴν θυγατέρα ἐνάτην ἡμέραν γεγαμημένην, *Hell.* ii. 4. 13, οὓς ὑμεῖς ἡμέραν πέμπτην τρεψάμενοι ἐδιώξατε, *Cyrop.* vi. 3. 11, καὶ χθὲς δὲ καὶ τρίτην ἡμέραν τὸ αὐτὸ τοῦτο ἔπραττον. Sometimes, as here, οὗτος is added, with the idea 'this is the nth day since . . .', e.g. Lysias xxiv. 6, τὴν δὲ μητέρα τελευτήσασαν πέπαυμαι τρέφων τρίτον ἔτος τουτί.

246–7 δέραια κτλ.: 'A necklace and some ornaments of that kind', i.e. of no special value. In comedy and in tragedy, and presumably sometimes in real life, pieces of jewellery were laid out with the exposed child, which was wrapped in some recognizable piece of stuff. The mother may have cherished a wild hope that if the child happened to survive and grow up they might establish its parentage; she may also have hoped that a finder in two minds whether to take up the infant might be swayed by the lure of some valuables.

248–9 λέγειν . . . λαλῆϲ: Although occasionally λαλεῖν is no more than λέγειν (886, *Perik.* 470), it usually retains, as here, some sense of 'chattering', 'babbling', or 'talking out of place'.

249 καὶ δικαίωϲ: Editors have all assigned this to Daos, in spite of *Samia* 389, where Demeas threatens to break the cook's head if he interrupts, and the cook replies καὶ δικαίωϲ. This is clearly a soft answer to turn away wrath, now further exemplified by *Dysk.* 602, where Getas, cursed for interference, replies καὶ μάλα δικαίωϲ.

252 ἐν νυκτὶ βουλήν: Proverbial (Zenob. iii. 97), hence the postponement of δέ is facilitated—'good counsel at night, however'. Cf. 'Menandri' Monostichoi 222 Jaekel, ἐν νυκτὶ βουλὴ τοῖς σοφοῖϲι γίνεται, Hdt. vii. 12, νυκτὶ δὲ βουλὴν δίδουϲ, *Carmen de Bello Actiaco* viii. 6, 'consiliis nox apta', Val. Flacc. vi. 16. V. De Falco, *Parola del Passato*, i (1946), 358, remarks that the proverb is as early as Phokylides frag. 8, νυκτὸς βουλεύειν, νυκτὸς δέ τοι ὀξυτέρη φρὴν | ἀνδράϲιν, and that, later at least, εὐφρόνη was derived from εὖ φρονεῖν, Cornutus c. 14 and *Et. Gud.*

254 παιδοτροφιάϲ . . . φροντίδων: For the (partitive) genitives, cf. 928 below; and *Iliad* xxi. 360, τί μοι ἔριδος; **ἐμοὶ . . . ἐγὼ . . . ἐμοί:** Cohoon and Keulen rightly call attention to the repetition as reflecting Daos' self-centred mind.

256 τοιουτοϲί τιϲ ἦν: 'Such, more or less, were my thoughts'; the use of an adjective (cf. 261 ϲύννουϲ) to describe a temporary state of mind or body is less common in Greek than in English (contrast, 'I am anxious, busy, sick' with ἀδημονῶ, ἀϲχολῶ, νοϲῶ) and I know no good parallel for this use of τοιοῦτος. Eur. *Or.* 1680, κἀγὼ τοιοῦτος may mean κἀγὼ οἷος πείθεϲθαι rather than 'such are my thoughts, too'.

261 τί ϲύννουϲ . . . Δᾶος; Not nom. for voc., but 'why is Daos so thoughtful?' The oblique question is tactful, for if Daos wished not to answer, he could parry it with a jest without being rude. cύννουc is found in [Isokrates] i. 15 (ἔθιζε cαυτὸν εἶναι μὴ cκυθρωπὸν ἀλλὰ cύννουν) i.e. ponder things but keep a pleasant look, don't frown over them, and in Aristotle, *Pol.* 1267ᵃ36; but cύννοια is in all three tragedians, Herodotos, and Plato, and the comparatively late appearance of the adjective may be accidental. Cf. frag. 722, τί cύννουc κατὰ μόναc cαυτῷ λαλεῖc; Plato, *Alcib.* 2. 138 a φαίνει γέ τοι ἐcκυθρωπακέναι . . . ὥc τι ξυννοούμενοc.

261 ἐγώ: A verb of saying is understood, cf. *Dysk.* 539.   τί γάρ; is used, as at *Dysk.* 553, 636, *Georg.* 85, *Aspis* 171, *Sam.* 129, to answer a question introduced by τί; and the meaning is 'you ask me why?'

262 περίεργοc: 'Busybody', not 'inquisitive' as in frag. 2 above and *Sam.* 300; cf. περιεργαcάμενον 575 below. In this sense the περίεργοc undertakes what it is absolutely unnecessary for anyone to do, whereas the πολυπράγμων minds other people's business. It is disputed whether περίεργόc εἰμι is to be taken as part of Daos' reply or with τὸ πρᾶγμα λέγω. In the first case the unnecessary action is that of rescuing the foundling (Capps); in the second that of telling Syriskos the story (Wilamowitz).

266 οὕτωc εὐτυχήc: Sc. γένοιο.

267–8 "γυναῖκά" φηcι "γὰρ ἔχω": γάρ cannot be the first word after a pause. It would seem that parenthetic φηcι could became part of the word-group in which it is included; the commas of some modern texts are misleading. Similarly with other parts of φημί, Xen. *Symp.* iv. 61, τοιοῦτοc μέντοι ἔφη μοι δοκεῖ Ἀντιcθένηc εἶναι, Plato, *Symp.* 174 a ὦ φάναι Ἀριcτόδημε, etc.

270 ἐδέου Cυρίcκε; The evidence of C is definite that Daos' speech ends at 269 (dicolon and paragraphus) and that Smikrines (named in the margin) begins 270. It has been objected that Smikrines did not know Syriskos' name and that as arbitrator he ought not to ask questions till he has heard the whole case; the latter objection, as Gomme said, trifles with the art of the theatre. Even if arbitrators did not intervene with questions—a matter of which we are quite ignorant— Menander was not compelled to observe niceties of legal procedure. Why should this street scene meticulously observe the rules of a public arbitration? We may imagine, if we like, that Daos pauses, impressively, at 269, and Syriskos, snubbed a little earlier (248), keeps his mouth shut till asked a question by Smikrines. The objection, however, that Smikrines does not know Syriskos' name is more serious. If Menander made him use it here, that cannot be shrugged off as a trifling oversight. It is an essential point of this scene that

Smikrines believes himself to be dealing with affairs of complete
strangers that are no concern of his, whereas in truth it is his own
grandson's future that is at stake. I find it incredible that Menander
could have forgotten this, and am more ready to believe that the
papyrus enshrines a very natural mistake. A dicolon after παιδίον,
intended to mark Daos' turning from Smikrines to Syriskos, has been
taken to mean a change of speaker and a paragraphus wrongly added
below the line. The names of speakers have no authority, and are not
part of the original text (introd. p. 40); I believe there is a similar
mistake at *Dysk.* 214. If we consider the question from the angle of
dramatic propriety, the same conclusion results. There is no reason
why Smikrines, who as yet has no idea of the point at issue, should
seize on this incident as particularly crucial to the case, and indeed
it is not crucial. But Daos feels that it is the heart of the matter that
Syriskos, who had *begged* to have the baby, should be grateful for it
and not now *demand* something in addition, i.e. the trinkets that had
been found with it, cf. 280–1, where he recalls the verb ἐδέου by the
participle δεόμενος. It is characteristic of the simple-minded thus to
challenge an opponent on a matter which is not vital. This consideration tells against any attempt to retain the question for Smikrines by
expunging the vocative Cυρίcκε as an intrusion (cf. perhaps the intrusion of Πάταικε supposed by some at *Perik.* 524); e.g. Sudhaus wrote
ἐδέου cὺ ⟨ταῦτα; (Cυ.) φημί⟩, and W. G. Arnott, *CQ* n.s. xviii (1968),
227, ingeniously proposes (Cμ.) ἐδέου cύ γ'; (Δα.) ἱκε⟨τεύων⟩ ὅλην τὴν
ἡμέραν κατέτριψε, pointing out that the phrase τὴν ἡμέραν κατατρίβειν
is frequently constructed with a participle. But a participle is hardly
necessary, since δεόμενος can easily be understood, and one would
expect Syriskos to answer Smikrines' question as he answers that in
274, ἐποίειc ταῦτα; :: ἐποίουν.

Further Syriskos takes up this incident at 297: οὐκ ἀντιλέγω·
δεόμενος, ἱκετεύων ἐγὼ ἔλαβον παρ' αὐτοῦ τοῦτ'· ἀληθῆ γὰρ λέγει. It is
rhetorically far more effective that he should thus admit the truth of
what his opponent had emphasized as if it were a trump card, than
that he should merely repeat an assurance he had already given to
Smikrines.

Körte argues that it is theatrically better that Smikrines should not
listen in silence throughout such a long speech as that of Daos. This
might be true of the modern stage, but Greek audiences relished long
uninterrupted speeches, and the force of his argument is blunted by
the fact that Smikrines will shortly maintain an unbroken silence
throughout an even longer speech by Syriskos.

A final point concerns the name Syriskos. This is the only place
extant where it occurs in this play. It could hardly have been put

into Smikrines' mouth by accident unless the charcoal-burner had previously been named. But it is *possible* that he had been, either in a prologue or in the lines, if there were any, lost at the beginning of the scene. The somewhat doubtful evidence of the Mitilini mosaic suggests that he was in fact somewhere called Syros. If that is so, the diminutive here must carry some significance, being used deliberately by the speaker. If Daos here insists on the charcoal-burner's past humility, he might well address him by the diminutive, intended to mark his inferiority. (In Ter. *Adelph.* 763 Syrus addresses himself as Syriscus; the diminutive is there used not derogatorily but in affectionate self-approval. Cf. also Lampadio/Lampadiscus, Plaut. *Cist.* 544/594 etc.)

273 κατεφίλει τὰς χεῖρας: Whether he 'kept on kissing' or 'tried to kiss' Daos' hands, Syriskos displayed an almost servile gratitude. It depends on the view taken of 270 whether the dicolon after χεῖρας is understood to indicate change of speaker, or that Daos turns from Smikrines to Syriskos. The two passages are clearly parallel. But again there is more reason why Daos should insist on the hand-kissing, a mark of respect he will not frequently have enjoyed, than why Smikrines should here interrupt.

275 ἄφνω is to be taken with what follows, not with περιτυχών. Daos' indignation breaks out in a breathless sentence. Lefebvre originally took μετὰ τῆς γυναικός with ἀπηλλάγη, but I think it clear that the woman was not present on this first occasion. The emphatic position of the phrase at the beginning of the sentence may be intended to suggest that Syriskos has been put up to his claim by his wife.

277 ληρός τις: 'Some frippery or other'. The later meaning of the word λῆρος, 'ornament of female dress', will have arisen from its meaning 'a mere trifle', through masculine disdain; and here we have probably a beginning of this, i.e. ληρός τις does not simply mean 'rubbish'. Daos, who has given a lot of unnecessary detail, glides rapidly over the objects in dispute, wishing to depreciate their value.

278 ἀπολαμβάνειν: 'To get as his due', ἀπο- as in ἀποδιδόναι etc. Cf. ἀπαιτεῖν, 304, 306, and 317.

280 ἐγὼ δέ γε: 'Yes, but I say . . .'

282 ἐξετασθῆναι: 'Be closely questioned', 'scrutinized'; a word used of a variety of official inquiries or investigations, but also in a wide range of private contexts.

284 κοινὸς Ἑρμῆς: A proverbial expression indicating that anyone present when something is found must share the profit, cf. Theophr. *Char.* 30. 9, τῶν εὑρισκομένων χαλκῶν ὑπὸ τῶν οἰκετῶν ἐν ταῖς ὁδοῖς δεινὸς ἀπαιτῆcαι τὸ μέρος, κοινὸν εἶναι φήcας τὸν 'Ερμῆν. Hermes was the god of luck, whence ἕρμαιον 'wind-fall, treasure-trove'.

287 τὸ πέρας: 'The final point', a colloquial phrase (below, 533; cf. *Dysk.* 117, Alexis frag. 261; Aischines i. 61 without the article). Daos ends by posing what looks like a neat dilemma. For his supplement ἑ[κών Lefebvre appeals to 291, which in fact tells against it. The final antithesis of Daos' speech is weakened if one half of it has been anticipated. His fondness for ἐγώ has been noted on 254: here we may have ἐμοί (283) . . . ἐγώ (285) . . . ἐμέ (286) . . . ἐγώ (287).

289 οὐκ ἀρέcκει is felt as one word ('unpleasing'), and οὐ retained after εἰ, as sometimes εἰ οὖ φημι, οὐκ ἐθέλω etc. Contrast 346, where the negative is separated from the verb.

290 μηδ' ἐλάττου: The change from ἀδίκει to ἐλαττοῦ is instinctive; Daos will not even imply that ἀδικεῖν can be used of *his* conduct.

291 κατιcχύcαντά με: An example of a verb compounded with κατα- taking a direct accusative, like καταβοᾶν τινα, κατασιωπᾶν τι. See Rennie on Ar. *Ach.* 160.

293 εἴρηκεν; 'He has finished his speech?'; the distribution of speakers given by C is quite possible. With the excuse of having been forbidden to interrupt, Syriskos can pretend to make sure that Daos has finished, the doubt implying a criticism of the speech. 'Can this be all he has to say?' Nothing is gained by giving the first εἴρηκεν to Smikrines, 'who must remind Syriskos twice that it is his turn to speak' (Lefebvre, Sudhaus). **καλῶς:** 'Thank you', see J. H. Quincey, *JHS* lxxxvi (1966), 139.

297 δεόμενος, ἱκετεύων: Daos had challengingly asked ἐδέου, Cυρίcκε; (270); Syriskos more than admits it; he adds ἱκετεύων. His honest candour is designed to win sympathy.

299 ποιμήν τιc: Notice the abrupt beginning with which Syriskos embarks upon his own version of the events. Similarly at 325, where he introduces the subject of tragedies on the stage. This is an oratorical device. **τῶν . . . cυνέργων:** partitive genitive.

302 αὐτὸς . . . οὑτοcί: The baby, which he takes from his wife. Syriskos brilliantly introduces the child as the real claimant. There is no easy way of translating γύναι, in the mouth of a husband. 'Wife' was once used in much the same contexts, mainly of command or criticism, but is now obsolete; the modern husband may use the universal 'dear'. **γνωρίcματα:** 'Tokens of recognition', this word is the key to the case Syriskos will develop. The trinkets' cash value may be small, but they are of great importance to the child, whose parentage they may some day establish. κύριος: Like a woman, a child had no legal personality, but its κύριος acted on its behalf, and administered its property.

307 cù δ' ἐποίηcάc με δούc: The aorist participle here not of an action previous to that of the main verb, but simultaneous with it—almost in fact the same action seen in another aspect; Goodwin, *MT* § 150, Barrett on Eur. *Hippolytus* 289–92. At this point (where the second asyndeton occurs) Syriskos hands the child back to his wife, with perhaps some little delay, and turns to Smikrines (βέλτιcτε).

312 τὸν λελωποδυτηκότα: Perhaps, as Gomme thought, governing a double accusative, 'who has robbed him of these things'; but ταῦτα may well be the object of ἔχειν. Properly speaking the λωποδύτηc stole, by guile or force, some or all of the clothes his victim was wearing. The same sort of odium attached to him as to the 'handbag snatcher' but a harsher penalty, since he was liable to summary arrest and to execution if he admitted the crime, Arist. *Ath. Pol.* 52. 1. Syriskos is quite unfair—Wilamowitz calls him impudent—in using the word.

313 εἰ πρῶτος εὖρε: Since there is no doubt about the fact, we might expect ἐπεί rather than εἰ. But in various circumstances Greek represents facts as hypotheses, the most familiar idiom being θαυμάζω εἰ, 'I am surprised that', not 'I wonder whether'. Here the expression suggests a generalization: 'if a man is the first to discover what belongs to another, is he therefore to keep it?' In Eur. *Andr.* 205, adduced by Wilamowitz, οὐκ ἐξ ἐμῶν cε φαρμάκων μιcεῖ πόcιc, ἀλλ' εἰ ξυνεῖναι μὴ 'πιτηδεία κυρεῖc, there is no doubt of the fact, but an underlying generalization 'if you are incompatible, your husband must dislike you.'

τί οὖν τότε; A fine rhetorical question, leading to a fine sophistic reply. Syriskos puts into Daos' mouth a question he had not asked, and makes not the obvious prosaic reply that he could not have asked for the trinkets because he did not know of their existence, but the more pathetic one that he had not then had the status of the child's guardian. Both C and O 14 have οὔπω παρ' ἐμοὶ τοῦτ' ἦν· ὑπὲρ τούτου λέγων ἥκω δὲ καὶ νῦν. But this gives a disjointed sense: 'This was not yet in my power; and it is as his advocate that I have came now too' (or 'even now'). Leo's emendations τότ' and λέγειν appear to me necessary: 'I was then not yet in a position to be his advocate; and now too it is not for myself that I have come to make a claim.' De Falco, like M. Weinstein, *HSCP* lxxv (1971) 137, supports τοῦτ', which can be translated; but the repetition of τότε is rhetorically effective, and the opposition of τότε and νῦν an advantage.

317 κοινὸc 'Ερμῆc: This is a fine piece of rhetorical effrontery. Daos had urged that this was *not* a case of a common find, in which the two parties should go shares. Syriskos speaks as if Daos, to further his own claim, had advanced the doctrine that one should go shares in such a find and rebukes him for 'stealing by finding'.

318 πρόcεcτι cῶμ' ἀδικούμενον: 'Where it involves a person's being wronged'. For cῶμα v. LSJ s.v. II. 2.

319 οὐχ εὕρεcιc κτλ.: The jingle, the rare words in -cιc (though such words were easily formed in Greek; they were much affected by Thucydides, who may have used some for the first time), and pretty antithesis are all nicely in the character of Syriskos. Naturally the line was quoted by itself, as something wonderful, in later times.

320 βλέψον δὲ κἀκεῖ: 'Look at this point, too', ἐκεῖ being used where ἐκεῖcε would be more accurate.   ἐν ἐργάταιc: ἐργάτηc is used mainly of workers on the land. Wilamowitz says that ἐργάται would be free men, μιcθωτοί, hired labourers, and so a cut above slaves, such as Syriskos and Daos themselves; and that Syriskos means: 'He might find himself out of place even among them, let alone among slaves.' There is nothing in this; ἐργάται were workers, and poor men, either free or slave, as fortune willed. Getas at *Dysk.* 608 applies the word to Gorgias and his slave Daos, Oedipus at Soph. *OT* 859 to a slave.

323 ᾄξαc: Restored by Leo, and confirmed by the discovery of the phrase εἰc δὲ τὴν αὑτοῦ (Früchtel: αὐτῶν MSS.) φύcιν ᾄξαc in Clement of Alexandria, *Stromateis* i. 153. 5 (p. 96. 3 Früchtel). This is no everyday word. Belonging mostly to epic and tragedy, where it is used of rapid movement, it is found in a metaphorical sense in prose, of eager turning to a thing, e.g. Plato, *Alcib.* i. 118 b, ᾄττειc πρὸc τὰ πολιτικά, Diog. L. x. 2 (of Epicurus, from the third-century historian Hermippos) ἐπὶ φιλοcοφίαν ᾄξαι, and other examples in LSJ s.v. ᾄccειν.

ἐλεύθερόν τι: ἐλεύθεροc often replaces the more precise ἐλευθέριοc, 'suitable to a free man'. In a slave-owning society the main social distinction is bound to be between slave and free, and ἐλεύθεροc has the colouring which 'gentleman' has in English, though not the same meaning, and ἐλευθέρα γυνή is 'a lady'.

The text of the scholion on *Odyssey* ii. 10, which quotes these two lines, does not give C's ποιεῖν, but πονεῖν, a word often used of difficult but rewarding labours (e.g. Eur. *Suppl.* 576–7, πράccειν cὺ πόλλ' εἴωθαc ἥ τε cὴ πόλιc :: τοιγὰρ πονοῦcα πολλὰ πόλλ' εὐδαιμονεῖ). It is hard to determine which is right, but the slightly high-flown ἐλεύθερόν τι πονεῖν is so appropriate to Syriskos' display of fine words here, that I have adopted it.

324 ὅπλα: The unusual scansion ὅπλα may be due to the atmosphere of tragedy, cf. τέκνον *Mis.* 215, μελάθροις *Sam.* 507, perhaps μίτρα *Perik.* 823. βαστάζειν, too, is a word from poetry.   **λέοντας:** Perhaps a romantic idea from tragedy; there were no lions to hunt in Greece, (Nausikrates frag. 6 K, ἐν τῇ γὰρ Ἀττικῇ τίς εἶδε πώποτε | λέοντας ἢ τοιοῦτον ἕτερον θηρίον, οὗ δασύποδ' (a hare) εὑρεῖν ἐστιν οὐχὶ ῥᾴδιον;), although such feats would be possible in the newly opened territories of the old Persian empire. Wilamowitz suggested that Syriskos might be thinking of the deeds of Herakles.

326 πάντα: Emphatic by position. There may be a flattering suggestion that Smikrines is better informed on this subject than Syriskos, who will not have had the same opportunities for seeing tragic acting. Syriskos can, however, be supposed to have seen the play he describes, perhaps Sophokles' well-known *Tyro*, which told how Neleus and Pelias, sons of Tyro by Poseidon, having been exposed, found, and reared in the country, were later recognized and able to rescue their mother from ill treatment. According to Aristotle, *Poetics* 1454^b25, the recognition was effected by means of the cradle in which they had been exposed, but this is not necessarily inconsistent with Syriskos' account, for Aristotle may mean a cradle and its contents, as is suggested by Pearson and strongly argued by Gudeman (ed. *Poetics* l.c.), who compares the ἀντίπηξ containing Ion's γνωρίσματα, which is produced at *Ion* 1337–8. Apollodoros, i. 90 ff., has a version of the story in which the twins were found not by a goatherd, but by a ἱπποφορβός, but there is no reason to suppose him to be following Sophokles. In any case, we do not know that Syriskos refers to Sophokles' play. A contemporary of Menander's, Astydamas the younger, also wrote a play on this theme; so did Karkinos, an author of the first half of the fourth century, who is quoted by the slave Daos in *Aspis* 417.   **τινα . . . ἐκείνους:** τινα suggests that not everyone has heard of Neleus, ἐκείνους that he and his brother are characters well known to Smikrines; a flattering touch.

333 τότ': Perhaps at the time when they were given the wallet. But ποτ' would be an easy change (the opposite mistake *Dysk.* 16), and if Dio Cassius, who has πρίν, was quoting from memory, his evidence would favour ποτε, since πρίν gives the same sense.

334 εἰ δ' ἐκλαβών: I.e. if Daos had extracted the tokens from the bag. The position of the twins would then be the more miserable than if the bag itself had been taken. Its presence would arouse the suspicion that tokens had been exposed along with them, its emptiness would mean that there was no hope of establishing their parentage. It is hard to say whether εἰ δ' ἐκλαβών or εἰ δέ γε λαβών, 'Yes, but if Daos had got them', is the right correction of C's ειδεκελαβων. On the one hand there is no mark of elision after δ (but the writer may have understood δὲ καί), on the other κ for γ is a mistake unique in this MS., and the repetition of ε may have been helped by the similar sequence of letters, εδωκεδα, in 331. The combination δέ γε is most common in answers or retorts (as *Dysk.* 845); the continuative use, that would be found here, is comparatively rare, and 'often has a tinge of repartee' (Denniston, *GP* 155) suitable here; but there are no other instances in the remains of Menander.

Capps suggests that Δᾶος means 'a Daos'. Rather Syriskos naïvely talks as if the Neleus and Pelias he had seen on the stage were contemporaries, whom this Daos might have robbed.

335 δραχμάς: The first syllable is usually short (or better 'light') in comedy, but occasionally long ('heavy') as here (frag. 951. 5, Ar. *Peace* 1201, Philippides frag. 1 K).

337 οἱ τηλικοῦτοι καὶ τοιοῦτοι: These words are often joined to reinforce one another, see LSJ s.v. τηλικοῦτος. **ἀγνῶτες:** Although not unknown in prose, e.g. Plato, *Rep.* 375 e, and several times in Aristotle, this word is found here only in comedy, and Syriskos intends it to lend distinction to his conclusion. In the whole of this passage consummate skill is displayed in the handling of language and metre. Syriskos' style keeps rising towards that of tragedy, as he talks of his romantic fictions and of mythology, but never quite maintains the tragic level (otherwise his lines would not be appropriate in a comedy); but when he thinks of the real world comic metre comes rushing back. Thus, as has been seen, ὅπλα βαστάζειν is poetic, but the movement, with τρέχειν | ἐν ἀγῶσι added in asyndeton and running over to the next line, suggests the comic style. Coming back to earth with the address to Smikrines, Syriskos has a line without caesura. Then he mounts again: 327 could stand in a tragedy, but the next line has comic rhythm, as he thinks of himself. 329 is tragic but for the infringement of Porson's law, 330 perfectly tragic, and distinguished by the anaphora of ὡς, but 331 has a non-tragic anapaest; this avoids four successive lines of tragic rhythm, for 332–3 would be unexceptionable in tragedy metrically, although 332 is undistinguished in language. With the mention of Daos we are back to the style of comedy; in language completely so, while metrically 334 would be unusual rather than impossible in tragedy, but 335 contains two non-tragic features. The return to the tragic twins brings a perfectly Euripidean line, but the final line, eloquent and alliterative as it is, just fails to make the metrical grade.

339 τοῦδε: coming so soon after τοῦτο, may cause surprise, but is to be taken as deictic: Syriskos calls attention to the baby, to stir pity for it. Gomme preferred to follow Sudhaus in reading τὴν αὐτοῦ δέ, but the order of words will not do; it should be αὐτοῦ δὲ τήν, cf. K–G i. § 564. 4.

340 λαβόντα . . . ἀφανίcαι: A colourless λαβόντα, as the English 'take and make away with'. ἀφανίcαι is especially appropriate because it is the disappearance of the tokens that would put an end to the chance that the child might escape from its humble condition. cωτηρία often connotes escape or deliverance from hardship or danger, cf. *Dysk.* 840 n.

342 ἐρρύcατο: Itself a word from epic and tragedy. No story of brother and sister nearly marrying (γαμῶν, 'on the point of marrying') is known from tragedy, but the motive appears in *Perikeiromene*, and Plautus' *Epidicus*; a mother is saved, after a recognition, in the stories of Tyro (above, 326 n.), Antiope, Melanippe, and Hypsipyle, and a brother in that of Iphigeneia, all subjects of tragedy.

343–5: 'Nature has made the life of all men precarious: we must use foresight to protect it for them, keeping an eye well in advance on the means whereby it is possible to protect it.' Once again Syriskos produces a rhetorician's *sententia*, this time elaborately turned in language.

348 οὐκ ἐcτι δίκαιον: Körte, to avoid a broken anapaest, assumes the shortening δίκαιον by the analogy of δείλαιοc (frequent: Ar. *Knights*, 130, etc.), Ἀθήναιοc (Polyzelos frag. 11 K) and φιλαθήναιοc (Ar. *Wasps*, 283); cf. also Πειραιᾶ below (752). Similarly δικαίωc is probable in Machon 293 Gow, νὴ τὴν φίλην Δήμητρα δικαίωc †τοιγάρ. De Falco objects that δίκαιοc is more difficult than the other shortenings of -αι- because they have a long syllable preceding, just as the common ποιεῖν, τοιοῦτοc (and ποίαν, Ar. *Wasps* 1369) have a long syllable after that shortened. Tragedy provides a closer parallel in γεραιόc (Eur. *Hipp.* 170 and five other places; also in the paratragic line *Sikyonios* 169), and possibly παλαιόc (Soph. frag. 870 N, 956 Pearson, Eur. *El.* 497, where see Denniston's note). For the sake of completeness, I add frag. 788, ὡράϊζεται (phonetically distinct, since the dipthong αι was here followed by the vowel ι), and two textually doubtful examples from *Dysk.*, παϊανιcτάc 230, and γύναϊα 568, both defended by Handley, but not generally accepted.

A broken anapaest is even more difficult to defend than correption of αι. There is no certain parallel in Menander for an anapaest broken after the first syllable, if that syllable belongs to a word partly contained in the previous foot (see introd. p. 38). Yet there is no parallel for frag. 397. 3. οἷον τὰ νηcιωτικὰ ταυτὶ ξενύδρια, which defies emendation, or, to take an instance from Latin, the hexameter ending 'fluminum amores' (*Am.* iii. 6. 101) is unique in Ovid, but inescapable. No likely emendation has been proposed for this line. Wilamowitz approved Sudhaus's οὐκέτι δίκαιον, but οὐκέτι would imply that Syriskos recognizes part of Daos' claims as just, a thing which he is far from doing.

348 ff.: Syriskos takes it as established that Daos ought to hand over the trinkets (εἰ does not imply any doubt, either here or in 351, but is equivalent to ἐπεί, cf. 313 n.), and then indignantly asks whether he is trying not only to keep them, but also to get the baby as well (πρός, adverbial). He goes on to suggest that Daos' object in asking to have the baby back is to be safe once again to commit his intended crime of robbing it of the possessions which Fortune has so far preserved for it, safe because no one will then be interested in protecting its rights. Körte prints the sentence as a statement, Jensen as a question; the latter is more effective.

357 τἀδικεῖν: A rare crasis of τῷ ἀδικεῖν (for its form cf. τἀνδρί for τῷ ἀνδρί), the more remarkable because the article does not grammatically belong to the infinitive. There is nothing like this elsewhere in Menander, and Sudhaus's emendation τ⟨οῦτ'⟩ ἀδικεῖν may be right.

359 νὴ τὸν Δία τὸν Cωτῆρα: Cf. *Sam.* 310, *Perik.* 759, frag. incert. 951 (Körte–Thierfelder ii. 275), *Pap. Ghôran* ii. 194, and ὦ Ζεῦ Cῶτερ, *Dysk.* 690, frag. 581, 656. The simple phrases νὴ Δία, ὦ Ζεῦ had lost force, and an epithet was needed if any personal appeal to Zeus was to be felt. Genuine belief in the aid of Zeus Soter in the hour of need is indicated by Aristophanes, *Plutus* 1175 ff., where his priest speaks of the sacrifices made by those who have had a safe voyage or been acquitted in the law-courts; and the Athenians must often have been reminded of him, for the third libation at a party or feast was made to him (Plato, *Rep.* 583 b).

360 περιέcπαcμ': 'I am robbed, stripped, of everything', a rare sense of περιcπᾶν, apparently derived fram an original literal meaning 'to strip off a cloak, etc.' μετὰ βίαc ἀφαιρεῖcθαι, Photios.

362 ἢ μηθὲν ἀγαθόν, κτλ.: I.e. 'May I be damned if it isn't.'

363 ὦ Ἡράκλεic: A common expression of surprise or dismay; Herakles is invoked as ἀλεξίκακοc. ἃ πέπονθα: 'Heavens, (see) what I suffer.' The relative ὅc does not (*pace* LSJ) introduce an exclamation. Cf. 367.

364 βραχύ: The dicolon before this word is to mark the change of person addressed, not change of speaker (introd. p. 41). Smikrines was about to go, without a word, in his usual surly way.

366 ἐργαστήριον: The word can be used of any kind of workshop; only here apparently does it have the sense of the Latin corruption *ergastulum*, namely a place of confinement for hard labour. Further the name of the place is transferred to the inmate; the insult means that Daos is one who should be in a place of punitive forced labour. Similarly in Ar. *Lysistr.* 372 an old man is addressed ὦ τύμβε. Cf. also Ter. *Phormio* 373, 'ain tandem, carcer?' Most editors assign this speech to Syriskos; like Capps, I incline to think it belongs to Smikrines, who is free with terms of abuse: 228, 1064, 1080, 1100, 1114, 1122.

368 τὴν δίκην ἐμοῦ λέγοντος: 'As I was presenting my case', cf. Ar. *Wasps* 776, ἦν δίκην λέγῃ μακράν τις.

369 ὡς ἡλίσκετ': 'When he found he was losing'.   **οὐκ ἂν ᾠόμην:** 'I would not have thought it', i.e. that such an unjust decision could be given, cf. Eur. *Alc.* 1088, οἷον εἶπας· οὐκ ἂν ᾠόμην, (similarly *Pap. Ghôran* ii. 103), Polybios x. 32. 12, τὸ μὲν γὰρ λέγειν ὡς "οὐκ ἂν ᾠόμην. τίς γὰρ ἂν ἤλπισε τοῦτο γενέσθαι;", Plut. *Mor.* 474 e, τὸ "οὐκ ἂν ᾠόμην" καὶ τὸ "ἀλλ' ἤλπιζον" καὶ τὸ "τοῦτ' οὐ προσεδόκων". W. G. Arnott, *CQ* N.s. xviii (1968), 229 wrongly gives the phrase to Smikrines, 'I shouldn't have thought he swallowed anything'.

370 εὐτύχει: Lit. 'farewell', is found at the end of letters (Plato, *Epist.* 321 c, and commonly in Egyptian papyri addressed to superiors) and on tombstones. It is a formula for parting, cf. *Dysk.* 576.

371 θᾶττον: Not closely with δικάζειν, but perhaps 'immediately' 'without delay', i.e. 'that is the sort of arbitrator we should have, and let us have no delay over introducing this reform', for the imperfect ἔδει shows that arbitrators are not all of that sort. Otherwise θᾶττον may be taken as the equivalent of μᾶλλον. Mazon compared Soph. *Phil.* 631, θᾶσσον ἂν . . . κλύοιμ' ἐχίδνης, but the parallel is inexact.

373: *CYP*/ was added in the left-hand margin, as a reminder that Smikrines has left the stage at 370. At 369 the same indication in the right-hand margin must be a mistake.   **ᾔσθας:** Cf. *Perik.* 290 and οἶσθας 481 below, frag. 286. These forms are due to a feeling that the second person singular should end in -ς; it is an accident that ᾔσθας occurs in Menander only before a vowel; οἶσθας stands before a consonant in 481, *Mis.* 250.

374: Körte prints von Arnim's supplement, taken from 311, αὐτ[ά, ἕως ἂν ἐκτραφ]ῇ⟨ι⟩; this supposes an unusual *scriptio plena* in the papyrus, but may be right. If the final η has been wrongly read, the way lies open for many other suggestions.

376 βάδιζε: This imperative often has the sense 'get along', 'get a move on', and is often addressed to slaves. But the impulsive Polemon can use it to Pataikos, 'come along' as he hurries him into his house, *Perik.* 525, cf. *Sik.* 147, 267, and *Sam.* 154 n.

(iii) **376–418:** *Syriskos (with wife) and Onesimos*

377 τὸν τρόφιμον: See frag. 1 note. As Wilamowitz urged, the word does not necessarily imply that Chairestratos lived with his father, only that he is still young enough for the old name to stick. Similarly in *Aspis* Kleostratos is Daos' τρόφιμος at 2, 34, 106, δεσπότης at 214. Later Syriskos speaks of himself as Chairestratos' οἰκέτης (408); but he is living on his own (χωρὶς οἰκῶν in the legal phrase) and working for himself, paying his master a regular fixed sum (ἀποφορά). He is independent enough *de facto* to have a wife and to be able to bring up a child without obtaining his master's permission.

379 ἐπ' ἔργον ἐξορμήσομεν: 'We will set out back to work', i.e. leave the village for the woods.

381 ἔχεις κοιτίδα τινά; Being a *persona muta*, Syriskos' wife does not speak, but it is quite natural that she should indicate by an upward movement of the chin, the standard gesture of negation in ancient as in modern Greece, that she has no box.

381: This line is unique in Menander as having three dactyls. According to J. W. White, *Class. Phil.* iv (1909), 158, there is only a single instance in Aristophanes.   ἀπαρίθμησαι, the earliest instance of the use of the middle for the active in this compound, but cf. ἠριθμησάμην Plato, *Phaedr.* 270 d, ἠριθμοῦντο, Thuc. iii. 20, καταριθμησαίμεθα [Isokr.] i. 11.

382 προκόλπιον: A fold, serving the purpose of a pocket, made by drawing up some of the chiton through the belt in front. Wilamowitz thought that Theophrastos, *Char.* vi. 8 and xxii. 7 showed it to have been improper for a man to carry anything in the προκόλπιον and that the same would apply to freeborn ladies. But the passages collected by Gow on Theokr. xvi. 17 show this to be a false generalization as regards both sexes. Theophrastos observes only that a man who is a bit 'cracked' turns up with his προκόλπιον bulging with papers, and that the ἀνελεύθερος so brings his vegetables home instead of employing a slave to carry them for him; this does not imply that *nothing* should ever be carried there.

382: Onesimos comes out from Chairestratos' house. He does not immediately notice Syriskos and his wife, nor is he observed by them. But as soon as he does see them, the inquisitiveness of his nature

makes him approach. Wilamowitz observes that his entry on the stage
is unmotivated. Menander did not bother himself about the motivation of entries, any more than did Molière or Shakespeare. If a good
reason is to hand for a character's appearance, it may be given or
suggested; if there is not, the author knows that the best way of
handling the matter is to say nothing (Gomme, *Essays*, p. 254). It is part
of the conventions of Menander's theatre that the audience may
expect the characters to come out and keep them informed of what is
passing inside. Here Onesimos' relation is cut short by his catching
sight of the others.

383 τηνικαῦτα κτλ.: 'At this hour yesterday they had long been
at their wine'; i.e. the dinner was over, for *at a banquet* the Greeks
drank after the meal. We might say in English, 'over their port'.
I believe the point of this is to suggest that a good deal more than half
the day is past, and so to prepare for the lapse of a night between
Acts II and III (see the introductory note to that Act).

385 στριφνός: Normally means 'tough', either for praise or censure.
Perhaps here 'lean' (Wilamowitz) rather than 'tough', for toughness
as such could hardly be inferred in a toy figure made in bronze or
clay. But I prefer Capps's suggestion that Syriskos playfully pinches
the cock, as if testing it for tenderness (cf. Ar. *Birds* 530), and finds it
as hard as rock. Moiris (a grammarian, second century A.D.) says that
στιφρός is Attic, whereas the κοινή uses στριφνός, and *Pap. Oxy.* 1803,
a lexicon of Attic words, makes the same distinction, quoting
Menander's Cυναριστῶσαι (frag. 389) for the Attic form στιφρός. We
are unfortunately not in a position to say whether Menander here
used the word through imperfect command of Attic Greek, of which
Phrynichos accuses him (s.v. cύccημον), or deliberately put a non-Attic
word in Syriskos' mouth, either as not being Athenian-born, or as
thinking it 'smart' to use the word from the κοινή. Or C may have
substituted the new for the old unfamiliar Attic form, as has probably
been done with other words at *Sam.* 394, ἄχρις, and (in B) at *Sam.* 98,
ἰχθύες, *Dysk.* 192, Διόσκουροι.

386 διάλιθον: 'Set with stones'. Cf. the temple inventory, *IG* i². 289,
[ὅρμος] ῥόδων διάλιθος χ[ρυσοῦς (fifth century), and 387, δι]άλιθον
χρυσία ἔχον (latter fourth century).   πέλεκυς: Similarly in Plaut.
Rudens 1158 a toy axe is a recognition-token.

387 ὑπόχρυσος: 'Gilt'; Körte, *Hermes* lxiv (1929), 267 ff., showed
that whereas originally adjectives compounded with ὑπο- were used
to denote the underlying material and those with ἐπι- to denote the
covering, later ὑπόχρυσος came to be used for ἐπίχρυσος (*Inscr. de Délos*,
298, 240 B.C.), no doubt under the influence of ὑποχρυσοῦν 'to gild',

cf. *SIG*² 588, δακτύλιοι cιδηροῖ ὑποκεχρυcώμενοι, and of adjectives in ὑπο- that mean 'not fully so-and-so', e.g. ὑπαύcτηρος. γλύμμα is the engraving in the semi-precious stone (e.g. onyx) which the ring carries, for use as a seal. οὐκ ἂν διαγνοίην: cf. *Perik.* 769. To illustrate the difficulty of recognizing the likeness intended, Wilamowitz compares an indeterminate animal on a Cretan stone of the Mycenean period, illustrated by Furtwängler, *Antike Gemmen,* i, pl. iv. 27. But fourth-century engravers attained a greater realism. It may be more relevant that it is easier to recognize a figure on the impression made by a seal than on the seal itself.

389 Κλεόcτρατος δέ τιc: Nothing is known of this Kleostratos. Comparatively few gems bear the engraver's name; when they do, it may be in the form *Δεξαμενὸc ἐποίει*, or just the name may be inscribed, G. M. A. Richter, *Catalogue of Engraved Gems,* p. xxxii. Syriskos is here playing the connoisseur, as before he played the orator and patron of the theatre. Onesimos recognizes the ring as his master's from the description; it is easy to believe that the inquisitive personal servant of Charisios was familiar with it; and he knew that it had been lost (406–7, 472–3); thus Syriskos' nice vanity, and Onesimos' περιεργία combine to set in train the recognition of the baby's parents.

Gomme here wrote as follows:

> It is a convention of our texts to accent oxytones at the end of iambic verse as barytones when the sentence runs on to the next line, as though there was never any pause even of the slightest, even where there is hiatus. We should perhaps distinguish, writing e.g. at 346 γάρ, at 364 βραχύ, at 401 ἤ, at 426 καί and at 430 κακά; but not ἐγώ at 359 nor perhaps ἀνήρ at 327; to make the rule universal suggests that trimeters were not trimeters. Can we believe that here a Greek pronounced τιc oxytone, with ἐcτιν in the next line enclitic?

I do not believe it, but for a different reason. It is improbable that in a series of enclitics two successive syllables could, contrary to the general rule, carry the raised pitch. The Greek will have said *Κλεό-cτρατος δέ τιc ἐcτίν*, not *Κλεόcτρατος δέ τίc ἐcτιν* (see Euripides, *Hippolytos,* ed. W. S. Barrett, pp. 426–7).

391 ἐπιδεῖξον: Cf. Ar. *Ach.* 765. ἀποδεῖξον (Richards) is supported by *Perik.* frag. 2. Syriskos hands the ring over, as one might to anyone showing interest in an *objet d'art.*

392 ὁ ποῖος; Not the scornful ποῖοc without the article, but 'what ring do you mean?' Cf. *Sik.* 378, Ar. *Ach.* 963, *Clouds* 1270.

393 χολᾷc: 'You are mad', cf. *Sam.* 416. Mental derangement was supposed to be due to biliary disturbance, see *Dysk.* 89 n.

395 coì θῶ; A nice ethic dative—'put it down to please *you*?', 'because you tell me to?'

396 Ἄπολλον καὶ θεοί: The exclamation is one of surprise or dismay. Apollo is appealed to as ἀποτρόπαιος, averter of evil. When the oath lost force through repeated use and familiarity, it was strengthened by adding καὶ θεοί (e.g. 400 and *Dysk.* 151), as was also done with the oaths by Poseidon, Athene, and Earth.

398 ἁρπάζειν βλέπει: The accus. of noun or adjective (e.g. νᾶπυ or ὀξύ) after βλέπειν denotes the nature of the look. The infinitive, denoting the purpose inferred from the look, ('looks as if he'd grab it') is less common, e.g. Ar. *Wasps* 847, τιμᾶν βλέπω, Alexis frag. 97 K, ὀρχεῖσθαι μόνον βλέποντες.

398: The division of speakers here is uncertain. C has a dicolon after βλέπει. If that is explained as a mistake or as indicating a change, not of speaker, but of person addressed, as Syriskos turns from his wife to Onesimos, a tolerable sense results, and this is Körte's text. But thinking that προσπαίζεις ἐμοί; 'Are you having a game with me?' suits Syriskos better than Onesimos, Gomme preferred to interpret the dicolon after βλέπει as marking a change of speaker in the normal way and to assume the omission of a dicolon at the end of 399. This gives (*Ov.*) τὸν δακτύλιον θές, φημι (*Cv.*) προσπαίζεις ἐμοί; (*Ov.*) τοῦ δεσπότου κτλ. Onesimos must then be supposed to adopt Syriskos' phrase τὸν δακτύλιον θές (394). This is, however, unlikely, since there is no sign that he had surrendered the ring at Syriskos' earlier bidding.

402 καθυφείμην: A favourite word (but usually active) of Demosthenes for conceding, giving way weakly or treacherously (e.g. xix. 6); or for a prosecutor's letting his case drop collusively (e.g. xxi. 151)); for the middle see iii. 8, εἰ καθυφείμεθά τι τῶν πραγμάτων. Syriskos is talking to himself or his wife (τούτῳ not coí), rallying his spirits, frightened of the determined Onesimos.   ἄραρε: 'It is settled, my mind is made up'; as in Eur. *Or.* 1330, cf. *Med.* 321, μὴ λόγους λέγε, ὡς τοῦτ' ἄραρε. Lipsius, *Attisches Recht* iii. 797²⁸, and A. R. W. Harrison, *The Law of Athens*, i. p. 168 n., think that δικάσομαι, together with 417, δίκας μελετᾶν, provides evidence that a slave, if μισθοφορῶν, would be competent to bring certain suits in court. Whatever the legal position may in fact have been, it cannot be deduced from this play: Syriskos can use δικάζομαι and δίκαι of any informal procedure such as he has just engaged in before Smikrines, cf. 229, δίκας λέγοντες περιπατεῖτε;

403 παιδίου: Without the article, like a proper name; cf. *Perik.* 262 n. These words are probably addressed to Onesimos, in further protest. Then he turns to his wife. To prevent Onesimos from claiming anything more he hastily checks the rest of the things and hurries her into the house. To his wife at least he can give orders peremptorily; and his authority thus re-established, he turns again to Onesimos. But that authority soon crumbles.

404 στρεπτόν: A twisted metal collar, see Hdt. iii. 20. 1; there στρεπτός as in Plato *Rep.* 553 c and Xen. *Cyr.* i. 3. 2; the neuter is found in *IG* ii². 1388. 28 (Attic, fourth century) and Plutarch, *Artaxerxes* 15. πτέρυξ is called by Pollux (vii. 62) the half of a χιτωνίσκος, i.e. the front or the back, cf. Plut. *Numa* 25 (of the Spartan girls), τοῦ παρθενικοῦ χιτῶνος αἱ πτέρυγες οὐκ ἦσαν συνερραμμέναι κάτωθεν, ἀλλ᾽ ἀνεπτύσσοντο καὶ συνανεγύμνουν ὅλον ἐν τῷ βαδίζειν τὸν μηρόν. In this case it was probably used to wrap the child in. Such a πτέρυξ is a token by which Stratophanes is recognized in *Sikyonios* 280.

405 πάραγε: 'Go along in', as 411 below, *Dysk.* 556, etc.

407 μεθύων ἀπώλες᾽, ὡς ἔφη: He had not told Onesimos all the truth.

407–18: Syriskos' agreement to allow Onesimos to keep the ring is, on reflection, a little easily given. He does not know him (391), nor has he seen him come out of Chairestratos' house, nor does he know that Charisios, whose slave Onesimos has declared himself to be, is a guest there. Nevertheless he takes it for granted that Onesimos and he are both going to enter that house (411). A movement in that direction by Onesimos might serve to explain his belief. The spectators know the facts that Syriskos does not know, and will not notice that he is less well-informed than they. For them the emphasis lies in the last eight lines, which suggest that Onesimos will do nothing till the next day, and that Syriskos will willingly wait: significantly he repeats the word αὔριον.

412 συνάγουσι: 'There is company'; Athen. 365 c, ἔλεγον δὲ συνάγειν καὶ τὸ μετ᾽ ἀλλήλων πίνειν, a sense for which he quotes frag. 146 K–T. Besides this intransitive usage, the verb is used transitively, 'to collect guests', cf. *Perik.* 175, *Dysk.* 566, frag. 384.

415 ὅτῳ βούλεσθ᾽ ἐπιτρέπειν: Syriskos, intending to maintain his claim to the ring, offers to accept any arbitrator that Onesimos and Charisios may name. ἐνὶ λόγῳ ἕτοιμος: I.e. 'I say without ado that I am ready.' The word εἰμί is frequently omitted with ἕτοιμος, e.g. *Dysk.* 361 n., 370, At this point Onesimos will enter Chairestratos' house, leaving Syriskos to address the audience before following.

416 οὐδὲ νῦν κακῶς: 'I did not came off badly this time, either', i.e. in the arbitration conducted by Smikrines. For the understatement of οὐ κακῶς compare 510. [Gomme proposed to read οὐδὲ νῦν καλῶc (or κακῶν) 'even now I have not got away safely' (or 'from my troubles') 'but must etc.' This is to my mind no improvement on the traditional text.]

417 δίκαc μελετᾶν: 'Practise the pleading of cases'. The Athenians were still able to smile at their own fondness for litigation, but the absurdity that lies uppermost is that of a slave's training himself in oratory.   **διὰ τουτί:** Many editors (but not Allinson, van Leeuwen, De Falco or Del Corno) have adopted Croiset's conjecture διὰ τούτου. But the distinction between the genitive to express the means by which something is done and the accusative to express the cause of its being done was less rigid than might be gathered from e.g. LSJ. That dictionary acknowledges the use of διά+acc. of a person to mean 'by the agency of'. Here we may translate: 'It is due to this that anything is kept safe to-day.' The immediate means of preserving things is to plead one's case well, a less immediate cause of their preservation is training in litigation.

XOPOY: This time there are no verses, as there were at the end of Act I (169 n.), to introduce the chorus.

ACT III

The interlude represents the passing of an indefinite period of time. We may therefore suppose with van Leeuwen that the morrow (414) has come with Act III, or follow the more usual view that the time is later on the same day. The internal evidence of the play strongly favours the former view. (1) Onesimos suggests at the end of Act II that he will not show Charisios the ring until the next day; when he reappears in Act III, he says that he has several times been on the point of showing it. (2) In Act II Syriskos expresses himself quite ready to wait till the next day (414); in Act III he appears in a state of perturbation because Onesimos has not yet done anything about showing the ring (442). (3) It fits in with this that Habrotonon says in Act III that she has been in Charisios' company on the two previous days (440). We know from Onesimos (383) that there had been a drinking-party on the day preceding Act II. There may, of course, have been one also on the day before that, but we have no evidence of it. On the information given we are bound to suppose the two previous days to have been the one before the opening of the play and the one to which the first two acts belong. The audience could refrain from drawing this conclusion only if somewhere in the lost part of the play there was something to forbid it, *or* if there was a recognized convention that the action of a play should not extend over more than a single day. It is certainly true that most Greek plays are either explicitly so limited (e.g. *Dyskolos*) or bear no suggestion that the events occupy two or more days. But there are exceptions. In tragedy *Eumenides* and Euripides' *Supplices* are clear examples; in Old Comedy *Lysistrata* and *Plutus*. It might be, however, that by the time of New Comedy it was established that the action should be completed within a day. At first sight there is disproof of this in *Heautontimorumenos*, where a new day begins at 410; but Terence in his prologue admits to having made some changes from the Menandrean original and it has been argued (Körte, *RE* xv. 747, H. Marti *Lustrum* viii [1964], 47) that one of these was to spread the action over two days. This is, however, nothing but speculation; K. Gaiser, *Wien. Stud.* lxxix (1966), 198, gives reasons for believing the time-scheme to be that of Menander. It must be allowed that the evidence, for what it is worth, as was also held by G. Jachmann, *RE* 2. ix. 634, shows that it was possible to exceed the limit of a single day. Plautus' *Captivi* certainly does so, but is also in other respects an abnormal play. A recently-published papyrus, *P. IFAO* 337 (*ZPE* vi [1970], 5), may bring further confirmation. It is a scrap from a catalogue of plays, very like that in *P. Oxy.* 1235 (see p. 694); the account of the play immediately preceding Δὶς ἐξαπατῶν ends with the words τοῦτο δυεῖν ἡμερῶν χρόν[.

(i) 419–429: *Onesimos alone*

419 ὥρμηκα: See 557 n.

419–29: Onesimos explains that he has several times been on the point of telling his master about the ring. But he has hesitated because his previous giving of information had brought him trouble. He means by that his action in telling Charisios of Pamphile's child. Charisios wishes he had been left in the dark, and Onesimos fears that if he should be reconciled with Pamphile he may want to get rid of the slave who knows the story they will both wish to forget. Now he sees that by returning the ring he may make further trouble for himself, becoming involved in another story that may embarrass his master. His hesitation, we discover, had led to the loss of most of the morning: later in this act the guests are about to have lunch (610).

421 καὶ πρὸς αὐτῷ παντελῶc: 'And indeed right up to him' (Gomme, as Capps, Del Corno, etc.). But I prefer 'and being absolutely on the point of it', i.e. of showing it, as in Soph. *OT* 1169, οἴμοι, πρὸς αὐτῷ γ' εἰμὶ τῷ δεινῷ λέγειν, 'on the dreaded brink of speech' (Jebb). Similarly cφόδρα ὢν ἐγγύc does not mean being 'very near my master', but 'very near showing it'. καί then adds a stronger expression by way of climax, as e.g. Plat. *Apol.* 23 a, ὀλίγου τινὸς ἀξία καὶ οὐδενός, and see K–G ii. 256. ἐπιεικῶς developed in meaning like the English 'fairly'; here one can render 'pretty often' or 'often enough', and in 429 'pretty big'. With verbs the meaning is 'fairly well', e.g. ἐπιεικῶς οἷοί τε ἦσαν κατέχειν, Plato *Phaed.* 117 c. πυκνά: *Heros* 4 n.

424 ὡς . . . ἀπολέcαι: The use of ὡς in wishes is familiar in Homer, sometimes with an optative, sometimes with ὤφελον (ἤλυθες ἐκ πολέμου· ὡς ὤφελες αὐτόθ' ὀλέσθαι says Helen to Paris, *Il.* iii. 428), but rare in Attic, see Jebb on Soph. *El.* 126. When it does occur, more often than not it is joined, as here, with ὄλλυμι; that may be a survival of an old formula.

427 ἀφανίcῃ: 'Make away with me', cf. 340. The imprecise word does not imply 'killing', any more than at Isokr. xvii. 11, ἀφανίζει Κίττον τὸν παῖδα: Onesimos might fear that he might be sold to undertake one of the less pleasant occupations. **καλῶc ποῶν:** A probable but uncertain conjecture by Wilamowitz, cf. *Perik.* 989, where by chance there is the same doubt about the tense of the main verb. L. Koenen, *ZPE* iv (1970), 156, revives Eitrem's proposal to read καλῶς ἔχει, in the sense 'No, thank you'. I find this unlikely.

428 κυκᾶν: Cf. 573, Ar. *Knights* 363, *Peace* 270. Onesimos sees danger in a step that may connect his master with an unwanted child.

ἀπεcχόμην gives good sense: 'I did well to refrain from a second piece of trouble-making'. Gomme here preferred a future, but did not suggest one, since the obvious ἀφέξομαι is contrary to the traces of letters which Jensen thought he saw at the edge of the hole that succeeds κυκαν in C. Gueraud, however, denied their existence. Nevertheless, if ἀφέξομαι or φυλάξομαι were right, one would expect to see the tail of φ.

(ii) 430–442: *Onesimos and Habrotonon separately*

430 ἐᾶτέ μ' ἱκετεύω cε: Note cε between the plural imperatives, one person being momentarily singled out, cf. *Dysk.* 123. It is natural to suppose that some of the young men were molesting Habrotonon, since Charisios had no use for her, but they may only have been trying to prevent her from leaving. If, contrary to what is argued in 142 n, Habrotonon is first seen here, it is to be observed that her name is not introduced until 497. Enough has been heard of her already for the spectators to recognize her immediately, and the absence of her name does not imply that she must have appeared before. In *Dyskolos* Sikon is not named until 889 or Simiche until 931.

431 ἀθλία: I.e. ἡ ἀθλία with an unusual crasis, as μὴ ἀλλά gives μᾶλλά, Ar. *Frogs* 103 etc. The article seems to be necessary, as with ὁ δυστυχής, e.g. *Perik.* 472, 778. Lefebvre and Körte saw a rough breathing on αθλ[but Jensen denied its existence (rightly I think).

432 χλευάζουςα: Wilamowitz compares Dem. (or pseudo-Dem.) xlvii. 34, of a debtor, οὐκ ἀπεδίδου . . . ἀλλ' ἐχλεύαζέ με. There is emphasis here on ἐμαυτήν; it might not have been surprising if she had made fools of others. For the position of words ἐμαυτὴν . . . χλευάζουςα, cf. 130 n. **προςεδόκων:** Sudhaus' conjecture μὲν ἐδόκουν, preferred by Gomme, gives an objectionable division of words in a fifth-foot dactyl. Capps' suggestion is based on Anaxilas frag. 22, 29, οἱ δ' ἐρᾶςθαι προςδοκῶντες. If the restoration is right, Habrotonon had had so much confidence in her own charms that she expected Charisios to became enamoured, not merely to use her for a night or two.

433 ἄνθρωπος: 'The man'; the phrase can be used in surprise, anger, irony, contempt; only the last is excluded here. **θεῖον:** 'Marvellous' as in Hdt. ii. 66. 2 (but not vii. 137. 1, 2 as LSJ; there it means 'divine', as Powell translates); the word was rarely so used of things, and did not degenerate into a mere alternative for θαυμάςιος in the same sort of way as 'awfully' has became a substitute for 'very'. There is probably still some feeling that it describes something that has no natural explanation.

434 τάλαν: Originally the vocative of τάλας, this has become a mere interjection, 'Oh dear!', used in comedy exclusively by women, and as C. Dedoussi remarks, in a good account of the phrase, Ἑλληνικά xviii (1964), 1–6, in Menander only by women of lower social level; but she adds that this may be accident, as upper-class women say little in our remains (and note *Dysk.* 438). The form ὦ τάλαν occurs just below at 439. **κατακεῖςθαι:** As is well known, the Greeks reclined upon couches to dine or take their wine. Many vase-paintings show hetairai thus sharing a couch with a man. By οὐδέ Habrotonon means that far from there being any love-making, she is not allowed even to 'sit' beside Charisios.

435: It may strain belief that the inquisitive Onesimos should be so engrossed in his own thoughts as not to notice the entrance of Habrotonon, even though the young men with whom she was having trouble remain in the house and do not accompany her. But it is an established convention of Greek comedy that characters may be on the stage together without observing one another; and Menander does not allow the situation to continue long enough to strain the convention: Onesimos' attention is shortly captured by the appearance of Syriskos (Gomme, *Essays*, 255).

436–7 τάλας οὗτος: 'Poor man: why does he throw away all this money?' *τάλας* is, as usual, sympathetic.

439–41 κανοῦν ἔμοιγε: A reference to the basket-carriers at the Panathenaia, who may be seen on the Parthenon frieze; they had to be virgins. Habrotonon is of course no virgin, but she declares that she is one, *τό γ' ἐπὶ τούτῳ* 'for anything that Charisios had done', since she has spent two days with him in unexpected chastity. *φασί* can be attached to any proverbial expression (cf. *Perik.* 291, *Dysk.* 433), but *ἁγνὴ γάμων* may be a phrase taken from the law concerning participation in some festival. Plato, *Laws* 840 d, says that animals live *γάμων ἁγνοί* until they mate; the plural *γάμων*, as England remarks, may denote sexual intercourse, cf. Eur. *Hel.* 190, Dem. xviii. 129. **κάθημαι,** 'sit about with nothing to do', see Ar. *Knights* 396, and Gomme on Thuc. iii 38. 7.

Menander wrote a play called *Ἀρρηφόρος ἢ Αὐλητρίς* (or *Αὐλητρίδες*) ; see frags. 59–67 K–T and Webster, *StM* 145. It is a pity we do not know more about it.

(iii) **442–463**: *Onesimos and Syriskos: Habrotonon listens*

442: A third person comes out of Chairestratos' house, Syriskos searching for Onesimos. The device of an unexpected entry in mid line has already been used at 382; *Sam.* 428 provides another instance. A mid-line entry of a character whose approach has been remarked is somewhat different: *Dysk.* 775, 402, *Aspis* 431.

444: We need not bow to the authority of Wilamowitz, who asserted that *ποτέ* belongs to *ᾧ* (cf. *ὅστις ποτέ*, etc.), 'whoever it is'. Syriskos knew that Onesimos intended to show the ring to his master. *ποτέ* with an imperative expresses impatience, as in 366, *δός ποτ', ἐργαστήριον*, *Sam.* 373, Soph. *Phil.* 816, *μέθες μέθες με* :: *ποῖ μεθῶ;* :: *μέθες ποτέ*. It is separated from its verb, as here, in *Aspis* 222, *λαβὲ τὰς μαχαίρας παιδάριον θᾶττόν ποτε*.

445 κρινώμεθα: Cf. 220. Syriskos demands the arbitration he had suggested at the end of Act II, because he has business elsewhere. This neatly motivates both his eagerness to get the matter settled and his departure at 462 below.

446 ἄνθρωπε: A form of address unavoidable, according to Wilamowitz, because they do not know each other's names. As if that mattered, or as if they would not have learnt them by now! The address is not in itself insulting, but it always implies some sort of a protest, 'now, look here, you!' and can be offensive. Here the protest is against Syriskos' impatience.

449 τοῦτον: The ring.

450 cυνεξέκειτο: Sc. τὸ παιδίον.

451 Ταυροπολίοιc: The Tauropolia was a festival in honour of Ἄρτεμιc Ταυροπόλοc, who was worshipped at Brauron and also outside Attica (L. Deubner, *Attische Feste*, p. 208). An inscription (Πολεμων i [1929], 227 and, more accurately, Ἐφημ. Ἀρχ. 1932 [publ. 1934]) shows that an important festival of this name took place at Halai Araphenides, a deme on the coast adjacent to Brauron; this festival must be referred to in Eur. *IT* 1450 ff. χῶρόc τίc ἐcτιν Ἀτθίδοc πρὸc ἐcχάτοιc | ὅροιcι, γείτων δειράδοc Καρυcτίαc, | ἱερόc, Ἁλάc νιν οὑμὸc ὀνομάζει λεώc. | ἐνταῦθα τεύξαc ναὸν ἵδρυcαι βρέταc, | ἐπώνυμον γῆc Ταυρικῆc πόνων τε cῶν, | οὓc ἐξεμόχθειc περιπολῶν καθ' Ἑλλάδα, | οἴcτροιc Ἐρινύων. Ἄρτεμιν δέ νιν βροτοὶ | τὸ λοιπὸν ὑμνήcουcι Ταυροπόλον θεάν· | νόμον δὲ θὲc τόνδ'· ὅταν ἑορτάζῃ λεώc κτλ. Cf. also Hesychios, Ταυροπόλια Ἁλαιεῖc (Deubner, ἃ εἰc MSS.) ἑορτὴν ἄγουcιν Ἀρτέμιδι. Probably this is the Ταυροπόλια of this play.

Wilamowitz says that παννυχίδοc οὔcηc καὶ γυναικῶν means that this festival was exceptional in admitting women to the παννυχίc. The contrary is the case; παννυχίδεc were particularly associated with the participation of women, cf. *Dysk.* 857, *Sam.* 46, Eur. *Helen* 1365, Ar. *Frogs* 371 and 409. Several night-festivals were mainly (Adonia) or wholly (Thesmophoria) celebrated by women. 'When the night-festival was held and there were women there', the implication being that they were naturally there; similarly in *Phasma* 95 παν]νυχίδοc οὔcηc καὶ χο[ρῶν.

Although there is nothing in the text to indicate it, no doubt Habrotonon would, as Wilamowitz remarks, show that the mention of the Tauropolia had caught her attention.

452–4 κατὰ λόγον ἐcτίν: 'It is reasonable, natural, to suppose' that here was a case of violence to a girl—reasonable because such a story was well known in tragedy and comedy, and sometimes in real life.

τοῦτον masc., by the normal attraction of τοῦτο to the gender of the predicate βιαcμόν. δηλαδή marks, as always, a likely presumption.

455: Onesimos means that if they can find a girl who recognizes the ring as one she had pulled off the finger of the man who had raped her, and later put out with the child she had exposed, then the ring will be good evidence that Charisios is the child's father. But without this woman's witness the ring will do no more than cast suspicion on him, and put him in a quandary of uncertainty.

457 ὑπόνοιαν . . . ἔχει: If the subject of ἔχει is to be determined, it will be τὸ προcφέρειν τὸν δακτύλιον. That brings *mere* suspicion and useless upset.

458 ἀναceίειc: The intransitive is unparalleled, but ἀναceίω and ἐπαναceίω are used with an object to mean 'threaten with so-and-so', a metaphor from brandishing an intimidating weapon, cf. Thuc. iv. 126. 5, ἡ διὰ κενῆc ἐπανάceιcιc τῶν ὅπλων ἔχει τινὰ δήλωcιν ἀπειλῆc. [Dem.] xxv. 47, has a figurative use of the blackmailer who was always threatening to bring actions against public men, τὴν κατὰ Δημοκλέουc εἰcαγγελίαν ἀναceίcαc. Here it would seem that Syriskos warns Onesimos not to try to blackmail him into buying the ring back by a threat to keep it and refuse arbitration. Pollux ix. 155 gives as synonymous ἐκπλήττειν, θορυβεῖν, ἀπειλεῖν, ἀναceίειν, and ἐκφοβεῖν. Phot. Berol. 121. 15 gives ἀπειλεῖν as one meaning of ἀναceίειν; another is ἐπηρεάζειν, which is not suitable here. It may be that the unusual word is chosen to characterize Syriskos as the possessor of 'a little learning'; similarly μεριcμόc (461 below) is apparently one of those new-fangled abstracts which in Hellenistic Greek so often replaced the verbs of a simpler (and to our eyes preferable) language; it is first found in Plato, *Laws* 903 b. 'To my mind no going-shares whatever is possible'. Wilamowitz notes that for ἀπολαβεῖν . . . δοῦναί τε it would have been more usual and more logical to say ἀπολαβόντα δοῦναι.

461 ταῦτα δή: C is difficult to read, but (Cv.) ταῦτα δή is probable. Wilamowitz joined ταῦτα δή with ἥξω, comparing Plato, *Prot.* 310 e, αὐτὰ ταῦτα καὶ νῦν ἥκω παρά ce; but Jensen (in his note but not his text), Körte, and Guéraud prefer to make the words independent, 'very well, then', cf. Ar. *Ach.* 815, περίμεν' αὐτοῦ :: ταῦτα δή, *Wasps* 1008, ταῦτα νῦν, εἴπερ δοκεῖ, cf. ibid. 142, *Peace* 275. This is more likely.

Wilamowitz thought that we may infer from ἥξω that Syriskos did appear once more. This is doubtful; the phrase explains why he is ready to leave the ring with Onesimos, and the audience will feel no surprise if all is settled before he gets back.

462 διαδραμών: 'Having run my errand', cf. *Dysk.* 557.

(iv) 464–556: *Onesimos and Habrotonon*

464 ἡ γυνὴ . . . ἔνδον: Syriskos' wife, in Chairestratos' house.

465 ναί, φηcίν: This is not strictly true. A slight carelessness, to avoid pointless complication, may plausibly be ascribed to the poet. Yet it is possible that he did conceive that Syriskos had avoided strict accuracy, thinking his claim to the ring would be more readily accepted if he were thought to be its finder.

466 ὡς κομψόν, τάλαν: τάλαν is an interjection, see 434 n., 'dear me, what a lovely thing it is!' On this use of κομψός as a vague word of praise, see *Perik.* 298 n. Wilamowitz, translating 'fein, elegant, geistreich', comments that Habrotonon, with feminine instinct, recognizes the baby's good birth. No: the Greeks were not so class-conscious as that.

468 τρόφιμος ὄντως ἐστί: In view of frag. 1, where Charisios is Onesimos' τρόφιμος, there may be some temptation to take the word to denote Charisios here too. But he has been called δεσπότης in the previous line, and it is clear that the sense required is 'if this baby is really your master's son'. Although in some contexts τρόφιμος may be translated 'the young master', it is regularly rendered in Latin by 'erilis filius'. The feminine τροφίμη is applied to a four-year-old child, *Sik.* 8.   **ἐν δούλου μέρει:** 'In the condition of a slave', cf. Isok. ix. 24, ἐν ἰδιώτου μέρει διαγαγεῖν.

470 ὅπερ λέγω: Gomme thought Wilamowitz was off the track when he suggested the sense 'all I mean is', 'what I am saying is', and preferred 'as I was saying'. Wilamowitz's view that Onesimos envisages Charisios' being upset if he found the mother was a slave is improbable, since Habrotonon is later, with his approval, to pretend to be the mother. Rather Onesimos is repeating his point that Charisios' paternity, without which the child could not be his τρόφιμος, is not to be determined without the evidence of the mother.

472 παροινῶν γ': 'Yes, up to some mischief after he had been drinking.'

473 παιδάριον . . . ἀκόλουθος: The young slave who was attending him on this occasion.

474 μόνας: Herwerden's correction of μόνος is necessary. Habrotonon surmises (δηλαδή) what happened, and there could be no point in surmising that Charisios was alone when he intruded on the women. If he had had other lively friends with him, they would have been as likely to abet and encourage as to oppose his adventure. What is to the point is that he found the women when *they* were by themselves and unprotected.

477 παισὶν . . . κόραις: Cf. Ar. *Lys.* 595, παῖδα κόρην γεγάμηκεν.

478 αὕτη θ' ὁμοῦ συνέπαιζεν: I adopt without complete confidence Capps's correction of C, which has συνέπαιζον. It is based on the argument that, since Onesimos proceeds to inquire about the girl who had been ravished, Habrotonon must have mentioned her. Gomme supported this by observing that Habrotonon's presence was adequately explained in the previous line—she had been hired to play for the young ladies—and there was no reason why she should add that she was joining in their games. αὔτη, 'this girl', is possible, although no girl has been explicitly mentioned; she is implicit in ἐγένετο τοιοῦτο ἕτερον. Wilamowitz's αὐτὴ . . . cυνέπαιζεν is less likely. The reading of C can however be understood if Habrotonon states, with pardonable pride, that she played not *for*, but also *with* the free-born girls. Her next sentence explains that she could thus take part because she was still a virgin. This is conceivable: we do not know what were the relations between slave and free at the Tauropolia. As for Onesimos' question about the girl (480) it was obvious that she was a leading figure in the story Habrotonon had begun to tell, even if not yet mentioned.

The decision between the alternatives is not easy; but the dialogue becames tauter if Capps's emendation is adopted. Habrotonon says 'I was making music for the girls' (that answers Onesimos' question 'you there?'), 'and *she* was playing among them' (that is relevant to the tale, whereas 'I was playing with them' would be merely incidental). Then thinking that this girl was so soon to lose her virginity, she continues: 'I, too, did not at that time know what a man was.' This sentence is about herself, but related to the story of the unknown girl. It is not merely self-regarding, and if it contains any element of self-pity, it must also contain pity for the other. This interpretation accepts Körte's punctuation οὐδ' ἐγὼ τότε, οὔπω γάρ, ἄνδρ' ἤδειν τί ἐcτι. The majority of editors (with whom Gomme sided) write οὐδ' ἐγὼ τότε—οὔπω γὰρ ἄνδρα κτλ. But why this aposiopesis? And what is suppressed? 'I too was not then a hetaira' (Gomme), 'I too did not expect any violence' (Capps)? Neither carries conviction. Wilamowitz proposed cὺν δ' ἐγὼ τότε, restoring the idea that he had banished from the earlier part of the line because he had felt the need for a mention of the other girl.

479 καὶ μάλα: This must be given to Onesimos in spite of the absence of dicola and paragraphus in C. It is in ironic, mocking assent to Habrotonon's claim; and her answer means, 'really I did not'. There is no paragraphus under μὰ τήν either, though the change of speaker is marked by the dicolon after Ἀφροδίτην.

480: I leave the current supplement, but think τὴν δὲ ⟨δὴ⟩ παῖδ' a little more likely. δὲ δή is often found in 'emphatic and crucial questions', Denniston GP 259.

482 γυναιξί: The young ladies' mothers, who had engaged Habrotonon to accompany them (so Wilamowitz, following Capps).

484 ὦ θεοί: The exclamation is characteristic of Habrotonon, cf. 489, 548. It is used by no one else in the surviving remains of Menander, except in the paratragic recognition-scene of *Perik.* (807) and *ibid.* 827, where see n.

485 αὕτη 'cτι τυχόν: 'She *might* be the mother of this child.' Literally, 'she (i.e. the mother) may be this one you are talking of'. *Not* 'could it be she, namely Pamphile, Charisios' wife next door?', as some have supposed; neither Onesimos nor Habrotonon has any reason for such an identification. It is possible that αὐτή should be written: 'perhaps she is the same (as the mother)'.

486 μεθ' ἡμῶν is to be taken with οὖca not with ἐπλανήθη.

489 ταραντῖνον: Described by Photios as a light diaphanous cloak. The cloth was woven, or originally woven, at Tarentum from the silky 'byssus' of *Pinna nobilis*. A gland in the foot of this shellfish secretes filaments which coagulate on contact with water; they were used for the manufacture of small articles, e.g. gloves, in Taranto and S. Italy until the eighteenth century, *Enciclopedia italiana*, art. Bisso.

Aelian frag. 12 tells a story of a woman whose ταραντινίδιον stretched and broke when she tried to use it as a noose to hang herself.

'The childish admiration for the beautiful garment and the sympathy for its loss is indicative of Habrotonon's uncorrupted youth', wrote Wilamowitz, who had a weak spot for the girl. Lord Harberton (Unus Multorum), who felt that she 'oozed vulgarity at every pore', a judgement that may be held to do its author little credit, thought it indicative of her values that she gives so much attention to Pamphile's clothes, so little to her misfortune. Habrotonon is attractive because she is young, warm, and clever. But her only deep feelings are for herself. Dr. Austin calls my attention to Mazon's words: 'Esclave, elle aspire avant tout à la liberté; pour l'obtenir, elle usera de ruse et de mensonge, mais avec adresse et prudence et sans perfidie inutile. Elle est franche par nature: elle a du cœur; c'est sans ironie qu'elle plaint Charisios des dépenses qu'il fait pour elle et c'est sincèrement qu'elle se réjouit du dénouement heureux que son intervention provoque' (*Extraits de Ménandre*, p. 275). This is well put; but notice that it is not unnecessary expense which provides the right reason for pitying Charisios.

491 τοῦτον: Sc. τὸν δακτύλιον.

493 ὅρα cὺ τοῦτ': 'It's for you to decide'.

495–6 ἐcτ' ἐλευθέρας παιδός: The genitive depends on τὸ παιδίον understood. If the child is the son of a free girl, the father (who may well be Charisios) ought to know what has happened. Habrotonon will have it in mind that he might wish to repudiate Pamphile (from whom he seems to be estranged) and marry the other girl, obtaining what was always important to a Greek, a male heir.

Wilamowitz with unnecessary elaboration supposes that ἐλευθέρας παιδός depends on τὸ γεγονός but, as that would be odd Greek, that Habrotonon had intended something like ἐλευθέρας παιδὸς βιασμός but then for propriety's sake substituted the colourless τὸ γεγονός.

497 ff.: Onesimos sticks to his point that until the *mother* has been identified it would be dangerous to take a step that might suggest that Charisios is the father: the mother might turn out to have had no connection with him. But Habrotonon, on her side, will not stir up trouble by looking for the mother until she knows who the *father* is; only that would justify reopening the unsavoury affair, and possibly damaging the girl's reputation. Thus a nice dilemma arises, for which she finds an ingenious solution. Note how the emphatic position of the words points the dilemma: ἐκείνην ἥτις ἐστίν)(τὸν ἀδικοῦντα . . . τίς ἐστιν.

The last word of 498 is uncertain. If the two unclear letters are ρα, the possibilities are ὅρα (Robert) or φράσον (Leo). In either case it must be supposed that Habrotonon interrupts Onesimos before he has completed his request; she must assume that whatever she is being asked to look to or explain will involve telling the girl's friends, that being something she ought not to do. If on the other hand the letters are εν, as Guéraud thought equally possible, γενοῦ seems to be necessary. Sudhaus, who proposed this, thought that Onesimos would have continued cυνεργός. It is likely that the interrupted speaker of *Fab. incert.* 19, γενοῦ γάρ, ἱκετεύω c' ἐγώ—, did intend to continue in such a way. But he is interrupted, not by someone who divined his meaning, but by an irrelevant exclamation: it does not matter for the progress of the dialogue what he intended to say. Here it does matter, it is necessary that the audience should take Onesimos' meaning, and it may be doubted whether such a curtailed sentence would be adequate. Moreover there is no apparent reason why Habrotonon should interrupt him. Headlam supposed that cυνυγγενου was indeed written, but in error for νυνcυνγενου, i.e. νῦν cυγγενοῦ 'help me with this'. Although this sense of cυγγίγνομαι is not paralleled in comedy, the suggestion may be right; it is supported by Arnott, *CQ* N.s. xviii (1968), 230, and I have ventured to put it in the text.

499 οὐκ ἂν δυναίμην . . . πρίν: Notice how οὐκ ἂν δυναίμην, like the English 'I could not', means 'I would not think of . . .' The construction of πρίν with infinitive (instead of ἄν and subj.) after a negatived verb, repeated in 508, is unusual in Attic, although normal in Homer.

Contrast Soph. *Trach.* 630 f. δέδοικα γὰρ μὴ πρῴ λέγοις ἄν . . . πρὶν εἰδέναι τἀκεῖθεν and ibid. 2, οὐκ ἂν αἰῶν᾽ ἐκμάθοις βροτῶν πρὶν ἂν | θάνῃ τις.

503: Note the order of words. τῶν παρόντων is thrown in as an explanatory afterthought, and then, as another, ἕτερος, to drive home Habrotonon's point: 'Someone got the ring from him as a pledge, one of the people at the festival, and then lost it, someone else, not Charisios.'

504–6: Here are two reasons for which Charisios might have given his ring to someone else, pledging it not for its money value, but because its device was personal to the owner, using it as a promise to pay. Among the Greeks, the ring performed many of the functions of the signature in the modern world. Unfortunately an unfamiliar vocabulary is used in giving the reasons, and the following explanations are offered with some reserve. ὑπόθημα is a variant, known elsewhere only in inscriptions (*AJP* lvi [1935] 374, cent. iv. B.C., *SIG*² 976. 13–14, cent. ii. B.C.), for ὑποθήκη 'pledge'. εἰς cυμβολάς may mean 'as a contribution to the jackpot'. The word is known in the sense of subscriptions to a dinner or party, of which the expense was shared. In such a case, too, rings might be pledged, cf. Ter. *Eun.* 539 ff., 'heri aliquot adulescentuli coiimus in Piraeo, in hunc diem ut de symbolis essemus . . . dati anuli', etc. cυντιθέμενος 'making an agreement', perhaps not a bet, for which the *vox propria* would be περιδόμενος. We can only guess at the meaning of περιείχετο; LSJ give 'was hard pressed', Capps 'embarrassed', presumably in a financial sense. Perhaps rather 'was held to the bargain, caught by it without a way out', like the inhabitants of a beleaguered city or a military force surrounded by the enemy (Hdt. viii. 80. 2). In either case Charisios would have given the ring as surety that he would fulfil his obligations.

τυχόν: Lit. 'it so chancing', 'perhaps', not found in Plato's genuine works, but in Isokrates and Demosthenes, becomes frequent in New Comedy. The combination τυχὸν ἴcωc, common in Menander, appears to occur first in Timokles frag. 14 K. (The fragments of Epicharmus and Euripides adduced by LSJ are falsely ascribed to those poets.)

510 μέντοι: Wilamowitz, by a convention of his own, printed μέν τοι *separatim*, to mark that this is not adversative, but emphatic assent; Denniston, *GP* 401. The same use is certain in *Dysk.* 151, probable in *Sam.* 12 and 566, the only instances as yet of the word in Menander.

θέαc᾽: This substitute for ὅρα or cκόπει is unparalleled in New Comedy (but θέαcαι is to be found in Ar. *Ach.* 366, ἰδοὺ θέαcαι, *Peace* 906 θέαc᾽ ὡc προθύμως ὁ πρύτανις παρεδέξατο, *Thesm.* 280, ὦ Θρᾷττα, θέαcαι) and its exact force cannot be determined; perhaps 'look attentively'.

511 ποήcῃ τιc: Deliberative questions, in the subjunctive, are always in the first person, except when τιc is substituted for the first person (as *on* might be in French); cf. *Perik.* 928, *Dysk.* 517.

512 ἂν cυναρέcῃ . . . ἄρα: The postponement of ἄρα, ('as it may do', cf. *Dysk.* 665 n.) gives emphasis as in Ar. frag. 150 (from his *Gerytades*), ὡc cφόδρ' ἐπὶ λεπτῶν ἐλπίδων ᾤχειcθ' ἄρα, where ἄρα means 'as it turns out'. **ἐνθύμημα:** 'Idea', almost 'plan', a favourite sense with Xenophon, e.g. *Anab.* iii. 5. 12, but Thucydides so uses the verb, e.g., viii. 68, κράτιcτοc ἐνθυμηθῆναι.

514 τὸν δακτύλιον λαβοῦcά τε: τε in fourth place because 'to take the ring' is treated as one thought; the postponement is unusual, see *Perik.* 128 n.

515 λέγ' ὃ λέγειc: Cf. *Karch.* 14, ὅτι λέγειc λέγε. **ἄρτι γὰρ νοῶ:** Cf. Ar. *Lys.* 1008, ἄρτι νυνὶ μανθάνω, 'I am just beginning to understand', Plato *Polit.* 291 b, νῦν ἄρτι δοκῶ κατανενοηκέναι. What does Onesimos claim he is beginning to see? If he is not simply pretending to be quick in the uptake, he must see that Charisios, observing Habrotonon to be wearing his lost ring, will if guilty of a rape on the night of the Tauropolia suspect her to be his victim and may give himself away: he could not possibly divine any more of the plan she is about to unfold.

518 τά τ' ἐκείνη . . . ποουμένη: The anacoluthon (for ποήcομαι) is strange, but may be psychologically due to the presence of a participle in the preceding clause, cf. Lysias xiii. 40, πυθομένη δ' ἐκείνη ἀφικνεῖται μέλαν τε ἱμάτιον ἠμφιεcμένη, where, as Denniston says (*GP* 502), τε does not couple the participles. Headlam's emendation τἀκείνη may be right.

520 ἄριcτά γ' ἀνθρώπων: Wilamowitz saw a scurrilous meaning which Habrotonon was, in his view, too modest to notice. But this is a will-o'-the-wisp. Onesimos' words are meant as a compliment on her plan, 'first-rate!', cf. Plat. *Theaet.* 148 b, 163 c. ἀνθρώπων strengthens the superlative, as πάντων might, lit. 'of all men (you speak, best'. **οἰκεῖον:** 'To do with him'.

520–1: The sense of Habrotonon's sentence is complete, so that none of the additions proposed to restore the metre of 521 (e.g. εὐθὺς ⟨μέν⟩ Sudhaus, εὐθὺς ⟨μάλ'⟩ van Leeuwen, εὐθὺς ⟨τόδ'⟩ Ellis, πρᾶγμά ⟨γ'⟩ Lefebvre) seems anything but otiose. The one exception is Robertson's neat πρᾶγμα. ⟨(Ον.) εὖ γ'. (Ἀβ.)⟩ εὐθύc. But it is not clear why Onesimos should be moved to interrupt by the preceding words. Wilamowitz's proposal to read ἥξει φερόμενος εὐθέως introduces in εὐθέως a form found only once in Menander to date (*Sik.* 148). The most plausible solution is Arnott's transposition of δέ, which I adopt with due reserve. ἥξει φερόμενος: Cf. Lykurgos *in Leokr.* 59, ἥξει δ' ἴcωc ἐπ' ἐκεῖνον τὸν λόγον φερόμενος, and *Perik.* 278.

522 μεθύων: Not 'drunk', which is too strong, see *Perik.* 142 n.

524 τοῦ διαμαρτεῖν μηδὲ ἕν: 'In order to make no mistake by speaking first'; what she has in mind is mistakes of detail; she will confine herself to τὰ κοινὰ ταυτί, generalities that will fit all such occasions.

For the genitive of purpose, without χάριν or other preposition, see *Perik.* 156 n.

526 ἀκκιοῦμαι: LSJ translate 'I will dissemble and talk commonplaces', but the word connotes affectation. Habrotonon will affect a flattering pretence of being impressed by Charisios' brutal virility.

531 κλαῦcαι . . . καὶ φιλῆcαι: Wilamowitz remarks that these words need mean no more than 'lament and hug', but tears and kisses surely need not be excluded.

532 Ἡράκλεις: Onesimos is astonished at Habrotonon's resourcefulness.

534 ἔcτι: Gomme thought ἤδη preferable, as well as more probably C's reading; it would mean not 'at this moment', but 'at this stage of the story': 'You now find yourself with a child.' Wilamowitz, however, maintained that the participle without a copula is intolerable, and Headlam too thought that ἤδη γέγονεν would be necessary. Although Lefebvre inclined to read]η, in which he was supported by Guéraud, he thought]τι 'far from impossible'.

535 πανούργως καὶ κακοήθως: Literally πανοῦργος means 'ready to do anything', hence 'villainous, unprincipled'. But like English 'up to anything' it may become a compliment, e.g. Dem. i. 3, Plato, *Rep.* 409 c, *Theaet.* 177 a, and is so meant by Onesimos, who is impressed by Habrotonon's artfulness. κακοήθης usually means 'malicious' or 'malignant' (in Ar. *Rhet.* 1389ᵇ20 'putting a bad construction on things'), but that does not suit here, where the sense required is 'sly', 'playing a double game', cf. frag. 588, οὐδέποθ' ἑταίρα τοῦ καλῶς πεφρόντικεν, ᾗ τὸ κακόηθες πρόσοδον εἴωθεν ποεῖν, Theophilos frag. 1. 17 K, Dem. xviii. 11, xxxvii. 15. The same sense belongs to the verb κακοηθεύειν at 551.

540 λύσετ': 'He will redeem you', i.e. buy you from the πορνοβοσκός (cf. Ar. *Wasps* 1353), with the intention of manumitting you. A man of some sentiment might not wish his child to be brought up to be a slave.

541 οὐ γὰρ οἶσθα cύ; Onesimos' question is sarcastic, cf. Xen. *Oec.* 19. 2, οὐκ ἐπίσταμαι :: οὐ γὰρ cὺ . . . ἐπίστασαι;

542 ἀλλ' [ἦ]: I am doubtful whether to prefer this to *ed. pr.*'s ἀλλ' [οὐ]. Jensen affirms that there is room for only one missing letter, but even if he is right, a vertical stroke is reported above the space—an obliterating smudge makes it impossible to see anything on the photograph; hence there may have been a letter added. ἀλλ' ἦ is normally used in surprised or incredulous questions that answer some statement (Denniston, *GP* 27), and that is not true here. If right, the phrase must here mean, not 'Why, do I get any thanks?', but 'Well, do I get etc.'.

543 πάντων: There seems to be no sufficient reason for accepting Vollgraf's emendation πάντωc, as many editors do.

544 τούτων: The intrusive c' that C has after this word was due to the taking of ἐμαυτης in the previous line for the genitive (hence it has no apostrophe in C) instead of ἐμαυτῇ cε.

545 ἐξεπίτηδεc: According to Wilamowitz this strengthened form gained ground against ἐπίτηδεc (*Dysk.* 501) from the end of the fifth century.

545 ἐᾷc: 'Let it drop'.   **παρακρουcαμένη:** The verb is common in the orators in the sense 'mislead', 'cheat'. Literally it means 'knock aside': the origin of the metaphor is from wrestling, *Et. Magn.* 652. 48.

547: Wilamowitz, Körte, and others, unlike Capps, Jensen, and others, have no stop after ἕνεκεν, to the detriment of the sense. 'Goodness me, why should I do that? Do you think I long for children?' If she gets her freedom by her trick, Habrotonon is bound to look for the child's mother, since she has no wish to be saddled with a baby that is not even hers.

550 διαφόρωc: 'Exceptionally', 'extremely', cf. *Perik.* 262.

551 κακοηθεύcῃ: 'Play a double game', cf. 535 n. The verb is not quoted from any other author, except Galen (of malignancy in the medical sense), and a scholiast, but Plutarch, *Pompey* 37, has κακοήθευμα, which implies the verb's currency in Hellenistic times.

552 δυνήcομαι γάρ: He will be able to make trouble by denouncing her trick over the baby.

553 εἰ τοῦτ' ἔcτιν: 'If this is really so', i.e. if the baby is Charisios' child.

553 ἀποδίδου: Not 'give back', but 'give as you should', what you are bound to, because you have agreed to the plan.

555–6 φίλη Πειθοῖ κτλ.: The elevated style, sharply contrasted with the opening words of the next speech, is most effective in winning sympathy for Habrotonon; reinforcing 541 and 548–9, it stresses the importance of the issue for her. In fifth-century Attic literature Πειθώ is predominantly the goddess of rhetorical persuasion, whereas in lyric she is associated with love. But on many Attic vases of that century, and also of the fourth, she appears as the companion of Aphrodite and Eros. Her two aspects, separated in modern treatments like that of Pauly–Wissowa's *Realencyclopädie*, did not constitute two distinct divinities, and we can see them united in Habrotonon's mind. When she addresses the goddess as a familiar, φίλη Πειθοῖ, it is as a goddess of love that she knows her, but she now wants her help in the field of persuasion. Wilamowitz, it is true, denies that, whatever may have happened in Lesbos, Πειθώ was a goddess by whom an Athenian hetaira would swear (presumably *qua* hetaira); but we should not forget that she was worshipped at the foot of the Acropolis in association with Aphrodite Pandemos, a foundation said to be based on a revenue from brothels (Pausanias i. 22. 3.; *Kolax* frag. 1 n.).

(v) 557–582: *Onesimos alone*

557 τοπαστικόν: Found only here, but a familiar type of adjective in nonce-formations, satirized by Aristophanes, *Knights* 1378–81, and *Clouds* 1172, ἐξαρνητικός. τοπάζω means 'make a guess', but here something rather different must be intended, perhaps 'hit on a solution'.   **ἤϲθηθ'**: From the mid-fourth century there was a tendency for the perfect to replace the aorist as a past tense; the perfect envisages the present result of the past action, whereas the aorist expresses only the action itself. It has been held that the perfect of a transitive verb may express the resultant present state of the object; this is, however, denied (rightly I think) in a recent survey by K. L. McKay, 'The Use of the Ancient Greek Perfect down to the second century A.D.' (*Bull. Inst. Class. Stud.* xii. 1); he thinks it always refers to a continuing or subsequent state of the subject. The choice of tense depends upon which aspect is in the speaker's mind. The use of the perfect here is correct, 'now that she (has observed and) is aware that . . .'; the main clause contains a true present, πορεύεται. Contrast 329, where ὡϲ ἤϲθετ' stands in plain narrative, and the main clause has a *historic* present. There are in fact few passages in Menander, if any, where the present aspect is absent from the perfect: speaking in general of the fourth-century Greek Chantraine writes: 'Aucun exemple n'est décisif parce que chaque texte peut être interprété différemment par des lecteurs différents. Il n'est jamais possible d'affirmer que le parfait soit l'équivalent d'un aoriste, mais la nuance qui sépare ces deux temps devient de moins en moins sensible' (*Le parfait grec*, 189). At 419, τὸν δακτύλιον ὥρμηκα πλεῖν ἢ πεντάκιϲ τῷ δεϲπότῃ δεῖξαι, the aspect of result is hard to see, but one might say that the speaker claims present credit for his attempts, as in English 'I have tried' differs from 'I tried'. This is a variety of the common use of the perfect to mark continuing responsibility for a past act, e.g. ἠδίκηκα. Another difficult expression is the recurring phrase ἐψόφηκε τὴν θύραν (875), *Sam.* 669, *Dysk.* 204, frag. 766); the reason for the use of the perfect ἐψόφηκε must be that the speaker is not interested so much in the past noise as in its present sequel; the man who made the noise is coming on the stage.

(The later grammarians denounced the misuse of the perfect and Wilamowitz thought that the mistake ηϲθεθ' in the papyrus was due to a conscious or unconscious correction of a 'wrong' perfect to the 'correct' aorist. This is very unlikely; a simple *lapsus calami* is sufficient, or a misreading of the original—it may be noted that Lefebvre originally misread the first η as ε.)

559 ἀλύει: See frag. 3 n., again there may be doubt of the meaning— either 'is distressing herself in vain' (= ἀδημονεῖ, Wilamowitz), or 'is wasting her pains' (LSJ).

561 λέμφος, ἀπόπληκτος: 'Drivelling, and paralysed'. λέμφος is properly μύξα, 'snot', but by transference used of a man, cf. Hesychios, λέμφος· ἄνθρωπος μυξώδης καὶ μάταιος. Latin has a similar but reverse usage in *emunctae naris*, 'keen-sighted'. For ἀπόπληκτος cf. *Perik.* 496 n.

564 καὶ διαλογίζομαι: I.e. even my calculations are pointless, like my actions.

566 νῦν ἐπιϲφαλῆ: Note the asyndeta, 563, 565 and here, probably marking pauses in utterance.

There is an instructive treatment of 564–6 in Stobaios. The sentence is adapted to form three complete trimeters by omitting ὡϲ κενά, and by adding after προϲλάβοιμι the phrase καὶ κάλλιϲτ' ἔχει. Then a fourth line is added from some other source, οὐκ ἐν γυναικὶ φύεται πιϲτὴ χάριϲ. Here is one more warning against relying on the accuracy of anthologies.

568 ταχέως κτλ.: A difficult sentence. (1) Since it is hardly possible to attach ταχέως to the preceding sentence ('and that right soon' Capps, Allinson) it must by its position before ἐάν be emphatic; 'if she is *quickly* found to be of free birth and mother of this child, he will marry her and repudiate his present wife'. Perhaps this could be explained as meaning that if such a discovery were postponed, Charisios might in the meantime have became reconciled to Pamphile, who would thus be in less danger of repudiation. No editor seems to have envisaged this possibility. Wilamowitz mentions as conceivable two other interpretations: (*a*) ταχέως ἐάν = ἐπειδὴ τάχιϲτα; (*b*) ταχέως = 'perhaps', a meaning thought by some to occur in one or two passages in Polybios, but denied by Schweighäuser (see his index). He confesses, however, that even were either meaning admissible, the position of ταχέως would remain a difficulty. I suspect that ταχέως is an error for τελέως, which would belong to the preceding sentence, strengthening ἐπισφαλῆ, PCPS 1967, 46. This change was hesitantly suggested by Capps. For this position of associated words, cf. 130 n. (2) Wilamowitz supposed the subject of εὑρεθῇ to be unexpressed, and κόρη to be the predicate, 'if she (i.e. the woman Charisios ravished) is found to be the daughter of a free citizen and mother of this child'. Gomme thought the suppression of the subject likely to prove obscure, although a good actor might convey the meaning. He argued that κόρη is the subject, and defended the omission of the definite article by κεκτημένη, 'the mistress', e.g. Perik. 262, βασιλεύς 'the King of Persia'. One could add δεσπότης, 'the master', Perik. 359. But these are not parallels, and it is perhaps better to translate 'if a girl is found who is of free birth and mother of this child'. In that case Onesimos will overlook a third necessary condition, namely that she was ravished by Charisios.

570–1 ταύτην . . . ἀπολείπειν: Since Guéraud reports that no letters between these two words can be discerned except ν at the end of the lacuna, with no balance in favour of the earlier attempts to read επειξ[εται or επειξ[ομαι] την ναυν, it is idle to print a restored verse. Gomme withdrew his own proposal ἐπείξεται τὴν ναῦν ἀπολείπειν, recorded by Körte: it had been based on the report that the traces favoured τὴν ναῦν. His final view was that certain things may be said: (1) ταύτην must refer to Pamphile (whether or not further defined by [τὴν ἔνδο]ν in the next line), for we need something about her; and since the next letter is probably α or δ, ἀφείς or δ' ἀφείς is plausible; (2) Jensen's δ' ἐγώ is not possible—no one could write 'he will take the latter, and I will desert the former and leave the sinking ship'; (3) ἐπείξομαι τὴν ναῦν ἀπολείπειν (Jensen) is also inadmissible, for we should not, by a conjecture, introduce into a man's character something quite new that is nowhere justified in the rest of the play, and that does not fit well with the succeeding lines. (4) Sudhaus's conjecture, ταύτην δ' ἀφεὶς ἐπείξεται τὴν ἔνδον ἀπολείπειν (in itself the best, because the simplest, that has been made) is not to be rejected as *contra usum Atticum* because Bekker, Anecd. 421 has ἀπέλιπε μὲν ἡ γυνὴ τὸν ἄνδρα λέγεται ἀπέπεμψε δὲ ὁ ἀνὴρ τὴν γυναῖκα· οὕτω Μένανδρος (frag. 823), cf. Lucian, Soloecista 9. Normally the family house was owned by the husband; in consequence, in a separation, if the initiative was the wife's, she would leave him (going back to her father or other relative); if it was the husband's, he would send her away (again to her father); but this would not prevent Menander or any other writer from using ἀπολείπειν, not in itself a technical word, of a man's leaving his wife, if he has in fact done so, as, for the time, Charisios has done in this play; just as in English we can use 'desert' in a non-technical sense, even though the word has a legal meaning as well; cf. Lucian, *Bis Accusatus* 29, τὴν μὲν νόμῳ γαμετὴν . . . οὕτως ἀτίμως ἀπέλιπε, Plut. *Mor.* 1034 a. Elsewhere doubtless Menander wanted to make use of the two words each in its more technical usage; he may have done so in this play, e.g. at 625 and 930; or in the later scene in this act between Smikrines and Pamphile; we can even guess, if we like, at some such dialogue as: 'You must leave him, Pamphile.' 'Alas, that is what he has done to me.' 'Nonsense, a man doesn't leave his wife; he can only send his wife away, and that when he has good reason to; and this husband of yours has no reason.' (Gomme, *CQ* xxx [1936], 64–5.)

Post's conjecture, ταύτην (sc. Habrotonon) ἀφείς, ἐπεύξεθ' ἡ γὰρ ἔνδον ἀπολείπειν (*AJP* lxii [1941], 461), which is an attempt to get over this imaginary difficulty, is anyhow misguided. (He wrote ἐπεύξεθ' because the fourth letter was thought to be υ rather than ι; obviously, for a conjecture in this sense, ἐπείξεθ' is alone possible).

572–3 καὶ νῦν χαριέντως ἐκνενευκέναι: If καί, as seems likely, goes with νῦν, the meaning is 'now too I have neatly escaped danger by reason of the fact that the present complication of affairs is not being effected by me' (but by Habrotonon). This suggests that the previous sentence had some such sense as 'I shall do well not to concern myself with Pamphile's difficulties', e.g. ἐμοὶ δ' ἐκεῖν' ἄμεινον ἀπολείπειν ὅλως. Wilamowitz takes ἐκνενευκέναι to be from ἐκνεῖν and quotes Eur. *Hipp.* 470, εἰς δὲ τὴν τύχην πεσοῦσ' ὅσην σύ, πῶς ἂν ἐκνεῦσαι δοκεῖς; Capps and van Leeuwen supposed it to be from ἐκνεύειν, 'dodge aside', a word used in later prose to mean 'avoid' (see LSJ). This latter seems more likely, since Onesimos has just dodged possible danger; he has not, like Phaidra, been immersed in a sea of troubles from which he has swum to safety. Further, Onesimos uses the language of the κοινή rather than that of poetical metaphor.

575–644: This leaf has been reconstituted from five fragments (MNT) (VX). NT fit together to make the complete lines 575–7; hence 575–82 and 609–15 are established. M fits N at the beginning of 582, showing the tail of ρ, of which N has the head. This establishes the position of the beginnings of 583–99 and the ends of 616–33, contained in M. The ends of 583–99 and the beginnings of 616–33 are on VX, two fragments whose edges fit together: they have, however, no physical connection with M. Lefebvre first thought from their appearance, namely their colour and wear, that they belonged to the same sheet as MNT, but later changed his mind (for an insufficient reason, inability to understand how τέτοκε (639) could be said by anyone at this point of the play). Robert, however, in *SB Akad. Berlin* 1912, 402, argued that the top of VX corresponded to the foot of T much as the west coast of Europe and Africa correspond to the east coast of America; and that if VX were placed one verse earlier than Lefebvre had thought of putting them, it was possible to fill many of the gaps between them and M with convincing supplements. Robert's placing of VX has been generally accepted by subsequent editors, although 'after much hesitation' by Allinson, who thinks it merely more probable than any other solution. It must be confessed that Robert's geographical simile exaggerates the likeness of VX to T and that his supplements have met with little favour. Nevertheless Lefebvre's original feeling that these fragments all belong to the same page is strongly supported by the marginal name of the speaker at 622 in VX, which as Gueraud maintained is indubitably καρ, i.e. Karion. It is hardly credible that the cook, on stage at 610–13, should appear again after 759 or 1023, the only other places where room could be found for VX. If we must accept, then, that VX belong to the same page as M, their relative position is still not fixed. C has on the average 35 lines to a page, never fewer than 33 (I³ = *Sam.* 280–312) nor more than 38 (J³, ⁴ = *Perik.* 331–68, 369–406). If Robert's placing is adopted, one side of the page would have 34 lines, the other 36. Alternative placings with 33 and 35, or 36 and 38, lines would give pages of unusual (but paralleled) length. To drop VX by one line would give 35 and 37 lines, by no means unlikely figures. But so to do brings no visible advantage, and I place the fragments in the position assigned by Robert, with the warning that it cannot be regarded as more than probable.

575 περιεργασάμενον: Note the tenses; literally 'if anyone finds me to have been meddling or talking', not 'if anyone catches me meddling'. Hence μέ τι (Wilamowitz) is better than μ' ἔτι (Lefebvre).

576 τοὺς ὀδόντας.—οὑτοcί: Here is a notorious puzzle. C has ἀλλ' ουτοcι, but not, as most editors have believed, γαυc for τουc. The new photograph (*Preface* p. ix) shows Lefebvre to have been right in transcribing τουc. The metre may be mended by deleting ἀλλ' with von Arnim; for examples of ἀλλά added to avoid asyndeton see Jackson, *Marginalia Scenica*, 103 and probably *Sam.* 48. (Körte reads ὁδί for οὑτοcί, in order to preserve ἀλλά, an improbable change, of which its author, Wilamowitz, later repented, *Schiedsgericht*, 87.) But the deletion satisfies the demands of metre better than those of sense. Teeth are knocked or pulled out, not cut out. Groeneboom (*Mnem.*

xliv [1916], 315) tried to defend ἐκτέμνειν ὀδόντας by referring to the poem Εἰς νεκρὸν Ἄδωνιν (Gow, *Bucolici graeci*, 166), where the boar says (33) τούτους (sc. τοὺς ὀδόντας) λαβοῦσα τέμνε. But to cut *off* a boar's tusks is a natural idea, to cut *out* a man's teeth not so. Again one would expect Onesimos to sacrifice either his tongue (in punishment for talkativeness) or some vital organ. Hence it was suggested by Capps and Robert that τοὺς ὀδόντας stands παρὰ προσδοκίαν for τοὺς ὄρχεις. This is perhaps not impossible; it is no objection that the substitution gives the strange idea of 'excising teeth'—that might be part of the joke. τοὺς ὄρχεις cannot be *expected* in this line at the point where τοὺς ὀδόντας might be substituted; metre forbids. But metre did not bar Aristophanes from such jokes. If ἀλλ' οὑτοcί is retained, οδοντας must be corrupt; it has been explained as an intrusive explanation of μύλους, 'molars', or a mistake for διδύμους (Knox, *C.R.* xxvii [1913], 121) or γόνας (Arnott, *Rh. Mus.* cviii [1965], 269). As a curiosity it may be mentioned that Coppola, De Falco, and Del Corno bravely defend the unmetrical verse as giving an indication that Onesimos stutters over the sentence.

578–9 πάλιν . . . αὖτις: Just our 'back again' and not simply pleo-nastic. Cf. *Od.* xiv. 356. The form αὖτις for αὖθις (1110) recurs *Sam.* 626, perhaps 637, *Dysk.* 962 n.

For the plural, τὰς ἀληθείας (possibly 'the details' of the true story), cf. *Theophor.* 25, *Sam.* 525, *Aspis* 372 (where the plural seems to be purely *metri gratia*), frags. 81 and 775. The plural is found already in Isokrates xv. 283, καὶ ταῦτα ταῖς ἀληθείαις οὕτως ἔχει. On the question what Smikrines had learned, see the note on the beginning of Act II.

581–2 ποιεῖν κτλ.: It is best not to restore. The new photograph eliminates the proposals δοκεῖν or ἔχειν for the end of 581, but con-firms the possibility of Gueraud's λαλεῖν, so 'I do not want to speak to him' may be the sense; and as Onesimos is not present, apparently, in the following scene, 582 may have said, 'I must therefore make myself scarce'. Wilamowitz's restoration of 581, ποιεῖν ἐμαυτὸν οὐδὲ πράγματ' ἀλλ' ἔχειν or οὐδ' ἰδεῖν αὐτὸν δοκεῖν, like De Falco's οὐδὲ πρὸς τοῦτον λαλεῖν, is anyhow suspect because of the use of οὐδέ = 'and not' after a positive clause, a use common in epic, lyric, and tragedy, but absent from Aristophanes (who, however, occasionally so uses μηδέ), as from Attic prose (Denniston, *GP* 190); Gomme could find only one instance in Menander, and that in a quotation by Clement, frag. 276. 7 K–T, 'a moralizing passage in fine style'; no great reliance can be placed on textual details of quotations.

(vi) 583–602: *Smikrines alone*

583–602: These lines, with the conceivable exception of 601, are a monologue by Smikrines, which may extend further, to 608. So little is left of them that only tentative guesses about their content are possible. Smikrines has perhaps returned because he has learned something that makes his son-in-law's conduct appear even worse than he had thought. He may have in mind to take his daughter away, but it is also possible that this step occurs to him later, when he learns that Charisios has got a child by Habrotonon. What had he heard? The word ἄcωτ[οc (or ἀcωτ[ία) in 584 was one applied to spendthrift profligacy, Arist. *EN* 1119ᵇ31, τοὺς γὰρ ἀκρατεῖς καὶ εἰς ἀκολαcίαν δαπανηροὺς ἀcώτους καλοῦμεν, διὸ καὶ φαυλότατοι δοκοῦcιν εἶναι. Smikrines will have heard a story, perhaps exaggerated, of Charisios' doings—maybe that he is living with Habrotonon. It must have put the young man in a worse light than had the information with which he came primed in Act I.

583 ff.: Robert's insertion in 584–5 of frag. 882 Kock is attractive. For the phrase, cf. Plato, *Lysis* 205 c, ἃ δὲ ἡ πόλιc ὅλη ᾄδει περὶ Δημοκράτους.

Jensen's restoration of 583–92 (using some suggestions by others) is sufficiently ingenious to be quoted: ἐξηπ[άτηκεν οὗτος ἡμᾶc ὁ μιαρόc·] | ἄcωτ[όc ἐcτι καὶ δαπανηρόc· ἡ πόλιc] | ὅλη γὰ[ρ ᾄδει τὸ κακόν· ὀργιcθεὶc δ᾽ ἐγώ] | εὐθὺc [ἐπανῆλθον ταῦτα πάντα δηλαδὴ] | cαφῶc [πυθέcθαι βουλόμενοc· λέγουcι γὰρ] | πίνειν [ἀπόκοιτον ὄντα καὶ τῶν cυγγε]νῶν | τοὔνομ[α καταιcχύνοντα μετὰ τῆc] ψαλτρίαc | ζῆν αὐτό[ν· ἀλλ᾽ ὁ χρηcτὸc οἰκέτ]ηc ἔφη | πλέον ἡμ[ερῶν τριῶν ἐν οἰκίᾳ μένειν] | αὐτὸν διαλλ[αγέντα.

Down to ζῆν αὐτόν this gives a fairly acceptable sense, although δηλαδή is wrongly used (it always supports a surmise, as at 473) and τῶν cυγγενῶν is unlikely. Yet the restoration is hardly right. Smikrines had said something very like this at his first appearance. He would not repeat himself, especially as he would seem to have learned something fresh on his visit to the town. Jensen's 590–2 introduce an idea for which there is no other evidence.

593 οἴμοι: This is probably not the beginning of someone else's speech, since there is no paragraphus. How long Smikrines' monologue went on we cannot tell; but χαιρέτω (602) would be a suitable close, and a new speaker (Karion) has arrived at or before 609 (see below).

594 κοινωνο[: Cf. 920 below. (Perhaps Pamphile is the subject here—Smikrines may be protesting: 'She came here to share his life; *I* brought her, and see what has happened').

598–9: Jensen conjectured φιλάργυρος with the idea that Charisios had been approved as a son-in-law because Smikrines had thought him fond of money. Gomme preferred Webster's φιλόςοφος (*StM* 38 n. 2), although thinking that his completion of the lines, φιλόςοφος ὥςπερ ὤν τις, ἀλλὰ τῷ τρόπῳ ἐναντίως ἔχων δίαιταν τὴν ἁπλοῦν ἀφῆκε, was unconvincing.

601 κύβοι τυχόν: Robert's restoration of the line, γέλως, βοή, πότοι ςυνεχεῖς, κύβοι τυχόν, which incorporates frag. 659, πότοι ςυνεχεῖς, κύβοι (quoted without naming the play), is ingenious, perhaps right, but obviously very uncertain.

602]λα χαιρέτω: Either ἀλλά or πολλά. Jensen supported the latter from frag. adesp. 554 Kock, οὐκ ἔςτ᾽ ἐμὸν τὸ πρᾶγμα· πολλὰ χαιρέτω: Gomme felt that Körte's further suggestion that the line comes from this passage was wide of the mark, even with a necessary change of οὐκ ἔςτι to ἀλλ᾽ οὐκ. Charisios must be the subject of χαιρέτω if Smikrines is still the speaker, and not even for a moment would Smikrines say that the affair, Charisios' way of life, was no concern of his.

(vii) **603–631:** *Smikrines and Karion*

603–36: From 609 to 631 both Smikrines and the cook Karion are on stage. There is nothing to determine whether they converse at any point, or whether Smikrines merely comments on what Karion says. Nor is it clear whether Karion enters at 603 (Wilamowitz) or at 609 (Körte, who thinks he speaks into the house as he comes out; it is, however, hard to see how this half-line could be enough to make Smikrines describe the lunch as ποικίλον). Finally the speaker of 631 νὴ τὸν Ἥλιον to 636 may be Karion, in spite of his eagerness to depart; if it is not he, then Chairestratos is perhaps the most likely person, since by a marginal *XAIP* C records him as speaking at 690. (Guéraud, it is true, preferred to read *ABP*, but Habrotonon has no place here, see 690 n.)

Many editors have supposed the person who may enter at 631, and is certainly addressed at 645, to be Simias, mentioned in 630. They imagine him to be another friend of Charisios, contrasted as a man of high moral tone with an easy-going Chairestratos, in whose house the young husband carouses with a *hetaira*. Wilamowitz restored 630 as ὦ Ἡρ[άκλεις, Χαιρέςτρατος καὶ] Ϲιμίας, and thought that Karion beat a retreat at the approach of these two characters. Webster pointed out, however, in *StM* 36, that the name Simias suggests a slave. The only other persons of this name in comedy are slaves, (Plautus, *Pseudolus*, Act IV and Dionysios frag. 2 K; if ςημιαν in Menander frag. 451. 5 is a corruption for Ϲιμία, the person there didactically addressed by the cook may well be a slave). Webster originally guessed Simias to be an elderly slave of Chairestratos's and gave him a speaking part at 664, restoring μὴ δές[ποτ'. Later, however, he inclined to suppose him to be an assistant of Karion's and a κωφὸν πρόϲωπον, *CR* n.s. xv (1965), 17. This seems to me the most likely solution, and 630 might then run e.g. ὦ Ἡρά[κλεις, οἷον τὸ κακόν· ποῦ] Ϲιμίαϲ; ἀπίωμεν. It is to be noticed that if Simias enters with Chairestratos at 630 or thereabouts he cannot have a speaking part unless four actors are employed, an assumption not to be lightly made (introd. pp. 16–19). The parts that have been assigned by some editors to Simias at other places in the play, as indeed his very presence there, are entirely speculative (see notes on 142 ff. and Act V init.).

C spells Ϲιμμιαϲ, the Boeotian form of the name, made familiar by Plato's *Phaedo*, which has led to the mis-spelling here. Attic inscriptions show ϲιμιαϲ, and the corruptions in Dionysios frag. 2 K (καὶ χάριϲ αἰεὶ μία for κεχάριϲαι, Ϲιμία and ϲημεια for ϲιμία) also point to the form with one μ.

607 εἶναι ϲ[: Guéraud denies that any letters can be deciphered after ϲ but agrees that Jensen's ϲτάϲιν is possible.

609 οὐδείϲ, κτλ.: Sudhaus's δύναιτ' ἄν in the gap is, according to Guéraud, impossible; and no other worthwhile suggestion has been made.

609 ff.: C names the speaker of 615b, 621 as Smikrines, that of 622 as Karion. It is practically certain that they are the speakers of 609–14, where there are dicola and paragraphi. ὦ τρικάθλιοϲ κτλ. seems to suit Karion; he must therefore end his previous speech with ἕτεροϲ ὑμῖν. Smikrines' interjection, 'they are having variety in their lunch!', will refer as Wilamowitz saw, not to the food but to incidents to which the cook has referred. What these were we can to some extent guess: they will have been the result of Habrotonon's declared intention to flaunt Charisios' ring. She *may* be meant by μόνη in 606. Smikrines' interjection can hardly have been based on the words οὐδείϲ . . . ὑμῖν alone, however the gap is to be filled. Körte's suggestion that Karion comes on the stage at 609, speaking back into the house, is therefore improbable. Jensen supposed that two or three lines were missing between 608 and 609. These might have been enough to contain the beginning of Karion's speech. Körte, however, rightly rejects this supposition. VX 'recto', giving the ends of 586–608, show part of the lower margin of the page, TN 'verso' (609 ff.) show the upper margin of the next. At the most, as Lefebvre argued, one line is missing from the foot of VX. This is probably not enough for Karion's speech, which Wilamowitz may be right in starting with 603: the word ἐγώ suits this theory, for it can naturally occur at or near the beginning of a soliloquy, cf. 908 below, *Samia* 616, perhaps *Dysk*. 489. In 612 διασκεδάννυντ' ἐκτός is a reading made almost certain by the new photograph and it yields a reasonable sense. Karion, one may imagine, came out at 603, expressing indignation at the interruption the lunch had suffered; then at 609, e.g. 'no other cook would have put up with such treatment from you, (i.e. from the guests). For some reason the party is breaking up, but if any of you wants a cook again, you can go hang for all I care.'

614 βαλεῖτ' ἐc μακαρίαν: ἐc μακαρίαν is a substitute for ἐc κόρακαc or εἰc ὄλεθρον in imprecations. In Ar. *Knights* 1151 the Paphlagonian says ἄπαγ' ἐc μακαρίαν ἐκποδών, which suggests that the substitution was a well-used one, and not in itself funny any longer. The scholiast says there that ἐc μακαρίαν means εἰc ὄλεθρον because the dead are called οἱ μακαρῖται. βάλλ' ἐc μακαρίαν is found in Plato, *Hippias Major* 293 a, cf. Antiphanes frag. 245 K, ἐc μακαρίαν τὸ λουτρόν.

C had εἰc, but Attic retained the old form ἐc in ἐc μακαρίαν and ἐc κόρακαc; e.g. Helladios in Photios *Bibl.* 535, 2. οἱ Ἀττικοὶ κατά τι πάτριον ἔθος οὐ χρῶνται τῷ εῖ διφθόγγῳ ἐν τῷ λέγειν "ἐc κόρακαc" ἢ "ἐc μακαρίαν". The Bodmer papyrus writes ηc at *Dysk*. 112, εις ibid. 432, and these forms are often used in the MSS. of Aristophanes; but C has εcκορακαc at *Heros* 70, B at *Sam*. 353, 370.

615: cμι in the right-hand margin suggests that Smikrines began speaking in the middle of this line; if so Karion's speech continued into its beginning, possibly with some such words as τίνα δ' αὖ βλέπω; (cf. 932). There is no dicolon at the end of 614. τινοc is not inevitably to be read at the end of the line: ἐcτὶν ὅc is also possible.

615–21: At 645 Smikrines shows that he has learned that Charisios had had a child by Habrotonon. This he has presumably heard, or overheard, from Karion, and these lines seem the likely place for it; 621 might be a surprised or indignant exclamation, e.g. Χαριcίῳ παῖc γέγονεν ἐκ τῆc ψαλτρίαc; Sudahus and Körte's restoration Χαρίcιοc ἔνδον ἐcτὶ μετὰ τῆc ψαλτρίαc gives a statement of little significance; and as Thierfelder points out (K–T ii. p. 280), it has a broken anapaest in the second foot, an anomaly too rare to be permissible in a restoration (see 348 n.). Jensen's Χαρίcιοc προῆλθε is very improbable—it was based on reading ΧΑΡ in the margin before the next line. The true reading is ΚΑΡ, confirmed by Guéraud.

629: The sense may be 'Habrotonon seems to be the mistress of his household'. Either Karion or Smikrines could say this. The line ends in C with a colon, not a dicolon. ὦ Ἡράκλειc may be more likely in

Karion's mouth than in that of Smikrines, although the belief held by some that this was an oath confined to the lower orders is incorrect (*Sam.* 435, 552).

(viii) 631–699: *Smikrines and Chairestratos* (?)

632 ff.: These lines, which in view of what has been said in the note on 603–36 should perhaps be given to Chairestratos, are difficult to restore. 633–4 would seem to mean 'only the other day he was austere and virtuous': Sudhaus not improbably suggested πρώην ἄρ᾽ εἶχε τοῦ μετώπου τὰς ὀφρῦς ἄνω, after Alexis frag. 16 K, τὰς δ᾽ ὀφρῦς ἔχοντες ἐπάνω τῆς κορυφῆς. For ὀφρῦς so used of the 'high-brow' or the philosopher, cf. frag. 34, εὑρετικὸν εἶναί φασι τὴν ἐρημίαν οἱ τὰς ὀφρῦς αἴροντες, frag. 395, οἱ τὰς ὀφρῦς αἴροντες . . . καὶ "σκέψομαι" λέγοντες, *Sik.* 160. But the eyebrows are also lifted in pain or anxiety, e.g. frag. 634, ἐὰν ἀνασπάςας τις τὰς ὀφρῦς "οἴμοι" λαλῇ, *Dysk.* 423, Ar. *Ach.* 1069. In 632 ταύτην may indicate Habrotonon. But what was said of her? 'I was almost bowled over by her story'?

It is not clear whether after the appearance of the new character Smikrines does not speak until 637; no paragraphi are now visible, but the papyrus is very worn. Nor is it clear whether at 637 he speaks to himself or addresses the other character. It is a likely guess that he expresses an intention to remove his daughter now that her husband has got a child by the *hetaira* he is keeping.

637: U. E. Paoli, *Aegyptus* xxxiii (1953), 284, argues that a father's right to withdraw his daughter from her marriage would be ended as soon as she had became the mother of a son, and suggests that we could restore [παιδίον γὰρ οὐδέπω] τέτοκεν. This would certainly provide a pleasant piece of irony.

641 παρακαλ[ες: παρακαλεῖν is a technical word for calling witnesses, although that is not its only use. Smikrines may here threaten to bring a complaint before the archon, demanding a divorce and the return of Pamphile's dowry, because of Charisios' misconduct. He would presumably call Charisios' friends as witnesses for it. On the legal procedure see A. R. W. Harrison, *Law of Athens*, i. pp. 40–4, 55–6.

642: If the paragraphi are all preserved, either the latter part of this line or part at least of the next must have been spoken by Smikrines' companion on the stage; Smikrines then continued from the beginning of 645 at the latest. In 646 πόρνης is a harsh word, 'a whore'.

645–713: Very little remains of these lines. The fragment Y gives 645 and the beginnings of 646–50, 655–65, and on the other side

680–1 and the the ends of 682–5, 690–9. The fragment R gives the ends of 648–59 and the beginnings of 684–94. The two fragments are not physically joined, but their relative position is assured because 692 is quoted by Harpokration: some of the shorter gaps can also be convincingly supplemented by conjecture. The assignment of YR to this part of the play is determined by their matter, and their position, by which 645 (Y) immediately follows 644 (X), is certain, because 644 is the last line of a page and 645 the first of another.

649–54: It is impossible to follow the changes of speaker here. Clearly Smikrines speaks 655 from ἀλλ' ἴcωc at least, and as there was no paragraphus below the line we may infer that the whole of it belongs to him. The preceding repetition δυcτυχοῦc, δυcτυχῇ suggested to Gomme that his interlocutor, who may have spoken the whole of 649–53, said something in defence of Charisios, and called him δυcτυχήc, and that Smikrines indignantly replied, e.g. ἐκάλεcαc τὸν πονηρὸν δυcτυχῇ | τοῦτον; But this solution is inconsistent with the dicolon read by Jensen and regarded as possible by Guéraud at the end of 654, and the paragraphus below the line (omitted in Körte's text). Those who believe both Chairestratos and Simias to take part in this scene may think that 654 might be spoken by one of them to emphasize the idea, expressed by the other in his speech, that Charisios is δυcτυχήc.

655 ff.: Smikrines asks sarcastically whether he is interfering or over-stepping his rights, when he has every reason (κατὰ λόγον) for removing his daughter. He continues that that is what he will do—his mind is just about made up. cχεδόν carries little emphasis; it is often used without implying any real modification of the verb, see LSJ s.v. He then calls upon Charisios' friends to witness something, perhaps Charisios' bad behaviour, that justifies the removal of Pamphile. ὁμολογεῖν, if right, probably depends on μαρτύρομαι, cf. Aesch. *Eum.* 643, ὑμᾶς δ' ἀκούειν ταῦτ' ἐγὼ μαρτύρομαι. μαρτύρομαι, if standing alone, calls witnesses to an imminent assault, Ar. *Ach.* 926, cf. *Samia* 576, Page *GLP* 48, 17 (p. 234).

664–5: Jensen at times thought that he saw traces of C[.]M in the left-hand margin, at others that he did not. The margin is so torn that if there were any letters there, only minimal remains can survive.

680–2: Wilamowitz, Körte, Webster, and others supposed that a friend of Charisios here defends him from the charge of debauchery, saying that he hates the so-called 'life of pleasure'. But it is not clear how this defence would be aided by 681–2, which seem to record his drinking and perhaps wenching. Wilamowitz suggested that these were mentioned as the bygone activities of his bachelor days, and that

they were not the end of the story. It is hard to see how αὔριον could
be fitted into a context of this sort.

Nothing rules out a quite different interpretation, namely that
these lines are spoken by Smikrines, being preceded by e.g. οὐ λέγειν
ἔχοις ἂν ὡς. 'You couldn't say that he hates this so-called life of
pleasure. He was drinking with what's-his-name, then at night he
had some woman or other, and he was going to have her or someone
else tomorrow.' Smikrines, to whom Chairestratos is a stranger, is
unaware that he is speaking to the man he calls 'What's-his-name',
the host of the party, although he knows him to have been there.
This solution adopts Sudhaus' restoration of 681–2, ἔπινε μετὰ τοῦ
δεῖνος, εἶχεν ἑσπέρας | τὴν δεῖν', ἔμελλεν δ' αὔριον τὴν δεῖν' ἔχειν (but
Sudhaus divided the words between two speakers). The new photograph shows that he was right to see an apostrophe, not a dicolon,
between δειν and εχει. But ἔχειν is an emendation: there is no final ν,
and a thin horizontal line visible on the facsimile above the iota is
probably not ink.

690 ἡμῖν κεκήδ[ευκ': 'He has become connected with us by marriage'
can only be spoken by Smikrines, who for all we know may have
spoken continuously since 683. Letters in the right-hand margin have
been read as *XAIP* confidently by Jensen, dubiously by Lefebvre,
who was, however, almost sure of *X* and sure of *P*. Guéraud was
extremely uncertain and preferred *ABP*. But the supposition that
Habrotonon appears here has nothing to recommend it; one may feel
confident that the second half of the line was spoken by Chairestratos.

691 ff.: The assignment of these lines is not easy. Wilamowitz gave
691 to Chairestratos, 692 ff. to Smikrines. He thought that it was
difficult to see in καταφθαρεὶς κτλ. and ὑψηλὸς ὤν . . . οὐκ οἰμώξεται
sentences that could be joined by τε, and supposed that τε joined
καταφθαρείς and κεκηδευκώς of 690. But there is no dicolon at the end
of 691, and no paragraphus below it; the proposed distribution was
therefore not intended by the writer of the codex. He must have
meant either Chairestratos or Smikrines to speak the whole of 691–5
(at least). Since the end of 690 is lost, we cannot tell whether there was
a dicolon there; if there was, Smikrines is meant, if not, Chairestratos.

I do not think that a decision between these alternatives can be
more than a guess, but favour the former because the indignation
shown by the speaker is readily intelligible if he is Smikrines. There
is no *evidence* that Chairestratos felt indignation with his friend. Del
Corno suggests that he may have been moved to it by jealousy over
Habrotonon, but that is mere speculation. The text seems to be compatible with either alternative. If Smikrines is the speaker, τε in 692

may join two indignant questions: Shan't this high-and-mighty fellow suffer? and Shall he, gone to the bad, spend his life in a brothel? The same may be true if Chairestratos is the speaker; or, the first question may end with καταφθαρείς τε or ἐν ματρυλείῳ and τε join καταφθαρείς to another participle or adjective that stood in the second half of 690. At 694 ἡμᾶς will in Chairestratos' mouth mean 'me and my friends', in that of Smikrines 'me and my daughter': since Charisios has as yet made no attempt to hide his relations with Habrotonon from Chairestratos, the latter interpretation may be more likely. At 691 οὐκ οἰμώξεται recalls Smikrines' use of the phrase οἰμώξει μακρά at 1068 and (as I guess) 160.

Harpokration quotes οὐκ οἰμώξεται . . . τὸν βίον, to illustrate the word ματρυλεῖον. (His MSS. either omit τε, or write καταφθαρεῖσθε). I do not see how these 7 (or 8) words can be construed, since τὸν βίον required βιώσεται to govern it. Perhaps the grammarian who originally quoted the passage gave it in full.

691 ὑψηλός: 'High-and-mighty', 'superior'. The word is used again by Charisios of himself at 922, apparently meaning that he had given himself airs of moral superiority. It does not occur elsewhere in the remains of New Comedy, but see Phaidra's phrase in Eur. *Hipp.* 730, ἵν' εἰδῇ μὴ 'πὶ τοῖς ἐμοῖς κακοῖς ὑψηλὸς εἶναι.

692 ματρυλείῳ: A rare word, perhaps of non-Greek origin. Ancient grammarians and lexicographers probably had to guess at its meaning. Harpokration writes: Ἡρακλέων καὶ Δίδυμος (grammatici) τόπον τινά φασιν εἶναι ἐν ᾧ γράες διατρίβουσαι δέχονται τοὺς βουλομένους καταμεθυσθῆναι and gives references to *Epitrepontes* and the late fourth-century orator Deinarchos. Plutarch has the word twice, *Amatorius* 752 c, τὸν θεὸν (sc. Ἔρωτα) ἐκ γυμνασίων καὶ περιπάτων καὶ τῆς ἐν ἡλίῳ καθαρᾶς καὶ ἀναπεπταμένης διατριβῆς εἰς ματρυλεῖα καὶ κοπίδας (καλπίδας Kronenberg from Antiphanes frag. 106 K, 'cosmetic boxes', κοιτίδας Post) καὶ φάρμακα καὶ μαγεύματα καθειργνύμενον ἀκολάστων γυναικῶν, and *non posse suauiter* 1093 f, τὰς ἐκ τῶν ὀπτανίων καὶ ματρυλείων ἡδονὰς ἐκείνας (where Wilamowitz saw a line from comedy, presumably Menander, ἐξ. ὀπτ. κ. μ. ἡδονάς). On the whole the meaning 'tavern-cum-brothel' is indicated.

693 ἐπεισάγει: This word is used of bringing a second woman into one's home, e.g. [Andokides] iv. 15, ἐπεισάγων εἰς τὴν αὐτὴν οἰκίαν ἑταίρας, καὶ δούλας καὶ ἐλευθέρας, ὥστ' ἠνάγκασε τὴν γυναῖκα . . . ἀπολιπεῖν, ἐλθοῦσαν πρὸς τὸν ἄρχοντα κατὰ τὸν νόμον.   **καλῆς:** Sarcastic, cf. *Sam.* 353.

699: The end of the act must have followed shortly: only about 14 verses are missing (see introd. p. 44), some of which are needed for the beginning of Act IV. Smikrines entered Charisios' house, if he had not already done so, to interview his daughter; Chairestratos left the stage either by returning to his own house or, as I think more likely, by going to the city or on some errand that will keep him out of the way during the next act.

ACT IV

(i) 714–759: *Smikrines and Pamphile*

714 ff.: Act IV opened with the appearance of Smikrines and Pamphile. During the interval between the acts he must be supposed to have urged her to leave her husband and she to have refused. They came on the stage continuing the argument. From the point of view of realism, such a conversation would have taken place entirely indoors. It was, however, a limitation of the Greek theatre that indoor conversations could not be represented as such. Rather than forgo them entirely, dramatists would at times bring their characters out of the house without giving a reason. Provided that the dialogue was interesting enough to rivet the audience's attention, the improbability would pass without being noticed. As the opening of Act IV is lost we cannot say whether Menander found any way of motivating the appearance of Smikrines and his daughter. Gomme supposed at least 8 lines to be missing, 4–5 from Smikrines urging Pamphile to leave with him, 2 from her showing reluctance, 2 more from him to the effect that he was trying to *save* her from a disastrous situation. But most of this is unnecessary: the previous act had shown that Smikrines intended to remove his daughter (657), and Pamphile's reluctance would be implied in the second speech (itself very plausible) suggested for him by Gomme. Menander was an economical writer, and no more than a line or two is necessarily lost here. That is not to deny the possible loss of more.

This is doubtless Pamphile's first appearance on the stage, but her father may after his earlier visit have said something about her surprising refusal to take sides against Charisios.

714 τοῦτο μὴ πείcαιc ἐμέ: τοῦτο, 'this course', i.e. to leave Charisios. Persuasion is constantly opposed in Greek thought to force and constraint. Pamphile clearly envisages the possibility that her father could force her to come away, but argues that he would then be acting like a master to a slave. 'We have always been told that Greek fathers, especially Athenian ones, were complete masters of their children, especially of their daughters; and I do not know that the discovery of Menander any more than the reading of Sophocles has weakened a strange conviction' (Gomme). One must distinguish between a father's rights *de jure* and his behaviour *de facto*.

716 λόγου δέ: δέ in the question marks impatience, Denniston, *GP* 173. cύμπειcιc only here (πεῖcιc is quite unknown) and first registered by LSJ in the supplement. But the verb cυμπείθω is common, e.g. 1067, *Perik.* 330, 718, *Dysk.* 790, 818, 837, 855, and means 'persuade to agree'.

717 ἐπιπόλαιον: 'Obvious'; Jensen's brilliant (but not indubitable) restoration of this word is based on Aristotle's phrase, *Rhet.* iii. 10, 1410^{b}21, ἐνθυμήματα ἐπιπόλαια, which he explains by ἐπιπόλαια γὰρ λέγομεν τὰ παντὶ δῆλα.

Wilamowitz's αὐτό is an equally good restoration, 'the thing itself gives tongue, cries aloud'; he compares for the whole sentence, Ar. *Wasps* 921, αὐτὸ γὰρ βοᾷ, and Dem. i. 2, ὁ καιρὸς μόνον οὐχὶ λέγει φωνὴν ἀφιείc.

718 κἀμὲ δεῖ λέγειν: Gomme thought that καί must be taken with δεῖ λέγειν (for similar misplacing of καί see Denniston, *GP* 326–7), and wished to read καί με (*CQ* xxx [1936], 65). But καί may quite well go with ἐμέ, 'if (it is not enough for the facts to speak, but) I too must speak'.

719 τρία δέ cοι προθήcομαι: Wilamowitz states the three possibilities as 'you leave him now, at once, with me'; or (2) 'you wait, and he soon sends you away, divorces you on some pretext' (cf. n. on 571); or (3) 'the marriage continues, on the surface, but Charisios will lead a double life, with double expenses'. There is, however, nothing in what survives to support the view that Smikrines advanced these three alternatives, and the line οὔτ' ἂν ἔτι cωθείη ποθ' οὗτος οὔτε cύ (720) 'disaster is certain for both of you' is a strange way of introducing them. τρία προθήcομαι need not mean 'I will put three alternatives'; it may equally mean 'I will put three considerations before you'. This is Körte's view (*Praefatio* xxii); he thinks them to be (1) Charisios will not be able to meet the expense of two establishments, (2) Pamphile will come off second best in comparison with her rival, who has a *hetaira*'s advantages, (3) Pamphile will come off second best in comparison with a rival who has borne Charisios a child. There is evidence (749 ff., frag. 7) that Smikrines advanced the first two arguments, the third is a guess.

749–50 Θεcμοφόρια δίc: Smikrines imagines Charisios having to pay twice for the expenses of a women's festival, for both Pamphile and Habrotonon. Note the characteristic pettiness of his calculations. The Skira were a festival of Athens, celebrated by women (Ar. *Thesm.* 834), on the 12th day of the summer month Skirophorion. Poseidon and later Demeter and Persephone were associated with this festival, which took place at Skiron on the left bank of the Kephisos. See Pfister in *RE* 2nd series iii. 1. 530 ff., Farnell, *Cults* iii. 39 ff., L. Deubner, *Attische Feste*, 40–50.   τοῦ βίου: 'His means', a common sense, e.g. *Perik.* 806. In the next line ἀπόλωλεν, picking up ὄλεθροc, will refer to financial disaster.

753: 'When he has got there he will sit there' must mean 'He will be in no hurry to come back'.

754 περιμενεῖc: Guéraud's re-examination of the papyrus seems to be decisive against πολὺν χρόνον (Wilamowitz), which was in any case rather weak. His own hesitant suggestion, παννυχίδα cύ, is not convincing; if Pamphile's solitary night is to be ironically called a 'night-festival' some additional word, e.g. τινα or καλήν would be needed. It is doubtful what weight is to be given to his reading παννν[. Is πεινῶcα καί impossible? For the wife left at home, waiting for her husband's return for dinner, cf. Plaut. *Mercator* 556 (a play from Philemon), 'uxor me expectat iamdudum essuriens domi'.

754–8: These lines are badly damaged, and only 755 can be confirmed from the facsimile. In 754 the third letter has been read by all scholars who have seen the papyrus as υ, and this must be accepted, although on the facsimile it appears to be λ. If ὀδυνήcει is right, the word is probably 2nd person future passive, as in Teles frag. 2, p. 9 Hense. The small remains of 756–7 are so uncertain that attempts to supplement them are a waste of time. For the length of the gap that follows, about 93 lines, see introduction, p. 44.

Fragment 7. ἐλευθέρᾳ γυναικί: 'A lady', cf. 323 n. It is not certain that the fragment belongs to this play; other young women in comedies probably bore the name Pamphile (cf. Terence, *Adelphoe* 619), and a situation which could call for such lines may have occurred in other plays than *Epitrepontes.* However, it is likely enough that Smikrines spoke thus bluntly to his daughter, and it may be noted that he had earlier called Habrotonon a πόρνη (646).   πλείονα κακουργεῖ: 'She (the prostitute) uses more unfair tricks'.

Fragment 8. ἐξετύφην: The scholiast on Eur. *Phoen.* 1154, to explain τυφώc, writes τύφεcθαί ἐcτι τοὺc ὀφθαλμοὺc cυγκεχύcθαι, quoting these lines, and another from Φιλάδελφοι, viz. νὴ τὸν Δία τὸν μέγιcτον ἐκτυφήcομαι (frag. 439 K–T). Gomme translated 'my eyes swim with tears', 'my eyesight is blurred with weeping', and rejected Hesychios' interpretation ἐκτύφεcθαι· ἡcυχῇ ἐκκαίεcθαι. But μὲν οὖν (= immo uero), ὅλωc, and νὴ τὸν Δία τὸν μέγιcτον all point to an emphatic sense: 'I was burned out with weeping'; this accords with the meaning of τύφεσθαι, 'smoulder'. Wilamowitz imaginatively observes that Pamphile has cried since the birth and exposure of her child, and long even before that. But the aorist must refer to some particular point in the past: translators who use such phrases as 'I have cried my eyes out', 'my face has swelled up' (LSJ) miss this. Perhaps Pamphile is speaking of her distress at parting with her child.

The fragment may come from a soliloquy uttered by Pamphile after Smikrines has left to return to the town. G. Rambelli, in *Comica graeco-latina*, 157 (which I know only from Del Corno's edition), maintained that in this soliloquy she recounted the story of her rape. The reason, that Charisios knows of her ἀκούσιον ἀτύχημα at 914 (cf. 898), is inadequate. He knew of her illegitimate child, and would not suppose her to have been a consenting partner; he could guess the child to be the result of an ἀκούσιον ἀτύχημα. Pamphile presumably said something after Smikrines' departure, but it need not have been much.

Previously she must have refused to leave with her father, and expressed her refusal in striking terms, for it struck Charisios' conscience as he overheard it, and caused him to exclaim ὦ γλυκυτάτη τῶν λόγων οἵους λέγεις (888). Her speech was not a short one. This is implied by Onesimos' account of Charisios' behaviour as he listened to it, and confirmed by the length of the gap in which it was contained. The scene between Smikrines and Pamphile must have continued for 70 lines, perhaps more, after 759, at which point Smikrines had already spoken for about 40 and must therefore have said the larger part of what he had to say. D. S. Robertson put forward the theory that Pamphile's reply was in fact preserved in the 44 lines of the Didot papyrus (*CR* xxxvi [1922], 106). He may have been right (although even this is disputed) in arguing that these lines are an extract from a play by Menander. But the situation, although similar to that of *Epitrepontes*, is not the same, since the Didot rhesis replies to a father who wants to take his daughter from a good husband who has met with financial disaster. Nevertheless the daughter's speech, which can be found in OCT, pp. 328–30, may give some idea of the kind of reply made by Pamphile, firm and reasonable, yet modest and gentle.

(ii) 853–877: *Pamphile and Habrotonon*

853 ἔξειμ' ἔχουσα: Either Habrotonon here first comes on the scene, or she has already been out for some time, observing Pamphile without herself being seen, ('Can that be the girl I saw at the Tauropolia?') and now announces (to the audience) that she will go in and come out again (? πάλιν] ἔξειμι) with the baby, which she has heard whimpering

for some time, as if in distress of some kind. Gomme objected to the first alternative that, assuming τὸ παιδίον to be the lost object of ἔχουςα, the words explained the obvious. If a woman comes on the stage with her supposed baby in her arms, she need not say 'I am coming out with the baby'. The second alternative may appear preferable, provided that a space of one line (855) will serve to cover the time used by Habrotonon in fetching the baby. It is not impossible, however, that Habrotonon, leaving the house with the baby, to quieten it by taking it a walk, should tell someone inside that she is going out; what the audience would learn from 853–4 would be, not that she was coming out with the baby, a fact which they could of course see for themselves, but why she came out at all. An advantage of this view is that it makes a much better theatrical coup if Habrotonon comes out with the baby to quieten it and unexpectedly finds herself facing its mother.

The matter might be settled if 856–7 could be certainly restored, for they might show whether Habrotonon had previously seen Pamphile. Unfortunately C is so worn and torn from 856 to 863 that it is almost miraculous that anything has been read in it at all, and it is very doubtful how much has been genuinely deciphered.

854 μοι: So-called ethical dative, expressing the speaker's concern for the baby.

856: According to Guéraud nothing is certain between φίλτατο[ν and μη[τέ]ρα. The question ὦ φίλτατον τέκνον, πότ' ὄψει μητέρα; makes good sense. The statement ὦ φίλτατον παιδάριον, ὄψει μητέρα, printed by Körte, is impossible, for clearly Habrotonon is not yet, on any view, *certain* of Pamphile's identity; that certainty comes only at 860, when she has seen her face to face. This consideration rules out Sudhaus's extremely flat restoration of 857, καὶ γὰρ προςῆλθε (προῆλθε Jensen) καιρία. Apart from that, Pamphile, who has been on the stage a long time, has not 'come forward' or 'come up'. Guéraud says that there is nothing to be read in this line between καί and πορεύcομαι ('I will go in', cf. *Perik.* 184, 298).

859: It has been objected to the usual reading, ἐναντίον βλέπ' εἴ με γινώcκεις, γύναι, that Habrotonon could not expect Pamphile to recognize her, the poor harp-player, just because she recognizes Pamphile. This is pedantic: Habrotonon is eager, and looking for every possible proof that she has found the girl who had suffered a misfortune at the Tauropolia. There is, however, a further difficulty. There is a dicolon after γύναι, and a paragraphus below the line. Gomme suggested giving αὕτη ἐcτὶν ἣν ἑόρακα to Pamphile, but that will not do; Pamphile stands out for Habrotonon among all the girls she had seen at the festival, whereas Habrotonon can have no such uniqueness for Pamphile. If we are to respect the indications of the papyrus we must find a way of giving the second half of 859 to Pamphile, e.g. ἐναντίον βλέπε. (Πα.) ἦ με γινώσκεις, γύναι; (Merkelbach, *Mus. Helv.* [1966], 184). This sense was desiderated by Guéraud.

860 χαῖρε: This word is used in other scenes of recognition, *Perik.* 824 n.

The forms of address in this scene deserve attention. Habrotonon begins (858) with γύναι, a usual polite form, 'madam'. In 859 Pamphile replies in the same form (but perhaps with a colder politeness). On recognizing Pamphile, Habrotonon breaks out with the warm φιλτάτη (860) and γλυκεῖα (862). Naturally Pamphile does not respond to this, although Wilamowitz may go too far when, ever careful of the proprieties, he thinks it impossible that she could give her hand to a girl 'whose calling she must recognize from her dress'; thus are Greeks turned into modern northern Europeans (cf. Gomme, *JHS* lxxvii [1957], 255). At 864 we have the only place in Menander where the vocative γύναι begins a sentence. The effect is abrupt and arresting. Pamphile has to her astonishment seen one at least of the γνωρίσματα on the baby that Habrotonon is carrying; perhaps it is wrapped in the πτέρυξ (404). Habrotonon replies with an eager φιλτάτη (865), but seeing that Pamphile is bewildered and needs reassurance, returns to the proper, formal ὦ γύναι (866). Then Pamphile in her turn, in gratitude and appealing for confirmation of the good news, uses φιλτάτη (871). But Habrotonon is not encouraged thereby to any further liberties; her emotions more under control now, she reverts to γύναι (873).

863: Jensen completed the line with ἐν ταραντίνῳ καλῷ from 488, and Körte accepts this. Such a repetition is possible, but not very likely.

869 προσεποιησάμην: Sc. τεκέσθαι.   **ἀδικήσω ... εὕροιμι:** Although some deny that there is always a distinction of meaning when final subjunctive and optative are thus combined (Goodwin, *M.T.* § 321), it seems possible to find one here. Habrotonon declares that her object in pretending the baby to be hers was not a criminal one, which would have been an immediate wrong to the real mother, but the intention, necessarily more remote in execution, of discovering that mother.

κατὰ cχολὴν εὕροιμι: Habrotonon repeats a phrase she has used earlier (538), but it could not convey much to Pamphile. Her deception had been intended to discover not the mother but the father; that done, she had promised to look for the mother κατὰ cχολήν. In neither place will this mean 'in a leisurely manner', but rather 'undistracted' by the complications that might arise in looking for the mother without knowing the father.

874 θεῶν τιc ὑμᾶc ἐλέηce is the answer to Pamphile's despairing τίc ἂν θεῶν κτλ. (855), but perhaps an unconscious one. It does not follow that Habrotonon must have heard this other line (see 853 n.).

875 ἐψόφηκεν: See *Perik.* 316 n. The two young women must leave the stage for Habrotonon to tell the whole story, for the audience already know it. Onesimos comes out of the other house, that of Chairestratos.

(iii) 878–907: *Onesimos alone*

879 μαίνεται: Onesimos is at a loss for further words to describe his master's state, and can only repeat himself. Till now he has been going up the scale, ὑπομαίνεται, μαίνεται 'is acting madly', μεμάνηται 'is out of his mind' (this form of the perfect, instead of the usual μέμηνα, recurs in Theokr. x. 31). He would like a word still more emphatic, but can think of none.

880–1 χολὴ μέλαινα: An excess of black bile was believed to cause madness, see *Dysk.* 89 n.

883–4: The supplements may not give the exact wording, but the general sense is not in doubt.

888 δέ: Note the connecting particle of the narrative here incorporated in the quoted speech. This construction is common in Ovid (e.g. *Met.* iii. 644, 'obstipui capiatque aliquis moderamina dixi') but rare in other Latin authors. γάρ is sometimes so treated in Greek, e.g. Lucian, *Vit. Dem.* 11, εὐθὺς ἐν ἀρχῇ τῶν πρὸς αὐτοὺς λόγων τραχυτέρῳ ἐχρήσατο τῷ προοιμίῳ. ἄνδρες γὰρ ἔφη Ἀθηναῖοι, Plut. *Romulus* 19, τί γὰρ ἔφασαν δεινόν, Plato, *Laws* 681 e, κτίcce δὲ Δαρδανίην γάρ που φηcίν. Wilamowitz sees another instance in 894 below, but there γάρ may be part of what Charisios said. The usage is discussed by Haupt, *Opuscula*, iii. 510 ff., who has instances of the same placing of δέ from Herodian i. 6 and [Phalaris], *epist.* 71. It is not clear whether he intends to claim Leonidas, *A. Plan.* 236 as a further example: he prints "τοῦτο δ'" ἐρωτᾷc | "τῶν ὀλίγων λαχάνων εἵνεκα;" and since δέ is common in surprised questions, this seems defensible; but Gow and Page, *Hellenistic Epigrams*, i. 134 print "τοῦτο" δ' ἐρωτᾷc.

884 διακύπτων: Leaning forward through the half-opened door of Chairestratos' house to eavesdrop on Smikrines and Pamphile, who were talking in the street, cf. Ar. *Peace* 78.

885 περὶ τοῦ [πράγματοc: Wilamowitz notes that, although we might have expected some more precise word for the subject of Smikrines' conversation, Charisios' exclamations, as quoted by Onesimos, are equally imprecise. He explains that nothing is allowed to anticipate the import of Charisios' own speech, which is to follow so soon, and that the audience have themselves witnessed the scene between Smikrines and Pamphile.

887 ἄνδρες: Cf. *Sam.* 271 n.

888 τῶν λόγων οἴους λέγεις: Van Leeuwen and Wilamowitz take τῶν λόγων as a partitive genitive, quoting Ar. *Plut.* 1051, ὦ Ποντοπόσειδον, . . . ἐν τῷ προσώπῳ τῶν ῥυτίδων ὅσας ἔχει, and Hdt. vii. 233, λέγοντες τὸν ἀληθέστατον τῶν λόγων, ὡς κτλ., cf. ibid. 104, λέγειν τῶν λόγων τοὺς ἀληθεστάτους. Wilamowitz supposed that Pamphile might have expected to choose quite differently from the stock of possible speeches, while Gomme interpreted 'of all your gentle words to me since our marriage, these are the most kind and gentle'. These interpretations seem artificial by comparison with that of taking the genitive as one of cause dependent on γλυκυτάτη, cf. Plato, *Phaedo* 58 e, εὐδαίμων μοι ὁ ἀνὴρ ἐφαίνετο τοῦ τρόπου καὶ τῶν λόγων, ὡς ἀδεῶς καὶ γενναίως ἐτελεύτα, Eur. *Hec.* 661, ὦ τάλαινα σῆς κακογλώσσου βοῆς, ὡς οὔποθ' εὔδει λυπρά σου κηρύγματα.

889 ἀνεπάταξε: Only here except in Hesychios, who has two irrelevant glosses. Perhaps Charisios knocked his head backwards by a blow on the forehead.

890 αὐτοῦ: Is this just an instance, as Wilamowitz says, of a personal pronoun that is quite unnecessary and would have been avoided by earlier writers, or does its position, separated from κεφαλήν and isolated at the beginning of the line, give an emphasis and a comic effect, as Gomme thought? For τὴν κεφαλὴν . . . αὐτοῦ instead of the normal τὴν αὐτοῦ κεφαλήν see *Dysk.* 26 n.

891 ὁ μέλεος: A word from tragedy. Charisios' language holds a wavering course between that of comedy and that of serious poetry. With ἔργον ἐξειργασμένος (895) compare Aesch. *Pers.* 759, Soph. *Ant.* 384, *Trach.* 706. Line 897, οὐκ ἔσχον οὐκ ἔδωκα συγγνώμης μέρος, could as well belong in a tragedy as here. ἀνηλεής (899) first occurs here, next in Kallimachos, but [Andokides] iv. 39 has ἀνηλεῶς. When Charisios appears in person, his speech opens in high style (see notes on 910, 912) but gradually sinks so as to pass without abruptness into the colloquial exchanges with Onesimos.   ἠτύχηκα: 'What a wife I married, only to be in this wretched fix!' Probably ἀτυχεῖν is here used euphemistically for ἁμαρτάνειν. Kalbfleisch's conjecture ἠδίκηκα, which he supported by frag. adesp. 221, Kock, οἵαν ἀδικῶ γυναῖχ' ὁ δυσδαίμων ἐγώ, was accepted by Körte, *Hermes* lxxviii (1943), 285.

It gives something which Charisios might have said, if he had not preferred to say ἠτύχηκα.

892 βρυχηθμός: 'Gnashing of teeth' LSJ, as if from βρύχω, but the correct derivation is from βρυχάομαι, 'roar'. The word is used elsewhere of the noise of lions and of the sea, and of the distracted Deianeira, Soph. *Trach.* 904. τιλμός: Aesch. *Suppl.* 839. Onesimos favours nouns in -μός, cf. βιασμός for βία (453), ἀναγνωρισμός for ἀναγνώρισις (1121).

893 ἔκστασις: Cf. frag. 136; probably short for ἔκστασις φρενῶν, a medical term found in *Aspis* 422.

894 ἀλιτήριος: ἀλιτήριος 'sinner', but like ἱερόσυλος, τοιχωρύχος, the word became a term of abuse, frag. 746, οἷος δ᾽ ἀλάζών ἐστιν ἀλιτήριος, Dem. xix. 197, τῶν θεοῖς ἐχθρῶν, τῶν ἀλιτηρίων Ὀλυνθίων αἰχμάλωτον. Eupolis frag. 96 Κ, ὁ Βουζύγης ἄριστος, ἀλιτήριος, and frag. 146 Κ, Πρωταγόρας . . . ὃς ἀλαζονεύεται μὲν ἀλιτήριος περὶ τῶν μετεώρων, show a half-meaningful, half-abusive use as here.

898 ἀτυχούσῃ ταὐτά: Again the euphemistic use of ἀτυχεῖν may be present. Charisios can conceive of his crime in getting Habrotonon with child (as he thinks) as an ἀτύχημα: whereas Pamphile had no responsibility for her motherhood, which was an ἀτύχημα in the proper sense of the word.

899 ἐρρωμένως: Ar. *Wasps* 230, χώρει, πρόβαιν᾽ ἐρρωμένως, *Fab. incert.* 23, 57.

900 ὕφαιμον: A word frequently used in later authors of blood-shot eyes; Wilamowitz thinks that when Plato applies it at *Phaedr.* 253 e to the untamed horse of his myth, he has its eyes in mind. Blood-shot eyes are a sign of madness in Eur. *HF* 933. ἠρεθισμένος, not 'under provocation' (LSJ), for no one has provoked him, but 'worked up to a state of excitement'.

901 ἐγὼ μέν: μέν *solitarium* is common after personal pronouns (Denniston, *GP* 381); the usual implicit contrast, 'whatever may be true of others', can be understood here.

αὗος εἰμι: Cf. *Perik.* 352 n., *Sam* 515.

902 αὐτόν . . . με: An emphatic expression for '*me*' (LSJ s.v. αὐτός, I. 10 b); it is not idiomatic in English to add 'myself'. Contrast 916 αὐτόν . . . σ', where 'you yourself' is a possible translation.

903 τὸν διαβαλόντα: If the unexpressed object is αὐτούς, the meaning is 'set them at variance', if αὐτήν, 'informed on her'; the latter is the more obvious interpretation.

904 ὑπεκδέδυκα: 'I have slipped out'; cf. Herodotus i. 10. 2, ὑπεκδὺς ἐχώρεε ἔξω.

905 καὶ ποῖ τράποιμί γ': 'Yet where am I to *turn*?'

906 πέπληχε: See *Sam.* 300 n.

907: Onesimos probably bolts into Charisios' house. For the view that he hides himself somewhere outside, see 932 n.

(iv) **908–932**: *Charisios alone*

908: Charisios' coming out is not explained, see 714 n. But if a reason is to be imagined, one may suppose him to be on his way to make amends to Pamphile. This appears to have been Charisios' first appearance—perhaps also his last, but see n. on 1120 ff.—as Pamphile's shortly before 714 was her first (Gomme, *Essays*, 267). That is why Onesimos has to remind the audience that his master is Charisios (v. 880). It has been objected that earlier in the play Charisios must himself have appeared and said something corresponding to ἀναμάρτητος κτλ. (Zuntz, *Proc. Brit. Acad.* xlii [1956], 241); but we have had this from others, who all show us different aspects of his conduct and character—from Onesimos, Habrotonon, Chairestratos, even from Smikrines; probably, most sympathetically, from Pamphile herself in her monologue. The mistake is like that of saying that Achilles does not appear in the *Iliad* between books i and ix (e.g. Monro, ed., vol. i, p. 339), which is to ignore his appearance for an audience, or a reader, in Andromache's speech in vi. 407 ff. (see also ii. 377, 674, 875). Charisios and Pamphile dominate the play from the beginning, although for three acts they do not appear.

908 δόξαν: Charisios denounces his past priggish self-righteousness, and in the context the statement that he had looked to reputation is to be taken as one of the counts against him. Although the Greeks generally regarded 'honour' as a proper goal of ambition, the contrast between appearing to be good and being good is familiar, e.g. Plato, *Rep.* 361 b 7, κατ' Αἰσχύλον (*Septem* 592) οὐ δοκεῖν ἀλλ' εἶναι ἀγαθὸν ἐθέλοντα. ὅτι πότ' ἐστι suggests impatience with philosophical inquiries into the good; αὐτός implies that he had been ready enough to see other people's faults.

910 ἀκέραιος: An echo, perhaps unconscious, of Eur. *Or.* 922, ἀκέραιος, ἀνεπίπληκτον ἠσκηκὼς βίον; Menander's familiarity with this scene is evidenced by *Sikyonios* 176 ff. ἀκέραιος is uncommon in this moral sense, 'untouched by vice'. ἀνεπίπληκτος, 'beyond reproach', was used by Eupolis (frag. 397 K).

911 προϲηκόντωϲ: Only here in New Comedy, but in Hypereides, iv. 16, 17 Kenyon, a passage in a plain style.

912 τὸ δαιμόνιον: A vague term for 'a supernatural power', not found elsewhere in Menander or the remains of New Comedy, and therefore no banal phrase; it is common in Plutarch, who may reflect the language of Hellenistic historians. The 'prosopopoeia', by which words are put in the mouth of the Power, is a rhetorical device that elevates Charisios' ϲpeech above the everyday level. Editors disagree about the point at which the Power begins to speak. Van Leeuwen, Jensen, Sudhaus, and Wilamowitz in his note interpret ἔδειξ' as ἔδειξα, 'here I showed myself a (mere) man', and so cause the Power to begin with ὦ τριϲκακόδαιμον. Wilamowitz in his text, Körte, and Del Corno take ἔδειξ' as ἔδειξε, making the Power start with ἄνθρωποϲ ὤν. The latter is excellent if ἔδειξε can stand without an object, or with a reported speech taking the place of an object. This appears doubtful. On the other hand the construction ἔδειξα . . . ὤν is familiar, e.g. Thuc. iv. 73, ἔδειξαν ἕτοιμοι ὄντεϲ. Where the Power's speech ends is hard to determine. Charisios may pass imperceptibly from imagining that he is addressed to addressing himself. The Power certainly speaks in 915 and therefore continues to the end of 918 at least; but Charisios speaks in 929. The change, if there was a clear one, may have come immediately after 918 or (this is less likely) at the point where there is a gap in the text; I do not find it easy to put it, as Wilamowitz and Körte do, at χρήϲεται in 928.

Webster, *CR* n.s. xv (1965), 17, suggests that the whole of Charisios' speech from ὦ τριϲκακόδαιμον (913) is self-allocution. This is not compatible with 915–17, sentences which are certainly imagined to have been spoken at some previous time by someone who knew more than Charisios then did.   **μεγάλα φυϲᾷϲ:** 'Give yourself airs', probably to be explained as a more vivid variant of μεγάλα πνεῖν, Eur. *Andr.* 189, οἱ γὰρ πνέοντεϲ μεγάλα. φυϲᾶν occurs in a number of phrases indicative of pride or conceit; e.g. Dem. xix. 314, τὰϲ ὀφρῦϲ ἀνέϲπακεν . . . τὰϲ γνάθουϲ φυϲῶν, Ephippos frag. 5. 20 K, παύου φυϲῶν, and more in LSJ.

915 ἐπταικότα: 'To have stumbled'; Charisios must use a somewhat euphemistic word since he is representing himself, as he did in 898, as being in the same position as his wife. He had had bad luck, like her, and she, as appears in 921, was prepared to treat his situation as a misfortune, not a crime.

916 ἠπίωϲ: ἤπιοϲ is in general a poetic word, although the adverb occurs in Herodotos and ἠπιωτέρωϲ in [Dem.] lvi. 44.

917 θ': 'and so', see *Dysk.* 36–9 n. ἀτυχήϲ first because he had not been really responsible but could blame drink for his act, secondly because a child had resulted from it.

918 cκαιὸc ἀγνώμων τ' ἀνήρ: cκαιόc is 'clumsy', i.e. clumsy in mind; ἀγνώμων is all that a brute or a brutish man is, who lacks both mental and moral sensibility. Sometimes the moral, sometimes the mental element is emphasized; in Herodotos ἀγνωμοcύνη denotes the obstinate folly of the Ionians in not surrendering to the Persian threat (vi. 10) and the cruel obstinacy of the Aeginetans towards Epidauros (v. 83. 1: Powell, writing his quaint English, translates both passages 'hardened their hearts').

919 ὅμοιά γ' εἶπεν: A similar sarcastic use of γε is found in the orators: Dem. xviii. 136, xxiv. 181, etc. (Denniston, *GP* 128–30).

920 κοινωνὸc ἥκειν τοῦ βίου: To those brought up in the belief that to the Greeks marriage was nothing but a practical arrangement, this will sound a modern ideal. For the view that it is as old as Homer, see Gomme, *Essays*, 89–115. κοινωνόc fem. as in Aesch. *Ag.* 1037.

921: Wilamowitz's ἔφαcκε is adopted by Körte, but φάcκειν is always used elsewhere by Menander to mean 'allege', 'say falsely', *Perik.* 356, *Sam.* 79, 636, *frag.* 265. No verb of saying is necessary, since ἥκειν may depend on εἶπεν, but there is room for λέγουcα. **τἀτύχημα:** Pamphile forgivingly used this euphemism for Charisios' fault.

922 ὑψηλόc: The very word that Smikrines or Chairestratos had used of Charisios at 691.

923: It is not certain that this line followed immediately on 922; there may be a gap of a line or two.

925–7: Wilamowitz argued that Charisios only here takes the decision to return to Pamphile, when struck by the thought that her father will come and take her away. Accordingly he restored, *exempli gratia*:

> χρῆcθαι δ' ἐπίcταc' οὐδὲ ν]ῦν ταύτῃ cοφῶc,
> cκαιότατε, καί cέ ποτ]ε μέτειcι διὰ τέλουc,
> ἂν ᾖc τοιοῦτος, δαιμ]όνων τιc.

Although Körte prints this, it is far from certainly the right sense, and in the last line the supplement appears to be too long (13]ονων Hunt).

928: Körte prints προπετέcτατ' at the beginning of the line, but Hunt was right in doubting this, his own, conjecture. True though it is that when Smikrines later comes to remove his daughter, his action is twice called προπετέc 'precipitate' (1064, 1112), here the phrase 'her father will treat her very precipitately' is not plausible. **τί δέ μοι πατρόc:** Cf. 254 n.

931 τί cυνταράττειc: cυνταράττω may be used of upsetting one person, e.g. Ar. *Lys.* 7, τί cυντετάραξαι; But the text is uncertain; O 4 may have had τιουν, i.e. τί οὖν;

(v) 932–978: *Charisios, Onesimos, Habrotonon*

932 τί c' αὖ βλέπω 'γώ; It seems likely that this is correctly read. But editors can hardly be right in supposing Charisios to address Onesimos, who now comes forward, for the slave could not disregard the question, to converse with Habrotonon. And if he did converse with her, ignoring his master, the next question would not be 'Are you standing there eaves-dropping?' τί c' αὖ βλέπω 'γώ; must be part of the imaginary plain speaking to Smikrines. He had been once to bother Pamphile without succeeding in his plans. If he turns up to renew his efforts, Charisios will say 'Why do I see you here again?'.

There can be little doubt that Wilamowitz and Körte are right in supposing that Onesimos here comes out of Charisios' house talking to Habrotonon, and that ἀρτίωc ἐξῆλθον in 936 is nothing but the truth. Gomme found a difficulty in that Onesimos thinks himself in a dangerous position, whereas if he had been inside he would know that the child's identity had been discovered and all was going to end happily. Further he observed that Charisios does not notice Habrotonon until 942, when her intervention is so unexpected that he asks 'who are you?', an impossibility if she had been under his eyes for some time. Hence he supposed, with van Leeuwen, that Onesimos had not entered Charisios' house at 907, but hidden himself; now, seeing Habrotonon appear, he starts forward to address her; his movement attracts the attention of Charisios, who, however, does not see Habrotonon, who had caused it. (Van Leeuwen differs by regarding τί c' αὖ βλέπω 'γώ; as addressed to Habrotonon by Charisios).

Although Gomme's explanation of the scene is unacceptable, his difficulties need answering, and an answer may throw light on what happens. First, the discovery of the truth about the baby does not necessarily free Onesimos from his fears. He had been responsible, through his tale-telling, for the estrangement of Charisios and Pamphile, and as an accessory to Habrotonon's deception he had helped to put Charisios into an embarrassing situation. All that could be said for him was that his quickness in recognizing Charisios' ring had been the point from which the discovery of the happy truth had sprung. Habrotonon is his witness for the fact that it was he who had found the ring, and hence comes his appeal to her not to let him down.

Why do the pair come out? Clearly in order that they may go to Charisios and tell him what has happened; they share this errand because both had been concerned in the discovery. But why does Charisios see only Onesimos? Either Onesimos, as the man, comes forward while Habrotonon modestly waits in the doorway; or it may even be as Allinson thought, that Onesimos speaks 932–4 before she has appeared at all; there is no evidence that Greek manners required a gentleman to allow a lady to precede him through a door.

936–49: Restoration is impossible, and it may be that the papyrus was occasionally at fault in marking changes of speaker. 936 ἀλλ' ἀρτίως ἐξῆλθον belongs to Onesimos. No change is marked after ἐξῆλθον and there is no paragraphus below this line or the next. According to this he should continue to 938, where there is a dicolon after ἐπακροάcει, and a paragraphus below. This would mean that Charisios now speaks until we have another dicolon after βροντῶντα in 940, and again a paragraphus. But ἐγώ cε λανθάνειν of 939 and βροντῶντα seem much better suited to Onesimos, and so a change of speaker in 937 as well as 938 is likely. If Onesimos had originated all the trouble by overhearing something that revealed the secret of Pamphile's child, Charisios' question πάντ' ἐπακροάcει; will have greater force.

Habrotonon apparently speaks 941 (and perhaps the latter half of 940) in view of τίc εἶ c[ύ (probable, but τί cειc[άμενοc is just on the cards) from Charisios at the beginning of 942. Wilamowitz supplemented e.g. ἀλλ' οὐθὲν ὀφθήcε[ι cὺ τῶνδ' εἰδὼc cαφέc, which may give the sense; but ὀφθήcει is odd, unless it takes up a previous ὀφθήcομαι. Habrotonon must have spoken some part of 942 or 943, unless Onesimos struck in, since there are paragraphi under each. In 944 Körte's οὐκ ἦν ἐμόν follows from οὐκ ἦν cόν; (945). For 943 Gomme ingeniously proposed (*CQ* xxx [1936] 65) οὐκ ἐc [κόρακαc cύ τε καὶ τὸ παιδίον τὸ cόν (εἰc being written for εc as at 160, cf. 614 n.); the divided anapaest could be eliminated by omitting τε.

Since Habrotonon may or may not have spoken the second part of 945, the speakers of 946–9 are uncertain. The assignments in Körte are quite speculative. Lefebvre thought that there was stichomythia from 941 to 951, but this paratragic way of writing, although conceivable, is by no means necessary. It looks as if Onesimos spoke in 949, but even that is not beyond dispute, since the next line might run e.g. τί φηc', 'Ονήcιμ'; ἐξεπειράθη[τέ μου;

949: Körte prints Sudhaus' ἔδεια. But something like ἔδει cε [πατέρ' ὄνθ' ὁμολογεῖν τοῦ παιδίου seems more appropriate to the reply.

950: For the evidence that β_1 and Q_2 are rightly joined here see n. on p. 370.

952 περιcπᾷc: 'Distract, divert', common in Hellenistic Greek, see LSJ, who, however, give to this instance the unusual sense 'vex'. But 'mislead' seems to be required. The abusive ἱερόcυλε can be applied to a woman, (frag. 138, probably also frag. 192, and with γραῦ 1065 below), so this may be directed at Habrotonon (so LSJ). Then καὶ cύ μ]ε περιcπᾷc, ἱερόcυλε will mean 'you as well as Onesimos'. But this seems unlikely. Charisios must first see Habrotonon as having deceived him. Then he learns that Onesimos was in it too. Körte, *Gnomon* i (1952), 21, remarks that abusive ἱερόcυλε is peculiar to Menander. Too little is preserved of writing between Aristophanes and Menander for us to say when it became current. **μὴ μάχου:** Körte quotes Donatus on Ter. *Andr.* 543, 'ah neme obsecra : τῷ ἑλληνιcμῷ, μὴ λιτάνευε, μὴ μάχου, pro ne obsecres'. This is quite irrelevant to the meaning of μὴ μάχου. Donatus is explaining the rare Latin construction ne+imperative as an imitation of the normal Greek μή+imperative, of which he gives two examples: the first, μὴ λιτάνευε, translates 'ne obsecra'; the second, μὴ μάχου, which may have followed in a Greek trimeter, is not to be thought synonymous.

954 εἰ γὰρ ὤφελεν: Menander may well be the author of the similar line, frag. adesp. 584 Kock, οὗτος πατὴρ τοῦ παιδός; εἰ γὰρ ὤφελεν. Naturally Charisios hears the statement that the baby is Pamphile's with incredulity: it is so improbable that it hardly penetrates his mind. But at Habrotonon's reaffirmation, he begins to grapple with it, τίνα λόγον λέγεις; Then he passes through the bewildered logic of Παμφίλης τὸ παιδίον; ἀλλ ἦν ἐμόν, if that restoration is right, to the dawning hope of Παμφίλης; This is as finely conceived as it is simple in words.

954: Wilamowitz held to his τουτί at the beginning of the line, although Jensen and Körte agree that it is too short, on the ground that τέκνον is too poetic; yet he had defended his restoration of the word at 856 as an endearment. It has also been argued that οὑτοcί is used by Menander only of persons on the stage, and Habrotonon can hardly be thought of as carrying the baby now; but *Dysk.* 559 provides an exception to the rule.

855 νὴ τὴν φίλην Δήμητρα: Men and women alike swear by Demeter, but women always add the epithet φίλην. **τίνα λόγον λέγεις;** 'What story is this you are telling?'

956 τίνα; The restoration is not entirely convincing, but none better has been proposed. Jensen's ἐγώ; printed by Körte, is no improvement.

957 ἀλλ' ἦν ἐμ]όν: Although Jensen and Körte confidently agree in reading]ιν, this is not confirmed by the new photograph, which seems rather to show]ον. Jensen's cὺ φῃc ἔχειν is not convincing and too long. ἔχειc λέγειν is even longer.

958 ἀναπτέρου: 'Excite with hopes', 'give me wings to fly' like Ikaros. Cf. Aristophanes' witty use of the word, *Birds* 433, where the chorus say ἀνεπτέρωμαι. But fear can also lend wings, Eur. *Suppl.* 89. There are similar uses of ἀναπέτομαι: Soph *Aj.* 693 (περιχαρής) and *Ant.* 1307 (φόβῳ).

Charisios is not yet convinced, and there were twenty more lines in the scene; but little can be made of them, except that 970–2 were spoken by Habrotonon, 'how could I help doing thus and thus, and so deceiving you, until I had learned all the truth?' to which ὀρθῶc λέγειc is Charisios' assent. Whether Onesimos had sufficiently re- covered his spirits to take part in the talk, we cannot say; but he may have spoken the final lines after his master rushed into the house to find Pamphile.

ACT V

A modern audience might suppose the play to be over; the reconcilia- tion of Charisios and Pamphile can be left to the imagination, since nothing stands in its way. But there is still an act to come, an act of which the second scene is mostly preserved. In it Smikrines, unaware of the new turn events have taken, arrives to remove his daughter, and is met with insolent ridicule. The play thus gets a hilarious ending, appropriate to comedy, and Smikrines, the only objectionable character in it, suffers a most satisfactory humiliation. No doubt, as a matter of literary history, the hilarious ending and the discomfiture of Smikrines can be traced back to Old Comedy. The latter part of Aristophanes' plays frequently contained farcical scenes in which 'impostors' were driven away, or defeated adversaries made the butt of mockery. We can also adduce parallels from New Comedy, to show that it was no uncommon thing to end with a light-hearted scene in which folly received its deserts; e.g. *Dyskolos* and, if in this they are true to their originals, Plaut. *Miles Gloriosus* and *Bacchides*.

But quite apart from the question of what was traditional and might meet a Greek audience's expectations, this ending is dramatic- ally right. Although the whole play is set in motion by the affairs of Charisios and Pamphile, and they are at the centre of the action, neither has been on the stage in person for more than a couple of scenes. Their story has been played out largely in the lives of other people. And so their reconciliation, which, as has been said, might be thought by a modern to be the end and very climax of the story, is not directly represented on the stage at all. In place of that we are shown an effect of that reconciliation in the circle that revolves around them; and the two persons principally concerned, Smikrines and Onesimos, are suitably chosen to come on the stage again, since both had played large parts in all three acts preceding that in which the 'hero and heroine' had made their comparatively brief appearance.

The place in the whole play of the second scene of the last act is therefore intelligible. But another scene preceded, and sets a tantalizing problem. It probably contained about 80 lines, of which the fragmentary remains arouse and cheat the hope of divining their drift. Part of the difficulty is to see what could be demanded here by the structure of the play. The various guesses put forward may be described as offering either something that is irrelevant or something that is obvious. It is unlikely that Menander's scene was either.

There is not enough evidence to solve the problem, but we can put down what we have. First, what is the material on which to work? As set out by Körte, the scene is represented by 3 scraps of papyrus, Q, U, and β, and by the first two lines of the page H$_3$. The position of β in the codex is fortunately assured, since it overlaps with *P. Oxy.* 1236, which in its turn overlaps with the pages H$_1$ H$_2$. β is in fact from the central sheet of the quaternio, preserving a small part of each leaf, and its place on that sheet is certain. Q was placed by Sudhaus, who showed that it served to complete the two last lines of β_1 and β_2; it can hardly be chance that, by bringing Q and β together, he obtained for 950 ('verso') τί φής, Ὀν[ήϲιμ'] ἐξεπειράθη[ϲ or η[τε and for 982 ('recto') ἤδη τὸ μετὰ τα[ῦ]τα ϲκεπτέ[ον, where the letters in square brackets fill the gaps between the two pieces. Guéraud, it is true, expresses hesitation. He was unable to assure himself that if the lines on the 'verso' of Q and β were brought opposite one another, those on their 'recto' would also be opposite. But the comparison was a difficult one to make, since the fragments were so mounted that they could not be brought close together, and his doubts may be disregarded, even though similar ones were independently expressed by F. G. Allinson, *AJP* xxxvi (1915), 185. Guéraud raises a more serious objection to the placing of U in this scene. This scrap, which is of some importance, as showing the presence of Onesimos, has been assigned by Sudhaus and others to the same leaf as β_3 β_4. The reason is that the words on the recto ἀλλ' ἐξαπατ[, followed by Onesimos' reply ἀπέϲωϲε, look as if they must come from this part of the play, when it is known that Habrotonon's deceit had led to the restoration of

Charisios' happiness. In itself U 'recto' (U$_1$) might provide the beginnings of some of the later lines on β_2 but U 'verso' would then have to be associated with β_1, where no place can be found for it, as is demonstrated by Allinson, loc. cit. Thus the only home that can be found for U appears to be in the leaf to which β_3 β_4 belong. The objection raised by Guéraud is this. U$_1$ and β_3 are on this theory parts of the same page. Now the distance from the initial letters of β_3 to the fold at the centre of the sheet, beyond which lies the opposite page β_2, is 2½ cm. (Lefebvre, *Papyrus de Ménandre*, xiv) ; but the left-hand margin of U$_1$ is considerably more (at least 3 cm. to judge by the facsimile), without there being, accordingly to Guéraud, any trace of a fold. If the absence of the fold is established, this is a disturbing discrepancy, since vertical alignment in this codex is generally accurate. Although it is improbable, it is not utterly out of the question that the fragment U should belong to some other play, which contained another Onesimos, or to the conclusion of this play, after 1131 ; it is printed here with some reserve.

Interpretation of the opening of the scene has proceeded from a suggestion contained in its final lines (1060–1), namely that someone will not have (amatory) dealings with (presumably) Habrotonon. By a compelling restoration the scene begins with an address to Chairestratos about Habrotonon, and it is generally assumed that he receives a warning against making advances to her. This is conceivable, but it cannot possibly have formed the main topic of the scene, which must have contained something more positive than this. Moreover, it is not easy to understand the situation implied.

Wilamowitz argued that the speaker is Simias (621 ff. n.) whom he supposed to be a sober-minded friend of Chairestratos. Charisios intends to secure Habrotonon's freedom ; as a freedwoman she will need a προϲτάτηϲ, and it is not proper for him to act as such himself, out of respect for Pamphile ; he has therefore asked Simias to undertake the task, and the latter warns Chairestratos to keep his hands off the girl, if he wishes to retain Charisios' friendship. Wilamowitz restored vv. 979–82 *exempli gratia*

> ἔγνωμεν ἄρτι διὰ τέλουϲ ἀφειμένον
> τῆϲ Ἁβροτόνου Χαρίϲιον ταύτην ὅμωϲ
> ἐλευθερῶϲαι μαρτύρων ἐναντίον.
> Χαιρέϲτρατ᾽, ἤδη τὸ μετὰ ταῦτα ϲκεπτέον.

All this is very strange, and based on a romantic view of Habrotonon's essential innocence and purity. If Habrotonon's freedom is bought, what will she live on? Wilamowitz saw this point, but failed explicitly to imagine that Charisios provided her with an allowance, to be drawn so long as she lived chastely! Clearly she would continue her profession as a *hetaira*, but with the very important difference that she would be her own mistress, not subject to the orders of a πορνοβοςκός. There is the further difficulty that we cannot see how Simias learned of the events of the last act and of Charisios' intention to reward Habrotonon with her freedom. Wilamowitz claimed that the playwright may ask his audience to assume that anything he liked had happened during the interval between acts, and that he wisely did not waste time on explanations. It would be hard to find a parallel for such a proceeding, and Jensen more reasonably supposes that Simias and Chairestratos know nothing of recent events. His interpretation is as follows. Chairestratos had begun to take an interest in Habrotonon at the time when she was neglected by Charisios. Now he believes that Charisios, having found she had borne him a child, will make her his wife (by 'uxorem' he presumably means παλλακήν) and feels jealousy. Simias therefore exhorts him not to be disloyal to his friend. As an *exempli gratia* restoration Jensen wrote, incorporating as his first line monostich. 341,

> μὴ φεῦγ' ἑταῖρον ἐν κακοῖςι κείμενον·
> ὁρᾶς γὰρ αὐτὸν νοῦν ἔχειν. αὐτῇ λόγον
> δέδωκε πολλῶν μαρτύρων ἐναντίον,
> Χαιρέςτρατ'. ἤδη τὸ μετὰ ταῦτα ςκεπτέον,
> ὅπως διαμενεῖς ὧν Χαριςίῳ φίλος,
> οἷός ποτ' ἦςθα, πιςτός. οὐ γάρ ἐςτί που
> ἑταιρίδιον τοῦτ' οὐδὲ τὸ τυχὸν πρᾶγμ', ἐρᾷ
> ςπουδῇ δέ, καὶ παιδάριον ἤδη τέτοχ'· ὁ νοῦς
> ἐλεύθερος. πάξ. μὴ βλέπ' εἰς τὴν ψάλτριαν.

Although some details of this are impossible, it is more in accord not only with what has preceded but also with the facts of Greek social life. Friends might share the use of a ἑταιρίδιον (the diminutive is derogatory) but a man would keep a παλλακή to himself. Jensen supposes that the scene continued with the appearance of Onesimos, who informed the young men of the deception played on Charisios and its happy results. This cannot have been all, for there is no reason for taking up the audience's time with what they already know.

Sudhaus supposed the speaker to be Onesimos, who began by announcing that he had been freed—ὁρᾶτέ μ' ἔνδον ἀρτίως ἀφειμένον (perfect passive, not as for Wilamowitz middle) and continued ταύτην ἐπεὶ ςοὶ παραδίδωμι μαρτύρων ἐναντίον. He imagined that Charisios (using Onesimos as intermediary) gave Habrotonon into Chairestratos' protection, with injunctions to treat her well, and that the scene concluded with a vow by Chairestratos to 'abstain from her'. This bristles with problems. Who are the witnesses? How have Onesimos and Chairestratos got into contact? What happened in the rest of the scene?

Körte followed Wilamowitz in supposing that during the interval between the acts everyone but Smikrines had been made *au fait* with what had happened. But he adopted in part Sudhaus's method of disposing of Habrotonon, writing

$$\tau\alpha\acute{\upsilon}\tau\eta\nu\ \acute{\epsilon}\pi\epsilon\grave{\iota}$$
$$\sigma o\grave{\iota}\ \pi\alpha\rho\alpha\delta\acute{\epsilon}\delta\omega\kappa\epsilon\ \mu\alpha\rho\tau\acute{\upsilon}\rho\omega\nu\ \acute{\epsilon}\nu\alpha\nu\tau\acute{\iota}o\nu.$$

For him the speaker is Simias, and during the interval Charisios has freed Habrotonon and put her under Chairestratos' protection. He has no suggestion about how the rest of the scene can have been filled up.

Webster, *StM* 40, thought that when the scene begins Simias and Chairestratos are unaware of the changed situation. Simias, whom he believed to be a slave, Chairestratos' former *paidagogus* (see n. on 621 ff.), is persuading his master to keep off Habrotonon, who is now seen to have a closer relation with Charisios than had been thought. Onesimos comes on the scene and tells them the truth. This is a more possible situation, and it may be noted in its favour that S. Zini, *Il linguaggio dei personaggi nelle commedie di Menandro*, has argued that the exclamation $\pi\acute{\alpha}\xi$ and the word $\acute{\epsilon}\tau\alpha\iota\rho\acute{\iota}\delta\iota o\nu$ are better suited to a slave than to a gentleman. On the other hand the greater part of the scene cannot have been taken up by the posting of Chairestratos in what the audience already knows. There is little probability in Allinson's idea (loc. cit. 199) that the vocative $X\alpha\iota\rho\acute{\epsilon}\sigma\tau\rho\alpha\tau\epsilon$ was in a *reported* speech, and does not imply Chairestratos' presence on the stage. But a possibility not to be overlooked, and in fact recently revived by Webster, *C.R.* n.s. xv (1965), 17, who quotes Leo, *Der Monolog*, 102, is that the scene opens with a monologue by Chairestratos, who apostrophizes himself, as do Demeas at *Samia* 326, 349 and (perhaps a close parallel) Moschion in *Sikyonios* 397 ff. This is to my mind the most likely explanation. Perhaps Chairestratos said something like this: 'When he neglected her, I cast eyes on her: now the situation is the opposite of what it was. You must see to it that you remain a loyal friend. This is a serious affair between them. Keep your eyes off her. And first of all, let her have a private talk with her "dearest, sweetest Charisios".' A guess about what followed will be found in the note on 1018 ff.

984 $\mathring{\eta}\sigma\theta\alpha$: This is a probable rather than certain conjecture for C's $o\mathring{\iota}\sigma\theta\alpha$, cf. the reverse error, 337. $o\mathring{\iota}\acute{o}\varsigma\ \pi o\tau$'—$o\mathring{\iota}\sigma\theta\alpha$, $\pi\iota\sigma\tau\acute{o}\varsigma$ is *per se* possible; but I see no reason for the aposiopesis.

985 τοῦτο is the subject ('she') attracted to the gender of the predicate. τὸ τυχόν must have been followed by some noun. Sudhaus's παίγνιον can be supported by Anaxandrides frag. 9 K, ἦν ἐκείνη τις φίλη Ἄντεια—καὶ τοῦθ᾽ ἡμέτερον ἦν παίγνιον. For Jensen's πρᾶγμα, 'creature', cf. Antiphanes frag. 7 K, ἄμαχος, πρᾶγμα μεῖζον ἢ δοκεῖς, and perhaps Xen. Cyr. vi. 1. 36.

986: Körte prints Wilamowitz's cπουδῇ δὲ καὶ παιδάριον ἥδ᾽ ἔcωcε· ὁ νοῦς ἐλεύθερος. In this cπουδῇ seems over-emphatic, ἥδε (which ought to be deictic) is dubious Greek, while ἔcωcε is not true: Habrotonon may have claimed the child, she certainly had not saved it. But Wilamowitz had a soft spot for Habrotonon. Guéraud supports Sudhaus in reading ημμ rather than ηδε or ηδι. ὁ νοῦς is in itself not improbable, cf. frag. 722, εἰ δ᾽ ἡ τύχη τὸ cῶμα κατεδουλώcατο, ὅ γε νοῦς ὑπάρχει τοῖς τρόποις ἐλεύθερος, Sophocles frag. 854 N (940 Pearson), εἰ cῶμα δοῦλον, ἀλλ᾽ ὁ νοῦς ἐλεύθερος, Eur. Helena 730.

987 πάξ: 'Enough said!', only here in Menander; also Diphilos frag. 96 K, Ter. Heaut. 290, 717, Plaut. MG 808. Schwartz's μὴ βλέπ᾽ εἰς τὴν ψάλτριαν and Webster's μὴ βλέπ᾽ εἰς ταύτην ἔτι are both possible, cf. Sikyonios 397, νῦν οὐδὲ προcβλέψαι cε, Μοcχίων . . . πρὸς τὴν κόρην. But Guéraud denies that there was any apostrophe after π of βλεπεις, and omission of the apostrophe is rare in this papyrus. Parenthetic βλέπεις is read by some (as an emendation) in Sikyonios 188. But the construction μὴ βλέπεις, 'surely you are not looking', is also possible here (cf. e.g. Sam. 530), and βλέπω is often used by Menander with a noun, adjective, or verb to indicate the nature of the look, e.g. Aspis 454 ἐκφορὰν βλέπει, Dysk. 147 φιλάνθρωπον βλέπειν, Epitr. 398, ἁρπάζειν βλέπει.

988–9: Wilamowitz, arguing that τὸν φίλτατον must be a different person from τὸν γλυκύτατον, restored κατὰ μόνας Χαιρέστρατον τὸν φίλτατον καὶ τὸν γλυκύτατον Cιμίαν οὐ δεῖ προcειπεῖν: he seems to have overlooked the fact that Simias is, by his account, the speaker. The sense is also hardly compelling. Webster rightly maintains that the two adjectives may refer to the same person (K–G ii. 612), and prefers to adopt Sudhaus's Χαρίcιον at the end of 988. The sense 'she must have a private talk with her dearest, sweetest Charisios' is not unreasonable, if Chairestratos is unaware of what has transpired in the last act.

1003–17: Nothing can be made of these scraps. There were many proverbial expressions in which a wolf or wolves occurred (1006, see LSJ), several being concerned with cheated expectations, as λύκος χανὼν ἀπέρχεται, Aspis 372.

1018 ff.: A possible interpretation of this fragment is that Charisios, indignant at the deception practised on him, is disinclined to reward Habrotonon by purchasing her freedom: Onesimos urges her claims to recognition (so Allinson, *AJP* xxxvi [1915], 199). Onesimos had earlier expected that the intrigue would win Habrotonon freedom, and she had hoped it; it would be not unlike Menander to baulk those expectations temporarily, and the liberation of Habrotonon (and perhaps Onesimos) would be more dramatic if only reached after some difficulty and struggle. Such a development would supply the tension so lacking in most suggestions about the subject of this scene.

1060–1 are two of the most puzzling lines in the play, and no satisfactory explanation of them has been put forward. τοιαυτηϲί surely refers to Habrotonon, but nothing else is agreed—who is the speaker (Wilamowitz chose Simias, van Leeuwen Charisios, others Chairestratos), who is, or is not, ϲώφρων (Habrotonon? Charisios? Chairestratos?), what characteristic is meant by τοιαυτηϲί, why should the speaker say that he will steer clear of Habrotonon? No combination of answers seems to yield any plausible sense, and it would waste time to discuss them in detail.

(ii) **1062–1131**: *Smikrines (with Sophrone) and Onesimos* (enters 1088)

1062: Smikrines enters in mid-conversation with Sophrone, a name given elsewhere to an old family nurse (Ter. *Eun.* and *Phormio*, and presumably by Menander himself in *Heros*). Possibly, as Wilamowitz suggests, the audience had been prepared for her appearance by something that Smikrines said in his last scene with Pamphile, e.g.: 'I shall have to get old Sophrone to help me to persuade her.' Perhaps Sophrone had been privy to the child's exposure, and some have supposed that her function in this last scene was to confirm its identity. But that identity is not in any real doubt; her evidence could bring only marginal confirmation—and so would be of no dramatic interest. I believe, moreover, that the part was played by a *muta persona*, see n. on 1119–20.

1065 καταφαγεῖν: Cf. *Odyssey* iii. 315, μή τοι κατὰ πάντα φάγωϲι κτήματα, frag. 287 K–T, εἴ τιϲ πατρῴαν παραλαβὼν γῆν καταφάγοι. Smikrines shows himself to be less concerned for his daughter than for the safety of her dowry; he wishes to be sure of getting it back if the marriage is to break up. To mend the metre the change of ἀλλά to ἀλλ' ἦ (Körte, Wilamowitz) has generally been accepted. The alternative ἀλλὰ περιμείνω (Croenert, Headlam) introduces a dubious aorist, but cf. Soph. *El.* 81, θέλειϲ μείνωμεν αὐτοῦ; Smikrines regards the dowry as his, because in the event of a divorce it must be returned to him.

1066 λόγους λέγω: 'Do nothing but talk' (cf. Eur. *Med.* 321): contrast λόγον λέγειν (955, Ar. *Ach.* 299), 'pitch a tale'.   χρηστόν: Ironical as in *Sam.* 408.

1068 ὀξυλαβῆcαι: 'Strike quickly', a rare word, also found in Xen. *Hell.* vii. 4. 27.

1069 κρίνομαι πρὸς Cωφρόνην: Wilamowitz argues that Cωφρόνην is an error for Παμφίλην; his reason, that Smikrines could not put himself on a level with his slave but must take her agreement for granted, seems to overlook the possibility of sarcasm: 'Am I at law with Sophrone?' The meaning, however, is probably not this but: 'Am I put on trial before Sophrone as my judge?', see LSJ s.v. πρός C. II. 7. It must be confessed that a reader may find the reference to Sophrone in the third person to be oddly sandwiched between the second persons, λαλῆc and μετάπεισον. But stage action could make it clear. Smikrines' remonstrance with Sophrone ends with the threat οἰμώξει μακρὰ ἂν ἔτι λαλῆc τι. They will have been stationary during most of 1062–8. Smikrines now puts himself into motion again, with Sophrone behind him, and as they proceed he speaks to himself. On arriving at Charisios' door, he turns to Sophrone as she follows, and thinking that they will shortly be inside gives her her orders: 'Persuade Pamphile to change her mind, when you see her.'

1071 γάρ: 'Persuade her to change her mind, for (if you do not) etc.' For the placing of the post-positive γάρ after the vocative, which would show that in such a case at least our conventional commas round vocatives misrepresent Greek utterance, there seems to be no better parallel than the doubtful πάτερ δὲ of *Pap. Did.* i. 33. Hence E. Fraenkel, 'Noch einmal Kolon u. Satz', *SB Bay. Akad. Wiss.* (1965), 49, revives a suggestion made, but later abandoned, by Wilamowitz, namely to read Cωφρόνην γάρ. But the position of γάρ, in the second clause instead of the first, is then strange, and if the meaning is 'persuade her, *because* otherwise I shall drown Sophrone . . .' one would have expected Smikrines to address Sophrone throughout, not momentarily refer to her in the third person. Fraenkel shows that vocatives normally follow or precede a word or phrase that is emphasized. Here οὕτω τί μοι ἀγαθὸν γένοιτο may be emphasized. In usual prose order γάρ would be placed after οὕτω. Colloquially it is added as an afterthought, and if the text is right has here found a place after the vocative.

1073 τὴν νύκτα: It is supposed that evening is now coming on: it will be night by the time they are on their way home.

1074: Headlam objected to κἀγώ as unnecessarily emphatic.

1075 ἡ θύρα παιητέα: Normally a door was not bolted in the daytime, cf. Theopropides' surprise, Plaut. *Most.* 444, occlusa ianua interdius. We may suppose, if we like, that Charisios (Wilamowitz) or Onesimos (Capps) had purposely fastened the door to keep Smikrines out, should he come. But Menander may not have expected anyone to speculate on the reasons for the door's being bolted. The dramatic purpose is to allow the following scene to take place in sight of the audience; Smikrines would otherwise have walked into his daughter's house without knocking, just as he did at 163.　　παιητέα: 'Bang on the door': the word may suit Smikrines' bad temper; the usual verb for knocking on a door is κόπτειν. But παιητέα δ' ἐϲθ' ἡ θύρα recurs at *Aspis* 499 in the mouth of Kleostratos, who is not in the least angry; see the note there.

1081 λογιϲτικοῦ: Not 'practised in arithmetic', but 'one who uses his brains, calculating', cf. Plato's τὸ λογιϲτικὸν τῆϲ ψυχῆϲ, *Rep.* 439 d, and Xen. *Hell.* v. 2. 28, οὐ μέντοι λογιϲτικόϲ γε οὐδὲ πάνυ φρόνιμοϲ. The unusualness of the word increases its irony.

1082–3 τό θ' ἅρπαϲμα: Jensen and Guéraud agree that Lefebvre was mistaken in seeing a dicolon after ϲπουδή. Believing that there was a change of speaker at that point, Wilamowitz altered θ' to δ' (as would be necessary); he interpreted ἅρπαϲμα to refer to Charisios' supposed making away with Pamphile's dowry. On this last point he was probably right, only he failed to recognize the irony of the phrase τό θ' ἅρπαϲμα θαυμαϲτὸν οἷον. Onesimos, pretending to approve of Smikrines' conduct, says: 'And (Heaven help us!) this malversation is something extraordinary.' The view that by ἅρπαϲμα Onesimos means Smikrines' removal of his daughter is surely wrong: such an opprobrious word is out of place in his mocking approval. In 1083 πρὸϲ θεῶν καὶ δαιμόνων (for this adjuration in a protest cf. *Dysk.* 622) must be given to Smikrines, although C shows no change of speaker. H. Fränkel's proposal (*AJP* lxii [1941], 354) to give the whole of ἔγωγε . . . δαιμόνων to Smikrines is unconvincing; moreover, he disregards the dicolon before καὶ μάλα.

1084 ff.: It need hardly be said that it would be absurd to look for any expression of Menander's own opinions in Onesimos' philosophizing. He uses scraps of various current ideas with the object of exasperating Smikrines. This is a comic scene not a sermon. A. Barigazzi, *La formazione spirituale di Menandro*, 198–212, surveys the many attempts that have been made to find philosophy in it, and himself attempts to associate it with Aristotelianism.

1088 ὅμοιον εἰπεῖν: Lit. 'to give a number is all one', i.e. 'the exact number does not matter', 'to give a round number'; the phrase is Hellenistic. For ὅμοιον, 'it is all one', cf. Aesch. *Agam.* 1403, Hdt. viii. 80. 2. A speaker at Ar. *Eccl.* 1132 thinks that there were more than 30,000 citizens in the city: the number of *male citizens* of Athens at the census conducted by Demetrios of Phaleron was 21,000; [Dem.] xxv. 50 estimates them at 20,000 (Gomme, *Population of Athens*, 3); since Athens was a state of more than average size, rationalists may suppose Onesimos to give a figure for average population. But it was so usual to reckon a city's size by its adult male citizen population (figures for the whole population would not exist), and the concept of a 'city of 10,000' as a norm for democracy was so common in the fourth century (H. Schaefer, *Historia*, x [1961], 292), that Onesimos' mention of 30,000 would probably strike the audience as meaning adult males and as being therefore an absurd overstatement. '1,000 cities' is also an exaggeration, but perhaps not one that would be detected, see Ar. *Wasps* 707, εἰσίν γε πόλεις χίλιαι αἱ νῦν τὸν φόρον ἡμῖν ἀπάγουσιν.

1090 ἐπιτρίβουσιν: Cf. frag. 796, ἐπιτρίβουσι δ' ἡμᾶς οἱ θεοὶ μάλιστα τοὺς γήμαντας. Traditionally the gods send both good and evil, *Iliad* xxiv. 527–8, Hesiod, *Theog.* 219.

1091 ff.: The idea that if the gods concerned themselves with human beings their life would be a laborious one is Epicurean, e.g. Cic. *ND* i. 52, 'siue in ipso mundo deus inest aliquis qui regat, qui gubernet . . . hominum commoda uitasque tueatur, ne ille est implicatus molestis negotiis et operosis', but not necessarily solely Epicurean. At any rate there is nothing Epicurean about the sequel that the gods do care for the world, but by the mediation of men's own characters. This is an adaptation of a belief (on which see Rohde, *Psyche*, ii. 316, Eng. trans. p. 514) that every man had associated with him a daimon, or spirit, that was the vehicle of his fate. The identification of this daimon with a man's own character is as old as Herakleitos, frag. 119, ἦθος ἀνθρώπῳ δαίμων, and there is something very like Menander's phrase in [Epicharmos] frag. 258 Kaibel, ὁ τρόπος ἀνθρώποισι δαίμων ἀγαθός, οἷς δὲ καὶ κακός. A different line of thought about the daimon, making it always beneficent, is represented in frag. 714 (q.v.), and is closer to the developments found in later Stoic writers, but Seneca writes in *ep. mor.* xli. 2 'sacer intra nos spiritus sedet, malorum bonorumque nostrorum obseruator et custos. hic prout a nobis tractatus est, ita nos ipse tractat.' Onesimos' philosophy here will not stand up. He has confused two ideas: (1) a man's character brings him good or ill fortune, (2) man has in him a guardian spirit which will reward good deeds, but punish offences.

1090 πῶς; In C there is a dicolon before this, indicating a change of speaker, but the paragraphus under the line was omitted, as again at 1104. The division of speakers adopted here (with most editors) seems certainly right (C has no dicolon after πως). Del Corno follows Coppola in giving 1091 to Onesimos, finding its tone unsuitable to Smikrines' fury; it is then difficult to account for γάρ.

1092 οὐκ ἆρα φροντίζουϲιν κτλ.: Frag. 752 Kock runs οὐκ ἆρα φροντίζει τιϲ ἡμῶν ἢ μόνοϲ θεόϲ. It is quoted by Theophilos, Bishop of Antioch in the late second century A.D., and may be Menander's line altered, consciously or unconsciously, by Theophilos or before him, under the influence of Jewish and Christian thought.

1084 φρούραρχον: Just 'captain' or 'commandant', without any thought of a φρουρά for him to command (not, for example, a 'garrison' of our desires and passions), but nevertheless a natural word to use in an age when foreign garrisons were common and their commanders had the specific charge of preventing 'subversive movements' and keeping a right-thinking government in power. Even Athens was for periods controlled by a Macedonian garrison at Munichia.

1099 ἄτοπον: 'Bad', cf. *Dysk.* 288 n.

1102: The absence of the article with ἀνδρόϲ emphasizes the relationship of husband and wife, cf. *Dysk.* 240 n.

1104 θεᾷ: 'Are you watching this spectacle?', presumably addressed to Sophrone, although E. Fraenkel, *Mus. Helv.* xxiv (1967), 192, supposes an imaginary spectator to be meant. ὁρᾷϲ and ἰδού are common in such situations, θεᾷ is unexampled and surprising, but see 511 n.

1106 τοῦτόν τιϲ ἄλλοϲ: The authority of Wilamowitz has caused editors to write τίϲ interrogative; he stated that the indefinite τιϲ would necessarily be followed by ἤ not οὐ. Cf. also *Pap. Ant.* 15. 1.

1108 ταὐτόματον ἀποϲέϲωκε: Onesimos is not satisfied with the familiar ἡ τύχη, but uses a grander word. One would like to think that he was making play with the Aristotelian distinction by which τύχη was a subdivision of τὸ αὐτόματον, applicable only where a rational cause of action led to an unexpected and unintended good result: the generic word τὸ αὐτόματον must be used for the good fortune of an irrational creature. Smikrines here is acting irrationally. But this may be reading too much into Onesimos' words.

Popular ideas of the relation between ταὐτόματον and τύχη were confused and fluid. Sometimes they were identified. Then because τύχη was elevated into a divine power of Luck, to which one might pray, ταὐτόματον was used for 'mere chance', e.g. Philemon frag. 137 K:

> οὐκ ἔστιν ἡμῶν οὐδεμία Τύχη θεός,
> οὐκ ἔστιν, ἀλλὰ ταὐτόματον. ὃ γίγνεται
> ὡς ἔτυχ' ἑκάστῳ, προσαγορεύεται τύχη.

But it could also itself become a supernatural power, *Sam.* 163:

> ταὐτόματόν ἐστιν ὡς ἔοικέ που θεός,
> cῴζει τε πολλὰ τῶν ἀοράτων πραγμάτων.

In the previous generation Timoleon dedicated an altar at Syracuse to Αὐτοματία, to whom he ascribed his successes (Plut. *Timol.* c. 36). **καταλαμβάνεις**: 'You arrive to find'.

1112 ἀφεῖco: Perfect middle (like πέπαυco, *Sam.* 350, 612, Dem. xxiv. 64), 'drop your complaints for good and all'. The belief, which has the authority of Jebb on *Antigone* 1165, that the word must be passive, 'you stand relieved of these charges' (so LSJ), and therefore unsuited to the context, has led to a widespread acceptance of Lefebvre's emendation ἀφίεco. This is not only unnecessary but, if a broken anapaest is to be avoided, involves an improbable short ι, cf. *Dysk.* 111 n.

1114 παχύδερμοc: The word is not found again in the meaning 'insensitive, stupid' until Lucian, *Timon* 23, ἀπειρόκαλοc καὶ παχύδερμοc, but cf. Plaut. *MG* 235, 'elephanti corio circumtentust . . . neque habet plus sapientiae quam lapis'. Wilamowitz suggests that Onesimos makes a retort to the word μαcτιγία, 'even if my skin has been thickened by beating, you are thick-skinned too'. But καὶ cύ may mean 'you are stupid as well as other people to whom you have thought yourself superior'.   **ἦcθα**: 'turn out to be', Goodwin, *MT* 39. Even if Onesimos has been manumitted, his language is remarkably bold.

1116 πεντάμηνα: In Attic such compounds are made with πεντε-, Meisterhans³ 158, Rutherford, *New Phrynichus*, p. 490, but πεντα- predominates in the κοινή. One cannot be sure which Menander wrote. A premature child born at five months that lived would be a prodigy (τέρας).

1119–20: C marks off Cωφρόνη and αιcθανειγε by dicola and has a paragraphus below 1119; the intention must be to assign these words to Smikrines. But αἰcθάνει γε in his mouth is meaningless: it must be Onesimos who says to Sophrone 'do you see it?', thereby avoiding completing his sentence with, e.g., ἐβιάcατο. Sophrone knew all along about Pamphile's misfortune at the Tauropolia; she now learns who its author was. Perhaps the dicola were intended to mark that Onesimos turned from Smikrines to Sophrone and back again, and once more to her with αἰcθάνει γε, the paragraphus alone being a mistake.

1120 ff.: The assignment of speeches is not easy. That adopted by Körte must be wrong. (1) The quotation from Euripides' *Auge* in 1123–4 and the subsequent threat to recite a whole speech must belong to Onesimos, not Sophrone; they are part and parcel of his impertinence towards Smikrines, and suit his previous characterization as a man with a smattering of education. As the reaction of the old nurse to the discovery that her child's misfortunes have been happily ended they are quite out of place. (2) The phrase τί μῶροc εἶ; (1124) must be addressed to Smikrines, not to Sophrone. The fact that μῶροc is once used as feminine in tragedy (Eur. *Med.* 61) is inadequate support for such a use here; moreover μῶροc means 'dull, stupid' and admirably fits Smikrines, who is slow to see the truth, but is not applicable to one who unexpectedly bewilders you with a quotation from tragedy.

If we follow the indications of the papyrus, it will be necessary, having given the quotation to Onesimos, to assign τί μῶροc εἶ; to Sophrone. But 1119–20 show that the papyrus is not always to be trusted, and I believe that here too it is mistaken, and that the phrase belongs to Onesimos. Sophrone in fact has no speaking part at all in this scene, and will have been played by a super. Observe her complete silence when she arrives with her master, although there are pauses in his speech (1069 n.); observe too that when Smikrines addresses her here, it is Onesimos who replies (1122–3, as argued above; 1128, the same will be true if οἶδεν is the correct reading). A probable implication of this is that the third actor was wanted to play another character, perhaps Charisios, who will have appeared upon the scene. One may guess that the discomfited Smikrines was finally brought to share his son-in-law's rejoicing.

If this is right, we can see how Menander extracted dramatic profit from restriction to three actors. Sophrone will receive the news with gestures of joy (cf. note on παθαινομένη, 1127); she may be imagined to be too overcome for speech. Smikrines' failure to get any answers out of her then serves to increase his frustrated and bewildered irritation; and Onesimos, by answering for her, is doubly annoying.

In 1120 the papyrus makes Sophrone answer νή (ναί edd., but affirmative νή is now confirmed by *Karch.* 33 n., *Sam.* 385) to the question Onesimos puts to her. It is perhaps possible that a super was allowed on occasion to utter a single word, but it is also possible that she nodded and Onesimos translated her assent into the word. On the interpretation of 1117–31 see *PCPS* N.S. xiii (1967), 44–6.

1121 ἀναγνωρισμός, for the more usual ἀναγνώρισις, is found in Arist.

Poetics 1452ᵃ16. Onesimos favours nouns in -μός, cf. 453 βιασμός, 893 βρυχηθμός, τιλμός, *Entretiens Hardt*, xvi. 134.

1123 ἡ φύϲιϲ κτλ.: This quotation is shown by 1125 to be from Euripides' *Auge* (see n. on *Heros* θη 'recto'). This play was particularly apposite if according to it, as seems probable, Herakles ravished Auge while she was taking part in a night festival, and left a ring with her; this ring later enabled him to recognize as his the child she bore. The first line is frequently cited (frag. 920 Nauck), once as from 'New Comedy', i.e. from this passage. It was neatly parodied by Anaxandrides (apud Arist. *E.N.* 1152ᵃ23), ἡ πόλιϲ ἐβούλεθ', ᾗ νόμων οὐδὲν μέλει.   **ἐπ' αὐτῷ τῷδε**: To bear children.   **γυνὴ . . . ἔφυ**: Probably 'a woman is born for this' rather than 'she was born a woman', cf. Eur. frag. 322, ἔρωϲ γὰρ ἀργὸν κἀπὶ τοιούτοιϲ ἔφυ, and *Med.* 928, γυνὴ δὲ θῆλυ κἀπὶ δακρύοιϲ ἔφυ. The latter line was spoken by Medea, and so Auge may have spoken this in her speech of self-defence to Athena, from which frag. 266 comes.

1124 τί μῶροϲ εἶ; Wilamowitz thought it impossible that Sophrone could address her master so rudely. This cannot, however, be confidently added to the reasons for not assigning the phrase to her. Old slaves may take liberties and the *paedagogus* of Soph. *El.* addresses Orestes and Elektra as ὦ πλεῖϲτα μῶροι (1326).

1127 παθαινομένη: 'With your display of emotion'. The word is otherwise found only in later authors, e.g. Plut. *Mor.* 447 e, τοὺϲ ῥήτοραϲ ἐν ταῖϲ ἀριϲτοκρατίαιϲ οἱ ἄρχοντεϲ οὐκ ἐῶϲι παθαίνεϲθαι, ibid. 1101 a of maudlin sentiment, 713 a of emotional playing of the αὐλόϲ, Lucian, *Erotes* 29, Dio Cassius li. 12, and other passages collected by Headlam on Herondas v. 29. Here it must refer to Sophrone's actions. Note that it is not at all appropriate to the mocking speech that Körte puts in her mouth, τραγικὴν ἐρῶ ῥῆϲιν κτλ.

Hesychios has παθαίνεϲθαι· δεινοπαθεῖν (complain exaggeratedly) and Photios παθαίνεϲθαι· οὐ (? τὸ Gomme) δεινοπαθεῖν. Naber thought these entries derived from an accidentally reversed note of some Atticist who recommended the use of δεινοπαθεῖν (Dem. xl. 53) instead of the Hellenistic παθαίνεϲθαι.   **ϲφόδρ' οἶϲθα**: 'You know very well' is an unparalleled phrase, ϲφόδρα being normally used only with verbs that admit of degree. But cf. Plato, *Phaedo* 73 a, οὐ γὰρ ϲφόδρα . . . μέμνημαι, Ar. *Thesm.* 613, ϲκόπει . . . ϲφόδρα.

1128: C omitted a word (or two words) occupying one long (or two short) syllables in this line. Although the facsimile seems to show οιδα (so Lefebvre), Guéraud says that οιδε is as likely (Jensen's transcript agrees) and that the space left is excessive for a dicolon (as the facsimile seems to confirm). Accordingly he read οἶδεν; de Falco, accepting

this, fills the line with ⟨ἀλλ'⟩ εὖ ἴςθι (an alternative would be οἶδε·
τ⟨οῦτ'⟩ εὖ ἴςθι). This reading has been adopted in OCT as palaeographically slightly superior and as suiting the view that Sophrone has
maintained silence since her one word νή (if it is hers) in 1120;
Onesimos still does all the talking. Gomme thought the subject ἡ
γραῦς for the verb ςυνῆκε was unnecessary if οἶδεν had dispensed with
a subject; he therefore preferred to read οἶδα and to add νῦν rather
than Wilamowitz's πάντ'.

The mention of Euripides' *Auge* serves to make Smikrines see what
Onesimos has been telling him—that his daughter had borne an
illegitimate child, but he does not immediately take in the further
and more improbable point that his son-in-law was its father. In his
anger at the idea of his daughter's shame he turns on Sophrone, who
is showing delight. 'Your display of emotion turns me to anger—for
you know very well what Onesimos is now saying' (i.e. in 1123–6).
To which Onesimos replies: 'The old woman understood me before
you did.'

1130–1: In accordance with the view that Sophrone does not speak,
Sudhaus has been followed in assigning 1130 to Onesimos; this is
suitable since it is a reply to πάνδεινον λέγεις, which is undoubtedly
addressed to him.   εὐτύχημα (also *Sam.* 618) is, as Wilamowitz
noted, not an everyday word (not in the orators, nor elsewhere in
Comedy). It suits Onesimos' style of talking. Sudhaus has also been
followed in giving 1131 to Smikrines, in spite of the fact that there is
no dicolon visible at the end of 1130; in the absence of the sequel, one
cannot be certain here.

Nearly 160 verses of the last act have passed. There cannot be much
more to come. Some have supposed that Sophrone gave evidence to
confirm that the child really was that exposed by Pamphile. Since
the rules of drama and of courts of law are not identical, I think this
unlikely. The audience are adequately satisfied of the baby's identity,
and need no supplementary evidence from her. If, as I have argued,
she is a *persona muta*, perhaps Charisios himself appeared, for there
would be room for a third speaking character, and invited his father-
in-law to stay for a party to celebrate the good news.

Fragment 9. This line was frequently quoted in antiquity, sometimes as
Menander's, but only once (Orion vii. 8) with the name of the play,
and then as from *Georgos*, but with a marginal note ἐκ τῶν ἀποτρεπόντων (*sic*) in the same hand as the main text. It may have stood in
either play or in both. It would be easier to find a use for it in *Georgos*
than in *Epitrepontes*; Gomme guessed that it might have been addressed
to Smikrines either in the scene that breaks off at 665, or after 1131.

ἂν μὴ προϲποῇ: 'If you pretend that it is not so', cf. Thuc. iii. 47. 4, δεῖ δέ, εἰ καὶ ἠδίκηϲαν, μὴ προϲποιεῖϲθαι. Philemon had the lines (frag. 23 K),

> ὁ λοιδορῶν γάρ, ἂν ὁ λοιδορούμενος
> μὴ προϲπόηται, λοιδορεῖται λοιδορῶν,

which, if at all typical, would not make us regret his loss. But a quotation cannot be judged out of its context; and the lines may have been intentionally absurd.

Fragment 10. These lines also cannot be placed. Wilamowitz suggested that they were spoken in the last scene by Smikrines to justify his continued indignation, but ὀδυνᾶϲθαι seems inappropriate. Gomme more plausibly supposed them to be lines in Smikrines' argument with Pamphile: she had said that it would be torment to leave Charisios and he answered that it is better to suffer pain, as all human beings must, than the disgrace of ridicule and insult.

Wilamowitz guessed that the two final lines of the play were

> ἡ δ᾽ εὐπάτειρα φιλόγελώϲ τε παρθένος
> Νίκη μεθ᾽ ἡμῶν εὐμενὴϲ ἔποιτ᾽ ἀεί.

They are quoted as from an unnamed comedy by the scholiast on Aristides, Dindorf p. 301. He also guessed, as has been strikingly confirmed, that they concluded many of Menander's plays; for the evidence see *Dyskolos* 968 n. The second line was adapted by Dioskoros, the owner of the Cairo papyrus, in one of his own poems, and Wilamowitz inferred that he had borrowed it from one of the plays in that codex (*SB Berl.* 1916, 66).

HEROS

C *P. Cairensis* 43227. See intro. pp. 42–6.

P. E. Sonnenburg, *Rh. Mus.* lxix (1914), 80 ff. ; G. Jachmann, *Hermes*, lvii (1922), 107 ff. ; A. W. Gomme, *CR* lxi (1947), 72 ff. ; A. Barigazzi, *Athenaeum*, xxxiv (1956), 325 ff.

Plot

The scene is laid in Ptelea, an Attic deme of which the situation is uncertain (22 n.), and on the stage are represented the houses of Laches, married to Myrrhine, and Pheidias, a young man whose father does not appear in the play, and may have been dead or abroad. When Myrrhine had married Laches, some eighteen years previously, she did not know him to be the father of twins that she had borne as the result of a rape. The children, Gorgias and Plangon, had been given to Tibeios, a freedman shepherd of Ptelea, to bring up. Falling on evil times, he had been forced to borrow money from Laches, and when he died Gorgias and Plangon entered Laches' service to pay off the debt. Plangon was ravished by Pheidias, and became pregnant. Daos, one of Laches' slaves, fell in love with her and hoped that she would be given to him; in order to further this desire, he represented himself as father of her child, to Myrrhine's great distress and anger. The further complications of the plot are unknown (for guesses see p. 398), except that on Laches' return home from abroad the true relations were discovered, and Pheidias married Plangon, now found to be a suitable match for him.

Hypothesis

The metrical hypothesis is, like that of *Dyskolos* (q.v.), of twelve lines but, unlike that of *Dyskolos*, does not claim Aristophanes the grammarian as its author. Its reliability as a guide to the plot is not above suspicion. The hypothesis to *Dyskolos* is inaccurate, and here doubt attaches to the statement in line 3 that the man who had taken charge of the twins (ἐπιτρόπῳ) had *pledged* them (ὑπέθετο, in Classical Greek ὑπέθηκε) against a debt; nothing is said of such a pledge in 28–36 (see n. on 36). Nor did Daos *believe* (διαλαβών is late Greek in this sense, exemplified in Josephus etc.) that the girl was a slave.

2 ἔδωκε: Capps supposes that Myrrhine will, like other unwilling mothers in New Comedy, have exposed the twins. The hypothesis may, of course, have misrepresented the play, but Capps's guess is gratuitous.

3: The active γαμεῖν is normally used only of the bridegroom, the middle γαμεῖcθαι of the bride; but γαμεῖν of the bride is found in the New Testament.

9: The writer unfortunately does not specify what it was that the children's mother did not know. She may have been ignorant that they were her children (Jensen) or, as is more likely, that it was Pheidias, not Daos, who had seduced her daughter (Sonnenburg etc).

Dramatis personae

The list of characters will be, as for *Dyskolos*, in the order of their appearance. This may be inferred from the order of the first three names. After the scene between Daos and Getas, the hero will have spoken a 'deferred' prologue (intro. p. 20), to put the audience in the possession of facts necessary to their enjoyment of the play. A hero was to the Greeks a being intermediate between god and man. By origin some heroes had been minor deities, others had been men of note, others were inventions, like the eponymous heroes of tribes and demes. But most of them, at least, were thought of as having been living men, whose spirits survived at their tombs, where offerings were made. It is characteristic of the hero to be helpful to men, and in the words of S. Eitrem, 'nothing is too humble, nothing too elevated or difficult for him; he helps in sickness as in love, in family affairs as in those of the state . . . he knows hidden secrets and reveals the future' (*RE* viii. 1112). The hero of this play may have been a tutelary spirit of Laches' household, such as we meet in Kallimachos, *epigr.* 24, cf. E. Rohde, *Psyche*², i. 197 (E.T. p. 137) but it is possible that he was a less private figure, perhaps even Pteleon, the eponymous hero of the deme. In *Aulularia* a postponed prologue is spoken by the Lar Familiaris, who has been thought to replace a hero in the original play (F. Leo, *Plaut. Forsch.* 211 n. 2, W. E. J. Kuiper, *The Greek Aulularia*, 36); but Wilamowitz, *Schiedsgericht*, 136 n., *Glaube d. Hellenen*, ii. 16, enjoins caution and Webster, *StM* 123, argues for Hestia. See also W. Ludwig, *Philologus*, cv (1961), 46–7, and W. Kraus, *Serta Phil. Aenopontana* (1962), 186, who favours an anonymous θεὸc ἐφέcτιοc.

The other characters are easily identifiable, because their names are conventionally assigned to certain types. Myrrhine is a middle-aged matron in *Perik.*, *Dysk.*, *Georg.*, Plautus, *Casina*, Terence, *Hecyra*; here she will be the mother of the twins, and Laches (an elderly man, as in *Fab. incert.*, *Perinthia*, *Kitharistes*, *Plokion*, Terence, *Hecyra*) her husband. Pheidias is a young man, as in *Kolax*, *Phasma*, and will be the seducer.

HEROS

Sophrone is the name of an old nurse, as in *Epitr.*, Terence, *Eunuchus*, *Phormio*. Sangarios, named after the river Sangarios or Sagaris in Anatolia, is probably a slave, like Sanga in Terence, *Eunuchus* (776), Sagaristio in Plautus, *Persa*, and Sagarinus in *Stichus* (cf. K. Schmidt, *Hermes*, xxxvii [1902], 204); he might belong to either household, that of Laches or that of Pheidias.

Getas and Daos are common slave-names; the former name comes from the Γέται, a Thracian tribe which supplied many slaves, the latter is probably Phrygian, *Aspis* 206, 242. Getas may be a slave from Pheidias' household. Whether he played any part after the first scene is not known. He may have been a πρόσωπον προτατικόν, a character who is used only for the exposition, after which he disappears. Chaireas in *Dyskolos* is one such, and they are familiar in Terence: Sosia of *Andria*, Davos of *Phormio*, Philotis and Syra of *Hecyra*. Getas is no lay figure, a mere recipient of information, but has life of his own, being painted as a curious, good-natured, bantering, slightly cynical fellow. He speaks the majority of the first seventeen lines, so that when his turn comes to be the listener, he retains enough weight to balance the dramatically more important Daos.

3 μυλῶνα . . . καὶ πέδας: Slaves were sent to work in a mill as a punishment, presumably being rented to the mill-owner. The rotary mill not having yet been introduced, the laborious work consisted in pushing a saddle-quern backwards and forwards; this explains why the slave could be secured by leg-irons (πέδαι). See L. A. Moritz, *Grain-Mills and Flour in Classical Antiquity*, 34–61, 67 n. 6.

4 πυκνά: This word occurs four, perhaps five, times in the remains of Menander, once or twice in the singular (*Epitr.* 894 and perhaps *Aspis* 453) and always adverbially, meaning 'frequently', but it is used adjectivally by other writers of Middle and New Comedy.

5 ἐπιστάς: 'Coming to a halt', cf. Plato, *Symp.* 172 a, ἐπιστὰς περιέμεινα.

6 ὦ πόνηρε σύ: πονηρός often connotes wretchedness (πολλὰ πονῶν) as much as wickedness, cf. *Dysk.* 587. Ancient grammarians are not at one over the accentuation of the word, πόνηρος or πονηρός; similarly μόχθηρος or μοχθηρός. But the evidence of MSS. favours proparoxytone accent in the vocative. Schwyzer, i. 380, considers that this retracted accent (characteristic of vocatives, e.g. πάτερ/πατήρ, Ζεῦ/Ζεύς) was at times extended by analogy to other cases.

7 κερμάτιον: Small savings, such as a slave was allowed to keep as an act of grace and with which he might eventually buy his freedom. Cf. Terence, *Phormio* 43, 'quod ille unciatim uix de demenso suo | suom defrudans genium compersit miser'.

9–15: No restoration of these lines can be more than speculative, although the general sense is clear. Van Leeuwen suggested ἔως ἂν εὖ θῆς τὰ κατὰ ςεαυτόν, but Vollgraff, Χάριτες Leo 58, maintained that the middle θῆ would be required. In 11 the first and third surviving letters are uncertain; if they are rightly read as η and α, Körte's text εἰ προςδοκᾶς (Herwerden) πονηρά (Jensen) is not impossible, even if a little flat. In 14 it is agreed that there was no dicolon before εφθαρμαι; Guéraud saw either an apostrophe or a trace of δ; καὶ μάλ' ἔφθαρμαι would suit this. A privative adjective with πράγματι is suggested by Theophylaktos Simokates, *ep.* 36, ἀλογίςτῳ πάθει ςυμπέπλεγμαι. Theophylaktos (*floruit c.* A.D. 625), who has many echoes from Menander, seems to have known this scene: in *ep.* 15 he has πέπονθα τὴν ψυχήν (cf. 18) and in *ep.* 77 ὑπερμαζᾷ . . . μὴ παρέχου δυοῖν χοινίκων τῷ παιδὶ περαιτέρω (cf. 16–17).

16 δυοῖν χοινίκων: A slave would not expect to receive as much as two χοίνικες, which was the generous daily ration of barley-meal allowed under the armistice to the Spartans on Sphakteria (Thuc. iv. 16. 1), when their servants (Helots) received only one χοῖνιξ (about one litre or roughly 1⅗ lb.). One χοῖνιξ of wheat, which is a little more nourishing than barley, was regarded by Herodotos (vii. 187) as the minimum ration for a soldier: in Polybios' time the Roman legionary received ⅔ of a *medimnus* or thirty-two χοίνικες a month, as well as a messing allowance (vi. 39. 13). In the absurd Utopia of Aristophanes' *Ecclesiazusae* (424) the poor are given three χοίνικες for dinner. Menander's phrase became proverbial and is quoted by Choiroboskos (*in Theodos.* i. 293. 30 Hilgard) without its author's name.

17 πονηρόν: 'A bad thing, Daos. Probably you dine too well.' Euripides' line ἐν πλησμονῇ τοι Κύπρις, ἐν πεινῶςι δ' οὔ (frag. incert. 895 Nauck) became proverbial. Cf. also frag. 322 Nauck, οὐδεὶς προςαιτῶν βίοτον ἠράςθη βροτῶν, and frag. adesp. 186 Nauck, πλήρει γὰρ ὄγκῳ γαςτρὸς αὔξεται Κύπρις, and the dubious frag. 9 of this play.

18 πέπονθα τὴν ψυχήν τι: 'My heart has been touched.' Cf. Plutarch, *Amatorius* 749 d, ἔπαθέ ⟨τι⟩ πρὸς τὸ μειράκιον αὐτή, Xenophon, *Symp.* i. 9, οὐδεὶς οὐκ ἔπαςχέ τι τὴν ψυχὴν ὑπ' ἐκείνου.

19 κατ' ἐμαυτόν: 'Suited to me', 'of my own station in life', cf. *Perik.* 710, κατ' ἐμέ, Aesch. *PV* 890 (of Io), ὡς τὸ κηδεῦςαι καθ' ἑαυτὸν ἀριςτεύει μακρῷ, Kallimachos, *AP* vii. 89, νύμφη καὶ πλούτῳ καὶ γενεῇ κατ' ἐμέ. Gomme proposed to suppress the comma after ἄκακον and translated 'an innocent girl for my part', but it is more likely that Daos should ascribe unqualified innocence to his beloved. The heroine of *Dyskolos* is also ἄκακος, 'of simple, uncorrupted goodness' (222).

20 οὕτως: 'Just so', cf. Xen. *Oec.* I. 9, modified by ἡςυχῇ, 'more or less', 'in some measure': the word is usually no more than 'slightly', as in Plut. *Alexander* 4, αὐχένος εἰς εὐώνυμον ἡσυχῇ κεκλιμένου, Theophrastos frag. 159, ἡσυχῇ θερμόν. **δούλη**: The normal words for 'slave' in New Comedy are θεράπων, οἰκέτης (masc.), θεράπαινα (fem.). δοῦλος is used only where the emphasis is on the legal status, as at *Epitr.* 469 and here.

21 Τίβειος is said by Strabo vii. 3. 12 to have been a frequent name in Paphlagonia and hence given to Paphlagonian slaves; it is derived from Τίβειον in Phrygia (the evidence in Kock, *CAF* i. 704). Menander used it again in *Messenia* (*BCH* lxxxvi [1962], 877), *Perinthia* 3, and *Thettale* frag. 194. The next line implies that Tibeios had been freed, but that would not necessarily show that his children were also free. Yet their names, Plangon and Gorgias, are always citizen names in comedy, and the story, as Daos develops it, leaves no doubt that they are *not* slaves.

22 Πτελέασι: There is no cogent evidence for the situation of the deme of Ptelea. E. Meyer in *RE* xxiii. 1479 concludes that it was either near the Sacred Way not far west of Athens, perhaps near the modern Daphni, or more probably to the east, in the Thriasian plain.

24 ὡς ἔλεγεν αὐτός: The phrase alerts the audience to the probability that Tibeios did not tell the truth. Is it also in character for Daos? Yes; wishing to establish the quasi-servile status of Plangon, he appeals to the testimony of her supposed father. It is probable that Gorgias and Plangon possessed some token of their citizen birth; one could imagine that some hints of this had transpired.

25–7: There is no dicolon at the end of 25, nor was there one originally before οὗτος in 27. This gives a possible text: the whole passage belongs to Daos; οὗτος (after which there would be no punctuation) refers back to Tibeios, who is then named in 28, by a clarifying afterthought. However, the indication ΔΑ(ος) stands in the right-hand margin at 27, and to accord with this a corrector has added a dicolon (above the line) before οὗτος; he has failed to see that this implies a change of speaker at the end of 25 also. This division gives a livelier dialogue and is doubtless right. But it probably requires the further change of ἡμῖν to ὑμῖν, for Getas, unlike Daos (29, 31, 42), does not belong to the household of Laches, for whom Gorgias works; it is, however, just possible that ἡμῖν might be retained, if Laches had rented some pasture on the land of Getas' master.

30 ἀπέσκλη: 'Withered away', i.e. died. Cf. Ar. *Wasps* 160, Lucian, *Dial. Mort.* 27. 7, λιμῷ ἀπεσκληκέναι, and σκελετός, 'dead body'.

31 οὐκ ἀπεδίδου: Wilamowitz's clever suggestion, οὐκέτ' ἐδίδου, 'would not go on to give a third loan', is accepted by Körte, but it is possible that Getas, in his burlesque way, wishes to imply that Laches *ought* to have made the third loan to Tibeios; ἀποδίδοναι can mean to pay what you should pay. W. G. Arnott, *CQ* N.S. xviii (1968), 225, points out that the smaller change to οὐκ ἐπεδίδου yields excellent sense, 'would not bestow'; ἐπιδίδωμι is sometimes used of benefactions, LSJ s.v. B. 3.

32 προσλαβών: Borrowing a small sum in addition to the two minae. By τὰ νόμιμα may be meant a funeral meal and sacrifices at the grave; the ritual that preceded the burial being implied by θάψας.

36 ἀπεργαζόμενος: Cf. *Suda* (= Harpokration) s.v., ἀπεργασάμενος ἀντὶ τοῦ ἀποδοὺς ἐξ ὧν εἰργάσατο. οὕτως Ἰcαῖος ἐν τῷ πρὸς Ἀπολλόδωρον (Isaios frag. 3).   ἡ **Πλάγγων δέ τί;** 'And what of Plangon?' No particular verb is in the speaker's mind in this ellipse.

All that is here said is that Gorgias was working off his father's debt, presumably being kept but receiving no wages. There is nothing to show that the repayment had not been undertaken voluntarily as a debt of honour. On the other hand he may have been under some legal obligation or practical compulsion.

The hypothesis says that Tibeios had pledged his children for his debt, and in verse 20 of the play Daos, asked whether the girl is a slave, answers οὕτως, ἡcυχῇ, τρόπον τινά. This may be interpreted to imply some legal status that is neither fully free nor fully servile. There is an obvious difficulty. This interpretation and the hypothesis appear to conflict with the well-known legislation of Solon forbidding loans on the security of the person (Arist. *Ath. Pol.* 9). Yet Isokrates can write at *Plat.* 48 that the Plataeans at Athens see τοὺς παῖδας . . . πολλοὺς μὲν μικρῶν ἕνεκα cυμβολαίων δουλεύοντας, ἄλλους δ' ἐπὶ θητείαν ἰόντας. This suggests that it was not impossible for children to be, in some sense, enslaved for a parent's debt. It may be that the law of Solon admitted exceptions, perhaps regarding non-citizens; we do not know.

A situation similar to that of this play figures in Ter. *Heautontimorumenos*, and is not less good evidence for Athenian life because it is a fiction invented by the slave Syrus. His story had to be a plausible one. The tale was (500 ff.) that a Corinthian woman living at Athens had borrowed 1,000 drachmas from the *hetaira* Bacchis, and died leaving a daughter; this daughter had been 'left' to Bacchis as a pledge for the loan. The word *arrabo* must here mean 'security' not, as is usual, 'deposit'; later the phrase *oppignerare filiam* (793) is used. It is proposed that Bacchis should be paid 1,000 drachmas and hand the girl over to a youth who is in love with her. It is not clear whether

she is intended to be a slave *de jure*, so that Bacchis can legally dispose
of her, or merely a woman who will have no practical alternative but
to submit to an arrangement that she might after all be able to turn
to her advantage.

We must reckon with the fact that in practice the laws do not cover
all situations and are not always obeyed. The legislation of Solon
would not prevent a contract by which a man undertook in return
for a lump sum in advance to work without pay for a fixed time; and
no doubt he could commit his dependent children also. What would
be the sanctions if he or his children failed to honour the agreement?
Again we do not know, but they would not necessarily be the same
against a citizen and a non-citizen. In particular it is to be observed
that a freedman who failed to fulfil the conditions of his manumission
could be re-enslaved; it is conceivable that this was extended to cover
failure to stand by subsequent contracts with his former master. But
if we consider the realities of the situation in this play, they may alone
be enough to account for what is said. Gorgias and Plangon passed
as the children of a manumitted slave. Manumission of a slave did
not automatically or even usually carry with it the freedom of his
or her children. If Laches had maintained that the brother and sister
were in fact slaves, they might have had difficulty in establishing their
status. This danger could provide a sufficient motive for their making
no trouble about paying off the debt. On this explanation Daos'
answer (20) will have nothing to do with legal niceties, but it is
hesitatingly evasive of the issue. He knows that Plangon is no slave,
but sees that effectively her condition is not very different.

Among the Greeks of Egypt a man might be temporarily enslaved
without giving the owner a right to sell him; see J. Modrzejeński,
Recherches de papyrologie, ii. 75. B. Adams, Παραμονή, collects labour-
contracts, often very restrictive of freedom, from Egypt.

37 τῆc ἐμῆc κεκτημένηc: 'My mistress'. κεκτημένη has come to be
treated as a noun; hence ἐμῆc not ἐμέ.

38: C gives the word παιδίcκη to Getas, as an interjection or question;
this seems impossible. Even if the sense *liberane puella servili fungitur
officio?* (van Leeuwen) could be extracted from it, why should Getas,
who knows nothing of Plangon's birth and has been told that she is
in a way a slave, make such an interruption? Although Ammonios
(380 Nickau; p. 110 Valck.) writes παιδίcκη ἡ ἐλευθέρα παρ' Ἀττικοῖc,
παῖc δὲ ἡ δούλη, the word clearly has no such connotation for Daos
(cf. 18–20), and presumably not for Getas either. Ammonios is in
fact wrong: as LSJ shows, Attic authors use the word of any young
girl, free, slave, or prostitute. For other attempts to find a sense for

the word in Getas' mouth see Del Corno's edition, Vollgraff in *Χάριτες* Leo 59 f., W. G. Arnott in *CQ* n.s. xviii (1968), 225.

40 ἐλευθέριος: 'Carrying herself as a free woman', 'a lady in her ways'. κοςμία: 'Well-behaved'. The words may be intended to give the audience another hint that the girl is really of good birth, but they are in character for Daos, who is shown to admire and respect, as well as desire, her. They would seem to imply that he is, as yet, ignorant of her pregnancy, and there is nothing to show that Getas knew any more.

41 Ἡράκλεις: The exclamation expresses Daos' dismay at the very thought of an underhand affair.

43: 'He promised that after speaking to her brother he would—', do what? Lefebvre's cυνοικιεῖν is usually adopted: if rightly, it is remarkable that Laches should so readily undertake to dispose of a free woman, whose brother was at hand, in *contubernium* with a slave. But he might use such language, since his consent would be required as Daos' owner, and he might assume that young Gorgias, being in his debt, would show no recalcitrance.

A union between a citizen woman and a slave would be shocking to Greek sentiment. Plangon, however, is in the eyes of the world not a citizen, but an orphan of uncertain, perhaps servile, origin. Her future would be utterly precarious, and by living with Daos she might obtain a somewhat more stable and secure position. He may have had prospects of manumission (cf. 7), and he certainly intended to look after her. Plautus' *Persa* offers an interesting parallel for an association between a slave and a free woman; Toxilus, a slave who holds a position of influence in his household, there pays a *leno* to free the girl with whom he wishes to consort.

U. E. Paoli, *Aegyptus*, xxxiii (1953), 284, denies that cυνοικεῖν, cυνοικίζειν can be used of anything but lawful citizen marriage, but this can be disproved by Satyros, *Vita Euripidis* 39. xiii. 4, where Euripides is said to have made his wife live with (cυνοικεῖν) a young slave, or [Dem.] xlvii. 55 where a manumitted slave cυνῴκηςε ἀνδρί. Confusingly enough cυνοικεῖν can mean 'live together purporting to be legally married' as in [Dem.] lix. 122, τὸ γὰρ cυνοικεῖν τοῦτ᾽ ἐςτίν, ὃς ἂν παιδοποιῆται καὶ εἰςάγῃ εἴς τε τοὺς φράτερας καὶ δημότας τοὺς υἱεῖς, 126, ξένην οὖςαν ἀςτῷ cυνοικεῖν.

44 λαμπρὸς εἶ: 'You're in a splendid position'; for this colloquial use cf. *Perik.* 149, *Mis.* frag. 7, frags. 508, 627.

45 τρίμηνον is a likely supplement, τριταῖος possible. If the latter is right, something must have occurred to cause Laches to break off his journey and return unexpectedly.

46 ff.: It is likely that the noun with τῆc αὐτῆc was ἐλπίδοc. Good sense is given by Wilamowitz's supplements: εἰc Λῆμνον οὑμὸc δεcπότηc (Robert). ἐχόμεθα τῆc αὐτῆc ἔτ᾽ ἐλπίδοc· μόνον cῴζοιτο. (Γετ.) χρηcτὸc εἶ cύ. (Δα.) τῆc τ᾽ ἀποδημίαc ὄνηcιc εἴη. Yet this cannot be called certain, and οὑμὸc δεcπότηc must be admitted to be an unnecessary piece of line-filling. Gomme thought possible an exclamatory τῆc ἀποδημίαc, 'what a sad thing this foreign travel is', after which either Getas or Daos might continue ὄνηcιc εἴη. There are no paragraphi under 50, 51; so unless there was a second change of speaker in 49, whoever began with πολυ continued without a break. It is uncertain whether he habitually carries wood, a hard occupation (cf. *Dysk.* 31), or is carrying wood on this occasion, perhaps for a sacrifice.

Among the scraps from the Cairo codex are eight which belong or may belong to *Heros*. They have been fitted together by Lefebvre and Jensen to form three fragments: δεζ (53–7 on verso, 74–81 on recto), θη (57–64 on verso, 82–8 on recto), and γΟ (65–73 on verso, 90–7 on recto). The last comes from the bottom of a page and it is probable from the contents that the verso precedes the recto. δεζ is certainly from *Heros*, since 76–7 are quoted by Stobaios as from that play. The occurrence in γΟ of the name Myrrhine and of a shepherd makes it highly likely that this fragment, too, belongs to *Heros*. Nothing in the words of θη suggests that it should be attributed to this play, but Lefebvre thought it possible, from its appearance, that it belonged to the same page as δεζ. Sudhaus, although he expressed confidence that all three fragments were from the same page, confessed himself unable to give any cogent reason for his belief. The normal number of lines to a page in the Cairo codex is 35; the three fragments between them contain on the recto 24 and on the verso 21, together with a space of three lines occupied by the word ΧΟΡ[ΟΥ]. If, therefore, they all belong to the same page, as is now usually supposed, only about eleven lines are missing on each side; these eleven lines must be distributed between three gaps, one before each fragment (assuming that neither δεζ nor θη contains the top line of the page; δεζ, at least, appears to have the foot of a descending letter above 53). This leaves uncomfortably little room for the transitions between γΟ verso and δεζ or θη recto, and between one or other of the latter and γΟ recto. The belief that all the fragments belong to the same page should not be too readily accepted.

δεζ **verso:** This fragment contains the beginning of a new act, and *if* it belongs to the same page as γΟ, the recto of which seems to be leading up to a recognition-scene, that must be either the fourth or the fifth act. The first line was restored partly by Jensen, partly by

Körte, to read ὦ Ἡρά]κλεις, ἔα μ' ἁμάρ[τυρον λέγειν, and supposed to be a soliloquy; they thought the speaker to be Pheidias, who then in θη verso reproached himself with his bad conduct (ἄςωτος, 60). If he is to stay for the intimate conversation, in their view between Laches and Myrrhine, which follows in γO verso, it can only be as a somewhat improbable eavesdropper. Webster, *StM* 33, more reasonably believes the speaker to be Laches, who possibly recalled his own wild oats, and talked of arranging a marriage for Plangon or for his other daughter (δίδωμι νύμφην, 56). But the belief that the act opens with a monologue rests on a poor foundation. The invocation of Herakles to allow privacy is unconvincing; one would expect ὦ Ἡράκλεις to be the usual exclamation of surprise or dismay, and ἔα μ' ('let me be', cf. *Sam.* 460, 465) to be addressed to another character with whom the speaker enters in mid-conversation or to whom he addresses some final words as he leaves the house. As for the end of the line some form of ἁμαρτάνειν or ἁμαρτία is quite possible, e.g., 'let me make a mistake for once!' or 'can you call it a mistake if I—?', e.g., ἁμαρτάνειν με φῄς | εἰ τῇ κόρῃ δίδωμι νυμφίον (or εἰ νῦν ἐγὼ δίδωμι νύμφην Πλάγγονα). All that can be said for certain about this fragment is that the speaker of 55 must be a man, since he uses a masculine oath.

   θη verso: this is too fragmentary for rational comment.

   γO verso: a conceivable explanation is that one speaker is Laches, who knows or suspects that Gorgias and Plangon are Myrrhine's children. He has just informed her that he intends to give Plangon to Daos, and now reveals his belief that she is Plangon's mother (cὺ τάλαινα, 68). Then at 72 he will express his view that Tibeios was the father, who had got the better of him, as if he had been a bleating sheep. Webster, *StM* 33, thought that Laches here turned Myrrhine out of doors, having discovered her to be the mother of the twins; he took the shepherd to be Gorgias, who could care for a bleating sheep, but not for his own sister. I find this hard to reconcile with the tone of ὦ γύναι, ὦ Μυρρίνη, which is formal perhaps but not angry, and do not see how Laches' mind could have been 'long made up' to turn her out. But it had been long made up to give Plangon to Daos (43).

68 τὴν Θρᾷτταν: Robert (*Gött. Gel. Anzeiger* [1915], 282) and van Leeuwen suggest that this was Tibeios' wife.

69: C has τι: at the end of the line. The most probable correction is to transfer it to a position after τάλαινα; metre is thus restored in a manner. But the change of speaker between two short syllables that represent a single long syllable is suspicious, although Ar. *Ach.* 1023 has πόθεν :: ἀπὸ Φυλῆc and Menander, *Fab. incert.* 25, αὐτός :: ὑπόμεινον, both in first metron; see Handley, *Dyskolos* 67. C. Dedoussi,

Ἑλληνικά xviii (1964), 3, is exercised because elsewhere in comedy the vocatives τάλαν, τάλαινα are used only by women, although a man may call himself τάλας (οἴμοι τάλας etc.). The scenes, however, in which a man might address a woman as τάλαινα are so few that I think it rash to assume that because no man does use this vocative it was restricted to women. Dedoussi suggests that either the speaker here is a woman, possibly the Thracian woman of 68, or Laches is echoing a use of τάλαινα by his wife, cf. *Sam.* 370. Neither suggestion has more than an outside chance of being correct. For the writing of an omission at the end of the verse cf. Hypothesis 1, *Sam.* 304.

70 ἐς κόρακας: There is no parallel for a woman's using this imprecation, nor can it be addressed to Myrrhine for her to hear, as it is not in keeping with the preceding ὦ γύναι and τάλαινα. It will then be a comment on the situation, 'devil take it', as at *Dysk.* 112, or an aside. ἱδρώς, ἀπορία also seems to be an aside (Körte). Can both phrases be asides by some third party? More likely that Laches curses his wife under his breath, and then remarks to himself that she is sweating in confusion. The dicolon to mark change of speaker has been misplaced, perhaps because ἐξέστηκας and κόρακας both end in -κας.

δεζ recto: ὡς οἰκτρόν . . . ἔχει must be assigned to Myrrhine, the only suitable female character. With whom does she converse? Sonnenburg, *Rh. Mus.* lxix (1914), 80, suggested Sophrone: if Myrrhine was upset at Plangon's pregnancy, Sophrone might answer: 'You exaggerate the calamity; were you not yourself once ravished?' But it is not clear why she should then continue with 'Do you suspect who he was?', a plausible restoration of 80. An alternative interlocutor is Laches; yet one would suppose that when Myrrhine complains that her troubles are unique, this must be the prelude to something more than a confession that she had been ravished nearly twenty years before. May not her distress rather be that she finds her own daughter pregnant, apparently by a slave, and perhaps to be given to him, and that she dare not tell her husband the facts? If this is the situation, Sophrone is the most probable second speaker here. This would imply that δεζ and γ0 do not belong to the same page; if they do belong together, the conversation must be with Laches.

θη recto: a very puzzling fragment. One speaker is a man, since only men swear by Poseidon (87). Athene Alea (84) had a famous shrine at Tegea and at other places in the Peloponnese, and the Doric form of her name points to some non-Attic reference. Körte objected to the improbability of the view (Sudhaus, Jensen) that Myrrhine confessed to having been ravished in a Tegean temple, and supposed that there was an allusion to the story of Auge, mother by Herakles of Telephos. He imagined a dialogue in which Myrrhine mentioned a shrine as the scene of her misfortune. 'Did the man not respect the god's holy place?' 'Well, did Herakles respect the shrine of Athene Alea?' 'Of course he did not.' This very ingenious idea has been much approved. Auge seems to have incurred Athene's anger by giving birth to Telephos in her shrine at Tegea; it is now known from a recently discovered hypothesis to Euripides' *Auge* that she was ravished while washing the goddess's raiment at a spring, which may of course have been within the temple precincts (*P. Colon.* 264, *ZPE* iv [1969], 7). I know no case where an Attic author uses a non-Attic name for a god merely because he is recounting a mythological tale with a foreign setting; this is Körte's explanation of the form Ἀθάνα. It is perhaps more likely that there is a quotation from or allusion to tragedy, in which Ἀθάνα or Ἀθηναία is used, never Ἀθηνᾶ, the ordinary form of current speech. Euripides' play began Ἀλέας Ἀθάνας ὅδε πολ[ύχρυσος δόμος (*P. Colon.* 264, supplemented from Favorinus, *de exilio* iii. 2 [p. 378 Barigazzi]).

γ0 recto: the division between speakers is uncertain; the line-ends are so faint that it is difficult to be sure that there were not any dicola. Jensen suspected a dicolon after δοκεῖ (95) and traces of a paragraphus under the line; with some reserve the division has been accepted. (There was certainly no dicolon before ἔστω.) There can be little doubt but that this is part of a scene between Myrrhine and Laches, in which their joint parenthood of the twins is revealed. Laches asks: 'Is it eighteen years since you were ravished (or bore twins)?' What does she reply? Gomme thought that, too overcome to answer and expecting to be repudiated by Laches, she exclaimed: 'I cannot support all this in solitude (e.g. οὐκ ἔστιν μόνη φέρειν τοιαῦτα).' Jensen and Sudhaus thought the meaning might be 'I am not the only one to whom such things happened at that date', sc. 'and if you violated a girl then, it was not necessarily me?' Neither suggestion is obviously right, but both are preferable to Schroeder's reconstruction, *Hermes* lxxxviii (1960), 123, οὐκ ἔστιν μόνη λαλεῖν; (Λα.) τί ταῦτα; κτλ. 'Can't I talk in private?—What's this? Have your way, if you will' (signs to slave to depart).   **96:** The supplement ϲαφέϲ may be too short; Körte suggests the synonym τρανέϲ, for which cf. Polybios iv. 78.

96–7: Cf. Soph. *Phil.* 46, μὴ καὶ λάθῃ με προϲπεϲών. For elided δέ at the line-beginning cf. *Perik.* 351 n.   **πηνίκα:** Presumably 'at what hour did it happen?' The preceding word has defied restoration. Körte hesitantly proposed ἄπειϲι, which would have to be present, not future, in meaning, contrary to Attic usage. Gomme, also hesitantly, suggested ἀπῆλθε, if that could be reconciled (as it hardly can) with the traces of the letter after π. ἀπέλιπε may be possible.

HEROS

Fragments from other sources

Fragment 1. 'I will act as a guide for the huntsmen round the wild pears'; for the construction cf. Hdt. vii. 214, περιηγησάμενοι τὸ ὄρος τοῖϲι Πέρϲῃϲι. This looks like an exit-line. Did these huntsmen form the chorus (Capps)? If so, the fragment is probably from the end of the first act.

Fragment 2. Presumably spoken by Daos in his own defence to Myrrhine, but conceivably by Sophrone. The lines have a tragic ring, whether that was intended to move or to amuse the audience. A similar sentiment is expressed in Eur. frag. 431 N., καὶ τόνδ' (sc. Ἔρωτα) ἀπείργειν οὐδ' ὁ παγκρατὴϲ ϲθένει | Ζεύϲ, ἀλλ' ὑπείκει καὶ θέλων ἐγκλίνεται. δέϲποινα for the everyday κεκτημένη is paralleled in the anonymous comedy, *Pap. Ghôran* ii. 1 (Page, *GLP* p. 298).

Fragment 3. The second verse is found alone (with δεῖ, not δέ) in an alphabetic collection of single lines from an Egyptian schoolboy's notebook (*Pap. Bouriant*, ed. Collart p. 25, Ziebarth, *Aus d. antiken Schule*, Kleine Texte 65, no. 46), in *Menandri monost.* 768 Jaekel, and (in a corrupt form) in a collection of such lines published in *Sitz. Bericht. d. bayer. Akademie* (1890), 366 by W. Meyer, who maintained, perhaps rightly, that the two lines have been wrongly joined in Stobaios.

Fragment 4. A χοῦϲ was over five pints. Water was normally mixed with wine in the proportion of 1½ or two parts of water to one of wine; but exceptionally the mixture was made stronger or weaker (Athenaios 426 b–f).

Fragment 5. γλυκύτατε is elsewhere used by women (*Epitr.* 143, 653) and absurdly by Dikaiopolis to Euripides at *Ach.* 462, 467. The presumption then is that, unless part of a reported speech, the line was spoken by Myrrhine, perhaps to Laches, or by Sophrone. It is quoted to illustrate the use of ἀναλυθῆναι in the sense of being purged of a poison, τὸ καθαρμῷ τινι χρήϲαϲθαι φαρμάκων, and should, I think, be translated 'you were in a poisoned (or 'drugged') state and have only just been cured of it'. The aorist participle indicates what is in past time for the speaker, although not in regard to the main verb; Goodwin, *MT* § 152. The version 'only just cured, you had become poisoned again', although supposing a more usual use of the participle, seems to me a less likely sense.

Fragment 9. The alteration of Μένανδροϲ προποιήϲειϲ κτλ. to Μένανδροϲ Ἥρῳ "ποιήϲειϲ κτλ." is uncertain and, as Körte remarked (*Addenda*, p. 151), not even necessary.

Fragment 10. This fragment is not assigned by Hermias to any play. Since the joke, such as it is, was made by Getas at line 16 of *Heros*, it is not likely that he made it again later. Meineke (*Fragmenta Poetarum Comicorum* iv. 170) assigned the fragment to *Misumenos*, where it would fit the opening scene between Thrasonides and Getas.

The lost part of the play

Little can be done to reconstruct the remainder of the plot. It may be presumed that Myrrhine did not know, when the play opens, that Laches was the father of her twins. Whether she knew what had become of them is not certain, but it is not improbable that she did. Tibeios must have given Gorgias and Plangon some evidence of their free birth, but need not have told them who their mother was.

Webster's reconstruction is in outline as follows (*StM* 28–34). In the opening scene Daos does not know of Plangon's pregnancy; somehow he learns of it with Getas, who does not know that Pheidias is responsible, and hatches the plot by which he will take the blame, hoping that Myrrhine will give him the girl. Myrrhine, knowing her to be her own daughter, is furious and may reveal her knowledge. If this is so, and Pheidias learns of it, he cannot consider that his father would approve his marrying the bastard. Gorgias arrives at the moment when Plangon gives birth to a child and his anger must be pacified by Laches, who returns home. Laches discovers that Myrrhine is mother of the twins, and interrogates her; from this it transpires that he is the father, and the recognition is clinched by evidence from Sophrone or Sangarios. In the last act there had to be an arrangement for Pheidias to marry Plangon, and perhaps for Gorgias to marry a half-sister who had previously been destined for Pheidias. We hope that Daos is freed.

Gomme's suggested reconstruction was this:

'Pheidias and Plangon were in love, but there were apparently legal and social obstacles to marriage. Gorgias knows that Plangon and he are Myrrhine's children. He has kept silent from pride and because Myrrhine, and probably Laches, have been kind to them, as they had been to Tibeios. He learns, perhaps from Sophrone, that Pheidias, not Daos, is his sister's lover, and is determined that Pheidias shall know that he has wronged a free and gentle girl. If Myrrhine did not previously know that the children were hers, she may learn it from Gorgias, who wishes to secure her help for his sister. Laches, returning from abroad is told (? by Getas) that the twins are Myrrhine's. Great indignation: what is the world coming to? Is no woman honest? Who was the scoundrel who wronged you?

The children must be sent packing. In great distress, she confesses all, and with the help of details in her story, the truth comes out. Joyous reunion; and the children are not only found but as good as legitimate. The hypothesis treats the marriage of Pheidias and Plangon as a case of conventional morality ("he made an honest woman of her"), but Menander may have done something more. Daos is too sympathetically treated for us to lack interest in what happened to him. Was he just pushed aside? If so, one would suppose that Menander treated the situation with understanding.'

Daos is, indeed, treated with sympathy in the one scene we have. His absorption in his love and his appreciation of the girl's character render him likeable. Webster insists that 'his motives are entirely selfish', a judgement that is a little harsh. His acceptance of the child's paternity was no doubt intended to secure him Plangon without waiting for Laches' return, but it was also an action that would seem to him to be in the girl's interests. It did in fact imperil them, and it may be that a Greek audience would be less well disposed than we towards a slave who by a lie attempted to obtain a free girl as his 'wife'.

THEOPHORUMENE

Twelve lead theatre-tokens are known with legend *ΘΕΟΦΟΡΟΥ-
MENH*. Pickard-Cambridge, *Dramatic Festivals*[2], 271[6], suggests that
they were made for a performance shortly before the sack of Athens
in A.D. 267; presumably he assumes that in normal quiet times such
tokens were melted down and re-stamped.

F 2 *PSI* 1280. Two columns, each of fifteen lines, from Oxyrhynchus; of the first column only a few letters are preserved.

Latest discussion, E. W. Handley, *BICS* xvi (1969), 88.

The internal reasons for ascribing *PSI* 1280 to Menander's *Theophorumene* are strong. He alone is quoted by the ancient grammarians
for the form παράcτα (28, in place of παράcτηθι), as for ἀπόcτα (frags.
110, 158, 317); he alone is known to have written a Θεοφορουμένη
(although Alexis was the author of Θεοφόρητοc), and here we have a
woman who θεοφορεῖται. Any doubt must be removed by the mosaic
from Mitilini (illustrated *Ἔργον* [1962], 156, *BCH* lxxxvii [1963], 819,
Antike Kunst, Beiheft 6 [1970], Plate 4), which represents a scene from
Act II of Θεοφορουμένη. One of the characters, a young man who
dances with small cymbals, is labelled *ΛΥCΙΑC*, and another young
man is labelled *ΚΛΕΙΝΙΑC*. In our fragment one of the speakers is
Lysias (23, 29), a name elsewhere unknown in comedy, and before
the mosaic was found Webster had suggested reading Κλ[⟨ε⟩ι]νια in
14 (*StM* 51). In the centre of the picture a third and dominating
personage is a slave labelled *ΠΑΡΜΕΝΩΝ*, and there is a fourth
form, of small size, to one side.

Explanation of the fragment is difficult and hazardous. The most
plausible attempt is that of Handley, whom I follow in the main and
to whom the reader may be referred for a full discussion. Körte's
view (*Hermes*, lxx [1935], 431) was forcibly criticized by Page, *GLP*
256–7, who was sceptical of his own version also. Both these scholars
printed texts which have been made obsolete by Bartoletti's revised
readings of the papyrus (*Pap. Soc. It.* xii [1951] 135).

Del Corno (*Menandro*, i. 431), associating the mosaic with this scene
(perhaps a probable assumption, but no more than that), thought
that Parmenon must be one of the speakers, and assigned to him
17b–21 and 22b. He gave the repeated μαίνει (22a, 23a) and 24b–29a
to Lysias, 23b–24a and 29b–30 to Kleinias, and 16–17a to the girl

who was possessed. This makes an intelligible dialogue, but one hesitates to accept a solution that demands four speaking characters in a single scene, a thing as yet unparalleled in Menander. Moreover the girl seems to be indoors, since it is said at 26 that she will come bounding out, if she is really possessed. Although a voice off-stage was not unknown in the Greek theatre, see *Aspis* 299 n., it was not a common device.

Handley suggests that the whole of 16–23a is a quoted dialogue, and that there need not therefore be more than two speakers on the stage, Lysias, who gives the narrative, and someone else, in whom it is tempting to see Kleinias, since the young men were probably in conversation shortly before (8, 14). The mosaic may represent an earlier moment in the scene, and Parmenon may now have left; he must remove himself in order to change costume to come on as the demented girl. Handley prefers, however, another alternative, according to which the narrator of 16–23a is Parmenon. Kleinias replies: 'That is nonsense: isn't she pretending to be mad, Lysias?' Parmenon then proposes a test of the girl's madness, and once again Kleinias speaks, welcoming the proposal, which Lysias has not hastened to accept. Neither of these arrangements can be eliminated as impossible, although I find it unlikely that 29, νὴ Δί', εὖ γε, Λυςία, should be a reaction to a plan not proposed by Lysias himself. Accordingly I should prefer to retain him as the speaker of 24b–29a, even if 16–23a belong to Parmenon.

16: In the absence of context the meaning is impenetrable. καταςτάζω is a word found mainly in tragedy, although in some MSS. of Xen. *Cyr.* v. 1. 5; ὄμματα is also a word 'rare in prose' (LSJ), although used by Alexis frag. 112 K, ἦςαν κόραι θυγατέρες αὐτῷ; :: τὰς μὲν οὖν τῶν ὀμμάτων. Elevated language is perhaps more likely in speech, whether reported or not, by an excited girl than in the man's narrative, but one can hardly make a firm decision.   οἶδ' is very uncertain. Parenthetic οἶδα is normally graced by a second word, e.g. cάφ' οἶδα, εὖ οἶδα, οἶδ' ὅτι, or οἶδ' ἐγώ. The papyrus has a small gap between οι and δ, whence Bartoletti proposed to read οἱ δ'. [οἱ μὲν . . .] καταςτάξαντες, οἱ δ' ἀπ' ὀμμάτων is conceivably right, and, if so, the sense is probably 'and some were dripping from their eyes', cf. Eur. *Hec.* 240, ὀμμάτων ἄπο | φόνου cταλαγμοὶ cὴν κατέςταζον γένυν. But at *Med.* 216 ὀμμάτων ἄπο means 'out of sight', as does ἀπ' ὀμμάτων at *Alc.* 1064. With this latter sense οἶδ'. ἀπ' ὀμμάτων ἔπληςα is conceivable.

17 ἔπληςα is as good as certain. The verb is mainly poetic; prose used πληροῦν. ἔπληςα cannot govern δῶρα, for as Page saw, following Beazley, τἀμὰ δῶρα is repeated in reverse order as δῶρα τἀμά and both must be governed by ἐξεῖλον(το). For such arrangement of words, cf. *Perik.* 506, *Sam.* 465. Perhaps the meaning is 'I filled the cups', and the narrator is the subject.　ἀκούεις; is either part of what the girl said or an interjection by the narrator to call attention to her sentence.

18 ἐξεῖλονθ', ὁ δέ: This is Handley's interpretation of ἐξειλοντοδε. Failure to aspirate a final consonant before a word with rough breathing is not uncommon in papyri. 'They took my gifts from me' is a credible sense. It could also be given by ἐξεῖλοντο δή; the change of speaker would then have to be indicated by the actor's voice alone, as at *Sam.* 255, 256, *Sik.* 264, 265, *Mis.* 298. If ἐξεῖλον is read, the meaning must be 'My gifts destroyed me'. This, however, leaves an awkward isolated τόδε. Could it mean 'this is what she says'? Bartoletti would read τόδε τί δ' ἔλαβες, citing Eur. *IA* 821, τήνδε τίνα λεύσσω; But the cases are not parallel, in that here there is δέ, which should be placed after τόδε. If ὁ δέ is correct, who is this speaker? There is complete freedom to speculate. The only male character known from this play besides Lysias, Kleinias, and Parmenon is Kraton, the speaker of fragment 1.

19 ἱππόπορνε: Feminine; some have thought it improbable that Menander should use this word. But it is no coarser than λαικαστρία, *Perik.* 485. That to be sure is in the mouth of a drunken slave, but we do not know the status of the speaker here. If Del Corno is right in thinking him to be Parmenon, the word might suit him. It is used three times by Alkiphron (iii. 33, 50, iv. 11), who often imitates Menander, always of a 'gold-digger', an implication which may be present here too. ἱππο- seems to mean 'great', as in ἱπποσέλινον, 'giant parsley', ἱππόκρημνος, 'tremendously steep', Ar. *Frogs* 929. Thus the *Suda* explains the word, ἀντὶ τοῦ μεγαλόπορνε· σπανίως ('occurs rarely'). But an anecdote about Diogenes the Cynic (Athen. 565 c) suggests that the meaning was not obvious in the fourth century: πρότερον μὲν ἔφησε ζητεῖν τί ἐστιν ὁ ἱππόπορνος.

20: Several restorations have been suggested; none is more than a guess without foundation.

21: The girl probably has a wreath as taking part in a religious ceremony; she walks about outside, whereas she should, if a respectable girl, stay modestly in her home.

22: Handley follows Grassi, *Atene e Roma* N.s. vi (1961), 146 in believing the dicolon after μαίνει to be mistaken, anticipating the dicolon correctly placed after μαίνει in 23. He suggests as an alternative that the second dicolon may also be a mistake; then one could read "μαίνει;" φλυαρεῖς. It is clear that other punctuations could be found.

Del Corno supposes that Parmenon speaks 17–21 indignantly, and that Lysias asks him μαίνει; 'are you mad?' Parmenon, however, continues by asking why she does not prosecute her nefarious trade inside with doors bolted. Del Corno suggests that the verb is suppressed to avoid a coarse expression. Lysias repeats his question, and is backed up by Kleinias, φλυαρεῖc. But Kleinias thinks that the girl's conduct is put on, 'is not this a pretence?' I do not find this altogether convincing so far as τί οὖν οὐκ ἔνδον ἐγκεκλειμένη; is concerned; I should expect τί; or ἀλλὰ τί; not τί οὖν; and moreover it would not be usual for a prostitute to be locked up.

25 θεοφορεῖται: This play gives the first surviving instance of the verb, but Aesch. *Agam.* 1140 has φρενομανής τιc εἶ θεοφόρητοc, addressed to Kassandra. **ταῖc ἀληθείαιcι:** For the plural cf. *Epitr.* 403 n.; for the long form of the dative *Perik.* 268 and frag. 541, ὅcτιc δὲ διαβολαῖcι πείθεται ταχύ, Philemon frag. 130 K, εἰ ταῖc ἀληθείαιcιν οἱ τεθνηκότεc αἴcθηcιν εἶχον. The title Θεοφορουμένη suggests that the girl really was possessed.

27 μητρὸc θεῶν . . . κορυβάντων: The 'mother of the gods' will here be Kybebe, as she was called by the Greeks who came into contact with her through the Lydians: she was originally a Phrygian goddess, whose name was more closely represented by the form Κυβέλη; daemons from Asia Minor, whose name was slightly corrupted by the Greeks to Korybantes, were early associated with her. Worship of both was known in Athens by the second half of the fifth century at latest. The worshippers of the Korybantes were said κορυβαντιᾶν, to be possessed by the Korybantes. The rites were marked by shrieking, wild dancing, beating of cymbals and drums, and the playing of the αὐλόc (Plato, *Crito* 54 d). The mania thus induced sometimes led to prophecy (Arrian frag. 47, μέγα βοῶντεc καὶ ὀρχούμενοι προθεcπίζουcι τὰ μέλλοντα, θεοφορούμενοι καὶ μαινόμενοι), and it also served as a cure for insanity: the temporary μανία of the beneficent δαίμων drove out the μανία implanted by an evil δαίμων; there is a good account in E. R. Dodds, *The Greeks and the Irrational*, 77 ff. In the fourth century at least these procedures were apparently regarded with some reserve by the majority of Athenians. But the goddess herself had become respectable, perhaps aided by identification with some local mother-goddess. She was the divinity of the Metroön, where state documents were kept and laws were posted. Poets identified her with Gaia, Aphrodite, and particularly Rhea, an obscure goddess whom mythology had made wife of Kronos, and therefore mother of several gods, Zeus, Poseidon, Hera. On the Korybantes see *RE* xxii. 1441, Farnell, *Cults*, iii. 301; on Kybebe *RE* xi. 2250.

27: Körte and Bartoletti accept Maas's supplement πλέα; the adjective πλέωс is not yet known elsewhere in New Comedy, but that is not a fatal objection. Yet perhaps both genitives are, as Handley suggests, constructed with αὔλει, cf. *Dysk.* 433, αὔλει . . . Πανός. If so, there are many ways in which the line might be completed. A vocative addressed to the piper, cύ μοι or a proper name, is as likely a suggestion as any. Some particular tune or tunes were connected with the Korybantes, Plato, *Ion* 536 c, οἱ κορυβαντιῶντες ἐκείνου μόνου αἰcθάνονται τοῦ μέλουc ὀξέωc ὃ ἂν ᾖ τοῦ θεοῦ ἐξ ὅτου ἂν κατέχωνται. Whether to write αὔλει, imperative, supposing that Lysias has brought a flute-player with him, or αὐλεῖ indicative, with subject (αὐλητής τιc) understood (cf. *Dysk.* 879 n.), is doubtful. It is possible that some fluteplayer connected with the cult of the Korybantes here strikes up conveniently for Lysias. But the former alternative seems to fit better with the context, especially with πεῖραν ἔξεcτιν λαβεῖν of 24.

28 παράcτα: Cf. frag. 110, ἐμοὶ παράcτα, quoted by the *Suda* as a parallel to ἀπόcτα for ἀπόcτηθι; 'stand by me here, coming to the inn-door'.

30 καλὴ θέα: Cf. Xen. *Anab.* iv. 8. 27, καὶ καλὴ θέα ἐγένετο.

The fragment may have been immediately or almost immediately followed by a scene in which the girl sang, while possessed. This scene is referred to by the scholiast on Eur. *Andromache* 103, μονῳδία ἐcτὶν ᾠδὴ ἑνὸc προcώπου θρηνοῦντος, ὥcτ' οὔτε τὸ "Ἀcιατίδοc γῆc cχῆμα" (*Andr.* 1) μονῳδία ἐcτί· τραγῳδεῖ γάρ, οὐκ ᾄδει· οὔτε τὰ ἐν Θεοφορουμένῃ ᾀδόμενα· οὐ θρηνεῖ γάρ. A. Lesky, *Hermes*, lxxii (1937), 123, argues that the girl must have danced in the orchestra, in order that she might have room enough for her wild gyrations; hence passage between the stage and orchestra must have been possible, as it was in the fifth century (P. D. Arnott, *Greek Scenic Conventions*, 38–9, discusses the passages where the entry of an actor into the orchestra is possible). Lesky's inference, although widely accepted, is far from necessary. There is no evidence that the girl danced as well as sang, or that if she danced her movements were too wild to be confined to the stage.

Handley suggests (*BICS* xvi [1969], 95) that a text to appear in *PSI* vol. xv gives a fragment of this scene. It consists of the ends of 27 lines, of which apparently 18 were iambic comic trimeters, 9 dactylic hexameters, addressed to Korybantes and to the Mother goddess. Other, much less likely, metrical interpretations are criticized by C. Pavese, *SIFC* xxxviii (1966), 63, and Handley, op. cit. 97. I think it is probable, although not certain, that the fragment is from a comedy. Opinions may differ on the probability of its being from *Theophorumene*. I have printed it, with reserve, in OCT and here give a brief annotation. The *editio princeps* is by V. Bartoletti, *Dai papiri della Soc. Italiana* i (1965).

If it is rightly guessed that this scene is from *Theophorumene*, it would appear that the girl first addresses the company in iambics (τοῖc παροῦcι, ? Lysias and Kleinias) and urges them to accompany her with wild cries. She then invokes the gods, Korybantes and Kybebe, in hexameters. Whether in the later part it is she, or the 'audience', who utters the interspersed iambics must be uncertain.

6 μεγίcτα: The lyric hexameter uses the long α for the Ionic–Attic η.

7 cειcικάρηνοι: A new compound. Why not -κάρανοι? A copyist's mistake, due to the Homeric ὑψικάρηνοc? Or the poet's intention?

8 ἀδυπρόcωποι: Known to LSJ only as comically applied to χόνδροc, 'porridge', by Matron, *Convivium*, 102; it is also an epithet of the Horai in *Orphic Hymn* xliii. 5, Ὧραι ἀειθαλέεc περικυκλάδεc ἡδυπρόcωποι.

9 κλειτὰν ἑκατόμβαν: Also *Il.* iv. 102, and in the plural Pindar *Pyth.* x. 33. The v.l. κλεινὰν is a commoner word, and so probably not the original text.

11 μᾶτερ ὀρεία: If the supplement is right, cf. Soph. *Phil.* 391, ὀρεcτέρα παμβῶτι Γᾶ, Eur. *Hipp.* 143–4, ἢ cεμνῶν Κορυβάντων φοιτᾷc ἢ ματρὸc ὀρείαc.

After this line are two in a smaller hand, only partially legible. All that is certain is cτεφαν εχετω and παρα χειρα. If cτεφαν means cτεφάνουc, they may be hexameters; if cτέφανον, they may be a stage direction (Pavese); for a fuller discussion see Handley op. cit., p. 98.

15 ἐπιτίθει τε πῦρ: 'Put fire on the incense', cf. *Sam.* frag. 1, φέρε τὴν λιβανωτόν· cὺ δ᾽ ἐπίθεc τὸ πῦρ, Τρύφη.

20: The metre is doubtful since, as Handley remarks, one cannot exclude, e.g., χαῖρ᾽, Ἄγδιcτί, ⟨μοι⟩. Ἄγγδιcτιc, also spelled Ἄγδιcτιc, was an Asiatic goddess often identified with Kybebe, see Roscher, *Lexikon* s.v. Pausanias vii. 17. 10–12 records a myth, according to which she was an androgynous offspring of Zeus and Earth; she fell in love with Attis and at his intended marriage to the daughter of the king of Pessinus sent him mad and caused him to castrate himself.

24 Φρυγία Κρηcία: The Phrygian and Cretan mother-goddesses were early identified; each was associated with a Mount Ida, and this may have helped.

27 Λυδίουc: It was the expansion of Lydian power that made it easy for the worship of Kybebe to reach Greek cities on the coast of Asia Minor.

It remains to consider the relation of the Mitilini mosaic to *PSI*

1280, and to the appearance of the girl, which probably followed. Another work of art must here be brought into account. Handley maintains, not without reservation, that a Pompeian mosaic by or after Dioskurides of Samos (Pickard-Cambridge, *Theatre of Dionysus*, fig. 85, M. Bieber, *Hellenistic Theatre²*, fig. 346, Webster, *Hellenistic Art*, Plate 33, in colour) also illustrates this play. A companion mosaic by the same artist illustrates *Synaristosai* (intro. p. 12), and C. Robert's view, *Masken der neueren attischen Komödie*, 76, that this one represents a street scene, and not a stage-performance, must now be regarded as untenable. It shows two masked young men, one with cymbals, the other with a tambourine, dancing to the music of a masked αὐλητρίc; there is a fourth small figure without a mask. The young man with cymbals has a strong resemblance to the Lysias of the Mitilini mosaic, where Kleinias *may* be holding a tambourine. The small figure at Mitilini *may* be a female slave holding an αὐλόc. Handley suggests that the Mitilini mosaic shows a point slightly earlier than that from Pompeii, where Parmenon has withdrawn and the two young men have begun to dance to Korybantic music, which will bring out the girl. The increase in size of the αὐλητρίc, supposed by this interpretation, is no objection: the artists' principles of composition allowed only three full-sized figures in a picture.

This scheme, although tempting, is not certainly right. (1) There is no suggestion in *PSI* 1280 that the young men intend to dance; the phrase καλὴ θέα suggests rather that they will watch someone else. παράcτα δ' ἐνθαδὶ πρὸc τὴν θύραν τοῦ πανδοκείου gives no clear guidance. If the girl is in the inn, then either Kleinias or the piper may be summoned to make a noise where she will hear; if she is not, then Kleinias and Lysias are to stand away from her house, presumably to watch unseen. (2) Perhaps the girl was somewhere brought on by the piper's music (? in Act I), and the dancing of the young men in Act II was for some other purpose (Handley p. 90 recognizes this possibility). (3) The temporal sequence by which the Mitilini mosaic precedes that from Pompeii may be wrong. Parmenon may interrupt the dancing: Kleinias has stopped but Lysias still continues. (4) The Pompeian mosaic may represent a scene from some other play: Handley himself notes the possibility of *Menagyrtes*. None of these considerations are fatal to Handley's scheme, but as he candidly confesses, it is speculation, however probable it may appear.

Fragment 1. **1:** Kraton is an old man, since Plutarch, *QC* 739 f, quotes 18–19 as τὰ τοῦ κωμικοῦ γέροντοc.

2: An anecdote told by Suetonius, *Vespasian* 23, introduces this line: 'de Cerylo liberto, qui diues admodum ob subterfugiendum quandoque ius fisci ingenuum se et Lachetem mutato nomine coeperat ferre, ὦ Λάχης, Λάχης [frag. 663 K–T], | ἐπὰν ἀποθάνῃς, αὖθις ἐξ ἀρχῆς ἔcει | cὺ Κηρύλος.'

6 ἅπαντα: 'Anything whatever' : for this sense cf. Ephippos frag. 15 K, ἀγόραcον εὐτελῶc· ἅπαν γὰρ ἱκανόν ἐcτι.

12 ἐν ἑτέρᾳ τροφῇ: The noble cock has different, i.e. better, food.

15 ἐν τῷ νῦν γένει: 'In the present generation'.

17 τρίτα λέγει: 'Takes the third part (i.e. the least important) in the play', cf. Dem. xix. 246, οὗτος τὰ τρίτα λέγων διετέλεcε, Plut. *Mor.* 816 f, τὸν μὲν ἐν τραγῳδίᾳ πρωταγωνιcτήν . . . τῷ τὰ τρίτα λέγοντι πολλάκιc ἕπεcθαι. Such passages support the view that in tragedy at least there were three actors only, Pickard-Cambridge, *Dramatic Festivals at Athens*[2], 136.

Fragment 2. For the sentiment cf. Eur. *Hel.* 757, γνώμη δ' ἀρίστη μάντιc ἥ τ' εὐβουλία. Perhaps the remark was made to depreciate some prophecy or divination uttered by the girl in her state of possession, since Alkiphron, *Ep.* iv. 19. 21 makes Glykera write to Menander : καὶ μαντεύcαιτο ἡ Φρυγία (a prophetess in Phrygia) τὰ cυμφέροντα κρεῖccον τῆc θεοφορουμένηc coι κόρηc.

Fragments 3 and 4. Fragment 4 comes from a description of a drinking scene (possibly in the inn of line 29) ; such scenes are well represented in surviving fragments of Middle and New Comedy. The same is probably true of fragment 3.

περιcοβεῖ: Cobet's alteration to the imperative περιcόβει is arbitrary. The accent of Athenaios' MS. has, of course, no authority, but there is no sufficient reason for preferring the imperative to the (historic) present indicative. περιcοβεῖν, 'push round the wine-cup', is found in a letter attributed to Hippolochos (third century B.C.), Athenaios 130 c, and in Alkiphron, i. 22, iii. 55, who probably took the word from New Comedy.

Θηρίκλειον: Therikles was a famous Corinthian potter, whose name is frequently mentioned in the comic fragments (Athenaios 470 e– 472 e) and became attached to certain types of pottery. The noun to be supplied here is probably κύλικα.

Fragment 6. **δεύτεροc πλοῦc:** Leutsch–Schneidewin, *Paroem. Graeci*, i. 359, cf. frag. 205, ὁ δεύτεροc πλοῦc ἐcτι δήπου λεγόμενοc, ἂν ἀποτυχών τιc οὐρίου κώπαιc πλέῃ.

Fragment 8. Nikadias and Artios seem to be commentators on *Theophorumene*; they are not otherwise known. It is possible that the adjective εὐάντητοc was applied to Rhea in this play.

KARCHEDONIOS

O 9 *P. Oxy.* 2654 and *P. Col.* 5031. That these fragments belong to the same roll was recognized by L. Koenen, *ZPE* vi (1970), 60.

Although the material is so slight it serves to show that this play was not the model of Plautus' *Poenulus*, which may therefore be connected with Alexis' *Καρχηδόνιοc*. In the only piece that is preserved in a good state someone records that his mother was daughter of the Carthaginian general Hamilcar, and is asked how he can then hope to get a citizen woman as wife. This suggests that the scene is Athens, where a citizen woman could not marry anyone but a citizen, i.e. a man with citizens for both parents. The occurrence of the word cκάφη (26), used at Athens in connection with resident aliens (*Sik.* 167), supports this. It is possible that the person involved was mistaken about his parentage and proved to be a full Athenian: there may be a hint of this in frag. 227 K–T, αὐτὸν γὰρ οὐθεὶc οἶδε τοῦ ποτ' ἐγένετο, ἀλλ' ὑπονοοῦμεν πάντεc ἢ πιcτεύομεν. Plautus' *Poenulus* is located in Kalydon, where the laws concerning the family are represented as less strict: the hero was a Carthaginian adopted as son by a Kalydonian who had him from a slave-trader; such an adoption was impossible at Athens.

4–11: Hearing the opening of a door A draws back; B comes out, and reflects that long-standing folly cannot be cured in a day. A recognizes him as someone's slave, and probably adds: 'He is talking about me.' οὐ κεχείμαcται, 'he's not been badly buffeted', seems more likely than οὗ κ., 'where a man's been buffeted'. For metaphorical use of χειμάζομαι cf. frag. 335. 7, χειμαζόμενοc ζῆι, *P. Ghoran* ii. 166, χειμάζομαι γὰρ οὐ μετρίωc ὑπὸ τοῦδε, Soph. *Ant.* 391, ἀπειλαῖc αἷc ἐχειμάcθην.

8: Stobaios gives μεταcτῆcαι, which seems to be required if Handley's supplement οὐ τοῦ τυχόντοc is right. But if the sentence begins with ἔργον, μεταcτῆναι is possible: 'It is a job for folly to change.' Frag. 438, οὐ ῥάιδιον ἄνοιαν ἐν μικρῶι μεταcτῆcαι χρόνωι, and frag. 544, ἔργον ἐcτί, Φανία, μακρὰν cυνήθειαν βραχεῖ λῦcαι χρόνωι, support the transitive verb.

12–30 appear to contain a conversation between A and B, who are then joined by C. B says: 'You have come under a misapprehension about yourself.' It is possible, however, that A and C are identical.

33: For confirmatory νή cf. *Dysk.* 510, *Epitr.* 1120, *Sam.* 385.

34 νόμιζε: 'Imagine', cf. *Dysk.* 1, τῆc Ἀττικῆc νομίζετ᾽ εἶναι τὸν τόπον.
ποιεῖν ἐγγραφάc: Arist. *Ath. Pol.* 42 describes the procedure. Candidates for enrolment in the deme must be eighteen years of age and of
citizen parents (ἐξ ἀμφοτέρων γεγονότεc ἀcτῶν). All the men of the deme
vote to approve or disapprove their qualifications.

35: The name Hamilcar (abd Melkart, 'servant of Melkart') was
common at Carthage, and three generals so called had come into
contact with the Greeks of Sicily. The first was defeated at the battle
of the Krimisos, which is dated 343 or 339 B.C.; the second occupied
Syracuse in 319 B.C. and acted as an intermediary between Agathokles
and his enemies in 313, in which year he died; the third overran
most of Sicily between 311 and 309, when he was captured in an
assault on Syracuse and put to death. Since the date of *Karchedonios* is
unknown, it is impossible to be sure which Hamilcar would be understood by the original audience. But the second and third probably
overshadowed the first, who had been prominent at least twenty
years before them. Either of them, provided that he was not known
to have been too young to have a grown grandson when the play
was performed, is therefore more likely. I know no reason to suppose
that Hellenic feeling made Carthaginians unpopular at Athens at
this period. The Carthaginians of Plautus' *Poenulus*, probably from
Alexis' Καρχηδόνιοc, are sympathetically drawn, and an inscription
to be dated between 336 and 318 (*IG²* ii. 1. 418) records a friendly
embassy from Carthage. Aristotle gives a moderately favourable
account of the Carthaginian constitution, beginning πολιτεύεcθαι δὲ
δοκοῦcι καὶ Καρχηδόνιοι καλῶc, *Politics* 1272ᵇ24.   δραπέτα: A term
of abuse; there is no reason to suppose the man addressed really to
have been a runaway slave; cf. *Aspis* 398, Plaut. *Curculio* 290.

36 τί βλέπειc; 'What does that look mean?': an accusative after
βλέπω indicates the nature of the look, e.g. *Aspis* 464, θανάτουc
βλέπειc, 'you look like death', *Dysk.* 147, φιλάνθρωπον βλέπειν, 'to
look kind'.

39: It is not certain that there is a dicolon after αcτην. If not, one
should perhaps read ἐπειδή c᾽ ἐγγράφω, 'because I'm enrolling you
as the laws prescribe (and therefore rejecting your application)'.

40 κῆρυξ: Probably an official who will make announcements at the
meeting of the deme. At the beginning of the line it is possible that
a small detached fragment should be added, giving αγναγα[; this
would necessitate ἀγνά.

P. Col. 5031 is too fragmentary to yield any sense: there is mention of
marriage; someone will be a follower, carrying a sack, a wallet, and

a helmet; there are proper names, Daos and Ikonion, a town in Lykaonia, scanned here with a short first syllable ἰκ-, a scansion recorded by *Et. M.* 370. 45 as Menandrean and wrong (frag. 852 K–T).

Fragment 1. ὀψάριον, whence modern Greek ψάρι, 'fish', was originally an unrestricted diminutive of ὄψον, but came to be used particularly of fish, as here. In Mnesimachos frag. 3 K it is still general: τοὺς μὲν ἰχθῦς μοι κάλει ἰχθύδια, ὄψον ἂν λέγῃς ἕτερον κάλει ὀψάριον. If Bentley's emendation λιβανίδιον is right, the speaker seems to be a fisherman who has made only a tiny offering of incense to the stormy North Wind and so caught nothing: he will have to make do with boiling some lentil-porridge, proverbial as the poor man's dish, Ar. *Plut.* 1004, ἔπειτα πλουτῶν οὐκέθ᾽ ἥδεται φακῇ, Athenaios 156 e–158 d.

Fragment 3. λιτυέρςης was, according to Athenaios 619 a, a reapers' song. The mythological figure Lityerses, son of the Phrygian king Midas, who challenged passers-by to a reaping contest, was probably a fiction derived from the song. Gow on Theokritos x. 41 collects the material.

Fragment 7. Toup suggested that this fragment might come from Menander's *Karchedonios*; Meineke proposed to read Καρχηδονίῳ, as the name of the play from which it comes. It seems to be a conflation of a line from Euripides' *Telephos*, χρεία διδάςκει κἂν βραδύς τις ᾖ coφόν (frag. 715 Nauck), and a much more famous quotation from his *Stheneboia*, ποιητὴν δ᾽ ἄρα | ἔρως διδάςκει κἂν ἄμουςος ᾖ τὸ πρίν (frag. 663).

KITHARISTES

B 1 *P. Berol.* 9767. Three columns, the upper parts of which are much worn: the dotted letters in the OCT are mostly invisible on an excellent photograph, kindly lent me by Dr. Austin; they were read by Schubart from the papyrus.

Menander's *Kitharistes* contained a character named Phanias (frag. 1); this papyrus mentions a Phanias, who is a *kitharistes* (96–9). It is therefore highly probable that the papyrus, despite the doubts of Wilamowitz, who first published it, contains part of that play. The style seems worthy of Menander.

From the first column only a few words are preserved; they come from ends of lines. Someone, perhaps a young man, perhaps the Moschion who appears later, is talking to a woman (ὦ φιλτάτη, 2), perhaps about the violation of a girl (ὕβρει τὸ γεγονός, 19, cf. *Dysk.* 246, 298, and βίᾳ, 20). The woman is more probably the girl's nurse (Del Corno) or mother (as Austin suggested to me) than his own mother (Webster). He may have protested that he wanted to marry the victim (γάμου, 7). After 27 a gap of three lines' space, where no letters remain, made Sudhaus suspect that the lost centre of the column was occupied by the word *ΧΟΡΟΥ*, indicating the end of an act. Certainly four to five lines later the beginning of the second column shows that a new scene, with new characters, has begun. Körte suggests that this is the beginning of Act II; this can be true only if the first appearance of the chorus was not introduced by the formula of *Epitr.*, *Perik.*, *Dysk.*, *Aspis*, since the lines preceding the gap end οὐθενός, ουνεδει, λαθραι, and]ρων.

The new scene is said by Körte to be between two young men, but since neither speaker is Moschion, this is to overfurnish the play with young men. There is in fact no positive reason for supposing either to be young. The one tells the other that he does not know what has become of some woman, whose arrival by sea is long overdue. There is some trouble over property, and he proposes to ask the other man's advice. Unfortunately the details of the situation are obscure; they will be discussed in the notes.

The stage is left empty by the departure of these characters. Moschion's father appears: his son has unexpectedly sent for him from their farm in the country; usually the young man keeps out of his way. Moschion then arrives, anxious to meet his father. Here we reach the third column, of which only the left-hand side survives. After some uncertain exchanges, Moschion declares that his intended bride is the daughter of their neighbour Phanias, the harpist; he had met her, or seen her, in Ephesos. Mutilated as it is, this can still be recognized as a delightful scene. When we ask its relation to what precedes, little more than guesswork is possible. Since characters named Moschion are given to rape or seduction, one may suspect that he is the man concerned in the first column. One may also guess that the man in the second column, who is awaiting the woman from overseas and has himself come from some other place, had himself also been in Ephesos and was in some way connected with the events there concerning Moschion. He seems to belong to a house on the stage: hence either there were, unusually, three houses represented or he belongs to Phanias' house. Wilamowitz guessed him to be Phanias' son, but he may, as van Leeuwen suggested, be Phanias himself, who, being a widower, has found a new woman to share his home.

35–8: Schubart claimed to read on the papyrus the letters dotted in OCT, but the obscurity of the result advises caution. In 35 τήν may have been followed by a name in the genitive case, indicating parentage, but then the parent must have been the mother (e.g. τὴν Κλεοῦc), for there is no masculine name that will fit. λαβών would accordingly mean, as so often, 'having taken to wife'. Del Corno argues that this is impossible: speaker B has brought his daughter with him, but not his wife. This is not certainly right: speaker A may assume that B has brought with him the woman he has married, for he need not at 42 say, as Körte makes him, τί γὰρ οὐκ ἤγαγεc . . . τὴν γυναῖκα; A very small change gives τί γάρ; οὐκ ἤγαγεc . . . τὴν γυναῖκα; and there are other possibilities.

Nevertheless it is tempting to suppose that B has brought home this 'daughter', who is *his* daughter, and also the girl that Moschion loves. Against this is the strangeness of an Athenian's reckoning his daughter rich, and himself not. Del Corno, it is true, wishes to dissociate θυγατέρα and ταύτην, making λαβών . . . δεῦρο a parenthesis, but the co-ordinating particles τε . . . θ' prevent this.

B's reply to A, as constituted by Schubart, means 'I count everything as hers and hers alone and count my wife as mine', λογίζομαι being taken ἀπὸ κοινοῦ. This is clumsy, but the letters μαιτεμ are clear, so that Herwerden's suggestion λογίζομ' ἅττ' ἐμαυτῷ 'κτηcάμην (*Mnem.* xxxviii [1910], 221) implies corruption in B 1.

39: If the speaker is Phanias, he is an Athenian. An alliance with a woman who was not the legitimate daughter of an Athenian citizen, but merely 'a free woman from a Greek city', would constitute her, not a γαμετὴ γυνή, but a παλλακὴ ἐπ᾽ ἐλευθεροῖc παιcί. It has been guessed that the woman proved to be of legitimate Athenian parentage, perhaps Moschion's sister. Although there is nothing to prove the guess wrong, it is no more than speculation.

40 πάντα ταῦτ᾽ ἐκτηcάμην: If the speaker has just returned from his travels, on which he has allied himself with a rich woman, by ταῦτα he may refer to his luggage, which at 51 he probably orders to be taken into his house. But it is not certain whether that luggage is her property or something else which he has acquired himself. Further, if the speaker *is* Phanias, he has been in Athens long enough for his neighbour, who has been in the country for some time, to be aware of it (100–1).

41: The meaning *may* be 'I do not need to buy (or hire) a woman from a πορνοβοcκόc', since I have made a much better provision for myself by acquiring this free Greek woman. But there may be a reference to some specific circumstance, to which the fragments that survive give no clue. Jensen's θυγατέρα appears incompatible with the traces.

42–3: The traces of letters after εcτιν (*sic*) and before ηγαγεc are indeterminate. Editors suppose εcτιν to be an error for εcτι and write πῶc δέ, or τί γάρ, οὐκ ἤγαγεc: this may be right; at least it fits the space. So does ἐcτὶν ἄλλο; οὐκ ἤγαγεc. In 43 καὶ τὴν οὐcίαν is not improbable.

44–5: As an alternative to Körte's text, the friend may ask οὐκ ἐλήλυθεν; and the other reply οὔπω γε, γε being frequent in answers.

χρόνων: The plural is surprising, since it normally means 'points of time', i.e. dates, or 'periods of time', while here only a single period appears to be involved. But a single period may be divided in thought into a number of periods, and so appear even longer. The plural is often used in Greek of a single mass that can be divided into like parts, e.g. ἅλεc, ὕδατα, αἵματα, καπνοί may have the same denotation as ἅλc, ὕδωρ, αἷμα, καπνόc.

46 λογίζομαι πᾶν: 'I take everything into account, think of every possibility.'

47: περὶ λῃcτάc is a supplement giving good sense, as is Körte's περὶ ναύταc, since the honesty of sailors was not above suspicion. But B 1 has]ζαc or]ξαc, not]ταc.

48: B 1 has μημαθωc, usually interpreted as μὴ 'μαθῶc, 'Isn't that perhaps silly?' or 'Don't talk in a silly way.' But the prodelision is paralleled in Menander only by *Sam.* 580, ἰὼ 'νθρωποι, and the danger of sea-voyages is too well known for fears to be foolish, although a would-be comforter might, to be sure, depreciate them. Moreover ἀμαθής has not yet been found in New Comedy and is 'absent from papyri, N.T. and Septuagint' (Moulton–Milligan, *Vocab. of Gk. Testament*). I believe that μηθαμῶς (Maas, *Rh. Mus.* lxvii [1913], 364) = μηδαμῶς, 'don't talk like that', should be read; for the spelling cf. μηθαμῶς *Phasma* 87 and in B at *Sam.* 573, [μη]θαμου in *Pap. Arsin.* of Plato, *Phaedo* 67 b 3; for the word cf. *Sam.* 134, 562, 663, 723, *Dysk.* 502, 617, 751.

49 εἰκός τι πάcχειν: 'It is natural that you should be upset.' **οὕτωc** may be quasi-inferential: '*So* if you come along with me to the market-place, you shall hear the rest of the story, about which you must give me your advice.'

53: Moschion's father enters, from the country. Körte calls him Laches, taking the name from frag. 4. The guess is not unlikely. **οὐχ αὑτοῦ . . . ἔργον**: 'An uncharacteristic action', cf. such phrases as frag. 584, ἔργον γυναικὸc ἐκ λόγου πίcτιν λαβεῖν, 'it's like a woman to believe what is said'.

57: *Ed. pr.* read ἔπινε, G. Manteuffel from the published photograph ἔτεινε (*Charisteria Przychocki*, 1934); the new photograph unambiguously shows ἔπινε, which has the advantage of explaining why the son kept out of the father's way, and of leading up to the imputation of extravagance contained in 59–60. Manteuffel's argument that elsewhere in Menander πίνειν has an object expressed does not survive *Dysk.* 858, 902.

58–61: The general sense is clear, the exact wording uncertain. For γαρ ην (clearly written) Arnott plausibly suggests παρῆν. Nothing altogether satisfactory has been proposed for 59: Körte prints οὐ μὴν ἐπλήγην, 'I was not hurt by his conduct', quoting Plato, *Epist.* 347 d; but the word seems more suited to being wounded, as in Plato, by a single act than by a continued course of conduct. Wilamowitz suggested οὐ μὴν πρὸς ὀργήν (sc. νουθετῶν), but that, probably even with κατ' ὀργήν, is too long. Körte originally proposed δι' ὀργήν, but if the sense is 'angrily' this preposition elsewhere takes the genitive, ὀργῆς. In Aischines ii. 2, οὐ δι' ὀργήν means 'not because he was angry'. Jensen wrote οὐ μὴν ἐπέcτην, 'I did not stand over him', or 'I paid no attention (LSJ s.v. ἐφίcτημι, V)', excellent for sense, but]γην is certain. At the beginning, however, ουμ[is unconvincing, ουκ[more probable. Hesitantly I suggest οὐ παρῆν ὁ νουθετῶν· πατὴρ | οὐκ [εἶχον ὀρ]γήν, 'There was no one there to reprove him. I was his father, but I was not angry with him.' In 61 there is little to choose between ἠδίκηκεν and αἰτία 'cτιν; acid remarks made by old men at the expense of their wives are traditional in comedy.

62 'cτιν . . . ποεῖ: Sc. Moschion.

64 ἄρτι: This seems a necessary restoration. Phrynichos and Lucian, *Pseudosophistes* 1, condemn its construction with the future. Here it may be taken with what precedes, 'if he is not in at the moment', although Wilamowitz, who proposed the word, took it with πορεύσομαι, citing Antiphanes frag. 26. 7 K, τίc ποτε, ὦ Καλλιμέδων, cε κατέδετ' ἄρτι τῶν φίλων, where Meineke thought, not very probably, that ἆρα should be read.

65 πρὸς Ἑρμαῖc: These statues of Hermes were near the Stoa Poikile; in Mnesimachos frag. 4 K they mark a place where young men serving in the cavalry may be found. The father may therefore here suggest that his son will be in the company of rich young friends.

66: As the father is about to enter, or more probably actually enters, his house, Moschion arrives from somewhere in the town, eager to know whether the old man has arrived, for his business will brook no delay. The mutilated third column begins at 69, and for more than twenty lines little can be made out with regard to their sense. Improbable supplements are to be found in Sudhaus's edition; grotesque ones in an article by G. Manteuffel, *Eos*, xlii (1947), 63. At 73 father and son meet, and the question of marriage is soon introduced.

76 ἀνδρεϊcτέον: 'I (or 'you') must be brave.' The usual verb is ἀνδρίζομαι. ἀνδρεΐζομαι, from ἀνδρεῖος instead of ἀνδρ-, recurs in Clem. Alex. *Strom.* ii. 81. 3, iv. 48. 1. Austin recalls *Sam.* 63, ἀλλ' ὅπωc ἔcει ἀνδρεῖος, in a similar context.

79 γῆμαί με βούλει: It is not a necessary inference that the father has any particular girl in mind, as Del Corno concludes him to have.

80–92: These lines may all be spoken by the father; but equally well some may belong to Moschion. The absence of paragraphi from this MS. makes it impossible to say.

93: Note the jingle of Ἔφεcον ἔπεcον. Körte supplements cυcτρ[όφωc ἐρῶ· μολὼν] εἰc τὴν Ἔφεcον ἔπεcον [ἔρωτοc εἰc πέδαc. cυcτρόφωc and cύcτροφος are words otherwise unknown, although cυcτροφή, 'terseness', occurs in the literary critics; the rest is too poetical. In any case the word appears to begin cπ[or cτ.[. In 94 ἔπεcον γὰρ εἰc ἔρωτ' ἐγώ is probably the sense required.

95 δειπνοφορία: A processional carrying of food was part of some Attic festivals also, e.g. Oschophoria, Plut. *Thes.* 23. Wilamowitz inclined to think that the poet invented this Ephesian festival, rather than that he knew of the celebration there called Δαιτίc, at which youths and maidens offered meals to the goddess Artemis (*Et. M.* s.v.). This seems over-sceptical.

97 Εὐωνυμέωc: Euonymon was an Attic deme to the south side of the city. The father naturally supposes that a girl seen at an Ephesian festival where maidens carried offerings was herself an Ephesian, and is surprised that the demotic name Euonymeus was also used in Ephesos. Moschion explains that the girl's father was an Athenian temporarily in Ephesos because of debts. It remains surprising if she, as a foreigner, took part in a civic procession; but perhaps she was only a spectator.

It is odd that settlers from Euonymon were supposed to have gone to Ephesos, where one of the five tribes was named Euonymoi. It can hardly be a mere coincidence that Phanias is represented as belonging to that deme. But nothing in this passage depends upon these facts.

98: χρέα [πράξων παρῆν] or [ἦλθεν φυγών] were both suggested by Wilamowitz. Debt-collecting is a common reason for being abroad—Mnesilochus in Plaut. *Bacchides* spent two years in Ephesos collecting a debt—but he preferred the second of his alternatives, believing that Phanias must have once been poor, and that he would have left his daughter in Athens if he had gone to Ephesos to collect, not to escape, debts. There is nothing in our fragments to show this, any more than there is to support his belief that the father did not welcome the son's interest in Phanias' daughter. We simply do not know what Phanias' financial circumstances had been, nor how he was regarded by Moschion's father.

99 ἐντεῦθεν: Either he had come 'from here', i.e. from Athens, or he was collecting debts 'from there', i.e. from Ephesos.   κιθαριcτοῦ: The playing of the κιθάρα was widely taught, and reckoned as one of Apollo's customs. A κιθαριcτής might teach young people, but by Menander's time there were many competitions at which success was highly prized. Some performers sang as they played, and were specifically called κιθαρῳδοί.

Fragment 1. There is no means of telling who the speaker is, nor what trouble has lighted upon Phanias. Del Corno hesitantly suggests that a false report had arrived that the ship carrying the woman and her riches had been lost. Philemon, frag. 96 K, is a less lively treatment of the same theme.

2 μή is used because freedom from debt is represented as a *characteristic* of the rich, K–G ii. 185. The order of words, μὴ τὸ δανείζεcθαι not τὸ μὴ δανείζεcθαι, implies that the speaker has in mind the opposite of borrowing, i.e. (presumably) having funds of one's own (ibid. ii. 180).

3 cτρεφομένουc ἄνω κάτω: Cf. Plato, *Ion* 541 e, ὥcπερ ὁ Πρωτεὺc παντοδαπὸς γίγνῃ cτρεφόμενος ἄνω καὶ κάτω, but whereas that is meta-phorical, here the phrase is literal.

5 ἀλλὰ τῶν πτωχῶν τινα: Sc. ταῦτα ποεῖν. τινα is suspect, being possibly repeated from the previous line. If right, it must mean 'any poor man'.

6 μακαρίους: For this use of the word to mean 'prosperous, well-to-do', cf. Arist. *EN* 1157ᵇ21, 1169ᵇ24, 1170ᵃ2.

8–10: The meaningless play on cύνεcτιν, πάρεcτιν, the triple repetition of βίῳ, and the metaphorical cυγκαταγηράcκει raise the level of style, and are probably intended to provoke a smile, even if the auditor approves the sentiment.

Fragment 2. This *may* be part of Phanias' reply to frag. 1. It was not unusual for friends to club together to provide funds for another who had fallen on evil days; their contributions were called an ἔρανος. There may have been occasions when a single friend put a man on his feet. Cf. *Sam.* 16 n.

Fragments 3, 4. The nature of the ἀδικία is not determinable, and may not be the same in both fragments.

Fragment 5. The elision of the infinitive in -ναι has no certain parallel in Menander, although introduced by some editors at *Perik.* 343, *Dysk.* 895 (and see Ar. *Clouds* 1357, *Frogs* 692) and the postponement of τε to fourth place is paralleled only at *Sam.* 445. The chapter of Athenaios from which the fragment comes has suffered cuts and confusion, and it may be that some verb, that governed ἀκούcματα, has fallen out, e.g. φιλόμουcον εἶναι ⟨κἀγαπᾶν⟩ αὐτὸν πάνυ | ἀκούcματα.

εἰς τρυφήν τε παιδεύεcθαι: Like εἰς ἀρετήν or εἰς τέχνην παιδεύεcθαι. The verb is probably passive, but the middle, 'cause to be trained', not absolutely excluded.

Fragment 6. **οἰκοcίτους:** The word means 'providing their own meals'. The point may be to suggest that this performer (? Phanias) gets his audience by asking them to dinner. But if the line is a question this interpretation is wrong.

Fragment 7. **οὕτω τι . . . ἐπίπονον:** τι is adverbial, cf. Alexis frag. 210, Fraenkel on *Agamemnon* 884, Hdt. iii. 12, οὕτω δή τι ἰcχυραί.

Fragment 9. Ancient scholars were uncertain of the meaning of the word cκοῖδος. According to Pollux x. 16 he was ἐπὶ τῶν cκευῶν or ἐπὶ τῶν cιτίων, Hesychios believed him to be concerned with law-courts, Arkadios p. 47. 28 explains him as ὁ οἰκονόμος. L. Mancaleoni, *RFIC* xcii (1964), 422, calls attention to Sophocles' phrase τὸν ταμίαν

Ἴακχον, *Ant.* 1152. It is prudent to refrain from speculation about Menander's use of the word.

Two other fragments may come from *Kitharistes*. The name Φανίας recurs in frag. 797:

> καλὸν τὸ Κείων νόμιμόν ἐςτι, Φανία.
> ὁ μὴ δυνάμενος ζῆν καλῶς οὐ ζῇ κακῶς,

quoted by Strabo x. 486, who explains that at Keos there was a law that men over sixty should take hemlock, in order that there should be food enough for the younger. Frag. 544 appears in Körte–Thierfelder as

> ἔργον ἐςτι, Φανία,
> μακρὰν ϲυνήθειαν βραχεῖ λῦϲ᾽ ἐν χρόνῳ,

but the MSS. of Stobaios have πανία, except Br, which offers παπία, an emendation as probable as Φανία.

KOLAX

O 1   *P. Oxy.* 409. Three consecutive columns, each of thirty-four lines, from a roll of the second century A.D. At the time of the original publication the tops of the first and third columns were missing, together with a few letters from the top of the second. They were found by E. G. Turner and published in 1968, together with the beginnings of eighteen lines from a fourth column, as *P. Oxy.* 2655, in *Oxy. Pap.* vol. xxxiii. The roll did not contain the whole play, but extracts only. (1) Below line 54 it had a *diple* and goes on with 85, but *P. Oxy.* 1237, which here overlaps, continues the scene with at least sixteen more verses; (2) a space after 13 probably marks an omission; and (3) it is conceivable that 119 and 120, between which there is a line, were not consecutive in the play (see n. ad loc.). It is also possible that 95 did not follow immediately on 94 (see n. there). Strictly speaking, only the extract that occupies 15–54 (I take it to be a single extract, although there is no proof) is known to be from *Kolax*, 43–5 and 50–1 being quoted elsewhere as from that play; but the other passages suit the play so well that in all probability they too are from it. The purpose of this well-written roll can only be guessed. D. Del Corno, *Dioniso*, xxxviii (1964) = *Selezioni Menandree*, 36, recalls the practice of reciting scenes from Menander at symposia. Two explanatory notes with lemmata are a feature as yet unique in Menandrean papyri; notes without lemmata occur in B at *Dysk.* 113, 944, *Sam.* 325, 656.

Grenfell and Hunt, the original editors, transcribe as certain many letters of which no sign can be seen on their plates; in general Turner's re-examination of the papyrus, which he caused to be cleaned, confirms their readings.

O 5   *P. Oxy.* 1237. The tops of two columns, badly damaged, and five scraps. The first line is 52. Except that in 66 it contains the names Daos and Gnathon, it contributes nothing intelligible, and is therefore not commented on here.

Professor Handley informs me that an unpublished Oxyrhynchus fragment contains an insignificant scrap of *Kolax*, identified as such by interlinear names βιαϲ and ϲτρουθιαϲ.

Plot

The remains of *Kolax*, although not inconsiderable, are difficult to interpret. Little help is given by the known fact that Terence made use of the play for his own *Eunuchus*. His own words, in the prologue, are

> Colax Menandrist: in east parasitus colax
> et miles gloriosus: eas se non negat
> personas transtulisse in Eunuchum suam   (30–2)

These characters he calls Gnatho and Thraso, but it is disputed whether they brought with them any part of the plot of *Kolax*. Wehrli, *Motivstudien*, 104 ff., argues that Menander's Εὐνοῦχος, the basis of Terence's play, also contained a soldier and his parasite, and that Terence did no more than add to their roles the purely episodic scenes 230–64, 391–430 (adding to this the asides by Parmeno); these scenes do not affect the plot, but serve merely for characterization. No doubt he is right that they are based upon scenes in *Kolax*, but it is difficult to assert with confidence that no other part of *Eunuchus* is so based. Other scholars (e.g. Leo, *GGN* 1903, 690, Jachmann, ibid. 1921, 70) have supposed that the young man's rival in Εὐνοῦχος was not a soldier, and that the siege scene of *Eunuchus* (771 ff.) must be adapted from *Kolax*, where it was prepared for by the speech of the πορνοβοσκός preserved in our fragments (120 ff.). For all Wehrli's criticisms, this remains a possibility. Yet even if the rival was not a soldier, the origin of the siege scene is a matter for debate: A. Klotz, *Würzburger Jahrbücher* i (1946), 23, maintains that it is not Menandrean at all.

A further difficulty is that the parasite who in *Kolax* is attached to the soldier is named Strouthias (frag. 2), but that a Gnathon, who must from his name (even though it was not unknown in real life, *Pros. Att.* 3050–2) be a parasite, also occurs in the remains. Did *Kolax* contain two parasites, or was Strouthias a *nom de guerre* assumed by Gnathon in his dealings with the soldier (Kuiper)? The latter solution is on the whole easier. Terence's Gnatho boasts himself to be the inventor of a new technique of flattery (247 ff.), which he later exercises on Thraso; this technique was exercised in *Kolax* by Strouthias on Bias (frags. 2, 3). Gnatho also says that he will found a school of 'Gnathonici', a word generally supposed to suggest 'Platonici' (264). If Terence took the implied play on words from Menander, it is hard to resist the conclusion that Gnathon and Strouthias were identical. But there is no proof that the word Πλατωνικοί was applied to members of the Academy in the late fourth century B.C. K. Büchner indeed guessed (*SIFC* xiv [1937], 156 = *Stud. z. röm. Lit.* i. 12) that Terence

substituted Gnathonici (Platonici) for Ϲτρουθίειοι (cf. Ἐπικούρειοι);
but this is no more than a fancy with a remote chance of truth. If
such guesses have any value, why not Γναθώνειοι∽Ζηνώνειοι, a name
known to have been used in Menander's lifetime (Epicurus frag. 198
Usener)? For the adoption of a false name by a parasite there is a
partial parallel in Plautus' *Curculio*, where Curculio adopts the name
Summanus in order to trick a *leno* and his soldier-client (413). On the
other hand Lucian, *Fugitivus* 19, speaks of τὸν Γναθωνίδην ἢ τὸν
Ϲτρουθίαν; but is Gnathonides identical with our Gnathon? Körte
did not see how a single parasite could adhere to and harm both the
young lover and his rival the soldier; but this is to underrate the
ingenuity of the poet, who might have delighted in contriving that
situation. Although the balance of probability favours, in my view,
the identity of Gnathon and Strouthias, one must keep an open mind.
An argument, supposed by some to be cogent, namely that the title
Κόλαξ, being singular, excludes two parasites, overlooks the possibility
that Gnathon's part, although not identical with that of Strouthias,
was not remarkable for flattery.

The analysis of Terence's *Eunuchus* might lead to some conclusions
about *Kolax*; but they would not carry universal conviction, and the
task is far too complicated to be attempted here. The hope of reconstructing the plot of the latter play must be abandoned so long as our
evidence remains as inconclusive as it is. What can be said with
confidence is that the situation round which the plot revolved was
that a young man, Pheidias, wished to get possession of a girl who
was in the hands of a πορνοβοϲκόϲ; that he had a rival in a soldier,
Bias, who was attended by a flattering parasite, Strouthias; and that
the soldier was worsted, perhaps as the result of some action by
Strouthias. A marriage of Pheidias and the girl seems unlikely; 117
strongly suggests that she was actively a *hetaira*; in no surviving play
does this fate befall a girl of citizen birth, although it may be narrowly
averted. The conclusion of the play may be preserved in *Eunuchus*.
There Phaedria and Thraso will share the favours of Thais, for which
the latter alone will pay. This is not in harmony with the earlier part
of the play, where Thais is a woman of strong character, whose assent
to such an arrangement could not be taken for granted, and Phaedria
demands that she should be faithful to him. It seems less likely that
Terence invented this conclusion than that he transferred it from
Kolax, which, so far as we can see, it may have suited. Pheidias here,
unlike Phaedria, was probably short of funds (109 ff.) and the girl
a slave, whose personal inclinations need not be consulted. But further
knowledge might upset this theory. For attempts to reconstruct the
plot see Webster, *StM* 67, Kuiper, *Mnem.* lix (1932), 165.

Κόλαξ is conventionally translated 'flatterer' or 'fawner': the latter is better. Essentially the κόλαξ makes himself agreeable or useful to another man, not out of goodwill but to serve his own ends. The various forms this 'fawning' can take are illustrated in Plutarch's essay, *Quomodo adulator* etc., i.e. how to distinguish a κόλαξ from a φίλος. There was a tendency to replace the word by παράϲιτοϲ, properly applicable to the κόλαξ whose reward was to be fed at his patron's table. This name was apparently first given, perhaps by Alexis, by way of a joke, since it originally denoted certain religious functionaries (Athenaios vi. 234 d ff.; W. G. Arnott, *GRBS* ix [1968], 161). Frequently the κόλαξ is found undertaking actions that would be beneath his patron's dignity, or that involve deceit (e.g. Phormio and Curculio in the plays named after them); this may be relevant to the part played by the κόλαξ of this play. The poets of Middle and New Comedy used their ingenuity to depict varied and new types of κόλαξ or 'parasite' (Athenaios vi. 236 b–262 a), and no doubt Menander's κόλαξ was a striking and original creation.

Date

Certain indications point, not very conclusively, to a date not long after 315 B.C. Most important is the mention of the pancratiast Astyanax, whose fame was at its height in the 126th Olympiad (316–313 B.C.). Then the soldier has been in Kappadokia, where we know of military operations in 322 and 315 (Beloch, *Griech. Geschichte* iv. 1. 79, 123). The list of *hetairai* whose favours he is said to enjoy is hard to interpret, since their identification is uncertain (frag. 4 n.). But Chrysis and Antikyra are probably the women whom Demetrios Poliorketes established in the Parthenon in 304/3 (Plut. *Demetr.* 24). Hence K. Büchner, *SIFC* xiv (1937), 151 (= *Stud. z. röm. Lit.* i. 7), argues that the play is to be dated towards the end of the century. This builds on the shaky assumption that a *poule de luxe* necessarily has a very short career. The mention of Pyrrhus' customary tactics in *Eunuchus* 783 hardly belongs to *Kolax*, since his reputation was made after Menander's death; see A. Klotz, *Würzburger Jahrbücher* i (1946), 23, against E. Bethe, *Hermes*, xxxiii (1902), 278.

The question must be regarded as open, since Astyanax's reputation, like that of W. G. Grace, may have lived on; and there may have been later unknown wars in Kappadokia (cf. Plaut. *Mil. Glor.* 52; the date of the original is unknown, but 299 B.C. and 287 B.C. have been suggested). F. A. Steinmetz, *Die Freundschaftslehre des Panaitios*, 166, suggests that Bias had been with Seleukos at his winter quarters in Kappadokia in 302/1 B.C.; Seleukos was then βαϲιλεύϲ (cf. Ter. *Eun.* 397) and had a large force of Indian elephants (ibid. 413).

Timachidas of Rhodes (*c.* 100 B.C.) composed a commentary on the play, see Körte–Thierfelder, *Menandri quae supersunt*, vol. ii, Testimonium 52.

1–13: Körte adopts a current view that here Pheidias explains in a monologue that his father had gone abroad and left his estate in the hands of administrators (7), providing only enough money for the son's bare support. This makes good sense, but is quite uncertain. If δεcπότηc is right in 12, the speaker is probably a slave. Turner guesses that 1 may have been an entrance-line, e.g. ὡc οὐδέν ἐcτ' ἄπιcτον ἐν τῷ νῦν βίῳ.

7 διοικηταῖc: διοικεῖν is used of the management of anything from a state to a household, but διοικητήc is elsewhere found only of important public officials.

8: κακόδαιμον is a necessary restoration. Does the speaker address this vocative to himself?

12 ἑcτιάτωρ: Many scholars connect this with frag. 1 and suppose that Pheidias is one of the tetradistae, and responsible for their entertainment.

The second half of the line that succeeds 13 is blank; the first half may have had some words. The first extract therefore ends here. There is no telling how much has been omitted: Körte believed that the next extract begins with the end of the supposed monologue, but it seems rather to belong to a new scene.

19–54: The vocative Φειδία (20) shows that one character here is Pheidias, the young man who must be the hero of the piece. The unmetrical word Δωρίc at the end of 19 may be explained as the name of a speaker that has been falsely included in the dialogue; but it must be observed that nowhere else does this MS. give a speaker's name. There are other possibilities, e.g. Δωρίc may be misplaced, having been omitted at its correct position earlier in the line. To the question who Doris may be, there is no clue; possibly she is an attendant of the girl whom Pheidias desires.

The second speaker here may then be Doris (Robert) or another. Later, at 68–9, Daos is present and probably Gnathon also; Leo and Körte suppose Pheidias to converse here with the former, Kuiper and Jensen with the latter. If Doris speaks, she must at once depart, for she is not suited to a part in what follows: this is most plausibly interpreted as being a harangue by Gnathon (Kuiper, Webster, Del Corno), who apparently alleges that the gods help the wicked, illustrating this by the success of Bias, and boasts how he would have upbraided him in the market-place, but refrained because his insults might have been put down to drunkenness, since he had been followed by a slave with wine-jars. The whole of this is, however, assigned by Körte to Pheidias, as the second half is by Jensen, cf. A. W. Gomme, *JHS* lix (1939), 312; van Leeuwen assigned the first half to Pheidias, the second to an unnamed 'amicus'. But both the impiety and the boastful protestations suit the 'parasite' better than the 'hero'; see further note on 40 ff.

20 θαρρεῖν; A high point after the word justifies this punctuation.

22 φλήναφον: Either 'idle talk' or 'talker of nonsense', frag. 97 n.

23 δεσποῖν' Ἀθηνᾶ: This would seem to be a citizen's appeal: Pheidias or Gnathon speaks, not Daos or Doris. ὦ δεσποῖν' Ἀθηνᾶ is used by Theron, the parasite, at *Sik.* 144, but cῶζέ με would suit a despairing lover, as does οἴχομαι in 39.

27–8: A probable sense is: 'The gods favour rascals, while we who are well behaved never fare well.'

29: In the right-hand margin there is a note: διμοιριτ(ης)· ὁ διπλουν λαμβανων των στρατιωτ(ων) μισθον. Arrian, *Anab.* vii. 23. 3, reports that Alexander recruited Persians and formed sections of sixteen men, twelve of whom were Persian and four Macedonian; one of the latter was in command, and of the others one was a διμοιρίτης and two δεκαστάτηροι, so called from their pay, which was less than that of a διμοιρίτης but greater than that of τῶν οὐκ ἐν τιμῇ στρατευομένων. A δεκαστάτηρος would receive 10 staters = 40 drachmas a month, so that it is likely that an ordinary soldier received 30 dr. and a διμοιρίτης 60 dr. In Lucian's *Dial. Meretr.* 9. 5 a soldier who claims to be a χιλίαρχος is said by his rival to have possibly been a διμοιρίτης. This evidence shows that a διμοιρίτης was in Menander's time of no exalted rank, but something like a corporal. Earlier, among the Ten Thousand, a λοχαγός, commander of a hundred men, received only double the pay of a ranker, Xen. *Anab.* vii. 2. 36, 6. 1.

30: Diphilos frag. 55 K enumerates a soldier's burdens as κλίνην, κάδον, στρώματα, c⟨ίγ⟩υνον, ἀσκόπηραν, θύλακον, 'bed (?), water-bottle, blankets, spear, bag, haversack'. *P. Colon.* 5031 (*ZPE* iv [1969], 170), probably from Menander's *Karchedonios* (ibid. v [1970], 60), has a line that ends θ]ύλακον, πήραν, κράνος.

31 διβολίαν: In Plut. *Amat.* 754 f the word seems to mean some kind of garment, but may be corrupt. Elsewhere it denotes some missile weapon: Aristophanes frag. 476, καὶ τῶν πλατυλόγχων διβολίαν ἀκοντίων, Plut. *Marius* 25, ἀκόντισμα δ' ἦν ἑκάστῳ διβολία, Herodian ii. 13, τάς τε διβολίας καὶ τὰ δόρατα ἐπισείειν. LSJ's 'double-pointed lance, halbert' is unhelpful, since a lance is quite unlike a halbert and a double-pointed one an improbable missile, since it would have less penetrating power than one with a single point. I suspect that the word means 'a *pair* of javelins'.

32: Körte prints νῦν πάντα ταῦθ' ὁ δυςτ]υχὴς ὄνος φέρει, but other senses are at least as possible, e.g. ἄχθος ὅςον οὐδὲ δυςτ]υχὴς ὄνος φέρει.

33: Wilamowitz in proposing ὁ δέ ποτε Βῖθυς γέγονεν ἐξ]αίφνης Βίας may have had in mind Ar. *Wasps* 49, ἄνθρωπος ὢν εἶτ' ἐγένετ' ἐξαίφνης κόραξ. There is, however, no evidence that Βῖθυς would be regarded as a barbarian name; it was borne by a Macedonian general in the later third century.

34–9: All this is quite uncertain.

40 ff.: Although most editors give the bitter words about Bias to Pheidias, they suit Gnathon better. (1) A parasite is at least as likely as the young hero to think of brawling in the market-place; (2) it is unusual for characters in dialogue to utter *sententiae* like that of 43–5, grammatically independent and completely generalized; one may suspect the speaker of insincerity, cf. Chaireas' *sententiae*, *Dysk.* 62–3, 128, 129–30; (3) Gnathon might suitably go to buy wine for the meeting of the tetradistae (Kuiper, *Mnem.* lviii [1931], 172).

40: 'The space seems too short for the exigencies of the verse', Grenfell–Hunt.   κατέπτηκεν: This is known only as the perfect of καταπτήςςω, 'cower'. LSJ suppose that it here comes from καταπέτομαι, which seems better suited to the context. The correct form of the perfect, which would be πέπτηκα, is not in fact found, being replaced by πεπότημαι; an irregular form might have arisen under the influence of the active aorist that is found in compounds such as ἀνέπτην, κατέπτην, etc.

41: Cf. Plato, *Rep.* 615 b, ἢ πόλεις προδόντες ἢ ςτρατόπεδα. The restorations are far from certain.

48 τὰ Θάςια: Cf. Machon 266, παρῆν ἔχων δύο Χῖα, Θάςια τέccαρα. Thasian wine was, along with Chian and Lesbian, among those most frequently imported at Athens, cf. Athenaios 28 d–29 e. Hermippos frag. 82 reckons it second only to Chian. The noun here omitted will probably be the name of a jar, e.g. ςταμνία (Ar. *Lys.* 196) or ἀμφορείδια (id. *Eccl.* 1119), or κεράμια (*PSI* 438. 3) or possibly οἰνάρια, cf. Alexis frag. 275, Θαςίοις οἰναρίοις.

50 νεκρός: As we might say 'a skeleton'; for this colloquial use cf. Sannyrion frag. 2 K, Μέλητον τὸν ἀπὸ Ληναίου νεκρόν. This Meletos is included by Aristophanes among the ἀδοφοῖται (frag. 149), a word Hesychios explains by οἱ λεπτοὶ καὶ ἰςχνοὶ καὶ ἐγγὺς θανάτου ὄντες.

53: Leo's μιcῶ cε interrupts the series of questions fired (in imagination) at the soldier; and ἐκ τῆc ὁδοῦ (Petersen) does not altogether suit the scene, which is not in a street but in the market-place. *Ed. pr.*'s ἑτέρωcε is probable, being paralleled by Ar. *Ach.* 828, εἰ μὴ 'τέρωcε cυκοφαντήcειc τρέχων.

55–70: *P. Oxy.* 1237 preserves a few letters from the line-ends from 53 onwards. Daos is named at 68 as uttering the words οὐκοῦν Γνάθων, and in the next line we have ὦ Γνάθων, an address which does not prove him to be present, cf. *Dysk.* 220, *Aspis* 14. After this there is a gap of at least ten verses, and then the next column gives the beginnings of half-a-dozen lines; 72 begins τον πορνοβοcκο[.

85 ff.: In this, the third extract given by *P. Oxy.* 409, the speakers are a slave and his young master (τρόφιμε, 86). The latter may fairly confidently be identified with Pheidias, for it is not likely that there was a second young man who stood in danger. The slave may be Daos of the preceding scene, but a second slave is by no means impossible. He announces that he has discovered the universal cause of great disasters, the unexpected attack of a pretended friend. It is interesting to compare a similar passage from Diphilos, frag. 24 K, ὁ γὰρ κόλαξ καὶ cτρατηγὸν καὶ δικαcτὴν καὶ φίλουc καὶ τὰc πόλειc ἀνατρέπει λόγῳ κακουργῷ μικρὸν ἡδύναc χρόνον . . . αἱ κρίcειc θ' ἡμῶν νοcοῦcι. How much tamer than Menander!

85 εἷc: The 'one man' is probably identical with τοῦτον of 89. τὰ πάντα . . . πράγματα, 'this whole affair of yours', cf. *Sam.* 548.

87: c[οἱ λόγο]ν and c[οἱ πάλι]ν are restorations both made doubtful by traces, two places before ν, that look like the base of δ, μ, or ω (Rea), or α (Turner).

88 ἑόρακαc fills the space better than ἑόρακα.

89 διὰ τοῦτον: τοῦτον is presumably a parasite-flatterer, Strouthias or Gnathon alias Strouthias. Through watching him, the speaker has discovered his general rule.

91 οἰκιcτὴc τόπου: The age of Alexander and his immediate successors was one in which many new cities were founded.

92: Sudhaus's πάντ', printed by Körte to fill the gap, is certainly too long. There is room for πᾶc, but this seems to spoil the rhetoric (? deliberately). Although οὐ μὴν ἀλλά is not known in verse, it is common in the orators (Denniston, *GP* 29) and would be effective here: 'I mean those who have been utterly ruined, and what I say is true.' Grenfell and Hunt's οὐ γὰρ ἀλλά, a phrase found in Old Comedy and Plato, 'I really mean those who have been utterly ruined', gives a similar sense.

93: If Grenfell and Hunt's supplement νῦν is right, it is better taken with what follows than with what precedes; the point will be that destruction is *nowadays* so caused, whatever happened in the past.

94: It seems impossible to read anything but οἱ κόλακεϲ· οὗτοι (or οὕτω, Handley) δ᾽ εἰϲὶν αὐτοῖϲ ἄθλιοι, which can perhaps be translated: '... flatterers. But they (their victims) are wretched by reason of them.' The line is exceedingly feeble, and could with advantage be dispensed with. The next line means: 'That speech is violent, but I don't know what this thing is you are talking about.' But how could the young man be ignorant, if the slave had just explained that the thing that caused disaster was flatterers? I suspect that 94 is an explanatory interpolation, although as such unique to date in our texts of Menander. It is surely, even so, unsatisfactory, for the sequel shows that the cause of disaster is not simply the existence of flatterers, but the ill-founded security of those who are overthrown.

The above takes it for granted that 94 and 95 are consecutive. This may be wrong; Webster supposed that 95 begins a new extract; that cannot be disproved, and may be supported by the absence of a dicolon after αθλιοι, just as there is none after ταδικειν (54).

95 ϲοβαρόϲ: Although the primary meaning is 'violent', there may be a secondary connotation of pompousness or showing off, see LSJ.

97 τὸν ἐπιβουλεύοντα: The definite article may refer to some individual who is known to be plotting, or it may be generalizing, 'anyone who is plotting'.

98 δύνηται: Absolute, 'if he has no power'.

99 φυλάττῃ may be 3rd person active or 2nd person middle. The active, with the object αὐτόν understood, is possible here if κακῶϲ ποεῖν governs τὸν ϲφόδρ᾽ ἰϲχυρόν. Unfortunately a decision on that point is impossible until a satisfactory supplement has been found for 100. After the letters θεν there is a colon. The following word is not οιον. It looks like γιον, the ι having a projection to the left which can be interpreted as the joining right-hand stroke of an unusually narrow υ, cf. that in ϲυντριψαι, 102. After ον Turner transcribes a colon, but the spot is unusually large and high, and may be an accidental blot. Without confidence I suggest the sense: 'A son of Astyanax's could smash his nose as he lay at rest.'

100 Ἀϲτυάνακτοϲ: Astyanax of Miletos is said by Athenaios 413 a to have won the pancratium at the Olympic Games three times running. A scholion at the foot of the column in O 1 runs:

αϲτυανακτοϲ· του μιληϲιου [αϲ]τυαν[ακτ]οϲ πολλοι ϲφοδρα [τ]ων κωμω-
διογρ(αφων) μεμν[ην]τ[αι. εγενετο γ(αρ) παγκρατιαϲτ(ηϲ) κρα[τιϲτοϲ

τω]ν καθαυτον ηγων[ιc]ατο δ(ε) καὶ πυγμη⟨ι⟩. ερατοcθενηc δ' ε[ν τω .]
των ολυμπιονικ(ων) προθειc ρῑε ολυμπ(ιαδα) φ(ηcιν)· αcτυαναξ ο μιληcιοc
s̄ την περιοδον ακονιτει.

γ' was rightly expanded by Grenfell and Hunt to γ(αρ). Handley
prefers to see a numeral and interprets as τρίс, which goes somewhat
awkwardly with κράτιcτοc τῶν καθ' αὐτόν. It is one thing to say that
a man was the best pancratiast among the men of his time, another
that he was at three contests the best pancratiast among the men of
his time. Austin notes that over both his other numbers the scribe
writes a horizontal bar, absent here. Eratosthenes, librarian at
Alexandria after Apollonius Rhodius or c. 246 B.C., and a prolific
scholar, compiled an Ὀλυμπιονῖκαι, or list of Olympic victors, Diog.
L. vii. 51. His entry for the year 316 B.C., given above, included the
phrase: 'Astyanax of Miletos won the circuit [i.e. won at the Nemean,
Isthmian, Pythian, and Olympic Games] six times ἀκονιτί [i.e. by
a walk-over].' The numeral s (6) is written with a flourish and could
be mistaken for Γ (3); perhaps at some stage a copyist read a Γ as s,
the note having originally agreed with Athenaios. Three victories are
more credible than six: it can hardly be believed that a man could
retain his title as champion unchallenged for 20 years. Even the famous
pancratiast Dorieus won only three successive Olympic crowns
(Pausanias vi. 7. 1); Chairon won the wrestling there on four occasions from 356 to 344 B.C. (Pausanias vii. 27. 7), but that was a less
punishing event than the pancratium.

A walk-over win is recorded with surprising frequency. A con-
tributory cause may be that it was possible to reach the final by a
series of 'byes'; if the other finalist had had hard fights, he might be
unwilling to meet an opponent who was still fresh. But reluctance to
risk serious injury in fighting a man thought certain to win might
operate in every round, and so give a famous champion a walk-over
(see H. A. Harris, *Greek Athletics*, 116, 162).

The general sense is: 'If Astyanax were lying flat on his back you
could break his nose with a pestle; but a man secured for five minae,
who came with the intention of killing (?) him, could not easily do
it if he were looked out for.' I see no way of determining whether to
read cυντρίψαιμι or cυντρίψαι (optative) or cυντρῖψαι (infin.).

103–8: A line below 102 may indicate the beginning of a new extract.
But forms of φυλάττομαι in 106, 108, compared with φυλάξῃ in 99,
may show that the passage is continuous. No complete sense appears
until 115; here someone (? Pheidias) is told that he has now got
someone off his guard and (probably) out of the way.

Jensen and Körte wrongly disbelieved Grenfell and Hunt's report of a paragraphus below 119, and, since 120 ff. are clearly spoken by the πορνοβοςκός, supposed him to be the speaker of 110–19 also. This was impossible, even before the discovery of the missing lines: the speaker of 110–19 is confident that some stratagem is going well; the *leno*, on the other hand, is in a dilemma and unhappy.

105: Turner restores τοῦ[το ἐ]ποήςατ᾽, since τοῦ[το] ποιήςαι is too short. But the middle is hard to explain.

114 παῖδες will by analogy with *Perik.* 188 be a call accompanying a knock on the door, that of the soldier or that of the πορνοβοςκός. Less probably it summons slaves to follow the speaker somewhere.

ἐκτριβήςεται: 'Will be utterly destroyed'; the metaphor is from uprooting trees or plants. But the word is not otherwise known in comedy in this metaphorical sense and the restoration uncertain.

117 ἀφύλακτον: 'Off his guard', Dem. iv. 18, ἵνα . . . ἢ παριδὼν ταῦτα ἀφύλακτος ληφθῇ, Arist. *Rhet.* 1372ᵃ18, οἱ μὲν γὰρ φίλοι ἀφύλακτοι πρὸς τὸ ἀδικεῖςθαι.

120–32: The πορνοβοςκός speaks of penniless starvelings, among whom are included his neighbour: this must be Pheidias. He fears that if he gets wind of something, he will come with sixty friends, accusing him of having sold his girl to someone with more money. Well, he will not sell her. The girl is very profitable, earning three minae a day from the ξένος (probably the soldier, conceivably some other 'foreigner'). But this is dangerous: 'they' (? Pheidias and his friends) will kidnap her in the street, and he will have to go to law to recover her.

Previous interpretations of the speech need not be considered, since they were based on the erroneous reading ὠνεῖθ᾽ for ὧν ἐςθ᾽ in 122.

The πορνοβοςκός may have entered immediately after the departure at 119 of the characters previously present. But if what Grenfell and Hunt took to be a paragraphus is really a 'diple obelismene', his speech forms a new extract and did not necessarily immediately follow the passage that would then end at 119.

120: Turner's ῥαχιςτής is possible, but the remains are exiguous. The word occurs in Theopompos (a poet of Old Comedy), frag. 43 K, τούτων ἁπάντων ὁ ῥαχιςτὴς Δημοφῶν. Photios, who quotes the fragment, explains that ῥαχιςτής means ἀλαζών, and Hesychios gives that and similar meanings (ψευςτής, μεγάλα κακουργῶν, μεγάλα ψευδόμενος) for ῥαχιςτήρ.

There is space for a letter before ον, with which the line begins. With some plausibility, Austin suggests χ]οῦ[τος ῥ]αχιςτής, but it must be admitted that this does not fit well with what follows, and makes a strange phrase with which to open either an extract or a speech.

λιμοί: 'Starvelings', cf. Poseidippos frag. 26. 12 K, κυμινοπριστὰς πάντας ἢ λιμοὺς καλῶν. Körte completes the line with μόχλους, supposing that Pheidias' companions are ready to help him to break down a door to get at the girl he wants, cf. *Dysk.* 60 n. Can the missing word be τύλους, 'calluses'? These starvelings have had to take manual jobs to keep alive.

122: Grenfell and Hunt's ὅμ[ως fits the traces better than Körte's ὅδ̣[ε. Pheidias may be penniless, but all the same he'll make a row. If ὅδε were right it would accompany a gesture indicating Pheidias' house.

124: There may be an allusion to some unknown tragedy (so Jacques on *Dysk.* 159) which gave point to this line. According to the Homeric catalogue Odysseus took twelve ships to Troy, but the complement of one ship, if a penteconter, might be a little more than fifty (cf. *Il.* ii. 719).

125 μαστιγία: One who bears the scars of flogging, cf. ϲτιγματίας, 'one who has been branded', τραυματίας 'one who has been wounded'; the implication is that the πορνοβοσκός was once a slave. G. Zuntz, *Mnem.* 3rd ser. v (1937), 60, guesses that the person so addressed in a fragment, perhaps of Alexis (Page, *GLP* no. 48), is of the same trade, like the Cappadocian, addressed as *mastigia* in Plaut. *Curc.* 567. The word μαστιγίας is used also in contexts where its function is to suggest that a slave deserves the whip, *Dysk.* 473, *Epitr.* 1113, *Sam.* 324.

162: Plaut. *Pseud.* 344, 'meam tu amicam uendidisti?', cf. *Rud.* 839, suggests supplying ἐμήν, but the absence of the article may make that impossible. ὅϲτις, τί γάρ; and the girl's name are all on the cards. At the end of the line Turner is uneasy about the ι of χρυϲιον or χρυϲιδα; unnecessarily, I venture to think. The apex of the letter is preserved and its bottom half; what he sees as a curving upper half is a detached line, probably accidental.

127: The girl's name *may* have stood at the beginning of the line, but Körte's [τί Φιλώ]τι[δ'] ἆρα πωλῶ; is admittedly *exempli gratia*.

128 τοῦτον: Probably Pheidias. At the end of the line O 1 has ηνιαλαμβανεν, for which Leo suggested ἡ μία λαμβάνει. The divided anapaest is dubious, and perhaps ἢ μί᾽ ἐλάμβανεν (*ed. pr.*) should be read; the elision would justify the division.

129 τρεῖς μνᾶς ἑκάϲτης ἡμέρας: Such a rate seems fantastically high, yet even modern experience shows that huge sums may be spent for a woman's favours. In an anecdote told by Machon (333 ff. Gow) Gnathaina asks a rich foreign commander ten minae for Gnathainion for a single night, and compromises on five. But he, like Bias here, was paying an inflated price; see Gow's note.

131: For kidnapping in the street, cf. Lysias i. 27, iii. 37, Andokides iv. 14.

132 δικάcομαι: He would have to bring an action for the recovery of the girl. So in Ter. *Adelphoe* 195 Aeschinus offers Sannio the option of taking twenty minae for the girl stolen from him or of bringing an action: 'nunc uide utrum uis, argentum accipere an causam meditari tuam.'

The remains of the fourth column are too small to allow anything to be learned from them.

Fragment 1. τετραδιcταί, cf. Alexis frag. 258, are members of a *thiasos* who meet for a celebration, including a dinner no doubt, on the fourth day of every month. Similarly there were νουμηνιαcταί, Lysias frag. 153, and δεκαδιcταί (see LSJ). The fourth day of the month was sacred to Aphrodite and these τετραδιcταί celebrate Aphrodite Pandemos. This title, found also outside Attica, indicates 'one who is worshipped by the whole people', and she seems to have favoured political unity: the ephebes swore by her, as ἡγεμόνη τοῦ δήμου, that they would defend their country. But there was a current misapprehension, encouraged by Plato, *Symp.* 180 d (cf. Xen. *Symp.* viii. 9), that she was the goddess of sensual love and connected with the world of courtesans and prostitutes; Solon was supposed to have built her temple ἀφ' ὧν ἠργυρίcαντο αἱ προcτᾶcαι τῶν οἰκημάτων (Athen. 569 d). On all this see Farnell, *Cults*, ii. 658 ff.

In this passage the cook's religious formulae are comically interrupted by his orders to his subordinate. For the thrice-repeated cπονδή, which accompanies the pouring of a libation, cf. Ar. *Peace* 1104–10; there the interfering priest asks for the tongue, which, as a delicacy, the cook here reserves for himself, cf. Ar. *Peace* 1060, *Birds* 1704, *Plut.* 1110. The attendant is ordered to offer the cπλάγχνα to the participants in the sacrifice; so in *Peace* 1102, ἔγχει δὴ cπονδὴν καὶ τῶν cπλάγχνων φέρε δεῦρο; 1105, ἔγχει δὴ κἀμοὶ καὶ cπλάγχνων μοῖραν ὄρεξον. The third libation was to Zeus Soter; Plato, *Rep.* 583 b and Adam's note.

καλῶc ἔχει: εὔχου, given by the primary MS. of Athenaios, is universally rejected, as an anticipation of εὐχώμεθα. ἔγχου, a form without authority, and ἔγχει are said to disregard the fact that the pouring of the libation is done simultaneously with the word cπονδή (cf. H. Dohm, *Mageiros*, 39–42, where the fragment is expounded at length). Nevertheless it is possible that ἔγχει is right, being an order to Sosias to fill the participants' cups. καλῶc will then stand by itself: 'Well done!'

'Ολυμπίᾱcι: This formula retains an old form of the fem. dat. plural. The ending -ᾱcι, properly a locative, cf. θύραcι, had taken on the functions of the dative. Apparently by the influence of the masculine -οιcι this became -αιcι, and then -αιc, Schwyzer, i. 559. Attic inscriptions change from -αcι to -αιc c. 420 B.C., Wade-Gery, *JHS* li (1931), 78 ff.

πᾶcι πάcαιc: Similar inclusive phrases are found elsewhere, e.g. *SIG*³ 1150, Ἀσκληπιῷ καὶ Ὑγιείᾳ καὶ τοῖς ἄλλοις θεοῖς πᾶcι καὶ πάcαιc, Dem. xviii. 1, τοῖς θεοῖς εὔχομαι πᾶcι καὶ πάcαιc, cf. H. Kleinknecht, *Gebetsparodie in der Antike*, 37, who discusses this passage.

τῶν ὄντων νῦν ἀγαθῶν ὄνηcιν: 'Enjoyment of the good things here present', above all of the food and drink. But similar formulae could be used more generally, e.g. *SIG* 1219. 20, ἐπεύχεcθαι τοῖς ἐμμένουcιν . . . εὖ εἶναι καὶ τῶν ὑπαρχόντων ἀγαθῶν ὄνηcιν, and other examples quoted by Fraenkel on *Agamemnon* 350.

Fragment 2. Athenaios 477 f describes the κόνδυ as ποτήριον Ἀcιατικόν, quoting this and several other passages. Since a κοτύλη was nearly half a pint, Bias' feat involved drinking a dozen pints. In Plato's *Symposium* 214 a, Alkibiades, already tipsy, fills and drains a wine-cooler containing more than eight κοτύλαι. Not knowing with what proportion of water the wine was mixed, we cannot compare these feats with those of modern times.

ἐ⟨πέ⟩πιον: 'I drank on top of my food': this is a common sense of ἐπιπίνειν, e.g. Plato, *Rep.* 372 b, Ar. *Knights* 354, Xen. *Cyr.* vi. 2. 28. Bentley's ἐξέπιον, 'I drained the cup at a draught', is at least as good in sense, but involves a slightly less likely mistake. Without the context, a confident choice is impossible.

Fragment 3. What Bias had devised with regard to the Cypriote was probably the insult 'Cypriote bullock', frag. 8. This was a substitute for the common insult ϲκατοφάγε (*Dysk.* 488, *Perik.* 394), since cattle in Cyprus were supposed to eat dung; cf. Antiphanes frag. 126 K, ἐν τῇ Κύπρῳ . . . ϲκατοφαγεῖν τοὺς βοῦς ἠνάγκαϲεν. The allusion would not be intelligible to a Roman audience, and so Terence substituted a Latin proverbial expression, *Eun.* 426 and 497, 'lepus tute's, pulpamentum quaeris? . . . quid rides? . . . illud de Rhodio dictum quom in mentem uenit.'

Fragment 4. Spoken, no doubt, by Strouthias to Bias. Χρυcίc and Ἀντίκυρα were the names of mistresses of Demetrios Poliorketes; Νάννιον was a common name among *hetairai*; one mentioned in Middle Comedy was mother of a *hetaira* called Κορώνη (Athenaios 587 b);

perhaps *Ναννάριον* was another daughter (cf. *Γνάθαινα* and *Γναθαινίδιον*, mother and daughter). On the suitability of the name *'Ιςχάς* for a *hetaira* see V. Buchheit, *Rh. Mus.* ciii (1960), 201.

ἔcχηκαc: 'You have got (and still have)'.

Fragment 5. This is uncertainly assigned to Menander's *Kolax.* Meineke's reasons for so doing are (1) that it might be the origin of a line spoken by Gnatho's friend in Terence, *Eun.* 238, 'em quo redactus sum. omnes noti me atque amici deserunt'; (2) that Philemon, to whom Erotianos ascribes the line, is not known to have written a *Kolax.*

Fragment 6. This also is an uncertain fragment. But the iambic line *πρόcειcιν οἷον ἀψοφητὶ θρέμματος* is likely to be a quotation rather than accidental, and Plutarch quotes from *Kolax* in the same passage. Hesychios' entry *ἀψοφητί· ἠρέμα, ἡcυχῶc, κολακείᾳ* was not improbably emended by Meineke to conclude ⟨*Μένανδρος*⟩ *Κόλακι.*

Fragment 7. **κωβιόc:** 'Goby', see Gow on Machon 31. **ἡλακατῆνεc:** Athenaios says that these fish were *κητώδειc. κῆτος* is the zoologist's word for a whale, but it was applied in common speech to any large fish, from tunny to dogfish (*κύων*).

These words come from Mnesimachos *Hippotrophos*, frag. 4. 35 K, (Athen. 403 b), where they form part of a long list of fishes such as the Middle Comedy loved; if Athenaios made no mistake in ascribing them to Menander at 301 d, the later poet may have either borrowed them deliberately or repeated them unconsciously. They might have a place in the scene where Gnathon recounted his popularity with the fishmongers, cf. Ter. *Eun.* 256–7.

Fragment 8. See frag. 3.

Fragment 9. Pollux vii. 86 notes that Menander used the word *cανδάλιον.* Thierfelder suggests that he may have done so in this play, comparing Ter. *Eun.* 1028, 'utinam tibi commitigari uideam sandalio caput'.

KONEIAZOMENAI

Z *P. Ross-Georg.* i. 10 (Pap. Zereteli). Sudhaus suggested that this is a fragment from the latter part of *Fabula incerta* (q.v.): the guess is improbable; nothing favours it except the name Chaireas, which is common to both texts. The difficulties are well set out by Del Corno, *Menandro, Le Commedie,* i. 508. Mette, *Lustrum* x (1966), 149, tries to associate it with *PSI* 1176 (Page, *GLP* 276).

Nothing can be learned of the plot of this play; and the 'Women who take (or threaten to take) hemlock' may have been only incidental rather than the principal characters, cf. ᾽Επιτρέποντες. The scrap from the Zereteli papyrus must come from the latter part of the play. Zereteli thought that it may have been preceded by the word *XOPOY*; if this was so, it will have stood at the beginning of the fifth act, and although all seems to have turned out happily, there is still some unforeseen twist to come.

The conversation appears to be between a young man and another person, who is possibly, but not necessarily, a slave. It may be guessed that a girl's father, who had been supposed ill or dead, has returned unexpectedly: he is now preparing for her marriage. Editors perhaps rightly suppose that this young man is the bridegroom, who may, however, be Chaireas, to whom the girl's father is talking; the young man may be a friend who has been attempting vainly to promote the marriage.

3: U. E. Paoli, *Aegyptus,* xxxiii (1953), 270, points out that Körte's text, προῖκα δὲ δίδωσι τρία] τάλαντα, πένθ᾽ ἅμα [μνᾶς εἰς στολὴν καὶ] κόσμον, gives a most unusual relation between dowry and personal possessions. Normally a bride's clothes, jewellery, etc. are valued at half or one-third of her dowry. Five talents is an exceptional sum for a dowry, but only one talent more than that in *Epitr.,* and only half of that brought by a rich but ugly wife in *Plokion* (frag. 333).

6: There was a proverb ὑγιέστερος κροτῶνος ('a tick'), used by Menander in his Λοκροί (frag. 263). Zenobios vi. 27 explains that this animal is all smooth, without scratch or other harm. But Strabo vi. 1. 12 believes the proverb to be ὑγιέστερος Κρότωνος, the healthiness of Kroton being testified to by the multitude of athletes it produced. Zereteli saw a note in the right-hand margin which he dubiously read as τί λ[έγεις;] ὑγι[αι]ν[ει]. Sudhaus supposed that the sense was: 'Is he well?—Fit as a fiddle.—What's that?—I say he is as fit as a fiddle.'

It is probably right that somebody is in the best of health, and that must be the girl's father.

7: Adverbial τὸ δειλινόν, 'during the afternoon', is used by Lucian's Lexiphanes (c. 2), apparently as a rare phrase. δειλινόν can be an adjective used predicatively, as in *Com. adesp.* 609, δειλινὸς γὰρ ἤρξατο (? sc. ὁ ἄνεμος), but a neuter noun is improbable here.

9 Χαιρέᾳ: Chaireas is a young man in *Aspis*, *Fabula incerta*, Ter. *Eunuchus*, possibly young in *Dyskolos*. He may here too be young, whether the hero or the hero's friend.

10: A very grand house might have an ἐξέδρα, a hall with fixed seats (see F. W. Deichmann in *Reallexikon f. Antike u. Christentum*, s.v. Exedra), but this ἐξέδρα, if ἐγγύς is right, is hardly in a house. But ὄψομ᾽ εἰσιών, if given to the young man, as it is by Körte, suggests that he expects to see the conversing pair indoors. A possible escape would be that the seat is in some sort of precinct, that he will enter.

Zereteli thought there is a dicolon after δεξιας. Then the young man might ask, e.g., ἔνδον τί νῦν ποιοῦσιν; and the slave reply that he would go in and find out. Zereteli also saw a dicolon after εισιων, so that the reflection on Luck belongs to the young man, who will then soliloquize before going off to see the others. Körte, however, having seen a photograph, firmly rejected both dicola, and so gave both ὄψομ᾽ εἰσιών and the soliloquy to the young man. It must be confessed that ὄψομ᾽ εἰσιών looks like an exit-phrase, to which a soliloquy is an unexpected sequel.

13: The general sense of these lines seems certain, but the supplements must be regarded as *exempli gratia*. On the large place taken by Τύχη in Menander's time see *Aspis* 148 n.

20 πρόφασις: The sense 'cause', not 'pretext', most familiar perhaps from Thuc. i. 23, occurs several times in comedy: *Aspis* 11, Philemon frag. 194 K, Diphilos frag. 106 K, ἄνθρωπός εἰμι· τοῦτο δ᾽ αὐτὸ τῶι βίωι | πρόφασιν μεγίστην εἰς τὸ λυπεῖσθαι φέρει, probably Menander frag. 193, μικρὰ πρόφασίς ἐστι τοῦ πρᾶξαι κακῶς. Cf. also Dem. xviii. 156, τὴν ἀληθῆ πρόφασιν τῶν πραγμάτων . . . ἀπεκρύπτετο. The dicolon after γινεται may indicate that the speaker leaves the stage, or that he is here joined by someone else.

MISUMENOS

Fragments of this very popular play are preserved in eight papyri:

—	*P. Oxy. ined.*	vv. A1–A18
I	*P. IFAO* 89	vv. A1–A16
O 11	*P. Oxy.* 2567	vv. 1–92
O 10	*P. Oxy.* 2656	vv. 101–466
B 2	*P. Berol.* 13281	vv. 167–78, 210–21
O 3	*P. Oxy.* 1013	vv. 244–64, 276–99
B 3	*P. Berol.* 13932	vv. 132–44, 160–72
O 7	*P. Oxy.* 1605	vv. 418–44.

I use the arbitrary line-numbers adopted in *Oxyrhynchus Papyri*, vol. xxxiii. The subscription to O 10 is μεναυδ[ρου] θραϲωνι[δηϲ. That this is an alternative title for Μιϲούμενοϲ is certain, because the remains include (364) the first line of Körte's frag. 8, cited as from Μιϲούμενοϲ, and Thrasonides was well known as the principal character of that play. That O 11 belongs to the same play is shown by its containing characters named Getas and Krateia and an 'old foreigner', who must be Demeas.

O 11 consists of three fragments, written on the back of a lease, which serves to show the relation of frags. 1 and 2. It belongs to the third century A.D. Frag. 1 has the ends of thirty-nine lines of one column and remains of forty-four of the next; frag. 2 has the beginnings of seventeen lines of the first column; eight of the lines are common to the two fragments. Frag. 3 is only two letters wide and cannot be placed.

O 10 consists of nine fragments from a single-quire codex, assigned by Turner to the late third or more probably fourth century A.D. When joined, they form four damaged leaves, which followed one another in immediate succession. The surface is badly damaged, so that reading of what would otherwise be a clear hand is generally made very difficult. A second hand has made some alterations.

B 2 is the lower part of one leaf of a codex of the third century A.D.

O 3 is the lower part of one leaf of a codex of the fifth or sixth century A.D.

B 3 is a fragment of a parchment codex of the fifth century A.D., thought by Schubart to have contained also *PSI* 126 (*Aspis*).

O 7 is a narrow strip from a roll of the third century A.D., containing the beginning of twenty-seven lines from one column and a few fragments from the ends of the lines in the preceding column.

I is a fragment from the top of a column from a roll of the third century A.D.

Editiones principes:

O 11: E. G. Turner, *Oxyrhynchus Papyri,* xxxiii (1968), with photographs.

O 10: E. G. Turner, *BICS* Suppl. xvii (1965), with complete photographs.

B 2: U. von Wilamowitz-Moellendorf, *SB Berlin* 1918, 747.

O 3: A. Hunt, *Oxyrhynchus Papyri,* vii (1910), 103.

B 3: W. Schubart, 'Griechische literarische Papyri' (*Berichte d. sächs. Akad.* xcvii [1950], 47).

O 7: Grenfell and Hunt, *Oxyrhynchus Papyri,* xiii (1919), 45.

I: B. Boyaval, *ZPE* vi (1970), 1, with photograph.

Revised texts are to be found as follows:

O 10: *Oxyrhynchus Papyri,* xxxiii (1968), 20.

B 2, B 3: Koerte–Thierfelder, *Menander Reliquiae* (1959), ii. 286, H. Maehler, *Lustrum* x (1966), 154, C. Austin, *Oxyrhynchus Papyri,* xxxiii (1968), 17.

O 3: E. G. Turner, as for O 10.

I: L. Koenen, *ZPE* vi (1970), 99, viii (1971) 141 (new photograph).

In spite of all this material, much about the play remains a tantalizing puzzle. The only part that is really intelligible (and even here there are unsolved problems) is 176–325. But this is first-rate, full of incident and surprise and variety.

Characters

The characters known are:

> Thrasonides, a soldier
> Krateia, a captive taken in war, enslaved to him
> Demeas, her father
> Getas, Thrasonides' slave
> Kleinias, a young man (?)
> Old woman, slave of Kleinias
> A woman whose name contains the letters $\rho\upsilon$
> Krateia's nurse
> A cook

The last two characters do not speak, in what is preserved at least, unless the woman]$\rho\upsilon$[is Krateia's nurse. Seven speaking characters is a small number, but *Samia* has six only.

The name Thrasonides, appropriate for a soldier, was in use at Athens, Kirchner, *Prosop. Att.* 7396–9; so was Krateia, *Prosop. Att.* 8732a, 8733. The latter was used by Alexis in his play Κράτεια ἢ Φαρμακόπωλις.

The scene may be at Athens but, as Turner says, the arguments for it are frail. The marriage-formula is used in *Perik.* as well as plays set in Attica, and if ἱκετηρία (122, 132) indicates a legal process known to Athenians, the poet might have supposed (or known) that process to be used elsewhere also.

Plot

The publication of O 10 and O 11 has made earlier discussions of the plot out of date. Later articles: Q.Cataudella, *SIFC* N.s. xxxviii (1966), 135, with supplement ibid. xli (1969), 56, is profitless. R. Merkelbach, *Rh. Mus.* cix (1966), has some good observations. A. Borgogno, *SIFC* N.s. xli (1969), 19, has much that seems probable and does not conceal difficulties. See also K. Kumaniecki, *Eos* lv (1965), 58, C. Gallavotti, *Riv. di fil.* xciv (1966), 88, D. Del Corno, *Gnomon* xlii (1970), 256, W. Kraus, *Rh. Mus.* cxiv (1971), 1.

A professional soldier, Thrasonides, had as a result of a war come into possession of a girl prisoner, Krateia (frags. 1, 9; 235). At the beginning of the play he came out of his house while it was still night (frag. 2; A1), followed later by his servant Getas, who came unwillingly and urged his master to return to bed (frags. 3, 4). Thrasonides explained that he was madly in love with Krateia but that, since she hated him, he refrained from taking her (A10–A12). Chorikios (frag. 1) suggests that the reason for her hate was his conceit and boastfulness, but these characteristics do not appear in the remains of the play. He could also be understood to mean that Krateia had at one time been favourably disposed towards Thrasonides, but this is not a necessary interpretation of his words.

The next known incident in the play was that Thrasonides asked for his sword, with the apparent intention of committing suicide, and someone (perhaps Getas) refused to give it to him (frag. 2). On the contrary this person appears to have collected all the swords in the house (frag. 6) and deposited them in the keeping of a neighbour, Kleinias (178).

Meanwhile Krateia's father, Demeas, has arrived in the town, coming from Cyprus (231), where Thrasonides had recently served with distinction (frag. 5). Demeas' home was probably in Cyprus, and probably he knew that it had been destroyed in a war, causing his household to be scattered (233 f.). But he had apparently not known that Krateia was in this town, to which he had come for some other purpose (Simplicius ad Arist. *Physica* p. 384. 13 Diels, ὅταν λέγωμεν ὅτι ἀπὸ τύχης ἦλθεν ὁ ξένος καὶ λυτρωσάμενος τὸν αἰχμάλωτον, ὡς ὁ παρὰ Μενάνδρῳ Δημέας τὴν Κράτειαν, ἀπῆλθεν). In some way he became the guest of Kleinias (176 ff., 270, 286, 301), whose part in the play remains obscure, but who was closely involved, being in a state of great agitation and most anxious to find some woman whom he knows to be in the town (270 ff.).

Borgogno, taking the scene to be Athens, argues that both Demeas and Thrasonides are Athenians. He thinks this to be shown by the use of the customary marriage-formula (444–5). Krateia must have been taken prisoner during an invasion of Attica, perhaps Ptolemy's raid of 313 B.C., transported to Cyprus, and there bought by Thrasonides. Demeas had been to Cyprus in search of her, and on his return unexpectedly discovered her in his home town. Attractive as this is in some respects, it is not I think consistent with Simplicius' phrase ἦλθεν ὁ ξένος καὶ λυτρωσάμενος τὸν αἰχμάλωτον . . . ἀπῆλθεν, nor with the frequent references to Demeas as ξένος, nor above all with 31 f., ποδαπὸς εἶ, ξένε . . . σώματ' οὖν λυτρούμενος ἥκεις. At the most, Demeas might be an Athenian by birth, but not resident in Athens. The marriage-formula cannot be used as evidence, for it is employed in *Perikeiromene*, where Polemon is a Corinthian.

The first papyrus fragment gives what are probably the lines with which Thrasonides opened the play; the next remains, from Act I or II, contain the end of a scene between Thrasonides and his slave Getas (8–9). Soon after a ξένος, presumably Demeas, is conversing with someone, possibly Kleinias, but more probably Kleinias' slave. The scanty remains offer little certain hold, but the name of Krateia is introduced by one or the other. The principal MS. (O 10) begins (101) early in Act III, but only the most uncertain guesses can be made about its contents until 168 is reached. The speaker here seems to be Getas, who expresses his suspicions of some man; he then goes in with the intention of keeping an eye on what is happening (173). A woman emerges from Kleinias' house (176); her name is given by an interlinear note above 184, but illegibly (perhaps γ[ρ]αυ[ς]). She expresses astonishment at the actions of their guest, who is taking an interest in the swords in their house (178 ff.), which belong to the neighbours. It looks as if Demeas had recognized a sword as belonging to himself or some member of his household; it will have come into Thrasonides' possession as booty. She is shortly followed out by Demeas himself (184 ff.), who seems to ask her to knock on Thrasonides' door (188). What follows is doubtful, but the old woman leaves the stage, either returning to her own house or entering that of Thrasonides. Demeas now goes to Thrasonides' door and calls παῖ παῖδες (206).

But at this very moment someone is coming out, and he draws back. There emerge Krateia and her nurse (211 n.). Krateia speaks and her words may have explained why she has come out; the sight of her utterly astonishes Demeas. The nurse, probably by gestures, calls her attention to her father, and the two fall into an embrace, interrupted by the entrance of Getas, who comes out in search of Krateia. Getas believes that he has caught red-handed the man of whom he had been suspicious (who must have been young), but quickly realizes that this is someone else. It is soon established that Demeas is Krateia's father, and Getas runs to fetch Thrasonides, who is not at home. There follows a tantalizing scrap of conversation. Someone has been killed by the last person, says Demeas, who should have done the deed. Father and daughter now go into Thrasonides' house. No sooner have they done so than Getas arrives with Thrasonides, who in a short speech explains that his happiness depends on whether Demeas will give him Krateia in marriage. They go in, and then Kleinias comes home with a cook, whom he is bringing to provide a meal for a ξένος (Demeas?) and an unnamed woman; but he does not know whether she will be present.

Act IV opens with Kleinias' appearance. He speaks to someone (presumably the woman who had conversed with Demeas in the previous act), who had told him that his guest, having recognized 'the' sword, had gone to Thrasonides' house, on learning that it belonged there. His speech is interrupted by the appearance of Getas who, refusing to notice Kleinias' interjections, recounts to the thin air the scene that has passed between Thrasonides, Demeas, and Krateia. Thrasonides had asked for Krateia in marriage and protested his love for her; she would not listen, and all that Demeas would say was that he demanded to ransom her. Since Getas says: 'I would not have ransomed her' (315), it seems that Thrasonides did do so. At the end of this scene Getas recognizes Kleinias.

After some 35 hopelessly fragmentary lines Thrasonides appears to be on the stage; he seems to reflect that drink would be an undesirable comfort, for it would cause him to reveal the hurt that he would rather conceal. It is possible that a long monologue followed. Then there is a gap in the papyrus, which preserves nothing more but the last page of the play. Here someone (? Getas) tells Thrasonides that all is well, 'they' are giving him Krateia and she is willing to have him. Demeas then appears, promises a dowry of 2 talents, and he (or perhaps Kleinias) issues an invitation to dinner.

The part played in this plot by Kleinias is a puzzle. The only other bearers of the name in New Comedy are young men (*Theophorumene*, Ter. *Andria*, *Heautontim.*, cf. Lucian *Dial. Mer.* 10), and it is therefore likely that he is another. The girl in whom he is interested may be Krateia. It would lend itself to dramatic effect if she proved to be in fact his sister. The triangle Kleinias–Krateia–Thrasonides would then in some respects be like that of Moschion–Glykera–Polemon in *Perikeiromene*. Now an attractive interpretation of 246–9 is that Krateia and Demeas believe her brother to be dead and to have been killed by Thrasonides. If Kleinias turned out to be her supposedly dead brother that would exonerate Thrasonides and clear the way for her acceptance of him as a husband. It would also explain the plural in διδόασί coι γυναῖκα (431), which could refer to father and brother.

The obvious difficulty is that Demeas is described as Kleinias' guest, and the plot as sketched above provides no reason why they should not immediately recognize one another as father and son; the implication of 231 ff. indeed is that Demeas' family had only recently been broken up. The difficulty would be surmounted if Demeas in some way came as a guest to the house of a supposed stranger, and arrived when his host was out or away, so that the two have not met before Act IV, and need not meet until Act V. Such an absence on the part of Kleinias is all but required by the fact that he is unaware that Thrasonides' swords have been deposited in his house (278 ff.); and this ignorance is convenient if, as has been guessed, one of those swords is in fact his own. This hypothesis is untenable if Demeas is in converse with Kleinias at 31 ff., but that is at least uncertain and to my mind improbable. Borgogno, *SIFC* xli (1969), 41, suggests that Kleinias had been kidnapped or exposed when a child. This would account not only for his being unknown to Demeas, but also for his not knowing Krateia to be his sister. Kidnapping is more likely, since it would be strange to expose a son and keep a daughter. But in either case the sword is hard to fit in. Even if a sword were for some reason picked up with a child, it would be absurd to take it for granted that the child would have the sword when a grown man. A more probable solution is one suggested by Turner, *BICS* suppl. 17. 14–15. Kleinias will be Krateia's half-brother, the offspring of an irregular union between Demeas and some girl with whom he left his sword as a token and a gift to his son. Thus Aigeus left his sword with Aithra, and was enabled by it to recognize their son Theseus (Plut. *Theseus* c. 3. 6, 12. 4). Pelopia took his sword from Thyestes as he raped her, and it was carried by the child that was born to her, Aigisthos, and led to his recognition by his father (Hyginus 88). If Kleinias is an unfamiliar illegitimate son of Demeas many difficulties are surmounted. But at least one remains: Krateia would seem to know of the existence of the person whose death is presumed, and one would not expect her to know that she had an illegitimate brother.

The considerable remains of the play do not allow of more than a very imperfect apprehension of the plot. But clearly the relation between Thrasonides and Krateia lay at the centre of it, and was one of great interest. Thrasonides wins sympathy by his self-denial and Krateia by her determination not to succumb to her captor. But the surviving scenes are only enough to tantalize with their glimpses of what seems to have been a cleverly constructed, economically written, and imaginatively conceived comedy.

A1–A16: These lines stood at the top of a column in I, without any suprascription. This is no argument against their being, what they seem, the opening lines of a play; there is no heading to *Aspis* in the Bodmer papyrus. But to Turner the writing suggests that they are a schoolboy's exercise, not part of a complete copy of the play. They are here numbered A1–A16 to avoid changing the numeration of his edition, in which 1–16 belong to later lines. They contain an address by Thrasonides to the goddess Night; of the first twelve nine are complete and none of these would be metrically out of place in tragedy. Nor is there anything non-tragic in what remains of the other three, if *cov* in A8 can be treated as enclitic.

Other plays that opened with an address to Night were Eur. *Andromeda* (ὦ Νὺξ ἱερά, Σ Ar. *Thesm.* 1065) and *Pap. Ant.* 15 (ὦ δέσποινα Νύξ). Euripides' Elektra enters with the words ὦ Νὺξ μέλαινα (*Electra* 54). Plaut. *Mercator* 3, has: 'non ego item facio ut alios in comoediis | ⟨ui⟩ uidi amoris facere, qui aut Nocti aut Dii aut Soli aut Lunae miserias narrant suas.'

A1–2: Euripides' satyr-play *Skiron* began Ἑρμῆ, σὺ γὰρ δή (*P. Oxy.* 2455). Night has of all gods the greatest share in Aphrodite because night is the time *par excellence* for love-making.   τούτων cannot refer to the only preceding plural, θεῶν. It must mean τὰ τῆς Ἀφροδίτης, to be understood from the previous line.

A4–5a: I has superlatives ἀθλιώτατον and δυσποτμώτατον; the former is also given by most MSS. of Plutarch *Moralia* 534 a, where the comparative appears only in a few of little faith. Confusion between the two grades became common in late Greek and mistakes are often made in MSS. I think Koenen right in maintaining that Menander will have written the comparative. K–G i. 26 ff. give no support for the superlative (their quotation from Eur. *Andr.* 6 has a corrupt text). That the lover should declare himself more miserable than all mankind is a commonplace, *Perik.* 535, *Sam.* 12, *P. Ant.* 15, Ter. *Hec.* 293, etc. (Austin on *Aspis* 287).

A4 Ἄπολλον: The word must have become a mere exclamation, 'Heaven help us!', without any sense that Apollo is addressed, since it is embedded in a sentence directed towards Night. Handley, *ZPE* vi (1970), 97, proposes ἆρ' ἄλλον, suggested by 3 MSS. of Plutarch, which have τίνα ἄλλον for τιν'. [This emendation is now confirmed by *P. Oxy. ined.* See Addenda.]

A6: Apollonios quotes the line and explains that ἐμαυτοῦ is emphatic. A rejected lover outside someone else's door is a familiar figure; Thrasonides stands outside his own.

A8: It is difficult to be certain about the first two surviving letters, but re-examination of the papyrus has convinced Koenen that they are almost certainly εχ (κ being excluded) and the third probably ω (*ZPE* viii [1971], 141). His supplement πόθον τε κατέχω may be right. An alternative is ποθῶν τε κατέχω, with intransitive κατέχω: 'though I long for her, I restrain myself'. Austin suggests αὐτόν τε κατέχω, with αὐτόν = ἐμαυτόν.

It is disputed whether a new sentence begins with νῦν, or whether A8–A9 form a single sentence. In the former case there seems to be an anacoluthon, no main verb being reached.

A9: The line is completed from frag. com. adesp. 282 K, quoted in this form by Chariton iv. 7, who clearly expects it to be recognized. This quotation is therefore from some well-known play and probably from this passage. The line is quoted also by Eustathios 236. 32 and Schol. Eur. *Phoenissae* 481 with the reading τὴν ἐρωμένην ἔχων, which Eustathios calls an 'apparent solecism' (cολοικοφανήc) for ἔχοντ', and defends as a grammatical licence. It is easier to regard it as a corruption.

A12: οὐ ποιῶ δέ: Cf. Diog. L. vii. 130, τὸν γοῦν Θραcωνίδην, καίπερ ἐν ἐξουcίᾳ ἔχοντα τὴν ἐρωμένην, διὰ τὸ μιcεῖcθαι ἀπέχεcθαι αὐτῆc.

ὑπαιθρίῳ δ': The papyrus is damaged, but ὑπαίθριοc δ' seems a much less likely reading, unless it was written υπαιθριωc, δ being omitted.

A1–16: *Several of the preceding notes need modification in view of the evidence of P. Oxy. ined. See Addenda.*

Six fragments come from an early part of the play. The first four belong to the opening scenes; the other two may have come before lines 1–90.

Fragment 1. That Thrasonides aroused Krateia's hatred by boasting of his exploits is supported by Plutarch, *Mor.* 1095 c–d, where cτρατιωτικὰ διηγήματα are associated with Θρασωνίδαc τινας καὶ Θρασυλέοντας. It is impossible to determine whether this boasting was represented on the stage or only, as I guess, reported.

Fragment 2. μικρὰ εὐημερήcαc: This 'slight success' I take to be his obtaining Krateia as wife. To the Stoic Epiktetos nothing was of importance but morality, and so what was for the dramatist the climax of the play would be regarded by him as a trifle. He is not concerned to give an accurate account of the plot. εὐτελέc: Lit. 'cheap, inexpensive', and Thrasonides may not have paid much, if he paid anything, for Krateia. But the word also means 'paltry', and he probably used it in that sense.

Fragment 3. Choiroboskos, *Gramm. Graeci* iv. 1. 177 Hilgard, quotes, as from *Dyskolos* (to which it does not belong) ὦ δυcτυχήc, τί οὐ καθεύδειc; It is likely enough that his quotation should be amalgamated with this fragment. Getas speaks. Austin recalls that at the beginning of Ar. *Thesm.* the old man, tired by Euripides' walking up and down, complains ἀπολεῖ μ᾽ ἀλοῶν ἄνθρωπος ἐξ ἑωθινοῦ (2).

Fragment 4. κἄν sometimes seems to replace καί without any difference of meaning, K–G i. 244. Ordinary Greeks would have been puzzled to know whether in this locution καί was joined with the particle ἄν or with ἄν = ἐάν. But when κἄν is joined with a word or words to an imperative, it is probably right to see the influence of similar sentences with a καὶ ἐάν clause. Soph. *El.* 1483, ἀλλά μοι πάρες κἄν cμικρὸν εἰπεῖν, Ar. *Ach.* 1021. μέτρηcον εἰρήνηc τί μοι, κἂν πέντ᾽ ἔτη (where it would be easy to supply μετρήσῃς), Theokr. xxiii. 41, κἂν νεκρῷ χάρισαι τὰ cὰ χείλεα, Rufinus *AP* v. 92, κἂν ὑμεῖc πείcατε τὴν 'Ροδόπην. As early as Solon frag. 22 Diehl, κἂν νῦν appears without real justification, if the transmission can be trusted, ἀλλ᾽ εἴ μοι κἂν νῦν πείcεαι. The scholiasts who quote this phrase from Menander agree that his use of κἄν was condemned by grammarians.

Fragment 5. Körte states, with unjustifiable certainty, that Thrasonides is the speaker. ἦν may be either first or third person. If there was a postponed divine prologue, the sentence could belong there.

ἐν παραβάcει: Lit. 'in a digression', i.e. in parenthesis. ὡc should perhaps be deleted as a dittography of the preceding ωι. Körte accepted Wilamowitz's hazardous rewriting of the passage: ὡc ⟦ἦν παρὰ βαcιλεῖ⟧ ἐκ Κύπρου | πάνυ λαμπρὰ πράττων· ἦν ἐκεῖ γὰρ ὑπό τινι | τῶν βαcιλέων. For ὑπό+acc., 'under the command of', see LSJ s.v. ὑπό II.

1–90: These lines, contained in O 11, must come from Act I or Act II, since O 10 has the greater part of Act III and there is no overlap. Act II is the more probable, since room must be found in Act I for a considerable amount of other material. Being very fragmentary, the lines give little information, and in OCT only those remains have been printed that offer any hope of interpretation.

The vocatives δέσποτα and Γέτα in 8, 9 indicate a conversation between Getas and Thrasonides. A little later someone addresses a foreign stranger (ξένε, 24, 31), probably identical with an 'old man' addressed in 37, and almost certainly Demeas. The other cannot be either Getas or Thrasonides, who first meet Demeas later (219). Hence they must have left the stage at 9 or soon after. It may be guessed that Getas went indoors (Turner suggests the supplement εἰ]ϲιών, Γέτα at 9) and Thrasonides out into the town, whence he is fetched at the end of Act III. Who then does talk with Demeas? A guess ready to hand (Turner) is that it is Kleinias, but since there is some reason for assuming him to have been absent in the earlier part of the play, it may be considered whether the speaker is one of Kleinias' servants, perhaps even the old woman who appears later (176), and refers to Demeas as ὁ ξένοϲ. It may be noted that whereas Kleinias, naturally, knows his guest's name (301), this speaker addresses him as ξένε (twice) and γέρον.

30–3: The restorations printed are plausible, at least. In 33 Handley originally suggested τυ[χὸν ἴϲωϲ, but it seems impossible to recognize τ among the ill-formed letters before the gap. Austin in a letter suggests that ηκειϲϲϲυ, with a superfluous ϲ, can be read. λυτρούμενοϲ is presumably middle, 'ransoming', rather than passive; and the present tense is possible: 'you are here ransoming people' rather than 'you are here with the intention of ransoming people'. Demeas' denial suggests that he had not come in the hope of finding his daughter, and frag. 2 supports this. But what his purpose was cannot be guessed with any confidence.

35–46: Does Demeas reveal his daughter's name, or does the other person tell him that there is a girl called Krateia living here, and perhaps ask his help (τοῦτό μοι ϲυμπρᾶξον, 36)? The news surprises Demeas (46), and possibly he conceives the notion that this Krateia could be his daughter, although 210, ὄψιν οὐδὲ προϲδοκωμένην, tells against this.

45 ὦ Ζεῦ τροπαῖε: Soph. *Trach.* 303, Eur. *Heraclidae* 867 have this appeal. Ζεὺϲ τροπαῖοϲ is the giver of victory in battle, and Deianeira prays to him not to allow her own children to become captives and enslaved. Was there something similar here?

65–78: These lines offer some material for guesswork. It is possible that the speakers are still the same as in 35–46, but not certain. The phrase εἰς τὴν ὁδόν (69) suggested to Turner that Demeas asked the other (whom he guessed to be Kleinias) to get the girl into the street, so that he might identify her, if she were his daughter.

74 cυνβρα (not c᾽ ἐν βρα[χεῖ) is puzzling, since the preposition cὺν is in New Comedy restricted to a few phrases, cὺν θεῷ, cὺν κακῷ, etc. cυμβραβεύc or cυμβραβεύω are conceivable words.

101–31: These lines are so tattered that they are not reproduced in OCT. In 109 ξί[φος] (Austin) is probable, since a suprascript *nota personae*, perhaps γ]ρα[ῦς or κ]ρα[τεια or θ]ρα[ςωνίδης, indicates that ξ begins a word. In 122 the word ἱκετηρίαν may refer to the practice by which anyone with a public or private grievance might be heard at the second meeting of the Athenian ecclesia in each prytany. To obtain this hearing he had to deposit a ἱκετηρία (sc. ῥάβδος), a rod bound with wool; Arist. *Ath. Pol.* 43. 6, Pollux viii. 96, cf. Ar. *Plut.* 383, Andok. i. 110, Aischines ii. 15, Dem. xviii. 107, xliii. 83. There are, however, other possibilities, e.g. ἐπιστολὴν] ἱκετηρίαν, a phrase used by Aristainetos ii. 1, whose letters are full of reminiscences from comedy, this play included (i. 17 has ὄνος λύρας and οὐδὲ γρῦ, cf. 295, 291).

132–43: This passage is obtained by combining the two papyri O 10 and B 3; there is just enough overlap to establish their relation: namely 134 ιπωροντ, 135 ηλωτον, 140 ουτος, 141 ηθε. Although the words of the first four lines are nearly all known, ignorance of the situation makes it impossible to choose with confidence among the many combinations of possible supplements and assignments to speakers, of whom there may be either two or three. Some of the alternatives may be found in the critical notes in OCT. Handley has introduced a further complication by pointing out that one speaker may be reporting the words of someone else.

132 λέγουc᾽ may be λέγουcι or λέγουcα.   τάλαν: The speaker is a woman, or reporting a woman's words.   δεινὸν κτλ.: Cf. Plut. *Nic.* 5, ἐπίπονόν τινα καὶ ταλαίπωρον . . . ζῶντος αὐτοῦ βίον.

134–6: The text is uncertain but a possible meaning is 'Why, when he was happy and envied, did she stop his course?' 'She knows her own business better than anyone else.' This proposal is Handley's; one may have doubts about the verb ἔστηςε and the phrase οὕτω τις for τοιοῦτός τις; the persons spoken of are presumably Thrasonides and Krateia.   ἄμεινον . . . τινος: Cf. *Dysk.* 679 n.

139–55: It looks as if the speakers were interrupted and after some final exchanges leave. There is mention of a ring (146), of garments (θαιμάτια, 149), and of stamping or beating on the ground (τὴν γῆν κροτοῦϲαν, 151), of some future pouring of libations (ϲπείϲονθ', 152). ἱκε]τηρίων is a probable supplement in 153. The remains are so fragmentary that 142–5, 147–8 have not been printed in OCT.

Who are the speakers, who may have been conversing throughout the whole passage from 101 onwards? Turner suspected that Krateia was one of them; Merkelbach thought they were Krateia's nurse and another servant from Thrasonides' house, that they went to Kleinias' house to ask for help, and that the nurse there caught sight of Demeas, whom she recognized, and returned to inform Krateia. He may be right in seeing Krateia's nurse in one of the characters; the rest of his construction appears unlikely. In my view there is not sufficient ground for guessing either who are the speakers or what is the subject of their conversation.

140 παρά τινος: Probably 'from a certain person', not 'from someone', a quodam not ab aliquo, cf. Perik. 344, προϲέξει ϲοί τιϲ, Sam. 454, πρεϲβεύεταί τιϲ πρὸϲ ἐμέ. **ἀπαλλάγηθ':** Either ἀπαλλάγηθι or ἀπαλλάγητε.

155: In the nota personae v is certain, ρ probable. This gives a name that does not appear elsewhere in the remains of the play; Turner suggests Χρυϲίϲ or Τρύφη, even Φρυγία; δούλη is unlikely. θύραϲ, suggested for the end of the line, cannot really be read on the photograph, is doubtful because of the lack of the article τῆϲ, and not apparently suited to the context: the speakers here go off the stage entirely, leaving it to a man, probably Thrasonides' slave Getas, who delivers a soliloquy. Does he enter here, or has he been talking to the woman? Of 156–9 only a few letters remain; from 160 O 10 is again supplemented by B 3.

160–75: Getas, if it is he, appears to be recounting how someone, of ugly features, had been singing; he had every right to do so, as he was drinking. But the slave suspects him of some evil designs against his master; he ends by saying that he will go in and keep an eye on what is going on. I think it improbable that the singer is Demeas, who is apparently not yet known to Getas or to Thrasonides. He may be Kleinias.

160–1: The repetition of ανθρωποϲ at the same point of the line raises suspicion. In 161 B 3 shows the rough breathing. It is tempting to suppose the sense to have been 'he had a fat face; the man's a pig', with reference to ugliness perhaps rather than stupidity, as Turner thinks. But frag. 23 K–T, παχὺϲ γὰρ ὗϲ ἔκειτ' ἐπὶ ϲτόμα, causes one to consider such possibilities as ἤρειδεν παχὺϲ τὴν ὄψιν ὗϲ.

162: Metre may be corrected by writing either ἔξωθεν θεωρεῖν (Austin) or ἔξωθ' ἐπιθεωρεῖν (Merkelbach). ἔξωθε is known to LSJ only from Diog. Oen. 18, but ἔcωθε for ἔcωθεν is found in Eur. *Heracl.* 42, and there only.

163: No probable suggestion has been made for restoring this corrupt line.

164 θάτεροc: This is a back-formation from the correct θάτερον = τὸ ἔτερον. Its use by Menander is censured by [Herodian], *de soloecismo*, frag. 710 K–T, ὁ θάτεροc μὲν τοῖν δυοῖν Διοcκόροιν. The masc. accusative θάτερον is found in the spurious line Eur. *Ion* 849.

165: Before ὦ B 3 has ὁρᾶν, unmetrically; O 10 has γαρ. One may guess the correct text to be τὸν ἄνδρ' ὁρᾶν γάρ.

166 ἐπὶ πᾶcι ... δικαίοιc: Cf. Dem. xx. 88, ὡc ἀληθῶc ἐπὶ πᾶcι δικαίοιc ποιούμεθα τοὺc λόγουc, 'with complete fairness and justification', Aischines i. 178, τοὺc μὲν νόμουc τίθεcθε ἐπὶ πᾶcι δικαίοιc, iii. 170, ὁ λογιcμὸc ἔcτω ἐπὶ πᾶcι δικαίοιc. I do not know whether there are any other examples of this 'proverbial phrase'; for τὸ τοῦ λόγου cf. 303, *Dysk.* 633, and Headlam on Herondas ii. 45, where he collects examples of the expression.

168: Cf. frag. 732, οἷον πατάγημ' ἥκειc. 'You're something worth listening to that has now arrived'. The slave seems to address, in imagination, the man of whose singing he has been speaking.

169: The first word is uncertain; if the reported traces in B 3 are to be trusted, μαθών is excluded. ἐπικάμπτειc is possible, but the meaning 'make a flank attack' does not prima facie go well with πάλιν cτέλλει 'go back again'. Perhaps ἔτι κάμπτειc 'still turn round'. The imperfect suggested by B 3 is not attractive.

170 τὰc cυμβολάc: Quite obscure. Wilamowitz, *SB Berlin* 1918, 749, thought of some commercial agreement, Thierfelder of a δεῖπνον ἀπὸ cυμβολῶν, a dinner to which the guests all contributed; Webster now suggests that some kind of means of identification, carried by Demeas, is intended (normally cύμβολον).

171 λῆροc: 'Nonsense!' cf. Ar. *Plut.* 23. Does the slave mean thereby his own suspicions, or the actions of the suspect? If the former, the following sentence may be a statement, not a question.

174: Wilamowitz' supplement κρύπτων is generally approved, but may not Getas' intention have been to *join* the company? E.g. παράγων (hardly εἰcφρῶν) ἐμαυτόν (for transitive παράγω cf. *Sam.* 252).

176: A woman comes out of Kleinias' house, to report the strange behaviour of his guest, who has shown a great interest in the swords from Thrasonides' house, which are being kept in that of Kleinias. One would guess her to be a slave; but the *nota personae* at 184 cannot be read with confidence as γραυ[c, although that is plausible.

178 ff.: E.g. ἐν τῷ γὰ]ρ οἴκῳ τὰς cπάθας τῶν γειτόνων | [ἰδὼν παρ' ἡμῖν εὐθὺς a]ὐτὰς εἰς μέcον | [φέρειν ἐκέλευε κἀξετάcac πο]λὺν χρόνον.

183 ff.: Hereabouts the guest, who is Demeas, follows the woman on to the stage. After some conversation he asks her to knock upon Thrasonides' door on his behalf; apparently she tells him to knock for himself, and proposes to take herself off. A paragraphus under 206, however, suggests that the conversation continued.

188: For ἀποτρέχω (uncertain), cf. *Dysk.* 918, *Sam.* 464, *Aspis* 217.

193 τὴν ἐμήν: Perhaps cπάθην. There is a dicolon at the end of the line. It is more likely that the old woman says, of Demeas, κόψει τὴν θύραν (or e.g. τί δ' οὐχὶ κόψει τ. θ.), than that he says it of her, prompted by some very short remark by her at the beginning of 194a. At the end of 194a Handley, taking the other view, suggests κόψας' ἔτι; there seems to be a letter, δ or a, after c.

204 ἐνθύμιον usually means what 'lies on the heart', by way of conscience for the past or scruple for the future. But here, according to the Lexicon that quotes the line, it refers to calculation rather than conscience, and is more or less synonymous with ἐνθύμημα.

206: Demeas knocks upon the door, but immediately retreats, hearing someone inside about to come out. The request to the old woman to knock (189) suggests that he was for some reason diffident about approaching the house. But his retreat is necessary for reasons of stage-craft. The ensuing scene, involving four persons, would be intolerably cramped if they were all clustered in the doorway; indeed Getas, the last to appear, would hardly be visible.

207: On the tendency of post-positives to come second in a sentence, as αὐτῶν does here, see K. J. Dover, *Greek Word Order*, p. 14.

208: Krateia comes out of Thrasonides' house in conversation with her old nurse, who is a *muta persona*, although she is twice addressed as though she had spoken (211, 228). At both places her implied words would have been uttered simultaneously with those of another speaker, who was at that moment holding the audience's attention. Here the imaginary words coincide with Demeas' exclamation of wonder; at 228 she is supposed to have addressed her master during Getas' question to Krateia and the girl's reply. Thus illusion is preserved. The clever technique here employed in handling the *muta persona* is worth attention. It would not be plausible if the old nurse took no share in this scene, especially if, as is possible, she had earlier appeared in a speaking part. Now she cannot speak if the 'three-actor rule' is to be observed, as apparently it is. But though she does not open her mouth, the impression is created that she does speak, as is to be expected of her.

Some, e.g. H. J. Mette *Lustrum* x (1968), 157–8, A. Borgogno *SIFC* n.s. xli (1969), 34, suppose that this old woman is identical with the old woman who is Kleinias' slave, and that she entered Thrasonides' house at about 200; she will bring Krateia out to meet the stranger. I cannot disprove this, but much prefer my own interpretation, which is also that of Merkelbach and Del Corno. Kleinias' slave-woman comes out (176) to speak to the audience, not to go to Thrasonides' house. Her conversation with Demeas, so far as it remains, is not very amicable, and contains nothing to suggest a reason for fetching Krateia. A slave ought not to enter another person's house unbidden. It is a far finer *coup de théâtre* that neither Demeas nor Krateia should expect their meeting, each having come to the spot for some other purpose. Finally, why if this servant of Kleinias' has been present at the unexpected meeting of Demeas and his daughter, which she had herself arranged, should she tell Kleinias nothing of it, but merely inform him (276–8) that Demeas had gone next door on learning that a sword belonged there? Krateia's opening words, 'I could not have put up with . . .', or conceivably 'I could not wait', if this use (Plutarch, *Dion* 51, Arrian, *Anab.* iv. 8. 9) was already established, will have contained a clue to the reason why she leaves Thrasonides' house. They can hardly have contained any hint of where she was going; that must have come from a preceding scene.

210–15: The heightened emotional level of these lines can be seen from the absence of resolved feet and the keeping of the rules of tragic iambics. In 214 τέκνον is tragic prosody, cf. ὅπλα, *Epitr.* 324 n. τίν' ὄψιν . . . ὁρῶ; recalls Eur. *Hel.* 557, τίc εἶ; τίν' ὄψιν cήν, γύναι, προcδέρκομαι; parodied by Aristophanes *Thesm.* 905, ὦ θεοί, τίν' ὄψιν εἰcορῶ; τίc εἶ, γύναι; ὦ ποθούμενοc φανείc, ὁρῶ cε recalls Eur. *El.* 578, ὦ χρόνῳ φανείc, ἔχω cε. ἔχω cε is a standard formula at such reunions, *Aspis* 508, Soph. *El.* 1226, Eur. *Alc.* 1134, *Ion* 1440, *IT* 829, cf. Ter. *Heaut.* 407, 'teneone te?'

210 οὐδὲ προcδοκωμένην: Cf. frag. 136, πάντα δὲ τὰ μηδὲ προcδοκώμεν' ἔκcταcιν φέρει. 'Not even expected' would in English be nonsensical, because 'I expect this' usually means 'I think that this *will* happen'; προcδοκᾶν must be weaker than this, meaning 'look for', 'wait for', with hope or apprehension. Demeas did not think it even on the cards that he would meet his daughter at the house which he was approaching with some quite different intent.

τηθία is otherwise known only from Eustathios, 971. 43, who equates it with τήθη, properly 'grandmother'. Krateia's companion will hardly be her real grandmother; rather some old slave-woman thus affectionately addressed, probably her nurse or even her mother's or father's nurse. This slave will have come into Thrasonides' possession along with the captive girl. His motive for taking or keeping her would be to provide Krateia with the personal attendant that she would expect.

212 πατὴρ ἐμός: 'My *father*?' On the absence of the article see *Dysk.* 240 n.

216: Getas' first words as he comes out from Thrasonides' house suggest that he is looking for Krateia, who has been missed. Since there is nothing to show that he is accompanied by anyone whom he could address as παῖ, the phrase παῖ, τί τοῦτο; seems to be a fossilized exclamation of surprise; compare *Sam.* 691, 715 and the discussion *Dysk.* 500 n. Turner says that in O 10 the letter after ω is 'not π as this scribe usually writes it'. Hence Del Corno, *Gnomon* xlii (1970), 257, following Merkelbach, *Rh. Mus.* cix (1966), 104, would write ἔξω γ'· αἴ. Even if this was the reading of O 10, γε is unwanted.

217 τί ποιεῖc οὗτοc; οὗτοc with a question, as again in 221, meaning 'you there' is familiar, e.g. Ar. *Wasps* 1, οὗτοc τί πάcχειc; Normally it comes first in the sentence, but cf. [Dem.] lviii. 15, ἀκούειc οὑτοcί; τί λέγει;

223: Does Getas suspect that he has made a ridiculous mistake in taking Krateia's father for a lover (e.g. [ἦν ἐγὼ] οὕτω γελοῖοc) or protest that he has never heard such an absurd story (e.g. [τίc λόγοc] οὕτω γελοῖοc;)?

K. Kumaniecki, *Eos* lv (1965), 57, restores 223–9, not plausibly.

230: Demeas wishes he had come from home, because he no longer *has* a home, his family in Cyprus having been scattered. ἀλλὰ τυγχάνειc ἀπόδημοc ὢν ἐκεῖθεν: 'But you are in fact away from home, it is the case that you are away from home'. The verb τυγχάνω often throws an emphasis on the participle or participial phrase with which it is constructed. Thus Plato, *Phaedo* 73 a, εἰ μὴ ἐτύγχανεν αὐτοῖc ἐπιcτήμη ἐνοῦcα, 'if they did not in fact have the knowledge within them', 86 c, εἰ οὖν τυγχάνει ἡ ψυχὴ οὖcα ἁρμονία τιc, 'if the soul is in fact an "adjustment"', 91 b, εἰ μὲν τυγχάνει ἀληθῆ ὄντα ἃ λέγω, etc. Any idea of chance, of 'happening to be', is excluded in such instances.

230–3: Demeas, speaking with emotion, keeps the metrical rules of tragedy. The verb cπείρω, although common in verse, is used in prose and in particular of the 'scattering' of people, e.g. Thuc. ii. 27, ἐσπάρηςαν κατὰ τὴν ἄλλην Ἑλλάδα. To call war 'the common enemy' is a striking personification.

In spite of the absence of the article, I think πρῶτον τῶν ἐμῶν must mean 'what is first, i.e. most valued, of my possessions'. τινάς shows that Demeas supposes that *some* others of his household will have been driven or carried away, like Krateia, but others may have been killed; hence he does not say τοὺς οἴκοι.

239–45: Only a few letters can be made out. Perhaps Demeas' suspicions that his son is dead, because Thrasonides has his sword, are confirmed by finding that his daughter has fallen to the soldier as a captive. Some inquiry by the daughter about her brother may have been met by the reply that he is dead.

246–50: These lines are put together from O 3 and O 10. The overlap is clearer on the recto of O 3, of which frags. 1, 2, 3, 4 partially coincide with O 10 in 276–9, 282–5. If the evidence for change of speakers preserved in O 10 is regarded, it looks as if Krateia asks who has told her father of her brother's death. He probably does not directly answer the question, for all that remains of his reply is ἀπόλωλα, before which there is little room. When, after uttering a lamentation, she asks again, 'He is dead?', he replies 'Yes, and at the hands of the last man who should have killed him'. 'You know who it was?' 'I know etc.'. Assuming that his daughter is living with Thrasonides as his wife, Demeas views the situation with horror.

Although this seems the most likely interpretation, one cannot exclude an alternative, namely that Krateia tells her father that her brother is dead and that *he* asks her the source of her information, and then, convinced by the evidence of the sword in Thrasonides' possession, adds what she does not know, namely that he is aware of the identity of the man who killed him. Although O 10 clearly has απολωλα, it is tempting to suspect an error. εὖ οἶδ', ἀπόλωλεν would make a possible reply to τίς λέγει coι τὸν λόγον;, provided that the word ἀπόλωλεν, 'he has come to grief', is specific enough to convey the meaning 'he is dead'.

There is a third possibility, supported by Mette, Merkelbach, Borgogno, and Kraus. O 3 has dicola after both πεπονθαμεν and τεθνηκε, from which it would be gathered that Krateia speaks the words ὑφ' οὗ γ' ἤκιστ' ἐχρῆν. Then the *nota personae* Δη in O 10 will be mistaken. If this is accepted, an attractive hypothesis is possible. Krateia's hate for Thrasonides is not based merely on the tedium of his stories, but on a belief that he has killed her brother. He will have boasted to her of having killed the owner of the sword that excited Demeas' interest, and she will have recognized that sword.

This scheme has great advantages, not the least of which is that the conclusion that Thrasonides had killed her brother is much more plausible than if reached by Demeas on nothing more than the discovery that Thrasonides possessed his son's sword. A possible objection is that a girl would perhaps not be familiar with her brother's sword. Moreover, Del Corno urges that Krateia's exclamations in 247–8 suggest that she has just learned of some disaster, and I incline to accept his view that father and daughter combine to reach their conclusion. Krateia knows that Thrasonides claims to have killed the owner of the sword, Demeas that the sword is that of his son (*Gnomon* xlii [1970], 257). See further p. 441 above.

Since Thrasonides must be cleared of the charge of killing the brother, it is a plausible guess that the sword had been used by someone else. *Aspis* may provide a parallel; there Kleostratos is reported killed because his shield was found by an unrecognizable dead man.

248: For the restoration and position of ἐγώ cf. *Dysk.* 189, οἴμοι τάλαινα τῶν ἐμῶν ἐγὼ κακῶν.

249 ὑφ᾽ οὖ γ᾽ ἥκιϲτ᾽ ἐχρῆν: Cf. Lysias xxxii. 10, ὑβριϲμένουϲ ὑφ᾽ ὧν ἥκιϲτ᾽ ἐχρῆν, i.e. close relations. H. J. Mette, *Lustrum* xi (1967), 141 notes *Christus Patiens* 1663, τοίγαρ τέθνηκεν ὧν ἐχρῆν ἥκιϲθ᾽ ὕπο, perhaps from Euripides' *Bacchae*, and there used of the death of Pentheus at the hands of his mother and her fellow Bacchantes. Other places where similar phrases are used of close relations are *Aspis* 92 (see Austin's note), Eur. *El.* 1012, *Bacch.* 26, *IA* 487, Hdt. iii. 52, Neophron frag. 2 Nauck.

251: I can make nothing of ἀλοῦϲ᾽ ἄμιλλά τ᾽ οὖϲα του[, which Turner prints in *BICS*, nor of Austin's suggestion ἀμίλλαι (dative). Perhaps the very illegible line has not been correctly read.

252: Webster suggested e.g. φέρετε . . . κλάδουϲ, supposing that Krateia had left Thrasonides' house intending to take refuge in a holy place as a suppliant.

256–7: Uncertainty over readings makes restoration difficult. O 3 was deciphered by Grenfell and Hunt as having ζῆνευπρε[, but Turner denies that ευ is recognizable, and sees the feet of two verticals. In O 10 ζ is the only visible early letter, and it was second in the line. As a long shot, I suggest ἀλλ᾽ ἦ κἄμ᾽ ἔδ[ει], | [ἔ]ζην. τί πρέπει κτλ. 'I lived in the way I had to live. How can it suit . . .?' For the form ἔζην (not ἔζων) cf. *P. Didot* ii. 4.

Demeas and Krateia here leave the stage. The sequel shows that they entered Thrasonides' house. This is natural, since Demeas must wish to treat with him about her ransom. To take her into Kleinias' house would put Demeas in the wrong, for she still belongs to Thrasonides. He is, of course, not at home at the moment; Krateia had taken advantage of his absence to try to run away; but father and daughter will wait for his return.

258–9: O 3 assigns 258 to Thrasonides, but O 10 has a paragraphus below 258 and none below 257, and is, I think, right (so also Del Corno, *Gnomon* xlii [1970], 258¹). Thrasonides and Getas enter at 259, the stage having been momentarily empty after the departure of Demeas and Krateia at 258. Although the news that Krateia's father had appeared might make Thrasonides reflect on the unexpectedness of life, it would not cause him to regard it as 'distressing' or 'hard'. He hopes, on the contrary, that this event may be the key to his happiness, although he fears it may bring ruin. Demeas, who imagines he has lost a son and has certainly found his daughter a captive, has much more reason to use the adjective ταλαίπωρος. There is, as it happens, no parallel in Menander for ὤ and exclamatory genitive in an entrance line: but *Perik.* 360 gives one in an exit-line. φῄς in an entrance line is found below 276 and at *Dysk.* 50, 456, and when two characters enter in conversation they often come straight to a point of fact, one recounting what the other has said or done, *Sam.* 61, *Perik.* 267, *Sik.* 150: similarly, for what it is worth, Plaut. *Bacch.* 109, 405, *Cist.* 1, 631, *Aul.* 40, 120, 682, Ter. *Andr.* 301 ('quid ais?'), *Adelphoe* 517 ('ain patrem hinc abisse rus?'). Although there is not much left of ταλαιπώρου, I can find no alternative that suits the remains: τὰ λοιπά or τὸ λοιπόν is excluded. Possible nouns for the line-end are suggested by Soph. *OC* 91, τὸν ταλαίπωρον βίον, Alexis frag. 144 K, (A.) ὅσον οὐ τέθνηκα. (B.) τοῦ ταλαιπώρου πάθους.

260 μακάριος: A word often used of the happy bridegroom, *Sik.* 379 n.

261 δείξεις: Thrasonides may apostrophize Demeas in the second person, and then, turning to Getas, speak of him in the third as οὗτος.

262 κυρίως is to be taken with δώσει; the two words go closely together, so that τε may be postponed, cf. *Perik.* 128 n., Dem. xxxvi. 32, κυρίως δόντος τοῦ πατρὸς τοῦ σοῦ κατὰ τοὺς νόμους αὐτὴν γεγαμῆσθαι.

264 ὃ μὴ γένοιτο: Cf. *Sam.* 728.

266 ἅπαξ γνῶναι: 'Get to know once for all' is good for sense, but not altogether suitable to the traces, which seem better to fit απαξα-παντα. If that is right, it is not said what is βέλτιον, but 'to go in and have a show-down' can be easily understood.

269 οἰήσεως: 'Vague notion'. In this sense the word is cited by LSJ only from philosophers, elsewhere it means 'self-conceit'. Following

opinions expressed by Webster and Turner, I disregard the assignment
by O 10 of πῶc κτλ. to Getas, attach πωc (enclitic) to the previous
sentence, and suppose Thrasonides to express his surprise at what has
occurred. It would be surprising if Getas should at last break his
silence; one would have expected him to be a *muta persona*. To assign
these words to him involves a breach of the alleged 'three-actor rule'
since, unless the stage is left empty for a time after 258, he cannot be
played by either of the actors who took the parts of Demeas and
Krateia. If O 10 is right, Getas must say: 'What does he mean? I'd
be surprised at this.'

At the end of the line there are traces of a marginal note, in which
I should like to see ειcερχ΄ i.e. 'they go in', rather than αγνοια (Turner,
who inclined to reject ειcιαcι, but later reckoned ειcιον[τ]ι as possible);
but I do not assert that it can be read.

270: The stage is left empty as Thrasonides enters his house with
Getas. His neighbour Kleinias now appears with a cook, to whom he
gives instructions before taking him into his house. These lines refer
to some strand in the plot to which there is no clue.

Who are to be the guests at the party? The ξένοc is presumably
Demeas, so called by Kleinias' servant at 176, rather than the mer-
cenary soldier Thrasonides. But the woman? It could be Krateia, if
Kleinias had knowledge that she intended to run away from
Thrasonides, and hoped that she would seek shelter with him. But
Del Corno notes that he does not seem to connect her with the soldier;
otherwise he would show more agitation when he overhears Getas'
story of the dispute between Thrasonides, Demeas, and a woman.

271: It is not necessary to suppose the omission of any noun, since
ἐμή τιc could mean 'a woman belonging to me'; but some noun, of
which the missing parts of the play would provide a hint, may be
suppressed.

272 καὐτόc seems to imply that someone else also was in an agony of
suspense.

274 ἀλλὰ πάραγε cύ: Again at *Dysk.* 556.

275 τοῦ ταχέωc: Turner quotes frag. 558, τοῦ καλῶc . . . πεφρόντικεν,
frag. 648, ἐν τῷ καλῶc, *Dysk.* 63, ἐν τῷ ταχέωc. The traditional cook
of comedy is loquacious; this one says not a word. His unexpected
silence is necessary, because he must, if the three-actor rule is kept,
be played by a *muta persona*.

ACT IV

276: Only a short passage of time is represented by the choric interlude. Kleinias re-emerges, talking to his old servant, perhaps through the door; but she may have accompanied him on the stage, as a *muta persona*, and this may be more likely in view of the length of what he says to her. ἐπιγνούc: 'having recognized', as Soph. *El.* 1296, ὅπωc μήτηρ cε μὴ 'πιγνώcεται.

281: Except for the first three letters, probably the whole of this line has been cancelled and another version written above, but only the first half is legible. λῆμψιc is a form commonly found for λῆψιc from the second century B.C., due to the influence of λαμβάνω; similarly λήμψομαι, Mayser, *Gramm. Gr. Pap.* i. 194–5.

282 εὔδηλοc εἶ: Cf. *Heros* 3, *Dysk.* 94. The space in O 10 suggests that, like O 3, it may have had the corrupt προcιων for προιων; earlier in the line some correction has been made before ψοφει, whether by cancelling a letter or overwriting it with ε (?). I guess that O 10 finally offered ψοφεινδεπροcιωνφαινεται. Turner's abandoned ἐψόφηκε (cf. *Epitr.* 875, *Sam.* 540) cut the knot. There is no parallel for ψοφεῖν without an expressed subject (τιc or ἡ θύρα).

284: Getas comes out and pours forth his indignation at the unfeeling conduct of Demeas and Krateia (ἀμφοῖν 285), who have refused to consider Thrasonides' suit. He disregards all Kleinias' attempts to attract his attention until 323. No attempt is made to motivate his coming out of the house, nor does he explicitly address his story to the audience; contrast on both points Sostratos in *Dysk.* 666 ff. and Onesimos in *Epitr.* 878 ff. There is a slight disregard of realism also in Kleinias' phrase πάντ' ἀκούcομαι cαφῶc; to get a clear account of all that has happened from someone unknown who emerges from a house is an occurrence more likely in a play than in real life. But in a play the expectation will pass as natural. Menander then, with his gift for the unexpected, cheats the expectation: Getas' talk bewilders rather than enlightens Kleinias.

285 ἀπανθρώπου: 'Inhuman', *Dysk.* 6 n. **ἀμφοῖν:** Demeas and Krateia.

287 αὐθαδίαc: αὐθάδεια is defined by Theophrastos, *Char.* 15 as ἀπήνεια (discourtesy) ὁμιλίαc ἐν λόγοιc, and the αὐθάδηc or 'surly' man is said to be one to snub a questioner and not reply to a greeting. Demeas, it will appear, has refused to talk with Thrasonides except to ask for his daughter's return.

291 οὐδὲ γρῦ: It is impossible to know whether this is correct or the reading of O 10, μηδὲ γρῦ. But Aristainetos i. 17 has οὐδὲ γρῦ and ὄνος λύρας (cf. 295).

293–4: Turner's restoration ἧς ἐρᾷς ἐγὼ ταύτης πατὴρ καὶ κύριος has the disadvantage that the sentence cannot be referred to by the following ταυτὶ λέγει . . . κλάων ἀντιβολῶν. Demeas is harsh and inhuman; it is Thrasonides who is emotional and engages in entreaty (cf. ἀντιβολῶ 307). I think more likely something on the lines of φιλῶ Κράτειαν αὐτός, ὡς ὁρᾷς, ἐγώ, σὺ δὲ δή (or σὺ δ' εἶ) πατὴρ καὶ κύριος.

295 ὄνος λύρας: According to Photios the complete proverb was ὄνος λύρας ἤκουε καὶ σάλπιγγος ὗς, and was used of τῶν μὴ συγκατατιθεμένων μηδὲ ἐπαινούντων. The last word is ambiguous, 'praising' or 'saying "no thank you"', but probably means the latter; that sense would suit this passage, where Demeas says neither yes nor no to Thrasonides' proposal, but concentrates, like an αὐθάδης, on his own subject.

296: ὡς ἐμοὶ δοκῶ of O 10 means 'as I think', cf. Plato, *Apol.* 36 a 7, *Crito* 43 c 7, ἣν ἐγώ, ὡς ἐμοὶ δοκῶ, ἐν τοῖς βαρύτατ' ἂν ἐνέγκαιμι. ὡς ἐμοὶ δοκεῖ of O 3 means 'as it seems good to me to do'. Either is possible here.

297 εἴρει: No satisfactory alternative to the word εἴρει has been suggested. εἶπε would introduce a lone aorist into the series of historic presents in which Getas tells his story. O 3 seems to have ειρημετη (Hunt and Turner); if εἴρηκε was intended, that is unmetrical and might be a 'synonym' for εἴρει. εἴρειν is often used of stringing words together in speech (hence λέξις εἰρομένη 'continuous style'); for a collection of instances see W. G. Arnott, *BICS* xv (1968), 122. ἐν τοῦτο δ' εἴρει may mean 'he makes a string of this one sentence', i.e. he repeats it over and over again. But I should find it easier to understand 'he (Demeas) attaches this one reply only'. συνείρω, which normally is used much like εἴρω, can be so employed: Lucian, *Dial. Mort.* 2. 2, ὀδύρεσθε μὲν ὑμεῖς, ἐγὼ δὲ τὸ "γνῶθι σαυτὸν" πολλάκις συνείρων ἐπάσομαι ὑμῖν, where the meaning must be that the speaker will keep 'tagging on' γνῶθι σαυτόν to the dead kings' lamentations.

300 ἄνθρωπος: The word expresses Kleinias' bewilderment at Demeas' action: 'The fellow's gone into their house?'

302 λάβοι: Demeas is the subject. 'Can't he take what's happened like a human being?' Cf. frag. 650, ἀνθρωπίνως δεῖ τὰς τύχας φέρειν, *Aspis* 165. But whereas there the idea is merely that it is a part of human life both to suffer and to endure misfortunes, here, as at *Aspis* 260, there is a further suggestion that a human being will behave reasonably and with understanding, not with the savagery of a wild animal. With some hesitation I accept O 10's change of the original reading δ' οὐκ ἂν λάβοι to ἂν οὐ λάβοι, with the consequent unusual order of words (ἂν οὐ for οὐκ ἄν); the writer may have had some good reason for making it. But δ' οὐκ ἂν λάβοι is in itself perfectly good, δέ frequently being used in indignant questions, Denniston, GP 174–5.

303 ὗc ὄρει: The proverb is unknown, but the wild boar on the mountain might be a type of unsocial ill-temper. In a similar sense Theokritos xiv. 43 has ἔβα ποκα ταῦρος ἀν' ὕλαν. The locative use of the dative is almost entirely poetical, K–G i. 441–2, but perhaps possible in a proverb. Krates frag. 29 K has a corrupt line, which may contain the expression, ὗc ὄρ⟨ε⟩ι †μαχεῖν† ἄνδρεc οὐρανοῦ καττύματα (H. J. Mette, *Lustrum* xi [1967], 140). Unfortunately the passage, which seems to be an intentional conundrum, has not so far as I know been explained. The paroemiographers, e.g. Ap. xvii. 14, know a proverb ὗc ὀρίνει ('makes a commotion'), ἐπὶ τῶν βιαίων καὶ ἐριστικῶν. Alkaios, Z 70 Lobel–Page, uses it, πάλιν ἁ cῦc παρορίνει. J. H. Kells suggested ὗc ὀρεῖ, 'pig to mule'; if there was some fable to which this could allude, the mule must have been a 'good' character in it, since Getas' sympathies seem to be entirely with his master.

304–5: Austin's suggestion, ἀλλ' αὐτή (or αὕτη) πάλιν ἀφορᾷ λέγοντος, is tempting, and the rare sense of ἀφορᾶν, 'look away', is to be found in Xen. *Cyr.* 7. 1. 36, ἀφορῶντας παίειν. No other possible proposal has been made. Turner rejects it on the grounds that the vertical stroke of φ should be visible and that the writer did not normally add ι adscript. Austin replies that ink has often disappeared completely from this papyrus, that there is hardly a trace of *any* letter where φ should be, and that ι adscript appears from time to time (167 ηιcεν, 228 γραιδιον, 234 αλλαχηι, 372 ειζηι or ειπηι, and falsely at 266 οκνηιρωc).

307 ἀνὴρ ἐκλήθην is almost certain, cf. Eur. *HF* 150, ὡc ἀρίcτου φωτὸc ἐκλήθηc δάμαρ. It shows that Thrasonides and Krateia were believed to be living as man and wife, although that was not in fact the case. For ἀνήρ used of the partner of a παλλακή, cf. *Perik.* 186. πρῶτος is better joined to ἐκλήθην than to ἠγάπηcα as by *ed. pr.* Many people may have felt affection for Krateia before—her parents, her brother, etc. ἀγαπᾶν is frequently used of feeling love for children; it has no connotation of sexual desire.

311 ff.: Eur. *Med.* 1342 λέαιναν οὐ γυναῖκα. Turner's supplement ἀνηλεήc may be supported by *Epitr.* 898, βάρβαρος ἀνηλεήc τε, but cannot be right if the next word is, as seems likely, οὐχ. At the end the line the second hand has substituted παλαι for γετα; before παλαι there is a horizontal stroke, which may indicate a change of speaker. There is a dicolon before ουχ in 313, but no paragraphus visible

below the line. There seems to be a *nota personae* in the margin before
314; it can be interpreted as γε]τ′. With these uncertain and perhaps
incomplete indications, assignment of speakers is difficult. οὐχ ὑγιαίνει
παντελῶc could be said by Kleinias of Getas or by Getas of either
Demeas or Krateia. Could he also say it of Thrasonides? If his master
has agreed to ransom Krateia without the promise of her hand, he
too could be 'quite out of his mind'. That he had done so is not said,
but may be implied in Getas' next sentence: '*I* would not have
ransomed her.' If this is the case, the next lines must be a conversation that Getas imagines might have taken place, had he been in
Thrasonides' shoes.

313 ἀπροcδόκητον: 'This is something I would never have expected.'
Kraus suggests that the word is wrongly assigned to Kleinias, and
belongs to Getas.

314 μὰ τὸν Ἀπόλλω τουτονί: Cf. *Dysk.* 659 n.

315 πανταχοῦ: On the ground that there should be some trace of *v*,
Coles prefers πανταχῇ, perhaps rightly, but the form does not appear
elsewhere in Menander or Middle or New comedy. Kraus's punctuation, Ἑλληνικόν; καὶ πανταχοῦ γινόμενον; ἴcμεν is lively and perhaps
right.

317: ἀντελεεῖν occurs nowhere else, but the initial *a* is all but certain
here, and there is no reason for doubting the compound.

318: This line is quoted in two books of etymology to illustrate the
use of λόγοc in the sense of φροντίc, 'thought' (frag. 687 K–T).
ἐπιcτροφή, 'regard', 'attention'; a word not found elsewhere in comedy,
but in prose (Xenophon, *Hell.* v. 2. 9, Dem. xix. 306) as well as tragedy.

319: A puzzling and not altogether convincing line. ατοπονωcεγω is
a correction by a second hand of an obliterated first version. Most
scholars accept ὡc ἐγώ—, as an aposiopesis. This seems strange to me,
and Mette's attempt to read δο[κῶ] at the beginning of 320 is welcome,
but unfortunately not certain; δοκῶ is on the short side for the space.
Austin suggests δεινόν, as an exclamation that marks the end of Getas'
imaginary remarks. 'But it's impossible (i.e. to pay no regard) Why?
Nothing odd there to my way—(sc. of thinking). Terrible!'

Kraus supposes οὐθὲν ἄτοπον κτλ. to be Thrasonides' imagined reply
to οὐκ ἔcτι coι; 'You can't do it?' 'Nothing is as odd as I am.' I do
not find this convincing.

320 βοήcεται has Thrasonides as subject. For what follows I see no
alternative to Webster's βουλεύcεται κτανεῖν ἑαυτὸν cτάc. Yet uncompounded κτείνω is unknown in New Comedy, although found in
Thucydides and Aristotle, and cτάc is difficult. Perhaps it means

'coming to a standstill'; one may imagine that previously he had been moving about as he entreated first father, then daughter. Thoughts of suicide by the despairing lover are not unusual, 309 above, *Perik.* 976, Plaut. *Cist.* 639, Donatus on Ter. *Adelphoe* 275. I cannot explain the future tenses; possibly Getas at first imagines himself at the time when Krateia was surrendered; then Thrasonides was 'going to shout'. But at βλέπει he describes the scene as present.

321 βλέπει δὲ πῦρ ἅμα: Probably Thrasonides, who is not depressed but raging. The loss of the beginning of 322 must, however, dictate caution. Possibly οὐ[δὲ] τ[ότ'] ἐκεί[νη, 'not even then did she say anything'.

322 δράττεταί ⟨τε⟩ τῶν τριχῶν: No doubt Thrasonides, like Stratophanes (probably), *Sik.* 220, or Charisios, *Epitr.* 893. There is no occasion for a display of emotion by Krateia.

323 κατακόψεις: *Sam.* 292 n.

324: It seems to me likely that Kleinias says 'my guest's arrival seems to be causing a scene'; *ed. pr.* prefers Getas to say 'my master seems to be causing a scene'. There is no firm basis for reconstruction. Turner restores πόθεν πάρεσθ'; as an aside—'where has he come from?'

The next page (D ↓) is almost completely illegible. Paragraphi and *notae personarum* indicate that the conversation between Kleinias and Getas continued for 17 lines, when εἰσέρχο[μαι points to the departure of one or the other (341). At the bottom of the page Thrasonides is apparently on the stage and soliloquizing. (It is conceivable, but unlikely, that the soliloquy is reported by someone else.) He declares that he will conceal his disease: drink will uncover the wound that has been dressed and wishes not to be seen (364). 30 lines later, on the next page (D →) the monologue appears to be continuing still; Thrasonides addresses and answers himself in short lively phrases.

364: Cf. Asklepiades *AP* xii. 135, οἶνος ἔρωτος ἔλεγχος, Theokr. xxix. 1 and Gow's note.

388–403: Thrasonides' monologue continues, but little can be made of it. He seems to regard himself as ill-treated by Krateia, and asks whether he is right to defend her. He speaks of dying, but may reflect that her hate for him is not likely to be affected by pity. He examines his own way of life, and seems to recognize something in it which she thought to be a subject for reproach. Finally he recalls his own kindness to her.

418–65: The remnants of these lines are combined from O 10 and O 7; the latter has a few letters from some preceding lines. How much has been lost after 403 is uncertain. At least one sheet, i.e. 4 pages, of O 10 is not preserved: this would have contained a maximum of 160 lines, within which would fall the division between Acts IV and V. Since what remains of Act IV amounts to 130 lines, and of Act V to 38, the two acts would have totalled *c.* 325 lines. The last two acts of *Samia* total 317, but one act is in tetrameters. The last two of *Dyskolos* totalled about 350, of which nearly 160 are in tetrameters. If the loss of two sheets from O 10 is assumed, the two acts would have had about 480 lines; that is long, but *Epitrepontes* probably had a similar number. These calculations suppose that all pages of O 10 carried a text: the Bodmer papyrus is a reminder that pages might be left blank.

418–28 are preserved in O 7 only. After them Getas addresses Thrasonides, having come out with news. Thrasonides must therefore have been on the stage before, and may be the speaker of these lines. But they may belong to someone else, who at 428 expresses his intention of retiring (ἀνάγε[ιν) and past whom Getas brushes in 429. O 7 has a *nota personae* Γε either before 428 or before 429. That the right place is before 429 is suggested by the fact there is a paragraphus below 428 and none below 427.

429 ἄνθρωπε *tout simple* can hardly be addressed by Getas to his master, and it would be surprising if he spoke so to Kleinias, out of whose house he must come, since Demeas and Krateia will have left Thrasonides' house before the end of Act IV, and moved to that of Kleinias. We do not know of any other man who could be addressed as ἄνθρωπε, and although it is not an impossible way of speaking to a woman, it is unusual. Getas might, however, address his master as e.g. ἄνθρωπε μακάριε.

429–44: O 7 has paragraphi below 429, 430, 431, 433, 435 (where Grenfell–Hunt did not record it), 437, 438, 440, 441; the beginnings of many lines are in a bad state in O 10, from which, however, the paragraphi below 435 and 441 can be confirmed. In spite of these paragraphi the assignment of speeches is here and there uncertain, for there may have been more than one change in the missing part of a line. Where, as at 431 and 438, the text printed does not account for the paragraphus, it may be supposed that the other speaker made some interjection at the end of the line.

Getas appears to bring good news (430); he announces that 'they' are giving Thrasonides the wife he wants (431). Perhaps he says he has prayed for this, and protests the truth of his report, 'so may I prosper' (433). When Thrasonides demands to hear the very words that had been used, he reports how Demeas had asked Krateia whether she wanted to have the soldier, and she had assented (439). Demeas comes out and formally pledges his daughter's hand. After some remarks on the part played by chance in this happy result, thoughts turn to the wedding-feast (450), for which it may be supposed the cook engaged by Kleinias came in handy. The play ends with a call for torches and wreaths and applause, as do *Dyskolos* and *Sikyonios*, and with the same final couplet as concludes those plays.

437 λέγων τάχα τρέχει[: *Kitharistes* 17 ends λέγων τρέχεις, and the phrase must mean 'go at a gallop in what one says'. If it belongs to Thrasonides, he may have said: 'If you tell me every word, you will seem to me to be galloping through the story.'

438: Perhaps the paragraphus is mistaken; an interjection by Thrasonides is hard to accommodate.

439: If Krateia's last word is βούλομαι, Getas might continue e.g. ταυτὶ μόνον ἤκουσα. But O 10 may have εκουσα, and it would be appropriate for Krateia to insist on her willingness.

441: γελῶσα or γέλωτα could both be read and both would yield sense. γέλωτος is, according to Turner, impossible.

443: If the broken word is πρόαγε, Demeas will bring Krateia out, a *muta persona*, cf. *Sam.* 725. (Webster's οὐκ ἀπάγξομαι; is misconceived; *Perik.* 978 is no parallel, for Polemon considered suicide when he thought Glykera was lost to him, not after he had heard that she would take him back.) But Krateia's presence is not here necessary, and Demeas' words might be e.g. πρός σε νῦν ἐξέρχομαι. Thrasonides' καλῶς ποῶν would then be the equivalent of 'thank you for doing so'.

444–6: For this marriage-formula see *Perik.* 1013 n. For the amount of the dowry, *Epitr.* 134 n. It would be interesting to know how Demeas' wealth had survived the war in which his children had suffered.

447 μόνον ἀπόδος: Who speaks? If Thrasonides, he may say 'I want no dowry, just give me back Krateia', e.g. σύ, Δημέα, τὴν θυγατέρ'. But if Thrasonides thanked him for the dowry at the end of 446, Demeas might reply 'Just give in return what is due . . .', and that could be 'what a husband should'.

449 ταὐτομάτου: Cf. *Sam.* 163.

464: The wording of the appeal for applause is not that of *Dyskolos* or *Sikyonios*. The previous line may have ended μειράκια, παῖδες καλοί. πρεπόντως fits the traces better than anything else that has been suggested. Austin compares Plaut. *Cas.* 1015, 'manibus meritis meritam mercedem dare'.

465–6: See *Dysk.* 968 n.

A scene from the fifth act is illustrated in one of the mosaics from Mitilini, published by S. Charitonidis, L. Kahil, and R. Ginouvès, *Antike Kunst*, Beiheft 6 (1970), 57, colour-plate 8. Unfortunately the three personages shown are not named, and only one, a woman, can plausibly be guessed—she must be Krateia. Of the others one is probably a slave: he has round his neck a thick band of some material, of which the other end is in, or near, his raised hand. A central figure has been identified as Demeas or as Thrasonides. Interpretation is quite uncertain. It has been guessed that the slave attempts suicide, or describes an attempt by Thrasonides to commit suicide; but speculation is fruitless.

Several fragments cannot be placed with certainty.

Fragment 7. This may come from the opening scene, and in view of the large number of quotations that survive from that scene, that is perhaps likely. But the lines may be from some later point, e.g. from the lost beginning of Act V.

Fragment 8. Λακωνικὴ κλείς: Ar. *Thesm.* 421, οἱ γὰρ ἄνδρες ἤδη κλειδία αὐτοὶ φοροῦσι κρυπτά, κακοηθέστατα, Λακωνίκ' ἄττα, τρεῖς ἔχοντα γομφίους. The scholiast there talks of securing a door by a beam on the outside, so that people inside could not open it. Such a device is irrelevant, for Aristophanes is talking about locking up larders. Here too someone must mean that he must keep something under secure lock and key; was it Thrasonides when he discovered the disappearance of his swords? But if Spartan keys were also used, as the scholiast seems to think, to lock persons up inside a house or room, the object may have been to prevent Krateia's escape. μοι does not go in sense with ἔοικε, on which it is enclitic, but with περιοιστέα.

Fragment 9. W. G. Arnott, *CR* N.s. xviii (1968), 11, shows admirable scepticism about attempts to restore this fragment. Toup and Körte suppose that Thrasonides could be called Thrason. K. Mras, *Wiener Studien* lv (1937), 78 gives a number of examples where a man with a simple name, Kallias, Xanthippos, Simon, is also called by the patronymic Kalliades, Xanthippides, Simonides. Since the latter appear to be 'grander' forms, Kraus suggests that Thrasonides was derogatorily called Thrason.

Fragment 10. cπαθᾶν: Literally this word means to use the cπάθη (a broad wooden slat) when weaving, to bring the threads of the weft close together; metaphorically it elsewhere means 'to squander' e.g. Diphilos frag. 43, τὰ πατρῷα βρύκει καὶ cπαθᾷ, Plutarch, *Pericles* 14, Σ *Clouds* 53, cπαθᾶν τὸ ἄγαν κρούειν τὴν κρόκην and cπαθᾶν δὲ τὸ ἀφειδῶc ἀναλίcκειν καὶ παρὰ τοῖc ῥήτορcιν (e.g. Dem. xix. 43) εἴρηται πολλάκιc.

It is not clear how it should mean 'to tell grand lies', but the same sense seems likely in Page, *GLP* p. 316, cὺ δ᾿ ἀλαζονε]ύηι πρός με καὶ cπαθᾶιc ἔχων. Perhaps the idea is one of 'overdoing it', 'laying it on too thick'.

Fragment 11. ἐνερόχρωc: 'With ghost-like hue' (*BICS* suppl. 17, p. 13) perhaps described the despairing Thrasonides.

Fragment 12. This exchange may have come from the opening scene, but it is no more than a guess that it belongs to *Misumenos* at all.

PERIKEIROMENE

C   *P. Cairensis* 43227 contains 121–90, 261–406, 480–550, 708–25, 742–60.

H   *P. Heidelberg* 219 contains the ends of 162–79.

L   *Membranae Lipsienses* 613 contain 467–527, 768–827. The text of this vellum MS. differs in eight places from that of C, six times for the better (486, 492, 496, 520, 521, 524).

O 15   *P. Oxyrhynchica* 2830 has the beginnings of 473–92 and a few letters from the preceding column.

O   *P. Oxyrhynchica* 211 has 976–1026. A second hand added punctuation and stage directions, made some corrections to the text, and added and deleted a few paragraphi. It may be supposed that he used another MS.

A wall-painting from a house at Ephesos (F. Eichler, *Anzeiger d. österreich. Akad. Wiss.* 1968, 88, L. Kahil–R. Ginouvès, *Antike Kunst*, Beiheft 6, p. 100, plate 27) shows an unidentified scene from *Perikeiromene*. There are three figures, one in a cloak, one with yellow hair or headgear, and one with a raised arm.

Dramatis Personae

   Polemon, a professional soldier
   Sosias, his retainer
   Glykera, his concubine, later his wife
   Doris, her maid
   Moschion, a young man
   Daos, his servant
   Pataikos, an old man
   Ignorance, a divinity, speaker of the prologue
   Habrotonon, a flute-girl (not a speaking part)

Three other persons are mentioned by name: [Hil]arion, slave of Polemon; Myrrhine, supposed mother of Moschion, who has an important part in the plot, but who did not necessarily appear on the stage; and Philinos, conceivably Myrrhine's husband (see 951 n.), to whom reference is made at 364, 714. This husband may have played some part in the action.

    As is usual the names of the characters were all in use at Athens but, with the possible exception of Pataikos, are chosen to indicate their status or nature. This is obvious in the case of *Polemon*. *Sosias* is mentioned by Schol. Ven. on Ar. *Ach.* 243, along with Xanthias, Tibeios, Daos, Getas, as a typical slave-name of comedy. Although the name was in fact occasionally borne by citizens, there is no reason why this Sosias should not be a slave, like his namesakes in *Wasps* 136, *Kolax* frag. 1, Plautus, *Amphitruo*, or Terence, *Hecyra*; at the most he could be a freedman, like the Sosia of Terence, *Andria*. [There is no evidence about the status of characters with this name in Menander frag. 63 K–T, Com. anon. (Page, *GLP* p. 234), Philemon frag. 96 K, Stephanos frag. 1 K, but nothing to suggest that they are not slaves.]

Glykera is a name frequently borne in real life by *hetairai* (including Menander's own reputed mistress, Athen. 594 d), but also by respectable married women (Pape–Benseler, *Wörterbuch d. gr. Eigennamen* 2605). The status of Glykeras in frags. 87 and 280 is not certain, but it is very possible that the first was, like the Glykera of this play and the Glycerium of Ter. *Andria*, married by her lover when found to be of citizen birth.

Doris is a maid in frag. 951 (cf. Dorias in Terence, *Eunuchus*), and perhaps in *Kolax*.

Myrrhine recurs as the name of a married citizen woman in *Dyskolos*, *Heros*, *Georgos*, Plaut. *Casina*, Ter. *Hecyra*.

Moschion, 'Little Bull-calf', is a young man's name. Chorikios 71 alludes to some character of this name who ravished a young woman; the Moschions of *Samia* and *Fab. incert.* would fit, and the one in this play lacked the opportunity rather than the will for seduction.

Daos is a common name for a slave, perhaps the ethnic name of a Phrygian people, *Aspis* 206, 241.

Habrotonon is a harp-player in *Epitr.*; the name must be associated with the supposed aphrodisiac qualities of wormwood (see p. 291).

Pataikos (Kirchner, *Prosop. Attic.* 11676–80) occurs in no other play, so that one does not know whether it was a name with a conventional significance in comedy. Evidence accumulates that not all Menander's names were thus significant, since Knemon of *Dyskolos* and Kichesias of *Sikyonios* are, like Pataikos, unique. No help can be had from the fact that dwarfish deities, used by the Phoenicians as ships' figure-heads, were called πάταικοι (Hdt. iii. 37), although the name, of widespread occurrence in Greece, may originally have been derived from them, as a nickname (F. Bechtel, *Abh. Gött.* 1897, 11).

The lost opening scene

The first surviving page of the play (p. 99 of the Cairo codex as reconstructed on pp. 44–5 of the introduction) finds us in the middle of a 'prologue' by the goddess Ignorance. Perhaps Misapprehension would be a better translation of her name. In the absence of knowledge, the mind tends to be filled by false opinion, and the word often connotes this, cf. *Sam.* 705 n. (A scrap of papyrus, *P. Oxy.* 2652, has a drawing of a female figure labelled αγνοια. It is probable that it comes from an illustrated copy of *Perikeiromene*; *P. Oxy.* 2653, *PSI* 847 have other illustrations of dramatic texts.) It appears from what she says that at least one scene has preceded this prologue. How much has been lost? On the assumption that the play began on a new page, the reconstruction of the codex shows that page to have been 95 or 96. A start on p. 97 would hardly allow enough space, especially if the play itself was preceded, like *Heros*, by a hypothesis and list of characters. Allowing 20 lines for these preliminaries, and reckoning 35 lines to the page, we can calculate that about 120 or about 85 lines are missing.

Not much of the goddess's speech appears to be lost. She must have explained who she was, and then have narrated that a man (she may have named him, Pataikos) had caused his new-born twins to be exposed, his wife having died. The children were found by an old woman, who kept the girl (Glykera) and gave the boy (Moschion) to a rich woman (Myrrhine) whose house is represented on the stage. From this point the prologue survives.

The old woman, before she died, had given the girl (Glykera) to a professional soldier (Polemon), and told her of her relationship to Moschion. The soldier had recently bought a house near that of Myrrhine, and established Glykera in it. One evening Moschion, seeing Glykera on her doorstep, as she was sending a maid on an errand, ran up and embraced her; she, knowing him to be her brother, made no resistance. At this point a third party came on the scene, and Moschion retired, saying he hoped to see her again undisturbed, while she stood there lamenting her inability to meet him freely.

Reconstruction of the preceding scene or scenes is more difficult but not hopeless. We know from the goddess that Polemon and Glykera had both appeared, and it looks as if the audience were expected to recognize Sosias when he comes on at 172; he may well have been seen before. The crucial point to decide is the identity of the third party who surprised the embrace of Glykera and Moschion. Most scholars have supposed it to be Polemon. Surely this is most unlikely. Throughout the play he is represented as a man of quick impulses, and the goddess has described him as cφoδρóc, 'impetuous'. He was not the sort to let Moschion retire unimpeded after expressing the hope of an assignation. Nor, if it was the appearance of this third party that put a stop to the embrace, would Glykera greet her returning 'husband' by standing and bewailing her inability to meet her brother. If, on the other hand, the third party watched without being

seen, that does not suit Polemon's impetuosity; he would have intervened immediately. That the third party did remain unseen is indeed
suggested by the tenses: the present ὁρᾷ (not εἶδεν), which frequently
means 'watch', and the imperfects ἐδάκρυε and ὠδύρετο, which indicate that after Moschion had gone, Glykera remained for some time,
weeping and lamenting. These considerations point to the third
party's being Sosias (Webster, *StM* 5). There are other plays in which
a slave precedes a master who returns from abroad (e.g. Chrysalus
precedes Mnesilochus in Plaut. *Bacchides*). But Plaut. *Amphitruo* provides a close parallel; there Sosias, the servant of the *condottiere*
Amphitruo, returns one evening, ahead of his master, to find Alcumena
engaged with Juppiter.

It was Sosias, then, who observed and later, in a scene of the play,
recounted the events upon the doorstep (158). It is hardly hazardous
to guess that he recounted them to Polemon. And when? Although
there are exceptions to the rule (*Epitr.* 419 n.), the presumption must
be that the action of a play is confined to one day, and no difficulties
are raised by supposing that the scene took place early in the morning.
Again, *Amphitruo* provides a parallel, for Amphitruo gets home at
daybreak (546–51). On hearing Sosias' story, Polemon immediately
in a fury of jealousy (987–8) hacked off Glykera's hair as a humiliating
punishment. After this, it is not surprising that Polemon did not wish
to stay in the same house as Glykera; the situation would have been
a difficult one. He went off, just as he had returned, probably from
some campaign, wearing his sword and military cloak (179, 354–5), to
attempt to forget his troubles in the company of his friends. Polemon's
act of violence was not necessarily performed on the stage. Although
Glykera had been seen by the audience before the prologue, she may
have been hustled indoors, or, less likely, have appeared after the
outrage. But if the outrage was done *coram populo*, it would be more
calculated to induce revulsion in the audience (167).

This reconstruction appears to create no difficulties, to meet all the
indications of the text, and to offer scenes of dramatic force and
interest. It also has the merit of making the title of the play refer to
part of the action. Many titles which consist of a present participle
have such a reference, e.g. *Epitrepontes*, *Theophorumene*, *Misumenos*,
Diphilos' *Klerumenoi* (the original of Plautus, *Casina*). This may,
however, not have been an absolute rule: however much Terence may
have altered Apollodoros' *Epidikazomenos* to make his *Phormio*, the legal
process to which the title refers appears to have preceded the opening
of the play. It must also be noted that Agathias, *AP* v. 218 may imply
that the shearing of Glykera took place within the play; τὸν σοβαρὸν
Πολέμωνα, τὸν ἐν θυμέλῃσι Μενάνδρου κείραντα γλυκερούς τῆς ἀλόχου

πλοκάμους: similarly Schol. Bemb. Ter. *Eun.* 61, 'Periceiromenen Menandri . . . in qua fabula miles . . . gladio amatae amputat crines'. But both may have written loosely.

Since no reconstruction can be regarded as absolutely certain, some other theories may be recorded. Körte supposed that the play opened in the morning with the appearance of Polemon, who recounted the scene of the previous evening, abused Glykera's faithlessness, and went off with Sosias. Then Glykera appeared, complained of her treatment, and planned to take refuge with Myrrhine. He rejected Jensen's guess that there were also scenes between Pataikos and Polemon and Moschion and Glykera. Gomme thought that the play may have opened not, of course, with the events on the doorstep, but with what in his view immediately succeeded them, the cutting off of Glykera's hair, and that this may have been followed by a scene in which Pataikos persuaded Polemon to come away: the postponed prologue then marked the lapse of time before the next morning. This at least has the advantage over Körte that it envisages scenes with dramatic possibilities (and accounts for that sword and cloak). Other reconstructions may be found, by those who are interested, in the essays of Sudhaus, *Rh. Mus.* lxiii (1908), 292, Robert, *Hermes* xliv (1909), 283, Leo, *Hermes* xliii (1908), 142, and in Capps's edition. None of them seem to me to have any likelihood.

(i) 121–171: *End of prologue by the goddess Misapprehension*

121: It is not impossible that the old woman was 'eager to give the boy to a rich woman', but more likely that the missing part of the sentence contained a verb to govern δοῦναι, e.g. (to adapt Capps's supplement) τὸ μὲν | αὐτῶν ἐβούλετ' ἐκτρέφειν, ἔχειν τέκνον | αὐτὴ προθυμηθεῖσα θῆλυ, κτλ.

123 τὴν οἰκίαν ταύτην: One of the houses represented by a door in the cκηνή. The other to which the goddess refers (145–6) is that of Polemon. The problem whether Pataikos' house was also shown is discussed on 466.

124 ἐγγενομένων: Cf. Aisch. iii. 221, χρόνων ἐγγεγενημένων. Jensen was positive that the letter preceding μ was α or λ. Hence he proposed ἐνιcταμένων, which has been often accepted. Lefebvre, however, reported that the traces were so insignificant that he could not confirm this reading. ἐνίcταcθαι normally means to 'impend' or 'arise' or 'be present' (hence ὁ ἐνεcτώc, 'the present tense') or 'be an obstacle'. Here, if rightly restored, it must abnormally mean 'occur' or 'intervene'.

125: It is not possible, in view of the vagueness of the reference and the deficiency of our historical information, to identify the 'war and distress at Corinth'. Capps associated the words with the events of the last decade of the fourth century. Cassander took Corinth in 304 B.C. from Demetrios Poliorketes, who had somehow obtained it from Ptolemy, who had 'liberated' it in 308 B.C. Demetrios recaptured the place in 303 B.C. Lenschau (*RE* s.v. Korinthos, suppl. IV. 1030) suggested the troubles which started in 315 B.C. with an attack by Cassander, who ravaged the countryside, and continued until Ptolemy's 'liberation'; and Schwartz (*Hermes*, lxiv [1929], 3) thought that this reference was made certain by 281 (see n. there) in which he found an allusion to an incident of 314 B.C.

125: It has been argued that the phrases τὰ Κορινθιακὰ κακά and γένει Κορινθίου (129) show that the scene of the play is not Corinth, but Athens, since if Corinth were the scene they would be replaced by e.g. τὰ ἐνθάδε κακά and ἀϲτοῦ. This overlooks the fact that Ignorance is not thought of as being in Corinth; she is on the stage, addressing the spectators of the town, whatever it may be, where the play is performed. Moreover, if Athens were the scene, there would be three features of the story hard to explain. First, why should the troubles of Corinth bring distress to an old woman in Athens? Second, how was Polemon, although an alien, able to buy a house at Athens? It is well known that aliens were debarred from buying land or houses. Third, how was he able in the final scene to marry a girl of citizen birth? One would expect this to make him liable to enslavement and Pataikos to a fine (Lipsius, *Attisches Recht*, ii. 418). To be sure, a foreigner could be relieved of these disabilities by the grant of ἔγκτηϲιϲ and ἐπιγαμία, or indeed of citizenship. Even if these difficulties are all surmounted by some ingenious assumptions, we still have the curious and apparently pointless coincidence that the old woman, distressed in Athens by Corinthian troubles, gave Glykera to a Corinthian soldier. On the other hand, nothing stands in the way of Corinth's being the scene, and the characters all Corinthians. The insistence that Polemon is Corinthian by birth (129) can be explained by the consideration that a mercenary soldier may well not be a citizen of the town where he is resident. O. Fredershausen, *Hermes* xlvii (1912), 205, discusses marriages in comedy with a non-citizen, and finds that they are all in states other than Athens.

Several other plays of the New Comedy are placed in towns outside Attica, Menander's Ϲυναριϲτῶϲαι in Sikyon, Diphilos' Ἔμποροϲ at Corinth, etc. The reason for this is unknown; in some cases it may be that they had a non-Attic first performance.

127 τεθραμμένης: 'Now that the girl was grown-up'; this need suggest no greater age than 15 or so. But at the time of the play she can hardly be less than 18, for it is difficult to suppose her twin brother younger than that.

128 ἐραστοῦ γενομένου τε: Postponement of τε, although not very frequent in Menander, is more common than once appeared: *Dysk.* 7 οὐ χαίρων τε, *Epitr.* 338 τὸν δακτύλιον λαβοῦσά τε, *Mis.* 262 κυρίως δώσει τε, *Sam.* 445 ἐπ' ἀγαθῇ τύχῃ τε, *Sam.* 560 οὐ προήσεσθαί τε, *Sik.* 262 τραγωδίᾳ κενῇ τε, frag. 718 γαμηλίῳ λέχει τε. In all these instances the words preceding τε form a group, and here ἐραστοῦ γενομένου is the equivalent of ἐρασθέντος. Menander is more sparing than some authors with the postponement of τε after article and noun or preposition and noun; but it is found at 136 below, τὸν ἀγνοούμενόν τε, *Dysk.* 311 αἱ Νύμφαι τε, 719 τοὺς λογισμούς τε (by emendation), *Aspis* 5 ἐν βίῳ τε, 45 κατὰ σκηνάς τε, 109 τοῦ μειρακίου τε, *Kolax* frag. 1. 6 τῶν ὄντων τε, *Sam.* 672 εἰς ἀθυμίαν τε, *Mis.* A2 ἔν σοι τε, *Kith.* frag. 5 εἰς τρυφήν τε, *Dis Exap.* 21 εἰς μέσον τε, and in one MS. at 163 below, where I accept εἰς ὀργήν θ'. σφοδροῦ: 'Impetuous, vehement' rather than 'violent'.

131 ἀπειρηκυῖα: From the meaning 'renounce', 'resign', ἀπειπεῖν acquired the intransitive meaning 'fail', 'tire', and so in the perfect 'be exhausted, at the end of one's tether'. 'Failing', in the sense of 'near death', would do for a translation here. ἔχειν: To keep as his παλλακή. If law or custom were the same at Corinth as at Athens, there could be no question of his marrying a girl who was not known to be of citizen birth, but there was nothing disreputable in this union, and Polemon later protests that he regarded her as a 'wedded wife' (487). On the status of the παλλακή see intro. pp. 30–1.

132 τοῦ ζῆν καταστροφήν τινα: The goddess's style is matter-of-fact, and there is hardly any intentional reminiscence of Soph. *OC* 102–3, βίου καταστροφήν, but the three following lines all have a rhythm possible in tragedy, and one may think that she allows herself a slight elevation of language at this important and solemn incident.

134 μείρακα: 'The lass', a word always feminine in classical writers, among whom it is confined to comedy, but its diminutives μειράκιον and μειρακίσκος are used only of boys. ἀνείλετο: The *vox propria* for rescuing exposed children, cf. *Epitr.* 330, Ar. *Clouds* 531, Soph. *OT* 1035.

135: I.e. τά τε σπάργανα ἐν οἷς ἀνείλετο δίδωσι—the clothes in which the infant had been wrapped when found. The antecedent noun is attracted into the relative clause, Schwyzer, ii. 641. But the emendation διδοῦς' ἅμα (Croenert, Herwerden) is attractive and supported by W. G. Arnott, *CQ* n.s. xviii (1968) 232. By a convention of the theatre, in tragedy as in comedy, the clothes were preserved in good enough condition to be recognizable. Sometimes they were supplemented, or replaced, by trinkets laid out with the child (e.g. *Epitr.* 331–3). The classic instance in tragedy is Euripides' *Ion* 1351–1436.

136 τῇ φύcει: 'Her unknown brother-by-birth'; sometimes, when there are two attributes to a noun that has the article, one is placed after the noun, e.g. Xen. *Hell.* iv. 3. 15, τῶν ἐν τῇ Ἀcίᾳ πόλεων Ἑλληνίδων. Jebb on Soph. *OT* 1199, τὰν γαμψώνυχα παρθένον χρηcμῳδόν, suggests that the noun and second attribute are viewed as a unitary phrase.

137 τι τῶν ἀνθρωπίνων: 'Some mischance such as human beings are liable to', cf. Epicurus frag. 217, ἐάν τι τῶν ἀνθρωπίνων περί τινα γένηται.

139 τοῦτον: Moschion.   **ἀναγκαῖον:** 'Relative', the tie of blood being an inescapable one. The usage is common, e.g. Dem. xix. 290, cυγγενεῖc καὶ ἀναγκαῖοι ἄνθρωποι.

141–2 τι . . . ἀκούcιον: I.e. marriage or liaison between full brother and sister, cf. *Epitr.* 341–2. Athenian convention allowed marriage between half-brother and half-sister, if the father was the common parent.

142 μεθύοντα: 'Drinking', not 'drunk'. The verb does not imply any great degree of intoxication. When Alcibiades, in Plato's *Symposium*, breaks in cφόδρα μεθύων, he is only less well-mannered and much less discreet than he would be if sober; he is not less clear-headed.

144 βέβαιον: Masculine; οὐθέν acc. with βέβαιον—'that the man to whom she was being left (i.e. Polemon) was reliable in nothing'. Polemon, being a soldier of fortune, might be off to the wars again at any time, leaving Glykera—at least alone, possibly in the lurch.

145–6: The kind of remarkable coincidence frequent in Greek comedy, but kept by Menander to the preliminaries to the play.

146 ταύτην: With a gesture towards the other house, see 123 n.

147 ἐν γειτόνων: An example of a common form of ellipse, like our 'at Mr. Smith's'; but the phrase developed the sense 'in a neighbouring house', 'next door', so that the householder himself can be said οἰκεῖν ἐν γειτόνων, e.g. *Aspis* 122, where see Austin's note. Here the genitive τἀδελφοῦ is dependent on it, 'next door to her brother'.

149 λαμπρόν: See *Heros* 44 n.

150 ὄναcθαι δέ: To be constructed with ἐκεῖνον βούλεται, but by an

anacoluthon ἐκεῖνον here is subject of ὀνᾶσθαι whereas it was object of
ἀγαγεῖν. μέν of 147 is answered, not by this δέ, but by that of 151.

It is often said that Moschion has been adopted by Myrrhine and
her husband. This cannot be true if legal adoption is meant; legal
adoption of a foundling of unknown birth was not possible at Athens
(A. R. W. Harrison, *Law of Athens*, i. 87) and there is no reason for
supposing it possible at Corinth. But if it was allowable and Moschion
was legally adopted, there was nothing for Glykera to hide for fear
of ruining him. Moschion passes as this rich couple's real son, but
whether with the connivance of both, or whether Myrrhine alone
knows the secret, is not clear. The latter view was maintained by
van Leeuwen, and such a situation would certainly add to the possible
dramatic tensions. It has been objected (H. Sauer, *De Circumtonsae
Menandreae argumento*, 7³, cf. E. Ulbricht, *Krit. u. exeget. Stud. zu
Menander*, 40) that, according to a widely accepted restoration,
Moschion possesses some trinkets exposed with him (817–18), and
that if she had been concealing the truth from her husband, Myrrhine
would have destroyed any such incriminating evidence; but it may
be hypercritical to demand such logical action by her ἔξω τοῦ δράματος.
In any case, even if her husband was a party to the deception, it would
still have been prudent to destroy the tokens.

151 ὥσπερ προείρηκα: Inaccurate, if the reference is to 142.

153 φοιτῶντος: Going regularly to a place, as a student to a school
or college. Here 'hanging about' Polemon's house; for he has not
been invited inside. Though they are 'neighbours', their houses need
not be supposed to be literally next door to one another.

155 εὐθύ: 'Straight up'; the sense 'straightway', nowhere frequent,
is not found in Menander.

156 τῷ προειδέναι: 'Because she knew'; the use of the infinitive, both
in causal constructions (in the dative) and in final (in the genitive),
becomes common in later Greek (Schwyzer, ii. 369).

157: The supplement ἅτερος is possibly right, and has the advantage
over any other of leaving open the decision who this third person
was. That it was Sosias, not Polemon, has been argued in the introductory note to this play.

160 ἰδεῖν αὐτήν τι: Since ἰδεῖν can have the sense 'talk to', *Dysk.*
236 n., there seems no reason why it should not be modified by τι,
'have some talk with'. Editors have adopted the conjecture ἔτι
βούλεται, importing what is a metrical rarity for Menander, an ana-
paest, not in the first foot, divided ∪ ∪ | –, and in which the dissyllable

is not a preposition; cf. 374 n. Handley, however, on *Dysk.* 107–8, keeps τι.

163 εἰς ὀργήν θ' ἵνα: I accept C's reading rather than that in H, which omits θ', since omission of τε is a more common fault than its insertion. This necessitates taking the whole of ἐγὼ γάρ . . . λοιπά as a parenthesis, as Capps did; δέ then becomes more intelligible: 'I led him to his anger, not because he is naturally irascible, but in order to set going the train of discovery.'

164 οὐ φύcει τοιοῦτον ὄντα: Impulsive he might be and vehement, but not naturally brutal.

166 τὰ λοιπά: An imprecise phrase, perhaps meaning 'all that is still to be revealed'; all that is to 'get a start towards being revealed'.

167 εὕροιεν: If there is any difference between the force of the subjunctive λάβῃ and the optative εὕροιεν, it is that the latter refers to an event subsequent to the former (K–G ii. 387 and *Epitr.* 869 n.).

ἐδυcχέρανε: There is nothing to choose for sense between this reading, 'reacted in disgust', and the imperfect (more usual with this verb) of C, meaning 'had a (continuing) feeling of disgust'. An Athenian audience's protests at an unseemly incident or sentiment could in an extreme case stop a performance (examples in Pickard-Cambridge, *Dramatic Festivals²*, 272–4).

169 διὰ θεοῦ: διά with gen. frequently indicates an agent who executes the wish of another, e.g. δι' ἀγγέλου. Eitrem proposed to emend here to διὰ θεούc. But διά with gen. does not always indicate an intermediary, e.g. Aesch. *Agam.* 1485, ἰὴ ἰή, διαὶ Διὸς παναιτίου, Plat. *Rep.* 379 e, cπονδῶν cύγχυcιν ἦν ὁ Πάνδαρος cυνέχεεν, ἐάν τιc φῇ δι' Ἀθηνᾶc τε καὶ Διὸς γεγονέναι, οὐκ ἐπαινεcόμεθα οὐδὲ θεῶν ἔριν τε καὶ κρίcιν διὰ Θέμιτόc τε καὶ Διόc. K–G ii. 485 hold that διά with gen. indicates a stronger and more immediate action than διά with acc.

The claim that god turns evil to good may seem a sentimental one; that it is put forward by such a dubious deity as Misapprehension may excuse the spectator from taking it altogether seriously: he may half believe it, half enjoy the paradox. If chronology allowed, it would probably have been alleged that Menander was here reflecting Kleanthes' address to Zeus, τὰ πέριccά τ' ἐπίcταcαι ἄρτια θεῖναι (*SVF* i. 537).

170 γιγνόμενον: 'Even as it occurs'.   **ἔρρωcθε:** Lit. 'be in good condition', i.e. 'farewell'. The singular ἔρρωcο is commonly found as a formula at the end of letters, e.g. Xen. *Cyr.* 4. 5. 33, [Plato], *epist.* 1, 2, and 10, and is used by Daos in *Georgos* to say good-bye (84).

171 ἡμῖν: The company of actors.   **cῴζετε:** Lit. 'keep safe', i.e. pay attention to, do not hiss off.

(ii) 172–180: *Sosias*

172 coβαρόc is an interesting word. Aristophanes uses it of a blustering, rushing wind, *Clouds* 406, *Peace* 944; and of a *rousing* song— coβαρόν . . . μέλοc ἔντονον ἀγροικότερον, *Ach.* 674, 'a swaggering, rustic, lusty song' (Rennie). Of persons it generally means, in the fourth century, 'swaggering' or 'haughty', e.g. coβαρὸc καὶ ὀλίγωροc, [Dem.] lix. 37. The word is a favourite with Plutarch: both 'important' and 'self-important', 'impressive', and 'would-be impressive', 'pompous'. So here one might translate 'our swaggering soldier an hour ago'. He is now the very opposite of imposing—κλάει κατακλινείc, he has thrown himself down to weep. There is a reminiscence of this line in Heliodoros vii. 25. 1, see E. W. Whittle, *Cl. Phil.* lvi (1961), 178.

173 τὰc γυναῖκαc: A plural of scornful exaggeration, cf. δίκαc λέγοντεc, *Epitr.* 229.

175: This theme of the unhappy lover who tries to drown his sorrow among his friends is more fully developed in *Epitr.* In both plays there is a Habrotonon, but there she is important, here barely mentioned. Where are we to imagine this party, for whom lunch (ἄριcτον) is being prepared? A misunderstanding of 361 ff. led earlier editors to suppose Polemon to have retired to his farm in the country, unlikely though such a possession would be for an active professional soldier. We must conclude that he has gone to some place in the town; and this is confirmed by the fact that Sosias, who must have left with him before the goddess's speech, returns within the same act. The convention of comedy seems to have required a journey to and from the country to be spread over two acts; the intervening performance by the chorus indicated an adequate lapse of time.

175 τοῦ φέρειν: Cf. 156 n.

178 ἐκπέπομφε: ἐκπέμπειν is used of dispatching an expedition or embassy and, since the word is not elsewhere used by Menander except at *Sik.* 281, it is probably intended to recall such serious contexts, in ridiculous contrast with ἱμάτιον οἴcοντα. Whereas the aorist ἐξέπεμψε would merely give the fact that Polemon had dispatched Sosias, the perfect indicates that he 'is in the state of having dispatched him', he is still affected by having sent him, because he is anxiously waiting for the news he will bring. C's split anapaest (γινόμεν' ἐκ) may be palliated by the elision. The only certain parallel in Menander is frag. 620. 10, ὀργιζόμεθ'· ἄν. There may have been another at *Sik.*

420, if that line is to be completed μειράκι', ἄνδρες, παιδία, but μειράκια, παῖδες καλοί (Austin) is also possible. *Epitr.* 286, ἐμὲ δ' οὐδὲ ἕν, is different, since there is no word that overlaps from the preceding foot. H's γενόμενα, metrically normal, appears inferior in sense.

179 ἐξεπίτηδες: 'Deliberately', almost suggesting malice, cf. Dem. xxi. 56, 187. Although he knows that Polemon's object is to get news, Sosias irrationally grumbles (like Parmeno at Ter. *Hec.* 435) that he has no intention but to cause his servant unnecessary journeys.

180 οὐδὲ ἓν δεόμενος ἀλλ' ἤ: This idiom, in which ἀλλ' ἤ can be translated 'except that', is discussed by Denniston, *GP* 24–7. It *may* have arisen by a confusion between οὐδὲν . . . ἄλλο ἤ and οὐδὲν ἄλλο . . . ἀλλά. Here it would be logical to say either οὐδὲν δεόμενος ἄλλο ἤ περιπατεῖν ἐμέ or οὐδὲν δεόμενος ἄλλο ἀλλὰ περιπατεῖν με βουλόμενος. This passage differs from all those adduced by Denniston in that the negatived verb is a participle and that following ἀλλ' ἤ is finite; in his examples either the two clauses are co-ordinate, or the second is subordinate to the first. Körte finally adopted the view of his pupil C. Meister that a colon should be placed after δεόμενος, and the remaining words read as a question introduced by ἀλλ' ἤ, as at *Epitr.* 542, 1065, a combination which introduces a lively, anxious question, K–G ii. 528–9, Denniston, *GP* 27.

(iii) **181–190:** *Sosias and Doris, separate*

181 προελθοῦσα: 'I will go out' (or 'first') 'and see'. *Dysk.* 879 has ἐγὼ προσελθὼν ὄψομαι. It is not necessary to make the two phrases identical, yet the confusion of προ and προς is familiar, and common in the papyrus (B) of *Dyskolos*. If it were desired to bring the two passages into line it would be hard to decide which to follow; in both 'I will approach him (her) and see' is possible. But C is in general more trustworthy on such points than B.

181 ff.: Since Doris, as she emerges from Polemon's house, is speaking to her mistress inside, it is easier to accept the fact that she does not see Sosias. He must still be at the side of the stage where he entered. She then moves away from him, with her back to him, while he speaks 182–3. When he says πορεύσομαι, 'I will go on in' (cf. 298, *Epitr.* 857), she has reached Myrrhine's house. Doris' errand, of course, concerns Glykera's taking refuge there, but Sosias suspects nothing, nor does Doris know that she is observed—perhaps the goddess Ἄγνοια is at work. If a correct reconstruction of the opening scene was given above, the project of Glykera's taking refuge with Myrrhine has not yet been put before the latter. Doris may be entrusted with that mission, when her words will mean 'I will go first and see her'.

What they do *not* mean is 'I will go first and see if anyone is about who might observe your removal', for then her failure to see Sosias would be inexplicable (cf. Gomme, *Essays* 256).

182 οἷα γέγονεν: This implies that Polemon and Sosias have been away for some time. ἐρρωμένη, a word which may be used colloquially in a variety of extended meanings (*Epitr.* 899 n.), here has its proper sense 'strong and healthy'. ζῆν sometimes means 'live as life should be lived', e.g. Dio Cassius lxix. 19, βιοὺς μὲν ἔτη τόca, ζήcac δὲ ἔτη ἑπτά, Alexis, *Pannychis* frag. 2, οὐκ ἐπίcταcαι ζῆν. 'These women have a good life of some kind; that's clear enough.'

186 cτρατιώτην: A professional soldier; similarly γεωργός, τέκτων, κάπηλοc describe a man's profession. Aristotle, *EN* 1116ᵇ6 uses the word so when he says that οἱ cτρατιῶται appear to be brave, whereas the truth is that their experience prevents their falling a prey to false alarms. The ordinary Greek citizen was not this, but served in the army or navy when called up in time of war; 'When I was a soldier, when I was in the army (or navy) under Demosthenes' is, normally, cτρατευόμενος μετὰ Δημοcθένουc, not cτρατιώτηc ὤν (though Aristophanes can say cτρατιώτας καταλέγειν of citizens, *Ach.* 1065, and Nikias ἄνδρεc cτρατιῶται Ἀθηναίων, Thuc. vii. 61. 1, cf. Thuc. vi. 24. 3, ὁ πολὺc ὅμιλοc καὶ cτρατιώτηc, Isaios v. 46, ἀλλ' ὡc cτρατιώτηc ἀγαθόc; ἀλλ' οὐκ ἐcτρατεύcαc, Lysias ix. 4, κατελέγην cτρατιώτηc.) So many Greeks, however, in the fourth century, and especially after the conquest of Asia, had served as mercenaries in foreign or Greek armies abroad, had made soldiering their profession, or at least their road to fortune, that cτρατιῶται, 'soldiers of fortune', were common; and the word is often used in practically a technical sense, of any group of mercenaries, e.g. of those employed by the Greek states, e.g. *IG*² ii. 1. 450, 682. ἄνδρα: Gomme thought that, although the word can in some contexts, like the Latin *uir*, mean 'lover', it would here be best translated as 'husband'; 'Glykera and Polemon were living as husband and wife, although without benefit of the ceremonies that constituted a legal marriage.' This may be misleading because the English words do not correspond to the Athenian concepts. For 'legal marriage' one might substitute 'valid marriage', meaning thereby the union of a pair whose children would be citizens and have legal rights in the property of the families of both parents. The essential condition for such a union was that both parties should be of citizen birth on both sides. Although there were traditional ways of arriving at the union, there is no evidence that these forms were necessary to make a valid marriage. Further, there was no kind of public registration of such marriages. See intro. p. 28.

187 οὐδὲν πιστόν: Cf. the phrase οὐδὲν ὑγιές, applied to persons, e.g. Ar. *Thesm.* 394, τὰς οὐδὲν ὑγιές, *Plut.* 37, Eur. *Andr.* 446, Cπάρτηc ἔνοικοι . . . μηχανορράφοι κακῶν, ἑλικτὰ κοὐδὲν ὑγιές, and οὐδὲν ἱερόν, Men. *Aspis* 242.

188 παῖδεc: To call for the servants is the normal way of demanding attention when knocking at a door, whether the caller is himself a servant or not, cf. *Dysk.* 459 ff. παῖ and παιδίον (190) are not distinguishable in sense (see *Samia*, 226 n.), except that the latter is more friendly.

188–90: Who speaks the words εὐφρανθήcεται . . . αὐτός? Doris or Sosias? Scholars are divided, but Jensen and Körte give them to Doris. This is probably what is intended by C, which has no paragraphi. It has, however, dicola after παῖδεc and αὐτός. The dicolon (without paragraphus) is sometimes used to indicate change, not of speaker, but of person addressed, and a particular case of this is when the speaker addresses himself. Here the dicola may indicate that εὐφρανθήcεται κτλ. is soliloquy, and not addressed to the servant within. Since this interpretation makes sense, it has been adopted in the text of OCT. It is, however, possible that C is in error in not having paragraphi, and that the words should be assigned to Sosias, (Schwartz, *Hermes* lxiv [1929] 6, followed by Webster *StM* 7 and Del Corno). At some point in this scene he must have come out of Polemon's house again, and the interval of four lines between 184 and 188 would, by convention, give him time enough to collect a cloak (cf. 310–16, *Samia* 297–301, 664–9). The speech εὐφρανθήcεται κτλ. is slightly more appropriate to him than to Doris, since he *knows* that Polemon will learn of Glykera's tears, of which he will carry the news, whereas Doris could only *surmise* that Polemon will somehow hear of them.

189 νῦν: To be taken with κλάουcαν, by separation from which it gains emphasis; Glykera's first reaction to the outrage was doubtless anger.

(iv) 261–266: *Daos alone*

261: One leaf, i.e. about 70 verses, is missing. After the gap Daos, a servant of Myrrhine's household, assigned to Moschion, is alone on the stage. (The slaves whom he addresses [παῖδεc] are probably indoors, and the vocative may have been attached, not to μεθύοντα κτλ., but to a foregoing sentence.) He sees a band of revellers approaching in the orchestra. This is the chorus, who have no connection with the plot, and who were mentioned, if analogy with other plays may be trusted, only at this, their first appearance, which ends the first act. That is all that is left of the old close connection of chorus and actors, once so essential in comedy. πάμπολλα: The number of the chorus in the late fourth century is not known. It may still have been as many as 15, the number suggested by Aristotle, *Pol.* 1276ᵇ1, who implies that tragic and comic choruses were equal. See intro. p. 12.

What has happened in the gap between 190 and 261? At 190 Doris is just going to ask for Myrrhine; at 262 Daos knows of the latter's decision to welcome Glykera to her house; in the second act Glykera is with Myrrhine. Most scholars have drawn the obvious conclusion that Glykera's transfer took place in the gap, although there is room for disagreement about the way in which it was arranged. Körte thinks that Myrrhine came out to talk to Doris and later received Glykera; Schwartz, *Hermes* lxiv (1929), 5, and Wilamowitz, *Gnomon* i (1929), 467, argue that Myrrhine was never seen. There is no basis on which to attempt to adjudicate on this dispute. It is possible that Moschion left his house at some point in the gap, since after it he is not at home; a conversation in which he confided to Daos his belief that he had made a conquest would be appropriate; such a conversation is implied by 262 ff., and if it had not taken place on the stage, must be imagined.

Gomme felt certain that the conversation between Doris and Myrrhine took place on the stage, and that Daos was present during part of it. Glykera's removal may, he thought, have followed, but may have not been presented on the stage at all, being supposed to have occurred in the interval between the acts (*CQ* xxx [1936], 67). It must be observed that such an imaginary movement between acts is neither paralleled in Menander nor likely. The house doors remained in full view of the audience; there was no curtain to fall and hide them.

262 πάμπολλα: The word is written without elision, conceivably to indicate a pause; but such 'scriptio plena' occurs without reason, e.g. *Epitr.* 366 δοςποτεεργαςτηριον. **κεκτημένην:** 'Mistress', used without the article, as if it were a proper name; similarly δεςπότην at 359 (but τὸν δεςπότην at 264).

263 ἡμᾶς: This is a necessary correction of ὑμᾶς. The confusion is familiar in all kinds of MSS. η and υ had long been pronounced alike by the time the Cairo codex was written.

264 ὁ τρόφιμος: 'The young master', see *Epitr.* 134 n.

ACT II

(i) **267–353**: *Daos and Moschion*

267–93: The papyrus is everywhere difficult to read, being much rubbed and worn and in parts badly torn. It is impossible to test by Lefebvre's facsimiles the readings (which do not always agree) of the experts who have examined the papyrus itself. The text printed in OCT has been formed from a consideration of the evidence provided by Lefebvre's transcript, and the reports of Sudhaus, Jensen, who reproduced in *Hermes* xlix (1914), 410 his own drawing from the papyrus, and Guéraud, whose sober caution inspires confidence in his positive assertions. The passage is discussed by K. F. W. Schmidt in *Χάριτες F. Leo dargebracht*, 45–54.

Moschion and Daos enter from the town. The latter pretends that he is responsible for Glykera's having come to Myrrhine's house. He seems to be unaware of the soldier's return and violent treatment of the girl (cf. 361, ὁ ξένος ἀφῖκται), and Moschion shares his ignorance. The metre, the trochaic tetrameter, is characterized by Aristotle, *Rhet.* 1408ᵇ36 as κορδακικώτερον, and is suitable for a lively scene, cf. the latter part of *Samia* Act IV. *Dyskolos* has shown that it can also be used where the tone is serious and indeed emotional, see n. on 703–10 of that play.

268 ἀλαζών:'A liar', cf. *Georgos* 26 n.   θεοῖcιν ἐχθρός: In this phrase the long form of the dative, familiar from poetry (e.g. Hesiod, *Theog.* 779), persisted in comedy alongside the newer short form found in Dem. xix. 95, xxiv. 195, e.g. Ar. *Knights* 34, *Peace* 1172, Plato Com. frag. 74 K, Anaxippos frag. 6, 4 K, against 294 below and Diphilos frag. 60 K.

269 κρέμαcον: Probably 'tie me up to receive a beating', see *Dysk.* 249 n.

270 ἥμερον λέγειc τι: 'A mild suggestion'. This reading is likely rather than certain. Lefebvre thought there might be space before η for another letter; Jensen denied this, but Guéraud was prepared to admit that room can be found for a narrow c, projecting into the margin. But cήμερον would need emendation, for Menander uses the Attic form τήμερον (which Körte² printed); if that is right, the word must be taken with εἰ πλανῶ. It may be noted that Lefebvre believed there to be a colon before λεγειc. To read (*Mo.*) λέγειc τι is possible: 'There is some sense in that.' The opposite οὐδὲν λέγειc is more common, but cf. 341, Soph. *OT* 1475, λέγω τι; and LSJ s.v. λέγω III. 6.

πολεμίου τοίνυν τρόπον: 'Treat me to all the horrors of war', Post. The restoration is not certain; adverbial τρόπον with genitive is not found elsewhere in Menander except 812 below, where it may be paratragic. τοίνυν: See *Dysk.* 783 n.

272 δεδιῳκηκώς: The reduplication of the prefix, combined with internal augment, is found in Ar. frag. 429, and the passive δεδιῳκημένα in Antiphanes frag. 155 K, etc., cf. πεπαρῴνηκε, *Dysk.* 93; Plato has διῳκηκός, *Tim.* 19 e. Gomme's note on this line runs as follows: ' "In no one of Menander's plays (in the original) is there a sign of the slave who holds the will and the conscience of his master, to whom the latter not only defers, but is helpless without him" (Gomme, *Essays*, 287); for Menander, unlike Plautus, does not like exaggeration. This was too sweepingly said. This line is a hint of the type so admirably developed by Plautus; but it is only Daos' description of himself, and Moschion, though neither clever nor vigorous, is not helpless.' Had Gomme lived to know *Aspis*, he would have found that in Act II of that play Chairestratos is helpless without Daos, whose plan he accepts without modification. But Daos is not Chairestratos' slave.

276–82: The whole of this passage is very uncertain. The ink has almost entirely disappeared in places and papyrologists have been guided by depressions in the surface caused by pressure of the pen or by chemical action of the once-existent ink. The surface itself is dirty. It is therefore prudent to distrust any reading over which there is no unanimity.

276: The evidence of Lefebvre's transcript, Jensen, and Guéraud seems to establish the absence of a dicolon after ἀρέσκει. Guéraud thinks the gap that follows too short for πάντ' and prefers τοῦτ'. OCT has τοῦτ' ἐπιβλέψας λέγε, which is consistent with these opinions, but cannot be regarded as certain. Of other proposals, Jensen's πάντ' ἐπιβλεψώμεθα introduces a middle form for which there is no adequate warrant, while conversely Sudhaus's ταῦτ' ἐπιβλέψω should be ταῦτ' ἐπιβλέψομαι.

277–8: Testimony is unanimous that there are dicola after κράτιστον and before μηδαμῶς. Körte printed (*Mo.*) ἆρα τὸ μυλωθρεῖν κράτιστον; (*Δα.*) εἰς μυλῶν'; (*Mo.*) ἐμοὶ δοκεῖ οὑτοσὶ φερόμενος ἥξειν. (*Δα.*) μηδαμῶς τέχνην λέγε. In the addenda (ed. 1957) he suggested εἰς μυλῶνα; (*Mo.*) φαίνεται οὑτοσὶ κτλ., since Guéraud is confident that μυλωνα must be read, not μυλων'. 'Would it be best to keep a mill?' 'I'm to go to a mill?' 'This fellow, I think, will land there double-quick.' 'Don't suggest a manual trade.' The phrase φερόμενος ἥκειν is not uncommon, cf. *Epitr.* 521, Aischines iii. 89, Lykurgos 59, Plut.

Sertorius 586 a, but it cannot be said that this is an altogether plausible piece of dialogue, and Sudhaus and Guéraud agreed in denying that ἥξειν is possible. They both saw ἡμῖν, as Jensen originally did, an unwelcome reading, as an ethic dative is surprising; yet no other construction for ἡμῖν appears possible.

The tentative conclusion reached on 276 makes it plausible to give ἆρα . . . κράτιϲτον to Daos, as there is a paragraphus below that verse. This suggestion, made by K. F. W. Schmidt, *Hermes* xliv (1909), 413, has been unjustly disregarded, but is appropriate; however 276 is restored, whether Moschion tells Daos to review possible ways of life or Daos expresses an intention of doing so, one would expect the first suggestions to come from the slave. The word οὑτοcί suggests that Moschion's reply is either scornful or an aside; if the latter, one might consider εἰϲ μυλῶνα γ' ἐμπέϲοι οὑτοcὶ φερόμενοϲ ἡμῖν, cf. Eupolis frag. 348 K, εἰϲ ζητρεῖον ἐμπεcών (ἵνα κολάζονται οἱ δοῦλοι, μυλῶνεϲ καὶ ζητρεῖα, Pollux iii. 78), Lysias i. 18, μαϲτιγωθεῖϲαν εἰϲ μυλῶνα ἐμπεϲεῖν. For φερόμενοϲ 'with all speed', see LSJ, s.v. φέρω B. 2, and Theophilos frag. 11 K, ἐμπεϲεῖν εἰϲ Λαΐδα φερόμενον. μυλωθρεῖν occurs here only; a μυλωθρόϲ is the overseer of a mill, and would have slaves under him, some of whom might have been sent there as a punishment (cf. *Heros* 3 n.). If the suggestion that he should manage a mill comes from Daos, a counter-suggestion by Moschion (280) that he should 'manage the affairs of the Greeks' would follow effectively. In between, Daos adjures Moschion not to suggest a manual craft (τέχνη): he thinks of occupations followed by slaves who had been manumitted or allowed to live independently; manual work does not appeal to him. Shop-keeping is more attractive (283).

It must be admitted that there is no paragraphus below 277, so that the dicolon after κράτιϲτον may mark the beginning of an aside, not a change of speaker. If that is right, ἆρα . . . κράτιϲτον belongs after all to Moschion. The end of the preceding line might then be, e.g. πάντ' ἐπίβλεψον. (Δα.) βλέπω. [The passage is discussed at length by E. W. Whittle, *CQ* n.s. ix (1959), 57. He well explodes an absurd notion that φερόμενοϲ ἥξειν is an echo of Eur. *Bacch.* 968, but is handicapped by misunderstanding μυλωθρεῖν as '*work* in a mill'.]

280 διοικητήν may have been suggested by Daos' own phrase ὁ δεδιωκηκὼϲ ἐγώ ϲοι. The end of the line is quite uncertain. Körte prints Sudhaus's proposal: (Δα.) οὐ μέλει ξένων ἐμοί (ξένοι are mercenary soldiers). But Guéraud thinks the first letters are αλ or αμ, not ου.

280–1: Widespread approval has been given to Schwartz's conjecture (*Hermes*, lxiv [1929] 3) that these lines refer to Alexander son of Polyperchon, who was made ϲτρατηγὸϲ τῆϲ Πελοποννήϲου by Cassander in 314 or 313, but was shortly afterwards treacherously murdered by some Sikyonians, whose object seems to have been to recover Sikyon's independence. The conjecture may be correct, but its basis is flimsy.

282: Körte prints Sudhaus's proposal: (*Mo.*) ἀλλὰ κλέψεις ἐκδότης ὤν· ἐκδόσει λήσει λαβὼν ἑπτὰ τῶν ὀκτὼ τάλαντα. ἐκδότης is known from inscriptions in the sense of 'one who farms out a contract or tax-collection', and the suggestion is that Daos would be able, as an official, to retain seven-eighths of what the contractors paid him; Sudhaus thought there must be some allusion to a *cause célèbre*. This is all very ingenious but too hypothetical to be part of the accepted text; among the assumptions made is that C had ωνεκδοτης by mistake for εκδοτησων.

283 παντοπωλεῖν: Many slaves, when freed, set up as small shop-keepers, *IG* ii². 10, 1553–78, Gomme, *Population of Athens*, 41–2. But Daos need not have immediate freedom in view; slaves were often established in some craft or business, paying their master a fixed sum (ἀποφορά), and keeping the balance of their earnings, *Epitr.* 380.

285: Sudhaus's ὀμνύω μηδὲν μέλειν μοι πλουσίῳ καθεστάναι (πλουσίῳ Körte) is printed by Körte and makes excellent sense.

286–7: Jensen suggested ἀνόσιον λέγεις· | οἶδ' ἐκεῖνο· μὴ γένοιτο μελιτόπωλις εὐσεβὴς | γραῦς, i.e. 'You suggest a godless way of life; I know the saying "I hope no pious old woman ever comes to selling honey" (or "Let no seller of honey become pious in her old age").' He compared Xenarchos frag. 7 K, τῶν δ' ἰχθυοπωλῶν φιλοσοφώτερον γένος οὐκ ἔστιν οὐδὲν οὐδὲ μᾶλλον ἀνόσιον. The alleged saying is an odd one, if to mean 'shopkeepers are all rascals'. Sudhaus's εἰ δ' ἐκεῖνο μὴ γένοιθ' ὃ μελιτόπωλις εὔχεται γραῦς fits the traces, but is inexplicable in the absence of any knowledge of what aged female honeysellers prayed for. No plausible reconstruction of these lines has been offered. Sudhaus's earlier suggestion (*Hermes* xlvii [1913], 145), ἀλλὰ ταῦτα μὲν οὐδὲ Κρὴς ταπεινὸς οὐδὲ λαχανόπωλις εὔξατ' ἂν γραῦς, seems not to fit the traces.

288: Jensen's δ]ές[ποτ' is unlikely, for 'the master' is Moschion's father; Moschion would normally be addressed as τρόφιμε, as in 292. Lefebvre transcribed merely]ε[. But γ]εγ[ονέναι δέ γ' ἄξιος gives a good sense and is probably consistent with the traces.

289–90: Gomme thought Sudhaus's restoration of 289 and Jensen's of 290 possible:

(*Mo.*) μᾶ[λλον ἀδύνατος τρυφᾶν]
ἦσθας· ἀλλὰ τυροπώλει καὶ τὸ λ[ο]ι[πὸν εὐτύχει.]

'Be a grocer, as you don't know how to live like a gentleman.' Sudhaus compared *Sam.* 376 (which is, however, spoken in a very different tone) ; and for the end of 290 suggested καὶ ταλαιπώρει. (Δα.) καλῶс. But there are possibilities as good, e.g. μὰ [Δία, Δᾶ', οὐ δυcχερὴc] ἦcθαc. For the form ἦcθαc see *Epitr.* 373 n.

291: Aristainetos, ii. 1. init., after quoting *Epitr.* 555 continues : ταῦτα μὲν δή, φαcιν, εὐξάcθω (εὔχθω Hercher), whence Sudhaus's convincing restoration here. εὔχθω, third person, perfect imperative—'let that stand as my prayer'. Cf. *IG* ii². 112. 12, ταῦτα μὲν ηὖχθαι. For the line's end Körte accepts *exempli gratia* Sudhaus's suggestion δεῦρο δ' ἦλθεν ἦν ποθεῖc, which may be thought abrupt.

292 ἄνοιγε: Moschion must carry a key, and the door be fastened. This was unusual during the daytime, but conceivably Daos had ordered it, in the verses lost before 261, because of the approach of the revelling youths. In *Dysk.* the suspicious Knemon orders his door to be bolted (427) in his absence and so has to order it to be opened (454, ἄνοιγε . . . τὴν θύραν), cf. Plaut. *Aul.* 103.   **οἰκίαν** may, as at 342 and *Epitr.* 165, be used without the article, much as is κεκτημένη, 'the mistress', in 262.

293 παραμυθεῖcθ': Not 'console', for Moschion is unaware of Glykera's ill-treatment, but 'talk persuasively to her', cf. Plato *Rep.* 476 e, παραμυθεῖcθαι αὐτὸν καὶ πείθειν, Ar. *Wasps* 115, λόγοιcι παραμυθούμενος ἀνέπειθεν αὐτόν, or 'reassure her', cf. Men. frag. 951. 20, θαρρεῖν λέγε . . . παραμύθηcαι τε, *Aspis* 301.

294 πτεροφόρα̣: The meaning probably is that Polemon wore a plume in his helmet, perhaps as a mark of rank (cf. Ar. *Peace* 1172). Hesychios says that πτεροφόροι (πτεροφόραι W. Otto) were military officers, διὰ τὴν ἐν τοῖc λόφοιc πτέρωcιν, and that the name was also given to some of the Egyptian priests. These are known in Ptolemaic times from papyri (Preisigke, *Wörterbuch d. gr. pap. Urkunden*, iii. 383, G. Ronchi, *Parola del Passato* 1968, 290) ; they wore a hawk's wing or wings upon their heads. For the termination cf. βακτροφόραc in Kerkidas 2. 1.

   J. Taillardat, *Les Images d'Aristophane* 135, argues that πτερο- here refers, not to a crest, but to the 'wings' of the military cloak, the chlamys, usually called πτέρυγεc. Pausanias Θ10 Erbse quotes the phrase Θετταλικὰ πτέρα, perhaps from a comic poet, and explains it by διὰ τὸ πτέρυγαc ἔχειν τὰc Θετταλικὰc χλαμύδαc. Taillardat thinks there is a similar play on words in Ar. *Peace* 1177 ff. and *Birds* 1415 ff. This interpretation, although speculative, cannot be ruled out.

297: Note the post-position of πῶc; as in *Dysk.* 893, ἔχει δὲ ⟨δὴ⟩ πῶc; ἐμὲ εἰc τὸ προcδοκᾶν πῶc ἔχουcι; would not be a surprising order, in a prose author, to give emphasis both to ἐμέ (Moschion is an egoist) and to the whole phrase ἐμὲ . . . προcδοκᾶν. Can we also place an emphasis on ἔχουσι, as on ἔχει in *Dysk*., or is this rather a neutral word, separating the emphasized phrase from the interrogative, which also has emphasis through Moschion's anxiety?

298–7 μέρος is pleonastic, cf. *Epitr*. 234 n.   ἀκριβῶς: 'In detail'.

κομψὸς εἶ: The original sense of κομψός is uncertain, but it came to be used, like 'nice', as a general term of praise; it is so employed at *Dysk*. 415. But it frequently has the sense 'clever, ingenious, smart', as here; cf. *Sam*. 614.

300: Moschion begins a short monologue, thinking to himself. '*But* it is not so surprising that Glykera should have come to our house—she showed some hint of the kind last night.'

301: The letters at the end of the line are not enough to fill out the metre; above there are very dubious marks which may have been suprascript letters, correcting the error, as at 319. Sudhaus's ἐφίλησε is accepted by Körte, but although dactyls occur in trochaic tetrameters (see 340 n. and *Dysk*. 774 n.), they are so rare that one should be chary of introducing them conjecturally. His alternative, ἐπέσχε με, was approved by Guéraud, but Lefebvre, Jensen, and Körte all read]cε, which suggests alternatives, for which see the apparatus criticus of OCT; Leo's ἐπέσπασε seems the best.

302–3: Moschion's self-satisfaction is that of a very young man. ἑταίραις προσφιλής, if not the right words, must give the right sense, cf. Aristainetos i. 8, περιπόθητος (τριπόθητος Ruhnken) . . . ταῖς ἑταίραις. To boast of success with women was a habitual feature of the soldier of comedy, see Plaut. *Miles* 1265, 'nepos sum Veneris', and Terence, *Eun*. 424, a trait here transferred to the soldier's 'rival'. If ἐντυχεῖν is right, cf. [Plat.] *Epist*. 360 c, οὔτε ἄχαρίς ἐστιν ἐντυχεῖν, and Theophrastos, *Char*. xix. 3, δυσέντευκτος εἶναι καὶ ἀηδής.

304 τὴν δ' Ἀδράστειαν: To pay respects to Adrasteia (who was sometimes identified with Nemesis, but distinguished in frag. 266, from the early play Μέθη: Ἀδράστεια καὶ | θεὰ σκυθρωπὲ Νέμεσι) was supposed to avert the punishment that boastful words might otherwise incur, cf. *Sam*. 503 n., Aesch. *PV* 936, οἱ προσκυνοῦντες τὴν Ἀδράστειαν σοφοί, Plato, *Rep*. 451 a, προσκυνῶ δ' Ἀδράστειαν . . . χάριν οὗ μέλλω λέγειν, (see Adam's note), Dem. xxv. 37, Ἀδράστειαν μὲν ἄνθρωπος ὢν προσκυνῶ. Wilamowitz's supplement ἄραρε προσκυνεῖν gives a grandiloquent phrase, that would be in character, but ω after the gap, not ν, is almost certain.

305 ἡ μὲν λέλουται καὶ κάθηται: A suitable description of a *hetaira* waiting for her lover, and so Daos means it, cf. Ar. *Peace*. 868, ἡ παῖς λέλουται κτλ.

308: The end of this line is uncertain. Jensen's καὶ πάλαι γὰρ εἶπον is good sense, but Guéraud thought γάρ inconsistent with the traces, preferring Sudhaus's δή. The latter's suggestion πάλαι δὴ θρύπτομαι, 'Look, I've long been coy', is unlikely; coyness is not Moschion's fault. οὐκ is placed by the papyrus at the beginning of 309; cf. *Sam.* 308 n. For a negative at the end of the line, cf. *Kolax* frag. 2, οὐ | μὰ τὴν Ἀθηνᾶν; to place a prepositive word at the line-end is more common in iambic trimeters than in trochaic tetrameters, but see *Samia* 555, cτρόβιλος ἢ | cκηπτός.

Capps took the view, not recommended by the word-order, that εἴμ᾽ ἀήδης is a question, and that οὐκ should be suppressed as a mistaken addition by someone who misunderstood it as a statement. He suggested καὶ πάλαι μένουc᾽ ἐμέ. (μεν is consistent with the traces as recorded by Guéraud.) Retaining οὐκ, this could be adapted as καὶ πάλαι μένουcί μ'; οὐκ | εἴμ᾽ ἀηδής.

309: I see nothing to choose between νῦν παρόντα and cυμπαρόντα.

310 μὰ Δία: 'I did not', in some indignation at the suggestion that he was wanting in finesse.

312 παρακαλύψεται τ᾽· ἔθος γὰρ τοῦτο: Körte so restored, comparing Aristainetos ii. 2, cὺ δέ με θεωροῦντά cε κατιδοῦcα, τοῦτο δὴ τὸ cύνηθες ὑμῖν ταῖς ἐλευθέραις, ἠρέμα παρεκαλύψω. One might understand Moschion to mean that it is the manner of the superior *demi-mondaine* to show she can behave like a lady, cf. Aristainetos ii. 8, προcχήματι cώφρονος ἐπὶ τοὺς ὀφθαλμοὺς καθέλκουcα τὴν ἀμπεχόνην. But is this right here? Is it not rather 'She will be shy (or pretend to be) after that last meeting of ours. That is the way of women'?

313 ἀνακτήcαcθαι: 'Win over'.   **κολακεύειν** *need* carry no connotation of insincerity, see *Dysk.* 37 n.

315 ὡς οἰκείως: This was defended by Sudhaus as the pleonastic use of ὡς seen in ὡς ἑτέρως, ὡς ἀληθῶς (Soph. *El.* 1439 has ὡς ἠπίως). It would be simpler to make ὡς exclamatory, as in 317. But in either case οἰκείως must mean 'with proper feeling', cf. frag. 639, cυναγανακτοῦντ᾽ οἰκείως, frag. 276, ἀποθανόντα τε | ἔθαψε, περιέcτειλ᾽ οἰκείως. οἰκείῳ earlier suggested by Sudhaus and adopted by Körte, is an easy change and gives a good sense, 'handled the affair as if it were her own'.   **μηδὲν ἔτι:** Note the unusual division of the tribrach after the first short syllable; μηδὲν ἔτι must have been regarded as cohering words, cf. *Sam.* 593 n., *Dysk.* 752.

318 ἀτόπως: Sc. ἔχει. So *Dysk.* 102, ὡς ὀργίλως (sc. ἔχει). But Arnott, *CQ* N.s. xviii (1968), 234, may be right in resurrecting Sudhaus's conjecture ἄτοπον. Menander liked such neuter adjectives without a verb. Since the situation is both 'odd' and 'bad', it is hard to say which meaning predominates.   εἶπα: this form is common in Ionic prose, and predominated in the κοινή: even in Attic the usual form of the second person singular was εἶπας, not εἶπες.

320 ὅτι φοβηθεῖϲα: Note the emphasis, slight but definite, given to the participle by the order of words: 'It was because she was frightened that she came here', not in order to see Moschion.   λελάληκας, with the connotation of *unnecessary* talk.

321–2 μὴ ὥρας ϲύ γε: I keep the reading of the papyrus which, though suspect, is not indefensible. The original form of this imprecation seems to have been μὴ ὥραϲι ἵκοιο, where ὥραϲι is an old locative (cf. *Kolax* frag. 1 n.), 'may you never come betimes', i.e. may ill success attend you. Körte (on *Phasma* 43) thought that ὥραϲι should be restored here, on the analogy of Ar. *Lys.* 391, ἔλεγεν ὁ μὴ ὥραϲι μὲν Δημόϲτρατος, Alexis frag. 266, μὴ ὥραϲι μέν . . . ἵκοιθ', and accepted Schwartz's ὥραϲί γε. But whereas ϲύ γε is natural, cf. *Georgos* 53, it is not certain that ὥραϲί γε can be substituted for ὥραϲι μέν (emphatic). A complication is added by the existence of a phrase εἰϲ ὥρας ἱκέϲθαι ('reach this time next year', T. W. Allen, *Rev. de philol.* 3rd series ix [1935], 289), *Hymn. Hom.* xxvi. 12, δὸϲ δ' . . . ἐϲ ὥρας αὖθιϲ ἱκέϲθαι, Babrius liii. 7, μὴ ϲύ γ' εἰϲ ὥρας ἵκοιο, cf. Theokr. xv. 75 and Gow's note. Perhaps ὥρας ἵκοιο, found only here, since *Phasma* 43 is uncertain, is a hybrid, in which ὥρας was understood as an accusative of destination; such an intermediate form might have been due to misunderstanding of an elision, μὴ ὥρας' ἵκοιο, as is written by editors in Ar. *Lys.* 1037. Note the hiatus in the familiar phrase, in which μή is not shortened.

322: Sudhaus fills the gap with ἐκφθάρηθι καί: Körte prefers ἀϲχολῶ γάρ, νῦν (adapted from Schwartz's ἀϲχολῶ νῦν, καί), on the ground that ἐκφθάρηθι is an expression unsuitable for a lady to use. Our evidence is hardly sufficient to make this certain; Demeas can say θᾶττον εἰϲφθάρηθι ϲύ to Chrysis, with no intention of being offensive (*Samia* 574 n.). The active form ἀϲχολῶ is itself suspect, in view of *Suda* s.v. ἄϲχολοϲ· "ἀϲχολοῦμαι" καὶ "ἀϲχολεῖται" καὶ "ἀϲχολεῖϲθαι"· πάντα ταῦτα Μένανδροϲ λέγει, Φιλήμων δὲ καὶ "ἀϲχολεῖ".

323: Restoration is quite uncertain. One might think that the strong expression πάντ' ἀνήρπαϲτ' ἐκ μέϲου should be given to Moschion, and the milder οὐ ϲφόδρ' ἤκουϲεν παρόντα ϲ' ἡδέωϲ to Daos. But Jensen stated that there is no dicolon after μεϲου. The ink at the line-end is very faint, however, and it may be safer to leave open the possibility that there was once a dicolon there.   ἐκ μέϲου: 'From under our noses', cf. Euphron frag. 8 K, Anaxippos frag. 1 K, Dem. x. 36, xviii. 294.

325–6: It is, I think, impossible to determine with certainty what stood at the beginning of 326. τί φῄς; 'what are you saying?' shows that the line must contain a summary of what Moschion feels to be implicit in Daos' words 319–24. Van Leeuwen's οὐ φυγεῖν ἑκοῦςαν and Körte's ἣ φυγεῖν ἄκουςαν; both mean 'she didn't run away willingly'. (Similarly διὰ φόβον γ' ἤκουςαν would be 'she came here because she was *frightened*'; K–G ii. 72).

I do not think there is anything in Arnott's argument (*CQ* n.s. xviii [1968], 235) that the mother, not Glykera, is the expected subject of any infinitive to be supplied. He proposes οὐ λαβεῖν ἑκοῦςαν (after Capps's εἰςάγειν ἄκουςαν), but does not specify which woman was unwilling.

325 κατακέχρηςαί μοι: A very possible restoration. Commonly this verb is constructed with acc. of person, meaning 'destroy', e.g. frag. 403, εὐθὺς καταχρήςεθ' αὐτόν, and dat. of thing, meaning 'misuse'; but Aischines i. 122 has καταχρήςαςθέ μοι, 'do as you will with me'.

μὲν οὖν: Corrective, 'Ridiculous! rather, it was your mother who—' sc. behaved unexpectedly.

327 ἐγὼ δ': Indignant rejection of an imputation, cf. *Dysk.* 891–2, where a phrase is similarly repeated, ἀρτίως ἔπαςχες :: ἐγὼ δ' ἔπαςχον ἀρτίως; For δέ in indignant questions, see Denniston, *GP* 173.

329–30: Jensen and Körte print οὐκ ἂν ἦν ψεῦδος, τρόφιμέ μου, coῦ καταψεύδεςθ' ἔτι | μεῖζον, but I do not see how this can fit the context, since it appears to mean 'it would have been impossible to tell a still greater lie about you'. In fact I do not see any way to give a suitable sense to coῦ καταψεύδεςθαι since καταψεύδομαι and gen. means 'tell lies against a person'. Some corruption is possible: it is noteworthy that C originally had μεπολυ for μουcου. But it would be idle to conjecture a remedy when the line is so fragmentary and the required sense unknown: either 'I would not tell you a lie' (coì καταψεύδεςθ') or 'you are accusing me falsely' would suit.

In 330 Sudhaus's restoration cannot be far out.

331–2: In iambic trimeters a word placed at the beginning of a line with a heavy stop following may be either emphatic or unemphatic. If it is the latter, emphasis falls on the last word or group of words in the preceding line. The same rule appears to be true of trochaic tetrameters, so that ἐμοῦ is here emphasized, as τοῦ γάμου in *Dysk.* 765, τοῦ γάμου | ἔνεκα. Other examples are provided by *Sam.* 554 ὀπτώμενον | ὄψομαι, 580 ἀποκτενῶ | εἰςιών, 683 ἐᾷ | ἀπιέναι.

332–4: The addition here, by a later hand, of marginal and inter-linear notes of the speakers' names seems quite capricious, since there is no reason for doubt; that intended for 332 is wrongly placed against 331. **ἔπειθον:** Daos no longer claims to have persuaded Myrrhine, only that he had urged the course she had adopted. **δεῦρο δὴ βάδιζε:** There is an implied threat of punishment.

334–5: The text cannot be established with confidence. There is no dicolon after ποι. Jensen claimed to see one after μακραν, but I do not think there is room. Lefebvre had no doubt that there was one after ειcει; it cannot be confirmed on the facsimile, but there is space. If it is assumed that there should be a dicolon after μακραν, a possible piece of dialogue results. Daos (in a desperate attempt to treat the situation lightly): 'Where? Not far, I hope.' Moschion (threaten-ingly): 'You'll find out.' Daos (playing for time): 'I tell you what, Moschion; I—'. τὸ δεῖνα, 'You know what', 'I tell you what', is frequently used as an interjection to introduce an idea that suddenly comes into the speaker's mind, as at *Dysk.* 897. On its etymology see A. C. Moorhouse, *CQ* N.s. xiii (1963), 24.

Jensen and Körte disregard the dicolon after ειcει and suppose one to be omitted after ποι: thus they print (Δα.) ποῖ; (Mo.) μὴ μακράν. (Δα.) εἴcει τὸ δεῖνα. Here the *prohibition* μὴ μακράν seems strange, whether it means 'Do not come a long way' or 'Do not speak at length'. 'Not far', as an *answer* to ποῖ; would be οὐ μακράν. But εἴcει τὸ δεῖνα, 'You shall hear, I tell you what', is possible Greek, since τὸ δεῖνα is sometimes found as an object.

Gomme preferred the reading of Sudhaus and van Leeuwen: (Mo.) μὴ μακράν. εἴcει— (Δα.) τὸ δεῖνα, κτλ. One may suppose that Moschion had intended to continue: 'You will learn what comes of cheating me.' Although any of the three interpretations of εἴcει appears credible, no good parallels have been quoted. W. G. Arnott's suggestion ἐκεῖ, i.e. 'stop there' (CQ N.s. xviii [1968], 235), is worth consideration, and could be combined either, as he combines it, with Sudhaus's division of speakers, or with that suggested at the beginning of this note. Later (ibid. N.s. xix (1969), 205) Arnott preferred an anonymous proposal to give ἐκεῖ; to Daos as a question.

338 ἐξ ἐπιδρομῆc: The phrase may mean 'cursorily, summarily' or, in military contexts, 'by a sudden attack' (see LSJ s.v. and ἐπιτρέχειν).

ὡc ἔτυχε: 'Anyhow'; the aorist, properly belonging to sentences with a past main verb, became a fixed phrase used without any time-relation, *Sam.* 294 n.

339 πρὶν τάδ᾽ εἰδέναι cε: 'Before you know she is here for your sake'. Wilamowitz's restoration is better than πρὶν cυνειδέναι cε (Jensen) which would presumably mean 'before you know what her feelings are'. Jensen indeed translated 'before she makes you her lover' (*Hermes* xlix [1914], 414), but without adducing any parallel for such a meaning of the word. τὰ παρὰ coῦ γε: 'What *you* have to say', or 'offer', cf. Xen. *Mem.* iii. 11. 13, Plato, *Symp.* 219 a.

340 αὐλητρίc: A probable restoration. Flute-girls, who went to men's parties, often slaves hired for the occasion, were also prostitutes. πόρνη is always abusive and the diminutive is contemptuous. The dactyl in πορνίδιον τρισάθλιον is unusual, but the phrase (which recurs Com. Adesp. 120 Kock) has the stamp of genuineness. There are 6 such dactyls in Aristophanes' trochaic tetrameters, attacked by M. Platnauer, *CQ* N.S. i (1951), 132, but defended by M. A. Dale, *Lustrum* ii. 40, who points out that in all but one the group – ∪∪ – is contained in a single word (or the equivalent thereof, e.g. article+noun), a result unlikely to be achieved by textual corruption. See also *Dysk.* 774 n., *Sik.* 135, *Sam.* 731.

341 λέγειν . . . τι: 'To talk sense'.

343: Editors in general print οὐ φλυαρία. μεταcτῆν' εἰ cὺ τρεῖc ἢ τέτταραc ἡμέραc βούλει, and understand 'No nonsense there! if you will go elsewhere for three or four days, someone will pay you attention'. There are, however, serious difficulties: (1) except for Sudhaus, the author of μεταcτῆν', no palaeographer can accept the first τ. Lefebvre and Guéraud had no doubt that C has εραcτην with no apostrophe; the facsimile seems to show the round top of ρ, and also the characteristic long descending tail, remarked on by Guéraud and Jensen. Sudhaus's restoration, then, involves emending the papyrus; (2) the elision of an infinitive in -ναι, though found in Aristophanes, is perhaps unparalleled in Menander, cf. *Dysk.* 895 n.; (3) in the event, Moschion does not go away (349), and he does nevertheless expect to receive an immediate approach from Glykera (549). ἐραcτήν, on the other hand, which seems to be given by C, may be possible. Schwartz suggested καταλέλοιπεν οἰκίαν (οὐ φλυαρία γ'), ἐραcτήν. This is disjointed Greek, but perhaps not impossible in the mouth of the agitated Daos. Körte in his second edition printed οὐ φλυαρῶ, ⟨τόν⟩ τ' ἐραcτήν, which normalizes but may weaken the language. That Polemon should be spoken of as an ἐραcτήc, not an ἀνήρ, is quite right, for Moschion must see himself as a rival, an ἀντεραcτήc, not as an adulterer, a μοιχόc. εἰ cὺ τρεῖc ἢ τέτταραc ἡμέραc βούλει will then mean 'if you want to enjoy her for three or four days', i.e. if you want something more than the few hours you might want from an αὐλητρίc. Some infinitive e.g. cυνεῖναι will be understood, perhaps politely suppressed, with βούλει, and ἡμέραc be accusative of duration. One may compare the proposal made by the bawd to the young wife in Herondas i. 39, [πάπτ]ηνον ἄλλη κἠμέρας μετάλλαξον [τὸν] νοῦν δύ' ἢ τρεῖc.

344 τιc, like 'someone', can be substituted for a name which one does not wish, for some reason or other, to use (LSJ s.v. II. 3). Here Daos archly replaces 'Glykera' by 'someone'. For other examples see *Mis.* 140 n.   ἀνεκοινοῦτο: Middle or passive? and if the former, who is the subject, Myrrhine or Glykera? Probably the middle, and Daos leaves the subject purposely vague, for he is lying. The imperfect may be that of the action which is not the end of the story (K–G i. 144), 'she imparted this to me (and now I tell it you)'.

345 ποῦ ce δήcαc καταλίπω; I.e. 'where can I keep you out of mischief?'

346 περιπατεῖν: The meaning of this would be obvious if Daos, having brought his master home, now sent him away again. But it has been argued that this is not so. The phrase must be metaphorical: a long discussion has been needed to arrive at the truth.

347: To determine the reading and the meaning is not easy. Either μὲν οὖν or μὲν οὐκ and either ἀλ]ηθέc or ἔπ]ειθεc (Arnott, *CQ* xviii [1968], 236) are palaeographically possible. Thus four alternatives are to be considered. To start with what is certain, νῦν δὲ λελάληκαc πάλιν cannot mean, as Körte believed, 'now you have told me a (false) story again'. It is true that λαλεῖν is in Menander almost always at least slightly depreciatory, and to substitute λέγειν would change the colour of the word, just as in English 'have a chat with' is not the same as 'have a talk with' (although the former expression may be used, e.g. by a blackmailer, with a kind of irony). So there are passages where λαλεῖν clearly connotes unnecessary or pointless talk, e.g. *Dysk.* 512, 797, *Epitr.* 248, 1069, *Perik.* 523, *Sam.* 285, 380, etc. But I do not think there is any where the word actually denotes, as it would have to here, the telling of lies. Moreover, what is even more cogent, Moschion does not disbelieve Daos' last statement: he goes into the house fully expecting his mother immediately to bring him Glykera's terms for the affair he wants (547). The phrase νῦν δὲ λελάληκας πάλιν must therefore mean 'now you have talked sense again', and the verb λαλεῖν is used because Moschion wishes to express his contempt for the manner in which Daos has revealed the truth. As it is necessary to understand ἀληθὲς λελάληκας, it is very desirable that the word ἀληθές should be found in the first half of the sentence; hence ἀρτίως μὲν οὐκ ἀληθές is preferable to ἀρτίως μὲν οὐκ ἔπειθες, giving an echo of λόγους οὐκ ἀληθεῖς in the opening sentence of the scene. What Moschion rejects as false is the story that Daos had told in 318 ff.

To the accusation 'Lies a moment ago, but now you've babbled sense again', Daos excuses himself by saying that he had been rattled.

348: There is nothing to choose between με θορυβῶν and ἀθορύβωc, but the latter occurs in Eur. *Orestes* 630, a play well known to Menander. Wilamowitz proposed to restore μεταβαλοῦ, 'change your plan, up to a point', i.e. enter in the character of a respectable youth, not an impatient lover, although your final intentions will be unchanged. Jensen maintained that the traces he believed he saw better suited περιβαλοῦ, which he understood to mean 'pull your cloak around you' (it may have been disarranged at 334 ff.). In support of this Sudhaus quoted Aristainetos, who is fond of applying Menander's words to quite different situations: ἄπιθι τοίνυν καὶ cὺ παρ' ἐκείνην ἐν γειτόνων οἰκοῦcαν, μεταμφιεcαμένη μέντοι κοcμίωc ἡμιφάριον ἀλουργέc (i. 19), but the similarity is not so striking as to be decisive. Post's παραβαλοῦ, 'draw alongside', is not to be forgotten in a situation where no supplement is clearly right.

350: Restoration here is uncertain, since the traces are variously interpreted. Sudhaus thought that the last word was παιδιον, formed by correcting καιμαλα, erroneously repeated from the previous line, and that it was preceded by αγε; he suggested παῦε (or πάνυ γε), πάραγε, παιδίον. This is supported by Guéraud, who read π.υ... ραγεπαι. But it involves a change of speaker after ἔχοντα, and there is neither dicolon there nor paragraphus below the line. Jensen read, not ραγεπαι, but ραζει, and Körte, following Robert, prints ἐφόδι' οὐχ ὁρᾷc μ' ἔχοντα παραγοράζειν; οἴομαι κτλ. thus following C in giving the whole of καὶ μάλα . . . cυνδιορθώcαιc to Daos. Jensen himself supposed a change of speaker, writing (*Mo.*) παραγόραζε, παιδίον and explaining that Moschion gives Daos money, a gesture perhaps more suitable to a Shakespearian than a Menandrean master.

So much for the palaeographical evidence. To turn to the interpretation of the surviving words: (1) the phrase 'don't you see that I have (*or* can buy) provisions for the journey' appears to be a poor jest, the point of which is that Daos has *not* the wherewithal; (2) it is at first sight more likely that Moschion should say that he thinks he could have some help from Daos in putting through his plans (cf. 542) than that Daos should suggest in this slightly hesitant manner that Moschion, whom he has already bidden to enter, might come in and give a hand to secure success. It is also to be noted that an invitation to Daos to come in follows well on his jesting words about being ready to run away. I therefore suppose that C has failed to mark a change of speaker at the end of 350.

351: There are two possibilities: either (1) C writes δ' at the beginning of the line (cf. Ar. *Eccl.* 351, *Birds* 1716, A. Körte, *Glotta* iii [1912], 155), in accordance with medieval practice (see e.g. G. Zuntz, *Enquiry into the Transmission* etc. 232) but contrary to our convention by which such an elided word is placed at the end of the previous line, and has also omitted a monosyllable, or (2) δ' ειϲιων is an error for ειϲιων δ'. Change in word-order is a common fault, yet this change is an unlikely one. On the other hand, elision at the end of a line is as yet unparalleled in Menander. The final word may be ἑκών, which could be taken either with ὁμολογῶ, if the previous speaker is Daos, or by itself, ϲυνδιορθώϲαιμ' ἄν being understood, whether he is Moschion or Daos. If the previous speaker is Moschion, as I believe, I should prefer ἐγώ; This will lead up to ὁμολογῶ νικᾶν ϲε. Daos, asked to assist, simulates surprise that he, who had been so recently distrusted, should now be counted on for aid; Moschion then has to admit that his slave has talked him round.

352 δέει αὗος: This phrase recurs at *Epitr.* 901, cf. Ar. *Lys.* 385, αὖόϲ εἰμ' ἐγὼ τρέμων, Theokritos xxiv. 61 and Gow's note. It is a familiar experience that fear causes the mouth to dry up, but Gow prefers the explanation that the reference is to numbness, thought of as caused by lack of moisture in the tissues; this has the support of *Sam.* 515, αὖόϲ εἰμι καὶ πέπηγα.

353: Editors adopt Wilamowitz's εὐκρινῆ. Of the various uses of this word the most relevant seems to be one found in medical writers, who apply it to symptoms which foretell a favourable outcome (LSJ s.v. IV, who suppose a medical metaphor here). There is only one possible alternative, εὔκριτα, which might mean 'easy to decide on', i.e. 'easy to interpret'.

(ii) 354–397: *Daos and Sosias*

Daos has clearly remained on the stage to deliver his comment on the situation after Moschion's departure. Sosias now enters again, and Daos remains, unnoticed, by the door of Myrrhine's house, which (as has been explained in the note on 181 ff.) is at the opposite end of the stage to that where Sosias comes on. That Daos does not go in is shown by the fact that, after Sosias has entered Polemon's house, 361–5 are spoken by a man, as is proved by the oath νὴ τὸν Ἀπόλλω: this man can only be Daos, who is on the stage shortly after.

354: Polemon, having got his civilian ἱμάτιον, has no use for his military χλαμύϲ, and has sent Sosias home with that and his sword. On χλαμύϲ as characteristic military costume, see *Samia* 659 n.

355 ϲπάθην: ϲπάθη, the standard word in New Comedy for 'sword', properly means 'blade', as in Eur. frag. 373, σπάθη φασγάνου, hence 'sword', cf. the same development in Latin *mucro*.

356 ἀκαρὲς δέω κτλ.: ἀκαρής, lit. 'too short to be cut', i.e. minutely small. Here we have an acc. of extent with δέω, 'I miss by a fraction', cf. Plat. *Men.* 71 a τοσοῦτον δέω εἰδέναι; the more normal construction is with gen., e.g. μικροῦ δέω, 'I need but a little so as to . . .' Oddly enough, ἀκαρής is usually and illogically constructed as a nom. in agreement with the subject of a verb, e.g. *Dysk.* 695, ἀκαρὴς νῦν παραπόλωλας, *Aspis* 307.

358–60: This sudden volte-face by the grumbling Sosias is a clever way of enlisting sympathy for Polemon.   ἐνύπνιον may either be in apposition to δεσπότην, 'even as a figure in a dream', or adverbial as in Ar. *Wasps* 1218, ἐνύπνιον ἐστιώμεθα.   ἐπιδημίας: 'Home-coming'; although the noun seems to be used elsewhere of a foreigner's stay in a city not his own, e.g. Plat. *Parm.* 127 a, the verb ἐπιδημεῖν is used not only of this, but also of a citizen's being at home (*Georgos* 19, Plato *Symp.* 172 c) or coming home (Xen. *Mem.* ii. 8. 1), the opposite being ἀποδημεῖν, 'to be abroad'; there is no reason why the noun should not have been used in both the senses of the verb.

361 ὁ ξένος: Many scholars have taken this to mean Sosias, and have argued that in spite of his name and his own use of the word δεσπότης (359), he is a mercenary soldier, even an 'N.C.O.' But this gives Daos a remark of pointless obviousness. In fact, Daos infers from Sosias' words that Polemon (ὁ ξένος) has come back to the country, and observes that this puts a difficulty in the way of Moschion's intrigue. He then reflects that the fat will really be in the fire if his master, Moschion's father, comes back from their farm in the country. Myrrhine may, rather surprisingly, have been prepared to indulge her son in prosecuting an amour under her roof; her husband is not likely to be so accommodating.

362 νὴ τὸν Ἀπόλλω: A typically masculine oath, hence at Ar. *Eccl.* 160 the woman rehearsing a speech to be delivered in man's disguise, reproved for swearing μὰ τὼ θεώ (a feminine oath), corrects herself to ὤ, νὴ τὸν Ἀπόλλω. The only exception to the rule seems to be *Lys.* 917, where Myrrhine, opposing her husband's desires, swears μὰ τὸν Ἀπόλλω: is she 'wearing the trousers'? Some MSS. (not RV, the oldest) give a part at *Frogs* 503 ff. to a θεράπαινα, as do the scholia in RV; but a second scholion in V assigns it to a θεράπων, and since the person in question uses the oath μὰ τὸν Ἀπόλλω is probably right to do so; the rest of the words are at least as suitable to a man as to a woman.   ταῦτά γε: this restoration seems inevitable, although no real parallel for the repetition of ταῦτα has been adduced, unless one is to be found in *Aspis* 224–6. If only four more letters had been lost, every one would confidently have written νὴ τὸν Ἀπόλλω τουτονί, with a reference to the statue of Apollo Agyieus which stood outside the house, cf. *Dysk.* 659 n.

364 τὸν δεσπότην: The absence of Myrrhine's husband clearly facilitated the transference of Glykera, although it may not have been an essential condition; it also makes more dangerous the threat to attack his house to recover the runaway; it may have played some further part in scenes now lost. These lines create some presumption that he *will* appear before the play is over, but not more than a presumption. θᾶττον: 'Quickly', 'soon'.

365 παραφανείς: 'Coming on the scene'. ἀναφανείς or ἐπιφανείς would be a more usual compound, but cf. Plato *Theaet.* 199 c, δεινότερον μέντοι πάθος ἄλλο παραφαίνεσθαί μοι. Dr. Austin calls my attention to the hypothesis to Kratinos' *Dionysalexandros*, *P. Oxy.* 663. i. 10, παρα-φανέντα τὸν Διόνυσον, and that to Aristophanes' *Knights*, οἱ Ἀθηναίων ἱππεῖς . . . παραφαίνονται.

366: As Sosias reappears from Polemon's house, he abuses other servants, who may or may not accompany him on to the stage. Doris is on stage at 397, and could, but does not necessarily, already come on here.

368 ὑπαποστήσομαι: For this, if correctly restored, cf. *Samia* 368.

369 δηλαδή: As usual, in a surmise, and as usual at the line-end.

371 μάντιν: One or more seers were regularly attached to every army; hence the jest here. They are more prominent in some historians than others, in Herodotos, Xenophon, or Plutarch than in Thucydides or Polybios. Daos believes Sosias' suspicions to be well founded; but he will shortly lie stoutly to his face.

373: As Sosias marches to knock on Myrrhine's door, Daos comes forward to intercept him. ἐντεῦθεν εἶ; 'Are you from this house?' is, of course, said to someone found outside, not to a servant answering the door. Similarly in *Dysk.* 913, ἐντεῦθέν τις εἶ; is addressed to Knemon when Sikon 'finds' him outside his house.

374: Notice the anapaest beginning with a dissyllabic word that is not a preposition. This is rare outside the first foot. Here, as in *Epitr.* 296, 456 (where σαφὲς ἄν is justified by post-positive ἄν), *Samia* 312, a stop precedes, but not in *Heros* 22. τί πολυπραγμονεῖς; To be meddlesome or officious was a prominent fault of the Athenians, in public as in private affairs. The character who in the original of Terence's *Heautontimorumenos* uttered the sentence, later so famous, 'homo sum: humani nil a me alienum puto', did so to rebut a charge of being πολυπράγμων.

375: Lefebvre records a dicolon after θεῶν; if he is right, the papyrus must have been in error.

376 τοῦ κυρίου: A husband was his wife's κύριος, a position making him her representative in law. Sosias, although he knows quite well that Glykera has gone to her neighbours of her own accord, wishes to put them in the wrong; he therefore accuses them of detaining a free woman against her will, and forcibly preventing her κύριος, who would assert her rights, from releasing her. Was the 'husband' of a παλλακή in fact her κύριος? I have found no evidence, but see 497 below.

377–8: There is a barely legible marginal note of the speaker, which Jensen and Sudhaus interpreted as Δ]Ω. If the speech is given to Doris, it is in character and could be spoken aside. Guéraud considers Δ]Α more likely, and observes, for what it is worth, that Doris's name is abbreviated ΔΩΡ at 754. It is more in accord with usual dramatic technique that Sosias and Daos should wrangle without interruption, and Doris intervene only on Daos's departure at 397. ὡς πονηρὸς εἶ καὶ cυκοφάντης: regular terms of abuse in the orators, cf. Lysias xii. 5, Dem. xxv. 45, 97. The cυκοφάντης, a common figure in Athenian public life, was a πολυπράγμων with extra energy and with malevolence into the bargain—always prosecuting or threatening to prosecute prominent persons. As some would accept money to desist (or so their enemies said), the term often comes near to meaning 'blackmailer'. According to speaker and circumstance, they were either pestilent scoundrels or the watchdogs of the people. The *word* cυκοφάντης was of course always a term of abuse: it usually, as here, carries the connotation of 'trumper-up of false charges'. Dem. xxv (*in Aristogeitonem*) is the best example of an attack on such folk. Jensen's ὃc τοιαῦθ' ὑπολαμβάνεις, is an attractive suggestion for filling the line; Körte prints it, but notes 'locus nondum sanatus'.

379 ἔχειν χολήν: χολή, 'gall, bile', was supposed to cause anger, hence this popular phrase, first in Archilochos frag. 96 Diehl, χολὴν γὰρ οὐκ ἔχεις ἐπ᾽ ἥπατι. Demosthenes asks indignantly, xxv. 27, καὶ οὐδεὶς ὑμῶν χολὴν οὐδ᾽ ὀργὴν ἔχων φανήσεται ἐφ᾽ οἷς ὁ βδελυρὸς καὶ ἀναιδὴς ἄνθρωπος βιάζεται τοὺς νόμους; Cf. also Ar. *Lys.* 464, Eubul. frag. 61 K, οὐκ ᾤου cύ με χολὴν ἔχειν, Menander frag. 270, τίθημ᾽ ἔχειν χολήν cε καλλιωνύμου (a kind of fish) πλείω.

380–1: The difficulty of these lines is increased by the uncertainty of reading in 381; in 380, however, the restoration of τετρωβόλους is

certain, because of 393, κἂν τετρωβόλουc καλῇc. 4 obols a day was the
pay of some mercenary soldiers; Eustathios 951. 54, κεῖται παρὰ τοῖc
παλαιοῖc καὶ τετρώβολον, cτρατιωτικόc τιc μιcθόc, cf. 1405. 29, and
[Plut.] *Mor.* 233 c tells how when Lysimachos (? early third century)
asked one of his mercenaries if he was a Helot, he got the reply cὺ δ'
οἴει ἐπὶ τὸ παρὰ cοῦ τετρώβολον Λάκωνα ἥξειν; Menander frag. 297, μετ'
Ἀριcτοτέλουc γὰρ τέτταραc τῆc ἡμέραc ὀβολοὺc φέρων, probably refers
to a naval expedition of 314/13, but the pay may have been that of
a citizen or a rower, not of a mercenary soldier. G. T. Griffith,
Mercenaries of the Hellenistic World, 297 ff., concludes that about
350 B.C. the Athenians paid mercenaries not less than 4 nor more than
6 obols (including rations), that Alexander paid 4 obols plus rations,
and that rates probably rose after his death. This makes it possible to
accept the apparent implication of the passage before us that men
receiving 4 obols must be of inferior quality.

In 381 C appears to have τετραδραχμοιc. This is usually emended to
τετράδραχμοc, and Jensen maintained that the ι was in fact cancelled.
The resultant sense, 'when a four-drachma man takes command of
the likes of you, we'll easily fight you', is explained by the assumption
that Polemon's pay as a chiliarch would be 4 drachmas. For this
there is no firm evidence, although at the beginning of the fourth
century it was expected that a cτρατηγόc among the survivors of the
Ten Thousand would be paid four times as much as a ranker; his
command would have been of something between 500 and 1,000 men
(Xen. *Anab.* vii. 2. 36, 6. 1, 6. 7). Even recognizing that mercenaries
soldiered for booty as much as pay, a rate of 4 drachmas looks low
for a chiliarch, in comparison with the 2 drachmas paid to citizens
serving in the ranks in 303 B.C. It seems to me at least as likely that,
if τετράδραχμοc is right, it is a further insult, implying that Polemon
is no chiliarch, but of much humbler rank. There is a parallel of sorts
in Lucian, *Dial. Meretr.* 9. 4–5, where a Polemon who claims to have
been a chiliarch, and even to have commanded 5,000 men, threatens
to attack a house to recover his love, and his rival scornfully grants
him that he may have been a διμοιρίτηc, a sort of N.C.O., who received
twice the ranker's pay (see *Kolax* 29 n.).

Sudhaus suggested τετραδράχμουc, 'when he gets the likes of you
at 4 drachmas,' i.e. even if you were paid like an élite, instead of a
sum for which no one could be expected to fight, you would still not
be worth reckoning with as soldiers. This is a conceivable insult, but
ὅταν does not suit it: εἰ καί+optative would be needed. Körte gives
ὅταν δὲ . . . ὑμῖν to Sosias and Ἡράκλειc . . . ἀcελγοῦc to Daos. 'We
may be 4-obol men, but when our commander comes, we shall easily
fight you.' This retort, improbable in itself, implies two errors in C:

omission of a paragraphus below 383, and (as Capps saw) omission of the article before τετράδραχμος.

383 ἀcελγοῦc: Another word included in the orators' vocabulary of abuse, 'an outrageous action!'

384–5: The reconstruction printed in OCT is possible, but not more. In 384 Körte prefers to follow Sudhaus in writing πάρελθ', ἄνθρωπ', which he gives to Sosias. Certainly in the latter part of the line it is likely that Sosias calls to another servant whom he wishes to cite as a witness; as in 375–7, he tries to intimidate Daos by suggesting that the law is on his side; only when he makes no impression does he proceed to threaten to take the law into his own hands. Ἱλαρίων appears to be the only name that fills the gap, although if it is right the copyist should have written ανθρωφ', not ανθρωπ'.

In 385 restoration is uncertain. Körte prints, after Sudhaus, ἐκεῖν]οc [ἔτυχε] μάρτυ[c ὤν] λέγει τ' ἔχειν. μαρτυ[was read also by Guéraud. But the following gap is probably large enough for four letters (Lefebvre, Guéraud) and the facsimile supports Lefebvre's confident transcript]λογειτ'. Also ἔτυχε μάρτυc ὤν is doubtful Greek, for a μάρτυc is 'a witness' in the sense of one who gives testimony, not of one who is present. Perhaps οἴχεται (sc. Glykera), ὡc οὗτ]οc [ἔcται] μάρτυ[c· ὁμο]λογεῖτ' ἔχειν;

386–7: Jensen's hesitant restoration fits the sense well: (Δα.) οὐκ ἔχομεν αὐτὴν ἔνδον. The direct lie is in character and for the sense cf. 391, 395; but Menander need not have made Daos repeat himself. Indeed 395 may have been the first downright literal lie; here, as at 377 and 391, the lie may have been one of prevarication or implication.

388 τίc ὁ λῆροc; The phrase recurs *Dysk.* 872, and must be felt as a unitary group, justifying the broken anapaest.

389 οἰκίδιον: Myrrhine was wealthy, and the diminutive is to be understood as expressing Sosias' contempt, 'wretched house', rather than as a factual description of the house as small. For the quantity οἰκίδιον, see *Dysk.* 23 n.

390–1 πονηρόν: 'A bad case, yours', cf. *Heros* 17, *Dysk.* 220. Jensen (ed. p. xxxv n.) suggests that Daos quibbles by saying 'you wait for her as if she were with us', because Glykera is with Myrrhine, but not with his master, who is not at home. This is surely far-fetched.

392: The reading of this line has been much debated. Sudhaus wished to read οἱ παῖδεc· ἐπὶ τὰ πελτία, 'slaves, to arms'. But Guéraud was certain that C gives οἱ παῖδεc οἱ τὰ πελτί' οὗτοι πρὶν πτύcαι. This is by no means impossible; with τὰ πελτία we can understand an ellipse of ἔχοντες, 'these lads with the πελτία', cf. K–G i. 318 n. 22; Sosias must be supposed to make a gesture towards Polemon's house, suggesting that his servants are accustomed to the use of arms. The πέλτη was a light shield; the diminutive πελτίον occurs only here. From πέλτη is derived the noun πελτασταί, originally Thracian mercenaries, but later widely recruited. Unlike the ὁπλίτης, the πελταστής had no metal breatplate, and he was armed either with a pair of javelins or with a long thrusting spear (cάριca) as well as a sword. The Macedonian infantry was all peltast; see J. G. P. Best, *Thracian Peltasts*.

πρὶν πτύcαι: Cf. Epikrates frag. 2, 26 K, ἰδεῖν μὲν αὐτὴν θᾶττόν ἐcτιν ἢ πτύcαι, *Theokr.* xxix. 27, γηραλέοι πέλομεν πρὶν ἀποπτύcαι.

394 ἔπαιζον: 'I was joking'; Daos starts as if to retract the word τετρωβόλουc, but replaces it with cκατοφάγος, which can indeed be used to denote one who will stick at nothing, (*Samia* 550 n.) but is an insult when applied to a man to his face.   πόλιν οἰκοῦντεc: 'Here, in a civilized country!' sc. to act like savages.

395 αἰβοῖ: The exclamation seems in Aristophanes to indicate either laughter, *Peace* 1066 (αἰβοιβοῖ), sometimes a bitter laugh, *Peace* 544, *Clouds* 829, or disgust ('pshaw!'), *Wasps* 37, *Acharn.* 189.

396 cάρicαν: The long Macedonian pike (the second syllable is long and often written, especially in Latin, with a double *s*). Gomme thought that Sosias claims to be a member of the phalanx, 'the crack troops'. Perhaps it would be better to say 'the regular troops', for Alexander at least won battles as much by the use of cavalry and, when conditions were suitable, of hypaspists as by the phalanx. I am not sure that Sosias is not thinking that a *sarisa* will be a useful tool for forcing open the door of Myrrhine's house. The most recent account of this weapon is by M. Andronikos, *BCH* xciv (1970), 91; it had a heavy point and a metal foot, and the largest were according to Theophrastos, *H.P.* iii. 12. 2, of 12 cubits' length. But after his time they appear to have become longer: Polybios says that they were 14 cubits (6 metres), having once been as much as 16 (xviii. 29. 2), a figure confirmed by Polyainos, *Strat.* ii. 29. 2, and Arrian, *Tact.* 14. 2.

397: αὐθεκάcτῳ (Jensen) will hardly do for the gap; see *Samia* 550 n. for the meaning of this word. Körte's ἀπονοήτῳ is worth considering ('madman', cf. 375 and Theophrastos' character of the ἀπονενοημένοc) but the word is not found elsewhere, and appears to be too short by one letter. Daos goes in, and Doris comes forward, hoping to pacify Sosias.

(iii) 397–406: *Sosias and Doris*

400 οὕτωc ὄναιο: 'So may you be advantaged', used in making an appeal, like οὕτω τί coι ἀγαθὸν γένοιτο, (e.g. *Epitr.* 264), cf. Dem.

xxviii. 20, οὕτως ὄναιϲθε τούτων; similarly in a protestation, Ar. *Thesm.* 469, οὕτως ὀναίμην τῶν τέκνων, to be compared with οὕτω μοι γένοιθ᾽ ἃ βούλομαι in 403.

404 ὁρᾷϲ ἵν᾽ οἴχεται: ἵνα, 'whither', is unusual, but found in tragedy, e.g. Soph. *OT* 687, ὁρᾷϲ ἵν᾽ ἥκεις. That Sosias' phrase is intended to sound high flown is supported by the fact that τὸ μέλημα, 'her darling', is a word from poetry (Sappho, Pindar, Aeschylus); at *Ecclesiazusae* 905, ὦ γραῦ, τῷ θανάτῳ μέλημα (cf. 972), Aristophanes deliberately uses it for comic effect.

405–6: 'She's not now doing anything of what you have in mind.' Cf. Plat. *Rep.* 362 e, ἵν᾽ ᾖ caφέcτερον ὅ μοι δοκεῖ βούλεcθαι Γλαύκων, 'to make clearer what I believe Glaukon has in mind'. This is a reply to the implication of Sosias' last remark. νῦν is contrasted with Glykera's possibly imprudent conduct of the previous evening.

Körte follows Sudhaus in writing μηδὲν πόει νῦν ὧν cὺ βούλει. This is possible, but (*a*) it does not attach itself to what immediately precedes, (*b*) the force of νῦν is far from obvious.

In 406 Körte prints Jensen's ἐπεὶ ψευδῆ λέγειν—. This does not impose itself; for instance, one could have ἐμοὶ ψευδῆ λέγειc;

407–66: After 406 about 60 lines are lost. One leaf (2 pages) of the Cairo papyrus is missing, and will have contained about 70 lines. The loss is less than this because the first Leipzig fragment (L) overlaps its next surviving page, preserving 13 lines which precede the first line of that page.

The end of Act II fell in the lacuna. Since 140 lines of this act are preserved, it is not likely to have exceeded 180 lines in all—but one considerable scene is in tetrameters, longer lines than the normal iambics. Act IV of *Dyskolos*, which is mostly in tetrameters, contains only 164 lines. Act II of *Samia* had about 150, of *Aspis* not more than 145, of *Dyskolos* 194, of *Epitrepontes* about 240.

All that is certain about the missing scenes is that Sosias must have departed before the end of the act to fetch his master and that they returned at the beginning of the next act. Gomme's hypothetical reconstruction was as follows:

> After presumably more wrangling between Doris and Sosias, in which the latter will have maintained his stout-hearted resolution to get Glykera away from Myrrhine's house by force, Doris will have gone back to Polemon's house, and Sosias, in a monologue, declaring himself as brave as ever, have weakened, and decided to go first to Polemon to tell him Glykera has fled and to consult with him as to further action. This, however, will hardly have taken more than 25 to 30 lines; Menander was an economical writer; and some

other short scene has gone too, at the end of [Act] ii or the beginning of [Act] iii. At 467 Polemon reappears with Sosias and some of the companions, fellow-soldiers and a flute-girl, with whom he had vainly tried to forget his sorrows. Pataikos, his old friend (whom we had perhaps seen in Act i before the Prologue) is with him when our MS. [i.e. L] begins; either he had been with Polemon, or arrives having heard of the quarrel—perhaps summoned by Doris. A statement by Doris that she will send for him may have helped to weaken Sosias' resolution at the end of the last Act. If we like to take Sosias' words in 467 literally, we may suppose that Pataikos has called at Myrrhine's, and comes on to the stage from her house; but perhaps 486 makes it more probable that he came with Polemon. In any case before 467 he has already been trying to quieten and soothe his friend (who has only now heard of Glykera's flight, which must seem to confirm his worst suspicions), and especially to get rid of the noisy Sosias and his troop.

ACT III

How much is lost at the beginning of the act cannot be determined, but probably between 20 and 40 lines. At the first preserved line there are on the stage Pataikos and Polemon, accompanied by Sosias, Habrotonon, and some slaves. Pataikos has already begun to attempt to dissuade Polemon from recovering Glykera by a forcible entry into Myrrhine's house; Sosias is in protest against his intervention. How has he become involved in the events? All that is certain is that he is a friend of Polemon's. Sosias' words προδίδωςίν ce καὶ τὸ ϲτρατόπεδον might suggest that he was one of Polemon's party, coming from the gathering of friends mentioned in 176. But this is not easily reconcilable with the suspicion that he is 'a paid agent, come from the enemy's camp' (467). ἐκεῖθεν ἥκει may be as false as χρήματ' εἰληφώς, so that he need not have entered Myrrhine's house since his arrival; but the accusation could hardly be made if he had been constantly in Polemon's company. Hence it seems likely that he has arrived independently, and that his alleged 'treachery' is that of a friend, not of a member of the attacking party.

If he arrived independently it may be that, possibly disturbed by the noise, he came out of his own house, which was represented on the stage. This view is adopted by Körte, who therefore holds that after Glykera has been recognized as his daughter they enter that house, where they are both to be found in the final scene, 976 ff. On the whole, I think this likely; but one interpretation of 715 ff. would make Pataikos a relative of Myrrhine or of her husband, in which case he might here have come to visit his relatives and later use their house to marry his daughter from. The evidence of the prologue is, however, against this. He must have figured in its lost opening, and so, if he were connected with Myrrhine, one would expect a mention of the fact where she is introduced. This tells strongly against K. F. W. Schmidt, *B. ph. W.* 1921, 718, who argued that Pataikos was Myrrhine's husband, on the ground that if he were merely Moschion's natural father and not also his legal father, he would not have the right to arrange his marriage (1026). The point is a serious one. But if, as I believe, Moschion was not a legally adopted child, but one falsely passing as the physical son of Myrrhine and her husband, they would have no rights in him or control over him, once the falsehood was exposed. At first sight, also, 708–22, particularly 719 and 722, could hardly be spoken to the head of the house in which Glykera had taken refuge; yet on consideration it is not impossible: ἄπιθι in 722 *may* be no more than 'leave me', without any implication that Pataikos is to leave the house.

No other play by Menander is known to require the representation of more than two private houses, although there may have been three in Ἀδελφοί α', as there are in Plautus' adaptation *Stichus* (H. J. Mette, *Lustrum* x [1966], 24).

(i) 467–525: *Polemon, Pataikos, Sosias* (exit 485)

467: According to Körte (and Gomme) the siege-party includes, besides Polemon, Sosias, and Habrotonon, friends of Polemon's, who have arrived with him. There is no indication of this in the text, which only mentions slaves, whom Sosias is leading (477). If there had been any such friends, they must have been referred to; they could not just go away without a word.

467–8 χρήματ' εἰληφὼς . . . προδίδωσιν: The regular charge recklessly brought throughout Greek history against any person, especially politician or soldier, who has done something you disagree with, or has failed to carry out what you supported.

468 στρατόπεδον: Sosias absurdly elevates a few slaves to the dignity of an army, cf. Terence, *Eun.* 814, where Thraso swallows the malicious Gnatho's reference to his handful of followers: 'GE. iam dimitto exercitum? TH. ubi uis.'

469 ὦ μακάριε: 'My friend'. The phrase has an ironical tone; see *Dysk.* 103 n.

470 οὐχ ὑγιαίνεις: 'You are not in your right mind', cf. *Dysk.* 150.

470 coì λαλῶ: 'I am talking to *you*' (Polemon), a good instance of the now colourless use of this word (cf. *Epitr.* 248 n.). The distribution of speeches in the next dozen lines has been variously done; but that of Körte, followed in OCT down to 479, is the most satisfactory.

471–3 ὅc: See *Dysk.* 868 n. Although Polemon's indignation and self-pity may cause a smile, this speech simultaneously registers a point in his favour: he has not taken the easy way of drowning his sorrows in drink.

474 κελεύεις ἐμοί: The construction of κελεύω with dative is found in Homer and in late prose, e.g. (with infinitive) Diod. Sic. xix. 17. 3, Lucian, *Dial. Mort.* i. 1, (with neuter acc., as here) Aelian, *Hist. An.* ix. 1, *Cόλων τοῖc μὲν λέουcιν οὐ κελεύει ταῦτα.* διακελεύω is always at all periods followed by the dative. [Körte read ἐμε̣, but accepted Wilcken's correction ἐμοι. It is not I think possible to confirm either reading from the photograph.]   **ἐμοί:** The emphatic form; Pataikos has told Sosias to go away; now what will he tell *Polemon* to do?

475 τἆλλ', read by Gomme on the photograph (where it is quite clear), is accepted by Körte; τἆλλα are what Pataikos still had to say when previously interrupted by Sosias. In his *editio princeps* Körte punctuated after ἐρωτᾷc, in his later editions after νῦν. Either is possible, but the first dramatically better: νῦν | ἐγὼ δὴ | τἆλλ' ἐρῶ makes a slow and impressive introduction to Pataikos' intended speech, rudely shattered by Sosias' interruption.

476 ἐπιcήμηνον: Cf. Photios, *cημαίνειν καὶ ἐπιcημαίνειν· τὸ cφοδρῶc αὐλεῖν, ὥcπερ οἱ cαλπιγκταί· οὕτωc Μένανδρος·* (frag. 1011 Kock), which edd. take as a reference to this passage. So: 'Sound on your pipe the signal for attack.' A unique use of the word, which in the active generally means 'to set a mark on a person', as a disease, or, intransitive, 'to appear as a symptom' (Thuc. ii. 49. 7). Habrotonon is the flute-girl whom Polemon has had with him.

478: There are variant readings here between which the choice is hard. (*a*) L originally had διαλυεται, to which the second hand added a c after διαλυ. Either διαλύεται or διαλύcεται gives unexceptionable sense: 'he is putting an end' or 'he will put an end to the war'. The middle is frequently used in such phrases (LSJ s.v. 4). I accept the future, in the hope that the second hand had good reason for the change. The subject is probably Pataikos, but Polemon is not out of the question, although addressed in the first part of the line: Sosias might turn from him and speak to the 'troops'. If the present διαλύεται is maintained, it could be passive, ὁ πόλεμοc being understood as subject. (*b*) L originally had κακωcδιοικειcτονπολεμον; the second hand wrote γεπολεμειc above διοικειc, which he cancelled, and this seems also to be the reading of O 15, which Turner interprets as κακωc-γεπολεμειcτο. Since διοικεῖν can be used absolutely (see Arist. *Pol.* 1313ᵃ2, τυραννικώτερον πειρωμένων διοικεῖν and Bonitz's index), and πόλεμον πολεμεῖν is a common phrase, this leaves four possible ways of constituting the text: (i) κακῶc γε πολεμεῖc τὸν πόλεμον· διαλύcεται, (ii) κακῶc γε πολεμεῖc· τὸν πόλεμον διαλύcεται, (iii) κακῶc διοικεῖc τὸν πόλεμον· διαλύcεται, (iv) κακῶc διοικεῖc· τὸν πόλεμον διαλύcεται. I see nothing to choose between γε πολεμεῖc and διοικεῖc. Turner argues that πολεμεῖc is a pun on Polemon's name, but could an audience notice the alleged pun, when Polemon's name had not occurred in the previous eleven lines at the least? Without confidence I follow Gomme in accepting διοικεῖc with previous editors; γε πολεμεῖc may be a more explicit substitute. (c) A third hand in L altered αι of διαλύεται to ε: he may have been unnecessarily offended by the change to third person from the second person of πολεμεῖc or διοικεῖc.

Gomme declared that Sosias here acts the soldier, the man on the spot, who sees his plans frustrated by the appeasing politician.

479 ἐξόν: the reading of O 15, may also have been in L, although Körte thought the second letter more like ε than ξ and D. Mueller claimed to see δεον, which is inferior in sense.

O 15 has a dicolon after κρατοc, and L probably had one (the upper dot being lost in a hole). But whether this indicates a change of speaker or a change of person addressed is less certain. The margin in L is destroyed, but O 15 has no paragraphus below the line, which suggests the latter alternative. But there is a paragraphus below 478, where it seems unwanted. Has it been placed there by mistake, its proper place being below 479? At the end of the line Wilcken's reading μεγαρ is dubious. At the beginning of 480 the definite article ὁ is not in O 15, and can have been in C only if the lost initial letters were exceedingly crowded; its presence in L cannot be regarded as certain. With these doubts it is impossible to constitute the text with confidence. ἐξόλλυcιν is a strong word, 'is bringing utter disaster', and it seems impossible that Polemon could so speak of Pataikos, whose advice he has just asked. The word must belong to Sosias (Gomme, *CQ* xxx [1936], 66), and will be addressed by him to Polemon. Then he turns to the rest of the company, a change marked by the dicolon that follows both in O 15 and in L, and declares οὐκ ἔcθ' ἡγεμών, 'he (sc. Polemon) is no leader', or 'we have no leader'. The previous words offer more difficulty. The best solution seems to be to suppose οὑτοcί με γάρ— to be spoken by Polemon, whose meaning will be something like 'the reason for not storming the place is that this man is advising me—'; Sosias interrupts: 'Pataikos? he is bringing disaster!' Other solutions are possible. Turner suggests (Πο.) οὗτος— (Cω.) ἀλλὰ γὰρ Π. ἐξ. This supposes that ι of ουτοcι is a mistake for a dicolon.

481: The first part of the line is better assigned to Pataikos (Gomme, following Sudhaus) than to Polemon (Körte).

Gomme wished Habrotonon to have a speaking part and assigned her κακῶc . . . κράτοc, οὐκ ἔcθ' ἡγεμών, and ἀπέρχομαι. His ground was that if Habrotonon has not spoken, cέ in 482 would naturally be taken to refer to Polemon, whereas the latter half of the line shows that *she* is addressed. There is, however, no real difficulty; Sosias leaves the pair to whom he has been speaking (ἀπέρχομαι): his next remark is there- fore addressed to a member of the group in the background which he joins, and that member is quickly identified by the name Ἁβρότονον in the next sentence. There is thus no dramatic necessity to give Habrotonon a speaking part, so making four speakers on the stage at once, a thing unparalleled in Menander. Although it may be granted to Gomme that ἄνθρωπε *could* be addressed to a woman (and that ἡ ἄνθρωποc is not always contemptuous, see e.g. Antiphon i. 17, Isaios vi. 20), there is no example to be found in comedy.

485 ἀναβαίνειν, περικαθῆcθαι: These are the only jests in the surviving Menander that involve a sexual *double entendre*, with possible excep- tions at *Dysk.* 858, 892, see nn. In military language περικαθῆcθαι means 'blockade', ἀναβαίνειν probably 'scale a wall', cf. frag. 745 where a soldier gets a wound ἐπὶ κλίμακι πρὸc τεῖχοc ἀναβαίνων. I know no parallels for the sexual meaning, although βαίνειν and ἀναβαίνειν are used of the male, cf. Ar. *Lys.* 60, *Wasps* 501, etc.   **λαικάcτρια:** Obscene abuse, see Hesychios s.v. λεcβιάζειν· πρὸc ἄνδρα cτοματεύειν· Λεcβιάδαc γὰρ τὰc λαικαcτρίαc ἔλεγον, and *Dysk.* 892 n. These jests are not here merely for their own sake, although they are in character for a slave excited by drink. They serve the dramatic purpose of clearing the stage for a serious talk between Polemon and Pataikos. For Habrotonon takes herself off, insulted; Sosias' troop of slaves probably melt away too. But Sosias apparently remains, for he is referred to at 531 by the deictic οὑτοcί. As he plays no further part, it may be supposed that after ineffectively following Habrotonon he sits down and falls asleep, as it had been suggested he should (469).

487 γαμετὴν γυναῖκα: This phrase was used of what may be called a true wife as opposed to a concubine. The 'wedded wife' bears children who have rights in her husband's family, both of inheritance and of qualification for religious and political associations. She must be of citizen birth, and will have been married according to the customary forms, by which her κύριοc (father, brother, or uncle) 'gives' her to the bridegroom, usually with a dowry. Nothing of the kind had happened in the case of Polemon and Glykera, for she had no κύριος (τίς ἐςθ᾽ ὁ δούς; 490). When Polemon says that he has thought of Glykera as his wedded wife, he must mean that he thought of their union as permanent, and that he regarded her with the same sort of respect as he would have had for a true γαμετή. Since Glykera was not married in this way, she was free to leave him, as Pataikos points out. Had she been a γαμετὴ γυνή, Polemon would have become her κύριος, and to leave him against his will, she would have had to be transferred to the guardianship of a male relative with the knowledge of the archon basileus, see *Epitr.* 641 n.

488–9: L, originally followed by Körte, assigns to Polemon all from οἷον to ταύτην. Later Körte, with Jensen and Sudhaus, preferred the evidence of C, which gives to Pataikos διαφέρει δέ τι (as the phrase must then be accented in place of δὲ τί; that is required by L.) This is supported by O 15, which has a paragraphus below 488. C omits the dicolon which should have been placed after τι.

489 μὴ βόα: 'Don't shout' is perhaps too strong, for βοᾶν need be no more than 'talk loudly' (*Dysk.* 149) or 'cry out'. There is no rudeness, only deprecation of excitement.

493 τουτί με: This sentence exemplifies two points in which the order of words in a Greek sentence may differ from what we are tempted to call 'natural'. (1) τουτὶ . . . εἰπών; words closely connected are placed first and last; for other examples see *Dysk.* 236 n.; (2) the placing of the post-positive με after the first word, and its consequent divorce from λελύπηκας, with which it is logically connected, cf. Dover, *Greek Word Order*, 14.

494 ἐρᾷς: After much hesitation I accept this, van Leeuwen's correction of ἐρεῖς. τοῦτ᾽ οἶδ᾽ ἀκριβῶς is a phrase found elsewhere, *Epitr.* 871, τοῦτ᾽ ἴςθ᾽ ἀκριβῶς (cf. τοῦτ᾽ ἀκριβῶς οἶδα, *Aspis* 434) and the punctuation ἐρεῖς τοῦτ᾽, οἶδ᾽ ἀκριβῶς is therefore suspect. But ἐρεῖς alone is bald; one would expect e.g. ἐρεῖς καὶ cύ. ἐρᾷς gives good sense, as is well maintained by Arnott, *CQ* N.S. xviii (1968), 237, who exemplifies the cliché to which Pataikos alludes: love brings madness. 'You are in love, I know for certain; so your present course is a mad one: the only course open to a badly-placed lover is that of persuasion.' If ἐρεῖς is maintained, ὥστε must be regarded as continuing in sense from 492, the exchange τί φῄς; . . . ἀκριβῶς being a kind of parenthesis. Wilamowitz's alteration to ὡς, dependent on ἐρεῖς, is unnecessary.

496: C's paragraphus below the line must be wrong; that it had (erroneous) dicola after εcτι and γαρ was thought possible by Lefebvre, but denied by Jensen. There is no reason for supposing that L had dicola, although a hole before ποι does not allow one to assert that it did not. ἀπόπληκτον, used by medical writers to mean 'paralysed', 'struck by apoplexy', has a popular usage 'senseless, crazy', e.g. [Dem.] xxxiv. 16, μὴ γὰρ οἴεσθέ μ' οὕτως ἀπόπληκτον εἶναι καὶ παντελῶς μαινόμενον, Dem. xxi. 143.

497 ἑαυτῆς κυρία: I.e. she has no κύριος, is her own mistress. Persuasion is Polemon's only course, for he has no legal right to control her. It is not, however, to be supposed that Glykera has any positive rights that a woman with a κύριος lacked; she would be completely without standing in a court of law, since she had no man to represent her.

499–503 διεφθαρκώς: διαφθείρειν, like 'seduce', often connotes sexual intercourse. Polemon has no evidence of that, but the removal of Glykera to Moschion's house strongly suggests it. The word, however, does not commit him; it may indicate only the 'moral' corruption, of which he has no doubt. **ἀδικεῖ:** This is another word of wide meaning; it covers both wrongs for which there is legal redress and acts which, though unfair, are not specifically against the law. Pataikos does not attempt to decide into which category Moschion's supposed offence falls, for both ἔγκλημα and τιμωρία are ambiguous words. The first can be used either of instituting an action at law, 'lodging a complaint' (LSJ s.v. II) or of private complaint; the latter may mean either legal punishment or private retaliation, which was sometimes allowed, e.g. in the case of the adulterer caught *flagrante delicto*. The points on which Pataikos is clear are (1) that Polemon has a cause for private complaint at least, 'if he can discuss the matter with Moschion', (2) that Moschion's offence is not one that can be redressed by forcible means but that if Polemon uses force to recover Glykera he will be acting illegally and be condemned when brought to trial. His language does not exclude the possibility that some legal means of redress are open, but no form of action for enticing away a παλλακή is known, and it is improbable that any existed at Athens.

511 ὁρᾷς: Parenthetic, as perhaps at *Sam.* 461 and frequently in Aristophanes; similarly μανθάνεις 338, *Sam.* 378.

513 αὕτη: By the usual attraction for what we should find more logical, viz. τοῦτο.

515 φιλοτιμούμενος: Here used either in the sense 'showing a love of honour' (not 'love of honours', i.e. ambitious, or rivalling others), or more probably to mean 'in earnest endeavour', sc. to treat her well: πάντα is acc. of respect, cf. Xenophon, *Oecon.* 4. 24, ἀεὶ ἕν γε τι φιλοτιμούμενος. The dicolon at the end of the line in L (Jensen reads a single stop only, but the facsimile seems clear) must be intended to mark not change of speaker (there is no paragraphus), but the sudden abandonment of protestations to be conveyed to Glykera, and the introduction of a new project, that of showing Pataikos her finery.

516 τὸν κόcμον: Polemon means by this all the jewellery and dresses he has given Glykera and which will be evidence of his devotion. This leads to the discovery of ὁ κόcμοc in the narrow sense in which it was often used, e.g. 816 below, and *Epitr.* 247, 301, namely the small pieces of jewellery and the like put out with an exposed child.

καλῶc ἔχει: A formula of polite refusal, cf. *Dysk.* 829; J. H. Quincey, 'The Greek for Thank you', *JHS* xxxvi (1966), 133. Pataikos shows a natural reluctance to fall in with Polemon's naïve whim; but Polemon's insistence—all part of his simple and eager character— persuades him; and this leads to the solution of the play.

519 ἐνδύμαθ': Although the word occurs in an inscription (*IG* xii (5). 593^A. 4) of the fifth century B.C., this is its first appearance in literature; it recurs in later prose (Strabo, Plutarch).

520 λάβῃ: 'Puts on', cf. frag. 754. 4. **ἑοράκειc,** pluperfect, should refer to a state of affairs at some given point in the past. I do not understand why the perfect is not used: 'you have never seen her in her finery' seems the obvious thing to say. If the pluperfect is right, the meaning must be: '(At the time she left me, and there has been no later opportunity), you had never seen her in her finery.'

521 τὸ μέγεθοc: 'Grandeur' Allinson, 'magnificence' Capps, whom Gomme followed, suggesting that Polemon had in the opening scene reproached Glykera with all he had given her. But there can be little doubt that van Leeuwen is right in referring the word to Glykera's height, quoting Hdt. iii. 1, κάρτα μεγάλη καὶ εὐειδήc. Tallness was admired in women; a few passages among many may be quoted: *Od.* xv. 418, Theophilos frag. 12 K, κάλλει καλῆc, μεγέθει μεγάληc, τέχνη cοφῆc, Herakleides frag. 7, αἱ δὲ γυναῖκεc αὐτῶν (sc. τῶν Θηβαίων) τοῖc μεγέθεcι, πορείαιc, ῥυθμοῖc εὐcχημονέcταταί τε καὶ ἐκπρεπέcταται τῶν ἐν τῇ Ἑλλάδι γυναικῶν, Aristainetos i. 4, ὡc εὐμήκηc, Lucian *Dial. Meretr.* i. 1; further examples in W. J. Verdenius's article *ΚΑΛΛΟC ΚΑΙ ΜΕΓΕΘΟC, Mnem.* 4th ser. ii (1949), 294.

523 ἐμβρόντητοc: A strong word, lit. 'thunderstruck', and thus 'knocked silly', 'stupid'; it is found in Xenophon, *Anab.* iii. 4. 12, Ζεὺc δ' ἐμβροντήτουc ποιεῖ τοὺc ἐνοικοῦνταc, Plato, *Alcib.* 140 c, ἠλιθίουc καὶ ἐμβροντήτουc, and several times in comedy. **ὑπὲρ ἄλλων λαλῶν:** Since λαλεῖν is nearly always used by Menander of unimportant, desultory, idle, unnecessary, or even foolish talk, it is best to understand it so here. Then ἄλλων must have the not very common sense of 'unimportant, irrelevant', more familiar in the adverb ἄλλως, 'vainly'. ὑπέρ is the equivalent of περί, and the whole phrase means 'chattering about things not to the point'. Those who suppose that Menander would use λαλεῖν as a straight equivalent of λέγειν, as do some later authors (LSJ s.v. 3), may interpret it as 'when I am talking about other subjects'.   φέρω εἰc μέcον: Dem. xviii. 139, *Sam.* 270; originally 'put before the public' or 'the meeting'; here in a weakened sense, 'bring into the conversation'.

524: C has a line a foot too long, μὰ τὸν Δί', οὐδέν :: οὐ γάρ; ἀλλὰ δεῖ, Πάταικέ, cε, whereas L is metrical, ending δεῖ γε cε. Körte follows L, but the repetition of the vocative Πάταικε is a feature of the last part of this scene (507, 512 twice, 517), an indication of Polemon's desperate longing for the support of his friend. It will therefore be better to retain Πάταικε and drop some other word, either τόν (Sudhaus) or οὐδέν (Wilamowitz, who thought it a false variant for οὐ γάρ; [*Kl. Schr.* i. 253]; and now cf. the intrusive οὐδείς at *Aspis* 429). If οὐδέν is dropped, μὰ τὸν Δία will negative and reject the idea of chattering irrelevantly. οὐδέν, if kept, must be taken with ἐμβρόντητοc, 'in no way thunderstruck' (cf. βέβαιον οὐδέν at 144); μὰ τὸν Δία will then negative the same idea of being thunderstruck.

525: The OCT text follows L; 'lead on, I'm coming in'; C's dicola give (Πα.) πάραγε. (Πο.) εἰcέρχομαι. Körte prints (Πο.) . . . πάραγε (Πα.) εἰcέρχομαι, which flouts both manuscripts and gains nothing over L's division.

(ii) **526–550:** *Moschion*

526–31: As Pataikos and Polemon enter the latter's house, Moschion swaggers out of his own and, all danger past, launches unheard insults at his retiring enemies; he can safely disregard the sleeping Sosias (531, 485 n.). Gomme suggested that the lines should perhaps be given to Daos, on the grounds that otherwise the transition after 531 is very abrupt and that the humour suits Daos better than his master. The writing in C is very indistinct, and one cannot be positive that there was no dicolon or paragraphus after 531. But the abruptness of transition is quite natural. Moschion's entry is motivated by his desire to cock a snook at the departing Polemon; having struck that attitude, he turns to the audience and strikes another. It may also be noticed that if Daos were also on the stage, Moschion would, in view of 542 ff., deliver a monologue without being aware of his presence; this is not likely since they would both have issued from the same house within a few lines of one another, and Daos would have no reason for concealing himself. Körte strangely maintained that by ὑμεῖς in 526 Moschion must mean Sosias and his troop, not Polemon and Pataikos, whom it would be improper for him to address so rudely ('sic adulescens in senem invehi non potuit'); he added that Pataikos would not have a spear. It need hardly be said that if *one* of the attacking party had carried a spear Moschion could exaggerate that into a plural (cf. 173, τὰς γυναῖκας οὐκ ἐῶν ἔχειν τρίχας), and that the subject of ἐκπεπηδήκασι is the whole party, not just Pataikos and Polemon.

526 εἰσφθερεῖσθε: See *Dysk.* 101 n.

527 λόγχας: The line, like the next, has tragic rhythm, and the word λόγχη is mainly tragic; it is used by Aristophanes in comically high-flown passages, *Frogs* 1016, frag. 404. But it occurs in a list of very ordinary words, Men. frag. 282, χλαμύδα, καυςίαν, λόγχην, ἀορτῆρ', ἱμάτια. **ἐκπεπηδήκασί μοι**: 'They have scuttled out of my way', μοι being an ethic dative. *Perinthia* frag. 6, ἐκ τῆς πόλεως . . . ἐκπήδα.

529: C's οἷοι πάρεις', 'being such as we see here', is a strange phrase, since the persons spoken of are not present, with the exception of Sosias. As C has, according to Lefebvre, an accent on εις, the right reading may be οἷοίπερ εἷς', 'being such as they are' (Dem. xxiv. 185, οἵοισπερ cὺ χρώμενοι cυμβούλοις.) But I prefer οἷοι γάρ εἷς', cf. *Dysk.* 559, 'for what creatures they are, the malicious pests!' **βάσκανοι**: βασκαίνω means both 'to slander' (so *Aspis* 153), and 'to bewitch'; βάσκανος is not uncommon in Demosthenes as a term of invective with a connotation of slander and malevolence. If it is here more than a vague term of abuse, it carries the meaning of malevolence.

530 φησί: Sc. Daos, who will have reported to his master, and perhaps embroidered, his brush with Sosias; οἱ παῖδες οἱ τὰ πελτία may in the telling have become a troop of mercenaries. To suit his suggestion that Daos is the speaker of these lines Gomme supposed the subject of φησί to be Polemon.

530: 'The famous mercenaries are—Sosias here and no one else'. This, of course, does not imply that Sosias was in fact a mercenary soldier and a free man.   **533 φορά**: Conceivably a *rush* of misery, but more probably a *crop*, as Philoponos interpreted it. One may compare Dem. xviii. 61, φορὰ προδοτῶν, Aischines iii. 234, φορὰ ῥητόρων.   **τούτου**: neuter, referring to the idea of 'misery' contained in the adjective ἀθλίων.

534 δι' ὅ τι δή ποτε: 'For some reason or other', a common elliptical phrase as in ὅ τι δὴ εἰπών, etc., 'saying something or other' (cf. e.g. Hdt. iii. 121. 1). Denniston, *GP* 221.

535–6 ἄθλιον . . . **οὕτως ὡc**: Normally Greek does not use οὕτως ὡς = 'as much as': οὐδένα . . . ἀθλιώτερον ἐμοῦ would be the commoner expression. But οὕτως ὡς in this sense is found: frag. 572, οἰκεῖον οὕτως οὐδέν ἐστιν . . . ὡς ἀνήρ τε καὶ γυνή. Note the unusually artificial order of words; Moschion talks for effect. The whole sentence has a literary flavour, recalling some famous passages: Eur. frag. 282, κακῶν γὰρ ὄντων μυρίων καθ᾽ Ἑλλάδα, οὐδὲν κάκιόν ἐστιν ἀθλητῶν γένους, and Dem. *de corona* 61, παρὰ γὰρ τοῖς Ἕλλησιν, οὔ τισιν ἀλλ᾽ ἅπασιν ὁμοίως, φορὰν προδοτῶν καὶ δωροδόκων καὶ θεοῖς ἐχθρῶν cυνέβη γενέcθαι. E. Fraenkel remarks also that in both oratory and tragedy speeches often open with a formula like Moschion's, πολλά or πολλοί being opposed explicitly or implicitly to some other idea (*Glotta* xxxix [1961], 4).

537–9 οὐδὲν . . . **οὐδὲ** . . . **οὐ**: Cf. *Sam.* 510–11, μηδὲν . . . μήτε . . . μή.

540 οἶκον: 'Room', as probably in *Mis.* 178. Cf. the plural οἶκοι = 'house', plural like the Latin *aedes*, *Od.* xxiv. 417 and often in tragedy (LSJ s.v. I. 2). Either ἀλλ᾽ or τιν᾽ is intrusive; for examples of ἀλλά added to avoid asyndeton see J. Jackson, *Marginalia Scenica*, 103.

541 cυνεcτηκώc: 'Absorbed in thought', LSJ, but there is no real parallel. The meaning is uncertain, perhaps 'composed'. That would suit Moschion's character; he had been cravenly keeping out of his mother's way, but he restores his self-esteem by remarking how calm he was. Then he goes on to a day-dream of how his mother would bring him proposals from Glykera.

543 τοcοῦτον αὐτό: In apposition to the clause ὅτι ἥκω, 'just so much', 'so much and no more'.

550 ἐμελέτων: Similarly in *Samia* Moschion intended to practise a speech to his father (94), but failed to do so (120–6).

To guess what was contained in the gap of nearly 160 lines which are missing is extremely difficult, in spite of the fact that the sequel contains some hints. When Moschion reappears at 774 he has some reason for suspecting that Glykera is his sister, but does not know for certain. He appears to believe her to be a foundling. Further he may know himself to be a foundling. This follows from two passages. First, when he overhears Glykera say (786) that she had been exposed along with a brother, he seizes on this as answering one of the questions in his mind; clearly, if he knows himself and Glykera to be foundlings and suspects that Glykera is his sister, the information that Glykera was exposed along with a boy makes it more likely that they are in fact brother and sister. If this interpretation is correct, by τὴν ἐμὴν τεκοῦcαν μητέρα (775) he must mean, not Myrrhine, but his real mother. Secondly, it appears that the enumeration by Glykera of certain objects possessed by her brother (if Sudhaus's restoration of 815 ff. is on the right lines) finally convinces him that he is that brother. These objects are of such a nature that they would hardly have been preserved by a young man, unless thought to be tokens of some kind. Since there is no reason for supposing Moschion to have known himself to be a foundling when the play begins (see 150 n.), we may suppose that the knowledge of his origin and the tokens that went with it had come into his possession at some time after his leaving the stage at 352. He must also after that point have been informed that Glykera was a foundling, and have been led to entertain the suspicion that she was his sister.

At first sight it might be thought that all this had transpired before Moschion's monologue beginning at 526, and that it accounts for his expressions of despair. Gomme objected, with some plausibility, that there is no reason to assume that Menander used a long monologue to recount Moschion's discoveries and suspicions, when they could have been put more effectively into a dramatic scene between him and his mother. Accordingly he supposed that Moschion's despair at the beginning of his monologue is due, not to his hopes' having been destroyed through the possibility that Glykera is his sister, but simply to the fact that events have delayed the prosecution of his amour. When he calls himself the unhappiest man in Greece, that is no more than an extravagant *façon de parler*. This reconstruction may be correct, but cannot be regarded as certain. We are, to be sure, not bound to assume that Moschion's discoveries were put in a monologue, but equally we are not bound to deny it. Monologues were not objected to in principle by Menander, for whom they were an accepted dramatic convention, and he may have thought that a monologue here (we know of no others in the play) would lend variety and offer an actor the opportunity of displaying his skill. One may compare the long speech in *Samia* 206–82, where Demeas recounts to the audience how he had learnt some facts and come to harbour suspicions. Moreover, it might not have been easy to find a plausible excuse for bringing Myrrhine into the street to make her revelations.

Whatever the truth may be, whether Moschion got his information in a scene acted on the stage or recounted the manner of his getting it, it is a puzzle to guess how this step in the plot was motivated. Gomme, as has been said, supposed a scene between him and Myrrhine, and imagined that it proceeded somewhat as follows. 'Myrrhine tells him decidedly that Glykera is virtuous and respectable. Moschion protests that he means rightly by her, that he is seriously in love. But she insists that Glykera is not for him. "But why is she not for me?" "She hinted at something that makes it impossible. She is a foundling." "Oh, a foundling!" "Don't despise foundlings, Moschion; you are one yourself. Yes, I adopted you when you were a baby. I was told you had a sister who was exposed with you. I don't know what became of her; but Glykera hinted something—it is not certain—but I wondered; perhaps she was that sister?" Thus Moschion's arguments and protestations led him to the discovery of the unwelcome truth.'

Webster (*StM* 13), taking the view that Myrrhine did not appear on the stage, makes Moschion get his information from two sources. First, in a scene with Daos he learns that the latter had heard Glykera swear to Myrrhine that she would tell no one of her relationship to him; secondly, he consults his father, who has returned from the country, and learns from him that he is a foundling.

Gilbert Murray in his *Rape of the Locks* avoided all complications: Myrrhine of her own accord tells Moschion that Glykera is her daughter and his sister.

Körte's final view was that Myrrhine told her son that Glykera was not to be regarded as a light woman; she was of citizen birth and a foundling. She added that he too was a foundling, and gave him his birth-tokens. This seems to me as likely a reconstruction as any.

ACT IV

If Act III was of average length, some 50 lines may be lost at the beginning of this act, enough to contain another scene. Where our text resumes, Pataikos, who was last seen entering Polemon's house, is found in conversation with Glykera. To meet her, he must have gone to Myrrhine's, but this he could have done either at the end of Act III or early in Act IV. In the former case the interval would cover the earlier part of his supposed talk with her, as that between Acts IV and V of *Dyskolos* covers the earlier part of talk between Sostratos and Kallippides. A scene in which Polemon urged Pataikos to plead for him could be more easily accommodated in Act IV, but no such scene need have been represented; it could have been implied by a line or two from Pataikos. We must resign ourselves to ignorance and the reflection that, however Menander developed his plot, it was probably not in a way that anyone would now think of.

(i) **708–760**: *Pataikos, Glykera, Doris* (enters 754)

708: Glykera is defending herself against an imputation of having pursued Moschion into his mother's house. Körte suggests that this conversation was supposed to have begun inside the house, and that she and Pataikos entered the stage in the middle of it. This is not unlikely, as Menander often managed a dispute in this way, giving only one side of it, the other being understood (e.g. *Dysk.* 784 ff.; *Epitr.* 714 ff., 1062 ff.; W. Görler, *Μενάνδρου Γνῶμαι*, 78). Glykera and Pataikos will conclude their conversation outside the house, instead of indoors, not for any naturalistic reason, but for the audience's benefit. One may compare the scene between Pamphile and Smikrines, *Epitr.* 714 ff.

708 ff.: Many modern writers testify to the vivid impression made by Glykera; it is remarkable that it rests mainly on the following 18 mutilated lines. Her words come tumbling out in a flood of remonstrance, yet she clearly grasps the arguments that prove her conduct to show her innocence and the falsity of the suspicions to which it had given rise. Her indignation at being misjudged and still more at the treatment received from Polemon, which she regards as unforgiveable, are excellently portrayed. The self-respect and self-confidence (749) with which in the subsequent surviving fragment she rejects Pataikos' attempt at mediation prove to be the medium to the play's happy ending. Her refusal to return to Polemon necessitates her asking Pataikos' assistance in recovering her birth-tokens; he thus sees them, recognizes them, and finds that she is his daughter.

709 οὐ σκοπεῖς; Körte follows von Arnim and others in writing οὐ, σκοπεῖς, ἵνα. Parenthetic σκοπεῖς is, however, not paralleled. σκοπεῖν is not equivalent to ὁρᾶν, but means 'look into', 'inquire', as in the familiar phrases ἂν σκοπῇς, 'if you look into it', and σκόπει, 'consider'. Here οὐ σκοπεῖς may be the main verb on which the preceding words depend: e.g. 'are you not asking yourself what I could hope to gain by introducing myself into my lover's house?' Otherwise, if the words stand alone, as suggested by C's punctuation before and probably after them, they must mean 'don't you ask yourself that?', with reference to the same question.

710 κατ' ἐμὲ γάρ: 'He is quite in the same station of life as me', words intended to be taken as sarcastic, conveying their opposite. Moschion is apparently the son of rich parents, she is a foundling, without any fortune, seemingly a soldier's cast-off. But the sentence appeals to the Greek love of dramatic irony; although Glykera expects Pataikos to understand her to be somewhat bitterly contrasting her status and that of Moschion, she knows that in fact her words are literally true—κατ' ἐμὲ γέγονεν, Moschion was born in the same station as herself.

711 ἀλλ' οὐ τοῦτο: Note the rhetorical, argumentative style. This is ever-present in Greek; frequent in Euripides (from whom comedy learnt so much), kept well in control by Menander. Cf. *Sam.* 616 ff., *Epitr.* 718 ff., above all *Pap. Didot* I (if that is his). The rhetoric of Daos and Syriskos in *Epitr.* is conscious parody, which is something quite different: we smile or laugh at it, we are not meant to be moved by it.   **ἑταίραν:** 'To be his mistress'. Glykera does not mean a relationship like that she had with Polemon, with whom she had set up house, but a more casual, passing affair. The existence of such affairs was openly recognized in Greece, but it was not considered proper, at Athens at least, to carry them on inside the family house.

712–14 εἶτ' οὐ λαθεῖν κτλ.: 'Then should I not have done all I could to conceal the affair from the family (τούτους = Myrrhine and her husband), and he too the same? But (you suppose that) he recklessly established me under his father's roof?' Glykera's indignation causes her sentence to be a little disconnected.   **τάλαν:** See *Epitr.* 434 n.

κατέστης': Might in itself be third person, as translated above, or first, με being used instead of ἐμαυτήν, cf. Eur. *Andr.* 256, ἐκδώσω μέ cοι, K–G, i. § 454 n. 8. But the pronoun ἐγώ in the second clause suggests a change of subject, and the resultant chiasmus of 712–14 (Glykera, Moschion :: Moschion, Glykera) suits the rhetorical style.

Are we to suppose from this that Myrrhine's husband had in fact come home in the gap after 550, or is Glykera merely envisaging an expected return that would have resulted in her being under the same roof with her lover's (supposed) father? Wilamowitz, *Schiedsgericht*, 140 n. 1, confesses himself puzzled, but denies that Myrrhine's husband can be at home at this point. Yet there is some likelihood that Daos' fear that his master might return from the country (364) was more than a passing thought, and was a dramatic preparation for an actual return, which would certainly have created complications that might help to fill the long gap at the end of Act III.

715–18: Supplements here are far from certain, but in 715 editors seem to be on the right lines with ἔχθραν τε πρά[ττειν Μυρρίνῃ], 'promote a feeling of hatred in Myrrhine'.

In 716 ὑμῖν θ' ὑπόνοιαν καταλιπεῖν [ἀκοςμίας] (Körte) makes good sense; ὑμῖν will mean Pataikos and his household, 'leave you with a suspicion of misbehaviour', the misbehaviour being perhaps not only Glykera's but also that of Moschion's parents, suspected of conniving at the affair. This will be more readily intelligible if Pataikos is a neighbour of Myrrhine's and Polemon's.

In 717 C must be interpreted as giving ἣν ἐξαλείψαιτ' οὐκέτι, and editors have accepted this, keeping silence about any doubts they may have felt. It must be supposed to mean, as some translators think, 'which you could never efface (from your minds)'. But this would require ἄν with the optative, and one would expect οὐδέποτε, not οὐκέτι. Gomme, arguing that it is more likely that Glykera should say that *she* could never efface the suspicion than that the others would not, very hesitantly suggested emending to read ὑμῖν δ' ὑπόνοιαν καταλιπεῖν [ἣν οὐδαμῶς] ἣν ἐξαλείψασθ' οὐδέποτ'; for the middle ἐξαλείφομαι cf. Eur. *Hec.* 589–90, πάθος | οὐκ ἂν δυναίμην ἐξαλείψασθαι φρενός. (The broken anapaest could be justified by the elision, cf. 178 γινόμεν', ἐκπέπομφέ με. Perhaps with an excess of metrical scruple, he thought of substituting οὔποτ' for οὐδέποτ'. Although this form is found mainly in epic and tragedy there are occurrences in comic fragments, where, however, it is impossible to be sure of the tone— parody of elevated style might be involved.) As an alternative he suggested καταλιπεῖν [ἀκοσμίας] ἣν ἐξαλείψετ' οὐκέτι, assuming the familiar confusion of αι and ε, which is, however, not paralleled in C. This is a simple cure for the grammatical fault, but leaves a strange order of words; why should not Menander have written ἣν οὐκέτ' ἐξαλείψετε? Perhaps he did; mistakes in word-order are fairly common in C. Then οὐκέτι could be explained as indicating idiomatically that, although suspicions of improper behaviour might be suppressed so long as Moschion kept a mistress elsewhere, there would no longer be any possibility of effacing them once she had been brought under the family roof.

Another possibility to be reckoned with is that Pataikos is related to Myrrhine or her husband, and that Glykera means that suspicion of misbehaviour would have attached to the whole family group (ὑμῖν). Unfortunately our ignorance of Pataikos' position and the mutilation of the text make it quite impossible to reach any firm conclusion on this line.

οὐδ' αἰσχύνομαι: '(I act thus) and show no shame?' This seems more likely than οὐδ' αἰσχύνεται, sc. Polemon (Sudhaus), 'he is not ashamed to tell you such a cock-and-bull story'. But οὐδέ is difficult; after the positive εἱλόμην the correct connective would be καὶ οὐ. Perhaps οὐδέ here introduces an indignant question, cf. *Aspis* 415, οὐδὲ παύσεται; Ar. *Knights* 1302, οὐδὲ πυνθάνεσθε ταῦτα; Otherwise one must suppose an anacoluthon, illogically due to the influence of the immediately preceding negative word οὐκέτι.

723: The final letter partially preserved is more probably χ than λ, which makes likely Sudhaus's restoration, suggested by Eur. frag. 265 (from *Auge*), τὸ δ' ἀδίκημ' ἐγένετ' οὐχ ἑκούςιον. Even a deliberate action done under a misapprehension about material circumstances, as was Polemon's, might be regarded by the Greeks as 'involuntary', cf. Aristotle, *EN* 1110ᵇ18, τὸ δὲ δι' ἄγνοιαν οὐχ ἑκούςιον μὲν ἅπαν ἐςτίν.

724–5: Körte, modifying a suggestion of Sudhaus, prints ἀνόςιον δὲ χοῖον ἂν οὐδ' ἂν, τάλαν, θεράπαιναν ἐργάςαιτό τις; possibly the right sense, but far from certainly so.

In the missing lines Glykera's indignation with Pataikos must have moderated. When the fragments resume she is telling him, with the intention of engaging his assistance, that she possesses some tokens of her parentage.

742–3: Van Leeuwen restored ἐγὼ παρ' αὐτῆς (sc. the old woman of the prologue) λαμβάνω γνωρίςματα | τοὐμοῦ πατρὸς καὶ μητρός, ἐκέλευςεν δ' ἔχειν κτλ., Sudhaus ἐγὼ δ' ἐκεῖνα λαμβάνω τὰ χρήματα | τοὐμοῦ πατρὸς καὶ μητρός, εἴθιςμαι δ' ἔχειν κτλ., Körte, taking elements from both the foregoing, ἐγὼ δ' ἐκεῖν' ἐλάμβανον γνωρίςματα | τοὐμοῦ πατρὸς καὶ μητρός, εἴθιςμαι δ' ἔχειν κτλ.

745–6: ἀπέγνωκας ςὺ γάρ: Cf. *Sam.* 484, ἀπεγνωκώς με τυγχάνεις, Dem. vi. 16, ἀπεγίγνωςκε Θηβαίους and (if genuine) *epist.* ii. 17, οὐ γὰρ ἀπεγνωκὼς ὑμᾶς. γάρ seems preferable to γε (Jensen). To Pataikos' question, Glykera gives no answer—in her heart she has not altogether given up Polemon. In spite of the absence of a paragraphus it seems likely that Pataikos' speech begins after ταῦτα, since there is no dicolon after ἄνθρωπον, and τί βούλει; must be his.

747 διὰ ςοῦ: 'By your agency'.

748: A possible alternative to the text in OCT is πραχθήςεται (τοῦτό γε γελοῖον.) ἀλλὰ κτλ. or πραχθήςεται τοῦτό γε. γελοῖον· ἀλλά (Arnott). Why does Pataikos call the request ridiculous? It is a very natural one. He must wish to imply that it is absurd of Glykera to refuse conciliation and to send for her belongings. ὑπέρ = περί, cf. 523 n.

751 καλεςάτω τις: To whom is this order addressed? Have some of Myrrhine's servants come out with Pataikos and Glykera? Or are some of Polemon's sitting outside his door?

753–4: C is here not only mutilated but also corrupt, so that restoration is difficult. The doubtful letter after λόγος was read by Jensen as χ, but subsequently by Lefebvre as δ or λ. Since this copyist does not normally write *voces nihili*, the latter was probably right. If δεγω (i.e. δ' ἐγώ) was originally written, the following λέγω may be a correction. λόγουϲ λέγειν is a favourite phrase with Menander (*Dysk.* 822, *Epitr.* 566, 1066, *Sik.* 99, ? frag. 552, *Pap. Didot* I. 1), so that I favour ἐφ᾽ οἷϲ λόγοιϲ νυνὶ λέγω. The general sense is probably 'be reconciled on the terms that I now propose'. νυνί may refer to something in the gap before 742, or to a proposal that Pataikos is on the point of making, but which the appearance of Doris interrupts.

754–60: Doris' distress is at her mistress's misfortunes (van Leeuwen), and serves to emphasize Glykera's own courage. Like M. Hombert, *Revue belge de philologie et histoire* vi (1927), 26, I see no evidence to support the view that when inspecting Glykera's finery Pataikos had removed (under what pretext?) either the box in which the *crepundia* were kept (Gomme) or some piece of embroidery (Körte), and that Doris has already discovered and now laments the loss. It is easier (although possibly false) to suppose that Pataikos had looked absent-mindedly at Glykera's belongings, but now when he learns that among them were tokens of identity, he remembers that something, seen in Polemon's house, was very like his memory of what had been put out with his own children when they were exposed. For that reason he must now have asked to see Glykera's tokens, a thing which he would have had no cause to do but for his kindness in humouring Polemon in the previous act (525).

756: It is not certain what Doris is sent to fetch, the mention of which, on the assumptions of the preceding note, excites Pataikos' interest. Some have supposed a box (τὴν κιϲτίδ᾽ or τὴν κοιτίδ᾽), Körte (with unwise economy) the only thing that is later described, i.e. an embroidered garment (τὴν ξυϲτίδ᾽), quoting Harpokration, ξυϲτίϲ . . . γυναικεῖόν τι ἔνδυμά (cf. 519) ἐϲτιν πεποικιλμένον. τὰ ποικίλα would then have to mean 'embroideries'; but its only known sense, 'embroidered or figured cloths or clothes' (C. Dedoussi, Χάριϲ Βουρβέρη 289), is in favour of the problematical article's being a box, such as plays a part in the recognition scenes of the *Rudens, Eunuchus,* and *Cistellaria.*

760 ἄπιϲτον οὖν: Körte's supplement, for which he compares frag. 466, οὐκ ἔϲτ᾽ ἄπιϲτον οὐδὲν ἐν θνητῷ βίῳ is more likely than that of Sudhaus, ἄελπτον οὖν, which introduces a word of poetic colouring, (see LSJ).

In the very short lacuna Pataikos may have said e.g. 'I believe I have seen the garment in that box before', but there is no need to suppose this; an alert audience would realize that to be his thought, even though it was not expressed. Doris returned, and Pataikos and Glykera began to look at an embroidered piece of stuff.

(ii) **768–827**: *Pataikos, Glykera, Moschion* (enters 774)

768 ὃν καὶ τότ' εἶδον: A figure embroidered on or woven in the cloth; this figure he had seen when Polemon had shown him Glykera's possessions (τότε). For elaborate woven figures among birth-tokens cf. Eur. *Ion* 1417 ff. (Gorgon and snakes).

772 τῆς γυναικὸς κτλ.: Spoken to himself, or half to himself. ποικίλματα (Dedoussi) is probably not too long, ὑφάσματα (printed by Körte) certainly too short.

774–6: Pataikos falls silent, overcome by memories and surmises; while the old man pauses, Moschion enters, whether from Myrrhine's house or from the town we do not know, owing to the gap between 550 and 708, but the latter is more likely, since if he had been in her house, he would probably have known that Glykera and Pataikos had recently gone outside. He talks to himself, uttering his reflections. For the interpretation of Moschion's part in this scene, see Gomme, *CQ* xxx (1936), 68, importantly modified *ibid.* 193. If it has been correctly maintained in 551 n. that Moschion has been told that he is a foundling, it is necessary to restore οὐ τῶν ἀδυνάτων, not ἐν τῶν ἀδυνάτων (for which cf. [Dem.] lx. 1, Arist. *de caelo* 271ᵇ4) in 774.

776: Jensen read ἐφθαρμ', and the last four letters are strongly suggested by the facsimile; but Wilcken doubted whether the traces suited φθ.

779 ff.: From this line, at any rate to the intervention of Moschion at 824, the scene is written in the style of serious drama. Not only are there phrases borrowed from Euripides (notably 788, 809), but the versification is that of tragedy; caesura and 'Porson's Law' are observed and, with the possible exception of 783, anapaests excluded from all feet but the first. Resolution of long syllables is infrequent by comparison with what is normal in comedy. There are passages of stichomythia, which has the result that some half-lines (780, 785, 799, 805) are, in the manner of tragic stichomythia, no more than padding. Even outside the stichomythia there is a tendency for end of verse and clause to coincide. Körte in his original publication of this scene rightly said, after calling attention to these features, that Menander was deliberately approaching tragic style as closely as the limits of comedy allowed. He was less adequate in explaining this by saying that the recognition-scene was a device borrowed from tragedy. That is too simple, too mechanical an explanation. Menander wanted this crisis of his play to be taken seriously, wanted his audience to share his characters' excitement and joy.

But one may also believe, if modern experience is any guide, that the audience might be touched by the emotional level of a scene such as this, and yet not take it entirely seriously; feel with the characters, yet be amused by an incongruity between their poetic diction and their familiar everyday background. I am not convinced, as Gomme was, that there can be no question of parody. 788 must call to mind a line from Euripides' well-known play *Melanippe the Wise*, ἐπεὶ δ' ἐχωρίσθηcαν ἀλλήλων δίχα (frag. 484. 3), where it was applied to the cosmological separation of heaven and earth, and its transference to the human separation of twin babies must be intended to raise a smile. But perhaps more important is the presence throughout of Moschion, more obvious to the spectator than the reader. He is a figure who has never been taken seriously, and five colloquial lines from him, in comic metre, immediately precede and contrast with the opening of the stichomythia. The fact that he is eavesdropping on the exchanges is a constant reminder that they are being conducted in language that is not that of the workaday world to which he belongs. But the element of parody is restrained, there is none of the gross absurdity that an Aristophanes would have introduced.

Scenes of the recognition of lost children by means of tokens were common: they occurred in *Sikyonios*, in Plautus' *Cistellaria*, *Rudens*, *Vidularia*, and probably in *Pap. Ant.* 15. It was natural that a dramatist should look for some new way of composing them. Here in *Perikeiromene* Menander has been bold in introducing the recognition by a half-serious half-comic passage in stichomythia. But the contrast with the rest of the play may be too abrupt, too startling to be satisfactory. It must, of course, be remembered that different ages have different requirements as regards homogeneity of style. A prose-writer of the classical period, whether in Greek or Latin, would have regarded as barbarous our habit of verbatim quotation, whereas the audience of New Comedy may have liked elevated recognition-scenes. The fragment of such a scene in *Sikyonios* (280 ff.) has a touch of tragic style; yet its manner does not differ, so far as can be judged, so sharply from that of the rest of the play as does this scene in *Perikeiromene*. I have discussed the problem in *Entretiens Hardt* 1969, 126–8.

779 ὦ Ζεῦ τίν': The restoration is as good as certain, since the traces do not allow of ε]cτιν. The recognition of the *crepundia* does not prove that the children had also survived. Pataikos asks, 'what now is still existing of my family?'

780: τε joins τοῦτο πυνθάνου to [πέραι]ν' ὃ βούλει, cf. 128 n.

783–4: Moschion addresses himself, with the advice to draw back. He does not wish to interrupt the conversation that may bring him news of his own position. Körte prints ὡc ῥοθ[ίῳ] τ[ινὶ] ἤ[κ]ω τύχης εἰc καιρὸν οἰκείαc [ἐγώ. This should be an exclamation, preceded by a full stop; it cannot be a clause dependent on ἐπάναγε cαυτόν, for the change from second to first person would be awkward. The metaphor of ῥόθιον (breaking wave, surf) is not very obviously fitted to the context, since Moschion has not come like a rushing wave, but may be possible; the fifth-foot anapaest involved is, however, contrary to the metrical practice of tragedy, generally followed in this scene. Yet Moschion may be less deeply committed to tragic metre than the other two: in 787 he uses the non-tragic form τουτί.

The letter τ (of τινι), given by Körte as certain, is doubtful. Jensen recorded τ, Sudhaus said he 'thought he glimpsed the head of an ε', and the facsimile shows that any trace must be minimal.

Arnott, *CQ* N.s. xviii (1968), 238, has a useful discussion, but I do not find convincing his suggestion ὡc ῥόθῳ τινὶ ἦλω ('you jumped') τύχης εἰc καιρὸν οἰκείαc cφόδρα, 'Move back a little, for you gave an impetuous surging start at the moment when your personal fortune became involved.' Nowhere else in this scene does Moschion use such poetic language.

787: Körte originally doubted the possibility of ἔν μοι τῶν ἐμοί and suggested ἔτι for ἐμοί, a change Gomme tended to favour. But emphatic ἐμοί is good: Moschion's interest is in his own problems. The present tense of ζητουμένων is in point; his inquiries are still proceeding.

789: Gomme suggested emending coι to coῦ. 'I *might* tell that when I have heard *your* whole story; but ask me first about myself.' There does not seem, however, to be anything against C's text.

791 αὐτῇ: Whom does Glykera mean? Körte originally thought it was the old woman who had found her: he argued that she would have promised Myrrhine that the boy's origin should be concealed, and therefore have sworn Glykera to secrecy. But Glykera's silence was in the prologue put down, not to any oath, but to her generous desire not to hurt Moschion; moreover there is no reason why the old woman should now be in Glykera's mind, every reason why Myrrhine should be. In his last edition (p. xxxiv) Körte seems to think that Myrrhine is meant.

792 cύccημον: A word used by Aeneas Tacticus in the sense 'signal'; the Atticist Phrynichos, 393, pedantically stigmatizes its use by Menander as κίβδηλον ('false coin'). The word, correctly formed to mean 'corroboratively significant', is none the worse for appearing in no other Attic author.   τῇ μητρί: This must be 'to my (supposed) mother'.

796 μνημόνευμα: Although found in Aristotle and late prose, the word may have tragic associations, as it occurs in Moschion frag. 6. 33 Nauck. The historic present λέγει is formal rather than colloquial.

797 καὶ τόπον γ': This is the simplest way of restoring metre; the combination καὶ . . . γε, 'yes, and . . .', is common in all styles; καὶ . . . δέ, adopted by Körte, is not very frequent in verse, and some critics have even tried to exclude it from tragedy, Denniston, *GP* 157.

798, 800 ὁ τιθείς: The imperfect participle (Goodwin, *MT* § 140); line 800 is the equivalent of ἐτίθει μὲν παῖς, τρέφειν δ᾿ ὤκνουν ἐγώ. 'The man who exposed you was a slave.'

799 εἰ θέμις, κἀμοὶ φράσον: Not only a 'filling' (see 768 above), but θέμις belongs to the language of tragedy (Antiphanes frag. 89 K is high-flown). Similarly ἐκλείπει βίον (803) is tragic, e.g. Soph. *El.* 1131, also πότμου (804, if rightly restored).

798 εἴρηκε: Chantraine, *Le Parfait grec*, 182, notes the contrast with the banal narrative aorist εἶπε of 797; he claims that the perfect is more emotional. It does not leave the man's report in the past, but makes it operative for Pataikos in the immediate present. Two good examples of the pointed alternation of aorist and perfect are Soph. *Ajax* 1142 εἶδον, 1150 ὄπωπα, *Antigone* 442 δεδρακέναι, 443 δρᾶσαι.

801: To break the line, as Körte and van Leeuwen do, into two questions gives a lively effect, but it may exaggerate Glykera's surprise and add an unwarranted tone of reproof.

805: Körte, although reading ταλαγ[, follows Jensen in printing τὸ λανθάνον, but this is hardly credible; τὸ λανθάνον is not 'what I have yet to learn'. Wilcken's τάλαιν' ἐγώ, if it suits the traces, is more likely. Exclamatory τάλαν would not suit the tragic style.

806 βίον: A *good* livelihood, as in Eur. *Supp.* 450, κτᾶσθαι πλοῦτον καὶ βίον τέκνοις, frag. 198, εἰ δ᾿ εὐτυχῶν τις καὶ βίον κεκτημένος.

808 τὴν ναῦν: Pataikos may have been the owner either of the ship or of the cargo or of both, or again he may have lent all his capital to the owner. A merchant who owned his one ship would be accounted a well-to-do man by the modest standard of the Greeks (ὡς τὰ παρ᾿ ἡμῖν, Solon said to Croesus, Hdt. i. 30. 4). These conditions remained unchanged, practically, in the Mediterranean till the sixteenth century, cf. *The Merchant of Venice*, Act I, sc. i. 177–9: 'Thou know'st that all my fortunes are at sea; Neither have I money, nor commodity To raise a present sum.'

809: Cf. Poseidon's words in Eur. *Tro.* 88, ταράξω πέλαγος Αἰγαίας ἁλός.

810–12 ἐφόλκια: The division of the line between speakers marks the beginning of a less tense section of this scene. Although the metre remains that of tragedy, there is nothing elevated about the language. ἐφόλκιον is the small boat that was towed behind a Greek merchant-man at sea; figuratively ἐφόλκια are 'dependent burdens'. Euripides used the synonymous ἐφολκίς similarly; Andromache speaks (*Andr.* 200) of possible bastards as ἀθλίαν ἐφολκίδα, cf. *HF* 631, ἄξω λαβών γε τούσδ' ἐφολκίδας χεροῖν, ναῦς δ' ὡς ἐφέλξω. In Leonidas, *AP* vii. 67, the Cynic Diogenes, speaking to Charon, says that his ἐφόλκια ('impedimenta') are his staff, his scrip, his cloak, and the obol for his fare.

Gomme held that ἐφόλκια is the predicate and that τρόπον is used adverbially, translating: 'I thought that for a poor man to bring up children would be a drag: I was a fool to think so.' In favour of this it is to be noted that ἄβουλος, like ἀγνώμων, may connote lack of feeling, and in particular failure of paternal feeling, Soph. *Trach.* 140, *Electra* 546, where Clytemnestra asks of Agamemnon's conduct to Iphigeneia, οὐ ταῦτ' ἀβούλου καὶ κακοῦ γνώμην πατρός; Yet it seems more likely that ἐφόλκια is a description of the children than of the business of rearing them, and Menander may not use τρόπον elsewhere to mean 'in the manner of' (270 n.). τρόπος meaning 'character', 'mode of behaviour' is, on the contrary, frequent. The probable sense is: 'I thought that for a beggar to bring up children who would be a drag on him, was the conduct of a man completely ill-advised.'

ἡγησάμην δή: It is of some importance to decide the force of δή here. What is the emotional emphasis it gives to the verb? Is it indignant, 'forsooth', or explanatory, 'you see', or even 'of course'? If the latter, Pataikos replies to Glykera's cry of self-pity with a justification of his action; if the former, he admits a mistake. Choice between the alternatives may be determined by the view taken of the disputed question whether it was a common practice in the late fourth century not to rear unwanted children (intro. pp. 34–5). Would the audience most naturally regard Pataikos' decision as what was to be expected, or as foolish and pusillanimous?

813–14: Restoration here is very doubtful: to the end of this fragment the ink has faded even since the discovery of the parchment; and it is impossible to check what Körte, Wilcken, Sudhaus, and Jensen claim to have seen. None of the suggestions yet made are convincing. Clearly the sense of 813 cannot be recovered with certainty; but somewhere in 813–14 Pataikos inquired about other γνωρίσματα that had been exposed along with the embroidery.

815 διάλιθος: 'Set with stones', as in *Epitr.* 386, frag. 437. Other suggested words, κατάλιθος and ἀνάγλυφος, are first found in the Septuagint.

817–19: Sudhaus's brilliant restorations, although not absolutely certain even as regards the sense, are very probable: Glykera's use of the past tense in mentioning the articles shows that they are not in her possession; δηλαδή always indicates a surmise, and the surmise that her brother had the missing things is most likely; moreover if Moschion did in fact possess them, their enumeration would give him the required proof that he was Glykera's brother and Pataikos' son.

822 οὔκουν cυνῆκαc; A dicolon at the end of 821 is probable, one after cυνῆκαc is possible; the words are therefore better not given to Glykera. Jensen, Allinson, and Körte, writing οὐκοῦν, give them to Moschion, in whose mouth they seem to be addressed to Pataikos: 'Ah, you recognized *that*?', the solution favoured by Gomme. But cυνίημι will hardly bear this sense. It is better to write οὔκουν and take the words as a question put by Moschion to himself. 'Don't you understand?' sc. that this evidence clinches my paternity. Denniston, *GP* 431–5, concludes that interrogative οὐκοῦν is very rare outside Plato and Xenophon and that οὔκουν should probably always be written in oratory and drama.

822: Sudhaus's probable supplement δ[ιάφαν]έc τε χ[λανί]διον is based on Ar. *Lys.* 48, διαφανῆ χιτωνία. A χλανίc was an upper garment, cloak or mantle, worn by both sexes, and of fine manufacture. One so thin as to be transparent would be elegant rather than practical.

823: Jensen's νῦν seems to be too short for the space, but his claim to have read ειρηκαc[.]ι is probably more trustworthy than Petersen's ειρημενα. If εἰρημένα is correct, πάντα καθ' ἐν εἰρημένα could as appropriately be given to Pataikos as to Glykera.   **χρυcῆ τε μίτρα:** The first syllable of μίτρα would normally be short in comedy; it may here be lengthened according to the rules of tragic scansion (cf. *Mis.* 214 n., *Epitr.* 324 n.), but since the emotional temperature has fallen, as is indicated by the increasing number of resolved feet and the end of stichomythia, this is a doubtful explanation, and it may be right to transpose to read μίτρα τε χρυcῆ (van Herwerden). μίτρα can mean either 'belt' or, more commonly, 'head-band'. Whichever object is here intended, it will not have been of solid gold, but brilliant with gold-leaf or gold-thread.

824–5: In the first half of 824 Pataikos, satisfied that the *crepundia* of Glykera and her brother tally at all points with those of his own children, holds back no longer, but embraces his new-found daughter. καθέξω intrans., cf. Hdt. vi. 129, οὐκέτι κατέχειν δυνάμενος εἶπε, Soph.

OT 781, τὴν μὲν οὖcαν ἡμέραν μόλιc κατέcχον. The four-letter gap after φιλτάτ[η] can be filled with χαῖρ', which is the standard word in a scene of recognition, *Mis.* 213, *Epitr.* 860, Eur. *Ion* 561; *salue* in Latin adaptations, Plautus, *Rudens* 1172, 'contineri quin complectar non queo; filia mea, salue', *Menaechmi* 1124, *Poenulus* 1259, *Epidicus* 558, 649.

825–6: Sudhaus and Körte agree that the note μοc′ in the right margin belongs to 824, not 825 (as Jensen would have it). There is no good reason for supposing it to be mistaken or misplaced. But no satisfactory reconstruction of Moschion's speech has been suggested. The lines seem to be beyond recall. In the latter part Körte reports μ......α.ῦο and Jensen μ.........ῦο. Both these editors write εἰ δ' ἐγὼ [ἄπειμ]ι, τί προcέχεcθέ μ[οι; (which I find unintelligible), followed by [τὸν δι]άλο[γον] πάρειμι τοῦτον πά[ντα παρακούc]α[c] (or πα[ραλαβὼν ἄπ]α[ντ']) ἐγώ. I hesitantly suggest εἰ δ' ἐγώ (sc. τούτου υός εἰμι)— κἀμοὶ τί προcέχεcθ' ἐμποδών; τὸν διάλογον κτλ., 'why shouldn't they embrace me too?' Cf. Plaut. *Poenulus* 1262, 'quis me amplectetur postea?', spoken by Agorastocles as Hanno embraces his long-lost daughters.

827 ὦ θεοί: If θεοί has, as in 807, the usual disyllabic scansion of comedy, this line must start a scene in trochaic tetrameters. It may, however, exhibit tragic synizesis, so that the scene continues to have a paratragic flavour. I see no way of deciding, but feel that a lively scene in trochaics would both suit the intervention of the rather ridiculous character Moschion and provide an admirable contrast with the previous comparatively serious recognition-scene. ὦ θεοί is not common in comedy, being outside this scene used in the extant remains of Menander only by Habrotonon in *Epitr.* (see there 484 n.). Nor, although this may be accident, does it anywhere else express real astonishment, its commonest use being to give emphasis, as twice in *Epitr.* and e.g. Antiphanes frag. 58 K, καλὰ δῆτ', ὦ θεοί, frag. 163 K, ἐπαγωγόν, ὦ θεοί, frag. 183 K, λιπαράc, ὦ θεοί. I see no way of being certain who speaks 827 init., Glykera or Pataikos. Of course Glykera is acquainted with Moschion, but for all we know Pataikos may be also. Either could say these words as they break from their embrace, before there is time to recognize the interrupter, cf. *Epitr.* 942.

ACT V

The gap before the next (and last) fragment is of uncertain length. It may be supposed to have included a large part of Act V as well as the end of Act IV, since the fragment appears to come from near the end of the play. From the first to the last surviving verses of Act IV there were 120 lines; if 40 lines are lost at the beginning of that act, and Acts IV and V contained between them 400 lines, the gap might amount to about 150 lines, the majority of which would, if the division were an equal one, belong to Act V. It is unlikely that the missing lines are fewer than 100, even if these last two acts were, as in *Dyskolos*, shorter than the average. I have allowed in the numeration for the loss of 150 lines.

Gomme reconstructed the plot as follows: 'It is not too fanciful to suppose that in the last scene of Act IV, after the mutual embracings of Pataikos, Glykera, and Moschion, the young man turned to Glykera and explained that doubtless, now that she had discovered herself to be Pataikos' daughter and (what is more) *his* sister, she would have nothing more to do with the soldier fellow; and that it was the vanity and conceit of her brother, no less than Pataikos' genuine regard for Polemon (as well as her own suppressed inclination), that caused her to turn once more to her lover. She would realize again his worth by contrast with Moschion. Pataikos of course at once promised that she should be formally married to Polemon.' Although Gomme placed all this in Act IV, making it the longest of the play, and leaving little for Act V ('it only ties up some loose ends'), that would not be an essential part of his theory. Webster, *StM* 15, also assigns to Act IV three entirely lost scenes and to Act V little beyond what is preserved of it. In his imagined scenes the characters inform one another of what the audience already knows—not a likely hypothesis.

976–1026: The termination of each line is lost. Editions differ only slightly in choice of supplements, yet the text is less certain than this unanimity might suggest. But the doubt affects details only, not the general sense.

(i) **976–1005:** *Polemon and Doris*

976: Polemon and Doris are in conversation. The former speaks of his suicidal intent. The optative in the final clause ἵν' ἐμαυτὸν ἀπο-πνίξαιμι shows that this intent was either in the past or hypothetical. ἀποπνίγειν may mean 'drown' (*Dysk.* 668), but the context, if recovered, might show that some other form of strangulation was in Polemon's mind—'hanging', if ἀπηγχόμην is to be restored in 988.

976, 978: The ends of these lines could be filled in many ways. The common expression χωρὶς οἰκῶν suggests that χωρὶς ὤν need not necessarily be followed by a genitive.

981 ἐνλίποιμι: Attic inscriptions of all periods not infrequently fail to assimilate *v* to a following consonant in compound words (Meisterhans[3] 112), and so Menander may have written ϵνλ- here. We cannot tell, and there is no case for 'correcting' the papyrus.

981: I hesitate to adopt Weil's supplement, ὦ φίλη. Like that of Wilamowitz, it ignores the paragraphus added by the second hand below 981. The corrector can fall into error, as when he deleted the paragraphus at 1024, but it is disturbing to reject his evidence here. The difficulty in making a change of speaker is that it seems necessarily to involve abandoning the likely progression from ϵὖ to ὑπέρϵυ in one sentence. Otherwise one might write e.g. (Δω.) ϵὖ τοῦτ'. (Πο.) ἀλλὰ cὺ | ὑπέρϵυ λέγϵιc. It is possible, but unlikely, that a spot of ink below *v* of ουθϵν is the remains of a dicolon.

982 ὑπέρϵυ: Cf. ὑπέρϵυγϵ, *Aspis* 412, *Epitr.* 525, *Theoph.* 30. Polemon characteristically passes in a moment from despair to enthusiasm.

ἐλϵυθέραν . . . ἀφήcω: Striking services by slaves are in the New Comedy frequently rewarded by manumission, e.g. Trachalio in Plaut. *Rudens*, Syrus in Ter. *Adelphoe*. Doris has done nothing more than act as bringer of good news, for which Polemon promises her a reward that must seem excessive; his generosity is almost comic, but betrays the depth of his relief. For the hiatus after Δωρί, cf. *Samia* 382 n.

984 ϵἰcϵλήλυθϵ: Doris, guessing that she knows enough to satisfy Glykera, has gone in without waiting for any detailed message.

At the end Aristainetos ii. 20, ἔχϵ μϵ κατὰ κράτοc ἑλοῦcα τὸν παcὶ καὶ πάcαιc ἀνάλωτον, if a reminiscence of this passage (which is doubtful), would support a simple supplement like Sudhaus's φιλτάτη rather than the more fanciful φθονέρ' Ἔρωc (Wilamowitz). It is not, however, fully convincing; one might expect Polemon to recognize Misapprehension or Chance as his victor, if this sentence refers to what follows.   ἀλάcτωρ: Originally an evil spirit that leads men to destruction; the word came to be used of the man himself who commits a criminal folly, perhaps through an intermediate stage in which he was regarded as 'possessed' by the evil spirit, Soph. *Ajax* 373, Dem. xviii. 296, xix. 305. The Berlin Photios, p. 71. 15, seems to allege that the word had only recently been introduced into Attic speech (προcφάτωc ἦν ἐπιχωρία sc. ἡ λέξιc); but the evidence of Demosthenes is against this, and the interpretation of Photios' entry uncertain, see Körte–Thierfelder ii. pp. 294–5.   ἀπηγχόμην, 'I was for hanging myself', is a plausible supplement. καλῶc ποῶν, 'and a good thing, too', cf. *Dysk.* 629, *Mis.* 444, *Sik.* 178, Neil on Ar. *Knights* 1180.

990: The first hand of *P. Oxy.* 211 (O) used paragraphi, but not dicola, to indicate change of speaker; he also left short spaces to show pauses. The second hand, which may be contemporary, added punctuation, dicola, some names of speakers, and three stage directions, namely ἐξέρχ(εται) δωρις here, εἰcερχ(εται) πολεμων in the middle of 1003, πολε(μων) εἰcειcι at 1024; he also added some paragraphi, and bracketed some of the original ones, see 995 n.

992 ἐπεξήταζε: Gomme followed Capps in thinking this a military metaphor—'Pataikos was holding a review' and that Doris was poking fun at him. LSJ gives as an alternative 'was feasting his eyes'; Allinson has 'looked and looked'. But the simple 'was asking her further questions' (van Leeuwen) suits the situation. See Addenda.

εὐαγγέλια … θύειν: Internal acc., 'to make the good-news sacrifice', as διαβατήρια θύειν, ἐπινίκια θύειν. Sometimes internal and objective accusative are combined, e.g. Ar. *Knights* 656, εὐαγγέλια θύειν ἑκατὸν βοῦc τῇ θεῷ. Cf. also ibid. 647, ἐcτεφάνουν μ᾽ εὐαγγέλια, 'gave me the good-tidings wreath'.

995: The first hand placed a paragraphus below this verse and the next, and left a space after λέγεις. He therefore probably intended (Δω.) ὁ δὲ … μάγειρος ἔνδον ἐcτί. (Πο.) τὴν ὗν θυέτω, although there is no space after εcτι. The corrector bracketed the paragraphus below 995, and added δω(ρις) to 997. This gives the text printed in OCT.

ὁ δ᾽ … μάγειροc: The professional chef or caterer, who was hired by Athenian households to cook anything more than a simple meal. Gomme thought that his presence here was not necessarily accounted for, and that the audience might, if they liked, suppose Polemon to have retained his services from the party described at 174-6. This seems to me unlike Menander's technique, which does not leave loose ends of this kind. Moreover, if the cook came from the lunch of 174, he must have been seen to come; the door of Polemon's house was continually in view. He, and his pig, would have made a nicely comic adjunct to the siege-party at the beginning of Act III. Curiosity, a stock characteristic of the cook in comedy, might account for his following Polemon. Then the soldier, or Sosias, might have ordered him into the house. This is, of course, no more than a guess, but the presence of the cook and the pig in Polemon's house can hardly have been left unexplained. Other plays show and account for the entry of the cook, *Dysk.* 264 and 393, *Epitr.* fragments 1–5, *Mis.* 270, *Sam.* 194 and 283, Plaut. *Aul.* 280, cf. *Cas.* 720, *Men.* 219, *Merc.* 697 and 741, *Pseud.* 790; at *Aspis* 216 he appears unexpectedly *from* Chairestratos' house, but his presence there is at once accounted for.

997 κανοῦν: See *Samia* 222 n. Polemon is so impatient to get on with the sacrifice that he refuses to wait to do the ritual acts in the right order.

999 μᾶλλον δὲ κἀγώ: The sacrificer wore a garland; Polemon announces that he will not leave the sacrifice to the cook, and that as no garland has been prepared for him (it was normally among the contents of the κανοῦν), he will take one from an altar.   **πιθανώτεροc:** Presumably Doris means that he will be more likely to win Glykera over if he shows himself to be taking part in this ceremony of celebrating her good fortune. But πιθανός developed a sense something like 'attractive', see Asklepiades, *AP* v. 53, 158, (with Gow's note, *Hellenistic Epigrams,* ii p. 120) and perhaps Plut. *Phoc.* 3, οὐ πιθανὸν ἔcχε τῷ ὄχλῳ ἦθοc.   **γοῦν** 'introduces a *pro tanto* reason for following a suggested course', Denniston, *GP* 452. The late position of the word is unusual, but may be on the model of postponed γάρ. The second hand wrote ν above φ and ηc above γ, wishing to read πιθανώτεροc πολλῶν ἂν εἴηc (or possibly φανείηc). This is presumably a variant reading from some other MS.; its sense is poor.

1003 τί γὰρ πάθῃ τιc: 'What can happen now?' this is the equivalent of τί γὰρ πάθω;, τιc being substituted, as 'one' sometimes is in English, for the first person singular, cf. *Dysk.* 517, ἐφ' ἑτέραν θύραν ἔλθῃ τιc; If we accept a supplement like δεῦρ' ὅ τε πατήρ, γάρ must be understood as explaining the alarmed *tone* of αὐτόc rather than the word itself. Polemon is as nervous of meeting her father (who will of course take his daughter's part) as of meeting Glykera herself. The scene has become farcical. It must be observed, however, that the restoration is not absolutely certain; one might have e.g. δεῦρ'. (Πο.) ὑπανάγω | αὐτόc. In that case, Pataikos' appearance with Glykera at 1006 will be unexpected and the more effective.

1003–4: Körte and Jensen print ὦ τάλαν, τί δρᾷc; | ἔφυγεν· κακὸν τοcοῦτον ἦν θύραν ψοφεῖν; This makes good sense, but is suspect. (*a*) τί δρᾷc; for τί ποεῖc; has no certain parallel in Menander; (*b*) ἔφυγεν cannot be right: the second letter of 1004 has no descender (? ν), and the third is not υ (η or ν G–H).

1006 ff.: It is almost impossible to reconcile this passage, as it stands in O and in all editions, with the belief that there were only three actors. Polemon enters his house at 1003, Doris follows him at 1005; Pataikos comes out of another house at 1006, accompanied by Glykera, and Polemon returns at 1009. All these are speaking parts. If only three actors are available, the only methods of playing this seem to be:

(*a*) actor A goes in as Polemon at 1003, and emerges from another door as Pataikos, having changed masks, at 1006; actor B goes in as Doris as 1005 and returns as Polemon at 1009, having changed masks and substituted a masculine costume for a feminine.

(*b*) actor B goes in as Doris at 1005 and returns as Glykera from another door at 1006 or possibly at the end of 1008, the intervening lines being addressed to her through the door.

Neither of these alternatives is attractive and I think neither is feasible unless there is a pause, with empty stage, between 1005 and 1006. But not only would this be awkward by delaying the action at a moment when it should proceed rapidly, but 1004 strongly suggests that the new characters are in the act of coming out. With regard to (*a*), the protagonist might be expected to play Polemon, and his performance in this part would be his principal claim to win the acting prize: it would be odd if in the final scene he surrendered it to another actor. But it may be noticed that the remark on Doris' fine physique (182) may be an indication that the actor who played Doris also played a male part; similarly Glykera's tallness (521) may be a virtue made of necessity.

But the assumption, apparently made by the second hand who added names of speakers, that Glykera has a speaking part may not be correct. The letters κε, read by Grenfell–Hunt in the margin at 1021, indicate that he assigned to her 1021–1022a, and 1023. This is very natural after the appeal to her in 1020. But it is conceivable that she kept a modest silence and, like a respectable Greek girl, let her father speak for her. That he was not misrepresenting her sentiments would be known from 1006. Observe that Polemon's reply is made to Pataikos, and that there is no reason for supposing that she said anything more before the end of the play, that is not far distant. If, of course, 1023 ended, as in all our editions, τετύχηκα[ϲ ἐξ ἐμοῦ, that must be spoken by Glykera, but the supplement is by no means inevitable. One could have e.g. τετύχηκα[ϲ εἰκότωϲ, or τετύχηκα[ϲ. (*Πο.*) εὖ λέγειϲ. (*Proc. Camb. Phil. Soc.* 1967, 40).

(ii) 1006–1026: *Polemon, Pataikos (with Glykera)*

1006 τὸ "νῦν διαλλαχθήϲομαι": The quotation (your 'I will now be reconciled') is introduced by the article. (LSJ s.v. ὁ, ἡ, τό, B 5). Elsewhere Menander has διαλλαγ- not διαλλαχθ-, e.g. 1020 below. He may not have been consistent; the MSS. of Aristophanes give διηλλάγητε at *Lys.* 1161, διαλλαχθῆτε ibid. 900.

1007 δέχεϲθαι τὴν δίκην: 'Accept the proffered satisfaction'; the formula δίκαϲ δοῦναι καὶ δέξαϲθαι (Thuc. v. 59) means 'submit disputes to peaceful settlement'. The first hand placed paragraphi below 1006, 1008, thus assigning this speech to Glykera: the second hand was certainly right to cancel them.

1008: For this feeling of Greek superiority cf. *Pap. Hibeh* 6. 36 (Page,

GLP p. 290), "Ελλην βεβαίως φαίνεταί τις τοὺς τρόπους ὁ Δημέας ἄνθρωπος.

1009 ἀλλ' ἐκκαλείτω τις: Slaves may be supposed to have followed father and daughter on to the stage.

The OCT text accords with the indications of the original hand, which placed a paragraphus below this verse. The second hand may have added πολεμ in the left-hand margin opposite 1010 (the traces are doubtful), but if so, did not necessarily take Polemon's speech to start with ἀλλ' ἔθνον.

1010 εὐπραξίας: Both εὐπραξία and εὐπραγία are found in the MSS. of fourth-century authors (LSJ). Photios has εὐπραξία· οἱ παλαιοὶ κωμικοὶ διὰ τοῦ ξ, Θουκυδίδης δὲ διὰ τοῦ γ. **γνησίων παίδων ἐπ' ἀρότῳ coὶ δίδωμι:** This is the formula of betrothal, recurring in other plays, but with slight differences in wording and in the way it is introduced into the trimeter: frag. 682, and *P. Oxy.* 2533 (cf. *Mis.* 444 and *P. Oxy.* 1824), παίδων ἐπ' ἀρότῳ γνησίων (δίδωμί coι), *Fab. incert.* 29, γνησίων ἐπὶ σπορᾷ παίδων, *Dysk.* 842, ἐγγυῶ παίδων ἐπ' ἀρότῳ γνησίων. The mention of the dowry follows in *Dysk., Sam., Mis.* and *P. Oxy.* 2533 as here, but without interruption from the prospective husband. Polemon is too eager to let Pataikos finish his sentence. On the amount of the dowry see *Epitr.* 134 ff. note.

1015: καλῶς ἔχει (Grenfell–Hunt), like French 'merci', can be a formula of polite refusal or, as it would be here, of grateful acceptance. But there are unambiguous alternatives, καλῶς λέγεις or καλῶς ποεῖς, that are possible supplements and in OCT I print the latter. See J. H. Quincey, *JHS* xxxvi (1966) 138, whose punctuation I adopt, to show that καί joins the phrase to λαμβάνω.

1016: Grenfell and Hunt's ὧν, ὅπως must be adapted by writing ὧν, ἵνα, since Menander nowhere else uses ὅπως and subj. without ἄν for final clauses, a construction that is fairly uncommon in Attic inscriptions before the second century B.C., Meisterhans³, 254. But the supplement is not certain.

1019 μέμψομαι with dative means 'find fault with'. The restoration seems to be imposed if the dative γλυκεραι of O is kept. But Grenfell and Hunt supposed that to be an error for the vocative, as φιλτατηι is mistakenly written for φιλτατη.

1021 γάρ marks an anticipatory reason. For the possibility that this speech and 1023 should be assigned to Pataikos see note on 1006 ff.

1024: Paragraphi under this line and the next have been cancelled by the second hand, erroneously it would seem so far as the first of them is concerned.

1026: It has been suggested (Körte, *Berichte Abh. Akad. Leipzig.* 1908, 172⁴) that Philinos is Myrrhine's husband, and this is not impossible; when she took over Moschion she may have been childless but have borne a daughter later. (A daughter older than Moschion would be an unlikely bride for him.) But Philinos may as well be some friend of Pataikos here mentioned for the first time, like Phanocrates and Archonides in the similar passage at the end of Terence's *Heauton-timorumenos*, or Callicles in Plautus' *Trinummus* 1183.

ὦ Γῆ: The addition of καὶ θεοί is possible (cf. Nikostratos frag. 5 K), but ὦ Γῆ stands alone at *Fab. incert.* 63. It is difficult to decide to whom the exclamation should be assigned; hardly, with Grenfell and Hunt, to Glykera. An expression of surprise (or consternation) by Moschion (R. Kauer, *Wiener Stud.* xxvi [1904], 205) is improbable, for nothing suggests his presence. The second hand of the papyrus may be right in indicating that Polemon goes indoors at 1024, (πολ' εισισι) to continue his sacrifice: if so, his reappearance at 1026 to speak these words, although possible in view of his volatility, would be unexpected. Most editors, wishing to give the exclamation to him, suppose the stage direction to be a mistake. But some reflection by Pataikos on his surprising good fortune is not out of the question; the absence of a paragraphus below the line supports this solution (it is uncertain whether there was a dicolon after θυγατερ'). A very few more lines would suffice to complete the play, as is shown by the end of *Misumenos*.

Fragment 1. Jensen suggested that this line may have been spoken by Polemon with reference to Pataikos.

Fragment 2. Sudhaus supposed these words to have been spoken by Glykera to Doris early in the play, when sending her to Myrrhine: she is to show her the γνωρίσματα, which might arouse her interest and pity. An objection to this is that if the tokens of birth have been prominent just before Glykera's flight, her failure to take them with her is less natural. Gomme, attempting to account for ὅμως, 'in spite of that', suggested that the line comes from the latter part of Act IV and that Pataikos said: 'All is clear, you are my children. Still show the γνωρίσματα to Myrrhine; she can compare them with Moschion's.'

PERINTHIA

O 2   *P. Oxy.* 855, now in the Bodleian Library (Gr. Class. g 99 (P)), where I have inspected it. The writing is very well preserved.
In the prologue to his *Andria* Terence claims that the plots of Menander's *Andria* and *Perinthia* were not unalike, although language and style were different, and that he had transferred elements of *Perinthia* to his own play. Although it would suit Terence's book to exaggerate the similarity of plot, there can be no doubt that there was a resemblance. Donatus said that the first scene of the two plays was 'almost in the same words', except that in *Andria* the old man delivered a monologue, whereas in *Perinthia* he spoke to his wife, as in Terence's *Andria* he confides in his freedman Sosia. Two later short passages, one of 20, the other of 11 lines, were also identical. 'Cetera dissimilia sunt', by which must be meant that the words were different; it is not implied that there was no similarity in plot.

Plot

The situation expounded in the first scene of Terence's *Andria* is that an Andrian woman, Chrysis, had settled in Athens and adopted the trade of *hetaira*. Some of her lovers used to take Simo's son Pamphilus to her house, but he never lay with her himself. Chremes, struck by Pamphilus' virtue, suggested to Simo that the youth should marry his daughter. The match was arranged, when Chrysis died, and at the funeral Simo saw a lovely young girl, said to be her sister. In her grief this girl was about to throw herself on the pyre, when Pamphilus prevented her; it was clear to Simo that the two were in love, and next day Chremes indignantly called the marriage off, having learned that Pamphilus was treating the girl as if she were his wife. In this situation Simo proposes nevertheless to tell Pamphilus that he is to marry Chremes' daughter that very day: if Pamphilus makes no difficulty, he will be able to assure Chremes that the boy is not really in love with the other girl.

The development of the plot depends on Simo's slave Davus who, guessing that the alleged marriage is a mere blind, advises Pamphilus to accept. This leads unexpectedly to a change of mind by Chremes, who once again favours the match. Meanwhile the girl gives birth to a boy. Davus causes the child to be laid on Simo's doorstep, and arranges a scene in which Chremes overhears him wrangling with the

girl's maid, who convincingly denies his allegation that the child is
not the girl's nor Pamphilus its father, and also declares the girl
herself to be of free Athenian birth. Once again Chremes decides to
call the marriage off; no sooner has he gone than Chrysis' cousin
turns up, with evidence that the girl is a free Athenian. When Davus
reports this, Simo is enraged, thinking it an invention to prevent the
marriage between Pamphilus and Chremes' daughter, and has Davus
carried away and bound. But the actual evidence of the cousin is
irrefragable and shows that the girl is in fact a long-lost daughter
of Chremes: the lovers may therefore be united, to universal satisfaction.

How far is it likely that this plot was reproduced in *Perinthia*?
(1) In *Perinthia*, as in *Andria*, Daos discovered that the proposed
marriage was a blind. One of his reasons was that there were no preparations at Chremes' house for a marriage feast. Frag. 2 refers to this.
It is therefore probable that he also advised his young master to meet
deceit with deceit and pretend to fall in with his father's proposal.
(2) There was probably a midwife in the *Perinthia*. The midwife of
Terence's *Andria*, as doubtless of Menander's, comes and performs her
task without fuss, but she is described at 229 as follows: 'sane pol illa
temulenta est mulier et temeraria, nec sati' digna quoi committas
primo partu mulierem'. It may be guessed that this characterization
is borrowed from *Perinthia*, in which a bibulous old woman played a
part, frag. 4. Although a child will have been born in that play too,
it was not necessarily used in the same way on the stage. (3) The
motive for his master's rage with Daos may have been the same,
namely a belief that the slave was falsely passing the girl off as free-
born, but the immediate incidents cannot have been identical, since
in the fragment preserved from *Perinthia* Daos takes refuge at an altar,
from which preparations are made to burn him out. From this predicament he may have been rescued either by surrender (as Webster
suggests, *StM* 82), or by the appearance of confirmation of his story.
(4) Sosia, who never appears again in Ter. *Andria*, is not a plausible
confidant for Simo, and the reasons offered for telling him the long
story are unconvincing: he is to keep an eye on Pamphilus' conduct,
and deter Davus from mischief. On the other hand Laches of *Perinthia*
would naturally confide in his wife, whose co-operation he would
need in pretending that there was about to be a marriage. Why did
Terence replace her by Sosia? Is it possible that in *Perinthia* she played
some active part, and that Terence found it easier to substitute a
totally new character than to modify her figure (F. Leo, *Plautinische
Forschungen* 220[6])? (5) Terence's *Andria* contains two figures, Charinus
and his slave Byrrhia, who on the evidence of Donatus were not in

Menander's play; they are so loosely connected with the plot that this might have been guessed, even had he not said so. Charinus is a friend of Pamphilus, in love with Chremes' daughter: he somewhat ineffectively complains when Pamphilus appears to be about to marry her, and at other times asks him to use his influence on his behalf. It has been maintained that Charinus comes from *Perinthia*, where he may have played a more decisive part. If this is so, *Andria* 301–35 are probably based on *Perinthia*. (His presence in the next scene, in which he contributes nothing but banal comments, may be due to Terence). On this presumption a further possible element from *Perinthia* is 412–31, Byrrhia's scouting expedition, which in turn leads to the scene between Charinus and Pamphilus, 625–65 (F. Schöll, *SB Heidelberg. Akad. Wiss.* 1912, 7). Donatus, however, at least in the form to which his commentary has been reduced, says nothing of these characters' having been taken from *Perinthia*, a play he seems to have read carefully to discover what it has contributed to Terence's *Andria*. At 301 the note runs: 'has personas Terentius addidit fabulae —nam non sunt apud Menandrum'; and at 977: 'binos amores duorum adulescentium et binas nuptias in una fabula machinatus est —et id extra praescriptum Menandri, cuius comoediam transferebat'. Neither note, as it stands, is compatible with knowledge that the characters were taken from Menander's *Perinthia*. Two further points, made by W. Beare, *Roman Stage*[2], 89 ff., that in Athens Charinus would have had no opportunity of falling in love with the wealthy Chremes' daughter, who must have lived in seclusion, and that it is not explained why he could not be an open suitor, are of less importance. There is nothing to show that Charinus had ever spoken to Philumena; he might for example have seen her taking part in a procession (cf. *Kitharistes* 94), and been overcome. And Menander, if Charinus is his character, could have somewhere explained why he was not a welcome match.

1 ff.: Daos has taken refuge from his master Laches by sitting on an altar (cf. Plaut. *Most.* 1094), possibly that of Apollo Agyieus which stood outside every house. To drag a suppliant from an altar by force was impious, but it was legitimate to force him to leave by lighting a fire round it. This Laches plans to do, aided by three slaves, Getas, Tibeios, and Pyrrhias. Although the official object of such a procedure was not the death of the suppliant, it might be the result, and the intended result. In Ar. *Thesm.* 726 f., 749, the angry women threaten to burn Euripides' kinsman at the altar. In Plaut. *Rudens* Labrax first intends to get possession of the suppliant girls (760–1), but later declares 'hasce ambas hic in ara ut uiuas comburam, id uolo' (768). Daos, therefore, fears that Laches may not give him the chance to leave, but 'burn him up'. Besides Daos and Laches there is a third speaker, whose name appeared above the second half of 21. Grenfell and Hunt read it as π]υ[ρ]ριας, but the last letters are ϲιαϲ. Schroeder's ϲῳϲιαϲ, although not recognizable, will give the right name. It recurs in the form ϲωϲ (neither ϲω' as Schroeder has it nor βωϲ as G–H) to the left of 17, where it is generally thought to be in the right-hand margin of the previous column, that is anything from 30 to 50 lines earlier. Körte supposes the speaker of 21b to come on the scene at that verse, bringing news that effects Daos' release. Although possible, that is speculative. If we accept the most obvious interpretation of the dicola before and after εκνιϲθηϲ in 16, that word must belong to this third speaker, who could be a slave who is taking a malicious pleasure in Daos' plight; the coarseness of 17–18 might suit such a character better than Laches. (From its position, it is not certain that ϲωϲ belongs to the previous column; does it go with 17?)

1: The letters τιβ are preserved on a detached scrap of papyrus. Leo expanded them to make Τίβειε καὶ Γέτα, φυλάττετ' αὐτόν, which he placed before cὺ δ' ἀκολούθει.

Schöll suggested that Pyrrhias is not Laches' slave but, as Byrrhia in Ter. *Andria* is the slave of Charinus, the slave of the character in *Perinthia* whom he believed to be the origin of Charinus.

2 κληματίδας: 'Brushwood'; the restoration is supported by Ar. *Thesm.* 728, ἵωμεν ἐπὶ τὰς κληματίδας, and 740, παράβαλλε πολλὰς κληματίδας; there the women propose to burn Euripides' kinsman at the altar where he has taken refuge. The speaker may be Daos, but if a malicious Sosias is present, the words would suit him.

Körte ends the line τὸ πῦρ φέρε. But a man who is to carry a huge bundle of wood (8) cannot well carry fire also, and in fact it is Laches himself who will bring the torch. Arnott's τὸ πῦρ, Γέτα (*CQ* n.s. xviii [1968], 240) is also unsatisfactory, since Getas remains on the stage (3). The correct supplement must be uncertain; possibly (Δα.) βοᾷ | καὶ πῦρ. Notice that τὸ πῦρ must be spoken off-stage, and therefore loudly.

4 ἔπειτα introduces a surprised question, cf. Ar. *Clouds* 226, ἔπειτ' ἀπὸ ταρροῦ τοὺς θεοὺς ὑπερφρονεῖς; *Thesm.* 188, ἔπειτα πῶς οὐκ αὐτὸς ἀπολογεῖ; ἀφείητ' ἄν conveys a suggestion rather than an open command; Goodwin, *MT* § 237, K–G i. 233. For the plural verb with singular vocative cf. *Epitr.* 254 n. Tibeios and Getas cannot answer, for they are *personae mutae*, but their silence is dramatically effective.

5 cύνδουλον: Although Moiris declares that the Attic form was ὁμόδουλος (which could also be restored here), both forms were in fact used in Attic (see LSJ). An opinion recorded by Pollux iii. 82, ὁμόδουλον τὸν τῆc αὐτῆc τύχηc, cύνδουλον δὲ τὸν τοῦ αὐτοῦ δεcπότου, may be excessively precise.

At the end ν[and ι[are equally possible. If Grenfell and Hunt were right in reading διαcωcαν[τ᾽, Daos must have previously saved Getas from some danger: a reminder of his services would be relevant to this appeal for help. At the end of the line read εὖ πάνυ rather than οὐ πάνυ, which is not known in New Comedy as an independent phrase (Arnott, *CQ* N.s. xviii [1968], 240), and would go awkwardly with what follows. I am not, however, attracted by Arnott's view that εὖ πάνυ is ironical, and the following four words 'a cynical affirmation of the position'. Rather εὖ πάνυ is to be taken with ἀφείητ᾽ ἄν (for this position of words see *Dysk.* 236 n.), and then οὐκ] ἄν μ᾽ ἀφείητ᾽; is a despairing question.

But my preference is for διαcωcαι[τ᾽ (Herwerden, *Mnem.* xxxviii [1910], 222). With that reading one can continue εὖ πάνυ | νῦν ἄν μ᾽ ἀφείητ᾽. ἀλλά will then introduce a shocked question, Denniston, *GP* 8.

8 ὅcον γε: γε is exclamatory, 'What a load!' Denniston, *GP* 127, 129.

9 αὐτός, 'the master' (*Sam.* 258 n.), would be an adequate subject; the addition of Λάχηc at the beginning of 10 may be right, but is not necessary.

13–15: Laches must have overheard Daos' words preserved in frag. 3. There the slave said that there was 'nothing magnificent in cheating an easy-going empty-headed master.' Here Laches seems to substitute for 'nothing magnificent' φλύαροc, 'nonsense, tomfoolery', i.e. something that no self-respecting rascal would take seriously. Daos may, of course, have used that very word in the lines following frag. 3. G. Luck, *Rh. Mus.* cviii (1965), 269, has a different interpretation, proposing to break off the sentence after δεcπότην, and to accent ἔcτι: 'You can "cheat your empty-headed master".' What nonsense that was!' Abuse seems to me not in tune with the sarcastic manner in which Laches here plays with Daos. Moreover it is improbable that Daos regarded his master as ἀπράγμονα καὶ κοῦφον after discovering his intrigue that involved the pretence that a marriage was in train.

ἤήν is an exclamation of embarrassment, on which see *Dysk.* 465 n.

15–16 cτακτή is the best kind of oil of myrrh (Pliny, *NH* xii. 68), here used metaphorically for a superlative intelligence. Perhaps Daos had applied the phrase to himself. In Plaut. *Most.* 309, by a play on words, *stacta* is used of an outstanding woman: 'uin unguenta? :: quid opust? cum stacta accubo.' φρένεc, in the sense 'mind', is poetical, except in some phrases, e.g. ἔξω τῶν φρενῶν. ἡ τῶν φρενῶν cτακτή is high-flown language, which would be suitable in a slave's boasting speech. **ἐκνίσθης:** 'Did that sting you?' A dicolon before the word should imply that the speaker is not Laches, but it may be mistaken. Daos' reply is a little puzzling. Van Leeuwen understood it to mean 'this is not like you, not your way', cf. e.g. Eur. *HF* 585, πρὸς coῦ μέν, ὦ παῖ, τοῖς φίλοις εἶναι φίλον. This is, I think, right, although the absence of τοῦτο is perhaps surprising. The alternative is that πρὸς coῦ means 'at your hands' (Grenfell–Hunt). Then it must be supposed that Daos gave a start on hearing the phrase τὴν τῶν φρενῶν cτακτήν, but pretends that something else caused his discomfort.

17 μέν: The absence of the sequel makes explanation uncertain. If this is a μέν *solitarium*, the unexpressed contrast may be 'but the loyal ones are all right'.

18 κατὰ τῶν cκελῶν: Ar. *Peace* 241 describes War as ὁ δεινός, ὁ ταλαύρινος, ὁ κατὰ τοῖν cκελοῖν, which the scholiast interprets by ἀπὸ τῶν διὰ δειλίαν ἀποτιλώντων. It appears that Daos has in his fright fouled himself. The verb is omitted as a concession to decency.

κληρονομίαν: At. Ter. *Andria* 796 Crito arrives with the intention of claiming the dead Chrysis' estate, but that may be a false clue. τὴν κληρονομίαν could be metaphorical, and may belong with the preceding words. At the end of the line Grenfell and Hunt correctly read φι[λ]τατο[. Schmidt's φίλτατε is an improbable emendation. No explanation seems possible.

23: Del Corno remarks that one meaning of κύκλος is 'place where slaves are sold' (Hesychios s.v., Pollux vii. 11).

Fragment 1. In a marginal note *P. Hibeh* 181, a mutilated scrap of comedy, containing a list of foodstuffs, has the word προστάτης. Hence Barigazzi suggested that it comes from *Perinthia* (*Hermes* lxxxviii [1960], 379). In that play the word προστάτης occurred 'at the beginning', an unlikely place for such a list.

Fragment 5. **εἰς τὸν ἴσον ὄγκον:** Both will become, in the words of Soph. *El.* 1142, cμικρὸς ὄγκος ἐν cμικρῷ κύτει.

Fragment 6. **μαλακά** are light, easily transportable goods. If the person here addressed corresponds to Crito of Ter. *Andria*, who foresaw that his claim to Chrysis' estate might be successfully contested, he is here advised to seize what he can lay hands on and make off with it, a bird in the hand being worth two in the bush.

Fragment 9. **ὑπόξυλος:** Pollux iii. 56 says that in New Comedy the word was applied to one who passed as a citizen, but was not one. This may be, but is not necessarily, the meaning here.

SAMIA

C P. Cairensis 43227 contains 216–416, 547–686.
B P. Bodmer 25 contains 1–245, 254–406, 411–54, 458–605, 612–737.
   P. Barcinonensis 45 contains 399–410, 446–57.
O 16 P. Oxy. 2831 (ii A.D.) contains small fragments of 385–90.
O 17 P. Oxy. 2943 (ii/iii A.D.) contains the ends of 120–5 and the beginnings of 134–42 and 13 succeeding lines.

P. Barcinonensis and *P. Bodmer* are parts of the same codex. Where the line numbers given overlap, each papyrus has a part of the line. The same codex included *P. Bodmer* 4 and 26. Both it and the codex of *P. Cairensis* are described in the introduction, pp. 42–8.

Apart from general editions of Menander, see the commentary (on C only) by C. Dedoussi, Μενάνδρου Σαμία, Athens 1955 (in demotic Greek), and the edition of C. Austin, *Menandri Aspis et Samia* (Kleine Texte für Vorlesungen und Übungen), vols. i (1969) and ii (commentary, 1970). Wilamowitz, 'Die Samia des Menandros', *SB Berlin* 1916, 66 (= *Kl. Schr.* i. 415) is stimulating although out-of-date at many points. J.-M. Jacques's valuable edition in the Budé series (1971) appeared too late to allow more than a few references.

Other articles (a selection): W. G. Arnott, *Gnomon* xlii (1970), 10, *Arethusa* iii (1970), 49, C. Austin, *ZPE* iv (1969), 161, A. Barigazzi, *Riv. di fil.* xcviii (1970), 148, 257, E. W. Handley, *BICS* xvi (1969), 102, H. J. Mette, *Lustrum* xiii (1969), 535, F. Stoessl, *Rh. Mus.* cxii (1969), 193, M. Treu, *Rh. Mus.* cxii (1969), 230.

Title

That this play is *Samia* is established by the subscription in B and by the Mitilini mosaic, reproduced by Dedoussi and in colour by *ed. pr.* of P. Bodmer 25, which illustrates beneath the heading Σαμιας με(ρος) γ the scene in Act III where Demeas turns Chrysis away in the presence of the cook. Five lines, however, (140–2, 163–4) that are quoted by Stobaios appear in Körte–Thierfelder's edition of the fragments as from *Knidia* (248, 249). The title *Knidia* is not known from any other source, and even here is conjectural. The MSS. of Stobaios give Κνηδία for frag. 248 and Κηδείᾳ or Ἀκηδεία (with rubricated initial *A*) for frag. 249. With some probability, Lloyd-Jones suggested reading Κηδεία, 'Connection by Marriage', supposing this

to be an alternative title for *Samia*, cf. *Dyskolos/Misanthropos*, *Misumenos/
Thrasonides*, etc. Although many comedies end with a marriage, this
is one where the marriage is envisaged in the first act, arranged in
the second act, and obstructed in the third, fourth, and fifth acts.
Therefore it deserves the title Κηδεία better than most.

Plot

In Athens there lived next door to one another a rich citizen
named Demeas and a poor one named Nikeratos. Demeas had
adopted a boy Moschion, who at the time of the play, was a young
man (a μειράκιον, perhaps 21), and Nikeratos had a daughter named
Plangon (630). Demeas, who was unmarried, had fallen in love with
Chrysis, a Samian *hetaira*, and been encouraged by his son to take her
into his house to avoid the inconvenience of young rivals. While the
fathers were away on a journey to Pontos, from which they return at
the end of the first act, Moschion had come home from the country
and found the women of the two households, who had made friends,
celebrating the Adonia in his own house along with certain others. In
the confusion he had violated Plangon, but later confessed his deed
and promised to ask his 'father', when he could, for permission to
marry her. The girl bore a child before Demeas' return, but it was
transferred to the care of Chrysis, who had lost a baby born about the
same time. All this was recounted by Moschion in a long speech,
which opened the play (1–57). Chrysis then appeared. Moschion had
probably already left, but he shortly returned with the slave Parmenon, who has been his helper (61). Parmenon announces that he
has seen Demeas and Nikeratos and tries to stiffen Moschion's resolution to ask for Plangon in marriage. Chrysis is brought into the conversation and confirms that she will say the child is hers; she does not
wish to part with it and it is expected that Demeas will soon accept
it (61–85). The three characters go their ways, Moschion to practise
the speech he will have to make to his father. The two old men now
enter and after some travel reminiscences declare themselves entirely
at one on the question of Moschion's marriage (96–118). Although
it is not said in so many words, at least in what is preserved, it must
be supposed that they intend to marry him to Plangon. Why, we do
not know; but he is agitating himself vainly. Hereabouts will have
come the end of Act I.

Act II is represented by inadequate scraps only. Apparently Demeas
entered and then Moschion, recounting how he had been acting out
the marriage in imagination; he is interrupted by catching sight of
Demeas, who complains that he has got a 'married *hetaira*', but
declares he'll turn both her and the child out (133). Moschion pro-

tests, and no doubt won Demeas over; after a gap of some 28 lines they are discussing the arrangements for Moschion's marriage, which Demeas agrees shall take place that very day. Parmenon is dispatched to hire a cook and buy food, after Nikeratos has been brought to consent. The act is almost finished; everything seems to have gone with the greatest ease.

The third act is almost completely preserved. Demeas in a long monologue confides in the audience that he has overheard talk by Moschion's nurse that indicates the baby to be not his own, but his son's (206–79). Parmenon enters with the cook and is terrified by his master into admitting that this is true, and then takes to his heels (280–324). Demeas tries to keep calm: it must be Chrysis who has seduced his boy, for whose sake the fact must be kept quiet; but she must be sent packing (325–56). He turns her out, bewildered by his sudden unexplained rage, and she is given asylum by Nikeratos (369–420).

The fourth act opens with the appearance of Nikeratos, intent on tackling Demeas. Moschion, who has been away in the town, returns and learns of Chrysis' expulsion (421–39). He remonstrates with Demeas, who after a great attempt at self-control tells him that he knows him to be the child's father. Moschion does not react to this as Demeas expects and Nikeratos now joins his friend in a tirade of denunciation, then enters his house to turn out the wicked Chrysis. Moschion sees the misunderstanding and has just had time to tell his father the truth when Nikeratos returns distracted: he has seen his daughter suckling the child. Moschion takes to his heels in alarm (452–539). Nikeratos in a passion re-enters his house, determined to discover who the father is. When the women refuse to tell him, he threatens to kill the child, and Chrysis appears, carrying it, in terror. To her surprise Demeas protects her and sends her into his house; then he tries to persuade Nikeratos that some god must be the father, assuring him at the same time that Moschion will marry the girl (540–615).

In the fifth act Moschion explains that the more he has thought over what has happened the more indignant he has become at being suspected of an affair with Chrysis. He will punish his father by pretending to leave home to enlist as a mercenary soldier (616–40). Parmenon returns, having thought better of flight, and is sent in to fetch Moschion a sword and cloak; he comes out with the report that the wedding-feast is ready. Nevertheless Moschion persists in his plan, but then wonders what will happen if his father does not, as expected, beg him to stay (641–86). Demeas comes out to look for his missing son, admits his own fault but reproves him for forgetting all the years of good treatment he had known, and for being ready to advertise his father's mistake: he, Demeas, had done all he could to conceal what he had believed to be his son's crime (692–712). Moschion is saved the embarrassment of finding a reply to this by the appearance of Nikeratos, looking for the bridegroom, and he is soon in possession of his bride (729).

The third and fourth acts of the play are not only the longest but also excellent; the character of Demeas and the difficulty of the position in which he believes himself to be are well portrayed in his two monologues, admirably contrasted with the lively scenes between him and first Parmenon, then Chrysis. The difference between him and Nikeratos is well kept in view during their exchanges, packed with incident, in the fourth act; and the earlier part of the act, in which father and son are in turn bewildered by the other's talk, is most ingeniously contrived.

The first two acts seem, by contrast, to have been lacking in dramatic tension. The fact that only parts of these survive may lead to an underestimate. Nevertheless it would seem that they were inferior. In the second act the possible obstacles are easily overcome; Demeas' unwillingness to keep the child is the most serious; Moschion and Demeas quickly discovered that each was equally set on an alliance with the neighbour's daughter and Nikeratos needed little talking over to agree to a quick marriage. All seems to proceed very easily towards an obvious happy ending. The first act does no more than explain the situation and draw Moschion's character: a nice youth fundamentally, but a little spoiled and somewhat weak; he seems not to do anything in this act or even take any new resolve, so that he is not dramatically effective here. The goodness of writing in certain passages cannot conceal the fact that dramatic material is short for the first two acts and the play does not get under way until the third.

Date

The play is usually supposed to be early; Körte (Praef. xl) even puts it 'inter primas Menandri adulescentis'. The reasons are the mention of contemporary figures, of whom Chaerephon was certainly and Androkles probably ridiculed by poets of the Middle Comedy; the use of trochaic tetrameters; and the almost farcical nature of the scene that ends the fourth act. The last is clearly an insecure argument; one cannot presume that Menander's style consistently grew more serious as he grew older. A number of plays from which we have trochaic fragments are early, but others are undated; this, too, is an argument of no cogency. The jests at the expense of individuals are more relevant; but although such gibes certainly were frequent in Middle Comedy and became rare in New Comedy, we cannot give any year as a *terminus ante quem* for their occurrence, or say that they indicate a date among the very earliest of Menander's plays. Androkles at least is an old man (606), so that his probable appearance in Middle Comedy is a frail argument. The suggestion of Moschion that he might serve as a mercenary in Baktria or Karia might be of use in dating the play if a time could be found in which mercenaries were required in both places. As regards Baktria, however, Moschion might take it for granted that soldiers would always be needed in that distant frontier province, especially after the insurrection of 323 B.C. had led to the slaughter of so many mercenaries unwilling to remain there. There is no record of fighting in Karia before 315 to 313 B.C., when the region was secured by Antigonos; Ptolemy occupied it in 309 B.C., and may have required garrison troops. Seleukos may also have been recruiting there for his eastern campaigns (? 308–306 B.C.), which involved Baktria (Beloch, *Griechische Geschichte*, IV. i. 124; Cary, *History of the Greek World 323–146 B.C.*, 31, 40, 66). Moschion's plan is therefore consistent with a date *c.* 309, but an earlier one, 315–313, is not excluded.

There is certainly nothing immature about the writing. The monologues, whose length and frequency have oddly enough been advanced as a reason for believing the play to be early, are composed with complete mastery: they are so designed that they reveal far more about the speaker's thoughts and feelings than he intends to communicate. There are scenes, too, which show a command of dialogue that outdoes anything in *Dyskolos*. It would be hard to better the passage 369–88 for the economy of the rapid exchanges with which it opens, and the contrast of the tirade with which it ends; nor could incidents succeed one another more rapidly or more logically than in 555–88. This is the hand of an assured master, and since Plutarch testifies that the later plays were much superior to the early ones (*Mor.* 853 f), it would be rash to place the *Samia* very early. For similar reasons Dedoussi suggests *c.* 310 B.C. Jacques, liv–lxv, argues for a date before that of *Dyskolos*.

Dramatis Personae

        Moschion, a young man
        Demeas, his father
        Parmenon, their slave
        Chrysis, Demeas' mistress
        Nikeratos, his neighbour
        A cook

Scene: Athens.

Except for *Nikeratos* (a common name of real life, *Prosop. Attica* 10730–46), the characters bear names familiar in comedy, and indicative of their status. Even Nikeratos recurs in the anonymous comedy *Pap. Ghôran* II, but there seems to be a young man.

For *Moschion* as a young man's name see *Perik.* p. 466.

Parmenon is a slave-name in *Theophorumene, Plokion, Hypobolimaios, Pap. Hamburg* 656, Terence, *Eunuchus, Adelphoe, Hecyra*. Since it suggests παραμένων, Menander perhaps used it ironically for one who would in fact take to his heels.

Demeas is an elderly man in *Dis Exapaton, Imbrioi, Misumenos*, Terence, *Adelphoe*, and middle-aged at least in *Pap. Hibeh* 6, *Pap. Argent.* 53.

Chrysis is a *hetaira* in *Eunuchos*, Terence, *Andria*.

(i) 1–56: *Monologue by Moschion*

1–56: This monologue discharges the functions of a prologue; it formed the opening scene, since it begins on the first page of the codex. *Ed. pr.* claim that about 5 lines preceded the first letters preserved. They do not give their reasons, but Dr. Kasser now considers them inadequate. A comparison of the fibres of the first leaf with those of the second suggests to him as an alternative that about eleven lines are missing. This seems more like the space required, even if the play was, like *Aspis*, given no title. In what is lost Moschion must have mentioned his adoption by Demeas, referred to at 346, 698.

Why did Menander make Moschion Demeas' adopted son, not his son by birth? Before the end of the play was known, some scholars accepted the guess of van Leeuwen, that the intention was that in some recognition scene Chrysis might be found to be Moschion's sister, and so fit to become Demeas' wife. This was always very improbable, and is no longer tenable. There seems to be nothing in the plot that *requires* Moschion to be an adopted son. Are there any advantages in making him one? There are some possibilities. First, an adopted son has not the same claim on his father's affections as a son by birth. Demeas' indulgent treatment of Moschion, described in 7–17, and his attempt to preserve his reputation (352) are therefore the more creditable, and he has the greater reason for reproaching him for ingratitude (698–710). Secondly, it may have seemed more suitable for an old bachelor than for a widower to take up with a *hetaira*; although in real life widowers may have entered on such arrangements, there was perhaps some expectation that they would look for a second wife.

Although so much remains of the first lines preserved, it is hard to be sure of their sense. They cannot be restored with any confidence. In 4]ο seems certain, excluding Austin's once suggested ὅμως φέρω τοῦτ' εἰς μέσον (cf. ἐcομενον for εἰς μέcον at 270). τοῦτο is written in full, so perhaps γε or δέ has fallen out after it, e.g. νῦν αὐτ]ὸ τοῦτό ⟨γ'⟩ ἐcόμενον λογίζομαι. Moschion says that he has erred and something is therefore painful (3), perhaps to tell his story. I guess him to continue that he will be thought by the audience to tell the story more reasonably if he first gives an account of his adopted father's character. He clearly remembers his own luxurious early childhood but will say nothing of it; he was not then old enough to appreciate what his father was doing for him (9). He had not been brought up like everyone else, one of the crowd—but he was now more wretched than the average—; he had been wealthy and ambitious, hunted, served brilliantly in the cavalry, helped his friends financially.

3–6 ἡμάρτηκα: Presumably by his rape of Plangon.   **ὑμῖν:** The audience.   **ἐκείνου:** Demeas. The OCT text may be translated: 'I calculate that to tell my story will be painful, as I say, but that I should do it more reasonably in your eyes if I first give an account of my father's character.' λογίζομαι is constructed first with a participle, then with an infinitive.

7: There is a choice between μὲν ἐτρύφηcα and ἐνετρύφηcα, 'revelled in'; the word usually has a connotation of self-indulgence. Supplement is doubtful with either choice: perhaps the best are οἷc μὲν ἐτρύφηcα or cφόδρ' ἐνετρύφηcα; with the latter cαφῶc ⟨δ'⟩ is desirable.   **τῷ τότ' εὐθέωc χρόνῳ:** 'The time immediately following thereon'; one may guess that this means 'immediately after my adoption', and the remains of the play do not offer any hint that might suggest any other time. It is sometimes thought that because Moschion's wet-nurse had been Demeas' servant (236–47) Moschion must have been adopted as an infant. This is not necessary, since she might have passed to Demeas along with Moschion when he was a small boy and already capable of memory, having looked after him until that time.

9: Contrast Aischines i. 39, ἤδη φρονῶν καὶ μειράκιον ὤν.

10: Possibly εἶτ' ἐνεγράφην, 'I was enrolled in my deme'. It is hard to see how there could at this ceremony be any opportunity of *not* being one of the crowd. If the supplement is right, Moschion must mean that as a citizen he was on a par with all other Athenians, although financially he was far above the average. But I cannot fit line 12 into this context. Kassel suggested emending to ἐτράφην and some have written ἀλλ' ἐξετράφην. I do not see how a man who is describing his luxurious youth could say that he was not reared differently from anyone else, and would prefer οὐκ ἐξετράφην: 'I was not brought up like anyone else, "one of the mob", as the phrase goes.'

11 τῶν πολλῶν τις: *Dysk.* 484 n.   τὸ λεγόμενον δὴ τοῦτο: cf. Plato, *Gorgias* 514 e, τὸ λεγόμενον δὴ τοῦτο ἐν τῷ πίθῳ τὴν κεραμείαν ἐπιχειρεῖν μανθάνειν, *Soph.* 241 d, Aristainetos i. 11, τὸ λεγόμενον δὴ τοῦτο ἐδόκει τῇ κεφαλῇ ψαύειν τοῦ οὐρανοῦ, Men. frag. 689 K–T, τὸ δὴ λεγόμενον τοῦτο, frag. 333. 8 K–T and frag. adesp. 120 Kock, τοῦτο δὴ τὸ λεγόμενον, *Phasma* 42, τὸ δὴ λεγόμενον, Denniston *GP* 235.

12: Perhaps ᾧ γέγονα, with the meaning that the greater the height, the greater the fall. νῦν γέγονα is too long.   μέντοι will be affirmative, as probably in all other instances in Menander, *Epitr.* 510 n.

13: A word to mean 'rich' suggests itself as a supplement, but nothing convincing has been found (χρηστοί, πρῶτοι, ἄκροι). λαμπροί is a poor best. αὐτοὶ γάρ ἐςμεν is perhaps possible: 'I confess this, because we are alone.' Cf. Plut. *Amat.* 755 c, νεανικὸν μὲν τὸ τόλμημα καὶ Λήμνιον ὡς ἀληθῶς (αὐτοὶ γάρ ἐςμεν) ςφόδρ' ἐρώςης γυναικός, Herondas vi. 70, Lucian, *Dial. Deor.* x. 2.

χορηγεῖν: The association here with φιλοτιμεῖςθαι and ἐφυλάρχηςα probably confirms that the word has its usual meaning of acting as *choregos,* that is paying the costs of a dithyrambic or dramatic chorus, and in some measure organizing it. Austin quotes Aristotle, *EN* 1122ᵇ21, ὅσα πρὸς τὸ κοινὸν εὐφιλοτίμητά ἐςτιν, οἷον εἴ που χορηγεῖν οἴονται δεῖν λαμπρῶς ἢ τριηραρχεῖν. Cf. also Plut. *Nicias* 3, χορηγίαις ἀνελάμβανε . . . ἑτέραις τε τοιαύταις φιλοτιμίαις τὸν δῆμον.

It is surprising to find a young man, whose father is alive and controls the family property, acting as *choregos,* and surprising also that he should hold the responsible military office of φύλαρχος, commander of the cavalry supplied by his tribe (15). Under the constitution of the Five Thousand this office was reserved for men over the age of 30 (Arist. Ἀθ. Πολ. xxx. 2), and in Aristotle's time a *choregos* of a boys' chorus had to be over 40 (ibid. lvi. 3). But a change of the verbs to read διέφερεν and ἐφυλάρχηςε, making Demeas their subject, would be temerarious. These age-rules may have operated for a period only, and they suggest that there was already a tendency, thought undesirable by some, to appoint young men. In the decade after 320 B.C. the cavalry will have been intended for ceremonial parades rather than military action, and wealth, giving the ability to provide a smart turn-out, may have been more important in its commanders than experience. Much later, rich young men held offices that in the classical age would have been reserved for seniors: in 38/37 B.C. an ephebe is recorded as γυμναςιαρχήςαντά τε . . . καὶ φυλαρχήςαντα καὶ ποιηςάμενον τὴν χορηγίαν ἐπὶ τρεῖς ἡμέρας (*I.G.* ii².

1043); but it is not known how rapidly this tendency developed. Notice how Demosthenes boasts, xviii. 257, ἐμοὶ μὲν τοίνυν ὑπῆρξεν . . . παιδὶ μὲν ὄντι φοιτᾶν . . . ἐξελθόντι δ᾽ ἐκ παίδων . . . χορηγεῖν τριηραρχεῖν εἰσφέρειν, μηδεμιᾶς φιλοτιμίας μήτ᾽ ἰδίας μήτε δημοσίας ἀπολείπεσθαι, ἀλλὰ καὶ τῇ πόλει καὶ τοῖς φίλοις χρήσιμον εἶναι.

14: For γαρετρεφε Jacques proposes παρέτρεφε, suggested by Plutarch (quoted in the next note). φιλότιμος and its derivatives often have a connotation of munificence, public or private, and although lines 15 and 16 may be seen as explanatory of a claim to much munificence, the keeping of hounds is less obviously relevant. Yet φιλοτιμία can also be used of luxury that serves to increase the figure cut in the world by its owner.

15: A high stop after μοι at the end of 14 shows that the first word of this line was not an adjective (and in any case κύνες, hunting-dogs, are usually grammatically feminine). ἵππους is suggested by Plut. *Mor.* 830 b, ἵππους παρατρέφουσι, κύνας, πέρδικας, κολοιούς. Cf. also Ar. *Plut.* 156–7, αἰτοῦσιν οὐκ ἀργύριον οἱ χρηστοί (sc. παῖδες) :: τί δαί; :: ὁ μὲν ἵππον ἀγαθόν, ὁ δὲ κύνας θηρευτικάς, Ter. *Andr.* 55, 'quod plerique omnes faciunt adulescentuli . . . aut equos alere aut canes ad uenandum.' ἵππους leads on naturally to ἐφυλάρχησα, 'I was a cavalry officer'. λαμπρῶς: Cf. Xen. *De Re Equestri* xi. 10, ἤν γε μὴν τότε συμβῇ τινι τῶν τοιοῦτον ἵππον κεκτημένων ἢ φυλαρχῆσαι ἢ ἱππαρχῆσαι, οὐ δεῖ αὐτὸν τοῦτο σπουδάζειν ὅπως αὐτὸς μόνος λαμπρὸς ἔσται, ἀλλὰ πολὺ μᾶλλον ὅπως ὅλον τὸ ἑπόμενον ἀξιοθέατον φανεῖται.

16 τὰ μέτρια: 'I was able to give them the help that was adequate', commensurate with their needs. The 'righteous man' of Ar. *Plutus* says that, having adequate means from his father, ἐπήρκουν τοῖς δεομένοις τῶν φίλων (829); Demosthenes xviii. 268 claims that in his private life he was φιλάνθρωπος καὶ τοῖς δεομένοις ἐπαρκῶν.

17 δι᾽ ἐκεῖνον ἦν ἄνθρωπος: 'Through him I was a human being.' The idea that man is by nature admirable, pride in being human, and the belief that to be human means to be humane, are concepts more than once expressed by Menander's characters. They lie behind the use of the adverb ἀνθρωπίνως, *Aspis* 260, *Mis.* 302, and the line frag. 484, ὡς χάριέν ἐστ᾽ ἄνθρωπος, ἂν ἄνθρωπος ᾖ. This can be combined with the thought that man cannot expect everlasting success, so that it is part of humanity to tolerate misfortune, *Aspis* 166, frag. 650, ἀνθρωπίνως δεῖ τὰς τύχας φέρειν. But in 22 we are carried a stage further: human beings have their weaknesses; such a thing is ἀνθρώπινον, and for that reason pardonable.   ἀστείαν: The exact sense here is not certain; ἀστεῖος is properly what suits the refined ways of the town, but it became a general term of praise, 'smart', 'pretty', 'nice', and the original sense may here be no more than faintly felt in the background. **κόcμιοc**: Demeas later twice testifies to his son's *κοcμιότηc*, 273, 344. **ὅμωc**: An adversative is difficult here, and Jacques' *ὅλωc* is a possible correction. But perhaps seemly behaviour is unexpected in a rich and indulged young man.

19: I.e. *δίειμι ἅμα πάντα*, 'in telling the story, I shall go through everything all together'. The details about his father's passion, important for the play, are not over-relevant to the story of his own love-affair and misconduct.

21 ἐπιθυμίαν: Not infrequently in Plato of sexual appetite, e.g. *Rep.* 390 c, *τὴν τῶν ἀφροδιcίων ἐπιθυμίαν*, *Critias* 113 d, *αὐτῆc δ' εἰc ἐπιθυμίαν Ποceιδῶν ἐλθὼν cυμμείγνυται*, and elsewhere, e.g. Parthenios 24, *εἰc ἐπιθυμίαν ἀφίκετο πάνυ καλοῦ παιδόc*. **τινὰ**, if right, must tone down and apologize for Demeas' appetite. Jacques's emendation *τινὸc* is attractive, cf. Antiphanes frag. 212 K, *ἐν γειτόνων αὐτῷ κατοικούcηc τινὸc ἰδὼν ἑταίρας εἰc ἔρωτ' ἀφίκετο*.

22–3: B's *με* in 23 is shown by the metre to be an explanatory addition; *δε* in 22 is perhaps another, but a mistaken one, indicating that a new sentence begins with *πρᾶγμα*. The *πρᾶγμα ἀνθρώπινον* must be the act of falling in love, not that of concealing one's emotions: this sense is most effectively given by attaching the phrase in apposition to the preceding words. It can also be obtained, with the retention of *δέ*, by understanding 'but he tried to conceal this maybe human act'. This, however, seems to me less probable, and to leave *ᾐcχύνετο* somewhat isolated. Webster's belief that Demeas' human act was to conceal his love (*BICS* 1969, 104) is untenable; the reflection that it is human to fall in love is too common in Greek literature. To Austin's passages (Eur. *Hipp.* 439, Heliod. vii. 21. 1, Ach. Tat. v. 27. 2, Herodian v. 6. 2) add e.g. Philodemos, *AP* v. 112, *ἠράcθην· τίc δ' οὐχί*; and Menander frag. 198.

24 ἄκοντοc αὐτοῦ: 'Although he did not want (me to know of his passion)'.

25 ἐγκρατήc: *Sik.* 3 also has the word in the sense 'be in control of another person'. It is unnecessary to infer that Chrysis was a slave; in fact she is later stated to be free (577); a free woman in Demeas' house would be 'under his control', even though she would also be in theory free to leave him.

28: There is hardly room for more than two letters before ω, hence *εἴcω*, with ει ligatured, would suit the space; but without the context restoration is frivolous.

30–4: These lines are quite obscure. In the gap before them (*c.* 20–25 lines) Moschion must have recounted how the *hetaira* had been taken into Demeas' house, and how Demeas had gone abroad with his neighbour, who had a daughter (τῆc κόρηc, 36).   -ηcθε: The 2nd person plural must be addressed to the spectators.   cυνθλάcαc τὸ cημεῖον perhaps 'smashing the seal' that had been placed to secure or mark some property (LSJ s.v. cημεῖον I. 7; so Austin). I guess that Moschion had removed Demeas' mark from some property or produce and caused it to be added (προcετίθην) to Nikeratos' share for the benefit of his family while both fathers were away.

35–8: For the most part the Samian woman went next door, where her neighbour had kindly feelings (φιλανθρώπωc) for her; the neighbour returned the visits at times (ποτε); gadding about would less befit a married woman with a grown daughter.

38 ἐξ ἀγροῦ: 'From our farm'.   καταδραμών, 'hastening down'; the reason for the haste may have appeared in the lines lost before 30.

39 Ἀδώνια: The festival of Adonis, imported from Cyprus, was popular among women at Athens as early as the late fifth century (Plut. *Alcibiades* c. 18, Ar. *Lys.* 389, Pherekrates frag. 170 K). A well-known feature was the sowing of seed in trays to spring up quickly and symbolize the rebirth of the dead Adonis (Plato, *Phaedr.* 276 b); these trays were taken up to the house-roofs. L. Deubner, *Attische Feste*, plate 25, 1, shows an Eros handing such a 'garden' to a woman who is climbing up a ladder to her roof; cf. W. Atallah, *Adonis dans la littérature et l'art grecs*, figs. 39, 40, 44–8, 51. The account here given by Moschion may support Deubner's view (op. cit. 220) that Athenian women lost sight of the original meaning of the festival, but treated it as an occasion for jollification. The festival was much kept by *hetairai* (Diphilos frag. 43, 50), because of the association with Aphrodite, and we may see the occasion as one likely to arouse Moschion's passions. N. Weill, *BCH* xc (1966), 677–97, clearly establishes that the date of the Adonia was in the summer, and probably in the latter part of July. Atallah, like A. D. Nock, *Gnomon* x (1934), 291, thinks there may have been a subsidiary spring festival (op. cit. 227–58). Turner suggested the supplement περυcινά γ', attractive for sense; but γε gives excessive emphasis to περυcινά, and although the names of festivals dispense with the article, if a determinative phrase is added, it has the article, e.g. Lysias xxi. 4, Παναθηναίοιc τοῖc μικροῖc, K–G i. 600. Perhaps ὡc ἔτυχέ γ', 'as chance would have it'.

43 οἶμαι: B has οιμε. Confusion of αι and ε, identical in pronunciation at the period of its writing, is common. At the Adonia not only were there participants but there might also be spectators, cf.

Theokritos xv. 23, θαϲόμεναι τὸν Ἄδωνιν. Moschion did not intend to be a spectator, but he found himself in a position which he thinks was that a spectator would have occupied. The emendations οἴκοι (Kassel hesitantly) and οἴμοι (Jacques) suppose a confusion of οι and ε, cf. the previous line where εχουϲηϲ was originally written οιχουϲηϲ. Jacques explains that all Moschion's troubles had begun on this night, hence his sigh, οἴμοι. We might consider reading οἶμ᾽ ἐνθεαϲτήϲ, 'I became, I think, possessed'. The word ἐνθεαϲτήϲ is quoted only from *Glossaria* (where it is corrupted to ἐνθεατήϲ), but ἐνθεαϲτικῶϲ ἔχειν describes the lover's state at *Dysk.* 44. Moschion's rape of the girl will be palliated by his having been under the influence of a supernatural power. The following clause ἀγρυπνίαν κτλ. would then explain ϲυμπαρών, his presence at the proceedings.

46 ὠρχοῦντ᾽: Dancing at the Adonia is implied by Ar. *Lys.* 391 ff., ἔλεγεν ὁ μὴ ὥραϲι μὲν Δημόϲτρατοϲ | πλεῖν εἰϲ Ϲικελίαν, ἡ γυνὴ δ᾽ ὀρχουμένη | "αἰαῖ Ἄδωνιν" φηϲίν: a middle verb in asyndeton is probable, and no alternative recommends itself.

47: Since ὀκνῶ, 'shrink from', often has a connotation of 'be ashamed to do', it can hardly be followed by a corrective ἴϲωϲ δ᾽ αἰϲχύνομαι. Hence Austin prints ἴϲωϲ δ᾽—αἰϲχύνομαι, i.e. 'But perhaps (I must). I am ashamed, but there's nothing to be got by being ashamed'. Another possibility is offered by Lowe's supplement οἷϲ: 'But perhaps I am ashamed over what it does no good to be ashamed of'. ὅτε, the disregarded suggestion of Post, may be right: 'But perhaps I am ashamed when it does no good.'

48: αλλ seems to be written above ομωϲ in B. I take this to be an addition to avoid asyndeton; for other examples see Jackson, *Marginalia Scenica*, 103, and probably *Epitr.* 400. Jacques suggests ἐϲτιν· ἀλλ᾽, deleting ὅμωϲ, and Arnott ὄφελοϲ· ἀλλ᾽ ὅμωϲ.

51 τὴν αἰτίαν ϲχών: 'Having incurred the responsibility', as in Soph. *Antigone* 1312, ὡϲ αἰτίαν γε τῶνδε κἀκείνων ἔχων. For the scene described, cf. Ter. *Adelphoe* 471, 'ad matrem uirginis | uenit ipsus ultro lacrumans orans obsecrans | fidem dans, iurans se illam ducturum domum.' On the necessity of a father's consent to his son's marriage see intro. p. 32.

53: Kassel's ἐπώμοϲα causes an unusual word-division of the dactyl in the third foot θη ποθ᾽ | ὁ, but the elision palliates it; and cf. *Dysk.* 386, 476. Hence many accept ἂν νῦν ἐπανέλθῃ ποθ᾽ ὁ πατήρ. ἐπώμοϲα i.e. 'if my father returns some time now'. If this is right, it will give the audience a hint that his return is imminent. Unfortunately I have no parallel for νῦν ποτε, and one would expect a promise to marry whenever the father returned, not if he returned at about the time of the play. Possibly, then, Menander wrote ἂν cυνεπανέλθῃ ποθ', 'if he returns with his travelling companion, the girl's father'.

ἐπόμνυμι, 'swear an oath confirmatory of a statement', is not often used absolutely, but see Plato, *Laws* 917 b, ὁ κιβδηλεύων τι ψεύδεται ... καὶ τοὺς θεοὺς παρακαλῶν ἐπόμνυcιν.

54 εἴληφα: Sc. εἰc τὴν οἰκίαν; the phrase occurs in full in frag. 352 K–T, Straton frag. 1 K (Page, *GLP* p. 264). οὐ πάλαι modifies both γενόμενον and εἴληφα. The perfect is used because the result of the action persists and is of prime importance; the same is true of cυμ-βέβηκε in the next line. Since little more than 9 months have elapsed since the Adonia of late July, the action of the play may be thought of as taking place at the end of April. Demeas and Nikeratos, who will shortly appear, must have set out from Pontos soon after the beginning of the sailing season.

55: This sentence must have told that Chrysis had also given birth to a child. καὶ μάλα is strangely placed if it refers to what precedes, and of dubious good sense; how can the birth have been *very much* a matter of chance? Is a line lost? Or is Jacques's supplement καὶ μάλ' ⟨εὖ⟩, adopted in OCT, right?

56: Restoration is uncertain; ὥcτ' ἔ⟨τε⟩κε]ν is possibly right (Austin and Arnott). The tense of ἔτικτε]ν, printed in OCT, has raised doubts, but the imperfect ἔτικτον is sometimes used with no clear difference of meaning from the aorist; so frag. 685, ⟨ὑπ⟩εδεξάμην, ἔτικτον, ἐκτρέφω, φιλῶ (cf. Plat. *Menex.* 237 c, τῆc τεκούcηc καὶ θρεψάcηc καὶ ὑποδεξαμένηc), frag. 740, εἰ γὰρ ἐγένου ... ὅτ' ἔτικτεν ἡ μήτηρ cε, Kratinos frag. 323 K, εὐδαίμον' ἔτικτέ cε μήτηρ. The explanation may be that the present τίκτω can be used to indicate the result of giving birth, i.e. 'I am a mother', e.g. Eur. *Ion* 1560, ἥδε τίκτει cε, 'she is your mother'. The imperfect will then mean 'was a mother' (Goodwin, *MT* §§ 27, 34). If ἔτικτεν ἡ Χρυcίc is right here, the force will be 'Chrysis was a mother' or 'Chrysis had given birth to a child'.

The missing conclusion of the monologue must have explained that Chrysis' child had died and that she had taken Plangon's in its place. Thereafter Moschion probably left the stage, perhaps with the intention of going to the harbour to discover whether there was any news of the ship on which his father was returning, cf. Plaut. *Stichus* 151. The gap is one of *c.* 25 lines.

(ii) **58–86:** *Chrysis, joined by Moschion and Parmenon*

58 ff.: After Moschion's departure Chrysis came on and delivered a short monologue. At 61 Moschion and Parmenon enter in conversation, and are at first unaware of her presence.

59 cπουδῇ πρὸc ἡμᾶc: Chrysis here announces the approach of Moschion and Parmenon. Does πρὸc ἡμᾶc mean 'towards our house', cf. 40, or is she accompanied by some servant, a *muta persona*? If the guess was right that Moschion had gone off to visit the harbour, the audience will not have expected to see him again during this act. His unforeseen return will then be the first of a long series of incidents in this play that cheat the expectations that have been aroused.

61: In other plays a man who returns from abroad is seen, and his arrival announced, by some other character before he actually appears on the stage: Plaut. *Mostellaria* 352, *Stichus* 274 ff., *Trinummus* 1121, Ter. *Phormio* 199.

63 εὖ γ' ἐπόηcαν: Cf. Eur. *Med.* 472 εὖ δ' ἐποίηcαc μολών; the Greeks frequently expressed gratification (as here) or gratitude by phrases expressing praise of the person who was its cause, see J. H. Quincey, *JHS* lxxxvi (1966), 133. **ὅπωc ἕcει:** This construction, the equivalent of an imperative, is common in Aristophanes. It may have arisen from the common use of ὅπωc and future indicative after verbs signifying *plan, take care* etc., Goodwin, *MT* §§ 271 ff. It is convenient as a substitute for the imperative of εἶναι, e.g. Eur. *Cycl.* 595, ὅπωc ἀνὴρ ἕcει. In comedy ἴcθι is always imperative of εἰδέναι.

64 ἐμβαλεῖc περὶ τοῦ γάμου λόγον: A similar phrase in *Dysk.* 352.

69 ὅπωc: This can be explained by supposing an aposiopesis; the sentence might have continued e.g., ὅπωc οὐκ αἰcχυνεῖ καταλιπὼν λέγε, 'tell me how you will not be ashamed if you desert the girl you have wronged'. Or, as Jacques has suggested to me, ὅπωc μὴ ἐγκαταλείψειc, 'see that you don't leave them in the lurch'. The mention of the girl and her mother is enough to throw Moschion into agitation, and Parmenon breaks off to continue: 'Are you trembling? You are no man.' But Austin's suggestion οἴμ' ὡc may be right. The phrase, however, common in Old Comedy, is not paralleled in Menander.

ἀνδρόγυνε: The word means 'hermaphrodite' in Plat. *Symp.* 189 e, but is used elsewhere of 'womanish' i.e. cowardly men, e.g. *Aspis* 242, Aischines ii. 127, ὁμολόγηcον ἀνδρόγυννοc εἶναι; Plato himself adds, νῦν οὐκ ἔcτιν ἀλλ' ἢ ἐν ὀνείδει ὄνομα κείμενον. The vocative is used as an insult or reproof in [Plut.] *Mor.* 219 e, ἀνδρόγυνε, τί δ' ἂν πάθοιμεν δεινὸν θανάτου καταφρονήcαντεc; **δύcμορε:** See 255 n.

71 γελοῖον: 'That's ridiculous', cf. 579, 654.

72 τουτονί: Moschion. **ταύταιc,** with a gesture towards Nikeratos' door.

73 ἐκεῖνα ὧν ὤμοcεν: Parmenon is particularly and personally interested in the feasting that will go on at the marriage. This was implied in the promises made by Moschion to the girl, but was not their whole content. So Parmenon can say he wants Moschion not to forget these elements in what he had sworn to do.

74 cηcαμῆν: A mixture of honey and sesame seeds, a symbol of fertility, eaten at Athenian weddings; Ar. *Peace* 869, cηcαμῆ cυμπλάττεται, where a scholiast explains cηcαμῆ· πλακοῦς γαμικὸς ἀπὸ cηcάμων πεποιημένος, διὰ τὸ πολύγονον, ὥс φηcι Μένανδρος. The seeds were pounded and crushed, hence κόπτειν. Photios, s.v. cήcαμον, says that the mixture was in old times sent round to friends, but now (νῦν) people gave a dinner at home and there distributed it to the guests.

74–5: The infinitives θύειν etc., although explanatory of ἐκεῖνα, may be felt to be grammatically dependent on βούλομαι and like the preceding infinitives to have τουτονί as their subject: 'I want him not to forget these points in his promises: (I want him) to sacrifice, etc.' If this is so it may be necessary to change παρελθών to παρελθόντ', unless an anacoluthon may be seen, occasioned by the intervention of the verb ὤμοcεν, of which Moschion is the subject. παρελθών (or παρελθόντα) would mean 'coming to help the servants'. But I know of no evidence that it was part of the bridegroom's duties to help in the making of the sesame-cake.   **αὐτός:** Moschion wants the marriage to take place, but Parmenon himself has reasons enough of his own for wanting it also.

77 ἐγὼ μὲν οἴομαι: 'I imagine he will'; this seems to be said by Chrysis rather than by Parmenon. The succeeding exchanges are hard to allot to their speakers. But since ὁ πατὴρ χαλεπανεῖ must belong to Moschion, it seems to me likely (although Austin disagrees) that the speech it explains, i.e. τὸ παιδίον οὕτως ἐῶμεν κτλ. is also his. If coι is rightly added in 80, the question τὶ δὴ γὰρ οὔ; must be put by Chrysis; otherwise it could be Parmenon's. 84–5 look like Chrysis' declaration that she will not abandon the child. The preceding lines 80b–83 can be assigned to her also, following B, which has no paragraphus or dicolon at 83; the *hetaira* can no doubt speak from experience of the mollifying effects on men of the passion of ἔρως.   **τὸ παιδίον:** B has τοδεπαιδιον, whence some would read τό γε παιδίον, but γε seems pointless and the broken anapaest in fifth foot is unusual, although not unexampled (*Epitr.* 299); cf. *Dysk.* 846 n. For other instances of intruded δε in this codex see 22, 356, *Dysk.* 187, 242, ? 678, 729.

81 ὦ βέλτιcτε: This is a polite form of address, and if the speech belongs to Chrysis, may recognize Moschion's concern for her interests. Although βέλτιcτε is usual in Menander, ὦ βέλτιcτε recurs at *Dysk.* 338, *Aspis* 251. Alkiphron *Ep.* iv. 8. 4, ἐρῶ γάρ, ὦ Πετάλη, κακῶς, cf. ibid. 14. 7, is probably an echo of New Comedy.

85: The child is already too old to be exposed. Chrysis considers no worse possibility than that Demeas should refuse to have it in the house and insist on its being put out to a nurse, some poor woman living in a tenement-house. A cυνοικία is a house in which several families live, LSJ s.v. III, Aischines i. 124, ὅπου μὲν γὰρ πολλοὶ μιcθωcάμενοι μίαν οἴκηcιν διελόμενοι ἔχουcι, cυνοικίαν καλοῦμεν.

What happened in the gap of about 21 lines after 86 is uncertain, but Chrysis must have gone in, and probably Parmenon also, for he seems to be at hand to be summoned in the next act (189). The scene ended with a monologue by Moschion of which the end remains, in a fragmentary state.

(iii) 87–95: Moschion alone

91 οὐκ ἀπάγξομαι ταχύ; Cf. Polemon in *Perik.* 505. But Moschion has no reason for despair. He has, it is true, a tendency to dramatization, illustrated in the last act, which may here make him exaggerate his distress. Perhaps, however, his question is hypothetical: 'if I don't persuade my father, shan't I hang myself?' Or Moschion may here imagine himself to be addressing his father, and threatening suicide if he does not get his way. Then at 93 he may say (to himself now) that his present oration is inadequate; he must go away to some quiet spot to practise it.

92 ῥήτωρ, a word used especially of speakers in the *ecclesia*, looks likely, but I know no plausible supplement.

95 γυμνάζομαι: A possible but not certain supplement. The present would be used for the future, to express intention, Goodwin, *MT* § 32. The word, properly applied to physical training, was frequently used of training for any kind of contest, including dialectical and rhetorical (Arist. *Topica* 108ᵃ13, 164ᵇ1, etc., *Rhet.* iii. 1410ᵇ8).

(iv) 96–119: Demeas and Nikeratos

96–7: Moschion retires to solitude to practise the speech that he will have to make to his father. For such practice in a retired spot cf. Ter. *Andr.* 406, 'uenit meditatus alicunde ex solo loco: orationem sperat inuenisse'. The stage is left empty for the entry of Demeas and Nikeratos. Demeas addresses his first remark to servants or poor followers (αἰcθάνεcθε, 96, is plural) as well as Nikeratos.

98–101a: The staccato speech, in brief phrases, is very like that used by Nikeratos later (399–420), and it is odd that the wealthy Demeas should praise Athens as the home of true blessings for the poor (100). I suspect that all this, perhaps with the exception of the cry Ἄπολλον, an expression of dismay used twice elsewhere by Demeas (567, 570), belongs to Nikeratos. See *Entretiens Hardt* xvi. 121. Πόντος: This name of the Black Sea was also applied to the countries round it, particularly those on the South shore, cf. 417 note, *RE* suppl. ix. 955–85. The abundance of fish in the Black Sea, a spawning-ground, is frequently mentioned, e.g. Arist. *HA* 598ᵃ30, Plut. *De Soll. An.* 981 c, Oppian, *Halieutica* i. 597 ff. (see Mair's note), Theophylaktos Simokates, *Dial.* i. 19, περὶ τὸν Πόντον τοίνυν τοὺς ἰχθύας ἅπαντάς φασιν ἐνδημεῖν. Diphilos frag. 17 K, speaks of τὸ πλῆθος ἰχθύων with the inhabitants of Byzantium.

98 παχεῖς: Perhaps 'dense, stupid', as well as 'fat', old men, cf. Ar. *Clouds* 842, ἀμαθὴς καὶ παχύς. According to Theopompos in Athenaios 526 e the Byzantines spent their time drinking in taverns; Phylarchos said the same, ibid. 442 c. Men. frag. 61, πάντας μεθύσους τοὺς ἐμπόρους ποιεῖ τὸ Βυζάντιον. This may have made them fat. Jacques prefers a third possible meaning, 'rich', found several times in Aristophanes (LSJ s.v. II). ἰχθῦς ἄφθονοι: The papyrus has ιχθνες, with a broken anapaest. The Attic form is ἰχθῦς, guaranteed by metre in Antiphanes frag. 236 K, ἰχθῦς Cικυῶνος, Αἰγίου δ' αὐλητρίδες, Alexis frag. 261, and almost guaranteed in Eubulos frag. 109 K, πηδῶςι δ' ἰχθῦς ἐν μέςοιςι τηγάνοις, where ἰχθύες would give a broken anapaest; in all these passages the MS. A of Athenaios preserves the correct ἰχθῦς. ἰχθύες is, however, presented in *anapaests* in Teleikleides frag. 1 K. Similarly Attic has ῦς, μῦς contrasted with ςύες, μύες of the κοινή; e.g. Antiphanes frag. 193 K, Βοιώτιαι μὲν ἐγχέλεις, μῦς Ποντικοί. These forms arose by analogy with the accusatives ἰχθῦς etc., which show a normal development from *ἰχθυν-νς etc.; K–B i. 439, Schwyzer, i. 564. Why are 'plentiful fish' one of the curses of the Pontos? Presumably because one can tire even of a good thing.

The prevalence at Byzantium of the herb ἀψίνθιον, wormwood, is referred to by Diphilos frag. 17 K, ἂν Βυζαντίους (sc. κέκληκας), ἀψινθίῳ cπόδηcον (Dindorf: cφοίη δεῖξον A) ὅcα γ' ἂν παρατιθῇς. Demeas (or Nikeratos) complains that its bitterness infected everything: similarly Philostratos, *Vit. Apoll.* i. 21, says that the great quantity of wormwood in Babylonia makes all the wild edible plants ἀηδῆ καὶ πικρά. Infestation of Pontic regions by wormwood is mentioned by Plaut. *Trin.* 934, Ovid, *Tristia* v. 13. 21, *Ex Ponto* iii. 1. 23, 8. 15.

100 καθαρά: 'Undiluted'.

101 Ἀθῆναι φίλταται: An address to one's homeland on return to it occurs elsewhere: frag. 1, χαῖρ' ὦ φίλη γῆ, διὰ χρόνου πολλοῦ ς' ἰδὼν ἀςπάζομαι, frag. 287, ὦ φιλτάτη γῆ μῆτερ, ὡς ςεμνὸν ςφόδρ' εἶ τοῖς νοῦν ἔχουςι κτῆμα κτλ., *Aspis* 491, Plaut. *Stichus* 649, 'saluete Athenae, quae nutrices Graeciae'; probably frag. com. adesp. 340 Kock. The prayer that Athens may have what she deserves may have had some topical allusion to a danger or misfortune in which she was involved.

105 ἀπόπληκτε: *Perik.* 496 n.; here the sense 'paralysed' is present, as in Amphis frag. 23 K, ἔνδον κάθητ' ἀπόπληκτος; the word is addressed to a servant, who has not moved quickly at the command to enter the house (εἴσω παράγετε); cf. Herondas v. 40, ἕστηκας ἐμβλέπων σύ; iv. 44, ἕστηκε δ' εἴς μ' ὀρεῦσα, and perhaps *Dysk.* 441.

107: For absence of sunshine in Pontos, cf. Greg. Naz. *Epist.* 4. 4, τὸν ποθούμενον ἥλιον, ὃν ὡς διὰ κάπνης αὐγάζεσθε, ὦ Ποντικοὶ Κιμμέριοι. Nikeratos gives a characteristically down-to-earth explanation, Demeas lets his fancy play, ascribing human motives to the sun. He no more seriously believes this than he will believe the story he later tries to impose upon Nikeratos, that a god was the father of Plangon's child.

110 οὐδὲν σεμνόν: Lit. 'nothing majestic, or noble'; we might say 'nothing very wonderful'.   αὐτόθι: 'On the spot', similarly used of a foreign country, Philemon frag. 47 K, οὐ γὰρ γίγνεται τοῦτ' αὐτόθι (in Seleukos' kingdom).

111: With ὥστ' αὐτὰ τἀναγκαῖ' ἐπέλαμπε compare Diphilos frag. 4 K, ἵν' αὐτὰ τἀναγκαῖα δυστυχῆς μόνον. Austin quotes also Eur. *Suppl.* 855, *Pap. Hibeh* VI a 30 (Page, *GLP* p. 288). J. Tate, 'The Greek for "Minimum"', *CR* lxii (1948), 7, illustrates the use of ἀναγκαῖον to mean what is (*a*) well above zero, (*b*) hardly up to pass-mark.

114: It is remarkable that no reason is revealed for Demeas' intention to marry his son to his poor neighbour's daughter. Menander probably thought that such marriages between rich and poor should be natural and usual, *Dysk.* 308 n. Here he appears to recommend the practice by representing the wealthy Demeas as treating the match with the poor family next door as if it were the most ordinary thing in the world. Whether Demeas explained or defended his intention in the lines lost after 118 must be uncertain. Even if he did not, his action may have appeared more credible to those who remembered 15–16, his encouragement of Moschion in financial generosity to friends in straitened circumstances.   τῷ μειρακίῳ σου: The dative is dependent on τὰ περὶ τὸν γάμον, 'the marriage for your young man'. The Greeks were sparing with this construction of noun+dative, unless the noun is derived from a verb that would govern a dative, but enough examples (e.g. *Aspis* 130, μακροτέραν ὁρῶν ἐκείνῳ τὴν ἀποδημίαν, Xen. *Hell.* vii. 4. 8, εἴ τινα ὁρᾶτε σωτηρίαν ἡμῖν) occur to make it unnecessary to change with Austin to the genitive τοῦ μειρακίου (K–G i. 426–8).

115–7: Although the assignment of speeches in B gives a possible text, it seems improbable that Demeas, having asked Nikeratos his intentions, should not wait for an answer, but assume his consent. For this reason Kassel, following Blume, assigned ταῦτ᾽ ἀεὶ λέγω . . . θέμενοι to Nikeratos, in whose style (it may be added) the short phrases are. He also accepted Fraenkel's suggestion to read (Δη.) δέδοκται ταῦτα; (Νι.) ἐμοὶ γοῦν. For the question Fraenkel compared Soph. *Phil.* 1277, οὕτω δέδοκται; and Ar. *Eccl.* 457, καὶ δέδοκται;

118: It is tactful of the rich Demeas to insist that the idea of the match between his son and the poor neighbour's daughter originated with himself. It seems that Nikeratos now goes in; if so, it is not clear why the date for the marriage is not first fixed. Perhaps Nikeratos expects Demeas to obtain Moschion's consent for it, and then to call him out (παρακάλει) to make the arrangements. In any case, both old men will soon be gone, each into his own house, leaving the coast clear for the entry of the chorus, composed (if analogy with other plays is trustworthy) of a company of young men who have been drinking.

The conversation of Demeas and Nikeratos about their travels most unexpectedly turns to some exchanges that show them to intend a matrimonial alliance between their households. Moschion's reluctance to propose such a thing to his father thus turns out to be quite unnecessary. It looks as if nothing stood in the way of a rapid happy ending. The next act brings a complication in that Demeas falls into the expected rage on learning that Chrysis is bringing up his child, but it seems that he was talked out of it without great difficulty, and by the end of the act the marriage is once again on the point of taking place.

ACT II

(i) 120–166: *Demeas and Moschion*

120: A new act has begun. Moschion, returning from the solitary place where he should have prepared his speech to win over his father (cf. Ter. *Andr.* 406), recounts how he had instead imagined himself to be eagerly preparing for the marriage that had not yet even been arranged. It is probable Demeas has come out from his house but, being absorbed in his own thoughts, does not notice his son.

121: For μελετᾶν, 'to run over or prepare a speech in one's mind', cf. *Perik.* 550, Dem. xix. 255, xlvi. 1.

124 λουτρά: Both bride (cf. 713) and bridegroom (cf. 729) took a bath before marriage, Photios, s.v., Ar. *Lysistr.* 378, Menander frag. 52; the water was fetched from the fountain Kallirhoe, Pollux iii. 43. The supplement γ[υναῖκας is supported by 730.

125 cηcαμῆν διένεμον: Cf. 74 n.

126: B marks no change of speaker here, and it is quite possible that Moschion acknowledges his own folly. But one should not leave out of account another possibility. If Demeas had spoken earlier—and this seems likely, since otherwise he must have come on the stage without a word—he might say ἦν ἀβέλτερος in continuation of his previous speech, declaring himself to have been foolish to take Chrysis into his house. For a similar continuation, after a pause during which another character speaks unnoticed, see *Epitr.* 435. Then Moschion will break off his monologue because his father's remark has, somewhat slowly, penetrated his mind and made him aware of his presence. ἐτερέτιζον is an onomatopoeic word, like 'twitter'; it is often used of quiet singing, Theophrastos *Char.* xxvii. 15, cf. xi. 11, Euphron frag. 1 K. It can have an object, as in Phrynichos frag. 14 K τερετιῶ ⟨τι⟩ πτιστικόν, and so might govern ὑμέναιον; but B separates the words by a colon; the latter will then be the object of a verb (? ᾖδον) in the previous line. If it is used absolutely it may mean 'I prattled pointlessly', as in Zeno, *SVF* i. 78. Aristotle called the Platonic Forms τερετίσματα, *An. Post.* 83ᵃ33.

It is to be presumed that the bridegroom would not at his wedding himself sing the wedding-song. Whether there was any standard form for this song at Athens is not known: the literary version at the finale of Ar. *Peace* may give an idea of the sort of thing that was sung: see Maas, *RE* ix. 130–4.

127 ἐνεπλήcθην: 'Had my fill' of imagination. δ' οὖν marks that the speaker is returning to what is really essential, Denniston, *GP*, 462–4. What that was we do not learn, for he is interrupted by catching sight of his father outside the house.

128 ἀκήκο' ἆρα: 'Then he has heard!' ἆρα is a metrically convenient substitute for ἄρα, Denniston, *GP* 45. Moschion rightly guesses that Demeas has heard the story that Chrysis had borne him a son. Austin points out that the interrogative particle ἆρα does not always stand first in the sentence; but in none of Denniston's collection of examples (*GP* 49) does it come last. Moreover when ἆρα occurs late in an interrogative sentence, it may be, not the particle of interrogation, but equivalent to ἄρα, 'then'. χαῖρέ μοι, πάτερ: This is the first meeting of father and son, but Moschion, who must guess why the other looks grim, comes straight to the point with τί cκυθρωπάζεις;

129 νὴ καὶ cύ γε: Cf. *Georgos* 41 n.   τί γάρ; must be given with B to Demeas, cf. *Dysk.* 553, 636. 'You ask why?'

131 ἀγνοῶ ⟨γὰρ⟩ τὸν λόγον: Soph. *Trach.* 78, Eur. *Phoen.* 707, both have τὸν λόγον γὰρ ἀγνοῶ. A γαμετὴ ἑταῖρα is, of course, a paradoxical contradiction in terms. Similarly in Aischines i. 111 a speaker uses a puzzling phrase and continues ἀγνοεῖτε ὅ τι λέγω;

132 λάθριός τις υός: The supplement is tempting, but if Demeas said this, he was unreasonable. He had been abroad at the time of the birth and for some period previously; he had been told of the child immediately on his return. The word λάθριος is used in frag. 718, but mainly by poets, prose authors employing λαθραῖος.

133 ἐς κόρακας ἄπεισι: Demeas will use the same phrase to Chrysis at 369, ἄπιθι . . . ἐς κόρακας ἤδη.

134–42: O 17 nowhere overlaps B, but is firmly placed with regard to it because each contains a part of lines 140–2, which are quoted by Stobaios. In 134 ἤδη λαβοῦca is more probable than Handley's ἡ διαλαθοῦca, since it is an essential point that Demeas wants to be rid of the baby. It may be assumed that Chrysis had refused, as she had promised at 84, to part with the child; hence Demeas says that she will have to go and take it with her. An object for λαβοῦca is desirable: good sense would be given by τὸν δ'] ἐc κόρακαc . . . λαβοῦca, but there is hardly room for four letters. Turner thinks ὅν] not too short.

135: Turner understands 'am I to rear a bastard for the sake of someone else?', i.e. for Chrysis. For the masculine adjective, which would lay emphasis on her 'otherness' rather than her sex, cf. Eur. *Andr.* 712, οὐκ ἀνέξεται | τίκτονταc ἄλλουc, *Alc.* 634, παρεὶc ἄλλῳ θανεῖν, K–G i. 82. I think this is right. But the words have another, dangerous sense, which Demeas cannot intend, but of which Moschion (and the audience) must be aware: 'am I to rear another man's bastard son?' The ambiguity adds to the tension.

139: Cf. Heliodoros ii. 30. 4, παίζειc ἡμᾶc :: οὐ παίζω . . . ἀλλὰ καὶ cφόδρα cπουδάζω.   cὺ μέν: μέν *solitarium* often follows pronouns, Denniston, *GP* 381. But it is probable that Demeas, intending to continue with a δέ-clause, was interrupted.

140 γένος: Perhaps 'offspring', but more probably 'descent, ancestry'.

141 ἐξετάcαι: *Sik.* 277 suggests that ἐξετάζειν was the *vox propria* for the inquiry into claims for citizen birth.

141–2: 'The good man is legitimate, the bad illegitimate as well as bad'; this is a *sententia* on legitimacy more striking than any that can be quoted as parallels, e.g. Eur. *Andr.* 638, νόθοι τε πολλοὶ γνηcίων ἀμείνονες, Soph. frag. 84 N, ἅπαν τὸ χρηστὸν γνησίαν ἔχει φύσιν, Eur. frag. 141 N, ἐγὼ δὲ παῖδας οὐκ ἐῶ νόθους καλεῖν (Hense: λαβεῖν), τῶν γνησίων γὰρ οὐδὲν ὄντες ἐνδεεῖς, νόμῳ νοσοῦσιν.

Moschion must have persuaded his father to allow the child to be brought up, although illegitimate; when the fragments resume, Demeas is in the act of realizing that his son is eager for a quick marriage. Moschion tells him to ask no questions but to help (151–2).

146 ἐρῶ: Probably 'I am in love', not 'I shall say'. But the sense of 146–50 is irrecoverable.

150: The particle τοι is, apart from καίτοι and μέντοι, very rare in the manuscript tradition of Menander, and always dubious. The only examples are 342 below (C, but not B), frag. 276. 8 (τι Weil), frag. 348 (τὰς Blaydes) and frag. incert. 949 (a grammarian's quotation, not ascribed by him to Menander, and not necessarily correct). There is only one example in all the other fragments of New Comedy, Diphilos frag. 1. 6. See also *Dysk.* 460 n. Lowe suggests ἂν διδῶς' οὗτοι, γαμεῖς. Although Nikeratos has given his consent to the marriage, perhaps Demeas does not wish Moschion to know it yet. He may want to avoid giving the impression that everything has been arranged behind his son's back. But when he finds how keen Moschion is for the marriage, he drops the pretence that Nikeratos' consent is still needed (155).

151–3: The exact import of these exchanges must be doubtful unless the beginning of 151 can be supplemented with certainty, which does not seem possible. Kassel's πῶς ἂν is, however, not unlikely; the question is the equivalent of a wish (cf. 102 and K–G i. 235): 'Can you manage to ask no questions but realize that I am in earnest?' Demeas then repeats three words interrogatively: 'In earnest? Ask no questions?'

Kassel himself understands his text in a different way: 'How can you see that I am in earnest if you don't make inquiries of Nikeratos?' Stoessl, *Rh. Mus.* cxii (1969), 200, thinks the meaning is 'How can you know I'm in earnest when you know nothing of the affair?', that Moschion intended to confess about the child, and that Demeas cuts him short, expecting only a protestation of love for Plangon.

153 κατανοῶ τὸ πρᾶγμα: The meaning is not, I think, that Demeas guesses that Moschion has got the girl with child, and wishes to marry her before her parents find out, but that he understands the urgency of love, cf. 335, οὐκ ἐρῶν γάρ, ὡς τότ' ᾠόμην, ἔσπευδεν.

155 τουτονί: Nikeratos. A gesture will indicate his house.

156–9: The hole after ταυ[in B is not large enough to have swallowed the last word of the line; perhaps it was omitted. If ἅ μοι λέγεις is right, Moschion must have asked, in the gap before 145, for some of the concomitants of a wedding. B has paragraphi below 156 and 158, but a dicolon after ποειν in 156 has been cancelled, and another after λεγειc in 157 converted to a single point. The loss of the ends of 156 and 158 makes the ground uncertain, but if it is supposed that there was a dicolon after ἐπιθειc in 158, and none after ταυτα in 156 (so that the paragraphus below that line should also have been cancelled), the corrector of B intended the text adopted in OCT, which gives the whole passage down to ἐπιθείc to Demeas. This may be right. Demeas shows his willingness to hasten on the marriage (already indicated by τρέχω in 154) by telling his son to start the preparations at once: he assumes, again as in 154, that Nikeratos will agree. But when Moschion unexpectedly completes his sentence by speaking of fetching the bride, he realizes that it would be tactlessly premature to do *that* before her father has in fact given his consent to an immediate marriage. I hesitate, however, to accept this without reserve. Moschion does not go in to begin preparations, but goes away, only to return at the beginning of the fourth act: his absence is required by the plot, for he cannot be at home when Chrysis is turned out. He gives no reason for not doing what his father, according to B, suggested he should do: apparently he explains why he should not do something quite different, i.e. remain with Demeas when the latter talks to Nikeratos. Hence I think that the correct distribution may be to give the whole sentence from περιρρανάμενος to μέτειμι to Moschion, who proposes a speeding-up of action that Demeas sees is quite unacceptable. At one time I supposed him to reply μήπω δή, negativing the whole of Moschion's proposal, and to add βάδιζε ἄχρι ἄν, 'take yourself off until etc.', cf. 258, *Epitr.* 376, οἴμωζε καὶ βάδιζε, *Sik.* 267, 269, Ar. *Eccl.* 144, cὺ μὲν βάδιζε καὶ καθῆco. But Austin rightly objected that 161–2 do not follow naturally if Demeas had told Moschion to take himself off. It is better to take μήπω δὴ βάδιζε as a single phrase, 'don't hurry off yet'.

157 περιρρανάμενος: Lit. 'having given myself the ritual sprinkling'. In view of his haste, Moschion minimizes the washing that preceded a wedding (124).   παραγαγών: 'Having gone in'. παραγενοῦ 'be at hand' (M. L. West and myself) is unlikely because B has παρ'α[, indicating elision of the prefix.

158 λιβανωτὸν ἐπιθείς: 'Having put incense on the fire on the altar'. For burning of incense before the bride is fetched, see 674.

162: Moschion departs to kill time until the arrangements have been made; he will not return until the opening of Act IV. Demeas remains to soliloquize.

164: 'Accident secures many things one has not seen', e.g. here Demeas did not know of Moschion's love, but he chanced to take the action that would allow its continuance. It was common to recognize Τύχη as a goddess, but unusual to see divinity in τὸ αὐτόματον. Timoleon, however, had set up a shrine of Αὐτοματία, Plutarch, *Timoleon* 36.

166: A colon after ερωτικως forbids ἐρωτικῶс ταύ[της, which might be suggested by Plato, *Symp.* 222 c, ἐρωτικῶс ἔχειν τοῦ Cωκράτουс and Aristainetos i. 13, ἧc εἶχεν ἐρωτικῶc.

(ii) 167–205: *Demeas, Nikeratos, Parmenon* (enters 190)

167: There is a gap of about 27 lines before the text resumes, and then in a fragmentary form. It is useless to attempt to guess what Demeas can have said if what is lost was a monologue, or what action can have been introduced. The plot does not seem to require anything. The general run of 167–87 can be established with some probability. Nikeratos is either called out or comes out (168), perhaps wondering why Demeas has not yet called him. The warm greeting χαῖρε πολλὰ cύ (169) probably comes from Demeas, who is going to ask a favour of his friend. He continues 'you remember' either 'that we did not fix a day' or 'that we fixed such and such a day'; if Nikeratos went in at 118, the former alternative is necessary. Next he proposes that the day should be today. Nikeratos replies by bewildered questions and then a refusal: 'it is impossible' (176). At 181 he may object that there cannot be a wedding before friends have been invited. But at 187 he gives in, and is congratulated by Demeas (νοῦν ἔχειc, cf. 605).

168: Handley's suggestion, (Νικήρατ'), ἔξελ]θ' εἰc τὸ πρόcθεν [δε]ῦρό μοι, is excellent for sense. B ends μαι, but something was written above the α. Kasser, however, is certain that]θ is impossible, and the photograph supports him. He also regards]υ as impossible and is sure that whatever is above α is not ο. On these points the photograph tends to confirm his view. Accordingly I retain Austin's text.

183: The correct text must remain doubtful. ἤν· πῶc γνώcομαι; is not unlikely, ἤν being an exclamation of embarrassment, cf. 313 n. Before that ἄχαριc would be metrically regular, but the suprascript οι is left unaccounted for. ἐμ]οὶ (or c]οι) χάριc gives a broken anapaest with change of speaker, unexampled in Menander, but occurring in Aristophanes, *Lys.* 731.

189–205: Nikeratos' consent having been secured (187) Demeas calls for his slave Parmenon (189) and sends him to procure necessities for the feast, including a cook to prepare the dinner (194). The old men retire to instruct their households, and Nikeratos must have left to procure a sheep for sacrifice.

190 cήcaμa: Sesame-seeds to make the wedding-cake, cf. 74 n.

191: Perhaps 'buy absolutely everything to be had in the market'.

193 καὶ ταχέωc is a supplement to the imperative lost in 101–2; cf. Ar. *Frogs* 166, τὰ cτρώματ' αὖθιc λάμβανε :: πρὶν καὶ καταθέcθαι; :: καὶ ταχέωc μέντοι πάνυ.

194–5: I doubt whether μάγειρον can be the object of πριάμενος, since a cook must be 'hired' not 'bought'. A joke by Parmenon, pretending that he had been told to buy a cook, is not in itself out of question, but would not bring the simple assentient reply πριάμενος. The sense must be 'Am I to get the cook after I have made the other purchases?'

195 ff.: Austin supposes, I think rightly, that Parmenon enters Demeas' house at 195. When he returns at 297 from his expedition to the market he has a basket, which he will here fetch. Whether he is supposed also to collect money in the house, or whether Demeas carries a purse from which he supplies him, must be uncertain. He may come out again at 198, speaking back into the house (Stoessl, *Rh. Mus.* cxii [1969] 201). But it is more likely that 198–200 are spoken off-stage, audible because the door has been left open, and that he does not reappear until 202, when he is immediately criticized for his slowness. Nikeratos must reappear before the end of the act, to leave for the market, while Demeas retires into his own house. Once again, as at the end of Act I, the way seems clear for the desired marriage.

195: Cf. Antiphanes frag. 68 K, cὺ δ' ἀγοράceιc ἡμῖν λαβών, | Πίcτ', ἀργύριον, Plaut. *Cas.* 490.

196 cὺ δ' οὐδέπω, sc. εἰc ἀγορὰν ἀπῆλθεc.

198 διώξομαι: 'I shall follow', as in *Dysk.* 372, *Sik.* 384. Parmenon remarks that he does not understand the situation; he must guess that a marriage-feast is to be prepared, but who is to be the bride or why it is so hurried, he cannot know. His ignorance means that he would be unable, even if willing, to answer the cook's questions at 287–90. **cυντείνω τ' ἐκεῖ:** 'I am hastening thither', cf. Plut. *Nicias* 30, δρόμῳ cυντείναc εἰc τὸ ἄcτυ. But Parmenon still dawdles, and Demeas has to speed him on at 202.

201: 'We must not allow argument or delay.' Nikeratos' wife never appears on the stage, but there are other indications that she is not a nonentity (421, 558).

ACT III

(i) 206–282: *Demeas*

Demeas comes out of his house and in a long monologue confides in the audience that as all seemed set fair, he had been struck out of the blue by a catastrophe. By a brilliant piece of writing the hearer is kept waiting for some 40 lines before he learns the nature of the blow, which is revealed, when it comes, as unexpectedly as it had hit Demeas. The talk of an old servant had showed her to believe that Chrysis' child was not his but Moschion's.

207–9: Punctuation is uncertain, but B has a stop after ἐλθών.

209 θέοντας: The verb θεῖν is used not only of ships but also of men at sea 'running before the wind', Xen. *Hell.* vi. 2. 29, εἰ μὲν αὖρα φέροι, θέοντες ἀνεπαύοντο; similarly Soph. *Ajax* 1083, πόλιν . . . ἐξ οὐρίων δραμοῦσαν.   **ἐξήραξε:** 'Shattered'; the verb was used by Aristophanes, *Knights* 641, *Thesm.* 704.   **κἀνεχαίτισεν:** 'Capsized'; the verb is properly applied to a horse that rears and perhaps throws its rider, and metaphorically of various kinds of upset. In Eur. *Bacchae* 1072 Dionysus is careful, as he allows the bent tree to straighten, that it shall not throw Pentheus, φυλάccων μὴ 'ναχαιτίcειέ νιν. In *Hippolytus* 1232 the bull caused Hippolytus to be thrown from his chariot, ἔcφηλε κἀνεχαίτιcεν.

Favorinus, *De Exilio* col. 23. 24, has οὐρίῳ ποτὲ πνεύματι θέοντας . . . τὸ πνεῦμα κατὰ πρύμναν λάβρον ἐμπεcὸν αὐτάνδρους κατὰ τὸν Μένανδρον ἐξήραξε καὶ ἀνεχαίτιcεν. It was supposed that he quoted a verse that ran αὔτανδρον (sc. ναῦν) ἐξήραξε κἀνεχαίτιcεν (frag. 701 K–T). That could be true, in spite of this passage of *Samia*, for Menander may have repeated the image in some other play.

213 οἶδα . . . καλῶc is possible for εὖ οἶδα, cf. Soph. *OC* 269, καλῶc ἔξοιδα, but εἰ βλέπω . . . καλῶc ἔτι seems preferable, 'whether I am still seeing straight', see *Dysk.* 236 n.

214–15: Restoration of these lines is hazardous. B seems to have ἐπιο in 214, which I suppose to be a misreading of εἰcτο. The phrase εἰc τὸ πρόcθεν with a verb of motion is not infrequent: 168 above, *Mis.* 209, αὐτῶν προϊών τις εἰc τὸ πρόcθεν, *Theophorumene* 26, εἰc τὸ πρόcθεν ἐκπηδήcεται. Meaning literally 'to the place in front of the house', it is almost equal to 'out on to the stage'. The final word or phrase appears to begin with π or τ; but nothing very satisfactory has been found. Possibly προάγομαι (Austin).   **ἀνυπέρβλητον:** 'Unsurpassable', a word found in several of the orators.

216 ἦ 'cτ[ι] πιθανόν; 'Is it persuasive?', i.e. 'can I believe it?', cf. Ter.

Andr. 625, 'hoccinest credibile?' But the reading is uncertain. The first letters are lost from B and damaged in C, where a vertical stroke seems to precede ϲ. Koenen, after inspection, denies that the first letter is ε, but thinks η possible. Turner suggested ἧϲ τἀπίθανον ϲκέψαϲθε, *CR* N.s. xxi (1971), 352, but since B accents πιθανόν, ἧϲ τὸ πιθανὸν would be better. But it is neither 'pain' nor 'a blow' that has persuaded Demeas, but the whole set of circumstances that he will recount. Can it be that Menander wrote εἰϲ τὸ πιθανὸν ϲκέψαϲθε, 'just look at the probability of it'?

217 εἰϲ ἀκρίβειαν: 'Interpreting nothing with accuracy', cf. Plato, *Laws* 967 b, οὕτωϲ εἰϲ ἀκρίβειαν, Arist. *Politics* 1331ᵃ2, εὑρημένων . . . εἰϲ ἀκρίβειαν.

218 ἐπάγομαι μέγ' ἀτύχημα: 'Bring a great misfortune on myself', cf. Lysias iv. 19, ϲυμφορὰν ἐμαυτῷ . . . ἐπαγαγέϲθαι.

219 ὑπερεϲπουδακώϲ: A rare and emphatic word, found in frag. 780, but otherwise not recorded by LSJ before Lucian. Another instance, probably from Menander, of a marriage that takes place on the same day as that on which it is arranged is *Aulularia* 261, and the double marriage of *Dyskolos* may be fixed for the next day (851). In Ter. *Andria*, when Simo said 'uxor tibi ducendast, Pamphile, hodie' (254), Pamphilus did not object that this was improper haste—on the contrary he could not think of any reason to advance against the unwelcome order. Although it was presumably unusual in real life to push a marriage on so fast, it would be rash to suppose it an impossibility. But, like another unusual event, the discovery of a foundling's true parents, it was a convenient feature for comedy, since it enabled the incidents of a plot to be compressed within the single day to which the action was usually confined. In *Samia* the hurrying on of the marriage serves another dramatic purpose: the eagerness of Demeas, and everyone else, to see Moschion and Plangon married is frustrated by successive obstacles.

220 ἁπλῶϲ: He gave a simple, direct explanation: 'I did not fuss them: I only explained [the original meaning of φράζω, as in Homer] that they must get everything ready for a wedding in an hour or so.'

222 ἐνάρχεϲθαι κανοῦν: A formular phrase, denoting the preparation of the sacrificial basket by placing in it the requisites for a sacrifice; here the sacrifice preceding a wedding, cf. *Perik.* 922, Ar. *Peace* 948, τὸ κανοῦν πάρεϲτ' ὀλὰϲ (barley groats) ἔχον καὶ ϲτέμμα καὶ μάχαιραν. The basket was carried round the altar (Ar. *Peace* 956, Eur. *HF* 926, *IA* 1471–3, 1568), the barley-grains scattered on the victim, and the ϲτέμμα (garland?) placed on it; Humborg, *RE* Suppl. iv. 871.

πέττειν: Sc. ἄρτους, 'wheaten loaves', and πέμματα, 'cakes', which were eaten at the wedding feast. πέττειν is regularly differentiated from μάττειν, 'make barley-dough, μᾶζα', eaten by all on occasion, but the ordinary food of the poor and of slaves, Hdt. i. 200, Plato, *Rep.* ii. 372 b, Neil on Ar. *Knights* 55.

223 ἀμέλει: 'Of course' (by origin imperative of ἀμελῶ, 'never mind'). **ἑτοίμως:** 'With a will', as at 395.

225 ἔρριπτο: The pluperfect expresses a past state, 'was lying on the couch where it had been dumped'; the perfect κεκραγός functions as usual like a present participle, cf., e.g., κεκραγὼς καὶ βοῶν, Ar. *Plut.* 722. Either ἔρριπτ' or εὐθύς must be an intrusion into this line. Although at first sight ἔρριπτο might be thought to have been added to supply a verb left to be understood, εὐθύς is out of place in view of the preceding and following imperfects ἐνεπόει, ἐβοῶν. It would not be part of the *continuing* confusion that the baby had *immediately* been put out of the way; that it was lying and yelling *was* part of it.

226 αἳ δ': The women servants. αὐτοῖς of 224 covers both men and women.

228 καὐτός: Gomme supposed that Chrysis, as mistress of the house, supervised the servants, while Demeas went to the store-house to give out what was wanted. In the conventional rich man's house of comedy, and perhaps in reality as well, especially in the country (see Xenophon's *Oikonomikos*), large quantities of such things as flour, oil, and wine, some from the estate itself, were kept in stock; there was no day-to-day buying, as with us, from a shop. That was one reason why the master of the house might keep control of the stores. Though his 'wife', naturally, distributed them in the ordinary way, Demeas lent a hand on this important day (cυλλαμβάνων). It must, however, be pointed out that there is no *evidence* that Chrysis was in this sense mistress of Demeas' house or that on this occasion she supervised the servants, whose orders indeed came from Demeas (221 f.). A *hetaira* would not necessarily acquire this position, even by a long stay.

230 προαιρῶν: For this word used in connection with stores, cf. Ar. *Thesm.* 419, αὐταῖς ταμιεῦσαι καὶ προαιρούcαιc λαθεῖν | ἄλφιτον, ἔλαιον, οἶνον, and Theophr. *Char.* iv. 6 (the ἄγροικος), καὶ προαιρῶν δέ τι ἐκ τοῦ ταμιείου δεινὸς φαγεῖν. According to Guéraud nothing is visible in C after cκοπουμενος. On the infra-red photograph there appears what looks like c. Sudhaus suggested cχολῇ. Another possibility is cυχνά (Hense, Wilamowitz). Jensen thought he read παλιν, which Körte rashly prints.

233 ταμιειδίου: No significance need be given to the diminutive (elsewhere known only from the *Suda*, and plausibly restored here for C's ταμειῖον) in contrast with ταμιεῖον (229, 236). There was a tendency in Greek from early times for a diminutive to take the place of the simple form, as in ἀργύριον (originally 'a piece of silver'), παιδίον, etc. Such diminutives are often met in later Greek, including the New Testament, and in modern Greek the diminutive has often excluded the primary noun, e.g. παιδί, ψάρι, 'fish' (from ὀψάριον, dim. of ὄψον), γίδι, 'goat' (from αἰγίδιον).

234 οἴκημα: 'Room'. **ἱστεών:** 'A weaving-room', lit. 'a loom-room'; the suffix -ών denotes 'room of', 'place of', as in ἀνδρών, Παρθενών (room of the Maiden), ἱππών. In Ionic the suffix -εών was used (e.g. ἀνδρεών, cf. Hdt. i. 34 etc.), perhaps by false analogy with such words as χαλκε[ϝ]ών, 'smithy', and this spread into the κοινή. Phrynichos (144) says that the Attic form was ἱστών, although as it happens this survives in no author but the Roman Varro. In the MSS. of Attic authors there are a few other words that end in -εών, without justification—περιστερεών (Plato), 'dove-cote', κεγχρεών (Demosthenes), 'place where ore is thrown', βολεών (Deinarchos, Philemon), 'place for disposing of κόπροc' (but κοπρών).

237 τίτθη: A nurse who had been Moschion's foster-mother. It has been suggested, 7 n., that Moschion may not have been an infant when adopted; if that is so, γεγονυῖ᾽ ἐμὴ θεράπαινα must mean 'one who had become my slave', probably coming with Moschion to Demeas' household.

Although she was freed, she was, it would seem, still in Demeas' service; it was not unusual for the conditions of freeing a slave to provide that he or she should perform certain stipulated services for the former master. But other circumstances can be imagined. For instance the speaker in [Dem.] xlvii. 55 tells how his old nurse (τίτθη τιc ἐμὴ γενομένη πρεcβυτέρα) had on being liberated gone to live with a man, who had later died. Having no one to support her, she had returned to the speaker's household.

240 ἔνδον: 'At home', 'in the house', as at 256. We now see the point of the information that she had come downstairs from the upper story. Being upstairs, she had no knowledge of Demeas' movements.

241 λαλεῖν: Although in Menander's time the word is sometimes all but indistinguishable from λέγειν, cf. *Epitr.* 248 n., *Perik.* 470, it more usually has the connotation of idle or unnecessary chatter, as here. The genitive τοῦ λαλεῖν defines the field of reference of ἐν ἀcφαλεῖ, 'safe with regard to chattering', being similar to the gen. in such phrases as ὡc γνώμηc ἔχω, cf. Xen. *Hell.* vi. 2. 9, ἐν καλῷ . . . τοῦ τὴν χώραν βλάπτειν. Slightly different are expressions like *Cyr.* iii. 3. 31, ἐν ἀcφαλεῖ εἰcι τοῦ μηδὲν παθεῖν, 'safe so as not to suffer'.

242 ταῦτα δὴ κοινά: 'The usual things' cf. *Epitr.* 526, Ter. *Hec.* 117, 'et haec communia omnium quae sunt patrum'. δή indicates the half-contemptuous tone of the speaker—'the sort of things an old nurse would say'.

244 ἐφίληce: 'Kissed', see *Epitr.* 531 n.

245 ὦ τάλαιν' ἐγώ: This common phrase, like τάλαν, does not mean 'wretched that I am'; it is scarcely more here than 'dear me', spoken with a sigh.

246 πρώην: This word, which in Homer means 'lately', can in Attic mean 'the day before yesterday', but it is commonly used (often in the phrase χθὲc καὶ πρώην) in the sense of 'only the other day'.

248 ἤδη: Sudhaus and Guéraud so read C, I believe rightly. 'Now I'm already fondling this baby, too' is also better sense than is given by Lefebvre's ἄ[λ]λη: 'Another woman, i.e. Chrysis, actually nurses this child.'

251 θεραπαινιδίῳ: The sense of the diminutive is here probably 'a young servant-girl', but at *Dysk.* 460 it is contemptuous. The dative depends on φηcίν (253).

252 ὦ τάλαν: See *Epitr.* 434 n.

254 τὸν μικρόν: According to Gow on Theokritos xv. 12 (τῶ μικκῶ) this is the only example in Attic of ὁ μικρός to mean 'the child'. One would expect it to have been a common phrase; its rarity in surviving literature is probably an accident.

255 δύcμορε: A word of epic and tragic provenance, rare in prose (LSJ quote only Antiphon, iii. 2. 11, where it is intended to be very moving), and not found in comedy outside Menander, who puts it in the mouth of women: this girl, Chrysis at 67 above, 347 below, Habrotonon in *Epitr.* 427. ἡλίκον: 'How loud', cf. 424.

256 ἔνδον: 'At home', cf. Theokr. xv. 1, ἔνδοι Πραξινόα; αὐτός: 'Himself', the master; so αὐτή in 258 is 'the mistress'. The word shows Chrysis' position in the household, but as she is not legally married to Demeas, she can be unceremoniously turned out, as shortly happens. οὐ δήπου γε: 'Surely not!' cf. Dem. xx. 167.

257 παρεξήλλαξέ τι: 'With a change of voice', i.e. she raised her voice. This compound is cited by LSJ only from here (except that the scholiast on Soph. *Ant.* 849 uses παρεξηλλαγμένον to explain ποταίνιον, 'different'). The force of παρα- is 'by comparison with what went before', cf. παρεξίcταcθαι, 'to undergo a change'.

258 καί: With βάδιζε, 'move off' (cf. 159 n.), the girl drops her voice again; the intermediate καί will help the actor to indicate this.

265 τὴν Caμιάν: Significantly Demeas does not call her Χρυcίδα, but more coldly 'the Samian'; this is indicative of the suspicions which he is about to disown, somewhat unconvincingly.

266: The reading of B, ἔξω καθ' αὐτὴν ⟨καὶ⟩ διδοῦcαν τιτθίον, is easy: that of C, ἔξω διδοῦcαν τιτθίον παριὼν ἅμα, more difficult; the absence of καί, to join ἔχουcαν and διδοῦcαν, is strange. παριὼν ἅμα must mean 'as I was going by while she was feeding it'. This is not, however, a case where a *lectio difficilior* is to be chosen. καθ' αὐτήν may have fallen out through some copyist's jumping from καθ to και, and C's reading may be an attempt to restore the line.

267 τοῦτο γνώριμον εἶναι: γνώριμον is not exactly a synonym for δῆλον, but as at 473 means 'known' or 'knowable' (the common sense 'well-known', e.g. *Aspis* 185, *Epitr.* 865, is unsuitable here). Aristotle sometimes uses the word in this sense, e.g. *Anal. Post.* 83ᵇ36, εἰ δὲ τόδε διὰ τῶνδε γνώριμον, 100ᵇ9 αἱ ἀρχαὶ τῶν ἀποδείξεων γνωριμώτεραι. Here Demeas means 'that this is her child is something that can be *known*', as opposed to the mere hypotheses about paternity. It is comic irony that he is mistaken on the one point he believes to be certain.

269 ἄνδρεc: For this form of address to the audience cf. 329, 447, 683, 734, *Epitr.* 887, *Dysk.* 194, 659, 666, *Sik.* 405.   **τοῦτ':** I.e. that Moschion is the father. Demeas tries to deceive himself by saying that he does not *suspect* this.

270 οὐχ ὑπονοῶ, given by B, is easy: the syndeton is suitable to Demeas' tense state. C's οὔθ' is more difficult, and has been thought impossible by most editors. Yet it cannot be rejected without hesitation. οὐ . . . οὔτε is given by the MSS. in a number of passages not only of tragedy but also of prose, a number that Denniston, *GP* 509, thinks may be too large to justify alteration everywhere to οὐ . . . οὐδέ. It is conceivable that the irregularity here is right and intended to mark Demeas' suppressed agitation.

270 τὸ πρᾶγμα δ' εἰc μέcον φέρω: 'Put the matter before you', cf. Dem. xviii. 139, φέρειν εἰc μέcον τὰ τούτων ἀμείνω.

272 cύνοιδα: '*Know* something *about* a person, especially *as a potential witness for* or *against* him' (LSJ).   **μειρακίῳ:** This suggests an age not much over twenty, see *Dysk.* 27 n.   **κοcμίῳ:** Like Eng. 'moral', the word is often used in the field of sexual behaviour, although not of course confined to it, e.g. Lysias i. 26, xiv. 41.

274 περὶ ἔμ' . . . εὐcεβεcτάτῳ: The separation of the words throws emphasis on περὶ ἐμέ; Demeas is the last person Moschion might be expected to injure. εὐcεβής may indicate filial respect as well as reverence for the gods; Plato, *Rep.* 615 c, εὐcέβεια εἰc θεοὺc καὶ γονέαc, *Symp.* 188 c, ἀcέβεια . . . καὶ περὶ γονέαc . . . καὶ περὶ θεούc.

275 τὴν λέγουcαν: She who said what I reported above. 'When I consider that she is Moschion's former nurse, and then that she was talking where [as she thought] I should not hear; and then again think of the woman who shows such love for the child . . .' The repetitions of sound, as Demeas' anger rises, are noteworthy: λέγουcαν, οὖcαν, λέγουcαν, εἶτ', εἶτ'. Notice also the slight disorder of the sentence: πρῶτον does not head its clause, but comes in by way of afterthought, as the second clause presents itself to the speaker's mind; the second εἶτα is not parallel to the first. Demeas' feelings overcome his assumed calm, until he breaks out with ἐξέcτηχ' ὅλωc.

278 βεβιαcμένην: Middle, 'has insisted on rearing it'. Used with an infinitive but no object, βιάζομαι may mean 'use every effort to', as in Lysias ix. 16, βιαζόμενοι βλάπτειν ἐξ ἅπαντοc λόγου. The distinction between aorist and perfect, which expresses the present aspect of a past action (cf. *Epitr.* 557 n.), is, I believe, always maintained in Menander. The perfect is appropriate here, since the results of the insistence persist, to stare Demeas in the face.

Demeas' speech is a kind of 'messenger's speech', recounting incidents which have taken place off the stage but are essential to the plot. Such speeches are not uncommon in comedy: *Dysk.* 522–45 and 666–89, *Epitr.* 878–907, *Mis.* 284–322, Ter. *Hecyra* 361–408, and another was converted by Terence into the duologue *Eun.* 549–606. Although in some sense forced on the dramatist by the conditions of the Greek stage, they were exploited as offering the actor an opportunity of displaying his virtuosity. Experience of modern productions shows how effective are the 'messenger's speeches' of tragedy, and these speeches in comedy, delivered by characters who, unlike the tragic messengers, had played a part in the scenes they describe, were doubtless no less effective. Demeas' speech is brilliantly written, with plentiful detail to give a vivid picture; yet very little of that detail is irrelevant to the central theme, the ghastly suspicion that has been aroused in his mind. For example the screaming child, put out of the way (225), seems at first sight to be just another noise along with the shouts for meal, water, etc., but had it not been for its screams the nurse would not have been tempted to pick it up and talk indiscreetly. Again, her commonplaces, 242 ff., provide a background of banality against which her bombshell explodes, 248; at the same time they are made dramatically tense by the ominous phrase which introduces them, ἐν ἀcφαλεῖ εἶναι νομίcαcα τοῦ λαλεῖν. The clarity and order of the narrative are of the highest. These are merits in a messenger's speech, but they are merits consistent with Demeas' character. He is represented as holding himself in control as he refuses to commit himself to the natural conclusion from what he has seen and heard. This self-control extends to the quiet, orderly narrative. But it ends with the sudden, unexpected explosion of ἐξέστηχ᾽ ὅλως. This is characteristic of the man, a pattern to be repeated when his quietly threatening approach to Parmenon suddenly turns to fury, and when his reflections on Moschion's possible innocence end in the violence of the language in which he resolves to throw Chrysis out, ἐκ τῆς δ᾽ οἰκίας | ἐπὶ τὴν κεφαλὴν ἐς κόρακας ὤσον τὴν καλὴν | Σαμίαν. Here he quickly recovers himself at the entrance of Parmenon with the Cook, whom the former had in the previous act been dispatched to fetch for the wedding feast. The Cook is attended by at least one subordinate (282, 295). Demeas finds Parmenon's arrival opportune (εἰς καλόν, cf. Dysk. 773, Xen. Anab. iv. 7. 3, εἰς καλὸν ἥκετε, Plato, Symp. 174 e, εἰς καλὸν ἥκεις, Lucian, Lexiphanes 18, ἀλλ᾽ εἰς καλὸν γὰρ τουτονὶ . . . ὁρῶ . . . προσιόντα) because he wants to question him about his newly aroused suspicions—but not, of course, in the presence of the strangers, who must first be taken inside.

280 τουτονὶ προσιόνθ᾽: B's reading is much easier than that of C, τοῦτον εἰσιόνθ᾽, which cannot be defended with conviction. There is no parallel for εἰσέρχομαι in the sense 'come on the stage'; as a stage-direction at Perik. 928 εἰσέρχεται means 'enters the house'. That meaning is conceivable here, if Demeas' house is to the audience's right. He will have moved to the centre of the stage; Parmenon comes on from the right, as returning from the market, and is seen by Demeas to be 'about to enter'. He pauses, however, to chaff the cook, while Demeas stands, perhaps lost in his reflections. But this defence is unsatisfactory. For what is timely (εἰς καλόν) in Demeas' view is not the entry of Parmenon into the house, but his arrival, which allows him to be questioned.

282: Elsewhere in Menander παράγειν is always intransitive, 'go indoors'. The transitive sense, 'introduce', is found in other fourth-century authors (see LSJ s.v. III), and so is not out of the question here. Lloyd-Jones obtains an intransitive by the easy alteration τούτους θ᾽ οὓς ἄγει. But Demeas does not intend to allow Parmenon to go in, except momentarily to put down his basket.   **τούτους:** The Cook and his assistant or assistants, whom Parmenon had been dispatched to hire (194).

(ii) 283–324: *Demeas, Parmenon, and Cook* (exit 295)

283: It is a common convention of comedy, aided by the great width of the stage, that characters entering may fail to see those already there. But those who wish may suppose that Parmenon is so absorbed by the Cook that he does not notice his master Demeas, or else that he pretends not to notice him. The cook of comedy is traditionally loquacious and Athenaios (290 b–293 e, 376 e–380 c, 660 e) preserves many long, and usually boastful, speeches by these characters: ἀλαζονικὸν δ᾽ ἐστι πᾶν τὸ τῶν μαγείρων φῦλον (290 b). The cook of Plautus' *Pseudolus* is true to the type, *multiloquus, gloriosus, insulsus* (794). Menander here keeps the characteristic of loquacity, but hints at it instead of representing it at length.

285 κατακόψαι: Metaphorically κόπτω and κατακόπτω ('make mincemeat of') can mean 'weary, bore'; and the play on the literal and metaphorical senses is a stock joke at the expense of cooks, Alexis frag. 173. 12, μὴ κόπτ᾽ ἔμε ἀλλὰ τὰ κρέα, Anaxippos frag. 1. 23 K, ἐμὲ κατακόψεις, οὐχ ὃ θύειν μέλλομεν. In Sosipatros frag. 20 K, ἆρα σύ με κόπτειν οἶος εἶ γε, φίλτατε, the pun is not so much made as alluded to, as is the case in *Dysk*. 410 (cf. n.). Here the jest is given a new turn: the Cook's tongue is so powerful that he could dispense with knives. The familiar pun lurks in the background, and emerges at 292: 'You are certainly making mincemeat of (boring) me.' **ἄθλιε ἰδιῶτα:** The cook stands on his professional dignity as a skilled craftsman; the ἰδιώτης is by contrast the man who is uninstructed, unskilled, lacking in technique. Σ Ar. *Frogs* 891 explains the word by ἀμαθής.

287 πόσας τραπέζας: Small light tables were used, each being sufficient for a few guests. The verb ποεῖν might wrongly suggest that the word τράπεζα here has the sense of 'course', as in the phrase δεύτεραι τράπεζαι. But a τραπεζοποιός is not a cook, but one who sets out or lays tables, and the sense 'table' is required in the similar passage, frag. 451 K–T, πόσας τραπέζας μέλλομεν ποιεῖν, τρίτον ἤδη μ᾽ ἐρωτᾷς. χοιρίδιον ἓν θύομεν, ὀκτὼ ποήσοντες τραπέζας, δύο, μίαν, τί σοι διαφέρει τοῦτο. It would matter to the Cook whether he had to make eight courses or one out of the piglet; what is of no concern to him is how many guests there will be to share the food. Cf. also Euangelos frag. 1 K, τέτταρας τραπέζας τῶν γυναικῶν εἶπά σοι, ἐξ δὲ τῶν ἀνδρῶν.

288 γυναῖκες: Women, unless *hetairai*, were not usually present at dinner-parties, but wedding-feasts formed an exception.

290 τραπεζοποιόν: See *Dysk*. 647 n. **προσλαβεῖν:** 'Get in from outside'; probably sometimes hosts made do with their own household servants. **κέραμος:** 'Whether you have enough crockery'; there may be a touch of impertinence about this, but cooks did sometimes hire crockery if the host had not enough, Alexis frag. 257. The next question is more obviously tiresome: in poor houses the kitchen might be nothing but a part of the open courtyard, but hardly in Demeas' house: it was under cover even in Philokleon's (*Wasps* 138 ff.) and he was not accounted a rich man. Compare with all this Alexis frag. 173: (*Μαγ.*) ὀπτάνιόν ἐcτιν; (*A.*) ἔcτι. (*Μαγ.*) καὶ κάπνην ἔχει; (*A.*) δηλονότι. (*Μαγ.*) μή μοι "δῆλον". (*A.*) ἀλλ' ἔχει κάπνην. (*Μαγ.*) ἔχει; κακόν, εἰ τυφοῦcαν. (*A.*) ἀπολεῖ μ' οὑτοcί.

292–3 περικόμματα: Cf. the sausage-maker in Ar. *Knights* 372, περικόμματ' ἐκ cοῦ cκευάcω.   **οὐκ ὡc ἔτυχεν:** Cf. *Perik.* 338, 'in no casual fashion', 'not just anyhow', but μαγειρικῶc (Ar. *Ach.* 1015), like a professional (LSJ s.v. τυγχάνω, A. 3). B has ἔτυχεc: this personal construction is found in some similar phrases (ibid. A. 4), but no example is quoted that replaces the fairly frequent ὡc ἔτυχεν.

294 οἴμωζε :: καὶ cύ recurs at *Sik.* 167.

295 τοῦτό γε παντὸc ἕνεκα: An example of what Denniston, *GP* 138, calls epexegetic γε: 'The speaker reaffirms his preceding words.' Here τοῦτο = οἴμωζε: 'Yes, bad luck to you, on all counts.'

296 ἐμέ τιc κέκληκε: 'Did someone call *me*?' Perfect tense because the effect of the call continues into the present; the phrase means: 'Am I wanted?'

297 cφυρίδα: A cφυρίc, more commonly cπυρίc, is a large basket; it will contain the shopping, and Parmenon is told to 'dump it', by implication in the house. Cf. *Pap. Hibeh* 6. 2 (Page, *GLP* 286), τὴν cπυρίδα ταύτην ἐν ᾗ | ἐνταῦθα τοὺc ἄρτουc ἐκόμιcαc ἀπόφερε.   **ἀγαθῇ τύχῃ:** A formula of consent, *Epitr.* 223 n.

297 ff.: Dedoussi supposes that Demeas' tone of voice alarms Parmenon, who then says ἀγαθῇ τύχῃ because he needs to wish himself luck, and that the instructions the slave gives to Chrysis (301–3) 'awkwardly conceal his uneasiness'. No doubt the passage could be so acted, but there is nothing in the words to suggest it. It will be more effective if Demeas, who gave no hint at 281 that he intended to examine Parmenon, should speak quietly with his characteristic self-control. Parmenon remains full of self-satisfaction; he had helped to arrange Moschion's affairs, he has just scored off the Cook. Inside the house he importantly gives orders, and when he returns with an 'At your service, sir' (τί δεῖ ποεῖν, δέcποτα) the ground suddenly opens under his feet. But for the audience's full enjoyment, they must see that he is walking blithely towards disaster, and they are given the necessary hint by Demeas' words (298–300), spoken while the slave is out of hearing.

300 περίεργος: 'Meddlesome and inquisitive', cf. *Epitr*. frag. 2 n.

300–1 ἀλλὰ τὴν θύραν προϊὼν πέπληχε: 'He has struck the door': this is a variant for the phrases with ψοφεῖν (e.g. ἐψόφηκε τὴν θύραν, 'he has caused the door to make a noise') which are often used to mark the coming of a character from a house. The function of such phrases is to explain why the characters who utter them cease to address the audience and turn with expectation towards the door from which the other person will emerge. The old fable that the Greek house-door opened outwards and that a man emerging knocked upon it to warn passers-by has been exploded by archaeological evidence and common sense (see W. Beare, *Roman Stage*, 279 ff.). The Greek house normally had a double door (hence the plural θύραι), opening inwards; the leaves met in the centre and turned on sockets at the side, doubtless often squeaking as they did so. But the phrase τὴν θύραν πέπληχε, which recurs at 366, 555, *Dysk*. 188, *Epitr*. 906, is a puzzling one. The number of occurrences being small, explanation is hazardous. In all three instances from *Samia* the person who comes out has just gone in with the intention of returning: he will not therefore have fastened the door, but is likely to have left it ajar. Similarly in *Epitr*. Onesimos, the last person to come out previously, may not have closed the door, wishing to make as little noise as possible. (But Knemon in *Dysk*. is not likely to have failed to shut his door.) A door that is half open can be fully opened by striking its outer side, and a man coming out in a rage or a hurry is as likely to do this as to pull it. Even if the door is shut, he may, having partially opened it by pulling, strike it with the other hand. This explanation suits the passage of *Epitr*. and the other passages of this play. But here Parmenon is not angry or hurried. Perhaps the gesture reveals a certain insolent self-confidence, also expressed in the words in which he gives Chrysis and the other servants their orders; that confidence is in a moment rudely shattered. In *Dysk*. the verb may serve to indicate the hurry with which the girl comes out. The phrase is discussed by C. Dedoussi, Ἑλληνικά xviii (1964), 6–10, who is probably right in thinking that *pepulit fores* at Ter. *Ad*. 788 represents another occurrence; Demea rushes out of the house into which he has burst a moment before. But her conclusion that the phrase indicates that the person emerging has slammed the door shut behind him hardly fits *Sam*. 555 or *Dysk*. 188. See Addenda.

301: Parmenon, by a common device, speaks through the open door, out of which he has come, to persons in the house, giving instructions in the tone of a privileged servant, and showing no haste to attend to his master. Observe the familiar way in which he addresses Chrysis by her name, not as κεκτημένη.

304: Both B and C have lost a word after ποεῖν. Sudhaus and Guéraud thought that in C traces of ϲε were visible at the end of the line after θύρας (cf. *Heros* 69); I cannot confirm this on the infra-red photograph. Austin quotes Fraenkel as preferring ⟨ἴθι⟩ δεῦρο (Leo and Mazon) to ποεῖν⟨ϲε⟩, on the ground that when words are indignantly repeated, nothing is added. Even if this is universally true, on my reading of the passage Demeas does not speak indignantly; he does not show his hand until 306. Certainty is impossible, but ϲε seems to me the more likely loss.

302 τὴν γραῦν: Wilamowitz suggests that she is identical with the γραῦϲ of 373, and is a servant who had belonged to Chrysis before her association with Demeas. But the only old woman of whom the audience have heard is Moschion's former nurse, and they will necessarily identify her with the woman of whom Parmenon speaks. The κεράμια from which she is to be kept contain wine: the bibulous old woman is a stock comic figure, here used by Menander not primarily for her own sake but to depict Parmenon's self-importance.

305 ἤν: 'There now', complying with a request, as *Epitr.* 391, frags. 135, 319. Photios explains the word by ἰδού, which is similarly used, e.g. 312 below, Ar. *Knights* 157, *Clouds* 825. **ἄκουε δή νυν:** Denniston, *GP* 218, quotes thirteen instances of this locution from Euripides, two from Aristophanes; it 'expresses an increased urgency in command'. Whether to accent νυν or νῦν is uncertain; usually, at least, medieval MSS. give the latter. C's δή μου (cf. *Fab. incert.* 27) is marginally inferior.

308 ϲυγκρύπτειϲ τι πρόϲ μ': 'You are helping to conceal something from me', lit. 'with regard to me', cf. Soph. *Phil.* 588, λόγων κρύψαι πρὸς ἡμᾶς μηδέν' ὧν ἀκήκοας. Here B's πραγμ' for προϲμ' is clearly an error due to a misreading. The end of the line is lost, but ἐγώ stands extra metrum at the beginning of the next. If it has been erroneously transferred there (cf. *Perik.* 308, and the opposite error at 587 below) it is more likely to have suffered this removal if taken to be part of Parmenon's speech. Sudhaus suggested ᾔϲθημ'—(*Πα.*) ἐγώ; but like other editors printed ᾔϲθημ' ἐγώ.

309: A string of oaths is an old comic effect, Ar. *Birds* 194, μὰ γῆν, μὰ παγίδας, μὰ νεφέλας, μὰ δίκτυα; Antiphanes frag. 296 (= Timokles frag. 38), μὰ γῆν, μὰ κρήνας, μὰ ποταμούς, μὰ νάματα, is alleged to be a quotation from Demosthenes, Plut. *Dem.* 9. The slave Chrysalus in

Plaut. *Bacchides* 892–5 swears by eighteen gods, possibly developing a passage in Menander's *Δὶς Ἐξαπατῶν*, the original of *Bacchides*.

τουτονί: For this reference to the Apollo who stood outside the house's door see *Dysk.* 659 n.

311 παῦ: This form is attested by Photios, who regards it as shortened for παῦcαι. Modern grammarians see a shortened form of παῦε (Schwyzer, i. 799), which is used intransitively and almost entirely replaces παῦον, although in the plural παύεcθε is always used (Rutherford, *Babrius* 28). There is no parallel for such an apocope of -ε. In Latin *dic(e)*, *duc(e)* a stress accent facilitated the dropping of the final -*e*.

312 ἢ μήποτ' ἄρα—: Sc., e.g., ἀγαθόν μοι γένοιτο μηδέν. ἄρα is a metrically useful equivalent of ἄρα, see *Dysk.* 665 n.; perhaps it adds liveliness to the wish.   **οὗτος βλέπε δεῦρο**: Similarly Soph. *Trach.* 402: the messenger says to the evasive Lichas οὗτος βλέφ' ὧδε.

313 ἤν: An embarrassed and puzzled exclamation. For the breathing, which distinguishes it from ἤν = ἰδού, see *Dysk.* 465 n.

315 cόν, φηcίν: This old reminder that only the mother knows the child's father must infuriate Demeas. One would hesitate to make the supplement, which is more pointed than Sudhaus's φαcίν, did not Guéraud report the fourth letter to have been a tall one, φ or ψ.

316 εἰδότα γ' ἀκριβῶc πάντα: Demeas is prepared to stretch the truth in the hope of frightening Parmenon into a confession. When Parmenon asks who has told him of these alleged facts (τίc φηcι; 319), he returns a plain lie, πάντεc. It is interesting that this readiness to lie, or at the best to trifle with the truth, with the best of motives, shown by Demeas and by Moschion, determines the course of the play. First Moschion allows his father to believe that the child is his own and the mother Chrysis; on this depend Acts III and IV. Then Demeas tries to persuade Nikeratos that Moschion is not the father. Finally Moschion pretends that he is not going through with the marriage to Plangon.

320 ἀλλὰ λανθάνειν—: The suppressed continuation would be something like: 'It was hoped that we could keep quiet the fact that Moschion was the father and had wronged Plangon.' Demeas, however, would understand 'keep quiet the affair between Moschion and Chrysis', and would naturally be enraged at this attempt to conceal from him what so intimately concerned him.

321 ἱμάντα: A leather strap, Lat. *scutica*, commonly used to punish slaves, cf. Antiphanes frag. 74 K, ἔξω τιc δότω ἱμάντα, *Dysk.* 502, τὸν ἱμάντα δόc, γραῦ. It might be used as a whip, but also to tie the hands,

Plaut. *Capt.* 658 ff. ('lora'). παιδων is the reading of B, while C has παιδ. [.]. Austin reads the letter after δ as ω (no more than a part of the left-hand upright remains); previous scholars had taken it to be ε. Either reading looks possible, and the vocative παῖδες would be suitable here, since Demeas must speak, or shout, in a way that will attract the servants' attention.

322 ἀceβῆ: Perhaps not mere abuse, since Parmenon has perjured himself in denying that he has deceived his master; or he may be regarded as sharing in the supposed ἀcέβεια of Moschion, being his accomplice.

323 cτίξω ce: The face of a runaway slave was often tattooed, as a combined punishment and precaution against a repetition of the offence, cf. the abusive word cτιγματίας and the Latin *homo trium litterarum*, i.e. F(ugitiuus) H(ic) E(st). Other faults might be dealt with in the same way; in Herondas v. 65 a jealous mistress sends for the tattooer with his needles and ink to punish her slave-lover for his infidelity. (Headlam's notes on 66, 67, 79 collect much material.) Ar. *Wasps* 1296, ἀπόλωλα cτιζόμενος βακτηρίᾳ is metaphorical, but not merely—'beaten black and blue' (LSJ); rather Philokleon used the point of his stick, the slave was 'piqueté' (van Daele in the Budé edition), cf. Plaut. *Men.* 951: 'Ego te pendentem fodiam stimulis triginta dies.'

(iii) **325–356:** *Demeas alone*

325 λάβ' αὐτόν: Perhaps addressed to a slave who has come out with a strap, but perhaps to the world at large and no one in particular.

ὦ πόλιcμα: B has a marginal note οιδιπους ιριποδοῳ (*sic*). It seems then that ὦ πόλιcμα Κεκροπίας χθονός κτλ. is a quotation from Euripides' *Oedipus*, and that the latter part of that play dealt with Oedipus' refuge in Athens after his blinding (cf. perhaps frag. 98 Austin (*Nova fragmenta Euripidea*) = Stob. iv. 5. 11, frag. 1049 Nauck). We may also compare Eur. *Med.* 771 and *IT* 1014, πτόλιcμα Παλλάδος, *Hipp.* 34 and *Ion.* 1571, Κεκροπίαν χθόνα, *Orest.* 322, τὸν ταναὸν αἰθέρα. Demeas breaks out into quotations or adaptations of Euripides, the favourite poet of the fourth century. Similarly the distracted Demea of Terence's *Adelphoe* breaks out 'o caelum, o terra, o maria Neptuni' (790); here, however, there is a further effective touch: Demeas' swelling passion proceeds outwards from Athens to Attica, from Attica to the sky—and then he suddenly recalls his runaway thought to himself. Should we speak of tragic parody here? Hardly: Demeas is represented as so overwrought that he resorts to quotations from tragedy. This is funny for the audience because they know that his emotion is due to a mistake. The contrast is not between the language of tragedy and ordinary life, but between the language of emotion and the situation to which it is unsuited.

326 βοᾷς: *Perik.* 489 n.

328 παράβολος: 'Venturesome, hazardous'. Longinus, *Subl.* 32. 4, uses the word of a hazardous combination of metaphors (cf. θρασεῖαι μεταφοραί and τόλμη μεταφορῶν just before) that may be justified by the orator's passion, e.g. Dem. xviii. 296. The contrast with ἀληθινός may be explained by paraphrasing 'it may seem a wild thing to say, but it is true'.

330 κεκνισμένος: 'Provoked'; the verb is commonly used of the effect of sexual passion, LSJ s.v. II. 2.

332 ἐπὶ τῆς αὐτῆς διανοίας: Cf. Dem. iv. 7, ἄν . . . ἐπὶ τῆς τοιαύτης ἐθελήσητε γενέσθαι γνώμης, xxi. 213. **παρατεταγμένος:** Lit. 'drawn up to do battle', cf., e.g., Thuc. iv. 43. 3. The metaphorical use is found in Ar. *Wasps* 1123, Epicurus frag. 489 Usener, 184 Arrighetti, παρατετάχθαι δὲ πρὸς τὰ δοκοῦντα εἶναι κακά. The force of the dative here is not, as sometimes, 'alongside of me', but 'against me', as in Isokr. xii. 92, στρατοπεδευσάμενοι μεθ' ἡμῶν . . . καὶ παραταξάμενοι τοῖς πολεμίοις, Xen. *Hell.* iv. 3. 5, ὡς παρετάξαντο ἀλλήλοις.

334 ἀπολελόγηται: A true perfect, 'his defence stands good'. **τὸν φανέντ' αὐτῷ γάμον:** 'The plan of marriage with Plangon then sprung on him'.

336 ἔσπευδεν: Moschion had shown eagerness for the marriage, and declared himself to be in love (?146, 151).

337 Ἑλένην: Phaidra would have been in some respects a better mythological parallel, but Helen is the most notorious unfaithful wife. **φυγεῖν . . . ποτε:** 'To get away at last'. **ἔνδοθεν:** 'Out of this house.'

339 παρέλαβε μεθύοντα: 'She got hold of him when he had been drinking', cf. *Perik.* 142 n. **ἐν ἑαυτοῦ:** A strange but well-attested idiom, 'in control of himself': *Aspis* 307, Soph. *Phil.* 950, Plato, *Charm.* 155 d, Ar. *Wasps* 642. In the last three places some MSS. regularize the construction (Jebb on *Phil.* 950 would follow them). Analogy with ἐκτὸς ἑαυτοῦ and ἐντὸς ἑαυτοῦ may provide the explanation.

340–2: The most probable explanation of this sentence is that of Austin, *ZPE* iv (1969), 167, who supposes that the subject of λάβῃ is an indefinite 'someone' (K–G i. 35–6). 'Wine and youth work many silly deeds, when a man finds by him one who has contrived a plot with these as aids.' Demeas casts his reflection in the most general form; hence the masculine cυνεπιβουλεύcαντα, although in the particular instance the plotter was a woman.

To make 'wine and youth' the subject of λάβη (for the singular verb cf. K–G i. 72) would require a change of τούτοιc to γ' αὐτοῖc (Jacques), or one could write cυνεπιβουλεύονθ' ἑαυτοῖc (Oguse). For the combined effect of youth and strong drink, cf. Plaut. *Aul*. 795, 'per uinum atque impulsu adulescentiae', *Bacch*. 88, Ter. *Ad*. 470.

341 ἄκρατοc: Wine taken neat; the normal practice in classical times being to drink it diluted with up to twice its bulk of water, hence the proverb ἢ πέντε (3:2) πίνειν ἢ τρί' (2:1) ἢ μὴ τέccαρα (3:1).

The drinking of wine neat was associated with barbarians and with drunkenness, but the not infrequent mentions of the practice in the comic fragments suggest that it became more common in the fourth century. Menander frag. 443 has τοῦτο δὴ τὸ νῦν ἔθοc | "ἄκρατον" ἐβόων, "τὴν μεγάλην" (? sc. κύλικα), Alexis frag. 255 τιμωρίαν οὐ προcδοκῶντεc τῆc μέθηc | ἥξειν προχείρωc τοὺc ἀκράτουc πίνομεν.

345 ἀλλοτρίουc: Persons not belonging to the family.

346 ποητόc . . . μὴ γόνῳ: The same opposition in Lysias, xiii. 91, τόν τε γόνῳ πατέρα . . . ἔτυπτε . . . τόν τε ποιητὸν πατέρα ἀφείλετο ἃ κτλ. τρόποc is character as revealed by customary behaviour.   **δεκάκιc:** Cf. Eur. *Andr*. 635, κεἰ τρὶc νόθοc πέφυκε. The still more emphatic δεκάκιc belonged to common speech, e.g. Dem. viii. 37, οὐδ' ἂν δεκάκιc ἀποθάνῃ.

Demeas' generosity towards Moschion and desire to protect his reputation are the more creditable since Moschion is not his own son; at the same time, although Demeas here denies it, it does probably cross his mind that an adopted son might not feel the same loyalty as a real one.

347 ὑόc: BC have υιοc, but the form without an ι is universal in Attic inscriptions of the fourth and third centuries (Meisterhans[3], 60), and often preserved in Menandrean papyri. The vowel υ is long.

348 χαμαιτύπη: 'A common whore', a most insulting term, a word of the Attic dialect according to Moiris; it first appears in literature in Theopompos frag. 225 Jacoby. For ὄλεθροc as a term of abuse, cf. frags. 186, 612, *Dysk*. 366.   **ἀλλὰ τί;** 'But why waste breath on her?' ἡ ἄνθρωποc frequently, as here, carries a derogatory sense; the word is often applied to slaves.

349 οὐ γὰρ περιέcται: Capps and van Leeuwen suppose this to mean 'I'll get nothing by it', but that would be easier with a subject: οὐδὲν περιέcται. LSJ quote the passage under the general rubric 'to be superior to another', and presumably take it to mean 'she shall not get the better of me'. But the context makes at least as likely 'she shall not survive this'.   ἄνδρα χρὴ εἶναί ϲε: 'You must be brave', cf. Eur. *El.* 693, ἄνδρα γίγνεϲθαί ϲε χρή.

350 πόθου: πόθοϲ is longing for a person from whom one is separated, as Demeas has been separated from Chrysis. Similarly at 495 Moschion has been separated from Plangon in effect, even if we suppose he had occasionally been able to see her during her father's absence.   πέπαυϲ' ἐρῶν: 'Be finished with your love.'

351–2: μὲν . . . δέ clauses are less common in Menander than one might expect, probably because they require a degree of foresight which is found only occasionally in unpremeditated colloquial speech. Observe that here μὲν . . . δέ is possible just because Demeas has brought his indignation to heel, and speaks calmly—until he breaks out at 353 with a clatter of k's, and stinging word after stinging word. But with ἔχειϲ δὲ πρόφαϲιν κτλ. (354) he drops back into flat simplicity.

352: Cf. Lucian, *Timon* 38, ἐπὶ κεφαλὴν ἐξωϲθεὶϲ τῆϲ οἰκίαϲ, Plato, *Rep.* 553 b (quoted by Austin).

354 ἔχειϲ δὲ πρόφαϲιν: 'You have got a reason', as in Eur. *Hec.* 340, not 'a pretext'. Demeas had originally thought the child provided ground enough for turning Chrysis out (133).

353 τὴν καλὴν Ϲαμίαν: Perhaps, as at 265, Demeas avoids the proper name Chrysis, and substitutes the ethnic, with an Athenian's contempt for the sexually unrestrained Ionian. Aischines, the Socratic pupil, declared τὰϲ ἐκ τῆϲ Ἰωνίαϲ γυναῖκαϲ ϲυλλήβδην μοιχάδαϲ καὶ κερδαλέαϲ (Athen. 220 b). But καλήν is not merely ironic; Chrysis was probably a beautiful woman, and Demeas will simultaneously have in mind both that and *also* her supposed moral turpitude. Editors before Austin read κακην in C; he has no doubt that, like B, it gives καλην, and he is, I think, right.

355 ἀνείλετο: 'Kept'; ἀναιρεῖϲθαι is the *vox propria* for taking up an exposed child (*Perik.* 134 n.), but here is used, as at 374, 411, of the decision to keep, and not expose, one's own baby, cf. Plut. *de fortuna Romanorum* 320 e, μέχρι δὲ πολλοῦ διεφύλαττον οἱ περὶ τὸν τόπον ἐκεῖνον κατοικοῦντεϲ μηδὲν ἐκτιθέναι τῶν γεννωμένων, ἀλλ' ἀναιρεῖϲθαι πάντα καὶ τρέφειν. Dedoussi maintains that in classical Greek the only words for keeping a baby were τρέφειν, ἐκτρέφειν, and that it was only later that ἀναιρεῖϲθαι lost its necessary association with foundlings, being used to denote the specifically Roman practice by which a father accepted a child by raising it from the ground; the Latin words are *suscipere, tollere.* But although Plutarch in the passage quoted above refers to Romans, as also at *Antony* 932 c, *Romulus* 19 c, 20 c, there are other places in authors of the Greco-Roman period where the word is used like τρέφειν, without any restriction to Romans: Plut. *de fraterno amore* 489 f, παιδίον οὐδὲ ἓν ἠθέλησεν ἐκ τῆς γυναικὸς ἀνελέσθαι τεκούσης πολλάκις (Attalus), Epictetus i. 23, attacking Epicurus, τολμᾷ λέγειν ὅτι "μὴ ἀναιρώμεθα τέκνα". Whether purists would have countenanced it or not, this usage must on the evidence of this play have begun at least by the late fourth century.

356 εὐγενῶς: 'Bravely', cf. *Dysk.* 281 n.; 'set your teeth (lit. bite the lip) and hold up: see it through bravely', Ar. *Clouds* 1369, τὸν θυμὸν δακών. In Soph. *Trach.* 976, ἴσχε δακὼν στόμα σόν means 'keep quiet, say nothing'.

(iv) 357–368: *Cook and Demeas* (exit 360)

357 : Demeas must now be off the stage for a short time, to represent the period necessary to find Chrysis, the child, her personal possessions, and a couple of servants. It cannot be left empty, and the gap is filled by the appearance of the Cook, an appearance which, however convenient, is well motivated. He comes out, baffled to know why Parmenon has not followed him indoors; he expected help from him as the chief servant of the household. While he calls for him and complains, Demeas stands collecting his resolution for the coming scene with Chrysis; then with a shout of 'Out of the way!' rushes into the house. The Cook's reactions of surprise, assumed indifference, and alarm may be comically punctuated by repeated shouts for Parmenon, but see 360 n.

359 ἀλλ' οὐδὲ μικρόν: On internal ἀλλ' οὐδέ see Denniston, *GP* 23, who explains that the speaker 'begins as if he would mention something of trifling importance and then corrects himself by saying that even that is too much'. Thus here the Cook starts as if he were going to say that Parmenon had run away *in the middle of the job*, but improves on that with, 'Why, he hasn't even lent a hand at all!', cf. Dem. *Prooem.* 48, τῶν μὲν ὑμετέρων ψηφισμάτων ἀλλ' οὐδὲ τὸ μικρότατον φροντίζουσιν, Diphilos frag. 61 K, τοῦτό μοι τὸ δεῖπνον ἀλλ' οὐδ' αἷμ' ἔχει.

360 τί τοῦτο, παῖ: It is hard to say whether the words should be so taken together, 'What's all this?', or punctuated τί τοῦτο; παῖ, 'What's this? Boy!', supposing παῖ to be a call for Parmenon. It is becoming clear that the word παῖ (or was it παί of which παπαί was a fuller form?) was used as an exclamation without its being necessary that anyone should be present who could properly be addressed as παῖ; see the discussion at *Dysk.* 500 n. and C. F. L. Austin, *Gnomon*, xxxix (1967), 125. T. Williams, *Philologus*, cxv (1962), 218, argues that the phrase τί τοῦτο, παῖ; is so common (*Perik.* 316, *Dysk.* 82, *Mis.* 216, frag. 100) that the words cannot be separated here. I am inclined to think he is right, although this involves treating 363, τί δέ μοι τοῦτο παῖ, in the same way: here an exclamatory παῖ is a little less attractive.

361 μαινόμενος . . . τις γέρων: The cook has not yet been introduced to Demeas and does not know that this apparent maniac is his employer. Gomme, *Essays*, 264, regards Demeas as not yet turned fifty. Similarly Dedoussi argues that New Comedy divides men into νέοι and γέροντες, so that Demeas, whom she thinks of as in his forties, must yet be a γέρων. This seems artificial; and the supposed sharp distinction between young and old is improbable: Chairestratos in *Aspis* seems to be neither. Probably Demeas' exact age was nowhere stated. All we can say is that he makes on the Cook the impression of being a γέρων, which cannot mean early middle-age. The Cook must use the word in its everyday sense, so that it will suggest a man of sixty, cf. *Mis.* 219–20. Attempts to minimize Demeas' age are due to modern ideas of propriety: the elderly ought not to be moved by ἔρως. In the Mitilini mosaic, for what it is worth, Demeas seems to be white-haired. It is easy to collect elderly lovers from ancient literature, e.g. Ibykos frag. 7, of which Plato, *Parm.* 137 a, says ἔφη . . . πρεσβύτης ὢν εἰς τὸν ἔρωτα ἀναγκάζεσθαι ἰέναι. Men. frag. 198 K declares that those who put off love to old age, εἰς τὸ γῆρας ἀναβολὰς ποιούμενοι, have to pay interest for the delay.

363 μαίνεθ': In the previous line the Cook envisaged some alternative explanation of Demeas' action; now hearing yells indoors he decides that the 'old man' must be mad.

364: Cf. Aischines ii. 106, ἀναβοᾷ παμμέγεθες Δημοσθένης.   **ἀστεῖον**: 'A really pretty thing it would be if he were to smash the dishes I've set out in there into fragments—the whole lot alike.' But B has ετοιμ[, and πάνθ' ἕτοιμα, 'everything is ready for him', i.e. there is nothing to stop him doing anything, would be possible. For the ironic use of ἀστεῖος cf. frag. 384, ἀστεῖον τὸ μὴ | συνάγειν γυναῖκας μηδὲ δειπνίζειν ὄχλον, ἀλλ' οἰκοσίτους τοὺς γάμους πεποηκέναι, *Dysk.* 569.

365 λοπάδας: Shallow dishes in which it was usual to cook fish, e.g. Euphron frag. 8 K, μεστὴν ζέουσαν λοπάδα Νηρείων τέκνων, Philemon junior frag. 1 K, ἄν τις εἰς τὰς λοπάδας ἰχθὺς ἐμβάλῃ, etc. See *Dysk.* 520 n.; μου separated from λοπάδας, cf. *Aspis* 420 n.

366 ποιῆσαι: C (unusually) accents the word, to mark it as an aor. optative, not infinitive.

368 ὑπαποστήσομαι: The Cook withdraws to the back or side of the stage, so that he may see and hear without being observed, a common manœuvre in New Comedy, e.g. (to take plays of Menandrean origin) Ter. *Adelphoe* 635, 'concedam huc', Plaut. *Bacch.* 610, 'sed huc concedam'. His presence, caught up in bewilderment in the scene between Demeas and Chrysis, lends a comic element to what would otherwise be an encounter too serious for the tone of this play. To understand his attempted interventions, one must remember that he is a free man and self-important, even though he is one of humble calling, who can be treated with familiarity by Parmenon.

(v) **369–398**: *Demeas, Chrysis, and Cook* (exit 390)

369 ὦ τάλαν: Cf. 252 n.

370 δύςμοροc: Does Chrysis mean herself or Demeas? The former is more likely.

371 ἐλεινὸν ἀμέλει: This may be harshly sarcastic, 'affecting, to be sure, to cry like that'. C (but not B) has a dicolon after δάκρυον. A change of speaker is so obviously nonsensical that one may suspect that there should be another dicolon after ναί, δύcμοροc, making ἐλεινὸν . . . δάκρυον an aside to indicate the feelings that Demeas must suppress. Dicola are not infrequently omitted in C at the ends of lines, e.g. 369, 375. Since, however, ἀμέλει, 'of course', strongly suggests sarcasm, it is more probable that the dicolon after δάκρυον is a mistake. On the Attic form ἐλεινόc see *Dysk.* 297 n.   **παύcω c' ἐγώ**: The thought in Demeas' mind is 'I'll put an end to your games with my son—', but he checks himself as he remembers that this is what he wants to keep dark, for the sake of his son's reputation and his own relations with him.

373 τὴν γραῦν: Cf. 302; probably the τίτθη of 237, who might accompany Chrysis of her own free will, but possibly some old slave woman, not necessarily identical with one of the θεράπαιναι of 382; she might have belonged to Chrysis before the association with Demeas.
    ἀποφθείρου: Cf. *Dysk.* 101 n.   ποτέ with an imperative indicates impatience, as in *Epitr.* 366; C's ταχύ is a correct interpretation.

374–5: The division between speakers has been much discussed, since C's only dicola are after each καὶ in 374. B turns out to support Jensen's division of 374. Chrysis guesses that she is being turned away because she had taken up the child to rear; Demeas accepts the reason, and is about to add some more, when he checks himself, as in the previous line, remembering the need for dissembling. When Chrysis tries to make him go on (τί "καί";) he will not. After διὰ τοῦτο, B has a dicolon and then gives the unmetrical τουτηντιτοκακον-μανθανω (C is also unmetrical, with τοιουτηντοκακονμανθανω). The easiest correction is τοιοῦτ' ἦν τι τὸ κακόν· μανθάνω. B assigns the speech to the Cook and Austin rightly accepts this. He has pointed out to me that the Cook was at first puzzled, 362, τί τὸ κακόν ποτ' ἐcτί; Now he finds that the trouble is to do with a baby, and says: 'I understand; the trouble is (and was all along, ἦν) an affair of that sort.' It is interesting that C suggests a text that, but for the evidence of B, there would be no reason for doubting, viz. (Δη.) διὰ τοῦτο. τοιοῦτ' ἦν τὸ κακόν. ⟨Χρ. οὐ⟩ μανθάνω.

376 τρυφᾶν γὰρ οὐκ ἠπίcτασο: 'You did not understand how to lead a life of luxury' and not, as one might expect, 'You did not know when you were well off', which would require τρυφῶca. Demeas must mean that Chrysis' τρυφή did not take the legitimate form of enjoying lady-like ease in his comfortable home, but that of illicit love. Again his language baffles Chrysis.

378 cινδονίτῃ: Photios explains the word by χιτὼν λινοῦc. cίνδων means cloth of flax or other vegetable fibre, not necessarily thin, but possibly so, as in Aesch. frag. 153, λεπτὸc δὲ cίνδων ἀμφιβάλλεcθαι χροΐ; in Plut. *Mor.* 340 d a poor gardener is ἐν εὐτελεῖ ('cheap' or 'shabby') cινδονίcκῃ.　　**μανθάνεις:** 'Do you follow me?', parenthetically, cf. *Perik.* 338, *Dysk.* 949.

379 λιτῷ: 'Plain, simple', cf. frag. 375 (*Sik.* frag. 3), λιτόν ποτ' εἶχεc χλαμύδιον καὶ παῖδ' ἕνα. These seem to be the earliest occurrences in literature, apart from the metaphorical use in Arist. *Rhet.* 1416^{b}25, of this adjective, which later became common; but the adverb is in Sotades frag. 1 K (Middle Comedy).　　**ἦν ἐγώ coι πάντα:** 'I was everything to you', cf. Dem. xviii. 43, πάντ' ἐκεῖνοc ἦν αὐτοῖc. Capps well observes that this reveals Demeas' true motive: jealousy and hurt at the loss of Chrysis' affections.　　**νῦν δὲ τίc;** The innocent question seems to Demeas to be effrontery: for him the answer is obvious—Moschion. Yet he cannot speak the word; he can only refuse to reply.

381–2 τὰ cαυτῆc: This will mean any clothes and jewellery that she had brought with her and gifts that she had received from Demeas. Clothes and jewellery belonging to a bride are often enumerated alongside her dowry, e.g. Dem. xvii. 13, xli. 27, and would be taken away by her if she were later divorced. Similarly Chrysis must take away her own possessions.　　**θεραπαίναc:** That Demeas should give Chrysis one servant is plausible; more than one is surprising, although no doubt possible, generosity. But it is improbable that, as some suppose, Demeas should exaggerate his gift; the plural must be taken literally. Körte prints Sudhaus's emendation (later withdrawn and now not supported by B) θεράπαιναν. Guéraud firmly rejects Jensen's claim that in C the final ϲ is dotted, i.e. cancelled. **Χρυϲί:** The hiatus is justified by Ar. *Ach.* 749, Δικαιόπολι, ἦ, *Perik.* 908, Δωρί. ἀλλά, Herondas i. 84, v. 69. Lefebvre suggested reading χρυϲί, 'gold ornaments or coins', and this turns out to be the reading of B. But Demeas, who could not utter Chrysis' name while speaking of her (265, 337, 354), now when face to face keeps flinging it at her (378, 385, 392), and I think B is mistaken. Nevertheless a woman's servants and jewellery are often joined, Dem. xlv. 28, lix. 46, ἃ δ' ἐξῆλθεν ἔχουϲα . . . χωρὶϲ ἱματίων καὶ χρυϲίων καὶ θεραπαινῶν . . . ἀποδοῦναι, Plaut. *Men.* 120, 'tibi ancillas, penum, lanam, aurum, uestem, purpuram bene praebeo', Ter. *Heaut.* 252, 'ancillas aurum uestem . . . unde esse censes?' It is not unheard of for a man to claim that jewellery he had bought for his mistress to wear was not a gift to her, and Demeas might here generously make over to Chrysis valuables which were not part of her legal property. One can compare the advice given to the soldier in Plaut. *MG* 981: 'Iube sibi aurum atque ornamenta, quae illi instruxti mulieri, dono habere, abire, auferre abs te quo lubeat sibi.'

383 ὀργή: ὀργή was defined by the Stoics as ἐπιθυμία τιμωρίαϲ τοῦ ἠδικηκέναι δοκοῦντοϲ, *SVF* iii. 395–7. The dicolon in C after προϲιτέον indicates that the Cook's aside is ended; he now speaks to the angry man, whom he politely addresses as βέλτιϲτε, not knowing him to be his employer, Demeas, the master of the house, cf. τιϲ γέρων (361). βέλτιϲτε is a usual form for addressing one whose name is unknown; thus four times in the arbitration-scene of *Epitr.*, *Dysk.* 144, 319, 338, 342, 476, 503, *Sik.* 13, *Aspis* 431. Sam. 81 and *Aspis* 251 (ὦ βέλτιϲτε) are the only instances in the present remains of Menander where the name of the person so addressed is known to the speaker. Gomme proposed to read τί ⟨ϲύ⟩ μοι διαλέγει, but this is possible rather than necessary Greek.

384 μὴ δάκῃϲ: 'You needn't bite me', cf. *Dysk.* 467. Demeas ignores this, as he turns back to Chrysis.

385 νὴ καὶ τοῖϲ θεοῖϲ θύϲει: Van Leeuwen's interpretation is certainly right: 'Another woman will now be glad of what I have to give and will sacrifice to the gods in gratitude.' Cf. Herondas ii. 70, vi. 10, for this meaning. O 16's νη is clearly more lively than BC's νυν; 'yes indeed, and will etc.'; there is a similar use of νή at *Epitr.* 1120, cf. also *Karch.* 33, *Dysk.* 510.

386 τί ἐϲτιν: Editors before Körte gave this to Chrysis, as an exclamation of bewilderment. But stunned silence after the command μή μοι λάλει will be more effective than this banal question. Given to the

Cook, as is now confirmed by B, it may be an aside or, as following Körte I would suppose, another intervention; when it produces no reaction, the Cook remarks to himself οὔπω δάκνει, 'he isn't biting me yet', 'so far I'm safe'. B has τίc ἐcτιν; accepted by Austin. This can only be an aside, 'Who is she?', and does not lead up so well to οὔπω δάκνει. At *Aspis* 416 τιc in B is clearly a mistake for τι. At the end of the line O 16 has ἀλλὰ τί; 'but what importance has that?', a phrase used by Demeas also at 348 and 450, and perhaps preferable to ἀλλὰ cύ of BC.

O 16 was published by E. G. Turner, *Aegyptus*, xlvii (1967 [issued 1970]), 187. Since it has a small space before νη, and a trace of ink which he admits 'it would be hazardous to interpret as part of an intended dicolon', he wishes to ascribe the phrase νὴ καὶ τοῖc θεοῖc θύcει to the Cook, explaining it by professional interest. The following τί ἐcτιν; he assigns to Chrysis, supposing that the corruption of νη to νυν led to a change in part-allocation. This arrangement is not dramatically plausible. The Cook knows nothing of the causes of the quarrel and must not take sides, as he would with the assenting νή. Moreover it is far from certain that the papyrus intends a change of speaker before νή: the top of the line is broken away, and may have contained a single point, marking a new clause; this would account for the space below.

Turner argues that the length of lines in O 16 suggests that it had τι, not τιc. The final ι in 386 is immediately below the ι of χρυcι in 385. If we count a dicolon as equivalent in space to a letter, the ι of χρυcι is thirtieth, that of τι thirty-third if it had τιc, thirty-second if τι. Although the writing, so far as can be judged from a small scrap, is regular, the discrepancy is not large enough to build on.

387 ὐὸν πεπόηcαι: So B, while C has πεπόηκαc. The normal Greek for 'have a child' in the sense of 'give birth', or, of the man, 'beget', is παῖδα or ὐὸν ποιεῖcθαι (while παῖδα or, ὐὸν ποιεῖcθαι τινά means 'adopt so-and-so as a son'). The only example of the active ποιεῖν adduced by LSJ is Plut. *Mor.* 145 d (ibid. 312 a is a false reference), παιδίον μὲν γὰρ οὐδεμία ποτε γυνὴ λέγεται ποιῆcαι δίχα κοινωνίαc ἀνδρόc, where the emendation ποιήcα⟨cθα⟩ι is not improbable. **πάντ' ἔχειc:** Either 'that is all I have to tell you' (cf. Aesch. *Ag.* 582, πάντ' ἔχειc λόγον, Eur. *Phoen.* 953, τὰ μὲν παρ' ἡμῶν πάντ' ἔχειc) or 'you have all you want' (cf. Eur. *Med.* 570, Ar. *Birds* 1543, *Lys.* 929). The latter appears more probable to me: Demeas sarcastically pretends that Chrysis has bettered her position by exchanging a home for a son.

388 ὅμωc: Perhaps he intended ὅμωc ἄκουcον.

389 νὴ δικαίωc: 'Quite right, too', i.e. I deserve it for being so foolish

SAMIA 587

as to interfere, cf. *Dysk.* 602 n.; in *Epitr.* 249 and frag. 740. 13 the phrase is not in any way ironical, but a soft answer to turn away wrath. For νή cf. *Dysk.* 510, *Karch.* 33 n.

390 τὸ μέγα πρᾶγμα: 'A fine figure!'; unfortunately 'the big noise', 'the big shot' are too slangy, [Dem.] xxxv. 15, οἱ μὲν γὰρ ἀδελφοὶ οἱ τούτου ἔτι νεώτεροι ἦcαν, οὑτοcὶ δὲ Λάκριτος Φαcηλίτης μέγα πρᾶγμα, Ἰcοκράτους μαθητής, Eubulos frag. 117 K, εἰ δ' ἐγένετο | κακὴ γύνη Μήδεια, Πηνελόπη δέ γε | μέγα πρᾶγμα. Demeas must apply the phrase sarcastically to Chrysis; he goes on to say that she will find what she amounts to as 'a woman of the town', no longer sheltered in Demeas' house. ἐν τῇ πόλει is emphatic by position, opposed in thought to ἐν τῇ ἐμῇ οἰκίᾳ. This is better than to place the stop after πόλει (Sudhaus, LSJ), 'you were a fine figure in the town (as my mistress)'. Miltner, *Mitt. Ver. klass. Phil. Wien* iv, 60, supposed Demeas to refer to the Cook, but Demeas would waste no sarcasms on him. Gomme's suggestion, 'the great thing is to have the Cook out of the way', also makes Demeas honour him with more attention than is plausible.

392–3: 'Not in your style, Chrysis, other women run to dinner-parties, making ten drachmas only.' This is the meaning of B's text, and I think it is possible. By 'your style' Demeas means 'the style you have been enjoying while with me' or 'the style to which you pretend', cf. Chionides frag. 1 K, πολλοὺς ἐγῷδα κοὐ κατά cε νεανίας | φρουροῦντας †ἀτεχνῶc† καὶ cάμακι κοιμωμένους.

C gives αἱ κατὰ cέ, Χρυcί, πραττόμεναι δράχμας δέκα μόνας ἑταῖραι (B also had εταιραι before correction to ετεραι). Several scholars proposed ἕτεραι (and indeed the confusion of the two words is not uncommon, e.g. *Perik.* 1024): 'the others of your sort, Chrysis, etc.'. But the position of ἕτεραι, so far removed from αἱ κατὰ cέ, makes this unconvincing to me, although it is printed by Austin.

More radical remedies for C's text look less likely now that its general shape is supported by B. But Leo's complicated transposition is worth mention: αἱ κατὰ c' ἑταῖραι, Χρυcί, πραττόμεναι δέκα δράχμας μόνας. Körte followed Miltner in supposing ἑταῖραι to be an explanatory expansion of αἱ κατὰ cέ, which had ousted some other word (ἀεί Leo).

There is a difficulty in the word μόνας. It seems to imply that ten drachmae is poor pay, yet Charisios in *Epitrepontes* is called extravagant for giving twelve drachmae a day for Habrotonon. But it is argued in the note on *Epitr.* 139 that Charisios' 'extravagance' was solely in Smikrines' eye. Further a good payment for the services of a slave, even one trained in music, might be a poor one for a free woman of any pretensions. If ten drachmae is compared with the wage of a skilled workman, two drachmae a day at this time, it must be remembered that a *hetaira* could not count upon an invitation to dinner every day.

393 τρέχουσιν ἐπὶ τὰ δεῖπνα: Cf. the adj. τρεχέδειπνος, perhaps applied to parasites by Alexis (frag. 168 K), and *AP* xi. 208, ἐπὶ δεῖπνον | ἔτρεχε. ἄχρι ἄν: The statement of Phrynichos and Moiris that the Attic forms are ἄχρι, μέχρι is entirely borne out by inscriptions, including a metrical one of the third or second century B.C., which has ἄχρι ἄν (Kaibel, *ep. gr.* 48). It is less likely that Menander here used a non-Attic form than that copyists have substituted what was more familiar to them. The *traditio* gives ἄχρι or μέχρι ἄν in frag. 525, Diphilos frag. 3 K, Hegesippos frag. 1. 26 K, Phoinikides frag. 3 K, Machon 474 Gow.

395 πεινῶσιν: Indicative: *either* they jump at invitations to dinners and drink themselves to death, *or* they starve, if they do not respond willingly and quickly to such invitations, but try to act the grand lady. ἄκρατον: Cf. 341 n. The company at these dinners is disreputably hard-drinking. τοῦτο . . . ποιῶσιν, i.e. τρέχωσιν ἐπὶ τὰ δεῖπνα.

398 ἕσταθι: 'Stay where you are': probably Chrysis makes a movement towards Demeas, to detain him, as he goes (certainly not one to re-enter the house herself, as Allinson understands).

The short scene that ends here is written with masterly skill. In the opening section Demeas' real reason for anger is kept firmly before the audience, although never mentioned; but it affects his language in such a way as to increase Chrysis' bewilderment. The intervention of the Cook then brings a touch of comic absurdity; it is absurd when a man is interrupted in a moment of high passion by an interfering stranger. Demeas does not even inquire what the Cook wants; he brushes him aside as an irrelevance. Then, having reduced both him and Chrysis to silence, he relieves his feelings by the brief tirade in which he prophesies a squalid future for the mistress he is discarding.

398 τάλας ἐγώ is much more frequent than τάλας ἔγωγε; but cf. *Perik.* 810, τάλαιν' ἔγωγε τῆς τύχης, and frag. 724, τάλας ἔγωγε.

(vi) 399–420: *Chrysis and Nikeratos*

399: Chrysis being left alone with the baby and her attendants, Nikeratos enters with a small and skinny sheep. He is not intended to be miserly, as Gomme thought, quoting Theophr. *Char.* xxii. 4, where the ἀνελεύθερος is said ἐκδιδοὺς αὐτοῦ θυγατέρα τοῦ μὲν ἱερείου πλὴν τῶν ἱερέων (what is due to the priests) τὰ κρέα ἀποδόσθαι, τοὺς δὲ διακονοῦντας ἐν τοῖς γάμοις οἰκοσίτους μισθώσασθαι, cf. frag. 384. He is a poor man who can afford nothing better. At a wedding both households would perform a sacrifice, cf. Plaut. *Aulularia*, where the bride-groom's father provides the bride's miserly father with a lamb—'quid? hic non poterat de suo senex opsonari filiai nuptiis?' (294–5)—a lamb which the ungrateful recipient later describes as 'ossa ac pellis totus' (564). Other scenes in which a sacrificial animal provides an opportunity for jests occur in *Dysk.* 393 ff., Ar. *Birds* 901. Here they are given an original turn by their contrast with the situation of the weeping Chrysis: it is not a simple response that is required from the spectator.

Nikeratos is a foil to Demeas; poor, and slow-witted, with no great gifts of speech. He talks for the most part, as has already been made clear, in short phrases. Here even his opening remarks, although long enough to support a μέν-and-δέ sentence, are partially broken up by the device of asyndeton into small units: αἷμα γὰρ ἔχει, | χολὴν ἱκανήν, | ὀcτᾶ καλά, | cπλῆνα μέγαν, | ὧν χρεία 'cτι τοῖc 'Ολυμπίοιc. From 405 he utters a series of short abrupt sentences, so abbreviated at 411, ἐμβροντηcία. ἀλλ' ἔcτ' ἐκεῖνοc ἡδύc, that editors are uncertain of his meaning.

400 θυθέν: This form (for τυθέν) is found in an inscription from Delphi *c.* 250 B.C. (*BCH* vii. [1883] 65) and at Amorgos in the same century. Similar spellings, indicating an inaccurate pronunciation, are found in Athenian inscriptions from the fifth century, e.g. ανεθεθη (429 B.C.), ενθαυθα (396 B.C.), χιθωνιcκοc (*c.* 345 B.C.), Meisterhans³, 102–4. C has a colon after the word; since there is no grammatical reason for this, it may indicate a pause in delivery: Nikeratos remembers the god-desses and adds by afterthought that they too will get their due from the one skinny sheep. This suits his style of speech.

401 χολήν: As Dedoussi notes, Plutarch says that the gall-bladder was not sacrificed to Hera Gamelia, but thrown aside, symbolically he believes (*Mor.* 141 e, frag. 157. 2). This is not relevant to the present passage. The sheep is not intended as a sacrifice to Hera alone, but to 'the gods and goddesses'.   **cπλῆνα μέγαν:** An enlarged spleen is a sign of disease.

404 τὸ κῴδιον is kept to the end of the sentence for an effect of sur-prise. For the practice of sending portions of a feast to uninvited friends cf. Theophr. *Char.* xvii. 2, Ar. *Ach.* 1049, ἔπεμψέ τιc coι νυμφίοc ταυτὶ κρέα | ἐκ τῶν γάμων.   **ἔcτι:** The use of the present for the future is not common in Greek: 'That's what's left for me.'

405 πρόcθε τῶν θυρῶν: 'In front of my door'; she has been driven away from that of Demeas' house.

406 οὐ μὲν οὖν ἄλλη: μὲν οὖν is assentient, Denniston, *GP* 477. For the phrase cf. Alexis frag. 270, Διὸς Cωτῆρος; οὐκ ἄλλου μὲν οὖν, Lucian, *Timon* 54, ἀλλὰ τί τοῦτο; οὐ Θραcυκλῆς ὁ φιλόcοφοc οὗτόc ἐcτιν; οὐ μὲν οὖν ἄλλοc, *Menippus* 1.

408: A similar ironical use of χρηcτόc, in *Aspis* 75, ὁ ἡγεμὼν ἡμῶν ὁ χρηcτόc, *Epitr.* 1066, τὸν χρηcτὸν αὐτῆc ἄνδρα, cf. frag. 16, ὁ χρηcτὸc ... μοιχόc.   τί γὰρ ἄλλο; 'That is all.'

410 τῶν γυναικῶν: Sc. his wife and daughter.

411 ἀνελομένη: Cf. 374 n.   ἐμβροντηcία: Richards's correction ἐμβροντηcίαc is supported by Hesychios (ε 2321 Latte), ἐμβροντηcίαc· μανιάc, φρενοβλαβείαc, θάμβουc, which *may* allude to this passage. I know no other example of an exclamatory genitive consisting of a bare noun; usually the noun is attached to an exclamatory word, e.g. οἴμοι γέλωτοc, Soph. *Ajax* 367, or has an article or adjective: τῆc τύχηc, Xen. *Cyr.* ii. 2. 3, χρήcτω κοικτίρμονοc ἀνδρόc, Theokritos xv. 75. But Nikeratos is a man of few words. If the nominative is retained, it may find a parallel in *Heros* 72, where ἱδρώc, ἀπορία seem to be quasi-exclamatory nominatives. Van Leeuwen printed the dative ἐμβροντηcίᾳ, constructing it with ἀνελομένη, but the disjointedness given by the nominative (or genitive) better suits Nikeratos' style of speech. A more difficult and more important question is whether Nikeratos here characterizes Chrysis' action in bringing up the child (Wilamowitz), or Demeas' conduct towards her: Gomme believed it was the latter, and that the former, although possibly foolish, could not be described as ἐμβροντηcία. Unfortunately the connotations of the word are doubtful, since this is its first occurrence and it does not appear again before Plutarch, *adv. Colotem* 1119 b, where it is said of the Platonic Socrates that τὴν ἐμβροντηcίαν ἐκ τοῦ βίου καὶ τὸν τῦφον ἐξήλαυνε; in Sext. Emp. ix. 40, to think rivers are gods is the height of ἐμβροντηcία. The participle ἐμβρόντητοc occurs several times in comedy. Literally 'thunder-struck', or 'struck stupid', it may like the English 'lunatic' be used as an emphatic term for 'foolish, stupid', as in Ophelio frag. 4 K, βιβλίον Πλάτωνοc ἐμβρόντητον. Nowhere is it used of violent madness; it rather means 'crack-brained': at Plato, *Alcib.* 2. 140 c it is regarded as a little weaker than μαινόμενοc: τοὺς μὲν πλεῖcτον αὐτῆc (sc. ἀφροcύνηc) μέροc ἔχονταc μαινομένουc καλοῦμεν, τοὺς δ' ὀλίγον ἔλαττον ἠλιθίουc τε καὶ ἐμβροντήτουc. It would seem, then, that ἐμβροντηcία is at least as applicable to Chrysis, provided that her action could be regarded as folly, as to Demeas, whose madness takes a violent form. Moreover this provides an easily intelligible train of thought for Nikeratos: 'Because you kept the child? a crackpot thing to do: but he is normally an agreeable man (and one would not have expected him to object so violently).' Now could he regard Chrysis' action as quite stupid? Yes, for in her position, with no security, it was folly to saddle herself with a child and that without the previous consent of the father in whose house it was to be brought up (on the Greek attitude to rearing of children, see intro. pp. 34–5). Nikeratos is no sentimentalist; he has the realism of the poor. Nor is he one to mince his words (cf. 550), or to refrain from telling Chrysis what he thinks.

412–13: Nikeratos continues after ἐμβροντηϲία with his characteristic brief phrases; Chrysis answers his question with a confirmatory relative clause; compare *Dysk.* 867, ὁ Κνήμων δ' οὐδέπω; (Γο.) ὃc ἱκέτευέ με κτλ. B omits the dicolon after ἀρτίωc, but has a paragraphus below the line. Editors, except Lefebvre (1907) and Allinson, have disregarded C's dicolon and paragraphus, preferring to make the change of speaker after ἡδύc. There C has a high point; a lower one may have disappeared, but that is not likely as there is no paragraphus below line 412. It may be possible to understand ἡδύc as laudatory, 'he is a kind pleasant fellow (and so his action is inexplicable)', cf. Alexis frag. 365, ἔδει γὰρ ὅϲτιϲ χρηϲτὸϲ ἦν ἡδύc τ' ἀνήρ, and Arist. *Rhet.* 1381ᵃ30, ἡδεῖϲ ϲυνδιαγαγεῖν ἢ ϲυνδιημερεῦϲαι. But the word is often used sarcastically to mean 'simple, innocent', e.g. Plato, *Gorg.* 491 e, ὡϲ ἡδὺϲ εἶ. If the explanation of ἐμβροντηϲία adopted above is right, Nikeratos may be using the word in a double-edged way: Demeas is kind, but also easily imposed on, and therefore might be expected to swallow Chrysis' folly. Webster translates 'soft', which could be similarly ambiguous.

415 με: ἐπειϲπίπτω is constructed with the acc. in Eur. *HF* 34, τήνδ' ἐπεϲπεϲὼν πόλιν, but one can burst *into* a city, not into a person. Hence με must be the object of ἐκκέκλεικε. ἔξωθεν, as so often, is the equivalent of ἔξω and also goes with ἐκκέκλεικε, and ἐπειϲπεϲών is used absolutely as, e.g., Eur. *Hec.* 1042.

416 ἐκκέκλεικε: This suggests that when Demeas entered his house the noise was heard of the bolt's being rammed home, or even that Chrysis followed him and tried the door (Wilamowitz). It may be noted that if the play was performed by three actors, some action by Chrysis was needed after 398, in order that the actor who played the Cook might have time to change his mask and get round to the *parodos* from which he entered as Nikeratos. χολᾷ: 'He is out of his mind.' Although χόλοϲ and χολή, 'bile', in their transferred senses mean 'anger' and χολεῖϲθαι 'to be angry', the verbs χολᾶν and μελαγχολᾶν (*Dysk.* 89 n.) mean 'to be mad', e.g. *Epitr.* 393. Crönert's punctuation Δημέαϲ; χολᾷ is effective, but a straightforward statement Δημέαϲ χολᾷ quite intelligible.

417 Πόντος: πόντος in the sense 'sea' is poetic; this, combined with the word χωρίον, shows that Nikeratos means the region to the south of the Black Sea, cf. Xen. *Anab.* v. 2. 2, ἀνθρώπους πολεμικωτάτους τῶν ἐν τῷ Πόντῳ, ibid. v. 6. 15, Aischines iii. 171, Νύμφαιον τὸ ἐν τῷ Πόντῳ, Arist. *Meteor.* 367ᵃ1, Ἡράκλεια ἡ ἐν τῷ Πόντῳ, Theophrastos, *Hist. Plant.* iv. 5. 2, τὰ μὲν γὰρ ἐν τῷ Πόντῳ καὶ τῇ Θρᾴκῃ γίνεται. One may guess that Demeas has been there on a trading journey: the chief Greek towns were Sinope and Herakleia; from the former Diogenes had found his way to Athens, Heracleides Ponticus from the latter.

419 ἀπομανείς: 'When he takes account of what he is doing, he will come to his senses and stop.' The only example of ἀπομαίνεσθαι previously quoted is in Lucian, *Dial. Deor.* xii. 1, where it is not immediately clear whether the meaning is 'getting rid of madness' or 'going completely mad'. Austin at one time took it the first way, but I think LSJ rightly understand it in the second. There is, however, a clear instance of the first meaning, noted by R. Renehan, *Glotta*, xlviii (1970), 95, in Aretaios, *SD* i. 6, ἦν ἀπομανῶσι (Reiske for ἀπομένωσι), εὔθυμοι, ἀκήδεες. In the passage of *Samia* the aorist participle forbids the interpretation 'he will stop being quite mad'.

ACT IV

(i) 421–439: *Nikeratos and Moschion* (enters 428)

421–8: Nikeratos comes out of his house, prepared to have it out with Demeas over his conduct. But what angers him is not the ill-treatment of Chrysis but the fact that it has resulted in an ill omen for the marriage which is being prepared. The women have been crying and are upset.

421 παρατενεῖς is supported by the same word, again in Nikeratos' mouth, at 544. The word is several times used metaphorically in the passive by fourth-century authors to mean 'be racked, tortured, worn out' and in the active by Xenophon, *Cyrop.* i. 3. 11, ἕως παρατείναιμι τοῦτον ὥσπερ οὗτος ἐμὲ παρατείνει ἀπὸ σοῦ κωλύων. This usage seems suitable in both passages of this play. An alternative explanation is that since παρατείνω is used transitively to mean 'prolong', it might have an intransitive sense 'keep on, continue'; something like this is found much later in Philostratos, *Vit. Ap.* vii. 22, ποῖ παρατενεῖς δεδιὼς ταῦτα; 'To what point will you continue fearing this?' But whether the word here means 'You are going to wear me out' or 'Are you going to keep on?' its force is much the same. Austin points out that we have had a hint at 200 that Nikeratos' wife is 'rather formidable'. προcβαλῶν: 'To make an attack on him'.

422 οὐδ' ἂν ἐπὶ πολλῷ . . . ἐδεξάμην: 'I would not have willingly accepted the occurrence of what has happened even if paid highly for it.' Cf. LSJ. ἐπί B. III. 3. τὸ γεγονὸc μὰ τοὺc θεοὺc πρᾶγμα: The insertion of μὰ τοὺc θεούc into the combination article+ participle+noun is remarkable: it may be a sign of Nikeratos' agitation.

424 οἰωνὸc . . . ἄτοποc: The bad (ἄτοποc, see *Dysk.* 288 n.) omen is the weeping and confusion that followed Chrysis' arrival, cf. Eur. *Or.* 788, δάκρυα γοῦν γένοιτ' ἄν :: οὐκοῦν οὗτοc οἰωνὸc μέγαc.

425 τιc: Nikeratos knows Chrysis' name (191) perfectly well; he avoids its use in order to put at a distance the woman who had disturbed the preparations.

427 cκατοφαγεῖ: The word is of course abusive, but more than mere abuse; it indicates that Demeas is behaving without proper feeling in that he has spoiled the atmosphere for the marriage by throwing out his mistress; see 550 n. His conduct has been clumsy (cκαιόc).

428 οὐ μὴ δύῃ ποθ' ἥλιοc: Moschion enters. He was not at home during the events of the last act, and so has not heard of them; as appears from 432 he had been in the market-place, where he had met Parmenon, sent there to do the shopping (189–202). The bridegroom fetched his bride after sunset, see Photios s.v. ζεῦγοc ἡμιονικόν· ἄγουcιν εἰc τὰ τοῦ γαμοῦντοc ἑcπέραc ἱκανῆc. Moschion, who has been killing time by visiting a public bath-house, is waiting impatiently: 'The sun is never going to set.' The origin of the construction οὐ μή+aor. subjunctive, equivalent to a strongly negatived future indicative, is discussed by Goodwin, *MT* 389–97, who brings out the difficulties, but does not make out an adequate case for an alternative to the orthodox view that there is an ellipse of the concept of fearing: 'There is no (fear) that the sun will set.'

429: 'Night has forgotten herself', i.e. Night is not behaving as she usually does; she is slow to come. For bathing before a wedding cf. 729 n. But Moschion is not here speaking of the ritual bath, but of visiting a public bath-house as a way of killing time.

430: Nikeratos makes his presence known; Moschion was too self-absorbed to notice him, and even now does not return the old man's greeting, but abruptly asks why he should not come at once for his bride.

436 cου must, although separated by the diaeresis in the middle of the line, go with ὁ πατήρ, 'your father', not with ἔνδοθεν on which it is enclitic, nor with τὴν Χρυcίδα; cf. 709 n.

438 δεινὸν καὶ θαυμαστόν: A conjunction of adjectives found elsewhere, Ar. *Birds* 1471, Eur. *IA* 1538.

439: Perhaps the sentence would, if not interrupted by the appearance of Demeas, have continued '—join me in making him take Chrysis back', or 'in protesting'. Demeas too, it appears, has been having trouble with his household, who regret Chrysis' departure. 'If I get hold of a cudgel,' he says, 'I'll see that these tears are knocked out of you.' After telling them to help the Cook, he adds sarcastically that they have reason for weeping; they have lost someone who was much to their advantage, as the facts show, i.e. they had had an indulgent mistress and had grown idle. Demeas' phrase ἂν λάβω ξύλον κτλ. has a parallel in Plaut. *Aul.* 48–9: 'Si hercle hodie fustem cepero aut stimulum in manum, testudineum istum tibi ego grandibo gradum.' But whereas that is obvious, Demeas' threat is paradoxical: he will use the stick not to make his servants cry, but to stop them crying.

444 Ἄπολλον: Cf. 309 and *Dysk.* 659 n. He is addressed again as δέσποτα in 448, cf. Ar. *Wasps* 875, ὦ δέσποτ' ἄναξ, γεῖτον Ἀγυιεῦ, τοὐμοῦ προθύρου προπύλαιε. It is to be noted that for all his frivolity over Helios (110) and Zeus (590–5), Demeas here shows warm feeling for Apollo and a belief that the god can help him.

445 ἐπ' ἀγαθῇ τύχῃ τε πᾶσι: 'With good fortune for us all'. Cf. Ar. *Wasps* 869, ὦ Φοῖβ' Ἄπολλον Πύθι', ἐπ' ἀγαθῇ τύχῃ τὸ πρᾶγμ' ὃ μηχανᾶται, . . . ἅπασιν ἡμῖν ἁρμόσαι, com. anon. (Page, *GLP* 236, *P. Tebt.* 693), ἐπεὶ δοκεῖ περαίνειν τοὺς γάμου[ς . . .] ἐπ' ἀγαθαῖς ἤδη τύχαισιν πρός ϲε[.

447 καταπιὼν τὴν χολήν: 'Swallowing my anger'; the phrase recurs in Chrysippos, *SVF* ii. 891. Demeas then asks that his feelings shall not be seen by anyone. He must be forced to sing the wedding-song because in his circumstances he is not feeling inclined to make merry. εἰϲαναγκάζειν is a rare compound, Aesch. *PV* 290, and with a dependent infinitive, as here, Plato, *Tim.* 49 a.

450–1: There is nothing to show that Demeas, who has just been addressing the audience, is yet aware of the presence of the other two characters. The sense of the lines may be irrecoverable. In 450 the second letter is either ξ or aspirated (the second letter of a diphthong). Possibly ἄξομ' οὐκ ἄριστ' ἐγὼ γάρ (also suggested by Barigazzi); the middle ἄγεσθαι is used of a father who brings his son a bride, Hdt. i. 34, ἄγεται μὲν τῷ παιδὶ γυναῖκα. Webster's οἷον οὐκ ἄριστ' ἔγωγ' ἄν, 'a sort of thing I should not do very well', hardly fits the space, even if written οιονγανουκαριϲτεγω, as he somewhat improbably suggests.

SAMIA
595

Lloyd-Jones suggested ⟨κακ⟩ῶc ἔχω, but that robs the line of its diaeresis. Jacques's hesitant suggestion for 451, οὐκ ἂν ἐπανέλθοι (sc. Χρυcίc) is unlikely unless 450 contained something to call her to mind; she has been dismissed from attention at 444. Perhaps πάντα νῦν ἔλθοι: 'What does it matter? Let anything happen now.'

451: The dramatic technique here is noteworthy. The appearance of Demeas covers an imaginary conversation between Nikeratos and Moschion in which the necessity of remonstrating with the angry man was accepted. This conversation becomes audible at 451 when Nikeratos says to Moschion: 'You approach him before I do.'

452–6: If εἶέν is right, Moschion replies to Nikeratos, 'Well then, here goes', and then addresses his father as if for information rather than with open protest. But Demeas feels that he is interfering, suspects him of being Chrysis' emissary, and snubs his intervention. Of 454–6 only οὐχὶ cόν . . . φλύαρος is addressed to Moschion; the rest is an aside that he cannot catch. τί φῄς; 'What's that you're saying?', is a likely supplement, cf. 545.

454: Galiano proposes to add δηλαδή at the beginning of the line. δηλαδή is usually last in the sentence, but see Eur. *Or.* 789, δηλαδὴ cιγᾶν ἄμεινον. **πρεcβεύεταί τιc:** 'Someone is sending an intermediary'; LSJ s.v. II. 3 gives Thuc. v. 39 as a place where the middle means 'go as [not 'send as'] an ambassador', but this misinterprets the passage. Like Nikeratos, Demeas avoids using the proper name Chrysis and substitutes τιc.   **οὐχὶ cόν:** The restoration is supported by *Aspis* 254.

456 δεινὸν ἤδη: 'Really dreadful', cf. Ar. *Ach.* 315, *Wasps* 426, *Eccl.* 645.   **cυναδικεῖ μ' οὗτοc:** Contrast 328, οὐδὲν γὰρ ἀδικεῖ Μοcχίων cε.

457–8: ἀcμένῳ χρῆν γὰρ αὐτῶι . . . γεγονέναι: This is, I think, the required sense, 'this ought to have been a welcome event for him'; if Moschion had been seduced against his will, he should have been glad to see the last of Chrysis. For the construction of the dative participle ἀcμένῳ with γεγονέναι cf. K–G i. 425. Except perhaps at *Aspis* 92, Menander elsewhere uses the form ἐχρῆν, e.g. 499, 551; it indicates that something ought to have happened, but has not. The gap after γε[is too short to take enough words to fill the metre; something must have been omitted. Jacques's γεγονέ⟨ναι⟩ is palaeographically excellent.

459: Kasser's reading]κω looks probable; perhaps then π[ροcδο]κῶ ⟨'γώ] or ⟨μοι⟩ (Austin) τοὺc φίλουc.— Demeas intends to say 'I expect my friends to approve of my getting rid of an unfaithful

U

woman', but pulls himself up as he realizes this to be what he has determined to keep quiet.

461 τοῦθ', ὁρᾷς, ὑπερβολή: 'This beats all', cf. Dem. xxvii. 38, ταῦτ' οὐχ ὑπερβολή; The sentence is an aside by Demeas, who has not yet accused his son openly of anything: moreover it is clearly not heard by Moschion, who disregards it, continuing his own train of thought. If ὁρᾶθ' (Oguse) is right, it will be addressed to the audience. But parenthetic ὁρᾷς is familiar (e.g. *Perik.* 332, 511) and there is no reason why Demeas should not address the word to himself.

464 ff.: Reminded of Nikeratos' presence, Moschion tells him to go in and instruct Chrysis 'to run off home here'. Nikeratos, however, does not obey him. There now ensues a brilliant scene of cross-purposes; Moschion's innocent pleas exasperate Demeas, to whom they appear incredibly impudent, when he has warned his son that he knows all. At last he takes him aside (δεῦρο δή, 476) to tell him in plain words that he knows him to be the baby's father. Moschion's reply, 'If I am, what has Chrysis done to you?', reduces him to momentary incoherence, and the further statement that 'thousands have done the like' leads him to command the youth, who seems to have lost all sense of shame, to tell Nikeratos on whom he had got the child. This, of course, embarrasses him, but Nikeratos at last guesses what Demeas has been thinking—the child is the quasi-incestuous offspring of Moschion and Chrysis; he heaps abuse on the uncomprehending boy.

465 τρίτον: 'This third time I say it', cf. Eur. *Helen* 1417, αὖθις κελεύω καὶ τρίτον γ', εἴ σοι φίλον. **τουτογί:** This emphatic form of the demonstrative is familiar from Aristophanes, but not yet known elsewhere in New Comedy, except by uncertain emendation at *Georgos* 63. Even here the right reading may be τοῦτ' ἐγώ.

468 ποίαν χάριν: Not 'What kindness?' but indignantly, 'You call that a kindness?' This use of ποῖος is common in Aristophanes, see LSJ s.v. 2.

473 γνώριμα: Cf. 267 n. Here the word is more or less synonymous with σαφῆ; Moschion's words are 'open to understanding', i.e. plainly clear.

474 συνόμνυται: 'Is conspiring with my enemies'. The verb is normally active, but the middle is found in Plut. *Sertorius* 27. It is interesting that it can be taken for granted that Demeas has enemies, cf. 706. For ancient Greeks both friends and enemies loomed larger than they do to us. An anecdote recounted that the sage Chilon, hearing someone say that he had no enemies, asked whether he had no friends either (Plut. *Mor.* 86 c, 96 a). τιc: The name *Μοcχίων* is avoided. καὶ διαρραγήcομαι: 'I shall in very truth burst with rage', cf. Ar. *Knights* 340, οἴμοι, διαρραγήcομαι, and 519 below. Λοξία: Photios s.v. *Λοξίαc* says εἰώθαcι τὸν πρὸ τῶν θυρῶν ἱδρύμενον βωμὸν τοῦ Ἀπόλλωνοc *Λοξίαν* καὶ *Ἀπόλλω* προcαγορεύειν καὶ *Ἀγυιᾶ.* On the question whether what was addressed as Loxias etc. was an altar or a pillar representing Apollo that stood outside the house, see *Dysk.* 659 n. Frag. 807 runs καθεδοῦμαι δ᾽ ἐνθαδί τὸν *Λοξίαν* αὐτὸν καταλαβών; cf. also frag. 40 with Körte's note.

476 δεῦρο δή: Demeas draws Moschion aside: he still wishes to keep the truth dark; Nikeratos must not hear it.

477 ἀλλ᾽ ἐγώ: Sc. *ποήcω;* this is a new formula of assent, repeated at 733. οἶδα is not parenthetic, but isolated and emphatic, 'I *know*'. When used parenthetically, οἶδα is normally joined with cάφ᾽, εὖ, ὅτι, or ἐγώ.

480 ἀλλὰ τίc; requires Moschion to suggest who, if not Chrysis, is to blame. This use of ἀλλά generally follows a negative sentence by the previous speaker, Denniston, *GP* 9; but here Moschion's question is in effect a negation. See Addenda.

481 οὐδὲν ἐνθυμεῖcθε; Lit. 'Don't you think at all?', i.e. 'Have you and Chrysis no scruples?', cf. Plato frag. 106. 3 K, οἳ ζῆτε τερπνῶc οὐδὲν ἐνθυμούμενοι. B has τι φηιc: | ουδεν: ουδεν ενθυμειcθε, and Austin and Jacques write τί φήιc; (Mo.) οὐδέν. (Δη.) ἐνθυμεῖcθε. But how could Moschion reply that he was saying nothing? He is in dead earnest. Jacques sees in the word 'de la lassitude, du découragement'. But there is no other sign of such feelings: Moschion stands up firmly for what he thinks to be the right. It is more likely that after ουδεν had been accidentally doubled, a reader mistakenly supposed the first ουδεν to be Moschion's reply and marked it off with dicola before and after; no space was originally left for the dicolon after the word. ὅτι βοῶ: '(You ask) why I am shouting?' The use of ὅcτιc, ὁποῖοc, etc. to repeat questions asked with τίc, ποῖοc, etc. is familiar. κάθαρμα: Lit. 'what is taken out by cleaning'; the word was used as a term of abuse, Eupolis frag. 117 K, αἱρούμενοι καθάρματα cτρατηγούc, Dem. xviii. 128, cοὶ δ᾽ ἀρετῆc, ὦ κάθαρμα, . . . τίc μετουcία, Aischines iii. 211. The scholiasts on Ar. *Plut.* 454, ὦ καθάρματε, say that it was the equivalent of φαρμακόc, the criminal executed as a scapegoat, itself a term of abuse in Aristophanes.

484: 'Do you so completely reject and renounce me?', cf. *Perik.* 745 n. τυγχάνειc throws emphasis on the participle. Moschion is completely at a loss to understand his father's question. The absence

of median diaeresis in this line is unparalleled in Menander, although
such rhythm is not uncommon in Aristophanes. But the line is otherwise excellent and no plausible emendation presents itself: it should
be accepted, perhaps as representing Demeas' turmoil of spirit.

485: Cf. Ter. *Ad.* 687, 'humanum tamen: fecere alii saepe item boni.'

488: Austin defends the position of δή, a postpositive word, at the
beginning of the verse by reference to Soph. *Ajax* 986, where δῆτα is
so placed. The enjambement probably reflects Demeas' sudden plunge
into what he has been avoiding, the exposure of his son's conduct.
Since the only other person present is Nikeratos, οἱ παρόντες must be
the spectators, who are, as explained in the introduction, p. 14, more
closely associated with the action than the audience at a conventional
modern drama.

496: Just as it appears that Moschion will be forced to admit that
Plangon is the child's mother, Nikeratos at last guesses the reason for
Demeas' passion and bursts out into abuse of the young man. His
first two lines, however, do not indicate what he believes Moschion
to have done; and Moschion accordingly, taking them to be the
indignation of the wronged girl's father, responds in an aside that all
is up with him. He does not yet realize that he has in fact been saved
from confessing his crime to Nikeratos. ὑπονοεῖν . . . μόλις ποτε:
See *Dysk.* 236 n. τέλος ἔχω: 'I am finished', cf. 548. τὴν τύχην:
'What has happened'.

495 ff.: Nikeratos denounces Moschion as a worse criminal than the
most famous incestuous figures of mythology. In the circumstances
this is comic, and even if Moschion had been guilty, Nikeratos'
language might be thought overdone. Nevertheless it must be recognized that the simple fellow regards these characters as historical
personages, and that the Greeks were often ready to find in what we
call their 'mythology' parallels for contemporary behaviour, much as
at least until recently the English could talk about 'a Delilah' or
'a Jezebel'. When at 589 ff. Demeas reminds Nikeratos of the story
of Danaë, although the latter cannot believe it is relevant, he does
not know how to reject it, for he cannot declare it to be false, a mere
poetic invention.

The story of Tereus was that, having raped his sister-in-law
Philomela, he cut out her tongue to prevent her revealing his deed,
of Thyestes that he seduced his brother's wife and later raped his own
daughter. Tereus was treated in Sophocles' famous play of that name,
by Philokles (earlier than Ar. *Birds* 281), and perhaps by Karkinos
(frag. 4 Nauck). Euripides wrote a *Thyestes*. But Nikeratos does not

SAMIA

speak as if his knowledge of these stories came from seeing them on the stage.

497: Handley's suggestion ὅσα γέγον', ὅσ' ἡμῖν ἐστ' ἀκοῦσαι is a little nearer B's corrupt γεγονασ'. The restriction of the universal ὅσα γέγονε to such stories as were current is a little absurd, but Nikeratos is absurd. Also the short clauses suit his style of speech.   λέχη: 'Bed', always with a sexual connotation, is a word not used in prose. Nikeratos uses a poetic word for his poetic examples.

498 Ἀμύντορος: In *Iliad* ix. 447 ff. Phoinix tells how at his mother's instigation he lay with the concubine of his father Amyntor, who laid a curse on him and confined him, but on the tenth night he escaped and fled the country. Nikeratos has in mind another version, used and perhaps invented by Euripides in his *Phoinix*, according to which Amyntor blinded his son (Nauck, *TGF* p. 621). Aristophanes, *Ach.* 421, makes Euripides refer to this play, τὰ τοῦ τυφλοῦ Φοίνικος. Aischines quotes from it, *de falsa legatione* 152, and Demosthenes in his reply, xix. 246, suggests that there had been no recent performances of it (Μόλων ἠγωνίζετο καὶ εἰ δή τις ἄλλος τῶν παλαιῶν ὑποκριτῶν). Those of Menander's audience who knew the play would have the pleasure of knowing that Euripides' Phoinix was, like Moschion, innocent (Schol. A. *Iliad* ix. 453). In fact, all those who refer to the story of Phoinix' blinding believe that he was the victim of a false story put about by the concubine: Apollodoros iii. 13. 8, *AP* iii. 3, *Suda* s.v.   ἔτλης: τλᾶν is the poetic equivalent of the ordinary prose word τολμᾶν, but ventured on by Isokrates iv. 96 and Xenophon, *Cyr.* iii. 1. 3. Aristophanes has τλαίην three times in paratragic passages: *Clouds* 119, *Wasps* 1159, frag. 149; and ἔτλης, *Clouds* 1387, τέτληκα, *Plutus* 280, both in long iambics.

500 τούτῳ: Sc. Νικηράτῳ. Moschion has defeated Demeas' attempts to hide his supposed affair with Chrysis.

503 εἰς κόλπον: Spitting, often into one's bosom, to avert evil, was a common practice, cf. Theokr. vi. 39, ὡς μὴ βασκανθῶ δὲ τρὶς εἰς ἐμὸν ἔπτυσα κόλπον, and Gow's note. Adrasteia, associated or identified with Nemesis, was supposed to cheat extravagant hopes, and so was often spoken of with some deprecatory phrase, to make harmless words that might sound presumptuous, see *Perik.* 304 n. and Headlam on Herondas vi. 34. Spitting and Adrasteia are associated again in Lucian, *Apologia* 6, ἐῴκει ἡ Ἀδράστεια τότε κατόπιν ἐφεστῶσά σοι . . . καταγελᾶν . . . ὅτι οὐκ εἰς τὸν κόλπον πτύσας πρότερον κτλ. Here Nikeratos, making what seems to be the extravagant statement that he would rather have Diomnestos than Moschion as a son-in-law, wishes to avert any possible evil consequence, presumably the chance that his girl should have such a bad husband.

504 ἐπί: 'In the hands of' or 'in the power of', LSJ s.v. B. I. 1. g.

Διομνήϲτῳ: C. Dedoussi, *Entretiens Hardt* xvi (1970), 167, suggests a reference to the story (Heracleides Ponticus frag. 58 Wehrli) of an Eretrian Diomnestos, who deposited the fortune of a dead general with Hipponikos at Athens; this Hipponikos kept it for himself when the Persians killed or carried off all the Eretrians; it was squandered by his son Kallias. But if we have here a reference to a Diomnestos who was a proverbially unsatisfactory son-in-law, one would expect him to have been notoriously unfaithful rather than one who never enjoyed a dubiously acquired fortune. The name Diomnestos was borne by Athenians (*Lys.* xviii. 21, [Plut.] *Mor.* 836 e), and there may be an allusion to some contemporary scandal.

505 ὁμολογουμένην ἀτυχίαν: 'A recognized misfortune'; the internal accusative, expressing the result of the action denoted by the rest of the sentence, is admirably explained by Barrett's note on Eur. *Hipp.* 752–7; see also Schwyzer, ii. 86.

506 ἠδικημένος κατεῖχον: Perhaps 'although injured I controlled myself'. κατέχω, intrans., cf. *Perik.* 824 n. A man without spirit can be said to think of himself as an ἀνδράποδον, Xen. *Mem.* iv. 2. 39, πάνυ ἀθύμωϲ ἔχων ἀπῆλθε . . . καὶ νομίϲαϲ τῷ ὄντι ἀνδράποδον εἶναι, Plato, *Gorgias* 483 a, οὐδὲ γὰρ ἀνδρὸϲ τοῦτό γ' ἐϲτιν τὸ πάθημα τὸ ἀδικεῖϲθαι, ἀλλ' ἀνδραπόδου τινόϲ, Dio Chrys. xxxi. 109, οὐκ ἔϲτιν ὅπωϲ οὐκ ἂν ἀνδράποδον ἡγήϲαϲθαι εἶναι τὸν λέγοντα. Nikeratos will have declared that Demeas had acted like a slave in putting up with injury; e.g. ἀνδράποδ[ον εἶ, Δημέα.

507 λέκτρον is, like λέχοϲ (495), a poetic word. But whereas the latter might pass in its mythological context, the use of λέκτρον by a humble citizen of his own connubial bed must be absurd. Nikeratos outdoes this absurdity when at 517 he speaks of his house as μελάθροιϲ τοῖϲ ἐμοῖϲ. μέλαθρα is a word from poetry, usually applied to the palaces of kings. Its second syllable is often short in tragedy, but Nikeratos adopts the option of dividing the word μελαθ-ρα, making the syllable long, as in epic scansion. Other pieces of diction that do not belong to everyday language, although less extreme, are the following:

1. αἰϲχύνει λέκτρον: cf. Eur. *Hipp.* 944, ᾔϲχυνε τἀμὰ λέκτρα.
2. ἡ ϲυγκλιθεῖϲα: the word is rare and the only exact parallel quoted for this meaning is Eur. *Alc.* 1090, οὐκ ἔϲτιν ἥτιϲ τῷδε ϲυγκλιθήϲεται, although the word is used of the man in Hdt. ii. 181.
3. The use of φόνοϲ, 'murder', for a sexual offence. This puzzles

Moschion and even the explanation 'I call murder any acts committed in rebellion' implies that Moschion's supposed act was one of 'insurrection' against his father, a possible but imaginative word.

4. τοῖcιν: there is no other example in Menander of the old long form of the dative of the article (unless frag. 681 is in fact by him and τοῖc⟨ι⟩ is correctly restored). αὐτοῖc⟨ιν⟩ is a likely conjecture (but not certain) in frag. 711, and transmitted in *Pap. Ghôran* ii. 134 (possibly Menander). Nouns with the long termination are ἀληθείαιcιν, *Theophorumene* 25, διαβολαῖcι frag. 541.

All this elevated language is made more comical by the contrast with the prosaic lines that describe the men sitting to chatter in the barber's shop (510–12). One cannot say that it was impossible for an Athenian to resort to the language of tragedy if he had strong feelings to express. There may be some element of exaggeration here, but Menander may nevertheless still be 'representing life'.

507–13: Nikeratos is so moved by Moschion's supposed crime that he bursts out of his usual staccato style of speech to utter a long period, with eight (or nine) clauses.   εἰ ᾔcχυνε . . . οὐχ ὕβριcε: Not a past condition, see 623 n.

509 ἐπώλουν: Clearly a παλλακή who was a slave could be sold by the master to whom she had been unfaithful, but Chrysis was not a slave. Is it possible that a free non-citizen παλλακή could legally be punished by being sold into slavery? Or could she in fact have been so punished, if she lacked any protector? The precarious position of a foreign παλλακή at Athens is discussed by E. W. Bushala, *AJP* cx (1969), 65.   cυναποκηρύττων: The right of a father to 'expel' his son, thus barring him from a share in family worship and probably from inheritance (Dion. Hal. ii. 26), is stated by Demosthenes xxxix. 39, but it seems rarely to have been exercised, since there is no certain historical instance, see A. R. W. Harrison, *Law of Athens*, i. 75–6. Aristotle, *EN* 1163ᵇ22, thinks it would only be exercised against one of 'excessive wickedness', but Plato, *Laws* 928 d–929 d, lays down elaborate provisions for its use. Aelian, *ep.* 19, makes a rustic say τὸν μὲν καλὸν νυμφίον (his son) ἐc κόρακαc ἀποκηρύξω . . . τὴν δὲ νύμφην (a girl the son has 'freed') ἀποδώcομαι κἀκείνην ἐπ' ἐξαγωγῇ ('to be taken abroad'). The situation is quite different, but he may have known *Samia*.

510 μήτε . . . μή: This energetic anacoluthon (K–G ii. 289) is mainly found in tragedy, e.g. Eur. *Orestes* 1086, μήθ' αἷμά μου δέξαιτο κάρπιμον πέδον, μὴ λαμπρὸc αἰθήρ.   κουρεῖον: For the barber's shop as a place of gossip cf. Ar. *Plut.* 338, καίτοι λόγοc γ' ἦν, νὴ τὸν Ἡρακλέα, πολὺς ἐπὶ τοῖcι κουρείοιcι τῶν καθημένων, ὡc ἐξαπίνηc ἀνὴρ γεγένηται πλούcιοc, *Birds* 1440–5, Lysias xxiv. 20.

511 ἐξ ἑωθινοῦ: 'From (the period of) dawn' is an ordinary phrase: Ar. *Thesm.* 2, Alexis frag. 257. 4, Xen. *Hell.* i. 1. 5.

513 ἐπεξελθὼν τῷ φόνῳ: Possibly unusual. Normally the dative is used of the person prosecuted, the accusative of the crime, e.g. Antiphon ii. 1. 2.   **ποίῳ φόνῳ;** This question may be put either by Demeas or by Moschion. Austin supposes it to be the latter, and may be right. But 515 is an aside by Moschion, perhaps a little awkward if he has just received a reply. Moreover, B's indication that he speaks that line is odd if the previous question had been his. Further, Nikeratos' speech 506–13 is directed at Demeas, criticizing his mildness of action; hence it would not be unnatural for him to reply.

514 ὅcα τιc: With some probability Handley suggests ὅcτιc, referring to his note on *Dysk.* 766 ff. where he gives examples of 'illogical correlation between main clause and relative clause'. But B's text is defensible: 'I count as murder all such deeds done by someone who is aiming to take another's place.' ἐπανίcτημι is inadequately translated by 'rebel', which only suggests obtaining freedom from another's rule, for it often connotes a desire to substitute one's own rule for that of the one to be deposed. Nikeratos' language is far-fetched, but he means that Moschion has tried to replace Demeas as Chrysis' lord and master.

515 αὖοc: 'I am dry (with fright)', see *Perik.* 353 n., *Epitr.* 901.
   πέπηγα: 'I am frozen stiff.' At Eur. *HF* 1395 Herakles, in despair, says he cannot rise, ἄρθρα γὰρ πέπηγέ μου.

518: 'Think yourself wronged along with me as a genuine friend would be.' The implication is that Nikeratos *is* a genuine friend (LSJ s.v. ὡc ἄν is misleading). True friends have all things in common. Similarly at 702, φέρειν τι . . . ὡc ἂν ὑόν, not 'as if you were my son' but 'as a son should'.

Austin originally printed ⟨c'⟩ ἰδών, but Nikeratos means that he will explode when he sets eyes on Chrysis, of whom he has just been speaking. Hence in vol. ii ὃc διαρραγήcομ' ⟨ἐπ⟩ιδών (Lloyd-Jones) is preferred. For ὃc introducing an assentient sentence cf. 413.

519 διαρραγήcομαι: Cf. 475 n.   **βάρβαρε, Θρᾷξ ἀληθῶc**: For the supposed sexual appetite of Thracians see frag. 794; Strabo, who quotes it, says that Menander was not inventing the story but using a fact.

   οὐ παρήcειc; is the equivalent of the imperative πάρεc, 'let me pass', but has a threatening tone, K–G i. 176.   **ἐμβλέπειc;** 'Can you look

me in the face?', cf. 483, Dem. xix. 69, οἷc ἀπαντῶντας ἐμβλέπειν . . .
ἀνάγκη . . . τούτουc ἐξαπατᾶν ὑπέcτηcαν.

521: Page and Lloyd-Jones thought of transferring νὴ Δί' to the
beginning of the line, to form the first words of a sentence by Moschion,
interrupted by Demeas. But one would perhaps expect Moschion to
deny something (μὰ Δία) rather than affirm something; and after the
agitated πρὸc θεῶν, the comparatively weak νὴ Δία is not altogether
convincing. Austin hesitantly suggested, *ZPE* iv (1969), 169, εἰ δὲ
μηδὲν ὤν, which has the advantage of making it possible to keep
μηδὲ ἕν in 522. (But note the variant readings οὐδὲ γρῦ and μηδὲ γρῦ
at *Mis.* 291.) Arnott independently thought of οὐδ' εἰ μηδὲν ὤν, which
is nearer B's reading, and may be right.   **προcδοκᾷc:** Sc. γεγονέναι.

525 τὰc ἀληθείαc: *Epitr.* 578 n. The plural is defensible because there
are two statements: (1) the child is not hers, (2) she is doing me a
kindness. But at *Aspis* 372 the plural seems to be not so explicable.

527: Moschion means that if Demeas hears the full story, he will see
that his son's fault was a small one.

528 ἀποκτενεῖc: Like the Latin *enicas*, 'You'll be the death of me
before you've told me', i.e. 'Come on, answer the question!'

530 μή με βουκολεῖc ὅρα: 'See that you are not trying to pull the
wool over my eyes': 'μή with the present indicative expresses the fear
that something *is now going on*', Goodwin, *MT* § 369, cf. K–G ii.
394–5.

530–1 βουκολεῖc: 596 n. The division of speeches is that of B, and more
satisfactory than any alternative.   **οὖ:** 'Where'. Used of place the
word is not uncommon in comedy; it is less frequently used, as here,
of circumstances, but see Plato, *Symp.* 194 a, εἰ γένοιο οὖ νῦν εἰμι.

καὶ τί κερδανῶ; Sc. βουκολῶν cε.

532–4: It is necessary that the conversation of Demeas and his son
should cease and that they should attend to Nikeratos: the sound of
his door alerts them. The unfinished sentence is a sign of his precipitate
entry. In Nikeratos' speech ἄχει is the only word foreign to prose,
and even that is found in Xenophon, *Cyr.* v. 5. 6; but nevertheless
the whole atmosphere and vocabulary are those of tragedy.

There is intentional bathos in the very ordinary language of what
follows. There is also a contrast, probably intentional, between the
confused rage of Nikeratos on seeing his daughter suckling the baby,
and the self-control of Demeas when he saw Chrysis, also διδοῦcαν
τιτθίον.

536 τοῦτ' ἦν ἄρα: 'Then that's what it was', i.e. that was the terrible
sight referred to in 533–4. But it is not certain that the phrase is

Moschion's. There is, it is true, no dicolon after αρα, but the *nota personae* μοςχ΄ stands at the beginning of 537. If τοῦτ᾽ ἦν ἄρα belongs to Demeas, a possible alternative meaning is 'then this that you told me was true' (so Jacques). But 'father, d'you hear?' follows less convincingly on that.

537: The insertion of μ᾽ after ἀδικεῖc Μοcχίων is perhaps not necessary, but it is recommended by 456 cυναδικεῖ μ᾽ οὗτος, and an accusative pronoun is found with the verb at 328, 479, 583 also.

538–41: Moschion and Demeas have overheard Nikeratos, but he does not realize it; he comes over to the latter and repeats his words almost verbatim. First, however, Moschion retires in mortal fear of the injured father; cf. Demosthenes iv. 45, τεθνᾶcι τῷ δέει, xix. 81, δουλεύειν καὶ τεθνάναι τῷ φόβῳ. His departure is quite natural, but at the same time dramatically needed, if the following brilliant scene is to take the form it does. He does not go into his house, but away off-stage by a *parodos*. This is proved by the fact that when he returns at 616 he does not come out of the house, being unaware that arrangements for his wedding are in full swing within (670 ff.). Note, however, that Demeas encourages Moschion to remain (θάρρει, 539) ; that is to say, he has not at this point planned his action. In fact, he tries to suggest first that Nikeratos was mistaken in supposing his daughter to be suckling the child, and then that Moschion was not the father.

543 κατέπεσεν: 'Fell in a faint', cf. Xenarchos frag. 7 K, καταπίπτει καὶ λιποψυχεῖν δοκῶν ἔκειτο, and com. adesp. 3 K, κατέπεcον ἀκαρὴc τῷ δέει.   τυχὸν ἴcωc: Cf. *Epitr.* 504–6 n. Austin completes the line with cοι, but it is hard to see how Nikeratos could have 'imagined' that his daughter fell. Another possibility is that Demeas intended to advance a theory that the daughter imagined something, e.g. that the person entering was a stranger, but was interrupted before he could complete his sentence. My text adopts this alternative.

544 παρατενεῖc: See 421 n.   τούτων αἴτιος εἴμ᾽ ἐγώ: Demeas says this to himself, remembering that if he had not driven Chrysis and the baby from his home, Nikeratos would never have found his daughter suckling it. Nikeratos does not hear what it is that he is saying, and so asks τί φῄc;

546–7: κορυζᾷc: Lit. 'you have a running nose'; this was a metaphor to mean 'you are drivelling', Plato, *Rep.* 343 a, Polybios, xxxviii. 12. 5 ; the noun κόρυζα was used in the same way by Lucian (see LSJ s.v.). Hesychios has βουκόρυζος· ἀναίcθητος, ἀcύνετος. There was a similar usage of λέμφος, see *Epitr.* 561 n.   οὐκ ἐcτιν λόγος: 'Is not a mere tale', but an ἔργον, a fact; however, he will go back and confirm the

facts. Demeas tries to delay him, remonstrating (ὦ τᾶν, cf. *Dysk.*
247 n.).   τὸ δεῖνα, 'I tell you what', introduces an idea that has just
entered the speaker's head (*Perik.* 334 n., *Dysk.* 897), but Demeas
may here simply be playing for time, hoping that something *will* come
into his head.   μικρόν: Sc. ἐπίϲχεϲ, 'wait a moment'.

548: B and C both had πανταταπραγματ'. The dactyl in the first foot
cannot be rejected out of hand, see *Perik.* 301 n., but unlike the more
plausible examples there given is not contained in a single word of
the shape – ∪ ∪ –, nor does it include the syllable δι-, in which some
scholars think ι might become a semi-vowel: on the other hand it
can easily be got rid of by supposing a dittography of τα. πάντα τὰ
πράγματα would be 'all our affairs'; πάντα πράγματα is more vaguely
'everything', 'the lot', cf. Amphis frag. 14 K, οἶδα γὰρ ὅτι πάντα
πράγματ' ἀνατριαινώϲει κρότοιϲ, Lucian, *Dial. meretr.* xv. 2, ἀνατέτραπτο
πάντα.

549 τὸ πρᾶγμ' ἀκούϲαϲ: When he hears that Moschion is the father of
Plangon's child. Demeas foresees that Nikeratos will inveigh against
Moschion and him, since he expects that the women will admit the
truth. Menander cheats the expectation.

550 ϲκατοφάγοϲ: In *Perik.* 394 the word is used merely as an insult,
cf. *Kolax* frag. 8 and perhaps *Dysk.* 488; but here like ϲκατοφαγεῖ at
427 it clearly has a meaning, as in frag. 733, ἀλλὰ ϲκατοφάγοϲ ἐϲτὶ καὶ
λίαν πικρόϲ ('vindictive'). In both places 'one who will stick at nothing'
would suit. Dedoussi quotes Σ Ar. *Plutus* 706: ϲκατοφάγον. ἀναίϲθητον·
(i.e. 'without feeling' or 'without sense') εἴρηται δὲ ἀπὸ τῶν παρὰ
Βοιωτοῖϲ βοῶν, οἳ διὰ τὴν πολλὴν ἀναιϲθηϲίαν ϲκάτα ἤϲθιον.
      αὐθέκαϲτοϲ: Possibly lit. ὁ αὐτὸ ἕκαστον λέγων, 'the man who calls
each thing just what it is'; first found in Aristotle, *EN* 1127ᵃ23, where
it is stated that the virtue which is the mean between the two vices of
ἀλαζόνεια (claiming to be more than you are or to have qualities
which you have not) and εἰρώνεια (disclaiming qualities which you
have, popularly 'slyness') has not been given a name, but ὁ μέϲοϲ
αὐθέκαϲτόϲ τιϲ ὢν ἀληθευτικὸϲ καὶ ἐν τῷ βίῳ καὶ τῷ λόγῳ, τὰ ὑπάρχοντα
ὁμολογῶν εἶναι περὶ αὐτόν, καὶ οὔτε μείζω οὔτε ἐλάττω. Kleanthes, *SVF*
i. 557, has αὐθέκαϲτον as a characteristic of τἀγαθόν, next to αὐϲτηρόν.
But the word could also be understood to mean ὁ αὐτὸς ἕκαϲτα ποιῶν,
the man who goes his own way. Thus Ariston the Peripatetic (late
third century B.C.), summarized by Philodemos περὶ κακιῶν, Bk. x,
cols. xvii, xix, regards it as typical of the αὐθέκαϲτοϲ that he consults
no one over his actions and disregards criticism, thinking himself
the only sane man and able to live in isolation. Phrynichos, *Praeparatio*

Sophist. p. 28 de Borries, says Μένανδρος . . . ἐπὶ τοῦ πικροῦ καὶ ἀηδοῦς τέθεικε τὴν λέξιν· "πικροῦ γέροντος αὐθεκάστου τὸν τρόπον" (frag. 736).

It is clear that Aristotle uses the word (which may have been a recent coinage) in an etymological sense; the man calls everything just what it is (αὐτὸ ἕκαστον). But the τις which he adds shows that this is not exactly its ordinary meaning, cf. the ἀναίσθητός τις of 1104ᵃ24. Unfortunately there are only four examples of its use that may belong to fourth-century Athens: (1) this passage; (2) the similar frag. 736; (3) Philemon frag. 89 K inquires why men differ in character although animals do not: οὐκ ἔστ' ἀλώπηξ ἡ μὲν εἴρων τῇ φύσει ἡ δ' αὐθέκαστος; (4) Poseidippos frag. 40 K is said to have used the word ἀντὶ τοῦ ἁπλοῦ. The fox of (3) will be the fox of Aesop's fables rather than that of natural history; both in this passage and in (4) the adjective indicates straightforward truthfulness, a virtue. In (1) and (2) it does not indicate a virtue: it might be thought to denote excessive bluntness of speech, were it not for the addition of τῷ τρόπῳ, which suggests an element, at least, that is less an external mark. LSJ give 'self-willed' for these passages, but this is not very suitable either here or in any of the places adduced from later prose. In [Plut.] *Mor.* 11 d, applied to fathers who do not allow ἐρασταί to consort with their sons, it clearly means 'harsh', 'unsympathetic', τοὺς αὐθεκάστους καὶ τὸν τρόπον ὀμφακίας καὶ στρυφνούς, οἳ τῶν τέκνων ὕβριν οὐκ ἀνεκτὴν νομίζουσι τὴν τῶν ἐρώντων ὁμιλίαν; at *Mor.* 823 a, although combined with αὐθάδης, 'self-willed', it may be opposed to εὐπροσήγορος, 'easy to deal with'; in Lucian, *Phal.* 1. 2, the adjective is joined with βίαιον, σκαιόν, and ὑβριστικόν. These passages all suggest that a development took place from 'straightforward' to 'blunt' to 'harsh'.

551 ἐμὲ . . . τὸν μιαρὸν . . . ἐμέ: ἐχρῆν is probably used, as perhaps everywhere else in Menander, to indicate what ought to be done or have been done or ought to happen but is not or was not done or does not happen. Then Demeas will mean that he ought to have guessed that the child's mother was not Chrysis but some girl with whom Moschion had had dealings. His self-denunciation is strong because in full he is thinking: 'I ought to have guessed the truth, and not have entertained the suspicion that did possess me.' The force of γάρ is hard to understand. I incline to see what Denniston, *GP* 69, calls 'anticipatory' γάρ, where the explanatory sentence precedes that which is to be explained. If so, here Demeas explains his statement that he deserves to die by the preceding sentence, according to which he ought to have suspected something like the truth (and not, by condemning and expelling Chrysis, have brought about Nikeratos' discovery of his daughter's misfortune). But examples of this construction are rare unless some part of the 'main' clause, even if only an exclamation, precedes the γάρ-clause (see Denniston, *GP* 68–9). Hence perhaps one should try to find some ellipse to account for γάρ. This is difficult and I cannot improve upon Wilamowitz's idea that it refers to some stage-business: e.g. Demeas might strike his head and explain the gesture by saying ἐμὲ γὰρ κτλ. Perhaps more improbable is to suppose an ellipse of 'I am responsible', an idea which might be more easily supplied because it was explicitly expressed at 544–5.

553: B, like most modern editors, punctuates before and after τοῦτ' ἦν: 'this it was' must mean 'I was right' (Allinson). I do not know a parallel, since 536 has another meaning, and think there is much to be said for van Leeuwen's ἡλίκον κέκραγε τοῦτ'· ἦν, πῦρ βοᾷ. A certain amount of noise will have been heard from Nikeratos' house during the preceding lines: now there is a sudden startling yell that jerks Demeas away from his reflections. πῦρ βοᾷ, 'is calling aloud for fire', cf. Eur. *Phoen.* 1154, βοᾷ | πῦρ καὶ δικέλλας.

554 ἐμπρήσειν . . . ὀπτώμενον: A farcical colouring in the scene seems clear.   υἱδοῦν: 'My grandson'; the child was Nikeratos' θυγατριδοῦς. The absence of the article is due to the emphasis on the relationship, *Dysk.* 240 n.

555–6 στρόβιλος: 'Whirlwind'.   σκηπτός . . . τις: Possibly 'a kind of thunderbolt' (τῶν κεραυνῶν ὅσοι κατασκήπτουσιν εἰς τὴν γῆν, [Arist.] *de mundo* 395ᵃ28), but more likely 'a sort of sudden squall', as at *Aspis* 402 n. The separation of the words by ἄνθρωπος is noteworthy.

556 συνίσταται: 'Is in a conspiracy against me'. Since the women are unaware that Demeas knows the truth, it is to the interest of those of Nikeratos' household to hold to the old story. Chrysis shows herself loyal to them. This is not what Demeas had expected would happen (549 n.); it is characteristic of Menander thus to cheat expectation.   πάνδεινα . . . πράγμαθ': Cf. Dem. liv. 33, πάνδεινον . . . πρᾶγμα, *Dysk.* 954 n.   οὐ προήσεσθαι τ': Cf. *Perik.* 128 n.

561 τῆς γυναικός: 'My wife'; it is Chrysis who is holding the baby (559), is privy to the illegitimate birth (562), and shortly comes running out, with Nikeratos in pursuit (569). Hence it is Chrysis whom Nikeratos threatens to kill, not his own wife as some editors suppose. Again we have an approach to farce in the crazy way in which Nikeratos insists that he is hiding nothing of his intentions from his friend (563). ἀνήρ and γυνή can of course be used of those who live as man and wife, *Perik.* 186 n.   αὐτόχειρ: Originally used of doing anything with one's own hands, this word became particularly connected with suicide and murder. Although common in tragedy, it is found also in Isokrates and Demosthenes, and not only in elevated passages, see *in Meidiam* 116, ἀγνοεῖτ', ἔφη, τὸ πρᾶγμ', ὦ βουλή; καὶ τὸν αὐτόχειρ' ἔχοντες (λέγων τὸν Ἀρίσταρχον) μέλλετε καὶ ζητεῖτε καὶ τετύφωςθε; οὐκ ἀποκτενεῖτε; οὐκ ἐπὶ τὴν οἰκίαν βαδιεῖςθε; οὐχὶ cυλλήψεςθε;

564 τιc: Substituted for the first person, as in *Perik.* 928, τί γὰρ πάθη τιc;

566 μέντοι: Affirmative. Demeas cannot put his resolution to be frank into effect, for he has to deal with a more pressing problem, to rescue Chrysis. That crisis over, he reverts to being disingenuous. Once again an expectation is aroused in the audience and then cheated. τί δράcω; δρᾶν appears elsewhere in Menander only by conjecture. The unusual word is chosen here to mark how seriously Chrysis takes her plight. Her language could be found in tragedy, cf. Soph. *OC* 828, οἴμοι τάλαινα, ποῖ φύγω; *Ajax* 920, τί δράcω;

569 Χρυcί, δεῦρο . . . εἴcω τρέχε: Since Chrysis does not know that Demeas realizes he has misjudged and wronged her, this must be astonishing to her; she would naturally hesitate, so that Demeas has to step in to prevent her being caught, and must repeat his injunction to her to go (575).

570 μονομαχήcω: Armed duels as an entertainment, although uncommon in Greece, were not unknown. Ajax and Diomedes begin one at the funeral games in the *Iliad* (xxiii. 802 ff.). In Menander's day Cassander held funeral games in 316/15 in honour of Philip, Eurydike, and Kynna, which included μονομαχίαc ἀγῶνα, εἰc ὃν κατέβηcαν τέτταρεc τῶν cτρατιωτῶν (Diyllos ap. Athen. 155 a). This incident may lie behind this line, but Poseidippos frag. 22 K makes a sailor say τῶν μονομαχούντων ἐcμὲν ἀθλιώτεροι, which suggests that such duels were not quite exceptional. In later Greek μονομάχοc is the equivalent of the Latin *gladiator*.

The word μονομάχοc and its derivatives are also used in contexts where it is a question of armed combat between the champions of two sides, e.g. Eur. *Phoen.* 1220, 1325, *Heracl.* 819, and Plato uses μονομαχεῖν of the fight between Hephaistos and the river Xanthos in *Iliad* xxi (*Crat.* 391 e). Hence it is not *necessary* to see in this passage any allusion to 'gladiatorial' events, and I think Demeas means no more than 'I shall have to fight in single combat as champion of my side'.

572 τοῦ παιδίου ἐγκρατῆ: The device of threatening a child, to force its relations to some action they dislike, was used in Euripides' *Telephos* (parodied in Ar. *Thesm.* 689 ff.) and adopted by Themistokles

SAMIA 609

at the court of Admetos, king of the Molossians (Thuc. i. 136. 3):
'Let me get hold of the child and then I'll get the facts out of the
women.' **μηθαμῶc:** This, or rather η θαμωc, is written above
μαινομαι in B, perhaps as a *varia lectio*. I do not see that μαίνομαι gives
any likely sense. C has μαίνεται, which does. But it may be suspected
of being an 'emendation' of μαίνομαι. If it is accepted, it is probably
better to continue with Körte's allocation: ἀλλὰ τυπτήcειc με; (Νι.)
ἔγωγε. (Δη.) θᾶττον εἰcφθάρηθι cύ. ἀλλὰ μὴν κἀγὼ cέ.

572–6: The allocation to speakers has been much discussed, but that
given by B seems satisfactory. Demeas blocks Nikeratos' way, prepared to fight (cf. μονομαχήcω). Nikeratos uses the formula τυπτήcειc
με; which is effectively a warning against committing an assault, cf.
Dysk. 168 n. But Demeas stands his ground (ἔγωγε), and then, turning
to Chrysis who is still hesitating, impatiently bids her get inside his
house (for this use of φθείρομαι cf. 373 n.). C has a dicolon after ἔγωγε,
to mark the change of person addressed (as again after νυνί). Nikeratos
then cries, 'Then I'll hit you, too', and the two old men grapple; but
Nikeratos claims that Demeas struck first. Since an assault might be
resisted, but yet be the subject of a legal action, it was important to
establish that the accused 'began it'. The technical phrase was ἄρχειν
χειρῶν ἀδίκων, Xen. *Cyr.* i. 5. 13, Lysias iv. 11, see Cope on Arist.
Rhet. 1402ᵃ. **ταῦτ᾿ ἐγὼ μαρτύρομαι** is the standard formula to call
bystanders to witness wrongful treatment, above all an assault, cf.
Ar. *Clouds* 1297, *Frogs* 528, *Birds* 1031, *Plutus* 932.

575 κἀγὼ cέ (sc. τυπτήcω) of B has the advantage in sense over
κἄγωγε (sc. cε τυπτήcω) which most palaeographers have read in C,
because cέ is important: 'Are you going to *hit* me?' . . . 'Then *I'll* hit
you, too.' But Lefebvre was not certain that the fifth letter in C was γ
(the foot is lost) and I share his doubts.

576 πρότεροc ἅπτει: Cf. Arist. *Rhet.* 1402ᵃ1, . . . εἴ τιc φαίη τὸ τύπτειν
τοὺc ἐλευθέρουc ὕβριν εἶναι· οὐ γὰρ πάντωc, ἀλλ᾿ ὅταν ἄρχῃ χειρῶν
ἀδίκων.

577 ἐπ᾿ ἐλευθέραν γυναῖκα: Cf. *Perik.* 375. The law against ὕβρις,
roughly speaking assault, gave equal protection to men and women,
to free and slave (Dem. xxi. 47). But the penalty against a man con-
victed was for the court to settle, and it may be guessed that a woman
might arouse more pity than a man and a free woman than a slave-
woman.

578 cυκοφαντεῖc: 'You are making a vexatious accusation', to frighten
me out of my rights. Some form of blackmail or intimidation is usually
associated with cυκοφαντεῖν.

579 τοὐμόν: Gomme supposed Demeas to forget that he had recognized that the child was not his, but Moschion's. This seemed an inadequate explanation of a puzzle that has generally been neglected. Nevertheless it may not be far wrong. Demeas is excited and has not yet made up his mind on what line to take. But he may already be thinking of trying to exonerate his son, and so revert for the moment to what was the position before he had heard that Moschion was the father. Yet this would not be an attitude he could maintain. Another possibility is that by 'the child is mine', he means only that it is under his protection, since he is its paternal grandfather and it is in his house; Nikeratos then retorts 'it is not yours', meaning that Demeas is not its father.

580 ἰὼ 'νθρωποι: This cannot be an appeal to the spectators, who are always addressed as ἄνδρες or ὦνδρες; it must be a cry either to imaginary bystanders or to the world in general to witness his distress and his wrongs.   **τὴν γυναῖκα:** 'My wife', as τῆς γυναικός in 561 is 'my wife'. Some have strangely thought that the words mean 'your wife', i.e. Chrysis. She has disappeared into Demeas' house, and he stands in Nikeratos' way, barring any pursuit. Nikeratos, thus baffled (τί γὰρ ποήcω;), can think of nothing better than to return into his own house (the usual meaning of εἰcιών) and punish his disobedient wife, a plan which, in its turn (πάλιν), Demeas finds objectionable. Hence he tries to prevent the angry man's departure (ποῖ cύ;) and offers to reveal the truth, so that Nikeratos need not extort it from his wife. Nikeratos in this scene entertains a rapid succession of different intentions: his first idea is to get rid of the evidence of his daughter's disgrace by burning the baby up; then he suggests that he will have to kill Chrysis to get hold of the child; but when he appears in pursuit of her his object has altered slightly, since it is now to threaten the child in order to extort the truth from the women; foiled in this, he falls back on the idea of violence to his own wife. To suppose that he reverts to the idea of killing Chrysis, which had never been an end in itself, is not only contrary to the language of 581–3, but does not do justice to the fertility of Menander's dramatic invention and his ability always to give a *new* turn to events.   ἀποκτενῶ, as a threat, need not be taken quite literally, cf. *Epitr.* 1073, *Dysk.* 931.

583–6: Nikeratos, convinced that Chrysis and his womenfolk are in league, and finding that Demeas aids Chrysis, includes him in the conspiracy. When Demeas implicitly admits that he knows all about it, Nikeratos easily passes to the suspicion that Moschion is involved and will be the unknown father. He is, perhaps, somewhat slow to conceive this: Moschion had after all admitted paternity, although not in so many words, in Nikeratos' hearing. But Nikeratos had thought of the parents as being Chrysis and Moschion. When he saw that the child was Plangon's, the idea that Moschion was the father left his mind along with the idea that Chrysis was the mother.   ἐντεθρίωκεν: The verb is found only here in this sense, and only in Ar. *Lys.* 663 elsewhere in literature; there the chorus of old men propose to take off their tunics, ὡς τὸν ἄνδρα δεῖ | ἀνδρὸς ὄζειν εὐθύς, ἀλλ' οὐκ ἐντεθ-ριῶσθαι πρέπει, and the verb means 'be wrapped up' (θρῖον is a fig-leaf, and fig-leaves were used to wrap up foodstuffs for keeping or for cooking). Here, metaphorically, it must mean 'dished me'. Hesychios gives, perhaps with reference to this passage, ἐντεθρίωκεν· ἐνείληκεν ἢ ἐσκεύακεν (see 559 n.), ἀπὸ τῶν θρίων.   φλυαρεῖς: 'You are talk-ing nonsense. He will marry the girl, but it's not as you think', i.e. not because he is the father of her child. At 566 Demeas had been for frankness, but now he attempts to save Moschion's reputation by a suggestion that cleverly avoids throwing any hint of discredit on the girl. She had been honoured by being taken by a god. Nikeratos is clearly not convinced by this idea, but being unable to refute it, finds it convenient not to resist it. Later, when he thinks that Moschion is about to desert the girl, he reverts without ado to what he really knows to be the truth, since that is the way he can bring pressure on the young man.

The scene 589–608 is certainly farcical, since one cannot believe that in real life anyone should have adduced Chairephon and Androkles as persons clearly of divine origin, but the idea that a god might beget a human child was not as incredible to the fourth-century Athenian as to the twentieth-century Englishman, for whom this has happened at the most once, on a unique occasion. For many Greeks mytho-logical stories were records of fact or at least of what might have happened, and the gods had not lost their power of loving women. The stories that made Alexander the Great the son of Zeus were put about in his lifetime, and even if their originators did not believe them, they expected them to be widely believed.

588 μικρά: Both in B and in C the word stands at the end of the previous line (but C has μικρō = μικρον), cf. the similar displacement of ιδιον in O 14 at *Perik.* 316; 308–9 above exhibit the opposite error. μικρόν was in Menander's time the usual form of the adverb, but cf. Sosipatros (? third century B.C.) frag. 1. 22 K, μικρὰ διακινήσω σε περὶ τοῦ πράγματος, Plato, *Prot.* 316 a, cμίκρ' ἄττα διατρίψαντες; later μικρά is not infrequent, e.g. Plut. *Mor.* 150 d, Alkiphron iii. 5, μικρὰ προσπαίξας.

590 τραγῳδῶν: Cf. *Epitr.* 325 n. Sophocles and Euripides each wrote a *Danaë*; others may have done so too. Revivals of plays by Euripides were not infrequent in the fourth century, and there may be a topical allusion here. A possibly genuine 'hypothesis' of Eur. *Danaë* says that ὁ Ζεὺς . . . χρυςὸς γενόμενος καὶ ῥυεὶς διὰ τοῦ ϲτέγουϲ εἰς τὸν κόλπον τῆϲ παρθένου ἐγκύμονα ἐποίηϲεν (Nauck, *TGF* p. 716).

591 ἐμοίχευϲεν: The word μοιχός was used not only of the man who violated another's wife, but also of one who raped or seduced other free inmates of a man's house, his mother, sisters, daughters, or concubine. But the exact limits of μοιχεία as a legal term are hard to determine: women who 'openly offered themselves for sale' were excluded, and there was some provision that the husband must not have enticed the man into his house, Lysias i. 32, x. 19, A. R. W. Harrison, *Law of Athens*, i. 36.   **καθειργμένην**: B maintains the Attic form, C has κατειργ-, the Ionic form which prevailed in the *koine*.

592 εἶτα δή: Cf. Ar. *Clouds* 259, εἶτα δὴ τί κερδανῶ;

593 ῥεῖ: 'Leaks'; the word is used of ships and pots too, cf. Plut. *Mor.* 782 e, when one pours liquid into sound and worn vessels, φαίνεται τὸ ῥέον, 'the leaky one is shown up'.

594 χρυϲίον: Cf. Lucian, *Somn.* 13, ἀκούεις δήπου ὡς χρυϲίον ἐγένετο καὶ ῥυεὶς διὰ τοῦ τέγουϲ ϲυνῆν τῇ ἀγαπωμένῃ. Austin, following van Leeuwen, suggests that the diminutive is used 'ironically', and compares Horace, *Odes* iii. 16. 8, 'converso in pretium deo'—one meaning of χρυϲίον is 'gold coin'. Rather χρυϲός is the word used by poets for 'gold', and so appropriate when speaking of tragedy (500), χρυϲίον is the everyday word and so in place here, where Demeas, representing his solution as simple and obvious, employs the plainest of language. Any suggestion that Plangon had sold herself to Moschion is utterly out of place.

595 ὕδωρ: 'Rain', Ζεὺς ὕει.

596 καὶ βουκολεῖϲ με; βουκολῶ, lit. 'herd cattle', is a word for 'cheat', 'beguile', not too colloquial for Aeschylus to use, *Agam.* 669. One may compare ποιμαίνειν in the same sense (Eur. *Hipp.* 153). καί, i.e. as well as bringing shame on my house you are trying to make a fool of me. So Ar. *Wasps* 1406, καὶ καταγελᾷϲ μου; i.e. as well as assaulting me, a passage which indicates that this is to be punctuated as a question. *Phasma* 90 has καὶ παραϲκώπτεις με; :: ἐγώ ϲε; μὰ τὸν Ἀπόλλω' γὼ μὲν οὔ.

597 Ἀκριϲίου: Danaë's father.

598 εἰ δ' ἐκείνην ἠξίωϲε: 'If he thought well of' or 'gave honour to Danaë', cf. Soph. *Ajax* 1114, οὐ γὰρ ἠξίου τοὺς μηδένας, Eur. *Heraclid.*

918, ὦ Ὑμέναιε, διccοὺc παῖδαc Διὸc ἠξίωcαc, and perhaps 708 below. Austin supposes that ἠξίωcε μοιχεύειν is to be understood; the infinitive would have been expressed in the apodosis only.

599 ἐcκεύακεν: An unparalleled colloquial use. Capps argues that it must mean 'tricked' ('cheat, cozen' LSJ), and is derived from the common use of the word in the sense 'dress up'; cκευή is a regular word for theatrical costume. But to dress someone up is not to trick him. Perhaps the metaphor is really from cooking, 'has made a dish of me', cf. Ar. *Knights* 372, περικόμματ' ἐκ coῦ cκευάcω, *Wasps* 1331, ὑμᾶc φρυκτοὺc cκευάcω. 'To prepare (food)' is a very common meaning of cκευάζω. This fits Hesychios' use to explain ἐντεθρίωκεν, if that word was rightly connected (586) with the kitchen use of fig-leaves. The parallelism between the use of the two verbs is marked: each is followed by λήψεται μέν, succeeded by a δέ-clause that gives the idea 'but not because he is the father of her child'. Nikeratos' varied vocabulary of colloquialisms is no doubt part of his characterization.

600: Jensen's punctuation (τοῦτο· θεῖον), which is that of C, is to be adopted, because in τοῦτο θεῖον δέ the words τοῦτο and θεῖον would not form a unit, to explain the postponement of δέ, but would be subject and predicate. Van Leeuwen was probably right to withdraw his emendation τὸ γεγεννημένον. It is true that elsewhere in Menander 'what has happened' is always τὸ γεγονός, as in 602. The intricate relations between γέγονα and γεγένημαι are explored by P. Chantraine, *Le Parfait grec*, 110–18. γέγονα seems to be the proper Attic form, but the Ionic γεγένημαι (universal in Thucydides) is found in Aristophanes, and in inscriptions after 375 B.C., without any distinction of meaning. But the Attic genius for the elimination of synonyms got to work: τὸ γεγονός tends to the meaning 'what has happened', i.e. the present situation, while τὰ γεγενημένα are 'what took place', which may be old history, cf. Lysias i. 1, iii. 21. This distinction may be found here, τὸ γεγενημένον being Plangon's rape, τὸ γεγονός (602) the situation resulting from all that has happened. But it is also to be noted that γεγένημαι sometimes has the sense 'have come into existence', 'have been born', e.g. Dem. xviii. 205, ἡγεῖτο γὰρ αὐτῶν ἕκαστοc οὐχὶ τῷ πατρὶ καὶ τῇ μητρὶ μόνον γεγενῆcθαι ἀλλὰ καὶ τῇ πατρίδι; and it may be that τὸ γεγενημένον denotes the baby, as much as would τὸ γεγεννημένον, participle of a verb elsewhere unknown in New Comedy.

603 Χαιρεφῶν: A well-known parasite, also named by Alexis frags. 210, 257; he had been in his heyday before Menander's earliest plays, since he is mentioned by writers of Middle Comedy: Antiphanes frag. 199 K, Timokles frag. 9 K, Timotheos frag. 1 K. He also occurred in Menander's earliest play Ὀργή (frag. 304 K–T), in Μέθη which is earlier than 318 B.C. (frag. 265 K–T), and in Κεκρύφαλος (frag. 245 K–T) and Ἀνδρόγυνος (frag. 51 K–T), which are probably both early (Webster, *StM* 103–4, Körte, *Praef.* xl.) Anecdotes recounted by Machon (10, 17 Gow, Athenaios 243 e) and Lynceus (ibid. 584 e) bring Chairephon into connection with Diphilos and his mistress Gnathaina. Diphilos was slightly older than Menander and Gnathaina is made fun of in Middle Comedy (Anaxilas frag. 22 K, Timokles frag. 25 K). He may have become a legendary figure for his success in attending parties uninvited, since Athenaios reports (243 d) that Apollodoros of Karystos, who belongs to the generation after Menander, in his *Hiereia* frag. 24 K spoke of someone as 'a new Chairephon'. More difficult is a fragment (26 K) from the same author's Cφαττομένη: καλῶ δὲ Χαιρεφῶντα· κἂν γὰρ μὴ καλῶ, ἄκλητος ἥξει. It is hard to believe that Chairephon was still living and a good butt so late as this. Since the *Suda* ascribes a Ἱέρεια to Apollodoros of Gela, a contemporary of Menander's, a possible solution is that Athenaios made a mistake, confusing the two Apollodoroi. **πρώτιστος:** 'Is the foremost example'. The adverbial forms πρώτιστον, πρώτιστα are not uncommon in comedy, but I know no other clear example of the adjective outside poetry and late prose. **ἀcύμβολον:** 'Without a contribution'; Alexis frag. 257 K begins ἀεί γ' ὁ Χαιρεφῶν τιν' εὑρίcκει τέχνην, καὶ νῦν πορίζεταί γε δεῖπν' ἀcύμβολα: he explains that Chairephon discovers from cooks, who are hiring crockery, where the dinner is, and, if he finds the door open, πρῶτος εἰcελήλυθεν. It was a common practice for friends to share the expenses of a dinner which one of them would organize; their contributions were called cύμβολα, Ter. *Eun.* 539, 'heri aliquot adulescentuli coiimus in Piraeo in hunc diem, ut de symbolis essemus.'

604 οὐ θεός: Demeas' argument looks illogical, since both his examples to show that there are *children* of gods among the population are men whom he alleges to *be* gods. But the child of a mortal woman and a god could be a god: Dionysos, Herakles, Amphion and Zethos (Ar. *Ach.* 905), Alexander the Great. The evidence in the case of Chairephon is that, like the gods, he does not pay for his share of dinners, cf. Timokles frag. 8 K, χαίρουcι δείπνων ἡδοναῖc ἀcυμβόλοιc | τίc δ' οὐχὶ θνητῶν; ἢ τίc ἥρωc ἢ θεὸc | ἀποδοκιμάζει τὴν τοιαύτην διατριβήν; **τί γὰρ πάθω;** 'What can I do?', an expression of helplessness, see *Phasma* 8 n., Ar. *Birds* 1432, *Lys.* 884, *Eccl.* 860, Plato, *Euthyd.* 302 d. **διὰ κενῆc:** 'To no purpose', cf. Ar. *Wasps* 929, διὰ κενῆc ἄλλωc, Plato Com. frag. 174. 21 K, μάτην ... διὰ κενῆc, Thuc. iv. 126. 5, ἡ διὰ κενῆc ἐπανάcειcιc τῶν ὅπλων (like Livy's 'armorum agitatio uana', vii. 10). This is an instance of the use of the feminine adjective in adverbial phrases, e.g. ἐκ καινῆς, 'afresh', Thuc. iii. 92. 6, ἀπ' ἴσης, μακράν. The breaking of the anapaest after the first syllable *may* be excused by the close coherence of the two words; one may compare *Dysk.* 775, πά/νυ μὲν οὖν/, *Perik.* 337, τυ/χὸν ἴcωc/; Richards's transposition διὰ κενῆc cοι is not necessary, but may nevertheless be right, cf. the placing of the words in 672. Is Nikeratos persuaded? There is nothing to show it. The important thing is that his daughter will be married. It would be fruitless to argue with Demeas about who was her child's father.

606–11 were omitted by B; probably a copyist's eye jumped from νοῦν ἔχεις in 605 to νοῦν ἔχει[in 611.

606: Nothing is known of Androkles. He may have been another parasite; he may have been the subject of Sophilos' comedy Ἀνδροκλῆς, the date of which is unknown. It contained a suggestion that two or three ὀψονόμοι should be appointed. Dedoussi guesses that there was a reference to Demetrios of Phaleron's γυναικονόμοι, but this is speculative. The 'running and bounding' more probably describes his gait than refers to his continuing to take part in athletics. Dedoussi, believing him to be a parasite, thinks that he runs to dinners and jumps for joy at the food. πολὺ πράττεται would seem to mean 'makes a large income', cf. [Dem.] lix. 41 ἀργύριον πραττόμενος πολύ; the point is obscure. Can he possibly be Androkles of Sphettos, who is according to the μαρτυρίαι in [Dem.] xxxv the plaintiff who delivered that speech? He had lent money to a merchant for a voyage, and gives the impression of being one in the practice of making loans.

607 μέλας περιπατεῖ· λευκὸς οὐκ ἂν ἀποθάνοι: 'He walks around dark and swarthy; even if he were white-haired, he would not die, not even if murdered.' This, I suggest, is the meaning and the punctuation to be adopted. Androkles seems to have perpetual youth, so that even if his hair were to turn white, it would not be a sign that he was on the path to the grave; his vitality would still be there. Wilamowitz poured scorn on anyone who did not punctuate to make μέλας περιπατεῖ λευκός a single phrase. The scorn would be more justifiable if any convincing explanation of that phrase could be given, or even if C's punctuation indicated it to be a phrase; C has, in fact, a colon after πηδᾷ, but no other mark to aid the division of words.

I know the following attempts to explain the phrase μέλας περιπατεῖ λευκός. Capps supposed it to mean that he walks about with black dyed hair, when his hair is really white. As if this were not obscure enough, he suggested a secondary meaning, 'with a swarthy tanned skin when really effeminate', and this was approved (as the sole meaning) by Wilamowitz. But although an effeminate person who avoids manly outdoor pursuits may be fair-skinned, like Agathon, Ar. *Thesm.* 191, λευκὸς ἐξυρημένος γυναικόφωνος, it does not follow that λευκός can be applied to a dark man to mean that he is effeminate. As for Capps's primary meaning, if the point is that Androkles shares with the gods the secret of perpetual youth, it is weakened by adding that his black hair is a sham. The same objection applies to van Leeuwen's view that, being too old to take exercise in the palaestra, he artificially tanned his white body. A. Weiher, *Berl. Phil. Woch.* xxxiii (1913), 478, suggests an interpretation already rightly rejected by Capps: 'Though white-haired he walks about in the black clothes of a parasite' (for which see Pollux iv. 119). Even if anyone could so understand the words, the statement would be irrelevant to Androkles' alleged immortality. The meaning 'wicked' proposed for μέλας by A. C. Headlam, *Emendations in Menander*, 20, is inadequately supported as well as irrelevant. Professor Arnott allows me to quote his view, according to which it is a mistake to look for logic here. There are two jokes: (1) Androkles is an old man desperately trying to be young: he takes part in athletics and dyes his hair; (2) he has been around so long you would suppose him to be immortal.

608: C gives οὗτός ἐςτιν οὐ θεός, which must be read as a question. But although οὐ may, under certain conditions, follow the verb in statements (see A. C. Moorhouse, *Studies in the Greek Negative*), it does not normally do so in questions. Mr. Moorhouse suggested to me that ἐςτί που should be read, comparing 163, ταὐτόματόν ἐςτιν ὡς ἔοικέ που θεός. This is more probable than the transposition οὗτος οὐκ ἔςτιν θεός. But perhaps the *traditio* may be defended if Demeas is supposed to begin as if to make the statement οὗτός ἐςτι θεός and then convert this to a question, οὗτός ἐςτιν—οὐ θεός; Aristophanes, *Frogs* 637–9, has χὠπότερον ἂν νῷν ἴδῃς κλαύσαντα πρότερον . . . εἶναι τοῦτον ἡγοῦ μὴ θεόν. This is an imperfect parallel, since the words μὴ θεόν closely cohere.

609 θυμία: 'Burn incense' to accompany the prayer, or in preparation for the wedding (cf. 674), or in thankfulness that all is turning out well, cf. Hermippos frag. 8 K, καὶ θυμιάςω τοῦ τέκνου ςεςωςμένου (*leg.* ςεςωμένου).

610–11: B omitted 606–11 (see above). From 610 to 615 C is badly rubbed and its writing full of ligatures. Hence 610–11 are beyond certain restoration. At the beginning of 610 all supplements proposed are too short, but Jensen suggested that there was a flaw in the papyrus, which the scribe left blank. For sense, Edmonds's ςφάττε is as good as anything: it would involve a heavy stop after ςυμφέροντα, then: 'Burn incense, sacrifice; my son will come immediately for his bride.' For this meaning of μετιέναι, cf. 159, 433, 676, Alexis frag. 163 K, τοῖς νυμφίοις μετιοῦσι τὴν νύμφην.

The latter part of 611 is hard to read, but it seems to end with the words νοῦν ἔχεις (ἔχει cannot be excluded). This phrase is probably spoken by Demeas, as it is in 605. It may be a reply to something said by Nikeratos, but it is possible that Demeas assumes that he is sensible from his silence or a gesture. The latter alternative is supported by the apparent absence from C of dicola in 610 and 611; but too much should not be made of this, since C is fairly unreliable in this respect. The line begins with ἐξ ἀνάγκης ἐστί, probably followed by ταῦτα. If these words are a recognition by Nikeratos that he must accept the situation, they are suitably answered by Demeas' νοῦν ἔχεις; but it may be Demeas who insists that Nikeratos has no choice. The intervening words are a puzzle. They are probably separated from νοῦν ἔχεις by a single point. Körte, who assigns the opening of the line to Demeas, continues (Νι.) πολλ['εφ' ή]μ[ιν]. But the sense, 'much turns on us', is not altogether convincing; moreover, it is hard to accept the reading λλ[; more likely is μ[. I have thought, without much confidence, of ⟨ἀλλ'⟩ ἀπομ[εμυγ]μ[α]ι, 'but I've had my nose wiped', i.e. been tricked, cf. frag. 427, γέρων ἀπομέμυκτ' ἄθλιος. The word would suit Nikeratos' vocabulary, but Pollux ii. 78 says ἤδη δέ τινες τῶν κωμικῶν τὸ ἐπὶ κέρδει ἐξαπατᾶν ἀπομύττειν εἶπον, and if the verb was limited to cheating for financial gain it is not suitable here.

612: B and C have a paragraphus below the line; B has cancelled a dicolon before ποει; the end of the line is lost in C. B seems to have had the dicolon that is required after τοτε; only a high dot is visible on the photograph, but the surface below is damaged, and Kasser says that there is a faint trace of the lower dot. Nikeratos begins: 'If Moschion had been caught, then—' (as was seen by F. G. Allinson, *TAPA* xliv [1913], 65) and Demeas interrupts, 'have done with that', to prevent him from exacerbating himself.

Apart from the difficulty of extracting any good sense from the sentence εἰ δ' ἐλήφθη τότε, πέπαυσο, which must be assigned to Demeas, the hypothesis 'if he had been caught then' is not one that Demeas could entertain, since he has been arguing for Moschion's innocence. 'If he *was* caught then' is a supposition contrary to the whole story.

613: B's assignment of speeches is unexceptionable and must be followed. Nevertheless I do not feel sure that Menander intended this and not πόει τἄνδον εὐτρεπῆ, ποήσω τὰ παρ' ἐμοὶ δ' ἐγώ.

614–15: Demeas flatters Nikeratos, 'you are a clever chap', i.e. to accept the theory put forward and go on quietly with the wedding. The rest is not for Nikeratos' ears, and so marked off in C by a dicolon before χάριν. For κομψός see *Perik.* 298 n. Earlier interpretations are made obsolete by the evidence of B.

ACT V

616 ff.: Once again at the end of Act IV all seems arranged for the best, and the audience would wonder during the interval, if not entirely absorbed by the dancing of the chorus, how the play could continue. The new Act brings the answer. Moschion has slowly grown indignant that he had been held in suspicion, and comes back prepared to teach his father a lesson by pretending to abandon the proposed marriage in order to go abroad as a soldier of fortune. His speech is in an elevated tone, not because we are to take it seriously, but because Moschion takes himself very seriously. He opens with three colloquial lines, but as he warms to his wrongs he becomes purely rhetorical: observe the asyndeton ὅρκος πόθος χρόνος cυνήθεια, the grand phrase οἷς ἐδουλούμην ἐγώ, the poetic word αἰχμάζων, and the line ὁ τῆc ἐμῆc νῦν κύριος γνώμης "Ἔρως, which might well come from a tragedy (γνώμη occurs in three other passages only in Menander: once in the meaning 'gnome' (*Dysk.* 817) and twice in gnomes (*Her.* 80, frag. 582 K–T). From 623 to 629 every line keeps the metrical rules of tragedy.

617 ἐλεύθερος with metaphorical meaning is, as Dedoussi remarks, mostly a tragic usage; she gives as the only other example in comedy Heniochos, frag. 5 K, but even there the context is that of political liberty, πόλεις φορῶν ἐλεύθεραι. This is the first hint, in an otherwise plain sentence, of the elevated diction that is to come.

619 ὑπέλαβον: ὑπολαμβάνειν is often used of an erroneous supposition.
  ἔννους γίνομαι: ἔννους does not occur again in Menander, but this is a good prose expression, Dem. xxxi. 2, ἔννους γίγνεται, found also in Alexis frag. 85 K. In Eur. *Bacch.* 1270, γίνομαι δέ πως ἔννους, the sense is different, 'restored to my senses'.   **λαμβάνω λογισμόν**: Cf. 420, Dem. xxiii. 156.

620 ἐξέστηκα: The audience will appreciate the paradox, unintended by Moschion himself; normally a man falls into a rage and then reasons with himself and brings himself under control. With Moschion it is the opposite; reason leads him to fall into a passion. A sign that he is only feigning indignation can be seen in the fact that at the very moment when he says ἐξέστηκα τελέως ἐμαυτοῦ, 'I am quite beside myself', he is calm enough to analyse his feelings and the situation in long sentences, with balanced μέν- and δέ- clauses (616–19, 623–30). ἐξέστηκα τελέως brings to mind Demeas' real turmoil of spirit, ἐξέστηχ' ὅλως (279).

621 παρώξυμμαι: 'Irritated, provoked to anger', as probably in 612, 721, Polybios iv. 7. 5. The more normal sense is 'stimulated, spurred on', as in Lysias iv. 8, ὑπὸ τῆς ἀνθρώπου παρωξυμμένος, *Dysk.* 383, τούτοις παρώξυμμ' εἰς τὸ πρᾶγμα διπλασίως.

622 ἐφ' οἷς: I.e. παρώξυμμαι ἐπ' ἐκείνοις ἅ μ' ὑπέλαβεν ἡμαρτηκέναι. B has ἐφ' οἷς ὁ πατήρ μ', C ἐφ' οἷς μ' ὁ πατήρ.

623 εἰ εἶχε . . . οὐκ ἂν ἠτιάσατο might be taken as a past unfulfilled conditional sentence, but that is excluded by the context. This is an example of a construction, most commonly found in Plato, in which 'an aorist not referring to past time is found in the apodosis, after a protasis in the imperfect referring to the present' (Goodwin, *MT* § 414). The aorist excludes the idea of duration which an imperfect would express. Here, in the second half of the apodosis, where duration is essential, the imperfect is used (διέτριβον), Webster, *StM* 45. The verb in the aorist is normally one of saying, as ἠτιάσατο is in effect. A non-Platonic example is Soph. *Ant.* 755, εἰ μὴ πατὴρ ἦσθ', εἶπον ἄν c' οὐκ εὖ φρονεῖν. When Moschion says that, if the circumstances were not what they are, he would be soldiering in Asia, he falls into a natural exaggeration; in sober fact he might be no further than half way to the Peiraeus with the intention of finding a ship in which to cross the Aegean. It may also be pointed out, since at least one scholar has gone astray here, that he has no reason for supposing that Demeas might bring a second accusation against him: this is just the talk of an angry man.

625 cυνήθεια: Probably the word that Terence translated by *consuetudo* in *Hec.* 404: 'Amor me grauiter consuetudoque eius tenet.' We could render χρόνος, cυνήθεια as 'our long intimacy', cf. frag. 544 K–T, ἔργον ἐcτί, Φανία, μακρὰν cυνήθειαν βραχεῖ λῦcαι χρόνῳ, and P. *Ghôran* ii. 113 (Page, *GLP* p. 300), ἡ μὲν cυνήθει', ἡ φιλία, τὸ διὰ χρόνου.

ἐδουλούμην: The imperfect needs explanation. It indicates the length of the process by which he grew to be a slave, that is, unable to dispose his own life freely.

626 οὐ παρόντα γε: 'Not to my face'; the idea is repeated in αὐτόν με. **αὖτις:** See *Dysk.* 962 n.

627 ἀποφθαρείς: 373, *Dysk.* 101 n. This angry or impatient word is frequently used in the second or third person as a substitute for ἀπιέναι; I do not know of another instance where the speaker applies it to himself. **ἐκποδών:** 'Out of his way'.

628 Βάκτρα ποι ἢ Καρίαν: Βάκτρα is the name both of the satrapy (as here) and of its chief town. Bactria was just about the furthest place where a Greek might find service; after Alexander's death the

Greek mercenaries there, 20,000 infantry and 3,000 cavalry, revolted because they wanted to come home and were massacred by Macedonian troops. Moschion rather spoils the effect of the phrase by his alternative, Karia, which was the nearest. Karia is associated with mercenaries in *Sik.* 137, Ter. *Eun.* 126.

What light, if any, these lines throw on the date of the play is discussed on p. 543. That a son, unhappy at home, should take himself off and enlist as a mercenary is a motif that occurs elsewhere in New Comedy, as no doubt it did in the real life of the time. Such a step is the starting-point of the plot of Ter. *Heautontimoroumenos,* cf. Plaut. *Trin.* 598.

629 αἰχμάζων: A brave word, belonging to epic and tragedy, 'with spear in hand'. αἰχμή itself is rare in prose, although Herodotos uses it by metonymy for 'war', iii. 78, vii. 152. This is the culmination of seven lines of tragic rhythm; the next sinks back to a comic trimeter before Moschion rises again to the climax of 632.

633 οὐ μήν: 'Yet . . . not', found only here in New Comedy, although in Aristophanes (*Clouds* 53, *Wasps* 268) and the orators.

635 λόγῳ μόνον εἰ μηδὲν ἄλλο: There is a conflation here of two phrases: (1) λόγῳ μόνον, οὐκ ἔργῳ, (2) λόγῳ, εἰ μηδὲν ἄλλο ποιήcω.

636 ἀπαίρειν: 'Depart'; the word is not confined to 'setting sail', although Moschion would take ship for Asia.

637: Guéraud was uncertain whether C had αυτιc or ουτοc, the reading of B, which is quite satisfactory, cf. 665. Austin prefers αὖτιc, quoting Ar. *Lys.* 1277, εὐλαβώμεθα τὸ λοιπὸν αὖθιc μὴ 'ξαμαρτάνειν ἔτι, and *Epitr.* 1110. **ἀγνωμονεῖν:** Cf. ἀγνώμων, *Epitr.* 918 n. This is one of the worst of sins, to have no understanding, and *therefore* no sympathy, no pity for others. It was characteristically Greek to attribute want of sympathy and cruelty to stupidity.

638 μὴ παρέργωc: τὸ πάρεργον is what is secondary, subordinate to real business (ἔργον), unimportant; to do anything παρέργωc is not to take it seriously, as in frag. 397. 6. In *PSI* 1176. 2–3 we have ἔγειρ', ἔγειρε δὴ . . . cεαυτὸν μὴ παρέργωc, in Porphyry, *de abst.* ii. 61, μὴ παρέργωc, ἀλλὰ πάcῃ προθυμίᾳ.

641: Parmenon returns from his flight, just when he is needed. On this apparent structural *naïveté* see intro. p. 27. The convention that a character entering does not see one already on the stage is also used here. It must be confessed that from the point of view of realism it is strange (as is observed by F. Leo, *Der Monolog im Drama,* 88) that Moschion should allow Parmenon—just the man he has a use for (639)—uninterruptedly to recite his inward debate at such length.

Should we see here a sign of dramatic inexperience, Menander being unable to account for Parmenon's return without involving himself in this improbability? Hardly, since there would have been explanation enough if he had been interrupted at ἔφυγον (644). Rather Menander had an idea that could be effectively developed, and thought it worth a place in his play. The awkwardness would be less apparent on the stage than to the analytical reader: Parmenon, by addressing the audience, would rivet their attention on himself, so that Moschion's presence would be half-forgotten, and no spectator would ask why *he* didn't interrupt. The interruption will be the more effective when it does come (οὗτος, 657), surprising the audience as well as Parmenon.

642 εἴμ' εἰργαcμένοc: 'I am in the position of having done.' This is almost equivalent to the perfect εἴργαcμαι. Similarly in 644, τί ἦν πεποιηκώc; 'What was I then in the position of having done?' 'The periphrastic form [of the perfect] expresses more fully the continuance of the action of the perfect to the *present* time . . . although the simple form very often [this is cautious] implies the continuance of the result of the action down to the present time . . . it does so less distinctly than the compound form', Goodwin, *MT* §§ 45–6. The same applies *mutatis mutandis* to the pluperfect. Parmenon's opening lines are comically solemn: the impressive oath, the lengthy word εὐκαταφρόνητον, outdoing ἀνόητον, and the construction ἔργον εἰργαcμένοc, for which cf. *Epitr.* 895 n., and in the passive Soph. *OT* 1374, ἔργ' ἐcτὶ κρεῖccον' ἀγχόνηc εἰργαcμένα.

651–2 τῶν ἔνδον . . . τιc: 'One of the household'. Parmenon knows of course that this was Chrysis, but by calling her τιc he puts her at a distance, as it were. The aorist ὡμολόγηcε (B) is clearly right against C's perfect ὡμολόγηκε, according as it does with ἐξήμαρτεν, εἰcῆλθεν, and ἤνεγκε. **ἐνταῦθα:** 'In these circumstances'.

654–5 γελοῖον: Probably to be taken not with what precedes, 'ridiculous to run away', but rather with what follows, 'a ridiculous question: he threatened to mark me' (and so I had every reason for running away), cf. 71, 579, *Perik.* 325. At the end of the line a hole in B leaves it open whether ηπειληc'εμε or ηπειληcεμε was written. ἐμέ is more pointed: the crimes, says Parmenon, had all been committed by others, but he threatened to mark *me*. C has μοι, which is also possible, cf. Lysias iii. 28, ἠπείλουν αὐτῷ ἐγὼ ἀποκτενεῖν. **μεμάθηκαc:** 'You have found the answer.' **ἀλλ' οὐδὲ γρῦ:** The Greeks themselves were reduced to guessing the origin of the word γρῦ, which was explained as 'dirt under the nails', 'a small coin', or 'a grunt', see Σ Ar. *Plut.* 17. ἀλλ' οὐδέ means 'why, not even', 359 n., Denniston, *GP* 23.

657 οὐκ ἀcτεῖον: 'Not a pretty thing'; for this colloquial use of ἀcτεῖοc cf. 364. The word became a general adjective of praise, and was later adopted by Stoics and Cynics as an equivalent of cπουδαῖοc, 'good'.   οὗτοc: A common way of brusquely demanding attention, 'you there'. Parmenon's reply χαῖρε is a normal greeting, but it usually has attached to it a name, e.g. *Georg.* 41, χαῖρε πολλά, Μυρρίνη, or its equivalent, e.g. δέcποτα (*Sam.* 296), ἑταῖρε φίλτατε (*Pap. Ghôran* ii. 111). χαῖρε cύ is unparalleled, and may contain a half-concealed rebuke to Moschion for his failure to observe the civilities.

659 χλαμύδα: The soldier's mantle, cf. *Perik.* 354, frag. 282 K–T, χλαμύδα, καυcίαν, λόγχην, ἀορτῆρ', ἱμάτια, but it was also worn by ἔφηβοι, perhaps because of their military training, Philemon frag. 34 K, Antidotos frag. 2 K (LSJ s.vv. χλαμύc, χλαμύδιον).   cπαθήν τινα: Cf. *Perik.* 355 n., where cπάθη and χλαμύc are similarly combined, and Plaut. *Pseud.* 735, where to disguise a man as a soldier's servant 'opust chlamyde et machaera et petaso'. τινα shows that Moschion is so little of a soldier that he has no sword of his own. The motif of sending a slave to fetch weapons as a piece of play-acting is used again at Plaut. *Cistellaria* 283 ff., but there the intention is to suggest that the lover has been sent out of his mind by his passion.

661 cιωπῇ: 'Without a word to anyone'. Capps explains that by enjoining secrecy Moschion hopes to ensure that Parmenon *will* tell. Dedoussi thinks he means 'without any more talk'. I prefer to think that, if on his way in Parmenon were to reveal his errand, Demeas might forbid him to execute it. Moschion guards against this eventuality, which would make his threat to leave less instant.

662 εἰ λήψομαι ἱμάντα: The future indicative is often used in conditions that contain a threat (Goodwin, *MT* § 447): 'If I get a strap (you'll be sorry).'

664 πρόcειcι νῦν: One may compare the confidence of another Moschion that his mother would come to him, *Perik.* 547.

665: In OCT I print B's reading, without confidence. Elsewhere in Menander δηλαδή always occurs at a line-end (twelve times, including probable restorations), and C has, unmetrically, καταμενεινμου. An interpolated explanatory μου, surely unnecessary, would be more likely to find a place near δεήcεται. Sudhaus proposed to read δεήcεθ' οὗτος καταμένειν μου δηλαδή, supposing δεηcεθ' (or δεηcεται) to have been omitted by haplography and replaced at the end of the line. It is possible this is right.

667 πιθανόν: This has often been taken to mean that Moschion shows a sudden diffidence about his plan: 'I need only be plausible— the last thing I can do'. Guéraud, *Bull. Inst. français d'archéologie* *orientale*, xxvii (1927), 118, suggests a better alternative: 'The one need is that the last thing I can do, that is, go away, should seem a plausible intention.'

669 τοῦτ' ἐcτίν: 'This is the truth', cf. *P. Didot I.* 39. Moschion, who has been addressing the audience, with his back to the house, hears the door open and turns expecting to see his father emerge. Instead, Parmenon returns in excitement and a high good humour, marked by the change of metre to trochaic tetrameters. When he had run away, his master had discovered that the baby was Moschion's and was in a rage; now he finds all is going happily forward for Moschion's wedding. He cannot understand that Moschion does not share his own relief and hurry in to join the festivities.

When he had last seen the young man, the arrangements for the marriage had not been completed; Demeas had still to ask Nikeratos to give his daughter immediately (159–60). Moschion had taken himself off to wait. Parmenon must now suppose that the demand for a soldier's outfit must be due to an exaggerated despondency (ἀθυμίαν 672) about the result of Demeas' mission.

670 ὑcτερίζειν: 'You are not up to date with affairs here', see LSJ s.v.

671 εἰδώc τ': Moschion is not up to date with affairs *and so* is tormenting himself unnecessarily, not knowing what has happened. For this common sense of τε see K–G ii. 242. Fraenkel and Jacques adopt C's δέ and suppose it to be adversative. I do not understand this, and Austin has abandoned it.

672 διὰ κενῆc: Cf. 605 n.   **εἰc ἀθυμίαν τ' ἄγειc:** Parmenon has not been told why Moschion requires his cloak and sword, but must guess that it is in order to leave Athens, and that he would do that only if despondent, believing that his father would not consent to his marriage with Plangon.

673 κεράννυται: The wine is being mixed with the water.

674: B gives θυμιατ' ανηπτ' ανηρ[κ]ται cπλαγχναθ' ηφαιcτου πυρι and C Θυμιαματιθυμιατ'αναπτεταιθυμιατ'ηφαιcτουφλογι. (The dotted letters are Guéraud's guesses.) These readings seem to represent alternative versions: (B) θυμιᾶτ'. ἐνῆρκτ', ἀνῆπται cπλάγχνα θ' Ἡφαίcτου φλογί and (C) θυμιᾶτ' ἀνάπτεταί ⟨τε⟩ θύμαθ' Ἡφαίcτου φλογί, of which the first, and fuller, is preferable. It gives two pairs of verbs: the first, κεράννυται, θυμιᾶται, are in the present tense since they name activities that are still going on; ἐνῆρκται, ἀνῆπται are in the perfect tense because they name past activities of which the results remain.

For ἐνάρχομαι, 'prepare for the sacrifice', see 222 n., and for the perfect see Eur. *Electra* 1142, κανοῦν ἐνῆρκται, Aischines iii. 120, ἐνῆρκται μὲν τὰ κανᾶ, παρέστηκεν δὲ τὰ θύματα. For τε as third word after the phrase ἀνῆπται cπλάγχνα see *Perik.* 128 n. This instance of the postponed position of τε is avoided by Austin, who adopts for cπλάγχνα θ᾿ C's reading θύμαθ᾿. But θῦμα is a word as much used in prose as in verse, whereas cπλάγχνα, being mainly poetical, is probably original here.

Parmenon's language is paratragic, recalling Eur. *IA* 1601, ἐπεὶ δ᾿ ἅπαν κατηνθρακώθη θῦμ᾿ ἐν ῾Ηφαίcτου φλογί, and Aristophanes' tragic parody, *Plutus* 661, καθωcιώθη πελανὸc ῾Ηφαίcτου φλογί. θύμαθ᾿, if correct, is a poetic plural. The use of elevated language to describe a feast has its parallel in *Dysk.* 946 ff., and was traditional in comedy; but whereas for the early poets such language was simply employed for the sake of comic effect, it is here psychologically relevant: Parmenon is so happy that he bursts into poetic diction, almost as a modern might.

676–7: Parmenon's five brief insistent phrases are uttered as Moschion makes no reply, debating whether to carry through his plan. But the young man decides to stand firm, and advances on the slave in a threatening manner, causing him to exclaim in alarm τί βούλει; Gomme would have given μέλλεις; to Moschion, as at 681, making μετιέναι depend on περιμένουcι. There is, however, no good reason for departing from the distribution of speeches in the papyri, and it is not likely that Menander would have made Moschion repeat himself. Dedoussi argues that the sentence is a statement, 'you are expected to fetch the bride'.

678 παῖ· τί ποιεῖc: Cf. 690, 715, παῖ τί τοῦτο; Evidence grows that παῖ came to be used as an exclamation of surprise or consternation, see 360 above, *Dysk.* 500 n., *Mis.* 216. Moschion makes to strike the slave.   ἱερόcυλε as a term of abuse often stands alone (*Aspis* 227, *Epitr.* 935, 952, 1100) but is found joined to γραῦ in *Epitr.* 1064, 1122. Hence the majority of editors, who here join it to παῖ, have some warrant. But there is no justification for overriding the evidence of both B and C, which place a dicolon before, not after, παι.

679 διακέκομμαι τὸ cτόμα: LSJ give 'I am struck dumb', assigning the phrase to the meaning 'interrupt', sometimes borne by διακόπτω. Much more likely is 'you've cut my lip' (Capps and others, cf. *Georg.* 48, διέκοψε τὸ cκέλοc, Dem. liv. 8, τὸ μὲν χεῖλοc διακόψαι). Ter. *Ad.* 559 has *discidit labrum*, spoken by a slave who pretends that he has been drubbed. For cτόμα, cf. Plut. *Brutus* 988 a, cοῦ πάλιν ἐγὼ cυντρίψω τὸ cτόμα.

680 νὴ Δί᾿ ἐξεύρηκά γε τόδε κακόν: νὴ Δία . . . γε is common, e.g. in Aristophanes, *Ach.* 811, νὴ τὸν Δί᾿ ἀcτείω γε τὼ βοcκήματε, *Birds* 135, νὴ Δία ταλαιπώρων γε πραγμάτων ἐρᾷς, *Lys.* 1033, νὴ Δί᾽ ὤνησάς γέ με, *Thesm.* 20, νὴ τὸν Δί᾽ ἥδομαί γε, *Frogs* 1433, *Eccl.* 1045.

The phrase here is ironic, 'this discovery of mine is a bad thing'; Parmenon thinks that anyone would suppose his discovery that the marriage was being prepared was a very welcome one, but Moschion does not treat it as such. Austin and Jacques refer τόδε κακόν to the split lip.

681 μέλλεις: Parmenon hesitates at the door, from which he can see what is going on inside: ἄγουσι τοὺς γάμους ὄντως. **πάλιν:** Sc. λέγεις. Parmenon had already told Moschion this at 673. **ἕτερον . . . τι:** 'Bring me some other news'; I think this is merely ironical. Parmenon at last enters the house.

683 ἀπορρυγισθείς: This compound occurs only here outside the Septuagint; the force of the prefix may be either to indicate departure from a normal state or intensive, as in ἀπεχθαίρειν, ἀποθαυμάζειν.

684 παρέλιπον: 'Left out of my calculations', 'passed over'.

686 ἀνακάμπτων: 'Turning round and coming back', as in *Dysk.* 256.

687–91: C ends with 686, and some scholars attempted to guess how the scene proceeded. The discovery of B shows none to have been successful. It should have been presumed that neither of the alternatives envisaged by Moschion would be fulfilled: his father would neither beg him to stay nor fall into a rage and let him go. In fact it is not Demeas who appears, but once again it is Parmenon, who this time brings the sword and cloak. To the young man's confusion he declares that no one had seen him, and urges Moschion to be on his way. It looks as if the stratagem had entirely miscarried (690). But no sooner has the spectator been thus led not to expect to see Demeas than out he comes. His surprise at seeing Moschion equipped for travel shows that Parmenon had told the truth. His motive for coming out must therefore be to look for the son whose absence is impeding the wedding.

690–2: εἶτα ποῦ ᾽στιν; εἶτα with the question indicates surprise, perhaps impatience, even some indignation. **παῖ, τί τοῦτο;** Similarly Nikeratos at 715, and Getas at *Mis.* 216. In the latter case there is no one present to be called παῖ; so it is probably right to see in all three places a simple exclamation. παῖ will not be a vocative addressed to Moschion. See further 678 n. **τί τὸ πάθος;** 'What has taken you?' **ἡ στολὴ τί βούλεται;** 'What does this costume mean?', cf. Ar. *Eccl.* 753, τί τὰ σκευάρια ταυτὶ βούλεται; Ter. *Eun.* 558, 'quid sibi hic uestitu' quaerit?'

690 φλυαρεῖς: Perhaps Parmenon means that the inquiries whether he had been seen and the curse make no sense in the mouth of a man who is about to leave home. Austin suggests that the word is said *sotto voce*, in which case it might indicate a belief that the whole of Moschion's procedure is nonsense, a put-on act. Does the word perhaps belong to Moschion, who says that Parmenon is talking nonsense if he thinks he has any intention of leaving? For, of course, he has never had any such real intention.

693–4: Interpretation is difficult, but I think the following is possible. When Moschion does not depart on receiving the cloak and sword, but anxiously inquires whether these preparations have been observed and utters curses when he learns that they have not, Parmenon realizes that the departure is play-acting, and resolves to embarrass the young man by himself entering into the game, urging him to go quickly. Then he pretends that he too is going, although he has neither been asked to nor received Demeas' permission: he must, therefore, say good-bye to the household (for this use of προϲειπεῖν see *Dysk.* 884 n.). 'I, too, must say good-bye' is the way he puts it, wickedly assuming that Moschion must have taken leave before going. He knows that he has not done so, and, by calling attention to this point, hopes to suggest that there is something bogus in the affair.

Parmenon here goes in; if the play were to be performed by three actors, the same actor must come on again as Nikeratos at 713. Demeas is quick to understand that Moschion is angry at being suspected; but anger might be indicated by gesture as well as by the preparations for leaving home.

697: Demeas proceeds to put his son in the wrong. He candidly admits that he had wrongly accused him but reminds him of all he had done for him. Even now he had done his best to prevent the supposed crime becoming public knowledge. But Moschion has forgotten the gratitude he owes for years of good treatment and is publicizing the folly of a single day. This is a line that Moschion had not anticipated; he had hoped that his father would beg him to stay, feared that he might angrily let him go; he had not expected sympathetic reproof.

698 πατήρ, not ὁ ϲὸϲ πατήρ, for the emphasis is on the relationship, 'I am your *father*'; see *Dysk.* 240 n.

700 ϲε δεῖ: B has no sign of elision, and the present tense gives a better sense than the imperfect ἔδει. Demeas' immediate concern is with how Moschion is to act now, not with what he ought to have done in the past: 'You must put up with those acts of mine which pained you.'

702 ὡϲ ἂν ὑόν: Cf. 518 n.

703–4 ἠγνόηϲα is more than 'I did not know'; it means, 'I had a false belief', similarly ἠγνόουν, 705. Aristotle, *EN* 1111ᵃ11–16 gives as examples of ἄγνοια thinking that your son is a foreign enemy, that a pointed spear has a button on it, or that a stone is pumice, etc. At the end of 704 ἡλίκην is almost certain; an exclamatory word (cf. 255) so late in the sentence is improbable, so that it must be an adjective dependent on a verb at the end of 703, e.g. ῥητέον. If this is so, the combination of εἴς τε τοὺς ἄλλους ἁμαρτών with ἐν ἐμαυτῷ τ' ἐτήρουν is irregular (τε τηρῶν would be required). The easy change of εἴς τε to εἴς γε avoids this difficulty.   coῦ πρόνοιαν ἔσχον: Cf. *Pap.* *Ghôran* ii. 127 (Page, *GLP* p. 300), ἐμοῦ πρόνοιαν εἶχες; 'Did you care for my interests?', Eur. *Alc.* 1060–1, τῆς θανούσης . . . πολλὴν πρόνοιαν δεῖ μ' ἔχειν.   ἐτήρουν: 'I tried to keep it quiet.'   εἴς γε τοὺς ἄλλους ἁμαρτών: 'I acted wrongly towards all the others concerned', i.e. towards Chrysis and the infant, Soph. *OC* 968, τάδ' εἰς ἐμαυτὸν τοὺς ἐμούς θ' ἡμάρτανον.

705 ὃ δή ποτ' ἠγνόουν: 'Whatever misapprehension I had'. ὅστιςδήποτε in Attic invariably indicates inclusiveness. If ὃς δή ποτε has the same sense, the meaning here will be that Demeas kept absolutely all his misapprehensions to himself. Jacques, however, believes that δή gives a sense of vagueness. If that is right, Demeas must be trying to suggest that his misapprehension might be allowed to slip out of memory.

706 ἔθηκα φανερὸν ἐπιχαίρειν: 'Made it plain to rejoice at'; the infinitive is epexegetic. Notice the assumption that a man will have enemies to rejoice in his discomfiture, cf. Eur. frag. 460 Nauck, χρὴ περιστεῖλαι καλῶς κρύπτοντα καὶ μὴ πᾶσι κηρύσσειν τάδε· γέλως γὰρ ἐχθροῖς γίγνεται τὰ τοιάδε.

707 ἐκφέρεις: 'Publish', cf. Isokr. viii. 14, ἐκφέρουσιν εἰς τοὺς ἄλλους Ἕλληνας τὰ τῆς πόλεως ἁμαρτήματα. Demeas is not quite fair to Moschion, who had not told anyone that he was leaving because falsely suspected by his father; but he might reasonably assume that he had told or would tell.

708 οὐκ ἀξιῶ: 'I don't expect it.' The verb is normally followed by an infinitive, e.g. Thuc. iv. 86, οὐκ ἀξιῶ . . . ὑποπτεύεσθαι, but see Dem. xx. 12, ἐγὼ μὲν οὐκ ἀξιῶ. Merkelbach suggests the emendation οὐκ ἀξίως, 'unsuitably'.

709 μου τοῦ βίου: The position of μου before τοῦ βίου, not after, is unusual but not impossible, cf., e.g., 436, frag. 665, ἣν γὰρ κακῶς μου τὴν γυναῖχ' οὕτω λέγεις, K–G i. 619. The emendation μέν, which like Jacques I once suggested, now seems unlikely (and is unnecessary, Denniston, *GP* 165): it introduces an irregularly formed clause— μὴ μνημονεύσῃς ἡμέραν μέν for μὴ ἡμέραν μὲν μνημονεύσῃς.

710 διεϲφάλην: 'I was utterly wrong.'

712 πιθέϲθαι: This aor. 2 is rare in comedy (Diphilos frag. 32. 9 K, ὃϲ ἂν δὲ μὴ πίθητ᾽) and its sense approaches 'obey'.

713 ff.: Demeas' speech puts Moschion in a difficult position. There is no answer to the accusations that he has allowed one incident to outweigh many years' good treatment, and that he has been ready to injure his father's reputation, while his father had done all he could to preserve that of his son. Reason requires that he should abandon his dramatic pose and apologize. But this is a thing that Moschion, like many young men, would find very hard. He is saved by the sudden appearance of Nikeratos, which relieves him from the necessity of an immediate reply.

Nikeratos' first two lines are spoken to his wife, who remains in the house; she has been fussing and he comes out to escape. Then he catches sight, with surprise (παῖ τί τοῦτο;) of Demeas and Moschion; their attitudes may indicate that something is amiss, and a military cloak (χλαμύϲ, see 659 n.) is strange wear for a bridegroom. He assumes that Moschion intends to desert the girl he is to marry, and threatens, perhaps not entirely in jest, to restrain him forcibly. This is just what Moschion wants; if he can appear to be forced to stay, which is what he wishes to do, he need not explicitly give up his pose of leaving. So he bewilders Nikeratos by begging him to execute the threat. 'Stop your nonsense,' the old man replies, 'and put down that sword.' 'Put it down, for heaven's sake,' adds Demeas; 'don't irritate him.' This makes Moschion look more foolish than ever, but he tries to retain his dignity by pretending that the old men's 'entreaties' have persuaded him; he recalls the scene that he had imagined, in which his father would entreat him to stay (δεήϲεται 664, δεόμενοι 722). 'Entreaties?' replies Nikeratos, and orders the young man to come to his house. Moschion is now alarmed lest Nikeratos should really intend to secure him by physical bonds; since he has been forced to give in, that would no longer serve any purpose. Demeas intervenes, telling Nikeratos to fetch out his daughter. Father and son are for the moment left alone. Moschion still cannot admit that he was wrong, only that his love for Plangon is his strongest motive: 'If only you had had Plangon brought out at the start, you wouldn't have had the trouble of preaching a sermon to make me stay.'

713 λουτρά: See 121 n.   **προτέλεια:** Neut. plur., 'a preliminary sacrifice', particularly that which initiated a marriage, e.g. Eur. *IA* 718, προτέλεια δ᾽ ἤδη παιδὸϲ ἔϲφαξαϲ θεᾷ, Plato, *Laws* 774 e. Photios has προτέλεια· ἡ πρὸ τῶν γάμων θυϲία (frag. 903 K–T).   **οἱ γάμοι:** There was no particular point in the Greek ceremonies at which the marriage might be regarded as accomplished, unless it was the transference of the bride to her new home. Hence there is perhaps an absurdity in Nikeratos' view that the marriage has taken place and all that remains is for the bridegroom to come for the bride.

716 φησὶ γοῦν: Demeas is sceptical about his son's seriousness in intending to leave.

717–18 ἤδη . . . οὐκ εἰς μακράν: Cf. Ar. *Wasps* 453, δώσετον καλὴν δίκην, οὐκέτ᾽ εἰς μακράν, Dem. xviii. 36, τί οὖν cυνέβη μετὰ ταῦτ᾽ εὐθύς, οὐκ εἰς μακράν;

A μοιχός, caught with the woman, might be bound by her husband or other responsible relative, and then subjected to any physical revenge or even killed. Alternatively he might buy himself free, perhaps by a money-payment, perhaps, if the circumstances made it suitable, by undertaking to marry his partner. I think that Nikeratos may propose, somewhat late in the day, to treat Moschion as a captured μοιχός, and so force him to complete the marriage from which he appears to be trying to escape. He had in the last scene of Act IV finally not resisted Demeas' theory that a god, not Moschion, was responsible for his daughter's child; but it may be guessed that he had done so because it was a theory that eased the situation for all concerned, rather than because he believed it. Now, if Moschion wishes to evade marriage, it no longer serves any purpose, while Moschion's paternity is a lever to force him to abide by his promise.

720: I see no way of determining whether πρὸς τῶν θεῶν belongs to κατάβαλε or to μὴ παροξύνῃς (Fraenkel).

721 μὴ παροξύνῃς: B has παροξυνος, cf. *Dysk.* 211, καθοcαι for καθηcαι; 441, κεχοναc for κεχηναc. **καταλελιπαρήκατε:** This intensive compound was previously not recorded before Lucian: its rarity makes the falsity of Moschion's claim more absurd. ἀφείcθω is also dramatic in effect, 'let it go!', for the ordinary ἀφίημι or καταβάλλω.

723 μηδαμῶς: Sc. δῆcον, the marriage is to proceed at once. 'That's agreed?' asks Nikeratos, and, on receiving confirmation, hc goes in to fetch Plangon, with whom he reappears, saying, 'Come on out, you', πρόαγε δὴ cύ (δεῦρο is either a variant or an explanation; if a variant, inferior in view of δεῦρο in 722 and 723). In the short period of his absence Moschion tries, illogically but perhaps not altogether seriously, to put some blame on his father.

725 φιλοcοφῶν: To the ordinary man, philosophers are always slightly suspect and absurd. 'You would not have been put to the trouble of preaching just now.'

726: Nikeratos hands Plangon over to Moschion, uttering the usual marriage-formula, γνησίων παίδων ἐπ' ἀρότῳ, cf. *Dysk.* 842 n., *Perik.* 1010 n., and intro. p. 28. The 'witnesses' to whom he refers will be members of the two households, played by supers.

727 προῖκα: A μοιχός who married the girl he had violated could not expect a dowry (A. R. W. Harrison, *Law of Athens*, i. 19), so that Nikeratos, who probably could not afford one anyhow, will here seem comic rather than mean.

728 ὃ μὴ γένοιτο: This is a formula to avert an evil that has been mentioned as a possibility, cf. *Mis.* 264, [Dem.] xl. 56, *Pap. Didot* i. 28. εἰσαεί, if right, is a word from tragedy, see LSJ s.v.

729 στέργω: 'I cherish her', cf. *Dysk.* 309.   λουτρὰ μετιέναι: The bride has been bathed (713), but Moschion has as yet not received the ritual bath. Water must be fetched from the spring Kallirhoë (see 124). The λουτροφόρος was a young boy or girl, a relative of the bridegroom, who fetched it, with assistance of course. The αὐλητρίς will provide music to accompany the procession, cf. Ter. *Adelphoe* 904, 'uerum hoc mihi mora est, tibicina et hymenaeum qui cantent', Plaut. *Cas.* 798 f. Chrysis, played here by a super, may have followed Demeas on the stage, although possibly, as Austin supposes, Demeas calls his orders to her through the door.   καὶ στεφάνους: For the unusual dactyl cf. *Sik.* 135, *Dysk.* 774 n.

732 συμπροπέμπωμεν: 'Join in conveying Plangon to her new home', cf. Xen. *HG* iv. 1. 9, ποίαν γὰρ νύμφην πώποτε τοσοῦτοι ἱππεῖς καὶ πελτασταὶ καὶ ὁπλῖται προὔπεμψαν.   ὅδε: Some slave, a *muta persona*.   πύκαζε σὺ κρᾶτα: 'Put a garland on your head'; the verb is poetic. Demeas' language is slightly elevated, preparing the way for his final lines. Eur. *Tro.* 353, πύκαζε κρᾶτ' ἐμὸν νικηφόρον καὶ χαῖρε τοῖς ἐμοῖσι βασιλικοῖς γάμοις, Kratinos frag. 98 K, τῷ δ' ἀειφρούρῳ μελιλώτῳ κάρα πυκάζομαι.

733 ἀλλ' ἐγώ: Cf. 477 n.   παῖδες καλοί: The enumeration of different age-groups among the spectators is found also in the final lines of *Dysk.* and probably of *Mis.* and *Sik.* Here the boys are given a flattering adjective: they are 'lovely boys'. A verse from Plato Comicus (frag. 206 K), παῖδες γέροντες μειράκια παλλάκια, need not be from the end of a play.

734 πάντες εὐρώστως ἅμα: A traditional formula in asking for applause, found also in the penultimate line of a play by Antiphanes, Demiańczuk, p. 8, *P. Oxy.* 427.

735 Βακχίῳ: 'The Bacchic one' is Dionysos, who as god of the dramatic festival is pleased when a good play causes the applause that indicates the audience's favour.

736–7: The last two lines give a trochaic alternative for the iambic couplet that ended some other plays by Menander (*Dysk.*, *Mis.*, *Sik.*, and an unidentified one). The words εὐμένης ἔποιτο Νίκη ἀεί are common to both versions. In the last line the actor drops all pretence of being Demeas; the χοροί must be his own or those of the poet. But the word is used in a traditional formula. It is the play that wins the victory, and the χορός has no longer any part in the play, for which it provides no more than intervals.

The goddess Νίκη cannot be expected to attend every contest, but she takes her seat at the finest, among which of course are the dramatic contests at Athens. πάρεδρος frequently means an assessor, and it is possible that she is illogically but understandably represented as determining the result, deciding to which poet she shall be awarded.

All gods are ἄφθιτοι, but Victory may be deathless because the play's success will be preserved in the public records.

Fragment. This is a rare case where Phrynichos quotes Menander with approval, for calling incense λιβανωτόν, not (as ignorant people did) λίβανον, the name of the tree from which it was derived. But it seems probable that he was mistaken over the name of the play, since *Samia* contains no Τρύφη nor is there any vacant place where the burning of incense is likely. It is just possible, however, that Demeas found an occasion for such an offering to celebrate either his homecoming at the end of Act I or the arrangement of the marriage at the end of Act II. If this was so, Τρύφη must be the name of a slave of his household, a *muta persona*, told to put fire on the altar, while another is ordered to fetch the incense; cf. frag. 257 K–T, ἐπίθες τὸ πῦρ, ἡ ζάκορος ('temple attendant').

The only other instance in comedy of the name Τρύφη ('Morsel', cf. θρύπτω, ἐτρύφην) is Alexis frag. 230 K, μὴ παντελῶς αὐτῷ δίδου | ὑδαρῆ, κατανοεῖς; ἴσον ἴσῳ μικροῦ. καλῶς. | ἡδύ γε τὸ πῶμα. ποδαπὸς ὁ Βρόμιος, Τρύφη; | (Τρ.) Θάσιος. (Α.) ὅμοιον. καὶ δίκαιον τοὺς ξένους | πίνειν ξενικόν. It is likely that someone is talking to a *hetaira* who is about to entertain a foreigner or a mercenary soldier. In real life the name Τρύφη was probably not confined to *hetairai* (few names were), but in comedy names usually indicate status. There is no room in *Samia* for a second *hetaira*; so, if the fragment comes from that play, the name will not after all show the character's status. (A Τρύφη in Aelian, *ep. rust.* 11. 12, lives with her father, but is a forward minx; the only historical Τρύφη I have found was a member of a thiasos in the Peiraeus in the second century B.C. [*IG* ii². 2357]; was she a *hetaira*?)

SIKYONIOS

S: *P. Sorbonnensis* 72, 2272, 2273. These are all parts of a papyrus roll written in the latter half of the third century B.C. It was used by mummifiers to make papier mâché cases for their mummies. *P. Sorb.* 72, which contains 52–109, 206–13, 280–322, and parts of 382–6, 405–10, was found by P. Jouguet at El-Ghôran early in this century; *P. Sorb.* 2272 and 2273, which come from different mummies, were found in Paris by A. Bataille in 1962 and 1963. Bataille's technique for the separation of the sheets was brilliantly successful. The surviving columns of the roll contain from twenty-one to twenty-five lines apiece. Change of speaker is indicated by a paragraphus, and sometimes a space between speeches in addition; a dicolon occurs twice, perhaps as an afterthought. Offsets of ink, arising from the folding of the papyrus in making the mummy-case, may be misleading where letters are incompletely preserved.

O 6: *P. Oxy.* 1238. Beginnings of seven lines and a few letters from two more.

Discussions: R. Kassel, *Eranos*, xliii (1965), 1, E. W. Handley, *BICS* xii (1965), 38, P. H. J. Lloyd-Jones, *Greek Roman and Byzantine Studies*, vii (1966), 131. See also H. J. Mette, *Lustrum*, x (1966), 169, A. Barigazzi, SIFC xxxvii (1965), 7, and B. Marzullo, *Quad. it. fil. gr.* (Cagliari) ii (1967), 15.

Title: In eight places the play is referred to by other authors as Cικυώνιoc; at Stob. iv. 12. 4 and Alkiphron iv. 19. 19 the termination is lost. The subscription in S, however, has Cικυώνιοι and the plural also appears on a wall-painting at Ephesos, depicting an unidentifiable scene from the play, F. Eichler, *Anzeiger d. österreich. Akad. Wiss.* cv (1968), 79, L. Kahil–R. Ginouvès, *Antike Kunst*, Beiheft 6, p. 99, plate 27. Other plays are alternatively referred to in our sources by singular or plural titles, e.g. Αὐλητρίc or Αὐλητρίδεc, 'Εφέcιοc or 'Εφέcιοι. Usually the inconsistency will be due to scribal error (C. Corbato, *Studi Menandrei*, 64). Kassel prudently writes 'de titulo fabulae nihil affirmo'. It is unlikely that any Sikyonian appeared on the stage besides Stratophanes (and even he was really an Athenian); therefore the singular has some claim for preference.

Scene: Perhaps Eleusis or its neighbourhood. This location would be certain if Kichesias, who sets out in Act V for the house of the priestess there, returned with his daughter before the end of the act. But of that there is no certainty. Stratophanes goes to some part of Eleusis and returns therefrom in the interval between Acts III and IV. This suggests that the distance was not very great. There is no parallel for a long journey between successive acts. In *Epitrepontes* Smikrines does not necessarily go from a country deme to Athens and back between Acts IV and V. Those scholars, however, who suppose the scene of *Sikyonios* to be Athens cannot be proved wrong.

Dramatis Personae

A divine speaker of the prologue
Stratophanes, a *condottiere*, supposedly a Sikyonian
His true mother
His true father (? Smikrines)
Kichesias, an Athenian fallen on hard times
Philumene, his daughter
Dromon, his slave
Theron, a parasite
Pyrrhias, Stratophanes' slave
Donax, also Stratophanes' slave
Malthake, perhaps Stratophanes' mistress
A democrat (? Blepes)
Moschion, Stratophanes' brother

In what is preserved, at least, Philumene and Donax do not speak.

Stratophanes is a soldier again in *Truculentus*; the name is scratched on the temple of Osiris at Abydos, Preisigke, *Sammelbuch* 3761, and also occurs in the Zenon-papyri, *PSI* 526.

Kichesias, a name unique in comedy and uncommon in real life; it was borne by three members of a family of the deme Aixonai, *Pros. Att.* 8445.

Philumene occurs again in frag. 489; a common name in real life, *Pros. Att.* 14749–57, 14750a–f, 14751a.

Dromon, 'Runner', is a slave's name in Euangelos frag. 1 K, *P. Oxy.* 2329 (comedy), Plaut. *Aulularia*, Ter. *Andria*, *HT*, *Adelphoe*, Lucian, *Dial. mer.* 10. 4. But it was also borne by a writer of comedy, Athen. 240 d, 409 e, and is not necessarily a slave's name in Euphron frag. 10 K, Dionysios frag. 3 K, Lucian, *de merc. cond.* 25, *Timon* 22.

Theron, 'Hunter', a suitable name for a parasite, as predatory on the rich. It is also a name of real life, *Pros. Att.* 7239a, 7240–1, but best known as that of the tyrant of Akragas.

Donax: see *Dysk.* 959 n.

Malthake, a name borne by citizen women of the fourth century, *Pros. Att.* 9661–2, by a *hetaira* in Theophilos frag. 11 K (Ath. 587 f.).

Lucian, *Rhet. Mag.* 12, speaks of a Malthake who is a famous figure in comedy.

Pyrrhias: see *Dysk.* introductory note p. 131.

Moschion: see *Perik.* introductory note p. 466.

For Smikrines see *Epitr.* p. 291; but also the note on 156 below.

Plot: The plot of the earlier half of the play cannot be reconstructed in more than a very general way. The latter half, however, is fairly clear. Stratophanes, a successful captain of mercenaries, believed himself to be the son of Sikyonian parents. On returning from service in Karia, he had taken a house or lodgings in a house probably in or near Eleusis; in it was Malthake, probably his mistress, and with him was associated a parasite, Theron, who was probably an Athenian (144). We do not know how early in the play Stratophanes appeared; the first surviving scene to show him is in the third act; he there learns from Pyrrhias, who had been sent on to announce his safe return, that his supposed mother has died, at an advanced age, having first revealed that he was not her son nor that of his supposed father, news of whose death had already reached him in Karia. The supposed father had lost an action against a Boeotian, who would have been able to arrest Stratophanes and seize his property to obtain the sum adjudged, had it not been shown that Stratophanes was not the dead man's heir.

In the next scene Stratophanes turns up, not in search of his real parents—that they were Athenians has in fact not been revealed by him, although it will appear that he knows it from his 'mother's' letter, which Pyrrhias has brought (247–51)—but at an incident in Eleusis. His appearance there is recounted by a character (? Blepes) who seems to have no part in the play but that of a messenger and who tells his story to a man probably named Smikrines. We learn how a soldier intervened in a situation where a girl and a slave had taken sanctuary. The sight of the girl caused him great emotion—he claimed that she was a citizen and that he had saved her to restore her to her father; he hoped to marry her, since he too was a citizen. The slave was his slave, and he assigned him to the girl, who had then been sent off to the care of the priestess (? of Demeter). This solution had been opposed by a youth who had earlier been hanging around the girl and the slave, talking to the latter, whom he claimed to know. This youth later proves to be Moschion.

How is this scene to be explained? It is certain that the girl and the slave were Philumene and Dromon, who had been kidnapped from Attica at least ten years earlier, and sold on the slave-market at Mylasa in Karia to a Sikyonian captain (5–15). That captain was perhaps Stratophanes; if not, he had transferred his purchases to Stratophanes at some later time. It has been guessed that Philumene and Dromon, left in Greece while Stratophanes was in Asia Minor, had been seized, or had been in danger of seizure, by the Boeotian creditor, and had escaped to take refuge in sanctuary; that Stratophanes had in some way heard of their predicament (? 118) and gone to their rescue (Lloyd-Jones, *Greek Roman and Byzantine Studies*, vii [1966], 143). Moschion's presence is explicable by the fact that he was in love with the girl and hoped to secure her for himself, perhaps as a mistress. It is quite obscure how he had come to know her. An explanation suggested by Jacques (*REA* lxix [1967], 309) is that Moschion's father Smikrines had bought Philumene and Dromon from the Boeotian. But Smikrines gives no sign of recognizing the girl and the slave of Blepes' tale. This is odd if a girl and a slave had just run away from him.

Lloyd-Jones's theory is not supported by any surviving passage. The few clues point rather to the belief that Philumene, knowing herself to be of Athenian birth, feared that her master Stratophanes, who had just returned from Karia and made known his passion for her, would force her to be his mistress although he also knew of her birth. Accordingly she took refuge at an altar with Dromon, who declared her citizen status (97-8, 197, 241).

What follows on the narration by Blepes is obscure. I think that Stratophanes enters, now searching for his father, whose house is on the stage. That father was in fact Smikrines, the man to whom Blepes told the story of the events in Eleusis. Stratophanes is pursued by Moschion, who threatens to arrest him as a kidnapper; at this point there is a gap, after which Stratophanes is found to be Smikrines' son and Moschion's brother. The last act opens with the entrance of Kichesias and Theron. Kichesias is Philumene's father, although Theron does not know it, and has been reduced to poverty. Theron wishes to suborn Kichesias to declare Philumene to be his own long-lost daughter, and thus make possible a marriage between her and Stratophanes; he himself hopes to obtain Malthake (145). Kichesias reacts with indignation at first, and then with tears as he remembers the daughter he had lost. Theron thinks this a fine piece of acting on his part. Hereupon Dromon suddenly announces that Kichesias' child is safe, alive, and in the town; Kichesias almost faints at the news. Whether Dromon has been present at the previous scene or here enters and almost immediately recognizes his old master is not agreed, but it seems to me much more likely that he comes on the scene at this point. Stratophanes is now summoned, meets Kichesias, to whom he is presented as the man who has kept his daughter safe, and dispatches Dromon and the old man to the priestess, promising to follow. This he does, after giving instructions for transferring some of his luggage to his father's house. After his departure Moschion enters, saying that he must now have no eyes for Philumene; he will be his brother's best man. After a gap, there remain the first halves of the final thirteen lines of the play, which are hard to interpret.

1–24: This passage clearly comes from a prologue spoken by some divine personage. No character in the play could possess the necessary knowledge except Dromon himself, who seems to be the 'servant' twice mentioned here. The ends of lines 23–4 recall *Dyskolos* 45–6, which introduce the final verses of the prologue: no doubt, like the lines that end both plays, they are a standard formula. I assume, not necessarily correctly, that this prologue was not postponed until after the first scene but, like that of *Dyskolos*, opened the play. If only one column of text is lost before 1, the prologue had about the same length as that of *Dyskolos* or of the postponed prologue of *Aspis*. The postponed prologue of *Perikeiromene* must, however, have been longer, perhaps seventy to eighty lines.

3–7: This describes the kidnapping of Philumene and Dromon, probably from Halai on the coast of Attica (see 355 n.). The old woman, who was not worth transporting to the slave-market, was probably a nurse. Mylasa (*RE* xvi. 1048) was a large inland town in Karia, a district where there was employment at times for mercenary soldiers, see *Samia*, introductory note, p. 543. The name is always spelled *MYΛΑCA* in inscriptions, including those from Attica (Meisterhans³, 99), but often μύλαcca in MSS., as in S here; similarly μυλαccευc in the papyrus of Sosylos (frag. 1 Jacoby) from the first century B.C. The only evidence for quantity is *AP* ix. 671 (anon.), Ἀμβρόcιοc Μυλαcεύc, and Ausonius, *Mosella*, 215, Mўlāsena. The rarity of word-division in fifth-foot anapaests suggests that Menander too pronounced a single c. The name often has the article, τὰ Μύλαca, but not always, Arrian, *Anab.* i. 20. 4, 21. 1; Hdt. i. 171.

3 cωμάτων: cώματα, 'persons', originally used freely (e.g. Aischines iii. 78, τὰ φίλτατα cώματα), came to be used particularly of slaves, at first with a determinative adjective, e.g. Dem. xx. 77, αἰχμάλωτα cώματα, Aischines i. 16, οἰκετικὰ cώματα, but later absolutely, e.g. *Pap. Hibeh* i. 54. 20 (third century B.C.). Pollux iii. 78 protests cώματα δ' ἁπλῶc οὐκ ἂν εἴποιc ἀλλὰ δοῦλα cώματα. Phrynichos 355 allows cώματα to be used ἐπὶ τῶν ὠνίων ἀνδραπόδων, and it is to be noted here that from the kidnappers' point of view the three persons were articles for sale.

5: S seems to have τιν (Bataille, Coles, Austin) and there is no need to change this to τον. The servant (Dromon) will not have been mentioned before, since he was of no importance for the narrative so far. All that it had been necessary to say was that the girl was by the sea, in the care of an old woman. Note that the failure of the pirates to take this old woman contributes to the story: she was left as a witness, and Kichesias knows what had befallen his daughter (357).

7: Elsewhere the phrase ἀγορᾷ χρῆϲθαι is used of buyers, not as here of sellers, in the market: Xen. *Anab.* vii. 6. 24, Anaxandrides frag. 4 K, Plut. *Brut.* 47, *Coriol.* 16.

8 τὴν τροφίμην: 'His young mistress', cf. *Dysk.* 883 n.

9 ἡγεμών: A military commander, in this case doubtless of mercenaries. The word seems to indicate someone more important than a chiliarch, Lucian, *Dial. mer.* 15. 3, ἡγεμόνες εἶναι καὶ χιλίαρχοι λέγοντες, compared with *Kolax* 90, ἡγεμὼν μέγας, cατράπης, φρούραρχος, οἰκιϲτὴς τόπου, ϲτρατηγός. Strabo xiv. 2. 23 quotes the opinion of τῶν ἡγεμόνων τις on the situation of Mylasa.

Some have wished to recognize here and in 14 below a proper name Ἡγέμων. This is improbable because: (*a*) surviving prologues do not often give names, unless it be that of the central character: the alleged Hegemon would probably not even be a character in the play itself, but at the best a character's father; (*b*) ὁ Ϲικυώνιος . . . Ἡγέμων (13–14) would imply a namesake from some other town, and this seems pointless. Ἡγέμων is in any case an uncommon proper name: it occurs twice in *Pros. Att.* 6283 (a lost and badly copied inscription of unknown date), 6284 (coin of 176/5 B.C.), and very occasionally in Egypt (*P. Amherst* i. 128 of 128 B.C., possibly *P. Hibeh* i. 92 of 263 B.C.); also in the lemma to *AP* vii. 436. The common name was Ἡγήμων, *Pros. Att.* 6288–6301.

Is the Sikyonian captain identical with Stratophanes, or another soldier? My own view is that Sikyonian captains should not be multiplied beyond necessity, and that there is no necessity to suppose a second one (cf. B. Marzullo, *QIFG* ii [1967], 30 ff.). If the girl Philumene is now sixteen, she will certainly be marriageable; since she was four when kidnapped (355), we may guess that not more than twelve years have elapsed. Stratophanes' supposed mother has just died, as a 'very old woman' (216); he cannot, therefore, be a young man, but is perhaps in his later thirties. If twelve years earlier he was, say, twenty-five, could he already be a rich captain? It is not impossible. Chairestratos in *Aspis*, still a μειράκιον, has acquired booty worth nearly four talents. Frag. 3 (see n.) does not, as some suppose, show Stratophanes to have been poor when young.

If this Sikyonian captain is not Stratophanes, but someone else, he must soon have transferred the girl and Dromon to Stratophanes. Of this there is no hint elsewhere, but so much of the text is lost that the possibility remains. See also 226, τέτροφα μικρὸν παιδίον.

9 ἠρώτα "πόcου κτλ.": Cf. Diphilos frag. 66 K, ἂν ἐρωτήςῃς "πόcου ὁ λάβραξ", Alexis frag. 16 K, ἐὰν δ᾽ ἐρωτήςῃς "πόcου τοὺς κεcτρέας πωλεῖc δύ᾽ ὄντας;"

10: For the form of Handley's excellent restoration Kassel compares *Epitr.* 272, ὑπεcχόμην, ἔδωκ᾽, ἀπῆλθεν.

11 παλίμβολος: Harpokration 143. 11, ὁ πολλάκιc ἐμπολῇ μεταβεβλη-μένοc [παλίμπρατοc] παλίμβολος λέγεται, ὡc δῆλόν ἐcτιν . . . ἐκ τοῦ Μενάνδρου Cικυωνίου (frag. 379 K–T). Kassel would join τῷ θεράποντι with φηcίν (13), comparing *Sam.* 251 ff., but πλήcιον may be followed by a dative, as well as the more usual genitive, e.g. [Eur.] *IA* 1551, cταθεῖcα τῷ τεκόντι πληcίον, cf. Soph. *Ant.* 761, πληcία τῷ νυμφίῳ, Schwyzer, ii. 534.

12 τῶν αὐτόθεν τιc: A local character, cf. *Dysk.* 263. But if the right restoration is πωλουμένων, the meaning could be 'another of those who were being sold from the same place (in the market)'.

13 βέλτιcτε: In no other passage is a slave so addressed, although Sikon at *Dysk.* 497 says that he does so address a slave whom he wishes to get round; clearly it would be a piece of flattery. Sikon may be a free metic, so that a phrase that would be flattery on his lips might be politeness on those of another slave, but its use here must be noted as out of the ordinary. Kassel further observes that elsewhere θάρρει regularly *precedes* a vocative, quoting eight passages; Jacques, however, *REA* lxix (1967), 307, notes Ach. Tat. vi. 7. 9, ὦ γύναι, θάρcει.

14 χρηcτὸc καὶ πλούcιοc: Cf. *Aspis* 125. It may be worth remark that Athens and Sikyon were, at least when under democratic rule, friendly states, *IG* ii². 1. 448 (of 318/17 B.C.).

24: In the *editio princeps* it is stated that ητε is preceded by a letter with a descending tail, and this is also suggested by the photograph (Plate VI). But orally Prof. Bataille later withdrew the statement, and I have seen another photograph which shows no such descender. Nothing, therefore, stands in the way of recognizing here the formula of *Dysk.* 46.

25–35: The oath μὰ τὼ θεώ (33) and the exclamation τάλαν (34) show that these lines were spoken by a woman, but there is no clue to her identity (? Malthake) or to that of the interlocutor.

36–51: It looks as if a parasite with a hearty appetite is under discussion. τρέφειν (39) is a usual word in this connection, e.g. *Sam.* 603, Diphilos frag. 73 K, Diodoros frag. 2. 33 K.

52–109: These two scraps 52–61, 62–109 must come from the first half of the play, but it is quite uncertain which is the earlier or by what intervals they are separated the one from the other, or either from the preceding or following fragments. The first seems to concern a plan to suborn someone to bear false witness. Many scholars have accepted Legrand's suggestion, *BCH* xxx (1906), 122, that it is a question of evidence that will allege a girl to be free-born. A. Barigazzi proposes that the plan is put forward to Dromon by Moschion, who wishes to free Philumene from captivity in order to possess her himself, *SIFC* xxxvii (1965), 39. Later (343 ff.) Theron attempts to secure such false testimony; hence it is possible that it is he who here adumbrates the plan. But not enough is known of the plot for one to say whether either explanation is suitable.

57: Schröder's ἐνταῦθ' ἐν ἄϲτει τ', 'here at Eleusis and in the city', is quite uncertain, perhaps improbable, since οὐδ' Ἐλευϲίϲ ἐϲτι seems not to make sense. But τοῦδε is also difficult to account for, unless we accept Page's proposal μάρτυρα] τοιοῦτον . . . τοῦδε, *GLP* p. 308. I am not convinced that Ἐλευϲίϲ ἐϲτι is Greek for 'this is Eleusis'. To accent ἔλευϲίϲ ἐϲτι, 'there is a coming of people', would improbably introduce a rare noun, not known in comedy. Perhaps we should punctuate Ἐλευϲίϲ· ἔϲτι καὶ πανήγυρίϲ που. Ἐλευϲίϲ would then stand alone with a predicate to be supplied, like Πόντοϲ and probably Βυζάντιον in *Sam.* 98–9.

58: πανήγυ]ριϲ is probably too short, but so suitable that it is tempting to suppose that some mistake of writing or fault in the papyrus caused the word to take up more space than it should have done. Probably που— τίϲ . . .; rather than ποῦ τιϲ . . .;

59–60: Perhaps, e.g., εἰ ϲυνδραμεῖται δῆμοϲ, εἷϲ τιϲ οὐ ταχὺ | τὴν παῖδ' ἀφελκύϲαιτ' ἄν, 'a single person will not quickly drag the girl away (for himself)'; i.e. if a public claim is made that the girl is free, her present owner will not be able to carry her off from the collected crowd. ἀφέλκω, like ἕλκω, is normally used in the active, but the middle is found in Ar. *Acharnians* 1120. For the confusion of ϲ and τ cf. 121, 199, 249, 254, 282. This makes ἀφελκύϲαι γ' ἄν a less likely correction.

72–108: An obscure fragment; the latter part, 86 ff., is much damaged and difficult to read. If the paragraphi seen by some scholars below 95, 96, and 97 are really there, a conversation is in progress. But Coles regards them as uncertain, and it is possible that the speaker of a monologue reports or imagines some conversation. There is a paragraphus below 108; hence μειράκιον of 109 may be a vocative, and so suggest that the previous speaker is Moschion. It would appear from 102–5 that he has learnt from the words of a servant that a girl is of citizen birth, and therefore someone of concern to the citizens in general. The girl must be Philumene and the servant is presumably Dromon. This may be associated with 206–7, where Moschion says that he has heard most of the facts from a conversation between Dromon and his master, by which I take it he means Stratophanes. Since Stratophanes shows no sign of recognizing him, Moschion probably overheard the conversation. In the earlier part of the fragment, 72 ff., he may perhaps complain, as Kassel suggests, that Dromon has been ungrateful and wrecked his chances. This could be by taking the girl off to seek refuge at an altar. That Moschion knows of this move is almost certain, because he turns up there, hardly by accident (200). Then it may be guessed that the subject of φηcί in 97 is Dromon, and that this is the explanation he gave of his action in taking the girl away: she is afraid (or he is afraid for her) of her master, a foreigner (?), who is in love with her (cf. 241).

78 οἰκότριψ: A slave born and bred in the house. Like the Roman *uerna*, such might be both favoured (Aelian, *VH* xii. 15) and loyal. But the word was applied as a term of abuse to free persons, Ar. *Thesm.* 426, ᾠκότριψ Εὐριπίδης, [Dem.] xiii. 24, οἰκοτρίβων οἰκότριβας (foreigners). Some believed the word to denote a domestic slave, whether born in the house or not, see frag. 1 n.

80 ἀπολέcαι: Optative, cf. *Epitr.* 424, κακὸν κακῶc ὁ Ζεὺc ἀπολέcαι, *Sam.* 689.

82 ἀνῄρηκαc: Cf. *Dysk.* 595, ἀνῃρηκυῖά [με.

93: Kassel and Austin suggest τὴν παῖδα παρακάλει. Something of this sort would suit my proposed interpretation of the passage, if Moschion here addresses himself.

94–6: The damage to the writing is severe: attempts to read the first line have given varied and unintelligible results, but the text printed in OCT for 95 and 96 has some probability. δίδωμι and δέχομαι are often associated, as in frags. 358, 485.

97–109: There are no paragraphi, except below verse 108. Is the speaker Moschion, who reflects on something he has heard, or overheard? He rejects the idea that it is none of his business; he must pluck up his courage: the girl is of concern to all citizens.

97 δέδοικε: The subject is probably Philumene, but could be someone who fears for her.

98: Cf. *Pap. Ant.* 55 d recto 3, πρῶ]τον μέν, ἔςτι κύ[ριος ς]οῦ, δεύ[τερον
. . .]τος, ⟨τὸ⟩ τρίτον, ἐρᾶ. **ξένον:** As an Athenian of citizen birth,
Philumene would hope for a marriage to an Athenian : a foreign lover
could never become her husband.

100 ἐμοὶ δὲ καὶ τούτῳ κτλ.: Cf. *Dysk.* 114. **τούτῳ:** The subject of
φηςι, or the δεςπότης?

104: This line seems to have too many letters. Gallavotti's νὴ [{τὸν}
Δί]α is tempting (on the apparent broken anapaest see *Dysk.* 774 n.),
but the second or third missing letter seems to have had a flat base.
Barigazzi's ἦ[ν δῆλο]ν {τοις} meets this requirement, but τοῖς cannot
be dispensed with.

109 πορνη is very dubious : perhaps ...ρχη.

110–149: *Stratophanes, Theron, and Pyrrhias* (enters 124)

110–24: Stratophanes and Theron are in conversation. The latter
approves some plan of action decided by his patron. It seems to concern his preventing his possessions falling into other hands (118). This
may have something to do with the fact that his supposed father has
died owing a large sum through a decision of the courts, a sum for
which he would be liable (see 133 ff. and 138 n.). The conversation is
interrupted because one or the other sees the slave Pyrrhias approaching. He had been sent on ahead to announce their safe arrival on the
mainland after their sea-crossing, perhaps even after a campaign.
His return is unexpected.

The details are irrecoverable. Probably the enthusiastic phrases of
assent, εὖ γε νὴ Δία and εὖ γε νὴ τὸν Ἥλιον, with the next two lines,
belong to the κόλαξ Theron, perhaps more.

112 ἐπιπαροξυνθήσεται: 'He will be still further incited' or 'enraged'.
The compound is not recorded elsewhere before the end of the second
century A.D.

113 εἶτα μή is altered by Handley to εἴτε μή, perhaps rightly ; but
Jacques defends the solecism of μή for οὐ, quoting Xenarchos frag.
8 K, εἶθ' ἁλιεὺς ὢν †ἄκρος ςοφίαν† ἐπὶ μὲν παγούροις . . . γέροντα
βούγλωττον δὲ μὴ ταχέως πάνυ ςυναρπάςομαι; πεπράξεται is a more
likely correction of πεπράξεται than is πεπράςεται, 'will be sold', but
either is possible.

114 ἔςτ]ω is supported by the occurrence of ἔςτω, δεδόχθω in
Aristainetos i. 21 (Jacques).

115: διὰ λογιςμόν or διαλογιςμόν? The compound noun has the senses
'balancing of accounts', 'consideration', 'discussion'.

119–20: At the beginning of 120 one speaker must say something to indicate the approach of Pyrrhias. This leaves little space for a verb after οἵτινες; it may have been suppressed by the idiom exemplified in 265 n., 'whoever they may be'; but more probably the sentence was interrupted by an exclamation prompted by the arrival of Pyrrhias. If Pyrrhias was mentioned in the first part of 120, e.g. Πυρρίας, δοκῶ γε—, the reply may be (ὁ) ποῖος Πυρρίας; 'What Pyrrhias?' But I think more likely, e.g., μὴ προσέρχεται δ'— :: ὁ ποῖος; :: Πυρρίας: 'Surely this is not—?' 'Who?' 'Pyrrhias . . .'

121 cεcωμένουc: Convincing evidence that cέcωμαι, not cέcωcμαι, was the Attic form was assembled by Rutherford, *New Phrynichus*, 99; it is supported by διαcεcωιμενουc in *IG* ii². 435. 11 (here cωι—, paralleled in *P. Cair. Zen.* 240. 11 (cent. iii B.C.), is due to the influence of cωιζω; similarly ἔcωιcα is found in inscriptions from the fifth century B.C. The original forms, without -ι-, are from *cαο-ω).

122–4: Assignment of speakers can be no more than guesswork.

122: The spelling ὀλίοc for ὀλίγοc, repeated at 155, and perhaps 86, (cf. ὀλιαρχικόc 156), represents a pronunciation ridiculed by Plato Comicus frag. 168 K, ὁ δ' οὐ γὰρ ἠττίκιζεν . . . ὁπότε δ' εἰπεῖν δέοι "ὀλίγον", "ὀλίον" ἔλεγεν. Since in this play the speeches of at least three persons show this dropping of γ, it cannot have been used by Menander for characterization, and may be put down to the account of a copyist. Such spellings occur occasionally in inscriptions as early as Menander's time, e.g. ολιαρχια *IG* ii². 448 (318 B.C., Meisterhans³, 75).

123: It is tempting to join τί οὖν . . . μαθών, 'What's his idea in coming back?' But there is a space after τιουν, that suggests it is independent, as, e.g., *Dysk.* 363, 823.

124: Pyrrhias was presumably walking quickly, like the messenger in Eur. *Hipp.* 1151, cπουδῇ cκυθρωπὸν πρὸc δόμουc ὁρμώμενον, or like Parmenon at *Sam.* 59. His face carries bad news, cf. Eur. *Phoen.* 1332, cκυθρωπὸν ὄμμα καὶ πρόcωπον ἀγγέλου, Ar. *Ach.* 1069, Plaut. *Epid.* 608. In the Greek plays the character does not appear elsewhere, and may have been given a mask with the appropriate facial expression; but this cannot have been done for Plautus' Epidicus, who appears in a variety of scenes. It may well have been left to the spectators to imagine the expression, as they must imagine the tears to which dramatic texts often refer.

125: νεώτερον is a euphemism for a misfortune, as in frag. 774, νεώτερόν τι cοι cυμβέβηκεν; Jacques quotes Aristainetos i. 22, νεώτερόν τι cυμβέβηκε.

126: Unless Stratophanes' mother was referred to by name, it seems impossible to give the first words to Pyrrhias. One could, e.g., restore (*Στ.*) μὴ γὰρ ἡ μητὴρ τέθνηκε; (*Πυ.*) πέρυσιν (Kassel), or μὴ γὰρ ἡ μητήρ—; (*Πυ.*) τέθνηκε πέρυσιν (Handley). If the latter alternative is adopted, it would be better to punctuate τέθνηκε. πέρυσιν (sc. 'it happened'). It is doubtful whether τέθνηκε, a perfect with present meaning, 'she is dead', can be modified by the word πέρυσιν, 'last year'. **γραῦς σφόδρ' ἦν** may belong to any of the three speakers, but we do not *know* that Theron was aware of her great age.

128 ἀνελπίστοις: 'Unexpected'; in Plato, *Apol.* 36 a, Socrates calls the verdict οὐκ ἀνέλπιστον.

129: Clearly, 'You were not X's son', 'Whose then?' But was X the supposed mother or supposed father? For the immediate sequel the important thing is that Stratophanes was not his supposed father's son, and so escaped shouldering the debts that man had incurred. But I do not think this is decisive for the supplement to be chosen here.

130 ἐνθαδί: 'Here', on a tablet that he holds; Stratophanes calls it a γραμματείδιον at 141.

131 ἀποθνήσκων: The masculine participle must be explained by assuming a gnome, to which the present tense φθονεῖ is appropriate; contrast the adjacent ἔγραψεν and ἐβούλετο. If correctly restored, the gnome strikes a somewhat false note (it is not true, and it suggests that until she was on her deathbed Stratophanes' 'mother' did begrudge him the benefit of knowing his parents), and is probably most suitably assigned to Theron. This is the more likely if he spoke the beginnings of 127 and 130; an isolated interruption, although paralleled, is contrary to normal practice. The sentiment reverses that of Dionysios frag. 7 K, τοῖς οὐδὲν οὖσιν οὐδὲ εἷς ὅλως φθονεῖ.

132: ἑαυτοῦ for σεαυτοῦ, cf. frag. 59. 6 n., K–G ii. 572.

133–5: For the construction cf. Isaios vii. 6, τριῶν αὐτῷ ταλάντων δίκην ὀφλεῖν.

135 κατὰ σύμβολα: The reading of the papyrus gives a dactyl, which is not normally admitted in the trochaic tetrameter, *Dysk.* 774 n. One might emend to τὰ σύμβολα, and understand 'the contracts were of many talents'. But (1) it is not this that would be important, but the amount at issue in the lawsuit, (2) the plural 'contracts' is unexpected, (3) a contract is normally συμβολαῖον, whereas σύμβολον is used of 'unilateral' documents, e.g. receipts, see Kahrstedt *RE* 2. Reihe iv A. 1087. σύμβολα was the name given to treaties between states providing for the settlement of commercial disputes between their nationals, LSJ s.v. II. 3, and in view of the context this meaning is very probable here. It is best therefore to accept the dactyl, which has a parallel in *Sam.* 731, καὶ cτεφάνουc ἵνα. **Cτρατοφάνη**: The vocative form is not that recognized by grammarians, who give -όφανεc, -όμενεc, κτλ. Photios s.v. quotes frag. 3, with the remark that Menander uses the voc. Cτρατοφάνη throughout. W. Schulze, *Ἀντί-δωρον, Festschrift J. Wackernagel*, 245, collected evidence from tomb-stones that have an address to the dead man, to show that the forms in -η were standard practice in all parts of the Greek world except Attica, for which there is no evidence. His conclusion that the forms in -εc were literary and dead, those in -η in living use, is confirmed by the evidence of this play. One may see the force of analogy with a-stem nouns such as Cμικρίνηc, voc. Cμικρίνη. Terence, doubtless copying the Greeks of his time, even has Lache, Chreme, where the gen. is Lachetis, Chremetis.

136–7 ἦλθε . . . εἰc Καρίαν: For this position, first and last, of associated words see *Dysk.* 236 n.

138 τούτῳ: Kassel supports his emendation by Plut. *Solon* 13, ἀγώγιμοι τοῖc δανείζουcιν (cf. Dion. Hal. *Ant.* v. 69), *GDI* 1878 (second century B.C.), ἀγώγιμοc ἔcτω Cῶcοc Καλλιξένῳ αὐτὸc καὶ τὰ αὐτοῦ πάντα.

'In Egypt contracts often made a defaulting debtor ἀγώγιμοc, i.e. liable to be summarily hauled away to something like personal private bondage' (J. W. Jones, *Law and Legal Theory of the Greeks*, 243). At Athens the loser in certain commercial cases was liable to arrest until he paid the sum adjudged against him, [Dem.] xxxiii. 1, xxxv. 46–7, lvi. 4, Lipsius, *Attisches Recht*, ii. 633, but he was placed in the public prison.

Nothing seems to stand in the way of the simple assumption that Stratophanes' supposed Sikyonian parents lived in Sikyon. The action against his father will have been in the courts of that country; it was the usual provision of cύμβολα that actions should be in the court of the defendant, Lipsius, *Attisches Recht*, iii. 965 ff. Having lost the case, the father would by the laws of Sikyon become liable to arrest and his property to seizure by the Boeotian to secure the sum adjudged. On his death his son, as successor to his estate, would be in the same position. I do not know whether the Boeotian could exercise his rights of seizure anywhere except in Sikyon (and Boeotia), nor whether the supposed law of Sikyon was identical with that current at Athens. It is certainly true that at Athens a man who accepted an estate was liable for its debts, even though they exceeded the assets, but it is disputed whether a son had the right to renounce his father's estate. On the whole the evidence, discussed by A. R. W. Harrison, *Law of*

Athens, i. 125–9, suggests that he had not. [Andokides] iv. 18 speaks of cύμβολα that provide that foreigners should not be arrested in Attica; but it is not a speech on the evidence of which a wise man would rely.

139 τε joins τὴν οὐcίαν cου to cε.   προὐνοεῖτο . . . καὶ ἀπεδίδου: 'Tried to make this provision for you and to restore you your family'.

140 ἀπεδίδου: Imperfect, 'she tried to restore you'.   εὐλόγωc, 'as was reasonable', is sometimes added at the end of a sentence, e.g. Arist. *EN* 1153ᵇ15. Similarly εἰκότωc, 'as might be expected', *Dysk.* 737.

τοῖc ἑαυτῶν for τοῖc (c)εαυτοῦ is inexplicable, but no emendation is plausible. If two groups *ABΓ* and *KΛM*, related to one another, meet, it would be possible to say both that *ABΓ* cυγγίγνονται τοῖc ἑαυτῶν and that *KΛM* cυγγίγνονται τοῖc ἑαυτῶν. Thus οἱ ἑαυτῶν might be felt to mean 'the family', and be used illogically where οἱ ἑαυτοῦ would be correct. But there is no evidence that this did happen.

141 γραμματειδίον: A diminutive of γραμματεῖον, 'a writing-tablet'. This is the correct spelling, as in frag. 278 and in *Pap. Ant.* 55. S's γραμματιδιον should be from γραμμάτιον, itself a rare diminutive of γράμμα. Although the substitution of ι for ει becomes common only after 100 B.C., a number of instances are found in Attic inscriptions of the third century (Meisterhans³, 48³⁵⁷) and at 274 S has μιρακιον for μειρακιον. The mistake is probably that of the papyrus rather than of of the poet himself.   καὶ ταδὶ χωρὶc γ' ἔχω: 'The effect of γε in καὶ . . . γε is to stress the addition made by καί', Denniston, *GP* 157. S's λέγω is intolerably awkward both in sense and in word-order (= ταδὶ χωρὶc τῶν γεγραμμένων λέγω γνωρίcματα); the mistake may be due to λογωc (immediately above in the preceding line). Kassel's φέρω is also a possible correction, but palaeographically a little less likely than γ' εχω. The meaning is in any case the same.

142 ἐκείνοιc: This word can be explained as denoting the same persons as are referred to by the phrase τοῖc ἑαυτῶν in 140. Stratophanes' 'mother' had sent him a letter addressed to his real parents, to inform them of the identity of the bearer (A. Oguse, *Ant. Class.* xxxv [1966], 623). But I am not certain this is right. Letters and tokens would then be used in conjunction to establish the identity; why are they here distinguished (χωρίc)? One would rather suppose that the letter informed Stratophanes who he was, and that the tokens would have a meaning for his parents. Various corrections have been proposed. ἐκείνῃ or ἐκείνων would make sense, but neither accounts for the corruption. I have thought of ἐκεῖ coι; εκεισοιcτρ could become εκεινοιccτρ under the influence of εκεινην in the line below; for ἐκεῖ γεγραμμένων cf. ἐνθαδὶ . . . ἔγραψε (130–1).   γνωρίcματα καὶ τεκμήρια: A hendiadys, 'evidential tokens of identity'.

144 cαυτῆc πόει: 'Make him one of yours', i.e. an Athenian citizen, and so able to marry (λάβῃ) Philumene, who must already be known to be of citizen birth. Does Theron hope to *marry* Malthake, who may be a *hetaira*, or does he use the word in a different sense, hoping only to 'get' her? Pollux iv. 119 writes οἱ δὲ παράcιτοι μελαίνῃ ἢ φαιᾷ (sc. χρῶνται ἐcθῆτι), πλὴν ἐν Cικυωνίῳ λευκῇ, ὅτε μέλλει γαμεῖν ὁ παράcιτοc. If this refers to Menander's play (frag. 377 Körte), probably Theron did look forward to marriage with Malthake, since it is hard to see who else could have been the bride. It is improbable that he could enter into a marriage ἐπ' ἀρότῳ γνηcίων παίδων with Malthake, so far as membership of the Athenian state was concerned. But they may have been in a position to contract a marriage that would be recognized by the law of some other state, where conditions were less strict. During his speech, Stratophanes peruses the tablet, but keeps its content to himself. Without wasting any words, he gives the orders that the situation demands: he is accustomed to command.

146 οὐ λέγειc μοι; 'Aren't you telling me what's in the letter?' According to Plutarch, *quomodo adulator etc.* 50 e, a dangerous type of κόλαξ is the one who πράξεων μετέχειν οἴεται δεῖν καὶ λόγων ἀπορρήτων βούλεται κοινωνὸc εἶναι. Theron tries to insinuate himself into Stratophanes' confidence, and is snubbed by the reply, 'move on'. This illuminates the relation between soldier and parasite, but at the same time serves as an excuse for not letting the audience into the know about the letter's contents, which are first partially revealed at 247–51.

146 δεῦρο: 'This way', i.e. 'come with me', not 'to me', as in Ar. *Clouds* 505, οὐ μὴ λαλήcειc, ἀλλ' ἀκολουθήcειc ἐμοὶ | ἀνύcαc τι δευρὶ θᾶττον.

147 ἀλλ' ὅμωc: For this protesting phrase cf. *Epitr.* 230.   κἀγώ—: ? 'I too am interested.'

148 τὰ cύμβολα: 'The supporting evidence' in the shape of the γνωρίcματα and τεκμήρια. εὐθέωc, although fairly frequent in the comic fragments, has as yet occurred only here and at *Sam.* 7 in Menander, who frequently has εὐθύc.

ACT IV

(i) 150–168: *Smikrines* (?), *another*

150 ff.: That the act here beginning is the fourth is shown by the stichometric letter *H* (= 700) which stands in the margin against 151 and roughly indicates the number of lines so far copied. Two persons enter, and perhaps a third. The presence of a third person is suggested by the plurals βουλόμεθ' ἀκοῦσαι, 172 and ἡμῖν 175, but one man can use a plural of himself, cf. *Dysk.* 455, 562, etc.

One speaker is probably named Smikrines, and is probably the man who later proves to be Stratophanes' father. The identity of the other is quite obscure. Nothing favours or excludes the possibility that he is Kichesias. The subject of the two men's conversation is also obscure. Smikrines, as with slight reservation we may call him, criticizes his companion for supposing that a man who 'weeps and entreats' is in the right. It is more likely that this criticism arises from some specific incident than that it comes from an abstract discussion. In the scene, shortly to be recounted in full (188–271), that had taken place in Eleusis, Stratophanes had wept (219) and he *may* have uttered an entreaty in 224–34, lines which are mostly lost. It is therefore possible that the man criticized had been present at that scene, and is supposed to have told Smikrines something of it before they come on the stage. If this interpretation is right (but it is no more than a possibility), then he may not leave at 167, but embark upon a full account, introduced in paratragic style at 169. In favour of the identification of Smikrines' first companion with the 'messenger' is the fact that they both seem to be democratic men (156, 182; A. Barigazzi, *SIFC* xxxvii [1965], 18).

Kassel adopts, perhaps rightly, the alternative view that Smikrines' original companion leaves at 167, and is immediately replaced by another, who halts Smikrines on his doorstep and treats him to a long narrative about the incident at Eleusis; his story told, he abruptly departs (271). If this is correct, the effect must be strange, but can perhaps be understood as a kind of parody of speeches in tragedy, delivered by messengers whose entries and exits are often equally abrupt. It suits this explanation that the speech has a reference to that of the messenger in Eur. *Orestes*, see 176 n.

The reason for supposing that Smikrines is identical with Stratophanes' father is that the recital to him of the incident in Eleusis must lose in dramatic interest if he is not somehow personally concerned in its outcome, although apparently he is unaware of this concern. He is not the girl's father, whose name is Kichesias, but he may well be that of Stratophanes. There would then be comic irony in his judgement that right and tears do not go together: in his ignorance he will be condemning his own son.

Smikrines had appeared in a previous act (cf. B. Marzullo, *QIFG* ii [1967], 46), since his identity must be known to the audience if they are to appreciate the following scene. The person with whom he enters is not necessarily known, and probably unknown *if* identical with the man who introduces himself at 184.

150 ὄχλος: Dem. xix. 24, οἱ δ' ἀντιλέγοντες ὄχλος ἄλλως, 'a mere nuisance'; but here there must be overtones of being one of the mob, as well as tiresome. Cf. also Dion. Hal. *Ant.* v. 75. 1, ὄχλον ἄν τινι καὶ φλυαρίαν φανῆναι τὴν . . . σπουδήν, Dio Chrys. lv. 12, τὰ τοιαῦτα . . . ὄχλον ἄλλως καὶ φλυαρίαν ἡγοῦνται.   **ὦ πόνηρε cύ** is contemptuously pitying, as in *Heros* 6.

152 τὸν δεόμενον: δεῖcθαι is often used of appeals made to a jury's feelings. If the characters are not talking in general terms, but about the scene which is later to be described in detail, the reference here is not to a formal trial, but to the popular decision of a spontaneous meeting.   **δέ:** The use of δέ instead of a stronger adversative (καίτοι, ἀλλά, μὲν οὖν) to introduce a contradiction of the preceding sentence is not very common outside tragedy, Denniston, *GP* 166–7.

cυνεδρίῳ is not certain, but the word is applied by Aischines i. 92 to the Areopagos, a court which had the confidence of conservatives and a reputation for unemotional decisions.

156: At the end of 156 *ed. pr.* read πονηροιcγ[. The photograph leaves no doubt that S has πονηροccμ[; the only subject for hesitation is the last letter. ὁμ[ολογῶ is impossible. Provided, then, that S has made no mistake, there is no practicable alternative to a proper name beginning Cμικρ-, and Smikrines is a name familiar in comedy although not yet known from real life. But all other characters who bear it are close-fisted, to say the least, and there is no sign of that in this character; it would indeed seem an unsuitable trait in the man who will be discovered to be the hero's long-lost father. Accordingly one should not lose sight of the possibility that he was called, not Smikrines, but Smikrion, a name used in Attica, *Pros. Att.* 12746–8, or Smikrias, ibid. 12740–5.

157 ff.: The division between speakers causes difficulty, and is variously done. But the following points may be made: (1) ἀπολεῖτέ με, 'you'll be the end of me', is likely to be spoken by Smikrines, who has already accused his companion of being troublesome (150); (2) ὦ Ἡράκλεις often begins a speech, being a protest: hence the whole of 157 may well belong to the anti-oligarch (there is in fact no space in S after μεγιcτον); (3) Although there is a space after υμεις, τί γάρ μοι λοιδορεῖ; looks like a sequel to what precedes—moreover it suits Smikrines better than the other man, since that other has responded to a rational statement by calling Smikrines names; (4) 160 clearly belongs to the anti-oligarch, since it is Smikrines who has shown himself contemptuous of popular ideas; (5) There is no space after απαντας in 161, and no plausible supplement has been suggested by which ὄχλος ὢν δέ κτλ. could be given to Smikrines—moreover there is a paragraphus below 162: the change of speaker was probably not at the end of the line, so that the indications are that Smikrines says οὐκ ἂν γένοιτο τοῦτο; (6) Kassel's brilliant restoration of 167–8, cκάφηc ἐγὼ γὰρ ἄν c' ἐπόηcα cυνcτομώτερον, could be given to the anti-oligarch, who has started on a tirade of denunciation, which might have ended in Smikrines' having no word to say in self-defence; Smikrines, on the other hand, has done nothing to reduce the other to silence. Nevertheless Smikrines remains on the stage here and it may be that the other departs, thus saving himself from what would have been a crushing reply by Smikrines.

159 λοιδορεῖ: Second person middle, a correction of λοιδορειc: the dative seems not to be used elsewhere in classical Greek with the active, though regular with the middle. Tragedy uses the active only, New Comedy elsewhere the middle only, except in Philemon frag. 23 K, ὁ λοιδορῶν γάρ, ἂν ὁ λοιδορούμενοc | μὴ προcποῆται, λοιδορεῖται λοιδορῶν, where the active form is required for contrast with the passive. At the end of the line a quasi-tragic compound such as βαρύcτομε or βαρύcτονε would not be out of the question; but something simple, like βαρύc τιc εἶ, is equally possible.

160 τοὺc τὰc ὀφρῦc ἐπηρκόταc: 'Those who give themselves airs and disdain the common man'. Such phrases are sometimes applied to philosophers, as by Baton frag. 5 K, οἱ γὰρ τὰc ὀφρῦc ἐπηρκότεc καὶ τὸν φρόνιμον ζητοῦντεc ἐν τοῖc περιπάτοιc, by Amphis frag. 13 K (of Plato), probably by Men. frag. 34. But it is not necessarily philosophers who are so characterized: Alexis frag. 16 K, τοὺc cτρατηγοὺc τὰc ὀφρῦc . . . ἀνεcπακόταc. Kratinos frag. 355 K, ἀνελκταῖc ὀφρύcι cεμνόν, may have referred to Perikles.

161: At the end ω[is more likely than ου[or οι[, and ὄχλοc ὤν δ' ὁμολογῶ makes sense: the democrat is proud of being a nuisance to oligarchs. He might complete the line by, e.g., τιc χρήcιμοc, to which Smikrines retorts that he could never be of use.

162 ἐγώ cε: I doubt whether Smikrines' companion does anything more than hurl wild charges at him.

167 καὶ cύ: This retort to οἴμωζε recurs at *Sam.* 294. **cκάφηc . . . cυνcτομώτερον:** Photios s.v. cυcτομώτερον cκάφηc says that the phrase is used of those who keep quiet διὰ τὸ ἀγενέc, 'low-birth'. Theophrastos (frag. 103 Wimmer) in his περὶ νόμων explained that metics at Athens carried cκάφαι (bowls or trays) in the public processions, and that 'when they wished to indicate a metic, they would use the word cκάφη or cκαφηφόροι, and because the metic had not the right of free speech there was a threat (ἀπειλὴ ⟨ἦ⟩ν: ἀπειλὴν cod., ἀπειλεῖν Porson, ἠπείλουν Kassel) to make one tighter-lipped than a cκάφη'. S.v. cκάφαc Photios adds that the bowls contained honeycombs and cakes, and that Menander used the phrase; Zenobios Athoos i. 59 gives Εὐνοῦχος as the source (frag. 166 Körte).   cυνcτομώτερον: Conventionally we write the phonetic spelling cυc- not cυνc-, but inscriptions show both forms, Meisterhans³, 111–12.

169: On the problem whether the speaker is a new character who enters here, or whether the democrat suddenly turns back and detains the oligarch, see note on 150 ff. If the latter is correct, the oligarch's phrase cκάφης cυcτομώτερον will prove to have been wide of the mark: this could be a comic touch. If the 'messenger' is a new character who enters at 169, Smikrines cannot know that he is in a position to report about the meeting. But he seems to take that for granted at 172 and 175.   ὦ γεραιέ: The word is mainly tragic; it is, as here, scanned γεραιόc in Eur. *HF* 446 and Soph. *OC* 200, where Dindorf introduced the spelling γεραόν, now found in the papyrus of Timotheos, *Persae* 227.   ἐν παραcτά[cιν δόμων: This is a probable supplement, supposing the line, like the next, to be paratragic. παραcτάδεc are properly 'things that stand alongside' a doorway, perhaps pillars, Kratinos frag. 42 K, παραcτάδαc καὶ πρόθυρα βούλει ποικίλα. In Eur. *Andr.* 1121 a παραcτάc has pegs on which armour was hung. But the word is also used of the space between these παραcτάδεc, 'entrance, porch, vestibule', Eur. *IT* 1159, ἔχ' αὐτοῦ πόδα cὸν ἐν παραcτάcιν, *Phoen.* 415, Ἀδράcτου δ' ἦλθον ἐc παραcτάδαc.

170 θωύccειc: 'Shout', a purely tragic word.   τίνοc χάριν; occurs in the paratragic stichomuthia of *Perik.* 801.

171: This is completely mysterious. Kassel suggests, as a long shot, ὡc ἂν cὺ μικρὸν καὶ καπνὸν βλέψῃc πυρόc, 'ut saltem fumum incendii cuius ego spectator fui videre possis'. καπνόc, or καπνοί, is used metaphorically of what is unimportant or empty of meaning (see LSJ); one might think of, e.g., καὶ καπνοὺc μάθηc ἐμούc, the messenger paradoxically treating his story as not worth telling; in tragedy messengers often announce that they have good or bad news. But one suspects that there may be a parody of some lost play.

176 f.: There is an allusion to the speech of the messenger in Eur. *Orestes*, who begins ἐτύγχανον μὲν ἄγροθεν πυλῶν ἔcω βαίνων (866). Merkelbach suggested supplying οὐ[κ ἄγροθε πυλῶν ἔcω] βαίνων, but the similarity may not have extended beyond the initial words ἐτύγχανον μέν and βαίνων. In Lucian's allusion to this same speech, *Juppiter Tragoedus* 33, after an opening ἐτύγχανον μέν there is no echo of Euripides until six lines later there is reached ὁρῶ δ' ὄχλον cτείχοντα (= *Or.* 871, cf. ὄχλον ἰδών here, 188).

There is a parallel between this speech and that of the *Orestes* in that both give an account of a debate before a popular assembly that decides the fate of a man and a woman. The resemblance ends there so far as incidents go, but 182 contains a verbal quotation. The likeness was no doubt intended to catch the notice of a literary spectator, but it is fleeting and its importance not to be exaggerated.

178 καλῶc ποῶν: The Greeks frequently expressed gratitude by a laudatory formula, J. H. Quincey, 'The Greek for Thank you', *JHS* lxxxvi (1966), 133.

180 εἰc τριώβολον: It is tempting to see an allusion to the juryman's pay of three obols. But the word was often used, like 'sixpence', to indicate an insignificant sum of money, e.g. Eubulos frag. 88 K, Philippides frag. 9 K, Nikophanes frag. 12 K. The phrase φοβερὸc εἰc τριώβολον may, then, mean 'terrible' (or 'timorous'), 'down to the last sixpence'.

181 μέγα βοῶν οἶc ἂν τύχω: 'Calling loudly to those I meet' is a phrase that can stand alone; it need not be associated with the preceding words. The sense of 178–81 has unfortunately not been determined.

182: οἵπερ καὶ μόνοι cῴζουcι γῆν is from *Orestes* 920, where it is applied to an αὐτουργόc whose speech the messenger reports. This messenger appropriates it to himself. It is not certain how he describes himself. ἐργατικόc is on the short side, and anyhow Menander is likely to have substituted for αὐτουργόc some word of different meaning, to make a paradoxical line. δημοτικόc, having wider letters, is very possible, and suits the speaker's evident satisfaction in his report of the crowd's action.

183 ἐξ ἄcτεωc: Unlike the Euripidean messenger, who came from the country to the town.

184: The motif of the thin beast sacrificed to make a dinner for the members of a deme recurs in Theokritos iv. 20–2, λεπτὸc μὰν χὠ ταῦροc ὁ πυρρίχοc· αἴθε λάχοιεν | τοὶ τῶ Λαμπριάδα τοὶ δαμόται ὅκκα θύωντι | τᾷ "Ηρᾳ τοιόνδε. In Theophrastos, *Char.* x. 11, the μικρολόγοc is one to ἑcτιῶν τοὺς δημότας μικρὰ τὰ κρέα κόψας παραθεῖναι.

How many members of the Eleusinian deme were there to share an ox? Since Eleusis supplied six or seven *prytaneis* to the *boule* and representation was roughly proportional, one might suppose that in Menander's day, if there were 20,000 male citizens (intro. p. 22), there must have been something between 200 and 250 eligible Eleusinians. But some would be abroad and others might not trouble to come.

The name **Βλέπηc** is that of an Athenian from an inscription of 336 B.C. (*SEG* xix [1963], 149. 33). S has βλεπηιc. The addition of ι is an error to which the writer is prone (114, 214, 242, 252, ?280), but here he may have thought he was supplying its omission. Chantraine's parenthetic βλέπεις; lacks good parallels and supposes a corruption perhaps unlikely at the date of the papyrus, since ηι and ει were not yet confused in pronunciation: note, however, 82 ανειρηκας for ανηιρηκας. τόῦ τῆc θεοῦ κτλ. is such an elaborate way of saying, 'I belong to the deme Eleusis' that I suspect parody of tragedy. Blepes bears the name of Eleusis when he refers to himself formally by his personal name plus his demotic, which distinguishes him from any others who have the name Blepes but belong to other demes. To say that anyone is ἐπώνυμοc means that he is called after someone or something. Thus the Pelasgians are called after Pelasgos, Aesch. *Suppl.* 252, ἐμοῦ δ' . . . ἐπώνυμον γένος Πελασγῶν; Herodotos (ii. 44), having seen a shrine of Herakles Thasios ('of Thasos') in Tyre, speaks of ἱρὸν Ἡρακλέους ἐπωνυμίην ἔχοντος Θασίου εἶναι. In the same way Blepes is called Eleusinios after Eleusis.

188 ἐπέcτην: 'I came to a halt', cf. *Heros* 5.　　**ὄχλον ἰδών:** Eur. *Or.* 871, ὁρῶ δ' ὄχλον.

189 προπυλαίοιc: The great Propylaea at Eleusis were in the north wall of the sanctuary, to which they gave access. Opposite them stood a temple of Artemis and Poseidon.

190 καθημένην: Sitting as a suppliant, cf. Isaios v. 39, τὴν δὲ μητέρ' αὐτοῦ καθημένην ἐν τῷ τῆς Εἰλειθυίας ἱερῷ πάντες ἑώρων. The girl is Philumene.　　**τῶν κύκλῳ:** Since κύκλῳ is often used adverbially, this phrase is as possible as τῶν ἐν τῷ κύκλῳ.

191 δῆμος ἦν: Possibly 'I was the deme', i.e. I made myself its spokesman or representative. But this lacks any real parallel; δῆμον ἐόντα in *Iliad* xii. 213 means 'being a member of the common people', like Horace's *plebs eris* (*Epist.* i. 1. 59). There may be some corruption, but neither δημότην (Chantraine) nor ἐκ τε τούτων τῶν κύκλῳ γενόμενος εὐθὺς δῆμος ἦν, 'there was at once an assembly of the deme formed from those standing around' (Handley), convinces. Hesitantly I place a full stop after γενόμενος. It was not until he had got into the ring that Blepes could see the girl, but in telling his story he anticipates, and then adds the explanatory clause. Then εὐθὺς δῆμος ἦν will mean 'there was at once a popular assembly', or 'an assembly of the deme'. Perhaps an inquiry was made to discover who the girl's κύριος was.

193–5: Obviously spoken by Dromon, who probably takes up a suppliant's position himself with his final words. Whether καθέζομαι or καθίζομαι should be restored in 195 is uncertain. The sequel shows that in the missing verses he has explained that the girl is of Athenian parentage, but separated from her family. ὁ κύριος is the man under whose control the girl has been *de facto*: if her citizenship is proved she will acquire a κύριος *de jure* from among her male relations. The κύριος *de facto* is either the Boeotian creditor or Stratophanes. I incline to suppose the latter, since 241, ἀφεῖται τοῦ φόβου γὰρ ὑπό γ' ἐμοῦ, implies that she had been afraid of what he might do; cf. also 97–8. μεθ' ὑμῶν: 'Among you'.

196 ὠρεχθήcαμεν: Probably 'roared'. "πολῖτίς ἐcτιν ἡ παῖc" is then the cry that went up among the crowd. ὀρεχθεῖν occurs once in Homer, *Il.* xxiii. 30, and ancient grammarians were divided whether to connect it with ῥοχθεῖν and to suppose that it indicated a sound or with ὀρέγεcθαι and to see the meaning 'stretch'. In Ar. *Clouds* 1368, πῶc οἴεcθέ μου τὴν καρδίαν ὀρεχθεῖν; LSJ give the sense 'swell with anger'; but the Homeric κραδίη δέ οἱ ἔνδον ὑλακτεῖ shows that a verb of sound may be applied to the heart. Gow on Theokr. xi. 4 is dubious whether ποτὶ χερcὸν ὀρεχθεῖν means 'roar' or 'swell' towards the shore. The sense 'swell' is clear in Ap. Rhod. i. 275, ii. 49, Nicander, *Alex.* 340, but they may have been taking the less popular side in the grammarians' dispute rather than reflecting any actual usage in speech. In the present passage the meaning might conceivably be that a kind of surge went through the crowd, but some noise of approval or excitement seems more likely in itself and is supported by the following κατεcβέcθη ἦχοc. V. di Benedetto, *Maia* xviii (1966), 64, thinks that Menander may have had in mind ἐπερρόθηcαν in the messenger's speech of Eur. *Orestes* (901).

197 πολῖτιc: Aristotle *Pol.* 1275ᵃ1 ff. shows how difficult it is to define a πολίτης, even as regards one state. To give an exact meaning to πολῖτιc is equally difficult. But at Athens the word must indicate at least one who is the free daughter of a citizen father, and probably one who is herself qualified to be the mother of citizen children (see intro. p. 28).

198 οὐ⟨ν⟩ τῷ: The article ὁ is clearly required, and more neatly so introduced than by Galiano's ὁ τῶν.   **κατεcβέcθη** is a striking metaphor, cf. Soph. *Ajax* 1149, χείμων κατασβέcειε τὴν πολλὴν βοήν. (This passage supports the supplement πολύc.) For the metaphorical treatment of sound as a flame, cf. Bacchylides iii. 12, ὕμνοι φλέγονται, Virgil, *Aen.* x. 895, 'clamore incendere caelum'.   **ἦχοc:** The earliest instance of this word seems to be in a fragment of tragedy, perhaps Euripides, *P. Oxy.* 2746; it is then used by Aristotle, *de divinatione* 463ᵃ13, and Theophrastos, *de sensu* 19, of ringing in the ears. Later authors often use it of the sound of words. Probably it here suggests the confused noise of voices.

199 προcίcταται: 'Approaches and stands'.

200 μειράκιον . . . λευκόχρων: This is Moschion. [Aristotle], *Physiognomica*, i. 31, gives a pale skin (λευκόχρωc) as an indication of the λαγνόc, or lecherous man.   ὑπόλειον: A new word; such compounds, in which ὑπο- has the sense 'rather', are freely invented.   ἀγένειόν τι: τι probably not adverbial, but an adjective attached to μειράκιον, 'some lad'.

201: At the end of the line λαθυ is fairly clear. A reasonable sense is given by μικρὸν λαλεῖν or λέγειν, 'speak quietly', cf., e.g., Plato, *Lysis* 211 a, λάθρᾳ τοῦ Μενεξένου μικρὸν πρόc με λέγων, Philemon frag. 5 K, οὐκ ἂν λαλῇ τιc μικρόν. Handley's proposal to read μικρόν. λαθεῖν keeps closer to S, but can be right only if Moschion was short, a matter on which we have no evidence.

202 μεῖζον λέγε: Cf., e.g., Ar. *Wasps* 963, λέξον μέγα, 'speak up', *Ach.* 103, λέγε δὴ cὺ μεῖζον.

204–7: The final question τί λέγειc; points to an answer from the young man rather than from the servant, i.e. to punctuating after, not before, ὁ θεράπων. For φηcί at the beginning of the line cf. *Sam.* 256. But in neither case does the reply give an intelligible sense, and it may be doubted whether it would even if the plot were better known. οἶδεν οὗτοc is no sort of answer to τί λέγειc;—it is quite clear that both of them know; the crowd wants to know also, itself. Similarly the crowd cannot regard the words as any sort of answer to τίc ἐcτι; I think that we should emend to οἶδέ μ' οὗτοc ὁ θεράπων—πάλαι γὰρ οὖν βοηθῶ—. This will do something to establish the speaker's bona fides: he answers τίc ἐcτι; by saying that he is a well-disposed acquaintance, who has already tried to give his help. γὰρ οὖν is rare in comedy (Ar. *Thesm.* 164, parenthetic as here, Φρυνίχοc—τοῦτον γὰρ οὖν ἀκήκοαc—) but its sense, 'for in fact', is appropriate: the young man protests. κἄν τινοc δέητ' ἐρωτ[ῶ] (the first ω is probable) gives an excellent continuation, as an answer to τί λέγειc; if the phrase can mean 'I am asking him if he needs anything'. But ἐρωτῶ ἐάν . . . is ill attested (Hippokrates, *Steril.* 230 and Thuc. viii. 53, where MSS. are divided between εἴ τινα, ἤν τινα, and ἤντινα). Yet εἰ and ἐάν occur with other verbs of inquiry, e.g. *Od.* viii. 133, ἐρώμεθα . . . εἰ, i. 282, πευcόμενοc . . . ἤν τιc . . ., Xen. *Anab.* iii. 2. 22, cκέψαcθε εἰ . . . Who is Dromon's δεcπότηc? Kichesias cannot be meant, since at this point he has not been recognized. It must be Stratophanes, into whose possession Dromon had come. The meaning of 206–7 will then be 'I have heard' (perhaps 'overheard') 'the greater part of the facts as he was talking to his master'.

208 κόκκινοc: 'Scarlet'. κόκκοc means 'grain of seed', but is also used of the gall that grows on *Quercus coccifera* and was used to make a dye. Compare Dromon frag. 1 K, ἐρυθρότερον κόκκου περιπατοῦντα. ὑπανεδύετο: Not here 'withdrew secretly', but 'fell back a little'.

209–10: Since παντελῶc βδελυρόc is stronger than οὐ cφόδρ' ἤρεcεν, it must have been negatived; otherwise there would have been an anti-climax. βδελυρόc, 'loathsome', is sometimes joined with words meaning shameless, e.g. Ar. *Frogs* 465, ὦ βδελυρὲ καὶ ἀναίcχυντε. Moschion showed by his blushes that he was not entirely lost to shame. I see no alternative to ἤ]μῖν for]μειν at the beginning of 210; although this ι/ει confusion did not set in until the first century B.C., there are isolated examples in the third century, Meisterhans[3], 48[357], and cf. 274 where μιρακιον is written. Antiphanes frag. 68 K has ἤρεcεν cφόδρα | ἡμῖν ἅπαcιν. μοιχώδηc δὲ μᾶλλον κατεφάνη: Moschion's blushes are taken as a sign not only that he had some shame, but also that he had a guilty conscience. The crowd is more sure than before that his intentions towards the girl are dishonourable. His physical appearance had already given rise to suspicion; the Stratophanes of Plaut. *Truc.* denounces his rival as 'moechum . . . umbraticulum' (609).

214: For a discussion of the possibility that a whole column has been lost after 213 see R. A. Coles, *Emerita*, xxxiv (1966), 133. The column that succeeded 193–213 was ornamented in the top left-hand margin with a coronis; all the rest has been cut away. The function of the coronis is uncertain but, if the column is identical with that of which the ends are preserved as 214–35, it may draw attention to the entry, dramatically important, of Stratophanes and his followers. It is diffi-cult to see what material could have occupied a missing column at this point, and it seems safe to regard the surviving text as continuous. There are two other coronides: one marks the end of the play; that at 254 may mark the end of Stratophanes' speech. πεφευγῦ': S retains the correct spelling, universal in fourth-century Attic inscrip-tions, without an ι, Meisterhans[3], 59–60; cf. Herodian ii. 281 Lentz, οἱ Ἀθηναῖοι . . . τὸ τετυφυῖα καὶ γεγραφυῖα τετυφῦα καὶ γεγραφῦα λέγουcιν.

215: There now comes on the scene one who is 'very masculine', in contrast to the somewhat effeminate-looking Moschion. He must be Stratophanes, who is accompanied by Theron and Pyrrhias. The general run of the story is clear: on seeing the girl, Stratophanes fell into a passion of weeping and clutched ⟨his hair⟩; the onlookers ⟨were astonished⟩ and called on him to explain. He declared that he had reared the girl ⟨whom he had got⟩ as a small child ⟨and that he hoped to restore her to her parents who were citizens⟩. (Brackets enclose the elements supplied by conjecture.)

219 πόταμόν τινα [δακρύων: The exaggeration would be unlikely in fifth-century tragedy, which speaks in a more restrained and poetic manner of δακρύων νάματα (e.g. Soph. *Trach.* 919) or πηγαί (id. *Ant.* 803). But it can hardly have seemed violently absurd, for the display of emotion, although perhaps unexpected in a professional soldier, is intended to win him sympathy.

236 ff.: The soldier ends his speech with five short incisive sentences in asyndeton. Although Dromon belongs to him by purchase on the slave-market in Mylasa, he hands him over to the daughter of his original owner. He asks no reward for having reared the girl. He puts no obstacle in the way of her finding her parents.

235: E.g. οἰκέτης ἦν τοῦ] πατρὸς | αὐτῆς (Handley).

236 τροφεῖα: 'Return for nurturing' is more likely than τροφάς, which can have the same meaning, but is mainly poetic, LSJ s.v. II.

ἀφίημι: Remit that to which one has a right, LSJ s.v. II. 2. c.

ἀντιτάττομαι: 'Resist'; this sense was not previously met earlier than Polybios.

239 εὖ γε: 'Hear hear!' from the crowd. Cf. the applause for Praxagora's speech in Ar. *Eccl.* 213, εὖ γ᾽, εὖ γε νὴ Δί᾽ εὖ γε, λέγε, λέγ᾽, ὦγαθέ.

241 ὑπό γ᾽ ἐμοῦ: I.e. 'Whatever others may do, I deny having any claim on her person; she is not my slave, and has nothing to fear from me.'

242 θέςθε: 'Place for safe-keeping'; πρός may be used rather than παρά to suggest taking the girl to the priestess (cf. 258–382 below), or because πρός is often used of actions 'before' an official.

244 εἵλκυς᾽: 'Attracted', not a common metaphorical usage, except with personal objects, e.g. Plato, *Rep.* 458 d, πείθειν καὶ ἕλκειν τὸν πολὺν λεών. But Eur. frag. 419 has ἕλκετε . . . τιμάς.

245: Probably ἀνέκραγον πάλιν, not "λέγε" . . . πάλιν; cf. *Epitr.* 890, ἀνέκραγε . . . πάλιν δέ. For the position of the words, first and last in the sentence, see *Dysk.* 235 n.

247 οὑτοcί: Pyrrhias.

248: The absence of the articles τῆς and τοῦ is remarkable, and belongs to the style of tragedy.

249 καὐτός: I.e. 'I too, as well as the girl, am an Athenian citizen.'

252 ἀφέληςθ᾽: ἀφαιροῦμαι with double accusative, of person and thing, is common in Attic and in tragedy. With ἀφαιρῶ the construction used is dat. or gen. of person, acc. of thing (see LSJ s.v.). τῆς

παρθένου . . . πολίτης: 'The girl's fellow citizen'; the use of the genitive of a single person, not of the whole body of citizens, is unusual,
but cf. Plat. *Prot.* 339 e, ὦ Πρόδικε . . . còc μέντοι Cιμωνίδης πολίτης.

ἔcῳca: The correct form is ἔcωca, but inscriptions from the fifth
century onwards often have the iota adscript, introduced by false
analogy with the present cῴιζω.

254 λαβεῖν: 'Take as wife', as frequently in *Dysk.*   **τοῦτον**: I.e.
τὸν πατέρα, but λαβεῖν τὴν κόρην of course.

255 τῶν ἀντιπραττόντων: Is someone else besides Moschion trying to
get hold of the girl?

259 τε does not join this clause to the preceding sentence, but is
anticipatory of the following καί.

260 cυμπέποιθ': The word must be taken as ironical. The absence of
any particle to indicate irony makes it possible to suspect corruption:
cυμπέπεισθ' (Arnott, Galiano), 'are you convinced . . .?', may be right.

262: τραγῳδία and τραγῳδεῖν are sometimes used of speech or actions
that outdo reality and stir emotion. Here 'melodrama' might serve
as a translation.

263: 'Will take the girl away and then let go of her' or 'keep his hands
off her', cf. Soph. *OT* 1521, cτεῖχε νῦν, τέκνων δ' ἀφοῦ.

264: A cry from the crowd. Moschion's smooth skin and beardlessness
are unfavourably interpreted; to shave is a sign of effeminacy, and so
Agathon is described at *Thesm.* 191 as λευκὸς ἐξυρημένος.

265 μὰ Δία κτλ.: Mette, *Lustrum*, x (1966), 177, keeps S's reading, μὰ
Δί', ἀλλὰ coί τιc—, and supposes it to be an obscenity directed by
Moschion at Stratophanes, who replies with λάcταυρε. I do not think
that indecent insults suit either character, and, if an explanation of this
sort is correct, would prefer to see further cries from the crowd,
suggestively developing the implication of ἐξυρημένον. But one would
expect the suppressed verb to have a direct object in the accusative,
and it would be well to accept Handley's c' ὅcτιc. Then the meaning
would be: 'Not he, but whoever it is who —s you. That's right, isn't
it?' One could compare Virgil, *Ecl.* iii. 8, 'nouimus et qui te—',
Theokritos i. 105, οὐ λέγεται τὰν Κύπριν ὁ βουκόλος, Meleager, *AP* v.
184, οὐχ ὁ περίβλεπτός cε Κλέων; But such an explanation is not entirely
convincing. It is perhaps possible that the first shout (264) should be
addressed to Stratophanes and the second, which takes it up, to
Moschion. The position of cε before ὅcτιc is, however, hard to justify
('a rare type', Dover, *Greek Word Order*, 14); moreover this supposed
second intervener must intend the verb ἀποκτενεῖ, to be understood in

his truncated sentence, to have the weakened sense of Latin *enicare*, English 'be the death of', and although this occurs in other contexts, I can quote no parallel in sexual ones.

Another approach is to suppose μὰ Δία . . . οὐ γάρ; to be a reply by Moschion to the interrupter. 'No, he'll kill you, whoever you are, won't he?' For ὅcτιc cf. Ar. *Frogs* 39, ὡc κενταυρικῶc ἐνήλαθ', ὅcτιc. But this seems singularly devoid of point; why should Stratophanes have anything against a man who seems to be on his side?

Handley (*BICS* xii [1965], 53) toys with some interpretations that suppose τὸν ἐξυρημένον to be Stratophanes, clean-shaven because he was a soldier, but one cannot thus reject the obvious implication of the word, followed in 266 by λάcταυρε.

In this puzzling situation, I adopt without any confidence another solution, namely that Moschion replies to the interrupter, but is himself interrupted, e.g.: 'No, indeed, he won't, but whoever you may be—(sc. may the gods destroy you).' 'Oh, won't he? Out of the way, etc.', cf. Plaut. *Merc.* 434, 'hercle di illunc infelicent, quisquis est', and for οὐ γάρ; introducing a reply *Perik.* 524. An explanation of this kind would make possible the retention of coι τιc—, i.e. (may) some (misfortune fall) on you.

266: λάcταυροc· οἱ μὲν νῦν χρῶνται ἐπὶ τῶν πονηρῶν καὶ ἀξίων cταύρου(!), οἱ δὲ ἀρχαῖοι ἐπὶ τοῦ καταπύγονος, Phrynichos. The word is used in this obscene sense in Theopompos frag. 225a Jacoby, cf. the passage that there shortly follows, beginning οἱ μὲν ξυρόμενοι καὶ λεαινόμενοι.

There is no distinction of meaning between πολλὰ ἀγαθά and πολλὰ καὶ ἀγαθά; for the first cf. *Epitr.* 358, for the second Antiphanes frag. 163 K.

267 ἐκεῖνοc: Stratophanes, and his words are addressed to the girl. But Dromon, who seated himself as a suppliant (so it has been suggested) at 195, now rises and requires the authorization of the crowd before she will move. ναί, βάδιζε is the crowd's reply.

269 ἀνίcτατο: The use of the imperfect rather than the aorist may be due to the proximity of ἐβάδιζε. The imperfect is often used as a narrative tense with verbs of motion, since the action is a continued one. Here there is expressed not the *fact* of getting up, but the whole process of getting up and going. But the supplement is not certain: the imperative ἀνίcταcο is possible.

270: To support his supplement Austin quotes Eur. *Or.* 1498, τὰ δ' ὕcτερ' οὐκέτ' οἶδα.

271 ἀλλ' ἀπέρχομαι: Possibly there is a faint echo of the last words of the messenger in the *Orestes*: they are ἀλλ' ἀπώλεcεν.

272 ff.: The scene that begins here is a lively one. The opening line comes like a clap of thunder after the long narrative which has preceded. Unfortunately it is not clear what is happening. I give first my own view of what is most probable; a similar one is expressed by B. Marzullo, *QIFG* ii (1967), 89.

Not only does Blepes leave the stage at 270; Smikrines does so, too, entering his house, on the doorstep of which he had been detained at 169. The stage is empty, as at *Dysk.* 392 n. Then Stratophanes and Theron enter, with Moschion in hot pursuit. Stratophanes will be on his way to Smikrines' house, for the γένους γνωρίσματα have indicated that he is his father; Moschion has already shown that he suspects Stratophanes of an attempt to secure the girl by a false pretence that he is her fellow citizen, in search of her father, and now he threatens to arrest him and Theron as ἀνδραποδισταί. ἀνδραποδισμός was kidnapping, whether of another person's slave (cf. Plato, *Laws* 879 a) or of a free person (cf. ibid. 955 a).

It would obviously be impossible to keep the kidnapped person safely in Attica, and he or she would be taken abroad for sale; hence Lysias x. 10 argues that παῖδα ἐξαγαγὼν ληφθῆναι means the same as ἀνδραποδιστὴν εἶναι, cf. Dem. xxv. 55. The ἀνδραποδιστής was, like the λωποδύτης and τοιχωρύχος, liable to summary arrest (ἀπαγωγή) by any citizen who took him red-handed, and could be executed by the Eleven without trial, Lipsius, *Attisches Recht*, 78, 317, 330[46].

It is intelligible that Moschion should attempt to put this procedure into operation against Stratophanes, whom he suspects of planning to get hold of Philumene, whether she is the property of the Boeotian who has seized the assets of Stratophanes' father, or a free woman, as had been declared to the crowd; those suspicions he had expressed at 263. Although this would be an unjustifiable use of ἀπαγωγή, since Stratophanes was only a suspect, not a criminal caught ἐπ᾽αὐτοφώρῳ (Lipsius, op. cit. 320[14, 15]), stretching the laws was common enough at Athens: Epikrates in Hypereides' *in Athenogenem* says that he was urged to arrest the Egyptian Athenogenes as an ἀνδραποδιστής, although he seems not to have had a shadow of a case.

Lloyd-Jones supposes that Stratophanes enters, threatening to arrest Smikrines, whom he takes to be Moschion's associate in an attempt to buy Philumene, an attempt frustrated by her taking refuge at an altar. This reconstruction, which rests upon a story that is indeed conceivable, but is not supported by a single word in the extant remains, is much less plausible. (1) It was not an offence to buy a slave who was in fact an Athenian: it would only be an offence to keep as a slave one whose citizenship was known to you. The threat of a charge of ἀνδραποδισμός for the mere intention (and that thwarted)

of doing an act that would not be criminal even if done would be
arrant *cυκoφαντία*, such as one would not ascribe to Stratophanes.
(2) Since Moschion had been discomfited at the public meeting,
Stratophanes, who had got his own way, could neglect him. It was for
the defeated Moschion to make a move against his successful antagonist.
Stratophanes' urgent business was to establish his own Athenian
citizenship. (3) Until that citizenship was established. Stratophanes
would, it must be presumed in view of the general legal status of
foreigners, have had no right to arrest anyone. (4) The would-be
arrester is addressed as *μειράκιον*, a word applied to Moschion at
200. Stratophanes cannot literally be a *μειράκιον* (*Dysk.* 27 n.) since
his supposed mother had died *γραῦc cφόδρα* (126). Perhaps Smikrines
as his elder might insultingly call him *μειράκιον*, 'my lad', but this
is not to my mind very plausible. I have discussed the passage in
PCPS N.s. xiii (1967), 41 ff.; some objections, which I do not find
strong, are raised by J. M. Jacques, *REA* lxix (1967), 309. A fragment from an unknown author (Page, *GLP*, p. 234) has an attempt
to seize an alleged *ἀνδραποδιcτήc*: *δίωκε, Cωcία, cυνάρπαcον τὸν*
ἀνδραποδιcτήν, λαβὲ λάβ' αὐτόν.

The completion of line 272 is uncertain. The best suggestion seems
to me to be Austin's *ὑμᾶc ἐγώ—*. One may remain doubtful about how
Moschion would have proposed to execute the arrest. Stratophanes'
interruption cuts in before he can continue.

273 κορυβαντιᾷc: Lit. 'are you frenzied like a devotee of Kybebe?',
but here no more than 'are you out of your mind?', cf. Ar. *Wasps* 8,
ἦ παραφρονεῖc ἐτεὸν ἦ κορυβαντιᾷc; and *Theophorumene* 27 n.

274 ἐξαίφνηc πολιτ[: If, as is suggested in the note on 272, this is
spoken by Moschion, he reiterates his doubts, expressed at the meeting (260 ff.), of Stratophanes' sudden claim to be an Athenian. Then
at 277 he will challenge him to have his claim examined.

275 γενναῖον I take to be a sarcastic adjective, 'magnificent' cf.
Plato, *Rep.* 348 d, 363 a, 488 c, etc., standing alone as an exclamation,
as other neuter adjectives do in Menander, e.g. *Epitr.* 436, *Perik.* 325.

280 ff.: The extent of the gap after 279 is uncertain. But 137 verses of
the act preceded, and 32 more are to come, making 169 in all. If one
column (of 21 to 25 verses) is missing, the act would have just over 190
verses; if two are missing, about 215; if three, about 240. An act longer
than that is unlikely. A single column barely gives room for the opening of the recognition scene towards the end of which 280 must be
placed: therefore it may be supposed that *c.* 45 or *c.* 65 verses are lost.

There are three speakers in the recognition scene: Stratophanes

(309), Smikrines (286?, 310), and Smikrines' wife (290?, 306). Hence Moschion, if present at all, must be represented by a *muta persona*. He has therefore left the stage at some point in the gap. This would not be difficult to manage. If Stratophanes declared that he was looking for Smikrines, Moschion could reply: 'Why, he's my father! I will go and tell him that there is someone here who claims to be his son.'

Except that 280 has no caesura, the metre of the first seven lines appears to be that of tragedy; and the scanty remains of the next seventeen contain nothing that is not tragic. This recalls the recognition scene of *Perikeiromene*: see the last paragraph of the note on 779 ff. of that play.

280 πτέρυξ: 'A half', cf. *Epitr*. 404 n.   **διπλῆ:** Although adverbial διπλῆ is known (Eur. *Ion* 760, κεἰ θανεῖν μέλλω διπλῆ), the adjectival use of a folded article of dress is familiar (e.g. *Il*. x. 134, Apollod. Caryst. frag. 3, ἐπωμίδα πτύξας διπλῆν), and probable here. The addition of ι is a frequent error in S (6, 33, 60, 114, 129, 137, 188).

281 ἐξεπέμπομεν: Cf. Lysias xvi. 4, ἡμᾶς γὰρ ὁ πατὴρ πρὸ τῆς ἐν Ἑλλησπόντῳ cυμφορᾶc ὡc Cάτυρον τὸν ἐν τῷ Πόντῳ διαιτηcομένουc ἐξέπεμψεν. The speaker, Mantitheos, may have been a child, but cannot have been an infant. The reason for sending him away does not appear. Soph. *El*. 1130 has δόμων δέ c', ὦ παῖ, λαμπρὸν ἐξέπεμψ' ἐγώ. Elektra sent the young Orestes away for his life, which would have been insecure while he was in Aigisthos' power. There is nothing here to indicate why Stratophanes' parents had wished, or been willing, to part with him.

282 πρὸς τὴν ξένην: It is hardly possible to dissociate ξένην from αἰτοῦcαν; otherwise εἰc τὴν ξένην sc. γῆν (Körte), 'abroad', might be considered. Or is it conceivable that Sikyon, being for some reason short of children, invited gifts of children from citizens of other states? It is more likely that the Sikyonian was a guest-friend of Stratophanes' father, and his wife, being childless, asked their Athenian friends to give her their own child. The plural τέκνα is, however, then odd (? τέκνον Jacques).

283 ff.: Restoration here seems to be impossible. But in 285 Schroeder's πέριξ ἰώ]δουc τοὖν μέcῳ δὲ πορφυρᾶc may be on the right lines, but πορφύραc would be more likely, since a noun in 286 to agree with the adjective is hard to provide.

288 λαμπαδηφόρου: A runner in a torch-race (?), as in Ar. frag. 422, or an adjective attached to a noun such as δρόμου. Perhaps the word is used metaphorically.

311: Gallavotti's suggestion ἡμᾶς γὰρ ἔνδο[ν] προc[δοκῶνθ' εὑρήcομεν is not impossible. Although there is space for two letters in the gap before προc, the original text has been erased and another substituted, and the second one may have been shorter. If the suggestion is right, it would provide strong support for my account of Moschion's movements, in the notes on 272 ff. and 280 ff.

ACT V

(i) 312–360: *Theron, Kichesias*

312: Theron enters with Kichesias, whom he intends to bribe to bear witness that Philumene is the legitimate daughter of an Athenian citizen; he is quite unaware of Kichesias' identity, having picked him up as a complete stranger, whose obvious poverty is likely to make him ready to do what is wanted. In the first lines Kichesias seems to protest against having been brought a long walk; what project has Theron of adequate importance? Theron must be supposed to have lured Kichesias by vague talk of some possible advantage to be gained. He has not yet revealed what he wants, because he hopes that by inducing Kichesias to come with him he will establish a relationship that Kichesias will find hard to break when his proposal is made. Kichesias, on the other hand, a somewhat broken and bewildered old man, has so far succumbed to Theron's plausible manner. It was essential for the play that Theron's proposal should be made on the stage, and not when he originally found Kichesias; Menander's method of achieving this most skilfully illuminates the characters of the two men, and gives no suspicion of artificiality.

From 316 the remains have defied any plausible reconstruction. In 319 'chatting brutally (θηριωδῶc Schroeder)' is an odd phrase, and I see no occasion for an insult (θηρίον vocative, Lloyd-Jones). Who is this tax-gatherer or customs-man?

The suspicion presents itself that ἄξιον ἀκριβῶc ἴcθι is Theron's reply to Kichesias' ἄξιον in 313, just as cπουδαῖον in 318 corresponds to cπουδαῖο[ν in 312. Perhaps the paragraphi below 316 and 317 are misplaced and should be below 315 and 316; then the lines could have some such form as (Θη.) πάνυ | ἄξιον, ἀκριβῶc ἴcθι, γινώcκειν. (Κι.) τί οὖν; | (Θη.) τίc εἰμι, μὰ τὸν Ἥφαιcτον οὐκ ἠπίcταcο, | cπουδαῖον ἂν δέξῃ με μηδὲν ὑποβαλεῖν.

343 ff.: The key to understanding this scene lies in a similarity with Plautus' *Poenulus*. There Milphio wishes to procure someone to pose as the father of two girls, who are in the hands of a slave-dealer, and so secure their release. He lights upon Hanno, who is in fact the girl's father. Hanno does not reject the idea indignantly, but volunteers that he *had* lost two daughters, along with their nurse, by kidnapping. Milphio thinks that Hanno has fallen in with his game and is merely pretending: when he weeps at the memory, he praises him for being even more cunning than himself:

> filias dicas tuas | surruptasque esse paruolas Carthagine. | manu liberali caussa ambas adseras | quasi filiae tuae sint ambae. intellegis? | HA. intellego hercle. nam mihi item gnatae duae | cum nutrice una surruptae sunt paruolae. | MI. lepide hercle adsimulas. iam in principio id mihi placet. | HA. pol magis quam uellem. MI. eu hercle mortalem catum! | malum crudumque et callidum et subdolum! | ut adflet, quo illud gestu faciat facilius! | me quoque dolis iam superat architectonem (1100–10).

Although Menander's scene is much more subtle, there are obvious parallels: intellegis?~ἆρ' ὑπέλαβες, lepide hercle!, eu hercle! ~ εὖ γε, εὖ πάνυ, ἄριστα, mortalem catum! ~ ἀγαθὸς ἄνθρωπος, ut adflet ~ τό τ' ἐπιδάκρυον, me quoque superat ~ πολὺ cὺ βέλτιον λέγειc.

Here Theron has put to Kichesias some proposition which causes him to protest indignantly that 'Kichesias would never act so', whereupon Theron says: 'This is a much better plan; pretend to be Kichesias, for fortunately you are short and snub-nosed as he is said to be; and add that you lost your daughter from Halae when she was four years old.' It appears from this (1) that Theron had not originally asked Kichesias to pretend to be Philumene's father: he had not required of him what Milphio requires of Hanno; (2) that he had said that Philumene's father was called Kichesias, since otherwise he could hardly fail to be astonished that the stranger should pretend to bear that not very common name. One may guess that Theron's suggestion had been that his tool should pretend to recognize the girl as Kichesias' daughter.

The orators give examples of perjury to secure citizenship for those who bribe the witnesses: Dem. lvii. 52 speaks of citizens being bribed to say that they are relatives of non-citizens, Isaios xii. 2 of adopting rich foreigners (who, by implication, will be declared to be of citizen birth and so enrolled in the deme).

343: The text printed in OCT, ἀποφθερεῖ for αποφθαρει, supposes only the common error of S by which α and ε are confused: for the wording compare Ar. *Knights* 892, *Clouds* 789, οὐκ ἐc κόρακαc ἀποφθερεῖ; The alternative ἀποφθαρείc, taking οὐκ εἰc τὸν ὄλεθρον; as complete sense in itself, is palaeographically less likely, although independent οὐκ εἰc ὄλεθρον is to be paralleled in Soph. *OT* 430, 1146.

The parenthetic χαλεπὸc ἦcθα, suspected by Lloyd-Jones as 'singularly flat', can hardly be addressed by Kichesias to Theron, who may have been annoying or insulting, but not 'cruel', 'angry', or 'difficult to manage'. It must be spoken by Theron to Kichesias, possibly *sotto voce*. Kichesias turns out to be 'a difficult customer'. The imperfect of εἰμί is idiomatically used of what was true all along but has only just been discovered, Goodwin, *MT* 39. The absence of ἄρα is unusual, but cf. *Epitr.* 1114, παχύδερμος ἦcθα, Theok. v. 79, ἦ cτωμύλος ἦcθα.

345 λαβεῖν ἀργύριον: 'Take a bribe', as in Ar. *Eccl.* 186. χρήματ' εἰληφώς, *Perik.* 467, is a variant of the phrase.

346 ἀδίκου πράγματος: For this exclamatory gen. cf. *Epitr.* 371, where it is plausibly restored.

347: The division of speeches is difficult, and I am not confident that I have it right. Theron does not take Kichesias' indignation seriously. He believes that by assuming (as he thinks) the name Kichesias, the man he is talking to is indicating his readiness to impersonate that character. He may then repeat the name, Κιχηcίαν (346), with enthusiasm. Kichesias confirms it: 'Yes, born one of the Skambonidai.' 'Splendid,' replies Theron, 'have you got it, then? Take your pay for that, not for what I previously suggested.' But it is possible that Kichesias repeats his own name, and Theron replies: 'Yes, born one of the Skambonidai. Splendid etc.' I do not see how S's γενόμενος can be maintained. γενόμενον is the simplest change, but J. Martin's γε τὸ γένος supplies a welcome γε of assent. The deme Skambonidai belonged to the trittys Leukonoë, a town-trittys to the NE. of the city. Theoretically its members belonged to a single family, J. Toepfer, *Attische Genealogie*, 314.

348 πρᾶξαι: Imperative of the middle, as in Ar. *Clouds* 245, μιcθὸν δ' ὅντιν' ἂν πράττῃ με.

349 τοῦ τίνος: Cf. τὸ τί; Ar. *Peace* 693, 696, *Wasps* 818, etc. **Κιχηcίαc Cκαμβωνίδηc γε:** Theron repeats the name and demotic with relish. Handley's correction γ' εἶ is not necessary, and perhaps awkwardly anticipates οὗτος γενοῦ (352), 'become Kichesias!'

351: 'It's clear you see the outline of the affair', cf. Damox. frag. 2. 51 K, νοεῖc τὸν τύπον, Plato, *Rep.* 491 c, ἔχειc γὰρ τὸν τύπον ὧν λέγω.

353: Theron notices that his 'tool' is well equipped to impersonate Kichesias, having some of his physical characteristics. ὁ θεράπων must be Dromon, and the occasion of his having given the information in Theron's hearing may have been that alluded to in 207.

354: The paragraphus below 353 indicates that Kichesias' speech begins with γέρων, 'I have become the old man I am'. Kassel believes S to be mistaken, and gives the word to Theron. This has the advantage that ὅϲ εἰμι γέγονα has double point. To Theron it is a mere platitude, to Kichesias it means 'I have turned (in this man's sight) into the man I am'.

355 Ἀλῆθεν: There were two demes called Halai, both on the coast, so that either might be the scene of a piratical raid. Halai Araphenides lay on the NE. coast of Attica next to Brauron, Halai Aixonides on that between Phaleron and Sunium, which was the scene of the kidnapping of the girl in Terence's *Eunuchus* (519 ff.); both were named after the salt-pans that were exploited in their territory. See C. J. W. Eliot, *The Coastal Demes of Attica*, 25 ff. τετραετέϲ: Similarly Hanno's daughter was kidnapped at the age of four (Plaut. *Poen*. 85).

356: The allocation of speeches is difficult. Kassel gives Δρόμωνα . . . ἀπολέϲαϲ to Kichesias, which follows the model of *Poenulus*, where it is Hanno who mentions the loss of the nurse along with his daughters. But here I think that it is more probable that Theron, who imagines himself to be priming the other with the details of the story to be told, should give the name of Dromon. Perhaps it is also not very likely that Kichesias, reminded of the loss of his daughter, should react by naming the slave he had lost on the same occasion. With Kassel's division the second ἀπολέϲαϲ is awkward. I accept Austin's view that Theron's speech continues to Δρόμωνά τ' οἰκέτην, but not his change of ἀπολέϲαϲ to Ἄπολλον; Kichesias picks up the word ἀπολέϲαϲ, which he refers particularly to his daughter and utters with a deep emotion that elicits a 'bravo' from Theron; he continues with ἁρπαϲθὲν ὑπὸ ληϲτῶν, the participle agreeing with θυγάτριον, the person in his thought.

358 θυρᾶϲ is very improbable. Of the remedies proposed θυγατρόϲ (Post, Barigazzi) is the most attractive; οἰκτρόϲ is not elsewhere applied by Menander to a person, but it is so used in tragedy, e.g. Soph. *OT* 58, ὦ παῖδεϲ οἰκτροί.

(ii) **361–396**: *Theron* (exit 367), *Dromon and Kichesias* (exeunt 385), *Stratophanes* (enters 377).

361: Kassel supposes that Dromon has been listening and here comes forward. But a slave who has found his master after a dozen years' separation would not approach him with a sentence formally constructed with μέν and δέ clauses. Rather Dromon here enters, talking to himself and at first does not notice Kichesias. 'My young mistress is being safely taken care of; now I must look for her father.' If πάτερ is right, he must catch sight of Kichesias in the middle of 362, e.g. τὸν δεϲπότην δ' ἤδη—Κιχηϲία, πάτερ.

363 ἀνίϲταϲο: Similarly when Philokleon faints in Ar. *Wasps* 998, . . .

ἀλλ' ἀνίϲταϲο. Some scholars, e.g. Gallavotti, *Maia*, xix (1967), 202, keep S's ἀνίϲταϲαι as a question, but this is unconvincing; would not οὐκ be needed?

368 ἀναφέρεται γάρ: The intrans. active is more common, but cf. Theopompos Com. frag. 66 K, ἄφωνος ἐγένετο ἔπειτα μέντοι πάλιν ἀνενέχθη.

369 τί ἐϲτί; Kassel notes how, as Kichesias comes round, his sentences become longer. λόγου φήμην is poetical, cf. Soph. *Phil.* 846, but not periphrastic (LSJ); the λόγος is the sense of the statement, φήμη its utterance.

370 ἔϲτι . . . καὶ ϲᾠζεται: Cf. Heliod. ii. 2. 1, ἔϲτι Χαρίκλεια καὶ ϲᾠζεται.

371 καλῶϲ: The fate of a kidnapped girl might well be to become a *hetaira*; the fate that threatens the heroines of *Poenulus*, *Rudens*, and possibly *Eunuchus*.

372 αὐτὸ τοῦτο: 'Just that', 'that and no more', as again at 374. Plato's αὐτὸ τὸ καλόν is what is 'just beautiful', not also, e.g., a man or a building or a sound.

376 οὕτω must, if καλῶϲ is kept, mean 'if Philumene is safe'. But I believe that καλῶϲ is, as often happens, a mistake for κακῶϲ, when οὕτω will mean 'if a man is old, poor, and lonely'. The sentiment is like that of Philemon frag. 125 K, πῶϲ ἡμῖν ἔχεις; :: μηδέποτ' ἐρώτα τοῦτ' ἐπὰν γέροντ' ἴδῃϲ | ἢ γραῦν τιν', ἴϲθι δ' εὐθὺϲ ὅτι κακῶϲ ἔχει, and the couplet ascribed to 'Philistion' (i.e. Philemon) in *Comparatio Menandri et Philistionis*, ii. 44 Jaekel, ἐπὰν ἴδῃϲ γέροντα ⟨πενιχρὸν add. Studemund⟩ καὶ μόνον, μηδὲν ἐπερώτα· πάντα γὰρ κακῶϲ ἔχει.

377–82: The pace of these lines is extraordinary: no time is wasted over introductions, and Stratophanes is not allowed to develop his broad hint that he is a suitor for Philumene's hand. Dromon, whose excitement comes out in the repeated initial vocative Ϲτρατοφάνη, placed at the line-end to cut in on the previous speaker, is anxious to reunite father and daughter. Old Kichesias is too bewildered to say more than three words, and those he does not directly address to Stratophanes—an excellent touch.

377: The words with which Stratophanes comes on the stage may have the function of showing that his parents too have been informed of what has been reported.

379 πάτερ: Simply the well-known respectful address to a senior, as in 381, *Dysk.* 171.   **μακάριοϲ:** A word often used of the bridegroom, 400, *Aspis* 294, *Dysk.* 389, *Mis.* 260, Eur. *IA* 1405.

382: The letter after the gap is very uncertain: ϲ, π, ζ appear to be possible. νῦν βαδίζωμεν is doubtless the sense required.

383: Kassel's ἡγοῦ ϲ[ὺ τωιδε] does not fit the traces, nor is β[αδιζε] satisfactory. Perhaps λ[αβὼν ϲύ]. For the end of the line cf. Philemon frag. 79 K, ἐδίωκον κατὰ πόδαϲ ('on his heels').

384–5: The left-hand edge of the column, which sloped to the left as it descended, probably became vertical for the last lines, to judge by the next column, where it is preserved. If so, ἐγὼ δι]ώκω or ἐκεῖ δι]ώκω (*Dysk.* 378) fits better than ὑμᾶϲ δι]ώκω, and προάγ]ωμεν will be long enough in 385. τ[οῖϲ ἔνδο]ν is quite adequate to fill the gap in the later part of 384.

Kassel's reading ἡμερᾳ.κ seems to lead nowhere, and there is room for more than three uncertain letters. προάγωμεν ἡμεῖϲ seems called for, followed by δή or ὤ. Austin, however, who examined S for me, much preferred ρ to ι. Dromon departs with Kichesias, while Stratophanes attends to his personal affairs, calling a slave Donax out from his house.

386 ff.: It is odd that Stratophanes should go into such detail about the transference of his belongings from his hired house to that of his newly found mother. It must be supposed, of course, that he had warned her of his intentions. There may be some dramatic point of which we are unaware; but perhaps the lines are there to give an actor who had played Dromon or Kichesias time to change his dress and mask so as to appear as Moschion at 397.

A question hard to answer is whether the whole of Stratophanes' following is to remove, or whether, as Handley suggests, the barbarians, Theron, and the donkey-drivers are to stay in his house, ἐνταῦθα (394) having a different reference from δεῦρο (387, 391). ἐνθάδε of 390 might refer, with the appropriate gesture, to either house. On the whole, I think Handley is right. The emphatic αὐτήν τ' ἀπιέναι δεῦρο (391) suggests that the others are not to come. Moreover, if Theron is to marry Malthake, it would be fitting for them to be separated until the marriage.

388 κανδύτανας: Pollux vii. 79 (in a list of receptacles for clothes), παρὰ τοῖϲ νεωτέροιϲ καὶ ῥίϲκοι καὶ κανδύτανεϲ, ἴϲωϲ καὶ ἀόρται, may come from this passage; his doubts about ἀόρται are probably due to another passage, from Μιϲογύνηϲ (frag. 282) in which he knew variant readings: χλαμύδα, καυϲίαν (a hat), λόγχην, ἀορτήν (or ἀορτῆρ'), ἱμάτια. In that passage ἀορτῆρ' is probably correct (so Körte–Thierfelder), and means a sword-belt; the word may be eliminated from consideration here.

On κανδύτανες he says (x. 137) that they are a kind of box, mentioned by Menander in Ἀσπίς (frag. 76 K–T, 4 Austin), and that he thinks it is a Persian word, derived from κάνδυς (a sleeved garment), adopted by the Macedonians. Photios s.v. interprets as ἱματιοφορίδες. Aelian's use of the word for certain large 'mice', of whose skins Persians make coats, is irrelevant (xvii. 17). Other forms of the word occur: κανδυτάναι or κανδύλαι in Hesychios and κανδύταλις in Diphilos frag. 40, ὁ δὲ κανδύταλις | οὗτος τί δύναται καὶ τί ἐστίν; :: ὡςπέρει | εἴποις ἀόρτας. ἀόρτης (the accentuation may be ἀορτής) occurs again in Poseidippos frag. 10 K, ςκηνάς, ὄχους, ῥίςκους, ἀόρτας, †τάχανα†, λαμπήνας, ὄνους. Pollux, who quotes this (x. 139), takes the word as fem. from ἀορτή, but there is no evidence for this gender outside lexicographers, who may have been misled by the familiar ἀορτή = aorta. Fortunately there is no problems over ῥίςκοι, coffers or trunks, see LSJ. The word, which Donatus on Ter. Eun. 754 calls Phrygian, made its way into Latin.

390: What can be seen after μη does not suggest, nor quite exclude, μητερ; but that yields no likely sense. In a later papyrus ευρηςκοντας would probably be a mis-spelling of εὑρίςκοντας, but the ι/η confusion began, so far as is known, in the mid second century B.C.; Schwyzer, i. 186. εὑρήςοντας may be right.

394: Theron is condemned to nice company, sandwiched between foreign slaves, who have presumably not yet learnt Greek, and donkey-drivers, who were not highly regarded: we hear of one who fetched the low price of 140 dr., W. S. Pritchett, *Hesperia*, xxv (1956), 279. The Cynic Krates said that one should pursue philosophy until generals seemed to be donkey-drivers; Diog. L. vi. 92.

397: Stratophanes leaves, to follow Kichesias and Dromon to the priestess. Moschion, having learned that Philumene's father is found, and so assuming that Stratophanes will soon marry her, comes out of his parents' house. That he is alone and soliloquizes is shown by the address to the audience in 405.

Kassel supports his supplement ἔτι by reference to *Dysk.* 121, 268, 316, 686, etc. where ἔτι at the line-end follows an earlier negative. For προςβλέψαι πρός, 'look at a woman with interest', cf. Eupolis frag. 206 K, ὁ Φιλῖνος οὗτος, τί ἄρα πρὸς ταύτην βλέπεις;

398: Metre will be restored by suppressing ἐςτ' or more probably by transposing it after εὐόφθαλμος. Then Handley's οὐδὲν λέγειν neatly completes the line. For whiteness as admired in women cf. Ar. *Eccl.* 699, καλλίςτη καὶ λευκοτάτη, Alexis frag. 98 K, λευκόχρως λίαν τις ἐςτι, Theokr. xi. 19, ὦ λευκὰ Γαλάτεια. **εὐόφθαλμος:** Probably 'with beautiful eyes', rather than 'beautiful to look upon'; Kassel quotes Aristotle frag. 92, τὸ εὐπρόcωπον καὶ εὐόφθαλμον, where τὸ εὐόφθαλμον is defined as τὸ ἔχον ὀφθαλμοῦ ἀρετήν.

401: The aposiopesis need not be filled out, but perhaps 'for what a (joy he will have of her)!'. **οὗτοc ἔτι λέγειc;** cf. *Sam.* 680, ἔτι λαλεῖc οὗτοc; Moschion addresses himself.

403 οὐκ ἐρῶ: 'I won't *say* it' or 'I'm not *in love*'; the loss of the context makes it impossible to decide. **μὴ γάρ:** 'No, don't', cf. *Dysk.* 921 n.

ὅταν is difficult to accommodate, unless we have here an early instance of its construction with future indicative, occasionally found in the *koine* (see LSJ s.v.), or unless there is another aposiopesis, so that ὅταν's verb is suppressed; e.g. ὅταν ὅcον δύνῃ—, 'when you must (do) all you can to—'.

Austin suggests reading ὦ τᾶν, which is suitable in sense, see *Dysk.* 247 n; the same error is found in B at *Dysk.* 359. But the confusion of o and ω, common from Hadrianic times, is first recorded in the early second century B.C., Meisterhans³, 24.

404 παροχήcομαι: The bridegroom was accompanied on the cart or carriage that fetched the bride to her new home by a 'best man'. Paus. Att. s.v. πάροχοc· ὁ παροχούμενοc ἐκ τρίτων τῷ νυμφίῳ καὶ τῇ νύμφῃ ἐπὶ τῆc ἁμάξηc. καὶ παροχήcομαι· πάροχοc ἔcομαι. Photios s.v. ζεῦγοc ἡμιονικὸν ἢ βοεικόν says that the bride sat between bridegroom and best man, who was a friend or relation, and that the word πάροχοc was used, even if the bride was fetched on foot. Lucian, *Herod.* 5, describes a picture of the marriage of Alexander and Roxane, where Hephaistion plays the part of πάροχοc καὶ νυμφαγωγόc. Cf. also Ar. *Birds* 1740.

411 ff.: The speakers here are quite uncertain, as is the point of their conversation. *Perhaps* the woman who carries barley to the donkeys, if on the stage at all, goes out on that errand at 412 after πορείαc; she may not have a speaking part.

It may be that A extorts B's consent to something by the *fait accompli* of getting torches and garlands; and with this the play ends. This is probably not serious enough, and too late, to settle the fate of a principal actor in the drama. Perhaps the successful man is Theron, who gets Malthake from Stratophanes.

413 εὐχόμην: S spells ηυχομην at 48. Augmented forms of words beginning εὐ- disappear on Attic inscriptions after 300 B.C., Meisterhans³, 172. Moiris has ηὐξάμην διὰ τοῦ η Ἀττικῶc, διὰ δὲ τοῦ ε Ἑλληνικῶc. One cannot be sure that Menander was consistent.

415 ἐμμένειν is a word commonly used of adhering to an undertaking or decision.   ὁ βαθυ[: A compound is likely, but see frag. 830 (from the *Suda*): βαθύς· ἀντὶ τοῦ πονηρός· οὕτως Μένανδρος.

418 διακόψαις: Perhaps a military metaphor, 'break through his defences', see LSJ s.v. 2.

420 δώςω, read by Coles, I think certain.   **κατάνευσον:** The gesture of assent by nodding will reinforce the verbal promise of δώςω: cf. the Homeric phrases ὑπέστην καὶ κατένευσα, *Iliad* iv. 267, ὑπέσχετο καὶ κατένευσεν, ibid. ii. 112.

μειράκι᾽ ἄνδρες παιδία is a plausible supplement, the broken anapaest being justified, as at *Perik.* 178, by the elision. Although elsewhere παῖδες is found in the formula for inviting applause, Ar. *Eccl.* 1146 has καλεῖς γέροντα, μειράκιον, παιδίσκον; in an invitation to the audience to come to dinner. Another possibility here is παῖδες, οὐ | πρωράςετ᾽; which has the advantage of requiring no change of S's reading. Gallavotti suggests μειρακύλλι᾽, ἄνδρες εὖ | πρωράςετε. *Sam.* 733 indicates the possibility of μειράκια, παῖδες καλοί (Austin).

421 πρωράςατ᾽ ἐκτείναντες: Hesychios has the entry πρωράςαντες· κροτήςαντες. ἡ δὲ μεταφορὰ ἀπὸ τῶν νεῶν καὶ τῆς εἰρεςίας (C. Gallavotti, *Riv. fil.* xciii [1965], 443 would read πρωρά⟨ςετ᾽ ἐκτείν⟩αντες). The idea is that the clapping carries the play forward to success as the splashing oars drive the ship forward, cf. Aristophanes' Knights, who, in their appeal to the public at the end of their anapaests in the parabasis, mix the two notions, αἴρεςθ᾽ αὐτῷ (sc. τῷ ποιητῇ) πολὺ τὸ ῥόθιον, παραπέμψατ᾽ ἐφ᾽ ἕνδεκα κώπαις θόρυβον χρηςτὸν ληναΐτην (546–7). It is possible that, as Aristophanes explained αἴρεςθε τὸ ῥόθιον with θόρυβον, a common word for applause, so Menander explained πρωράςατε with ἐπ[ικροτήςατε ἐκτείναντες probably means 'stretching out your hands', as men do who clap enthusiastically. A similar phrase is quoted from Menander (frag. 771) by Σ *Plutus* 689: τὴν χεῖρ᾽ ὑφῄρει . . . ἐξέτεινε. καὶ Μένανδρος· ἐξείραντες ἐπικροτήςατε. (The paradosis here has ἐξείραντες, not ἐξάραντες, E. Fraenkel, *Beobachtungen zu Arist.* 155, cf. Hdt. iii. 87, ἐξείραντα τὴν χεῖρα.) Some have, however, found difficult the absence of τὰς χεῖρας, which Dindorf in fact wished to insert in frag. 771 before ἐξείραντες. An object could be provided for ἐκτείναντες by supplying μειράκ[ι᾽, ἄνδρες, τὰ σκέλη (Xen. *Anab.* v. 8. 14), or τὰ γόνατα, (Ar. *Wasps* 1212) in the previous line; and this is supported by Plaut. *Epidicus* 733, 'plaudite et ualete, lumbos porgite atque exsurgite'. But the separation of σκέλη and ἐκτείναντες is suspicious, and frag. 771 suggests that hand-clapping, not leg-stretching, is to be looked for.

422–3: These lines are known to conclude at least four of Menander's plays, see *Dysk.* 968–9 n. A subscription gives the title of the play as

Μενάνδρου Cικυώνιοι, and the number of lines it contains. The number is mutilated and its first element unfamiliar. The figure intended must be more than a thousand.

Fragment 1. ἄβραν: The word, perhaps of Semitic origin, is used of a slave who is a woman's personal attendant; in Plut. *Caesar* 10 Clodius speaks of Pompeia's ἄβρα, Lucian, *Toxaris* 14, 16, calls a married woman's confidential maid a ἄβρα, in the Septuagint, Gen. 24: 61, Rebecca's handmaidens, Exod. 2: 5, Pharaoh's daughter's hand-maidens are ἄβραι. Menander frag. 58, ᾤμην, εἰ τὸ χρυcίον λάβοι ὁ γέρων, θεράπαιναν εὐθὺς ἠγοραcμένην ἄβραν ἔcεcθαι, throws no further light. Photios rejects two interpretations as false: the word is neither a mere synonym for θεράπαινα nor does it mean a good-looking servant (this idea will have arisen through confusion with the adjective ἁβρά, 'graceful, pretty'). It means, he continues, a girl belonging to a woman, domestically employed and valued by her, whether born in the household or not. My guess as to the sense of this fragment, which may have come from the prologue, is that Stratophanes having conceived a love for Philumene did not hand her over to his mistress Malthake, for whom he bought a ἄβρα as a substitute, but had her brought up in a separate establishment in a manner suiting a free woman. To fall in love with a girl not yet marriageable and to wait for her to grow up is unusual, but not unheard of.

Marzullo would adopt a variant reading from Photios, αὐτωνού-μενοc, 'buying in his own person'. The verb is not known elsewhere, but cf. αὐτωνητήc, Deinarchos frag. 89.

Fragment 2. This may be from the lost early part of the play, but could have had a place between 279 and 280.

Fragment 3. The words also make a single complete trochaic tetrameter. The meaning, 'You once had a simple little soldier's cloak and one slave to follow you', could be reversed by writing πότε for ποτέ, 'When did you have only a simple cloak etc?'

Fragment 4. 'A sailor comes ashore; he is found in the courts to be a member of an enemy state, if he has any portable possessions; he is made over to forced labour.'

This may not refer to the fate of any character in this play; the lines could have occurred in a passage descriptive of the sort of thing that went on somewhere; they might even be part of a piece of moralizing.

Fragment 5. I think, perhaps wrongly, that the entry in Photios means that Menander used only the first three words of the proverb, allusively. Philemon frag. 21 (Stobaios iii. 8. 10) consists of the whole line, which Thierfelder guesses to be taken from some tragedy.

Fragment 6. There is no good reason for supposing this fragment to be from *Sikyonios*. The verses are ascribed by Stobaios to Menander, but not to any play. The scholiast on Plato, *Symp.* 195 b says that in *Sikyonios* Menander referred to the proverb ὡς αἰεὶ τὸν ὅμοιον ἄγει θεὸς ὡς τὸν ὅμοιον. Nauck, *Mélanges Gréco-Romains*, vi. 114, argued that the scholiast had these verses in mind. C. W. Müller, *Rh. Mus.* cvii (1964), 285, rightly maintains that this is not the most natural interpretation: 'God brings the like-minded together' and 'Choice of like-minded friends leads to harmony in life' are by no means the same sentiment.

Fragment 7. ἐμπρίϲαϲα might mean 'having bitten' and be explained by ὀργιζομένη. Although ἐμπρίειν properly means 'saw into', it is used of biting with the teeth, Diod. Sic. x. 17, xvii. 92, and ὀδόντας πρίειν, 'gnash one's teeth in rage', is familiar. For the absence of an object Marzullo compares *Sam.* 356, δακὼν δ' ἀνάσχου, 'bite (your lip) and bear it'.

One cannot guess what place this fragment can have had in the play. ἀπολείπειν is technically used of a wife who leaves her husband; that does not seem likely here.

Fragment 9. By Ϲικυωνίῳ without an author's name Photios is more likely to have intended Menander's well-known play than that of Alexis. He seems to mean that at some point Theron wore a white cloak in place of his usual dark one.

Fragment 11. The names of Theron and Malthake (and also of Pyrrhias, if the *nota*, of which only the initial letter π survives, refers to him) are adequate to identify this scrap as a fragment of *Sikyonios*. Unfortunately it is not intelligible nor to be brought into relation with the other remains.

PHASMA

P   *Membrana Petropolitana* (Petr. graec. 338). One of the surviving
      leaves of a fourth-century codex, described intro. p. 55, con-
      tains on one side twenty-seven lines, on the other twenty-five,
      of a play which can confidently be identified as *Phasma*, or *The
      Apparition*. Lines 50–6 are quoted as Menander's by Clement of
      Alexandria, and the matter fits the plot of the play as it is re-
      corded by Donatus.

O 12 *P. Oxyrhynchica* 2825. Parts of four columns, containing remains
      of verses quoted elsewhere as being from Menander's *Phasma*.
      I am indebted to Professor Turner for allowing me to make use
      of an advance proof of his publication in *Oxyrhynchus Papyri*,
      vol. xxxviii.

The remains are discussed by E. G. Turner, *Greek Roman and Byzantine
Studies*, x (1969), 307–24.

The play was revived at Athens in 254 B.C. and 167 B.C. (Pickard-
Cambridge, *Dramatic Festivals of Athens*[2], 111, 123) and produced upon
the Roman stage in a translation by Luscius of Lanuvium shortly
before 161 B.C. (Ter. *Eunuchus* 9).

Plot

A brief and unfortunately incomplete account of the play is given
by Donatus. A widowed man remarried, thus providing his grown son
with a stepmother. She had once borne a daughter, probably as the
result of a rape (*ex uitio*), and brought her up secretly. The girl was
hidden in the house next door to that of her mother's new husband,
and could be seen by her mother, without anyone's knowledge, by
the following device. The woman had made in the party-wall a hole,
to which she had given the appearance of a shrine, decking it with
garlands and greenery. There she often engaged in religious practices
and called the girl to come to her. The stepson noticed this and at the
first sight of the beautiful maiden was struck with fear, taking her to
be a divine apparition. But slowly the truth came out and he fell so
passionately in love that there was no cure but marriage. So the play
ended with a wedding that was to the advantage of mother and
daughter, fulfilled the lover's hopes, and had his father's consent.

It was clear that there must have been a great deal more to the play than this, a conclusion confirmed by the mosaic from Mitilini, which represents a scene from Act II of the play (*BCH* lxxxvi [1962], 876, lxxxviii [1964], 802). The girl appears in a doorway to the left; in the centre an old man moves towards her; to the right is a third figure of uncertain sex. Mme Kahil, who gives a full account in *Antike Kunst*, Beiheft 6 (1970), 60 (with a colour photograph, plate 8), hesitantly thinks it to be a young man; Turner, *GRBS* x (1969), 320, wonders whether it can be the 'apparition's' mother, surprised by the unexpected return of her husband. In any case it seems to be certain that the secret is out: the girl must be recognized as a human being. It follows, as Turner says, that the young man's vision of the girl and his mistake in taking her to be supernatural formed the starting-point of the play; they may even not have been in the play at all, but recounted in the opening scenes.

That Donatus gives little beyond the initial situation is confirmed by O 12, known to be from *Phasma* because it contains both the fragments of that play quoted by other authors. In one passage from this a slave informs his young master that the girl he loves has been exposed to the passionate kisses of another man, who looks like eating her face away. The young man says he will go in and get information from his sister, whom he expects to be despondent at the marriage that is in train. In an earlier passage there is a cook, and talk of a remarriage, or a marriage that is 'on again'.

It appears then that there were two young men in the play, and also two young women. The second young woman is probably mentioned in the prologue, where she is referred to as τῆς γαμουμένης, 'the bride-to-be' (10). This points to a situation like one of those envisaged by Turner, of which the more probable is:

The Son is known from the Petrograd fragment to be called Pheidias. The others I refer to as Brother, Bride, etc.

Perhaps the Apparition passes as the daughter of the house in which she lives. But, if so, the wife at least must be aware of the hole in the wall and therefore of her true parentage. Turner suggests that a marriage had been arranged between Pheidias and the Bride, that he fell in love with the Apparition (so far cf. K. F. W. Schmidt, *B. ph. W.* [1921], 739), and then, pretending melancholia, stayed at home, kissing her ferociously when she came through the wall. The Brother had been hoping to marry the Apparition, whom he may have believed to be his paternal half-sister, and was perturbed to hear of Pheidias' conduct. All this must have been early in the play, and the plot was complicated by the discovery made by Pheidias' father and illustrated in the mosaic.

Another fragment in O 12 probably comes from later in the play. It is concerned with the circumstances of a rape, and therefore probably looks forward to the discovery of the paternity of the Apparition. This must, of course, have been established to enable her to be legally married. Perhaps her father turned out to be Pheidias' father. The lovers would have the same father but different mothers, and so could marry. The girl who had been ravished will then have become the second wife of the man who had ravished her (as in *Synaristosai*, Plaut. *Cistellaria* 177). But, as Turner says, this is only one possibility. As another, he suggests that the father of the Apparition is the man in whose house she lives, and that his present wife is Pheidias' mother. Then Pheidias and his intended bride would have the same mother: their marriage would be impossible, and might be replaced by one between Pheidias and the Apparition. This brings an awkward and to my mind not very likely complication: Pheidias' father must have got rid of his first wife, Pheidias' mother, if she had been free to marry his neighbour. But it must be confessed that the remains of the play are far too scanty to allow any certain reconstruction.

The interpretation of the mosaic is disputed. Turner thinks (*GRBS* ibid. 322) that it must represent an indoor scene, the passage of the Apparition through the party-wall, and that this cannot have been shown on the stage. It must therefore have been described, not acted, and the artist has portrayed not what the audience saw, but what they were invited to imagine. This is tempting and I hope right. But there is no exact parallel, although Turner quotes some miniatures in the MSS. of Terence that simultaneously show stage action and what is to be imagined as passing indoors. Mme Kahil in *Antike Kunst*, loc. cit., argues that the mosaic shows what went on before the spectators' eyes. Either the doorway, drawn as equipped with double doors and not surrounded by greenery, represents the front door of a house; or the opening in the *skene*, that normally represented the front door, was temporarily made to represent the hole in the party-wall. The dispute cannot be settled without more evidence.

1–56: In view of the new evidence no doubt can remain that the leaf of the Petrograd codex that contains most of these lines is from an early part of the play. Nor can there be any serious doubt that those are right who see on one side of it part of a divine prologue. We are here typically given a brief outline of the situation (9–25) in a matter-of-fact manner; it is a situation not known to any of the principal characters other than those who are mentioned. Just possibly the secret had been entrusted to some reliable slave (although Donatus says *nullo conscio*) ; such a slave is the only alternative to a god as the speaker.

Although van Leeuwen had doubts, this prologue has generally been supposed to precede the scene on the other side. Some ten lines were thought to have been lost at the foot of the page, enough to conclude the prologue, but not enough to conclude that scene and introduce the prologue. Turner, however, has shown that codices of the age of P may have fifty lines or more to the page, so that we may imagine not ten lines, but twenty, or even more, to be lost. He supposed, moreover, that the prologue begins at 9, and that 1–8 are the end of a preceding scene: the prologue was a 'postponed prologue'. This enabled him to reconstruct this part of the play with 26–56 as the first surviving scene ; the slave advises the distrait young man, who has already seen the Apparition, to get the womenfolk to exorcize him. A gap of up to twenty-five lines follows, in which he asks his mother so to act, and her reply is to be found in 1–8, lines which certainly contain a conversation. Ingenious though this is, it is not quite convincing, because 9 ff. would form an astonishingly abrupt opening for a divine prologue. It would be extraordinary for a god to say nothing to introduce himself. The previous lines must then be part of the prologue, a conversation reported by the god. That being so, it is not likely that the twenty-five lines available if 26–56 precede the prologue would be adequate to contain its lost beginning. Accordingly I maintain the traditional order.

1–25: This side of the leaf is very hard to read, but Turner in general confirms Jernstedt's reports. Although previous editions, excepting Del Corno's, restore the missing half of the text, it is only in the latter part that there is any prospect of success; for there Donatus gives a clue to the sense. I confine supplements to that part, with the warning that they are *exempli gratia*.

1: Körte prints τῶν Διο]νυcίων, but Turner will not confirm the first ν, and envisages θυcιῶν, οὐcιῶν, or even, e.g., δεικνὺc ἰών.

2 ἐπιτελεῖν: The most likely meanings are 'complete, finish' or 'celebrate, perform' some religious ritual (LSJ s.v. II).

4: 'The girl's mother' will probably be the mother of the girl that the bridegroom of the previous line is to marry.

5 ἑτέρῳ . . . ὁμομητρίῳ τινί: 'Some other man who has the same mother', a phrase puzzling in its vagueness. Can ἑτέρῳ . . . τινί possibly not agree with ὁμομητρίῳ, but with, e.g., τρόπῳ?

Since in 9 the prologue-speaker seems to say 'this is no apparition, but a real girl', it is an easy guess that the person who is addressed in 1–7 believes her to be an apparition. He will, then, be Pheidias, and the person who is adjuring him will probably be his stepmother (K. F. W. Schmidt, loc. cit.). She may say to him: 'Do not show your interest in this apparition. Think of yourself as a bridegroom. Do not alarm the girl's mother, tell some other story to her brother, don't give any grounds for suspicion.'

7 οὕτω ποεῖ: Perhaps this should be imperative, οὕτω πόει, a phrase that recurs at *Mis.* 238 in the same position. All editors take it so, as part of the preceding speech. But it would be rather weak after the preceding entreaty, which makes an excellent climax. The historic infinitive is common in the narrative of prologues, and the reaction of the young man to the appeal must somewhere be stated (cf. Webster, *StM* 102).

8 τί γὰρ ἄν τις πάθοι; 'What else could anyone do?' Cf. Lucian, *Menippus* 3, τί γὰρ ἂν πάθοι τις, ὁπότε φίλος ἀνὴρ βιάζοιτο; This is a variant of τί γὰρ πάθῃ τις; *Perik.* 425. The common phrase τί πάθω; or τί γὰρ πάθω; 'what can I do?', 'how can I help it?' seems to have developed as an expression of helplessness from the original sense 'what's to happen to me?'. It is often difficult to say which sense is predominant, as in Ar. *Lys.* 954, *Plut.* 603. The subjunctive is 'prospective'; this is the only phrase in classical Greek to retain the common Homeric construction. It may have survived through false analogy with deliberative subjunctives like τί ποιῶ; K–G i. 222–3. Whereas τις attached to a deliberative subjunctive is always a substitute for ἐγώ, when attached to an optative with ἄν it often refers to a person previously mentioned, K–G i. 662.

9 φάσμα: An apparition is something that comes and goes, it has not the permanence of a natural object; but it is often thought of as having a real existence of its own, it is not dependent on the living being who 'sees the vision'.

10: Turner suggests that the right sense, 'living in the house of the bride', might be given by ἐν οἰκίᾳ τα]χθεῖσα τῆς γαμουμένης. All will share his doubt of ταχθεῖσα. Would στ]αθεῖσα, 'placed, established', be possible?

11 πρὶν ἐλθεῖν ἐνθάδε: Donatus' account suggests that when the mother became his father's second wife Pheidias was already a young man, and it would probably follow that her daughter was not an infant but at least approaching marriageable age. But if so, what had the mother been doing during the dozen years or more that must have elapsed since her rape? U. E. Paoli, *Aegyptus*, xxxiii (1953), 280, supposes that she had made a previous marriage. This passage of the prologue is consistent (unless 12 is to be restored, e.g., ἒξ καὶ δέκ' ἔτεϲιν) with her having married Pheidias' father not long after she had had her child. It would be simplest to suppose that, in spite of Donatus' language, Pheidias was then still a young boy. It need not be imagined that the device of the hole in the party-wall had been long in use at the time of the play: it may have been recently invented, to allow mother and child to meet.

13 ἐν τῶν γειτόνων: Sc. οἰκίᾳ, cf. *Dysk.* 25 n. I have followed Turner in supposing that this house next door is not occupied merely by the Apparition and an attendant, but belongs to a married couple. If this is true, the girl probably passes as theirs. A nurse and a parentless girl would be strange lodgers in a respectable Athenian house.

15–18: The supplements are *exempli gratia*.

19 ποθεῖτε: The audience.

20: Hypereides' speech *pro Lycophrone* defends a man who is known, from the fragments of another speech by an unknown orator (*P. Oxy.* 1607), to have been accused of an intrigue with a married woman to whom he gained access by a hole in the party-wall.

26–52: The other side of the leaf from P is easy to read. It contains part of a scene between Pheidias, the young man who has seen the Apparition, and someone who addresses him as τρόφιμε (41), 'young master'. As this person is affected by the price of wheat, he must be either a freedman or a slave who has to keep himself out of his earnings. The guess that he was once Pheidias' παιδαγωγός is no more than a possibility. The young man has been behaving with a purposelessness, which the other puts down to the boredom of a spoilt child. In fact, it is the vision of the girl that has affected him. He cannot yet know that she is human, for the audience has only just been informed of that (9). He has fallen in love with a being he supposes to be unattainable. His companion's words, ἵνα μὴ ἐπιθυμῆϲ τῶν ὑπὲρ ϲέ, either are a response to a hint that he has set his heart on something beyond him or fit the situation better than the speaker knows.

27 πῶϲ: 'At what price?', cf. Ar. *Ach.* 758.

28 δ' ἐμοί: Wilamowitz's change from δε ϲοι is inevitable, if 30 is correctly supplemented as δακέτω ϲ' ὑπὲρ ἐμ[οῦ.

30 τίμιοι: P has τειμιοϲ, which Sudhaus defends as an anacoluthon, cîτοϲ having replaced πυροί in the speaker's mind.   **δακέτω**: Cf. *Kith.* frag. 2, τὸ κουφότατον πάντων ϲε τῶν κακῶν δάκνει, πενία.

37 μαλακῶϲ ἐλούϲω: 'You take a luxurious bath', gnomic aorist, like εἰcῆλθεc (36). For μαλακῶc cf. Theophr. *Char.* ii. 10, ὡc μαλακῶc ἐcθίειc; there is probably a suggestion of softness, self-indulgence.

39 τὸ πέρας: Cf. *Epitr.* 111 n.

42: Cobet's supplement is based on Marc. Aurel. v. 12, οἰκείωc ἂν ἐπιφέροιτο τὸ τὸν κεκτημένον αὐτὰ ὑπὸ τῆc εὐπορίαc οὐκ ἔχειν ὅποι χέcῃ.

43 μὴ ὥραcι μέν: See *Perik.* 321–2 n.

45 ἀρρώcτημα, 'illness', and ἀcθενικόν, 'weakly', are neither very common words, and the latter is not found elsewhere in comedy; they may be in character for the speaker. With sarcasm he recommends a quack remedy as suitable for an imaginary disease: Pheidias is to submit to a ritual purification, washing and fumigation, sprinkling with water from three springs, into which salt and lentils have been thrown. This was the sort of thing which was done to avert the supposed effects of bad dreams, cf. Plutarch, *de superstitione*, 166 a, ἀλλ᾽ εἰ c᾽ ἔνυπνον φάνταcμα φοβεῖ | χθονίαc θ᾽ Ἑκάτηc κῶμον ἐδέξω, | τὴν περιμακτρίαν κάλει γραῦν καὶ βάπτιcον cεαυτὸν εἰc θάλαccαν; ibid. 168 d, a mild case of superstition sits at home περιθειούμενοc καὶ περιματτόμενοc. For taking water from more than one source cf. Theophrastos, *Char.* xvi. 2, οἷοc ἐπὶ γ′ κρηνῶν (Borthwick, *Eranos*, lxiv [1966], 106, ἐπὶ χρωνῆν V ἀπὸ γ′ κρουνῶν Diels) ἀπονιψάμενοc τὰc χεῖραc καὶ περιρρανάμενοc), Empedokles frag. 143, κρηνάων ἀπὸ πέντε.

46: The genitive ἐμαυτοῦ can hardly depend on βαρέωc ἔχω; it must be governed by the verb lost at the end of 45.

56 περίρραν᾽: I.e. περίρραναι, aor. middle imperative.

57–74: Who the speakers are is quite uncertain. Syros, who is twice addressed, could be a *persona muta*. 73–4 may be spoken by a cook, but all that is certain is that they have to do with a cook, since Athenaios quotes the words as illustrating the way in which Menander exalts (ἐκcεμνύνει) the art of cookery.

59 καὶ γαμεῖ πάλιν: The obvious meaning, 'he is going to marry again', i.e. remarry, does not suit the plot at which we have guessed; possibly 'his marriage is on again'. (A second person future, 'you will marry', is not excluded, nor even γάμει, imperative, 'marry again'.) One may guess that Pheidias, after seeing the Apparition, showed signs of melancholic madness; but that, following his stepmother's advice, recounted in the prologue, he had shown himself ready to go on with the marriage arranged with his neighbour's daughter; this had made it appear that his health was better.

62 οἴχομαι: It may be guessed that this is an exclamation of despair by someone hearing this talk of marriage to whom it is unwelcome since he hopes for the bride for himself. But this is speculative.

65: Turner suggests that the cook lacks some clean utensil.

67 βέλτιστε: A cook is addressed as βέλτιστε, Hegesippos frag. 1 K, as βέλτιστε σύ, Lynkeus frag. 1 K, and addresses his employer as βέλτιστε, *Sam.* 384.

73–4 ἐπισημαίνεσθ': This may be imperative, or infinitive, as it is written in MS. A of Athenaios. The word may mean 'signify, indicate', or 'show approval' (so LSJ interpret here, s.v. IV. 3). σκευασία, according to Turner, may refer to the tableware as well as to the cooking. Perhaps, but cooks are more interested in the preparation of food than in the dishes on which it is served. σκευασία, like σκευάζειν, is particularly used of prepared food (see LSJ s.v.); καθάρειος often occurs in connection with food, when it suggests refined simplicity, Eubulos frag. 110 K, μὴ πολυτελῶς ἀλλὰ καθαρείως, Plut. *QC* 663 c, where τὸ καθάριον καὶ τὸ εὐστόμαχον is opposed to τὸ ποικίλον. ποικίλη may then be a deliberately surprising adjective to join with it.

75–92: Trochaic tetrameters begin not later than 79, and perhaps already with 75. Whether any of the characters in this scene were already on the stage in the previous scene cannot be determined. But οἴχομαι in 79 might be spoken by the same man as used the word in 62, and he may be the Bride's brother. If the previous scene had indicated that Pheidias was going ahead with the marriage, this will cheat expectations by bringing news that he was passionately kissing another girl.

80 οὐκ Ἔμβαρός ἐστιν: Two opposed accounts of this name were given in antiquity, and are combined in the entry in Hesychios s.v., ἠλίθιος, μῶρος, ἢ νουνεχής. Pausanias, quoted by *Suda* s.v. Ἔμβαρος and by Eustathios *in Il.* ii. 732, told a story of Embaros' cleverness. The Athenians suffered from famine and Apollo promised them relief if anyone would sacrifice his daughter to Artemis. Embaros offered to do this, if the priesthood of Artemis were made hereditary in his family. He then hid his daughter and in her stead sacrificed a goat that he had dressed in her clothes. After the words εἰς παροιμίαν περιέστη the two versions diverge: Eustathios ends Ἔμβαρος εἶ, τουτέστι νουνεχής, φρόνιμος, while *Suda* has τάττεται δὲ ἐπὶ τῶν παραπαιόντων καὶ μεμηνότων (similarly Zenobios *epit.* i. 8). The story makes it clear that Embaros was a type, not of a fool or madman, but of a smart wide-awake fellow. Hesychios also has an entry οὐκ Ἔμβαρος εἶ· οὐ φρονεῖς. So here οὐκ Ἔμβαρός ἐστιν will mean 'he is not in his senses' as is to be illustrated by the conduct soon to be described.

ὑπενόουν . . . ὀρθῶс: It is more probable that the words are to be taken together as first and last in their sentence than that ὀρθῶс goes with what follows.

84 ἐπῆξε: Having met the girl (ἐνέτυχεν) in the previous line, here he 'rushes on her'.   ἀναφρόδιτοс: Here 'unlucky in love', as in Lucian, *Dial. Deorum* xv. 2, where Apollo complains of his failure to obtain Daphne and Hyakinthos.

85: I look on Turner's restoration with some reserve. He thinks it to mean 'you are one of those who offer him a locked-up girl for food', but was there such a group of people? Can the truth rather be τῶν διδόντων δ' εἰc τροφήν γ' εἶ, τρόφιμε, κατακεκλημένοιc, 'you are one of those who provide food for prisoners'? If Pheidias is shamming mad, he may be shut up in his house.

86: 'If the fit comes on him'. παραcτῆναι is mainly used of thoughts that 'occur' to one; here τὸ κακόν is the 'illness' from which Pheidias is supposed to suffer (cf. καμών).   τὴν ῥῖνα: Cf. Plaut. *Men.* 194: 'si amabas, iam oportebat nasum abreptum mordicus.'

87 μηθαμῶc: For the spelling cf. *Sam.* 573.

88 ἅμα φιλῶν τι: 'While he kisses her a bit'. Although there is no space before or after τι, there is a paragraphus below the line; hence Turner gives τί; to the young man, as a question. But there is no paragraphus below 87, where one is needed; so perhaps this is misplaced.

90: Cf. *Sam.* 596.

92: Perhaps the young man thinks his sister will be depressed at the prospect of marrying a man who is so madly in love with another.

93–107: The length of the gap between 92 and 93 is unknown. That 93–107 come from a later scene than 57–92 is only a probable guess. In this passage two persons at least talk about the rape of a girl at some religious festival. Turner at one time supposed them to be man and wife. Handley suggested that someone tells a husband how he should question his wife and forecasts the conversation. It is clear that a future conversation is imagined, but that the female who will take part in it is a wife is not certain, nor that it was she who was raped.

93 καταιcχύνει: This verb is used of dishonouring a woman in Lysias i. 49.

95: *Epitr.* 452 suggests that παννυχίδοc οὔcηc καὶ χορῶν (sc. ὄντων) is a genitive absolute. The phrase will not necessarily have been followed by a verb; rather the verb will have been suppressed for the sake of decency, as at *Epitr.* 1120.

96–8: It seems that the woman will by the word beginning βρ answer the question implied by the word ἐλέγξεις or ἐξελέγξεις. The latter is more probable, for ἐλέγχειν usually means 'refute', or 'show up', whereas ἐξελέγχειν may mean no more than 'ascertain by strict inquiry'. That βρ is to be continued as βραυρων- is made probable by βραυ[in 104. To find a plausible question and answer is not easy. Hesitantly I suggest τὴν ὁδὸν τίς ἦν τότε | εἶτ᾽ ἐξελέγξεις, ἡ δ᾽ ἐρεῖ "Βραυρωνάδε". In 98 Turner observes that Βραυρ]ωνίοις is too long, and suggests Ἀδ]ωνίοις, saying that the testimonies must disagree on the festival involved. This seems very difficult, since no notice appears to be taken of the supposed disagreement. Can it be that letters were omitted and we should write, e.g., βρ⟨αυρ⟩]ωνίοις?

99 πλανηθεῖς᾽ ἡ: Or πλανηθείσῃ. Cf. *Epitr.* 486, ἐπλανήθη.

Caesius Bassus, a metrist reputed to have perished in the eruption of Vesuvius in A.D. 79, says that the ithyphallic (– ∪ – ∪ – ⊻) often admits a tribrach, as may be illustrated from Menander's *Phasma* (*Gr. Lat.* vi. 255 Keil).

Wilamowitz, *Schiedsgericht*, 143 n. 1, suggests that frag. 740 might be placed later in this play: but one play is not likely to have contained two similar sermons preached by a slave to his young master. Webster, *StM* 102, would like to think that frag. 656 and frag. 722 belong to *Phasma*: the idea cannot be disproved at present. All three fragments may be found in OCT.

FABVLA INCERTA

Sudhaus, *Menanderstudien*, 49; Kuiper, *Mnem.* lviii (1931), 234;
Wilamowitz, *Gnomon*, v (1929), 9; Körte, *Hermes*, lxxii (1937), 50;
U. E. Paoli, *Aegyptus*, xxxii (1952), 267; Webster, *StM* 53

C *P. Cairensis* 43227

Three other papyrus fragments have been connected with this play:
P. Oxy. 429, *PSI* 1176 (Page, *GLP* p. 276), *P. Oxy.* 2533. Körte,
Hermes, lxxii (1937), 72 ff., shows that certainly the first and probably
the second do not belong to it. The third contains a betrothal scene
in which a Moschion and a Chaireas have a part; it may come from
the end of our play, but there is nothing but the names to recommend
that conclusion. Webster revived Sudhaus's suggestion that *Fab.
incert.* is Κωνειαζόμεναι, or *The Hemlock-Takers*, but that is based on
little more than the occurrence of a Chaireas in that play, too; in
*SLGC*² 207 he is more cautious. H. J. Mette, *Lustrum*, x (1965), 73
attempts to combine *PSI* 1176, *Fab. incert.*, and *Koneiaz.*, not I think
with an entirely convincing result. Nothing seems to favour identification with Ἀνέψιοι (Robert, *GGA* xxvi [1915], 271) or Κανηφόρος
(Kuiper).

Plot

Although much remains uncertain, Kuiper and Körte have given a
plausible explanation of the fragment. During the absence of his
father Laches, Moschion has taken as wife Kleainetos' daughter, whom
he had raped, and a child has been born. It was feared that Laches
would disapprove of the marriage, but on his return Moschion's young
friend Chaireas sets about a trick to extort his consent. At this point
the fragment begins. Chaireas tells Laches that the girl had been
given or promised in marriage to him, that Moschion had vainly
attempted to persuade him to surrender her, and finally raped her;
he had probably earlier told him that Moschion had been taken in
the act and imprisoned at the scene of the crime. By Attic law the
adulterer so taken was at the mercy of the woman's κύριος, who
might even kill him. Laches, horrified at his son's peril, offers Chaireas
his own daughter as a substitute for the damaged bride—it may be
guessed that the young man was in fact in love with this daughter,
although he pretends to hesitate. At this moment Kleainetos appears,
ignorant of the story that Chaireas has been spinning. But before he

can say anything that would spoil the plot, Chaireas assures him that
Laches confirms the marriage, and Laches sees himself obliged to do
so, and not only this but to give Chaireas his own daughter. Chaireas
departs to carry the good news to Moschion. The old men are left
together and each expresses surprise that the other has acted with
such mildness. This leads to the discovery of Laches' misunderstanding;
but, for all his indignation, it is clear that he will have to keep
his word.

This reconstruction is, I think, basically right. But there is no positive evidence that Kleainetos is the girl's father. Those who are supposed to have given or promised her in marriage are twice spoken of
in the plural τοῖϲ δοῦϲι (18), ἐξεδώκατε (51), and Kleainetos uses the
plural of himself throughout, thus associating others with himself,
ἠδικήμεθα (28), ἡμῖν ἔδοξε (46), ᾠόμεθα (48), εὐτυχήκαμεν (49). Was
he one of a number of relatives who had become responsible for the
girl in the absence of her father, who may have been dead?

Nor am I sure that Kleainetos is entirely innocent in the matter of
Laches' deception. He seems not to know that Chaireas had represented himself as an injured bridegroom, but when at 46–7 he tells
Laches that Moschion already possesses the girl, and had taken her
of his own free will, not been forced to it, he clearly knows Laches to
be under the misapprehension that force had been applied. He must
be referring to some sort of deceit, and it may be that he has in mind
the other half of Chaireas' story. In that case, when he cried ἠδικήμεθα
at 28, he was acting a part, that of a man who has suffered a recent
wrong.

Such duplicity would not suit an Areopagite, but the belief that
he held that honoured position rests on an uncertain supplement (11),
and even if the supplement is right, on confidence that of all Chaireas'
story this piece alone is a true statement.

1–6: Among the papyrus scraps from the Cairo MS. there is one (ι)
that contains on its 'recto' letters from the ends of six lines and on its
'verso' letters from the beginnings of six others. Sudhaus guessed that
these were the ends and beginnings of the lines fragmentarily preserved at the top of the sheet reconstructed from the fragments LPS,
and found that he could fill in the intervening spaces with words that
satisfied him. Körte does not accept all his supplements, but like
Jensen agrees that he placed the scrap correctly, and prints as follows
for lines 1–6:

```
          - - - - - - -  τε
  .  ι - - - - - - - - - - -  ν  ἔδει
  ___
```

(Χα.)   ἐπ - - - - - - - - - ξας ὄλ. ϲ
         ἔχ[ει - - - - - - - - τὸν μ]έγ᾽ ἄθλιον.
___

(Λα.)   ἔκϲωϲ[ον, ἱκετεύω ϲε πο]λλά, Χαιρέα.
___

(Χα.)   μαρτύρα[ϲ ἐκεῖνοϲ φαίνετ᾽1 ο̣ὐ̣κ̣ [ὀλίγουϲ ἔχειν.

And again for 33–9:

(Λα.)   - - - - - - - - - - - - ερα
         ἅ]παντ᾽ ἀκ[έϲαϲθαι βούλομ᾽ ἅπερ ἡμάρτανεν
         ἐκεῖνοϲ[εἰϲ ὑμᾶϲ· ἰταμὸϲ ἄνθρω]ποϲ ἦν.   35
(Χα.)   ἀναδέξομ[αι ᾽γὼ τοῦτο· ϲυλλαβεῖν] ἐμοὶ
         φί[λ]ῳ δίκαι[όν ἐϲτι γάρ. (Λα.) κα]λῶϲ ἔχει.
(Κλ.)   ἄπ[αντ]α μέλ[λει νῦν γενέϲθαι κα]τὰ τρόπον.
(Χα.)   π[ρὸϲ] τοῦτ᾽ ἀ̣[πέρχομαι· πολὺ] γάρ μοι διαφέρει.

This is ingenious, but there is nothing to connect the fragment ι with the rest except Sudhaus's guess and these invented supplements. It may be noted that whereas the reconstruction requires paragraphi below 35, 37, and 38, Lefebvre shows them below 36, 37, and 38, Sudhaus below 34 and 35, Jensen below 37 and 39, and Körte none at all. The facsimile shows nothing that can be confidently recognized as a paragraphus. Again, the *nota personae XAIP* in the *right*-hand margin at 36 strongly suggests that Chaireas' speech began in mid line (although the normal rule is not kept at *Epitr.* 1078), not at the beginning. It is also noticeable that Sudhaus's 35, although three letters shorter than his 34, ends at least five letters further to the right. In view of these facts it is prudent not to print fragment ι as part of lines 1–6, 33–9.

7: Jensen claimed to read ἐπ᾽ αὐτοφ[ώρωι, which would support the view that Chaireas alleged Moschion to have been taken red-handed. But I share Lefebvre's scepticism; the photograph seems to confirm his reading επαλλαϲ[. There is little ink left, but the diagonals of λα can be recognized.

10 παῖ: Although this vocative is normally addressed to a slave, *Dysk.* 741, *Sam.* 148 and 129 (ὦ παῖ) offer parallels for its use to a son. But the word may be an interjection of surprise, for which see *Dysk.* 500 n.

11 ἀρεοπαγίτηϲ: The duties of 'the Eleven' with regard to summary action against malefactors were transferred to the Council of the Areopagos by the reforms of 321 B.C., and not restored in 307 B.C., Ferguson, *Hellenistic Athens*, 24, 99. There is a possible echo of this passage in Alkiphron 3. 36. 2: ἐμὲ ... δήϲαϲα κατέϲχεν, εἰϲ τὴν ὑϲτεραίαν

δὲ παρὰ τὸν ἑαυτῆς ἤγαγε πατέρα, τὸν cκυθρωπὸν Κλεαίνετον, ὃc τὰ νῦν δὴ ταῦτα πρωτεύει τοῦ cυνεδρίου καὶ εἰc αὐτὸν ὁ Ἄρειοc πάγοc ἀποβλέπουcιν. The situation is, however, quite different concerning a thieving parasite. Van Leeuwen supposed that in this play it was not Kleainetos, but one of his witnesses, who was said to be an Areopagite. Although it is more likely to have been Kleainetos himself, one cannot be certain.

13: Cf. Eur. *Med.* 692, ἀδικεῖ μ' Ἰάcων οὐδὲν ἐξ ἐμοῦ παθών. The construction πάcχω ἐξ (for ὑπό) is poetical, and the line is intended to have a tragic ring, the more amusing because the audience knows the speaker's indignation to be feigned. Whether Menander consciously remembered, or hoped that some of his audience would remember, Euripides' line cannot be determined.

17 ἐξειργάcατο: ἐξεργάζομαι is often used of acts of crime or violence, cf. *Epitr.* 575 (of a rape, as here), Soph. *Ajax* 315, but it may also carry a sense of achievement of purpose, cf. frag. 462, ἅπαντα cιγῶν ὁ θεὸc ἐξεργάζεται. ἀναίνει: According to Harpokration 17. 16 (Menander frag. 378) ἀναίνομαι is particularly used of refusing a marriage or intercourse; its wider usage seems to be mainly poetical. As an offer to Chaireas of Laches' daughter the sentence is abrupt; it might be clearer if the play were complete. Chaireas' reply, 'what excuse can I offer to those who have given me my present wife?', means that he has no reason for repudiating her; Moschion had, according to his story, taken her by force; the fault was in no way hers.

18 τοῖc δὲ δοῦcι: The exact meaning of the words is uncertain, since a daughter may be 'given' either when she is promised or when she is actually handed over. It seems, however, that Chaireas presents himself as the girl's husband. This makes more intelligible his question, what reason is he to give for repudiating her? A prospective husband would have every reason for repudiating a prospective bride on discovering that she was not a virgin and could bear a child that might or might not be his. But when the marriage had taken place and the husband had accepted responsibility for the wife, her subsequent rape would be a misfortune that they must both share.

19–22: The assignment of speakers is difficult. There is a dicolon at the end of 19 and a paragraphus below the line. Körte neglects these, perhaps in order that τί ποήcω; of 20 should be spoken by Chaireas, as are the same words in 22. This repetition is not improbable, but it can be secured without refusing the evidence of the papyrus, if we accept a dicolon after Λάχηc, which Lefebvre considered possible. ἱκετεύω c' ἐγώ appears, moreover, to suit Laches, who is asking

Chaireas to do something difficult, better than Chaireas, who has merely put a question, perhaps a rhetorical question, to Laches.

Kleainetos enters at 20, curious to know who is making a noise outside his door: this refers probably to the cry οἴμοι, τί ποήcω; that immediately precedes. He is generally supposed to come out of his own house, as does Callicles in Plaut. *Trin.* 1093, 'quid hoc hic clamoris audio ante aedis meas?' But it is possible that he is returning home (Allinson) and finds the other two by his door. One of them seems to find his arrival opportune; it is perhaps more likely that Chaireas does, since he will in a moment use it to achieve his purpose; nor am I sure that Laches and Kleainetos know one another, since line 30 may be intended as an introduction of Laches to the other father. One may compare the way in which Chrysalus at Plaut. *Bacch.* 844 welcomes the arrival of the soldier, whom he uses to achieve his plan: 'per tempus hic uenit miles mihi.' If Chaireas speaks 21b–22a, the dicolon recorded by Lefebvre after με must, if it existed, have marked the end of his aside, not a change of speaker.

21 εὐκαιρότατά γε: Körte's supplement supposes that C had ευκαιροταγε by mistake. His earlier proposal εὔκαιρος ἧκε is improbable; ἧκει would be required. Wilamowitz's εὔκαιρος ἦλθε, *Gnomon*, v (1929), 467, is too long.

23 πείθωμεν αὐτόν: I.e. to take back his daughter and give her to Moschion instead (παραδοῦναι, 24). Lefebvre was convinced that αυτον is followed by ε, but the very indistinct traces must be of a dicolon.   **ἐρρωμένηc:** 'Formidable', lit. 'powerful', obviously a colloquial usage, cf. 57 below and Polybios iv. 17. 3, μανίας ἔργον καὶ ταύτης ἐρρωμένης. The rape (βίαc) was formidable, if it was to result in the injured husband's aiding the offender to get the woman for good.

25 νὴ τὸν Ἥλιον αἰcχύνομαι Λάχηc cε: Most editors give this to Kleainetos, whom they suppose to feel shame at having given his daughter to Moschion without having obtained Laches' consent. But such an opening does not lead naturally to his next protest, ἠδικήμεθα (28). Del Corno explains the change of tone as due to a signal from Chaireas. Allinson and Körte (originally) gave the phrase to Chaireas. This seems possible; the young man pretends that his sense of modesty makes him give in to the wishes of Laches, whom he regards as an elder and better. If this is right and the next speech begins τί βοᾷς; (Jensen's reading, unverifiable on the photograph) that will belong to Kleainetos, who here comes up to the others.

28 ἠδικήμεθα: Kleainetos has been wronged because Moschion has ravished his daughter (or relative). But the offence was an old one and had been condoned by the marriage, of which Kleainetos had approved. Perhaps he thinks attack is the best form of defence; but I suspect that he is acting the part of a man suffering a recent injury. In any case, Laches will so understand the word, with Chaireas' story in his mind.

29 γνηςίων ἐπὶ ςπορᾷ παίδων: Elsewhere the father, when giving his daughter in marriage, uses the *formula* παίδων ἐπ' ἀρότῳ γνηςίων, *Perik.* 1013 n. The phrase ςπορὰ παίδων or τέκνων occurs when it is not a question of uttering a formula, Plato, *Laws* 729 c, 783 a, Clem. Alex. *Strom.* 2. 23, ἐπὶ γνηςίων τέκνων ςπορᾷ. But the discovery of a new text might upset this distinction. In frag. 682 Porson's emendation of ςπόρῳ τῶν γνηςίων to ἐπ' ἀρότῳ γνηςίων is preferable to Mette's γνηςίων ἐπὶ ςπορᾷ.

30 ὁ πατὴρ αὐτοῦ Λάχης ὁδί: The elaborate phrase suggests, but does not prove, that Laches and Kleainetos were previously unacquainted; cf. *Aspis* 262 n., Χαιρέας ὁδί.

32: In the three or four verses that are lost, it is very possible that Laches promised Chaireas his own daughter. Kuiper suggested that the doubtful letters ερα at the end of 33 are the last letters of frag. 682, παίδων ἐπ' ἀρότῳ γνηςίων | δίδωμί coι 'γὼ τὴν ἐμαυτὴν θυγατέρα. Somewhere before 41 Chaireas left, perhaps to take Moschion the news.

49 ἀςτεῖος: This word, in opposition to ἀγροῖκος, connotes good manners and intellectual flexibility: perhaps here, 'you have turned out to be a man of the world', through not creating the scene that might have been expected of a less cultured character.

53 οὐκ ἀκήκοας: This may be 'didn't you hear what I said?', sc. in 45–7.

57 πρωί: 'Too soon', i.e. at 49. The Attic form is monosyllabic, πρῴ (cf. *Suda*, πρῴ· οὕτω μονοcυλλάβως), and the Ionic πρωί, with short final syllable, e.g. *Iliad* viii. 530, πρωὶ δ' ὑπηοῖοι. Machon 329 Gow also offers spondaic πρωί in the first foot: it is possible that the two instances support one another, yet the scansion is hard to explain. The alternation of -τῐ and -τῑ, e.g. *Soph. OC* 1251, ἀcτακτῐ, 1646, ἀcτακτῑ, is not parallel. I should prefer to suppose that a word has been lost, e.g. ⟨ἢ⟩ πρῴ γε c' or πρῴ γε ⟨τότε⟩ c'.

59: The predicative position of φίλτατος, if taken with the preceding words, is hard to justify. Körte hesitantly suggested emending to the vocative φίλτατε, but there is nothing in the surviving lines to show that Laches has any warmth of feeling for Kleainetos. I punctuate (Λα.) οὐδὲ ἕν ὁ Χαιρέας ἄρ' ἠδίκηται; ⟨Κλ.⟩ φίλτατος—τί γὰρ ἠδίκηται; —Χαιρέας. No dicolon is visible at the end of the line.

61 ἐβούλετο: There is no need to suppose that Menander had devised any way in which Kleainetos might have completed his explanation.

63–4: It seems that Laches is resigned to accepting defeat. The play may be near its close, although it is conceivable that some further twist of the action is still to come (Kuiper).

If the play preceded *Heros* in C, as is probable, a minor conclusion may be drawn. *Heros* begins on p. 29, a 'recto'. These fragments came from a leaf in which 'recto' preceded 'verso'. Hence the *latest* possible pages with which they can be identified are 25, 26. If no page was completely blank, they were followed by between thirty-five and seventy lines. If on the other hand they come from pp. 21, 22, then 175 to 210 lines, i.e. a whole act, are missing.

Fragmentum dubium. If this belongs to *Fab. incert.*, it is surprising that Kleainetos (= *B*), who had already given the girl to Moschion, should now at this late stage find it necessary to use the formula of ἐγγύηcιc. But not enough is known of this ceremony's conditions and legal effects for it to be declared impossible.

It is also not clear why Chaireas should only now, at this last minute, have learnt that he will get the girl he loves. Perhaps Laches, angry at the trick played on him, had withdrawn the offer he had made of her hand. It is moreover odd that Laches should not be present to dispose of his own daughter; it is tempting to believe the girl to be on the stage, indicated by αὔτη.

These difficulties mean that the fragment is not obviously the end of *Fab. incert.*, although they are not so insuperable as to rule it out.

FRAGMENTS CITED BY
OTHER AUTHORS

ΑΡΡΗΦΟΡΟΣ ἢ ΑΥΛΗΤΡΙΣ ἢ ΑΥΛΗΤΡΙΔΕΣ

The alternative titles (cf. *Dysk*. hypothesis 15 n.) are given by Athenaios 442 d, 559 d, and the same fragment (60) is referred to Αὐλητρίδες by the *Suda* and to Ἀρρηφόρος by Stephanos of Byzantion and Zenobios. The plural form Αὐλητρίδες occurs also at Athenaios 446 d, [Justin], *de monarch*. 152, and in the list of plays by Menander, *P. Oxy*. 2462.

On the festival named Arrephoria, see W. Burkert, *Hermes*, xciv (1966), 1 ff., and L. Deubner, *Attische Feste*, 9 ff., who, however, rashly accepts the ancient derivation from ἀρρητοφορία, 'carrying of secret tokens or offerings'. The word is found outside Attica in forms such as ἐρσηφορία, ἐρρηφορεῖν (cf. ἔρσην, Att. ἄρρην). Nine fragments of the play survive, but little can be deduced from them about the plot, Webster, *StM* 145.

Frag. 59

2 τοῦτον τὸν βίον: 'This life you now lead'.

4 ἀνερρίφθω κύβος: 'Let the die be cast.' The perfect imperative orders the acceptance of what has been done, cf. δεδόχθω, λελέχθω, εἰρήσθω, and Euclid's ᾐτήσθω, 'let it stand assumed'. Caesar used this exclamation on crossing the Rubicon, Plut. *Caes*. 32, *Pomp*. 60; in the former passage Plutarch calls the phrase 'the usual preface of those embarking on uncertain chances'. When the die is once thrown, the way it falls depends upon chance; the outcome is not in the thrower's control. ἀναρρίπτειν was used because the die was thrown up in the air, as we toss a penny, cf. *AP* v. 25, ῥίπτω πάντα κύβον κεφαλῆς αἰὲν ὕπερθεν ἐμῆς. The phrase occurs first in a fragment of Kritias, *P. Oxy*. 2078, πᾶς ἀνέρριπται κύβος, and Aristophanes frag. 673; but κίνδυνον ἀναρρίπτειν, clearly a derivative, is already in Hdt. vii. 50. 3. Both expressions are fully documented and discussed by M. M. Kokolakis, Μορφολογία τῆς κυβευτικῆς μεταφορᾶς, 5–41 (more briefly by J. Taillardat, *REG* lxiv [1951], 4–9). He points out that there is no evidence to support the belief of many modern writers that Caesar was consciously quoting Menander's play. It is *possible* that the play gave currency to the expression, but more likely, in view of the commonness of the conjunction κύβον ἀναρρίπτειν, that Caesar and Menander's character both used a well-established formula.

5 ἀληθινόν: The psychology of calling a metaphorical sea a 'genuine' one seems to be the same as that of the journalist who embellishes his metaphors with 'literally'. For 'the sea of troubles' cf. Aesch. *Pers.* 433, κακῶν δὴ πέλαγοc.

6 αὐτὸν for cεαυτόν is not uncommon in Xenophon, Plato, and the orators as well as in tragedy, where it is confirmed by metre, e.g. Aesch. *Agam.* 1297, μόρον τὸν αὑτῆc οἶcθα, K–G ii. 572.

8 οὗ . . . τρία: 'Where not three out of thirty ships are lost'. Some have taken οὐκ with ἀπόλλυται, 'three out of thirty are not lost' : this excessively pessimistic view of the dangers of navigation spoils the contrast with the certainty of disaster in matrimony.

9 οὐδὲ εἶς . . . ὅλωc: 'Absolutely not a soul'. ὅλωc goes with the negative, cf. *Dysk.* 861.

Frag. 60

1 κινήcῃ: κινεῖν with a personal object can mean 'stir to anger', or be used *sens. obsc.*, but here the meaning clearly is 'move to speech', as in Plato, *Rep.* 329 e, βουλόμενος ἔτι λέγειν αὐτὸν ἐκίνουν.

2 ἦν τίτθην καλεῖ: I print this, since it is not necessarily wrong. But Bentley's correction ἢ τίτθην καλῇ is plausible. The old wet nurse is encouraged in her loquacity by the reminder that she had once held this position of trust.　　**πέρας ποιεῖ λαλιᾶc**: 'Causes a perfection of loquacity', cf. Poseidippos frag. 26. 17 K, τῆc τέχνηc πέρας, Damoxenos frag. 3 K, πέρας τι κάλλους. Bentley's πέρας ⟨οὐ⟩ ποιεῖ, 'she makes no end of talking', is unnecessary, and introduces a rare, although not unexampled, break in the anapaest (see *Heros* 22, *Epitr.* 299).

3 τὸ Δωδωναῖον χαλκίον: The phrase was used proverbially, we are told by the *Suda*, Zenobios i. 2, Diogenianus viii. 32, of long-winded talkers. Two other explanations are recorded by Steph. Byz. s.v. Δωδώνη, neither of which agrees with Menander's. Demon, writer of a book about proverbs, active in the late fourth century B.C., said that there were many 'tripods' (holding bowls, cf. Xen. *Anab.* vii. 3. 21, where τρίποδεc are described as 'full of meat') at Dodona set up together in line round the sanctuary; if one was touched the resonance passed to the next and so on, and the sound continued until checked by laying a hand on the first tripod. Polemon, a century or more later, objected that the proverb referred to a single vessel; he described what was no doubt visible in his time, a single bowl standing on a column; it was made to sing by the lashes of a whip held by a statue on an adjacent column and moved by the wind. The ancient evidence is set out by A. B. Cook, *JHS* xxii (1902), 5 ff., and H. W. Parke, *The Oracles of Zeus*, 86–8, who think that Menander refers to Demon's story. One might suppose him to refer to neither story, but to imagine, rightly or wrongly, a single cauldron which was made to sing by human touch. If he was right, the cauldron may later have been mounted on the column alongside the statue, which was a dedication by the Corcyreans (Strabo vii. frag. 3). Kallimachos refers to it twice: *Hymn* iv. 286, ἀcιγήτοιο λέβητος, and frag. 483 Pfeiffer, μή με τὸν ἐν Δωδῶνι λέγοι μόνον οὕνεκα χαλκὸν | ἤγειρον.

6 νύκτα: For the absence of the article, cf. K–G i. 606.

ΔΕΙCΙΔΑΙΜΩΝ

According to Caecilius (? of Kale Akte, *floruit c.* 50 B.C.), reported by Eusebios, *PE* x. 3. 13, this play was a copy or a rewriting (μεταγράψαι) of Antiphanes' Οἰωνιcτής from beginning to end. Accusations of plagiarism were freely made in antiquity, and there is no telling what degree of similarity there may have been between the two plays.

Frag. 97

1–2: The omissions in Clement's text cannot be made good with certainty; in particular it is impossible to say where in the line ἀγαθόν τι μοι γένοιτο should be placed.

3–4 τὸν ἱμάντα τῆς δεξιᾶς ἐμβάδος: The ἐμβάc was a kind of boot, described by Pollux vii. 85 as being in shape like a low κόθορνος, fastened across the ankle by a thong (ἱμάc). It was a common form of footwear for men, frequently mentioned by Aristophanes; Isaios v. 11 speaks of it as characteristic wear of the poor; and it is no doubt part of the joke here that the superstitious person makes so much fuss over a cheap boot. But expensive ἐμβάδες were also made, Ameling, *RE* v. 2482. Evidence about the materials used is scanty, but the ἐμβάδες of a gardener in *AP* vi. 21 were ὠμοβοεῖς, i.e. of untanned cowhide. LSJ's view that ἐμβάδες were made of felt is perhaps no more than a guess, but felt 'uppers' are conceivable as one variety.

4 ὦ φλήναφε: Elsewhere φλήναφος means 'nonsense', but Pollux vi. 119 includes it in a list of derogatory adjectives applicable to bores, μακρολόγος, πολυλόγος, βαρύς, ἐπαχθής, φληναφῶν, φλήναφος, τὴν γλῶτταν ὀλισθηρός κτλ. E. Fraenkel, *Plautinisches im Plautus*, 185[1], thinks this speaker is not seen by the first.

Frags. 208, 209

The speaker of 209 (which comes from an unnamed play) imagines the horrors of a wedding-party where there are present many relations of the bride; a wedding-party, since this is an occasion when men and women drink together. Wilamowitz plausibly connected this with frag. 208, from Θυρωρός, where the speaker congratulates himself (or another) on getting a bride who has no relations (*SB Berlin* 1907, 10).

2: The form ἑώρακα for ἑόρακα (due to analogy with ἑώρων) occurs in papyri and inscriptions from the third century B.C. There is no other place in comedy where it is required by the metre, but there is no easy way of avoiding it here. 'Has not even heard of an uncle': for this construction of ἀκούω with acc. of person perhaps cf. Ar. *Thesm.* 164, καὶ Φρυνίχος· τοῦτον γὰρ οὖν ἀκήκοας. K–G i. 360, Schwyzer, ii. 107, understand it this way. But others suppose 'you have heard Phrynichos' to mean 'you have heard Phrynichos' songs'.

3: The reading of Photios, ὀλιγοστούς, is dubious in sense; 'low in the range of ordinal numbers' is not the equivalent of 'few'. The singular ὀλιγοστός may mean 'one of a few', but that is not to the point. Since ὀλιγοστούς would also be metrically exceptional in Menander, as violating the rule of median diaeresis in the trochaic tetrameter, everywhere observed except at *Sam.* 484, it is better emended.

4 τρίκλινον: Neut. noun, properly 'dining-room', hence 'dinner-party', as in Anaxandrides frag. 70 K, τρίκλινον δ' εὐθέως cυνήγετο. **cυγγενείας:** 'Kinsfolk', LSJ s.v. II.

6: The right reading is hard to find. The MSS. of Athenaios give παραίνεcιc πέπαικεν. Schweighauser proposed παραινέcειc πέπαικεν (is that Greek?). With πέπαιχε, the perfect of παίζω, the phrase would mean 'he has played the game of "Advice"'. No such game is known; could the speaker imagine one? A further difficulty is that πέπαιχα is, not surprisingly, very rare. The perfect indicates the present result of a past action, and so Plutarch can write, *Demosthenes* 9, Ἀντιφάνης τουτὶ πέπαιχεν, 'there is this jest by Antiphanes'. If πέπαιχεν is right here, it may indicate that the father remains conscious of the game he has played. πέπαικα is the perfect of παίω, and not known in classical Greek except in the compound ὑπερπέπαικα. If it were combined with Meineke's suggestion παραινέcαc, possibly the meaning might be 'having given his advice, he has thumped me on the back'. But again the perfect is odd, and it may be doubted whether the mother would also treat the guest so roughly. Meineke wrote πέπωκεν, but that word connotes the effects of drinking, which should not be apparent so early in the proceedings. An alteration perhaps no less likely than any of these would be παραινέcει πέπαιχεν, 'has used the giving of advice to make jokes'.

7 τήθη: 'Grandmother'. Meineke was perhaps right in changing to τηθίς, 'aunt', in view of the next line. But 'some grandmother' is intelligible as expressing impatience, and the MS. text is not impossible. **παραλαλεῖ:** 'Breaks in with some chatter': the word recurs in Dio Cassius lxix. 4, εἶπε τῷ Ἀδριανῷ παραλαλήcαντί τι ὅτι "ἄπελθε καὶ τὰς κολοκύνθας γράφε". Meineke's παρακαλεῖ, 'exhorts', brings no improvement.

8 γραῦc καλοῦcα φίλτατον: 'An old woman who calls you "darling" '. Since no relationship is stated it may be suspected that this is an old slave-woman, perhaps the bride's former nurse.

9 ὁ δέ: Apparently the father nods his approval. But there is another possibility, i.e. that 4–8 are part of a reported speech, and that ὁ δέ refers to the man to whom it was originally delivered.

ΙΕΡΕΙΑ

Körte, *Hermes*, lxxv (1940), 106; Kuiper, *Mnem.* 3rd ser. viii (1940), 283; Webster, *StM* 149.

The plot is partially known from a papyrus which seems to have contained summaries of Menander's plays in alphabetical order, together with information about their first performance. The plays are identified not only by their titles but also by quotation of the opening line: this was a standard procedure, cf. the summaries of Euripidean plays in *P. Oxy.* 2455, 2457 and *PSI* 1286 (C. Austin, *Nova Fragmenta Euripidea*, 88–103), and the fragments of similar Menandrean catalogues, *P. Oxy.* 2534 and *P. IFAO* 337 (*ZPE* vi [1970], 5). Körte guessed the papyrus to be part of the work of one Sellios or Sillios, alias Homeros, whom the *Suda* records (s.vv. Ὅμηρος Cέλλιος and Cέλλιος) as having composed prose summaries of Menander's plays.

The priestess of the title had given her son to a married woman who had passed him off as her own. Later this woman had had a son and a daughter of her own. The supposititious son's father, ignorant of his whereabouts, had in some way connected him with the priestess. One of his slaves agreed to pretend to be possessed by a spirit, and was sent to the priestess for exorcism: he 'discovered the truth', or rather part of it, namely that the missing boy passed as the other woman's son. Meanwhile that woman's younger, legitimate, son had fallen in love with the priestess's daughter, and caused his mother to go to the priestess to discuss a marriage. The old man, overhearing a conversation between the women, got a suspicion of the truth, and being told

by his servant that the two young men differed in features, jumped
to the conclusion that the younger was his son, and greeted him as
such. The young man rebuffed him, but, realizing the nature of his
mistake, warned his 'brother' that the old man was demented and
given to claiming all young men as his sons. The old man then found
out the truth and attempted to claim his real son; but he too rebuffed
him. (Körte thinks that these scenes were suggested by Eur. *Ion* 517 ff.,
but the likeness of situation is not striking.) After this the errors were
in some way dissipated, and the play ended with a triple marriage,
of the old man to the priestess, of his son to the girl he had supposed
to be his sister, and of the other young man to the priestess's daughter.

This summary leaves much unexplained. (1) It looks as if the
younger man acted against his own financial interest when he tried
to prevent the recognition of his supposed brother. His motive may
have been to spare his mother the discovery of her deceit; or he may
have thought him to be the old man's bastard and wished to save him
from that awkward and inferior position. (2) Under what circumstances had the old man got the priestess with child? Hunt's supplement of 37-9, accepted by Körte, makes him her previous husband.
This leads to difficulties. Why had they separated? Why could he not
ask her directly what had become of her child? It would be easier
to suppose that he had got the child by rape, that she had married
someone else by whom she had had her daughter, and then become
a widow. The old man would then be a stranger and unable to ask
her about a child, born out of wedlock, whose existence she had never
owned. His marriage to her at the end of the play would be necessary
to legitimize their son, and so make it possible (assuming the scene
to be Athens) for him to contract a full marriage.

Frag. 210

This is the only considerable surviving fragment from the play. Körte
thought the lines were addressed to the priestess by the old man; in
them he revealed the reason why he had left her—an unwillingness
to put up with her religious practices; the mention of cymbals shows
her to be a devotee of Kybebe. Thus to revive the old subject of
dispute seems out of place, and other interpretations of the fragment
are possible.

The rare name Ῥόδη recurs in frag. 592 (q.v.), which Clericus
wished to assign to *Hiereia*. If Ῥόδη of *Hiereia* is the priestess, Ῥόδη
of frag. 592 is hardly the same character; but both might be the
married woman, the priestess's neighbour. Kuiper, whom Webster
inclines to follow, guessed that both fragments were spoken to this

woman by her husband in an early scene, as he left for the country: frag. 592 reproves her for her conduct, frag. 210 criticizes her friend the priestess.

1: 'God does not preserve one man because of the intervention of another' is the required meaning, not 'by means of another as his agent'.

2 τινα: Ps.-Justin's 'some god or another' suits the contemptuous attitude of the speaker, and Clement's τὸν θεόν is *lectio facilior*.

3 κυμβάλοιc: Cymbals were used in the worship of Kybele, but not in hers alone.

5 βίαc: Bentley's emendation of βίου is not entirely convincing. To whom do these religious impostors do violence? Perhaps it is a case of pretended exertion of force upon the god. But the τόλμα with which it is joined is real, not pretended. βίου, however, is perhaps more difficult: the cymbals would then be instruments through which effrontery is *displayed*, and a livelihood is *gained*; the two genitives would express different relations. Yet, if this is possible, the resulting sense is excellent.

7 εἰc καταγέλωτα τῷ βίῳ: I find this as obscure as Meineke's translation, 'in seculi ignominiam'. Can it be 'inventions for the ordinary run of men to laugh at'? For this meaning of βίοc see LSJ s.v. III, who quote only authors of the Greco-Roman period.

Blaydes's emendation τῶν θεῶν, 'inventions to bring the gods into ridicule', gives a good sense.

ΙΠΠΟΚΟΜΟC

Frag. 215

Monimos is said by Diogenes Laertius vi. 82 to have been a Syracusan, the slave of a banker and later a follower of the Cynic Krates. The other biographical details, including an association with Diogenes, are regarded as apocryphal by K. von Fritz, *RE* xvi. 127. He was well-enough known to be represented as a skeleton, carrying a wallet, on a silver cup from Boscoreale, *Arch. Anz.* (1896), 82. Since he is spoken of in the past tense, he was dead or no longer in Athens when this play was written.

2 ἀδοξότεροc: The speaker must mean 'not very celebrated'; then after the interruption he continues 'but yet the author of a remarkable piece of wisdom'. Allinson translates 'a little too paradoxical', a meaning too unusual (LSJ s.v. II) to be understood without help from the context.

3 τρεῖc: The point is obscure, unless it is merely, as Meineke guessed, that the wallet (for alms) is the mark of the Cynic, and that one with three wallets is thrice a Cynic and an unconscionable beggar. The suggestion (Allinson etc.) that Monimos had a hunchback and a paunch as well as a wallet is quite unsupported.

5 βοωμένοιc: 'That get cried up'.

6 ῥυπῶν: Moralists who are suspicious of pleasure or set up to follow Nature may avoid bathing or even 'excessive' washing; but even apart from theory it would not have been practicable in ancient Athens for a beggar, sleeping rough, to keep clean.

Epikt. iv. 11. 9–30 inveighs against those who associate dirt and virtue, clearly with an eye to certain Cynics.

7 τῦφος, properly 'delirium', and popularly used of follies and delusions, cf. τυφογέρων in Ar. *Clouds* 908, *Lys.* 335, was a favourite word among Cynics, who applied it to all the vanities they ascribed to the mass of humanity; cf. Krates' parody of *Od.* xix. 172, Πήρη τιc πόλιc ἐcτι μέcῳ ἐνὶ οἴνοπι τύφῳ (frag. 4 Diels). Sextus Emp. *adv. M.* viii. 5 writes Μόνιμος ὁ κύων, τῦφον εἰπὼν τὰ πάντα, ὅπερ οἴηcίc ἐcτι τῶν οὐκ ὄντων ὡc ὄντων. ὑπολαμβάνειν means 'assume' (often of what is assumed without warrant or justification). Monimos seems to have advised sticking to known facts, and to have ridiculed all theorizing.

ΚΥΒΕΡΝΗΤΑΙ

Frag. 250

5 ἀθαναcίαc δ' οὐκ ἔcτιν: Sc. τιμὴν παραcχεῖν δυνατόν.

6: Zenobios vi. 4, διεβεβόητο ὁ Τάνταλοc ἐπὶ πλούτῳ, ὡc καὶ εἰc παροιμίαν διαδοθῆναι.

7: Stob. iv. 51. 8, which gives the name of the play, is more likely *a priori* to be right than iii. 22. 19, which does not. But apart from that, 'if you die' comes oddly after the statement that money cannot buy immortality.

In Stob. iii. 22. 19 *Dysk.* 254–7 are attached without a break.

Frag. 251

2 οἱ φυcῶντεc . . . μέγα: 'Those who puff themselves with pride at themselves', cf. *Epitr.* 913 n.

3 αὐτοί: I.e. whatever deficiencies they may despise in others, they themselves do not know what man's nature is.

5 τὰς θύρας: The singular τὴν θύραν is more common, but the plural frequent enough to make the majority reading acceptable; the phrase ἄνοιγε τὰς θύρας recurs at *Aspis* 312, ἄνοιγε τὴν θύραν at *Dysk.* 427, 454.

4–7: If these lines followed directly upon 1–3, the speaker must have been muddle-headed. The fact that X, who appears splendid in the outer world, is hen-pecked at home does not illustrate any universal aspect of human nature. The speaker indeed emphasizes that it does not, by drawing a distinction between X and himself, who has no cause for distress. The self-satisfaction of his final words goes ill with the opening οἷοι λαλοῦμεν ὄντες, 'how we talk when our state is what it is'. I think it likely that two extracts have coalesced in Orion; the first was on the topic 'pride goes before a fall', the second on 'the great have their troubles'. It is noteworthy that Stobaios quotes the first three lines alone, in his chapter headed περὶ ὑπεροψίας, On Disdain, Plutarch the last four alone, to illustrate the theme that those whom you may be tempted to envy have troubles of their own.

ΜΕΘΗ

The mention of Kallimedon in 14, with the implication that he is in Athens, shows this play to be earlier than 318 B.C., when he was condemned to death in his absence (Plutarch, *Phocion* 35) by the restored democracy. He is described by Plutarch, ibid. 28, as μισό-δημος. This is the only example in the remains of Menander of an attack on a political figure.

Frag. 264

1: 'Are not our fortunes in line with our sacrifices?', i.e. both poor. It is possible that this was the line with which a character came on the stage, leading his intended sacrificial victim; εἶτα is Knemon's first word as he enters, *Dysk.* 153.

2 τοῖς θεοῖς μέν is in thought opposed to ἐμαυτῷ δὲ καὶ τοῖς φίλοις.

3 ἀγαπητόν: A sheep with which I am well satisfied, bought for ten drachmas. W. K. Pritchett, *Hesperia*, xxv (1956), 256 ff., shows that sacrificial sheep usually cost somewhat more than this; in the famine year 329 B.C. the price rose as high as thirty drachmae. The diminutive προβάτιον is depreciatory. Kock proposes to read ἄγομεν and ἀνάπηρον, comparing Hermippos frag. 35 K, ἀνάπηρά σοι θύουσιν ἤδη βοίδια.

5 Μενδαῖον, sc. οἶνον. This was a favoured white wine (Kratinos frag. 183); Athenaios 29 f quotes Phainias of Eresos to the effect that it was smooth (μαλακός) because the grapes were drenched with the juice of the squirting cucumber. In [Dem.] xxxv. 18 3,000 jars (κεράμια) are worth one talent, i.e. two drachmae a jar. Mende was a town on the coast of the Thracian Chalkidike. Handsome coinage of the period 450–425 B.C. shows a vine laden with grapes. On Thasian wine see *Kolax* 48 n.

6 μικροῦ: Sc. δεῖ, 'almost a talent', clearly a violent exaggeration.

γίνεται τὸ κατὰ λόγον: 'There comes about what is proportionate (to our outlay)', i.e. ten drachmas' worth of good fortune at the best; λαβεῖν and ἀντανελεῖν are epexegetic of τὸ κατὰ λόγον.

9: 'And to deduct as a set-off against them (πρὸς ταῦτα) the expense on these things', i.e. the girls, wine, etc. In casting up our accounts we find ten drachmas on the credit side, provided the sacrifice has been accompanied by good omens, and all our expenditure on the other. τούτων and ταῦτα, somewhat confusingly to the eye, have different references; on the stage a gesture might help understanding. For ἀντavαιρεῖν as a term of business arithmetic see LSJ s.v.

10: Wilamowitz suggested the deletion of this verse; I do not understand it. Kock's interpretation, 'et pecunia perit et poena a sacrificantibus exigitur', does not suit 7–8.

11–12: See *Dysk.* 451 n.

13 τὴν ἔγχελυν: The definite article (for which Dobree proposed to substitute τιν') can best be represented in English by translating 'his eel', i.e. the eel which my regulations would require to be served to the gods at every sacrifice.

14 ἵνα with past indicative expresses the unattained purpose of an unaccomplished action or wish, Goodwin, *MT* 333, 336. The politician Kallimedon is frequently made fun of in Middle Comedy for his *gourmandise* over fish, e.g. Antiphanes frag. 26 K, Alexis frags. 112 K, 168 K, 193 K. The point here seems to be that he would be so horrified if an eel were made into a burnt-offering for the gods instead of a dish for human consumption that he would sacrifice his life in an attempt to save it. The joke can only have been intelligible to men who had heard previous more explicit jests in other comedies, such as that of Alexis frag. 193 K, ὑπὲρ πάτρας μὲν πᾶς τις ἀποθνῄσκειν θέλει, | ὑπὲρ δὲ μήτρας (*cervix uteri* of the sow, a great delicacy) Καλλιμέδων ὁ Κάραβος | ἐφθῆς ἴσως προσεῖτ' ἄν (the *traditio*, πρὸς ἰταλων, is corrupt: προσεῖτ' ἄν ἄλλον Arnott) ἀποθανεῖν. Kallimedon's passion for eels was also referred to by Alexis frag. 145 K, γενοίμην ἔγχελυς, ἵνα Καλλιμέδων ὁ Κάραβος πρίαιτο με. He is called one of the eel's relatives because he was nicknamed Κάραβος, 'langouste' (*Palinurus vulgaris*) from his squint—a far-fetched joke, since it does not need a modern zoologist to see that an eel and a crustacean have little in common.

In this piece the point is somewhat laboured and the concluding jests frigid. It is conceivable that this was intentional and characterized the speaker, but more likely that in this early play Menander was still feeling his way.

ΜΙCΟΓΥΝΗC

Pap. Ant. 55 (vol. ii. 196) gives some lines of a comedy which its editor, J. W. B. Barns, identified with Μιcογύνης, a play that Phrynichos s.v. γῦροc called τὴν καλλίcτην τῶν (sc. Μενάνδρου) κωμωδιῶν. We know of its revival in the first twelve years of the second century B.C., B. Snell, *Nach. Akad. Wiss. Göttingen* (1966), 32, Pickard-Cambridge, *Dramatic Festivals*[2], 110. Barns attempted to reconstruct the plot with the aid of the fragments quoted in literary sources. Unfortunately his identification is improbable, see K. Latte, *Gnomon*, xxxiv (1962), 152.

What the papyrus gives is too fragmentary to be worth treatment in this book. For a discussion see T. Williams, *Philologus*, cv (1962), 193.

Frag. 276

This fragment is composed of two passages 1–6, 7–16, which may have been separated by some lines, but which surely belong to the same speech. As Körte argues, the character on whom the advantages of marriage are urged is probably not a young man, to judge by his name. One passage of Stobaios gives it as Demeas, the other as Simylos. Demeas is in comedy always the name of a man old enough to have grown-up children; Simylos occurs only in Ter. *Adelphoe* 352, where it belongs to a dead father. Whether this character is being encouraged to bear with his wife or to take the plunge and marry is not certain from these lines. The idea of an old bachelor's marrying is not foreign to Menander, e.g. *Georgos*, Ter. *Adelphoe*. Nevertheless, other fragments suggest that he is a husband. Frag. 277 shows that the μιcογύνης (who is likely to be the same person) was or had been married; in frag. 279 someone threatens to bring an action for ill-treatment against a husband, who is again likely to be the μιcογύνης. This combination falls short of constituting proof, but the most likely conclusion is that Simylos is the μιcογύνης and is married.

5–6: *Ecl.* iv. 44 gives, and *Ecl.* iv. 41 does not give, the name of the play. The text of the former is, therefore, less likely to have suffered deliberate change (cf. W. Görler, *Μενάνδρου Γνῶμαι*, 111); the latter's unmetrical ὦ Δημέα looks like an attempt to avoid the unfamiliar name Cιμύλε.

7 πολυτελήc: The wife in question may have had expensive tastes, although frags. 283, 284, which mention luxuries, do not of themselves show this, and it would be rash to print Kaibel's otherwise attractive suggestion πολυτελέc ἐcτ', ὀχληρόν, 'a wife is a cause of expense, of trouble'. Observe that the passage seems, as it continues, to have any wife in mind (9 ff.) not only an extravagant one.   **οὐδ':** 'Not even' is hardly the sense: it looks as if, contrary to the idiom of Attic speech, οὐδέ is here used without a preceding negative, instead of καὶ οὐ. One may suspect that the lines should run γυνὴ πολυτελέc ἐcτ', ὀχληρόν, οὐκ ἐᾷ ζῆν τὸν λαβόνθ' ὡc βούλεται.

8: τοι is a rare word in Menander, and nowhere clearly right, see *Sam.* 150 n. Some support for τι here is to be found in a frag. ascribed to Euripides' *Antigone* (Nauck, *TGF* 828), ζευχθεὶc γάμοιcιν οὐκέτ' ἐcτ' ἐλεύθεροc· ἀλλ' ἕν γ' ἔχει τι χρηcτόν.

9 παῖδεc: This is suspect, for it is illogical to say '*one* good thing comes of her, children', and then to continue in the same breath to expound at some length another advantage that a wife confers, her care for the sick and the dead. παῖδεc was, however, already in Clement's text, for he paraphrases as follows: βοηθεῖ δ' ὁ γάμοc καὶ ἐπὶ τῶν προβεβηκότων τῷ χρόνῳ, παριcτὰc τὴν γαμετὴν ἐπιμελομένην καὶ τοὺc ἐκ ταύτηc παῖδαc γηροβοcκοὺc τρέφων. If the text is correct, the only explanation is that the speaker interrupts his sermon to knock upon a door and summon the slaves within; this must seem improbable, although there is something of a parallel at *Kolax* 114. Another possibility is that some reader, thinking that children were a desirable result of any marriage, added the word, and that it has expelled something else, metrically equivalent (? καὶ μέγ').

10 ταύτην: Sc. τὴν νόcον, if right, but I think Herwerden's correction necessary.   **ἐθεράπευcεν:** Gnomic aor.

16 προcδοκωμένων: Cf. *Mis.* 114 n.

ΝΑΥΚΛΗΡΟC

Frag. 286

The assignment of speeches is difficult. In 2 ὡc εἰc καλόν is perhaps an exclamation, 'at what a good moment!' and should be given to Straton, as suggested by Thierfelder; but 1–4 may all belong to speaker A. The last two lines, given to A by Meineke, were transferred to Straton by Körte. I agree with Thierfelder that this is unlikely; when

Straton has heard that the ship is safe, he has no obvious reason for meticulously identifying it; but without the context, it is impossible to be certain that he had none. Another possibility is that Straton is not the father but the messenger: then punctuate ὦ Cτράτων, ὡς εἰς καλόν. The unusual ὦ with the vocative would then be a sign of emotion; compare *Aspis* 19.

1: A takes the line from Eur. *Troades* 1, changing ἥκω to ἥκει. Aristophanes frag. 1 begins ἥκω Θεαρίωνος ἀρτοπωλίον λιπών.

2 Θεόφιλος: This is probably the ναύκληρος, or ship-owner; he is not necessarily the son, who may have been a passenger.

3 cεcωμένος, not cεcωcμένος, is the Attic form, *Sik.* 121 n.

4 κάνθαρον: A word of many meanings. Two are in play here: (*a*) a kind of ship, as in Ar. *Peace* 143 (again a pun), Nikostratos frag. 10 K; (*b*) a deep drinking-cup with handles; Athenaios 473 d–474 d gives thirteen examples, including twelve from comedy, of which this fragment is one. (Webster, however, *JHS* lxxv [1955], 160, seems to think its inclusion a mistake.) Speaker A must intend the word in the latter sense; the other replies: 'What kind of κάνθαρος? You mean the ship?' A sees that he knows nothing of the golden cup: the words οὐδὲν οἶcθας ἄθλιε may be either a statement or a question; whichever they are, the second speaker disregards them, wishing to have the safety of the ship confirmed.

6 ff: The text is uncertain and the meaning also. I have supposed that A elaborately and absurdly identifies the ship; this fits well with the way he used Eur. *Troades* 1 to announce Theophilos' arrival. Thierfelder's guess that he is a parasite is reasonable, although no more than possibly true. Kaibel believed that A was speaking metaphorically of the cup, of which Kallikles was the maker, Euphranor the previous owner; this also is possible. Körte thought that A said ἔγωγε μήν, and the other continued, to make sure that the right ship was identified. If this sense is correct, it could be attained with less alteration of the transmitted text by writing (A) ἔγω⟨γε⟩. (Cτρ.) τὴν | ἐμὴν ἐκείνην ⟨ἣν⟩ ἐποίηςε Καλλικλῆς.

8 †τὸν καλούμενον†: Heringa's ὁ Καλύμνιος gives a broken anapaest.

Frag. 287

This is probably the speech of a traveller, greeting his native land on his return from a voyage. Cf. frag. 1 (Plaut. *Stichus* 402), Plaut. *Bacchides* 170, probably *Aspis* 491.

4 ἤδη indicates that this punishment ought to follow 'without more ado'.

6 οὐκ ἐφείсατο: 'Did not use it thriftily', i.e. squandered it.

ΟΡΓΗ

This was Menander's first play, produced in 321 B.C. Not only do the two longer fragments preserved make fun of historical persons, but frag. 305 mentions the starveling Philippides. 'Οργή is presumably (like Μέθη, another title) the abstract noun, although it was also a proper name (Gow on Machon xix).

Frag. 303

A husband complains that he is being forced into an extravagance of living such as was not his even when he was a young man; in New Comedy (and no doubt sometimes in life) the sons of rich fathers spend lavishly on their pleasures.

3–4 χλανίδα: Cf. *Dysk.* 257 n.   βάψομαι: 'Will get my hair dyed'.

5 παρατιλοῦμαι: The removal of superfluous hair from the body, practised by women, was regarded as effeminacy in men (Epiktetos iii, 1. 27–45, treats the subject at some length), and luxury was by many associated with effeminacy.   νὴ Δία καί: The apparent broken anapaest can be removed by reading νὴ Δί, a form vouched for by ancient grammarians, see *Dysk.* 774 n.

6: According to Athenaios 165 e Ktesippos, son of the general Chabrias, was a spendthrift who sold the stone of his father's tomb, which had been paid for by the city, to meet the cost of his pleasures.

Frag. 304

1: Chairephon was a parasite and gatecrasher mentioned by several authors of the Middle Comedy, Timokles, Antiphanes, Timotheos, Alexis. See *Samia* 603 n.   διαφέρει . . . οὐδὲ γρῦ: *Sam.* 655 n.

2: ὅс probably refers back to Χαιρεφῶντος.

3–4: There is an involved order of words, such as Menander would not have used in his later writing; what is meant is πρὸс τὴν cελήνην τὴν cκιὰν ἰδών, ὄρθριοс ἔτρεχεν ὡс ὑcτερίζων.

3 δωδεκάποδος: There is an ellipse of cτοιχείου or cκιᾶς (Hesychios s.v.), cf. Ar. *Eccl.* 652, ὅταν ᾖ δεκάπουν τὸ cτοιχεῖον, λιπαρὸν χωρεῖν ἐπὶ δεῖπνον (see Rogers's ed.), Pollux vi. 44, τῇ cκιᾷ δ' ἐτεκμαίροντο τὸν καιρὸν τῆс ἐπὶ δεῖπνον ὁδοῦ, ἣν καὶ cτοιχεῖον ἐκάλουν. Although there is no explicit evidence, it is probable that this method of reckoning time depended on measuring the shadow of a vertical stick one foot high.

This character, whether Chairephon or one like him, outdoes Philokrates in Eubulos frag. 119 K, ὅν φασί ποτε κληθέντ' ἐπὶ δεῖπνον πρός τινος, εἰπόντος αὐτῷ τοῦ †φίλου† ὁπηνίκ' ἂν εἴκοσι ποδῶν μετροῦντι τὸ στοιχεῖον ᾖ, ἥκειν, ἕωθεν αὐτὸν εὐθὺς ἡλίου μετρεῖν ἀνέχοντος, μακροτέρας δ' οὔςης ἔτι πλεῖν ἢ δυοῖν ποδοῖν παρεῖναι τῆς σκιᾶς, φάναι δ' ἔπειτα μικρὸν ὀψιαίτερον δι' ἀσχολίαν ἥκειν, παρόνθ' ἅμ' ἡμέρᾳ. Menander's greater concision is noteworthy, and his story is hardly spoiled by the fact that the moon does not regularly set just before daybreak.

ΠΛΟΚΙΟΝ

The Roman dramatist Caecilius adapted this play, and Aulus Gellius ii. 23. 5 compares three passages: 'di boni, quantum stupere et frigere quantumque mutare a Menandro Caecilius uisus est.' This judgement makes it hazardous to reconstruct Menander's play with the aid of the fragments of Caecilius, but the attempt has been made by O. Ribbeck, *Com. Rom. Frag.* 68, and by Webster, *StM* 99 f., who boldly brings in Menander, *frag. incert.* 612. What is clear is this. One house in inhabited by a man and his wife Krobyle, an ugly heiress who wears the trousers, and her (perhaps their) son and daughter. Being suspicious, she causes him to sell a young slave-girl, an excellent worker of good appearance (frag. 333). Caecilius' phrase 'facie haut illiberali' suggests that this girl may have turned out to be of free birth, and perhaps the πλόκιον (necklace) of the title played a part in her recognition. The neighbouring house belongs to a poor man, who has a daughter and a faithful slave; they have moved in from the country less than ten months previously, perhaps quite recently. The daughter had been ravished at some night-festival, but this misfortune had been concealed from her father. Now she gives birth to a child (frag. 335), and her cries are overheard by the slave. Analogy with other plays suggests that the child's father proved to be Krobyle's son, whose mother probably wished him to marry some kinswoman (frag. 345). A scene from the second act is represented on one of the mosaics from Mitilini, showing Krobyle along with Laches and Moschion, probably her husband and son (G. Daux, *BCH* xci [1967], 475; L. Kahil and others, *Antike Kunst*, Beiheft 6 [1970]). Further details that can be deduced with more or less probability from the fragments of Menander and Caecilius do not affect the understanding of the passages printed in OCT.

Frag. 333

1 ἐπ' ἀμφότερα: Sc. ὦτα. *Paroem. gr.* ii. 409, ἐπ' ἀμφότερα καθεύδει τὰ ὦτα· ἐπὶ τῶν ἔξω φροντίδος. R. Foerster, *Hermes*, xii (1877), 214, cited Libanius, *Ep.* 490. 4 and *Chr.* 3. 24, for examples of the omission of ὦτα. As Krobyle was an ἐπίκληρος, she had presumably been married, according to the law, by her nearest male relative (intro. p. 29).

5 ἀποβλέπωσιν εἰς τὸ πρόσωπον: This vivid phrase is found as a cliché in the N.T., Matthew 22 : 16, Mark 12 : 14.

6 ἐμὴ γυνή, not ἡ ἐμὴ γυνὴ, because the relationship is emphasized; see *Dysk.* 240 n. The meaning will be 'so that it may be clear that it is my *wife* who gives the orders in my house'. But the reading is not certain. ἐμοί would give a good sense: 'My *wife* treats me like a slave.'

7 ἐκτήσατο: 'Has got herself', as if she were responsible for her own face.

8 ὄνος ἐν πιθήκοις: *Paroem. gr.* i. 439, ὄνος ἐν πιθήκοις· ἐπὶ τῶν αἰσχρῶν ἐν αἰσχροῖς.

10 κακῶν ἀρχηγόν: The speaker wrily uses high-falutin' language, cf. Eur. *Hipp.* 881, κακῶν ἀρχηγὸν ἐκφαίνεις λόγον.

12 τὴν ῥῖν' ἔχουσαν πηχέως: Kock's ingenious and plausible emendation is based on Lucian, *de mercede conductis* 35, εἰςὶ δ' οἳ καὶ ἐπὶ κάλλει θαυμάζεσθαι ἐθέλουσι . . . πηχέως ἐνίοτε τὴν ῥῖνα ἔχοντες. 'A nose of two feet', i.e. a two-foot-long nose. Such 'qualitative' genitives are more often used of time than of space, but cf. Xen. *Anab.* i. 4. 11, ὄντα τὸ εὖρος τεττάρων σταδίων.

13 φρύαγμα: Lit. 'whinnying', metaphorically 'airs'. Aristainetos ii. 12, φρύαγμα ὁμοζύγου πλουσίας, may be based on this passage.

ὑποστατόν: 'Supportable', another elevated word, elsewhere (according to LSJ) only in Euripides in this sense, although ἀνυπόστατον is in Xen. *Cyr.* v. 2. 33.

15–16: The restoration of these lines is difficult. The text in OCT (Thierfelder's, with a slight change) means: 'The girl is, to be sure, attentive to one's needs and a quick worker. But away with her! There's nothing to be said!' The sense is satisfactory, but τάχιον is suspect: nowhere else does Menander use ταχύς as an adjective, but always adverbially, and the Attic comparative is θάττων; ταχίων, found in authors from the first century B.C., is condemned by Phrynichos.

Frag. 334

1 Λάμιαν: A fabulous monster that ate human flesh, 'Vampire': one of Demetrios Poliorketes' mistresses was so called, no doubt as a nickname (Athen. 128 b, 615 a, etc.).

5 ἀργαλέα: The word occurs nowhere else in the remains of New Comedy, but several times in the Old. It may be added to the evidence of frag. 333 to show that a wide vocabulary is characteristic of this old man.

Frag. 335

3: 'Does not keep watchful guard over those close to him'; in the present instance the slave's master has not been able to preserve his daughter's virginity.

4: 'Nor on suffering a misfortune could he disguise it, so far as his life in the world goes, by the use of his money'; again the slave has in view his master's predicament over his daughter. A rich man might hush such an affair up.

Frag. 336

This was probably spoken by the same faithful but sententious slave as frag. 335. The opinion is very like that expressed by Daos at *Georgos* 79 ff.

4 τότ' αὐτόν ἐcτ' ἰδεῖν: 'Then he can himself see.' If we had the context, it might support this, but τόθ' αὐτόν, 'then he can see 'how he himself . . .', looks more likely.

8 μερίδοc: The word is used of a class (or of a faction) in the state, LSJ s.v. II.

9 παραπέταcμα: For the metaphor cf. Alexis frag. 340, τὰ χρήματα παραπέταcμα τοῦ βίου.

ΤΡΟΦΩΝΙΟC

Frag. 397

1: The distinction of speakers was made by Herwerden. Less plausibly Dobree supposed the cook to begin with τίνοc. The scene belongs to the numerous class in which a cook praises or explains his own art either to the slave who has come to hire him or to an assistant. The idea that the food should be adapted to the guests is developed at length in Anaxippos frag. 1. 28 ff. K (Dohn, *Mageiros*, 157 ff.) and more briefly by Diphilos frag. 17 K. Thierfelder argues that it is unnecessary to suppose a second speaker, since the cook might put the question ποδαποῦ; to himself. This is conceivable rather than likely.

3: The broken anapaest defies plausible emendation, and is thereby unique in the remains of Menander. Mette, *Lustrum*, x (1965), 113, boldly suggests οἷον τὰ μὲν ⟨× – ∪⟩ νησιωτικὰ ⟨× – ∪ – × – ∪⟩ ταυτὶ ξενύδρια. Is there any other reason for supposing the line to be corrupt? The deictic ταυτί is strange, but the context might explain it. Diminutives in -ύδριον are derogatory.

5 τοῖς ἁλμίοις: The word does not occur elsewhere, but must mean 'salted fish', more usually τάριχος, which the islanders, accustomed to a variety of fresh fish, do not much care for. The cook is inventive in the matter of vocabulary, cf. ἀθάλαττος (nowhere else in this sense) and πλούταξ (only Eupolis frag. 159 K).

6 οὕτως παρέργως: 'In a way that is simply off-hand', cf. LSJ s.v. οὕτως IV. Austin suggests spelling οὕτω, on the ground that Menander does not use οὕτως before consonants (Körte on frag. 154).

7 ὀνθυλεύεις: Another invention perhaps, since Pollux may have no other authority when he writes, vi. 60, αἱ δὲ περιτταὶ σκευασίαι ὀνθολεύσεις καὶ μονθολύσεις ἐκαλοῦντο, ὡς παρὰ Μενάνδρῳ αἱ ὑποστάσεις, ζωμὸς παχὺς ἀμύλῳ πηγνύμενος. ὀνθυλεύω (Phrynichos condemns as non-Attic the form μονθυλεύω) means to dress with stuffing. **καρύκη** was a spiced sauce of Lydian invention.

9 λοπαδίοις: 'Little stewpots'. The context shows that the cook means *fish*-dishes, which are a novelty for the inland Arcadians; this limited use does not seem to occur elsewhere, although λοπάδια containing fish can be adduced: *Pap. Cair. Ζen.* 82. 17, Alexis frag. 186 K, Eubulos frag. 9 K; and Mnesimachos frag. 10 K calls the great fish-epicure Dorion λοπαδοφυσητής. In the fragments of comedy the word λοπάς is primarily associated with fish. Madvig proposed λεπαδίοις: limpets were sometimes cooked, but the emendation is improbable.

10 Ἰωνικός is adj., πλούταξ noun. -αξ was sometimes used as a derogatory suffix, e.g. θαλάμαξ for θαλαμίτης, Cτόαξ for Cτωϊκός, βώμαξ for βωμολόχος.

11 κάνδαυλον: Cf. frag. 451. 6 n. **ὑποβινητιῶντα:** The Ionians were thought to be effeminate; on the meaning of βινητιῶ see *Dysk.* 462 n. ὑποβ. is a nonce-word, such as anyone might make up, but its application to βρώματα is bold; the meaning must be that these dishes encourage unnatural desires.

ΥΠΟΒΟΛΙΜΑΙΟC

Frag. 416

The arguments for dividing this fragment after line 7, a course first recommended by A. Heringa, *Observationum criticarum liber* (1749), have been most fully put by G. Zuntz, *Proc. Brit. Acad.* xlii (1956),

209 ff. Both parts offer a consolation for early death; but whereas the first urges that the greatest joy in life is the contemplation of the great phenomena of nature, which can provide no novelty, however long one lives, the second depicts life as a scene of unpleasant bustle and futility. Nothing is done to attach one part to the other: they stand side by side, self-contained inconsistent blocks. The only circumstance which could make a continuous speech of them would be if the speaker were represented as thoughtlessly reproducing commonplaces on life and death, without care for consistency. Such an explanation is at the best barely credible. A more recent attempt by M. M. Kokolakis, *Ἀθηνᾶ* lxvi (1962), 1 ff., to maintain the unity of the piece (*a*) argues that ὅν φημι must refer to something that precedes, which could be vv. 1–8—this shows *ignoratio elenchi*, (*b*) appeals to Dio Chrysostom xxx. 28–43 (*Charidemus*), where *some* men spend their time on earth in contemplating nature, *others* in gaming and quarrelling—this shows that it is possible to combine these two themes, but if anything underlines the fact that they are not combined here. M. van der Valk, *Ant. Class.* xxxvii (1968), 477, also maintains that the fragment is a unity, without facing the difficulties set out by Zuntz.

There are other places where Stobaios, or his manuscripts, by omitting a lemma, run together passages that should have been distinct, e.g. the last four lines of frag. 250 (attributed by Stobaios to Κυβερνῆται) are now known to be *Dyskolos* 284–7. If something similar has happened here, there is no reason for supposing that the second passage is from the same play as the first, or even by Menander. Gomme, *CQ* N.S. x (1960), 103 replying to Zuntz, admits that 8 cannot follow directly on 7, but suggests that a line or two, that would have formed a transition, have been omitted. This possibility cannot be excluded, but it is hard to imagine a plausible transition from the lofty philosophic sentiments, serious style, and reflective atmosphere of 1–7 to the loose grammar, staccato phrases, and didactic manner that rightly remind Zuntz of the Cynic diatribe. See also n. on 9.

2 ἀλύπωϲ: Zuntz well remarks that the aspiration for a life free of suffering is often met with in the fourth century, e.g. Aristotle *EE* 1215ᵇ6, Euphron frag. 5 K, and, in the form that λυπή is inescapable, Menander frags. 341, 622, *Kithar.* frag. 1, etc.

3 τὰ ϲεμνὰ ταῦτα κτλ.: The originality of the passage lies in its adaptation of a traditional piece of folk-pessimism ('it is best not to be born, next best to die quickly') by the recognition that life offers one fine experience, the spectacle of nature; but even that is quickly seen. There is no suggestion that nature is a subject for philosophic study, or (as in Aristotle's version of the tradition, *Eudemus* frags. 5, 6

Ross, 35, 40 Rose) that a truer life is to be found in death. These points are decisive, as Zuntz shows, against the view that Menander here reflects Aristotle's *Protrepticus* (E. Bignone, *L'Aristotele perduto*, i. 94, M. Tierney, *Proc. Roy. Irish Acad.* xliii. 242). ἀπῆλθεν ὅθεν ἦλθεν: Cf. Soph. *OC* 1227, βῆναι κεῖς' ὁπόθεν περ ἥκει, Eur. *Suppl.* 532, ὅθεν . . . ἀφίκατο | ἐνταῦθ' ἀπελθεῖν, Epiktetos i. 9. 14, ἀπελθεῖν ὅθεν ἐληλύθαμεν.

4 ὕδωρ: Prob. 'rain' (Gomme), and πῦρ perhaps 'lightning' (Kokolakis, who quotes frag. 614, Ἐπίχαρμος τοὺς θεοὺς εἶναι λέγει, ἀνέμους ὕδωρ γῆν ἥλιον πῦρ ἀστέρας, and Ennius, *Epicharmus* frag. VII, 'istic est is Iuppiter quem dico, quem Graeci vocant aerem; qui ventus est et nubes, imber postea, atque ex imbre frigus').

5: Cf. Lucretius' consolatory words: 'eadem sunt omnia semper . . . omnia si perges uiuendo uincere saecla' (iii. 945).

4 τὸν ἥλιον τὸν κοινόν: In frag. 740 the phrase ἐσπάσας τὸν ἀέρα τὸν κοινόν is characterized as τραγικώτερον. Cf. also frag. 737, ἅπανθ' ὅσα ζῇ καὶ τὸν ἥλιον βλέπει τὸν κοινὸν ἡμῖν, δοῦλα ταῦτ' ἔσθ' ἡδονῆς, where the epithet serves to underline the unity of all life. Here the point is that the best experiences of life are open to all.

8 πανήγυριν: Life is a 'festival', but the emphasis is laid not on any spectacle there may be (as it is by Epiktetos iii. 5. 10, ἠξίωσάς με συνπανηγυρίσαι σοι καὶ ἰδεῖν ἔργα τὰ σά) but on all the 'side-shows' and accompanying turmoil, 'the crowds, the market, thieves, games of chance, distractions'. This unpleasant side of the festival is emphasized by later authors, e.g. Dio Chrysostom viii. 9, Epiktetos i. 6. 26, iv. 4. 24. Hence Teles in the third century B.C. speaks of leaving life readily, ὥσπερ ἐκ πανηγύρεως (p. 10. 13 H). A more favourable aspect is seen in frag. 219 K of Alexis, which has some ideas in common with this fragment:

> ἔγνωκα δ' οὖν οὕτως ἐπισκοπούμενος,
> εἶναι μανιώδη πάντα τἀνθρώπων ὅλως,
> ἀποδημίας δὲ τυγχάνειν ἡμᾶς ἀεὶ
> τοὺς ζῶντας, ὥσπερ εἰς πανήγυρίν τινα
> ἀφειμένους ἐκ τοῦ θανάτου καὶ τοῦ σκότους
> εἰς τὴν διατριβὴν εἰς τὸ φῶς τε τοῦθ' ὃ δὴ
> ὁρῶμεν· ὃς δ' ἂν πλεῖστα γελάσῃ καὶ πίῃ
> καὶ τῆς Ἀφροδίτης ἀντιλάβηται τὸν χρόνον
> τοῦτον ὃν ἀφεῖται καὶ τύχῃ γ' ἐράνου τινός,
> πανηγυρίσας ἥδιστ' ἀπῆλθεν οἴκαδε.

9 χρόνον ὃν φημι τοῦτον: If correct, this must refer back to some preceding description which certainly is not to be found in 1–7. In view of the uncertainty of the text it is hard to determine whether τὴν ἐπιδημίαν is a possible apposition to χρόνον. In favour of his conjecture τῆς ἐπιδημίας Zuntz quotes [Plut.] *Consol. ad Apoll.* 117 F, βραχυτάτου τοῦ τῆς ἐπιδημίας ὄντος ἐν τῷ βίῳ χρόνου, [Plato], *Axiochus* 365, παρεπιδημία τίς ἐcτιν ὁ βίος.

10 κυβεῖαι: Zuntz, *Journ. Semitic Studies*, i (1956), 135 ff., maintains that the word has the sense 'frauds' that it later developed, e.g. Eph. 4:14. Epiktetos uses κυβεύω to mean 'cheat', ii. 1. 28, but *Epitr.* 328 provides good evidence for dicing at a festival.   **διατριβαί:** The word may mean 'passing the time' or 'amusement', but in this context it is likely to be 'time-wasting', cf. Thuc. v. 82.

11 καταλύcειc: It seems impossible to fit in the noun καταλύcειc. Gomme's καταλύcειc βελτίονας, ἐφόδι᾿ ἔχων gives an awkward asyndeton and the plural is unexplained, for a man has only one resting-place, death, on his journey from life. G. Murray had to translate: 'You have gone to find a better inn.' The easiest remedy is to read καταλύcειc (future) βέλτιον with Salmasius (for βελτῖον cf. Aesch. frag. 309. 3 Nauck, Eupolis frag. 20 Demiańczuk; other instances of comparatives with the scansion -ίων are collected by C. Austin, *Nova Fragmenta Euripidea*, 63). 'If you are the first to leave, you will get better lodgings, having money left to pay for them.' Yet, true as this may be of a real festival, it is not clear what feature of death is so allegorized. Little light is thrown on this obscure point by Thierfelder's suggestion that ἐφόδια are 'reserves of strength' for the journey to the next world (*Gnomon*, xxx [1958], 552). More plausibly Kokolakis, art. cit. 62–4, suggests that the meaning is 'you will die with some of your provisions for life's journey still unspent' (cf. frag. 407, χρηcτότηc . . . θαυμαcτὸν ἐφόδιον βίου). He further takes καταλύcειc to have no reference to inns, but merely to mean 'you will die', cf. Diokles frag. 14 K, ὅπωc | νέοc ὢν ἀγαθόν τι τῇ ψυχῇ παθὼν | ὥρᾳ καταλύcει μηδ᾿ ἀγόμφιόν ποτε | αἰῶνα τρίψει. Many have felt that to leave life *early* is more to be expected than to be the *first* to leave (which surely would be to die in infancy). Preller's πρῷοc (which might be followed by ⟨καὶ⟩ καταλύcειc) gives a reasonably good sense. Austin notes that the same mistake is likely in Eupolis frag. 278 K, εἰ πρῶτοc (πρώιοc W. Luppe) ἔλθῃc κἂν καθίζεcθαι λάβοιc. But there may be some deeper corruption (cf. the full discussions by Zuntz, art. cit. 213–15, and Kokolakis, art. cit. 22–4).

13: Zuntz rightly objects to the too ready acceptance of Porson's δ᾿ ἐκοπίαcεν ἀπολέcαc (sc. ἐφόδια) for δὲ κοπιάcαc ἀπώλεcεν, but nothing better has been proposed.

14 γηρῶ, first in Xen. *Cyr.* iv. 1. 15, is inceptive in meaning, 'grow old', like γηράcκω, which it never supplanted and which is the only form met in good Attic authors; M. S. Ruipérez, *Estructura del sistema de aspectos y tiempos* . . ., 131.

15 ῥεμβόμενος: 'Wandering', 'drifting'; the word does not occur elsewhere earlier than Plutarch. Whether it should be taken (as in most texts) with ἐχθροὺς εὗρε or, as I prefer, with ἐνδεής που γίνεται is a matter of taste.

16 εἰς χρόνον: 'Later', 'hereafter', Aesch. *Eum.* 484, Hdt. iii. 72.
εὐθανάτως: Pollux iii. 106 quotes this adverb from Kratinos (the comic poet).

Frag. 417

That success depends on luck as well as judgement is a simple truth that Greeks often reiterated; Cornford, *Thucydides Mythistoricus*, 104 ff. emphasizes the importance of the idea to Thucydides.

The temptation to exaggerate this and make luck mainly or solely responsible was one to which many succumbed; for Pindar Τύχη was the most powerful of the Μοῖραι (frag. 21 Bowra, 41 Schröder); Soph. *OT* 977, τὰ τῆς Τύχης κρατεῖ, πρόνοια δ' ἐστὶν οὐδενὸς σαφής, Plato, *Laws* 709 b, τύχας δ' εἶναι σχεδὸν ἅπαντα τὰ ἀνθρώπινα πράγματα, Dem. ii. 22, μεγάλη γὰρ ῥοπή, μᾶλλον δ' ὅλον ἡ τύχη παρὰ πάντ' ἐστὶ τὰ τῶν ἀνθρώπων πράγματα, Chairemon frag. 2 (quoted *Aspis* 411), τύχη τὰ θνητῶν πράγματ', οὐκ εὐβουλία (Nauck, *TGF* 782, where a collection of parallels may be found). The last line was given currency by Theophrastos in his *Callisthenes*, and was later found in 'libris et scholis omnium philosophorum' (Cic. *Tusc.* v. 25). The speaker here is therefore elaborating a platitude, and the seriousness with which he does so may have been comic. M. M. Kokolakis, Ἀθηνᾶ lxvi (1962), 82, urges that he may be a slave, comparing the philosophizing of Pseudolus on the same topic, Plaut. *Pseud.* 678–86.

The extract which succeeds this in Stobaios, without any lemma, runs as follows:

Τύχη κυβερνᾷ πάντα. ταύτην καὶ φρένας
δεῖ καὶ πρόνοιαν τὴν θεῶν καλεῖν μόνην,
εἰ μή τις ἄλλως ὀνόμασιν χαίρει κενοῖς.

Meineke and Kock assigned it, without good ground, to *Hypobolimaios*. Körte rightly regarded its authorship as uncertain.

1–3: This sentence has been much discussed and emended. As given by Stobaios, it must be interpreted as follows. Man's mind profits him nothing, what does profit him is Luck's mind, whether the right word for that is 'divine spirit' or 'mind'. Although one must not look for philosophical precision in this passage, I share the incredulity of many scholars with regard to that sense. Of all emendations that of Meineke gives the easiest Greek. He substituted μή for νοῦς in 3 : νοῦς will have been added as an explanation of ὁ τῆς Τύχης, and then taken as a correction of μή. 'Whether τύχη is a divine spirit or not, it is she who steers all things.' It is, however, surprising that Luck should be credited with νοῦς; it would be a paradox to give her rationality. Perhaps Bosius was right in reading ἄλλο for ἀλλ' ὁ; 'human thought adds nothing to Luck'. This sentiment is restated more vividly in 7–8.

I do not find satisfactory the suggestions of Weil, *REG* i (1888), 384 (ἀλλά) or Zuntz, *Proc. Brit. Acad.* xlii (1956), 237 (θερμόν for θεῖον).

5 καπνὸς καὶ φλήναφος: Cf. Plato, *Rep.* 561 d, καπνὸν καὶ φλυαρίαν.

7: Canter's emendation is supported by Xen. *Anab.* v. 6. 28, λέγων καὶ νοῶν καὶ πράττων, *Hipp.* i. 1, νοεῖν καὶ λέγειν καὶ πράττειν.

8 ἐπιγεγραμμένοι: 'We just append our names', cf. [Dem.] *in Neaer.* 43, τῶν παραβοώντων παρὰ τὸ βῆμα καὶ ἐπιγραφομένων ταῖς ἀλλοτρίαις γνώμαις, Aischines, *in Ctes.* 167, ἐὰν δ' αὐτόματόν τι συμβῇ, προσποιήσῃ καὶ σεαυτὸν ἐπὶ τὸ γεγενημένον ἐπιγράψεις. Guesses at the plot of *Hypobolimaios*, which had an alternative title Ἄγροικος, have been made (see particularly Webster, *StM* 100, Zuntz, art. cit. 236), but lack adequate basis (Gomme, *CQ* n.s. x [1960], 108) ; Kokolakis, art. cit. 104–9, is more cautious.

ΨΕΥΔΗΡΑΚΛΗϹ

Frag. 451

5 παράθες may conceal πάραγε 'go on in!', addressed to the cook, as in *Sam.* 295, *Mis.* 274. If σημίαν conceals the voc. Ϲίμια, that may be addressed by the cook to the slave. In *Samia* the cook knows Parmenon's name (357).

6 ff. κάνδυλος or κάνδαυλος was a Lydian dish, suggested as suitable for a rich Ionian in frag. 397 ; it was made, according to Hegesippos of Tarentum, of stewed meat, bread-crumbs, cheese, dill, and rich gravy (Athenaios 516 d).   **καρύκη** was a rich sauce, also of Lydian origin.   **σεμίδαλις**, a word of oriental origin, means fine wheat flour.

9 ff.: ἐγχύτους: 'Shaped cakes' (Athenaios 644 c).   **χόνδρον**: Oatmeal, cf. Ar. frag. 203, ἢ χόνδρον ἕψων εἶτα μυῖαν ἐμβαλών.   **θρῖον** is properly a 'fig-leaf', used to wrap eatables. The point of this piece is that everything is topsy-turvy : the cook makes cakes and other simple dishes that were normally the province of the household ; the cooking is done by the δημιουργός who, however, only does simple roasts, cf.

Ar. *Ach.* 1104, such as would not require a professional cook. Then the diner gets τραγήματα, dried fruits and sweets that should form the dessert, as his main course; but when he has been perfumed and has taken the garland that should mark the cυμπόcιον following the dinner, he is served with roast thrushes and honey-cake. This cook is even more paradoxical than Karion in *Epitr.* frag. 5.

12 ἀντιπαρατεταγμένη: 'Posted opposite him'. **δημιουργός:** Hesychios s.v., λέγεται δὲ καὶ γυνὴ δημιουργός, ἢ ἐν τοῖc γάμοιc πέμματα πέccει. For the contrast between δεῖπνον and τραγήματα cf. Alexis frag. 163 K, οὐδὲ φιλόδειπνός εἰμι, μὰ τὸν Ἀcκληπιόν, | τραγήμαcιν χαίρω δὲ μᾶλλον . . . τούτοιcι χαίρω, τοῖc δὲ κεκαρυκευμένοιc ὄψοιcι καὶ ζυμοῖcιν †ἠδ᾽ ὀμωθεοι† (οὐδάμ᾽, ὦ θεοί Jacobs). There are two speakers in this passage—the MS. tradition of Athenaios does not mark change of speaker in his quotations—a cook and his hirer, probably a slave in view of 6–8. I think the cook begins to speak at line 5, to boast of his newfangled methods; note the bombastic effect of the long words of 12, 14, 15, quite unlike the style of the first speaker. The passage is strongly reminiscent of the conventional loquacious cook of Middle and New Comedy, and seems to have no dramatic import. Webster may be right in thinking Ψευδηρακλῆc to be an early play (*StM* 104), since it mentioned Nannion, a courtesan also referred to by Amphis (frag. 23 K) and Alexis (frag. 223 K) and other authors of Middle Comedy. The cook's speech makes no reference to the preceding lines; some omission is possible.

FRAGMENTS FROM UNNAMED PLAYS

Frag. 538

This is not an original piece of moralizing: Diog. L. vi. 5, (Ἀντισθένης) ὥσπερ ὑπὸ τοῦ ἰοῦ τὸν cίδηρον, οὕτωc ἔλεγε τοὺc φθονεροὺc ὑπὸ τοῦ ἰδίου ἤθους κατεcθίεcθαι, Plato, Rep. 609 a, κακὸν ἑκάστῳ τι καὶ ἀγαθὸν λέγεις; οἷον ὀφθαλμοῖc ὀφθαλμίαν καὶ cύμπαντι τῷ cώματι νόcον, cίτῳ τε ἐρυcίβην, cηπεδόνα τε ξύλοιc, χαλκῷ δὲ καὶ cιδήρῳ ἰόν ... τὸ cύμφυτον ἄρα κακὸν ἑκάστου καὶ ἡ πονηρία ἕκαcτον ἀπόλλυcιν, and Polybios vi. 10.

3: The trustworthiness of Stobaios' text of Menander in those eclogues where he does not know the name of the play is not great; it is therefore likely that Dobree was right to emend this line to avoid the broken anapaests.

8 παράcταcιc: παρίcτημι means 'set before the mind'; so παράcταcιc will be 'suggestion'. The pompous line may have been in accord with the speaker's character, but it sounds very like an anthologist's addition, cf. frag. 581. 16 n.

Frag. 568

2 ὄψει: Perhaps 'to a woman's appearance' or even 'to a face', rather than 'to their own eyes', but it comes to much the same thing.

6 ἀπῆλθε καταγελῶν: Cf. *Dysk.* 52 n.

8: Unfortunately the unmetrical εἴcω δή of Stobaios cannot be corrected from the other passage, *Amat.* 763 b, where Plutarch quotes this line, for there the MSS. have a lacuna, co-extensive with these letters. Lacunae, seemingly due to inability to read a model, are frequent in the *Amatorius*. Later in the fragment of περὶ ἔρωτοc Plutarch, dilating on the truth of the last line and a half (εὖ καὶ ὀρθῶc) declares that love requires a suitable cause brought to bear at the right moment on a heart ready to be influenced—καιροῦ τῷ παθεῖν ἑτοίμῳ cυνάπτοντοc ἐν ἀκμῇ τὸ ποιεῖν πεφυκόc. From this I take my suggestion εἰς ἀκμήν, to be construed with πληγείc. I suppose ακ to have been lost after εις, and the verse to have been patched up by someone of limited metrical knowledge, who reflected that the lover's wound is an internal one.

Frag. 581

4 γαμεῖ has no express subject; a vague 'anyone' is to be understood.

7: The infinitive φέρειν never receives a construction: some such phrase as ἄλογόν ἐστι will be in the speaker's mind. There is a temptation to substitute ἄλογον for λάλον in 13, but the talkativeness of women is a common subject of complaint, e.g. frags. 60, 592, and λάλον comes pleasantly παρὰ προσδοκίαν as a climax after a number of faults that a hasty judgement might consider more serious.

8 δοκιμαστής: An assayer, synonymous with ἀργυρογνώμων, Arist. *Rhet.* 1375ᵇ5, Bekker, *Anecd.* 89. 7, Moiris 190. 15, probably an employee of a banker, see Bogaert, *Banques et banquières dans les cités grecques*, 45–6.

9: The dowry was regularly paid in cash, but would then often be invested in property.

11 δοκιμάζομαι, middle, for the usual active, is found in Xen. *Oec.* 8. 10.

16 ἀνάγκη . . . λαβών: These words have been added by an anthologist to round off the quotation. Compare Stob. iv. 22. 151–2, which similarly round off *Epitrepontes* 564–7. Menander rarely ended a speech with a gnome (W. Görler, *Μενάνδρου Γνῶμαι*, 80 ff.). This gnome does not even fit the context, since foreknowledge of *this* bride's faults will not enable anybody to secure the least objectionable of possible wives.

Frag. 592

The name 'Ρόδη occurs in a fragment (210) of *Hiereia*. That is not an adequate reason for asserting this fragment also to be from that play. Körte thought it was not (*Hermes*, lxxv [1940], 115), Kuiper believed it was (*Mnem.* 3rd ser. viii [1940], 292).   **αὔλειος θύρα:** αὔλειος ἡ ἀπὸ τῆς ὁδοῦ πρώτη θύρα τῆς οἰκίας, ὡς δηλοῖ Μένανδρος, Harpokration 40. 7. The phrase, known to Homer, *Od.* xi. 239, will be derived from the free-standing country house with a yard for animals (αὐλή) in front of it. In a town there was no yard and the door gave directly on to the street. Note that this fragment does not say that a married woman will not go outside her house, but that she will consider her house ends at the front door, and therefore not continue the private business of quarrelling with her husband so that it goes on in the street. Cf. Gomme, *Essays*, 99.

Frag. 612

2 τῇ φύcει προcόν: Lit. 'attached to their nature', i.e. belonging to themselves as themselves. The speaker (is it a son or a daughter?) thinks of persons who could not be described by Sophocles' words εὐγενὴς γὰρ ἡ φύcιc, κἀξ εὐγενῶν (*Phil.* 874).

4 μνήματα: 'Memorials', i.e. funeral stelae and the like.

13 ὄλεθροc: For this term of abuse cf. *Dysk.* 366 n. The punctuation of Cκύθης τιc; as a question is due to Porson and accepted by Meineke and Kock. Körte prints τιc·, making a statement of it. Either of these may be right, but there is a third possibility: Cκύθης τιc ὄλεθροc, 'a pestilential Scythian', might be a quotation, or a semi-quotation, the sort of thing people say, cf. Dem. ix. 31, ὄλεθροc Μακεδών, Plut. *Sertorius* 571 a, βαρβάρουc ὀλέθρουc, *Eumenes* 594 c, Χερρονηcίτης ὄλεθροc.

Ἀνάχαρcιc: Hdt. iv. 46, 76 knows Anacharsis as a wise man who travelled in Greece. A legend grew up about him, according to which he visited Solon, and Ephoros the historian made him one of the Seven Sages, in place of the shadowy Myson (Diog. L. i. 41).

Frag. 614

An example of how poets copied one another. Philemon frag. 65 has τὸ τῆc Ἀμαλθείαc δοκεῖc εἶναι κέραc | οἶον γράφουcιν οἱ γραφεῖc κέραc βοόc; | ἀργύριόν ἐcτι· τοῦτ᾽ ἐὰν ἔχῃc, λέγε | πρὸc τοῦτ᾽ †εἶ† βούλει· πάντα cοι γενήcεται, | φίλοι, βοηθοί, μάρτυρες, cυνοικίαι.

2 ὕδωρ, πῦρ: Cf. frag. 416. 4 n. The meaning is that Epicharmos *identified* the gods with these natural phenomena, not that he said that these phenomena were divine. Dobree's wish to read ὁ μὲν γὰρ Ἐπίχαρμοc θεοὺc εἶναι λέγει κτλ. was misguided.

6 εὖξαι τί βούλει: The use of τίc for ὅcτιc is illustrated by LSJ s.v. τίc B. II. b; the earliest certain example there quoted is Eur. frag. 773. 2, αἰτοῦ τί χρῄζειc ἕν (= *Phaethon* 46 Diggle, who rightly compares Soph. *El.* 316, ἱcτόρει τί cοι φίλον).

8 δικαcταί: The great size of Athenian juries and the elaborate arrangements for assigning jurymen to cases were supposed to eliminate the possibility of bribery.   μάρτυρεc: Cf. Eubulos frag. 74 K, πάνθ᾽ ὁμοῦ πωλήcεται | ἐν ταῖc Ἀθήναιc· cῦκα ... μάρτυρεc.

9: i.e. even the (traditional) gods can be bribed to serve you.

Frag. 620

There is a less lively expression of similar sentiments in Philemon frag. 93 K.

3 τουτονί: The word implies that there is a donkey on the stage, as in the opening scene of Ar. *Frogs*.

9 ἄν πτάρῃ τιc: Sneezing may be a good or a bad omen; but sneezing is not in place here. What is wanted is something that will form a pair with slander, just as in 10–11 we have a pair of bad omens that cause fear. It spoils the balance of the sentences to make one of the first pair also a bad omen, but the cause of grief. Perhaps read ἄν παρίῃ τιc: 'We are hurt if someone outstrips us (*or* passes us by, disregards us); we are angry if someone slanders us.' Cf. *Proc. Camb. Phil. Soc.* N.S. xiii (1967), 37.

10: It is well known that the Greeks tended to attach more importance to dreams than we do. On the whole subject see the fascinating pages in Dodds, *The Greeks and the Irrational*, 102–34.

11: Cf. Theophrastos, *Char.* xvi. 8, (the δειcιδαίμων) κἄν γλαῦκεc βαδίζοντοc αὐτοῦ ⟨ἀνακράγωcι⟩ ταράττεcθαι.

12 ἀγωνίαι: Acute worry, Arist. *Spir.* 483ᵃ5, ἐν τοῖc τῆc ψυχῆc φόβοιc, ἐλπίcιν, ἀγωνίαιc. **δόξαc:** 'Fancies', 'false opinions'. **νόμοι:** Körte interprets this as 'custom', but the Greeks recognized no hard and fast line between law and custom; both can be represented as interference with φύcιc, nature. That νόμοι needs no emendation is shown by a parallel passage from Philemon (frag. 93 K), ὦ τριcμακάρια πάντα καὶ τριcόλβια | τὰ θηρία . . . ἡμεῖc δ᾽ ἀβίωτον ζῶμεν ἄνθρωποι βίον. | δουλεύομεν δόξαιcιν εὑρόντεc νόμουc κτλ.

13 ἐπίθετα: 'Adventitious', cf. Antiphon, *VS* 87, B frag. 44 A col. i. 23, τὰ μὲν τῶν νόμων ἐπίθετα, τὰ δὲ τῆc φύcεωc ἀναγκαῖα, a passage that supports νόμοι in 12.

Frag. 656

5 ἐξέτριψεν: The ἐξέρριψεν of the MSS. hardly suits the action of a whirlwind. Herwerden's other suggestion, ἐξήρειψεν, is accepted by Körte, but the verb ἐρείπω is mainly poetical (ἐξερείπω trans. only in Pindar, *Pyth.* iv. 264).

6 cυγκλυcμόc: The word is rare ([Arist.] *mir.* 843ᵃ15), but the verb cυγκλύζεcθαι is used by Plutarch, *Mor.* 467 d, of the swamping of a ship at sea. **ἀναπνοὴν ἔχει κτλ.:** 'It gives a breathing-space to say "O Zeus, O Saviour".' The following imperative, 'hold on to the rigging', must be addressed to a fellow sailor.

8 τρικυμίαν: Properly a series of three waves (LSJ s.v.).

9 ναυαγίου: A piece of wreckage; the singular is unusual.

10 εἰμι . . . ἐν βυθῷ: The hyperbaton is notable. The intertwining of ἁψάμενος καὶ φιλήςας and εἰμὶ ἐν βυθῷ mirrors the simultaneity of the embrace with being drowned by love.

Frag. 714

1: Julian doubtless had his quotation from an anthology; the line of Euripides has got attached to the passage of Menander by some mistake.

2: Cf. *Epitr.* 109 n.

2 μυcταγωγός: Properly one who introduces an initiate to a religious 'mystery', but later the word was used of guides at temples, Cic. *Verr.* iv. 132, 'ii qui hospites ad ea quae uisenda sunt solent ducere— quos illi mystagogos uocant'. Strabo xvii. 1. 38 uses μυcταγωγῶν of a man who took him round Arsinoë. It is therefore not necessary to press the metaphor that life is a 'mystery'.

3 ἀγαθός is emphatic by position.

5 χρηcτόν is *lectio difficilior*. βίος χρηcτός seems to stand here for 'a man who leads a good life'.

7 ἐπιπλοκήν: 'Complication'.

8-9: Perhaps 'having frittered everything away through their own thoughtlessness'; but the text is doubtful.

10 γεγονότες: Sc. κακοί, but one may suspect that this extract has been mutilated at the end. It is possible that the sentiment was that men are responsible for their own misfortunes, *either* because they are wicked *or* because they are foolish.

Frag. 718

1 εἶτ' οὐ; Cf. *Dysk.* 153 n.

3 λαμπάς: There is a reference to the torch-race at Athens in honour of Prometheus, the λαμπαδηφορία.

5 γυναῖκας ἔπλαcεν: According to one story Prometheus fashioned the original human beings out of clay (Pausanias x. 4. 3, etc.). According to another, which may be at the back of the speaker's mind, Zeus made women to punish mankind for the deceit they had learned from Prometheus, who taught them to hide in fat when sacrificing (Hesiod, *Theog.* 535 ff.). It was for this or for stealing fire from heaven that he was fixed to the rocks of the Caucasus.

7 λάθριοι: A poetic word, but perhaps used also at *Sam.* 132. The line is suspect. By its position λάθριοι should be predicative, 'evil desires in future will be unseen'; this does not fit easily into the context. Edmonds suggests ἄθροι, 'incessant', which with γάρ (Jacobitz, as if in his MSS.) for ἄρ' makes a reasonable sense. But it is possible that 1–6 and 7–10 do not belong together, but had accidentally been combined in the anthology from which Ps.-Lucian took the lines (cf. frag. 714). In this context ἐπιθύμιαι will connote sexual desires, as in *Sam*. 21.

8 γαμηλίῳ λέχει: γαμήλιος and λέχος are both poetic words and perhaps the whole line will be a quotation from tragedy.

10: Körte's χρόνον for βίον appears to be an oversight.

Frag. 722

Published by W. Aly, *SB Heidelberg* 1914. Wilamowitz, *Schiedsgericht*, 107, saw that the lines were parodied by Lucian at the beginning of his *Juppiter Tragoedus*. This shows that the play was well known in his time, and therefore probably written by Menander. It is likely that, as in Lucian, the lines opened the play.

3–4: On the distinction between οἰκέτης and δοῦλος see *Heros* 20 n.

7: Cf. Soph. frag. 854 N, εἰ cῶμα δοῦλον, ἀλλ' ὁ νοῦς ἐλεύθερος.

Frag. 740

Deprived of its dramatic context, this sermon by a slave or freedman seems a fairly tedious piece of moralizing.

3 πράccων for πράττων must be suspect, but the whole line may be a quotation from tragedy. For the last three words cf. *Dysk*. 286.

6 ἄτοπον: 'Bad'.

8: The added καὶ has no authority, D being a MS. riddled with conjectural changes. The phrase ἀέρα κοινὸν cπάcαι is not known from any surviving tragedy; Aesch. *PV* 1092, πάντων . . . κοινὸν φάος, Eur. *Hel*. 905, κοινὸς οὐρανὸς πᾶcιν βροτοῖc, are similar. R. Kassel, *Untersuchungen zur Konsolationsliteratur*, 64, observes that the phrase was known to the author of Wisd. 7:3, καὶ γενόμενος ἔcπαcα τὸν κοινὸν ἀέρα: this suggests that it is an authentic quotation from tragedy.

9 λογιcτέον: The absolute use of λογίζομαι, except of numerical calculation, is a strangely rare construction (LSJ s.v. II. 6) and one or more lines may be lost. ταῦτα cannot be object both of οἰcτέον and of λογιcτέον, for as object of οἰcτέον it must mean 'these present troubles' but of λογιcτέον 'these considerations'. I have considered the punctuation οἰcτέον (ἄμεινον), ταῦτα καὶ λογιcτέον . . ., where ταῦτα would be anticipatory of the following line(s), but then τὸ δὲ κεφάλαιον τῶν λόγων would follow somewhat awkwardly. For isolated ἄμεινον, cf. *Dysk.* 149, βέλτιον. ἄμεινον is not found elsewhere in New Comedy, except in frag. 607 (the authenticity of which is not assured) and Alexis frag. 124, 18 K.

11 ὕψος, given by the interpolated classes of Plutarch's MSS., is a would-be correction of οἶκτον, in fact a corruption of ὄγκον.

14 οἰκονομεῖται: The middle is found in Arist. *Oec.* 1343ᵃ23, but the phrase 'runs his household by (?) most important things' is barely intelligible, and suspect. Perhaps ⟨ἐν⟩ πράγμασιν, 'manages for himself in most important affairs'.

15 καλά, the reading of the MSS., gives a possible sense, an extension of what must have been said in the previous clause: man's fall shatters many blessings. But this is not equivalent to extreme abasement (ταπεινότητα). καλός and κακός are often confused in MSS. and πλεῖστα cυντρίβει κακά, 'very many are the ills that shatter him', better suits the previous sentence. Cf. *Epitr.* 1101, (ὁ τρόπος) cυντρίβει cε, Plut. *de superst.* 165 b, δέουc ἐκταπεινοῦντοc καὶ cυντρίβοντοc τὸν ἄνθρωπον.

18: Nauck's alteration of μέcον to μέροc is accepted by Körte–Thierfelder, but spoils the argument. The young man has not lost any very great blessings nor met anything but moderate misfortune; he should therefore put up with what is presumably (που) also a middling grief; ἀνὰ μέcον goes predicatively with τὸ λυπηρόν.

Frag. 745

Körte supposed the speaker to be the malicious man who lures the soldier on to boast, Thierfelder thinks him to be the soldier himself. A soldier who recounted his own discomfiture would be an unusual figure. The man who is making fun of him can point out the wound in mock-seriousness. The truth is uncertain, but I side with Körte.

3 δεικνύω: An unusual form for δείκνυμι, found also in frag. 77 (δεικνύει).

4 ἐπεμυκτήριcαν: Perhaps 'turned up their noses' (LSJ); or can the word mean 'choked their laughter'? μυκτηριcμόc is described by Tryphon, *de tropis* 21, as 'something done along with a certain movement and contraction of the nostrils'.

Frag. 754

3 αὐτῶν ἀκραcίαν: 'Failure to control themselves'. ἀκραcία is a development from *ἀκρατια (cf. εὐεργεσία, ἀδυνασία). τοὺς πόδας τὴν γαστέρα: I suppose that this asyndeton was found strange and removed by inserting καί. Körte prints τὼ πόδε καί, but the split anapaest is suspect (see intro. p. 38).

4 cάκος, not cάκκος, was the Attic spelling, Photios s.v. The correct restoration of the line is uncertain; I have adopted the simplest method, supposing another asyndeton. ἔλαβον: 'They take', i.e. put on, gnomic aorist. For the meaning of ἔλαβον cf. Perik. 520.

5 τὴν θεόν: The best-known Syrian goddess is Atargatis of Hierapolis, with whom Lucian's de dea Syria is concerned.

Frags. 794, 795

2: The echo of the Homeric γένος εὔχομαι εἶναι is no doubt comic.

8: The change καταcτροφή γῆς is accepted by LSJ, to mean 'he's the undoing of his country', without parallel. Bentley confidently proposed ἀναφρόδιτος ('si de hoc dubitare audes, tota tibi ars critica erit abiuranda'), an ingenious suggestion, but ruled out metrically (ἀνᾰφ-) unless the scansion is to be defended as paratragic. Tyrwhitt's proposal τύχη καταcτροφῆς is highly probable, καταcτροφή being a common word for 'death', used by Menander in Perik. 132 in the full form τοῦ ζῆν καταcτροφή. An alternative would be τύχη καταcτρέφῃ, 'by chance die' (cf. Epicurus, ad Menoec. 126, τὸν μὲν νέον καλῶς ζῆν τὸν δὲ γέροντα καλῶς καταcτρέφειν), but τύχη τινί would be expected. ἀνυμέναιος, ἄνυμφος are used of those who die unmarried: Eur. Hecuba 416 (Polyxena), Soph. Ant. 876, 916. ἐπικαλεῖν means to give a nickname; therefore ἀποκαλεῖν 'to call disparagingly' (Dysk. 366) is needed here. In Lucian, de luctu 16, a dead man asks τί μοι λοιδορῇ καὶ ἄθλιον ἀποκαλεῖς καὶ δύcμορον; cf. Heliodoros i. 13. 3, τὸν ἄθλιον ἀποκαλοῦcα.

POSSIBLY MENANDREAN PAPYRUS
FRAGMENTS

Pap. Ant. 15

Ed. pr.: C. H. Roberts, *Antinoopolis Papyri*, i (1950), 30. Re-edited, with photographs, J. W. B. Barns and P. H. J. Lloyd-Jones, *JHS* lxxxiv (1964), 21.

This lively fragment is from a codex of the fourth century A.D. The name of the author and that of the play stood at the top of the sheet, but nothing can now be read with any certainty. It is highly probable that a MS. of this date contained Menander, and nothing speaks against his authorship. If the name of the play ended with the letters τος, as some think, the only suitable known Menandrean title is Ἄπιστος (C. Austin).

Since the list of characters includes a Kantharos, a portion of the same play may be found in *P. Berol.* 13892, in which a person of that name is addressed. Unfortunately the remains, of thirty-six lines, are too slight to allow any conclusions.

P. Ant. has the beginning of the play. A young man comes out of his house by night, complaining bitterly of his misfortune. He has been married for five months, during which time he has never left his wife for a single night, but loved her faithfully; and she cared for him. Before he can explain what is wrong, a female servant approaches, attempting to show him some objects, which only increase his grief. Here the text breaks off, the bottom part of the leaf being lost. The gap before the first line of the other side will hardly be of less than ten lines, probably more. When the text resumes the two persons are opening a box, which contains the moth-eaten remains of half a cloak, necklaces, a single anklet, and some form of writing on one of these objects or on something else. One of the pair, probably the husband, says that they must be a child's recognition-tokens, and 'the mother' was keeping them; they are to be put back as they were and he will seal them up. This is a mystery irrelevant to his present troubles, and may be postponed until he has settled them.

The scene was clearly intended to puzzle, as well as interest, the audience, and since its mutilation has removed some of the clues, it is unlikely that it can be solved today. The young man has presumably been left by his wife, whom we may guess to have been pregnant when she married him, like Pamphile of *Epitrepontes*. The box has probably been found among her belongings. How had she come by it?

For a full commentary see the article by Barns and Lloyd-Jones.

Didot Papyrus

A roll now in the Louvre at Paris—no. 7172, discovered about 1820 in the Serapeum at Memphis, and named after its one-time owner Alphonse Firmin-Didot. It contains various extracts from Greek poetry and some accounts for the year 160 B.C. Most of it is written by two brothers, Ptolemaios and Apollonios, who were catechumens in the temple. The first passage, of forty-four iambic trimeters, is however in the hand of some third person of rather better education. It was repeated on the verso by Ptolemaios, writing from memory. Among the passages written by Apollonios is a monologue of fifteen lines from an unknown comedy. *Editio princeps*: H. Weil, *Monuments grecs* (1879), i. 8, with photographs.

The wife's speech

Since both versions of the extract of forty-four lines ascribe it to Euripides, Weil, the first editor, felt bound to accept this authorship, although he observed that the style was more like that of Menander. Wilamowitz, *Herakles*, i. 41, rightly denied the Euripidean authorship but thought the verses a forgery fathered on Euripides. No further attention was paid to them until D. S. Robertson, *CR* xxxvi (1922), 106, not only claimed them for Menander, but found in them the reply made by Pamphile in the *Epitrepontes* to Smikrines' attempt to cause her to leave Charisios. Jensen accepted this, *Rh. Mus.* lxxvi (1927), 10 ff., but Körte, *Hermes*, lxi (1926), 141, while agreeing that the lines are by Menander, denied that they could be part of Pamphile's speech. In spite of a rejoinder by Robertson, *Hermes*, lxi (1926), 348, it would seem that the denial was right. The speaker of the Didot papyrus is a married woman who, like Pamphile, has been urged by her father to leave her husband. But the situation is not the same. This woman's husband has behaved towards her exactly as she would have wished him to do and has shown her unchanging affection (15–19); his only fault is that he has lost his money (19, 25–30). Pamphile could not talk like this of a husband who had deserted her for a *hetaira*, and who was at the most in danger of losing his money if he persisted in an extravagant way of life that he had only just embarked on. The counter-arguments of A. Barigazzi, *Athenaeum*, N.S. xxxiii (1955), 278 ff., do not convince me. The best reason for supposing the speech to belong to New Comedy is the domestic subject-matter. Fifth-century tragedy is excluded by the phrases τυχὸν ἴϲωϲ

(9), μέχρι πόϲου (32), by the position of δέ in 33, probably by the use of ἀπορεῖν, 'to be poor' (19), and by the accumulation of a number of metrical irregularities for which only isolated parallels can be found in tragedy: the violation of Porson's law (10, 20), the elision of -αι (44), the word-divisions of τῶν μὲν διὰ τέλουϲ (15) and τῶν μὲν ἀγαθῶν (25). Even if this list were somewhat shortened by emendations (a dubious resource, illiterate though the writer was), enough would remain to justify the conclusion. Nevertheless D. L. Page, *Greek Literary Papyri*, 180, includes the piece among the fragments of tragedy; so little, he argues, is known about tragedy in the late fourth century that we cannot deny the possibility that it belongs to a tragedy of that date. This is true, but it would be a matter for surprise if an extract from some obscure tragedian had found its way into this anthology, and for even greater surprise if it were discovered that tragedy ever dealt with themes like this. The number of violations of tragic metrical rules is not large, but as Tyrrell pointed out, *Hermathena*, iv (1883), 96, comic poets sometimes approached nearly to tragic metre: in seventy-eight iambics preserved from Damoxenos Porson's law is not once infringed. Estimation of probabilities in such a matter must be largely subjective, but I should be less surprised by a comedy which for one speech so combined comparative regularity of metre with a serious and impassioned tone than I should be by a domestic tragedy. It must be confessed that this piece is more tragic in rhythm, and stiffer and more formal than anything of Menander's that is preserved, apart from the exceptional stichomythia of *Perik.* 779 ff. There is no internal reason for ascribing it confidently to him rather than to a contemporary or a successor. Apollodoros is suggested by G. Coppola, *Riv. fil.* n.s. ix (1931), 247. H. Lucas, *Phil. Woch.* lviii (1938), 1102, doubtfully assigned the speech to Menander's Ἀδελφοὶ α'. In that play, which is distorted in Plautus' *Stichus*, the husbands have not been heard of for three years and lost their money in riotous living. These circumstances, though not absolutely excluded by this speech, are not suggested by it.

One cannot even argue that the young Egyptians are more likely to have had their piece, wherever they found it, from Menander than from a lesser-known comic author. They also knew an extract from Aeschylus' *Carians* and two otherwise unrecorded epigrams of Poseidippos. Neither of these belongs to the run of the mill. Nevertheless the rhesis is, with all due reserve, included here, since it has been so widely accepted and its humanity is worthy of Menander. I am less sure about its execution, although unable to agree that the lines are as flat and jejune as is maintained by W. Buhler, *Hermes*, xci (1963), 345. He thinks they are a bad imitation of Euripides by some third-rate author of comedy.

1–5: That men have more sense than women and that women should keep their mouths shut were common opinions among the Greeks: e.g. Soph. *Ajax* 293, γύναι, γυναιξὶ κόσμον ἡ ϲιγὴ φέρει, Demokritos frag. 274 VS, κόϲμος ὀλιγομυθίη γυναιξί, Aesch. *Septem* 232, ϲὸν δ' αὖ τὸ ϲιγᾶν, Eur. *Heracl.* 476, γυναικὶ γὰρ ϲιγή τε καὶ τὸ ϲωφρονεῖν κάλλιϲτον. But this woman's father has let pass his occasion for speaking (ἀφεῖκαϲ sc. λέγειν), and so she is forced herself to expound what is right.

6–11: 'If my husband has committed some serious crime, it is not for me to exact retribution, while if he has done me any wrong, I ought to be aware of it, and am not. I may be a foolish woman, but a woman may understand her own business.'

9 τυχὸν ἴϲωϲ: See *Epitr.* 504–6 n.

10 καίτοι γ': καίτοι occurs twice in Menander, *Sam.* 377, frag. 303. The combination καίτοι γε is rare anywhere, but cf. Eur. *IT* 720, καίτοι γ' ἐγγὺϲ ἕϲτηκαϲ φόνου.

12–18: 'Granted that you are right, tell me what wrong he does me. The rule of married life is that the husband should cherish his wife and that she should do what seems good to him. That rule is kept by us: he treats me well, as I expected him to, and I approve all his wishes.'

19–26: 'He is a good husband, then, but has fallen on hard times; you want to give me to a rich man, so that I shall not suffer poverty. What riches can be a substitute for my husband? Is it right that I should have shared his prosperity and now not share his poverty?'

20 ἐκδίδωϲ: 'Wish to give me in marriage'. Both texts have εγδιδωϲ, which may well have been the poet's own spelling, since the assimilation of κ to a following δ is normal in Attic inscriptions until the first century B.C., Meisterhans[3], 107.

27–33: 'Suppose this second husband, whom you have in mind, should lose his money, would you then give me to a third, and so on? Where would you stop?'

29 οὖν here modifies the negative οὐκ, 'certainly not with my consent'. It is therefore the negative of γοῦν, but that, as Denniston points out, *GP* 422, is οὔκουν . . . γε. Ibid. 424 he claims that, wherever in Attic γε is lacking after emphatic οὔκουν, it should be supplied. Here it can easily be added after θελούϲηϲ. For οὔκουν . . . γε attached to a participial clause, just as γοῦν may be, see Thuc. ii. 43. 1.   **θελούϲηϲ:** θέλειν is very rare in New Comedy, *Dysk.* 269 n. It is at home in tragedy, and the elevated tone of this passage may account for it.

δυναμένηϲ: Page translates 'nor while I can prevent it', which is no doubt the general sense; but κωλύειν can hardly be understood. Rather δυναμένης means 'while I can do anything', cf. Lysias xxiv. 12, ὡς εἰμὶ τῶν δυναμένων, 'that I am able-bodied'.

33 δέ: For the position after the vocative cf. *Epitr.* 1071 n. Weil, to maintain a possibly tragic style, supposed that δέ was a mistake for cú.

34–8: 'You chose my husband for me, but now that I am his wife, I must make my own decisions; and if they are wrong, it is my own life that will suffer.' I accept Blass's καλῶc for κακῶc. εἰκότωc, 'and reasonably so', is appended to the previous sentence, and then explained by the sentence introduced by γάρ. κακῶc can be defended only by supposing the meaning to be 'look to see that I do not by a bad judgement harm my own life'; but then εἰκότωc is awkward and γάρ intolerable (it could be removed by substituting 'γώ).

38 ἐμαυτῆc: For the position see *Dysk.* 26 n. Here it is obviously emphatic.

39 ταῦτ' ἐcτίν: 'That is the truth.'   πρὸc τῆc Ἑcτίαc: The appeal to the goddess of the household hearth is to the point here, contrast *Fab. incert.* 63, Strato frag. 1 K, Diphilos frag. 80 K, Anaxandrides frag. 45 K.

41: Since the law would allow him to break up her marriage, not to do so is 'an act of favour', but the favour is a 'just' one, i.e. enjoined by morality, and 'humane'.

44 μὴ μετ' αἰcχύνηc: 'Without doing anything that would bring me shame', e.g. actively resisting her father or second husband. The speaker does not challenge her father's legal right to break up her marriage, even though there is no question of making any complaint against her husband's conduct towards her. In Dem. xli. 4. a father removes his daughter, 'having quarrelled with' her husband, διαφορᾶc γενομένηc πρὸc τὸν Λεωκράτη.

At the end of the piece the young Apollonios added ευριπιδηc cποδρεγατηc. The latter word is interpreted by L. Radermacher, *Hermes*, lxi (1926), 350, as cπουδεργάτηc, 'a keen craftsman'. This would be more convincing if the word existed elsewhere or if other compounds with cπουδ- were usual (cπουδαρχία and its offspring are in fact the only ones known to LSJ, but cπουδεργόc is found in Anna Comnena, *Alex.* 483 c). Page suggested cπευδεργατηc = ψευδεργάτηc, 'spurious Euripides'; this word also is unknown.

The monologue

This speech was claimed for Menander by R. Herzog, *Philologus*, lxxxix (1934), 185 ff.; for earlier guesses—Philemon, Alexis, Theognetos—see *Rh. Mus.* xxxv (1880), 88, 255, 277. Edmonds assigns it to Poseidippos' Ἀναβλέπων (his frag. 1 A), E. Rechenberg in F. Zucker's *Menanders Dyskolos als Zeugnis seiner Epoche*, 149, would wish it to be from Middle Comedy, on the inadequate ground that the theatre is not elsewhere mentioned in our remains of New Comedy. One cannot be certain, but it is not unworthy of Menander. Herzog saw in the speech part of a prologue, but it is safer to call it a monologue, since it may well have occurred later in the play (G. Rambelli, *Stud. it. fil. cl.* N.S. xix [1942], 24). Nor is there any probability in his suggestion, supported by A. Barigazzi, *Athenaeum*, N.S. xxxiii (1955), 271–7, and M. van der Valk, *Ant. Class.* xxxvii (1968), 477, that it belongs to Menander's Ὑποβολιμαῖος: such similarity as there is with frag. 416 makes it, if anything, unlikely that the same play could accommodate both passages (cf. M. M. Kokolakis, Ἀθηνᾶ, lxvi [1962], 95, against Zuntz, *Proc. Brit. Acad.* xlii [1956], 240). There is a valuable discussion of the passage by K. Gaiser, *Gymnasium*, lxxv (1968), 193, who gives a photograph. He points out that the speaker is not certainly a young man, as has generally been supposed, but could be one converted late in life.

1 μέν: Speeches in tragedy often begin with μέν *solitarium*, and this device was also used by orators, particularly the earlier ones (Denniston, *GP* 383). Here it must mark the seriousness with which the speaker takes himself; the very sound of the opening lines is weighty, with the repeated assonance of ου and ων. It may be noted that the rules for tragic iambics are seldom infringed in this piece.

3–4: Some noun, meaning 'life', is needed as an antecedent for ὅν in 4. αἰῶνα has been suggested, as a substitute for ἄλλον (Kock) or ἄπανθ' (Weil). But this is a poetical usage, doubtful for New Comedy, in which the word occurs only in frag. 656 K–T, where it means 'an eternity'. It is more likely that the normal word βίον has been replaced by πάλαι, which Apollonios remembered too soon: it comes in 6. πάλαι is more easily dispensed with than either ἄλλον or ἄπαντα.

ἔζην: The 'correct' form is ἔζων and should perhaps be restored (Weil), but ἔζην, formed by assimilation to ἔζη, occurs in papyri from the second century B.C. and in most MSS. of Demosthenes xxiv. 7; it is perhaps not impossible for Menander.   **πιστεύετε:** The most likely correction of πιστευςεται; πιστεύςατε and πιστεύςετε are closer in sound, but the imperative πίςτευε is common.

3 ἄνδρες: An address to the spectators, as in *Sam.* 269, *Dysk.* 194, 659, etc. It is an interesting and perhaps intentional paradox that the man who is looking for solitude confides the secrets of his heart to the thousands of the audience. F. Leo, *Der Monolog im Drama*, 80, calls the proceeding naïve, but of course the poet was quite aware that a spectator can simultaneously recognize a dramatic convention and accord the play the make-believe acceptance that the theatre requires (cf. Gomme, *Essays*, 252 ff.).

5: Herzog read πανυδαυτο and wrote πάνυ ταὐτὸ τὸ καλόν, τἀγαθόν, τὸ cεμνὸν ⟨ἦν⟩, τὸ κακόν. Zuntz and also Gomme, *CQ* n.s. x (1960), 108, objected to the lack of balance, three words for the good and one for the bad. Whether this was right or wrong, Herzog's line is also suspect because, as Gaiser points out, the papyrus does not have πανυδαυτο. He himself thinks παντηκιο possible, and suggests πάντ' ἦ⟨ν⟩ cκιά, τὸ καλόν, τὸ cεμνόν, τἀγαθόν, τὸ κακόν. This is ingenious, but gives a line that neglects Porson's law, which is observed by all the rest, and also has a non-tragic anapaest in τὸ καλόν, paralleled however by τὸ θέατρον in 15. L. Koenen, *Zeitschrift für Papyrologie und Epigraphik*, iii (1968), 138, sees πανιλεκτο, which is in my view the most plausible reading of the very dubious three middle letters. But his restoration, ἐλέλεκτο πᾶν τὸ καλὸν τὸ cεμνὸν τἀγαθόν | κακόν, seems improbable.

9 ἐνθάδ' ἐλθών: Many have supposed that the speaker has recently come to Athens, and there had his eyes opened by some philosopher. It may be so, but *either* life in Athens *or* acquaintance with philosophy (or indeed something else, even love) could by itself be sufficient to work a change. The last lines are consistent, at the least, with the speaker's being long familiar with the Athenian scene. ἐνθάδε could mean, not Athens, but a house on the stage, the scene of his revelation. **εἰc Ἀcκληπιοῦ**: Edelstein, test. 419; the sick would sleep in the temple of Asklepios, and be healed in a vision. Cf. Ar. *Plut.* 411, κατακλίνειν αὐτὸν εἰc Ἀcκληπιοῦ κράτιcτόν ἐcτι. **cωθείc**: 'Cured', as often in medical writers, N. van Brock, *Recherches sur le vocabulaire médical du grec ancien*, 230.

10: Once again Apollonios has made a mess of his copying. He appears to have started with εα and then to have written ν below and over the α. κατακ is clear, but the next few letters are illegible; perhaps he intended κατακλιθιcωcνιcθε. Gaiser suggests ἂν κατακλιθῆιc cῶc ἦιc τε. This is closer to the written letters than Bücheler's ἐγκατακλιθεὶc cωθείc τε, but less convincing Greek.

11 περιπατῶ: This has no reference to the 'Peripatetic' school, who were originally called οἱ ἀπὸ τοῦ περιπάτου, because they taught in a 'walk', περίπατοc, not because they walked as they taught. To walk and talk is here simply a sign of being alive. That is not to deny that philosophers sometimes walked about as they talked; Alexis frag. 147, ἄνω κάτω τε περιπατοῦc' ὥcπερ Πλάτων, Men. frag. 722, ὠχρὸc περιπατῶν φιλοσόφου τὸ χρῶμ' ἔχων, Diog. L. vii. 5, ἀνακάμπτων δὴ ἐν τῇ ποικίλῃ cτοᾷ (of Zeno). Apollonios wrote περιπατων, and the participle is grammatically possible; but the triplet of verbs is in Menander's manner.

12: Gaiser writes περιπατῶν λαλῶν φρονῶ ἐν τηλικούτῳ καὶ τοσούτῳ ἡλίῳ. νῦν δ' οἷον εὕρημ', ἄνδρες, with an unacceptable hiatus. τηλικοῦτον καὶ τοιοῦτον: These words often reinforce one another, see *Epitr.* 337 n.; Plato, *Symp.* 177 a, τηλικοῦτος καὶ τοιοῦτος θεός, is an example to show that τηλικοῦτος may denote power and magnificence rather than physical size. There need not be any allusion here to philosophers' theories about the sun's magnitude.

13 ἐν τῇ τήμερον αἰθρίᾳ: 'In the clear light of today'. Because Lucian, *Nigrinus* 4, makes himself say that he had once carted round a blind 'soul' but through listening to the Platonic philosopher Nigrinus, ἔχαιρον ὥσπερ ἐκ ζοφεροῦ τινος ἀέρος τοῦ βίου τοῦ πρόσθεν ἐς αἰθρίαν τε καὶ μέγα φῶς ἀναβλέπων, Herzog claimed that he was adapting this passage, as he adapts frag. 722 at the beginning of *Iuppiter Tragoedus*. Not even the fact that there are in *Nigrinus* several references to drama makes this anything but fanciful, although it was accepted by Körte and others. There is a certain similarity between the images used by the speaker and those used by philosophers to represent philosophic education. Passages are quoted by K. Gaiser, *Antike und Abendland*, xiii (1967), 19, from Aristotle, *de philosophia* frag. 13 Ross, *Protrepticus* frag. 9 Ross, Diog. L. v. 19, but he develops what is actually attributable to Aristotle to make it more like what is said here. Later, in *Gymnasium*, lxxv (1968), 207, he argues that what has changed the speaker must be, not philosophy, but the whole educational influence of living in Athens. He shows that such a theme has many literary parallels. His interpretation may be right, but is less than certain.

There is a subscription by Apollonios, αριστων φιλοσοφος μαθηματα. What the illiterate boy meant is quite uncertain. One may doubt whether he had ever heard of either Ariston, the Stoic or the Peripatetic. Perhaps, as Gaiser suggests, he intended ἄριστον φιλοσόφοις μαθήματα, 'for lovers of wisdom the best thing is learning'. His words may have as little relevance to this piece as his addition to the 'wife's speech' has to that. It has been maintained that the lines have Ariston as their author (B. Hemmerdinger, *Aegyptus*, xxxvi [1956], 24, *REG* lxvi [1953], 11; M. K. Ohly, *Stichometrische Untersuchungen*, 51), but this need not be taken seriously; at the best they might have been quoted by the Peripatetic as illustrative, whatever their original context, of the change that can be worked by philosophy.

Pap. Ghôran ii (now *P. Sorbonne* 72)

Five pieces of this roll, written about 200 B.C., come from the same site as *Pap. Ghôran* i, which is now known to contain parts of Menander's *Sikyonios*. Whereas Blass denied that those fragments could be by Menander, he considered that *Pap. Ghôran* ii was his work; and in this he was supported by Jouguet, their discoverer, and Legrand. Later opinion set against a Menandrean origin, which was regarded as impossible by Körte, Schroeder, Wilamowitz, and improbable by Page. Their arguments from language and metre are, however, false or flimsy, and there are many phrases which now have their parallels in Menander's work. If there is a sound case against his authorship, it can be found only in the nature of the writing. It may be that the scene between the two young men (126–60) uses somewhat obvious motifs and does not display Menander's characteristic wit; but it is not to be expected that he always wrote at his best. Taking the fragment as a whole, I agree with Robert's verdict, *GGA* clxxx (1918), 193, that it is not the work of 'an unimportant poet'. Page calls the piece 'lively but inartistic'; I accept only the former epithet. I hope it may be noticed how economical and significant the writing is from 104 to 112, and how cleverly Phaidimos' language from 125 to 141 fails to give Nikeratos enough clues to grasp the underlying meaning. In the final scene the way in which Nikeratos shows that he is a little hurt at being suspected and the speed of the development on Chairestratos' entry are both worthy of Menander. Mette, *Lustrum*, x (1966), 192, places the piece among the 'Fabulae Incertae', and Jacques, *Bull. Assoc. G. Budé*, (1968), 221, considers Menander a possible author. (G. Capovilla, *Bull. Soc. Arch. Alexandrie*, iv. 205–29, and A. Dain, *Maia* N.S.xv [1963], 278, favoured identification with Δὶς 'Εξαπατῶν, now known to be out of the question.) But possibility is very different from certainty. There is no proof that Menander wrote this play. Webster, *Studies in Later Greek Comedy*², 240, makes something of a case for Apollodoros, a considerable artist, on whom Menander's influence is clear.

Plot

A young man Phaidimos was in love with a girl, probably a citizen, whose father did not intend to let her marry him (145–9). During his absence abroad his friend Nikeratos, with the knowledge or assistance of another friend, Chairestratos, looked after his interests. This involved some action that could arouse the suspicion that he intended to marry her himself (149–50). The girl appears to have left her father's house (101–4). Although it is not certain that this was at

Nikeratos' instigation or even with his knowledge, it is a very likely guess that she had taken refuge with him. On Phaidimos' return from his journey, Nikeratos sent Chairestratos down to the harbour, no doubt to inform him, if he should find him there, of what had been done on his behalf (107, 160–2), while he himself looked for him in the town (105) But Phaidimos, without being intercepted, arrived at the scene of action, where perhaps Nikeratos' house was represented (179) along with that of the girl's father. He had heard news that led him to believe that Nikeratos had betrayed him and on his arrival he rounds bitterly on a slave whom he suspects of complicity (80–2). The girl's father appears, and is told a story, true or false, of her present whereabouts (102). He departs and Nikeratos comes on the scene (105). Phaidimos upbraids his friend, who is about to defend himself (159) when Chairestratos comes back from the harbour; he declares that he knows the facts and will explain to Phaidimos what a good friend he has in Nikeratos—but not in the latter's presence.

The situation has some resemblance to that of Δὶς Ἐξαπατῶν, in that a young man acts, while his friend is abroad, to secure for him the girl he loves, and thereby causes that friend falsely to accuse him of disloyalty. But the circumstances are entirely different.

Position in the play of the surviving lines

The second verse of column II has the letter P prefixed, and this has been believed to indicate line 100 of the play. This is a little surprising, since so much seems already to have happened. If column V immediately follows column IV, there is another objection. It contains the end of an act, marked by the word *XOPOY*, but no verses to introduce the chorus, such as are found everywhere else at the end of the first act. This then is probably not the end of the first act. But it is not certain that columns IV and V are consecutive, see 180 n. Accordingly this objection has less importance. Another difficulty is that Nikeratos' appearance at 105 presupposes that he is known to the audience: he must have appeared before. The same considerations apply, although with less certainty, to Chairestratos' appearance at 160. One must therefore presume a scene in which Nikeratos sent Chairestratos on his errand. If after that he himself departed, it is somewhat surprising that he should be back as early as line 105 of the play, saying that he has been unable to run into Phaidimos anywhere.

K. Ohly, *Stichometrische Untersuchungen*, 81, expressed utter disbelief that P could stand for 100. In all other known MSS. marginal stichometry follows the principle that $A = 100$, $B = 200$, $\Gamma = 300$, and so on. Thus P should $= 1,700$. Professor Turner tells me that he would not rule out the possibility that in our papyrus a different method

A a

was used: such early MSS. are few; almost all the evidence is from
the imperial age. Already in the MS. of *Sikyonios* (third century B.C.),
although the marginal figures are in the usual style, the sum total of
lines at the end is given in the Ionic system (where $P = 100$). He is
unable to give any parallel for the continuous numeration of two
plays, which would be a possible explanation if $P = 1,700$, this being
about the 700th line of the second. It seems impossible to determine
the position in the play of the surviving lines. I preserve Schroeder's
numeration, which accepts the interpretation of the marginal P as
indicating line 100, although I should be surprised if it is right. But
any alternative would be arbitrary and therefore an unjustified
novelty.

The remains were first published by P. Jouguet, *BCH* xxx (1906),
123–49. The plot was largely elucidated by Körte, *Hermes*, xliii (1908),
38–57, and *Archiv f. Papyrusforschung*, vi. 230 ff. He, however, made
Phaidimos, not Nikeratos, send Chairestratos to the harbour. This is
supported by Page, who suggests that the object of the mission was
to delay the girl's father; he admits, however, that this leads to
difficulties, the absence of any reference to the mission at 163, and
the obscurity of 107. The view that Phaidimos dispatched Chairestratos
is in fact excluded by the warm exchange of greetings between the two
at 164–5, impossible if the two men had only recently parted. The
explanation that I have given was in essentials proposed by Robert,
GGA (1918), 190. I cannot accept the plot proposed by Webster,
Studies in Later Greek Comedy[2], 241.

Editions: Schroeder, *Novae Comoediae Fragmenta* (1915), 29, Demiańczuk, *Supplementum Comicum* (1912), 104, Page, *GLP* (1950), 296,
Edmonds, *Fragments of Attic Comedy*, iii. 336.

Dr. Colin Austin kindly lent me a photograph of the papyrus; he will
include the fragment in his *Comicorum Graecorum Fragmenta in papyris
reperta*.

72: The speaker is a slave. His opening words, ὦ δέϲποινα, do not show
that his mistress is on the stage. He may speak them back into her
house as he comes out, or he may apostrophize her in her absence, as,
e.g., Daos does Knemon at *Dysk.* 220. He is supposed by most to
belong to the girl's father, and this is not improbable, although it is
a little odd that he should speak of him not as τὸν δεϲπότην but as
τὸν πατέρα τουτονί. But the context may have made it necessary to
describe him as the girl's father, not the slave's master.

Restoration of 73 is uncertain. The best suggestions are that the
slave fears (δέδοικ᾽ ἔγωγε) or pities (ἐλεῶ ᾽πὶ τοῖϲδε) the father. At 77
he catches sight of Phaidimos; whether the young man is arriving or,

as I suspect, already on the stage cannot be determined. Phaidimos regards him as responsible for the supposed loss of the girl. If he is her father's slave, he may be thought to have facilitated her leaving home.

99–104: In this passage the girl's father learns of his daughter's whereabouts from someone, whom most scholars suppose to be the slave. Phaidimos they believe to stand aside unseen during the conversation. This may be so, but there is the difficulty that the slave's departure at 104 is neither mentioned nor accounted for. Phaidimos knows, or imagines he knows, what has happened to the girl, and it may be he who informs her father. This was Robert's view: he pointed out that the father could now take steps to recover the girl, and that Phaidimos would thus himself have ruined the plan devised by Nikeratos for his benefit. There would again be some similarity with the plot of Δὶc 'Εξαπατῶν, where Sostratos, suspecting his friend Moschos of disloyalty, ruins the plan devised for his own benefit by Syros.

104: The fourfold repetition of the vocative θύγατερ may strike some as excessive. Editors from Schroeder onwards give ἆρ' ἀφίcταται; to Phaidimos in the sense 'is he going?' There is no space before αρ to indicate a change of speaker, and it is possible that the father says τί ταῦτα, θύγατερ; ἆρ' ἀφίcταcαι; 'are you breaking with me?' The word ἀφίcταμαι is used by Aristotle, *EN* 1163^b23 of breaking the family bond, by Lysias xxiii. 7 of a runaway slave.

Jouguet and Blass could read nothing, except the final letter, after φ. Little confidence can be put in Schroeder's [. . .]τ[.]ι. Even if the doubtful letter is τ, c and τ are several times confused in the nearly contemporary MS. of *Sikyonios*.

105–12: Nikeratos speaks the first 3½ lines. 105–6 are addressed to the audience to explain his return, by the convention discussed in the note on 160; 107–108a, on the other hand, are spoken to himself and express a thought that is in his mind. This rapid passage from the artificial to the natural disguises the lack of realism in the first two lines. There is a paragraphus below 107; it must be erroneous and its comparative faintness suggests that an attempt has been made to erase it. Above it there is a darker diagonal stroke, such as is used in the Herondas papyrus to draw attention to textual difficulties; conceivably it was here employed by someone who doubted the correctness of the paragraphus.

Jouguet testifies that when discovered the papyrus, now illegible, had πεμψαc; and there is a paragraphus below line 108. Schroeder claimed to have glimpsed a paragraphus below 109; there is no sign of this on the photograph, although the surface of the papyrus seems to be well preserved immediately below the line's initial letter. It is also very doubtful whether there was a space and a dicolon before μετα. This suggests that Phaidimos speaks continuously from ἡμέτερος down to the middle of 111 before χαῖρε. But I have been unable to devise a plausible sentence for him. He may use ἡμέτερος φίλος in the sense 'our family friend'.

In 107 μή introduces a hesitant question, 'can it be that . . .?' It may be prompted by the fact that here Nikeratos catches sight of Phaidimos, at the other end of the stage; he is not immediately certain of his identity, but if this is Phaidimos, then it was a mistake to send Chairestratos to look for him at the harbour. As Phaidimos speaks, he crosses the stage towards him and, assured that this is his friend, breaks out in a warm greeting. Phaidimos does not reply, and has to be prompted to the embrace his friend expects. This action would appear more clearly from the words if Nikeratos said ἡμέτερος οὗτος φίλος· διάδηλός ἐστι (ἡμέτερος then would mean 'my friend and Chairestratos' friend'). But a mistake by the papyrus in the assignment of speeches, although not impossible, ought not to be assumed (as in OCT) without better cause.

106 αὐτὸς μὲν ἥκω is an excellent emendation. αὐτὸς μέν is opposed in thought to Χαιρέστρατος δέ.

108 εἰς λιμένα: Without the article, as in 160. Similarly an Athenian said εἰς ἀγοράν, 'to the agora', εἰς ἀγρόν, 'to the country', κατ' ἄστυ, 'in the town' (K–G i. 602).

113: Cf. Sam. 624, ὅρκος, πόθος, χρόνος, cυνήθεια.   τὸ διὰ χρόνου: 'The fact that ⟨we meet again⟩ after a long time' (Körte). This would be a reason for a warm greeting. But others think the meaning is 'the fact that ⟨we have been friends⟩ for a long time'. I cannot decide.

124 ὑπερηκόντικας: 'You have outdone', perhaps, as Körte suggested, the most famous models of friendship. The metaphor, from competitions in javelin-throwing, was used by Aristophanes, Plutus 666, κλέπτων τοὺς βλέποντας ὑπερηκόντικεν, Birds 363, Knights 659; Diphilos frag. 66.5 K uses the word without an object.

126 ὑπερεπιτηδείως: The exaggerated word is invented for the occasion. An ἐπιτήδειος is a friend seen in his function as a helper.

127 πρόνοιαν εἶχες; Cf. Sam. 704.   οἴομαί γε δή: 'I certainly think I did!' The effect is emphatic. If γε is limitative, the phrase is an ironic understatement. Denniston, GP 245, is perhaps unnecessarily ready to admit instances of straightforward emphatic γε δή in answers.

129 ἀντιβλέπειν: 'Look in the face', cf. Xen. Hell. v. 4. 27, τῷ ἐμῷ πατρὶ οὐδ' ἀντιβλέπειν δύναμαι. Menander has the verb constructed with the acc., frag. 598, ἀντιβλέπειν ἐκεῖνον οὐ δυνήσομαι | ἀδικῶν.

132 ἑκάτεροι: I.e. both sides in a battle.

133 ἐπιτρέπει: 'Allows'. Menander uses the word in this sense, *Dysk.* 611, *Aspis* 158, *Sam.* 460, but not elsewhere with an abstract subject like τὸ cυνειδέναι.

135 αὐτοῖcι: This form was made a reason for denying Menandrean authorship. But it is restored with high probability in frag. 711, οὐκ ἠρκέcαμεν αὐτοῖc⟨ιν⟩, ἤδη ⟨δ'⟩ εἰμὶ cῶc (compare the similar restoration in frag. 637, ταῖc ἀτυχίαιc⟨ι⟩ μὴ 'πίχαιρε τῶν πέλαc). *Sam.* 516 has τοῖcιν ἄλλοιc in a passage with other pieces of high-flown language. Here Phaidimos is speaking in an elevated emotional tone, which will account for the unusual form. The long dative endings -οιcι, -αιcι are found in nouns at *Perik.* 268, *Theoph.* 25, apparently purely *metri gratia*. In frag. 541 διαβολαῖcι πείθεται should perhaps be διαβολαῖc τι πείθεται. Frag. 681 is restored καὶ τοῖc⟨ι⟩ δούλοιc, but is of uncertain authorship. **cυνειδέναι αὐτοῖcι:** The construction, by which what lies on the conscience is not expressed, is unusual; the context will suggest cυνειδέναι αὐτοῖcι ἀδικοῦcιν. The use of the infinitive without an article as the grammatical subject is not very common, but well established, K–G ii. 3, Schwyzer, ii. 366, e.g. Aesch. *Agam.* 584, ἀεὶ γὰρ ἡβᾷ τοῖc γέρουcιν εὖ μαθεῖν, Xen. *Rep. Lac.* 9. 2, ἔπεται τῇ ἀρετῇ cῴζεcθαι. The uncommon construction may be an intentional feature of Phaidimos' rather high-flown speech. Blass added τό, accepted by the editors.

136 ὅcον διημάρτηκα τοῦ ζῆν: 'How completely have I missed living a real life!' Mere existence, without friends, is not life.

137: The papyrus gives τῶν φίλων μεῖζον ἀγαθόν. In the fifth-foot dactyl a break after the second syllable was avoided. Handley, *Dyskolos* p. 68, disposes of three apparent exceptions, but does not notice *P. Oxy.* 11. 5, ἀδόξῳ γὰρ ἐφάνη (author unknown). He suggests that μεῖζον ἀγαθόν is an 'ironical substitute' for μεῖζον κακόν, and therefore to be allowed as 'a special case'. But Phaidimos does not mean that friends are the greatest evil in life. They are the greatest blessing, but he, it seems, had not realized this and had therefore not learned how to recognize the man who would be a true friend. He has not, then, the clue to a happy life, and why should he live at all, if he must live unhappy? Transposition of words is a common error in other papyri, and is likely to have occurred here.

138 μήτ' ἐπίcταμαι ὡc δεῖ θεωρεῖν: 'I don't understand how to observe men as I should', cf. Arist. *EN* 1169ᵇ33, θεωρεῖν μᾶλλον τοὺς πέλας δυνάμεθα ἢ ἑαυτούς.

144 cυντεινόμενον πρὸc ἐμαυτόν: Phaidimos has not yet made any direct criticism of Nikeratos, and the meaning cannot be 'exasperated with me' (Page). Rather 'ranting to me'.

146 caυτόν: In Greek a reflexive pronoun in *oratio obliqua* can refer either to the subject of the introductory verb, as here, or to that of its own clause (K–G i. 561–2). Nevertheless the author was accused by Körte of bad grammar. Mette, *Lustrum*, x (1966), 16, would read c᾽ αὐτόν, but does not explain the intended meaning of this.

148 περίμενε: The scornful repetition of the other speaker's imperative is paralleled in *Dysk.* 503, if the right division of speakers there is Cικ. ἄφεc. Κν. ἄφεc;

150 οὐκ ἔμελλεc λαμβάνειν; λαμβάνειν, 'take as wife', as often. If Nikeratos had taken this citizen girl into his house, it would be expected that he would marry her. Phaidimos is incredulous at his denial.

151 ὦ μακάριε: Addressed to an angry man, cf. *Dysk.* 103 n.

152: Schroeder printed οὐκ οἶcθαc, mistakenly thinking he read οὐκ in the papyrus. The crasis (ὁ οὐκ) would be unparalleled in New Comedy, and the meaning obscure. **πρὶν μαθεῖν:** Cf. *Dysk.* 301 n.

154 ὦ τᾶν, Φαίδιμε: Cf. *Dysk.* 247 n.

155 ἐπ᾽ ἀρίcτερ᾽ εἴληφαc: 'You have given the matter a sinister turn', cf. frag. 276, ἐπαριcτέρωc τὸ πρᾶγμα λαμβάνειc.

158 ἀγνοούμενοc: 'Misapprehended', cf. *Sam.* 703 n.

159 τί ποτ᾽ ἐρεῖc; 'Whatever will you say?' But perhaps one should read τί ποτ᾽ ἐρεῖ; (cf. *Sam.* 535), as an aside.

Nikeratos is slow to guess why his friend is upset, especially since he must have been aware that he had himself acted in a way that might give rise to suspicion. But if his slowness may be overlooked, the scene is otherwise excellent. Phaidimos utters his complaints in terms that are at once general and high-flown, so that Nikeratos' initial bewilderment would be intelligible in anyone else. When he does see Phaidimos' mistake, he is just enough hurt at being misunderstood not to proceed directly to explanation. Then, as the audience expect the explanation to come, it is interrupted by the entry of Chairestratos. To him Nikeratos speaks half-humorously, 'I'm having a rough passage' (χειμάζομαι), but still with a shade of complaint.

160: Chairestratos enters and explains that he has not been to the harbour, having met one of Phaidimos' fellow passengers, who had informed him that the latter had set off long ago, to come 'here', i.e. to the scene of action. Körte, *Hermes*, xliii (1908), complained of the unrealistic nature of this speech, which is intended entirely for the benefit of the audience, and made this an argument for the non-Menandrean authorship of the play. There is now, however, a parallel in *Dysk.* 259 ff., where Sostratos explains for the benefit of the audience why he has returned alone. It can be seen that such passages are explicable by the relation between actors and spectators discussed in the introduction, p. 14. The presence of the latter is openly recognized by the former, who therefore need have no hesitation about artlessly explaining their movements. If more were known about the dates of Menander's plays it might be possible to show that he abandoned this device in favour of more naturalistic methods. In what remains of *Aspis, Epitrepontes, Samia,* and *Sikyonios,* such speeches as are made to the audience are made under the influence of emotion, and express thoughts that might be passing through the character's head at that moment. Contrast *Dysk.* 522 ff., *Perik.* 172 ff. and perhaps 537 ff.

162: It cannot be determined whether the second half of the line was spoken by Phaidimos or Nikeratos. Jouguet, Blass, Wilcken, and Schroeder all read απocαω. The second α is not visible on the recent photograph. If it was correctly read, it must have been a mistake. I suggest (*Νικ.*) ἀποcέcωκά c', ὥcτε μή—. Hearing him, Chairestratos interrupts τίc οὗτοc; 'Why, it is Nikeratos, and this is Phaidimos himself', the man I was looking for. The two greet warmly: for νὴ καὶ cύ γε cf. *Georg.* 41 n., *Sam.* 129.

166 χειμάζομαι: Lit. 'am storm-tossed'. Ammonios 511 Nickau says that χειμάζειν can mean ἐνοχλεῖν and that Menander so used the word in his Ἡνίοχοc (frag. 184 K–T). ἐνοχλεῖν would here be a colourless substitute.

167 ἠγνόηκε: Körte wrongly thought this perfect un-Menandrean. It is quite correct: 'Surely Phaidimos is not still under a misapprehension', i.e. has formed a false opinion and still holds it.

177 ff.: For some reason it suits the dramatist's convenience that Nikeratos should be separated from the other two: he is made to go into his own house on the excuse that he is not to be embarrassed by hearing a recital of his good deeds. It is not improbable that the act is near its end. If column V, which is on a detached piece of papyrus, followed immediately on column IV, there are only four lines after

Nikeratos' departure. Even if column V belongs to some other part of the play, the act-end may have been in the column that succeeded column IV. The facts to be imparted to Phaidimos may be already known to the audience; if so, he and Chairestratos must be removed from the stage before the story is told. But there can be no certainty about how the play continued after 179.

Frag. Incert. 951

Pap. Hamburg 656. Remains of two columns, probably of third century B.C. Change of speaker within the line is marked by dicola; that there were also paragraphi is a probable guess, since their absence from the second column, which preserves the beginnings of lines, is compatible with a long uninterrupted speech.

Ed. pr.: B. Snell, *Griech. Papyri d. Hamburger Staats- und Universitätsbibliothek*, 20 ff., with photograph (1954); A. Thierfelder, *Menander* (1959), ii. 274.

The attribution to Menander is uncertain. It is based principally upon the phrase ἀπὸ μηχανῆς τις τῶν θεῶν (12). The scholiast on [Plato], *Clitophon* 407 a, has "ἀπὸ μηχανῆς θεὸς ἐπεφάνης" . . . Μένανδρος Θεοφορουμένῃ καὶ Κεκρυφάλῳ. Snell suggested that the phrase occurred verbatim in Θεοφορουμένη only, and in a variant form in Κεκρύφαλος, from which this fragment could be taken. Clearly this is possible; on the other hand, there is no reason to suppose that Menander had a monopoly of the phrase ἀπὸ μηχανῆς θεός. There can be no a priori assumption that a MS. as early as this one is of a Menandrean play. The exchanges 15–21, which serve no purpose but to get the characters off the stage, seem somewhat clumsy, but Κεκρύφαλος, the suggested play, was early, perhaps soon after 320 B.C., if Del Corno, *Dioniso*, xxxvi (1962) 136, is right in arguing that the γυναικονόμοι (frag. 238) were introduced then rather than in 317 B.C.

A young man, Moschion, is interested in a girl called Dorkion. She is in need of money, and some woman offers clothes and jewellery, which she says can be pawned for 1,000 drachmae. This can be a loan or, if repayment proves impossible, a gift: she is ready to contribute that for Dorkion's σωτηρία, preservation from some danger.

Snell and Thierfelder suppose that the 1,000 drachmae (ten minae) are needed in order to buy Dorkion from her owner, but point out that this would be a low price by comparison with those asked in *Pseudolus* (twenty minae, 52), *Rudens* (thirty minae, 45), *Curculio* (thirty minae plus ten for clothes and jewellery, 344), *Epidicus* (forty minae, 52). They argue that ten minae must be either a deposit or a remainder, as yet unpaid, of a larger price. Another possibility is that Dorkion is a free woman who has engaged herself, like Bacchis in *Bacchides*, for a period in return for an advance payment, and now wishes to go back on the bargain, cf. U. E. Paoli, *Studi Calderini–Paribeni*, ii. 117. See also Webster, *JHS* lxxv (1955), 159. Because she is probably addressed as γενναία γύναι (10), the woman who lends the clothes and jewellery is taken by Thierfelder to be a married woman. It is surely not out of the question that she is a wealthy but noble-minded *hetaira*, like Bacchis of Ter. *Hecyra*, so far as this phrase goes. Yet it is possible that she *is* a married woman and that Dorkion turned out to be her long-lost daughter. Perhaps, as Snell guessed, something among the jewellery matched something in Dorkion's possession.

1: In the right-hand margin is *XNX*; unexplained. Cantarella's suggestion *X(ωρεῖ) N(ῦν) X(ρυcίc)*, recorded by Del Corno, *Dioniso*, xxxvi. 136, does not carry conviction.

3 Δορκίῳ: In Ter. *Phormio* 152 the name is that of a servant-girl, in *AP* xii. 161 of a *hetaira*. The status of Dorcium in Turpilius, *Leucadia* frag. 16 Ribbeck is unknown.

4 θέντεc: Either Moschion and Dorkion or Moschion and Parmenon.

5 δραχμάc: For the unusual long first syllable see *Epitr.* 335 n.

8 δύνῃ: Moschion alone is now addressed.

11: Supplement is uncertain: the best suggestion is Jachmann's ἄριcτα.

12–14: The speaker is uncertain; he might even be Parmenon, addressing himself (Thierfelder). Parmenon must have been charged with the task of raising the money (hence cοι).

17 φέρε: Thierfelder urges that whoever speaks will not intend the woman to carry the goods herself; that task is for the maid Doris.

18 ἀγαθῇ τύχῃ: Cf. *Sam.* 274, *Dysk.* 422. Gomme thought, not improbably, that there should be punctuation after the phrase. If so, the missing word might be εἴceιμ', but other guesses can be made.

21 τοῦτο βούλομαι: This is a guess, but likely, cf. *Theophor.* 30.

Incerti Auctoris Fabula

This play, nearly 400 lines of which are fragmentarily preserved in two rolls of the third century B.C., was thought by Blass to be by Philemon. His grounds were negligible, as was Schroeder's appeal to the word νομάρχ[οc, or νομάρχ[ηc, the title of an Egyptian provincial official found in *P. Grenfell* II 8, which is associated with this play by no more than a guess. (Philemon spent some time in Egypt and may have written comedies with an Egyptian setting. But Hdt. iv. 66 speaks of νομάρχαι among the Scythians and Arrian, *Anab.* v. 8. 3, among the Indians.) Austin suspects the play to be Menander's *Hydria*, since it contains a character named Libys. Frag. 404 K–T, from that play, runs οἱ Θρᾷκες, Λίβυ, Τρῶες καλοῦνται· πάντα νῦν ἤδη 'cθ' ὁμοῦ. But Kraus would emend to οἱ Θρᾷκες, Λίβυς, Τρῶες καλοῦνται.

I do not myself greatly favour Menander as its author, but it is too fragmentary to allow of a rational judgement. I have printed in OCT two passages where unusually complete lines are preserved.

(*a*) The speaker is probably the cook Libys, who appears elsewhere in the play. He regrets the way in which comic poets accuse cooks of petty theft. Whether his complaint is that their larceny is exaggerated or underestimated is not certain. It puts one in mind of a cook's monologue (Page, *GLP* 272) from some unknown comedy:

$$\mathrm{\mathring{a}}\pi\eta\rho\acute{\iota}\theta\mu\eta c\acute{a}\nu\ \mu o\iota\ \kappa\rho\acute{\epsilon}a\cdot$$
$$\mathring{\epsilon}\pi\acute{o}\eta c'\ \mathring{\epsilon}\lambda\acute{a}\tau\tau\omega\ \tau a\hat{\upsilon}\tau a,\ \tau\grave{o}\nu\ \mathring{a}\rho\iota\theta\mu\grave{o}\nu\ \delta'\ \mathring{\iota}ca.$$
$$\chi o\rho\delta\hat{\eta}c\ \tau\iota c\ \mathring{\eta}\nu\ \mathring{o}\beta\epsilon\lambda\acute{\iota}c\kappa o c\cdot\ \mathring{\epsilon}\xi\epsilon\lambda\grave{\omega}\nu\ \tau\acute{o}\mu o\upsilon c$$
$$\mathring{\epsilon}\kappa\ \tau o\hat{\upsilon}\ \mu\acute{\epsilon}c o\upsilon\ \tau\mathring{a}\pi'\ \mathring{a}\kappa\rho\omega\ c\upsilon\nu\acute{\eta}\gamma a\gamma o\nu\ .\ .\ .$$
$$c\tau\acute{\epsilon}a\rho\ \mathring{\epsilon}\mu a\rho\psi',\ \mathring{\epsilon}\lambda a\iota o\nu\ \mathring{\epsilon}\xi\eta\rho a c\acute{a}\mu\eta\nu,$$
$$\mu\acute{\epsilon}\lambda\iota\ c\upsilon\mu\pi a\rho\acute{\epsilon}\lambda a\beta o\nu.$$

δύ' ἐξ ἑνὸς ποιοῦcι: They divide one piece of meat into two and steal one half.   **χορδή** is a sausage: they steal slices from the middle and then join it up again. Cf. Antiphanes frag. 72 K, ἐκτεμὼν χορδῆς μεcαῖον.   **ἐπάγουcι** is a strange compound to use; cυνάγουcι would be expected.   **cφογγιαῖc:** This pronunciation for the more usual cπογγιαῖc, like cφυρίc for cπυρίc, *Sam.* 297, is Attic and not satisfactorily explained.   **οἰνόμελι:** An uncertain restoration, but liquid mead is more easily soaked up in a sponge than honey would be.

(*b*) The slave Strobilos puts on an act by which he pretends to take the person Δ for a god, recognizable by his divine perfume (cf. Eur. *Hipp.* 1391). The opening lines are less clear, but it is plausible to suppose that Γ urges Strobilos on to strain every nerve in his deceit, which is intended to get him out of some difficulty, and then departs. But these two lines may be self-allocution by Strobilos. Δ immediately enters, I guess through one of the openings in the *skene*, having just had evidence that something extraordinary has happened. For ὦ Ἡράκλεις as an entry-phrase cf. *Heros* 55. Strobilos somewhat artlessly emphasizes his words by saying things twice: ἀκριβῶς . . . caφῶς, ἐνθάδε . . . ἐνθάδε.

Page (*GLP* 292) follows Schroeder in supposing that Strobilos has found a treasure, of which he will shortly inform Δ (his master). He prints, five lines after the last words of OCT, the supplement *Κροί[cου* *cε γὰρ πεπόηκα πλουcιώτερον].* This reconstruction is conceivably right, but speculative.

Schroeder prints *νόμιζε Λά[μπ]ιδος τρέχειν κτλ.,* but Lampis is known only as a victor in the pentathlon in the eighteenth Olympiad (Pausanias v. 8. 7); although a foot-race was one of the events, there is no record of its having been crucial for him.

ADDENDA

Aspis

61 ὑπαϲπιϲταί: The latest treatment is by R. D. Milns, *Historia* xvi (1967), 509, xx (1971), 186, who follows W. W. Tarn, *Alexander the Great* ii. 153, in maintaining that Alexander's *hypaspists* had the same equipment as men of the phalanx; the difference between them was that 'the phalanx was the national Macedonian levy, while the hypaspists were King's troops' (Tarn, loc. cit. i. 10). Whatever the details of armour and weapons may have been, it seems to be established that hypaspists cannot be reckoned as light-armed troops. Their superior mobility was due rather to their higher standards. The hypaspists of the Greek army in Lykia must be seen as the élite of the infantry; they may have had a closer attachment than the main body to the commander of the expedition.

299: Del Corno, *ZPE* vii (1971), 29, argues further for his view that Chairestratos never enters his house, but collapses outside it; he modifies some details of his interpretation. Lloyd-Jones, *GRBS* xii (1971), 183, understands the scene much as I do, but thinks that the words μᾶλλον δ' ἄνοιγε τὰϲ θύραϲ are addressed to Chaireas.

316–9: In support of giving the whole of 317 to Daos, A. Lampignano, *ZPE* vi (1970), 220, quotes Ter. *HT* 677: 'at sic opinor—non potest —immo optime.' νὴ τὴν Ἀθηνᾶν is used in *PSI* 1176 by someone who may be a slave, and in Philemon frag. 79. 3 by a cook. It is unsafe therefore to argue that the oath shows that the phrase in which it occurs cannot have been spoken by Daos.

382: My conjecture μηδένα ἔξω γ' (for εξωτ') ἀφίετ' is supported by Ar. *Wasps* 922, μὴ νῦν ἀφῆτέ γ' αὐτόν, where γε emphasizes that it is important *not to let him go* (Denniston, *GP* 115, 126). Similarly the emphasis here lies on the importance of not letting anyone *out of the house*.

405: It has been pointed out to me that there is a vertical line in B immediately before 406. This might be the tail of a ρ preceding 405, the remains of a *nota personae*, i.e. ϲμικ]ρ'.

415 ἄπιϲτον ἄλογον δεινόν: It is not certain that these words are a quotation from tragedy. They may be Daos' own 'impassioned' description of what has 'occurred'; he will then correct it by the quotation from Karkinos, which denies that anything is unbelievable.

Georgos

60 : The meaning of ἐξέτριβεν, 'rubbed him down', is paralleled in Photios's ummary of Ktesias' *Indica* (*bibl.* 48 a), τὰς δὲ χεῖρας ἀπο-νίζονται, ἐλαίῳ δὲ χρίονται . . . καὶ ἐκτρίβονται δέρμασιν.

Dyskolos

P. 132: A schoolboy's exercise of the third or fourth century A.D. contains a number of names from comedy; one is Cιμικη, so spelt (Clarysse and Wouters, *Ancient Society* i [1970], 201). This may weaken the case for writing Cιμίχη in the text of Menander, but does not destroy it. Cιμικη may have appeared in many MSS. and yet have been a false spelling.

Epitrepontes

218: Another possibility is that a dicolon has been omitted before δυcτυχης, intended to show not change of speaker, but that the word is an aside. If so, Daos pities himself, 'my luck is out', just as at *Sam.* 370 Chrysis utters the isolated word δύcμοροc in reference to herself.

227: Lloyd-Jones has observed to me that O 14 probably had εἰ δή τι μή cε κωλύει, which looks preferable to C's εἰ δή cε μηδὲν κωλύει.

410: The new photograph makes it appear unlikely that the word αυτοc was followed by the letter φ. The supplement φυλάττειν must therefore be regarded with scepticism.

Heros

P. 386 : Helpful though the Hero of this play presumably was, I should have quoted some less favourable judgements on the activities of Heroes, e.g. Menander frag. 394, οἱ γὰρ ἥρωεc . . . κακοῦν ἕτοιμοι μᾶλλον ἤπερ ὠφελεῖν, Σ Ar. *Birds* 1490, οἱ ἥρωεc δὲ δυcόργητοι καὶ χαλεποὶ τοῖc ἐμπελάζουcι γίνονται . . . ἀποπλήκτουc μὲν ποιεῖν δύνανται, τὸ δὲ ὠφελὲc οὐ κέκτηνται.

Kolax

29: The *Suda* has an entry s.v. διμοιρίτης. τοῦτο ἐνίοτε τριώβολον (τετρώβολον Drachmann) ἀποδεδώκαcιν, ἐπειδὴ τοῦτο δίμοιρόν ἐcτι τῆc δραχμῆc. ὁ οὖν τοῦτο λαμβάνων cτρατιώτηc διμοιρίτηc ἐλέγετο. The first sentence must be emended, since δίμοιροc means 'two-thirds'; LSJ's alternative sense, 'half', is unwarranted. The second may be no more than a false guess; the other evidence is unanimous that the διμοιρίτηc received more than a ranker's pay.

Misumenos

A 1–A 18 : Professor Turner kindly allows me to refer to a fragment from Oxyrhynchus, to be published in a supplement to *Greek Roman and Byzantine Studies*. It removes several doubts and down to A 14 supplies most of the words previously missing. Turner does not necessarily agree with my interpretations.

Readings or conjectures confirmed by P.Oxy.: A 2 λόγοι A 3 πλεῖστοι (Kraus) λέγονται (Koenen) A 4 ἆρ' ἄλλον (Handley) and ἀθλιώτερον A 5 δυσποτμώτερον A 12 ὑπαιθρίῳ A 13 αἱρετώτερον (possible in P . IFAO). Text of P.Oxy. corrupt or suspect: A 7 περιπατωντε A 8 begins αμφοτερασμεχρ A 9 εξω and εχει A 12 ουτωωδε A 14 καλουντι A 15 τωθεω

A 7 begins ἐν τῷ στενωπῷ, probably to be taken with both ἔστηκ' ἐγώ and περιπατῶ. The narrow town-street (στενωπός) is represented by the stage, on which Thrasonides' house-door opens. In Hegesippos fr. I. 23 K στενωπός οὑτοσί will be the stage, for in it is the door of the house that the cook is about to enter. In Plaut. *Pseud.* 960, 971 the stage is an *angiportum*; on this word see W. Beare, *Roman Stage*, 248–55.

A 13: Although the space is inadequate, χειμ[ῶνος ὄν]τος (Turner) seems necessary, followed in A 14 by ἑστη[κέναι τ]ρέμοντι (Rea): 'it is preferable to stand out of doors in the winter, shivering.' χειμῶνος . . . ὄντος means 'in the winter' at Ar. *Thesm.* 67–8. Cf. also Aristophon fr. 10 K, ὑπαίθριος χειμῶνα διάγειν. Was *Misumenos* written for the Lenaia, the winter-festival?

A 15: A paragraphus below A 14 and a *nota personae* here show that Getas speaks, perhaps having emerged from Thrasonides' house, although Turner thinks he has been following his master up and down. In the darkness that the spectators must imagine they cannot immediately see one another. Getas' initial words may be τὸ δ[ὴ λεγό]μενον (Austin); what follows is much damaged and perhaps irrecoverable.

Perikeiromene

396: W. W. Tarn, *Alexander the Great* ii. 169–70, shows that there was a short Macedonian cubit of 13–14 inches and, supposing that to have been used in measurement of the *sarisa*, reckons that weapon, as used in Alexander's army, to have been 13–14 feet (*c.* 3½ metres) in length.

976–1026: G. M. Browne has re-examined the papyrus and is preparing to publish his findings. I owe him thanks for allowing me to see a first draft and an excellent photograph, both made available to me by Professor Turner. **992:** Browne considers that επεξ[ητ]αζε cannot be read, and interprets the damaged script as επεσκ[ευ]αζε. If ἐπεσκεύαζε is correct, I should understand it to mean 'he was giving her a new outfit'; Glykera had left her best clothes and jewellery in Polemon's house when she fled from it (519–20). ἐπισκευάζειν is the ordinary word for refitting a ship, and both it and its derivatives are often used of repairing or restoration. **1001:** It is clear that the fourth letter after αγετε is ξ. Hesitantly Browne suggests [γε ἔ]ξ[ω τὴν κόρην: *scriptio plena* occurs once elsewhere in O (1024), although there at change of speaker. γε is not commonly attached to an imperative, but Denniston says that 'the usage seems established' (*GP* 125). Without any confidence I suggest προ]ξ[ενεῖτέ μοι, 'plead my case for me'.

1009: Π[ολέμω]ν' of Koerte's text cannot be right; there is no apostrophe and the first letter seems to be δ not π.

Samia

300–1: H. Petersmann, *Wiener Studien* N.F. v (1971), 91, revives the view that the stage-doors in the skene opened outwards, unlike the normal house-door, and could therefore be struck on the inside by someone who was coming out. At several points his treatment of the evidence seems forced. B. Bader, *Antichthon* v (1971), 35, carefully surveys the passages where mention is made of the noise made by the stage-door. Incidentally he marshals the evidence, which he finds conclusive, that it opened inwards. He suggests that the phrase 'he has struck the door' means that the character who is about to come out has in reaching for the interior handle given the door a push, causing it to rattle against its frame.

480: The punctuation is difficult. In my note I accept Austin's ἀλλὰ τίς; σύ; 'Who wrongs me, if not Chrysis? Is it you?' But I now find this unsatisfying. Demeas has no doubt that Moschion has wronged him; he has decided that he is in the plot against him (474–5). Having told him that he knows the truth, he is unlikely to put to him the question: 'Are you the guilty party?' Further, if Moschion is guilty, that will do nothing to exonerate Chrysis; hence the questions ἀλλὰ τίς; σύ; are not what one would expect. In OCT I have therefore printed the single question ἀλλὰ τίς σύ; Demeas, who began the scene with Chrysis in mind, has become more and more exasperated with his son and by now is primarily concerned with *his* disloyalty, which is far more wounding than that of Chrysis. So now, when Moschion asks 'What wrong has she done you, if the child is mine?', he brushes aside the question of her guilt to demand 'Yes, but who (on that admission) are you?' He means: 'You are the seducer of your father's mistress.' Moschion, unable to recognize the point of the question, continues with the attempt to exculpate Chrysis.

A SHORT CONCORDANCE

TO CERTAIN EDITIONS OF MENANDER

K   Körte, *Menander quae supersunt*, pars prior, ed. 3 (Teubner 1938, corrected reprint 1957). This has the numeration commonly used during the last generation.

LSJ   Körte, *Menandrea* (Teubner 1912). References in Liddell–Scott–Jones use its numeration, as do Jensen, *Menandri reliquiae* (Weidmann 1929), and Wilamowitz, *Das Schiedsgericht* (Weidmann 1925).

J   Jacques, *Ménandre* I 1, *La Samienne* (Les Belles Lettres 1971).

OCT   Sandbach, *Menandri reliquiae selectae* (Oxford 1972). The numeration of this edition is used in the present commentary.

For the sake of brevity correspondences have been set out for every tenth line only, except that the first lines of each passage have also been noted. A user who wishes to discover the number given in this book to a line for which he has a reference to some edition other than the OCT will, if its number does not appear in the table, take the nearest *smaller* number and proceed by *addition*. For example, wishing to discover the OCT number corresponding to *Epitrepontes* 547 Körte, he will see that 540 Körte corresponds to 860 OCT; therefore 547 Körte corresponds to 867 OCT.

Aspis	**K**	**OCT**
(*Com. Flor.*)	1	120
	10	129
	17	145
	20	148
	30	158
	33	378
	40	385
	50	394
	60, 61	—
	62	404
	70	412
	80	422

Epitrepontes	K	OCT	LSJ
	1	127	Inc. 2, 1
	10	136	Inc. 2, 10
	20	146	Inc. 2, 20
	23	159	Inc. 2, 23
	30	166	Inc. 2, 30
	40	176	Inc. 2, 40
	42	218	1
	50	226	9
	60	236	19
	70	246	29
	80	256	39
	90	266	49
	100	276	59
	110	286	69
	120	296	79
	130	306	89
	140	316	99
	150	326	109
	160	336	119
	170	346	129
	180	356	139
	190	366	149
	200	376	159
	210	386	169
	220	396	179
	230	406	189
	240	416	199
	250	426	209
	260	436	219
	270	446	229
	280	456	239
	290	466	249
	300	476	259
	310	486	269
	320	496	279
	330	506	289
	340	516	299
	350	526	309
	360	536	319
	370	546	329
	380	556	339
	390	566	349

Epitrepontes	K	OCT	LSJ
	400	576	359
	410	586	369
	420	596	379
	430	606	389
	440	616	399
	450	626	409
	460	636	419
	470	646	429
	480	656	439
	489	666	448
	490	680	449
	500	690	459
	510	714	—
	520	724	—
	522	749	—
	530	757	—
	532	759	469
	533	853	470
	540	860	476
	550	870	486
	560	880	496
	570	890	506
	580	900	516
	590	910	526
	600	920	536
	610	930	546
	620	940	556
	630	950	566
	639	969	575
	640	970	576
	650	980	586
	660	1003	596
	670	1013	606
	680	1023	—
	681	1037	611
	690	1046	620
	700	1056	—
	702	1060	626
	710	1068	634
	720	1078	644
	730	1088	654
	740	1098	664

Epitrepontes	K	OCT	LSJ
	750	1108	674
	760	1118	684
	770	1128	694

Misumenos	K	OCT
	1	168
	10	177
	12	210
	20	218
	24	276
	30	284
	40	294
	50	248
	60	258

Perikeiromene	K	OCT
	1	121
	10	130
	20	140
	30	150
	40	160
	50	170
	60	180
	70	190
	71	261
	80	270
	90	280
	100	290
	110	300
	120	310
	130	320
	140	330
	150	340
	160	350
	170	360
	180	370
	190	380
	200	390
	210	400
	217	467
	220	470
	230	480

Perikeiromene	240	490
	250	500
	260	510
	270	520
	280	530
	290	540
	300	550
	301	708
	310	717
	319	742
	320	743
	330	753
	338	768
	340	770
	350	780
	360	790
	370	800
	380	810
	390	820
	398	976
	400	978
	410	988
	420	998
	430	1008
	440	1018

Samia	K	OCT	J
	—	1	10
	—	11	20
	—	21	30
	—	30	64
	—	36	70
	—	46	80
	—	56	90
	—	58	118
	—	60	120
	—	70	130
	—	80	140
	—	87	169
	—	88	170
	—	98	180
	—	108	190
	—	118	200

Samia	K	OCT	J
	—	120	216
	—	124	220
	—	134	230
	—	144	271
	—	153	280
	—	163	290
	—	167	321
	—	173	330
	—	183	340
	—	193	350
	—	203	360
	—	206	375
	—	211	380
	1	216	385
	10	225	394
	20	235	404
	30	245	414
	34	249	421
	40	255	427
	50	265	437
	60	275	447
	70	285	457
	80	295	467
	90	305	477
	100	315	487
	110	325	497
	120	335	507
	130	345	517
	140	355	527
	150	365	537
	160	375	547
	170	385	557
	180	395	567
	190	405	577
	200	415	587
	—	418	590
	—	428	600
	—	438	610
	—	448	620
	—	458	630
	—	468	640
	—	478	650

Samia	K	OCT	J
	—	488	660
	—	498	670
	—	508	680
	—	518	690
	—	528	700
	—	538	710
	202	547	719
	210	555	727
	220	565	737
	230	575	747
	240	585	757
	250	595	767
	260	605	777
	270	615	787
	280	625	797
	290	635	807
	300	645	817
	310	655	827
	320	665	837
	330	675	847
	340	685	857
	—	688	860
	—	698	870
	—	708	880
	—	718	890
	—	728	900

INDEXES

I. GENERAL INDEX

II. GREEK INDEX